Handbook of Research on Children's and Young Adult Literature

This landmark volume is the first to bring together the leading scholarship on children's and young adult literature from three intersecting disciplines: Education, English, and Library and Information Science. Distinguished by its multidisciplinary approach, it describes and analyzes the different aspects of literary reading, texts, and contexts to illuminate how the book is transformed within and across different academic figurations of reading and interpreting children's literature.

- Part 1 considers perspectives on readers and reading literature in home, school, library, and community settings.

- Part 2 introduces analytic frames for studying young adult novels, picturebooks, indigenous literature, graphic novels, and other genres. Accompanying each chapter are commentaries on literary experiences and creative production from renowned authors and illustrators including David Wiesner, Lois Lowry, Philip Pullman, Jacqueline Woodson, Markus Zusak, Joseph Bruchac, and M.T. Anderson.

- Part 3 focuses on the social contexts of literary study, with chapters on censorship, awards, marketing, and literary museums.

Editors' part-opener essays and chapter introductions point academic and practitioner colleagues to each field's histories, contemporary concerns, and research methods, while outlining the potential for intersecting research and scholarship in all three fields.

Chapter authors write from a combination of scholarly as well as personal perspectives. Readers—scholars, teachers, librarians, parents, publishers, editors, and those on the verge of entering the field—are invited to join the conversation, to raise their own arguments, contradictions, and questions, to look for personal reflections on their own lives and their lives among youth and their books.

The singular contribution of this *Handbook* is to lay the groundwork for colleagues across disciplines to redraw the map of their separately figured worlds, thus to enlarge the scope of scholarship and dialogue as well as push ahead into uncharted territory.

Shelby A. Wolf is Professor of Education at the University of Colorado at Boulder.

Karen Coats is Professor of English and Director of English Education at Illinois State University.

Patricia Enciso is Associate Professor of Literature, Literacy, and Equity Studies at The Ohio State University.

Christine A. Jenkins is Associate Professor at the Graduate School of Library and Information Science, University of Illinois at Urbana-Champaign.

Handbook of Research on Children's and Young Adult Literature

Edited by

Shelby A. Wolf

University of Colorado at Boulder

Karen Coats

Illinois State University

Patricia Enciso

The Ohio State University

Christine A. Jenkins

University of Illinois at Urbana-Champaign

Routledge
Taylor & Francis Group

NEW YORK AND LONDON

First published 2011
by Routledge
270 Madison Avenue, New York, NY 10016

Simultaneously published in the UK
by Routledge
2 Park Square, Milton Park, Abingdon, Oxon OX14 4RN

Routledge is an imprint of the Taylor & Francis Group, an informa business

Typeset in Times and Optima by EvS Communication Networx, Inc.
Printed and bound in the United States of America on acid-free paper by Sheridan Books, Inc.

Library of Congress Cataloging in Publication Data
Wolf, Shelby Anne.
Handbook of research on children's and young adult literature / edited by Shelby A. Wolf ... [et al.].
p. cm.
1. American literature—History and criticism. 2. Children's literature, American—History and criticism. 3. Young adult literature, American—History and criticism.
PS121.H22 2010
810.9'9282—dc22
2010016339

ISBN 13: 978-0-415-96505-7 (hbk)
ISBN 13: 978-0-415-96506-4 (pbk)
ISBN 13: 978-0-203-84354-3 (ebk)

For Ashley and Lindsey—You started me on this path
and have helped to guide me every step of the way.

Shelby A. Wolf

For Will and my girls, Emily and Blair—the three of you are my story—and
for Him who provides the work and the grace with which to do it.

Karen Coats

For Mary Ann Enciso, my mother; Susan Hepler, my first children's literature
teacher; and Brian Edmiston, my partner and colleague—storytellers and story
revelers whose words and teaching encouraged me throughout this book's journey.

Patricia Enciso

To my two best librarians: my mother, Marjorie Jenkins Wezeman, and my partner,
Susan Searing. "Books are friends. Come, let us read!"

Christine A. Jenkins

CONTENTS

CONTENTS

CONTENTS

PREFACE

In 1977 Margaret Meek, Aidan Warlow, and Griselda Barton assembled a collection of essays on children's and young adult literature entitled *The Cool Web*. The collection brought together the visions and voices of authors and scholars, blending classic pieces with new scholarship that would later become classics. Building on earlier understandings that "…writing and reading stories for children [is] an activity of creative significance which adults could take seriously" (p. 3), they took the argument further by bringing in the readers themselves. They asked: "What is the nature of the experience which gives a young reader a memory and a past not his [sic] own, or projects him into a future he might never have anticipated?" Furthermore they argued, "It is the responsibility of all those who play a part in teaching children to read to examine the nature of certain specific aspects of the reading experience, notably those concerned with narrative, story, or fiction" (p. 5).

In the decades following the publication of this groundbreaking book, research on children's and young adult literature and literary engagement has grown at exponential speed, but in the process branched off into a variety of fields. As a result, scholars often become isolated within a discipline. For example, scholars in English and literature tend toward a text-oriented approach that historically excluded the reader from view. Scholars in Education focus on the reader, but may well ignore the insights to be gained from the text being read. And scholars in Library and Information Science are often between intellectual worldviews of either end of the text–reader continuum, because their professional work is located precisely in the intersection between texts and young readers.

In the view of theorists Holland, Lachicotte, Skinner, and Cain (2003), the three fields we represent in this *Handbook of Research on Children's and Young Adult Literature* and the artifacts, practices, and relationships we construct operate as distinct "figured worlds." By figured worlds, Holland and her colleagues mean "…the socially and culturally constructed realm(s) of interpretation in which particular characters and actors are recognized, significance is assigned to certain acts, and particular outcomes are valued over others" (p. 52). We argue that the realms of interpretation for youth literature have, likewise, developed particular practices of reading, writing, and constructing audiences that carry accompanying values

for determining useful ways of describing and analyzing relations among readers, texts, and contexts.

We are interested in what is considered "normal" practice regarding the teaching of children's and young adult literature in our disciplines, how the book is transformed within and across different academic figurations of reading and interpreting children's literature. We ask, "What 'gets accomplished' and what is valued about books and readers from the locations of these different figurations of interpretation?" Thus, the purpose of this *Handbook* is to bring scholars representing all three disciplines to describe and analyze different aspects of literary reading, texts, and contexts.

For all of us the book is a central "pivot" (Holland et al., 2003, p. 61) through which it is possible for us to focus our conversations and examine what we know and how we know it. In general, we recognize the book as a place we can all turn to as we consider the changing forms, purposes, and social practices that accompany research and scholarship in children's literature. For example, we are all interested in award-winning books, but we differ in how, where, and with whom we value their inclusion in our scholarship. We argue that a view of our fields as figured worlds can help us begin to examine the continuities in our practices that create boundaries, as we also point to the edges and intersections that could be productively exploited for expanding our conversations—and the scholarship of children's and young adult literature.

In Part 1, we focus on the position of the reader, but in relation with changing forms of literature and contexts. As a way to understand the evolving meaning of reader and reading, we frame the meaning of childhood, adolescence, and reading in historical and contemporary contexts, describing ways youth read with adults and peers, both inside and outside school boundaries. Across this section, we engage the following questions: Where and how do young people become readers? How are youth and books defined and how are those definitions changing? In what ways can familial and institutional efforts influence or even boost access to and interest in literary reading? And how do youth, who recognize and celebrate their racialized and multilinguistic identities, move across different spaces to make sense of themselves as readers of literary texts? How do adults, in schools, libraries, and communities, assist youth in their efforts to reach out to new possibilities for themselves and others within the world?

Part 2 concentrates on the book, but again not in an effort to turn away from reader or context. Here we concentrate on literary criticism—various kinds, various genres, various sociopolitical lenses. Critical here will be the evolving nature of the literature—often to meet the needs of the changing reader and the changing view of what the reader wants and needs within a rapidly changing world. As Bruner (2005) explains: "We know all too clearly already that the world of the future will *not* be a stable and easily predictable one. It's such a world that we must have in mind in thinking about our pedagogy. How do we go about preparing a next generation for a world of expanding possibilities?" And this is certainly true of the kinds of books that children and young adults read to find sustenance and possible answers to their many questions while raising more questions in turn. To this end, these chapters, as well as a few in Part 3, feature the perspectives of tradebook authors and illustrators who describe what they perceive to be "points of departure" for new narrative and illustrative forms, new ways of including multimedia, and new topics.

Part 3 is devoted to the context and the larger world that surrounds the multiple connections among books and youth. How do books get into—or not get into—the hands and minds of youth? In what contexts do reader-book connections take place? Under what conditions do these connections flourish or languish? We'll acknowledge the critical translation of children's literature around the globe, the business of literature and the power of publishing houses and media, the grass roots and institutional connections with censorship, as well as the awards, review journals, websites, and museums that are devoted to the preservation and proliferation of literature. Children's and young adult books have multiple audiences that include not only young people and the adults around them, but also scholars who study the literature from an even wider range of research traditions.

Because the international scholars and tradebook authors and illustrators represented here come from widely diverse perspectives, we've asked them to raise arguments, contradictions, and questions—to trouble rather than settle issues in definitive ways. We've encouraged them to shift away from the isolation of normal practices within a discipline and up the ante on the theoretical possibilities that might result when knowledgeable people come together for good conversation. Most unique, perhaps, for a *Handbook of Research*, we've asked our authors to write from a combination of scholarly as well as personal perspectives. While some chose to remain more academic, others let us into the interior worlds of lives lived in books for the young.

Knowing that books can never lift off the page without readers, we ask *our* readers—scholars, teachers, librarians, parents, publishers, editors, and those on the verge of entering the field—to join the conversation, to raise your own arguments, contradictions, and questions, to look for personal reflections on your own life lived or about to be lived with youth and their books. Though we have carefully ordered the chapters in the sequence that made the most sense to us, we hope that as readers, you will move around the text as you will. To aid in this process and following the lead of Meek and colleagues (1977) in *The Cool Web,* we have provided introductions for each chapter—brief insights into the sights and sounds of particular arguments. We've set a course, but hope you will navigate your own way, stopping first perhaps at favorite places of interest, but then hopefully moving to other ports that may offer tantalizing ways to widen your own perspective.

For far too long the fields of English, Library and Information Science, and Education have pushed ahead in their various directions—exploring theoretical ideas, conducting wide-ranging research, writing books and articles, and attending conferences within our separate figured worlds. We've rarely journeyed out of the small spaces of our own circles. It is our hope that this *Handbook of Research on Children's and Young Adult Literature* will enable our colleagues across disciplines to redraw the map of our separately figured worlds so we may enlarge the scope of our scholarship and dialogue as well as push ahead into uncharted waters.

References

Bruner, J. (2005, October). *Aiming for the future: Cultivating a sense of the possible.* Presentation for the annual meeting of the National Academy of Education. New York: Teachers College.

Holland, D., Lachicotte, W., Skinner, D., & Cain, C. (2003). *Identity and agency in cultural worlds.* Cambridge, MA: Harvard University Press.

Meek, M., Warlow, A., & Barton, G. (Eds.). (1977). *The cool web: The pattern of children's reading.* London: The Bodley Head.

Part I

THE READER

The book may be at rest when found on a shelf, in an adult's hands, at home, or in a classroom, but young readers are on the move and they often pull the book out of its stillness into a whirl of play, voices, media, and memories. The image of the silent, isolated child-reader has dominated reading theories and pedagogies over the centuries, but as scholars show across this section on The Reader, that idyll was wholly constructed from the presumption that words on a page can exist only in the mind.

Along with the silent reader, another image usually springs to mind of a Madonna-like mother and child, at rest, leaning in toward a book. Such images have been popularized today by the "Read to your bunny" campaign, spearheaded by author and illustrator Rosemary Wells. A parallel campaign, aimed at young adolescents, featuring celebrity athletes and film stars happily looking up from their favorite novel, suggests that the child will grow beyond the reach of home and need a more peer-oriented, popular base for motivating a love of books. In fact, never mind the poster campaigns, publishers have already learned that "book trailers," styled after film trailers, can take the book to where many youth spend a great deal of time—on Youtube and social media internet sites.

The reader is moving, and educators, researchers, and publishers are in a hurry to catch up. But a single perspective on how reading should be experienced and what it should look like will be inadequate for understanding the histories, thought processes, and social relationships that inform all that makes reading an integral part of youth experience. The truth is, reading is as much a social, political, and embodied experience as it is cognitive and critical. Cognitive views on reading rely on the belief that the mind is schematically organized and seeks reason and form, while social, cultural, and political theories understand reading as an effort, and often a struggle, to establish one's vision and experiences as meaningful and valued. From both theoretical angles, the reader is active; but each has a different orientation to the person—the fully embodied and social being—who is interpreted along with the book.

Many teachers and educational researchers look to young people and their social worlds to understand what connects them to reading; but as national policies impose more restrictions on extensive literary reading and focus increasingly on testing outcomes, they often worry most about, and organize research and interventions around, the cognitive domains of reading (e.g., word identification, comprehension skills, fluency). So where does that leave younger readers who are subject to an ever-widening range of theories, practices, and policies—what Foucault (1988) would describe as "technologies of reading"?

For some, their school and public libraries remain the single most important places for them to discover a favorite author, picturebooks, nonfiction literature, and glorious shelves full of graphic novels and manga. For others, no book found in school has yet told their stories, so literary worlds become available in places that innovative and activist teachers create with youth: like the reading club at a community center for LGBTQ (Lesbian, Gay, Bisexual, Transgender, & Questioning) teens, young adults, and allies; or a class of first generation immigrant teachers who find the poetry and literary legacy of the Puerto Rican diaspora in the online archives of El Centro; and the second generation Filipino fifth graders in Los Angeles, who return to their family's oral narratives of migration and education to reconstruct a story of dignity for themselves and their classmates.

Vital places for reading, whether in community centers, online, or in classrooms, are usually structured by an emphasis on emergent understanding over finalized, predetermined meaning. Social psychologist, Lev Vygotsky (1987) suggested that two forms of sense-making are important to learning: the first, translated as "sense," can be understood as a storm cloud of thought and the second as "meaning" or what eventually becomes represented as a stable and unified idea or concept (Smagorinsky, 2001, p. 145). Given opportunities to engage in what Ricoeur (1983) calls "configurational acts" of reading, sense and meaning combine to create a composite understanding, distributed among readers that situates some of what is known about a story as changeable across circumstances, times, and people (sense), and other ideas about the story as articulated and held relatively constant (meaning).

Much of the pleasure and challenge of reading literature lies in finding out what sense and meanings can be made of another world, how that world intersects with one's own and others' worlds, and how it might be possible to think and move as someone in that world. These are exploratory, inquiry-oriented questions that rely on readers' willingness to risk being simultaneously engaged with their own life's memories and sensations, and "outside themselves," bringing their feelings to others' lives and to a temporary, imagined self.

An individual reader might find this configurational experience wholly enjoyable and engaging, but in a group situation, where diverse and differentially valued identities are also in play, many young people learn that unless they offer the predetermined meanings of a traditional literary analysis or go along with the prevailing valences of power and popularity in classroom interaction, they really have nothing to add to a discussion of literature. Reading experiences, even when they are supposed to be open to discussion, can become, again, isolating and exclusive instead of widening readers' approaches to sense and meaning. And even among those students whose voices are most often heard, the literature often becomes a site for rehearsing and reproducing dominant social norms and values rather than a forum for questioning assumptions or social status.

Too often, reading and literature education are restricted by finalized meanings that leave teachers and students on the outside of literary worlds, moving across words instead of through them; and missing altogether the many narratives and ways of viewing the world that youth bring to a story. Indeed, such narratives are not all that may be silenced. Eva-Maria Simms (Chapter 2) points out that although reading produces a wider net for understanding and imagining experiences, it also carries with it the loss of genuine interest we feel through our embodied experience of intense conversation and oral storytelling. When

reading and readers are regulated by implicit and sometimes explicit beliefs about what and how a reader should sound, sit, move, and even look, such losses multiply and categories of deficiency, illiteracy, and "at risk" become a taken for granted part of life with books.

Perhaps it is not surprising to find, then, that the most promising responses to disengagement in reading are those pedagogies that get everyone moving again—through image-making, dramatization, film-making, social advocacy, and creative writing. The "lived through experience" of a story as Louise Rosenblatt (1978) described it, does not have to be created alone. Stories were shared, enacted, and remembered long before they were written down; in part because a good story, well told and well acted, will hold an audience of peers over hours as they collectively step out of "here and now" and create "if." When a story becomes shared again through drawing, or as an enacted exchange between characters, it is possible to look together at the ways one moment holds many stories, raises questions, makes us feel, and makes us want to examine what we thought was true.

As several chapters on secondary students' reading and writing show, the pleasure of making stories has been revived with gusto, but not necessarily in school settings. While "disciplinary discourses" (Lewis & Dockter, Chapter 6) in contemporary classrooms reproduce the same reading lists, assignments, and forms of analysis instituted some 50 years ago, young people are moving to online spaces, where they can freely access the stories they care about and create their own book reviews, blogs, and fanfictions (Dutro & McKiver, Chapter 7). The question of equity and access, however, makes such creative endeavors online a mirror of the economics of literacy associated with early 17th- to late 19th-century homeplaces, where parents with economic resources were able to foster their youngsters' literary sensibilities with books, paper, art materials, and games. Those children creatively remade and invented new stories as they enjoyed the comforts of their familiar surroundings. They could run with stories.

Today, the pleasure of moving into and through stories is afforded to those young people whose adult caregivers, teachers, and communities recognize and support the inventiveness of youth narratives, whether these are in the form of digital videos, theatrical performances, or poetry slams. Those youth might also travel with their stories across the global economy of digital media. But other children, whose literary and digital experiences are more limited by availability or shortsighted use of media and literature, are not simply "out of the game" because of economic disparities; they, too, should have every opportunity to shake a story from its stillness, whether that story was made by their friend, an author, or their grandparent, and move it—out loud, in action, through images, and rhythm—into a place that invites them to shape life with others.

References

Foucault, M. (1988). Technologies of the self. In L. H. Martin, H. Gutman, & P. H. Hutton (Eds.), *Technologies of the self: A seminar with Michel Foucault* (pp. 16–49). Amherst, MA: University of Massachusetts Press.

Ricoeur, P. (1983). *Time and narrative* (Vol. 1; K. McLaughlin & D. Pellauer, Trans.). Chicago, IL: University of Chicago Press.

Rosenblatt, L. M. (1978). *The reader, the text, the poem: The transactional theory of the literary work.* Carbondale, IL: Southern Illinois University Press.

Smagorinsky, P. (2001). If meaning is constructed, what is it made from? Toward a cultural theory of reading. *Review of Educational Research, 71*(1), 133–169.

Vygotsky, L. S. (1987). "Lectures on psychology." In *The collected works of L.S. Vygotsky. Vol 1. Problems of general psychology* (pp. 339–349). New York, NY: Plenum.

I

Children Reading at Home

An Historical Overview

Evelyn Arizpe and Morag Styles

University of Glasgow and University of Cambridge

Evelyn Arizpe and Morag Styles, well known for their work together over the years, provide an historical account of parent/child reading. From a framework of connections, creativity, and critique, they demonstrate the similarities and differences in children reading at home over time—both children of privilege and those who had a hard time finding any books at all. The authors begin with their high adventure and close scholarly detective work in unveiling the reading lives of Jane Johnson and her family, and they end their chapter with modern day parents moving with their children into 21st century technologies. From "reading cards" to digital books, Arizpe and Styles offer us an insider's view into the reading patterns in homes across the centuries.

...the ephemera of childhood...reside almost entirely in memory. Blocks, card sets, small chips and game parts, pictures torn or cut from magazines...lose their value and are thrown out. But what might such ephemera tell us of what went on in the nursery, before the hearth, or in the corner of rooms where children were sent to be entertained or to entertain themselves. (Heath, 1997, p. 17)

Though the ephemera are often missing, other sources sometimes lead us into understanding of the relationship between children and books. For example, an essay by Robert Louis Stevenson (1992) drew attention to the Scottish poet Robert Burns's home-schooled education and the influence of his father on his reading. Although a poor man, William Burns took pains to educate his children by borrowing books for them "and he felt it his duty to supplement (their knowledge of theology) by a dialogue of his own composition, where his own private shade of orthodoxy was exactly represented." Stevenson wrote: "Such was the influence of this good and wise man that his household became a school to itself, and neighbours who came into the farm at mealtime would find the whole family, father, brothers, and sisters, helping themselves with one hand, and holding a book in the other" (p. 89).

This chapter seeks to celebrate, understand, and cast some light on other such enlightened parents as well as the practices of children's home reading between the 18th and the 21st centuries. Given the enormity of the field, we have had to be selective in the accounts discussed here. However, we were guided by the fact that there are relatively few longitudinal studies of children's development as readers, particularly before the 20th century. We were greatly helped by secondary sources such as biographies and histories of reading and literacy. Our primary sources included personal journals, letters, autobiographies, and other published texts; in some cases, there were also artifacts, such as drawings or teaching materials.

Given the sketchy and uneven corpus of research, we have tried to provide some structure by organizing accounts in terms of particular families for whom there exists more information, usually parents teaching their own children to read or encouraging, supervising, and observing children's early reading in the home context. However, we have also included some more individualistic accounts, particularly from selected writers in the 19th century, drawing on their early reading autobiographies and recollections of their own childhoods. The accounts from the 18th and 19th centuries have been patched together, some pieces larger and more colourful than others, some rather threadbare, but together providing a strong enough pattern to allow us to imagine what reading in the home was like for some families in the past. Accounts from the 20th century are easier to find with parent observers offering the most structured and detailed descriptions of their children's early reading, which is why we have given them a large section of this chapter.

While we do touch on schooling, our emphasis remains on childhood reading in the home. Inevitably, those who have taken the time and trouble to both educate their children at home and to document the process have been those who were economically and educationally advantaged. That means that most of our evidence is middle class in origin. We know, however, from Spufford's (1985) pioneering work on 17th century literacy, as well as the research of other historians and sociologists, that domestic literacy also went on in impoverished households, and we are keen to tell their stories, too. For example, there are fascinating accounts of the early reading experiences of working-class people in the home, but these tend to be less detailed and comprehensive than those we have consulted elsewhere.

The writers of this chapter have to own up to both the Anglocentric scope of this study and giving most space to British evidence. While wishing to offer an international outlook, to do justice to such wide scope would be hard to achieve in a single chapter. We also know the research coming from the UK much more intimately than elsewhere. We have, therefore, compromised by providing an account that includes data that was relatively easy to obtain from North America, Australia, New Zealand, and some parts of Europe, while concentrating on the UK. It is also important to bear in mind that not only do other cultures have different views on reading practices and the value of early literacy (e.g., Schieffelin & Cochran-Smith, 1984), but also that wide differences can occur within neighbouring communities in western societies, as Heath's (1983) seminal research has shown.[1] What follows is fairly typical of the history of domestic literacy in western countries elsewhere, and we hope that it will provide food for thought in considering reading in the home in other cultures as well.

Connections, Creativity, and Criticism

In their fascinating study, *The Braid of Literature,* Shelby Wolf and Shirley Brice Heath (1992) select three key characteristics shared by Wolf's daughters who had been closely observed reading in the home by their mother: connections, creativity, and criticism. The notion of *connections* was mainly concerned with the text-to-life associations spontaneously made by the young readers. The links that these readers spontaneously make reveal the deep impact of reading—almost like a lens through which we view our own lives, allowing us to reflect on our experiences and thereby deepen our enjoyment and our learning. An important part of *creativity* refers to the performative aspects of reading (using voice, gesture and movement), which were borne out again and again in our research as adults recalled their own or their children's fascination with storytelling, role playing, and toy theatres or puppets. However, our understanding of creativity also includes all the created "artifacts" related to play and learning that stem from reading, much of the "ephemera" which Heath refers to in the quotation that opens this chapter—a spontaneous re-working of narrative, characters, and language into other media, such as writing, drawing, artwork and, more recently, computer-generated images. Finally, *criticism* refers to the evaluative responses of children to the texts they read; indeed, we would question whether children are actually reading if there is not, in Dorothy Butler and Marie Clay's (1979) words, communication "between one mind and another" (p. 5). We believe that Wolf and Heath (1992) have not only identified some of the most important aspects of what it means to read, but also those features that young readers themselves think important. Therefore, in this chapter, we attempt to trace connections, creativity, and criticism throughout the accounts we have found of children reading in the home across three centuries.

Family Case Studies from the 18th Century

> She has a little Compendium of Greek & Roman History in her Head; & Johnson says her Cadence, Variety and choice of Tones in reading Verse are surpassed by nobody, not even Garrick himself. it was Pope's Ode to Musick that she read to him. (Hester Thrale Piozzi, cited in Hyde, 1977, p. 40, on her daughter Queeney, age six)

In this section, we discuss some early case studies of domestic literacy where either the mother or father took a special interest in the domestic education of their children and where there is enough data on which to draw. Apart from the special case of Jane Johnson, about whom the authors have a particular interest and for whom extensive archival material is available, each of these families has at least one person in it who is a published author; often there is more than one. We focus, therefore, on *family* portraits of reading in the homes of the Johnsons, the Mathers, Richardsons, Thrales, Edgeworths and, finally, the Taylors who take us into the first decade of the 19th century. While it can be argued that these were rather exceptional families (for different reasons), it is also true that they reflected the thinking of their time about the teaching of reading and in some cases, were themselves influential in developing reading practices in the home.

We start with a brief introduction to each of these families and then proceed to discuss the patterns that cut across them, such as the reading environment of the home, everyday literacy practices, and the books and other texts that were available, as well as broadly considering the notions of connections, creativity, and critique. Although we may not have much evidence of children's responses to books and methods of teaching, or even know whether they enjoyed the activities provided for them or became accomplished readers, the details that can be gleaned from these historical cases do provide some basis for a general description of the literacy teaching that was going on in homes in both England and the United States in the 18th century.

The Families

Our first historical case study has to be that of Jane Johnson (1706–1759) and her children, and in this account we will continue to refer to her by her first and second name in order to avoid confusion with Samuel Johnson who is mentioned below. As far as we know, it is the earliest and richest archive on domestic literacy in the 18th century and the authors' in-depth research has shown it is invaluable for understanding home reading during this period. Jane Johnson was a well read and pious woman, a "genteel lady," married to the clergyman, Woolsey Johnson who lived in Olney, in Buckinghamshire and later in Witham-on-the-Hill, in Lincolnshire.

As well as the Nursery Library, which contains the reading materials she made for her children, there are many other noteworthy documents in this archive, including a story she wrote for her children in 1744, "A Very Pretty Story" (2001) and family letters and journals. We will highlight the most relevant findings from this nursery library, but because we cannot do justice to this extraordinary archive in a couple of paragraphs, we refer the reader to *Reading Lessons from the Eighteenth Century* (Arizpe & Styles, 2006) and to the Lilly Library website.[2]

Of all the case studies in this section, Jane Johnson's is the only one that specifically points to methods for teaching reading. Letters reveal that Johnson not only taught her own children to read as soon as they could talk, but that she greatly enjoyed doing so and approached her task through a mixture of methods. As well as reading

and writing, "classifying, observing, and reflecting in the pursuit of understanding mathematics, botany, zoology, philosophy, and theology" (Heath, in Arizpe & Styles, 2006, p. 204) were part of Jane Johnson's curriculum for her children, all of which contributed to their becoming highly literate adults.

Slightly earlier than Jane Johnson is the case of Cotton Mather (1663–1728) and his family. Better known for his numerous sermons and other religious works, this Puritan minister in Boston was intensely interested in the education of his children. Although he had sixteen children, only two of them survived him; one of them, Samuel, was born in 1706, the same year as Jane Johnson. Mather's diaries, covering about 21 years of his life, provide a detailed description of both his methods for teaching reading and writing and his reflections on those methods. E. Jennifer Monaghan's study (1991) of his diaries examines these as well as the general literacy activities, which involved all family members, including the family's three slaves.

Although we do not know how his children learned to read, Mather had a clear idea of his role as instructor: giving specific assignments, modelling ways to comprehend text, and constructing "bridges between life, language and literacy" (Monaghan, 1991, p. 364). Even though he quite clearly directed their learning, Mather also allowed the children some choice and self-expression. We do not know what his children thought of his methods, but the few glimpses there are of those who survived to adulthood show that they also believed in the importance of reading and writing. Mather's case provides evidence of how connections, critique and, to the extent permitted by the religious context, some limited creativity were present in this family of readers and writers.

One of the most popular authors in Jane Johnson's generation and beyond was Samuel Richardson (1689–1761). Richardson's work as a writer and publisher, as well as his interest in pedagogy and children's reading (he composed a version of *Aesop's Fables* in 1740) must have influenced his own daughters' education. Naomi Tadmor (1996) draws on Richardson's correspondence to build up a picture of reading activities in his household that had religious and moral, as well as social, purposes.

A close friend of many writers of her day, Hester Thrale (later Piozzi, 1741–1821) started keeping a journal of her children's progress, originally called "The Children's Book," in 1766 when her first child, Hester Maria Thrale (known as Queeney) was two years old. It is likely that she was encouraged to keep this record of her children's progress by Dr. Samuel Johnson whom she met in 1765 and who soon became a keen family friend as well as tutor to Queeney. Mrs. Thrale's journal was kept over 13 years (sometimes with long gaps between entries) as she produced 10 more children. As she also recounted happenings of other family members, the name of the book was changed to the "Family Book" in due course.

While Queeney's intellect seems to have thrived in

the hothouse atmosphere created for her, the demanding educational expectations of her mother and her lack of sympathy with Queeney as a person clearly made the child most unhappy. This reminds us how much of the domestic literacy project is affective and contrasts keenly with Jane Johnson's approach to teaching her children where her interest in educating the child in the widest sense is evident and the word "love" predominates. There were few text-to-life connections made for poor Queeney in her rigorous educational schedule. Feats of memory seemed to be valued more than understanding, while creative aspects of learning and critical reading were not encouraged.

The Edgeworths were another exceptionally literate family whose practices are well documented and were made public through the writing of two of its most famous members: Richard Lovell Edgeworth (1744–1817) and his daughter, Maria Edgeworth (1768–1849). His four marriages resulted in 22 children with nearly 50 years between the birth of his first son in 1764 and his last son in 1812. Maria was the second eldest and, although she never married or had children of her own, through her siblings she had vast experience of children, which she drew on in writing textbooks with her father and in her own stories.

Edgeworth's initial project was to find a method for learning to read, but it soon went beyond this and he and his second wife, Honora, conceived a plan to teach scientific and technical knowledge as well as morality through stories for children. In a sense, they are a case of parent-observers, trying out their lessons on real children, which other educational thinkers of the period did not do and registering their reactions to new knowledge and experiences. In this way, they would gather empirical evidence to support their methods, thus "making education an experimental science" (Maria Edgeworth, quoted in Butler, 1972, p. 65). Perhaps for the first time, the actual responses of children—albeit not to imaginative literature but to didactic texts—was being taken into account. As Maria grew up and after the death of Honora, she and her father began to work as partners in this educational enterprise.

Another outstanding family were the Taylors of Essex and Suffolk that, like the Edgeworths, was busy with reading, writing, and educating children (Davidoff & Hall, 1987). Isaac Taylor (1759–1824) came from a family of goldsmiths who were "steeped in a literate, religious milieu" (p. 61). He married Ann Martin and they settled with their growing family in Lavenham, Suffolk, where their "two eldest bright and uninhibited little girls were much admired. The family had little capital but education, skill, and a formidable energy fuelled by active religion that centred on raising their children and enlightening their community" (p. 61). Later they moved to Colchester, Essex, where there were always apprentices and pupils living in the house alongside the family. The daughters of the family, Ann (1782–1866) and Jane Taylor (1783–1824), are now remembered for their poetry for children published in the first decade of the 19th century.

Literate Environments

There is evidence that in all these households, reading and writing were regular practices throughout the day and that these involved, to different extents, the aspects of creativity, connections, and critique. In the Mather family, reading aloud was part of the daily routine, from the reading of Scripture during morning and evening prayers to lessons and the reading of what the father deemed suitable devotional books before bedtime. Monaghan (1991) provides details from Mather's diaries, which show how literacy was a communal activity, and fostered interactions between Mather and his wife and children, but also among siblings as they read to each other. In the Richardson household, reading also took place at various times during the day, beginning before breakfast with Mrs. Richardson reading aloud from the Psalms and after breakfast, when she heard her daughters reading their lessons for the day. In the evenings, reading was often combined with other activities such as needlework or drawing (Tadmor, 1996). Children in the house would therefore be listening to a variety of texts during the day and in the evening—from magazines and plays, to Milton, Locke, and Richardson himself. We have speculated that conversation would probably have followed reading, thus allowing for making connections between texts and life, the moral and the literary.

Marilyn Butler (1972) describes a similar scene in the Edgeworth household in her detailed biography of Maria Edgeworth:

> At certain times of day—after breakfast, for example, and in the evening—the family gathered around the library table. The children were offered books to read (adult books, necessarily) on any desired subject—history, biography, travels, literature, or science. Short passages that were considered to be within a particular child's comprehension had already been marked for him [sic]. When the child had read the passage, the adult teaching him would go carefully over the sense of it, word-by-word and idea-by-idea. The atmosphere at these sessions was pleasant, and the child was encouraged to ask questions.... Intellectual work from breakfast time until the family went to bed was executed in the communal situation, and accompanied by the hubbub of questions and answers, or the steady flow of reading aloud. (p. 99)

One gets a slightly different impression from Mrs. Thrale's diary. She had been a prodigious scholar herself and she expected great things of Queeney, so she carefully supervised what would now be considered a taxing curriculum for a pre-school child. Although there must have been a great deal of reading and writing going on in this household, there is less of a sense of it being done as a communal activity and more as direct instruction in subjects such as geography and mathematics. At the age of barely three, her mother described Queeney as a "miserable poor Speller & can scarce read a word" (Hyde, 1977, p. 26), a comment that suggests the learning environment was neither relaxed nor entertaining for the children.

On the other hand, the description of the Taylors again stresses the familial literate atmosphere. As well as taking up the ministry and working hard at engraving, Isaac Taylor also managed to write books of travel, nature, and advice for young men, and produced learning aids such as flash cards with anatomical drawings to be coloured in. Even so, Isaac spent time with his children "at meal times, for lessons, in the workroom, on daily walks or special excursions, family evenings and amateur theatricals" (Davidoff & Hall, 1987, p. 61). The children also enjoyed the companionship of their mother who regularly read aloud at meal times. After raising a large family, Ann turned author in middle age writing popular books on domestic life. As the literary essayist, E. V. Lucas (1905), suggested, "It was practically inevitable that Ann and Jane Taylor were to write, for writing was in the blood" (p. v).

Books and Other Texts

We don't have a description of daily reading practices in Jane Johnson's family, but judging from the existence of the extensive hand-made reading materials and the books we know she was reading, it is likely that literacy events would have permeated this household as well. It was probably during the 1740s that Jane Johnson created her extraordinary "nursery library" for her four children: Barbara (1738), George (1740), Robert (1745), and Charles (1748). This library comprises more than four hundred "reading cards", most of them decorated with "scraps" painstakingly cut out of lottery sheets and coloured in by hand and then framed with Dutch floral paper. Some of them also have a threaded cord on the top probably in order to hang around the nursery. She also made a couple of little books that in the manner of primers of the day, included letters, simple words, and short sentences. Given that Jane Johnson used some of the material from published primers, we can assume that some of these were also available in this household.

It is probable that other mothers would have created similar artifacts for teaching their children to read because they were encouraged to do so by some of the pedagogues fashionable at the time, such as John Locke and Charles Rollin. Mrs. Thrale, for example, made her daughter a "little book" in 1766. Yet, Richard Edgeworth was dismissive of the books and primers available at the time except for Anna Laetitia Barbauld's *Lessons for Children from Two to Three Years Old,* which he liked for its simplicity, clarity, and familiar settings (Butler, 1972, p. 61). Following this method, two of his daughters apparently learned to read in six weeks, and this led Edgeworth to begin to formulate his own theories on the subject.

He was influenced not only by the Lunar society's notions on scientific inquiry, but also by the very early ideas on educational psychology. He proposed that texts for children must be pleasing and therefore founded on children's natural preferences for stories. Although the children did read some books by the new generation of women writers such as Mrs. Trimmer's *Fabulous Histories*, Edgeworth did not find them intellectual enough for his children, so he and Maria set out writing their own stories for them as well as for cousins and other family friends.

Performance, the Visual Image, and Other Creative Activities

In the case of the Thrale family, performance mainly took the form of recitation in front of adults as a way of displaying the child's prodigious learning. Nor was Queeney the only prodigy in this family as Mrs Thrale recounted how her son, Henry, then four years old, "reads the Psalms quite smartly, seldom stopping to spell his Way; can repeat the Grammar to the end of the Genders…& reads vastly better than his sister did" (Hyde, 1977, p. 45).

Fortunately, Jane Johnson's nursery library provides richer evidence of creative performance. Wolf and Heath (1992) distinguish between the creativity of moving from text to performance and the making of artifacts involving visual images; there are indications of both in some of the households in this section. Jane's nursery library was clearly intended not only for learning to read, but also for developing the genteel arts of conversation and performance. It is almost certain that this was extended to the reading aloud and enactment of some of these texts which would have involved gestures and other dramatic expressions, and the use of voice from the hushed rhythm of a lullaby to exclamations. Heath (in Arizpe & Styles, 2006) shows that the "play" in many of Johnson's texts is influenced by the public stage in the use of postures, expressions, and backdrops.

One of the many notable aspects of the Jane Johnson Nursery Library is the use of visuals, particularly the images on the cards. The cut-outs, which beautifully illustrate the cards, are not only eye-catching but are also full of potential for discussion and storytelling as they can be related either to the text or to other stories. Jane was aware of the importance of images in teaching reading, but was also using them to foster aesthetic awareness and creativity, which included drawing, painting, writing, and the careful construction of little books and paper games.

Text-to-Life Connections, Intertextuality, and Critique

Just as Wolf and Heath (1992) found in their portrait of modern young readers who made connections between their lives and what they read, the Jane Johnson archive reveals that there were many connections for the children to make as they read and played their way through their nursery library. The materials are distinctive in that they reflect everyday conversational language and also their inclusion of ordinary familiar experiences. The texts sometimes include the names of the Johnson children themselves and refer to particular events in the household. The inclusion of familiar stories and jokes, games, street-cries, and names of people the family knew encouraged connections between life and text and resulted in material that was more interesting and amusing for the children—and it made religious and moral topics more accessible as well. The children would also be able to recognize intertextual references, particularly to the Bible, but also to Aesop's fables, nursery rhymes, and chapbook tales.

The aspect of critique is also apparent in this archive. As her commonplace book shows, Jane Johnson herself could be very critical of other texts and given the nature of the narratives and images from the Nursery Library, we can assume that she encouraged her children to talk and write about the texts, ask questions, and express their opinions. The correspondence and journals that the Johnson siblings maintained throughout their lifetimes reveal them to have become critical and intelligent readers as well as can be seen in their frequent comments on books or poems which they recommended (or not) to each other. Their writing reveals a similar use of wit, humor, and irony to that which appears in both the personal and the didactic texts their mother wrote.

Although Mather's belief that "improving in Reading" meant "improving in Goodness" is similar to that of Jane Johnson, reading in his household seems to have been more limited to strictly religious material. However, he often assigned his children books or compositions that he considered were particularly relevant to their situation (for example, to deal with bereavement). Mather also encouraged his children to comprehend and reflect on their reading; in his case, he commented on the verses or passages, turning them into prayers or writing about them. Even when his children were at school, he continued with his own educational program and encouraged them to write their own prayers as well as "agreeable and valuable Things" in the equivalent of a commonplace book. He provided them with material from both devotional and scientific texts to copy but also encouraged them to transcribe passages that had "most affected" them.

While his motivation was different to that of Jane Johnson and Mather, Richard Edgeworth also proposed that children should be capable of understanding the experiences of the characters in the story and relating them to his or her own experience:

> So long as the child responded to what he met in his reading, he would himself, by the associative process of the human mind, combine that experience with an infinitely proliferating number of fresh impressions. He would relate the significantly chosen single instance to analogous cases: intellectually and imaginatively, what he read would become part of him. (Butler, 1972, pp. 62–63)

As we arrive at the end of the 18th century, we see that even though changing views of childhood and pedagogy led to variations in the way teaching occurred at home, those three aspects of reading—connections, creativity and critique—are still interwoven through the accounts from the 19th century.

Individual Accounts of Becoming Readers at Home in the 19th Century

> It gives my grandchildren so much pleasure to look at pictures and hear me tell stories about them; how natural therefore that I should go on to paste loose pictures, with appropriate texts, on to sheets of paper, either in the form of a letter, or like a book. (Adolph Drewsen, cited in Dal, 1984, n.p.)

By the beginning of the 19th century, efforts to create a literate population were evident in the Sunday School movement in England and the development of church schools from various religious groups that taught thousands of children to read and write. The rationale behind universal literacy was less founded on notions of equality of opportunity than the need for an educated workforce and the fear of their radicalization. In England the government established a national system of compulsory education for children between the ages of five and eleven in 1870. A similar growth of educational institutions occurred in Europe and the United States where schools were established for girls and women, for African Americans, and for aspiring teachers. By the late 19th century, the widespread belief in the power of education to mold individual character and improve human life was evident. Parents were encouraged to send their children to the professionals to be educated and to use commercial methods and textbooks rather than teach them at home.

Changes in technology and printing also influenced the materials that were available in the home. The beginning of the 19th century saw a growth of interest in print and a series of new inventions which enabled the printing process to operate more rapidly and efficiently, mainly through the application of steam-power to printing presses, which also made longer print-runs possible. This meant that all manner of commercial printing (newspapers, magazines, pamphlets, chapbooks, and broadsides) could reach a larger audience. Techniques for making and reproducing illustration also improved and added to the appeal of printed materials through finer and, in some cases, colored images. Even poorer families would have had the opportunity to acquire some of this printed material, thus increasing the opportunities for children becoming literate from an earlier age.

Writers as Young Readers

Detailed accounts of domestic literacy seem to be thin on the ground in the 19th century in comparison to what came before and after. However, there are rich pickings on reading in the home when one examines the memoirs, autobiographies, and accounts of authors' early lives.

"A verra takkin' (appealing) laddie, but ill (difficult) to guide" (Eisler, 1999, p. 22) was the astute verdict on George Gordon Byron (1788–1824) by his Scottish relatives. Byron spent his early years living above a shop in Aberdeen, a stubborn, fearless, "holy terror"! As a little boy, Byron was subject to a beloved and devout scripture-quoting nurse who "introduced him to the beauty of biblical language" (Longford, 1976, p. 6). His fellow Scot, Robert Louis Stevenson (1850–94), "suffered" the same advantage, and both were without siblings. We know something of Stevenson's interest in reading from his letters, essays, and his poems of childhood, *A Child's Garden of Verses* (1885). His formal education was extremely patchy—most of what he learned was at home from books.

John Clare (1793–1864) was a farm labourer who became one of the finest Romantic poets. He enjoyed a brief publishing success but finished his life in poverty, indeed, in a lunatic asylum. Clare's poetry was inspired by the countryside around him, but he did write about his early reading experiences for his publisher, John Taylor, on which we draw.

Charles Dickens (1812–70) wrote constantly about children, childhood, and schooling in fiction mainly aimed at adults. Dickens enjoyed little conventional schooling himself; when he was still a youngster, his father went into prison for debt and the young Charles was sent to work at a blacking factory for about a year. Dickens was outraged both at having to endure such treatment *and* being denied an education.

We could have provided many examples from Europe, but we will only mention one, known not only as a writer but also as a storyteller, performer, and creator of extraordinary paper cuts. Among the few factual details that Hans Christian Andersen (1805–1875) provides in his autobiography is that his father was fond of reading and among the books he owned were the *Bible*, Ludwig Holberg's comedies, and the *Arabian Nights*. Andersen went to school near his home in Odense around the age of five, having already been taught to read in the infant school and, like all the authors mentioned above, he soon developed into a voracious reader.

Charlotte Bronte (1816–1855) and her highly gifted siblings spent much of their lives isolated from wider society, partly because of the remoteness of where they lived, partly because their mother died young, and partly because their eccentric clergyman father was a loner largely leaving the children to their own devices. Another talented, highly literate family about which there is copious information are the Rossettis; the children (Maria, Gabriele, William, and Christina (1830–94) were quick to learn to read and soon became devoted to books. This is unsurprising as they were brought up in an affectionate, demonstrative, bookish Italian/English bilingual family. Three of the four children went on to become gifted writers.

Reading the Word and the World

Examples of writers using reading to reflect on their own lives and connect themselves sympathetically to wider humanity are legion. Books gave these children what they needed to develop wide knowledge of the world; imagina-

tion, tenacity, and natural talent did the rest. Indeed, Byron had most of the books of the Bible under his belt before he was eight, preferring the drama of the Old Testament "for the New struck me as a task, but the other a pleasure" (Eisler, 1999, p. 26). During Aberdeen's freezing, wind-lashed winters, the *Arabian Nights* offered escape into desert tents and palace harems. At the very end of his life Byron remembered Knolle's *Turkish History* as "one of the first books that gave me pleasure as a child; and I believe it…gave, perhaps, the oriental colouring which is observed in my poetry" (p. 26).

Byron and his mother were both avid readers, she a devourer of newspapers, periodicals, and novels and a passionate believer in the French revolution. As Eisler (1999) put it, "Byron literally learned his republican sympathies at his mother's knee" (p. 26). He probably picked up her reading habit, too. Later in life, he boasted that he had read four thousand works of fiction including Smollett and Scott before he was 10 years old. Clare, too, educated himself through reading; and although he is reputed to have said that he would rather have written *Babes in the Wood* than *Paradise Lost,* he certainly read Milton, Chaucer, Pope, Cowper, and Defoe as well as contemporary poets like Byron and Keats.

The adult neglect of the Bronte children, combined with the fact that their father was a scholar and shared his library with his offspring, led to precocious juvenile reading and writing on their behalf. There is clear evidence that the children's eclectic childhood reading included Aesop's fables, Shakespeare, Milton, Scott, Byron, plenty of history, periodicals, annuals, works of art, and Blackwood's magazine: "Maria read the newspapers, and reported intelligently to her younger sisters….But I suspect that they had no children's books and that their eager minds browsed undisturbed among the wholesome pasturage of English literature" (Gaskell, 1975, p. 93).

According to a contemporary, Mary Weller, Dickens was also "a terrible child to read" (Slater, 2007, p. 4):

> He constantly read and reread the books in his father's little library—the 18th C essayists, *Robinson Crusoe, The Vicar of Wakefield, Don Quixote,* the works of Fielding and Smollett, and other novels and stories…. These books became fundamental to his imaginative world, as is clearly attested by the innumerable quotations from, and allusions to, them in all his writings. (Langton, 1891, pp. 5–6)

Stevenson was another autodidact whose early education was provided by his nurse, Alison Cunningham, to whom *A Child's Garden of Verses* is dedicated. Although she looked after young Stevenson devotedly, Frank McLynn (1993) describes her as a religious maniac filling the child's head with terrifying stories: "When he was still an impressionable infant she read the entire Bible to him three or four times…Foxe's *Book of Martyrs* and from *Pilgrim's Progress*. Worst of all, she told stories…in which hell-fire and the noonday demon seeking all whom he could devour were living realities" (pp. 14–15).

Storytelling and Performance

The performative and creative side of reading was highly advanced in most of our chosen authors. Calder (1990) shows how Stevenson's writing, which came early, "went hand-in-hand with an addiction to stories and dramatising" (p. 8). Stevenson (1992) wrote, "Men are born with various mania: from my earliest childhood it was mine to make a plaything of imaginary series of events; and as soon as I was able to write, I became a good friend to the paper-makers" (p. 209).

Stevenson was particularly perceptive on the role of play and performance in children's learning as the following quotation shows. He was addicted to a stationer's shop in Leith Walk in Edinburgh, which sold Shelt's play theatres with books to paint and figures to cut out. Stevenson "handled and lingered and doted on these bundles of delight; there was a physical pleasure in the sight and touch of them" (p. 64).

> Indeed, out of this cut-and-dry, dull, swaggering, obtrusive and infantile art, I seemed to have learned the very sprit of my life's enjoyment; met there the shadows of the characters I was to read about and love…acquired a gallery of scenes and characters with which, in the silent theatre of the brain, I might enact all novels and romances. (pp. 128–129)

Calder (1990) notes how Stevenson not only relished this fantasy life, but also made every effort to stay in touch with it when he became an adult. Like Kipling, Stevenson was late to learn to read, so "until that age he was totally reliant on the stories that were told and read to him and the stories he invented himself" (p. 41). As Stevenson (1992) explained, "It is the grown people who make the nursery stories; all the children do, is jealously to preserve the text" (p. 58).

Clare's mother "knew not a single letter" (Robinson, 1986, p. 2), but she encouraged him to read and learn and she spent hard-earned money sending him to school whenever funds could be spared: "…every winter night our once unlettered hut was wonderfully changed in its appearance to a school room the old table…bearing at meal times the luxury of a barley loaf or dish of potatoes, was now covered with the rude beginnings of scientific requisitions, pens, ink, and paper" (p. 4). Clare described his pleasure in learning favourite passages of the Bible by heart, singing ballads with his father and reading "those sixpenny chapbooks hawked by pedlars from door to door which shaped (his) childhood imagination" (p. xii). He also remembered old village women telling story upon story of "Giants, Hobgoblins and fairies" (p. 2).

It is no surprise to learn that Dickens' mother was also "an inimitable storyteller" (Slater, 2007, p. 1) who taught him the alphabet and rudiments of English at home. Langton (1891) tells us that Dickens also enjoyed "games of make-believe with his friends and getting up magic-lantern shows, also performing…comic songs and recitations" (p. 26). Theatre, of course, remained one of the great passions of his life.

"When mere children, as soon as they could read and write, Charlotte and her brother and sisters used to invent and act little plays of their own" (Gaskell, 1975, p. 94). Indeed, it was for their juvenile writing and play-acting that the Bronte childhoods are now famous but it is unlikely that the well known little books (tales, dramas, poems, romances, plays), in which Charlotte penned her lively stories in miniature writing, would have come about without a childhood also devoted to reading.

Frances Rossetti was a fine storyteller. Indeed, Christina dedicated one of her own collections of tales to her mother "in grateful remembrance of the stories with which she used to entertain her children" (Marsh, 1994, p. 27). The Rossetti children often acted stories from history at home, and Christina started writing poetry herself at eleven. William Rossetti (quoted in Thomas, 1994) described a typical family evening as adults talking and the children "drinking it all in as a sort of necessary atmosphere of the daily life, yet with our own little interests and occupations as well—reading, colouring prints, looking into illustrated books, nursing a cat, or whatever" (p. 26).

Hans Andersen remembers his father reading aloud to him in the evenings and also making him a toy theatre. One of Andersen's stories is called "Godfather's Picture Book" (2006/1868) and in it he portrays himself as the creator of stories:

> Godfather could tell stories; so many and such long ones. He could cut out pictures and he could draw pictures; and when it was near to Christmas, he would take out an exercise book with clean white pages, and on these he would paste up pictures taken from books and newspapers, and, if he had not enough for what he wanted to tell, he would draw them himself. I got several such pictures when I was little.

Although this is a description by an expert storyteller, Andersen's story also provides a glimpse into the way in which grownups may have interacted with children when looking at a text which, in this case, contains pictures as well as words, and is both amusing and instructive: "'See, that's the title page,' said Godfather. 'That's the beginning of the story you're going to hear. It could also be given as an entire play, if one could perform it'" (n.p.).

Although "Godfather's Picture Book" may have only been fiction, Andersen made many real picturebooks, sometimes with little stories or verses, for the children of his friends. The only picturebook by Andersen to have been printed is one that he helped his friend Drewsen make for his granddaughter Christine for her third birthday in 1859, revealing a desire to entertain rather than to teach. Alderson and Drewsen (1984) suggest that the "pages may also have been compiled with an eye to the talk that could arise as Christine turned to them" (n.p.). There were many printed sources available at the time from which pictures could be cut out and pasted, such as calendars, periodicals and annuals, but the most common sources were the "Bilderbogen" or picture-sheets (sometimes known as "lotteries"), which were printed by the thousands in Europe, particularly in Germany and France. Jane Johnson used the same sort of sheets for her nursery library.

Critical Readers

From an early age our gifted young writers were also critical readers who knew their own minds and held strong opinions of the texts they read. While Byron was able to translate Horace's verse into English by the age of six, he didn't take to poetry at first. However, the lively stories in the Old Testament were relished and history was enjoyed for the sense of adventure and drama it offered.

On the other hand, Clare writes movingly about the moment he discovered poetry when he was thirteen before he understood "blank verse nor rhyme either" (Robinson, 1986, p. 9).

> I met with a fragment of Thomson's *Seasons*....I can still remember my sensations in reading the opening line of Spring. I can't say the reason, but the...lines made my heart twitter with joy: I greedily read over all I could before I returned it and resolved to possess one myself.

Frances Rossetti encouraged her children to read fiction by Maria Edgeworth and "tried to interest them in pious children's tales, such as *Sandford and Merton* and *The Fairchild Family*, but the little Rossettis were not impressed" (Thomas, 1994, p. 27). Christina claimed only to read what took her fancy—Perrault's fairy tales, Dante, Keats, Shelley, Byron, and other poets. Maria read Greek, loved Homer, and tackled Euripedes in translation, valiantly trying to keep up with her brothers once they went to school. Marsh (1994) explains: "Almost from the cradle the young Rossettis knew a true metre from a false one, in both English and Italian, and they grew up with a knowledge of couplet, lyric and ode, to add to the rhymes of the nursery and the hymns at church" (p. 35).

Working-Class Readers

It was in the 19th century that at last we begin to hear the voices of the men and women whose labour produced many of the luxuries that middle- and upper-class families took for granted. David Vincent (1982) argues that despite grinding poverty and harsh working conditions, there was an "established tradition of laboring men embarking upon the pursuit of knowledge. There was a sufficient availability of reading matter, a sufficient level of literacy… [and] a sufficient access to elementary education to endure that even in rural communities it would be possible to find two or three 'uneducated' men who were lovers of books" (p. 31). E.P. Thompson (1980) cites a typical example—the poet-weaver, Samuel Low from Todmorden whose work revealed knowledge of Virgil, Ovid, and Homer.

> For the first half of the nineteenth century, when the formal education of a great part of the people entailed little more than instruction in the Three Rs, [it] was by no means a period of intellectual atrophy. The towns, and even the villages, hummed with the energy of the autodidact. Given the elementary techniques of literacy, labourers, artisans,

shopkeepers and clerks and schoolmasters, proceeded to instruct themselves, severally or in groups. (p. 781)

Thompson goes on to talk about a working-class culture with its eager disputations around the booksellers' stalls, in the taverns, workshops and coffee-houses but, as Vincent (1982) pointed out, the autobiographical writings of working-class people, while almost always finding their way to books and valuing them highly, also emphasised the "general recognition of the subordination of education to the demands of the family economy" (p. 94).

Most working-class children received, at best, a basic and fragmentary elementary education and those who provided it were often barely literate themselves. As the miner John Harris recounts: "In those days any shattered being wrecked in the mill or the mine, if he could read John Bunyan, count 50 backwards, and scribble the squire's name was considered good enough for a pedagogue" (Vincent, 1982, p. 100).

And Sunday Schools apart, this education was almost always domestic—usually in the sitting rooms or round the kitchen table of people in the local community. The eight-year-old, Charles Shaw for example, remembered the bitterness of poverty, not so much because of hunger and want, but the injustice in terms of access and time for books: "I had acquired a strong passion for reading, and the sight of this [advantaged] youth reading at his own free will, forced upon my mind a sense of painful contrast between his position and mine…. I went back to my mould-mining and hot stove with my first anguish in my heart" (p. 91).

The fact that money, books, and a decent education were in short supply, however, meant that what learning was available often had to be shared; those with literacy skills were in close contact with those who were non-literate with the likelihood that sharing of access to print was a regular occurrence. Still, Vincent explores how the tensions between aspiration and opportunity were often more keenly felt by women who had few avenues in which to pursue emerging intellectual and literary interests. One thing many of these women did was to take a deep interest in the education of their children, particularly their sons. D. H. Lawrence's famous account of just such a mother in *Sons and Lovers* rings extremely true for the 19th century as well as the early 20th century. Vincent (1982) explains, "What was left to both men and women was the freedom of all those who survived the lessons in one-two and three-syllable words to travel outside the walls of their homes and beyond the streets of their neighbourhoods through the agency of the fiction" (p. 277).

This brief overview of the 19th century allows us some insights into what was going on in working-class homes. As the century turned, higher literacy levels among parents, wider availability of books, and new theories of development and education all influenced how children learned to read in the home. Despite universal state education, parents have not been discouraged from doing some pre-school teaching at home.

Contemporary Case Studies

> … our reasons for reading are as strange as our reasons for living. (Pennac, 2006, p. 174)

The most detailed accounts of children reading in the home in the 20th century are almost exclusively those of economically and educationally privileged families who, through their own academic training, become aware of the potentially rich data that are revealed through observing their own children's early literacy.

Although adults writing about their childhood memories of reading transmit strong impressions of particular books, pictures, or moments of reading, the most detailed observations of how children become readers in the home are provided by parents or carers who kept regular notes and diaries or made audio recordings of their children's language and interaction with books. These observations allow us access to the earliest stages of reading behavior, beyond most people's memories. Although some researchers have observed other people's children at home, the parental records show that in most cases the deeper understanding and interpretation of children's interactions with and responses to books (including play, performance, art and writing) is only possible through continuous, intimate contact with the young readers. There now exists a group of texts that have become classics in the literature on early reader response and pre-school literacy.

In this section, after briefly introducing each case study, we will discuss them as a whole, attempting to highlight the main features of this wealth of evidence through the three strands of connections, creativity, and criticism. It cannot be denied that these studies present a view limited to white, middle-class households in which book-loving adults (most of them academics) had the time and resources, as well as the firm intention to introduce their children to the world of books and reading (this also meant either limited or no access at all to television). Thus, the children in these studies were a-typical in this respect. With a few exceptions, they can all be considered pre-digital because, like television and videos, computers either did not exist or were used minimally.

Largely academics, the parents were familiar with the literature on the subject and therefore highlight observations related to current issues and controversies on literacy learning. The fact that most of the studies deal with children growing up in the second half of the 20th century and in English speaking countries, allows us to make useful comparisons.[3]

The Families

The pioneer among these studies is Dorothy Neil White's (1984/1954) *Books Before Five*. She records her daughter Carol's reactions to books from the age of two to the age of five, just before she begins school in New Zealand. The diary is informal and by no means comprehensive, yet White provides a clear picture of her daughter's reactions

to text and the context in which they take place and adds her own questions and interpretations to those responses. Curiously, Carol had little experience with books under the age of two, which perhaps is a reflection of earlier approaches to child-rearing where babies were considered too young to be given books (Dorothy Butler's *Babies Need Books* was not published until 1982).

Because of her granddaughter's special circumstance, Dorothy Butler (1980) does trace the responses of the child to books almost from birth in *Cushla and her Books*. Born in New Zealand in 1971 with several severe handicaps, Cushla developed a special relationship with books, which would sustain her and her parents through a difficult infancy (the record ends at the age of four). Despite Cushla's difficulties, Butler's record reveals that she went through many of the same response stages as other child-readers, and in some instances her understanding develops even earlier because of the intensity of her reading experiences.

Anna Crago was born in Australia in 1972. Her parents, Maureen and Hugo Crago (1983), recorded her reactions to particular books (and pictures), as well as observations on language and storytelling, from before the age of two up to the age of five in *Prelude to Literacy*. Also Australian, Rebecca (born in 1971) and Ralph (born in 1975) are contemporaries of both Anna and Cushla. Their mother, Virginia Lowe (2007), was inspired by White's book to keep a diary of her children's encounters with books, and she does this almost obsessively from when they are weeks old to the age of eight and even beyond. Her text, *Stories, Pictures and Reality,* presents the most detailed record to-date and includes evidence on particular cognitive developments occurring earlier than psychologists have believed were likely. She focuses in particular on topics such as reality, fantasy, and identification.

The conversation among these parent-researchers is further enriched by Wolf who co-wrote *The Braid of Literature* with Heath in 1992, based on records of her daughters' encounters with books and print, from their birth in the 1980s until 1991. Lindsey was born in Saudi Arabia but was three when the family moved back to the United States, where both she and her sister Ashley grew up. Wolf also looks at how the girls respond to and make meaning within "possible worlds" but, due to Lindsey's intense interest in performance, explores this aspect more fully than Lowe.

Among the other longitudinal studies that present some useful insights is Marcia Baghban's (1984) account of her daughter, Giti (born in 1976) whose pre-school literacy practices (in the U.S.) are recorded from birth to the age of three, but the focus is mainly on the development of oral language and writing/drawing and only more generally, on reading. Glenda Bissex's (1980) often quoted case study—*Gnys at Work*—is on her son Paul's developing literacy, mainly writing, from the ages of five to eleven years of age. Her records show the influence of reading on

Paul's writing, but it does not begin until Paul is already at school.

Brian Edmiston's (2007) case study of his son Michael's play between 18 months and 7 years has been published recently as *Forming Ethical Identities in Early Childhood Play*. Although he does mention reading where it is a source for early play, his particular focus is on play, myth, ethics, and identity. It is interesting to note that Edmiston's research was a way of making sense of his son's fascination with horror and violence in books, television, and videos because this is a response very much missing in the accounts of all the girl readers mentioned above. Two other boys have been the subjects of reading case studies published in the magazine *Books for Keeps*. In 2001 these were short, more impressionistic pieces by Gary McKeone (then Head of Literature at the Arts Council of England) on his son Jack's (born in 2000) interactions with books until the age of one year. These were followed in 2002 (and continue at the time of writing this chapter) by more detailed observations by Roger Mills on his son Hal from the age of 12 months. Mills's account presents the view of a psychologist and describes Hal's responses in terms of issues about security, predictability, and the development of self-consciousness, yet it also portrays the way in which the particular fascination of boys with machines and transport, for example, can stimulate their interest in books.

Finally, we include here extracts from Evelyn Arizpe's unpublished diary, which records the language and reading of her two daughters, Isabel (born in 1997) and Flora (born in 2000) from birth to the age of three in England. Children's books played an important role in this academic household because of Arizpe's particular interest in this area but her focus was on the development of bilingualism (Spanish/English). As well as books in Spanish, her daughters read many of the same English books read by the children in the case studies mentioned above and Arizpe's observations support much of the evidence obtained from them.

The Reading Environment and the Books

Despite different parental approaches to both child-rearing and research within their own families, and the different personalities of the children involved, it is interesting to note how similar some of their reactions are. However, it is not surprising that the children in these studies were so enthusiastic about reading at such an early age given that they were all born to parents already deeply involved with books, many in a professional capacity, and therefore into a print-rich environment that was extended by the purchasing and borrowing of children's books. As well as books, there were a plethora of other printed sources, from newspapers to maps, all of which provided impetus for talking, reading, and sometimes also writing. Books were clearly valued as objects and therefore they were to be looked after although they could be play objects at the same time. In this setting, book reading becomes a significant activity and "has special powers, since it demands the total cessation of all other activities by the adult. It centers exclusively around child and text, and language and lessons from this context are thus highly signalled for children as nonordinary" (Wolf & Heath, 1992, p. 80).

Another common element in these households was that reading occurred in an affective context where the children were in close contact with the reader, whether it be a parent or another adult. Mills (2002) stresses the "security" that reading together means for the child who at this stage is usually going through "separation anxiety" (p. 9). In this situation, dialogue and other interactions around the books arose naturally, as well as teaching, although this was not the objective of the reading session. Children knew that in this situation, they and the book had the full attention of the adults and that their comments and opinions would be listened and responded to.

These children had favorite books that they could stroke or even sleep with, and they were often given further texts by the same authors or illustrators who were part of the reading process and became household names. Older siblings encountered the same books again when they were read to younger siblings, and younger siblings were exposed to challenging books for older children. Children knew they had the power to initiate a reading, choose a book, or stop the reading when they were bored or frightened. They also knew they were allowed to ask questions and that they could openly say if they liked or disliked the text or pictures, the first steps towards becoming critical readers.

These children were fortunate in that their generation was among the first to benefit from developments in printing technology that allowed them to have access to a greater number of books than any generation before them. Yet although their reading was much more extensive than that of the children mentioned in the other sections of this chapter, it cannot be said that their acts of reading were any less intensive. Printing technology also offered them much higher quality image reproduction, particularly important in the now thriving genre of picturebooks. This allowed the children to peruse many more books on their own before knowing how to read print.

Despite the fact that some of the parent-researchers lived in rather isolated areas, they were able to provide their children with a wide range of books, including hand-made books such as cloth-books and scrapbooks which were so important to children in previous centuries. Indeed, Lowe (2007) made alphabet books and a series of "little readers" which included Rebecca's reading vocabulary (at the age of four) and adventures featuring her and her brother. In general, the parents were aware of new publications and endeavored to find books that would match the children's interests.

All the children in these studies seem to have been exposed to nursery rhymes from an early age and parents give examples of how these rhymes entered the children's early speech, sometimes in more than one language. Fairy tales clearly played a big part in the re-creations and performances that Anna, Lindsey, Ashley, Isabel, and Flora enacted in their everyday lives. They went through a prince and princess phase even before the Disney Corporation seized on the marketing potential of this fascination and turned it into a consumer craze. Rebecca and Ralph seem to have had less exposure to fairytales, and perhaps because they were taught from a very young age that fairies and dragons were "just pretend," they did not become a major part of their play. Michael based his pretend play on myths more than fairy tales, but these did include dragons and other fantastical beasts.

For the most part, the children in these studies were read texts that had already become or were fast becoming classics. Among the picturebooks that had the greatest impact were those by Beatrix Potter, Dick Bruna, Maurice Sendak, Ludwig Bemelmans, Margaret Wise Brown, Eric Carle, Dr. Seuss, and Anthony Browne. At a very young age, some of the children were also read chapter books that other parents might consider for older readers. As well as nursery rhymes, the children were read poetry, but prose was predominant. Personal circumstances and inclinations determined which books became significant, but all the children had their favorites that were repeatedly re-read.

Text-to-Life Connections, Orality, and Re-creations

Like the other children, Carol made constant connections between her books and her life experiences, not just weeks but even months after the reading. As White (1984) writes when Carol is two: "The experience makes the book richer and the book enriches the personal experience even at this level. I am astonished at the age this backward and forward flow between books and life take place" (p. 13).

Lowe and Wolf, in particular, were able to trace just how the experience of words, literary language, images, and character's actions became threaded through the lives of their children. In turn, these experiences were connected to other readings and texts, thus forming a familiar network that gave the children security and confidence in both life and books as well as double-fold enjoyment.

The children were well aware of the power of story language to engage both reader and listener or spectator. They could also imitate and reproduce "book talk" themselves which then developed into storytelling; in other words, they had a "sense of how to use language in literate ways" (Wolf & Heath, 1992, p. 228). Whether or not parent-readers dramatized the reading (Lowe's was undramatized compared to the Cragos's or Wolf's, for example), the children were aware of the differences between literary, poetical language, and everyday speech. Words from books appeared in the children's emergent talk, not only to convey meaning but also as sounds to be played and experimented with. They were fascinated by word play, mining it for humor and enjoyment and then trying it out themselves.

To what extent the texts were re-created depended on the children's personalities and interests. Most of them made up their own stories and some children, particularly Lindsey, also made up plays based on their reading. However, they all explored what it would be like to be others, either by taking on particular roles or attributes of characters. This form of identification allowed them to become other people or to explore alternative behavior and circumstances with the comfort of knowing they could go back to being themselves at any moment. Through these acts, as readers they were learning about characterization and empathy as well as exploring other potential ways of being.

Learning to Read

In all these households, reading was regarded not as the ability to decode words but as a pleasurable introduction to the world of literature, so none of these parents used early reading schemes or primers of any kind. Although none of them state it expressly, primers were clearly not seen as something that was necessary for their children's progress as readers and, presumably, not considered beneficial in a literary sense. As we mentioned above, some of the books parents provided would have been considered above the age level of the children they were read to. Curiously, Anna, Rebecca, and Isabel all had difficulties when it came to decoding, so we must be cautious about affirming that intense exposure to books before school will automatically guarantee the ability to read early. However, as Lowe (2007) points out, "the book exposure affected their vocabularies as one would expect, and acted as a framework for complex language structures" (p. 11)—and all three girls eventually became voracious readers. The influence of older siblings probably also plays an important role here, as the younger siblings in these studies did not seem to struggle as much. Certainly, Isabel (at the age of six) was responsible for introducing Flora (3.7 to 4.0) to letters and reading through rather intense instruction during a phase of playing school which went on for several months.

Baghban's (1984) account shows Giti at the age of 20 months beginning to distinguish letters from environmental print. Whatever we may think of the McDonald's fast-food chain, their logo introduces children to print long before school. For Giti, labels and logos became so important that her mother made her a homemade book with cut-outs of those she recognized from magazines and newspapers. Baghban cites various other small-scale studies that, like hers and those of other parent-researchers, show how by the age of two that children who are exposed to books are familiar with concepts of print such as directionality and also the idea that print triggers stories and certain types of interactions such as labelling and dialogue. Early pretend reading, a common activity among the children in these studies, seems to lead naturally to "real" reading. As Bissex (1980) writes: "Before a child can read, must he not have some global sense of what reading is about and what it feels like?" (p. 130).

To a lesser or greater degree, parents encouraged their children to question, to predict, to create hypotheses about the text, and thus to become critical readers. From these interactions, the child-readers knew that they could participate in the making of meaning with the adult readers and also in the evaluation of the texts.

Baghban (1984) emphasizes the interdependency of the language arts which also occurs before formal reading lessons take place: "Giti used oral language, reading, writing, and drawing as partners within a larger system of mutually reinforcing processes" (p. 97). There is no room here to discuss the development of writing (before school) that some of these case studies describe; however, it is closely linked to reading behaviors particularly because from an early age these children experimented with scribbles that they interpreted and read. Bissex (1980) puts her finger on the importance *meaning* has in the process of becoming readers and writers: "Paul, like his parents, wrote (and read and talked) because what he was writing (or reading or saying) had meaning to him as an individual and as a cultural being" (p. 107).

The Visual Image, Digital Literacy, and Popular Culture

Even before the 21st century, changes in media and technology were beginning to affect the ways in which children became readers in the home, and the visual image has perhaps been most influential in these changes. There are many references to the children's responses to visual images, not only in children's books, but also to "adult" art. Crago and Crago (1983), for example, record Anna's developing responses to shapes, sizes, incomplete objects, and representations of movement as well as her color preferences, visual memory, and the connections she makes among images. Lowe (2007) also has a chapter on her children's understanding of picture conventions while Wolf and Heath (1992) connect response to illustrations with other responses such as drama and play. Before the age of two, Isabel and Flora expected pictures on one page to be narratively linked to pictures on the next page and would point things out in the images as they read to their dolls. Clearly, the visual image was important to all the children in both functional and aesthetic ways and it helped them develop as readers by inviting them to predict, interpret, and make intertextual connections.

Crago and Crago (1983) suggest that Anna's high exposure to book illustrations resulted in her being more critically aware earlier than expected—such as using the realism of color as an evaluative criterion—a suggestion which applies to some of the other case studies as well. By the age of five, parents observed that the children were able to understand different versions of the same story and possessed an awareness of artistic style, which allowed them to recognize the work or the "stylistic signature" (p. 271) of particular illustrators. The importance of this exposure is confirmed in the Crago's conclusion that recognition and understanding depends on previous artistic experience, not just (or necessarily) life experience.

Although there are no studies on children responding to new types of media that are as detailed as the ones mentioned above, two articles in particular provide examples of observations of children in the home interacting with both books and some new technologies. One case study by Robinson and Turnbull (2005) is on their goddaughter Veronica (born in 1998) who, like Isabel and Flora, was exposed to popular culture in both English and Spanish. An enthusiastic reader of books (who evinces behavior similar to that of the other children mentioned in this section), she also watched television, videos (including home-made videos), and CD versions of stories as well as computer games. Robinson and Turnbull argue that all of these "have been truly porous as she has moved between them with little need to recognise media boundaries" (p. 69), and that they all contributed to enriching Veronica's connections and recreations. This also occurred with James whose exploration of CD-Rom storybooks led him to computer-based dramatic play (Smith, 2005, p. 2005).

Isabel and Flora loved watching the British program for toddlers *The Teletubbies*, which was taped so that they could watch them over again. Their first computer games, on the BBC website, were linked to this program, and by the age of three, they could manipulate the computer mouse on their own, both clicking and dragging objects. As soon as they mastered a few keyboard skills, they were writing their stories using word-processing software, selecting relevant images from Clip Art, and when Isabel began teaching Flora letters and numbers, she created the worksheets on the computer and printed them out.

As these and other studies show, new generations of children are more likely to be exposed to the electronic or digital version of books, sometimes before reading the original book and before starting school. Not enough research has been done on how this changes the ways in which children respond to the original text or on how the possibility of the repeated viewing of so many videos that are now available affects their understanding of, for example, narrative, character, and image. As Robinson and Turnbull (2005) point out, media boundaries have been broken and it now becomes more difficult, if not impossible, to follow particular connections children make between one media and the other. Yet, in a different but inseparable way from book reading, children's interactions with video, television, computers and other new technologies also have the possibility to lead them to make connections, evaluations, and re-creations of text.

Conclusion

> ...it is my inward autobiography, for the words we take into ourselves help to shape us... (Spufford, 2002, p. 21)

This concluding section begins with two contemporary writers, Frances Spufford and Daniel Pennac (2006). Pennac, whose *The Rights of the Reader* has been a publishing sensation, reflected honestly on himself as a caring and sometimes anxious and demanding father of emerging readers, whereas Spufford (2002), in a tour-de-force reading memoir, *The Child that Books Built,* documents his own domestic reading development.

Pennac (2006) reminds us of the sheer obsessiveness involved in deeply engaged domestic reading by making reference to his own boyhood when people were always trying to stop him from reading: "Stop reading for goodness' sake, you'll strain your eyes! Why don't you go outside and play? It's a beautiful day" (p. 15). He also points out the frequent discrepancies between what parents expect children to read and what children choose to read:

> It's interesting that even back then reading was rarely a matter of choice. So it became a subversive act. You didn't just discover a novel, you were disobeying your parents too. A double victory. The happy memory of reading time snatched under the bedclothes by torchlight. (pp. 15–16)

Thus, the subversive act becomes a creative act as children begin to make their own pathways through books, developing their own identities as readers and as human beings.

Spufford's (2002) account of what it means to be totally engrossed in reading as a child focuses on the transition from being part of real life to the journey into the imaginary world created between the reader and the writer. Like many of the young readers in our study, Spufford, read indiscriminately everything he could get his hands on but, at the same time, was forming intelligent critical judgements about the texts he encountered. He also reminds us of the powerful significance of the adults who first made us fall in love with books and of the lessons we learn from stories: "We tell stories all the time when we speak. Storytelling may be the function that made language worth acquiring….The medium of the first encounter is an adult voice speaking, and saying the same words in the same order each time the story comes around" (p. 46).

These lucid descriptions not only highlight the strands suggested by Wolf and Heath (1992), but also identify some of the common themes that link children from different centuries reading in the home. Despite the gaps in our knowledge before the 20th century, the accounts we have presented here allow us a glimpse into the connections, interpretations, and re-creations that were involved in children's readerly behavior as early as the 18th century. We will now briefly bring these insights together and point to possibilities for further research in this little explored field.

Although there were differences between the 18th century families described in our first section, there were also similarities. First, they show that in privileged, literate families, reading aloud was an important and frequent daily activity, which children encountered regularly from a very young age. According to Lorna Weatherill (1996),

estimates of time spent doing various household activities in the 18th century show that up to two hours daily were spent reading (p. 143). Conversation, questions, and reflections followed this reading, so that children would be encouraged to apply morals to their own lives and presumably link their reading from the Bible to other texts.

Mothers told children stories and usually taught them their first letters through primers or hand-made materials which began with the alphabet and continued with words and sentences of increasing length. Sometimes these materials included images, which would also be sources of conversation and storytelling. Like Jane Johnson, some of these mothers and fathers must have provided opportunities for their children to express their own interests and to find pleasure in these activities. In some families, games and toys also encouraged early reading. Drama and performance—where allowed—naturally followed the processes of reading and reciting. Finally, reading was linked to writing as children copied passages or lessons and, in some cases like the Taylor sisters, created their own poems and stories.

In the 19th century, individual accounts provide clues as to the development not only of voracious readers but also of gifted writers. Books provided knowledge but also the space for reflection, sometimes in economically deprived or in difficult emotional circumstances. In terms of books, quantity and quality did not seem to matter as much, nor did the extent of parental education and involvement or even the amount of schooling, as long as there was a strong will to learn. There is rich evidence for the links to storytelling, performance, and other creative pursuits.

These latter trends carried well into the 20th century. The detailed cases, which were often full research studies, reveal that, well before they can decode text, the children *behave like readers* as they make links between books and reality (and among texts), interpret, and re-create literary elements in their ordinary life and use these links and interpretations to analyze and evaluate not only texts but life.

Some of the expectations with which we began this research clearly emerged in the data: that the roles of parent/carers would be different according to the views of childhood of their time, that the affective relationship between children and these parent/carers would be important, that storytelling would be central, that pictures would add to the pleasures offered by books, and that reading would be linked to some kinds of performance. However, other themes also emerged and proved to be significant factors in creating perceptive young readers:

- omnivorous reading of books for adults as well as those specifically aimed at children;
- popular fiction and comics (chapbooks in the 18th century) playing as strong a part in the domestic reading diet as rich literary texts of which adults were more likely to approve;

- the liberty to make one's own reading choices;
- the time to do plenty of reading.

These themes suggest directions that future research in the field of domestic literacy might take, but there also remain important areas that we did not have time to address fully here:

- the differences in the ways in which imaginative and information texts are offered and taken up;
- the ways in which the home context has changed given the more vital role of school;
- the impact of new methods of teaching reading;
- the question of close involvement of parents/carers versus children finding their own ways to reading;
- the influence of siblings;
- the importance of gender—of the reader and of the parent/carer;
- the incursion of new technologies into the very heart of the home and the ways in which television and other electronic media have changed perceptions of the act of reading itself.

And yet, we would venture, that despite all the future and past research—the histories, the memories, and reflections from autobiographies as well as the close, informed observation of contemporary children—there is still much about the process in which children become readers that will always remain highly personal and totally mysterious.

Notes

1. Heath (1983) provides the most detailed record of learning to read in working-class and/or ethnic minority households. Jonda McNair (personal communication) noted that pre-school reading practices in African American families changed when reading more African American literature because these books reflected their personal experiences. She referred us to Durkin's (1984) study of poor, black, fifth-grade students which found that successful readers were those who had been read to at an early age, had been provided with challenging materials, and had been encouraged by their families to love reading.
2. This archive is mainly divided between the Lilly Library at Indiana University, Bloomington, and the Bodleian Library, Oxford. The former can be accessed online at http://urania.dlib.indiana.edu/collections/lilly/janejohnson/index.html
3. As Wolf and Heath (1992) point out, "For a comparative perspective, it is necessary to ask also about what this book says for single-parent families, cultures incorporating oral story-telling habits, and extended families that must cram three generations into a one-bedroom apartment" (p. 192).

Literature References

Andersen, H. C. (2006, June 13). *Godfather's picture book*. Retrieved June 17, 2008, from http://www.andersen.sdu.dk/vaerk/hersholt/GodfathersPictureBook_e.html (Original work published 1868)

Andersen, H. C., & Drewsen, A. (1984). *Christine's picture book* (B. Alderson, Trans., E. Dal, Ed.). London: Kingfisher Books.

Johnson, J. (2001). *A very pretty story*. (G. Avery, Ed.). Oxford:

Bodleian Library, Oxford University. (Original manuscript 1744)

Academic References

Arizpe, E., & Styles, M. with Heath, S. B. (2006). *Reading lessons from the eighteenth century*. Lichfield, UK: Pied Piper Press.

Baghban, M. (1984). *Our daughter learns to read and write*. Newark, DE: International Reading Association.

Bissex, G. L. (1980). *Gnys at work: A child learns to read and write*. Cambridge, MA: Harvard University Press.

Butler, D. (1979). *Cushla and her books*. London: Hodder and Stoughton.

Butler, D. (1995). *Babies need books*. London: Penguin.

Butler, D., & Clay, M. (1979). *Reading begins at home*. London: Heinemann.

Butler, M. (1972). *Maria Edgeworth*. Oxford: Clarendon Press.

Calder, J. (1990). *Robert Louis Stevenson: A life study*. Glasgow: Richard Drew Publishers.

Crago, M., & Crago, H. (1983). *Prelude to literacy*. Carbondale, IL: Southern Illinois University Press.

Dal, E. (1984). Postscript. In H. C. Andersen & A. Drewsen. *Christine's Picture Book*. (B. Alderson, Trans., E. Dal, Ed.). London: Kingfisher Books.

Davidoff, L., & Hall, C. (1987). *Family fortunes: Men and women of the English middle class 1780–1850*. London: Routledge.

Edmiston, B. (2007). *Forming ethical identities in early childhood play*. London: Routledge.

Eisler, B. (1999). *Byron*. London: Penguin.

Gaskell, E. (1975). *The life of Charlotte Bronte*. Harmondsworth, UK: Penguin.

Heath, S. B. (1983). *Ways with words*. Cambridge, UK: Cambridge University Press.

Heath, S. B. (1997). Child's play or finding the ephemera of home. In M. Hilton, M. Styles, & V. Watson (Eds.), *Opening the nursery door. Reading, writing and childhood 1600–1900* (pp. 17–30). London: Routledge.

Hyde, M. (1977). *The Thrales of Streatham Park*. Cambridge, MA: Harvard University Press.

Langton, R. (1891). *The childhood and youth of Charles Dickens*. London: Hutchinson.

Longford, E. (1976). *Byron*. London: Weidenfeld & Nicolson.

Lowe, V. (2007). *Stories, pictures and reality*. London: Routledge.

Lucas, E. V. (Ed.). (1905). *'Original poems' and others by Ann and Jane Taylor*. London: Wells, Gardner, Darton & Co.

Marsh, J. (1994). *Christina Rossetti: A literary biography*. London: Jonathan Cape.

McKeone, G. (2002). Jack's first books—November 2001. *Books for Keeps*, 131.

McLynn, F. (1993). *Robert Louis Stevenson: A biography*. London: Pimlico.

Mills, R. (2002). Hall's reading diary—May 2002. *Books for Keeps*, 134.

Monaghan, E. J. (1991). Family literacy in early 18th-century Boston: Cotton Mather and his children. *Reading Research Quarterly, 26*(4), 342–371.

Pennac, D. (2006). *The rights of the reader*. London: Walker Books.

Robinson, E. (1986). *John Clare's autobiographical writings*. Oxford, UK: Oxford University Press.

Robinson, M., & Turnbull, B. (2005). Veronica. An asset model of becoming literate. In J. Marsh (Ed.), *Popular culture, new media and digital literacy in early childhood* (pp. 51–72). London: RoutledgeFalmer

Schieffelin, B. B., & Cochran-Smith, M. (1984). Learning to

read culturally. In H. Goelman, A. Oberg, & F. Smith (Eds.), *Awakening to literacy* (pp. 3–24). Exeter, NH: Heinemann Educational Books.

Slater, M. (2007). *Charles Dickens.* Oxford, UK: Oxford University Press.

Smith, C. R. (2005). The CD-ROM game. In J. Marsh (Ed.), *Popular culture, new media and digital literacy in early childhood* (pp. 108–125). London: RoutledgeFalmer

Spufford, F. (2002). *The child that books built.* London: Faber.

Spufford, M. (1985). *Small books and pleasant histories: Popular fiction and its readership in seventeenth-century England.* Cambridge, UK: Cambridge University Press.

Stevenson, R. L. (1992). *Robert Louis Stevenson: Essays and poems.* (C. Harman, Ed.). London: Everyman, Dent.

Tadmor, N. (1996). "In the even my wife read to me": Women, reading and household life in the eighteenth century. In J. Raven, H. Small, & N. Tadmor (Eds.), *The practice and representation of reading in England* (pp. 162–174). Cambridge, UK: Cambridge University Press.

Thomas, F. (1994). *Christina Rossetti: A biography.* London: Virago.

Thompson, E. P. (1980). *The making of the English working class.* London: Penguin.

Vincent, D. (1982). *Bread, knowledge and freedom: A study of nineteenth century working class autobiography.* London: Methuen.

Weatherill, L. (1996). *Consumer behaviour and material culture in Britain 1660-1760.* London: Routledge.

White, D. N. (1984). *Books before five.* New York, NY: Oxford University Press. (Original work published 1954)

Wolf, S. A., & Heath, S. B. (1992). *The braid of literature: Children's worlds of reading.* London: Harvard University Press.

2

Questioning the Value of Literacy

A Phenomenology of Speaking and Reading in Children

Eva-Maria Simms

Duquesne University

It may seem odd, in a handbook that studies and celebrates the written word for children, to include a chapter that attends to the losses involved in the child's acquisition of traditional literacy. But as we are reminded in Betsy Hearne's essay, our first introduction to literature is through oral stories; thus we need to consider what it means that our young readers were first speakers and listeners, and how that transformation from orality to literature fundamentally changes perceptual frameworks. Phenomenologist Eva-Maria Simms asks readers to consider the embodied contexts of language use in children and how these contexts change with the advent of alphabetic literacy. Such understanding can help us discern what's at stake for the "reluctant readers" we encounter in our classrooms, as well as in Campano's and Ghiso's discussions of immigrant children learning to read books from cultures other than their own, or in the arguments Bradford highlights surrounding the inscription of indigenous narratives.

Reading as Technology

The Chirographic Bias

Reading and writing seem to be harmless, innocuous skills, mere addenda to the basket of natural skills that children develop throughout their formative years. At least, this is the impression promoted by handbooks and research reports on early childhood education (Spodek, 1993; National Reading Panel, 2000; Hall, Larson, & Marsh, 2003; Rasinski, Blachowicz, & Lems, 2006). The contributions by psychologists consist of discussions of cognitive/information processing abilities, memory strategies, Piagetian stages, and Vygotskian proximal zones—all presented as part of the cognitive/developmental scaffolding that makes learning to read possible. But how does the acquisition of literacy affect the child's consciousness? There is a surprising silence on this topic. Even among authors who are critical of the power relations in the educational system (Burman, 1994; Canella, 1997; James, Jenks, & Prout, 1998; Popkewitz & Brennan, 1997; Soto, 1999) the value of reading *per se* is rarely questioned. One of the few instances where the value of literacy is problematized occurs in the clash between indigenous cultures and the U.S. education system: The Native American Cochiti people have denied the transcription of their language into alphabetic notation and refused to have the written language taught to their children in schools (Martinez, 2000).

Our mainstream cultural belief in the desirability of literacy is what the phenomenological tradition calls a "natural attitude" (Husserl, 1952): Everyday phenomena are accepted without question and the opportunity for reflection does not arise. The phenomenological method attempts to bracket or suspend the unquestioned belief in the obviousness of what is given to our experience, and the researcher *suspends assent* (Gurwitsch, 1974). This withholding of assent does not mean that the *phenomenon* is suspended, merely that the researcher creates openness for a deeper exploration of what is there (Ihde, 1979). Husserl's (1969) call "to the things themselves" (pp. 12–13) is a challenge to direct our attention more fully to what phenomena themselves can disclose through a process of faithful description. What was taken for granted before appears now as strange and interesting. Phenomenology is a philosophical method that, by suspending assent, awakens wonder (Held, 2002).

The intent of this chapter is to suspend the belief in the goodness of literacy—our *chirographic bias*—in order to gain a deeper understanding of how the engagement with texts structures human consciousness, and particularly the minds of children. In the following pages, literacy (a term which in this chapter refers to the ability to read and produce written text) is discussed as a consciousness altering *technology*. A phenomenological analysis of the act of reading shows the child's engagement with texts as a *perceptual* as well as a *symbolic* event that builds upon but also alters children's speech acts. Speaking and reading are both forms of language use, but with different configurations of perceptual and symbolic qualities. Children's literature uses textual technology and, intentionally or not, participates in structuring children's pre-literate minds. Some of its forms, such as picture books and early readers, are directly intended to bridge the gap between the pre-literate listener and the literate reader and ease the transition into the literate state. It is my hope that the phenomenological analysis of the experiences of speaking and reading might help us understand more clearly how children's literature impacts the minds of children. Such an analysis can awaken a critical awareness of the power that letters wield as they shape the reader's psychological reality, and it can sharpen our sense of wonder about the metamorphosis of language from speaking to writing.

The question of the value of literacy is not an academic issue for me. As a parent and as a teacher of parents and therapists, I am often confronted with the issue of what children (and the society as a whole) *lose* by taking on literacy. One day my eight-year-old son and I wandered through the glass rooms of the botanical conservatory. Hundreds of plant species lined the banks of our path, spilled down from baskets, pots, and ledges, reached through the humid air towards the glass-filtered sunlight

or the shade of their companions. I tried to read as many identification tags as I could, but Nick was more interested in the markers for the treasure hunt, which the staff had hidden among the roots. He did not like reading. We entered a long glass room which was lined with a dozen topiaries representing Aesop's fables. Assuming that this could be a "teachable moment," I stopped before the first one, and told Nick that this was the fable of the fox and the stork and started to tell him the story. "You left out the good parts," he interrupted me, and proceeded to recite Aesop's tale from beginning to end. Then he rushed to the next topiary, and, standing before the exhibit, declaimed the next fable, exactly with the wording and intonation of his second grade teacher. And the next one. And the next one. At the end of the hallway he had told me six fables, metered and formulaic, with coherent plots, interesting details, and varied voices for the animal protagonists. I marveled at his ability to remember. Here was a child who recalled the words of a teacher verbatim. And he could not read.

This rhapsodic feat of memory, which recalls lengthy story lines and the details of content and delivery, is typical of pre-literate, oral people (Goody, 1968). Memory changes when people learn to read, and Nicholas was no exception: His recall prowess fell by the wayside a few years after he became literate. I have always wondered what other abilities of our children's perception, imagination, feeling, and cognition we have sacrificed when we taught them how to read.

Textuality as Technology

Literacy is deeply entwined with the structures of human consciousness, and it changes the culture that embraces it, as well as the individual who learns how to read. This has been documented by historians and philologists (Eisenstein, 1979; Havelock, 1982; Parry, 1971) as well as authors with a historical and cultural interest in anthropology (Goody, 1968), psychology (Luria, 1976; Ong, 1982), education (Egan, 1988; Sumara, 1998), and communication (McCluhan, 1962; Postman, 1994). On the cultural level, the phenomenon of textual literacy appears in sharper outline when it is contrasted with the literary and educational practices of oral cultures, which transmit their knowledge and traditions without texts, or with cultures that have pockets of literacy practices that are very different from our own.

Illich and Sanders (1988) have argued that alphabetization, i.e., the translation of the phonetic sound system into visual alphabetic notation, is an epistemological practice with far-reaching impact on mind and culture.[1] Illich (1996) has traced the creation of the "bookish" (p. 5) mind to the monastic reading and writing tradition of the 12th century, which built the foundation for new thinking practices, the founding of schools and universities, and the dissemination of ideas through the printing press in the following centuries. Reading is a mind-technology. The word "technology" is generally defined as the application of tools and methods, particularly the study, development, and application of devices, machines, and techniques for manufacturing and productive processes. On a deeper level, however, technology is the disclosure and manipulation of the essence of things (Heidegger, 1993). Technologies extract the essences out of human abilities by instrumentalizing them and by depriving them of their original lived context. An example is the invention of the automobile: The essential ability of human movement is extracted and intensified through the technology of the car, which, in turn, reduces the lived and embodied context of human motility. When we sit in the speeding car, our senses are insulated from the heat, smell, and touch of the places we pass, and we do not notice their details anymore. The adoption of automobile technology, in turn, has required changes in infrastructure, which have deeply altered the landscapes and social fabric of American cities. According to Illich (1996), when human experience becomes technologized, a double process of intensification of some experiential elements and the de-contextualization *and* reduction of others can be observed. Literacy as a technology extracts the essence out of human speech—the content of what is said—and instrumentalizes and intensifies it through the process of alphabetic notation and textual practices. The lived context of oral language is reduced and restructured. In the following sections we will trace this process of reduction and intensification as language becomes written text.

Introducing literacy into non-literate cultures has had profound effects on their cultural practices (Eisenstein, 1979; Goody, 1968; McCluhan, 1962; Ong, 1982). Some of the Pueblo peoples of New Mexico, as we saw above, have refused to allow their languages to be written and taught in schools as recently as the 1990s. They argue that written language is sacrilegious, gives indiscriminate access to esoteric religious practice, and is an imperialist tool that undermines the cultural identity and political sovereignty of Pueblo peoples (Martinez, 2000; Webster, 2006). This echoes Ong's (1982) statement that "writing is a particularly pre-emptive and imperialist activity that tends to assimilate other things to itself…" (p. 12).

The Phenomenology of the Speech Act

A Visit to the Kindergarten

Pre-literate children engage in language all the time, and their oral culture and the variety of the language forms they use is surprisingly sophisticated. It would go beyond the scope of this chapter to discuss the research in the field of language acquisition, but the consensus of the experts is that by the age of four pre-schoolers use grammar almost as well as adults (Bruner, 1993; Chomsky, 2002; Hirsh-Pasek & Golinkoff, 1996; Pinker, 1995). The complexity of young children's speech practices is apparent in the conversation between five children, which were recorded by Vivian Paley (1981) in her kindergarten classroom. Even though Paley's children are exposed to written language in the form of story books or reference works fetched from the library, textual material comes to them in the oral form: It is read aloud and explained by the teacher. The following analysis of a typical kindergarten conversation is guided by the ideas of the French philosopher Maurice Merleau-Ponty (1962) and his discussion of the phenomenology of speech.

Paley's (1981) kindergarten class had soaked and planted lima beans in milk cartons, but after a few weeks only two sprouted. When Wally sifted through the dirt in his planter he could not find any lima beans—and neither could the other children. They were puzzled by the mystery of the vanished lima beans and for weeks argued and theorized that robbers had stolen the beans. Here is one of their typical conversations:

Andy: My father has two cactus plants in the big windows in his office. You know why? When robbers come in at night they touch the cactus plants and have to go back where they came from. To get the prickles out. That's why my daddy has those plants.

Deana: What if you got stuck in the desert when you weren't stealing anything?

Eddie: What if he stole the whole cactus plant?

Andy: Then he might fall on it and get stuck by it.

Tanya: How about if the robber came in another way except by the way the cactus are?

Andy: He can't. The doors are locked.

Tanya: Does he have a cactus in all the windows? The robber could come through another window.

Andy: Only if he has a ladder. And how can he open the window if the lock is on the inside? And if he tries to break the window he could cut his arm.

Wally: They take him to jail if he breaks the window.

Eddie: He could break through the door.

Tanya: Then he might fall on the cactus.

Andy: I am going to tell my daddy to get more cactus plants for every window. And also one by the door.

Wally: Hey, here's a great idea. Let's put a cactus by the lima beans the next time. (p. 61)

Merleau-Ponty (1962) points out that speech is always situated in an interpersonal field and a particular location, with a speaker and a listener taking turns exchanging language: The children have their conversations in the classroom, from which the lima beans disappeared mysteriously. This provides the lived context for the conversation and the stimulus for what is talked about. The children are embodied and share the same environmental and historical context (they are in the here and now). This particular conversation refers to conversations the children had in the previous weeks, and it is part of the historical stream of speech, which spans a temporal frame that recalls the past and sets up themes for future conversations. In oral cultures, as with these children, the context of the conversation is clear and shared and does not need to be filled in (Ong, 1982): Wally's indignation when he found the lima beans gone from the dirt in his container is remembered by all, and so are other things lost over the weeks before this conversation. In his study of illiterate people in Uzbekistan and Kirghizia, Luria (1976) documented how the exclusive immersion into conversational contexts affected the kinds of thinking and speaking his participants engaged in: They refused to give definitions or comprehensive descriptions of things because situational events are obvious, and because a description or definition would miss many essential (non-visual) experiential aspects of things. Paley's (1981) children do not have to describe or define "cactus," but have an immediate grasp of the spiny, dangerous plant and its world, and they weave it into their conversation.

Speech is profoundly interpersonal and social and makes it possible "to think according to others which enriches our own thought" (Merleau-Ponty, 1962, p. 179).[2] The children have an implicit understanding that turn-taking makes speech generative: The cactus theme suggested by Andy is picked up by Eddie, Tanya, and Wally, who spin it forward. On the other hand, Deana's introduction of "cactus in the desert" falls flat because it leads too far away from the present location and the urgency of solving the mystery in this room. In oral conversation there is an immediate feed-back loop between speaker and listener in the service of the conversation. It is surprising to notice how well the children listen and take up, or "think according to," the ideas suggested by their conversation partners. They excitedly contribute their ideas, which link up closely with what the other child said but also amplify and modify and add to the other speaker's expressions. When we listen to a conversation partner we are "taken over by the other's speech, it fully occupies our mind," "we are possessed by it" as if under a "spell" (p. 180). Andy's story of the cactus on his father's windowsill has power, and the children become deeply engaged in the images and speculative thoughts it suggests. Only Deana drops out of the conversation because the other children were not willing to follow the spell of her speech, and she was unable or unwilling to change tack.

There is a profound connection between thinking and speaking, but Merleau-Ponty (1962) points out that language is not a simple utensil of cognition, as the constructivists claim (Piaget, 1955): It is not thinking that clothes itself in the garb of language, but the process of linguistic exchange produces and sustains thinking. Thought urges toward expression in language, and expressive speaking moves thinking forward. We do not know what we think before we speak it. "Thus speech, in the speaker, does not translate ready-made thought, but accomplishes it" (Merleau-Ponty, 1962, p. 178). Andy's idea of connecting the cactus to the mysterious robbers is a wonderful conver-

sational gambit. It has so much potential for speculation, and it intersects with the emotional puzzle of missing things that has occupied the children for a while. We could say that speech awakens thought and even accomplishes it by gathering and directing it and combining old thoughts into new ones in order for the language exchange between speakers to flow. The thought processes that Andy, Deana, Wally, Tanya, and Eddie produce are not individual but communal: Thought is born and accomplished in the evolving of their conversation. It flows through them, augmented (or stifled) by each individual contribution. Together they think better and more creatively than alone. The children speak to each other not in order to exchange information, but to re-live and approach the mystery of vanishing things. The excitement of their conversation lies not in its conceptual content, but in how much of the imaginary world they can open up.

At the beginning of the children's conversation, they are not sure where it will go. Andy introduces the themes of "robbers" and "protection against robbers," but it is by no means sure that the conversation will connect the themes to the missing beans. And yet it seems that the conversation tends that way. Before our own words are spoken, we reach for them. Words have a "near presence," they are "behind me," and come to realization in the act of speaking (Merleau-Ponty, 1962, p. 180). This emergence becomes particularly clear in Wally's final statement, as he discovers what everyone was reaching for: "Let's put a cactus by the lima beans the next time." Cactuses protect against robbers in a physical and magical way. "Cactus," "robbers," and "lima beans" are intuitively connected from the beginning, but it takes the children a while to consciously see the associative chain. It is as if they are working from the emotional complex of "protection against robbers" towards the final cognitive connection between cactus and lima bean, but need the bridge of speech to get there.

The conversation about the cactus allows for an imaginary participation in thoughts that are not connected to the here and now. The cactus does not reside in the room and is not present to their senses. It exists for all but Andy—who probably saw it in his father's office—outside their field of sensory experience. It is a purely imaginary object, which Andy introduces into their thought processes. However, the conversation partners treat it as completely real, as real as the lima beans to which it is linked. Language forms an "organism of words," which establishes a linguistic world and a new dimension of experience alongside the perceptual world. The word "cactus" has a location in the linguistic world for which the children reach, and some do it more successfully than others. Every human language, spoken or read, is a symbolic form of communication, in which the secondary world of invisible symbols is experienced as compelling and as real as the world of the senses. Luria (1981) succinctly summarized the power that language gives to the human child:

The enormous advantage is that their world doubles. In the absence of words, humans would have to deal only with those things which they could perceive and manipulate directly. With the help of language, they can deal with things which they have not perceived even indirectly and with things which were part of the experience of earlier generations. Thus the word adds another dimension to the world of humans....animals have only one world, the world of objects and situations which can be perceived by the senses. Humans have a double world. (p. 35)

The coming of words in the conversation between the children is based on the activity of trying to affect the world shared with the other. Speech has an expressive substructure that is deeply emotional, rather than conceptual. Through their speech, they want to draw each other in and create a common world, where everyone contributes to the complex cactus/robber/lima bean problem. Speech is a fundamental activity whereby human beings project themselves towards a "world" that can be illuminated and shared with the other. Paley (1981) does not tell us what happens after this conversation, but I am sure that if the class plants beans again, the children will want to "put a cactus by the lima beans the next time," as Wally suggests. The linguistic/symbolic world and its gestures are intermingled with the structure of the sensory/experienced world, which they outline and concur with. If a speech act is too far removed from the experienced world and does not fit into the emotional substructure of shared concerns, the conversation ends or the speaker's interjection is ignored. Not every thought is generative. Language, ultimately, is not a tool for expressing thought, but "it is the subject's taking up a position in the world of his meaning" (Merleau-Ponty, 1962, p. 193). The positions, even within the same conversation, can vary: Andy's role is that of an eye witness and defender of cactus-power, Deana's that of a silenced fool, and Wally's that of the synthesizing genius.

Throughout the year the children talk about the same theme of robbers when matchbox cars, coats, sweaters, and rugs disappear mysteriously. The intention to speak resides in an open experience, which leads to the productivity of speaking and is not merely repeating the memorized stack of words stored in the speaker's memory. The young child's desire for speech arises from "the ever-re-created opening in the plenitude of being" (Merleau-Paley, 1962, p. 197), and it is this plenitude that lets these kindergarteners approach the vanishing of the beans repeatedly and speak to each other over and over again. The conversations in Paley's kindergarten are productive, and we get a glimpse of the many possible themes and directions for thinking and speaking that open up when the children speak with each other: They discuss the nature of the man in the moon, if mothers collect bones and water and put them into their unborn babies, the functioning of pulleys, and how sugar comes from sugar beets. There is always more that could be said: The silence of the "more" is the fertile ground for all speaking.

Key Themes/Constituents of Oral Language Experience

Our brief phenomenology of the speech act highlights some key themes in the structure of oral language experience (we should keep in mind, however, that the following descriptions of the features of spoken language are written as positive descriptions, but that each of them also contains the possibility for failure and distortion within it).

1. The Embodied Context:
   Speech is situated in an interpersonal field and a particular location, with a speaker and a listener taking turns exchanging language. There is a lived context for the conversation, which is also the stimulus for what is talked about. Conversation partners are embodied and share the same environmental and historical context (they are in the here and now.) Engaged in a conversation, we think according to others, which, in turn, enriches our own thought. Moreover, we are taken over by other's speech, it fully occupies our mind, and we are possessed by it as if under a spell.

2. Speaking and Thinking:
   Thought urges toward expression in language and expressive speaking moves thinking forward. We do not know what we think before we speak it. Thus speech, in the speaker, does not translate ready-made thought, but accomplishes it. Before our own words are spoken, we reach for them. Words have a near presence; they are "behind me" and come to realization in the act of speaking. Language is not a simple utensil of cognition. It is not thinking that clothes itself in the garb of language, but the process of linguistic exchange itself produces and sustains thinking.

3. Sense and Symbol:
   Language provides us with an organism of words, which establishes a linguistic world and a new dimension of experience alongside the perceptual world. Every human language, spoken or read, is a symbolic form of communication, in which the secondary world of invisible symbols is experienced as compelling and as real as the world of the senses.

4. Shared Worlds:
   Speech is a fundamental activity whereby human beings project themselves towards a world that can be illuminated and shared with the other. The linguistic/symbolic world and its gestures are intermingled with the structure of the sensory/experienced world, which they outline and concur with. Language, ultimately, is not a tool for expressing thought, but it is the subject's taking up a position in the world of his or her meaning. Speech has an expressive substructure that is deeply emotional, rather than conceptual.

5. Language is Generative
   The intention to speak resides in an open experience, which leads to the productivity of speaking and is not merely repeating the memorized stack of words stored

in the speaker's memory. Language arises out of the ever-re-created opening in the plenitude of being. There is always more that could be said: The silence of the "more" is the fertile ground for all speaking.

Reading and Perception

To Be Alphabetized

Language enters the child's life as a powerful and transformative event. It begins as a sensory-musical presence in the womb (DeCasper & Spence, 1986), develops alongside the toddler's symbolic play, and undergoes a radical transformation when the young child learns how to read. The musical, the symbolic, and the textual aspects of language are all manifestations and possibilities inherent in language itself. Reading is rooted in human speech, but it also deviates from oral speech practice. Learning how to read requires that children change the way they perceive and think about the world. Textuality, in particular, reduces certain aspects of the language experience and intensifies others.

In their research on oral and literate competencies of children from kindergarten through third grade, Torrance and Olson (1985) discovered that children who are better readers use more psychological verbs that reflect cognitive processes (*think, know, decide, wonder, etc.*), but do not use a greater variety of affective verbs (*like, hate, love, care, etc.*). They argue that the predominance of cognitive verbs in young readers indicates their mastery of de-contextualization: The children understand that there is a difference between what a person means and what is actually said, i.e., that words and sentences per se mean something independent of a speaker. In order to understand the word on the page, the child must be able to recognize that words are words and can be represented in different media. "This is a basic move in coming to recognize 'words' as constituents of utterances, and it is a move that may be prerequisite to 'reading' any words at all" (p. 268). On the other hand, the researchers found that good conversational skills and oral competence, such as turn-taking and holding up one's end of a conversation, does not relate to success in learning how to read. This discovery indicates that successful engagement with text requires that the child achieves a reflective distance from the speech act. Language for these readers is no longer an intuitive, unconscious extension of their bodies, but a consciously, reflectively used tool.

Speech, in the conversation between Paley's (1981) children, was woven into a full sensory field. As Andy spoke about the cactus on his father's window sill, the children were sitting or standing together in close proximity. They saw each other, heard Tanya's breath as she got ready to interject her "how about" into the conversation, and sensed each other's gestures and facial expressions. The oral speech act is performed in a synesthetic sensory environment, where seeing, hearing, smelling, tasting, and

touching together make sense out of the flow of conversation and its context.

Before phonetic/alphabetic writing systems were invented, many cultures used pictograms as signs for objects, but the drawback of pictographic systems is that a vast number of signs are needed to code the many words of a spoken language (Goody, 1968). Alphabetization, on the other hand, is the translation of the sound system of a language into a small set of pictographic signs, which in the current Western alphabet means 26 symbols that code 5 vowels and 21 consonants (with some standard combinations between them). The invention of the alphabet created an economical and convenient instrument for recording languages, and we often forget what a momentous achievement this was: Goody (1968) remarked that the notion of representing a sound by a graphic symbol is "a stupefying leap of the imagination" (p. 38).[3]

While pictographic notation in general maintains its connection with the visual world by imitating it in pictures, alphabetic notation imitates language itself, and not what it refers to. Reading alphabetic notation means to decipher the sound of language from an abstract letter pictograph and then translate it into linguistic references. Alphabetic signs encode the symbolic system of spoken words, which are already one step removed from the world of the senses. The difficulty that many children have with this system is that the visual letters on the page have no intrinsic pattern relation with the phonemes they represent. They are arbitrary and have to be learned as a system. We could even argue that discrete phonemes do not exist in the flow of language that children use, and that a system of phonemes is an artificial and unintuitive construct, which then has to be linked to the artificial system of the alphabet. Before writing can make sense, beginning readers have to submit themselves to the rules of a senseless, arbitrary system of letters and phonics. Meanwhile teachers hope that each child will somewhere undergo Goody's "stupefying leap of the imagination" in which the chicken scratches on the page suddenly come together as a referential text.[4]

Alphabetic notation, then, is the visual representation of language sounds (as determined by cultural conventions). Engaging with texts, child readers have to restructure their perception: Language that existed primarily as an intuitive, oral event must be translated into a reflective, visual happening, where the visual spectacle of letters on the page has nothing to do with the multifarious visual experience of the perceptual field surrounding the reader. A written text is a visual abstraction which represents sound and context by eliminating it. Here we have the first example of the insertion of writing technology into oral discourse and the dynamic of intensification and reduction which it brings. The very structure of alphabetization, which is the foundation of Western reading practices, intensifies the representational capacity of language while at the same time unmooring it from its sensory anchor in the perceived world.

Reading in an Oral World

In the history of literacy there is an interesting chapter which describes the transition between reading as an oral and a visual event. Long after the invention of the alphabet, the written word remained closely tied to the ear and the voice: Until the 13th century most European literate people could not read silently. When you entered a medieval scriptorium, you would not find a hushed, silent library, but a community of mumblers and munchers (Illich, 1996). The readers would softly read out the words from the page, the scribes would dictate the words to their hands as they copied the text, and all would have intense bodily experiences as the sound settled into their senses and bones; some readers, like Talmudic scholars today, would rock back and forth. It is almost unimaginable to us that most people in the 12th century, even highly learned scholars, did think it impossible to read silently without moving their lips. When Peter the Venerable had a cough, he could not read a book, neither in the choir nor in his cell to himself. True silent reading was occasionally practiced in antiquity, but it was considered a feat: Augustine was amazed that his teacher Ambrose sometimes read a book without moving his lips. For the mumbling reader, the page was a "sounding page," a "soundtrack picked up by the mouth and voiced by the reader for his own ear. For the medieval reader the page is literally embodied, incorporated" (p. 54). This medieval oral reading practice was still closely related to the embodied, synesthetic speech act that we discussed above. The written text maintained its deep sensory connection to the spoken word, and reading was a slow recapitulation of an earlier speech act. Compare this carnal, oral, "deep view" of the written page to our contemporary understanding of texts as primarily *visual* events: "The modern reader conceives of the page as a plate that inks the mind, and of the mind as a screen onto which the page is projected and from which, at a flip, it can fade" (p. 54).

The text as a purely visual event is a historical invention with far reaching consequences, and it appeared in the late Middle Ages when silent reading and a new technology of text-production took over. The late 12th century invented (for the Western world) page lay-out, chapter division, the consistent numbering of chapter and verse, indices, tables of content, introductions, library inventories and concordances. Illich (1996) points out that this change in the technology of textuality fostered a change in the way reality is conceived. It created a new kind of reader who could read silently and swiftly, "one who wants to acquire in a few years of study a new kind of acquaintance with a larger number of authors than a meditating monk could have perused in a lifetime" (p. 96). The new kind of readers and writers looked at the page and experienced the exteriorization of a *cogitatio*, a thought structure, a thought outline of reasons. It became the foundation for the study practices of European universities and the production of bodies of knowledge in academic disciplines.[5]

The new relationship between text and mind, the ability to conceive of the written word as an abstract and inaudible record of thought, was the psychological foundation for the print culture, which began with Gutenberg in the 15th century. The elimination of sound intensified and sped up the reading process and involved the mind in a different way. The field of sound, as Ong (1982) pointed out, is not spread out before human beings but is diffuse and all around them. The visual field, however, is focused and laid out before the eyes. In the oral world human consciousness experiences itself surrounded by sound and enveloped by a cosmos. In the visual/textual world the cosmos is spread out before the eye: "Only after print and the extensive experience with maps that print implemented would human beings, when they thought about the cosmos or the universe or "world", think primarily of something laid out before their eyes, as in a modern printed atlas, a vast surface or assemblage of surfaces (vision presents surfaces) ready to be explored" (p. 73).

Pre-school age children experience their books in a way that is much closer to the oral, meditative reading of the mumbling monks. Our son, from the time he was 18 months old, insisted that we read the same book every night. For years we read Alley's *Busy People All Over Town* (1988), a picture book with extensive descriptive text. (Even though the book has been out of print for 20 years, there are still three current reviews on the Amazon website: Parents report that their young children want to "read" the book "over and over," "a hundred times"). Sitting together on Nick's bed, my husband or I read the text to him and we talked about the pictures. We were not allowed to abbreviate or change the wording because even as a toddler Nick knew the text by heart. The repetitive reading of the book was not an act of gathering information or new experiences, but it served to re-evoke a familiar world, which soothed him before sleep. Ong (1988) points out that in the oral world the word is essentially a call or a cry to the other, and that speech is not a reification of concepts or information, "but an event, an action" between people (p. 267). Every night we—and the other parents and children who have loved this book—enacted and performed the same story-event because it made our child feel safe, comfortable, and protected.

Synesthesia

Reading restructures the perceptual experience of human beings. We saw that the alphabet requires the translation of the language field into phonemes, which then are represented by symbols on the page. As a perceptual event alphabetization reduces the surrounding soundscape to the words that the reader can recreate in the mind, and the field of vision to the linear progression of letters on the page. While the medieval reader maintained the close connection between letter and sound, silent reading practice suppresses auditory perception and language becomes less and less a matter for the voice and ear. Visual perception, as well, is altered: The reader must see through the letters on the page in order to conjure up the invisible presence that the text encodes.

In his phenomenological analysis of alphabetization as a perceptual phenomenon, Abram (1996) shows how perception changes in the transition from oral to textual engagement with the world in non-literate, animistic cultures. His analysis, however, also applies to the restructuring child consciousness undergoes in the transition from orality to literacy. Prior to the immersion into textuality, the creative, synesthetic interplay of the senses with the perceived world creates a sense of magical envelopment. The earth is experienced as alive and meaningful and full of messages to the perceiver: "Direct, prereflective perception is inherently synesthetic, participatory, and animistic, disclosing the things as elements that surround us not as inert objects but as expressive subjects, entities, powers, potencies" (p.130). Abram's description of direct perception parallels Piaget's findings that young children's thinking is participatory, magical, and animistic (Piaget, 1929/1951).

Synesthesia works by bringing all the senses into play in the act of perception. We see something and know what sound it will make when we knock on it, how its texture should feel to the touching fingers, or how heavy it is when we pick it up. Even very young infants have this ability of cross-modal, synesthetic perception (Meltzoff & Borton, 1979; Stern, 1985). When one sensory mode is evoked the others come into play as well.

> In learning how to read we must break the spontaneous participation of our eyes and our ears in the surrounding terrain (where they had ceaselessly converged in the synesthetic encounter with animals, plants, and streams) in order to recouple those senses upon the flat surface of the page. As a Zuni elder focuses her eyes upon a cactus and hears the cactus begin to speak, so we focus our eyes on these printed marks and immediately hear voices. We hear spoken words, witness strange scenes or visions, even experience other lives. (Abram, 1996, p. 131)

Abram's analysis of the relationship between alphabetization and perception makes clear that the magical synesthesia, the evocation of all the senses, is relocated from the world to the text. When the eye perceives something, the other senses participate, even if they do not perceive directly. This is the virtual, imaginary dimension of perception (Merleau-Ponty, 1962). As the eyes read through the signs on the page, the mind brings all the senses into play to create a whole virtual world complete with sensory resonances. The magical power of books has its roots in the phenomenon of synesthesia: As we read, the world of the book is as compelling and sometimes more real to us than the actual world of the senses. "As nonhuman animals, plants, and even 'inanimate' rivers once spoke to our tribal ancestors, so the 'inert' letters on the page now speak to us! This is a form of animism that we take for granted, but it is animism none the less—as mysterious as a talking stone" (Abram, 1996, p. 131). And Abram is correct: We are animists when it comes to textual signification. We give ourselves over to the mysterious voices and beings that arise through the letters on the page and take them seriously—and among literate people we take the world of texts more seriously than the world of the senses: Most children spend more time in the text-centered symbolic discourse of school than in exploring and talking about the world they directly perceive.

The introduction of literacy changes children's relationship to the world because it shifts their attention from the animated, meaningful context of their perceived worlds toward the purely symbolic and *unperceived* dimension of the text's virtual world. Abram argues that the magic of full, synesthetic perception, the spell that it casts upon us and the force with which it draws us into a connection with the world, has changed its direction when we enter a literate world. Literacy is a technology that distances us from the life world and dulls our ability to attend to and "read" fully the expressions of the world of minerals, plants, animals, and the elements: "It is only when a culture shifts its participation to these printed letters that the stones fall silent" (p. 131). Here we have a second instance of the structural intensification and reduction which chirographic technology brings: The synesthetic intensification of the virtual/symbolic dimension of language and the reduction of the body's engagement with a plentiful, signifying, sensory environment.

Reading and the Symbolic Order

The Loss of Context

In order to perform the act of reading and to make the strange restructuring of auditory and visual perception possible, the young reader's experiential field of speech must be reconfigured. As long as children pay attention to the fullness of the perceptual field around them, the magical transportation into the world of the text cannot happen. In order to be a reader, a child has to let go of the lived context of the situation they find themselves in. Vygotzky (1986) noted that the young child's entry into literacy introduces an abstract process that is removed from the child's actual situation. Attention must focus through the visual process of decoding to the world of meaning the text transmits. This world of the text has no relationship to the child's here and now. The lived context for the conversation between speakers has to be eliminated: The room must be forgotten, other children must be blocked out, and the only one speaking is the text. Other bodies, and even the child's own body, are intrusions and must be restrained to a chair behind a table so that they don't occupy the space in social and disruptive ways. This is a change in the situatedness of language (Theme 1: *The embodied context* from our analysis of the speech act above). Andy, Deana, Eddie, Tanya, and Wally must stop talking to each other. Postman (1994) puts it succinctly:

But with the printed book another tradition began: the isolated reader and his private eye. Orality became muted, and the reader and his response became separated from a social context. The reader retired within his own mind, and from the sixteenth century to the present what most readers have required of others is their absence, or, if not that, their silence. In reading, both the writer and reader enter into a conspiracy of sorts against social presence and consciousness. Reading is, in a phrase, an asocial act. (p. 27)

When we are teaching children how to read, we should be aware that reading requires a profound change in the child's language experience. Speech is a very social and embodied activity, which has its own momentum and rewards. Most children love to talk to each other, and as we saw with Paley's (1981) class, they draw each other forward into the world of ideas that they talk about. Reading as an "asocial act" requires the child to engage with a speaker, the author, who is disembodied and unresponsive and does not create openings for the child's own introjections into the web of language and thought. The conversation, from the child's perspective, is passive and receptive, and the reader has no power to shape and alter the course of the conversation other than to disagree or put the book down. The child moves from the dialogue of oral exchange to the monologue of the text (Vygotsky, 1986). This is especially difficult for beginning readers, who cannot yet reconstitute the symbolic world behind the letters on the page, and have not yet tasted the pleasure that a good text evokes. Even though reading also requires an active mind, its activity is virtual, solitary, and disembodied. The very power of texts comes from their reduction of the actual, social, and embodied dimensions of language experience. The loss of the immediate social context opens the reader to the new context that the text offers. From a lived sociality the child moves into a virtual sociality that promises encounters with fictional characters. These encounters are powerful, disembodied, and invisible to others, which intensifies the reader's sense of privacy and interiority.

The Phenomenology of Entering a Text

Most children love stories. As an adult I remember being spellbound by one of David Abram's lectures about the gestural connection between humans and animals. He mesmerized us with words and movement, and as I glanced around the auditorium I saw my colleagues unconsciously bob their heads in imitation of a sea lion, which they clearly saw in their imaginations. The virtual reality created by language is extremely powerful. Oral story telling is supported by the physical presence and the shared context of narrator and listener. This is also the case when an adult reads aloud to children. In reading to oneself, however, this context is missing. The full magic of the written text can only come alive when the child overcomes the resistance of body and senses and enters into the particular symbolic structure that the web of sentences creates.

In his phenomenological analysis of the literary work of art, Ingarden (1973) suggests that out of the component parts of textuality (phonemes, words, sentences, and the textual unfolding as a whole) a particular *world* arises, and it is this world (which transcends the author's intended meaning) which the reader finds compelling—or not. The child has to be able to "climb aboard" and "accept the given perspectives" (Iser, 1972, p. 282), while at the same time be willing to collaborate with the text to allow it to come to fruition in the imagination:

The literary text activates our own faculties, enabling us to recreate the world it represents. The product of this creative activity is what we might call the virtual dimension of the text, which endows it with its reality. The virtual dimension is not the text itself, nor is it the imagination of the reader: it is the coming together of text and imagination. (p. 284)

The world displayed by the text refers to Merleau-Ponty's (1962) idea of the organism of words, which creates a new dimension of experience alongside the perceptual world (Theme 3: *Sense and symbol*). The child's imagination fills the gaps in the text, supplies what is not there. The text, on the other hand, allows the child to live and experience worlds that could never come to his or her immediate, embodied senses. A book takes on its full existence only in its readers (Poulet, 1969). If it receives their full participation, it allows them to absorb new experiences:

As soon as I replace my direct perception by the words of a book, I deliver myself, bound hand and foot, to the omnipotence of fiction. I say farewell to what is, in order to feign belief in what is not. I surround myself with fictitious beings; I become the prey of language. There is no escaping this take-over. Language surrounds me with its unreality. (p. 55)

The reader's thoughts and feelings are occupied by the thoughts of the author, and these in their turn draw new boundaries in our personality. The consciousness of the reader "behaves as though it were the consciousness of another" and "on loan to another" who feels, suffers, and thinks in it (pp. 56–57). Here we have another intensification and reduction of speech: The possibility of thinking according to others (Theme 2: *Speaking and thinking*) is intensified in the monological exposure to the text's voice. While in the oral speech act, the child participates momentarily in the speech of the other and then takes his or her turn; however, the written speech act requires the sustained immersion in the fictional world created by an author. The writer extends his or her own being by displaying a world with the hope that readers will share it (Theme 4: *Shared worlds*). The silence of the reader and the temporal structure of the continuous, uninterrupted voice of the author preclude the reader from interjecting and changing the direction of the language exchange. The world of the book worms its way into the consciousness of the reader. All a reader can do is close the book and refuse participation in the symbolic world the text promises.

The Symbolic Order

The conversations in Paley's (1981) class revealed how language gave the children a linguistic/symbolic world, which contained things (like the cactus) that were not actually present. This second order symbolic reality which is created in ordinary conversations is intensified and amplified in texts. The term "symbolic order" refers to the organism of words and the new dimension of virtual experience beyond the senses that appear in human language exchanges (Theme 3: *Sense and symbol*). It influences young infants before they themselves engage in symbolic activities (Lacan, 2002) because their parents participate in and are shaped by the languages and values of their cultures. Reading, once the child has mastered the decoding system, allows the child "to think according to others" (Merleau-Ponty, 1962, p. 179) to have experiences not available in the immediate sensory environment, and to be immersed in the cultural symbolic order more intensely.

In oral conversations, children take up each other's thoughts and weave a shared web of mind processes. In textuality, however, others' thought processes, memories, and images are recapitulated and accomplished in the child's mind without the child's direct, embodied response. Silencing the back and forth of embodied conversations intensifies the reader's exposure to the author's thoughts, images, and feelings. The most significant change that literacy introduces is the amplification of the symbolic order in the minds of children. As soon as children cross over the threshold of alphabetic decoding, they enter a compelling wonderland of ideas and experiences *which are not their own*, but which powerfully shape the mind. Literate cultures know that they need this world and that they have to colonize it. Through this process, on a massive scale, literate cultures reproduce themselves over the generations by establishing canons of texts that have to be read and internalized by children. Cultural memory is transmitted by texts. We call this process "education."

We can get a better view of the significance of the symbolic order when we look at it from a cultural-historical perspective. Literate cultures have commerce in the realities that are created by texts: Books hold knowledge and cultural memory. Books (and electronic media today) are a storehouse for memories of all sorts—records of legal transactions, historical events, philosophical arguments, poetry, scientific inventions and ideas, religious texts and commentaries, maps and calendars. Book content is the cultural currency that is transferred in the conversations of literate people and determines the intellectual and moral climate. Mumford (1934) argues that the invention of the printing press and the ensuing spread of writing technology led to a radical transformation of Western culture. "More than any other device, the printed book released people from the domination of the immediate and the local.... Print made a greater impression than the actual events....To exist was to exist in print: The rest of the world tended gradually to become more shadowy. Learning became book learning" (p. 28).

The proliferation of the symbolic order is fueled by the desire of writers to share their language and virtual worlds with others (Theme 4: *Shared worlds*). Print technology multiplies the audience for texts, as well as the number of authors who want to occupy the reader's mind. In turn, the dissemination of ideas in print, as Mumford indicates, inserts itself into everyday life practices and changes them radically (Theme 5: *Language is generative*). The invention of the automobile, the telephone, and electronic media was possible because their inventors could acquire the sedimented knowledge of previous generations through reading. In turn, these inventions changed where and how people lived, how they attended to and perceived their environment, and what they talked about with their neighbors.

Books do not merely contain information, but structure the way we think about reality. Literacy makes it possible to erect a conceptual scaffold above our everyday experience, which then is disseminated and transmitted through the authority of media and education. This makes the virtual reality of texts believable and compelling, even if it contradicts our senses: To exist is to exist in print. The immediate and local experience has been sacrificed to the symbolic dimension of texts.

Historically, the invention of print and the symbolic world it produced led to the cultural appearance of childhood. Those who could read and were educated were altered by literacy. The invention of "the Literate Human" inaugurated a symbolic distinction between childhood and adulthood:

> From print onward, adulthood had to be earned. It became a symbolic, not a biological achievement. From print onward, the young would have to become adults, and they would have to do it by learning to read, by entering the world of typography. And in order to accomplish that they would require education. (Postman, 1994, p. 36)

Unlike biological adulthood, which comes with puberty, symbolic adulthood requires education and has to be culturally reproduced in children. We ask each child to make a series of sacrifices on the way to literacy: Bodies do not lie on the floor or skip through the streets, but must sit in rows; the speech of friends is forbidden and re-defined as idle chatter; the magic of the sense-world is drained until it becomes dulled and distant, like the flat piece of sky beyond the sealed classroom window.

Notes

1. In *Of Grammatology* (1974), Derrida argues that the alphabet should not be thought of in terms of visual notation of phonemes, but as a differentiated system of visual signs that relates to the differentiated system of phonetic signs without complete congruence between the two. This complicates Illich's (1996) and the philologist's argument since it makes the historical leap into alphabetization (and I would include here also ideographic systems of signs) even more surprising

as a feat of the human mind: The acquisition of the alphabet requires the translation of one arbitrary system into another. But essentially Derrida's argument does not challenge the observation that pervasive writing technology brings radical changes to a culture (see also note #3).

2. The debate over the nature of language has been one of the most important discussions in 20th century philosophy. Since the Greeks, the study of language had been divided into grammar, logic, and rhetoric, with logic taking the pride of place in the philosophy of language. Heidegger, Merleau-Ponty, the late Wittgenstein, and Derrida shifted the emphasis—which was still apparent in Husserl's work—away from language as a conceptual tool of the logical mind towards language as performance within a personal and cultural context. Here language is no longer the expression of a private subject, but a means by which thinking is possible (Garver, 1973). Heidegger (1971) speaks of language as "the house of being" (p. 132). Merleau-Ponty (1962) thinks of it as the grillwork through which we can catch our thinking, and Derrida (1974) states that "we can think only in signs" (p. 50).

3. Since Derrida's (1974) *Of Grammatology,* many post-structuralist thinkers have given primacy to writing over speech. However, Derrida's notion of writing does not refer to the distinction between the spoken word and symbolic notation, but refers to the complex and infinite web of signification that comes with every language act. Textuality for Derrida means that every language act exists within a context and requires interpretation (Caputo, 1997), and that language as text is a "heterogeneous, differential, and open field of forces" (Deutscher, 2005, p. 33). Language is never the tool of an interiorized subject, but is given to us by our culture and is a repetition of what came before. As such it pre-determines what is expressible on the one hand, and what cannot be said on the other. Its conventional forms structure human cognition, identity, and experience.

From the perspective of child psychology, however, language does not pre-exist in the minds of children: It does not burst forth fully fledged like Athena from the head of Zeus. *Developmentally,* voice and gesture come before speech, and speech comes before writing. Before infants are able to engage in the symbolic dimension of the language field that surrounds them, they are attuned to the music and mood of what is spoken. Speech is an embodied, co-existential phenomenon, and infants acquire speech only if they are given the opportunity to interact with other people of their culture. There is a developmental sequence to language acquisition, a sequence which goes hand in hand with the development of interpersonal relationships, perception, and cognition. Infants, for example, have to be about nine months old before they grasp that a pointing finger (signifier) refers to something beyond itself (signified), and they have to have relationships with others that allow them to want to engage in joint attention. Developmental changes also mean that language exists for the child in different ways than it does for adults.

This does not negate Derrida's (1974) notion of textuality, but it adds the bodily dimension to the human experience of language. Even though the language a child "bathes in" is culturally constructed and instituted, the child's understanding and use grows on a daily basis through bodily engagement with the world. Language—and particularly grammar—as contemporary linguists have recognized, is not taught by adults, *but acquired by children.* We cannot prevent children from picking it up as long as they live in a speaking environment. This attests either to a biological/genetic foundation for language acquisition, as Chomsky (1959, 1969) claims, or to the child's insertion into a complex existential ensemble of bodily, co-existential, spatial, and temporal structures,

complemented by the child's inborn capacities for attention and learning that allow him or her to construct their native language (Tomasello, 2003).

4. Spoken language encompasses other forms of symbolic expression, which do not use the human voice. American Sign Language (ASL), for example, is a form of speech and a full language that is not dependent on the modulations of the voice. As with hearing infants, deaf infants who grow up in signing households acquire the language of their parents almost effortlessly within the first three years of life (Meier, 1993) (while children who learn ASL past puberty rarely achieve fluency). Writing, for deaf and hearing children, is an often-difficult modification of their speech acts. In writing the primary speech/language system of a child, such as ASL, is translated into the alphabetic system. Deaf children, for example, have an easier time deciphering alphabetic visual notation if they also learn how to fingerspell (Alvarado, Puenta, & Herrera, 2008), which is comparable to hearing children being taught the relationship between phoneme and grapheme. For both groups of children the in-between step of translating speech into phoneme, and symbolic gesture into fingerspelling attests to the difficulty in transitioning from embodied, contextual, and unreflected language use to the conscious acquisition of alphabetic notation and writing.

5. I have argued elsewhere (Simms, 2008) that the late middle ages saw not only shifts in literacy, but also in the ways people thought about themselves and how they conceived of childhood. The (re-)invention of silent reading, the instituting of confession in the Catholic Church, prolonged adult pilgrimages, and the children's crusade happened within a few decades of each other. The literate adult, the interiorized self, and the concept of childhood were invented at this time, and they comprise a web of profoundly entwined historical and psychological phenomena.

Literature References

Alley, R. W. (1988). *Busy people all over town.* Chicago: Goldencraft.

Academic References

Abram, D. (1996). *The spell of the sensuous.* New York: Vintage Books.

Alvarado, J. M., Puenta, A., & Herrera, V. (2008). Visual and phonological coding in working memory and orthographic skills of deaf children using Chilean sign language. *American Annals of the Deaf, 152*(5), 467–479.

Bruner, J. S. (1993). From communicating to talking. In M. Gauvain & M. Cole (Eds.), *Readings on the development of children* (pp. 135–143). New York: W. H. Freeman.

Burman, E. (1994). *Deconstructing developmental psychology.* London: Routledge.

Canella, G. S. (1997). *Deconstructing early childhood education: Social justice and revolution.* New York: Peter Lang.

Caputo, J. (1997). *Deconstruction in a nutshell. A conversation with Jacques Derrida.* New York: Fordham University Press.

Chomsky, C. (1969). *Acquisition of syntax in children from 5 to 10.* Cambridge, MA: MIT Press.

Chomsky, N. (1959). Review of B.F. Skinner, verbal behavior. *Language, 35,* 26–58.

Chomsky, N. (2002). *On nature and language.* Cambridge UK: Cambridge University Press.

DeCasper, A. J., & Spence, M. J. (1986). Prenatal maternal speech influences newborns' perception of speech sounds. *Infant behavior and development, 3,* 133–150.

Derrida, J. (1974). *Of grammatology* (G. Spivak, Trans.). Baltimore: Johns Hopkins Press.

Deutscher, P. (2005). *How to read Derrida*. New York: W.W. Norton.

Egan, K. (1988). *The educated mind: How cognitive tools shape our understanding*. Chicago: University of Chicago Press.

Eisenstein, E. (1979). *The printing press as an agent of change: Communications and cultural transformations in early-modern Europe*. New York: Cambridge University Press.

Garver, N. (1973). Preface to Derrida, Jacques, 1973. *Speech and phenomena: And other essays on Husserl's theory of signs* (pp. ix–xxix). (D. B. Allison, Trans.). Evanston, IL: Northwestern University Press.

Goody, J. (1968). *Literacy in traditional societies*. Cambridge, UK: Cambridge University Press.

Gurwitsch, A. (1974). *Phenomenology and the theory of science*. Evanston, IL: Northwestern University Press.

Hall, N., Larson, J., & Marsh, J. (Eds.). (2003). *Handbook of early childhood literacy*. London: Sage.

Havelock, E. A. (1982). *The literate revolution in Greece and its cultural consequences*. Princeton, NJ: Princeton University Press.

Heidegger, M. (1971). *Poetry, language, thought* (A. Hofstadter, Trans.). New York: Harper Colophon Books.

Heidegger, M. (1993). The question concerning technology. In D. F. Krell (Ed.), *Basic writings* (pp. 311–341). San Francisco: HarperCollins.

Held, K. (2002). The origin of Europe with the Greek discovery of the world. *Epoché, 7*(1), 81–105.

Hirsh-Pasek, K., & Golinkoff, R. M. (1996). *The origins of grammar. Evidence from early language comprehension*. Cambridge, MA: MIT Press.

Husserl, E. (1952). *Ideas: General introduction to pure phenomenology* (W. R. B. Gibson, Trans.). London: George Allen & Unwin.

Husserl, E. (1969). *Cartesian meditations* (D. Cairns, Trans.). The Hague: Martinus Nijhoff.

Ihde, D. (1979). *Experimental phenomenology*. New York: Paragon Books.

Illich, I. (1996). *In the vineyard of the text: A commentary to Hugh's Didascalicon*. Chicago: University of Chicago Press.

Illich, I., & Sanders, B. (1988). *ABC: The alphabetization of the popular mind*. San Francisco: North Point Press.

Ingarden, R. (1973). *The literary work of art* (G. G. Grabowicz, Trans.). Evanston, IL: Northwestern University Press.

Iser, W. (1972). The reading process: A phenomenological approach. *New Literary History, 3*(2), 279–299.

James, A., Jenks, C., & Prout, A. (1998). *Theorizing childhood*. Cambridge, UK: Polity Press.

Lacan, J. (2002). *Ecrits: A selection* (B. Fink, Trans.). New York: W. W. Norton.

Luria, A. R. (1976). *Cognitive development: Its cultural and social foundations* (M. Lopez-Morillas & L. Solotaroff, Trans.). Cambridge, MA: Harvard University Press.

Luria, A. R. (1981). *Language and cognition*. New York: Wiley.

Martinez, R. B. (2000). Languages and tribal sovereignty: Whose language is it anyway? *Theory Into Practice, 39*(4), 211–220.

McCluhan, M. (1962). The Gutenberg galaxy. Toronto: University of Toronto Press.

Meier, R. P. (1993). Language acquisition by deaf children. In M.

Gauvain & M. Cole (Ed.), *Readings on the development of children* (pp. 144–157). New York: W.H. Freeman.

Meltzoff, A. N., & Borton, W. (1979). Intermodal matching by neonates. *Nature*, 282, 403–404.

Merleau-Ponty, M. (1962). *Phenomenology of perception* (C. Smith, Trans.). London: Routledge & Kegan Paul.

Mumford, L. (1934). *Technics and civilization*. New York: Harcourt, Brace.

National ReadingPanel. (2000). *Teaching children how to read: An evidence-based assessment of the scientific research literature on reading and its implications for reading instruction*. Washington DC: National Institute of Child health and Human Development

Ong, W. (1982). *Orality and literacy: The technologizing of the word*. New York: Routledge.

Ong, W. (1988). Before textuality: Orality and interpretation. *Oral Tradition, 3*(3), 259–269.

Paley, V. G. (1981). *Wally's stories*. Cambridge, MA: Harvard University Press.

Parry, M. (1971). *The making of Homeric verse: The collected papers of Milman Parry*. Oxford, UK: Clarendon Press.

Piaget, J. (1929/1951). *The child's conception of the world* (J. Tomlison, & A.Tomlinson, Trans.). Savage, MD: Littlefield Adams.

Piaget, J. (1955). *The language and thought of the child*. New York: Meridian.

Pinker, S. (1995). *The language instinct*. New York: Harper Collins.

Popkewitz, T., & Brennan, M. (1997). Restructuring of social and political theory in education: Foucault and a social epistemology of school practices. *Educational Theory, 47*(3), 287–313.

Postman, N. (1994). *The disappearance of childhood*. New York: Vintage Books.

Poulet, G. (1969). Phenomenology of reading. *New Literary History, 1*(1), 53–68.

Rasinski, T., Blachowicz, C., & Lems, K. (Eds.). (2006). *Fluency instruction*. New York: Guilford.

Simms, E. M. (2008). *The child in the world: Embodiment, time, and language in early childhood*. Detroit, MI: Wayne State University Press.

Soto, L. D. (Ed.). (1999). *The politics of early childhood education*. New York: Peter Lang.

Spodek, B. (Ed.). (1993). *Handbook of research on the education of young children*. New York: Macmillan.

Stern, D. N. (1985). *The interpersonal world of the infant: A view from psychoanalysis and developmental psychology*. New York: Basic Books.

Sumara, D. J. (1998). Fictionalizing acts: reading and the making of identity. *Theory Into Practice, 37*(3), 203–210.

Tomasello, M. (2003). *Constructing a language: A usage-based theory of language acquisition*. Cambridge, MA: Harvard University Press.

Torrance, N., & Olson, D. R. (1985). Oral and literate competencies in the early school years. In D. R. Olson, N. Torrance & A. Hildyard (Eds.), *Literacy, language, and learning* (pp. 256–284). New York: Cambridge University Press.

Vygotsky, L. S. (1986). *Thought and language*. Cambridge, MA: MIT Press.

Webster, A. (2006). Keeping the word: On orality and literacy (with a sideways glance at Navajo) *Oral Tradition 21*(2), 295–324.

3

The Book as Home? It All Depends

Shirley Brice Heath

Stanford University and Brown University

What is it to feel difference—to feel a sense of distance from the traditional happily-ever-after portrait of parent and child reading together at night? Such a narrative has been instantiated in the public mind as the *right* way to be. It's not just one possibility, but the predictive indicator not only of assured school success but also of a guaranteed, life-long love of reading. In Arizpe and Style's opening *Handbook* chapter on reading in the home, the literary world Jane Johnson crafted for her children clearly demonstrates this narrative. Yet, in this chapter, Shirley Brice Heath, ethnographer and author of the groundbreaking *Ways with Words*—deconstructs the romance and tells us in a highly personal way what no bedtime story means. The intertwining of her childhood identity with her evolving adult academic identity and community work braids together a tale of multiple surprises and serendipitous turns narrating the many paths we take to reading.

No Way to Read

He left our interview, puzzlement written on his face. He walked across the campus parking lot, crowded with students, speaking to no one. For more than a week, I heard nothing from him until he confronted me outside the classroom where I was about to begin teaching. "I don't believe you. What you tell me goes against everything we believe about learning to love reading."

Ken Macrorie, teacher, essayist, editor, and inspiration for so many young writers in secondary school English classrooms, had asked to interview me for a book he was writing on language educators. I was flattered. It was 1985, and we were both faculty members at the Bread Loaf School of English, Middlebury College. This program brought secondary English teachers together to study literature and writing toward a Master's degree. When I joined the Bread Loaf faculty in 1982, Ken was a legend in English education. His books had inspired the "I-search" paper, an approach to undertaking research essays that had taken a generation of high school students to success with the elusive school-favored genre (Macrorie, 1985, 1988).

In the summer of 1986, Ken expected to complete a book of biographical essays based on his interviews with scholars he viewed as key influences in the field of language education. He began our interview by telling me how much he had enjoyed the stories from eminent men and women who were to be in his book: James Britton, Janet Emig, James Moffett, and others whom I had long admired. Ken told me that each of his previous interviewees had credited childhood teachers and favorite works of children's literature with shaping their desire to become language educators. Now Ken turned to me.

"I really have no story about favorite books."

Ken prodded: "Tell me about a teacher who instilled your love of literature."

I shook my head and looked out the window of the classroom where we sat together with Ken's audio recorder. I searched my memory. Nothing came to meet Ken's expectations.

He persisted: "What about your favorite books as a child?"

"But, Ken, there weren't childhood books as favorites— my grandmother's Bible, and she could not really read."

Ken forged ahead, certain now that it must have been teachers who brought me to a love of children's literature during my elementary school years. They must be the inspiration for my life's work in language and literacy. I continued to shake my head, and the interview ended shortly thereafter.

I could not tell Ken the story he wanted—yet another in the chain of accounts from eminent academics whose childhoods had been worlds away from my own. I kept my dissent silent then.

This chapter breaks that silence. Now I tell my story— one sure to resonate with narratives similar in consequence if not in detail for some readers of this volume. My story does not belong just to me. It has much in common with the unique tales that I hope children all over the world will stand up and tell at some point in their lives.

Their stories and mine come not out of anger but from a sense of difference. Our childhood histories are not laced with bedtime stories, favorite books, academic ambitions, family models of reading, and a circuit of moral and personal valuations in support of children's literature. Our families have not traveled for leisure or lived in exotic parts of the world. Like me, these children have lived their early lives in small spaces, with few possessions of lasting worth, and with frequent moves from place to place. When asked where they live, they answer, "I stay at my grandmother's house some of the time, and other times, I'm…." Their addresses represent households, not homes; these households have few if any books.

Adults in their lives cannot step back from the demands of work to tell stories or to sing songs with children. Except for the occasional Golden Book or Disney-film-inspired book picked up at the grocery checkout, books have no real claim on the budgets of the households in which they live. Their neighbors and friends find it hard to believe that some people "collect" books. Children like me encounter books randomly, usually only when someone else has made the book selection for whatever reason. We are not guided to cherish books and the time they might allow us to demand from adults for reading together. If and when we do find our way to books written especially for children, it is likely to come later in life, when some

unexpected change of status or accidental acquaintance makes it possible for us to bond with such books. Someday these children with few books and bedtime stories in their early lives may, as I did, become enthusiastic converts and steadfast promoters of bedtime stories, book shelves, and collections of books for their own children and for the children of others. But perhaps not.

This chapter tells a counter story to that generally told by language educators, widely read authors of fiction and poetry, or scholars, illustrators, and authors of children's literature. Theirs is the enchanted tale of the literary culture of childhood, told and retold by parents and readers nostalgic for the pleasures that books brought them as children (e.g., Arizpe & Styles, this volume; Hearne & Trites, 2009; Scholes, 1989; Schwartz, 1996; Spitz, 1999; Spufford, 2002; Tatar, 2009; Tucker, 1981).[1] All these works tell us what reading is and what it should be. These are good people thinking good thoughts and wishing for others the good that children's literature has to give. They (like Ken Macrorie) want others to share their joy, passion, and convictions surrounding the moral, pedagogical, and enriching experiences of reading.

My childhood story reminds us that there is no one age or reason to read, value, and absorb these worlds of children's literature. In many households, space, time, work, and social relationships ensure that there is no way to read at will and in peace. Children's literature makes demands; it involves the "witchery" of story; it can lead to "addiction" (Nell, 1988; Rugg & Murphy, 2006). Avid readers, including booksellers, collectors, and scholars, underscore this point in the genre they have created of collections of quotations from others like them who have never recovered from being infected with the "venom of language" that left them in the joyful stupor of the fantasy worlds of early childhood literature (Breakwell & Hammond, 1994, p. 18).

Reading with young children requires time for snuggling and conversing. As children grow in their reading, they need ample space for sprawling bodies and books whose numbers and sizes may overwhelm the capacity of available bookshelves. Children who read books demand time for stop-action attention from adults willing to inspect drawings, watch dramatic re-enactments, and listen to retellings of tales. Childhood reading comes with a price, literal and figurative, in time, space, and commitment by intimates who love their children and value reading as part of the expression of that love.

My narrative reminds us that ways to meet and learn to love children's literature have always been divergent and multiple and have not necessarily come with attentive parents and grandparents who spend time reading and talking with children. Learning to feel at home and to want to fill one's home with objects, values, ideas, and even relationships not experienced in childhood comes for some of us only with adulthood. For some, neither the books nor the time and space for conversations about books will ever come. For others who have these gifts in childhood, the accidents of life can erase their promise.

Storied Romance

Literacy educators hold tightly to the long-standing happily-ever-after transformational effects of children's literature or the beloved teacher who instills a love of books. Since the opening of the 18th century, the Anglo world has repeatedly made use of this romance, weaving it into children's books and through ideals of family literacy (cf. Lerer, 2008). Chapters in this volume attest to the strong ties that children's literature holds now and has historically held in the values of middle- and upper-class families. The ideology that links books with leisure, literate identity, and well-roundedness encourages parents to "cultivate" their children in an extended production process (Lareau, 2003). They manage time, space, and talk to ensure their children's familiarity with books. They look for performances and films, as well as accessories, to extend the characters and contents of children's books. They take pleasure in their children's language play, metaphors, and humor derived from bedtime stories. Parents draw on children's literature to tease, praise, chide, and coax their children (cf. Wolf & Heath, 1992).

Some leisure time of parents goes to reading for pleasure. Family conversations reference books and films, and outings include art museums with paintings whose narrative origins lie in written texts. Parents often believe children can acquire a fondness for science or mathematics on their own, but reading and knowing books must be taught. Educators and child-rearing guidebooks urge parents to read to and with their children. Didactic recommendations proclaim the power of storybooks to *instill, inspire, enthrall, influence, teach, enable,* and *direct* the ways of children. Children's songs and musical experiences often echo the lessons of books—from shapes, colors, and letters of the alphabet to moral cautions. The cultural resources that early childhood experiences with books offer are believed to sustain lifelong habits of reading and even to change the lives of children forever (cf. Fox, 2001; Meek, Warlow, & Barton, 1977; Pennac, 2006)

For centuries, upwardly mobile and financially established families of European, Anglo, and Scandinavian societies have believed that reading instills discipline and morality and bears a special relation to ethical action (Miller, 1987). The stories of children's worlds reinforce religious, musical, and visual values, model and inspire performance, and define not only what to stand for but also how to stand up to the world.

Picture books and illustrated stories, as well as chapter books, demonstrate the wit, curiosity, tenacity, and shrewdness of the young. In all these accounts, the young consistently out-maneuver adults, make friends with non-human creatures, and enlist magic, fantasy, science fiction, and a host of spirits to reshape the world to their will. Children's literature enables its heroes and heroines to overcome risk, pursue and achieve the impossible, and reconcile contradictions—all the while underscoring visions of the world to which adults around them subscribe (Wolf, 2004). Children can be anything they wish and travel anywhere on the "story road" (Hildreth, Felton, Henderson, & Meighen, 1940). Parents, older siblings, grandparents, librarians, bookshop owners, formal educators, authors, and edutainers—teachers all—have faith in the "magic of reading." Thus, the romance of children's literature and the wondrous potential of children merge into a unified whole.

Work Narratives

All romances rely on expectation. Those that extol the promise of picture books and written texts for children expect children and adults to have abundant leisure time free from the time demands of work. Reading is the enemy of chores and household tasks, for unlike storytelling, reading stops all other actions. Literary authors speak of their need to "hide," "steal time," "disappear," or feign deafness to avoid having to stop reading and to obey an adult's call to tasks. In homes and communities where family members do craft work, gardening, home and yard maintenance, food preparation and clean-up, and animal care, time for reading must be stolen away from chores and responsibilities. To read to or with a young child, adults step aside from the demands of their surrounding work. When youngsters begin to read for themselves, they must do so as solitary beings making themselves at home in their chosen book, disassociated from surrounding demands.

As a child, I had little chance for such disengagement.

For me, stories were told either by my grandmother or created in my own head in the midst of chores on my grandmother's small farm. I was an only child, born to parents who had caught one another on the rebound from prior too-early marriages. My father was a traveling salesman and refrigerator repairman; my mother a traveling waitress fond of following her favorite customers home. I have never known the full story of their life before me, and by the time I was five, each had decided that for the most part their lives were fuller and freer when I was not around. For my part, their absence was normal, for my life was full of play in work, choice of adventures, and the freedom to create imaginary places, people, and narratives.

I spent most of my early life with my grandmother in rural Virginia (in counties identified in 2008 as those with the lowest life expectancy in the United States). The woman I called "Granny" was really my mother's aunt, the sister of my mother's birth mother, who had died giving birth to twins. My mother had the misfortune of being the female of fraternal twins. Her father took her twin brother, leaving my own mother to die. Granny rescued the 3-pound infant and raised her. As soon as possible, my mother left home, and I was a product of her wanderings that she brought home to Granny.

When my grandfather died, my grandmother and I moved to a two-room tarpaper house without electricity while a cinderblock house was being built between our temporary home and the dirt road that fronted the farm. Our cinderblock house seemed to me a mansion, complete with oil stove and electric lights. Granny had a bedroom; so did I. There was an extra bedroom for my parents on the rare occasions when they came independently or together. I raised pigs and calves; my grandmother took care of the chickens. We had a garden and a small orchard. The change of seasons, care of animals, and rhythms of planting and harvesting told their own stories—the narratives of life and work for Granny and me.

On Sundays and sometimes early in the morning, Granny sat in her chair at the window of her room, where she had a front-row seat to everything that passed. There she had "good light" for "reading" her Bible. Each day she also sat quietly before picking up one of her several small thin-lined notebooks. She bent her head close down over her work as she laboriously wrote bits of sayings she had learned from her parents and short poems memorized during her few years of schooling. When I sat on her lap, she retold the adventures of Daniel, Jonah, and other young risk-taking males from the Old Testament. My grandmother had barely finished elementary school, and she had gone to the local church up the road all her life. Her grip on reading was precarious beyond the stories she had heard again and again in Sunday School and church services. Bible School had instilled in her and passed on to me a joy in reciting Bible verses while we worked. We practiced to prepare me for the competitions of Bible School. Across the dirt road in front of our house was the local Black church that had services once a month. Granny and I went to stand at the back of the tiny church with too few pews for the congregation. There, a deacon taught me how to read a hymnbook. Granny and I held the book together and sang our hearts out. Years later I knew I had learned something else standing in the back of that church: the printed word cannot restrain the soaring stories of gospel music, testimonials, and sermons.

Before I started school, the only books that came into my grandmother's house arrived in our mailbox. They carried inscriptions that read "To Shirley, a little girl who likes to read." They were signed with names like "Chuck" and "Bob," acquaintances of my mother. As a child, I sometimes puzzled over how these people I had never met knew of my existence or why they thought I knew how to read or would even like to read. I remember an over-sized book with the strange title "Bambi," a very long thin book of Mother Goose rhymes, and several Little Golden Books about tailors, elves, brown puppies, and ducklings. As strange to my grandmother as they were to me, these books were slipped reverently into shelves behind the front door.

When or how I learned to read, I don't know. I learned to recite the alphabet song my grandmother sometimes sang as we picked string beans. Their shapes of lines and curls went into letters of the alphabet—a welcome diversion as Granny and I prepared beans for canning.

By the time I was old enough to go to school, my father, pressured by his two younger sisters to take some responsibility for me, hired as my foster family a couple that my mother and father had met during their residence in North Carolina. They lived in High Point, North Carolina, where I could walk to the red brick elementary school. I spent that first-grade year away from Granny, holding onto the promise that I could come back to her in the summer.

Sensed Memories

My foster mom, "Mi," worked in a patent-leather purse factory; my foster dad, Carl, was a milkman. They had one child, Dick, a year older than I. They became my family intermittently—at any point when my aunts pestered my father too much about the absence of any "real schooling" with my grandmother. There I could walk just up the road to a three-room school that ran on the agricultural yearly schedule, starting late in September after tobacco, the local crop, had been harvested. So far as I ever knew, none of the local White families included anyone who had ever finished secondary school. For most of us, school was a palace of play, with its surrounding forest and meadows and long recesses.

For the first grade, I lived with Mi and Carl and walked to school each day. Bookcases with books lined the first-grade room and the school library. Mi had bookcases in the front room, and she sometimes read in the early evenings, but Carl went to work at 3 a.m. each morning, and our tiny house offered no well-lighted spaces for escape with a book at night. In that first year of school, I discovered the thrill of reading little bits of print for unexpected details. My foster mother gave me my first spanking when, during a bout of the measles, she found me, shut away in the darkest area of the house, shaking the pennies from my penny bank to read their dates with a flashlight.

At school, we ended the year with a "second reader, level two" hardback book entitled *The Story Road* (Hildreth et. al., 1940), but we did not get to keep our readers. By early May when I knew I would have to part with that little orange-covered book filled with stories of barnyard and circus animals, I read the stories over and over again so as to take them with me back to the farm. I wanted to tell Granny stories from my book. As I prepared to leave Mi at the beginning of that summer, she gave me a package wrapped in brown paper and told me to open it when I got to Granny's house. The car ride with my father took forever. As soon as we reached the farm, the three of us carefully removed the wrapping. There was *The Story Road* (Hildreth et al., 1940). My father read the inscription:

"To a little girl who likes to read. From some one that loves her very much, Mi and Dick."

That summer I tried to interest Granny in the books that had been secreted away behind the door. The pictures of Bambi, Smoky the horse (James, 1926), and the wild creatures of Thornton Burgess' Old Mother West Wind Series entertained us on nights when we were not too tired to stay awake. On my birthday late that summer, Granny gave me a package wrapped in a paper bag. Inside was *Elsie Dinsmore* (Finley, n.d.). The book, with its faded green cover, carried an inscription in a handwriting I knew well: "Presented to Rosa May [sic] by Mamma Dec. 25, 1920. Besure [sic] to read it and tell me what you think of Elsie D." Granny had given this book to my mother (Rosa Mae) the Christmas of her 10th year. I had never seen the book. My own stories from my first-grade reader and our sporadic summer evening reading had resurrected Granny's memory of a long-forgotten gift she had given my mother more than two decades earlier.

For that summer's birthday, as though to meet some deep notion of what parents do when they cannot do what others might expect of them, my father gave me a bookend in the shape of a black Scotch Terrier. I did not go back to Mi's for school that year or the next or the next.

I spent most of my elementary school years with Granny. I walked to the three-room seven-grade school of forty-some pupils with its "library" of three shelves of books kept behind the desk of the head teacher. She taught seventh grade, and prize pupils in her classroom won book-borrowing privileges. Otherwise, "books" meant workbooks.

Black on White

Down the road from my grandmother's house lived two teachers at the local Black school, a large brick building boasting resources, bus transport, and a staff trained at Hampton Institute, the historically Black college in a nearby county. Aunt Berta was their mother and the matriarch who lived in the big wooden house with the detached kitchen in the backyard. From her porch, Aunt Berta could see the smaller brick homes of all her children set nearby under the large oak trees that surrounded her property. Aunt Berta always welcomed me with a bear hug and took me back to the kitchen for fresh corn bread and buttermilk. When my chores were done at home, Granny knew I might be down the road with Aunt Berta or back of the big house playing with her grandchildren. Music, talk, laughter, and an abundance of food and children marked frequent family celebrations—a sharp contrast to the quiet life Granny and I lived. Back at home, I had to tell Granny who had come home to see Aunt Berta, who was getting married, and who was building a new house. Then we could unwrap the packet of food Aunt Berta always sent home with me. Aunt Berta did not venture far from home, but her family members stopped by to see Granny and visit whenever they went up the road to the store. A decade later, I realized they never came to the front door.

My grandmother and I were one of the few White families in an area where Black farmers owned most of the land and raised tobacco, corn, and large gardens. We looked forward to late August when tobacco season began. In fields around the area, farmers pulled tobacco and brought it in large mule-drawn slides to curing barns. There, children handed bundles of tobacco to women who tied the tobacco onto sticks the men placed high in barn lofts where curing took place. We measured the weeks of tobacco season by the staged smells of green leaves fresh from the field to the pungent smoky odor of the yellowed dried leaves on the sticks taken down from barn lofts and hauled to tobacco auctions at the end of September. On water breaks, we splashed one another and played with tobacco worms fat from feeding on the green tobacco leaves.

By early October, the few White children watched their Black playmates board school buses for transport to the Black school 15 miles away. That school was a new sprawling brick building. But the small three-room elementary school for White students was plenty big for the few of us. Unlike the Black churches that held bi-weekly services, the two local White churches had circuit preachers who came only once a month except during the two weeks of summer Bible School. On Sunday mornings, White families collected either in the back of Black churches or in their own church to plan the annual Homecoming, clean the cemetery, or hold an informal Sunday School and sing-a-long.

White schoolteachers were "hired in" for the three-room school, given a small house, and watched with a cautious eye. Few stayed more than a year or so. A test of their adaptation to local ways came in the speed with which they honored our flexible attendance rules. They also had to learn quickly that we required long recesses to run home for chores or to complete our elaborate games based on comic book characters, such as *Batman* and *Wonder Woman*. How we got those comic books, I don't remember, for the nearest city was over 50 miles away. But the comic books we shared among ourselves incited vivid reenactments with weapons crafted from tree limbs cut from the forest that surrounded the school.

Beyond the seventh grade, I walked to the paved road intersection where a bus took me and the few White students to the county seat, location of the small regional secondary school. The school had no library, but it did have a jousting field adjoining the fair grounds. The year's highlight, the county fair, featured a jousting tournament, 4-H booths, and competitions for the best chocolate cake, biggest pig, and finest rooster.

Late in my secondary school years, my mother returned and decided to take Granny and me to south Florida. There my mother worked as a seamstress in winter months. In our small town—said to be the tomato capital of the world—Blacks lived on the other side of the tracks, attended their own high school, and almost never crossed the tracks except to work in the tomato fields. The house where we stayed was very near the tracks on the "White" side. I sometimes rode my bike to the tracks where I could hear muffled voices and laughter and catch refrains of songs I had learned in the Black church at home in Virginia. Now that my mother was around much of the time, my grandmother told no stories and our household lived in silence.

At high school, I met my first Puerto Ricans, Cubans, Filipinos, Jews, and self-proclaimed atheists. Outsiders all, individuals from these groups became my friends, and I learned the stories of the Alvarado, Spitzer, and Mendoza families and the travels that had brought them to south Florida. My fitful peripatetic schooling left me woefully behind all my classmates in every subject. I studied every spare moment. My Spanish class, taught by a Puerto Rican woman who spoke little English, topped my list of terrifying experiences, for I had had no contact with any foreign language other than a bit of Latin from the secondary school in Virginia. I sought out more opportunities to be with Puerto Rican and Cuban friends, confessing my fear of the teacher and the language, and, most of all, of being called on to speak in class. As though to prove to myself that I was not an utter failure at this language, I turned more and more to reading Spanish literature, which I did with ease. My best-spoken phrases were those I used in private with the teacher to ask to borrow books in Spanish, so I could "practice" the language. She started me with children's books and allowed me to graduate to novels and classics from Latin America and Spain. My practice with the language remained largely restricted to silent listening and solitary reading.

At 16, I went to work as a grocery store clerk, and I occasionally baked pecan pies to sell to neighbors. I never remember going to the school library, though I found my way to the town library, which was near the grocery store where I worked. There I found the resources I needed to write research papers to meet class requirements. I became editor of the school newspaper, and in the days when typesetting and "going to press" were literal activities, I spent most nights of my senior year after work at the small press that published local small-town newspapers. There the typesetter talked to me of books, asked about my reading, and gave me ideas on how to edit, inspire younger writers on the newspaper staff, and read beyond the headlines and obvious stories of newspapers.

Never wanting to displease or disappoint, I thought I should turn all the typesetter's questions into action. One of my self-identified atheist friends was a reader, and one day I found my way to her house to ask her about what she read. She drew from the pile of paperbacks: "Start with these." I found solitary reading for pleasure outside of class assignments or religious contexts strange and recalled the times when as a young child, my grandmother and I leafed through the gift books sent to me by my mother's acquaintances. If Granny found me reading alone, she would ask: "Don't you have something you should be doing?" Her "should be doing" never included reading without instrumental purpose. Her disapproval and cautionary tone stayed with me through my senior year of high school. I read alone, but with guilt, for now I was reading books I could not share with her.

By the middle of my senior year, the guidance counselor asked what I was doing about college. I looked at her in puzzlement. She called in my mother, having recognized the need to convince her that college was a possibility for me. A friend was applying to the University of Chicago; I decided to do so as well. My father, who weighed in at that point from afar, nixed that idea by declaring any college north of the Mason Dixon line off limits for me.

The college I would attend came down to a choice between a small women's college in Georgia and Wake Forest in North Carolina. My mother heard that the Georgia college would feed me well (I weighed 99 pounds and stood 5'8" tall), and Wake Forest was a Southern Baptist school. But in the choice between food and God, the latter won. I headed to Winston Salem in the first year that Wake Forest admitted females. The campus banned dancing, required that dating be only double-dating, and insisted female students wear hats to compulsory Sunday chapel.

The summer before I was to enter Wake Forest, a single event shaped the course of my life's work and my future of trying to understand families and children in relation to language, literacy, culture, and belief systems. Thomas Mendoza, my Filipino friend from high school, was driving through Virginia on his way to college in the Northeast. I wrote to ask him to come by my grandmother's farm in Virginia. When my parents learned of the invitation, they issued a definitive "no," explaining that his dark skin proscribed such a visit. On this denial pivoted all the accumulated observations of exclusion, racism, and discrimination I had seen but not fully reckoned with in Virginia or Florida. I had been too busy just playing and working to sort out any analysis of the strangeness of the givens and the choices that made up my unique world.

Perhaps my blindness came because in Virginia I had neither witnessed nor felt exclusion. Blacks and Whites went to different schools, but the Black schools were better. Blacks and Whites worked together, but the Blacks owned most of the land and hired us White children to work as "hands" in tobacco season. Granny and I went in and out of our neighbors' houses and shared garden bounty. We gathered with friends in the back of Black churches to hear sermons and sing hymns. The Mendoza denial brought all that I had *not* seen into glaring detail in my memory. Uneasy in spirit and full of shame, I left for college that fall.

After a year of immersion in European history and Spanish literature, and a host of courses in mathematics, I left Wake Forest. The precipitating event came in the spring of my freshman year when I declared mathematics as my major. My professor called me to his office a week later. He counseled against my decision: "You cannot enter what is a man's world." Denial and discrimination had twice cut short my choices. Now I made my own choice. I ran away to Mississippi to work in the Civil Rights movement.

There I lived on the generosity of Black families. I tutored children in Black schools and took part in meetings and protests. Now I began to seek out children's books that related to the lives of the children, families, and churches that took me in. The few books I could find carried little of the richness of oral stories or the relevance to contemporary times I sought. Wonderful as Ezra Jack Keats' *The Snowy Day* (1962) was, neither the children in Mississippi nor I found much there in common with our experience of either climate or environment. Night after night, Sunday after Sunday, I listened to grandmothers, aunts and uncles, and parents tell stories, stage performances of their neighbors' lives, and plead with and sing for a god they believed knew them as characters and shaped the plotline of their days ahead.

From Mississippi, I went to southern California to work as a part-time substitute teacher in "special education" with migrant farm workers' children with whom my spoken Spanish now flourished. By now, I knew the work of my life would be to understand the shaping of cultural differences and the place of language(s) within everyday ways and values. Finances meant that I moved often, each time enrolling in a different college along with correspondence schools. As a result, I finished college with concentrations in Anthropology, Sociology, Education, Spanish literature, and English. Readings required across these fields provided some answers to a few of my many questions. But none acknowledged the role of stories, oral and written, for children and adults hard at work shaping and reshaping their lives and trying to make words and ideas do things for them and the social world around them.

Searching Stories

Forces that mold what goes into our memories and values remain largely hidden from us. Only from time to time do we believe we know what defined who we now are. For most of us, any such revelatory insights bear little definable relationship with who we were yesterday or will be several years hence.

Ken Macrorie and others whose livelihoods are made in industries that surround children's reading (from publishers to librarians and educators) urge consistency in the course of each individual's history with language and literacy. They trust in the causal and directional powers of socialization into literary culture. Yet reliable patterns based on single chains of influence are more often wished for than achieved. A generalized trajectory cannot account for the variation of routes that may lead at any point to respect, reverence, and fascination for books.

After college, doctoral work in anthropological linguistics and Latin American Studies at Columbia University took me to Mexico to study the history of language and literacy from the arrival of Cortés until the mid-20th century. From 17th-century archives through contemporary practices in indigenous villages, the power of oral stories for children came through again and again. Friars sent from Castile to Mexico learned the indigenous languages by collecting children within the walls of the monasteries and then listening through the thin walls of the children's dormitory to the stories and legends the older children told the younger ones to calm their fright. Language policies of the Castilian Empire in the New World resonated with expectations that children and their stories were the best teachers for the missionaries (Heath, 1972).

In the 1980s, my teaching at the Bread Loaf School of English fed my anthropological interest in how readers and writers of contemporary American fiction connected with one another throughout the 20th century. I began that work by hanging out in workshops that creative writers attended and by observing readers and writers in their separate environments. In the fiction sections of bookstores in 27 cities across the United States, I loitered, asking every fifth client who bought a work of fiction what led them to the purchase and if I might phone them at set intervals in the coming months to see how their reading had gone. Writers from creative writing workshops I attended allowed me to observe them over a full week at random times during a single year. I followed this pattern for eight years, socializing in literary events across the country with major contemporary writers reading and talking with their devoted readers.

One of the young novelists I met during the course of my study was Jonathan Franzen. Initially, he had resisted my project and "the whole idea behind it." Several years later, he entered the national scene with his award-winning novel *The Corrections* (2002). Critics saw him as a young writer to be reckoned with in the future.

In April of 1996, Jonathan published an article in *Harper's Magazine* entitled "Perchance to Dream: In the Age of Images, A Reason to Write Novels." A major New York newspaper had asked him to write a piece on the topic of "the great American novel." When he undertook the task, he remembered my research. With my blessing, he wove my findings into his reflections on his own life as reader and writer. He noted that novelists dislike social scientists and the idea that anyone could poke into matters of readership. He described me as a "beacon in the murk" that inadvertently jarred him from his depression about the state of the literary world and of his place as writer in that world. Most meaningful to Franzen from my poking about in the ways of readers and writers of American fiction was the fact that I could give names and reasons to his own childhood discovery of literature. I had found two key factors in the lives of readers who habitually read "serious" fiction as adults. The first was experience as a child with reading models—intimates who valued reading and encouraged others to take up this good habit. Franzen solemnly reported that he could not remember seeing either of his parents read a book, except when they read to him as a child. He could not declare them good models of reading or even promoters of the habit. He smirked, thinking he had demolished my social science "findings."

I continued: "But there's a second kind of reader. There's the social isolate—the individual who from an early age feels different from everyone else and who may or may not read as a child, but will, if fortunate, later discover literature and find others sorting out their unique destiny in life." His silence permitted me to go on. I said to him: "Readers of the social isolate variety are much more likely to become writers than those of the modeled-habit variety. You, Jonathan, are one of those socially isolated individuals desperately wanting to connect with your own past, a substantive imaginary world, and your intense lonely existence. You want these to be of some consequence in the future."

Franzen's piece for *Harper's Magazine* argued that writers, almost by definition, feel estranged from the world around them and most comfortable constructing and inhabiting an imagined world (1996, reprinted 2003; see also Franzen, 2007). The writer Don DeLillo had told me, as he later wrote to Franzen, that "the writer leads, he doesn't follow." This is because the dynamic behind the creative act will always live in the writer's mind and not in questions the writer ponders about acceptance or readership. In response to his article for *Harper's Magazine,* Franzen received many supporting testimonies to confirm the ties between loneliness and imagination in the lives of writers.

Readers wrote to say that they too were lonely and found joy, solace, and togetherness in reading the complexity of the lives of others. Echoing through these letters were voices railing against the death of either the novel or of book reading. Readers and writers both do what they do to fill a need—generally unexpressed though keenly felt and certainly denied to the individual's harm (Fox, 1992). Society simply had to keep books and reading alive. Though romance, mystery, and even compulsion surround ideas of literature, whether for children or adults, reality lies in the cultural apprenticeship they afford and the company they provide for lonely writers who will be society's keenest critics.

Uncommon Readers

In 2007, the British playwright Alan Bennett fictionally portrayed his monarch, Queen Elizabeth II, as a reader who came quite late in life to reading fiction and poetry. As she did so, four changes came over her that she attributes to her new self-identity as reader. First, she wants to talk about her reading with others. Then, she wants to meet with the authors themselves to probe their motivation

and inspiration for writing. Along the way, she organizes principles of her reading that derive from to-do and do-not-do lists, for she wants to read all the works of authors she comes to admire. For a long time in her reading, she tells herself to avoid the writings of authors whose characters live their lives in social classes with which she has little familiarity but considerable responsibility, but she overcomes this limitation. Ultimately, she determines that she will co-mingle in the world of writers by becoming a writer herself. She moves from recording her reading in her diary to wishing to shape her responses and her own creative worlds into written texts.

Despite the overdrawn humor and satirical framing of his book, Bennett hit a nerve for those among us who see something of our own later immersion in the world of books in the Queen's march of revelations. Like her, we have experienced the disdain of those who equate reading with shirking other responsibilities. Like her, during our daily routine duties, our thoughts remain on pages in the middle of a chapter cut short by the call of responsibilities others thrust upon us. And like the Queen, we have lost consciousness of outward appearance and relished curling up before the fire in our favorite baggy clothes and warmest socks. We have expanded the comfort zone that the escape of reading offers so that we may distance ourselves from the intruding world. Ultimately, we have come to decide we too can write, and we have turned out our own books or found ways to promote books to others[2] (cf. Gilbar, 1989).

Like Bennett's Queen, I too took up writing books. But I did so early in my career with an eagerness to explore and express what I learned about language and its uses in oral and written forms. Unlike the Queen, however, I was fascinated by more than words: I was drawn also to the powers of visual illustration. During fieldwork in Mexico, I spent time with not only archival remnants of Mexico's past but also in sites of excavation of monuments, settlements, and religious centers in Oaxaca, Puebla, the Federal District, and the Yucatan Peninsula. There texts came along with sculptured profiles of individuals and events carved into the stonework of panels that surrounded temples and public buildings.

Having completed my book on Mexico (Heath, 1972), I settled in the Piedmont Carolinas to teach in the midst of the initial turmoil of desegregation, busing, and laments by White teachers that they could not understand the language of their Black students. At first I spent my out-of-school time between Black and White working-class communities, working in gardens, gossiping on front porches, helping can food, and attending church and Bible School. I gradually wore a natural pathway into Black and White middle-class communities, where parents followed the romantic idea that early experiences with books would ensure their children's school success and establish lifelong reading habits.

In White working-class communities, I watched parents

read religious stories for children, point to illustrations and letters in alphabet books, and talk through books that recounted simple "true" stories written for children about pets, farm animals, and birds and small animals of the fields and forests. For these families, reading in and about the Bible held highest place in time and honor. Their questions asked for straight and familiar answers—no opinions or chases into imaginary places.

In Black working-class communities, I relived my years in the family compounds just down the road from my home with Granny. I heard gossip laced with jokes, family stories, and tales full of fun and moral lessons. Entire families used newspapers, letters, and circulars as prompt and props for stories.

For White working-class families, the exaggerated stories of their Black counterparts seemed to be nothing but lies. For Black working-class families, the stories their White counterparts told were just plain boring. My book, *Ways with Words* (1983), about the ways of reading and telling stories in these two communities laid bare just how uncommon some readers are.

In the decade in which my book was published, academics in fields from anthropology to religion began to study what being literate could mean across cultures and situations. Again and again, these works showed the intertwining of literate habits with different norms of time, space, relationships, as well as religious, academic, and commercial incentives (Barton & Hamilton, 1998; Boyarin, 1992; Scribner & Cole, 1981; Street, 1984, 1993; Taylor, 1983). Books, their accompanying artifacts and values, and their relation to children's socialization and adult habits of child-reading could not be considered apart from socioeconomic class, geographic location, religious beliefs, or cultural milieu. The only "common readers" were, in fact, those created out of the cultural habits and ideals elevated in Western societies where reading held a place right up there with morality and advancement in class status. The majority of the world was filled, instead, with "uncommon readers," albeit of a very different sort than the Queen Elizabeth of Alan Bennett's fiction.

By the early 1990s, the unquestionable importance of sociocultural context to the structures and uses of language was firmly established by social scientists and historians. Professional educators acknowledged the idea, but generally could not fit the wide-ranging differences into their fixed curricula and assessment tools for teaching reading. Educational policy, texts, and tests in the United States generally ignored the unique language and cultural patterns of African American communities in the South as well as the North.

Meanwhile, in both the United States and other economically advanced nations, migrations, relocations of refugees, and absorption of asylum seekers further challenged fixed normative ideas of routes to literacy and academic achievement. Motivations behind migration varied greatly for newcomers, as did the extent and type of their prior experience with either written language or formal schooling. Some read in non-alphabetic scripts, some only in a non-Indo-European language. Others had little experience with schooling or literate expectations.

Yet the norms and modes of teaching reading narrowed. The appeal of phonics accelerated while arguments for children's literature that had previously held for homogenous populations fell away as inappropriate and ineffective. Decoding became the goal. Comprehension according to formulaic dictates of "main idea" and "supporting evidence" became the primary purpose of such pedagogical practices. Education policymakers viewed interpretation and imaginative language, along with creative learning, as impossible with children vastly different in oral language fluency and background experiences. Learning to read mattered more than reading to learn. Surveys of book buying and reading for pleasure showed that both were on the decline. The "death of literature" was sure to come with the reduction of print and growth of images, technological shortcuts in communication, and shifts in habits of work and leisure (Kernan, 1990).

Nevertheless, children's literature and its power to inspire learning and to initiate a lifelong love of books and reading lived on in the intuitional wisdom of confident teachers and many middle-class parents whose family life was increasingly feeling pressure from the information economy and its partner technologies. Literary and art critics continued to hold onto the Western-model-tells-all-we-need-to-know framework. Books on reading and its values across the ages of individuals and of Western history proliferated (cf. Manguel, 1996). Romance is a difficult thing to dislodge.

Making Images, Expanding Modes, Shrinking Words

Particularly challenging to established thinking about children's reading and their literature have been picture books and illustrated books, comics and graphic novels (Eisner, 1996; Fox, 2008; McCloud, 1993). In such works, image often dominates word. As images expand in their conveyance of meaning, words shrink in their own power or work in sync to retain it. Authorities beyond the child reader lose control over interpretation. Through images, young readers can take charge.

Once the child has learned to speak, picture books engage child and adult relatively equitably. Infant laughter, gesture, and imitation are soon followed by the child's growing takeover of the story beyond the written words. Characters and their moves and motivations belong to the child who now reads images to take them beyond the written words. Adults *read* for meaning while children *look* for meaning. With the discovery of comics, children carry their expertise in reading images further into imitation of entire scenes with their friends and sometimes into their own attempts to draw graphic narratives. The visual can quickly outpace the verbal. For decades, young readers have charged into the "plague" of comic books and all that it represents by its open inclusion of readers of the lower classes, derision of social norms, promotion of consumerism, and representation of the horrors of "man's inhumanity to man" (Gordon, 1998; Hajdu, 2008; Spiegelman, 1986, 1991, 1994). With graphic novels, the imagined world within the page and beyond belongs almost entirely to the young (Adams, 2008). The intimacy of the adult-child reader dyad fades away.

Concern over the graphics of narrative derives from the long-standing linkage of children's literature with control over the moral, behavioral, and linguistic futures of children. Children's literature developed and has continued in relatively few regions of the world—the majority of those steeped in Anglo traditions, Judeo-Christian values, and often the tying of nationalism to moral certainty.

Early in their history, Scandinavian nations enlisted religious leaders to reinforce the habit of parents reading with their children, withholding services of the Church to resisting parishioners. Along with their empire, the British spread a high estimation of reading with children and entrusted books to build foundations for commitment to hard work, individualism, academic promise, and commercial success. American colonies, more than any others, renewed Protestant faith in reading the Word for life guidance and placed responsibility on parents to bring up their children as believers and practitioners of Biblical truths (see Stevenson, this volume). Sunday School books, pamphlets, daily devotional readings, and later video films, DVDs, and illustrated music books expanded meanings of ancient dicta in contemporary life.

The history of visual art in the Western world leaves little doubt about the spiritual convictions behind the idealized image of mother and child reading together in intimate pose with a book. European and American painters have given us the classic metaphor of the reading mother through Mary, the mother of Jesus, who becomes spiritual authority reading with her child as novitiate. The earliest now-familiar rendering of this narrative comes from Simone Martini's 14th-century depiction of the Annunciation. Medieval and Renaissance artists repeatedly portrayed the Virgin Mary startled from her reading by Gabriel's announcement of the forthcoming birth of Jesus, the Christ child. Uses of light, the cast of the eyes of the reader, and the positioning for the perspective of the viewer outside the paintings combine to reflect absorption, tranquility, and solitude in the presence of book as altar (Adler & Bollmann, 2005). The handling and elevated placement of the Bible as the Word during Protestant church services echo these sentiments of Judeo-Christian art. Such visual narratives portray the duality of being both outside the mundane world and inside the sacred realm of certainty, loving care, and promise. The family Bible in quiet times of intimacy leads to reenactment. Granny had never seen a work of Western visual art, but she knew how to take her Bible and sit me on her lap where our reading encircled us.

Women Who Read Are Dangerous

However, an oppositional genre of painting has told another story. From the Middle Ages forward, artists have suggested that reading may lead the weak and innocent away from the sanctity of home and into danger, foul play, and wrongly-placed passion. The romance of reading has, until recently, largely ignored any such idea. But by the late 20th century, art critics began to deconstruct details of classical works of art. This scholarship, along with the growing body of research on women readers by feminist writers, revealed images of women reading letters and other materials that could lead women into danger or even, more menacing, make them dangerous influences. The book as home, retreat, and reliable source of knowledge could be inciting resistance or rebellion.

These paintings suggest the potential of book reading, especially for women weak in resolve, to disrupt their devotion to family, their home, and their chastity. Images in these paintings show that reading stops time and action and allows viewers to read into images the secret desires of women. Jacob Ochtervelt's *La Requête amoureuse* (1670) and Johannes Vermeer's *The Love Letter* (ca. 1669–1670) tell more than is seen. When these artists portray facial expressions of women reading book or letter, viewers across the centuries have imagined lovers, plans of escape, and inclinations to temptation beyond the bonds of propriety. *Les femmes qui lisent sont dangereuses* [Women who read are dangerous] is a volume of paintings of women lost in reading through the ages (Adler & Bollmann, 2005). The images remind viewers that books and their secrets may stir in women the disobedient nature and weakness of will of their progenitor Eve. They may step out of place and wish to be "the woman on top" (Davis, 1965). Yet the message is that they must not succumb to either the temptations of others or their own ambitions (Liedtke, 2001). They must not lose themselves in nature, a favorite suggestion artists have repeatedly made in their paintings of women reading in open fields, on park benches, and before a window looking out onto a garden of rambunctious flowers (cf. Updike, 2005 on "looking").

Reading invites self-knowledge as well as exploration of distant places and unsanctioned behaviors. Reading takes one away from home to places where authority, ownership, and responsibility differ. Maps and legal documents, along with instruments for measuring and recording, figure in the background of many paintings of individuals reading and hint of multiple forms of "accounting." We must take measure of ourselves, but there are many ways to do so. Reading books can dislodge the weak and uninitiated—women and children—from received values that seem not to account for love or desire for freedom. Books introduce subversive ideas and lead women and the young to imagine behaviors and relations unaccountable in society's ways of measuring us. Reading may give women pleasure when their lives offer little else. *La Liseuse*, a Renoir (1877) portrait entitled "The Reader," became synonymous with a *woman* reader "lost in a book" and likely therefore to shirk her responsibilities as wife and mother.

Some painters portrayed women with books as resistant to the world of external power. Impressionists often juxtaposed the woman's inner world of peace in a book with the external world of upheaval (see, for example, Claude Monet's *La Gare Saint-Lazarem*, 1877). Female artists, such as Gwen John (1911), perhaps best known for her *Girl Reading at the Window*, made women reading a favorite theme in their work. The 1970s awakening to the subject of female artists consistently points to their serene portrayals of "the reading woman" (with her child or children) (cf. Barlow, 1999; Fine, 1978/1995; Schur, 1991).

But the quiet world of women reading changed after World War I when women were vitally needed in the workplace. Once called upon to work outside the home, women no longer had to read books to enter the world of dangers and temptations. They were now in the middle of them in a world of war and work. Throughout the 20th century, the realities of women in the workforce eroded the ideal of mothers having time and place to read at home with their children. By the end of the century, infants and toddlers went off to caregivers outside the home for much of each day; their evenings and mornings with parents held little time for reading. The image of mother at leisure to read with her child disappeared from Western art and norms of family life.

Dislodged and Dislocated

The idea that written texts undermine authority through alternative readings began well before the printing press. Storyboard narratives within medieval illustrated manuscripts and stained glass windows of cathedrals took readers and worshipers beyond Biblical text. In illustrated manuscripts of the Middle Ages lie the origins of comic books, graphic novels, books with illustrations, and children's picture books. This era established the ability of images to expand modes and shrink the power of words and bears examination when we turn to the question of what contemporary children read and the relative extent of image, print, and talk in their everyday worlds (Kress, 2003). Here the issue is not so much that written texts may lead the weak away from duty, morality, and ethical behavior, but that images, even more than words, explode with unpredictable meaning.

Borders of illuminated manuscripts, as well as sidebars to the Biblical narratives depicted in stained glass windows of medieval churches, tell of artistic license. *Vignettes*, the term used for borders of medieval illustrated manuscripts, contained images that suggested stories that only sometimes related to Biblical texts (Watson, 2003). Vignettes that ap-

peared alongside the text and within initials that opened textual materials included scenes of everyday life along with fantasy and foolhardiness. Monkeys covered their ears, grotesque animals frolicked, children teased dogs, and wives berated their husbands (cf. Stallybrass & White, 1986). Monks and scribes who illustrated manuscripts slipped into their images license to let the mind wander, question, and turn cynical (Heath & Wollach, 2007).

Illustrated manuscripts and stained glass windows of cathedrals may be the first crossover texts of Western history. For example, the windows gave parishioners in cold medieval cathedrals incentive to look up to find well-known Biblical characters moving through their narratives in grouped story-board-like panels. For children, the appeal must have been in the floating images—the butterfly, industrious squirrel, and bird on its way to build a nest. These designs were child-like and child-ready as were embellishments buried in garment folds and background scenes of distant castles. Cathedral windows were the kind of text and image artists believed children and adults might like to read. Text and illustration worked together and yet apart from one another.[3]

Chapbooks of the 18th century continued the pesky trend of working text and illustration into intimate partnerships that sometimes quarreled with one another and at other times joined peacefully. Chapbooks used the license of image to let young readers see the lives of the poor, the renegade, and the miscreant. Picture books and illustrative didactic materials created by educated mothers in the home to support their children's reading sustained the inclusiveness of chapbooks (see Arizpe & Styles, this volume; Heath, 2009). Children could look through the visual lens of the stories of their less fortunate counterparts.

Comic books of the 20th century do the same, telling stories of war, racial and ethnic divisions, violent crimes, and supernatural powers that contrast dramatically with the relatively tame stories of discovery and adventure rendered only in print (Hajdu, 2008; Heath & Bhagat, 1997). American, British, and European illustrators differ in use and extent of detail, suggesting national variation in assessment of when and how young readers can work out ambiguities and draw judgments on their own from images and text. In the 21st century, comic books joined graphic novels in their appeal to the shrinking attention spans of young people. Films and video games animated images and added sound effects, further reducing words—even in the spoken mode. Hand wringing over the dominance of image over text was inevitable. Official reports, such as *Reading at Risk* (National Endowment for the Arts, 2004) and *To Read or Not to Read* (National Endowment for the Arts, 2007), declared the decline in both amount of time youngsters spent reading and their comprehension skills with extended texts. Public media and educational reports lamented that young people not only read less now than in the past; they understood less of what they read.

Debates continue, with extremists certain that not only

is literature "dead," but the entire publishing industry is in peril. Still, moderates and advocates of images in every learning life view the widening range of modes and media young people use to read, write, and act in the world as a welcome though drastic change (Kress, 2003; Spitz, 1999). They argue the need to view the current rise of image, performance, and autonomy—as well as imagination—among young people as a desirable challenge and expansionist opportunity for educators (Buckingham, 2003; Doherty, 2002; Flood, Heath, & Lapp, 2008; Hobbs, 2007).

But this opportunity comes with a price. Adults trained in guided reading and interpretation of print have little understanding of how the young actually see and interpret images and print in relation to one another and layer meanings through multiple media. A sense of dislocation prevails for adults who hesitate to invest in learning how to navigate visual texts from comic books to on-line multi-party role-playing games. On the other hand, young people see themselves as disconnected from resources and identities that might guide them in ways to deepen skills and knowledge. The most astute young feel the dislocation coming for them in a world where their skills with entertainment and diversion via the internet will be no match for rapidly increasing computing power and electronic control over their lives (Heath & Wollach, 2007). Adults feel their past disconnects them from the present; young people see their present dislocated from the future. The romance of children's literature seems distant indeed.

Why Do We Care?

In the history of literacy studies, few topics have generated as many words of confession and conviction as reading and writing. Aristotle and Plato held strong views, based on their own lives and protections of the State. Religions of the world have celebrated vision as our greatest sense, and their evocation of the eye as the soul of human essence reminds us that we are knowledge makers and interpreters. We speak of cognitive understanding as "seeing," "gaining a perspective," having a viewpoint," and "glimpsing meaning." Scientists, artists, philosophers, and theologians have let us look over their shoulder as they read and left us their accounts of transformation brought about through their reading of words and interpreting of visual images that reveal narratives fundamental to life.

Judgments such as these lead individuals to be unduly self-conscious about their lives of reading and writing. How much? What kind? And for what?

When I ask these questions of myself, I admit that my life with reading started late. In the anger and violence of Civil Rights in Mississippi, I felt helpless. It was the same when I confronted in California educational institutions' exclusion of migrants from their language and culture. All I could see to do was learn; perhaps books could prepare me to know how to change things. I had to catch up for lost time.

It took me more time to overcome the silence of my childhood and to learn that conversations about ideas had to come along with book reading.

I threw myself into literature and the social sciences, burying any memory of my exclusion in college from further study of mathematics. Research on people and their ways of living and thinking came naturally to me. I liked listening and looking in silence. Fieldwork in Mexico and archival discoveries opened to me past and present contrasts in values and uses of literacy across languages and cultures. A keen observer of human behavior, I was never satisfied with only what I could see in the present scene before me. I had been fooled by that complacency in my childhood. Now I questioned every form of exclusion and use of language—oral and written. I searched for origins, reasons, and consequences. What were the personal pains and joys, the current shaping forces and those of history? A career in linguistic anthropology and social history fell into place gradually and certainly without long-term goal-directed planning. My reading was eclectic and frantic, the need to know relentless. Yet my life of scholarship was still void of extended talk about books. I read alone.

Extended conversations with books came in my head as I wrote books. I typed *Telling Tongues* (1972), based on archival research and fieldwork in Mexico, on an unfurling roll of shelf paper fed into the typewriter so as not to have to stop to insert separate sheets of paper.

When bilingual education became a national possibility in the mid-1970s, I wanted to help. I spent time in Washington, D.C. with fellow sociolinguists and educators. Slowly my writing and reading became less dependent on my solo conversations with my reading and writing. Expanded opportunities for conversation came when desegregation of Carolina schools raised questions about relations, linguistic and behavioral, between Whites and Blacks. I spent time in local communities and classrooms talking with teachers and children about their learning. I traveled to state capitals of South and North Carolina to lose myself in letters and diaries of plantation owners and small-town people whose lives centered on farming and raising tobacco and evolved into millwork with the coming of textile mills in the 1920s.

I filled the lives of my young children with books but without knowing good from bad, rich from shallow. Grocery store racks and the school library provided their books. Marriage, divorce, remarriage, and a move to Stanford University just as my children ended primary school brought possibilities I had never imagined. My husband, Charles Ferguson, was a prominent linguist whose love of language, distant places, and cultural supports for literacy was as intense as my own. Also an only child, he had grown up in working-class Philadelphia. As a young boy, he had been free to explore the city's many bookstores, hear other languages, and explore language in the many religions of the city. Our household was filled with children's literature and talk of politics, travel, and languages. Visitors from around the world came to our home in Palo Alto, and we traveled to parts of the world where numerous languages and cultures competed for political and social legitimation.

At Stanford University, I met Shelby Wolf, a young mother of two girls whose early childhoods with literature differed immensely from anything I had ever imagined. Together we talked for hours about how to interpret her fieldnotes documenting her children's talk about literature, dramatic reenactments, and entry into solitary reading. We discovered together the writings of other scholars who had also documented their children's lives with books. We brought this work together in our analysis of children's worlds of reading (Wolf & Heath, 1992).

Children's literature presented itself as another field in which I could feel simultaneously the panic and joy of catching up. By happenstance, several years later, I learned of the existence of an early 18th-century manuscript collection of children's literature in the Lilly Library at Indiana University. Over nearly a decade, I studied British history while analyzing the nearly 500 pieces in the "Nursery Library" (see Arizpe & Styles, this volume). I was "possessed" by the quest to learn about Jane Johnson, the maker of the collection (cf. Byatt, 1990). British scholars of children's literature Morag Styles, Victor Watson, and Evelyn Arizpe joined me in the search to know more about Johnson's life. Occasions for conversation, debate, and museum exhibitions, conferences, and books followed (Heath, 1997; Hilton, Styles & Watson, 1997; Styles & Arizpe, 2009).

Simultaneously, I was immersing myself and young ethnographers from Stanford in the lives of urban youth living in under-resourced neighborhoods across the United States. Theirs was a world different from my own and from any romantic notions about books in early childhood as essential to learning in later life. We studied young people who found their way to community organizations in their early teens to join theatre and music groups, artist cooperatives, and community service projects. They took up reading for pleasure, often motivated by the collaborative work of the group. But they also relished risk-taking, challenge, and long conversations. Talking about what they had read or were learning became socially acceptable among peers and adults who shared their interests. Talk motivated reading that they could take into action, contemplation, and further accumulation and testing of information (Heath & Roach, 1999; Heath & Smyth, 1999; Heath & Soep, 1998).

Meanwhile, I continued to follow the Black and White families of communities I had begun to study in the 1970s. The twists and turns of their lives took them far away from the South we knew in those days. Within two decades, their definitions of family, social life, religious values, opportunity, race, and work bore no resemblance to the lives I had captured in print in *Ways with Words* (1983/1996; Heath, 1990). I wrote and continue to write to document the dynamic of their mobile existence as individuals and families in "liquid times" (Bauman, 2000).

Knowing books, talking ideas, and seeing the world is sure to dislodge certainties—one's own and those that others try to force on us. For me, sweeping generalizations about language, culture, youth, childhood, race, gender, family, and tenets of socialization were boulders to be pushed away in order to open landscapes of difference, possibilities, and human capacities. The issue of difference is not that it is there, but how much difference we allow it to make for us.

When we are *in difference* as distinct from *indifferent,* we see that persistence of either children's literature or book reading as intimate parent-child dyads in quiet spaces of homes cannot take us where we now have to go. Families in economically advanced societies, those that have been the primary producers and consumers of books for children and young adults, have less and less time, space, and inclination to read with and for their children beyond the toddler years. Economic realities, two-working-parent homes, single-parent homes, and competing forms of home entertainment push interactions with print, image, music, and talk into layered mediated forms, places, and relationships. Recently, the number of hours libraries remain open across the United States has decreased, and many libraries have closed. Libraries and schools, as public institutions, are increasingly required to censor young learners' access to the internet and to new media, such as graphic novels and novels written for young adults.

Yet young people who learn that reading books may feed their special interests will find ways to get what they want. On buses, in community centers, and with special friends, they create for themselves mobile home-like atmospheres. The future of the book's home will be the "nonspaces" of supermodernity, away from private households into public spaces and in search of human company around and through technologies (Augé, 1995, p. 94).

Coda

What about Ken Macrorie's proposed collection of autobiographies of language educators? It never appeared. Whether or not my dissonant pattern moved him to set aside the project, I do not know. In the intervening years, I have resisted attempts to universalize ideas about literacy, language development, readers and writers, and modern childhood and youth. As individuals, we matter not in the ways we fit into categories or meta-narratives. Instead, we matter in the ways we experience and remember the emotions, expectations, and connections of our early lives and attempt to understand how those of others affect who they have become. "Each childhood is a nightlight in the bedroom of memories" (Bachelard, 1960, p. 140).

All childhoods of promise do not begin with reading as an archetypal activity. In this chapter, I have tried to shift us away from treasured reveries of childhoods with books. Through the lens of my life story, I have urged us to understand that people embody many different aspects of human potential—artistic, spiritual, economic, cultural, and intellectual; realized human potential does not depend on childhoods with favorite books. I hope to have disengaged us from constructions of single trajectories toward set destinations of literate lives. I have wished to heighten acknowledgement of difference not as deprivation but as incentive and inspiration to recognize that we are born to grapple—to observe and reflect on all that we experience.

From my life with books of all kinds, some written for children and the young, others about them, I have formulated two principles. The first recognizes that expectations embedded within metaphors of trajectory, pathway, and life course rely on a horizontal view to the past that precludes an open future. Such a perspective blinds us to differences of circumstance and will that lie beneath the shade of our skin and confines of our childhoods. The horizontal fails to account for the randomness of accident and serendipity.

A vertical perspective lets us see the intertwining of regional, racial, and gender origins with individual will and convictions of change. Verticality takes us deeper and higher and may even force us to return to places we think we have known before. We have to look up and down before we move ahead.

The second principle concedes that we cannot always move either ourselves or others—even those we love most—forward. The case in point is my daughter Shannon. In her childhood, we lived the romance of the book as home in our hours of reading, enacting, talking, collecting, and relishing books. When she was 18, on the cusp of adulthood, she suffered a severe head injury in a mountain-climbing fall. Memory, affect, engagement, and promise—all that had made children's literature part of the fiber of her being—left her. Today, a woman in midlife, her afflictions limit her to collecting and categorizing children's books and sometimes bringing their names into conversations she otherwise could not choose to enter. Her subterranean childhood passion survived brain insult to transform into the comfort and control that book names and taxonomies can give.

There is, to be sure, a correspondence here with the book as home. But resemblance is not sameness. Difference and an absence of predictability must summon in all of us a faith that goes beyond mere incidence to the certainty of awe in the motions of the mind.

Notes

1. Instances of this genre are numerous, and their forms range from substantive date books and journals designed for "the reading woman" (Schur, 1991) to the innumerable accounts by parents recalling their pleasures of reading as children or with their own children (Hearne & Trites, 2009; Tatar, 2009; Wolf & Heath, 1992).

2. Of those who collect essays or quotations about the powerful hold that books can have on life, women make up the vast majority. Of these, most have careers as scholars, writers, booksellers, small press directors, or collectors. See, for example, Bascove, 2001; Bettman, 1987; Hearne & Trites, 2009; Tatar, 2009. Alter (1989) analyzes the extent to which the ultimate complexity of reading for each individual will always ensure that no one else will ever replicate the process of another. This sense of "original creator" so inspires some readers that they cannot resist taking up the "many-voiced conversation" to write (p. 238).

3. Definitions of *crossover* texts abound and shift from year to year. As the genre of young adult fiction grew in popularity after the turn of the 21st century, debates raged over questions of appropriateness of topics and category assignment by award committees. When a thick volume, *The Invention of Hugo Cabret* (Selznick, 2007), won the Caldecott Medal for picture book, the matter of crossover took on new meaning, for here text and illustration announce themselves as partners in the progression of the story. The verbal and the visual never appear together on the same page; instead, the words and images take turns telling the tale. Within two years, other such books followed to complicate further the meaning of *crossover. The Selected Works of T. S. Spivet* (Larsen, 2009), described as "a boundary-leaping novel," tells the story of a 12-year-old cartographer who renders his adventures in both words and maps. The debate here is dual. Is the readership adult or young adult? And the medium—picture or word? T. S. Spivet leads us back to some of the earliest crossover texts—the accounts of explorers who could not tell their tales without lists, maps, drawings of plants and creatures discovered, and illustrations of fantasies imagined. He reminds us that rigid categories will never confine books, authors, and readers regardless of age.

Literature References

Bennett, A. (2007). *The uncommon reader*. New York, NY: Farrar, Straus & Giroux.

Byatt, A. S. (1990). *Possession*. New York, NY: Vintage.

Finley, M. (n.d.). *Elsie Dinsmore*. Chicago: M. A. Donohue.

Franzen, J. (2002). *The corrections*. New York, NY: Picador.

Hildreth, G., Felton, A. L., Henderson, M. J., & Meighen, A. (1940). *The story road*. New York, NY: John C. Winston.

James, W. (1926). *Smoky, the cow horse*. New York, NY: Grosset & Dunlap.

Keats, E. Z. (1962). *The snowy day*. New York, NY: Penguin.

Larsen, R. (2009). *The selected works of T. S. Spivet*. New York, NY: Penguin.

Selznick, B. (2007). *The invention of Hugo Cabret*. New York, NY: Scholastic Press.

Spiegelman, A. (1986). *Maus I: A survivor's tale: My father bleeds history*. New York, NY: Pantheon.

Spiegelman, A. (1991). *Maus II: A survivor's tale: And here my trouble began*. New York, NY: Pantheon.

Spiegelman, A. (1994). *The complete Maus. CD-Rom*. New York, NY: Voyager.

Academic References

Adams, J. (2008). *Documentary graphic novels and social realism*. Oxford, UK: Peter Lang.

Adler, L., & Bollmann, S. (2005). *Les femmes qui lisent sont dangereuses* [Women who read are dangerous]. Turin, Italy: Flammarion.

Alter, R. (1989). *The pleasures of reading in an ideological age*. New York, NY: Simon and Schuster.

Augé, M. (1995). *Non-places: Introduction to an anthropology of supermodernity*. London: Verso.

Bachelard, G. (1960). *The poetics of reverie: Childhood, language, and the cosmos*. Boston, MA: Beacon Press.

Barlow, M. (1999). *Women artists*. New York, NY: Hugh Lauter Levin.

Barton, D., & Hamilton, M. (1998). *Local literacies: Reading and writing in one community*. London: Routledge.

Bascove. (2001). *Where books fall open: A readers' anthology of wit and passion*. Boston, MA: David R. Godine.

Bauman, Z. (2000). *Liquid modernity*. London: Polity Press.

Bettmann, O. L. (1987). *The delights of reading: Quotes, notes & anecdotes*. Boston, MA: David R. Godine.

Boyarin, J. (1992). *The ethnography of reading*. Berkeley, CA: University of California Press.

Breakwell, I., & Hammond, P. (Eds.). (1994). *Brought to book: The balance of books and life*. London: Penguin.

Buckingham, D. (2003). *Media education: Literacy, learning, and contemporary culture*. Cambridge, UK: Polity Press.

Davis, N. (1965). Women on top. In N. Davis (Ed.), *Society and culture in early modern France* (pp. 124–151). Stanford, CA: Stanford University Press.

Doherty, T. (2002). *Teenagers and teenpics: The juvenilization of American movies in the 1950s*. Philadelphia, PA: University of Pennsylvania Press.

Eisner, W. (1996). *Graphic storytelling and visual narrative*. Tamarac, FL: Poorhouse.

Fine, E. H. (1978/1995). *Women and art*. New York, NY: Allenheld & Schram.

Flood, J., Heath, S. B., & Lapp, D. (2008). *Handbook of research on teaching literacy through the communicative and visual arts, Volume II*. New York, NY: MacMillan.

Fox, C. (2008). History, war and politics: Taking 'comix' seriously. In V. Ellis, C. Fox, & B. Street (Eds.), *Rethinking English in schools: Towards a new and constructive stage* (pp. 88–101). London: Continuum Press.

Fox, M. (1992). *Dear Mem Fox, I have read all your books even the pathetic ones*. San Diego, CA: Harcourt Brace.

Fox, M. (2001). *Reading magic: Why reading aloud to our children will change their lives forever*. New York, NY: Harcourt.

Franzen, J. (1996, April). Perchance to dream: In the age of images a reason to write novels. *Harper's Magazine*, 15–17, 38–54.

Franzen, J. (2003). *How to be alone: Essays*. New York, NY: Picador.

Franzen, J. (2007). *The discomfort zone*. New York, NY: Picador.

Gilbar, S. (1989). *The open door: When writers first learned to read*. Boston, MA: Godine.

Gordon, I. (1998). *Comic strips and consumer culture, 1890–1945*. Washington, DC: Smithsonian Institute.

Hajdu, D. (2008). *The ten-cent plague: The great comic book scare and how it changed America*. New York, NY: Farrar, Straus, & Giroux.

Hearne, B., & Trites, R. S. (Eds.). (2009). *A narrative compass: Stories that guide women's lives*. Carbondale: Southern Illinois Press.

Heath, S. B. (1972). *Telling tongues: Language policy in Mexico, colony to nation*. New York, NY: Teachers College Press.

Heath, S. B. (1983/1996). *Ways with words: Language, life, and work in communities and classrooms*. New York, NY: Cambridge University Press.

Heath, S. B. (1990). The children of Trackton's children: Spoken and written language in social change. In J. W. Stigler, R. A. Shweder, & G. S. Herdt (Eds.), *Cultural psychology: The Chicago symposia on human development* (pp. 496–519). New York, NY: Cambridge University Press.

Heath, S. B. (1997). Child's play or finding the ephemera of home. In M. Hilton, M. Styles, & V. Watson (Eds.), *Opening the nursery door: Reading, writing and childhood 1600–1900* (pp. 17–31). London: Routledge.

Heath, S. B. (2009). The deeper game: Intuition, imagination and embodiment. In M. Styles & E. Arizpe (Eds.), *Acts of reading: Teachers, text and childhood* (pp. 43–58). Stoke on Trent, UK: Trentham Books.

Heath, S. B., & Bhagat, V. (1997). Reading comics, the invisible art. In J. Flood, S. B. Heath, & D. Lapp, D. (Eds.), *Handbook of research on teaching literacy through the communicative and visual arts* (Vol. I, pp. 586–591). New York, NY: Macmillan.

Heath, S. B., & Roach, A. (1999). Imaginative actuality: Learning in the arts during the nonschool hours. In E. Fiske (Ed.), *Champions of change: The impact of the arts on learning* (pp. 20–34). Washington, DC: Arts Education Partnership.

Heath, S. B., & Smyth, L. (1999). *ArtShow: Youth and community development*. Washington, DC: Partners for Livable Communities.

Heath, S. B., & Soep, E. (1998). Youth development and the arts in nonschool hours. *Grantmakers in the Arts*, 9(1), 9–16, 32.

Heath, S. B., & Wollach, R. (2007). Vision for learning: History, theory, and affirmation. In J. Flood, S. B. Heath, & D. Lapp (Eds.), *Handbook of research on teaching literacy through the communicative and visual arts* (Vol. II, pp. 3–12). New York, NY: Erlbaum.

Hilton, M., Styles, M., & Watson, V. (Eds.). (1997). *Opening the nursery door: Reading, writing and childhood 1600–1900*. London: Routledge.

Hobbs, R. (2007). *Reading the media: Media literacy in high school English*. New York, NY: Teachers College Press.

Kernan, A. (1990). *The death of literature*. New Haven, CT: Yale University Press.

Kress, G. (2003). *Literacy in the new media age*. London: Routledge.

Lareau, A. (2003). *Unequal childhoods: Class, race, and family life*. Berkeley, CA: University of California Press.

Lerer, S. (2008). *Children's literature: A reader's history*. Chicago, IL: University of Chicago Press.

Liedtke, W. (2001). *Vermeer and the Delft School*. New York, NY: Metropolitan Museum of Art.

McCloud, S. (1993). *Understanding comics: The invisible art*. New York, NY: Harper.

Macrorie, K. (1985). *Telling writing*. Portsmouth, NH: Boynton Cook.

Macrorie, K. (1988). *The I-Search paper*. Portsmouth, NH: Boynton Cook.

Manguel, A. (1996). *A history of reading*. New York, NY: Penguin.

Meek, M., Warlow, A., & Barton, G. (Eds.). (1977). *The cool web: The pattern of children's reading*. London: The Bodley Head.

Miller, J. H. (1987). *The ethics of reading*. New York, NY: Columbia University Press.

National Endowment for the Arts. (2004). *Reading at risk*. Washington, DC: National Endowment for the Arts.

National Endowment for the Arts. (2007). *To read or not to read*. Washington, DC: National Endowment for the Arts.

Nell, V. (1988). *Lost in a book: The psychology of reading for pleasure*. New Haven, CT: Yale University Press.

Pennac, D. (2006). *The rights of the reader*. London: Walker Books.

Rugg, J., & Murphy, L. (2006). *A book addict's treasury*. London: Frances Lincoln.

Scholes, R. (1989). *Protocols of reading*. New Haven, CT: Yale University Press.

Schur, M. R. (1991). *The reading woman*. San Francisco, CA: Pomegranate Artbooks.

Schwartz, L. S. (1996). *Ruined by reading: A life in books*. Boston, MA: Beacon Press.

Scribner, S., & Cole, M. (1981). *The psychology of literacy.* Cambridge, MA: Harvard University Press.

Spitz, E. H. (1999). *Inside picture books.* New Haven, CT: Yale University Press.

Spufford, M. (2002). *The child that books built.* London: Faber & Faber.

Stallybrass, P., & White, A. (1986). *Politics and poetics of transgression.* Ithaca, NY: Cornell University Press.

Street, B. (1984). *Literacy in theory and practice.* Cambridge, UK: Cambridge University Press.

Street, B. (Ed.). (1993). *Cross-cultural approaches to literacy.* Cambridge, UK: Cambridge University Press.

Styles, M., & Arizpe, E. (Eds.). (2009). *Acts of reading: Teachers, text and childhood.* Stoke on Trent, UK: Trentham.

Tatar, M. (2009). *Enchanted hunters: The power of stories in childhood.* New York, NY: W. W. Norton.

Taylor, D. (1983). *Family literacy.* London: Heinemann Educational.

Tucker, N. (1981). *The child and the book.* Cambridge, UK: Cambridge University Press.

Updike, J. (2005). *Still looking: Essays on American art.* New York, NY: Knopf.

Watson, R. (2003). *Illuminated manuscripts and their makers.* London: Victoria and Albert Museum.

Wolf, S. A. (2004). *Interpreting literature with children.* Mahwah, NJ: Erlbaum.

Wolf, S. A., & Heath, S. B. (1992). *The braid of literature: Children's worlds of reading.* Cambridge, MA: Harvard University Press.

4

Reading Literature in Elementary Classrooms

Kathy G. Short

University of Arizona

Literature in elementary classrooms can be viewed as no more than filler that buys some free time or as a tool that sits alongside a skills worksheet. National policy trends lean heavily toward such limited visions of reading, and yet, as Kathy Short argues, it is possible to create practices of literary reading that support children's interest in reading processes, enjoyment in personal reading, and engagement in critical inquiry about the representations and themes literature presents. If literature opens an inquiry into life, then teaching must follow the curiosity and compassion that students are capable of bringing to reading. In this exploration of literature's place in reading education, Short recognizes the political forces that reduce reading to test scores, but provides a clear outline for framing literary reading in classrooms as vital to personal, communal, and intercultural understanding.

As a child, reading literature in the elementary classroom meant pulling a book surreptitiously from my desk when the teacher wasn't watching. My second-grade teacher once caught me sliding out a book between spelling words on the weekly test and reprimanded me for not paying attention. I *was* paying attention—to what was compelling for me. My life as a reader was fed by the school library, not by reading books in the classroom. In fact, I don't have memories of reading literature in school; my memories are of reading basal textbooks in round robin reading groups and completing comprehension cards to see who could get to the next color level first.

As a beginning classroom teacher, I struggled with the textbook programs and basal readers that were the heart of reading instruction. The significant role that literature played in my life outside of school was a constant reminder that I needed to somehow integrate literature into the life of the classroom. So while my first-grade students met in ability-leveled reading groups and read from inane stories in basal readers, I made time to read aloud from picture books and novels several times a day, created a classroom library, borrowed books from the school library, and set aside daily time for independent reading of self-selected books.

When I found myself falling asleep in the basal reading groups, I knew that it was time to rethink the curriculum. I was clearly the most active thinker in these groups and knew that my boredom was indicative of students' experiences. I noticed that the students who struggled most as readers never finished their worksheets and so rarely got to read. I became increasingly suspicious that the worksheets filling the majority of their time served only to keep them busy. In fact, I often felt that children were learning to read in spite of me.

Another tension occurred when my students and I gathered each afternoon to reflect on what they saw as significant learning for that day. They always talked about the afternoon experiences with our thematic units and never the morning instruction with the reading program. In the afternoons, we read literature for meaningful purposes, while in the morning we read stories designed to teach them to read. Children were clearly signaling which of those experiences were significant. The tension that finally caused me to take action was realizing that students rarely chose reading when we had "free choice" time on Fridays. Books had become "schoolwork" for them and not life work.

These tensions led me to engage students in books based on my goal that they view reading literature as integral to understanding themselves and the world. I immersed them in continuous experiences with literature through reading-aloud, independent reading, shared reading, book extension projects, and thematic units. These extensive experiences of reading many books encouraged children to enjoy books and to become proficient readers. I also observed, however, that while my students loved books, they did not necessarily think deeply or critically about what they read.

This observation led me to introduce literature circles where small groups of students met to share their responses to literature. Although they loved chanting the repeated language patterns in *Brown Bear, Brown Bear, What Do You See?* (Martin, 1968), this book did not invite the thoughtful sharing of feelings and experiences as did books such as *Stevie* (Steptoe, 1969). *Stevie* led them beyond chanting to discussions of quarrels and their complicated feelings of resentment and connection with siblings or cousins. Their sharing led to dialogue as students critically explored their understandings with each other. I also realized that students need support in developing their strategies as readers and in explicitly thinking about how literature and language function. I introduced metacognitive strategy instruction and individual conferences around the books students were reading. Instead of teaching isolated phonics skills through drills and worksheets, we talked about the books they were reading and looked at parts of the text where they were struggling to determine strategies they could use to figure out unknown words. These cognitive and social processes included making predictions based on context and letter/sound relationships, reading on to get more information, breaking a word into parts, examining the pictures for meaning cues, and thinking about a word that would make sense within the world of that story.

Over time, reading literature in my classroom reflected a balance of invitations to experience literature that included reading widely for enjoyment and personal inquiry along with in-depth dialogue about a few books, inquiries on content themes and topics, and discussions of reading strategies and literary elements. My changes as a teacher reflect similar shifts in the broader educational context as well. Schools in the United States have made major swings in how reading literature is viewed within elementary classrooms. For many years, reading literature was seen as supplementary, as something to do "when your work is done"—a time filler but not essential to learning about reading or literature. The 1980s and early 90s brought a major shift in reading instruction as many schools adopted literature-based curricular approaches that immersed children in reading literature across the classroom day for many different purposes (Huck, 1996). Literature was seen as a way to teach reading and to facilitate the learning of content across subject areas.

More recently, the pendulum has swung again; literature has been pushed to the margins within many elementary classrooms as politicized policies impose a return to teaching isolated skills through hierarchal, sequential reading programs and as stories are limited to excerpts in anthologies and controlled-vocabulary stories for reading schemes. Reading literature throughout the school day is not considered to be an "evidence-based practice for literacy instruction" with a stamp of approval from experimental research (Shanahan, 2003) and so has been relegated again to "free time" when other work is finished or assigned only to readers who have reached a level of fluent proficiency. This shift in reading literature is challenged by educators who are committed to deepening children's reading comprehension and engagement with literary forms (Peterson & Eeds, 1990; Lehman 2007) and by those who advocate for literature study that shows children how to locate, explore, and critique their own cultural identities and views of the world as the basis for social understanding and change (Lewison, Leland, & Harste, 2008).

My point in starting with a personal story is to illustrate that literature and its role in reading education in elementary classrooms are subject to changing political policies. The opportunities that children have to read literature, the literature that is available, and the types of experiences children have with that literature shift along with the sociopolitical context. The specific changes vary by country, but often those shifts in reading literature have less to do with educational theory and research than with political expediency and economic factors. For example, I was invited to Taiwan in 2001 to present several research seminars on the teaching of reading, particularly focusing on reading literature as a way to encourage critical thinking. Reading and discussing literature were seen as the key to shifting away from the General Method, which focuses on rote learning of Chinese characters and a centralized government textbook. The shift in reading pedagogy and philosophy was initiated, in large part, by a change in the Taiwan's economic development base from assembly-line mass production of trinkets to sophisticated electronic and technology industries that require workers who can think critically and creatively. Publishers created sets of books for use in schools including picture books and novels by

Taiwanese authors and illustrators that competed with the many translated books from other countries that had dominated Taiwanese markets. Ironically, the drive for more critical and creative education has recently been constrained by a conservative political shift seeking a return to a centralized textbook-based approach to reading.

An international perspective on reading literature in elementary classrooms must therefore address the politicized nature of reading across the world as well as the ways in which literature has been viewed in elementary contexts. Unlike secondary schools in which literature is a field of study, children's literature in elementary schools has primarily been viewed as a reading material that is used to teach something else, typically either skills or facts, or as a "free time" activity. This chapter begins with the argument that children's literature as a field of study can be opened up through a focus on literature as inquiry into life and that critical inquiry is central to dialogue and literary understandings. The practices of critical inquiry are made more complex when connected with issues of cultural relevance, identity, and authenticity and with a broad range of types of texts and ways of responding. Although critical inquiry is often constrained by political agendas, teachers can and do create conditions for critical literary study through strategic reading, personal reading and transformative reading.

Literature as Inquiry into Life

Inquiry as a stance toward reading literature can serve as a bridge between views of literature as an artistic, humanizing force and literature as an instrumentalist tool for learning to read. As a stance of uncertainty and invitation, inquiry supports a willingness to wonder and question as well as to seek to understand and think with others (Lindfors, 1999). Rather than settle for readymade answers, inquiry urges learners to reach beyond information and experience to seek an explanation, to ask why, and to consider what if. Learners, however, need to remain anchored in their own life experiences in order to generatively reach beyond themselves to create a productive tension between current understandings and new experiences. Tension and the state of being off balance during inquiry are the driving forces that compel learners to move forward, particularly when supported by a collaborative community (Dewey, 1938). Inquiry is thus a collaborative process of connecting to and reaching beyond current understandings to explore tensions significant to the learner (Short, 2009b).

Children need to have a voice in both identifying and pursuing the tensions and questions that matter to them within a literary study. In most cases, inquiry is conceived as problem-solving and guiding students through a process of research, with a predetermined outcome. This process of research usually begins with a form and focus for students' questions that has been predetermined by the teacher and curriculum. Freire (1972) argues, however, that the

person who poses the problem is the one who remains in control of learning; therefore, learners need to question the questions, not just answer questions. Students can learn to determine which issues are significant and worth investigating and which tensions are compelling and offer the potential for transformation and new understanding. Reading and responding to literature as problem-posing, as well as problem-solving, provides a critical frame through which multiple voices and perspectives can contribute to inquiry about oneself and the world. Inquiry through literature means understanding the particular contributions that literature makes to ways of thinking and knowing.

Literature as a Way of Knowing

In elementary classrooms, literature is rarely seen as a way of knowing the world that differs, for example, from ways of understanding science or history. Peterson and Eeds (1990) argue that educators have been so focused on using literature for purposes such as conveying information or teaching reading that they have lost sight of literature as valuable in itself. Peterson and Eeds believe that literature illuminates what it means to be human and that the aesthetic nature of literature makes accessible the most fundamental experiences of life–love, hope, loneliness, despair, fear, and belonging. If literature is the imaginative shaping of experience and thought into the forms and structures of language; children are the readers who reshape experience and use literary language to name and transform life. Living inside the world of a story may enable them to engage in inquiry that transforms their thinking about their lives and world (Rosenblatt, 1938). Huck (1982) argues that literature, whether in the form of fiction or nonfiction, creates the playing field of imagination and encourages readers to go beyond "what is" to "what might be." Literature expands children's life spaces through inquiries that take them outside the boundaries of their lives to other places, times, and ways of living. Hope and imagination make it possible for children to rise above their experiences in order to challenge inequity and envision social change. Transformation occurs as children carry their experiences and inquiries through literature back into their worlds and lives.

The Limits of Knowing Through Literature

Hunt (1994) argues that this view of children's literature as exploratory and mind-expanding is contradicted by adults' focus on the educational, psychological, and cultural influences of literature on children's development. Since adults are the ones who write and share literature with children, he argues, "children's books very often contain what adults think children can understand and what they should be allowed to understand" (p. 5). A particular culture's view of childhood is reflected in the books created for children. Because children are seen as being in the process of becoming, this literature can be viewed as manipulative—as adult writers create circumstances and characters that influence children's perspectives and actions. In this sense, adults are *problem-posers* who limit children's roles to problem-solving. Hunt's view, however, ignores the strategies that children have used through the ages to subvert adult control of their lives; neither does it acknowledge the stated intentions of many authors to invite children into inquiry, not determine their perspective and focus. On the other hand, many forms of media and literature do position readers as people who identify with stereotypic or passive perspectives. Children and teachers do not have to remain indifferent or unaware of such portrayals; rather, they can pursue questions about how they are positioned by texts in ways that make them feel less able than or even superior to others. Through such questioning, children develop an ability to critically analyze the ways things are in the world around them as they also view their world, their reading, and learning as part of a process of transformation and becoming.

Experiencing Literature as Democratic Life

Although teachers of literature in secondary schools and universities view literature as a field of study or content area, their focus has often been on teaching the formal art of words and structures and inducting students into a literary heritage, rather than on experiencing literature as life. Literary theorist Louise Rosenblatt (1938) posits reading as a transactional process through which each reader brings personal and cultural experiences, beliefs, and values to the reading of a text so that both the reader and the text are transformed. Although a text has particular potential meanings based on shared cultural codes, readers construct their individual interpretations as they engage in "lived through experiences" with that text. During and after reading, people construct understandings in light of their experiences and rethink their experiences in light of the text, thus bringing meaning to and taking meaning from a text through a process of inquiry. Further, as readers share their responses with others through dialogue, they are pressed to critique and take responsibility for these responses (Bleich, 1981).

Rosenblatt (1938) argues that reading literature encourages readers to put themselves in the place of others, to use imagination to consider the consequences of their decisions and actions. Imagination and the balance of reason and emotion are further developed when readers move from personal response to dialogue where they wrestle with their interpretations of literature with other readers. These discussions, therefore, are not just a better way to learn, but essential to democracy. Rosenblatt's vision of democracy is equitable social relationships in which people choose to live together by valuing individual voices within recognition of responsibility to the group. She believes that people need to have conviction and enthusiasm about their own cultural perspectives, while remaining open to alternative views and other's needs. Dialogue about literature provides a vital context through which students learn to live with the tension of recognizing and respecting the perspectives of others without betraying their own beliefs (Pradl, 1996). Through dialogue, students develop faith in their own judgments while continuing to inquire and remaining open to questioning their beliefs.

Literature as Inquiry into Life: *When My Name Was Keoko*

Reading literature to experience and inquire about life is not in opposition to literature as a way to learn and inquire about particular content. Literature can encourage interest in specific topics, develop conceptual understandings of issues, and provide insights into written language—all within the context of literature as a way of knowing and critiquing the world. Rosenblatt (1938), however, argues that readers need to first experience literature as life before examining that literature for other purposes.

A focus on literature as inquiry into life permeated the responses of fourth-grade students as they read *When My Name Was Keoko* (Park, 2002), a novel about the experiences of Sun-hee and her brother in Korea during the Japanese occupation and suppression of Korean culture in WWII. The teacher, Kathryn Tompkins (2007), read the book aloud to her students to support their overarching inquiry on culture. This classroom work was the focus of teachers' school-wide *action research* on intercultural understanding (Short, 2009a); a form of research that documents students' and teachers' perceptions of learning as well as analyzes and makes changes in the context for teaching and learning to challenge students' (and teachers') thinking. In Tompkins' classroom, issues of culture, identity, gender, war, freedom, courage, resistance, hope, and family relationships wove through students' talk, writing, and artistic responses as they engaged in critical inquiry around Park's novel. They particularly identified with Sun-hee's frustration at her lack of freedom. They connected her experiences with their own feelings of resentment toward adults who tell kids what to do and when to do it, but realized that her lack of freedom was based in fear and oppression of her culture and identity that went far beyond anything they had experienced. Their discussions naturally led them to insights into Korean culture, language, and history, and they pursued their tensions through inquiries using informational materials and web sites. Later, students returned to this book in a writing workshop study on the strategies that authors use to develop characterizations.

Literature and Critical Social Inquiry

Much of the research and classroom work around reading literature has focused on talk and writing as a means of responding to literature. Freire (1972) argues that dialogue is a tool for transformation and social change and his work has influenced educators to invite children into talk in which they think *with* each other and engage in collaborative inquiry and critique around critical social issues. Through practices of critical literacy, which encourage analyses and questioning of oppression and all forms of domination, readers are challenged to critique and question "what is" and "who benefits" as well as to hope and consider "what if." Through critical literacy, children learn to problem-pose and question the everyday world, to interrogate relationships between language and power, to analyze the images and messages conveyed through popular culture and media, to understand how and why power relationships are socially constructed and maintained, and to consider actions that promote social justice (Edelsky, 1999; Lewison, Flint, & Sluys, 2002).

Critical inquiry can grow out of a focused study such as described in relation to *When My Name Was Keoko* or children reading together may suddenly encounter a question that they know they must address. DeNicolo and Fránquiz (2006) describe such questioning as "critical encounters" and define them as a realization that can emerge when "a word, concept, or event in a story surprises, shocks, or frightens readers to such a degree that they seek to inquire further" and so sustain their dialogue and scrutiny of the text (p. 157). In their study, such a critical encounter occurred in reading *Felita* (Mohr, 1979) when students read about the main character's experience of a pejorative racial slur called out to her by another group of teens who rejected the presence of her Puerto Rican family in the predominately white community. The girls agreed, "You have to stand up for yourself," but disagreed on how they would respond to a racial slur. Several indicated they would "get all my friends and beat them up," while others argued that "fighting with them would make the problem worser" and would lead to being "scared of these kids" and that wouldn't solve anything (DeNicolo & Fránquiz, p. 165). Collaborating to make sense of the racism in this book led to a transformation of their relationships with each other as well as their understandings about racial issues. The group member who usually dominated discussions began to listen and consider alternative viewpoints; and a more careful, shy member spoke clearly and forcefully about the importance of questioning racism. Literature discussion provided a space for disagreement as it also supported the members in developing a critical lens to examine "values, beliefs, and events in personal and collective lives, and the recognition of literacy as an empowering rather than silencing force in classrooms" (p. 168). This space was influenced by the choice of literature that encouraged students to use their life experiences as linguistic and cultural tools as well as challenged them to deepen their understanding of social issues.

In another example, Martínez-Roldán (2005) documents the significance of an inquiry approach to dialogue for a group of bilingual children as they read *Oliver Button is a Sissy* (de Paola, 1979). They engaged in acts of inquiry in which "a speaker attempts to elicit another's help in going beyond his or her present understanding" (Martínez-Roldán, p. 23). For example, Amaury wondered, "What was so girly about playing dress-up?" to which Steve replied, "Probably he likes to play girls' games." Amaury explored another interpretation, noting that Oliver "says that he was pretending to be a star" and returned to his question about why dress-up is considered a girls' game. Steve later argued that "his dad wants him to play a boys' game instead of a girl game 'cause maybe his dad doesn't think he gets exercise," to which Ada replied, "I think he dresses up because boys dress up too." Their inquiry continued when Amaury commented that "Steve played dress-up before," and Steve immediately replied, "I know. I'm not a girl." (p. 26).

This authentic discourse did not resolve students' inquiries—Steve still wondered about boy/girl issues and Ada was not sure what to think—but their talk remained open and focused on the process itself. Martínez-Roldán (2005) notes that these students were able to engage in dialogue about gender because their focus was on their processes of thinking, not a final answer. She argues that an overemphasis on guidelines and procedures when talking about stories can instead force students to focus on product and performance.

Expanding Dialogue and Inquiry

Including Everyday Texts and Oral Narratives

Luke and Freebody (1997) argue that all texts represent cultural positions, ideologies and discourses and that all readers construct readings from particular epistemological stances. Critical literacy presses for an awareness of how, why, and in whose interests a particular text might work and an understanding of reading positions and practices for questioning and critiquing texts as well as oneself. In defining critical literacy, Luke and Freebody outline four key practices: (a) coding practices through which readers focus on developing their skills and resources as code breakers, (b) text-meaning practices that focus on developing meaning and participation in text production and interpretation, (c) pragmatic practices through which readers develop knowledge of how everyday texts (e.g., library card or cell phone contract) may work for and against their interests, and (d) critical practices that enable readers to question how a text shapes their point of view and challenges their assumptions. Their framework for reading that recognizes codes, meaning, pragmatic and critical practices is intended to initiate and guide a multi-voiced dialogue about texts in peoples' lives. Such a dialogue would value and extend each reader's right to be heard, critiqued, analyzed, and constructed in public forums. They argue that reading as a critical social practice could displace the cognitive emphasis on comprehension strategies in reading education and, instead, foreground concerns about the ways we understand power and change across personal, cultural, and social histories.

Luke and Freebody's outline of critical reading implies that literature should be defined broadly to include oral and written forms. The values that elementary schools place on written text have created deficit views of children from communities where oral traditions are integral to the culture. Children from these communities enter school with a background in oral literature and storytelling, rather than in written literature. They may not have been read to on a regular basis, but they do know story and have rich oral literature experiences (Dyson & Genishi, 1994; see Campano & Ghiso, this volume). In addition, children from families living in poverty frequently have many experiences with everyday print including family letters, newspapers, magazines, contracts, and bills (Dorsey-Gaines & Taylor, 1988). Children's success in reading literature in school contexts depends on whether teachers build from children's strengths in oral stories and critical insights about the materials they encounter every day.

In many countries, including Asia, Africa, and Latin America the dominant books available are translations from English-speaking countries, especially the U.S. and U.K. (Freeman & Lehman, 2001). Children do not find their own lives and cultural experiences within these books and are, instead, immersed in a constant diet of books that reflect dominant Western worldviews. As described in Chapter 31 of this volume by Michael Daniel Ambatchew, educators, authors, and publishers within these countries struggle with encouraging the writing, publication and distribution of literature from their cultural perspectives. Their debates about reading literature are often less about engaging children with books than about creating a body of literature from within the culture. Market forces work against their efforts since large corporations can provide translated books for lower costs than the small presses who work with authors and distributors to produce local literature.

Furthermore, as I discovered while teaching internationally, my Western, culturally specific view that reading for enjoyment should be a primary goal when creating a literature program, is not shared by educators around the world. My assumptions were met with puzzlement when I argued that they should immerse children in a wide range of literary reading so that they grow to love books and see reading as enjoyment. They valued, instead, reading widely for utilitarian purposes, to accomplish a task or to learn something of importance in their lives. Although we held different assumptions about reading for pleasure, we agreed, along with Luke and Freebody (1997), on the value of centering reading in children's questions, and supporting literacy in order to encourage personal lifelong inquiry. This difference in cultural perspectives speaks, again, to the importance of defining literature broadly in ways that include the texts and stories readers value and use in their daily lives.

Literature Relevant to Children's Cultural Identities

Building a democratic dialogue that includes the voices, questions, and texts of all students requires attention to and knowledge of culturally relevant and culturally authentic literature that connect to the reader's own cultural identity as well as to multiple ways of thinking and being in the world (Gay, 2000; Harris, 1997). Dialogue about culturally relevant literature provides a means for readers to not merely "look in on others'" lives, but more importantly, to critique and inquire into their own world views, cultural values and possible biases. Culturally relevant literature allows readers to "see themselves" within a book and provides opportunities for linking cultural knowledge and experiences to story worlds. In addition, reading books intended to represent the experiences and lives they know well can be the starting point for questioning how certain representations might offend, silence, or contradict their cultural knowledge and lived experiences (Brooks, 2006; Dutro, 2009).

Luke and Freebody (1997) suggest it is possible to create dialogues that develop insights into both literary forms and the issues implied within stories by foregrounding a social view of reading. However, discussions of social issues may be unfamiliar and, therefore, create a forum for resistance and confusion among many students. In discussions with fourth and fifth graders about picture books highlighting racism, Short with Thomas (in press) found that the students avoided difficult issues by simply evading the central premise that racism exists: "It doesn't matter what you look like on the outside, it's the inside that matters." They also believed that racism was only between Blacks and Whites in the U.S. and that racism ended when Martin Luther King, Jr. gave his famous "I have a dream" speech. We had to acknowledge that their perspectives were grounded in the discourses promoted by adults around them that emphasized racial harmony through events and experiences such as the school's celebration of Martin Luther King Day. To challenge these assumptions, we searched for picture books with a range of contemporary portrayals of racism and questioned children's narratives when they referred to clichéd explanations of their social life. We also spent time as teachers talking about how to discuss race with children and confronting our own hesitations and fears about openly addressing these issues.

Cultural authenticity is a critical issue for readers, both in identifying with and challenging the social worlds portrayed within literature (Fox & Short, 2003). Cultural authenticity goes beyond accuracy or the avoidance of stereotyping to include the cultural values and practices within a social group (Mo & Shen, 2003). Given the range of experiences within any cultural group and the unique transactions of each reader with a text, cultural authenticity is often interpreted through multiple, competing points of view. Reading literature from a critical perspective helps readers question the signs and structures embedded within texts, so that a story's construction and sources of meanings can be identified and examined. Amy Edwards (2008), a fifth-grade teacher, found that providing brief information about the background of authors and illustrators before reading aloud raised children's awareness about the significance of a critical inquiry stance while interpreting literature. Students realized that they needed to know if an author was a cultural insider, had visited the country, or had engaged in research or some kind of experience related to the content of the book. They saw a need for contextual information so they could imagine an author's perspective and consider how and why authors write about a particular topic as well as position themselves as authorities on a story world. Yenika-Agbaw (1998) argues that readers have the social responsibility to negotiate personal and cultural meanings from literature that create the possibility for social change in both their immediate and global communities.

Readers' responses to culturally relevant literature are not a simple matter of cultural identification because readers engage in continually negotiated cultural practices and have multiple cultural allegiances and subjectivities. For example, Brooks (2006) found that African American adolescents brought strong cultural connections to *Scorpions* (Myers, 1988), a novel about an African American teen struggling with gang membership, defending his need for a gun as a desire for respect and to keep others from "messing" with him. They rejected identification with *The House of Dies Drear* (Hamilton, 1968), a mystery involving an African American family living in a house inhabited by ghosts, stating "only white people would stay in a haunted house" (p. 388). Brooks argues that although the book is acclaimed as authentic culturally conscious African American literature, beliefs in the supernatural as a cultural practice was unfamiliar to this group of teens.

Enciso (1994) argues that students interpret literature based on their own cultural maps that "provide a framework for constructing the meaning of new events" and that include cultural resources and social allegiances drawn from popular culture (p. 527). She analyzes a discussion of *Maniac Magee* (Spinelli, 1990) by a small group of African American, Latino, and European American fourth and fifth graders. She particularly focuses on two boys (African American and European American) who were both thoughtful readers and transformers of culture but did not consider one another's interpretations because they drew from different cultural maps. Both enjoyed popular culture and were aware of heightened racial tension at the time, associated with the trial of white police officers accused of beating Rodney King, an unarmed Black citizen of Los Angeles. During their interpretations of the book (and related social life), Richard drew from his position as a "culturally conscious African American male," while Mark's allegiance was with "white liberal culture" (p. 530). Enciso argues that teachers and students need to examine who is included and excluded in interpretations

of literature and culture within these discussions. Furthermore, they need to develop knowledge and skills for mediating these discussions so that dominant perspectives that privilege White, middle-class interpretive resources are not assumed or taken for granted as the norm.

Learning to Read Interculturally

The increased availability of literature with settings in different cultures around the world has provided the opportunity for readers to immerse themselves as inquirers into story worlds that present unfamiliar ways of thinking and living. Teachers' and students' dialogue around these books make it possible to build intercultural understandings and global perspectives (Short, 2009a). Engaging children thoughtfully with this literature can be a struggle, however, because the books often focus on ways of living that seem far removed from children's immediate experiences. The danger exists that children will view this literature as exotic or strange, and thus, fail to connect in significant ways with the concerns and perspectives portrayed by the author and illustrator. Additional problems with reading cross-culturally will arise if teachers read past the culturally specific perspectives and details and instead focus only on the overarching themes (e.g., friendship, loyalty, loss) that are relevant, but become tangential, or even in opposition to intercultural understanding. On the other hand, too much attention paid to superficial features of cultural lifestyles can actually reinforce stereotypical perceptions (Case, 1991). Finally, a limited reading of culturally relevant literature could develop as teachers discuss the literature in terms of "we-they" dualisms that reinforce the normative assumption that "we" are inherently superior to those "others" who have not yet acquired a view of the world aligned with "my" view.

Iqbal (D'Adamo, 2001) is a fictionalized story of a boy who led an influential movement to protest child labor in Pakistani carpet factories. If read in isolation, with no continuous dialogue or reference to meaningful social change, this book could lead children to feel pity, rather than outrage and a sense of empowerment to change the world. A misinformed reading of the story might also lead to the misconception that all children in Pakistan are involved in child labor, chained to looms in carpet mills. If the book is instead read within a broader study of children's and human rights, and includes a collection of books representing Pakistan and Pakistani children's perspectives, as well as narratives from students' families and community members, children will have many more possible points of connection and opportunities to struggle over the voices and questions they raise through their inquiry.

Although researchers have provided many accounts of children's responses to multicultural literature, few studies focus on the use of international literature to build intercultural understanding—a major omission given our increasingly interconnected world. Children need to find their own lives in books, but if what they read only mirrors their views of the world, they cannot envision other ways of thinking and living and are not challenged to critically confront global issues.

From Dialogue to the Art of Representation

More recently, research and theory related to dialogue has expanded to consider the potential of a wider range of sign systems, such as visual art and drama as tools for thinking and interpreting literature. Siegel (2006) describes the process of *transmediation* as way to recast understanding about literature and its meaning for one's life. The concept of transmediation is taken from the work of the philosopher Peirce (1966), who argues that in moving an idea across sign or symbolic systems, such as from a written language to visual arts, we invariably discover new meanings and relationships between ideas, because the new sign system heightens attention to dimensions of a text that were otherwise difficult to isolate or describe. One form of transmediation is known as "Sketch to Stretch" and asks students to use the symbolic language of color, composition, and object relations to create a metaphor for a text's themes or character relations (Short, Kahn, & Kauffman, 2000). For example, Dan, one of the nine-year-old children in a class who read *Iqbal* (D'Adamo, 2001), created a sketch of a broken chain to represent the boy's literal escape from the looms, but he also recognized the image as a symbol of Iqbal's freedom, inner strength, and intelligence. Along the top third of his sketch, he created an arch of deep red and black colors to represent Iqbal's anger. Another student, Gabriela, responded to the same book with a sketch of the sky and a kite as symbols of freedom; the kite image was repeated in the bottom right and left corners of the page, with the added image of the kites breaking through a fence representing oppression (Bolasky, 2008; see Figure 4.1).

Edmiston and Enciso (2003) believe that drama is a forum for text interpretation that can reveal and mediate children's diverse cultural and social beliefs, through deliberate inclusion of multi-voiced, dialogic approaches that promote "an interplay of meaning among teachers and students across shifting social positions" within the drama (p. 868). They argue that these drama practices dialogize the discourses of literary texts to develop children's insights about themselves and the world.

Medina used drama practices, such as tableau, acting-in-role, and hot seat, around the picture book, *Friends from the Other Side* (Anzaldúa, 1987), a complex story of immigration, safety, cultural identity, and community. Through her use of dramatized dialogue, Medina encouraged students to move from interpreting text as outsiders to the experience of living on the Mexican/Texas border, to developing an active dialogue *as* and *with* the characters. Students used dialogue to explore multiple perspectives and questions around social issues that went beyond the limits of the story to the larger society. For example, students took turns occupying the hot seat and asking one another questions that concerned the status of undocumented immigrants. One student took on the perspective of the main character, Prietita, and was asked whether Joaquin and his mother, who were undocumented immigrants, should be returned to Mexico. Earlier, several students, drawing on images and stereotypes from the media, stated that Mexicans should be sent back because they had come across the border to steal and bring drugs. Their responses on the hot seat reflected their consideration of the different circumstances framing multiple points of view. One student who took the role of the immigrant official stated, "They have to make a decision if to let them in so they

Figure 4.1   Third-graders' Sketch to Stretch responses to Iqbal (D'Adamo, 2001).

can get work and they can get help. They have a very hard decision and it is mostly in their hands—all these lives to let them in or not" (p. 280). Another student argued that a border patrol officer who was also Mexican, probably knowingly passed the house where Joaquin and his mother were hiding because he did not want to put them in jail.

Dialogue, Literature, and National Reading Policies

These descriptions of critical dialogues within literary reading suggest that discussions of literature may be isolated from reading education. However, policy initiatives on the teaching of reading have long evolved from "pressures, tensions, and crises embedded in national and regional political contexts" (Openshaw & Soler, 2007, p. xiv), leading to national governments' involvement in specific decisions about reading instruction with the express aim of raising literacy standards. Perceptions of gaps in literacy achievement for particular cultural groups (i.e., Black and Latino youth in the U.S.) have further politicized these decisions and led to debates about whether these gaps reflect the need for more accommodation of cultural differences in instruction or for demanding adherence to national standards for all children, regardless of cultural differences.

Elementary reading programs, while accountable to national polices that restrict definitions of reading, can be organized so that children and teachers develop personal, social, and cognitive approaches to reading that will contribute to pathways for lifelong critical inquiry through literature. Teachers, working with librarians, can integrate wide reading for pleasure, reading for insights about oneself and the world, and reading to learn about literary forms, themes, and puzzles (e.g., metaphors, flashbacks, intertextual references). All of these ways of reading should be guided and motivated by inquiry—by investigations that, at times, are relevant to children's personal interests, at other times relate to the conditions and concerns of others' lives, and, still other times, focus on literary form, language, and interpretative possibilities. The following two sketches of reading across a day offer a sense of the integrative and interpretive work that can be developed for students in elementary classrooms.

Stepping Into an Upper-Grade Classroom. Nine-year-old Gabriela begins her day by finding her book, *To Dance: A Ballerina's Graphic Novel* (Siegel, 2006), so she can pursue her personal inquiry about becoming a ballerina. After independent reading, the class moves into reading instruction and guided reading. The teacher works with Gabriela and a small group of peers in a guided inquiry that helps them analyze how an author uses dialogue for character development in *Frog and Toad Together* (Lobel, 1979). They web the differences and similarities in the viewpoints of Frog and Toad based on their talk

and interactions with each other. After lunch, as part of a whole-class collaborative inquiry on human rights, the teacher reads aloud from *Iqbal* (D'Adamo, 2001). Students discuss the anger and fear in Iqbal's life and his willingness to take action for freedom for himself and others despite the risks. They talk about the ways in which he took action and their tensions about whether kids can really make a difference in a world controlled by adults.

Stepping into a Primary Classroom
In a classroom with younger students, Tim O'Keefe reads aloud a predictable book, *Bringing the Rain to Kapiti Plain* (Aardema, 1981), which has a cumulative rhyme about rain coming to a drought-stricken area of Kenya. He first reading encourages students to enjoy the story and build a shared sense of the story's meaning. After several shared readings, he and his students focus on the same book, with a discussion of letter pattern relationships, words that students recognize, and strategies that students are using to make, confirm, or revise their predictions about words and their meaning. The book then becomes part of the literature available for independent reading (Mills, O'Keefe, & Jennings, 2004).

In O'Keefe's classroom, reading experiences move from a sense of the whole story to its specific use of language and structure and then back to its whole experience and meaning again. His organization of reading literature challenges the approaches imposed by national standards and strictly guided reading programs that begin with isolated phonics skills and delay the long-term goal of whole text comprehension until later grades. Even when these skill-based programs finally focus on comprehension, the assumption is that comprehension is a form of meaning-making bounded by a predetermined summary of a story's purpose, theme, character relationships, and style. In contrast with O'Keefe's approach to shared reading, Larson (2002) documents how a shared reading of a predictable book becomes displaced by teaching isolated literacy skills, and meaningful discussion and inquiry are undermined by time restrictions, peer pressure, and district mandates to raise test scores. Literary reading is reduced to using a story as the springboard for drills on basic skills with any questions arising from children about the story or any interest generated by the story's themes relegated to learning outside of curricular timeframes and guidelines.

Locating Literature at the Heart of Reading Education

Roser (2001) argues that teachers like Tompkins and O'Keefe view texts as mediators of *both* literary reading and reading development. A literary text can become a touchstone for literary understandings, political contestation, content knowledge, and literacy strategies. Although this may be a lot of work for one book to carry, when teachers plan for a range of experiences with literature, students can learn to *read strategically* to learn about thought and imaginative processes when interpreting literature, *read widely* for personal purposes, and *read deeply* to think about life.

Reading Strategically to Learn about Literacy and Literature

Literary and literacy knowledge are distinct yet interdependent (Lehman, 2007) and can be taught together, throughout a school day. Literary knowledge relates to knowledge about literature as a narrative form (and way of knowing) and includes concepts such as sense of story, plot, themes, and language; while literacy focuses on reading and writing as processes and includes the related concepts of comprehension, sequence, main ideas, and vocabulary. Readers need both literary and literacy knowledge as they read in a range of genres so they are able to adjust their reading strategies based on their knowledge of the text structures for a particular genre. In addition, a critical perspective on both literary forms and literacy processes can be foregrounded in discussions and analyses of selected literature.

Strategic readers reflect on their reading processes and text knowledge; the strategies they use are general cognitive and social processes for constructing meaning during reading. For example readers need to make predictions based on context, read beyond a difficult word to get more information, break a word into parts, or reread a difficult passage. Other specific word-level skills, such as identifying letter-sound relationships or vowel rules, are taught as part of an overall approach to solving problems with words, rather than as isolated information to repeat and memorize. Teachers and children work together to explicitly identify and examine reading strategies and develop metacognitive awareness and control of the reading process through classroom routines, such as guided reading (Fountas & Pinnell, 1996), guided comprehension (Keene & Zimmerman, 2007), and conferencing and mini-lessons (Calkins, 2001).

Through these approaches to strategic reading, teachers take over the role of problem-poser and guide children's reflections on their reading processes, teach lessons on strategies and text structures, and choose literature to highlight particular reading strategies or text structures based on their insights about children's confusion or new experiences with literature. The teacher determines the focus of instruction based on careful assessment of students' needs, while students act as problem-solvers engaged in actively reasoning through reading strategies and text structures to develop generalizations they can use when interpreting the words, style, and structures of their current reading selection. For example, Diane Snowball and Faye Bolton (1999) describe a guided inquiry where students gather examples of different letter combinations for the long e sound by reading aloud to each other from familiar books. Whenever they hear that sound, they put the word on a large wall chart. After gathering examples for several weeks, students engage in problem-solving to organize the words into groups, each reflecting a specific letter combination, and create generalizations to explain that grouping.

These practices highlight instruction by adults who help children develop a repertoire of strategies to use when they encounter difficulty, as they figure out words, comprehend confusing plots or characterizations, or encounter new text structures and literary elements. Research by Gambrell (2000) indicates that if teachers and students depend entirely on a program of reading emphasizing the superficial skills of decoding and plot-based comprehension questions, they may know how to read but have little interest making reading a part of their lives. In the long run, teachers aim to develop students who know what it feels like to be engaged, knowledgeable, and strategic.

A Caveat about Strategic Reading. Instruction in comprehension strategies is based on the belief that cognitive processes, such as inference, connection, or visualization, need to be modeled and explicitly taught to readers who will then practice them whenever they read (Keene & Zimmerman, 2007; Moreillon, 2009). This focus on comprehension strategies is significant because it has expanded instruction beyond the basic skills of word recognition and identification of story elements and themes. But the promise of rigor in reading has sometimes led to a shift from deeply considering a range of meanings to learning the actual comprehension strategies. Atwell (2007) argues that this shift is problematic because readers are forced to approach literature from an efferent frame of mind, to read in order to acquire information, instead of to read to live within a literary world (Rosenblatt, 1978). Atwell believes that this emphasis teaches children to seek and carry away information about strategies when they read literature, rather than living through the stories and experiencing the journey. She found that directing her students to activate their comprehension strategies as they read interrupted their entry into a "reading zone." They were so focused on making connections, drawing conclusions, and identifying visual imagery as they read, that they lost comprehension. She argues that there may be occasional moments in a text when examining comprehension strategies is appropriate, but that "the story, the language, and the reader are all that matter" in other moments (p. 64). The issue is not whether or not comprehension strategies should be taught, but determining when they are appropriate and needed by the reader as well as their role within interpretation and response.

Relating Literary Form and Meaning. Often literary instruction in elementary contexts has taken the form of worksheets that require students to identify and list story elements, such as character, plot, and conflict, rather than a thoughtful consideration of how these elements influence their constructions of meaning. More recently, there has been a strong emphasis on genre studies, some of which are formulaic. An inquiry approach to genre study can support students' insights into the relationships between form and meaning. Instead of viewing a genre as a prescriptive set of rules, genre can be a flexible tool that readers use to identify social and textual structures for understanding their worlds (Wolf, 2004).

Cruz and Pollock (2004) invited their students into inquiry about fantasy through a touchstone text, *The Paper Bag Princess* (Munsch, 1988). Students then gathered many texts and sorted them into three piles—definitely fantasy, not fantasy, and maybe fantasy. This sifting process led students to develop a working definition of fantasy that they continued to explore through read alouds, independent reading, charting of elements, characters, and symbolism, and small group book clubs. Through this process, students identified six characteristics that cut across different kinds of fantasy and inquired into patterns, such as the relationship between the villain and the hero, the role magic plays in the fantasy world, the differing portrayals of dragons in stories from Western and Eastern cultures, and the changing roles of female characters. Ray (2006) argues that an inquiry approach to genre study repositions curriculum as the outcome of instruction rather than the starting point. The "noticings and questioning that students engage in and around texts determine what will become important content for the study, and depth rather than coverage is the driving force" (p. 238).

A guided inquiry approach to literary reading reflects a significant shift in the roles of students and teachers as they interact around literature. Although the teacher, as problem-poser, engages in explicit teaching around literary knowledge and reading strategies, this teaching is based on careful observation of students' needs and knowledge of literacy and literature, rather than a predetermined sequential curriculum. Within this focus, students as problem-solvers may explore their own inquiries about reading strategies and text knowledge as they read literature that engages them.

Reading Widely for Personal Purposes

Reading literature for personal purposes involves not only personal enjoyment of reading, but social opportunities to share and become interested in a wide range of genres, authors, styles, and themes. In personal reading development, the focus is on choice and extensive reading for purposes significant to the reader. Those purposes range from enjoyment and entertainment to personal inquiries on issues and topics that matter in a particular reader's life—often because friends are also interested in the topic and genre.

Extensive reading promotes positive attitudes about reading, expands students' literary knowledge and, thus, develops students' confidence in comprehension and interpretation, and encourages the development of lifelong reading habits. In addition, reading many materials with ease increases fluency as readers gain experience in effectively orchestrating a range of reading strategies within familiar texts (Morrow, 2003). As Galda (2001) points out, "children's books provide a reason to learn to read, as well as a reason to keep on reading" (p. 224), so that children become readers who not only *can* read, but who also will and do read across their lifetimes.

Children will have different purposes for their reading, and those interests and aims should be recognized and valued so everyone in a classroom can see that reading extends beyond the mandates of schooling. When developing a library for young readers, books and other materials (e.g., letters, class-produced books, annotated photo albums, postcards) should be accessible for independent reading. Among these books should be the stories that are read aloud in class, including patterned language books like *The Very Hungry Caterpillar* (Carle, 1968). Older children will be able to read and discuss different books in a series such as Lemony Snicket's "Unfortunate Events" series or the "Time Warp" series by Jon Sczeiska and Lane Smith. Many children prefer nonfiction literature and may resist an overemphasis on fiction; thus, books that address and extend children's interests in the natural world, world records, history, inventions, and sports should be available for reading and discussion with peers.

Reading widely develops through independent reading and read-alouds when adults provide a regularly scheduled time for these experiences, a variety of reading materials, and a place for reading alongside the child. While reading with children from a book of their choosing, the emphasis should be on meaning and interpretation of character relationships, plot, and connections with related stories and experiences. In this individualized time between the adult and child, it is possible to follow the child's questions and understandings about the story and about how text works. One to one conversations such as these inform a teacher's perspective on a child's reading development and can be recorded to supplement—if not supplant—standardized assessments of reading that discount the interests, questions, and contexts of children's reading.

The main focus of independent reading is immersion in reading, not writing reports or talking about this reading. These experiences with a wide range of self-selected texts help students explore personal purposes for reading within their lives. Research indicates that many adults stop engaging with books once they leave school and view reading as boring school work because of the lack of personal choice in reading materials in schools (Gambrell, 2000). Independent reading is supported by reading aloud to children and telling them oral stories to introduce concepts of print, book language, and story structures as well as open up new genres and encourage critical inquiry around literature (Galda & Cullinan, 2000). The recent political focus on evidenced-based reading practices has led to official discourse that questions the value of reading aloud in elementary classrooms. Reading aloud and discussing books with children is often pushed to the side or has become rushed with little time for children to explore their thinking with each other about a book. Copenhaver (2001) argues that the result is the silencing or marginalizing of children's inquiries as efficiency and control take away the extended time some children need to wonder about and talk back to a book.

Reading Deeply to Transform Understanding

Reading literature to think about and transform understanding about oneself and the world involves reading to inquire into issues in children's lives and in the broader society. These experiences support children in becoming critical and knowledgeable readers and thinkers. Through discussions of well-selected literature, readers are encouraged to engage deeply with the story world and then step back to share their personal connections and to reflect critically with others about the text and their responses. They engage in shared thinking about ideas based on critical inquiries that matter in their lives and world. These critical inquiries involve the types of discussion described earlier in children's dialogue and responses to *Oliver Button is a Sissy* (de Paola, 1979), *Iqbal* (D'Adamo, 2001), *Friends from the Other Side* (Anzaldúa, 1987), and *Felita* (Mohr, 1979).

This focus on the intensive reading of a few books to think deeply and critically, balances the extensive reading of many books. The books chosen by a teacher for intensive reading have multiple layers of meaning, and challenge readers to linger longer over ideas, words, characterizations, setting descriptions, and relationships among literary forms and themes (Sumara, 2002). Books such as *The Evolution of Calpurnia Tate* (Kelly, 2009) and *Fox* (Wild, 2001) invite social interaction and discussion as readers need others to think with as they struggle with interpretation and understanding. Because the focus is on children's thinking and dialogue, the literature may need to be read aloud to facilitate clarity and questioning during reading. Sipe (2008) found that the majority of young children's conversational turns occur *during* the reading of the book. He argues that expecting children to save their responses until the story is finished imposes an adult view of response that may not be productive for young children whose responses are often *of* the moment and *in* the moment.

Children may also engage with literature as part of a thematic study or inquiry within content areas, such as math, science, and social studies. They read critically to compare information and issues across these books and to learn facts about the topic as well as to consider conceptual issues. Literature becomes a tool for understanding the world and considering broader social and scientific issues as well as a means of facilitating children's interest in a topic. Sandy Kaser (2001) used fiction and nonfiction literature with fifth graders within a study of astronomy to explore conceptual understandings of "space," to examine a range of cultural theories about stars, and to support student inquiries into scientific issues and questions, as well as to read and discuss science fiction in literature circles.

Reading deeply to transform understanding focuses on collaborative problem-posing as teachers and students struggle together to identify and explore the issues they find significant within a text. This collaborative problem-posing and problem-solving balances the guided inquiry of strategic reading where teachers are the problem-posers and the personal inquiry of independent reading where students take on the role of problem-poser. These engagements and purposes for reading are connected by the belief that the reading curriculum should not be delivered *to* students but constructed *with* students as they engage in wondering and seeking insights into their own literacy processes and literary experiences.

Reading Education as a Political Act

Reading education has been one of the most controversial and contested areas of international debate among both educators and politicians. McCulloch (2007) argues that disagreements about teaching reading "swirl around and between rival camps and interests" to establish political narratives and alliances that form the basis for the power that can "undermine and challenge public policy directions and even entire governments" (p. ix). The intense debate over literacy has led to the imposition of one-size-fits-all models of national literacy standards and high stakes testing through legislation and policy initiatives such as the National Literacy Strategy in England, No Child Left Behind and Reading First in the United States, and the National Inquiry into the Teaching of Literacy in Australia. These initiatives and public debates over reading standards have shaped the political environments that are now highly receptive to centralized and prescriptive approaches to reading education—especially in elementary and primary schools.

These public debates and government initiatives have positioned teachers as objects of policy directives, rather than as active co-constructors of curriculum for their students. Ylimaki and McClain (2007) state that the "reading wars" have been contested within the political arena and not classrooms, and expressed through punitive legislation aimed at controlling teachers. Teachers are denied agency in the teaching process beyond selecting from approved instructional practices and packaged reading programs produced by approved textbook companies. At best, teachers and students are engaged as problem-solvers in their use of these materials, but not as problem-posers who inquire into tensions that are significant to their lives within the world or as literacy learners.

The politicized nature of decisions about the teaching of reading has created an ever-changing search for and imposition of single silver bullet solutions to the challenges of teaching literacy. The solution changes as governments, politicians, and policy makers move in and out of office and public approval but the focus on quick, easy solutions that can be imposed on schools and teachers remains constant. Soler (2007) argues that this emphasis on solutions reflects a shift from a discourse of liberal humanism in schooling toward a discourse of management based in "a view of the individual as a subject to govern and/or be governed" (p. 43). Child-centered views in elementary schools have been replaced with technocratic views that stress basic skills and prescribed methods and approaches to teaching. Indeed, the current national debates on literacy are not even how best to teach reading, but how best to teach phonics (Hall, 2007).

Polarities and oversimplification have won out over the realities and complexities of teaching reading in ways that are motivating, substantive, and relevant. And literacy research has been characterized as negative, inconsistent, and irrelevant for informing literacy instruction. Although literacy researchers, as social scientists, value debate, dialogue, critique, and multiple viewpoints across questions and directions for change, these cornerstone practices of well-developed research are dismissed because they cannot provide clear, simple solutions.

Since literature-based approaches are typically viewed as child-centered and as located within liberal discourse, literature is often not included in these discussions and is viewed as a mere accessory to children's learning and development. In addition, from an economic standpoint, the publishers of large textbook literacy programs and reading schemes have much to gain from the imposition of prescriptive approaches on schools and so maintain strong lobbyist positions (Shannon, 2007). Reading literature in elementary classrooms does not meet the political criteria of providing easy solutions to literacy instruction or of supporting large corporate efforts to maintain their positions in the school markets. The belief that children learn best in holistic contexts that strive to preserve the authenticity of materials and encourage inquiry is under attack or has been dismissed in many parts of the world, and many policy makers now view reading literature as a supplementary activity in elementary schools.

Conclusion

An inquiry stance to literature and curriculum invites children to make meaning of texts in personally and culturally significant ways to facilitate learning and to develop lifelong reading attitudes and habits. Children gain a sense of possibility for their lives and that of the society in which they live along with the ability to consider others' perspectives and needs. Engagement with literature thus allows them to develop their own voices and, at the same time, go beyond self-interest to an awareness of broader human consequences. An inquiry stance encourages this engagement through focusing on children as problem-posers who seek out the questions that are significant in their lives and world, as well as problem-solvers who investigate those problems to reach new understandings, take action, and pose more complex questions and problems.

Elementary educators value the role of story in children's lives and the ways in which children use story to construct their understandings of themselves and their world. This belief in the power of story as inquiry, however, has often focused on how to *use* literature to support the teaching of literacy and content, rather than on also valuing literature as a way of thinking and re-visioning life. In addition, many elementary educators are struggling with the politicization of reading instruction to the point that children are no longer able to meaningfully engage with literature. Research that investigates the complex roles literature can play within elementary classrooms and that challenges the current politicization of reading policies has tremendous potential for opening new possibilities for how literature is read within elementary contexts.

Literature References

Aardema, V. (1981). *Bringing the rain to Kapiti Plain* (B. Vidal, Illus.). New York, NY: Dial.

D'Adamo, F. (2001). *Iqbal.* New York, NY: Aladdin.

Anzaldúa, G. (1987). *Friends from the other side/Amigos del otro lado* (C. Mendéz, Illus.). San Francisco, CA: Children's Book Press.

Carle, E. (1968). *The very hungry caterpillar.* New York, NY: Philomel.

de Paola, T. (1979). *Oliver Button is a sissy.* San Diego, CA: Harcourt.

Hamilton, V. (1968). *The house of Dies Drear.* New York, NY: Simon & Schuster.

Huck, C. (1996). Literature-based reading programs: A retrospective. *The New Advocate, 9*(1), 23–33.

Kelly, J. (2009). *The evolution of Calpurnia Tate.* New York, NY: Henry Holt.

Lobel, A. (1979). *Frog and Toad together.* New York, NY: Harper Collins.

Martin, B. (1968). *Brown Bear, Brown Bear, what do you see?* (E. Carle, Illus.). New York, NY: Holt.

Mohr, M. (1979). *Felita.* New York, NY: Dial.

Munsch, R. (1988). *The paper bag princess* (M. Martchenko, Illus.). Toronto, Canada: Annick Press.

Myers, W. D. (1988). *Scorpions.* New York: HarperCollins

Park, L. S. (2002). *When my name was Keoko.* New York, NY: Clarion.

Siegel, S. (2006). *To dance: A ballerina's graphic novel* (M. Siegel, Illus.). New York, NY: Simon & Schuster.

Spinelli, J. (1990). *Maniac Magee.* Boston, MA: Little, Brown.

Steptoe, J. (1969). *Stevie.* New York, NY: Harper & Row.

Wild, M. (2001). *Fox* (R. Brooks, Illus.). LaJolla, CA: Kane/Miller.

Academic References

Atwell, N. (2007). *The reading zone.* New York, NY: Scholastic.

Bleich, D. (1981). *Subjective criticism.* Baltimore, MD: John Hopkins.

Bolasky, K. (2008). Encouraging symbolic thinking through literature. *WOW stories: Connections from the classrooms, 1*(1).

Retrieved January 22, 2009, from http://wowlit.org/on-line-publications/stories/storiesi1/6/

Brooks, W. (2006). Reading representations of themselves. *Reading Research Quarterly, 41*(3), 372–392.

Calkins, L. M. (2001). *The art of teaching reading.* New York, NY: Longman.

Case, R. (1991). Key elements of a global perspective. *Social Education. 57*(6), 318–325.

Copenhaver, J. (2001). Running out of time: Rushed read-alouds in a primary classroom. *Language Arts, 75*(2), 148–157.

Cruz, M., & Pollock, K. (2004). Stepping into the wardrobe: A fantasy genre study. *Language Arts, 81*(3), 184–195.

DeNicolo, C., & Fránquiz, M. (2006). "Do I have to say it?": Critical encounters with multicultural children's literature. *Language Arts, 84*(2), 157–169.

Dewey, J. (1938). *Education and experience.* New York, NY: Collier.

Dorsey-Gaines, C., & Taylor, D. (1988). *Growing up literate.* Portsmouth, NH: Heinemann.

Dutro, E. (2009). Children writing "hard times": Lived experiences of poverty and the class-privileged assumptions of a mandated curriculum. *Language Arts, 87*(2), 89–98.

Dyson, A. H., & Genishi, C. (1994). *The need for story: Cultural diversity in classroom and community.* Urbana, IL: National Council of Teachers of English.

Edelsky, C. (1999). *Making justice our project.* Urbana, IL: National Council of Teachers of English.

Edmiston, B., & Enciso, P. (2003). Reflections and refractions of meaning: Dialogic approaches to reading with classroom drama. In J. Flood, D. Lapp, J. Squire, & J. Jensen (Eds.), *Handbook of research on teaching the English language arts* (pp. 868–880). Mahwah, NJ: Erlbaum.

Edwards, A. (2008). Re-visioning the world through multiple perspectives. *WOW stories: Connections from the classrooms, 1*(1). Retrieved January 22, 2009, from http://wowlit.org/on-line-publications/stories/storiesi1/6/

Enciso, P. (1994). Cultural identity and response to literature: Running lessons from *Maniac Magee. Language Arts, 71,* 524–533.

Fountas, I., & Pinnell, G. (1996). *Guided reading.* Portsmouth, NH: Heinemann.

Fox, D., & Short, K. (2003). *Stories matter: The complexity of cultural authenticity in children's literature.* Urbana, IL: National Council of Teachers of English.

Freeman, E., & Lehman, B. (2001). *Global perspectives in children's literature.* Boston, MA: Allyn & Bacon.

Freire, P. (1972). *Pedagogy of the oppressed.* New York, NY: Herder & Herder.

Galda, L. (2001). High stakes reading: Articulating the place of children's literature in the curriculum. *The New Advocate, 14*(3), 223–228.

Galda, L., & Cullinan, B. (2000). Children's literature. In M. Kamil, P. Mosenthal, D. Pearson, & R. Barr (Eds.), *Handbook of reading research, Volume III* (pp. 361–379). Mahwah, NJ: Erlbaum

Gambrell, L. (2000). Literature-based reading instruction. In M. Kamil, P. Mosenthal, D. Pearson, & R. Barr (Eds.), *Handbook of reading research, Volume III* (pp. 563–607). Mahwah, NJ: Erlbaum.

Gay, G. (2000). *Culturally responsive teaching.* New York, NY: Teachers College Press.

Hall, K. (2007). Literacy policy and policy literacy. In R. Openshaw & J. Soler (Eds.), *Reading across international boundaries: History, policy and politics* (pp. 55–70). Charlotte, NC: Information Age.

Harris, V. (1997). *Using multiethnic literature in the K-8 classroom.* Norwood, MA: Christopher-Gordon.

Huck, C. (1982). "I give you the end of a golden string." *Theory into Practice, 21*(4), 315–321.

Hunt, P. (1994). *An introduction to children's literature.* Oxford, UK: Oxford Press.

Kaser, S. (2001). Searching the heavens with children's literature. *Language Arts, 78*(4), 348–356.

Keene, E., & Zimmerman, S. (2007). *Mosaic of thought: The power of comprehension strategy instruction.* Portsmouth, NH: Heinemann.

Larson, J. (2002). Packaging process: Consequences of commodified pedagogy of students' participation in literacy events. *Journal of Early Childhood Literacy, 2*(1), 65–95.

Lehman, B. (2007). *Children's literature and learning.* New York, NY: Teachers College Press.

Lewison, M., Flint, A. S., & Sluys, K.V. (2002). Taking on critical literacy: The journey of newcomers and novices. *Language Arts, 79*(5), 415–424.

Lewison, M., Leland, C., & Harste, J. (2008). *Creating critical classrooms.* New York, NY: Erlbaum.

Lindfors, J. (1999). *Children's inquiry: Using language to make sense of the world.* New York, NY: Teachers College Press.

Luke, A., & Freebody, P. (1997). Shaping the social practices of reading. In S. Muspratt, A. Luke, & P. Freebody (Eds.), *Constructing critical literacies* (pp. 185–223). Cresskill, NJ: Hampton.

Martínez-Roldán, C. (2005). The inquiry acts of bilingual children in literature discussion. *Language Arts, 83*(1), 22–32.

McCulloch, G. (2007). Forword. In R. Openshaw & J. Soler (Eds.), *Reading across international boundaries: History, policy and politics* (pp. ix–x). Charlotte, NC: Information Age.

Mills, H., O'Keefe, T., & Jennings, L. (2004). *Looking closely and listening carefully: Learning literacy through inquiry.* Urbana, IL: National Council of Teachers of English.

Mo, W., & Shen, W. (2003). Accuracy is not enough: The role of cultural values in the authenticity of picture books. In D. L Fox & K. G Short (Eds.), *Stories matter: The complexity of cultural authenticity in children's literature* (pp. 198–212). Urbana, IL: National Council of Teachers of English.

Moreillon, J. (2009). *Collaborative strategies for teaching reading comprehension.* Chicago, IL: American Library Association.

Morrow, L. M. (2003). Motivating lifelong voluntary readers. J. Flood, D. Lapp, J. Squire, & J. Jensen (Eds.), *Handbook of research on teaching the English language arts* (pp. 857–867). Mahwah, NJ: Erlbaum.

Openshaw, R., & Soler, J. (2007). Introduction. In R. Openshaw & J. Soler (Eds.), *Reading across international boundaries: History, policy and politics* (pp. xi–xxi). Charlotte, NC: Information Age.

Peirce, C. (1966). *Collected papers.* Cambridge, MA: Harvard University Press.

Peterson, R., & Eeds, M. (1990). *Grand conversations.* New York, NY: Scholastic.

Pradl, G. (1996). *Literature for democracy.* Portsmouth, NH: Boynton/Cook.

Ray, K. W. (2006). Exploring inquiry as a teaching stance in the writing workshop. *Language Arts, 89*(3), 237–247.

Rosenblatt, L. (1938). *Literature as exploration.* Chicago, IL: Modern Language Association.

Rosenblatt, L. M. (1978). *The reader, the text, the poem: The transactional theory of the literary work.* Carbondale: Southern Illinois University Press.

Roser, N. (2001). A place for everything and literature in its place. *The New Advocate, 14*(30), 211–221.

Shanahan, T. (2003). Research-based reading instruction: Myths about the National Reading Panel Report. *The Reading Teacher, 56*(7), 646–655.

Shannon, P. (2007). *Reading against democracy.* Portsmouth, NH: Heinemann.

Short, K. G. (2009a). Critically reading the word and the world: Building intercultural understanding through literature. *Bookbird: A Journal of International Children's Literature, 47*(2), 1–10.

Short, K. (2009b). Inquiry as a stance on curriculum. In S. Davidson & S. Carber (Eds.), *Taking the PYP forward* (pp. 11–26). London: John Catt.

Short, K. G. (1999). The search for "balance" in a literature-rich classroom. *Theory into Practice, 38*(3), 130–137.

Short, K. G., Kahn, L., & Kauffman, G. (2000). "I just *need* to draw": Responding to literature across multiple sign systems. *The Reading Teacher, 54*(2): 160–171.

Short, K., with Thomas, L. (in press). Developing intercultural understandings through international children's literature. In K. Whitmore. & R. Meyer (Eds.) *Revaluing reading.* New York: Routledge.

Siegel, M. (2006). Reading the signs: Multimodal transformations in the field of literacy education. *Language Arts, 84*(1), 65–77.

Sipe, L. (2008). *Storytime: Young children's literary understanding in the classroom.* New York, NY: Teachers College Press.

Snowball, D. & Bolton, F. (1999). *Spelling K-8: Planning and teaching.* Portland, ME: Stenhouse.

Soler, J. (2007). The Rose report: One step further in a managerialist approach to literacy education in England? In R. Openshaw & J. Soler (Eds.), *Reading across international boundaries: History, policy and politics* (pp. 43–54). Charlotte, NC: Information Age.

Sumara, D. (2002). *Why reading literature in school still matters.* Mahwah, NJ: Erlbaum.

Tompkins, K. (2007). Creating lifelong relationships: Children's connections to characters. *WOW stories: Connections from the classrooms, 1*(1). Retrieved October 19, 2008, from http://wowlit.org/on-line-publications/stories/storiesi1/6/

Wolf, S. A. (2004). *Interpreting literature with children.* Mahwah, NJ: Erlbaum.

Yenika-Agbaw, V. (1998). Images of West Africa in children's books. *The New Advocate, 11*(3), 303–318.

Ylimaki, R., & McClain, L. (2007). Curriculum leadership and the current politics of U.S.literacy education. In R. Openshaw & J. Soler (Eds.), *Reading across international boundaries: History, policy and politics* (pp. 71–86). Charlotte, NC: Information Age.

5

Readers, Texts, and Contexts in the Middle

Re-imagining Literature Education for Young Adolescents

Thomas P. Crumpler and Linda Wedwick

Illinois State University

Becoming a reader, as other authors in this section have shown, is often an unpredictable journey, usually marked by uncertainty and, if you're lucky, well-timed guidance. No time is more uncertain for being a reader than during the middle years of young adolescence, when engaged literary reading seems to wane for many youth, while becoming the refuge for others. Thomas Crumpler and Linda Wedwick open up the pathways to reading with an analysis of recent research on readers' approaches to literature, the literary content of particular relevance to this age group, and descriptions of the highly engaging forms of drama that can accompany reading in school and library settings.

When defining adolescence, a wide range of ages is typically included. For some researchers, the generally accepted age range for adolescence is 10 to 20. However, this generous age span is problematic when considering the changing nature of "physical and cognitive development on youth literacy practices" (Moje, Overby, Tysvaer, & Morris, 2008, p.110) and the changing contexts from primary school to middle school to high school that often mark significant shifts in adolescents' interests, experiences, and responsibilities. While we recognize that certain continuity exists between elementary and secondary-aged readers (such as identifying with characters in a story), there is value in focusing on a narrower age range, 11–14 specifically, for interpreting research and for considering how to engage young people in literary reading. In this chapter we focus on the dimensions of reading experience, especially social contexts and individual engagement, that can be formative for readers who are leaving behind episodic, humorous fiction and entering into a more critical and exploratory approach to book selection and interpretation. We begin with brief portraits of three readers and analyze these through the lenses of identity, social and cultural expectations, and motivational differences among readers.

The second section focuses on the characteristics of texts that have been viewed by critics, scholars, and educators as particularly well-suited to middle grade readers. We examine these characteristics in order to establish a sense of distinction for readers as they move into the transformative period of young adolescence.

Finally, we describe pedagogical approaches, especially dramatic processes, that support and extend readers' engagement in and interpretations of story worlds that may, at first, seem distant or confusing. Using several examples, we describe active, inquiry-based, social approaches to literary reading that enable young people to live inside worlds, rather than looking in from the outside.

Readers and Reading Inside Social Worlds

Some studies of adolescent readers have claimed that students' interest in reading declines in middle school. McKenna, Kear, and Ellsworth (1995), for example, found that students attitudes toward reading steadily declined from early elementary to middle school. More recently, Greenberg, Gilbert, and Fredrick (2006) claim the results of their study "indicate that middle school students show a significant lack of interest in reading and a lack of reading behavior" (p. 168). This survey research examined the responses of 1,174 middle school students from both rural and inner-city schools. Although their questionnaire was somewhat limited in complexity, participants' mean score for interest in reading was 2.42 on a 4-point Likert scale.

Despite this evidence, we know that middle school students' motivation to read is much more complex. Defining the parameters around a middle-level reader means taking into consideration the unique characteristics of early adolescence, their varied developmental characteristics, how they define reading, how they participate in reading as socially and culturally positioned people, and how they perceive their access to and comfort with unfamiliar ideas and perspectives represented in literature. For the past decade, researchers are more cautious in labeling adolescent students as unmotivated or non-readers. Not only do we need to consider both in and out of school practices; we must also consider their view of reading and their reader identity.

Ivey and Broaddus (2001) recognized that studies of young adolescents' attitudes toward and interests in reading were limited and few examined the instruction that may contribute to students' interest in reading. In their study, 1,765 sixth-grade students responded to a questionnaire about reading in their language arts classroom. The results suggest a mismatch between school structures, such as mandated curriculum and instructional approach. Additionally, they realized that motivation to read is not an "all-or-nothing construct" (p. 366).

More recently, in a study of 584 urban minority middle school students, Hughes-Hassell and Rodge (2007) found that 72% of the students reported that they engage in reading as a leisure activity. A majority of the students who engage in leisure reading report that they do it for fun, and magazines are usually their material of choice. Both of these studies confirm that readers' attitudes are

multidimensional and fluctuate based on the context. As the reading portraits presented below suggest, young adolescents' attitudes toward reading are deeply tied to contexts and purposes, as well as their beliefs about how books "talk" to you.

Katie, a seventh grader, says that "reading is something you do in your spare time, for enjoyment, to learn, and to find out what other people think about different topics." Katie reads for pleasure all the time. She likes contemporary realistic fiction the most, such as *The Lottery Rose* by Irene Hunt (1976) and *Walk Two Moons* by Sharon Creech (1996), but she admits that she will read anything. She rarely abandons books because even if she is not all that interested in the book, she "doesn't mind finishing it just to see what happens." In her language arts class, she is routinely finishing one book and checking out another. She also reads all the texts assigned in the other classes but only because she wants good grades. Katie's understanding of reading distinguishes between what she reads for school assignments and what she reads for pleasure. Her definition of reading does not include any reading that she might do for a school assignment.

Steven, on the other hand, understands that reading has a variety of purposes and exists in a variety of contexts, including both in and out of school. He defines reading as "a way of being communicated to. Sometimes reading is needed to find important information. Or, sometimes it is just for fun." Steven primarily selects fantasy texts for pleasure reading, including series such as the *Redwall* series by Brian Jacques.

In contrast, Bailey, an eighth grader, believes that "reading is when you are looking at words and saying what they are/say." Although he does not have a "reader" identity, and does not show much interest in reading novels, he uses a variety of comprehension strategies (such as making connections and asking questions) to understand texts that interest him. When asked, Bailey cannot name specific book titles of what he has recently read.

These three readers show three very distinct reader identities and three different definitions of reading. To complicate matters further, teachers and students may also conceptualize reading and what it means to be a reader differently. Williams (2004) suggests that young children believe that all reading both in and out of the classroom counts towards making them readers. However, by middle school, "reading becomes more connected to work and the demonstration and assessment of knowledge" (p. 687), so young adolescents' conceptions of their identities as readers change.

Describing oneself as someone who does not like reading does not necessarily mean that a young adolescent does not read or lacks fundamental skills for reading (Hughes-Hassell & Rodge, 2007; Strommen & Mates, 2004). According to Ivey (2001), middle-level reader differences can be viewed from two distinct and related dimensions: differences between readers and complexity within individual readers. Differences between readers include the wide range in ability that is both academic and cognitive. In addition, a multi-case study of sixth-grade students found that "individual middle level readers were multidimensional as readers, and their abilities and dispositions toward reading varied with different contexts" (p. 66).

Along with their perceptions of classroom-based reading, it is also important to understand how adolescents interpret reading in other parts of their lives. Moje et al. (2008) found that adolescents' social networks such as informal reading and writing groups and more organized reading groups became spaces "that allow racial or gendered identities to be constructed or enacted" (p. 132). Their longitudinal research challenges traditional views of reading practices among adolescents that describe them as indifferent or unmotivated. These findings help to explain why the readers described above think about reading very differently. Indeed, their reader identities are unique, multidimensional, and contextualized.

We take as further evidence of these nuances in reading interest, Tatum's (2008) analysis of the social and political contexts informing young African American males' reading choices. Tatum demonstrates, through interview data and evidence of students' literature-based writing, that racially based biases and judgments both in and out of school often collide and constrain reading interests for many students—particularly if they grow up in communities of high poverty.

In one case, Tatum (2008) focuses on a young man from Chicago whose choices of texts were mediated by racist experiences such as being pulled over by white police officers who assume the African American occupants possessed drugs or other illegal substances. These phenomena of "driving while black" and other "devaluing" situations are "often overlooked by literacy models that are solely grounded in cognitive reading processes" (p. 172). Tatum argues that these cultural experiences become texts that mediate other literacy practices (e.g. selection of books) for adolescent readers. Further, literate identities, for many African American males are informed by performative popular cultural texts such as hip hop music and rap lyrics. Tatum argues that these texts are key to the social networks that African American males inhabit, and that, as literacy practices, they exercise profound influence on the identities the young men enact as part of a more relevant and successful form of literacy experience outside of school.

Moje et al. (2008) contend that we need to know more about relationships between literacy practices outside of classrooms and school-based literacy, as well as how they are mutually constitutive. We believe this is particularly important for middle-level readers because they are involved in constructing and performing identities that are linked with, yet, challenge and transform traditional cultural understandings of literacy. What are the best contexts for successful literature instruction, and how are those spaces constructed and negotiated by and with middle-level students? As instructional walls become more porous through technology and students become more attuned to their roles in a global economy, how do constructs of middle-level readers, middle-level novels, and instructional practices shift?

Engaging Middle-Level Readers

From 2005 to 2007 nearly 80 articles appeared in *Reading Research Quarterly* and the *Journal of Adolescent & Adult Literacy* that specifically focused on adolescents' motivation and engagement in reading. According to Cassidy, Garrett, and Barrera (2006), literacy leaders agree "almost all the literature on adolescent literacy mentions the importance of motivation or engagement" (p. 35). Case studies included in the journal review may appear to be limited in scope or usefulness in making an argument for improving teachers' knowledge of engagement and motivation in reading the middle years, but according to Hinchman (2008), such perspectives have the potential to influence policy to consider a more diverse range of literacies and texts. Even the most recent studies on motivation indicate that school texts do not match what adolescents want nor need (Pitcher et al., 2007). Clearly, connectedness, or the transaction that takes place when a reader is engaged is imperative for students to develop as readers (Hunsberger, 2007).

Brozo, Shiel, and Topping (2007/2008) suggest that low motivation to read is not unique to young adolescents in the United States. Rather, "youth from across the globe exhibit a similar decline in performance and interest as they move from primary to secondary school" (p. 307). In a recent column of International Reports on Literacy Research, Botzakis and Malloy (2005) asked all International Reading Correspondents (IRCs) to identify the most pressing issues in literacy from their region. The disengagement with literacy of middle school students (grades 5–8; ages 11–14) was the issue most often identified. In response, each IRC sent out surveys to 20–25 people in their regions in order to gather more information about young adolescents' disengagement with literacy. The results across geographic regions showed that both gender and out-of school interests were reported as influential on literacy engagement. Girls were reported to be more engaged in school-approved literacies, but out-of-school literacies were rarely incorporated in classroom instruction. Further, students are more engaged and influenced by new technologies; however, these technologies are not used very often in classroom situations, particularly in areas of high poverty (Botzakis & Malloy, 2005).

In another recent International Report of Reading Research, Malloy and Botzakis (2005) summarize a longitudinal study of 370 students as they transitioned from childhood to adolescence. Schillings (2003) investigated the development of reading comprehension skills as well as motivation to read, metacognitive reading awareness, and reading achievement based on Guthrie and Alverman's (1999) framework of reading engagement. Participants consisted of 370 students at the end of Grade 6. Findings indicated support of the process of engagement adapted from Guthrie and Alverman (Malloy & Botzakis, 2005).

Finally, the Program for International Student Assessment (PISA) indicated that there is a link between engagement and achievement. PISA is a global effort that attempts to assess the reading literacy of adolescents. Based on the results of the PISA 2000 report, Brozo et al. (2007/2008) suggest that engagement is a critical factor in reading achievement and "keeping students engaged in reading and learning might make it possible for them to overcome what might otherwise be insuperable barriers to academic success" (p. 309). Highly engaged adolescents from the lowest socioeconomic indicators performed as well as two other groups in the study: (1) highly engaged youth from the middle socioeconomic status (SES) and (2) medium level engagement from high socioeconomic status. Socioeconomic status is figured by averaging the value for the dimensions of occupation, education, household income and family income. These studies along with the portraits of Katie, Steven, and Bailey suggest that readers are motivated to read in different contexts. The above study, specifically, calls for a need to change our approach for motivating and engaging students in schools, libraries, and other spaces for reading, especially when students have different goals and social values. With a clearly established link between engagement and achievement (Brozo et al., 2007/2008), we must focus on what we do in the classroom to motivate all students while accepting their unique reader identities and personal preferences.

Defining Middle-Level Narratives

From a policy makers' perspective, in the area of adolescent literacy there is tremendous need for researchers to assist with selecting materials and developing interventions for striving readers (Wise, 2007). Doubek and Cooper (2007) suggest that researchers find out not only why certain texts are chosen, but also explore the process of text selection. Instructionally, there need to be clear guidelines for selecting appropriate texts not just for educators but for non-educators in the community who work with young readers outside of the school context. Wedwick and Wutz's (2006) work with BOOKMATCH, a tool used for teaching self-selection strategies to middle-level students, is appropriate for both educators and noneducators. This tool scaffolds readers as they learn to match themselves to books that are just right for them rather than relying on a teacher, a publisher's assumption of what is just right for a grade level, or a scripted program, such as Accelerated Reader. Thompson, Madhuri, and Taylor's (2008) study of the Accelerated Reader program confirmed other studies that indicate students did not like the limited book selections associated with this program. Students also revealed

that they did not enjoy the book selections, and African American students felt there were very few books by black authors or with black protagonists other than books on slavery. Empowering students to choose their own books with a process like BOOKMATCH, may motivate them to continue reading rather than discourage them.

The literature for young adolescents is also evolving from children's literature to adolescent literature. At times, this transition may happen too quickly for some students. Additionally, middle school teachers are forced to consider the explicitness of some adolescent literature for whole class novels or even inclusion in their classroom libraries. In Wedwick's own teaching of middle school students, she had students every year who wanted to censor some books in the classroom. This inevitably led to a debate between those students who believed they should be able to read anything they wanted and those who believed that some books were inappropriate for everyone.

In selecting their own texts for independent reading, these students were expected to consider the topic appropriateness or their comfort zone for a particular text (Wedwick & Wutz, 2006). Students openly discussed that adolescent literature is often at a difficulty level appropriate for them, but that those books regularly have "touchy" topics which they may be uncomfortable reading. While choosing their own books, students ranked topic appropriateness as one of their top criteria for selection. Some students expressed that sometimes they are comfortable with a book's content, but their parents were uncomfortable with them reading a particular book and would not allow it. Of course, parents and adolescents may not have the same perception of what is appropriate. Nevertheless, young adolescents are quite aware of their comfort zone and must be allowed to choose books that match their comfort zone.

Having a way for both teachers and students to identify books in the middle of a children's literature and adolescent literature continuum could be beneficial. Trites's (2000) scholarship in adolescent literature helps to inform an argument for a middle-level genre. According to Trites (2000), the primary characteristic "that distinguishes adolescent literature from children's literature is the issue of how social power is deployed during the course of the narrative" (p. 2). For children's literature, "the action focuses on one child who learns to feel more secure" in his or her environment, "represented by family and home" (pp. 3–4). In adolescent literature, however, "protagonists must learn about the social forces that have made them what they are" (p. 4). In adolescent literature, the protagonist figures out how to "negotiate the levels of power that exist in the myriad social institutions within which they must function" (p. 4).

Appleyard (1990) explains what he understands to be the difference between books for children and books for adolescents:

> The difference is that the juvenile books all deal with an innocent world, where evil is externalized and finally powerless, where endings are happy. The adolescents' books

deal with sex, death, sin, and prejudice, and good and evil are not neatly separated but mixed up in the confused and often turbulent emotions of the central characters themselves. (p.100)

Books for the young adolescent, then, do not completely reflect the innocent world of children's literature, but also do not position the reader in explicit situational contexts as adolescent literature does. Although books can be a safe place for new experiences before adolescents try them out in the real world, young adolescents are not always prepared for the content of literature for older adolescents.

Drawing on the work of these scholars, and particularly Trites (2000) and Appleyard (1990), the chart in Figure 5.1 outlines a proposed set of criteria that distinguishes middle-level literature from children's literature and adolescent literature by the representation of sex/sexuality, power, and the innocent world.

We understand these criteria as guideposts for theorizing the genre of middle-level literature; they help mark explorations into the genre but are not meant to restrict them. Three texts are used here to help illustrate these distinguishing characteristics of children's literature, middle-level literature, and adolescent literature: *And Tango makes Three* by Justin Richardson and Peter Parnell (2005), *The Misfits* by James Howe (2001), and *Geography Club* by Brent Hartinger (2003).

In *And Tango Makes Three*, sex and sexuality are focused on the concept of family—specifically on same gender adults who are the caregivers in one family. Families are first described traditionally when a boy and a girl penguin become a couple. They build a home together, the girl penguin lays an egg, the couple takes turns warming the egg until it hatches, and the families become mama, papa, and baby. However, the male penguins, Roy and Silo, have no interest in the girl penguins, and the two of them do everything together, such as swimming, singing, walking, and nesting.

When the other penguins prepare their nest to hatch an egg, Roy and Silo follow their rituals, but without an egg, no baby penguin is hatched. The zoo keeper provides Roy and Silo with an egg, and the two penguins take turns sitting on the egg until it hatches. When Tango is born, the three of them live happily as a family. Tango has two daddies. Roy and Silo enact power by hatching the egg in their nest and taking care of Tango. Together they experience both a sense of self and a sense of family. The innocent world is represented in the plot as the focus is only on the happiness of all the characters. Roy and Silo do not experience ostracism by being a non-traditional family, and they experience the same happiness as all the other penguin families. There is essentially no evil in the story.

In the middle-level novel, *The Misfits* (Howe, 2001), sex and sexuality are evident in the harmless crushes the characters have on different people in their lives. For example, Bobby has a crush on the older Pam and the very shy Kelsey. Skeezie has a crush on Steffi, the older waitress at the Candy Kitchen. Joe has a crush on his classmate, Colin. Joe's gay identity is explicit, but he dreams only of

Sex/Sexuality		
Children's Literature	Middle Level Literature	Adolescent Literature
Focus is on gender roles/constructions; Implicit rather than explicit	Sexuality is viewed as innocent and harmless; perhaps even comical. The potential of its power is not fully understood.	Characters deal explicitly with issues of sex and sexuality; "experiencing sexuality marks a rite of passage that helps them define themselves as having left childhood behind" (Trites, 2000, p. 84).
Power		
The reader learns to feel more secure in immediate environment (Trites, 2000).	The reader learns that there are social institutions that have varying levels of power over them.	The reader learns to negotiate the levels of power in social institutions (Trites, 2000).
The protagonist's struggle enacts personal power and a sense of self (Trites, 2000).	The protagonist's struggle propels her/him forward on an identity quest and empowers him/her to continue the exploration.	The protagonist's struggle is more on an institutional level, and he/she is more likely to be disempowered by the social institutions in this struggle.
Innocent World		
Social injustice is rectified.	Social injustice may exist but individuals have the power to overcome it.	Social injustice is a fact of life and difficult if not impossible to eradicate.
Evil is externalized and powerless and endings are happy (Appleyard, 1990).	Evil can be internal and external. The protagonist learns to overcome the power of evil rather than understand it to be powerless.	"Deal with sex, death, sin, and prejudice; good and evil are not viewed as binary opposites but tied up in the turbulent emotions of the characters" (Appleyard, 1990, p. 100).

Figure 5.1 Characteristics of literature by category

holding hands with someone he likes. The comedic also plays a role in the characters' sexual awakening: DuShawn likes Addie so he hits her with spitballs and puts a whoopee cushion on her chair; Bobby finally works up the nerve to call Kelsey, but he hangs up twice when someone answers, and then keeps telling Kelsey that there is something wrong with his phone; Addie thinks she and Colin are going together because he showed up at the flagpole, gave her a compliment, and told her he'd get a soda with her another time; and Skeezie becomes speechless when the older Steffi flirts with him.

In terms of power, the gang of five experience struggles with the institutional powers of school and social status. They want to create a third party to run for student council, but they are repeatedly met with barriers from the teacher Ms. Wyman, the principal Mr. Kiley, and the larger institutional power of the two party governmental system of the country. However, the gang of five is granted permission to create their third party, the No-Name Party. The gang also believe themselves to be on the lower end of the social status, but they have each other, which empowers them. Even though they don't end up winning the election, they are still empowered by the experience and learn that each has "the freedom to be who you are without anybody calling you names" (p. 266).

Characters in *The Misfits* understand that evil exists. They have all been called names at least since the third grade. But, together, they learn to overcome this evil, or at least to fight against it. By not winning the election, they recognize that evil has power, but they learn that they can overcome it. They learn that they can stand up for themselves, and they believe that they have the power to make a difference.

In *Geography Club* (Hartinger, 2003), sex and sexuality become much more explicit. For example, Ms. Toles, the health teacher, teaches the students how to use condoms, demonstrating on a cucumber. The high school students in this novel describe sexual encounters as though sex in high school is a matter of fact. For example, Jared says, "she was begging for it, squirming around like a baby," and once he "started going at her, she couldn't get enough" (p.181). Russel Middlebrook, the novel's protagonist, is a gay teenager who occasionally visits gay chat rooms, and eventually experiences sex with another boy from his school. Russel's coming to terms with his sexuality is an explicit plot feature throughout the book.

However, while Joe in *The Misfits* does not hide who he is, the gay characters in *Geography Club* recognize the loss of power and social status should they reveal themselves. Russel learns that one's fear of exposure is more powerful than any other emotion. Kevin, Russel's boyfriend, knows that the power that comes with his social status as a popular jock is more important than being true to himself and being associated with the gay Russel. At the end of the novel, the institutional power seems to win. The Geography Club is defunct, and even though a Gay-Straight-Bisexual Alliance is formed, the gay members are content with the rest of the student body believing they are the "straight" members and Brian Bund is the one gay member of the club.

The innocent world is problematic in adolescent literature and injustices are prevalent. Topics like sex and drinking are positioned as sinful in the world of the novel, and characters deal with "real" consequences of their behavior. Russel learns that good and evil are not simply opposites. When Brian Bund is being tormented in the cafeteria, Russel says that he'd like to help him, but "it wouldn't have made any difference anyway" (p. 9) because he risked being a victim as well. Later, when Russel starts hanging around with the jocks, he too, teases Brian, even though he knows it to be wrong. When other members of the Geography Club invite Brian to join them, Russel votes no because he doesn't want to risk losing Kevin.

These three texts present unique characteristics and demonstrate the need for a middle-level genre. In children's literature, the protagonist experiences personal power. In the adolescent novel, protagonists struggle on more of an institutional level and they discover that they are more likely to be disempowered by the social institutions. The middle-level novel propels young adolescents forward on their identity quests and empowers them to continue that exploration. Trites's (2000) distinction between the *Entwicklungsroman* "which is a broad category of novels in which an adolescent character grows, and the *Bildungsroman*, which is a related type of novel in which the adolescent matures to adulthood" (p. 9) shapes our thinking about this identity quest. Middle-level novels are *Entwicklungsromane*, not *Bildungsromane*. Growth novels are not punctuated with graphic language and sexual how to, although there may be a sense of sexual awakening within the protagonist.

Overall, we believe work by these scholars and researchers, along with our newly defined characteristics, support our claim for recognizing texts for the middle-level reader as a viable category, situated between literature for children and literature for older adolescents. We acknowledge that the category we are arguing for may not encompass the experiences of all readers, and that particular groups of readers may find other types of texts engaging on a personal or political level (Enciso, Wolf, Coats, & Jenkins, 2010). However, we believe that identifying texts for middle-level readers has educational value. In the next section, we explore instructional contexts in which middle-level literature can be brought to life through meaningful, interactive experiences.

What Instructional Contexts are Most Likely to Engage Middle-Level Readers?

In this section, we focus on instructional research that suggests successful practices for teaching middle-level literature; we also argue for an expansion of research on teaching the middle-level novel that is informed by innovative pedagogy—particularly process drama. We believe that process drama, the practices of using dramatic structures as tools facilitate response to literature, offer new opportunities for thinking about research on teaching literature for middle-level readers. The work of the New London Group (1996) helped crystallize the notion of multi-literacies into a pedagogical frame that emphasized the concepts of design and literacy work for re-imagining "social futures" for learners. This approach offers a powerful heuristic for researchers and teachers who want to explore how middle-level readers draw on multiple sign systems (Siegel, 2006) as they respond to and construct understandings of literature. We argue that particularly promising are studies that draw on process drama to engage readers in complex meaning making around literature. In this chapter, we situate process drama in a larger context of reader response research; however, we also acknowledge that others would view it differently.

Readers Responding in the Middle-Level Classroom: Categories for Interpreting Middle-Level Reading Engagement

Early research by Appleyard (1990) discovered that becoming a reader and responding as a reader are developmental processes. He argued that to understand readers' responses to texts, we need to move beyond cognitive explanations of development and consider sociocultural factors. According to Appleyard, as readers mature, their attitudes, intentions, responses, and use of reading shifts along five roles: player, hero and heroine, thinker, interpreter, and pragmatic. He generated his concepts from a narrative analysis of three "instructive accounts" (pp. 23–25) of young readers and extrapolated his categories of role from these examples. Young adolescents fall between and among the characteristics of reader as hero and heroine and reader as thinker. The reader as hero and heroine imagines herself as the protagonist who solves the problems of the world through competence and initiative. The reader as thinker looks to literature to discover authentic roles for imitation, ideal images, and values and alternative values and beliefs. The shifting nature of these roles is related both to young adolescents' emerging identity and their cognitive development, as well as the situational context of middle school and their social practices.

This shifting of readers' responses is also documented in Galda's (1992) four-year study of students as they moved from fourth grade to seventh grade. The results showed significant differences in students' responses as they grew older. Students read two novels each year (one realism and one fantasy) and discussed those novels with the researcher leading the discussion with open-ended questions. Students' responses during these discussions and individual interviews with the researcher were classified into categorical and analytic responses. The results

indicated that students' responses changed from primarily categorical to more analytic, and "their preferences and understandings about reading literature became increasingly complex across the four years of the study" (p. 132). Although these students are not rereading the same texts, their experiences over time are contributing to the increasing complexity of their cognitive processes.

More recently, studies have concluded that adolescents have little critical response to texts (Beach & Freedman, 1992; DeBlase, 2003; Garner, 1999; Pace, 2003; Pearlman, 1995; Smith, 1992). Still, these findings do not imply that students lack the cognitive capacity for understanding ideology. The reader's social stance or subject position plays a salient role in the thinking readers do about the texts. Considering young adolescents' emerging identity, their need to explore alternative roles, the complexity and variability of their developing cognitive ability, and their shifting reader roles, these characteristics are distinctly different from those of childhood and those of later adolescence. This difference is related to the inchoate nature of young adolescent identities and a need to "try on" different selves in ways that are safe for middle-level readers. Therefore, middle-level texts will need to provide opportunities to interactively respond and explore some of these same distinct characteristics. However, young adolescent readers will also need instruction on how to read a novel and how to critically analyze ideology.

Shifting Practices

How middle-level readers respond to and engage with literature has been a trend in recent research (Almasi, 1995; Alverman et al., 1996; Lewis, 1997; Evans, 2002). These studies have established how understandings and interpretations of literature can be mediated successfully through literature circles and other discussion groups. Together, they are salient for recognizing the importance of highlighting social interactions as significant features of literature instruction for middle-level readers.

Recent scholarship has investigated how response to literature is culturally situated in specific contexts and how readers' responses to literature may be transformative—helping them see literary texts and their own meaning making practices differently. Galda and Beach (2001) chart the development of response to literature by reviewing scholarship in three areas—text, readers, and contexts. Based on their synthesis of work from the 1960s though the late 1990s, they contend that research on response has been informed by sociocultural theory. To deepen their pedagogical understanding of how middle-level readers respond, Beach and Meyers (2001) focused specifically on a group of 15 seventh-grade girls responding to a young adult novel in an after school book club. Their findings suggested exploring responses to the novel through dialogue journal entries helped these middle-level students unpack and question traditional roles of women in society.

Brooks's (2006) investigation of how African American middle-level readers respond to and interpret texts that include authentic representations of their own ethnic group was theoretically situated within a convergence of reader-response scholarship. She frames her inquiry by arguing for separating reader response categories proposed by Beach (1993): textual, experiential, psychological, social, and cultural; and selecting experiential and cultural as the most potentially generative for examining how this class of students responded to a group novels selected by the researcher and the librarian at the school where the research was conducted (Brooks, 2006, p. 375). Brooks defines experiential as significant for readers of African American literature because it focuses on "the value of life-text links" and cultural as how readers "draw from historical, discursive, ideological and social contexts (p. 376) in their responses. The list of novels for the study included *Scorpions* (Myers, 1988), *Roll of Thunder Hear my Cry* (Taylor, 1976), and the *House of Dies Drear* (Hamilton, 1968).

Brooks's analyses of responses during literature discussions indicated that textual features across novels (e.g., forging family and friend relationships, confronting and overcoming racism, surviving city life), could be used to augment effective literacy instruction with middle-level readers. What was particularly significant in Brooks's study was her implication that middle-level African American reader's responses to and understandings of the novels listed above were tied to student's culturally specific knowledge, yet were also complex. Pedagogically, this supports our argument that we need innovative instruction that both honors the cultural background of the middle-level reader and creates avenues to explore individual complexity across literary texts.

Other research (Juzwik & Sherry, 2007) has examined how the use of teacher oral narratives promoted specific categories of response in a seventh grade classroom and also enhanced class discussion of literature. Additionally, Stone (2006) looked at how students used the development of picture books as a way to mediate and respond to relationships between school culture and their communities and found that this type of genre-specific writing response opened dialogues for teaching critical literacy. These two studies suggest that culturally constructed textual features and a literacy practice like oral narrative foster more complex and potentially identity shaping responses in middle-level readers.

Others have built on this body of scholarship to consider how constructs of power, gender, and identity mediate reader's construction of meaning (Broughton & Fairbanks, 2003; Cherland, 1994; Smith, 1992). Clarke's research (2006), for example, investigated literature circle discussions as spaces where fifth-grade girls were positioned and positioned themselves along narrative and cultural story lines. Findings from this study challenge researchers to think more carefully and deeply about relationships within engagement with literature, and how teachers can "create

situations in which power and positioning become normalized" (p. 77). These patterns can reify traditional patterns of dominance in classrooms, and create opportunities for some students' voices to be squelched. In the next section we detail the power of drama and its pedagogical use with middle-level readers and argue that this approach brings together reader, text, and context in potentially powerful ways.

Drama and Readers' Response to Middle-level Literature

Identifying middle-level literature creates opportunities for teachers and students to select books that resonate for a particular category of reader; using drama as a pedagogical tool can shift instruction so that a student's "whole being" (Crumpler & Schneider, 2002) is engaged in the study of that literature. Wagner's (1998) survey and synthesis of research studies about using drama in language arts provided evidence for how process drama could impact students' learning and engagement. In the area of drama and literature instruction, the work of Rosenblatt (1938/1983, 1978) is conceptually salient. Scholars built on her theories and extended them to explorations of literary understanding (Steig, 1989), argued for how literary texts encouraged readers to enter fictional worlds (Benton, 1992), and developed performative theories of responding to and interpreting texts (Iser, 1989, 1993).

More recently, researchers have argued for the importance of literary theory for underpinning literature instruction with adolescents (Appleman, 2000; Soter, 1999; Sumara, 2002). Based on the works of these authors and others, researchers have explored how process drama can serve as a pedagogical tool to augment and enrich literature instruction and challenge traditional interpretive stances with readers (Crumpler, 2006; Gallagher, 2001; Medina, 2004; Wilhelm & Edmiston, 1998). In this chapter we conceptualize process drama as using methods of teacher in role, student in role, tableaux, and other dramatic structures to promote learning (O'Neill, 1995).

Heathcote and Bolton (1995), as well as more recent work, have investigated possibilities for drama as response to literature (Edmiston, 2003; Edmiston & Enciso, 2003; Wolf, Edmiston, & Enciso, 1997). Wolf (2004) delineates between "text centered" and "text edged" drama as interpretive work in which an author's words are either central to creating a performative event such as reader's theater and classroom theater or, on the other hand, tableaux and unwritten conversations, which stray further from the text. Key to both approaches is the concept of "critical space" in which teachers and students step out of a dramatic sequence of instruction with literature to examine how roles were taken up and critique the creation of the fictional experience.

Using such a framework, a teacher could use text edged drama to explore issues of family or perspectives suggested in the middle-level novel, *No More Dead Dogs*

(Korman, 2000). In this novel, Wallace, who refuses to lie under any circumstances, is an unexpected football success who gets suspended from the team after writing an unfavorable review of his English teacher's favorite novel, *Old Shep My Pal.* When he refuses to rewrite the report, he is forced to attend rehearsals of a school play based on the same book and directed by the same English teacher. Through drama, students working with their teacher in role, can use the fictional world of *No More Dead Dogs* to examine the real conflicts that might arise when someone sticks to their convictions. In other words, participants in a text edged drama can use roles they create to consider biases of teachers, the difficulties of telling the truth, and negotiating peer pressure.

Drama expands practices of literature instruction in classrooms in a variety of ways, including working in role, tableau, and other dramatic structures. Literature instruction that is informed by process drama provides opportunities for a teacher in role to de-center her or himself in the classroom and become a co-learner with students. For example, a teacher could move into role as Wallace, the main character. From this position, she can facilitate conversations between a character from a story and the students; and in this case explore how it might feel to have a group be angry at you, when they represent a group in which you really want to become a member. These (fictional/real) conversations allow the teacher and the students to activate background knowledge, draw on the text of the story, and re-access knowledge about texts they have read in the past while engaged in this interaction.

Crumpler's (2001–2002, 2006) research has argued for the theoretical power of drama for exploring issues of social justice in middle school classrooms and as a form of response to literature. In one study of a sixth-grade classroom (2001–2002), drama was used as a research approach to inquire into how students responded to *Encounter*, Jane Yolen's (1996) recasting of the story of Columbus from an indigenous boy's perspective. In this study, the teacher worked in role to become Columbus and invited the children to talk with her about plans for the island she had landed on in the story. Then stepping out of role, the teacher asked one of the students to become a reporter and interview the rest of the group in role as the ship's crew.

The sixth graders decided to put Columbus on trial so the teacher helped identify defense and prosecuting attorneys and jurors for the courtroom finale. In role as jurors, these children argued over what constituted proof of guilt, and challenged one another about who really understood the story that Columbus and his attorney told in the classroom court. Results from analysis of transcripts of the children's conversations in role indicated that "in *self-spectatorship,* participants' attentiveness to how they are developing a role, positioning themselves in relation to other participants, and the language choices that they make" (Crumpler, 2001–2002, p. 59) can be examined by adopting dramatic orientation to inquiry with students.

Crumpler (2007) has also conducted case study research to explore how a middle-level teacher used process drama to facilitate eighth-grade students' responses to and understanding of *To Kill a Mocking Bird* (Lee, 1960). Results of this study found that the use of the dramatic structures of teacher in role, student in role, tableaux, and writing in role as instructional tactics to foster response, helped students enter the world of the novel and then, as Galda and Beach (2001) recommend, critique and transform the world of Scout, Boo Radley, and the other characters in Lee's classic literary text. Particularly interesting was the teacher's use of tableaux, silent frozen images, which served as a mediator to help students access different meaning systems and tap into what the New London Group (1996) called "the resources for design" (p. 74). Through using these resources, students began to understand the "conventions of semiotic activity" (p. 74).

In other words, they internalized some of the structures of the novel (divisive opinions, the oppressive nature or racism, and the desire for freedom) and were able to translate them into their own literacy practices. In this study the students were engaged in a sequence of process drama activities with their teacher. The teacher, Gloria, stepped into role as a lady from the 1930s, and began to read from an imaginary book of manners, "Being a Lady." She stepped primly to the front of the room and read a passage from her "book," and it became a pretext (O'Neill, 1995) for the dramatic work on that day—its genesis and reason for coming into being. The pretext initiated the use of the tableau (singular for tableaux) in this case. She described the importance of manners and speaking when spoken to, the way legs should be crossed, and how a lady should dress.

After reading in role, the teacher stepped back into her role as classroom teacher and asked the students to write down what would be a gesture or behavior that they believed would represent or serve as an emblem or metaphor for how girls should act at the time in history portrayed in *To Kill a Mockingbird* (Lee, 1960). Five minutes passed as students wrote. She spoke as herself and asked the students to tell her what they had written down. The students called out their ideas, and she wrote them on the board. This is the list that was generated:

- Having tea with a group of elderly ladies
- Quietly reading a book
- Sitting on a porch waiting for father to come home
- Writing a letter to an aunt at a desk
- Curtseying

The teacher asked the group to choose one idea from the list, and they chose curtseying. She then divided the group in half, and they faced each other in the middle of the room. She explained to them that when she counts to three, they would all curtsey simultaneously. She acknowledged that there were boys in the room, but they were working in role to represent the 1930s. They created the tableau, as two groups of 10 faced each other and then asked them to "freeze," and then hold their position. The students were in two lines facing each other, trying to hold the concept of curtseying and looking intently at each other at first, and then slowly began to laugh. The teacher told them to relax and moved them into a second tableau.

Gloria invited them to think about a situation that would be totally opposite to curtseying that they could perform via tableau to show a polar contrast to this formal act/ gesture. After a few minutes of discussion in small groups, the students decided to present a tableau of a *mosh pit*. A mosh pit is something that happens at a punk or heavy metal concert. People attending a concert gather in front of the stage where the band is playing and will furiously push, shove and body slam each other. The goal is not to hurt one another but to enjoy the music in a less passive way.

For this tableau, the entire group worked together to wrap their bodies loosely around each other, some students were lying down, and some were kneeling, and others raised one leg off the floor to simulate flying through the air. The teacher asked the students to freeze into a tableau. The scene was intriguing as they concentrated to hold themselves still for less than a minute in this image of silent controlled mayhem. Process drama as a mode of response to literature can engage middle-level readers in learning through fostering complex interpretive decisions as they access the meaning system of a novel, their social interactions, and the imaginary world they construct using dramatic structures.

In other studies, research suggested that practices of process drama like tableaux, the creation of silent frozen moments, can act as an image to activate students' thinking and understanding about a particular literary work. Tableaux is a practice that has been used to enhance literature instruction with a variety of age learners (Downey, 2005; Wilson, 2003). Wilson's work with young children suggested that tableaux is a "way of thinking" (p. 375) and linked using tableaux to cognitive and language development literacy instruction. Downey (2005) worked with middle school students, and integrated tableaux into classroom instruction to explore issues of social justice and help students think critically about literature as well as social and historic episodes. She found that students creating tableaux moved to more abstract thinking, going beyond plot to an understanding of theme and metaphor.

Another area of inquiry with drama is performative critical literacy work (Medina, 2004). Medina (2006) draws on Sumara's (2002) work in literary interpretation to examine critical performance literacies with fifth-grade students who were recent Latino immigrants. These students were working in literature discussion groups reading *My Diary from Here to There/Mi Diario de Aquí Hasta Allá* (Peréz, 2002) and working through drama structures such as writing in role and tableaux. The discussion groups

provided opportunities for the students who are English learners to create a "common place" (p. 66) through drama where they could better understand characters through their own personal experiences. Clearly, process drama for working with middle-level readers and texts is an area of theoretical and instructional promise.

Reaching Middle-level Readers through Drama

Instructionally, process drama is a potentially powerful tool for engaging middle readers in rich explorations of literature. As we argued earlier in this chapter, research suggests that the identities of middle-level students are performed within various social networks and spaces— including classrooms—and the texts they engage with are mediated in specific ways within those contexts. Teachers who use drama as a tactic to explore literature can ask "what if" (Edmiston, 2003) when they are studying novels and create other possibilities for the direction of a story, bring in alternate characters, and build the "drama world" (O'Neill, 1995) so that learners can take up roles to try out language and perspectives within safe spaces of a classroom or an online environment (Carroll, Anderson, & Cameron, 2006).

Through this kind of work, middle-level readers use both cognitive and imaginary faculties to respond innovatively to texts because they are able to draw on textual, personal, social, and dramatic meaning systems to extend and deepen their understandings of literature. Teachers who bring process drama into their literature instruction create multiple contexts for middle-level readers to engage in rich conversations that generate new learning possibilities with texts. These possibilities may help middle-level students become more confident, critical readers who can re-imagine their own "social futures" (New London Group, 1996). The literature is mediated within the sequence of drama activities so that that the teacher and students co-construct the drama world through working in role, tableaux, and other dramatic structures. This allows possibilities for co-learning, and modeling, and it can involve students in reading, speaking, listening, and writing in response to middle-level novels.

New Directions for Research

In this last section, we consider new directions for research that will help detail and define instructional practices for teachers working with middle-level readers. The three constructs we identified at the beginning of this chapter intertwine, and while we recognize that studies can examine reader, text and context separately, we also call for research that integrates and probes their interconnectedness. Additionally, Hinchman and Chandler-Olcott (2006) have investigated researchers' representations of adolescent viewpoints about literacy and have argued for situating youth in central positions in research studies. However, their work is primarily theoretical, and empirical studies with middle-level readers are needed to flesh out theoretical claims.

How do we more carefully define middle-level readers in ways that bring their voices into that defining process? Studies that view middle-level readers as co-researchers (Egan-Robertson & Bloome, 1998) and examine how readers position themselves are important for deepening understandings of the literacy practices and preferences of this group. We need longitudinal studies that focus on individual readers as well as classrooms and unpack how and why a middle-level reader chooses books for himself or herself. Additionally, we need a better understanding how those texts figure into larger constellations of literacy practices. We need a more finely grained knowledge of of how middle readers use school-based and community-based practices to negotiate literate identities. Finally, we have theorized that process drama as a tool of literature instruction with young adolescents could help them discover intersections of reader interest and social positioning, and we believe such a line of research could provide evidence that would enrich learning in literature classrooms.

In this chapter, we have argued that middle-level readers need an interactive approach to literature education that engages their interests and shifting identities as they move into older adolescence. We also made claims for identifying literature that is particularly interesting and imaginatively evocative for middle level-readers, and we theorized characteristics of this new category of literature based on research with this age reader. These categories are dynamic, and we believe may help young readers choose literature that interests them and provides a catalyst for imaginative thinking. Finally, we see process drama as a mode of response that can help teachers of these young readers step into fictional worlds that they have created with students, and engage in interpretations of literature that are social, innovative, critical, and could transform classrooms into spaces where imagination fuels learning.

Literature References

Creech, S. (1996). *Walk two moons*. New York, NY: HarperCollins.

Hamilton, V. (1968). *The house of Dies Drear*. New York, NY: Macmillan.

Hartinger, B. (2003). *Geography club*. New York, NY: HarperCollins.

Howe, J. (2001). *The misfits*. New York, NY: Antheum.

Hunt, I. (1976). *The lottery rose*. New York, NY: Scribners.

Korman, G. (2000). *No more dead dogs*. New York, NY: Hyperion Paperbacks

Lee, H. (1960). *To kill a mockingbird*. Philadelphia, PA: Lippincott.

Myers, W. D. (1988). *Scorpions*. New York, NY: HarperCollins.

Peréz, Amada, (2002). *My diary from here to there/Mi diario de aquí hasta allá*. (M. C. Gonzalez, Illus.). San Diego, CA: Children's Book Press.

Richardson, J., & Parnell, P. (2005). *And Tango makes three*. New York, NY: Simon & Schuster.

Taylor, M. D. (1976). *Roll of thunder, hear my cry*. New York, NY: Puffin.

Yolen, J. (1996). *Encounter* (D. Shannon, Illus.). New York, NY: Harcourt.

Academic References

Almasi, J. F. (1995). The nature of fourth graders' sociocognitive conflicts in peer led and teacher-led discussions of literature. *Reading Research Quarterly, 30*(3), 314–351.

Alverman, D. E., Peyton-Young, J., Weaver, D., Hinchman, K. A., Moore, D. W., Phelps, S. F., et al. (1996). Middle and high school students' perceptions of how they experience text-based discussions: A multicase study. *Reading Research Quarterly, 31*, 244–267.

Appleman, D. (2000). *Critical encounters in high school English: Teaching literary theory to adolescents*. New York, NY: Teachers College Press.

Appleyard, J. A. (1990). *Becoming a reader: The experience of fiction from childhood to adulthood*. Cambridge, UK: Cambridge University Press.

Beach, R. (1993). *A teacher's introduction to reader response theories*. Urbana, IL: National Council of Teachers of English.

Beach, R., & Freedman, K. (1992). Responding as a cultural act: Adolescents' responses to magazine ads and short stories. In J. Many & C. Cox (Eds.), *Reader Stance and Literary Understanding* (pp. 162–188). Norwood, NJ: Ablex.

Beach. R., & Meyers, J. (2001). *Constructing social worlds in the English classroom: An inquiry based approach*. New York, NY: Teachers College Press.

Benton, M. (1992). *Secondary worlds. Literature teaching and the visual arts*. Buckingham, UK: Open University Press.

Botzakis, S., & Malloy, J. A. (2005). International reports on literacy research. *Reading Research Quarterly, 40*, 112–118.

Brooks, W. (2006). Reading representations of themselves: Urban youth use culture and African American textual features to develop literary understandings. *Reading Research Quarterly, 41*, 372–392.

Broughton, M., & Fairbanks, C. M. (2003). In the middle of the middle: Seventh-grade girls' literacy and identity development. *Journal of Adolescent & Adult Literacy, 46*, 426–455.

Brozo, W. G, Shiel, G., & Topping, K. (2007/2008). Engagement in reading: Lessons learned from three PISA countries. *Journal of Adolescent & Adult Literacy, 51*, 304–315.

Carroll, J., Anderson, M., & Cameron, D. (2006). *Real players? Drama, technology and education*. Stoke on Trent, UK: Trentham Books.

Cassidy, J., Garrett, S. D., & Barrera, E. S. (2006). What's hot in adolescent literacy 1997–2006. *Journal of Adolescent & Adult Literacy, 50*, 30–36.

Cherland, M. R. (1994). *Private practices: Girls reading fiction and constructing identity*. Bristol, PA: Taylor Francis.

Clarke, L. W. (2006). Power through voicing others: Girls' positioning of boys in literature circle discussions. *Journal of Literacy Research, 38*(1), 53–80.

Crumpler, T. (2001–2002). Scenes of learning: Using drama to investigate literacy learning. *Arts and Learning Research Journal* (18), 155–74.

Crumpler, T. (2006). Educational drama as response to literature: Possibilities for young learners. In J. Jasinski Schneider, T. Crumpler, & T. Rogers (Eds.), *Process drama and multiple literacies: Addressing social, cultural, and ethical issues* (pp. 1-14). Portsmouth, NH: Heinemann.

Crumpler, T. (2007, April). A drama of multiliteracies: Teaching that creates new worlds in a middle level classroom. Paper presented at the *American Educational Research Association*, Chicago IL.

Crumpler, T., & Schneider, J. (2002). Writing with their Whole Being: A cross study analysis of children's writing from five classrooms using process drama. *Research in Drama Education, 7*(1) 61–79.

DeBlase, G. (2003). Acknowledging agency while accommodating romance: Girls negotiating meaning in literacy transactions. *Journal of Adolescent & Adult Literacy, 46*, 624–635.

Doubek, M. B., & Cooper, E. J. (2007). Closing the gap through professional development: Implications for reading research. *Reading Researcher Quarterly, 42*, 411–415.

Downey, A. (2005). The transformative power of drama: Bringing literature and social justice to life. *English Journal, 95*(1), 33–38.

Edmiston, B. (2003). What's my position? Role, frame, and positioning when using process drama. *Research in Drama Education, 8*(2), 221–229.

Edmiston, B., & Enciso, P. (2003). Reflections and refractions of meaning: Dialogic approaches to classroom drama and reading. In J. Flood, D. Lapp, J. Squire, & J. Jensen (Eds.) *Handbook of research on teaching the English language arts* (pp. 868–880). Mahwah, NJ: Erlbaum.

Egan-Robertson, A., & Bloome, D. (Eds.). (1998). *Students as researchers of culture and language in their own communities*. Cresskill, NJ: Hampton Press.

Enciso, P., Wolf, S., Coats, K., & Jenkins, C. (2010). Children's literature: Standing in the shadow of adults. *Reading Research Quarterly, 45*(2), 254–265.

Evans, K. (2002). Fifth grade students' perceptions of how they experience literature discussion groups. *Reading Research Quarterly, 37*, 46–69.

Galda, L. (1992). Evaluation as a spectator: Changes across time and genre. In J. Many & C. Cox (Eds.), *Reader Stance and Literary Understanding* (pp. 127–142). Norwood, NJ: Ablex.

Galda, L., & Beach, R. (2001). Response to literature as a cultural activity. *Reading Research Quarterly, 36*, 64–73.

Gallagher. K. (2001). *Drama in education in the lives of girls: Imagining possibilities*. Toronto, Canada: University of Toronto Press.

Garner, A. (1999). Negotiating our positions in culture: Popular adolescent fiction and the self-constructions of women. *Women's Studies in Communications, 22*, 85–111.

Greenberg, D., Gilbert, A., & Fredrick, L. (2006). Reading interest and behavior in middle school students in inner-city and rural settings. *Reading Horizons Journal, 47*(2), 160–173.

Heathcote, D., & Bolton, G. (1995). *Drama for learning: Dorothy Heathcote's mantle of the expert approach to education*. Portsmouth, NH: Heinemann.

Hinchman, K. (2008). *Best practices in adolescent literacy instruction*. New York, NY: Guilford

Hinchman, K., & Chandler-Olcott, K. (2006). Literacies through youth's eyes: Lessons in representation and hybridity. In D. E. Alverman, K. A. Hinchman, D. W. Moore, S. F. Phelps, & D. R. Waff (Eds.), *Reconceptualizing the literacies in adolescents' lives* (pp. 231–254). Mahwah, NJ: Erlbaum.

Hughes-Hassell, S., & Rodge, P. (2007). The leisure reading habits of urban adolescents. *Journal of Adolescent & Adult Literacy, 51*, 22–31.

Hunberger, P. (2007). New directions in research "Where am I?" A call for connectedness in literacy. *Reading Research Quarterly, 42*, 420–424.

Ivey, G. (2001). Discovering readers in the middle level school: A few helpful hints. In J.A. Rycik & J. L. Irvin (Eds.), *What adolescents deserve: A commitment to students' literacy learning* (pp. 63–71). Newark, DE: International Reading Association.

Ivey, G., & Broaddus, K. (2001). Just plain reading: A survey of what makes students want to read in middle school classrooms. *Reading Research Quarterly, 36*, 350–377.

Iser, W. (1989). *Prospecting: From reader response to literary anthropology*. Baltimore, MD: Johns Hopkins University Press.

Iser, W. (1993). *The fictive and the imaginary: Charting literary anthropology*. Baltimore, MD: Johns Hopkins University Press.

Juzwik, M. M., & Sherry, M. B. (2007). Expressive language and the art of English teaching: Theorizing the relationship between literature and oral narrative. *English Education, 39*(3), 226–259.

Lewis, C. (1997). The social drama of literature discussions in a fifth/sixth grade classroom. *Research in the Teaching of English, 31*, 163–204

Lewis, D. (1990). *The constructedness of texts: Picture books and the metafictive. Signal, 61*, 131–146.

Malloy, J. A., & Botzakis, S. (2005). International reports on literacy. *Reading Research Quarterly, 40*(4), 514–518.

McKenna, M. C., Kear, D. J., & Ellsworth, R. A. (1995). Children's attitudes toward reading: A national survey. *Reading Research Quarterly, 30*, 934–955.

Medina, C. (2004). The construction of drama worlds as literary interpretation of Latina feminist literature. *Research in Drama Education. 9*, 145–160.

Medina, C. L. (2006). Identity and imagination of immigrant children: Creating common place locations in literary interpretation. In J. J. Schneider, T. P. Crumpler, & T. Rogers (Eds.), *Process drama and multiple literacies: Addressing social, cultural, and ethical issues* (pp. 53–69). Portsmouth, NH: Heinemann.

Moje, E. B., Overby, M., Tysvaer, N., & Morris, K. (2008). The complex world of adolescent literacy: Myths, motivations, and mysteries. *Harvard Educational Review, 78*(1), 107–154.

The New London Group (1996). A pedagogy of multiliteracies: Designing social futures. *Harvard Educational Review, 66*(1), 60–93.

O'Neill, C. (1995). *Drama worlds: A framework for process drama*. Portsmouth, NH: Heinemann.

Pace, B. (2003). Resistance and response: Deconstructing community standards in a literature class. *Journal of Adolescent & Adult Literacy, 46*, 408–412.

Pearlman, M. (1995). The role of socioeconomic status in adolescent literature. *Adolescence, 30*, 223–231.

Pitcher, S., Albright, L., DeLaney, C., Walker, N., Seunarinesingh, K., Mogge, S., Headley, K., et al. (2007). Assessing adolescent's motivation to read. *Journal of Adolescent and Adult Literacy, 50*(5), 378–396.

Rosenblatt, L. M. (1978). *The reader, the text, the poem: The transactional theory of the literary work*. Carbondale, IL: Southern Illinois University.

Rosenblatt, L. M. (1938/1983). *Literature as exploration* (4th ed.). New York, NY: Modern Language Association.

Schillings, P. (2003). Des profils de motivation pour la lecture en sixième primaire; une approché différenciée [Profiles of motivation for reading in primary sixth: A differentiated approach]. *Caractères, 10*(1), 13–21.

Siegel, M. (2006). Rereading the signs: Multimodal transformations in the field of literacy education. *Language Arts, 84*(1), 65–77.

Smith, M. (1992). Submission versus control in literary transactions. In J. Many & C. Cox (Eds.) *Reader stance and literary understanding* (pp. 162–188). Norwood, NJ: Ablex.

Soter, A. (1999). *Young adult literature and the new literary theories: Developing critical readers in middle school*. New York, NY: Teachers College Press.

Steig, M. (1989). *Stories of reading: Subjectivity and literary understanding*. Baltimore, MD: Johns Hopkins University Press.

Stone, J. C. (2006). Textual borderlands: Students' recontextualizations in writing children's books. *Language Arts, 83*(1), 42–51.

Strommen, L. T., & Mates, B. F. (2004). Learning to love reading: Interviews with older children and teens. *Journal of Adolescent & Adult Literacy, 48*, 188–200.

Sumara, D. J. (2002). *Why reading literature in school still matters: Imagination, interpretation, and insight.* Mahwah, NJ: Erlbaum.

Tatum, A. W. (2008). Toward a more anatomically complete model of literacy instruction: A focus on African American male adolescents and texts. *Harvard Educational Review, 78*(1), 155–180.

Thompson, G., Madhuri, M., & Taylor, D. (2008). How the Accelerated Reader program can become counterproductive for high school students. *Journal of Adolescent & Adult Literacy, 51*, 550–560.

Trites, R. S. (2000). *Disturbing the universe: Power and repression in adolescent literature.* Iowa City: University of Iowa Press.

Wagner, B. J. (1998). *Educational drama and language arts: What research shows.* Portsmouth, NH. Heinemann.

Wedwick, L., & Wutz, J. A. (2006). Thinking outside the bookbox: Using BOOKMATCH to develop independent book selection. *Voices from the Middle, 14*(1), 20–29.

Wilhelm, J. D., & Edmiston, B. (1998). *Imagining to learn: Inquiry, ethics and integration through drama.* Portsmouth, NH: Heinemann.

Williams, B. T. (2004). "A puzzle to the rest of us": Who is a "reader" anyway? *Journal of Adolescent & Adult Literacy, 47*, 686–689.

Wilson, G. P. (2003). Supporting young children's thinking through tableau. *Language Arts, 80*, 375–383.

Wise, B. (2007). Turning reading research into policy. *Reading Research Quarterly, 42*, 407–411.

Wolf, S. (2004). *Interpreting literature with children.* Mahwah, NJ: Erlbaum.

Wolf, S., Edmiston, B., & Enciso, P. (1997). Drama worlds: Place of the heart, head, voice, and hand in dramatic interpretation. In J. Flood, D. Lapp, & S. B. Heath (Eds.), *A handbook for literacy educators: Research on teaching the communicative and visual arts* (pp. 474–487). New York, NY: Macmillan.

6

Reading Literature in Secondary School

Disciplinary Discourses in Global Times

Cynthia Lewis and Jessica Dockter

University of Minnesota

While the preceding chapters on elementary and middle school literature demonstrate the dynamic change in classroom environments focused primarily on inquiry and response-based curriculum, Cynthia Lewis and Jessica Dockter redefine what literature and reading are becoming in secondary settings. Caught between the rock of unchanging text selection and the hard place of rigid curriculum based on testing expectations, secondary English teachers struggle to find room for movement in the face of cultural change. Yet, the authors lay out a vision for loosening the grip of disciplines that are consistently and ironically *disciplined* by tradition, and they argue for a more dynamic pedagogy that would highlight the potential of identity formation and transformation for youth within hybrid and multimodal "redefinitions of text, language, and global citizenship."

Nearly a decade into the 21st century, the teaching of literature in secondary school has finally reached the crossroads that some predicted in the early 1990s. In 1993 Robert Morgan proposed changes in secondary English that are still contested today because they call into question the purpose of "English" as a school subject. As scholars debated the merits of cultural literacy (Hirsch, 1987)—itself a rehashing of an age-old cultural heritage debate—versus more student-centered (e.g., reader response) or text-centered (e.g., new criticism) approaches to teaching literature, postindustrial nations in the last two decades of the 20th century were undergoing a social, economic, and digital revolution that would, inevitably, change the nature of teaching and learning. In arguing for

an English curriculum centered on approaches found in cultural studies, Morgan (1993) depicted debates about the purposes of literature as leading "not to border crossings into new disciplinary formations, but to staid reaffirmations of English as a curricular form (cf. Scholes, 1991, Dasenbrock, 1989)" (p. 21).

The form of English as a school subject that Morgan (1993) bemoaned is one in which texts are taught and read as bound objects of analysis or, in more reader-center models, a conduit in a text-audience circuit. The latter remains bound in its focus on the transaction of meaning between text and audience rather than on practices of articulation, which Laclau and Mouffe (1985) defined as "any practice establishing a relation among elements such that their identity is modified as a result of the articulatory practice" (p. 105). According to Morgan and the scholars he cites (cf. Radway, 1988), the subject of English should focus on practices of articulation rather than on a fetishizing of texts. In other words, students should learn how readers' identities are shaped not only by texts, but also by disciplinary and institutional discourses and by culture as it is produced and consumed in everyday life. In so doing, Morgan argues for English as cultural studies.

Fast forward to 2007, the publication year of an issue of *English Journal* that includes an article by Zancanella in which he asked eight educators, writers, and researchers to answer the question, "What should high school English be?" There were no arguments in favor of English as the purveyor of cultural literacy among the answers. Instead, most contributors offered impassioned pleas for the inherent worth of story in the lives of individuals and cultures. Although several mentioned 21st-century media as part of the mix, only one contributor, Kevin Leander, argued for a radical break with high school English as we know it. As first conceived by the Committee of Ten—a group of scholars that met in 1894 to determine appropriate high school subject preparation—the English of yesterday *and* today is primarily a course in "masterpieces" of literature. Despite the current attention and acclaim given to young adult literature within literary and academic circles—and despite the wide range of genres and diverse literatures represented therein—young adult literature is rarely included in secondary English classrooms.

According to Leander (Zancanella, 2007), English is currently bracketed around three outdated representations of the subject: first, it is bracketed around print literature; second, it is bracketed around English nations, especially the United States and England; and third, it is bracketed to exclude purposes for literature outside of a relatively closed text-reader circuit.

Leander's answer to the question of what English can be was strikingly different from the others, which were notable for their continuity with previous incarnations of progressive English education, particularly in their attention to the power of story and word to shape and be shaped by diverse human experience. As book lovers and English educators, we can't help but respond to the "call of stories" to borrow the eloquent words of Robert Coles (1989), but we believe that in the lives of many contemporary high school students this call is mediated by Web 2.0 technologies that not only incorporate sound and image, but also offer students transactions with literature that include text-making options unavailable to previous generations. Students can read and write fanfiction, discuss and create graphic novels, write scripts for YouTube productions, all the while receiving a steady stream of personalized commentary and critique. In short, distal technologies broaden Coles's "call" to include, crucially, "call *and* response" and open the notion of "stories" to narratives of any kind across texts, groups, and disciplines.

Secondary "English" as a subject remains, today, a stable category with changes being made only around its edges. What we need is to unhinge the brackets that Leander has rightly identified.

Global flows heightened by digital technologies and new economic structures (e.g., fast capital and neoliberalism) that benefit first world nations over the developing world and the affluent over the poor have resulted in fundamentalisms (Castell, 1996) that have led to new patterns of immigration and an increase in English language learners (ELL) in high school classrooms. As the sociologist Zygmunt Bauman (1998) explained:

> An integral part of the globalizing processes is progressive spatial segregation, separation and exclusion. Neo-tribal and fundamentalist tendencies, which reflect and articulate the experience of people on the receiving end of globalization, are as much legitimate offspring of globalization as the widely acclaimed 'hybridization' of top culture—the culture at the globalized top. (p. 3)

It is the "globalized top" that live the utopian dreams of globalization widely touted in the press and, at times, in scholarship focused on the Internet as a medium that promotes equity.

However, the globalization process as depicted by Bauman, Castell, and others underscores its consequences to those on the gendered, raced, linguistic, and socioeconomic margins. In a later section of this chapter, we will make the connection to the teaching and reading of literature in secondary school. For now, however, we want to make the point that times of monumental social and economic change produce the anxiety that leads to what Luke (2004a) has called "educational fundamentalism," a harkening back to what is perceived as "basic" (e.g., decoding, grammar), a limiting of what counts as knowledge (e.g., canonized Euro-American texts). This fundamentalism occurs at the same time that responsible teachers, concerned about the needs of English language learners, feel bound, ethically and pedagogically, to teach literature beyond the North American and British literary canon and to invite a wider range of responses to literature that allow ELL students to share their interpretations and demonstrate their understandings through artistic, performative, and digital mediums.

Research on reading literature in secondary school points to the tug and pull of transformative and fundamentalist moves in classrooms. Despite the transformative changes underway, federal and state mandates, including high stakes testing, have caused many English teachers to focus more intensely on what some call "the basics." In other words, teachers of secondary English need to account for the dramatically changing contemporary realities in the textual landscapes of their students, but at the same time they also need to attend to expectations that their classrooms will deliver instruction in "common culture" texts that have been canonized in the secondary curriculum and in the disciplinary apparatus.

What remains unchanged, then, is that a primary function of literature in secondary schools is to produce a particular kind of citizen. Whereas the kind of citizen considered desirable (i.e., religious, moral, empirical, personally engaged, socially conscious, culturally critical) changes with time, the use of literature and schooling to produce particular kinds of citizens is long-standing. This function of literature is evident in Caughlan's (2004) study of cultural models of literature teaching. Following Foucault (1982), she identified a pastoral function for the teaching of literature meant to control students' values and dispositions as individuals who will self-regulate for the common good. Caughlan (2007) briefly traced this tradition from Matthew Arnold, who promoted literature as a vehicle for refining the values of the working class (Hunter, 1988), through the expressive movement (Harris, 1991) in English education, best exemplified in the work of American and British scholars at the 1966 Dartmouth Conference advocating for personal expression in English as a school subject. John Dixon's (1967) influential report on the conference and the popularization of reader response English classrooms in the United States and Britain followed soon after. As Caughlan (2007) put it: "In contrast to the opaque text of New Critical Analysis, the text is transparent in this cultural model, a vehicle for the moral and ethical issues raised, and a representation of real people making real decisions" (p. 18).

As this history indicates, a primary function of literature as it is used in schools is to produce and reproduce particular values. However, we argue that the social, economic, and technological conditions that shape the teaching and learning of literature in secondary school today have led to value being placed on the production of the global citizen and, by consequence, a state of flux in English classrooms. Several excellent literature reviews provide an historical look at research on response to literature as well as the foundation of our knowledge base over the last 30 years (Beach & Hynds, 1991; Marshall, 2000; Probst, 1991). The same is true of the chapters on elementary and middle school learning in this handbook. Given the scant use of young adult literature in secondary classrooms, other chapters in this volume (especially Chapter 22) provide analyses of young adult literature beyond what we include in this chapter. Our chapter will take a different turn by considering how some of the following changes have shaped research and practice on literature in secondary school:

- New definitions of what counts as a literary text.
- New ways of responding to literature, using digital tools such as blogs and wikis.
- Influences of digital media and popular culture on young adult literature that fundamentally changes features of texts and reader response, including reader-text transaction, text structure, and text dissemination.
- Expectation among youth that the literature they read will serve the purposes of identity representation and affinity building (e.g., spoken word, fanfiction, zines, online journals).
- Greater linguistic diversity with the need for teachers to select literature that will build students' understandings of English in the dominant culture but also affirm the role of identity in language use and literary texts.
- More access to what Jenkins (2006a) calls "participatory culture" (usually online or through mobile technologies) that crosses race, class, gender, age, religion, and nationality as an outgrowth of globalization. This access also has consequences for young people's expectations about and responses to the books they read.
- Theoretical perspectives that view texts, readers, and contexts as socially, culturally, and politically constituted.
- Greater need for a critically literate public in the face of all of the above, including the changing economic and informational flows brought on by globalization.

The chapter is organized through the use of key terms to help communicate how the teaching and reading of literature in secondary school has been shaped by globalization. These terms—disciplinary discourse, identity/identification, hybridity, and multimodality—intersect and overlap, as will be clear in each of the sections. Nevertheless, they are distinct enough to be considered separately as important features of literature study in contemporary secondary classrooms. We have not attempted to be comprehensive in our review of literature, but rather have decided to draw on a few studies within each key category that we deem to be important in understanding secondary literature teaching and learning in a way that conceptualizes a field in transition and the promise of new directions. We begin with a brief explanation of why it is important to consider how globalization shapes the teaching and learning of literature in schools.

Globalization and the Teaching/Learning of Literature

Globalization, according to sociologist Arjun Appadurai (2000), is marked by increased "flows" of objects, images, persons, and discourses. Such flows expand the connectivity between ideas, bodies, and identities across local spheres, which are continually shaped by the global interdependence of economies, technologies, and politics. As such, locally manifested ways of being, producing, and interpreting are anything but local. As Pennycook (2005) observed, classrooms "can no longer be considered as bound sites, with students entering from fixed locations, with identities drawing on local traditions, with curricula as static bodies of knowledge" (p. 41). With the demise of neighborhood schools and the blend of students' racial, gendered, and transnational identities, the relevant unit of space has become the globe (Kress, 2007), and notions of stability and certainty have given way to fluidity and multiplicity (Bauman, 2007). Yet, the processes of globalization are also framed by a neoliberal logic that attempts to unify and standardize knowledge in the interest of the market (Luke & Carrington, 2002). Thus, globalization creates a push and pull between its desired outcomes of standardization and diversification.

We view globalization as a set of complex economic and cultural processes with both positive and negative implications on the teaching and learning of literature. First, while we argue that the goal of producing and reproducing certain kinds of citizens through the teaching of literature remains, we argue as well that globalization redefines who counts as a relevant, desirable, and global citizen. Although we may only guess at how global flows will shape selves over time, several authors envision the globalized citizen as enterprising (Apple, 2001), an ongoing project (Arnett, 2002), and shape-shifting (Gee, 2004). In turn, this redefinition of citizenship as fluid shapes students' expectations for the texts they read in English classes and the ways in which possible identities, discourses, relationships, and futures are represented and broadened by them. For example, in Demerath and Lynch's (2008) ethnographic study of students in an affluent, middle-class high school, students actively sought out and negotiated opportunities and texts that would allow them to develop the kinds of skills and capital, both social and academic, which would make them marketable to elite colleges.

Second, globalization expands the interpretive positions that students take up in the study of literature (National Council of Teachers of English, 2007). More and more, signs and images are mediated through distal interactions among geographically dispersed students. At the same time, the increased uncertainty that comes with increased movement creates intensely competitive notions of what counts as legitimate global knowledge (Apple, 2001) as nations, states, communities, and individuals vie for market niches. Thus, while globalization expands interpretive positions in literature classrooms, it expands their surveillance as well. Finally, while the new technologies of globalization redefine the selection, genres, and dissemination of literary texts, a reactionary anxiety calls for a return to the textual canon.

In part, this anxiety is ontological in that it is fueled by apprehension about the essence of adolescence, or, from a more postmodern perspective, the construction of adolescence in global times. Adolescence as a life stage is a sociohistorical and cultural invention that emerged at the onset of the industrial era when further education was needed to educate the job force, and thus young people were taken out of the work force to allow them to spend more time in school (Lesko, 2001). Tracing the evolving history of adolescence is beyond our scope, but characterizing the construction of adolescence in global times is central to this chapter. Naturally, secondary schools, in the hopes of addressing the educational needs of adolescents, are working from some normative assumptions about adolescents—who they are and the kind of adults they

"ought to" become (with differences between middle and high school). Teachers' assumptions about the adolescents they teach are fundamental to how they interact with their students, select texts to share with them, and raise issues relevant to them.

Global youth are often described in terms of their hybrid identities (Nilan & Feixa, 2006), shaped at the same time by seemingly opposing forces of nationalism, cultural traditionalism, transnationalism, ethnocentrism, blended ethnicities, multilingualism, digital culture, and consumerism. When cultural flows across the globe merge with local identities and ways of taking up these flows, new hybrid youth cultures emerge (Pennycook, 2005). Despite this generative view of the effects of globalization, some youth are restricted from taking up hybrid identities by processes of globalization that work to localize those with fewer resources rather than expand their spaces and repertoires. Thus, we have a "breakdown in communication between the increasingly global and extraterritorial elites and the ever more 'localized' rest" (Bauman, 1998, p. 3) who do not have the means to participate in the risks and benefits of global citizenship.

Bean and Moni (2003) argued that critical discussions of contemporary young adult fiction rely on understanding contemporary adolescence. Adolescent identity, they point out, is "a matter of self-construction amidst unstable times, mores, and global consumerism" (p. 642) with media and digital flows connecting macro and micro cultures in a postmodern landscape. In this landscape, institutions are viewed as "fragmented and unreliable" (Wyn, 2005, p. 45), causing adolescents to forge their own futures in risky and uncertain new economies. Young adult literature has shifted to address the needs and interests of this new adolescent (Dresang, 1999), yet global youth are normalized by the institutional discourse of education, according to Luke and Luke (2001), as the "uncivil, unruly techno-subject" (p. 8).

This way of characterizing adolescence—as dangerous other—has ramifications for the kinds of literature and forms of literary response found in school, with particularly detrimental effects on struggling readers and other marginalized students who are often engaged by out-of-school vernacular literacies and have the most to lose in the lethal atmosphere of high-risk economies and high-stakes testing. Indeed, most of the bullet points we listed earlier to describe changes that have shaped research and practice on literature in secondary school depend on a different construction of adolescence—one that views adolescents as savvy, resourceful, and, competent. Wolf and Maniotes (2002), for example, advocated the pedagogical use of literature that has typically been viewed as inappropriate for the classroom due to a focus on abusive sexual molestation, rape, and child abuse. These authors construct adolescents as capable of understanding the difficult world in which they live and benefiting from the chance to work through difficult issues through aesthetic experience and agentic discussion. The anxiety fed by new constructions of adolescence, then, can lead to particular disciplinary discourses in the study of literature. In fact, disciplinary discourse, discussed in the next section, plays a critical role in both the transformations and fundamentalisms associated with secondary school literature studies.

Disciplinary Discourse

Secondary school is commonly perceived as a space/time for learning disciplinary knowledge, with achievement in secondary school often measured by students' knowledge of disciplinary epistemologies and their attendant terminologies. Understanding the nature of disciplinary discourse over time in secondary school literature studies is central to understanding how literacy studies take up the function of producing and reproducing values and citizens for particular times. An unfortunate result of disciplinary discourse is that it often functions to "discipline" disciplines in ways that cause them to lose their dynamism. Literary canons, for example, change over time, but the changes come slowly to required text lists in secondary school, where budgets are constrained and where, as Luke (2004b) noted, teachers are attached to particular disciplinary traditions, and the institutional viability of a school is determined by public perception and standardized test scores. Thus, with the exception of a few titles, texts taught in the early 1960s, such as *Romeo and Juliet, Julius Caesar,* and *Huckleberry Finn,* remained constant in the late 1980s (Applebee, 1992). More recent studies (Hale & Crowe, 2001) have shown much of the same, with works by Shakespeare and other canonized authors dominating the top-10 list.

The static nature of disciplinary knowledge in the secondary classroom is reflected not just in text selection but also in approaches to instruction. In a study of classroom interaction in high school English classrooms (Marshall, Smagorinsky, & Smith, 1995), findings revealed that teachers took longer speaking turns than students, students responded with primarily informative statements, and teachers carried the interpretive agendas. Moreover, students generally cooperated with teachers in constructing this discussion pattern. According to Nystrand, Wu, Gamoran, Zeiser, and Long (2003), to promote student engagement and learning in literature classes, discourse must actively involve students in the production of knowledge and be highly interactive; students should be viewed as thinkers and, as such, asked to explain their thinking rather than simply report on the thinking of others. Importantly, they note that specific modes of classroom discourse engender particular epistemic positions for students, which, in turn, empower or constrain their thinking. The epistemic positions available to students in classrooms driven by district tests are explored in Anagnostopoulos (2003), a study of discussion in two English classrooms. Rarely did discussions approach the dialogic ones that

Nystrand et al. (2003) found to promote engagement and achievement. Even when one of the teachers joined with students to discuss racism in their lives related to *To Kill a Mockingbird* (Lee, 1960), the specter of the test would quickly cause the teacher to redirect the talk, thus "re-positioning students as minimally skilled readers and reading as producing details" (p. 200).

Despite the tenacity of teacher dominated discourse patterns, reinvigorated, now, in a ubiquitous testing climate, the move from New Criticism to reader response theory as a critical framework in more process-oriented classrooms over the last two decades has helped to change classroom interaction in many secondary classrooms. Although reader-response theory takes many forms, including the sociopolitical, the way that it has been practiced in schools—largely in opposition to New Criticism—is to highlight the life of the reader through personal response. Langer's (1995) research on the qualities of English classrooms that help students to enter the literary world of the texts they read found that students in such classrooms are invited to pose questions and are treated as capable of developing important understandings. Athanases (1993) pointed to important principles gleaned from a range of reader-response theorists, including moving students from private to public response, providing opportunities for student reflection, and transferring interpretive control from the teacher to the students to develop what Fish (1980) has called an interpretive community.

By the early 1990s, many scholars (cf. Corcoran, Hayhoe, & Pradle, 1994; Freebody, Luke, & Gilbert, 1991; O'Neill, 1993) argued that reader response as it had been applied to English education failed to acknowledge the sociopolitical constitution of textual interpretation and evaluation. These critics all shared the view that by valorizing the personal, educators ignored the ideological. Early on the scene to translate contemporary literary theory for use in high school classrooms were Mellor, O'Neill, and Patterson (1987) whose text leads students through activities with short stories that teach them how texts are constructed ideologically to position readers in particular ways. (The National Council of Teachers of English has reprinted these books from Australia's Chalkface Press to make them available to an audience of United States teachers.) By the late 1990s, many scholars wrote pragmatically about the pedagogy of cultural criticism in the teaching of literature, providing questions or issues meant to help students and teachers examine the social, cultural, historical, and political construction of texts and readers (cf. Apol, 1998; Lewis, 2000; Morgan, 1997).

Around this time, several influential books were published that offered preservice and practicing teachers ways to practically rethink high school literature instruction in a way that combined reader response with cultural studies and postmodern theory (Carey-Webb, 2001; Pirie, 1997). Perhaps the most explicit use of contemporary literary criticism for high school teaching is found in Appleman's

(2000) book focusing on what she calls "critical lenses" in the teaching of literature. In each chapter, she applied critical lenses such as feminist, deconstructive, archetypal, and so forth to literature commonly taught in high school classrooms in the United States, with accompanying materials for teachers to adapt for use in their classrooms. Critical theories also have been explicitly applied to young adult literature (Moore, 1997; Soter, 1999), but the disciplinary discourse of high school English situates canonized American and British literature as central to the high school literature curriculum despite calls from scholars of English education and adolescent literature to include more young adult literature.

An important component of Appleman's (2000) book is its persuasive argument that critical lenses invite readers to probe commonplace assumptions and ideologies in text, media, and life. This function of critical lenses prefigures recent work that links the goals of secondary school literature studies to social justice commitments. Several articles have put forth arguments for change in English education that call for an explicit relationship between English and social justice. Morrell (2005), for example, defined literacy development as a revolutionary tool "intended to challenge existing norms and disrupt existing power relations" (p. 314) and argued that English educators should act as activists and political agents. Kirkland (2008) described what he calls "New English Education" (p. 69), which seeks to transform society by understanding how the postmodern condition, particularly "postmodern Blackness" shapes the lives of youth and their popular media and culture. The disciplinary discourse Kirkland (2008) and Morrell (2005) offered is one of critical redefinition, both building on popular culture to extend the important critical literacy perspectives already discussed from analysis of language and image into the realm of social action.

Urban youth in Morell's study, for example, merged in- and out-of-school literacies by serving as critical researchers in their own schools and communities. After a five-week seminar, which prepared students as collaborators in praxis-oriented research, students collected field notes, wrote analytic memos, and produced critical memoirs chronicling their changing identities. This work stemmed from students' critical analysis of popular language and uses of literacy in their communities and involved them in presentations and publications at both national and local levels. Their results carried implications for practice, policy, and future research, and in this way, students developed critical literacies with a goal of social transformation.

This work builds not only on the traditions of scholars in critical literacy and cultural studies, but also on the traditions of those who have written eloquently on the subject of culturally-relevant pedagogy. Specific to culturally responsive teaching, Ladson-Billings (1995) has maintained since the early 1990s that classroom discourse and practices should include a range of cultural perspectives,

show the ways in which power relations have shaped the outcome of the production of knowledge, and legitimize students' previous learning and experiences, including linguistic experiences.

Lee (2007) has developed a theoretical framework and method she calls "cultural modeling" to help teachers recognize and value the contextualization cues and communication patterns that students bring from their speech communities and use those cues and patterns as a bridge to the study of literature and classroom tasks. This project marries culturally-responsive teaching with domain-specific instruction in literary analysis. For example, Lee shows how a class discussion of a song by The Fugees engages students in effectively using strategies for literary interpretation to order to understand the song's symbolism. Moreover, students commented articulately upon their own processes of interpretation, indicating a "form-function shift" (as cited in Saxe, 1991, p. 67) that suggests a transfer of conceptual knowledge from one context to another. Lee's (2007) research provides many examples of this kind of transfer, which extends, in the next stage, to applications of students' interpretive capacities to canonized literature. The role of the teacher is central to the process of marrying culturally-responsive teaching with domain-specific instruction in literary analysis in that the teacher must recognize students' developing interpretive strategies in order to make them explicit and to reinforce them as conventions that can be applied to other texts. This pedagogical skill is essential if the goal is for students to learn how to analyze literature in ways that are expected in school and on achievement tests that include literary reading.

Earlier we discussed Caughlan's work on the cultural models of English/language arts (ELA). In a 2007 study, after examining standards for ELA in two states, she wryly noted cultural models that could be but were *not* present in the standards. Given the changes in disciplinary discourse discussed in this section, we find Caughlan's insight about the absence of cultural models that reflect critical aspects of response to literature, such as the following, notable: "Literature expresses and reveals ideologies" (p. 188). Although this cultural model is very much present in the disciplinary discourse of the English education and literature scholars cited in this section, it is not typically the disciplinary discourse of literature study in secondary school. Yet, if students are going to become critical readers in the face of the changing economic and informational flows of global culture, it may well be this very disciplinary discourse they need most to learn. As Yagelski (2006) pointed out, English is a discipline that can help reshape society in the context of globalization. Through the analysis of language and image in new multimodal literatures, students can better understand the practices of articulation that create and sustain particular identities, which, in turn, have material consequences (such as the normalization of Whiteness through everyday images; see Dyer, 1997).

They can also participate with their teachers in developing a metalanguage based on the meaning-making potential of multimodal texts (Unsworth, 2006).

Students reading the graphic novel *Re-Gifters* by Mike Carey, Sonney Liew, and Marc Hempel (2007) might, for example, discuss the significance of Korean cultural heritage for the main character Dik Seong Jen—known as "Dixie"—as it is articulated through both words and image. Dixie is a master at the martial art of hapkido, but her flow, or "ki," is compromised when she falls for Adam, a California surfer-boy and her potential opponent. For Dixie, hapkido represents pride for the warrior spirit of her ancestors and also an obstacle to Adam's affection. This collision of worldviews expresses particular cultural ideologies in a rather explicit manner in the novel, but teachers might also encourage students to analyze how the images reveal their own set of ideologies, which at times may contradict those implied by the plot. Students might interrogate how race, class, and gender are depicted in the images and question why many of the White characters, including Adam, appear to be from upper middle-class backgrounds while Tomas, who we learn is from the "street" and to whom Dixie's affection ultimately turns, is drawn with Latino racial markers. The articulation of identity in this graphic novel takes place on the level of both word and image, and this shift in the discipline of English requires that teachers and students develop a language and practice through which to analyze such texts.

As important as it is to develop a metalanguage for transformative disciplinary discourse, secondary students also need to be competent in the ever-evolving established metalanguage of disciplinary discourse in the study of literature. We saw this at work in our recent research studying the discursive construction of critical engagement in an innovative high school English class that included the production of podcast memoirs and documentary films. Students needed to develop a language for talking about how narratives worked in order to analyze and eventually produce their memoirs and documentaries, which included new forms of layering and transitions that built on those found in print literature. In this vein, they analyzed excerpts from *Our America: Life and Death on the South Side of Chicago* (Jones, Newman, & Isay, 1997) and the related radio documentary *Ghetto Life* in order to learn the skills they would need to compose their own memoirs in the form of audio podcasts.

In a memoir about the importance of basketball in his life, one student began his podcast by dramatically placing himself in his bedroom waking up at 4:00 a.m. in order to travel the long distance from his home to morning basketball practice at school and show his determination to meet his goals in the face of difficult circumstances. He used background music with a consistent beat and repeated chords to communicate the repetitive nature of this aspect of his life, then shifted to louder music in order to introduce his transition from dramatic reenactment to traditional narration. In so doing, he modified narrative conventions related to cohesion and point of view and applied this disciplinary knowledge about literature to a format usually associated with out-of-school literacy practices (podcasts), but which is now becoming part of the established world of English studies.

In an article that examines response to literature as sociocultural activity, Galda and Beach (2001) contended that recent work on response to literature redefines earlier work by focusing more on "ways of integrating literature instruction within the development of students' larger language systems" (p. 64). As Willis (1997) explained in an article on exploring literature as cultural production in her course for preservice teachers: "I want the future teachers of my own children to understand that children bring with them rich and culturally mediated language, experience, and knowledge to the classroom" (p. 135). Certainly, the work on reader response, culturally-relevant pedagogy, cultural modeling, New English Education, and culturally critical English education described in this section fit the bill. All offer theoretical frameworks and pedagogical approaches for response to literature in secondary school that key into young people's uses of language (and other modes of representation) in family, community, and peer contexts, from formal to vernacular. Taken together they speak to the transformative potential of globalization—an expanded conception of what counts as literature, for instance—as well as the anxieties it creates about the identities produced through globalization and the kinds of readers produced through new forms of literature.

Identity/Identification

Conceptions of identity have long influenced the teaching and study of response to literature in secondary schools—albeit in varied and often competing ways. Whether texts are taught, for example, as bound objects of analysis or as conduits in the text-reader circuit, the teaching of literature has always been and remains tightly connected to readers' identities as it seeks to influence the "making" of particular kinds of people and particular kinds of readers. But literature shapes identities only to the degree that the reading transaction (which includes the reader, text, and context) involves a process of identification. This process is not necessarily one in which the reader's identity melds with the text, but may instead involve a connection between some aspect of the reader's identity and the text. Depending on the conception of identity in use, researchers define the making of selves with greater or lesser degrees of imposition and agency, stability and fluidity, consumption and production, legitimacy and resistance, to name just a few dichotomous classifications surrounding identity. Although identity can be interpreted differently depending on the interpreter (Gee 2000/2001), it remains central to studies on response to literature because texts have little meaning outside the contextualized lives and identities of their readers. Moreover, the social, cultural, historical, institutional, and political nature of identity carries with it material effects related to lived realities in the form of resources, goods, and emotional well being which influence students' motivations, access, and interpretations with regard to literature and response.

A central concern for researchers interested in how readers' identities shape their responses to literature has been the participatory or exclusionary nature of classroom practices. For example, in an important study on students' responses to multicultural literature in a secondary classroom, Spears-Bunton (1990) contended that culture is a source of conflict for readers "at the level of the text" (p. 567) and that the exclusion of African American literature left students in her study uninterested in literacy tasks which in turn negatively affected their performance in English classrooms. A "cultural mismatch" between students and the books they read, Spears-Bunton argued, pushed students to judge textual worlds negatively and to refuse to read, perpetuating the institutional identities of African American students as low readers. The inclusion of texts that represent varied cultural identities, on the other hand, has the potential to expand literary experiences, and according to Sims Bishop (1992), demonstrates a valuing of multiple identifications among students in school and society.

In a similar study, which analyzed the experiences of two African American female high school students, Pam and Natonya, in a traditional British Literature class, Carter (2006) found that the young women used nonverbal communication to challenge symbols and text that situated their cultural identities negatively. In one example, as a reference to the Confederate flag went unchallenged in a discussion, the two girls used their eye gazes to assert their gendered, racial, and cultural identities which stood in opposition to such a reference. Despite the assaults to their identities and the marginalization of their ways of knowing, the girls' social interactions, although often subtle, enabled them to master skills necessary to pass the class. Such a study demonstrates the need in literature classrooms to make the negotiation over knowledge and identity more visible, not as something students either possess or do not. When the experiences, perceptions, and relationships students value are not acknowledged, they often learn that literacy is an exclusive activity that diminishes their efforts to construct expanded identities (Enciso & Lewis, 2001).

Access to certain kinds of texts and ways of reading them demonstrate one significant aspect of identity making as it relates to response to literature. Yet, several researchers have taken up the question of how engagement with texts and the interpretive process do identity work as well. Sumara (1998) writes poignantly on this topic in the following way: "Because the reader's sense of identity emerges, in part, from perceived and interpreted knowledge about the world, response to reading alters a reader's sense of self. As the fictional text is interpreted by the reader, the reader is, at the same time, interpreted" (p. 205). In this way, the very act of interpretation of literary text becomes an act of negotiation of shifting and slippery identities as readers re-imagine and re-identify themselves, past, present, and future, and experience new self-possibilities in the process.

One of our own readings of Sherman Alexie's (2007) novel, *The Absolutely True Diary of a Part-time Indian*, serves to articulate this point. For Jessica, the understanding of the main character and narrator, Junior, was tied up in her own identity as a White reader. Junior, a Spokane Indian who decides to leave his reservation school to attend an all-White school, interprets his burgeoning relationships with White students in humorous and powerful ways: "And Roger, being of kind heart and generous pocket, and a little bit racist, drove me home that night. And he drove me home plenty of other nights, too" (p. 129). For Jessica, such statements not only revealed Alexie's keen insight into the complexities of White racial identities—kind of heart and a little bit racist—but also forced her to consider where she imagined her own White identity in the reading of the novel. Aligning herself with the kind White character could no longer be so simple. She, too, had been interpreted. Such practices of interpretation, Sumara (2002) argued, must be facilitated by "literary engagements" and "focal practices" (p. 150) with texts that require attention, energy, and interest. Literature still matters in school, he contended, because it seeks to interrupt familiarity and serves as a "commonplace" for readers to border cross into each other's interpretations.

Yet, readers do not necessarily depart on such border crossings on their own, nor do they make their literary journeys outside structures of social power. Lewis (2000) reminded researchers and teachers of literature that there are limits to identification when readers engage with texts, and that disrupting the "inclination to identify" may heighten the readers' consciousness of text and self, as well as status and power relations. Enciso's (1998) research with early adolescent working-class girls reading the Sweet Valley High series serves as a good example of how status and power frame responses to literature. The girls positioned themselves as "good" and "bad" girls according to dominant cultural discourses available to them, while at "carnivalesque" (p. 57) moments, they challenged authoritative expectations of school-based and masculine norms. Thus, the girls enacted positions that both inscribed their gendered selves with certain kinds of "good" and "bad" femininity embedded in literary texts while resisting those identifications at the same time.

Several authors consider the relationship between identity and response to literature in the teaching of multicultural texts, particularly when it comes to White students' responses to culturally diverse characters and experiences. Thein, Beach, and Parks (2007) and Thein (2006), for example, focused on the identity construction of working-class high school students as they read and discussed literature. Their work demonstrates how students mediate their identities through competing discourses related to the multiple social worlds they must negotiate and the textual world that is the object of discussion. Such mediation points to the tensions that often exist as part of response to literature, and the authors contended that trying on alternative perspectives is a "habit of mind" (p. 55) that helps students acknowledge other ways of understanding the world, even if they do not agree with those perspectives. It is the *capacity* to expand and imagine alternate realities that reading literature offers.

Given the tensions inherent in students' literary engagements, particularly with culturally diverse texts, Rogers and Soter (1997) advocated thinking about classrooms as "cultural sites" (p. 6) where interrogation, struggle, and social critique are commonplace. At the same time, they worry that students cannot distance themselves from the personal nature of their responses for a critical evaluation of text as disturbance instead of universal agent. Adult readers can also fall into the same universalizing stance. For instance, in previous research (Lewis, Ketter, & Fabos, 2001), Cynthia found that among a group of White teachers reading multicultural young adult literature, the members of the group often generalized across universal themes that they saw in the texts—such as the challenges of being a female adolescent—at the expense of examining oppressive structures outside their experiences. Vinz (2000), however, offered several pedagogical ideas for teachers in literature classrooms to encourage students' ongoing analysis of their own interpretive acts. She found that students are more likely to occupy the "spaces of others" (p. 43) and carefully attend to characters' textual motivations when they become those characters through drama and writing. Additionally, she argued, the juxtaposition of texts and the inclusion of popular culture creates spaces for students to recognize the plurality of meaning and to examine their own social, cultural, and ideological influences as text as well

Decades of work on identity and response to literature have brought researchers to important conclusions about literary access, interpretation, and tension. We argue, however, that these questions must be reframed as notions of identity continue to shift as adolescents confront a world in which the global economy demands constant negotiation of a multiplicity of texts (Moje, Young, Readence, & Moore, 2000). Questions remain as to how globalized redefinitions of nationalism, cultural traditionalism, multilingualism, technology, and consumerism will change notions of text and the teaching of literature. How, for example, will access (or lack of access) to digital forms of literature and other art forms transform students' literary engagements? And as students make identifications across a matrix of identities, relationships, and discourses, how might their insights and interpretations in relation to text be altered? The next two sections take up some of these questions.

Hybridity

Research in digital and transnational spaces demonstrates that literacy practices are evermore networked within local and global flows of activity (Leander & Lovvorn, 2006). Digital media, in particular, hold the potential for a more "participatory culture" (Jenkins, 2006a) for literacy and learning. At the same time, however, digital media can limit participation (i.e., digital divide) and control capital through commercial content. Given such a paradox, we think about hybridity in this section both in terms of the hybrid geographies that students bring to reading from their translocal identities, but also as productive, hybrid spaces where new youth cultures merge with "old" ways of teaching, learning, and knowing. We consider in the following paragraphs research that reframes response to literature through hybrid redefinitions of text, language, and global citizenship and start with a discussion of the acclaimed graphic novel, *American Born Chinese* (Yang, 2006), which provides an example of all three forms of hybridity.

Several studies included in this section focus on the classroom use of texts that are normally associated with youth culture outside of school or that combine elements of such texts with features of what teachers and critics might call "quality literature." *American Born Chinese* is a graphic novel that serves as an example of the latter because it combines comic book conventions, such as stock characters (the very stereotypical Chin-Kee) and fantastical characters (the transforming Monkey King and other gods) with the deep themes often associated with quality literature—identity, alterity, assimilation, and cultural affiliation. The novel tells the interrelated stories of three main characters, each trying to contest an identity imposed by others who, in the process, find an identity enriched by hybrid cultural and linguistic resources. There's a great deal of pain in this book, despite its built-in parody, humor, and comic pseudo-violence. The characters are unable to claim a comfortable space as cultural insiders or outsiders or as global citizens in the face of overt and subtle racism. In writing about the postcolonial dilemma of being at once a cultural insider and outsider, Minh-ha (1997) comments on the consequences of cultural and racial hybridity:

> Not quite the same, not quite the other, she stands in that undetermined threshold place where she constantly drifts in and out…. She is, in other words, this inappropriate other or same who moves about with always at least two gestures: that of affirming 'I am like you' while persisting in her difference and that of reminding 'I am different' while unsettling every definition of otherness arrived at. (pp. 415–419)

The pain of wanting to belong—to be accepted—while, at the same time, persisting in difference resonates throughout the book and speaks to young adult readers through hybrid genres (myth, fantasy, realism), languages (English and Chinese), and forms (comic strip, novel). In the process, the book tackles important themes related to the possibilities and perils of embodying and performing hybrid identities within oppressive frameworks.

Textual hybridity is conducive to pedagogical practices that invite students to respond critically from their own hybrid positions of global citizenship and multlingualism. For example, in her study of students' responses to postcolonial literature in a Canadian high school, Johnston (2003) set out to determine whether postcolonial pedagogy held potential for introducing deconstructive reading strategies for her students' reading of the "other" in canonized texts as well as new international literature. While postcolonial literature was appealing to both her immigrant students as well as those from mainstream backgrounds, Johnston found that postcolonial pedagogy demanded a commitment to helping students "cross borders constructed within discourses of race, class, gender, and ethnicity" (p. 144). Such crossings often led to anger as interpretations brought out tensions and contradictory viewpoints.

After reading Joy Kogawa's (1993) novel *Obasan*, Bob, a White student with German and Ukrainian heritage, began to question his vision of Canada as a fair and just society and asked in reference to the internment of Japanese-Canadians during World War II, "Was I one of many who was not aware of such horrific details, or do most know and not care?" (Johnston, 2003, p. 118). At the same time, Myka, a first generation Canadian whose parents had emigrated from China, reacted to *Obasan* with anger for other reasons. Collective memories of war and destruction at the hands of Japanese soldiers in China infuriated Myka and made him "sick" (p. 121). Yet, he refused to express such sentiments for fear that others would interpret his responses as racist. Given that feelings of vulnerability, anger, and exposure were common among students in her study, Johnston concluded that teachers must engage students both personally and emotionally through aesthetic readings of texts and critically through sociopolitical readings in order to create spaces where students might deconstruct repressive ideologies and "re-map" their cultural memories, painful and shocking as they may initially be. Although he continued to say little in class, Myka's initial reaction was mediated by other students' points of view, and, in a later interview with Johnston, he revealed that he had arrived at a more ambiguous conclusion about his inherited history after reading other, unassigned texts by Kogawa. Without erasing his own painful memories, a postcolonial pedagogy encouraged Myka to permit the hearing of other voices and histories as well.

In the new edition of her well-known text on literary theory, Deborah Appleman (2009) included a chapter on the teaching of postcolonial literature in which she offered examples of students re-reading and re-writing Conrad's *Heart of Darkness* (1902/1993) and other colonial texts through a postcolonial lens. Appleman (2009) argues that a postcolonial lens, with its focus on political and historical contexts, allows for interpretations of literature which move away from "universal" readings to readings which instill global significance to those whose experiences have been represented only as "the other" to the Western world.

Immigrant students must regularly cross the difficult discourse borders that Johnston found to be difficult even for students who were not immigrants. Sarroub, Pernicek, and Sweeney (2007) offered the reading experiences of Hayder, a Kurdish refugee student from Iraq, as representative of a "new type of immigrant" (p. 669) whose home life is often incompatible with school expectations that put him in a position to fail or drop out. Additionally, Hayder's arrival in the United States forced him to redefine masculinity and responsibility in light of assumptions about Iraqi men as dangerous in a post-9/11 world. The hybridity of Hayder's identity, then, as refugee, male, and student placed him in an often-confusing position. Despite his avid reading outside of school for purposes related to work and the navigation of day-to-day living, Hayder's success in school literacy tasks was mediated by varying degrees of support. Sarroub et al. argued that teachers and researchers must redefine reading and text in school contexts and make use of the multiple literacies that students like Hayder already practice in other contexts of their lives.

The literacy practices of youth in contexts outside of school have begun to productively merge with more traditional literacy practices in school, thus creating important hybrid spaces. Urban youth often engage voluntarily in literate practices through poetry and rap lyrics, which play an important role as social critique of poverty, violence, crime, and drugs (Mahiri & Sablo, 1996). English teachers interested in engaging students through non-school based literacies have begun to integrate such practices into their classrooms in powerful ways. Morrell and Duncan-Andrade (2002), for example, contended that hip-hop should be taught as subject of study in its own right, but also demonstrated how popular culture texts act as a bridge to engagement with traditional, "canonical" texts. In their study of high school English classrooms, teachers juxtaposed readings of poems such as Coleridge's "Kubla Khan" with Nas's rap lyrics for "If I Ruled the World." They found that the rap lyrics not only helped scaffold students' understanding of conventions such as metaphor, irony, and symbolism, but also helped students deconstruct dominant narratives in both poetry and their own lives (Morrell, 2002).

Building on such conclusions, Fisher (2005) and Jocson (2006) studied urban youths' literacy practices with poetry in spoken word and SLAM competitions in hybrid contexts where both in-school and out-of-school literacy practices merge. In Jocson's study, Antonio blended the musical genres and cultural forms as he mixed Bob Dylan and hip-hop in response to commercial manipulation of Black music and culture. In this move, Antonio negotiated his "multilayered social worlds" (p. 232) and redefined text as a hybrid form. Through his writing and performance of poetry, Antonio's literacy practices intersected in hybrid ways around both text and context. Jocson argued that researchers and teachers must redefine literacy as hybridity itself in order to embrace the cultural, linguistic, cognitive, and material resources, which characterize the relevance of a rich context for learning.

Medina and Campano (2006) also worry about the "marginalization of alternative literacy practices" (p. 332) and the impact it has on students in low-income, ethnically and linguistically diverse schools. They looked to drama, however, as the connection between school-based literacy practices and students' own identities. Because drama is a complex semiotic system, which allows for the embodiment of multiple social positions, students in their study were better able to reflect critically on various ways of knowing and to use fiction as a way of understanding their own mediated worlds. Through drama practices and *teatro*, political theater, students entered into spaces between characters' fictional lives and their own actual lives and identities. For example, students used drama to "fictionalize reality" (p. 333) by incorporating their own collective readings of unjust historical situations in a scene they called, "What the Teacher Didn't Know." Here, they offered alternative readings of fictional characters' lives and motivations by "freezing" text and inserting their own cultural experiences and understandings of how they are positioned by powerful others. As Edmiston (1998) argues in his work on drama and ethical imagination, drama can support the development of "dynamic relational selves that acknowledge and embrace internal contradictions in their views" (p. 83). As such, drama creates a hybrid, in-between space where students reshape text and self through their own critical readings.

Globalized processes, we argue, create increasingly hybrid identities, spaces, and literacies, and as such, notions of text, canon, and language have shifted. As we move beyond Western, dominant conceptions of literature and interpretation, studies of response in secondary schools continue to move toward an understanding of the hybrid merging of school and non-school-based literacy practices as well as the inclusion of multiple modalities. We take up a significant aspect of the redefinition of text in the next section.

Multimodality and Literature

Perhaps the most obvious effect of globalization on literature study in secondary school is the inclusion of multimodal texts, which often are shaped by global economic and cultural flows produced through digital media. These texts lead to transactions that involve readers not only in interpretation, identification, and critical analysis, but also in text production involving print and other modes such as sound, image, and gesture. We're using the term *multimodality* in the social semiotic tradition (Halliday,

1978; Kress & Jewitt, 2003) that focuses on the agency of individuals and groups to interpret and make signs within sociocultural contexts and transmediated across sign systems (Ranker, 2008; Siegel, 2006). Despite social and power structures that can be unyielding, these contexts have the potential for transformation through semiotic activity. It may well be this potential for change that attracts so many young people to "read" (read, in this case, means to consume, interpret, view, listen to) and create multimodal texts. As the sections on identity and hybridity attest, young people are motivated by the possibilities inherent in multimodal communication and expression. Moreover, multimodal texts are not a novelty to youth as they remain to many English teachers. Instead, they are an expected (and demanded) part of the literary landscape.

Young people expect that literature will speak to them in the way that rap, hip-hop, spoken word, graphic novels, zines, fanfiction, and other relatively new literary forms speak to many youth. They also expect that they can speak/write back to these texts, sometimes in the form of intertextual new creations (e.g., a new rap that speaks to an existing one; a serial fanfiction), and sometimes in the form of actual commentary, which they write and respond to. This commentary often initiates a chain of responses in a motivated exchange that is unlike most we see in schools relative to either teacher or peer response (Black, 2007). This process of speaking/writing back to texts makes it difficult to separate text production from text consumption when considering how multimodal texts work in the secondary classroom. However, given the scope of this chapter, we will limit our discussion to research related to multimodal forms of literature and response to these texts.

Multimodal texts and their attendant literacy practices can be daunting to English teachers, most of whom are not "digital natives," as millennial youth are often dubbed. Despite the persistence of a digital divide (Pew, 2005), youth of all demographics naturalize digital technology, often through the ubiquity of mobile technology even among low-income teens and the efforts of community-based organizations that provide Internet access. Moreover, not all multimodal texts require digital technology, as can be seen in the increasing popularity of the often community and performance-based texts of spoken word (Fisher, 2005; Jocson, 2006), and peer-culture texts such as graphic novels (Schwarz, 2006) and manga (Schwartz & Rubinstein-Ávila, 2006).

Daunting as this textual landscape may be, school-based and university-based educators, especially in England, where media education is part of the national curriculum, have been making multimodal texts and text production the center of their curricula for over a decade. In 1994, Buckingham and Sefton-Green (1994) argued:

> English teachers should be concerned with the whole range of cultural products, from Shakespeare plays to hamburger advertisements. Any text that we might choose to use in our

classrooms will come already surrounded by assumptions and judgements about its cultural value, which students themselves will inevitably articulate and wish to debate. (p. 5)

In nations that have required media education since the 1990s, such as England, Canada, and Australia, the responsibility for teaching students to interpret signs and symbols, not only in print literature but in a range of media texts, typically fell to secondary English. One of the striking conclusions that can be drawn from Buckingham and Sefton-Green's work in a working-class secondary classroom that focused on analyzing and producing popular media texts is the sophisticated level of analysis that resulted from students grappling with elements of composition and message as they produced their texts. Students' experiences with this process made it hard for them to either vilify or romanticize the process or the products, resulting in complex thinking about texts and readers' responses.

In the early years of the new millennium, Canadian scholars, Hammett and Barrell (2002), edited a collection to help teachers use texts and technologies not usually taught in English, including, for example, a chapter exploring popular culture texts using hypermedia and pairing them with canonized texts such as *Macbeth*. In 2004, Hammett and Barrell joined with United States scholars, Mayher and Pradl, to publish a volume that focused on developing new ways to conceptualize and teach English, given the sort of changes outlined earlier in this chapter, albeit with references to some now outdated technologies. For example, Mackey's (2004) chapter applied Thompson's (1987) levels of literary analysis among teens, which included empathizing, analogizing, and understanding of textual ideologies, to her own reading of a popular novel and film, suggesting, in the end, that the developmental levels Thompson described can be used to promote critical analysis of texts that students already know and enjoy. Hammett's (2004) chapter discussed ways to use technology in supporting response to literature (email, chat groups) and in understanding intertextuality through hypermedia links.

An interest in creativity related to literature and language arts has also fueled current attention to multimodality (Albers & Harste, 2007). In an article on working with preservice English educators in ways that encourage them to support their students' multimodal expression and representation, Albers (2006) suggested starting with a focus novel and inviting students to seek connections to other art or media in order to better understand the effects of transmediation across sign systems (for instance, the different effects of a Tupac poem as sung by his mother, in one case, and as a Power Point with sound and image, in another). This activity aligns with what Jenkins (2006b) called "convergence culture," which underscores intertextual connections that emerge from global flows and active participation across media formats on the part of audiences/consumers.

One form of multimodal literature that is beginning to find its way into the secondary classroom is the graphic novel. In recent years, some texts in this genre—such as *Persepolis: The Story of a Childhood* (Satrapi, 2004)— have acquired status through prestigious awards and curricular materials for use in the secondary classroom. Graphic novels such as these and the *Maus* (Spiegelman, 1986) series have, to some degree, achieved canon status, at least within their genre. Many scholars and educators argued that graphic novels benefit struggling readers and otherwise disengaged students by engaging them in texts that often communicate deep and complex messages, while allowing readers to imaginatively enter the text through different modalities (Carter, 2007; Frey & Fisher, 2007).

However, the graphic novels that have achieved literary status may not appeal to young people in the same way as those that young people exchange among themselves (e.g., graphic novel series books and manga), often creating new meanings and fashioning new identities by remixing elements of the books with videos and fanfiction. Despite recent research on how youth make meaning within transmedia frameworks (Ranker, 2008; Schultz, Vasudevan, & Throop, 2008), we still have little understanding to help guide our classroom teaching of new literary forms. The wide-reaching popularity of manga and Asian graphic novel series, across categories of nation, language, ethnicity, and gender, is more evidence of the effects of globalization on literary forms and hybrid youth identities, which then shape the meaning and method of literature study in secondary school. For instance, Schwarz (2006) pointed out that studying graphic novels can lead to discussions that challenge how literary canons are formed, so that the making of a discipline and the conflicts that are central to its formation are objects of study (Graff, 1993).

In some cases, forms of response to literature study in the classroom have changed more than the texts themselves. New forms of response, including weblogs and social networks, are expanding the boundaries of the classroom by providing students with wider audiences and conversational partners for their responses to literature. For example, Robyn Cook, who teaches in an urban high school program focusing on digital media, decided to use edmodo, a social networking program much like Twitter, during a class discussion of *Siddhartha* (Hesse, 1922/2007). She divided her class into two groups in preparation for a "fishbowl" discussion in which the inside circle discussed the text and the outer circle observed and commented on the discussion. Whereas in the past she asked students in the outer circle to take notes and prepare to talk about their observations, she decided this time to have all students in the outer circle use edmodo on individual laptop computers to comment on their observations related to the content and interactional dynamics of the inner circle's discussion. Cook (personal communication, March 2009) reported that every student in the outer circle was engaged in this process, with most making important observations that supported a deeper discussion than the class had previously experienced. She hypothesized that her students learned more by reading their peers' in-process thoughts, which then provided a reason for them to support, critique, and elaborate on each other's comments.

Responding to literature through weblog entries is another form of response that allows students to make use of the affordances of technology, in this case to fashion identities in relation to the texts and the classroom community. Each week, West (2008) invited her high school students to respond to what interested them most about the American literature they had been assigned to read. She found that students were not only eager to post their responses and read those of their classmates, but were motivated to write engaging blog entries to hold their classmates' attention. Having the authentic audience of their peers led them to leverage particular identities to establish their relationship to the text and to their peers. One student used her blog entries to leverage her cultural capital as someone knowledgeable about popular culture while simultaneously demonstrating her ability to analyze literature as expected in school. In the course of a paragraph, she referenced "The Illest Diva" from a song by the singer Missy Elliot before comparing her experience reading *Huckleberry Finn* (Twain, 1885/2002) to that of reading *The Great Gatsby* (Fitzgerald, 1925/1992) and ending with enthusiasm for "Hucky" and "Tommy" and their "loco" adventures. In this way, students in this Advanced Placement class managed to retain their positions as serious students, appealing to both their teachers' and their peers' sensibilities as well as taking up "hybrid social languages" (West, 2008, p. 588).

Transforming Literature Study in Secondary School

Hayles (2007) argued "the practices, texts, procedures, and processual nature of electronic literature require new critical models and new ways of playing and interpreting the works." In the examples of research included in this chapter, there are new practices worth underscoring. First, given an increasingly visual and global culture, it is important to develop in young people the capacity for critical citizenship so that they can "read" the linguistic, visual, and aural signs and symbols that inundate their lives, public and private. Second, because multimodal texts are not yet normalized, they tend to draw attention to themselves and, thus, allow readers to examine the process of reading involved in interpretation within and across media. Finally, given all of the new forms of texts and response that youth engage with in their communities, young people have come to expect that what they read will shape and be shaped by their social identities

and affiliations. Spoken word, for example, is both global and local, shaped by global economies and cultures, yet taken up in particular ways by different ethnic, racial, national, religious, and linguistic groups in various real-time and virtual locations. Sha Cage, a spoken word artist and activist in the area where the authors of this chapter live, incorporates local issues such as homelessness and poverty into her poetry while accessing connections to hip-hop, blues, and jazz and national figures such as June Jordan and Martin Luther King, Jr., who she refers to simply as "June and Martin." Her poetry draws on the local understandings of the live audience while connecting them to larger issues of social justice through globally known individuals and movements. Some secondary educators, aware of the multimodal texts that are at the center of youth culture, have begun to expand the textual landscape and response repertoires of their classrooms. As they do so, they create new disciplinary discourses for the future—discourses that have begun to transform the study of literature, the subject English, and the young people, all of whom are already world citizens. May others soon join their ranks.

Literature References

Alexie, S. (2007). *The absolutely true diary of a part-time Indian*. New York, NY: Little, Brown.

Carey, M., Liew, S., & Hempel, M. (2007). *Re-gifters*. New York, NY: DC Comics.

Conrad, J. (1902/1993). *Heart of darkness*. New York, NY: Knopf.

Fitzgerald, F. S. (1925/1992). *The great Gatsby*. New York, NY: Scribner.

Hesse, H. (1922/2007). *Siddhartha*. Los Angeles: Norilana.

Kogawa, J. (1994). *Obasan*. New York, NY: Anchor Books.

Lee, H. (1960). *To kill a mockingbird*. New York, NY: Warner Books.

Satrapi, M. (2004). *Persepolis: The story of a childhood*. New York, NY: Pantheon.

Spiegelman, A. (1986). *Maus: A survivor's tale*. New York, NY: Random House.

Twain, M. (1885/2002). *The adventures of Huckleberry Finn*. New York, NY: Penguin.

Yang, G. L. (2006). *American born Chinese*. New York, NY: First Second Books.

Academic References

Albers, P. (2006). Imagining possibilities in multimodal curriculum design. *English Education, 38*(2), 75–101.

Albers, P., & Harste, J. C. (2007). The arts, new literacies and multimodality. *English Education, 40*(1), 6–20.

Anagnostopoulos, D. (2003). Testing and student engagement with literature in urban classrooms: A multi-layered perspective. *Research in the Teaching of English, 38*(2), 177–212.

Apol, L. (1998). "But what does this have to do with kids?": Literary theory in the children's literature classroom. *Journal of Children's Literature, 24*(2), 32–47.

Appadurai, A. (2000). Grassroots globalization and the research imagination. *Public Culture, 12*(1), 1–19.

Apple, M. (2001). Comparing neo-liberal projects and inequality in education. *Comparative Education, 37*(4), 409–423.

Applebee, A. (1992). Stability and change in the high-school canon. *The English Journal, 81*(5), 27–32.

Appleman, D. (2000). *Critical encounters in high school English: Teaching literary theory to adolescents.* New York, NY: Teachers College Press.

Appleman, D. (2009). *Critical encounters in high school English: Teaching literary theory to adolescents* (rev. ed.). New York, NY: Teachers College Press.

Arnett, J. J. (2002). The psychology of globalization. *American Psychologist, 57*(10), 774–783.

Athanases, S. Z. (1993). Reader-response criticism and classroom literature discussion. In G. Newell & R. Durst (Eds.), *Exploring texts: The role of discussion and writing in the teaching and learning of literature* (pp. 259–282). Norwood, MA: Christopher-Gordon.

Bauman, Z. (1998). *Globalization: The human consequences.* New York, NY: Columbia University Press.

Bauman, Z. (2007). *Liquid times: Living in an age of uncertainty.* Cambridge, England: Polity Press.

Beach, R., & Hynds, S. (1991). Research on response to literature. In R. Barr, M. L. Kamil, P. Mosenthal, & P. D. Pearson (Eds.), *Handbook of reading research* (Vol. II, pp. 453–489). New York, NY: Longman.

Bean, T. W., & Moni, K. (2003). Developing students' critical literacy: Exploring identity construction in young adult fiction. *Journal of Adolescent & Adult Literacy, 46*(8), 638–648.

Black, R. W. (2007). Digital design: English language learners and reader feedback in online fanfiction. In M. Knobel & C. Lankshear (Eds.), *A new literacies sampler* (pp. 115–136). New York, NY: Peter Lang.

Buckingham, D., & Sefton-Green, J. (1994). *Cultural studies goes to school: Critical perspectives on literacy and education.* London: Taylor & Francis.

Carey-Webb, A. (2001). *Literature and lives: A response-based, cultural studies approach to teaching English.* Urbana, IL: National Council of Teachers of English.

Carter, J. B. (2007). Introduction—Carving a niche: Graphic novels in the English language arts classroom. In J. B. Carter (Ed.), *Building literacy connections with graphic novels: Page by page, panel by panel* (pp. 1–25). Urbana, IL: National Council of Teachers of English.

Carter, S. (2006). "She would've still made that face expression": The use of multiple literacies by two African American young women. *Theory Into Practice, 45*(4), 352–358.

Castell, M. (1996). *The networked society: Volume 1. The information age: Economy, society and culture.* Malden, MA: Blackwell.

Caughlan, S. (2004). *High-school teachers' cultural models of English as a school subject.* Unpublished doctoral dissertation, University of Wisconsin-Madison, AAT 3143227.

Caughlan, S. (2007). Competing cultural models of literature in state content standards. In D. W. Rowe, R. T. Jiménez, D. L. Compton, D. K. Dickinson, Y. Kim, K. M. Leander, et al. (Eds.), *56th Yearbook of the National Reading Conference* (pp. 178–190). Oak Creek, WI: National Reading Conference.

Coles, R. (1989). *The call of stories: Teaching and the moral imagination.* Boston, MA: Houghton Mifflin.

Corcoran, B., Hayhoe, M., & Pradle, G. (Eds.). (1994). *Knowledge in the making: Challenging the text in the classroom.* Portsmouth, NH: Heinemann.

Dasenbrock, R. W. (1989). Redrawing the lines. Minneapolis, MN: University of Minnesota Press.

Demerath, P., & Lynch, J. (2008). Identities for neoliberal times: Constructing enterprising selves in an American suburb. In N. Dolby & F. Rizvi (Eds.), *Youth moves: Identities in global perspective* (pp. 179–192). New York, NY: Routledge.

Dixon, J. (1967). *Growth through English.* Oxford, UK: Oxford University Press.

Dresang, E. (1999). *Radical change: Books for youth in a digital age.* New York, NY: Wilson.

Dyer, R. (1997). *White.* New York, NY: Routledge.

Edmiston, B. (1998). Ethical imagination: Choosing an ethical self in drama. In J. D. Wilhelm & B. Edmiston (Eds.), *Imagining to learn: Inquiry, ethics, and integration through drama* (pp. 55–84). Portsmouth, NH: Heineman.

Enciso, P. E. (1998). Good/bad girls read together: Pre-adolescent girls' co-authorship of feminine subject positions during a shared reading event. *English Education, 30*(1), 44–62.

Enciso, P. E., & Lewis, C. (2001). This issue. *Theory Into Practice, 40*(3), 146–149.

Fish, S. (1980). *Is there a text in this class? The authority of interpretive communities.* Cambridge, MA: Harvard University Press.

Fisher, M. (2005). From the coffee house to the school house: The promise and potential of spoken word poetry in school contexts. *English Education, 37*(2), 115–131.

Foucault, M. (1982). The subject and power. In H. Dreyfus & P. Rabinow (Eds.), *Michel Foucault: Beyond structuralism and hermeneutics* (pp. 208–226). Chicago, IL: University of Chicago Press.

Freebody, P., Luke, A., & Gilbert, P. (1991). Reading positions and practices in the classroom. *Curriculum Inquiry, 21*(4), 435–457.

Frey, N., & Fisher, D. (2007). Using graphic novels, anime, and the Internet in an urban high school. In J. B. Carter (Ed.), *Building literary connections with graphic novels: Page by page, panel by panel* (pp. 132–144). Urbana, IL: National Council of Teachers of English.

Galda, L., & Beach, R. (2001). Response to literature as a cultural activity. *Reading Research Quarterly, 36*(1), 64–73.

Gee, J. P. (2000/2001). Identity as an analytic lens for research in education. *Review of Research in Education, 25*(1), 99–125.

Gee, J. P. (2004). *Situated language and learning: A critique of traditional schooling.* New York, NY: Routledge.

Graff, G. (1993). *Beyond the culture wars: How teaching the conflicts can revitalize American education.* New York, NY: W. W. Norton.

Hale, L., & Crowe, C. (2001). "I hate reading if I don't have to": Results from a longitudinal study of high school students' reading interest. *The ALAN Review, 28*(3), 49–57.

Halliday, M. A. K. (1978). *Language as social semiotic.* London: Edward Arnold.

Hammett, R. (2004). Words and windows: Using technology for critical literacy. In B. R. C. Barrell, R. F. Hammett, J. Mayher, & G. Pradl (Eds.), *Teaching English today: Advocating change in the secondary curriculum* (pp. 117–131). New York, NY: Teachers College Press.

Hammett, R., & Barrell, B. (Eds.). (2002). *Digital expressions: Media literacy and English language arts.* Calgary, Alberta: Detselig Enterprises.

Harris, J. (1991). After Dartmouth: Growth and conflict in English. *College English, 53*(6), 631–646.

Hayles, N. K. (2007). Electronic literature: What is it? *The Electronic Literature Organization.* Retrieved June 25, 2008, from http://eliterature.org/pad/elp.html#sec

Hirsch, E. D. (1987). *Cultural literacy: What every American needs to know.* Boston, MA: Houghton Mifflin.

Hunter, I. (1988). *Culture and government: The emergence of literary education.* London: MacMillan Press.

Jenkins, H. (2006a). *Fans, bloggers, and gamers: Exploring participatory culture.* New York, NY: New York University Press.

Jenkins, H. (2006b). *Convergence culture: Where old and new media collide.* New York, NY: New York University Press.

89

Jocson, K. M. (2006). "Bob Dylan and hip hop": Intersecting literacy practices in youth poetry communities. *Written Communication, 23*(3), 231–259.

Johnston, I. (2003). *Re-mapping literary worlds: Postcolonial pedagogy in practice.* New York, NY: Peter Lang.

Jones, L., Newman, L., & Isay, D. (1997). *Our America: Life and death on the south side of Chicago.* New York, NY: Scribner.

Kirkland, D. (2008). "The rose that grew from concrete": Hip hop and the new English education. *English Journal, 97*(5), 69–75.

Kress, G. (2007). Thinking about meaning and learning in a world of instability and multiplicity. *Pedagogies: An International Journal, 2*(1), 19–34.

Kress, G., & Jewitt, C. (2003). Introduction. In C. Jewitt & G. Kress (Eds.), *Multimodal literacy* (pp. 1–18). New York, NY: Peter Lang.

Laclau, E., & Mouffe, C. (1985). *Hegemony and socialist strategy: Towards a radical democratic politics.* London: Verso.

Ladson-Billings, G. (1995). But that's just good teaching! The case for culturally relevant pedagogy. *Theory Into Practice, 34*(3), 159–165.

Langer, J. A. (1995). *Envisioning literature: Literary understanding and literature instruction.* New York, NY: Teachers College Press.

Leander, K., & Lovvorn, J. (2006). Literacy networks: Following the circulation of texts, bodies, and objects in the schooling and online gaming of one youth. *Cognition and Instruction, 24*(3), 291–340.

Lee, C. D. (2007). *Culture, literacy, and learning: Taking bloom in the midst of the whirlwind.* New York, NY: Teachers College Press.

Lesko, N. (2001). *Act your age!: A cultural construction of adolescence.* New York, NY: Routledge.

Lewis, C. (2000). Limits of identification: The personal, pleasurable, and critical in reader response. *Journal of Literacy Research, 32*(2), 253–266.

Lewis, C., Ketter, J., & Fabos, B. (2001). Reading race in a rural context. *International Journal of Qualitative Studies in Education, 14*(3), 317–350.

Luke, A. (2004a). Literacy and educational fundamentalism: An interview with Allan Luke. *English Quarterly, 36*(4), 11–17.

Luke, A. (2004b). At last: The trouble with English. *Research in the Teaching of English, 39*(1), 85–95.

Luke, A., & Carrington, V. (2002). Globalisation, literacy, curriculum practice. In R. Fisher, G. Brooks & M. Lewis (Eds.), *Raising standards in literacy* (pp. 231–250). London: Routledge.

Luke, A., & Luke, C. (2001). Adolescence lost/childhood regained: On early intervention and the emergence of the techno-subject. *Journal of Early Childhood Literacy, 2*(1), 97–103.

Mackey, M. (2004). Developing critical responses to stories in many media. In B. R. C. Barrell, R. F. Hammett, J. Mayher, & G. Pradl (Eds.), *Teaching English today: Advocating change in the secondary curriculum* (pp. 106–116). New York, NY: Teachers College Press.

Mahiri, J., & Sablo, S. (1996). Writing for their lives: The non-school literacy of California's urban African American youth. *The Journal of Negro Education, 65*(2), 164–180.

Marshall, J. D. (2000). Research on response to literature. In M. L. Kamil, P. B. Mosenthal, P. D. Pearson, & R. Barr (Eds.), *Handbook of reading research* (Vol. III, pp. 381–402). Mahwah, NJ: Erlbaum.

Marshall, J. D., Smagorinsky, P., & Smith, M. (1995). *The language of interpretation: Patterns of discourse in discussions of literature.* Urbana, IL: National Council of Teachers of English.

Medina, C., & Campano, G. (2006). Performing identities through drama and teatro practices in multilingual classrooms. *Language Arts, 83*(4), 332–341.

Mellor, B., O'Neill, M., & Patterson, A. (1987) *Reading stories.* Perth, Australia: Chalkface Press.

Minh-Ha, T. T. (1997). Not you/like you: Postcolonial women and the interlocking questions of identity and difference. In A. McClintock, A. Mufti, & E. Shohat (Eds.), *Dangerous liaisons: Gender, nation, and postcolonial perspectives* (pp. 415–419). Minneapolis, MN: University of Minnesota Press.

Moje, E. B., Young, J. P., Readence, J. E., & Moore, D. W. (2000). Reinventing adolescent literacy for new times: Perennial and millennial issues. *Journal of Adolescent & Adult Literacy, 43*(5), 400–410.

Moore, J. N. (1997). *Interpreting young adult literature: Literary theory in the secondary classroom.* Portsmouth, NH: Heinemann.

Morgan, R. (1993). Transitions from English to cultural studies. *New Education, 15*(1), 21–48.

Morgan, W. (1997). *Critical literacy in the classroom: The art of the possible.* New York, NY: Routledge.

Morrell, E. (2002). Toward a critical pedagogy of popular culture: Literacy development among urban youth. *Journal of Adolescent & Adult Literacy, 46*(1), 72–77.

Morrell, E. (2005). Critical English education. *English Education, 37*(4), 312–321.

Morrell, E., & Duncan-Andrade, J. (2002). Promoting academic literacy with urban youth through engaging hip-hop culture. *English Journal, 91*(6), 88–92.

National Council of Teachers of English. (2007). *Globalization and English education.* Report from the 2007 Conference on English Education Leadership and Policy Summit. Retrieved June 25, 2008, from http://www.ncte.org/groups/cee/129837.htm

Nilan, P., & Feixa, C. (Eds.). (2006). *Global youth?: Hybrid identities, plural worlds.* London: Routledge.

Nystrand, M., Wu, L., Gamoran, A., Zeiser, S., & Long, D. (2003). Questions in time: Investigating the structure and dynamics of unfolding classroom discourse. *Discourse Processes, 35*(2), 135–196.

O'Neill, M. (1993). Teaching literature as cultural criticism. *English Quarterly, 25*(1), 19–25.

Pennycook, A. (2005). Teaching with the flow: Fixity and fluidity in education. *Asia Pacific Journal of Education, 25*(1), 29–43.

Pew. (2005). Digital divisions. *Pew Internet and American Life Project.* Retrieved June 25, 2008, from http://www.pewinternet.org/Reports/2005/Digital-Divisions/03-Internet-Access-is-the-Norm-but-is-not-Universal.aspx?r=1

Pirie, B. (1997). *Reshaping high school English.* Urbana, IL: National Council of Teachers of English.

Probst, R. (1991). Response to literature. In J. Flood, J. M. Jensen, D. Lapp, & J. R. Squire (Eds.), *Handbook of research on teaching the English language arts* (pp. 655–663). New York, NY: Macmillan.

Radway, J. (1988). Reception study: Ethnography and the problems of dispersed audiences and nomadic subjects. *Cultural Studies, 2*(3), 359–376.

Ranker, J. (2008). Production in a fifth grade classroom composing across multiple media: A case study of digital video. *Written Communication, 25*(2), 196–234.

Rogers, T., & Soter, A. (1997). *Reading across cultures: Teaching literature in a diverse society.* New York, NY: Teachers College Press.

Sarroub, L. K., Pernicek, T., & Sweeney, T. (2007). "I was bitten by a scorpion": Reading in and out of school in a refugee's life. *Journal of Adolescent & Adult Literacy, 50*(8), 668–679.

Saxe, G. B. (1991). *Cognitive development and cultural practices.* Hillsdale, NJ: Erlbaum.

Scholes, R. (1991). A clock of cultures—A trivial proposal. *College English, 53*(7), 759–772.

Schultz, K., Vasudevan, L., & Throop, R. (2007). Adolescent literacy toward global citizenship. In B. Guzzetti (Ed.), *Literacy for the new millennium: Volume three, adolescent literacy* (pp. 21–36). Westport, CT: Praeger.

Schwartz, A., & Rubinstein-Ávila, E. (2006). Understanding the manga hype: Uncovering the multimodality of comic book literacies. *Journal of Adolescent & Adult Literacy, 50*(1), 40–49.

Schwarz, G. (2006). Expanding literacies through graphic novels. *English Journal, 95*(6), 58–64.

Siegel, M. (2006). Rereading the signs: Multimodal transformations in the field of literacy education. *Language Arts, 84*(1), 65–77.

Sims Bishop, R. (1992). Multicultural literature for children: Making informed choices. In V. Harris (Ed.), *Teaching multicultural literature in grade K–8*. Norwood, MA: Christopher-Gordon.

Soter, A. (1999). *Young adult literature and the new literary theories*. New York, NY: Teacher's College Press.

Spears-Bunton, L. A. (1990). Welcome to my house: African American and European American students' responses to Virginia Hamilton's *House of Dies Drear*. *The Journal of Negro Education, 59*(4), 566–576.

Sumara, D. (1998). Fictionalizing acts: Reading and the making of identity. *Theory Into Practice, 37*(3), 203–210.

Sumara, D. (2002). *Why reading literature in school still matters: Imagination, interpretation, insight*. Mahwah, NJ: Erlbaum.

Thein, A. H. (2006, November). Working-class girls' improvising flexible interpretive practices in negotiating lived and text worlds. Paper presented at the 96th Annual Convention of the National Council of Teachers of English, Nashville, TN.

Thein, A. H., Beach, R., & Parks, D. (2007). Perspective-taking as transformative practice in teaching multicultural literature to white students. *English Journal, 97*(2), 54–60.

Thompson, N. (1987). *Understanding teenagers' reading*. New York, NY: Nichols.

Unsworth, L. (2006). Towards a metalanguage for multiliteracies education: Describing the meaning making resources of language-image interaction. *English teaching: Practice and critique, 5*(1), 55–76.

Vinz, R. (2000). *Becoming (other)wise: Enhancing critical reading perspectives*. Portland, ME: Calendar Islands.

West, K. C. (2008). Weblogs and literary response: Socially situated identities and hybrid social languages in English class blogs. *Journal of Adolescent & Adult Literacy, 51*(7), 588–598.

Willis, A. I. (1997). Exploring multicultural literature as cultural production. In T. Rogers & A. Soter (Eds.), *Reading across cultures: Teaching literature in a diverse society* (pp. 135–160). New York, NY: Teachers College Press.

Wolf, S. A., & Maniotes, L. K. (2002). Silenced by sex: Hard truths & taboos in teaching literature. *New Advocate, 15*(3), 197–204.

Wyn, J. (2005). What is happening to 'adolescence'? Growing up in changing times. In J. A. Vadeboncoeur & L. P. Stevens (Eds.), *Re/constructing "the adolescent": Sign, symbol, and body* (pp. 249–270). New York, NY: Peter Lang.

Yagelski, R. (2006). English education. In B. McComiskey (Ed.), *English studies: An introduction to the discipline(s)* (pp. 275–319). Urbana, IL: National Council of Teachers of English.

Zancanella, D. (2007). Dripping with literacy, a jazz-fueled road trip, a place to breathe. *English Journal, 97*(2), 71–78.

7

Imagining a Writer's Life

Extending the Connection between Readers and Books

Elizabeth Dutro and Monette C. McIver

University of Colorado at Boulder

Annie Dillard once wrote a famous little masterpiece, entitled *The Writing Life,* in which she suggests that the writer "is careful of what he reads, for that is what he will write." In this chapter, Elizabeth Dutro and Monette McIver take Dillard's comment even further. They begin with the increasing role of literary texts as authorial mentors for young writers, emphasizing the intertwined nature of reading and writing. But then they up the ante by looking carefully at what kinds of mentor texts are valued both within and outside of school. They argue that literary borrowing does not simply supply a "model of skills, genre, and literary conventions," but can also serve individual expression as well as resistance to and transformation of the social status quo. The idea of how one's reading flows into "every scratch of the pen" will be echoed in Hammill's later chapter on how writing is preserved and serves as a transformational space within museums.

When we consider the relationship between reading and young writers we think of Jo March, the heroine of *Little Women* (Alcott, 2004), retreating to the privacy of her attic room and writing furiously in her notebooks. Filling page after page, she created the kinds of thrilling tales that she read in magazines and that she was sure were just what publishers wished to print. It took painful rejection, not to mention the burning of her manuscript by a vengeful little sister, to convince her that her own voice and story were more valuable than those she had so carefully modeled. But, those horror tales played an important, intertextual role in inspiring and motivating her to pursue a writing life (Dillard, 1989).

Most of us who spend time writing are well aware of the writers who have inspired us. If we caught the writing bug at an early age, we might have a mental bookshelf full of inspirational authors from childhood forward whose various styles, genres, characterizations, and themes have left their traces on our writing lives. Encountering young writers as educators, librarians, or parents, we know that children and youth are often inspired to write through their reading of favorite authors. Whether it is a first grader drawing her own version of Jaqueline Woodson's (2001) *The Other Side*, a fourth grader writing "Dragon Sky," his take on Laurence Yep's (1977) *Dragonwings*, a middle schooler adding a new chapter to her J.K. Rowling fan fiction novel, or high school poets performing at an open mic, literature provides a world from which new ideas can be launched. As Stephen King (2000) writes in recalling his own journey as a writer, "imitation preceded creation" (p. 27). Indeed, one of the powers of literature is how it can inspire a reader to reach for her pen and weave her own magic with words, imagining, imitating, creating, even rebelling.

Although successful authors are rightfully celebrated for their unique contributions, a writing life is informed by the literary voices that preceded and surround it. Well-known writers are often asked in interviews to name their literary mentors. *Newsweek* magazine recently began running a regular column, "A Life in Books," that asks famous authors to recount their five most important books. Several authors, including Stephen King, Beverly Cleary, and Anne Lamott, have penned memoirs that explicitly recount the reading that fueled their writing. Henry Louis Gates speaks eloquently about how seeing James Baldwin's pictures and reading his stories made his dream of becoming a writer a reality (Lamb, 1997). In addition, film portrayals of developing writers such as *Finding Forrester* or *Freedom Writers* often include scenes in which older mentors press a book into the hands of a young protégé that is certain to light his authorial passions. In short, the assumption of a powerful intertextual connection between reading literature and authoring texts of one's own is captured in the many and varied narratives that surround the art of writing.

However, even as that reading-writing connection functions as a collective assumption, and even though many writers are able to name their authorial muses if asked, the relationship between literature and writing is not often a tangible, visible one. The act of reading and writing are so intertwined that we do not often see the individual threads and how they come together. In this chapter, we will tease out some perceptible instances of the relationship between young writers and their reading. One of those tangible instances is how educators have harnessed the idea of authors as mentors through explicit attention to the modeling—of genres, voice, imagery, character development, and word choice—that published authors can provide for young writers. Thus, we devote a section of what follows to professional texts written for teachers, curricula, and research that address the relationship between literature and writing in classrooms.

Although the link between reading and writing is used as a pedagogical tool in schools, we also know that children and youth have long relied on authors as mentors for their own writing outside of the official world of the classroom and with or without the explicit guidance of adults. Therefore, we explore that territory as well, including the socially engaged work of youth, particularly youth of color, who draw on literary mentors to speak to and back to their communities and society. We also turn to the writing of young people who are employing new technologies to find outlets and audiences for their author-inspired writing,

particularly focusing on fan fiction, a genre that uniquely makes the author-writer relationship visible. As part of our discussion of fan fiction, we share examples from a fan fiction community devoted to Harry Potter where young writers critically engage and re-work the characters and plots of an iconic, beloved series. By following some of the tangible threads that tie the writing endeavors of children and youth to the worlds of authors and texts, we discuss the complex relationship between textual consumption and production and the opportunities as well as the inequities that are revealed through those connections.

Lenses on the Links between Reading and Writing

To claim a link between what is read and what is written is to evoke certain theoretical assumptions about texts and how they function. For one thing, such a relationship presumes intertextuality in the practices of reading and writing—encounters with any given text connect to memories of and meanings drawn from other texts one has engaged. The theories of Mikhail Bakhtin (1981), a Russian sociolinguist, have been influential in considering the intertextual nature of human engagement with language. Bakhtin argued that to communicate through language is to "appropriate the words of others and populate them with one's own intention" (p. 428). In this view, words are richly recycled—encountered, taken up, and re-shaped by people who imbue them with new meanings and embed them in new contexts. Therefore, no use of language or act of communication can be considered "neutral" or outside of the influence of the social and ideological contexts in which it is produced and received. The meanings woven from reading any given novel, for instance, are shot through with the experiences a reader has had with other texts. Similarly, when we sit down to write, the blank page we stare at is far from a void, for when the words appear they contain a history of encounters with words written by others.

When writing curricula for students in elementary or secondary schools draw on published authors as models for young writers, this intertextuality is made explicit. Teachers ask their children to be conscious of the process of drawing on one text to create another. The intertextual nature of writing, if always present, is also highly visible in the other reading-to-writing contexts we explore in this chapter. For instance, the work of youth poets may draw on canonical poets, rap and other hip-hop genres, and current events that they've encountered in the media. Writers of fan fiction also work visibly across texts, often infusing different genres into their re-workings of a favorite text or combining two or more texts in original ways. As Chandler-Olcott and Mahar (2003) write, "as a form, fanfictions make intertextuality visible because they rely on readers' ability to see relationships between the fan-writer's stories and the original media sources" (p. 562).

In addition to intertextuality, the connection between reading and writing also supposes an active reader, co-constructing meaning with the words on the page and, thus, dynamically creating the text as reader, rather than playing the role of passive sponge for an author's meaning. Reader response theories provide various conceptualizations of the active reader (e.g., Fish, 1980; Iser, 1989; Rosenblatt, 1994, 1995), but what the various approaches hold in common is a view of reader as integral to the potential of texts to convey meaning. In other words, an active reader response is not a quality of reading that one can switch on or off at will. Rather, these theories argue that it is only through a reader's transactions that texts can hold meaning at all. It follows then, that the dynamic reader, taking up the role of writer, consciously or not, re-visions the words, feelings, memories, and tone (to name but a few possibilities) evoked from the texts she has read.

A rich set of metaphors describes the ways that readers actively engage literature in their writing, including modeling, appropriating, drawing upon, inspiring, reworking, provoking, transforming, sparking, and poaching. That final term, "poaching," derives from the work of de Certeau. Jenkins (1992) draws on de Certeau's idea of poaching to theorize fan fiction writers' relationships to the texts on which they draw. Although the term may hold some negative connotations, de Certeau uses it to invoke a sense of readers boldly seizing meaning from texts and making them their own. In his argument, the metaphor of poaching infuses a sense of productive rebellion into the reader-writer relationship. Readers appropriate texts they encounter for their own purposes regardless of the "no trespassing" signs erected by theories of reading that have traditionally viewed authors' intentions with such sanctity. As Jenkins (1992) writes, "de Certeau's poaching analogy characterizes the relationship between readers and writers as an ongoing struggle for possession of the text and control of its meanings" (p. 24). Although this view of the reader is more confrontational than some, it paints an evocative image of how a reader wrests meanings from a text that she can then run with in her own writing.

Jenkins points out, again drawing on de Certeau, that this idea of readers poaching literary texts for their own purposes is at odds with the traditional ways in which readers are trained to read and respond to texts in schools—that is, with respect, if not reverence, for the plots, characterizations, and themes that are presumed to be directly conveyed by authors to readers. Although reader response theories position the reader as an active participant in constructing meaning from texts, reader as poacher positions the reader as more than just participant in meaning-making, but rather as one who finds something of interest in a text, takes it, and reshapes it for her own purposes.

This idea of the writer's own purposes driving the creation of a new text from those encountered highlights another important lens on the reading-writing connection. Written texts, particularly when they are published—bound and weighty on the bookshelf—do convey authority and importance. Yet, books are, of course, limited in the perspectives they include and experiences they represent. Further, as critiques of the predominance of White male authors in the traditional literary canon illustrate, some readers' experiences are far more likely to be left out than others (e.g., Bishop, 2007; Gates, 1992; Showalter, 1985). Therefore, it is sometimes the absences that the active reader notices in the literature she reads. Those voids can and do fuel the creation of new texts that allow for a wider range of experience and voices to be heard.

Theories of knowledge and power explain the absence of some kinds of literature in the school curriculum, particularly literature by and about marginalized groups. These gaps and omissions are evidence of the ways in which power is made visible and maintained. The dominance of some perspectives in a literature curriculum or in popular reading represents one instance of what Foucault (e.g., 1980, 1995) refers to as the disciplining nature of language. In this view, discourses, those large fields of meaning that are constituted through language, "enable and delimit fields of knowledge and inquiry, and govern what can be said, thought and done within those fields" (Luke, 1995/1996, p. 3). Although dominant perspectives in literature may influence what counts as valued knowledge and may reinforce power, resistance to such dominance is possible. As Foucault (1990) writes, "Discourse transmits and produces power; it reinforces it, but also undermines and exposes it, renders it fragile and makes it possible to thwart it" (p. 101). As we argue, such resistance is visible and made manifest in the work of both professional and student writers who insert their perspectives into the genres and texts they read.

Thus, writers' responses to the texts they read and the knowledge that those texts privilege reveal a fissure in the relationship between the assumptions embedded in the text and those brought to the text by its readers. Such rifts create opportunities for readers to critique the text's assumptions and their consequences. A young writer's re-working also represents, in and of itself, a "speaking back" to the original text or genre's positioning of characters, settings, and experiences or the absence of particular perspectives. As we turn now to a few specific examples of the reader-writer relationship, we will revisit these ideas of authorial mentorship, intertexuality, active readers, and young writers as social critics and transformative "poachers" of published literature.

Authors as Mentors in the K–12 Curriculum

Writing as apprenticeship grounds the increase of writer's workshop in American schools. The classroom writing practices central to writing process theory grew out of the work of researchers who studied the composing processes of experienced and novice writers. Chief among these studies were Emig's (1971) investigation of 12th graders and Hayes and Flower's (1980) analyses of adult writers. At the elementary level, Graves's (1983) work inspired many teachers to make writer's workshop a part of their daily classroom life. Though by no means exhaustive, these studies helped to define the conditions and the practices central to the writing process. Based on this work, other researchers and practitioners amended the process, and like the act of writing itself, writing process theory continues to evolve. Now, students in classrooms across the nation can describe the writing process (e.g., prewriting, drafting, revising, and editing for publication) with the self-assurance of published authors. Much of this can be credited to the work of Nancie Atwell (1987), Lucy Calkins (1986), Jane Hansen (2001), and Donald Murray (1985), who translated the practices of established writers to the everyday operations of K–12 writing classrooms. This work is further substantiated by the National Writing Project (NWP), which creates opportunities for classroom teachers to engage in the writing practices endorsed by these authors (Smith, 1996). Given the influence that the practices of professional writers have made on K–12 writing instruction, it is no surprise that turning to "authorial mentors" is gaining more prominence (Wolf, 2004).

As we emphasized earlier, students have borrowed ideas for writing from the books they have read and heard for as long as young readers have also put pencil to paper. Young writers routinely infuse their stories with opening phrases, dialogue, character sketches, and plot twists. One need only review the work of Dyson (1997) or Wolf and Heath (1992, 1993) for examples of how young writers have lassoed the personas of super heroes and princesses, capturing the lives of these characters in poetry, comic strips, and narrative stories. Young children often begin their stories with, "Once upon a time" as a result of the fairy tales they have heard or the movies they have seen. As we will discuss further in a later section, secondary students draw on myriad texts from their lives, including literature, to craft their own writing both within and outside of school settings. What is new at the K–12 educational level is the degree to which teachers use these examples, explicitly showing students how to transfer what they notice from the work of authors and incorporating these lessons learned into their own writing selections. Below, we discuss some of the research that supports the explicit use of literature as models for young writers.

Problem Solving

In process-oriented classrooms, writing is often equated with problem solving. In the course of writing, we determine what we know and don't know about a topic. Lindemann (1995) makes this connection noting that when writers practice the various phases of the writing process (e.g., prewriting, drafting, revising, and editing for publication), they are working their way through questions that they need to answer for themselves and for their readers. For example, a writer may change a word or phrase based on the audience, reorder sections of a manuscript to tighten an argument, or add an example to clarify a point. Thus, problem solving permeates the writing process. As questions—structural, logical, or lyrical—are answered, more arise, and writers must return to the step that will allow them to answer their new questions. Effective writers cycle through these steps to get a clearer vision of their message and the best way to convey it.

One of the ways that students can make their writing more engaging and effective is by eliciting the assistance of published authors. As Lancia (1997) explains, "Literature inspires, influences, and instructs young writers by providing the examples needed for effective writing" (p. 475). An advocate of infusing the writing workshop with literature, Harwayne (1992) suggests that "Children too need lots of influences. They need to feel free to take the bits and pieces they've learned from others and integrate them into their own unique ways of writing" (p. 160). Thus, young writers can read literature with the authors' process in mind. What issues might have arisen for the author while writing? How might a particular character have developed in the author's mind, and how does the author assist her readers in getting to know the character so intimately?

Children learn to lean on the literary examples they encounter through numerous interactions with literature. Even more, students can rely on literature to solve their own writing problems or to convey just the right guidance or message to a peer. To illustrate, consider the following conversation between Joseph and Richard, two fourth-grade students. Richard wrote a non-rhyming poem about football and has just solicited feedback from his classmate, Joseph:

Joseph: Okay, I have a question. Is this supposed to be like a story?

Richard: No, a poem. A poem doesn't have to rhyme.

Joseph: [agreeing] But it doesn't flow like a poem. You need to make it flow more like a poem.

Richard: [perplexed] You mean add a comma? You mean add a pause?

Joseph: [struggling to articulate his thinking] To where your words connect like a poem. Since it's not a rhyming poem, you words are kinda…

Richard: Choppy?

Joseph: Yeah, that's why I asked, 'cause it sounded more like a story.

Joseph, still not sure that Richard understood the message he was trying to convey, turned to a book of poetry, and together, the boys analyzed several poems. While the poems they reviewed were rhyming, the examples propelled the conversation forward, causing Joseph to offer Richard sage advice: "Some poems kind of stop. But then [they] will start flowing again. It's kind of like a waterfall when it gets plugged up. But then it unsticks and starts flowing again" (McIver & Wolf, 1999, p. 55)

Joseph and Richard's conversation exemplified what Lancia (1997) and others have encouraged for many years. Reading literature through the lens of the writing process can remove some of the mystique that so often surrounds the act of writing. If children and youth understand that even successful, beloved writers must problem-solve through the writing process, young writers may be encouraged to do the same. They too can engage in the writing process, working through sticky writing situations by turning to literary examples. Ultimately, students find themselves in multiple positions to read like writers.

Reading Like a Writer

One of the goals of a proactive approach to authorship is turning decision making over to students. To produce effective texts, students need multiple opportunities to reflect on the plot lines and techniques that they borrow from authors. Further, student authors gain command of their writing when they are clear about how and why they will incorporate what they learn from author mentors. Key to this is explicitly teaching students how to use published authors as resources. In other words, advocates of writing instruction that engages students in inspecting texts to identify authors' tricks of the trade seek to make explicit the intertextual connections that are implicitly present in the writing process. If student authors approach each reading and writing episode with the memories and meanings from their previous encounters with text, as Bakhtin (1981) contends, then the products that students produce are the external manifestations of these internal musings. Explicitly using literature as a model takes advantage of the implicit connections that readers make with all texts.

The distinction between explicit and implicit reading and writing links is an important one. Many of the interventions that researchers have studied reflected a casual connection to mentor texts. For example, the third-grade students in Bearse's (1992) analysis studied fairy tales for four weeks. Students engaged in a variety of activities, including comparing and contrasting, class-based discussion, and artwork. Then students wrote their own fairy tales based on a story map created by the whole class. Likewise, in a study conducted by Fitzgerald and Markham (1987), sixth-grade students were exposed to two revision interventions. Students in the "revision" group received direct instruction about how to make changes in their draft documents such as making additions, while the "control" group read literature such as an adaptation of O. Henry's "After Twenty Years" included in an anthology. Not surprisingly, students in the "revision" group made significantly more changes to their writing that positively affected the quality of their pieces.

Students in the "revision" group engaged with their writing from a problem-solving perspective. Working as writing detectives, these students read their writing, searching for instances of incongruence between their intended message and the actual message. Once identified, the students referred to a growing list of revision strategies, modeled by the classroom teacher, which might solve the writing problem and made appropriate changes. Thus, simply exposing students to exemplary texts does not mean that students will be able to transfer what they learn to their own writing. Students need explicit instruction from teachers, showing them how to incorporate what they learn from the reading of model texts to works of their own.

Writing experts have long encouraged teachers to explicitly make this connection between published models and students' writing (Atwell, 1987; Calkins, 1986; Smith, 1983). Harwayne (1992) recounts a discussion between a fourth-grade teacher and one of her students. As the teacher and her student, Mauricio, talk about a favorite author, Karla Kuskin, the teacher encourages him to notice the craft techniques that Kuskin uses (e.g., set in present time, many references to the sky, paring words). As a result, Mauricio not only envisions, but actually uses one of the techniques in his writing. However, Mauricio does not discuss why Kuskin might employ the techniques that he identified nor does he theorize appropriate instances to use the techniques in his own writing.

In fact, actually showing students how to incorporate a technique found in the works of a treasured author is a more recent phenomenon. Ray's (1999) *Wondrous Words* is primarily devoted to explaining how teachers can analyze craft with students and help them confidently transfer this knowledge to subsequent writing tasks. This transfer pays particular attention to how authors craft their texts and why a student may decide to include similar craft judgments. Toward this end, Ray advocates using the following model to support students as they analyze text and as they consider how to incorporate literary tricks in future writing tasks:

The Five Parts to Reading like a Writer
1. *Notice* something about the craft of the text.
2. *Talk* about it and *make a theory* about why a writer might use this craft.
3. Give the craft a *name*.
4. Think of *other texts* you know. Have you seen this craft before?
5. Try and *envision* using this craft in your own writing. (p. 120)

This model represents a significant shift from drowning students in a genre. Although students benefit from the exposure evident in the type of flooding technique conducted by Bearse (1992) and Fitzgerald and Markham (1987), they lack the explicit decision-making opportunities that Ray's (1999) framework provides. Following Ray's guidance, a student incorporates a popular phrase such as "melts in your mouth not in your hands" in a nonfiction piece describing the process for making chocolate. Having seen an author use a similar technique, and then envisioning how she might use it during her own writing process causes the student to make an informed decision. Intentionality is central to Ray's framework.

More recent studies documenting the strong connection between the texts students read and the written documents they produce give considerable credence to Ray's explicit instruction. In Corden's (2007) year-long study based in the United Kingdom, elementary teachers engaged students in a variety of interactions with mentor texts, including discussions of authors' writing strategies and teacher modeling of author-supported writing. Throughout the course of a year, teachers read aloud mentor texts, highlighting specific features the authors used. The teachers also showed students multiple ways to integrate the highlighted features in sample writing. In addition, students worked in small groups to discuss a variety of texts, and the teacher routinely joined their conversations. All of these strategies supported the students' ability to integrate what they learned from author mentors into their narrative writing. Predictably, the students made significant gains in the quality of their narrative writing samples. Corden's study exemplifies the need for students to assume the role of literary critics if they are going to analyze text as Ray (1999) advocates. Espinosa (2006) also argues that students need multiple opportunities to engage in critical analysis of written text. The bilingual students involved in her study used stories to identify the "seeds" for their own memoirs and as poignant examples of how authors captured small moments in meaningful ways. As these and other studies suggest, interacting with written text in a systematic and intentional manner sets in place a road map for young writers to follow (Urquhart & McIver, 2005).

Contexts for Explicit Engagement with Authorial Mentors

In what contexts does structured engagement with the idea of authors as mentors occur in K–12 classrooms? Although the answer to this question could be as various as the number of teachers in writing classrooms, the practice-oriented literature suggests some trends in recent approaches to the explicit link between published texts and student writing. For instance, genre study is evident in many K–12 schools. Through such structured investigations, students become familiar with the characteristics of different genres. Calkins (1994) describes genre study as an opportunity for students to "read and evaluate, muse over and analyze, learn from and model themselves after texts that are like those they will write" (p. 365). Although we make the argument that teachers should explicitly show students how to transfer the results of their analysis of text into writing selections, there is no substitute for exposing students to a plethora of examples illustrating possibilities for their own school-based writing. Selections might include phrases from a thought-provoking *New York Times* article or surprising character twists in a comic strip.

Teachers also are encouraged to point to the way pub-

lished authors employ language to convey meaning, share information, build characters, and paint rich descriptions. Building on Ray's (1999) example of how students can read like writers, Corden's (2007) study illustrates how students' command of language commandeered from authorial guides translated to powerful and poetic writing. Corden analyzes the difference between nine-year old Joel's beginning of school year writing and the product that he produced after 10 months of instruction. When the school year started, Joel's writing was characterized by little to no character development, a lack of suspense, and simple sentence structure. As the school year progressed, Joel's writing evidenced the depth of discussions and explicit instruction that characterized his writing classroom. Relying on works such as *One Stormy Night* (Brown, 1992) to build suspense and *The Butterfly Lion* (Murpurgo, 1996) to craft complex sentences, Joel effectively transitioned from lifeless writing the likes of "There was once a forest. There was lots of trees in and some animals," to "Late one night, the rain was pouring, the wooden gate opened furiously and the black cat purred" (p. 279).

Explicit instruction like the type that Joel experienced gives students the opportunity to see themselves as writers who have the tools and resources they need to move away from elementary and simplistic writing to the more imagistic and mature example that Joel exhibited. Implicit in this review of the role of literary mentors for student writing in schools is the degree to which "good writing" is the preferred model for students to emulate. It is clear that those texts deemed to be "quality" literature are the context through which students are explicitly shown how to use published literature to enhance their own writing. When teachers model analysis of text or reading text like a writer, the examples they select often represent tried and true literature. And while *Charlotte's Web* (White, 1952), *Where the Wild Things Are* (Sendak, 1963), and *The Moon* (Simon, 2003) may prove to be stellar examples by a variety of measures, these same texts may not have the same appeal for students. Indeed, young people's idea of "good writing" may include an exchange between the main characters in a Calvin and Hobbes comic strip, a plot idea from the virtual world of clubpenguin.com, or the predictable gender-based character roles evident in *The Princess Collection* from Disney (1999).

This discussion about explicitly teaching students how to rely on and use literary models throughout the writing process would be incomplete without addressing Lensmire's (2000) caution about such a direct approach to instruction. The opportunities for students' voices to be silenced abound. The proliferation of standards highlighting the genres that students should master by a given point in their academic careers, the narrow expectations for achievement on standardized tests and the literature choices deemed acceptable in classrooms like Joel's, Joseph's, and Richard's can render the voices of children and youth meaningless. However, we assert that providing students with the direct instruction suggested by Ray (1999) and evidenced by the students in Corden's (2007) study give voice to students. Indeed, as Joseph and Richard demonstrate, when students learn how to use the guidance that authorial mentors provide through the exemplary examples of an experienced other, they will rise to the occasion and assume the role of authors who want to write a more engaging story or help their poetry flow.

Educators can expose children to a variety of text, expanding their repertoire of writing possibilities and decision-making opportunities. However, it is possible that students' preferred texts will be overlooked. Toward this end, library and media specialists are in a unique position to bridge the potential gap between the texts that students admire and the examples that classroom teachers rely on to illustrate the panoply of literary devices and decisions that published authors use and make. In the end, educators strive to boost young writers, helping them see writing as a useful tool. Students can use writing to demonstrate compassion for another, to cause someone to reconsider a decision, or to illustrate deep understanding of a concept. To the extent that children can take ownership of their writing, shaping it in a manner that achieves their intended goals and meets the needs of their audience, they will view writing as a worthy endeavor and seek the models to support them along the way. Yet, direct instruction within school is but one context in which children and youth explicitly engage the reader-writer connection. In the next section, we address other instances of young writers drawing on authorial mentors.

Author Inspired Writing Outside of School

Although some teachers are beginning to harness the potential of the reading-writing relationship, children and youth have long drawn on favorite texts to inspire or prompt their own writing. We now turn to instances of how young writers have drawn on those reading-writing links outside of school. Children and youth engage in many unofficial writing practices beyond the hours of school (e.g., Hull & Schultz, 2002). Research has highlighted some of these practices, from keeping diaries to writing notes and emails to friends (e.g., Finders, 1997) to the textual work involved in the digital realms of blogging (Huffaker & Calvert, 2005) and personal networking sites such as My Space and Facebook (e.g., Lampe, Ellison & Steinfield, 2006). Our focus in this vast territory is on the writing practices that occur outside of the context of official school curriculum and that have an explicit connection to literature.

Within this focus, we concentrate on two primary areas in the research literature that provide useful insights. First, we examine youth poetry writing, both in written and spoken word forms. Our review of the research revealed several studies examining the experiences of youth writing and performing poetry, either individually or in organized programs. In both historical and contemporary accounts, published poetry, particularly socially engaged poems by authors of color, often served as models and inspiration for young writers. Second, we turn to the phenomenon of online fan fiction, a writing practice in which a clear link exists between published texts and young writers. Perhaps more than any other genre, fan fiction clearly showcases the reading-writing relationship as writers create new storylines that draw upon established characters and/or plots from a published source. Our discussion of these areas of research is not intended to be exhaustive, but rather to highlight some examples of how researchers in the disciplines of English, education, and cultural studies have engaged these writing practices in a few national contexts.

Poetry, Performance, and Socially Engaged Writing

The work of youth poets makes visible the links between literature and writing. We found examples of youth drawing on established poets as models for their own work in a range of research highlighting both traditional notions of the literary genre of poetry as well as programs that focused on the musical genre of hip-hop as a poetic form. (e.g., Fisher, 2005; Jocson, 2006b; Morrell & Andrade, 2002; Weiss & Herndon, 2001). Although this body of work addresses a range of literacy practices, in this section we showcase the research that explores the links—both contemporary and historical—between published poetry and the writing of urban youth.

Research emphasizes that youth engage in writing practices outside of school that are connected to their engagement with particular texts and genres. As Mahiri and Sablo (1996) found in their work with African American youth in urban communities, young people modeled their own poetry and rap lyrics on favorite writers and artists. The findings of these and other education scholars (e.g., Mahiri, 1998; Moje, 2000; Morrell, 2008) drawn from fieldwork with youth in the United States echoes the conclusions of researchers in English and cultural studies who have analyzed the textual productions of youth as both a contemporary and historical phenomenon (Dyson, 1997; Kitwana, 2003; Rose, 1994). This work traces contemporary youth cultural productions in various national contexts to literary traditions connected to social movements and cultural shifts, such as the Harlem Renaissance and the Civil Rights Movement in the United States (e.g., Chang, 2005), the Gay Liberation Front in England (Lent, 2001), and the rise of anime in an era of globalization in Japan (Yoda & Harootudian, 2006).

Writers and the texts they craft are always part of a legacy of life and language. Fisher (2004) captures this sense of literary inheritance in her exploration of the poetry and other genres produced by African Americans, including youth, in community venues such as Black bookstores and open-mic performance spaces. African American bookstore owners and operators purposefully nurtured relationships between established African American authors and members of the community who wished to share their experiences and ideas through their own writing. The purpose of the reading, writing, and performances fostered in these community spaces extended well beyond a desire to provide outlets for creative expression; such literary practices also functioned as political and social commentary and an important form of resistance to racial and socioeconomic oppression. As Fisher describes, "speaking was a natural outgrowth of reading and writing, but most important, all three were linked with a sense of purpose" (p. 292).

Such connections between published texts and amateur writers had important historical precedents and were often fostered by authors themselves. Of African American poet Elise Jordan and her contemporaries, Fisher writes that they understood "their place in a long line of literate and literary practices," an understanding "best summarized in one line [from one of Forman's poems]: 'we are new buds upon the highest branches'" (p. 291). Two well-known poets, Margaret Walker and Gwendolyn Brooks, cultivated writing and writers during the Civil Rights era. Brooks and Walker "would eventually be mentors in the Black Arts Movement that followed in the 1960s. Brooks, known for writing about the conditions of working-class Black Americans in Chicago, led writing workshops for poets and worked tirelessly with Black youth affiliated with gangs" (p. 296). Both the Black Arts Movement and the Harlem Renaissance that preceded it were dedicated to exploring African American experience through writing and other art forms and employing art to take social, political, and ideological stances against racism and other forms of oppression. Authors in these movements produced writing that became prominent mentor texts to the generations that followed.

In recent decades, the musical genres of rap and other forms of hip-hop have inspired some of the most socially and politically engaged writing among young artists of color. In the United States, researchers in several academic fields have focused on youth engagement with hip-hop. Cultural historians have linked the recent genres of rap and other forms of hip hop to their historical influences (e.g., Rose, 1994), while literary scholars have analyzed the social and political content and context of lyrics (Baker, 1987; Gates, 1998; Shusterman, 1991). Although the connections between the current authors of these cultural forms and the prior texts that paved their way are implicit in these analyses, they underscore the intertextual relations between production and consumption. As M. E. Dyson (1997) writes in an essay about rap music and African American youth culture, "Hip-hop still depends on existing black music even as it reshapes, often brilliantly, the groove it steals. Without its creative uses of past black music, rap would be a museum of speech with little to inspire us to conserve its words, much less heed its warnings and many lessons" (p. 122). As this passage emphasizes, new textual forms hearken back and pay homage in some way to those that precede them.

Some textual forms, however, are more valued than others in societies and their institutions. Such variance in the value placed on certain genres, forms, and content is one of the central concerns of education research examining the connections between the genres youth engage outside of school and school literacy practices. For instance, research points to out-of-school opportunities for youth to write from their experiences as providing important forums for young people to express and explore identities that are not always recognized, sanctioned, or safe to express in schools (e.g., Blackburn, 2005; Moje, 2000). However, a consistent finding in studies of the literacy practices of urban youth is that although youth use writing in their daily lives in powerful ways, their out-of-school writing is neither recognized nor valued in their school experiences (e.g., Mahiri, 1998; Morrell, 2008). Mahiri and Sablo (1996) argue that the provocative and engaged writing produced by youth provide opportunities to foster connections between students' lives and school literacies that are left largely untapped. In an attempt to actively engage those resources, Morrell and Andrade (2002) crafted a writing unit that used popular culture texts, such as rap and hip hop lyrics, as a bridge to literary analysis of more canonical literature and as model for literary elements that high school students could apply in their own writing. As they write, "Hip-hop texts are rich in imagery and metaphor and can be used to teach irony, tone, diction, and point of view. Also, Hip-hop texts can be analyzed for theme, motif, plot, and character development" (p. 89).

Public Enemy's "Don't Believe the Hype" is one example of a rap that Morrell and Andrade asked students to analyze in relation to the poem "Oh me! Oh life!" by Walt Whitman. Through literary analysis, students identified the connections between the lyrics of their favorite hip-hop artists and the poetry they commonly encountered in the school curriculum. In addition, they were encouraged to pay attention to how they applied literary elements in their own writing.

Other school and community-based programs have focused more explicitly on encouraging youth to write using established authors as models. For instance, Jocson (2006a) has addressed the changes in high school students' writing as a result of their participation in the program Poetry for the People (P4P). Founded by the late poet June Jordan and housed at the University of California Berkeley, P4P conducts poetry workshops in public schools, prisons, homeless shelters, and community centers. One of the program's central goals is to challenge "the so-called 'classics'" and emphasize the power of poetry to foster social transformation among oppressed groups whose voices have been excluded from the traditional literary canon" (Jocson, 2006a, p. 701). Although young people encounter canonical poets such as Walt Whitman, ee cummings, and Emily Dickenson through the high school curriculum, P4P's goal is to expose students to poets of color, such as Francisco Alarcón and Suheir Hammad, who may not appear on those official reading lists. Through its use of such published poets, as well as its emphasis on program participants serving as models for one another during its workshops, P4P explicitly engages connections between reading and writing. For instance, high school students were expected to write poems in response to topics that grew from their encounters with others' poetry. The students subsequently spoke in interviews about how those encounters impacted their writing (Jocson, 2006b). Damon, a 17-year-old biracial senior, wrote a poem called "Identity" in response to Ruth Forman's (1993) "Young Cornrows Calling Out the Moon" that explored his experiences as a Filipino/African American adolescent. Although Jocson's analysis is not focused on the specifics of Damon's use of Forman's poem, for our purposes we examined the two poems in relation to each other to better understand some of the specific ways that Damon drew on his mentor text (see Figure 7.1).

Examining excerpts from Forman's and Damon's poems in parallel reveal some of the ways that Damon drew inspiration from Forman for his own writing. His poem reflects Forman's in both content and form. For instance, he addresses the theme of racial identity and, even more specifically, the embrace of that identity as a source of pride and empowerment. In addition, the form and structure of his poem adhere quite closely to Forman's. He uses all lowercase, incorporates informal, vernacular language, and uses stanzas that hold together as sentences or related ideas, but do not include punctuation. Although the influence of Forman's poem is clear when placed beside Damon's, his use of those borrowed themes, form, and structure is original and creative. Damon's poem serves as a vivid example of how mentor texts can support young writers as they craft their own effective, personally meaningful work. Reflecting on his experience writing from mentor texts, Damon described his increased attention to revision in his writing, including attention to "better words" to express his ideas (p. 705).

Damon's engagement with Forman's work serves as a vivid illustration of one of the common themes in research on connections between poetic genres and the writing of urban youth: writing as a powerful tool for personal and social transformation. In both historical and contemporary examples, writing is introduced to youth as a mechanism for both self-expression and serving the larger goals of social justice. Although established authors provide models of a range of writing skills and purposes, they also demonstrate the importance of writing as a form of resistance and empowerment.

Fan Fiction: Devoted Readers as Writers

Fan Fiction represents another explicit manifestation of the link between reading and writing. The term "fan fiction," referring to unauthorized fiction written by fans of a particular text or genre that directly engages some aspect of the original text, appears to have arisen in the mid-1960s. However, writing by non-professional admirers of particular texts has been a recognized phenomenon for much of the last century and, some argue, has historical roots that extend as far back as the 17th century where unauthorized versions of texts such as *Don Quixote* are known to have existed. In recent years, fan fiction has been the focus of burgeoning interest among researchers in English, education, and library science. As one might expect, library science research has focused primarily on the literary-inspired aspects of fan fiction (e.g., Collins, 2006). On the other hand, researchers in both education and English have focused on a wider range of texts engaged by fan fiction writers, including movies, television, anime, and music in addition to novels (e.g., Hellekson & Busse, 2006; Pugh, 2005). Given the primarily literary focus of this volume, we have chosen to focus the bulk of our discussion on fan fiction inspired by written texts.

Forman's "Young Cornrows Calling Out the Moon"	Damon's "Identity"
1 we don have no backyard frontyard neither we go black magic and brownstone steps when the sun go down	1 half and half since the start of my path mixed wit the best of both worlds genetics turned my naps into curls
22 we got pretty lips we go callous feet healthy thighs n ashy knees we got fiiin brothas n we r fiiine sistas n we got attitude	10 i look deeper than the surface because i was not put on this earth to harm one soul i have no problems cause i was
31 so you know we don really want no backyard frontyard neither cuz we got to call out the moon wit black magic n brownstone steps	15 put here to contribute slice through edge of happiness and i ain't close to done

Figure 7.1

Fan fiction, as it exists today, emerged in the 1960s through the writing of fans of the television show *Star Trek.* Fans published fiction (called "fics" by those in the fan fiction community) based on the series in small-circulation fanzines, the first of which was *Spockanalia,* published in 1967. The practice of fan fiction grew through the 1970s and 1980s, particularly around other science fiction television shows and movies, such as *Man from U.N.C.L.E.* and *Star Wars* (Jenkins, 1992). Although fan fiction appears to have its roots in the United States, the practice is now a worldwide phenomenon. Japan, for example, has a thriving fan fiction community, including fans of manga. A distinctive style of comic that began in Japan, manga is now a common inspiration for fan fiction in the United States and other countries as well. Given variations in copyright law internationally, fan fiction takes different forms across national contexts. For instance, relatively lax copyright laws in Russia have meant that fan fiction authors can publish their work in book form, a practice that would be subject to legal action in the United States or England. Although Japan has stricter copyright laws, authors and publishers tend to look the other way when fans publish manga fan fiction, as fan writing can serve as effective advertising for established authors' work.

As might be expected, the dawn of the Internet transformed the practice of fan fiction. Whereas the authors of fan fics previously had to rely on ground mail to share their work or submit their writing to the few magazines devoted to fan fiction, writers can now instantly upload their pieces to one of many websites devoted to fan fiction. As Kustritz (2003) explains,

> By the mid-1990s, all types of fan writing had become, primarily but not exclusively, an Internet phenomenon.... Accessibility, combined with much lower costs (the cost of an internet connection versus the cost of printing and binding), made fan fiction reading a much more desirable activity for a much larger audience than it had been in previous years. (p. 372)

The community created by online fan fiction sites is an important part of the writing experience. Although they vary in their foci—with some including fan fiction across a range of texts and genres, while others focus on one author's work—the websites support interactions among authors, including discussion forums on a range of writing-related topics, opportunities to respond to others' writing, and space to share artwork related to the texts or genres. Some sites are international gathering spaces for fan writing, while others—due to common language, if nothing else—are created by and for fan fiction authors in particular countries. As Thomas (2006) emphasizes, "The online spaces devoted to fan fiction provide more than spaces for writing; they provide a supportive community for many young people" (p. 235).

Children's and young adult literature is highly visible on websites devoted to fan fiction. For instance, on the website fanfiction.net fans have built on the work of fa-vorite authors, such as C.S. Lewis's *Chronicles of Narnia,* Eoin Colfer's *Artemis Fowl,* Christopher Paolini's *Eragon,* Natalie Babbit's *Tuck Everlasting,* Ann Brashares's *Sisterhood of the Traveling Pants* and Stephanie Meyer's *Twilight* series. Fans also write in response to popular book series, including *A Series of Unfortunate Events,* *Animorphs,* *Gossip Girl,* and *The Jedi Apprentice.* However, J.K. Rowling's *Harry Potter* series has dominated young adult fan fiction in recent years. On fanfiction. net, the numbers of fan fics listed after each author and title speak to the prolific writing of Rowling's fans. For instance, as we write this, Colfer's popular *Artemis Fowl* series has 3,282 fan fics on the site and Meyer's *Twilight* books, a recent publishing phenomenon, boasts 55,322 fics. In contrast, *Harry Potter* has inspired 384,962. Given such numbers, it is no wonder that fan fiction devotees have launched thriving websites devoted exclusively to Rowling's books.

As the practice of fan fiction grows, scholars across disciplines explore this literary phenomenon and its implications. For instance, Jenkins (1992) argues that fan fiction functions similarly to traditions of oral storytelling, in which tales are passed through communities and down through generations, with each teller leaving her or his particular stamp on the story. Jenkins and others (e.g., Hellekson & Busse, 2006; Pugh, 2005) view fan fiction as a democratizing force within the profit-driven and often elitist world of literary publishing. Other scholars have engaged fan fiction as an emerging genre that uniquely combines features of traditional genres, such as the novel or short story, with features only available through new media (e.g., Jenkins, 2006; Stein, 2006). In addition, researchers in English and cultural studies have examined fan fiction as a space in which new associations between reading and writing are on display. For instance, Karpovitch (2006) describes the role of "beta readers"—readers who read, critique, and edit others' fan fics—in fan fiction communities. Finally, much research highlights the role of social identities, particularly gender and sexuality, in fan fiction (e.g., Bury, 2005; Lackner, Lucas, & Reid, 2006; Mazzarella, 2005).

In the field of education, some researchers have focused on the potential of fan fiction to support academic writing skills. For instance, Chandler-Olcott and Mahar (2003) discuss fan fiction as an opportunity for language arts teachers to "help students become more metacognitive about their compositions" (p. 564). In other words, the very self-conscious engagement with elements of favorite texts (e.g., character development, plot, setting) that is inherent in fan fiction may be instructive for other forms of composition. In another example of education-focused research, Thomas (2006) examines the fan fiction practices of one online community made up primarily of youth ages 13–17. The site was started by two girls in their early teens who wanted to create an alternative to the large fan-fiction sites that would allow them to focus on pairing two particular iconic texts—*Lord of the Rings* and *Star Wars*—and to engage more easily in collaborative writing. The girls Thomas interviewed believe that the collaborations they developed through their fan fiction greatly benefited their writing in ways that were tangible in their writing efforts in school. In addition, Black (2005) has argued that online fan fiction provides opportunities for young English language learners to receive valuable feedback on their English writing within a supportive community of fellow writers.

One of the reasons some scholars have cited for the appeal of fan fiction is that it allows readers to indefinitely extend their interactions with a beloved text (Harris & Alexander, 1998). Harry Potter fan fiction is a good example of this point. Although fans certainly mourned the end of the series following the publication of J.K. Rowling's seventh and final book, the fan fiction sites kept the story very much alive. Some authors write new plots into the time periods covered in Rowling's novels, as the fan fic author ObsidianEmbrace did through an elaborate subplot involving a murder mystery during the year depicted in *The Goblet of Fire* (2003). Other authors extend the books beyond the end of the series, writing new novels with Harry's children as protagonists.

However, fan fiction, at one and the same time, functions as both homage to favorite literary texts and critique of those texts. As research has emphasized, fan fiction authors are emotionally invested in the texts that inspire their writing (Jenkins, 1992). It is, indeed, that investment that fuels a desire by some young writers to recreate the original fictional world in ways that better reflect the lived realities and identities of a wide range of readers. As Thomas (2006) writes, "One of the features of most fan fiction is that fans of the text can take it and write in characters and plots that are relevant to their own identities and lives, giving them a voice in a text in which they might otherwise be marginalized" (p. 234).

In our view, perhaps the most important function of fan fiction for young writers is the opportunity for critical appropriation and transformation of favorite stories. Although little information is available about fan fiction authors' class status or racial identities (we could not find any large-scale surveys), scholars appear to concur that in the United States the vast majority are middle class and White, although some research focuses on Asian American youth actively engaging in fan fiction (e.g., Black, 2005). Anecdotally, we found that several fan fics that placed Anglo Asian characters from Harry Potter at the center of stories were authored by Asian Americans (however, this is based purely on authors' first and/or last names, a method of identification that is very limited due to the widespread use of pen names). Such moves to turn Cho Chang or the Patel twins into protagonists in the novels' plots serve as examples of fan fiction as a location of resistance to marginalization. Fan fiction offers the opportunity for writers to create stories that break with normative traditions,

even as they begin with affectionate relationships with established texts that reinforce those norms.

The importance of fan fiction as site of resistance has been cited by law scholars who argue that the creation of alternative versions of copyrighted texts should be allowed under "fair use." They base their arguments, in part, on the importance of opportunities for fans to recast their favorite stories in ways that challenge some of the exclusionary or stereotyped storylines or character portrayals. For instance, fans can place minor characters, those characters more likely to be female or non-White, at the center of stories or write into existence romantic relationships between same-sex couples or characters of different races that are absent in the original text. As law scholars Chander and Sunder (2007) write, "Theorists, both traditional and postmodern, affirm the discursive nature of creativity: all creators borrow from earlier masters. But contemporary cultural theorists recognize as an important discursive tactic the reworking of a *discriminatory* narrative to retell history and empower oneself" (p. 601).

One important way in which fan fiction writers re-vision their favorite texts is through the romantic storylines they create for characters. In a conversation with two 13-year-old writers of fan fiction, we were struck by how often the term "ships" arose in their talk. These were clearly not sea-going vessels the girls referred to, and these "ships" sparked heated debate and regular bursts of giggles. As the girls explained, "ship" is short for "relationship" and is a central focus of the online Harry Potter fan fiction community in which they were involved. Ships in Harry Potter fan fiction run the gamut from same-age, heterosexual pairings that challenge expectations based on the character relationships established in the books—such as imagining a romantic relationship between sworn enemies Hermione Granger and Draco Malfoy—to transgressive adult/minor pairings—between, for instance, the teacher Severus Snape and student Ginny Weasley. The centrality of ships in the writing and discussions of fan fiction communities makes sense given both the importance of romantic relationships to the plots of many of the popular narratives that serve as source texts and, simply, to the engaging and titillating nature of crafting such relationships. However, ships can also be viewed as key sites of resistance to the norms of gender, race, and sexuality that are embedded in many of the texts that serve as sources of fan fiction (Willis, 2006).

This leads us to one common category of ships in fan fiction and our focus for the remainder of this section: slash fiction. "Slash" refers to fan fiction in which a writer places two characters of the same gender into romantic relationships with each other. As Kustritz (2003) writes, "slash offers its own particular challenge to normative constructions of gender and romance" (p. 371). Slash fan fiction first emerged in writing by fans of the television series *Star Trek* in the 1960s. Slash fictions wove tales of romance between Captain Kirk and Doctor Spock. As

Kustritz explains, the term slash "comes from the '/' mark placed between the names Kirk and Spock at the beginning of a story to tell readers that it contained a romantic, sexual relationship between the two characters" (p. 372). The term is now common parlance across fan fiction communities and, although heterosexual ships predominate in most online fan fiction sites, slash stories are highly visible and easy to locate.

Because Harry Potter is by far the most prominent example of young adult literature that has inspired fan fiction, we turned to a popular Harry Potter fan fiction community for our specific examples of fan fiction generally and slash fan fiction specifically. FictionAlley.com is a large and well-established site for fan fiction, art, and discussion centered on the Harry Potter series. Although survey research has revealed that the majority of slash fan fiction is generated by heterosexual, White, middle-class adult women (Kustritz, 2003), the popularity of the Harry Potter series among children and adolescents indicates that a site such as FictionAlley includes a large number of fan fics authored by younger writers (though, still likely predominantly White and middle class). FictionAlley authors publish their fan fics according to genre/form: novel-length, romance, humor, or mystery/drama. Within those forms, FictionAlley also requires fan fiction writers to indicate features of their published stories, including rating (using standard movie ratings—PG, PG-13, etc.), spoilers (indicating which plot lines are revealed from across the seven Harry Potter books), genre (e.g., action/adventure), main characters, ships, and era (i.e., the years Harry attended Hogwarts or when his parents James and Lily were adolescents, etc.).

If a fic is "slash," the author indicates that under "ships" or, in some cases, includes that information in an "Author's Note" that precedes the story. In our relatively brief foray into FictionAlley, we found that many, but by no means all, authors of slash fiction did include author's notes that describe the romantic pairings in their fic. For instance, one author introduces her/his fic with: "written for the sirry slash Cookie Jar prompt number 14: Leather trousers. Dursleys. And. Um. This is my first Sirry. I really hope you like it, and please be gentle. Or give useful concrit, cause that's good, too." In addition to serving as an example of how authors introduce slash fiction, this note also illustrates some of the terms and language used within the fan fiction community. For instance, "Sirry" refers to a fic focused on a romantic relationship between Harry and Sirius. The "Cookie Jar prompt" refers to a discussion board on FictionAlley where writers can post previews or teasers for their forthcoming fics. This author's reference to "useful concrit" indicates the expectation that readers will respond to the fic with constructive criticism, a common and expected practice within fan fiction communities.

The slash fiction ratings on FictionAlley range from G to R (other sites include the NC-17 rating), with many falling into the PG and PG-13 categories. The stories are sometimes centered on romance, whereas others locate the slash relationships in the background. One PG-13 rated Harry/Ron slash story begins: "Harry Potter kissed four Weasleys before he got to kiss the one he had wanted all along" and centers on the developing romance between the two young men. The slash pairings on FictionAlley include almost any combination of characters one might imagine. Although most slash fiction seems to focus on relationships between male characters, some female pairings appear as well, such as Hermione/Ginny and Ginny/Cho Chang. Although the role and enactments of sexuality vary, all slash fiction challenges the heteronormativity of the original books.

The propensity for some readers outside of the fan fiction community to interpret slash fiction as transgressive is illustrated by an article by Collins (2006), a librarian who writes about a survey she conducted of 30 fan fiction authors who wrote from literary texts, primarily *Lord of the Rings* and *Harry Potter*. She writes that when asked about the features they found appealing in fan fiction, the most common responses included engaging plots, believable characters, vivid description, realistic dialogue, action and adventure, romance, and humor. Collins writes that fan fiction readers also cited as important writing style, pacing, setting, faithfulness to the original work, length and "oddly enough, homosexuality (or "slash" as it is referred to by writers of fan fiction)" (p. 38).

Unlike Collins, we do not find it at all "odd" that those involved in fan fiction cite "slash" relationships as an important and desirable feature of this genre. Slash fiction represents a particularly pointed rejection of the gender and sexual norms embedded in many mainstream texts and, along with the broader genre of fan fiction, serves as a powerful example of a critical, resistant relationship between reading and writing. Reader-authors poach from well-known texts in ways that subvert the characterizations or social norms such texts may reinforce, crafting an alternative, more inclusive fictional world.

Discussion and Conclusions

In this chapter we have attempted to explore a relationship that is intimate, but often intangible. Indeed, reading and writing are intricately woven processes, a fact not lost on any writer who has heard the influential whispers of the writers and writings she encountered as a reader urging her toward her own voice and purpose. Teasing out the many and varied ways that reading begets writing begets reading (and on and on) is neither possible nor necessary. In this final section, we consider some of the implications of those links for both research and practice.

Literature as "Model" and the Idea of Intertexuality
Those concerned with literature and its connection to writing in the lives of children and youth need to recognize

both how reading/writing connections can be explicitly fostered and how those connections are always and already inextricably linked. Taken together, these aspects of the reader-author relationship provide insight and opportunity for research and practice. The explicit use of literature as *model* for writing makes the interconnections of reading and writing visible, offering young writers insight into how the individual elements of the writing process add up to what can too often appear to be a mysteriously crafted whole. As emphasized in the scholarship on classroom practice, arbitrarily separating reading and writing through curriculum and instruction signals a misunderstanding of the critical connections that students should and do make as they engage in literacy processes.

Literature as Inspiration, Writing as Transformation, and the Idea of Critical Engagement

Although the notion of intertextuality supports the recent move in educational practice toward the explicit use of literature as models of various aspects of effective writing, it also points to the importance of providing children and youth with the freedom to build from and transform existing texts in ways that make sense to them. Viewed through the critical lenses we employ in this chapter, literature becomes far more than a model of skills, genre, and literary conventions for young writers. Rather, published texts serve as inspiration for expressions of identity, resistance to oppression, and movements toward social transformation. Literature also serves as a landscape of possibility for young authors who can reshape existing texts to reflect perspectives, experiences, or simply imaginative territories that are different from the original source.

As our review makes clear, children and youth are far from dependent on adults when it comes to bringing a critical eye to the texts they engage. Thus the disciplines of education, English, and library science can learn much from closer attention to the connections between children's and young adult literature and writing within and outside of formal educational settings. For instance, for education scholars to more fully examine the reading/writing relationship, the work must move beyond attention to function and include analysis of the literature itself. Such close readings would provide more intricate understandings of how young writers employ particular language and features of published literature in their own writing and, thus, lead to more specific implications for instruction. Conversely, scholarship in English could move beyond the text and consider how narrative structures, character development, and other features of literary genres function in the work of developing writers. Given the centrality of writing in university-level literature courses, young writers would almost certainly be well-served by increased attention to how the literature students read impacts what and how they write. In addition, research in English could employ methods common to Education and LIS that examine how young people use literary engagement in

expressions of identity, resistance, and social activism. In turn, if librarians had increased access to information about the function and potential of literary borrowing for young writers, they would be better equipped to guide children and youth to the literary mentors that will most inspire and nurture them as writers (the website of the National Writing Project, http://www.nwp.org/, is one important resource to which librarians might turn).

We posit that one of the most powerful ideas embedded in the research and practices we discuss in this chapter, and one that demands attention across disciplines, involves young writers re-working existing texts to include additional voices and perspectives. The writing of youth in urban poetry projects and that of writers in online fan fiction communities raise related, but somewhat different issues surrounding literature and young writers. In both contexts, writers pay homage to beloved texts, while also transforming them in their own image. In urban poetry projects, young writers build on mentor authors to insert their own voices in efforts to reveal and address social inequities. Fan fiction also often addresses absences and silences, but does so through transforming the original text. Although the foundational texts that inspire fan fiction do not necessarily serve as examples of critical writing, they serve as the launch for critical re-workings of text. As educators and librarians continue efforts to expand diversity in the books that children encounter in schools and libraries, we are struck by the equally important task of fostering critical tools that support children and youth in seeing and responding to the absences in literature.

The task for educators, librarians, and researchers, then, is twofold: children and youth should be encouraged to "poach" from the literature with which they engage in imaginative and generative ways; in turn, researchers across fields should recognize and learn from the creative poaching that is always and already practiced in children's and youth's writing. The contexts of school curricula, socially engaged writing, and fan fiction point to the kinds of inquiries researchers might pursue. What does close textual analysis reveal about how children and young adult literature influences youth writing and, thus, aspects of youth culture? What are the constraints and affordances of attempting to transfer particular relationships between reading and writing to classroom or library settings? How might educators and librarians positively foster and build on the inherent engagement and motivation of such reading-writing relationships?

Equity and Access in the Visible Links between Literature and Writing

As we write about youth's engagements with urban poetry projects and online fan fiction, we are very much aware of the different populations of youth on which the research focuses in these two areas. Studies of youth and poetry writing and performance often focus on the experiences of youth of color in urban settings. In contrast, research on fan fiction tends to focus on suburban, White, and sometimes Asian American youth. In general, the research on youth poetry includes more working-class teens or those from high-poverty neighborhoods, whereas the focus in online writing practices tends to be on middle- and upper-middle-class youth. As we have shown, both contexts afford stances toward literature that foster critically engaged writing. However, as new technologies gain increasing cache across the fields of education, English, and library and information studies, we worry that already entrenched class and racial disparities will become even more ingrained in both research and practice (Warschauer, 2004). Indeed, research on equity and technology suggests that not only would it be more difficult for some youth to acquire the tools that allow a high level of immersion in online communities, but that some online practices may be exclusionary in subtle ways that have nothing to do with access to the internet (e.g., Warschauer, Knobel, & Stone, 2004). We do not presume that rich online writing practices are absent in the lives of youth of color and those from less privileged socioeconomic circumstances; however, those practices are not as visible in the existing research. When such opportunities *are* described in research, the youth are often supported by extraordinarily technology-rich schools (e.g., Jocson, 2006b).

To be sure, the issue of access is complex and extends beyond the availability of technology (and updated hardware). For instance, McCarthey's (2008) research suggests that the increased focus on testing in the wake of No Child Left Behind has led some schools to jettison writing in favor of instruction in math and reading, the subjects on which a school's achievements are most often based. She found that this trend has impacted low-income schools the most, often resulting in the mandated use of pre-packaged curricula that emphasizes tested skills at the expense of rich engagement with literature and writing. Indeed, in our experiences teaching and observing in schools, a skills-based approach to literature emphasizes *naming* literary elements such as metaphor, rather than engaging with rich metaphors and having opportunities to employ them in one's own writing. Thus, the issue of equity includes access to quality reading and writing materials within and outside of schools, as well as knowledge of the variety of literacy communities available, subtle ways in which communities exclude and include potential participants, and exposure to the modes of communication necessary to engage with desired literacy communities. Although we do not contend that the presence of disparities should foreclose research into the technology-dependent literacies in which economically privileged youth engage, we do argue that the complexities surrounding issues of access and equity should be more often considered in this body of research.

Although a vast research literature exists on fostering a range of writing practices for children and youth, scholarship that specifically examines the connections between published literature and the writing of children and youth is much more limited. Although the idea of literature as mentor texts for young writers has gained momentum in recent years, the focus of the reading-writing connection has been primarily on the modeling of form and conventions. Our approach to this topic revealed that published texts do provide mentoring that extends far beyond skills, conventions, literary devices, voice, or genre, and such mentoring could be made much more explicitly available to children and youth. Provided with access to literature, the freedom and time to engage with favorite authors and, crucially, supportive communities of fellow readers/writers, young authors seize the opportunities literature provides to engage in critical dialogue with their mentors, appropriating, reforming and reshaping the texts they have encountered as readers. Like Jo March, young writers can write their paeans to their favorite authors and genres, seeing visions of their authorial selves reflected in the pages of published literature. And, like Jo, their writing can push back on those literary worlds, crafting stories that better reflect their own identities, social realities, imaginations, desires, and visions for a more just society. But always, as they write, the traces of all they have read are present in every keystroke, in each scratch of the pen.

Literature References

Alcott, L. M. (2004). *Little women.* New York, NY: Signet Classics.

Brown, R. (1992). *One stormy night.* London: Anderson Press.

Disney's princess collection: Love and friendship stories. (1999). New York, NY: Disney Press.

Forman, R. (1993). *We are the young magicians.* Boston, MA: Beacon Press.

Murpurgo, M. (1996). *The butterfly lion.* London: Collins Children's Books.

Rowling, J. K. (2003). *Harry Potter and the goblet of fire.* New York, NY: Scholastic.

Sendak, M. (1963). *Where the wild things are.* New York, NY: HarperCollins.

White, E. B. (1952). *Charlotte's web.* New York, NY: Harper and Row.

Woodson, J. (2001). *The other side.* New York, NY: Putnam.

Yep, L. (1977). *Dragonwings.* New York, NY: Harper Collins.

Academic References

Atwell, N. (1987). *In the middle.* Portsmouth, NH: Boynton/Cook.

Baker, H. (1987). *Blues, ideology, and Afro-American literature: A vernacular theory.* Chicago, IL: University of Chicago Press.

Bakhtin, M. M. (1981). The dialogic imagination: Four essays (M. Holquist, Ed.; C. Emerson & M. Holquist, Trans.). Austin, TX: University of Texas Press.

Bearse, C. I. (1992). The fairy tale connection in children's stories: Cinderella meets Sleeping Beauty. *The Reading Teacher, 45*(9), 688–695.

Bishop, R. S. (2007). *Free within ourselves: The development of African American children's literature.* Portsmouth, NH: Heinemann.

Black, R. (2005). Access and affiliation: The literacy and

composition practices of English language learners in an online fan-fiction community. *Journal of Adolescent and Adult Literacy, 49*(2), 118–128.

Blackburn, M. (2005). Disrupting dichotomies for social change: A review of, critique of, and complement to current educational literacy scholarship on gender. *Research in the Teaching of English, 39*(4), 398–416.

Bury, R. (2005). *Cyberspaces of their own: Female fandoms online.* New York, NY: Peter Lang.

Calkins, L. (1986/1994). *The art of teaching writing.* Portsmouth, NH: Heinemann.

Chander, A., & Sunder, M. (2007). The romance of the public domain. *California Law Review, 95*, 597.

Chandler-Olcott, K., & Mahar, D. (2003). Adolescents' anime-inspired "fanfictions": An exploration of multiliteracies. *Journal of Adolescent & Adult Literacy, 46*, 556–566.

Chang, J. (2005). *Can't stop won't stop: A history of the hip-hop generation.* New York, NY: Picador.

Collins, T. (2006, January). Filling the gaps: What's happening in the world of fan fiction. *Library Media Connection, 24*, 36–38.

Corden, R. (2007). Developing reading-writing connections: The impact of explicit instruction of literary devices on the quality of children's narrative writing. *Journal of Research in Childhood Education, 21*(3), 269–289.

Dillard, A. (1989). *The writing life.* New York, NY: HarperPerennial.

Dyson, A. H. (1997). *Writing superheroes: Contemporary childhood, popular culture, and classroom literacy.* New York, NY: Teachers College Press.

Dyson, M. E. (1997). *Race rules: Navigating the color line.* New York, NY: Vintage.

Emig, J. (1971). *The composing process of twelfth graders (Research Report No. 13).* Urbana, IL: National Council of Teachers of English.

Espinosa, C. M. (2006). Finding memorable moments: Images and identities in autobiographical writing. *Language Arts, 84*(2), 136–144.

Finders, M. (1997). *Just girls: Hidden literacies and life in junior high.* New York, NY: Teachers College Press.

Fish, S. (1980). *Is there a text in this class? The authority of interpretive communities.* Cambridge, MA: Harvard University Press.

Fisher, M. T. (2004). "The song is unfinished": The new literate and literary and their institutions. *Written Communication, 21*(3), 290–312.

Fisher, M. T. (2005). From the coffee house to the school house: The promise and potential of spoken word poetry in school contexts. *English Education, 37*(2), 115–131.

Fitzgerald, J., & Markham, L. R. (1987). Teaching children about revision in writing. *Cognition and Instruction, 4*(1), 3–24.

Foucault, M. (1990). *The history of sexuality, Volume 1.* New York, NY: Vintage.

Foucault, M. (1995). *Discipline and punish.* Toronto: Random House of Canada.

Foucault, M., & Gordon, C. (1980). *Power/knowledge: Selected interviews and other writings, 1972–1997.* New York, NY: Pantheon.

Gates, H. L. (1992). *Loose canons: Notes on the culture wars.* Oxford, UK: Oxford University Press.

Gates, H. L. (1998). *Signifying monkey: A theory of Afro-American literary criticism.* Oxford, UK: Oxford University Press.

Graves, D. (1983). *Writing: Teachers & children at work.* Portsmouth, NH: Heinemann.

Hansen, J. (2001). *When writers read.* Portsmouth, NH: Heinemann.

Harris, C., & Alexander, A. (1998). *Theorizing fandom: Fans, subculture, and identity.* Cresskill, NJ: Hampton Press.

Harwayne, S. (1992). *Lasting impressions: Weaving literature into the writing workshop.* Portsmouth, NH: Heinemann.

Hayes, J., & Flower, L. (1980). Identifying the organization of writing processes. In L. Gregg & E. Steinberg (Eds.), *Cognitive processes in writing* (pp. 3–30). Hillsdale NJ: Erlbaum.

Hellekson, K., & Busse K. (Eds.). (2006). *Fan fiction and fan communities in the age of the internet: New essays.* Jefferson, NC: McFarland & Co.

Hillegass, M. M. (2005). Early childhood author studies. *School Talk, 10*(4), 4–5.

Huffaker, D. A., & Calvert, S. L. (2005). Gender, identity, and language use in teenage blogs. *Journal of Computer-Mediated Communication, 10*(2), article 1.

Hull, G., & Schultz, K. (Eds.). (2002). *School's out!: Bridging out-of-school literacies with classroom practice.* New York, NY: Teachers College Press.

Iser, W. (1989). *Prospecting: From reader response to literary anthropology.* Baltimore, MD: Johns Hopkins University Press.

Jenkins, H. (1992). *Textual poachers: Television fans and participatory culture.* New York, NY: Routledge.

Jenkins, H. (2006). *Fans, bloggers, and gamers: Media consumers in a digital age.* New York, NY: New York University Press.

Jocson, K. M. (2006a). "Bob Dylan and Hip Hop": Intersecting literacy practices in youth poetry communities. *Written Communication, 23*(3), 231–259.

Jocson, K. M. (2006b). "There's a better word": Urban youth re-writing their social worlds through poetry. *Journal of Adolescent and Adult Literacy, 49*(8), 700–707.

Karpovich, A. (2006). The audience as editor: The role of beta readers in online fan fiction communities. In K. Hellekson & K. Busse (Eds.), *Fan fiction and fan communities in the age of the internet: New essays* (pp. 171–188). Jefferson, NC: McFarland & Co.

King, S. (2002). *On writing: A memoir of the craft.* New York, NY: Pocket.

Kitwana, B. (2003). *The Hip Hop generation: Young blacks and the crisis in African American culture.* New York, NY: Basic Civitas Books.

Kustritz, A. (2003). Slashing the romance narrative. *Journal of American Culture, 26*, 371–384.

Lackner, E., Lucas, B. L., & Reid, R. A. (2006). Cunning linguists: The bisexual erotics of words/silence/flesh. In K. Hellekson & K. Busse (Eds.), *Fan fiction and fan communities in the age of the internet: New essays* (pp. 189–206). Jefferson, NC: McFarland & Co.

Lamb, B. (1997). *Book notes: America's finest authors on reading, writing, and the power of ideas.* New York, NY: Times Books.

Lampe, C., Ellison, N., & Steinfield, C. (2006). A face(book) in the crowd: Social searching vs. social browsing. *Proceedings of the 2006 20th anniversary conference on computer supported cooperative work* (pp. 167–170). Alberta Canada: AMC.

Lancia, P. J. (1997). Literary borrowing: The effects of literature on children's writing. *The Reading Teacher, 50*(6), 470–475.

Lensmire, T. J. (2000). *Powerful writing, responsible teaching.* New York, NY: Teachers College Press.

Lent, A. (2001). *British social movements since 1945: Sex, colour, peace and power.* New York, NY: MacMillan.

Lindemann, E. (1995). *A rhetoric for writing teachers* (3rd ed.). New York, NY: Oxford University Press.

Luke, A. (1995/1996). Text and discourse in education: An introduction to critical discourse analysis. *Review of Research in Education, 21*, 3–48.

Mahiri, J. (1998). *Shooting for excellence: African American youth culture in new century schools.* New York, NY: Teachers College Press.

Mahiri, J., & Sablo, S. (1996). Writing for their lives: The non-school literacy of California's urban African American youth. *Journal of Negro Education, 65*(2), 164–180.

Mazzarella, S. R. (2005). (Ed.). *Girl wide web: Girls, the internet, and the negotiation of identity.* New York, NY: Peter Lang.

McCarthey, S. J. (2008). The impact of No Child Left Behind on teachers' writing instruction. *Written Communication, 25,* 462–505.

McIver, M. C., & Wolf, S. A. (1999). The power of the conference is the power of suggestion. *Language Arts, 77*(1), 54–61.

Moje, E. (2000). "To be part of the story": The literacy practices of gansta adolescents. *Teachers College Record, 102,* 659-690.

Morrell, E. (2008). *Critical literacy and urban youth: Pedagogies of access, dissent, and liberation.* New York, NY: Routledge.

Morrell, E., & Andrade, D. (2002). Encouraging academic literacy with urban youth through engaging hip-hop culture. *English Journal, 91*(6), 88–92.

Murray, D. M. (1985). *A writer teaches writing* (2nd ed.). Boston, MA: Houghton Mifflin.

Pugh, S. (2005). *The democratic genre: Fan fiction in a literary context.* Bridgend, Wales: Seren.

Ray, K. W. (1999). *Wondrous words: Writers and writing in the elementary classroom.* Urbana, IL: National Council of Teachers of English.

Rose, T. (1994). *Black noise: Rap music and black culture in contemporary America.* Middletown, CT: Wesleyan University Press.

Rosenblatt, L. M. (1994). *The reader, the text, the poem: The transactional theory of the literary work.* Carbondale, IL: Southern Illinois University Press.

Rosenblatt, L. M. (1995). *Literature as exploration* (5th ed.). New York: The Modern Language Association of America.

Showalter, E. (Ed.). (1985). *Feminist criticism: Essays on women, literature, and theory.* New York, NY: Pantheon Books.

Shusterman, R. (1991). The fine art of rap. *New Literary History, 22*(3), 613–632.

Smith, F. (1983). Reading like a writer. *Language Arts, 60*(5), 558–567.

Smith, M. A. (1996). The national writing project after 22 years. *Phi Delta Kappan, 77,* 688–692.

Stein, L. E. (2006). "This dratted thing": Fannish storytelling through new media. In K. Hellekson & K. Busse (Eds.), *Fan fiction and fan communities in the age of the internet: New essays* (pp. 245–260). Jefferson, NC: McFarland & Co.

Thomas, A. (2006). Fan fiction online: Engagement, critical response and affective play through writing. *Australian Journal of Language and Literacy, 29*(3), 226–239.

Urquhart, V., & McIver, M. (2005). *Teaching writing in the content areas.* Alexandria, VA: Association for Supervision and Curriculum Development.

Warschauer, M. (2004). *Technology and social inclusion: Rethinking the digital divide.* Cambridge, MA: MIT Press.

Warschauer, M., Knobel, M., & Stone, L. (2004). Technology and equity in schooling: Deconstructing the digital divide. *Educational Policy, 18,* 562–588.

Weiss, J., & Herndon, S. (2001). *The youth speaks guide to teaching spoken word poetry.* Portsmouth, NH: Heinemann.

Willis, I. (2006). Keeping promises to queer children: Making space (for Mary Sue) at Hogwarts. In K. Hellekson & K. Busse (Eds.), *Fan fiction and fan communities in the age of the internet: New essays* (pp. 153–170). Jefferson, North Carolina: McFarland & Co.

Wolf, S. A. (2004). *Interpreting literature with children.* Mahwah, NJ: Erlbaum.

Wolf, S. A., & Heath, S. B. (1992). *The braid of literature: Children's world of reading.* Cambridge, MA: Harvard University Press.

Wolf, S. A., & Heath, S. B. (1993). The net of story. *The Horn Book Magazine, 69*(6), 705–713.

Yoda, T., & Harootudian, H. (2006). *Japan after Japan: Social and cultural life from the recessionary 1990s to the present.* Durham, NC: Duke University Press.

8

Teaching Latina/o Children's Literature in Multicultural Contexts[1]

Theoretical and Pedagogical Possibilities

María E. Fránquiz, Carmen Martínez-Roldán

University of Texas – Austin

Carmen I. Mercado

City University of New York – Hunter College

Teachers, librarians, and community members have their favorite stories to share with young people; but many adults must find the stories that might matter most to them. Fránquiz, Martínez-Roldán, and Mercado describe the work they do with preservice and inservice teachers, whose identities as Latina and immigrant have been silenced or misrepresented during their school years. Now, as adults, they are asked to look back, to seek stories, poetry, and images in the words of their *comadres*, in archives, and in recently published children's literature that will return them to literacies and literature they had lost or forgotten. While deepening and expanding their literary heritage, teachers also learn that literacy development is not located in schools alone, but in all the places where adults create a sense of "us" for themselves and their children's futures.

Schools of Education in the United States prepare teachers for working with increasingly diverse student populations and thus have a responsibility for providing a coherent approach to educating culturally responsive teachers (Villegas & Lucas, 2002). One way to better prepare preservice and inservice teachers is to create spaces for discussing literary themes that address the authentic challenges, big or small, faced by persons of color in and outside the formal parameters of schools.

Building on the theoretical perspectives of caring, community, and cultural resources, we describe the ways identities of *literary belonging* can be developed in classrooms, especially among teachers who work with Latina/o students in the United States. Through the research we conducted in our teacher education courses, across three settings—Fránquiz in Texas, Martínez-Roldán in Arizona, and Mercado in New York—we show how it is possible to value students' hidden literacies, by showing the literary legacies and lived experiences of our undergraduate and graduate students. Fránquiz describes the written and creative work of undergraduate students in her course, Latino Children's Literature for the Bilingual Learner, taken by students interested in becoming bilingual elementary teachers; Martínez-Roldán draws on data from a graduate course, Latino Literature for Children and Adolescents; and Mercado draws on student writing and interviews from an undergraduate course on Literacy in the Content Areas, grades 1–6. We conclude by highlighting literary education practices that enable teachers to reveal, narrate, and renew their understandings of Latina/o students, families, and communities.

The Need for Resilient Student and Teacher Literacy Identities

Currently, over 40% of U.S. school-age youth are children of color, the majority of whom are Latinas/os. This diversity will continue to increase with a 2020 estimate of approximately 56% White, 23% Latina/o, 14% African American, 6% Asian/Pacific Islander, and 1% American Indian/Alaskan Native (United States Census Bureau, 2004). The bulk of the growth in the age 5 to 18 population can be attributed to students who are either immigrants or the children of immigrants; most of whom are presented with a less challenging literacy curriculum because of educators' beliefs about the students' heritage language, socioeconomic class, parents' educational attainment, and academic abilities. Studies show that English Language Learners (ELLs), in particular, find that teachers expect little of them academically (Cammarota, 2004; Olsen, 1997; Suárez-Orozco & Suárez-Orozco, 1995; Valenzuela, 1999; Vélez & Antrop-González, 2007), and their high school completion rates attest that "when little is expected, little is produced" (Callahan, 2005, p. 311). This persisting deficit view of students extends to U.S. citizens born in Puerto Rico whose parents migrate to the U.S. mainland. The challenge for activist scholars, then, is to demystify views held by some policy makers and educators regarding students from working-class immigrant families as emerging from households devoid of rich intellectual and social resources (González et al., 2005). Instead, students' resilient literacy identities must be nurtured in order to overcome negative experiences they may develop when viewed as a "nonreader" or "nonlearner" of school-based ways with words.

As demographic shifts impact our social worlds, teachers and policy makers must also address the pervasive view held by the U.S. public at large that children from Latina/o, African American, Asian/Pacific Islander and Native American homes need to be deculturalized. By deculturalization, Spring (1994) refers to a process of "stripping away of a people's culture and replacing it with

a new culture" (p. 1). When beliefs from their primary cultures are effectively silenced and ignored, children of color may believe it is best to adopt middle-class, Anglo-Protestant beliefs (Macedo, 1994; Spring, 1994). In contrast, researchers studying families' funds of knowledge or community cultural wealth (Yosso, 2005) propose that hidden funds of family knowledge and "nonacademic" literacies be used as resources for learning in schools from preschool to university, in libraries, in churches, in community-based organizations and in other educational settings. Because family and "nonacademic" literacies are for the most part hidden (Martínez-Roldán & Fránquiz, 2009), it is imperative to bring to light these funds of hidden literacies and make recommendations for ways to mobilize them for further learning.

Working within three distinct contexts and geographical locations, we have come to understand different, but related ways we can work with adults to recover hidden knowledge, narrate latent counterstories, and validate family and "nonacademic" literacies. These pedagogies are intended to support the personal liberation of our teachers, rather than their standardization, or domestication (Freire, 1970; Shor & Freire, 1987), into the broader teacher culture. By addressing teachers' reading, remembering, and writing, we hope to reverse the practices in literacy and literature education that continue to fail so many of today's Latina/o students.

Critical Caring, Cultural Resources, and Communities

Our review of the research literature and the examples from our classrooms are grounded in and interpreted from our personal and professional experiences as Puerto Rican/DiaspoRican scholars. The term DiaspoRican was popularized by Nuyorican poet Mariposa (a.k.a. María Teresa Fernández[2]) and refers to the increasingly diverse and dynamically evolving nature of Puerto Rican identity within the United States (Antrop-González & DeJesús, 2006; Torres-Padilla & Rivera, 2008; Valldejuli & Flores, 2000). We share combined experiences of teaching and researching in diverse settings from preschool through university, and we align ourselves with sociocultural theorists (Vygotsky, 1978) and critically caring theorists (Antrop-González & DeJesús, 2006; Valenzuela, 1999). Sociocultural theorists such as Moll (1990) show how cultural resources play an important role in the development of thinking and highlight the social mediation of learning that takes place in and through classroom social activity mediated by cultural artifacts or tools (Cole, 1990; Cole & Engeström, 1993). Initiated by Noddings (1992), caring theorists value an ethos of caring in and through social activity and are concerned when the curriculum and school do not actively promote a search for meaningful connections between teacher and student, between student and family, and among students themselves. These interpersonal connections are the ones that have profound consequences for Latina/o students' identity development in elementary through college and for their academic resiliency in meeting personal and communal learning objectives (Fránquiz & Salazar, 2004).

We base our teaching practice on the premise that when interpersonal relationships, curricular, and institutional structures do not place value on the native languages, histories and cultures of students, literacy resources for learning are subtracted (Nieto, 2002; Valenzuela, 1999) and academic resiliency suffers (Salazar, 2004). This has been one of the most consistent findings in research on Latina/o educational experience. As Thompson (1998) explains, educators working from this position, as we do, do not equate caring with emotionally laden practices of feeling pity for students' circumstances and lowering academic expectations. Rather, the goal is to build on educational scholarship on caring (Antrop-González & DeJesús, 2006; McKamey, 2004; Thompson, 1998; Valenzuela, 1999) because it seeks to uncover the existing knowledge base of students who are not academically validated in schools. We also operate on the premise that uncovering students' knowledge base means viewing learning not as a progression through predetermined standards of learning, but through the experiences and insights people acquire as they participate and communicate in a broad range of events and cultural worlds.

Locating Research and Directions for Literary Study

As *Diasporican* scholars of color, we are specifically acquainted with studies that show how the various waves of the Puerto Rican diaspora produced very important communities in the United States (Acosta-Belén et al., 2000; Whalen & Vázquez-Hernández, 2005) as well as the emergence of remarkable Puerto Rican literature (Flores, 1988; Torres-Padilla & Rivera, 2008). Our shared vision commits us to contribute to a body of promising scholarship in teacher education whose aim is to *Ricanstruct* (Irizarry & Antrop González, 2007) deficit myths about the capacities of Latina/o students, their families, and their communities. We aim to elevate the resilient writing within our own diasporic community while also defying colonial pedagogies that historically constrained the success of Latinas/os in the United States. To be clear, we do not offer monolithic views of Latinas/os nor advocate "best practices" for them. Instead, we highlight social science frameworks that identify and document the promising funds of knowledge (Moll, Amanti, Neff, & González, 1992; Vélez-Ibañez & Greenberg, 1992) in Latina/o students' homes, kinship networks, and locally situated communities.

The purpose of this chapter, then, is to describe research that makes visible some of the promising literacy experiences that can assist teacher engagement with issues of language, culture, literature, and literacy. We pay particular attention to the uses of languages and literacy practices that demonstrate potential for academic success but remain neglected and misunderstood hidden literacies (Villalva, 2006).

Literary Study and the Beginning of an Us: Discourse Matters

The following story offers an ideal, yet achievable model for the literary learning we aspire to in our teaching. Vivian Gussin Paley's (2001) main character, from the book, *In Mrs. Tully's Room: A Childcare Portrait*, reports, "When my babies do their stories, that's when they really see each other. That's what we need to go after in school, the seeing and the listening to each other" (pp. 10–11). The book's heroine explains that when two-year-old Alex told his classmates his one-word "Mama" story, they repeated it. "And then he returned the favor. Amazing, isn't it? The beginning of an *us*. A real community [where] everything eventually gets included" (p. 11). This literary network that comprised Mrs. Tully's classroom community was full of personal connections that emerged from the stories the class read such as *A Chair for my Mother* (Williams, 1982), and the stories repeated, retold, and dictated to an adult writer, such as Alex's story. In the space created for story a new child in the classroom, Allegra, shared, "Once upon a time there was a girl and no one noticed. Then someone noticed" (p. 18). Thea soon borrowed this opening line for her own version of *A Chair for my Mother*. Through the repetition of Allegra's story lines, Thea ensured that class members noticed the new girl, Allegra.

In Mrs. Tully's cultural group, children learned to read and produce stories through shared ways of participating in reading events. The texts produced in these events can be viewed as composed cultural artifacts that represent symbolic systems imbued with a potential for individual and community meaning. As the children talked about story, they developed more than the expression of ideas. They created discourses, defined by Gee (1990) as "ways of being in the world, or forms of life which integrate words, acts, values, beliefs, attitudes, social identities" (p. 142). Our identity, then, is shaped in and through discourse and the most advantageous course for learners is discourse that is inclusive and participatory as the *us* emerges. Thea's story functioned as a discourse that recognized Allegra as a member of *us* in Mrs. Tully's room.

Identity Matters

An identity of belonging matters whether one is two years old in Mrs. Tully's room, or an adolescent of color needing access to dominant discourses in order to speak and write forms of English recognized by many as a language of power (Delpit, 1988). Identity even matters to a teacher in training who is examining the influence of dominant discourse on her familial, cultural, ideological, and educational histories. Yes, identity matters and it is dynamically changing as social contexts provide opportunities to access participation in different situations. In the following section we describe three distinct educational contexts and the literacy practices that promoted the development of core and fluid identities via participation in literacy projects.

Three Cases: Literary Journeys in Teacher Education

As bilingual, bicultural, and biliterate educators, we are invested in assisting the teachers in our undergraduate and graduate classrooms as they talk back to tools of oppression that strip students of their self worth. For this reason our work heeds the call of Darling-Hammond, French, and Garcia-Lopez (2002) and Darling-Hammond and Baratz-Snowden (2005) who argue that teacher education must assist all teachers in acquiring the necessary knowledge and skills to teach for social justice. In the first case, Fránquiz taught an undergraduate course in Latina/o Children's Literature for the Bilingual Learner that introduced preservice teachers to the literary works of Latina/o authors appropriate for use in elementary schools and libraries. In this course she and her students co-constructed a community that discloses, reflects, conceptualizes, and transforms former monocultural and monolingual ways of being. In the second case, Martínez-Roldán provides examples that demonstrate the impact of teachers' new experiences with literature at the university on their elementary school students. In the third case, Mercado demonstrates how archival research on writers and their work enlightens teachers' perspectives on what constitutes a culturally responsive author study, whereby students' personal and cultural values are central to the assignments and goals for learning.

Memorias, Literacy Journey Boxes, and Deconstructing Dominant Discourses

With the goal in mind of assisting her majority preservice Latina students in developing consciousness of a new bilingual teacher identity (in Spanish, a *maestra* identity), Fránquiz believes that before teachers can build a positive sense of self in relation to ethnicity, race, class and gender, they must first identify and critique dominant assimilationist tales (Hurtado & Gurín, 2004). As such tales are analyzed, significance and value can be attached to newly found identities. Hurtado and Gurín argue for a new consciousness of personal identity which, "…refers to whether individuals are aware that the groups they belong to hold a certain status (either powerful or not powerful) in society and whether they will take action to change this status, not just for themselves, but for other members of the group as well" (p. xvii).

Fránquiz planned activities that presented her students with opportunities to exhibit consciousness of their growing identity. This goal was addressed by providing an assignment early in the semester that served as an exercise to "trigger both negative and positive memories" (Tello 1994, p. 59). The act of eliciting *memorias/memories* about oppressive moments in personal and collective educational histories served at least two purposes: (a) becoming conscious of cultural and linguistic oppression makes visible dominant assimilationist tales such as "Forget your native language and culture, and become part of the great American melting pot" and, (b) raising questions such as, "Does the American dream have to be dreamt in English-only?"

Eliciting consciousness through *memorias* (the mother of the muses according to Villanueva, 2004), can be understood as a scaffold offered to future teachers in a course on children's literature for the bilingual learner. A scaffold as a teaching strategy originates from sociocultural theory and proposes that social interaction with more knowledgeable or capable others significantly impacts ways of thinking and interpreting situations. In this case, the "more knowledgeable other" is located in memory, in the narratives of relatives, and in the literary and archival reading available to students. This scaffold was intended to deconstruct tales the teachers may have internalized and brought to their preservice educational experience regarding a single path to Americanization and also begins a libratory journey toward the construction of a bilingual *maestra* (respected teacher) identity.

Memorias were elicited from 56 Mexican American and 4 South American women enrolled in a children's literature course in a Hispanic Serving Institution. These *memorias* were the product of an assignment called, The Literacy Journey Box. In the research literature a journey box is "literally a box (e.g., suitcase, trunk, chest, cardboard container) that contains a themed set of photographs, selected artifacts, texts, journal entries, and an index that together tell a first-hand story of time and place" (Labbo & Field, 1999, p. 177). It is typical in the field of social studies to understand events or historical figures through the study of primary documents. For example, to construct the life of a heroine such as Emma Tenayuca who led a pecan shellers' strike in Texas in 1938, students have access to photos and articles from newspaper archives to learn more about her activism for better pay and working conditions. As an activist of color and survivor of oppressive conditions, there are many *records* of her statements both oral and written in libraries, museums, archives, etc. The heroine's biography is synthesized in an excellent rendition of her life in the children's book, *That's Not Fair!/No es justo! Emma Tenayuca's Struggle for Justice/La Lucha de Emma Tenayuca for Justice* by Carmen Tafolla and Sharyll Teneyuca (2008). As valuable as a journey box on Emma Tenayuca can be, in the class project that Fránquiz assigned for her class, the heroine is not Emma Tenayuca but the preservice teachers themselves, and the *memoria (remembrance)* is the story of their subordinated knowledge first represented in the literacy journey box (Figure 8.1), then in a timeline, and finally in their own autobiographies.

Spanish, English, or both languages appear in or on the completed literacy journey boxes that also include an index regarding the relics and artifacts placed inside or out. The lid, sides, and bottom are resplendent with cultural markers of life and death, children and parents, *quinceañeras* and weddings. There are personal literacy artifacts such

Figure 8.1 Examples of literacy journey boxes

as letters from Dad who was stationed in Kuwait or from *abuelita* (*grandmother*) in Jalisco, Mexico. They include primary documents of the self as a child, an adolescent, and an adult. Some students include artifacts that symbolize lessons learned with *lotería* cards and flash cards, of lessons acknowledged with school pins, awards, and certificates, of social memberships represented by library cards, prayer cards, employment identification cards, and obituaries of family members. They recreate and illustrate segments of *dichos*, proverbs, quotes, poems, and prayers and strategically paste them on the inside and outside of the journey box. Literacy *memorias* are also represented with sheets of music, books, and CDs.

As we share what is in the literacy journey box and discuss the process of putting it together, insights of students' similar and dissimilar material resources during the tender young years of childhood and adolescence bring the class community to tears, laughter, and applause. Our sharing, discussing, and discovering also marks the beginning of an *us*, a class community of future teachers. This beginning of an *us* is a critical moment because the professional development sequence known locally as "The Block" follows after the course is completed. As is customary in many U.S. teacher education programs for bilingual teachers, the literacy demands on each individual preservice teacher shift from majority English *before* The Block or Pre-PDS (pre-professional development sequence) to majority Spanish *during* The Block or PDS. Because most U.S. schooling is in English during middle and high school as well as in college, preservice teachers' academic Spanish language proficiency is rarely at par with English proficiency; consequently, bilingual linguistic identities

among the teachers I work with are often quite fragile. This is why establishing a safe environment for taking risks is significant for creating an *us*.

Once the literacy journey boxes are shared, the students make personal timelines and graphic organizers to gather ideas for writing their autobiographies. During these activities the preservice teachers reveal and examine personal literacy events such as listening to *Canciones de Cri-Cri* (Cri-Cri songs) that are important for honoring a history and heritage that for many had been subordinated. When students complain of uncertainties, failures or gaps in memories, they are encouraged to contact their parents, aunts, uncles, godparents, grandparents, close family friends, even former teachers in order to inquire deeply about their first reading and writing memories, their memories of language acquisition, the places and people that made them feel smart or dumb. In order to have a healthy *us* in the classroom, invitations for remembering and reclaiming are honored and respected by all.

Through the creation of literacy journey boxes, the timelines, graphic organizers, and auto-narratives, dominant assimilationist tales emerge in the consciousness of the class. For example, one student wrote in her autobiography: "On most nights my mother would read a story to my brother and me. Our favorite books were *The Little Engine that Could*, *Little Golden Books*, *Bible* stories, and most were read in English." Another student wrote, "My mother would read books in Spanish to me such as, *La Cenisienta, Pinocho, Blanca Nieve*, and *La Caperucita Roja* (*Cinderella, Pinochio, Snow White*, and *Red Riding Hood*)." While these stories have been popular for generations, they are normative in their praise of individualism, heterosexual mores, ingeniously passive roles for girls, and unambiguous in their presentation of issues of power and class (Nodelman & Reimer, 2003). Whether in Spanish or English, these stories are essentially monocultural. This realization prompted some students to question why their parents did not read culturally relevant books with them. For example, one student wrote:

> As I reflect back on my childhood reading experiences, some are positive and others are negative. I think back at different reading assignments and ask myself "Why wasn't I ever introduced to any literature in Spanish or assignments relating to my culture"? Reading the church missalettes and the prayers on holy cards were the only readings I did in Spanish. As a matter a fact, it wasn't until I began taking classes in my major that I became informed of the many books available in Spanish and relating to my culture. Our elementary school was predominately Latinos, so why wasn't our background enriched with these readings? I want to do for my students what my teachers didn't do for me and that is to introduce them to many books in Spanish that relate to our Latino culture.

While this student made a commitment to reclaim her heritage language and culture by immersing herself and future students in culturally relevant literature, other students included different memories in their autobiographies: "My beloved grandmother from Mexico was my inspirational model, known for her traditional storytelling like stories of 'La Llorona.' She encouraged me to learn words through games like 'La Lotería'." And another student wrote, "My parents read to me in Spanish—stories about *brujería, oro, y muerte (witchcraft, gold, and death).*"

Together the journey box, timeline, graphic organizers, and autobiography assignments served as scaffolds for future teachers to uncover layers of assimilation in some families and resilient ways of keeping oral traditions alive in others. One Mexican American aspiring teacher revealed a remarkable memory of liberating herself from an assimilative tale:

> In 2005 I took a Mexican-American course. This course was a challenge to me because many of the books were in Spanish and it had been so long since I had read Spanish. This is when I decided to change my degree plan from generalist to bilingual. I changed my mind because I realized that I had lost something that was very important to my heritage, and it was the ability to read and write in Spanish. I realized that I did not want my children and other peoples' children to grow up that way too.

Through her renewed commitment to the preservation of her heritage language for herself and others she challenged a common myth that, "if we focus on teaching the English language, learning in all areas will occur faster" (Samway & McKeon, 2007, p. 32). In a rebuttal to this myth, the young teacher clearly outlines and recognizes the price she paid by having to acquire English quickly.

Although the teachers in the class acknowledged the importance of learning English, they began to understand that erasure of the native language might not have been necessary in order for them to gain access to higher education. While many had experienced the shame associated with the home language with reprimands such as, "Speak Spanish correctly and cut out that Tex Mex language —that border talk!" other students remembered resisting English-only education by learning Spanish in after school or weekend activities. For example, one student wrote "*Cantos espirituales* (spirituals) in hymnals are divided by hyphens so I used English decoding skills to learn Spanish at church."

As they shared about their lives, influenced by dominant discourses, students learned about complying with language rules in certain contexts such as school and resisting these constraints in other social contexts of their lives. Such awakenings about language were also pertinent to the children's literature we read in class. For example, *The Tequila Worm* by Viola Canales (2005) was the touchstone text (Wolf, 2004) assigned to the class. *The Tequila Worm* is realistic fiction based on the author's memoirs of her youth in the border town of McAllen in South Texas. The main character, Sofia, lives on the poor side of town and aspires to be like the caring *comadres* (godmother, fictive kin) in her Mexican American community. When she is offered a scholarship to attend an elite boarding school away from her family and community, she must learn to make the people around her into a family as any good *comadre* would do. Crafting her *comadre* identity is at the heart of the narrative. Fránquiz selected this narrative to be studied closely in literature circles because the author is from South Texas as were 90% of the future teachers enrolled in the course. One student was so motivated to read a culturally relevant book about a girl from her hometown, McAllen, Texas, that she read the book ahead of the class schedule and did so in one sitting. She wrote in her autobiography, "I never liked reading and rarely read for pleasure. When I bought *The Tequila Worm* at the bookstore before classes started, I had to read it and I couldn't stop. I called my mom and we talked for hours about *comadres, sobremesa* (time spent talking during/after a meal), *canicula* (extremely hot weather/dog days of summer), and homesickness. I plan to translate the book for my mother." Clearly, the short chapters in this young adult novel facilitated profound connections with this student's core identity as a Mexican American woman from the borderlands and a future bilingual teacher.

Literature and the Mediation of Teachers' Learning, Pedagogical Practices, and Identities

Most of the teachers in Martínez-Roldán's seminar class had been exposed to children's literature in their undergraduate program not through a focused class on literature, but as integrated into their language arts classes. They were not so familiar, though, with Latino literature and were impressed, especially the Latina/o teachers, with the repertoire of Latino literature presented in the course. Approximately 40 teachers took the class across two years and Martínez-Roldán documented their responses to the literature. One group of six teachers discussed the novel *Before We Were Free* by Julia Alvarez (2002). The text addresses the topics of war, freedom, and immigration from the perspective of a girl who lived during the times of Rafael Trujillo's brutal dictatorship in the Dominican Republic and her eventual migration with family members to the United States. The teachers found themselves positioned by the text as insiders or outsiders in different and complex ways and yet all of them engaged in a transaction with the story of the protagonist, Anita de la Torre.

The diversity within the small group of six teachers was important to the mediation of their interrelated and recursive movement from exploratory to critical discussion. Across literature discussion during the semester, the more linguistically and culturally diverse the small discussion groups in the classroom were, the deeper they delved into a critical reading of the text and a negotiation of meanings and identities. Because of this pattern, Martínez-Roldán invited the small groups of teachers to come together to share their interpretations as a whole class group. The shift from small to whole group invited more learning and negotiation of meanings. In the whole class group, White, middle-class teachers typically stepped back to listen attentively to the insights of three immigrant peers—two Mexicans and a Serbo-Croatian. At the same time, both mainstream teachers and Mexican American teachers who had not experienced immigration in the same way as Bojana, a recent emigrant from Serbo-Croatian, asked for information and clarification of aspects taken for granted by U.S. cultural "insiders." For example, Bojana had experienced war in her native land. Thus she responded to *Before We Were Free* with a strong connection to the protagonist in this book as well as the protagonist of a book she read as a child:

> For me this book has a huge meaning because I could totally identify with the character because I also went through the war in my country and I also read the *The Diary of Anne Frank* when I was in fourth grade and that was when the war started in my country.

These intertextual connections between lived experiences in the text of her life and those of characters in the books led Bojana to respond to the historical novel with the composition of an identity poem:

Inspiration

I am not a white, middle class, female,
in a dominant culture of the USA.
I am a "Woman of the World"!
My roots that of indigenous mother, with my own culture, language, art, and ancestry.

I have my own folk tales and idols — a full coffin without the lid;
my own experiences of discrimination and religious separation,
in fact, I drag the whole civil war behind my feet.
I carry this culture's class division, imposed on my mother and father,
but don't underestimate the power of my nation,
and ability to move through the freedom of expression.
I am a child of the world. I demand a proper position!
No piece of flesh will dumb me down.
I move through my own literary expression,
reminded to always fly up high like the butterflies.

The historical fiction novel, *Before We Were Free*, afforded teachers with many opportunities to learn about themselves, about others, and about their own students. For example, during a different session of the course made up of a very diverse group of 18 students, most of them practicing teachers, they discussed *The Tequila Worm*. Across the chapters there are descriptions of many cultural experiences specific to South Texas that resonated with the lived experiences of students in the class. Interestingly, a teacher who identified as Yaqui[3] sought to understand the quest of the story's protagonist, Sofia, to become a good *comadre*. This teacher was specifically moved by the account of a Mexican American peer who talked at length about the profound link to a core ethnic identity she had experienced within a community of *comadres*. She connected with the Mexican teacher as she shared her understanding that to become a person you need your *comadre*; she is sacred. The Mexican teacher explained that in Mexico, the *comadre* is the child's Godmother and, in case the mother dies, the Godmother will automatically take her place for important decisions, especially those related to the education of the child.

The Yaqui teacher was impressed by the idea that although one may be asked to be a *comadre* in a very distinct *us,* there is also a personal responsibility for insiders to respect and protect each other like kin. Other teachers also acknowledged that their lived experiences were authentically depicted in a text used as part of their schooling experience. A Mexican American teacher, however, highlighted how the word *comadre* may have slightly different meanings as it had for her, and she alerted the group that as accurate as it can be a description of an experience by an insider, there would always be variations to the traditions and customs of all cultures. For the White European American teachers, the authentic and varied cultural perspectives validated by their Latina/o teacher peers had the potential of narrowing the cultural disconnect that some had previously reported feeling toward their Latina/o students.

The course was also designed to influence teachers' current classroom literacy practices. Changes in their practice were reflected in the kinds of reading they chose to initiate in their own classrooms, which in turn led young linguistically and culturally diverse students to move from exploratory to critical discussions about sensitive issues such as race. The course assignments provided a repertoire of reading engagements that the teachers could use to support their own students' reading and literacy development. Antonia, a mainstream teacher wrote:

As a teacher, I am always looking to enhance my lesson planning. Through the different styles of literature, I have found ways to use inquiry-based literature discussions, dramatizations, poetry interpretations, and many other styles of teaching... Working with the other students in the class has also given me intriguing thoughts for my next year's lessons.

A conundrum that some teachers experienced and discussed was how to integrate culturally authentic literature into their curriculum when they were forced to use a prescriptive phonics-based reading program that relies on sequential teacher-directed group instruction. The challenge is very real since "...scripted programs provide teachers with a script for what they are to say *verbatim* during instruction. Non scripted programs describe activities, provide examples, and expect teachers to choose activities that they judge to be most helpful to particular groups of children in their care" (Moustafa & Land, 2001, p. 10; emphasis in original). One of the teachers, Andrea, decided that although she did not have much instructional time for literature discussions she wanted to make Latina/o literature available to her kindergarten students (see DeNicolo & Fránquiz, 2006, for a case study of a teacher dealing with this dilemma in a fourth grade classroom). She decided to give a brief book talk every day about a new piece of Latina/o literature. After the talk she put the new book in a special basket to see if during Independent Reading the students would choose to "read" the books placed in this basket, which they did. This experiment opened up more opportunities for her students to see their lives reflected in books.

Once in a while Andrea also used the independent reading time in her classroom to organize literature circles (Short, 1997; Short & Pierce, 1998). In one of those literature circles, her students were discussing the book *The Subway Sparrow* by Leyla Torres (1997). It tells the story of a small group of passengers who, in spite of speaking different languages, managed to save a sparrow that was trapped inside the train. The teacher was surprised at the topics of racial and linguistic identities that engaged her kindergarteners during discussion. The following excerpt illustrates how the students engaged in a discussion of identity and language, trying to figure out what makes a person bilingual and in the process negotiating their identities and affiliations, while learning to participate in literacy events. In this excerpt the teacher posed a question about students' bilingualism:

Teacher: Do all of you know Spanish and English?
Mili, Iván, Bea: Yes!!!
Teacher: Why do you know Spanish and English?

Mili: Because we learn.
Bea: We learn at school.
Iván: Because we are Mexican.

The students made connections to issues of identity and to the teacher's surprise, began to negotiate what it means to be Mexican in terms of race and language. The children seemed to not only be reflecting on their own identities but they also positioned others in the group in particular ways, generating an intense discussion of identities. In response to Iván's former statement, the children responded:

Mili: We are not Mexican!
Bea: Yes!!!
Teacher: Why not, Mili?
Bea: Yes we are!
Mili: Some people is black, some is white.
Iván: I'm black.
Mili: You're brown.
Bea: I'm Mexican.
Mili: You're Mexican?
Bea: Yeah.
Mili: I remember someone told me I was Mexican, but I'm not.
Iván: You're a Mexican girl.
Mili: I'm not a Mexican girl!
Bea: What are you?
Iván: Or [maybe you are] just a kinder.
Mili: I'm not just a kinder!

Martínez-Roldán and Malavé (2004) have documented how very young children develop "embryonic ideological discourses" (p. 177) or cultural models about language and gender (Martínez-Roldán & Malaué, 2004). The children's responses here suggest that there was a sense of classroom belonging like in Mrs. Tully's classroom where the young children could safely discuss their developing understanding of racialized identities based on what they could see. Mili, who saw herself neither as Mexican nor Black, seemed perplexed with Iván's self-identification as Black Mexican. Her peers saw Mili differently than she saw herself and asked Mili to define herself. If she was not Mexican and was not Black, in what other terms could she be identified? What these youngsters saw was the obvious identity that she could claim—the schooling identity. Mili was a member of the *us* that comprised the kindergarten class, but her peers knew she had other social identities that she was not claiming. She certainly claimed to also see herself as something in addition to "just a kinder" student.

The teacher then prompted the students to continue thinking about the identity issues they had raised by expanding the meaning of Mexican:

Teacher: Mili, if you are not Mexican, what are you?
Mili: (Thought about it but provided no answer)
Teacher: What is a Mexican?
Bea: That means they talk Spanish.

115

Iván: Mexicans speak Spanish and English.
Teacher: So is Nurse Lynn Mexican? She speaks Spanish and English.
Iván: Yes [overlapping]
Bea: Yes [overlapping]
Mili: I'm white.
Iván: Your brown, I'm black.
Mili: You're not black, you're Mexican.
Iván: I'm a black Mexican.
Mili: No, you're not.
Iván: That's me, a black Mexican.
Mili: Okay, Iván, so are you a black, a white or a brown?
Iván: Black Mexican.
Mili: Stop acting like that, you're a brown Mexican.
Teacher: Mili, why do you say Iván is a brown Mexican?
Mili: Because of the color of his skin.
Teacher: So what am I? (she is a Mexican American white teacher)
Mili: You're white.
Iván: You're Mexican.
Bea: That means she speaks English and Spanish.

As this transcript shows, even very young children are curious about differences and are trying to figure out how they are an insider or outsider to a particular identifiable sociocultural group. Having the opportunity to find themselves represented in the literature, the kindergarteners produced language about real issues that affected their lives. The fact that there was an established *us* identity in Ms. Andrea's kindergarten class and that an argument could challenge the cohesion of the group made Bea ask Mili, "What are you?" Mili insisted, "I'm not just a kinder!" but also insisted she is not Mexican but White and that Iván was not Black but Brown. The challenges elicited in the discussion provided a space for children to weave together their understandings of racialized identities and to bring their questions and emerging connections among race, ethnicity, language, and phenotype.

While identity as a kindergartener was clear, a racialized identity was less clear. However, Ms. Andrea created a space for children to contest identity labels by recognizing "the students' experiences as a source of knowledge and a point from which to theorize practice" (Campano, 2007, p. 18). In this way, she invited students to inscribe their own individual experiences into the collective text about *us* in the kindergarten class. Encouraged by the thoughtfulness of students' responses to literature, Ms. Andrea decided to keep introducing Latina/o literature to her students every year.

Losing Ourselves and Finding Ourselves in the Archives

In this study, students were invited to examine the *us* that is shaped, not only by literature, but by author studies of local writers in New York. Mercado used an interdisci-plinary approach to literacy in the content areas in which undergraduates who are preparing to be elementary school teachers engage in archival research as a way to learn about writers from their local communities while also developing curricular applications. Teacher candidates in Mercado's classes were asked to transform information derived from historical documents that reside in the archives of the Center for Puerto Rican Studies of the City University of New York (El Centro http://centropr.org). They created original author studies of award winning writers from the literary renaissance known as the Nuyorican Movement inspired by Jesús Colón, and that flourished in the 1970s and 80s in New York City. Although Puerto Ricans have been migrating north from their Caribbean island to large urban centers such as New York since the post-Civil War period (late 1860s), and making important contributions to the economic, social, and cultural life of U.S. cities, educators in the United States and in Puerto Rico know little about the literary production inspired by this experience. Moreover, these literary legacies remain relatively invisible in the school curriculum and in commercially published texts produced for schools. Not surprisingly, Latino and non-Latino teacher candidates who enter teacher preparation programs in New York and across the nation have little, if any, knowledge of the historical experiences and literary contributions of Puerto Rican American writers. Addressing this serious gap is important because apprentice and novice teachers need support in meeting rigorous content area standards that challenge students to demonstrate competence in applying research methods in studying local communities and their writers. These competencies include using oral histories and memoirs as well as reading, interpreting, and synthesizing written information across multiple sources. While complex, the process of handling archival documents is a powerful educational experience precisely because it can bring the past to life. El Centro is just the place to both lose and find one's self.

El Centro, the leading research center on educational, language, and economic issues affecting U.S. Puerto Rican communities, houses a growing archival collection--a repository of historical documents that includes photographs, letters, newspaper articles, recordings, and manuscripts that encode the experiences and intellectual (including literary) contributions of U.S. Puerto Ricans since the 1900s. The archives of El Centro's collection, reflect the wisdom of their archive and library staff, who have deliberately sought out the voices and points of view of ordinary people, many early pioneers who ventured north seeking artistic freedom, and more recent migrants who came seeking a better life. From the very beginning, many of these migrants were intellectuals, writers, and musicians, from working-class backgrounds, such as the tobacco workers in Puerto Rico who inspired the intellectual development of a young writer, Jesús Colón (1961, 1993).

Although the wealth of information available in El Centro's collection is frequently used by social scientists nationally and internationally, it is rarely used by educators. Even educators from East Harlem, until recently the largest of the Puerto Rican communities in New York City, make infrequent use of the collection. For this reason collaborations with archivists and historians are especially promising so that educators—preservice and inservice alike—can understand the literary production of Puerto Rican writers and incorporate this knowledge into the literary experiences they share with students.

By involving her teacher candidates in what she calls the Local Writer's Project, Mercado invites future teachers to read about people and events to create an author study. The project has gone through distinct phases. However, the common purpose remains making accessible and creating resources for preservice and in-service teachers and faculty in schools of education. Although Puerto Rican writers are presented front and center, the course that includes this project does not focus exclusively on Puerto Ricans. Across the years students worked in teams or individually to create author studies in power point format, some of which are available on El Centro's website. All the power points include:

- A timeline of the writer's life showing key events that influenced her/his writing;
- A map showing where the writer lived/wrote, and how location and history influenced what the writer wrote about;
- Excerpts from and summaries of major writings/publications organized by dominant themes and values;
- Key quotes showing distinctive qualities of the writer, e.g., what compels her or him to write, the genres/styles/medium the author favors;
- Music capturing the mood and spirit of the writer;
- A summary of two lessons based on the New York standards for student performance in the language arts, one for primary grades (1–3) and one for upper elementary (4–6).

Though most of the works accessible through El Centro's archival collection are more appropriate and adaptable for children in upper elementary grades, two particular Puerto Rican authors address younger children directly—Pura Belpré and Nicholasa Mohr. The former was a talented storyteller who wrote and re-interpreted Puerto Rican folk tales. She was the first Puerto Rican librarian in the New York Public Library system. Belpré's life story was remarkably captured in the historical account, *The Storyteller's Candle/La Velita de los Cuentos* by Lucía González (2008). Her life's contributions are memorialized in the Pura Belpré Award, presented annually to a Latina/o writer and illustrator whose work best portrays, affirms, and celebrates the Latino cultural experience in an outstanding work of literature for children and youth. The award is co-sponsored by the Association of Library Services to Children, a division of the American Library Association (ALA), and the National Association of Library Science to the Spanish Speaking, an ALA affiliate. Nicholasa Mohr is an author of short story collections, novels, plays, essays, and numerous books for children, young adults and adults. Some of her young adult novels are published in both English and Spanish editions and are based on autobiographical details of ordinary life experiences of Puerto Rican immigrants in New York barrios such as *Nilda* (1973), which won the Jane Addams Children's Book Award, cited as a Best Book of 1973 by the American Library Association, and noted for the New York Times Outstanding Book of the Year Award in 1974.

Upon completion of her archival work on Nicholasa Mohr for the Local Writer's Project one of the preservice teachers in Mercado's class wrote, "Learning about Nicholasa Mohr…was a new experience. You should definitely continue to use this project in your classes. It is great to learn about minorities like us making such great contributions." These words acknowledge the authenticity of the writer's work while at the same time displaying the fact that in the 21st century many Puerto Ricans such as this teacher candidate are still being denied reading of and responding to culturally specific (Bishop, 1992) multiethnic literature (Harris, 1997) in their K–12 education.

Preservice teachers were also inspired by Pedro Pietri, one of the founders of the Nuyorican Poets Café. They reported that Pietri's poetry was "awesome," specifically his 1973 poem, *Puerto Rican Obituary*, a deceptively simple and powerful poem about social inequalities. From the study of the poem emerged an *us* among Puerto Ricans and non-Puerto Ricans in the university class and the poem was collaboratively adapted for 10- to 12-year-old children. Regarding the experience, students reflected, "My group fell in love with Pedro Pietri and his passion. It amazed us to even think we had not heard of him before." Another student wrote, "The writer's project was very powerful because I gained so much from it. Since I did the biographical information on Pietri, I learned so much about him that it was difficult to…keep it simple. I was fascinated by all the things I learned." As a group, the students formed an *us* in relation to the Puerto Rican artists and writers who had long been forgotten, but who were enlivened through inquiry as a vibrant resource for their own and their students' literary experiences. Through their author studies and archival adaptations for educational settings, preservice and inservice teachers discovered that although identities may be hidden, they are not lost. Indeed, identities in literary form must be recovered in order for youth and their communities to recognize and, when necessary, struggle and fight for, their right to be seen and heard—and read.

Conclusion

Téllez (2004/2005) points out, scholarship regarding the education and professional development of Latina/o

117

university students is scarce and initiatives designed to scaffold the professional development of bilingual teachers who will or do engage in teaching students in Spanish and English is lacking. We highlighted the literary practices/assignments used in our own teacher professional development courses in Texas, Arizona, and New York that effectively assisted bilingual teachers to reveal, narrate, and renew prior and new understandings about Latina/o students, their families, and their histories. While previous studies have shown how culturally specific Latina/o literature can bridge cultural gaps that mainstream teachers may have about their student constituents (Nathenson-Mejia & Escamilla, 2003), we showed how Latina/o teachers themselves also needed Latina/o children's literature as a tool for examining closely their own language and literacy (mis)understandings as well as for considering changes in pedagogy. Specific methods that had promising results in our teacher education classes were literacy journey boxes and autobiographies, poetry and literature discussion, archival research and author studies. It should be noted that for students with bilingual abilities, or desiring to improve bilingual abilities, Spanish and English were encouraged in our classrooms for engagement with reading, archival work, and writing. A common goal in our classes, then, was to encourage risk taking in classroom discourse participation and in individual or collaborative response-based projects.

We argued that reading, researching, and responding to the works of writers in local communities is invigorating and can be effectively accomplished through the following practices:

- co-constructing with students a safe learning space for risk-taking;
- employing inquiry methods with childrens' and adolescent literature to problematize official discourses and policies;
- inviting re-examination of one's own lived experience and underlying cultural assumptions;
- providing culturally engaged assignments where class members approach learning with profound respect for subjugated knowledge in their own and other's lives;
- practice becoming a *comadre/compadre* in and across groups so that all cultures, languages, and experiences are valued and included.

Ultimately, we concur that the quantity and quality of available literary resources in our local contexts can be improved. Such improvement ensures that students in the United States are exposed to culturally relevant books in their pre-k- to 12th-grade education. This improvement will have significant impact on the learning of all our students, Latina/o and non Latina/o alike, and is dependent on the continual refinement of the art of teaching, a task the three authors embrace.

Notes

1. The authors wish to express sincere thanks to the teachers who graciously shared their lived experiences in the classes reported in this chapter. The research in Texas was funded by the Academy for Teacher Excellence (ATE) in the College of Education and Human Development at the University of Texas in San Antonio.
2. Mariposa was born Maria Teresa Fernandez and is an award-winning Nuyorican poet from the Bronx. She is the author of *Born Bronxeña: Poems on Identity, Love & Survival*.
3. From first contact with the Spanish in 1533 to the present day, the Yaqui nation of Sonora, Mexico, has struggled successfully to maintain themselves as a distinct people in their homeland along the Rio Yaqui. Many Yaquis migrated from Sonora to the state of Arizona in the late 19th century.

Literature References

Alvarez, J. (2002). *Before we were free*. New York, NY: Knopf.

Canales, V. (2005). *The tequila worm*. New York, NY: Random House.

Colón, J. (1961, 2002). *A Puerto Rican in New York and other sketches*. New York, NY: International Publishers.

Colón, J. (1993). *The way it was and other writings*. Houston, TX: Arte Publico Press.

González, L. (2008). *The storyteller's candle/La velita de los cuentos*. San Francisco, CA: Children's Book Press.

Mohr, N. (1973). *Nilda*. New York, NY: Harper and Row.

Mohr, N. (1986). *Nilda*. Houston, TX: Arte Publico Press.

Pietri, P. (1973). *Puerto Rican Obituary*. Monthly Review Press.

Tafolla, C., & Teneyuca, S. (2008). *That's not fair!/No es justo! Emma Tenayuca's struggle for justice/La lucha de Emma Tenayuca por la justicia*. San Antonio, TX: Wings Press.

Torres. L. (1997). *The subway sparrow*. New York, NY: Farrar, Straus & Giroux.

Williams, V. B. (1982). *A chair for my mother*. New York, NY: HarperCollins.

Academic References

Acosta-Belén, E., Sjostrom, B.R., Santiago, C. E., Cruz, J. E., Santiago-Rivera, A., Benitez, M., Gonzalez-Rodriguez, Y., & Rodriguez, C.E. (2000). *"Adíos, Borinquen querida": The Puerto Rican diaspora, its history, and contributions*. Albany, NY: Center for Latino, Latin American and Caribbean Studies, State University of New York at Albany.

Antrop-González, R., & DeJesús, A. (2006). Toward a theory of critical care in urban small school reform: Examining structures and pedagogies of caring in two Latino community-based schools. *International Journal of Qualitative Studies in Education, 19*(4), 409–433.

Bishop, R. S. (1992). Selecting literature for a multicultural curriculum. In V. J. Harris (Ed.), *Using multiethnic literature in the K-8 classroom* (pp. 1–20). Norwood, MA: Christopher-Gordon.

Callahan, R. M. (2005). Tracking and high school English learners: Limiting opportunity to learn. *American Educational Research Journal, 42*(2), 305–328.

Cammarota, J. (2004). The gendered and racialized pathways of Latina and Latino youth: Different struggles, different resistances in the urban context. *Anthropology & Education Quarterly, 35*(1), 53–74.

Campano, G. (2007). *Immigrant students and literacy: Reading, writing, and remembering*. New York, NY: Teachers College Press.

Clark, E. R., & Flores, B. B. (2001). Who am I? The social construction of ethnic identity and self-perceptions in Latino preservice teachers. *The Urban Review, 33*(2), 69–86.

Cole, M. (1990). Cognitive development and formal schooling: The evidence from cross-cultural research. In L. C. Moll (Ed.), *Vygotsky and education: Instructional implications and applications of socio-historical psychology* (pp. 89–110). New York, NY: Cambridge University Press.

Cole, M., & Engeström, Y. (1993). A cultural historical approach to distributed cognition. In G. Salomon (Ed.), *Distributed cognitions* (pp. 1–46). New York, NY: Cambridge University Press.

Darling-Hammond, L., & Baratz-Snowden, J. (2005). *A good teacher in every classroom: Preparing the highly qualified teachers our children deserve.* San Francisco, CA: Jossey-Bass.

Darling-Hammond, L., French, J., & Garcia-Lopez, S. P. (Eds.). (2002). *Learning to teach social justice.* New York, NY: Teachers College Press.

Delpit, L. D. (1988). The silenced dialogue: Power and pedagogy in educating other people's children. *Harvard Educational Review, 58,* 280–298.

DeNicolo, C. P., & Fránquiz, M. E. (2006). "Do I have to say it?" Critical encounters with multicultural children's literature. *Language Arts, 84*(2), 157–170.

Flores, J. (1988). Puerto Rican literature in the United States: Stages and perspectives. *ADE Bulletin, 91,* 39–44.

Fránquiz, M. E., & Salazar, M. (2004). The transformative potential of humanizing pedagogy: Addressing the diverse needs of Chicano/Mexicano students. *The High School Journal, 87*(4), 36–53.

Freire, P. (1970). *Pedagogía del oprimido.* Mexico, DF: Siglo Veintiuno Editores.

Gee, J. P. (1990). *Social linguistics and literacies: Ideology in discourses.* New York, NY: The Falmer Press.

González, N., Moll, L., Floyd Tenery, M., Rivera, A., Rendón, P., Gonzales, R., et al. (2005). Funds of knowledge for teaching in Latino households. In N. González, L. C. Moll, & C. Amanti (Eds.), *Funds of knowledge: Theorizing practices in households and classroom* (pp. 89–111). Mahwah, NJ: Erlbaum.

Harris, V. (Ed.). (1997). *Using multiethnic literature in the K-8 classroom.* Norwood, MA: Christopher-Gordon.

Hurtado, A., & Gurín, P. (2004). *Chicana/o identity in a changing U.S. society. ¿Quién soy? ¿Quiénes somos?* Tucson: University of Arizona Press.

Irizarry, J. G., & Antrop González, R. (2007). Ricanstructing the discourse and promoting school success: Extending a theory of culturally responsive pedagogy for diasporicans. *Centro Journal, XIX*(002), 36–59.

Labbo, L. D., & Field, S. L. (1999). Journey boxes: Telling the story of place, time and cultural with photographs, literature and artifacts. *Social Studies, 14,* 65–73.

Macedo, D. (1994). *Literacies of power: What Americans are not allowed to know.* Boulder, CO: Westview Press.

Martínez-Roldán, C., & Fránquiz, M. E. (2009). Latina/o youth literacies: Hidden funds of knowledge. In L. Christenbury, R. Bomer, & P. Smagorinsky (Eds.), *Handbook of adolescent literacy research* (pp. 323–342). New York, NY: Guilford Press.

Martínez-Roldán, C. M., & Malavé, G. (2004). Language Ideologies mediating literacy and identity in bilingual contexts. *Journal of Early Childhood Literacy, 4,* 155–180.

McKamey, C. (2004, April). *Competing theories of care in education: A critical review and analysis of the literature.* Paper presented at the annual meeting of the American Educational Research Association. San Diego, CA.

Moll, L. C. (1990). *Vygotsky and education: Instructional implications and applications of sociohistorical psychology.* New York, NY: Cambridge University Press.

Moll, L. C., Amanti, C., Neff, D., & González, N. (1992). Funds of knowledge for teaching: Using a qualitative approach to connect homes and classrooms. *Theory into Practice, 31,* 132–141.

Moustafa, M., & Land, R. (2001). *The effectiveness of "Open Court" on improving the reading achievement of economically-disadvantaged children.* Paper presented at the annual meeting of the National Council of Teachers of English November 15–20, Baltimore, MD.

Nathenson-Mejia, S., & Escamilla, K. (2003). Connecting with Latino children: Bridging cultural gaps with children's literature. *Bilingual Research Journal, 27*(1), 101–116.

Nieto, S. (2002). *Language, culture, and teaching: Critical perspectives for a new century.* Mahwah, NJ: Erlbaum.

Noddings, N. (1992). *The challenge to care in schools: An alternative approach to education.* New York, NY: Teachers College Press.

Nodelman, P., & Reimer, M. (2003). *The pleasures of children's literature* (3rd ed.). Boston, MA: Pearson Education.

Paley, V. G. (2001). *In Mrs. Tully's room: A childcare portrait.* Cambridge, MA: Harvard University Press.

Olsen, L. (1997). *Made in America: Immigrant students in our public schools.* New York, NY: New Press.

Salazar, M. (2004). *Echándole ganas: The elements that support or constrain the academic resiliency of Mexican immigrant students in a high school ESL program.* Unpublished dissertation. University of Colorado at Boulder.

Samway, K. D., & McKeon, D. (2007). *Myths and realities: Best practices for English language learners.* Portsmouth, NH: Heinemann.

Shor, I., & Freire, P. (1987). *A pedagogy for liberation: Dialogues on transforming education.* South Hadley, MA: Bergin and Garvey.

Short, K. (1997). *Literature as a way of knowing.* Los Angeles, CA: Stenhouse.

Short, K., & Pierce, K. M. (Eds.). (1998). *Talking about books: Creating literate communities* (2nd ed.). Portsmouth, NH: Heinemann.

Spring, J. (1994). *Deculturalization and the struggle for equality: A brief history of the education of dominated cultures in the United States.* New York, NY: McGraw-Hill.

Suárez-Orozco, M., & Suárez-Orozco, C. (1995). The cultural patterning of achievement motivation: A comparison of Mexican, Mexican immigrant, and non-Latino White American students. In R. Rumbaut & W. Cornelius (Eds.), *California's immigrant children* (pp. 161–190). San Diego, CA: Center for U.S.-Mexico Studies, University of California.

Téllez, K. (2004/2005). Preparing teachers for Latino children and youth: Policies and practices. *The High School Journal, 88*(2), 43–54.

Tello, J. (1994). *Cara y corazón, Face and heart: A family-strengthening, rebalancing and community mobilization process.* San Antonio, TX: National Latino Children's Institute.

Thompson, A. (1998). Not the color purple: Black feminist lessons for educational caring. *Harvard Educational Review, 68*(4), 522–554.

Torres-Padilla, J. L., & Rivera, C. H. (2008). Introduction: The literature of the Puerto Rican diaspora and its critical practice. In J. L. Torres-Padilla and C. H. Rivera (Eds.), *Writing off the hyphen: New perspectives on the literature of the Puerto Rican Diaspora* (pp. 1–30). Seattle: University of Washington Press.

United States Census Bureau. (2004). *U.S. interim projections by age, sex, race, and Hispanic origin,* Washington, DC. Retrieved October 7, 2008, from www.census.gov/ipc/www/usinterimproj/

Valenzuela, A. (1999). *Subtractive schooling: U.S.-Mexican youth and the politics of caring.* New York, NY: State University of New York Press.

119

Valldejuli, J. M., & Flores, J. (2000). New Rican voices: Un muestraria/o sampler at the millennium. *Journal of the Center for Puerto Rican Studies, 12*(1), 49–96.

Vélez, W., & Antrop-González, R. (2007). Experiences of Latina/o students in large schools in drag: A critical analysis of an urban alternative high school. *Multicultural Learning and Teaching, 2*(3), 29–44.

Vélez-Ibañez, C., & Greenberg, J. (1992). Formation and transformation of funds of knowledge. *Anthropology and Education Quarterly, 23*, 313–335.

Villalva, K. E. (2006). Hidden literacies and inquiry approaches of bilingual high school writers. *Written Communication 23*(1), 91–129.

Villanueva, V. (2004). Memoria is a friend of ours: On the discourse of color. *College English, 67*(1), 9–19.

Villegas, A. M., & Lucas, T. (2002). *Educating culturally responsive teachers: A coherent approach.* New York, NY: State University of New York Press.

Vygotsky, L. S. (1978). *Mind in society: The development of higher psychological processes.* Cambridge, MA: Harvard University Press.

Whalen, C. T., & Vázquez-Hernández, V. (2005). *The Puerto Rican diaspora: Historical perspectives.* Philadelphia, PA: Temple University Press

Wolf, S. A. (2004) *Interpreting literature with children.* Mahwah, NJ: Erlbaum.

Yosso, T. (2005). Whose culture has capital? A critical race theory discussion of community cultural wealth. *Race, Ethnicity, and Education, 9*(1), 69–91.

9

School Libraries and the Transformation of Readers and Reading

Eliza T. Dresang

University of Washington

M. Bowie Kotrla

Florida State University

To transform means to change significantly for the better. How can school libraries transform readers and reading? What unique opportunities or perspectives does the school library provide for students that enhance and complement the students' classroom experience? What time-honored approaches, programs, and practices are still effective? What is the role of the school librarian in relation to 21st century literacies? How has technology modified the changes school libraries bring about in readers? Does the changing nature of youths' approach to reading and of the children's and young adult literature itself affect this transformation? In this chapter, Eliza Dresang and Bowie Kotrla examine these questions and point the way to answers and further questions for researchers who want to investigate the multiple roles of school libraries and librarianship in connecting students with children's and young adult literature.

Prologue

I walk into a brightly lit, inviting space. I'm hurrying to meet a friend; we're working on a collaborative project for our seventh-grade Language Arts class. The goal of our project, called a Visual Interpretive Analysis, is to demonstrate how illustrations in a book can convey as much (or more) information as words. We pull our draft website onto a large digital monitor, where we see pages 4 and 5 of a picture book, *Harlem,* written by Walter Dean Myers (1997) and illustrated by his son Christopher Myers. We found the book in the International Children's Digital Library (ICDL), and we have been studying it carefully to choose the pages we think will be most interesting to explore.

As we turn to our next task, we realize we are "stuck"— we need to find some help interpreting the conflicting information we've found about the Harlem Renaissance. Quickly we motion to Ms. Odema, one of our librarians, and request her help in interpreting these opposing points of view and assessing the trustworthiness of the websites we've located.

Nearby we see other students from our Language Arts class; they're building a Visual Interpretive Analysis of *I See the Rhythm*, written by Toyomi Igus (1998) and illustrated with paintings by Michele Wood, which they also located in the ICDL. We text them to see if they've found any resources we've missed and then get back to work on our project.

Another group of our friends is creating a book trailer for Suzanne Collins's (2009) *Catching Fire*. I liked her first book, *The Hunger Games* (2008), so I'd probably read that book without a trailer, but I like turning to these "quick ads for reading" for new suggestions. Our librarians and their student assistants post them for almost all new books that come into the library.

Our library is one of the most intensely used places in our school; it's definitely a favorite with students. It has lots of learning spaces, many different information technologies, and librarians to help us. We can download e-books onto our smart phones or other digital devices. If we don't own one, we can checkout a playaway. Or we can borrow an e-book reader and several books to take home. Our library is a space where students, librarians, and other teachers gather, learn, explore, and, yes, read together—even though there are no traditional handheld books in the collection! OK, now I have to turn this back over to Dr. Dresang and Dr. Kotrla—they just wanted my input into what a 21st century school library might be like.

Introduction

Does this scenario by a composite seventh-grade student sound like a fantasy or even a nightmare? It is neither; rather it is a 21st century reality, a rare reality that is a composite of several real life scenarios, but still a reality. It is a school library without printed books, but it is a school library with a great deal of emphasis on books and reading. As I (Dresang) scanned my online *New York Times* this morning before settling down to put the finishing touches on this chapter, my eye caught the title of an article that brought me full stop, "Do School Libraries Need Books?" (The Editors, 2010). The first person to respond in this article was James Tracy, Headmaster of Cushing Academy, a Massachusetts boarding and day school for 9–12 graders from the United States and 28 other countries. In the fall of 2009 his school made national headlines by announcing it was giving away its collection of 20,000 printed books, albeit some to classrooms.

Tracy maintains that now, much more than before, the library is the most vibrant place in the school with additional library staff and more reference and circulation stations. "It is immaterial to us whether students use print

or electronic forms to read Chaucer and Shakespeare," he states as he describes the library as a learning commons that accurately reflects how students learn in the 21st century. Although few school libraries have followed Cushing Academy's lead in entirely eliminating their print collections, many have reduced its size to make way for the numerous other forms and formats of reading materials, the funds to purchase them, and the space to read them. As Cushing and other schools turn to digital resources, the motive is not to save money but to transform reading and information seeking. Leading and implementing this change in readers and reading are school librarians and school libraries.

We have chosen the word "transform" for our title. To transform means to change significantly for the better. Drawing from our long-term association with school libraries and librarians, our knowledge of the research literature, and our own research, we maintain that school librarians have been a longstanding and significant force in changing readers for the better. This chapter will provide the evidence for this assertion.

Part 1 of this chapter is the foundation for the other two parts. We begin by looking at the numbers of school librarians in different types of schools; we trace the development in the United States of the transformational role from the end of the 19th century to the second decade of the 21st century, using national standards as our indicators. In this foundational part we also look at contemporary national legislation and policy that has an impact on school librarians and their role in reading transformation.

In Part 2, we take a deeper look at the time-honored role of the school library and librarians as motivators in the transformation process. There are hundreds of motivational activities, but we will focus on some of the best documented. They include collection development, providing advice to individuals about reading, and running school-wide reading events.

In Part 3, we examine the role of the school librarian as an individual and the school library as a place with responsibility for students and reading achievement. Despite the substantial body of research addressing these questions which we review, we have to ask ourselves, what do we really know?

Part 1: The Foundation of Transformation

The Presence of Libraries and Librarians in Schools

In the United States, upon which this chapter focuses, 90,760 public schools were in operation during the 2007–2008 school year, the most recent year for which data are available. Of these schools, 90.3% (81,920) have school libraries and 62.1% (50,910) of these libraries have full-time, paid, state-certified school librarians. Libraries in secondary schools are more likely to have a librarian (75.5%) than those in elementary (59.4%) or combined elementary/secondary schools (46.1%)

(Goldring, 2009). Although private schools were not included in this report, according to an earlier NCES (2004) report, based on 2000 data, 62.6% of the 27,223 U.S. private schools at the time had libraries.

These data demonstrates that school libraries in the United States are sufficiently prevalent to have a significant impact on the transformation of readers and reading. We will now seek evidence of quality by delving into the historical evolution of modern school libraries as documented in the standards of "best practices." The evolution of national standards for school libraries documents the change in function of the school library from warehouse to reading hot spot to social networking learning center.

School Library Standards and Guidelines

Standards of practice in school librarianship tell a story that makes Parts 2 and 3—what school librarians do—make more sense. It is unclear whether national standards provide a vision for best professional practice or simply reflect it. The fact remains that leaders at the building, district, state, and national levels, as well as educators in higher education, have developed standards that address school libraries and librarians. These standards provide the only consistent documentation of what has been considered to be best professional practice.

Initially, the school library, officially established in New York state in 1892 (Wofford, 1940), was not seen as a place to transform readers but rather as a more passive place where readers might locate books needed for schoolwork or for pleasure reading. School library standards go back to 1918. Both the 1918 standards and the subsequent 1925 standards were created by the National Education Association (NEA) during a time when school libraries were commonly under the auspices of public libraries. The emphasis was on the selection, care, and cataloging of books. This is not the school library we think of today (hopefully).

The next set of standards was drafted by an American Library Association (ALA) committee in 1945. During the previous two decades, most school libraries were no longer under the auspices of the public library system, but had instead become part of the administrative structure of schools. These new standards, *School Libraries for Today and Tomorrow* (Committees on Post-war Planning of the American Library Association, 1945), contained the first substantial directive for librarians to take responsibility for transforming readers. This was also the first time that the school library was described as an integral part of the educational program. The school library was to "to guide students in their reading to increase their enjoyment, satisfaction, critical judgment, and appreciation" (Gann, 1998, p. 164). We see the recasting of the school librarian's role beginning to take place.

After 1945, five additional sets of standards or guidelines appeared at the national level, and across these decades a marked change in focus occurred, as increasing emphasis was placed on the librarian's responsibility to create information-literate students, meaning students who could formulate questions, seek, find, use, and even create information. Students needed to be skilled readers in order to answer their questions, meet their needs, and/or solve their problems. And the responsibility of school librarians had become to produce an environment in which information literacy could flourish. However, in the end-of-century guidelines, reading is assumed but only fleetingly mentioned.

Near the end of the first decade of the 21st century, the story changes dramatically with the publication of a new set of national standards that brought reading front and center as a responsibility of the school librarian, and furthermore, not only as a motivator of reading but also as a teacher of reading skills. "Reading is a window to the world" (AASL, 2007, p. 2) is the first among nine statements of "common beliefs" upon which these new-century standards are built. What it means is further explicated:

> Reading is a foundational skill for learning, personal growth, and enjoyment. The degree to which students can read and understand text in all formats (e.g., picture, video, print) and all contexts is a key indicator of success in school and in life. As a lifelong learning skill, reading goes beyond decoding and comprehension to interpretation and development of new understandings. (p. 2)

In these 2007 standards, reading is not simply assumed to occur if the proper resources are provided as was the case in the early part of the previous century. The skill of reading is no longer left solely to the classroom teacher, but has moved to become a central focus of the school librarian as well. This is the transformational role of the 21st century librarian and library, and this belief is not merely articulated but is given a place of prominence. The challenge for the school librarian is to be both a teacher of reading skills and a motivational force for reading pleasure in the lives of students. In short, the school librarian is to be a transformational leader in helping young readers achieve a synergy of cognitive and aesthetics skills.

To achieve this, school librarians expect to teach reading skill development as well as to inspire personal growth and enjoyment in young readers. Moreover, 21st century school librarians are often held accountable for student assessment and achievement in tandem with the classroom teacher. School library collections reflect the radical change of literature itself in the digital environment. Ideally, the school library will be the place to find literature that may not yet be fully integrated into or accepted for classroom instruction. Thus, the commitment to 'text in all formats' as a part of reading refers not only to visual and audio text, but to notable and noticeable changes in the print medium as well. Finally, digital technologies and the digital environment permeate every aspect of librarianship, including literature and reading. School librarians are looked to for leadership and expertise in application and integration of these technologies.

National Board Library Media Standards

So far the story of school librarianship and the dramatic change of the school librarian's role from passive curator of collection to reading motivator and teacher of skills have been told solely from the perspective of the American Association of School Librarians (AASL) and its affiliates. However, another set of standards that affect the practice of school librarianship are those of the National Board for Professional Teaching Standards (2001, 2007, 2008). National Board Certification is the highest credential in the teaching profession

In the current assessment process, one of the four portfolios entries for National Board certification in Library Media is Appreciation of Literature. I (Dresang) conducted a research study in the fall of 2009, results of which are in the pre-publication stage, that illuminated a substantial difference in how teachers and school librarians approach the teaching and use of children's literature. The seven teachers with whom I worked were state-certified classroom teachers (K–12) who were within one semester of earning the Master's in Library and Information Studies degree. They were participating in the National Board's Take One! Program, which allows candidates to take one part of the certification exam early. The seven candidates were still classroom teachers when they prepared their portfolios for the Library Media Appreciation of Literature, and it was a struggle for them to think about the appreciation of literature from the perspective of a school librarian.

What I noted from observation and from their portfolios was their desire to use literature as a vehicle to teach a concept. They were pleased if children wanted to read the book or others like it, but that was not their chief concern when introducing literature to their students. School librarians, on the other hand, might use youth literature to teach a concept, but their primary concern is to motivate the child to read the book presented and to link that reading to a wide array of related literature available in the library. Thus I came to understand that the teacher perspective saw, first, the text to self relationship, and second, the text (book) to text (book). In contrast, the school librarian's perspective focused first on the text to text (this book to other books) relationship and second, the text to self.

It should be noted that the International Society for Technology in Education (ISTE) standards are extremely useful to school librarians in many of their roles but are not discussed in depth here due to their lack of focus on reading.

As the final topic in this part, we take a look at the national reading policies that have had a profound effect on the role of the school librarian and reading.

National Reading Policy Applicable to School Libraries in the 21st Century

The National Reading Panel. Although the results of the National Reading Panel (NRP) report have been widely adopted, many librarians are not aware of their origin. In 1997 Congress mandated the convening of a national panel to assess the effectiveness of different approaches used to teach children to read. The methodology and recommendations of the NRP Report (2000) have had a far-ranging effect on public policy in relation to reading and on the criteria by which the acceptability of research methodology is assessed. The influence of the NRP has set off waves of change that have swept into the school library as well as into every classroom in America. The most visible and far reaching effect is the No Child Left Behind Act of 2001 (NCLB), signed into law on January 8, 2002. NCLB reauthorized the Elementary and Secondary Education Act (ESEA, 1965), which has been the main federal law affecting education from kindergarten through high school since it was first passed in 1965.

The NRP based its recommendations on research published in peer reviewed journals. However, they decided to narrow their focus to include only (a) studies that were experimental or quasi-experimental in design and (b) research related to an earlier NRP report that identified what were believed to be the most critical skills relevant for gaining beginning reading skills. The result of this exclusive emphasis on "scientifically-based research," a term by which the experimental and quasi-experimental designs were known, limited the panel's scope to only those aspects of reading that could be quantitatively measured.

An implication for school librarians was that the qualitative research most common in school library studies was not consulted and that motivation to read was not a factor reflected in most of the research. The narrow focus on topics from the scientifically based research, i.e., alphabetics, including the issues of phonemic awareness instruction and phonics instruction; fluency; comprehension strategies; and vocabulary instruction, left many of the research studies to which school librarians had turned for validation of their practices without endorsement or even recognition. It meant that the essential function of readers' advisory work—that is, the librarian's recommendation of books to meet individual readers' reading interests and needs—and many other motivational reading activities were not supported by the definition of scientific research adhered to by the NRP.

Elementary and Secondary Education Act/No Child Left Behind. No Child Left Behind was due for reauthorization in 2008, but as of 2010 it had not been reauthorized. If changes to the legislation proposed by President Obama are passed, funding conditions for school librarians will worsen rather than improve. In addition, although the nature of high-stakes testing will change somewhat, the lack of emphasis on reading motivation versus skill building may continue. The good news is that school librarians do promote the NRP-identified skills and are becoming quite adept at imbedding skill instruction with reading for interest and pleasure activities as we will document in Parts 2 and 3 of this chapter.

Improving Literacy through School Libraries. The No Child Left Behind legislation prior to a reauthorization in the Obama administration included one program directly related to school librarians and literacy, "Improving Literacy through School Libraries" (LSL). It was celebrated as the first federally funded program directly aimed at school libraries in three decades. Even though the original allocation was to be approximately $300 million and it hovered at around $19.5M or less every year since authorization, it was a step in the right direction. In addition, only those local education agencies (LEAs, usually school districts) in which at least 20% of students served are from families with incomes below the poverty line are eligible to apply, a stricter standard than families eligible for free and reduced lunch. And only LEAs, not individual schools, can apply.

Four years after its initial authorization, the U.S. government evaluated LSL for its effectiveness by surveying the 400 recipients of grants. The government declared the results a success because of the positive outputs, e.g., more visits to the library by children, more collaboration, more technology, more after school programs (Whelan, 2006). According to the final evaluation report, "the percentage of students who met or exceeded the proficiency requirements on state reading assessments increased by an extra 2.7 percentage points among grantees, a statistically significant increase.... In addition, increasing the number of books was associated with significant increases in test scores. Because of the lack of a true experimental design, these findings cannot support causal inferences" (Michie & Bradford, 2009, p. 76).

Despite this apparent success, in the Obama administration's proposed reauthorization of ESEA/No Child Left Behind, no funding is designated specifically for school libraries. "Improving Literacy through School Libraries" would be consolidated with 11 other programs into funds that would go to state education agencies rather than local education agencies for a wide range of family literacy programs under the name "Effective Teaching and Learning: Literacy." The possibility for widespread positive impact on school libraries and their role in literacy education from the reauthorized ESEA is slim.

Having described the foundation upon which school librarians and libraries operate, we go to Part 2 to examine the intriguing question of how school librarians and libraries implement the prescribed (and perhaps not prescribed) roles of transforming students into passionate (or at least semi-passionate) readers.

Part 2: Motivation and Transformation

Part 2 of our transformation story continues by highlighting three key components of the reading motivation that librarians working with youth provide. All three are permeated with what has become known as the "library faith," the belief in the provision of library service to youth as a "just cause" that librarians pursue with all the passion of crusaders. The first role is that of school librarian as developer of collections, a role that has changed over time as young readers' interests and needs have changed. The second is a focus on the individual reader and advice given to him or her in an attempt to meet specific interests and needs. And the third component is the provision of reading motivation, a potpourri of school-based and national programs of which only a sample can be taken.

The Library Faith

The 1945 Standards stated that the school library was to "to guide students in their reading to increase their enjoyment, satisfaction, critical judgment, and appreciation" (Gann, 1998, p. 164). Clearly, the emphasis here was on motivation. It is not entirely clear what was meant by "critical judgment," but in this context, it most likely had more to do with 'making good choices' than with a skill that would fall under the rubric of today's expectations for critical thinking. From then until now, numerous articles have appeared in professional journals documenting best professional practices that school librarians have used to achieve this holy grail.

Such giants in the field as Frances Clarke Sayers in her *Summoned by Books* (Blinn, 1965) inspired librarians studying to work with children with their ideals of providing quality literature for young readers. According to Sayers and many other leaders, if books written for children were evaluated and selected against established criteria, the resulting selections were certain to capture the attention of young readers and motivate them to engage in reading. This belief was so strong that over time it came to be known as "the library faith." Hearne and Jenkins (1999) have documented this era of high ideals, noting that "power and glory...radiate from working with children and literature, especially literature for its own sake, freed of pedagogical requirements" (p. 536). Aside from historical accounts, academic studies that document the effect of this type of motivation on young readers in terms of concrete outcomes do not exist. At the time, prima facie evidence was sufficiently convincing that no one considered recording information about the outcomes of reading motivation activities as a necessary—or even a desirable—activity. For school librarians, the work of reading motivation was combined with the support for teaching and learning. However, an emphasis on the motivational factors remained.

Developing Collections Reflecting Societal Change

As soon as there was the profession of librarianship, librarians were in charge of developing and maintaining collections. In Umberto Eco's (1980) *The Name of the Rose* set in the 14th century, only librarians had access to the collections they built and protected. Today, in many large public library systems, a central coordinator does the collection development for all the system's libraries, taking into account the differing demographics, needs, and interests of the population served by each branch. In school libraries it is most commonly the local librarians who make the collection choices.

Representing All Children. As David Loertscher (1996) has noted, school collections should be what he refers to as "unbalanced." He advises school librarians to utilize a process he calls Collection Mapping to ensure that school libraries have not only a broad general collection but also "map" their collections with in-depth areas of emphasis that reflect current curriculum (Loertscher & Wimberly, 2009).

Another way in which school librarians over the past four decades have become adept at developing unbalanced collections is through their overview of the entire school population, their recognition of the needs of changing populations, and their assurance of who their users will be at any point in time. They have been able to view and accommodate to the needs and interests of changing populations and to align them with changes in the literature itself.

Children and society have changed over time, and their books and school library collections have also changed. One much-noted change occurred in "the new realism of the late sixties" as children's and young adult fiction began to reflect the often-harsh realities of the lives of many young people. There were still plenty of happy endings, but tidy outcomes and upbeat resolutions were no longer a requirement for stories for young readers. Other dramatic changes occurred in the ensuing three decades first in terms of increased gender equality, and in increasing, although still inadequate, presence of children of color and children with disabilities. School librarians were often in the vanguard of transforming their library collections to better meet the needs of their students by more accurately reflecting the larger society in which the students lived. Some librarians who work with youth see the process of diversifying their collections to represent the population of the United States, if not the world, as part of their library faith and their obligation to young readers. Others are still quite myopic in their vision of collection development.

Literature for Digital Age Readers. Another change that has had a huge impact on collections in school libraries and subsequently on readers and reading can be attributed to the pervasive nature of the digital environment. Over the past decade the theory of Radical Change (Dresang, 1999), which is based on the digital age principles of interactivity, connectivity, and access, has gained widespread recognition as a means to understand and explain the transformation of books as well as information behavior, including reading, for youth (Dresang, 2005a; 2005b; Whelan,

2007). These digital age principles can be recognized in books for youth by three sets of indicators that relate to Changing Forms and Formats, Changing Perspectives, and Changing Boundaries.

Radical Change was developed when I (Dresang) sought to explain the Caldecott Award picture book, *Black and White* (Macaulay, 1990), which I had helped select for the Medal as a member of the 1991 Caldecott Award Committee. Observing that reading hypertext and reading a handheld book such as *Black and White* required similar cognitive processes led to the development of the theory of Radical Change. Other books, I discovered, exhibited many of the same characteristics; their form and formats reflected the hypertextual, multilayered, and graphic interfaces of the computer and promoted interactive, non-linear, nonsequential reading. Subsequent reflection on the digital environment and the changes in literature for youth brought forth other characteristics. Changing perspectives had begun to appear, perspectives that incorporate previously marginalized populations, including youth themselves. Expanded boundaries in content encompassed new types of communities, characters, and subjects that had previously been taboo in children's books.

If you take a quick look through the lists of Newbery and Caldecott Award books over the past two decades, you will see many that can be identified by their Radical Change characteristics. For example, the 2008 Caldecott Medal, awarded to the most outstanding picture book first published in the United States annually, went to Brian Selznick's (2007) *The Inventions of Hugo Cabret*, a book that was deemed as radical as was *Black and White* in 1991. In the same year the Newbery Medal, awarded to the most distinguished contribution to American literature for children, went to another book with radical change characteristics, Amy Schlitz's (2007) *Good Masters! Sweet Ladies! Voices from a Medieval Village*, a story told through poetry reflecting a variety of perspectives from a 13th century village.

Picture books and fiction are not alone in exhibiting digital age characteristics. A pioneering publishing company, Dorling-Kindersley, created books that, according to founder Peter Kindersley, were intended to demonstrate that reading the pictures could convey as much information as reading the words (personal communication, 2001). Information books moved rapidly from sparsely illustrated linear texts to exciting portrayals of information to suit the needs of the rapid scanner as well as of the deep reader. And midst all of this change in traditional handheld books, graphic novels, formerly disparaged as comic books, invaded every genre from picture book to novel to information book.

School libraries and librarians have always been in the position of being in the vanguard regarding trends in children's literature, reflecting the changes in society and in children's interests in their collection; their impact in guiding the direction of non-textbook reading materials has been far broader than that of any single classroom teacher as they have collected and recommended books for the entire school population.

Readers' Advisory Services in a Digital Age. An integral part of the library faith is readers' advisory work. The term "readers' advisory" typically applied to guiding users to fiction reading for pleasure, often focused on certain genres such as mystery, romance, etc. For children, the component of choosing excellent, inspiring literature played a part in early readers' advisory work. In contemporary readers' advisory roles, librarians have moved from recommending the best books to recommending what best matches a reader's interests.

Often readers' advisory is thought to take place only in the public library, but literary recommendations occur also in school libraries (Moyer, 2007), a phenomenon that emphasizes a commonality between the two places where children and young adults read. And it is often the school librarian whom successful adults recall when they speak of the most important influence in their lives. Readers' advisory work is the library faith in action.

For librarians accurately to discern and understand readers' interests and advise them on books they might like, they must be attuned to the changes taking place in reader preferences. One of my Florida State University doctoral students, Kyungwon Koh, has developed a preliminary typology of youth information behavior indicators that parallel the changes observed in their literature (Dresang & Koh, 2009). Pantaleo (2004a, 2004b, 2007a, 2007b, 2009) has conducted a dozen studies in which she has documented how elementary age youth read and comprehend radical change books. Hassett (2005, 2006a, 2006b) has developed a theory of non-linear reading and has observed, like Pantaleo, that reading hypertextually, that is in a nonlinear manner as one does using hypertext links on digital device, helps rather than hinders comprehension. I have had many librarians over the past decade tell me that seeing the differences in books and in young readers through the lens of Radical Change has vastly improved their readers' advisory work.

Moreover, reading in the 21st century has moved far beyond the handheld book to the computer screen and to the numerous Personal Information Devices. Youth have delved into social networks in the 2.0 environment, connecting to other youth not only to socialize, but also to exchange information, often in the form of text and often about reading. Dresang and Kotrla (2009) have suggested that Rosenblatt's Reader Response theory not only must take into account the interaction between the reader and the book, but also and often, the interaction with online social network buddies. Social networking around books has becomes so prevalent that Howard (2010) has developed a taxonomy to describe the level of involvement of young readers with others. Because school libraries have traditionally been ahead of classrooms in incorporating the newest technologies and may be the only place some youth encounter them, youth often have the opportunity to first experience the changes in thinking and learning that are available in their school libraries. When advising young people about books and reading, the printed book is not the only or perhaps not even the primary source that the librarian will offer. This discussion leads to other more traditional but still social reading experiences.

Schoolwide and National School-based Reading Events. In their quest to provide motivation for readers, one of the best professional practices in which school librarians have provided leadership has been schoolwide events or events that involve a significant number of children across classrooms or grade levels. The librarian is, of course, uniquely positioned to oversee these types of events. Sometimes all children are involved; other times volunteers are sought or representatives are selected.

Perhaps one of the best known of these events is called Battle of the Books (2008), which is a nationally organized competition the aim of which is to encourage youth to read quality literature. The competition starts between or among classroom teams in a local school. Teams including school librarians select the books. Book fairs are another reading-related activity that school librarians often orchestrate in order to provide support for more books for the library as well as to encourage the ownership of books by youth. Paperback swaps may be arranged with the same goals.

If I Can Read, I Can Do Anything (2007) is a national reading club for Native American children. Through sponsorship at local schools, the program hopes to encourage Native American children to read, to use their school libraries, and to have access to relevant library collections. ALA past President Roy, the first Native American ALA President, is Director of this program.

School librarians initiate various configurations of book discussion programs. In the United States, these discussions may range from something as local and uncomplicated as a lunch bunch group to a collaborative effort by a public and school librarian known as Young Critics (Clark & McClelland, 1997) to something more highly organized such as the Junior Great Books program (Great Books Foundation, 1995–2008), which requires training and provides a scaffolded program for discussion from Kindergarten through 12th grade. One method of reading motivation particularly widespread among secondary school librarians is the short, pithy booktalk. In "On Beyond Book Clubs," one librarian shares how she has built upon the idea of booktalks and traditional book clubs by encouraging the teens with whom she works to share what they are reading as well as to give 'quickie reviews' to new books that have not yet publicly circulated (Honnold, 2008).

Another manner in which school librarians work to transform U.S. readers is through statewide reading choice programs. Many states have these, as will be seen in Junko

Yokota's chapter on awards in this *Handbook*. Typically, a group of teachers and school librarians choose the books to be considered for the award and teachers throughout the state register their classrooms to read and vote for the winner.

Almost none of these programs typically led by school librarians are associated with specific research linked to the role of the school media specialist or results for young readers. They are on the surface supported by the library faith of our foremothers. However, these programs on which school librarians spend so much time are backed up by a below-the-surface plethora of research that supports the principles behind them. For example, it is an undisputable fact that the more children read, the better readers they become. "In the United States, fourth-graders who read for fun every day or almost every day have higher average scores on the combined reading literacy scale compared to those who never or almost never read for fun, or do so once or twice a month" (NCES, 2001, para. 4).

Many school librarians look to Stephen Krashen (2004) for the evidence they seek regarding the power of reading per se—not reading for specific skills, not reading certain types of "good" literature, but just lots of reading. Krashen's review of reading research documents the value of time spent in free voluntary reading, a program initiated and supported by many librarians, during which the entire school sets aside minutes, usually around 15 minutes per day, for students to read uninterrupted and with minimum expectation for post-reading check-ups. He notes that "in-school free reading programs are consistently effective. In 51 out of 54 comparison studies (94%), readers do as well as or better than students who were engaged in traditional programs" (p. 2). He cites research that refutes the emphasis on direct instruction as more effective than time spent reading something that the reader chooses to read. Krashen concludes that "reading is the only way… we become good readers, develop a good writing style, an adequate vocabulary, advanced grammatical competence, and the only way we become good spellers" (p. 37). If Krashen's interpretation of research is accurate, it provides a powerful rationale for the many free, voluntary reading activities supported by school librarians and suggests that they do, indeed, transform readers.

But it is time now to examine this new role that we have alluded to throughout this chapter—the school librarian and transformation of readers through reading achievement. Just how does this happen and how do we know?

Part 3: Reading Achievement and Transformation

In the past, little was said about the librarian engaged in direct teaching of reading or as an essential direct support for achievement as measured by standardized tests—or for that matter as measured in any other manner. However, the topic is not an entirely new one.

Gaver (1963) conducted a groundbreaking quasi-experimental study involving 271 schools in 13 states, looking at the effect of centralized school libraries and academic achievement; she found that academic achievement was significantly higher when there was a centralized library that was well stocked and easily accessible to students and teachers. A few smaller studies followed in the wake of Gaver's. However, over the last decade of the 20th century and into the 21st century, the question of what role the school librarian plays in transforming youth into readers who score well on achievement tests rose to the forefront.

The School Library Impact Studies

The studies collectively referred to as School Library Impact Studies are the most extensive set of research projects to have attempted to associate school library characteristics with students' academic achievement. Beginning with what has become known as the "first Colorado study" (Lance, Welborn, & Hamilton-Pennell, 1993), these projects are analyses of survey responses and available data from individual states, data, including students' scores on standardized achievement tests, from individual states. Since the first Colorado study, similar studies were conducted in 18 other states and repeated in Colorado (see http://www.lrs.org/impact.php for links to these reports). Of the 20 studies, 14 included student's scores on reading sections of statewide standardized tests as one of the response variables. All 14 either were conducted by Keith Curry Lance and his colleagues at the Colorado State Library Research Service or were conducted by others using Lance et al.'s survey and methodology. A summary of study results through 2007 has been distributed widely in the pamphlet *School Libraries Work!* (National Commission on Libraries and Information Science, 2008).

Six of these 14 studies, all performed by Lance's research group, focused specifically on identifying predictor variables of standardized reading test scores of elementary, middle, and high school students. Variables reported as having a statistically significant positive correlation with higher reading scores are:

1. school library staff
   a. presence of a full-time, certified school library media specialist
   b. number of work hours/week/100 students
   c. amount of time spent teaching students and engaging in reading motivation activities
   d. amount of time spent collaborating with classroom teachers, individually as well as participation with them on policy-making groups
2. school library resources and services
   a. print volumes/student
   b. periodical subscriptions/student

c. availability of networked resources (e.g., library catalogs and licensed databases)
d. access to the Internet
e. availability of computer hardware
3. accessibility of school library to students
a. library service hours/week
b. number of library visits by individual students (distinct from scheduled class visits)
4. school library expenditures/student

A common factor that correlated with high achievement and was of particular interest to this research review was the level of reading motivation activities and reading incentives and support for ample resources in the collections.

The conclusions of these 6 and the 14 other School Library Impact Studies have been used as evidence of the importance of school libraries in an era of high stakes testing and funding provided or withheld based on the results of the tests. States as well as school districts and individuals have employed a variety of strategies to disseminate and make use of these studies. Among the questions posed at the outset of this research review was "What evidence exists, who has produced it, how confident can we be in its results, and what difference has it made?" The latter question was answered by The Colorado State Library Research in a survey posted to LMNET, a 16,000 member discussion group of school librarians. Eighty-one percent of the respondents shared this research with their principals and approximately half shared it with their superintendents, other administrators and/or parents, and two-thirds shared it with their teachers. Two-thirds stated that it improved their relationships with principals (Callison, 2005).

Although there is no doubt about benefits that have come from these studies, the question remains, "how confident can we be in the results?" In many of Lance's studies and the ones modeled thereon, the results and conclusions are questionable because of methodology or of omissions in the reports. For example, in reporting on the first Colorado study, Lance (1994, para. 5) states that "Ideally, schools included in a sample for a study like this would be selected on a random, stratified, or quota basis. None of these sampling designs was possible, however."

There is no evidence that any of the subsequent studies were based on random sampling. Without random sampling, no generalizations can be made, of course. Because data distributions were not presented and there were no discussions of the extent to which the data met the assumptions of the statistical tests used, the results' validity is questionable. Lance et al. argue in support of a causal relationship of the predictor variables to academic achievement on the basis of the consistency of the core results. Lance states,

> The cause-and effect claim associated with these correlations was strengthened by the reliability of the relationships

between key library variables (e.g., staffing levels, collection size, spending) and test scores when other school and community conditions were taken into account. (Callison, 2005, para 12)

Regardless of the number of data sets in which correlation is found, correlation alone never demonstrates causality.

Lance acknowledges that "in every Colorado-style study, the strongest available predictor of test scores has been socio-economic conditions, as indicated by the percentage of students eligible for the National School Lunch Program. This single variable has explained half to two-thirds of the variation in test scores in states where studies have been conducted" (Callison, 2005, para. 27). He concludes "In other words, because the economic variable is so strong, and because it confounds the effects of so many other variables of interest, it is time to explore new methodological options" (para. 28). Lance goes on to note that the U.S. Department of Education's emphasis on scientifically-based research, e.g., randomized samples with large populations and the trial of an intervention, makes 'acceptable' research difficult. It is not possible to intervene by, for example, withholding library services or funding for some children and not for others. This is a dilemma that remains to be solved.

Two Technologies and Transformation of Readers

It is impossible to discuss anywhere in this chapter all the many ways school librarians use technology to both motivate and promote achievement among students. However we have chosen two uses of technology, one a program using computers to measure and record results (electronic reading programs) and the other a digital format for books (e-books), and we placed the discussion here since the link to reading achievement is for many the most compelling reason for the use of these two technologies.

The use of electronic reading programs is one of the most controversial topics in school librarianship. Because these programs depend on large collections of literature in order to succeed, school libraries have become deeply involved with them. Renaissance Learning (2008) states that Accelerated Reader™ (AR) is used in 73,000 or roughly 60% of North American schools. Approximately 100,000 books are now in the AR database. The second most commonly used electronic reading program, Reading Counts!™ (Scholastic) does not keep statistics about how many schools use it.

We have conducted two of the very few library-related studies of AR. Our study of a random sample of several hundred grant applications for school library books from a national foundation found that librarians use the program, believing it to be transformational for readers, both to motivate and to create gains in achievement. One librarian told us that "since implementing Accelerated Reader™ a number of years ago we have seen our students' reading scores on standardized tests grow steadily" (Dresang

& Kotrla, 2003). Another research study we conducted showed the link between the Accelerated Reader™ program and national reading policy of No Child Left Behind and the National Reading Panel (Everhart, Dresang, & Kotrla, 2005), the broad implications of which are too complex to discuss here. One implication is that AR is linked to the student achievement that NCLB requires.

Counterbalancing the positive acceptance of some school librarians are the features that raise the ire of many other librarians, features that focus on the extrinsic rather than intrinsic motivation to read, the prominent labeling of books and therefore of readers, and the insistence of students as well as teachers and parents in some schools that young readers read nothing but books that will earn them rewards and are at their reading level as defined by the particular program. The measure of reading difficulty is unconvincing to many, and the separate shelving that occurs in some libraries, splitting authors' works from one another, is tantamount to denying access in the eyes of others. In our research, we also found out that the poorer the school, the more likely they were to use these programs, which raises another question of equitable access (Dresang & Kotrla, 2003). Often librarians have no choice but to administer the program and to participate in applying the results to students' grades.

Unfortunately, the questions on the basic Accelerated Reader™ quizzes are all at the lowest level on Bloom's Taxonomy, i.e., remembering. The following question is taken from a sample Basic quiz for middle readers on *The Adventures of Tom Sawyer:*

What did Tom offer to do if Jim would trade jobs with him?

- Give Jim a turkey wishbone
- Tell Jim where to find a dead rattlesnake
- Show Jim his sore toe
- Teach Jim how to whistle (http://www.renlearn.com/ar/quizzes.aspx)

They do not promote the kind of 21st century thinking, analyzing, seeking meaning that students need and for which they should be rewarded. When schools depend entirely on AR or mostly on AR Basic tests for their reading program, this is a serious downside. Reading Counts! has a somewhat higher level of questioning. Over dependence on these programs does not meet the 21st century national standards or best practices for school libraries.

Another large question looms for the future of technology and transformational reading—how readily will e-books be adopted by youth? With many more Personal Information Devices accommodating the download of books on the run, the possibility of e-book popularity replacing that of the paperback is entirely likely. If so, what will be the role of school libraries in this transformation? Some libraries, e.g., one of the Gulf Coast libraries severely damaged by Hurricane Katrina, 2006, rebuilt its collection, largely for lack of space, through the use of e-books that can be checked out just as traditional books have been.

Ultimately, as the *Standards for the 21st Century Learner* state, "the degree to which students can read and understand text in all formats (e.g., picture, video, print) and all contexts is a key indicator of success in school and in life" (AASL, 2007). Readers and reading can be transformed regardless of container of the text.

Teaching Skills for Transformation

The publication of a position paper to interpret and provide further guidance for the role of the school librarian in reading according to the new 2007 standards is an indicator of how important the role of the school librarian is in this best practices document. AASL produced both a position paper (AASL, 2009a) and a toolkit (AASL, 2009b) that describe the complexities of the dual role of the school librarian in relation to reading motivation and skill instruction and give examples of how to accomplish this. The new part of these items relates to the direct teaching of reading skills, although combining this with motivation is clearly part of the teaching skill.

Since comprehension is one of the National Reading Panel's top six skills, it presents a very compatible one for school librarians to emphasize. Judi Moreillon (2007) has demonstrated how school librarians can seize upon this new requirement by focusing on comprehension through the use of highly motivating literature in a collaborative relationship with a classroom teacher. Sharon Grimes (2006) has also written a book, *Reading Is Our Business,* that draws upon her experience as an elementary school librarian in Michigan. Her seven-step reading strategy is illustrated with examples of how to help students understand what they read. Study of the examples in the Moreillon and the Grimes books will provide a very concrete vision of how to combine the motivational and instructional roles expected of a 21st century school librarian in relation to changing readers.

The Value of School Libraries for Reading from the Students' Point of View

Another substantial body of research, another set of state studies, has been conducted under the auspices of Ross Todd (2008), Director of the Center for International Scholarship in School Libraries (CISSL) at Rutgers University and is in the process of replication by others. While the Library Impact Studies employ quantitative methodologies, Todd's research is qualitative.

His interest in the overall transformative nature of school libraries includes reading, and in fact, he has identified findings in relation to readings as perhaps the most important. No claim for generalizability is made for these studies because schools were chosen to participate based on best practices. To date, Todd has conducted studies in Ohio and in Delaware.

The survey employed by Todd and based on Brenda

Dervin's sense-making work contains blocks of questions, one of which has questions devoted to reading (Todd & Heinstrom, 2006, pp. 75–79), e.g., "The school library has helped me become a better reader" (in the Delaware study, 65% of the students said this was a help) and "The school library has helped me read more" (in the Delaware study, 63% of the students said this was a help). Most telling, however, were the open-ended comments from students. Looking at both the Ohio and Delaware study results, Todd found that "their perceptions of how school libraries support them on their wider reading interests and the development of reading literacies were lower than other dimensions in the studies." He goes on to note that library reading "initiatives center on book talks, literature displays, book promotions, and the like, all which seem to be fairly passive activities," while the students "valued such things as availability of latest releases; personalized, targeted, proactive service; identifying interests; developing self-esteem; using curriculum as link to reading enjoyment and enrichment; and being shown that academic success can be achieved through improving reading" (Todd, 2008, para. 6). In terms of recommendations, Todd concludes that "This means that school librarians must be much more astute in assessing the needs of students…reading environments, and being much more actively engaged in the literacy and reading policies and frameworks in the school" (para. 8). In other words, motivation is not enough, nor is simply providing services. Providing the synergy of aesthetic and cognitive skills, focusing on pleasure and skill and bringing the two together is essential if the 21st century librarian is to continue to transform readers and reading.

Epilogue

Dr. Dresang and Dr. Kotrla gave me their chapter to read and asked me to comment from a seventh-grader's point of view (not on whether it was interesting or boring but whether it seemed to describe what is important to me about my school library and librarian in relation to reading). Well, I'm a lot more positive about how much Ms. Odema helps me than those teens in Ohio. I couldn't do without her! I wonder if they are really aware of all the assistance they get! She did help my friend and me on that project we were doing—she demonstrated a systematic way to compare the sources on the Harlem Renaissance and taught us some strategies for seeing what we could infer about the contemporary pictures of Harlem we were analyzing. And she helped us locate a book that is cool in the ICDL in the first place.

What I don't get is why there is such a big fuss over whether printed books are important or not. What's the big deal? I'm actually reading (if you count comprehending and relating to a good story or needed information) all the time. All my friends are reading all the time also—and we read both words and pictures—that is the point of this Visual Interpretive Analysis. So I say school librarians are essential—I'm big on using their help on and off line (as we can ask a question any time of day or night). School libraries are also essential—I actually use this place more than I ever did when it was filled with printed books. There's more space available for us to hang out and talk about our projects and to learn from others. I don't necessarily go along with removing ALL the printed books, though—sometimes it would be a lot easier just to pick one up and READ and with the important ones scattered out in classrooms—well isn't that going back to the early 20th century way of things? And that stuff Dr. Dresang says about how printed books have changed—right on! No one I know would read, for example, an information book that had nothing but dense pages of text—we like the guiding boxes of extra facts or explanations. Like that Claudette Colvin book (Hoose, 2009) Ms. Odema recommended last week. I've read a whole lot of books about the Civil Rights days and didn't know what Jim Crow meant until I read the little insert clearly explaining it. So to answer Dr. Dresang's and Dr. Kotrla's question, no way school libraries and librarians or even printed books are becoming obsolete—both are needed. I'd definitely be a much poorer learner without all the help I get from the librarians and the resources they provide and the skills they teach me! But don't take my iPod or e-book reader away. I am addicted to marking my place and looking up words, and all the neat things I can do with digital books. And, hey, don't take away all my printed books either or make it harder for me to locate them. And most of all tell the world that we kids are reading more these days rather tha less. I'm sure of that. Well, just text me if I can help you again. Bye.

Literature References

Collins, S. (2009). *Catching fire*. New York, NY: Scholastic Press.

Collins, S. (2008). *The hunger games*. New York, NY: Scholastic Press.

Eco, U. (1980). *The name of the rose* (W. Weaver, Trans.). San Diego, CA: Harcourt.

Hoose, P. M. (2009). *Claudette Colvin: Twice toward justice*. New York, NY: Melanie Kroupa Books.

Igus, T. (1998). *I see the rhythm*. (M. Wood, Illus.). San Francisco, CA: Children's Book Press.

Macaulay, D. (1990). *Black and white*. Boston, MA: Houghton Mifflin.

Myers, W. D. (1997). *Harlem: A poem*. New York, NY: Scholastic.

Schlitz, L. A. (2007). *Good masters! Sweet ladies! Voices from a medieval village*. Cambridge, MA: Candlewick Press.

Selznick, B. (2007). *The invention of Hugo Cabret: A novel in words and pictures*. New York, NY: Scholastic Press.

Academic References

American Association of School Librarians. (2007). *Standards for the 21st-century learner*. Retrieved April 6, 2008, from http://www.ala.org/ala/mgrps/divs/aasl/guidelinesandstandards/learningstandards/standards.cfm

American Association of School Librarians. (2009a). *Position paper on the school library media specialist role in reading*. Retrieved February 14, 2010, from http://www.ala.org/ala/mgrps/divs/aasl/aaslissues/positionstatements/roleinreading.cfm

American Association of School Librarians. (2009b). *School library media specialist's role in reading toolkit*. Retrieved February 14, 2010 from http://www.ala.org/ala/mgrps/divs/aasl/aaslissues/toolkits/ALA_print_layout_1_561976_561976.cfm

Battle of the Books. (2008). *Battle of the books*. Retrieved April 6, 2008, from http://www.battleofthebooks.com/

Blinn, M. J. (Ed.). (1965). *Summoned by books: Essays and speeches by Frances Clarke Sayers*. New York, NY: Viking Press.

Callison, D. (2005). Enough already? Blazing new trails for school library research: An interview with Keith Curry Lance, director, library research service, Colorado state library & University of Denver [Electronic Version]. *School Library Media Research*. Retrieved April 6, 2008, from http://www.ala.org/ala/mgrps/divs/aasl/aaslpubsandjournals/slmrb/editorschoiceb/lance/interviewlance.cfm

Clark, M., & McClelland, K. (1997, July). Young critics with a passion for books. *Book Links, 6*, 23–35.

Committees on Post-war Planning of the American Library Association. (1945). *School libraries for today and tomorrow: Functions and standards*. Chicago, IL: American Library Association.

Dresang, E. T. (1999). *Radical change: Books for youth in a digital age*. New York, NY: H.W. Wilson.

Dresang, E. T. (2005a). Radical change. In K. E. Fisher, S. Erdelez, & L. McKechnie (Eds.), *Theories of Information Behavior* (pp. 298–302). Medford, NJ: Information Today.

Dresang, E. T. (2005b). The information seeking behavior of youth in a digital environment. *Library Trends, 54*(2), 178–196.

Dresang, E. T, & Koh, K. (2009). Radical Change theory and school media centers in the digital age. *Library Trends 58*(1), 26–50.

Dresang, E. T., & Kotrla, B. (2009) Radical Change theory and synergistic reading for digital age youth. *Journal of Aesthetics Education 43*(2), 92–107.

Dresang, E., & Kotrla, M. B. (2003). Breaking barriers with student-centred teaching and learning using library books in the United States' poorest schools. *Selected Papers from the 32nd Annual Conference of the International Forum on Research in School Librarianship, Durbin South Africa 7–11 July, 2003*. Erie, PA: International Association of School Librarianship.

The Editors. (2010, February 14). Do school libraries need books? *New York Times*. Retrieved February 14, 2010, from http://roomfordebate.blogs.nytimes.com/2010/02/10/do-school-libraries-need-books/#james

Elementary and Secondary Education Act. (ESEA). (1965). Pub. L. No. 89-10, 79 Stat. 27.

Everhart, N., Dresang. E. T., & Kotrla, B. (2005). Accelerated Reader and Information policy, information literacy, and knowledge management: U.S. and international implications. In S. Lee et al. (Eds.), *Information leadership in a culture of change. Selected papers from the 34th Annual Conference of the International Association of School Librarianship and Ninth International Forum on Research in School Librarianship*. Hong Kong, China, 8–12 July 2005. [CD-ROM]. Erie, PA: International Association of School Librarianship.

Gann, L. (1998). School library media standards and guidelines: A review of their significance and impact. In K. H. Latrobe (Ed.), *The emerging school library media center: Historical issues and perspectives* (pp. 153–194). Englewood, CO: Libraries Unlimited.

Gaver, M. V. (1963). *Effectiveness of centralized library service in elementary schools* (2nd ed.). New Brunswick, NJ: Rutgers University Press.

Goldring, R. (2009). *Characteristics of public and bureau of Indian education elementary and secondary school library media centers in the United States: results from the 2007–08 schools and staffing survey (NCES 2009-322)*. National Center for Education Statistics, Institute of Education Sciences, U.S. Department of Education. Washington, DC. Retrieved February 13, 2010, from http://nces.ed.gov/pubs2009/2009322.pdf

Great Books Foundation. (1995–2008). *Great books foundation*. Retrieved April 6, 2008,, from http://www.greatbooks.org/

Grimes, S. (2006). *Reading is our business: How libraries can foster reading comprehension*. Chicago, IL: American Library Association.

Hassett, D. D. (2005). Reading hypertextually: Children's literature and comprehension instruction. *New Horizons in Learning*. Retrieved April 13, 2007, from http://www.newhorizons.org/strategies/literacy/hassett.htm

Hassett, D. D. (2006a). Technological difficulties: A theoretical frame for understanding the non-relativistic permanence of traditional print literacy in elementary education. *Journal of Curriculum Studies, 38*, 135–159.

Hassett, D. D. (2006b). Signs of the times: The governance of alphabetic print over 'appropriate' and natural reading development. *Journal of Early Childhood Literacy, 6*, 77–103.

Hearne, B., & Jenkins, C. (1999). Sacred texts: What our foremothers left us in the way of psalms, proverbs, precepts, and practices. *The Horn Book Magazine, 75*(5), 536–558.

Honnold, R. (2008). Beyond book clubs. *Voice of Youth Advocates, 31*(1), 19–21.

Howard, V. (2010). Peer influences on young teen readers: An emerging taxonomy. *Young Adult Library Services, 8*(2), 34–44.

If I Can Read, I Can Do Anything. (2007). *If I can read, I can do anything: A national reading club for Native American children*. Retrieved April 6, 2008, from http://www.ischool.utexas.edu/~ifican/index.html

Krashen, S. D. (2004). *The power of reading: Insights from the research* (2nd ed.). Portsmouth, NH: Heinemann.

Lance, K. C. (1994). The impact of school library media centers on academic achievement [Electronic Version] *School Library Media Research, 22*. Retrieved April 6, 2006, from http://www.ala.org/ala/mgrps/divs/aasl/aaslpubsandjournals/slmrb/editorschoiceb/infopower/slctlancehtml.cfm

Lance, K. C., Welborn, L., & Hamilton-Pennell, C. (1993). *The impact of school library media centers on academic achievement*. Castle Rock, CO: Hi Willow Research and Publishing.

Loertscher, D. V. (1996). *Collection mapping in the LMC: Building access in a world of technology*. San Jose, CA: Hi Willow Research and Publishing.

Loertscher, D. V., & Wimberly, L. H. (2009). *Collection development using the collection mapping technique: A guide for librarians*. San Jose, CA: Hi Willow Research.

Michie, J., & Bradford, W. (2009). Second evaluation of the improving literacy through school libraries programs. U.S. Department of Education, Office of Planning, Evaluation and Policy Development, Policy and Program Studies Service, Washington, D.C. Retrieved February 13, 2010, from http://www2.ed.gov/rschstat/eval/other/libraries/libraries09.pdf

Moreillon, J. (2007). *Collaborative strategies for teaching reading comprehension: Maximizing your impact*. Chicago, IL: American Library Association.

Moyer, M. (2007). Books alive: Reading incentive programs for high school students. *Library Media Connection, 25*, 10–12.

National Board for Professional Teaching Standards. (2001). *NBPTS Library media standards*. Retrieved April 6, 2008, from http://www.nbpts.org/the_standards/standards_by_cert?ID=19&x=36&y=8

National Board for Professional Teaching Standards. (2007). *Library media scoring guide.* Retrieved April 13, 2008, from http://www. nbpts.org/for_candidates/scoring?ID=19&x=31&y=9

National Board for Professional Teaching Standards. (2008). *National Board for Professional Teaching Standards.* Retrieved January 25, 2008, from http://www.nbpts.org/

National Center for Education Statistics. (2001). *Reading outside of school for enjoyment.* Retrieved April 1, 2008, from http://nces.ed.gov/pubs2004/pirlspub/12.asp

National Center for Education Statistics. (2004). *The status of public and private school library media centers in the United States: 1999–2000.* Retrieved April 1, 2008 from http://nces.ed.gov/pubsearch/pubsinfo.asp?pubid=2004313

National Commission on Libraries and Information Science. (2008). *School libraries work!* . Retrieved April 8, 2008, from http://www2.scholastic.com/content/collateral_resources/pdf/s/slw3_2008.pdf

National Reading Panel. (2000). *Summary report.* Retrieved on April 13, 2007, from http://www.nationalreadingpanel.org/Publications/publications.htm

No Child Left Behind (NCLB) (2002). Act of 2001, Pub. L. No. 107-110, § 1251, 115 Stat. 1425, 1567-1571.

Pantaleo, S. (2004a). Exploring grade 1 students' textual connections. *Journal of Research in Childhood Education 18*(3), 211–225.

Pantaleo, S. (2004b). Young children and Radical Change characteristics in picture books. *The Reading Teacher 58*(2), 178–187.

Pantaleo, S. (2007a). Everything comes from seeing things: Narrative and illustrative Play in Black and White. *Children's Literature in Education 38*(1), 45–58.

Pantaleo, S. (2007b). How could that be? Reading Banyai's *Zoom* and *Re-Zoom. Language Arts 84*(3), 222–233.

Pantaleo, S. (2009). *Exploring student response to contemporary picturebooks.* Toronto, ON: University of Toronto Press.

Renaissance Learning. (2008). About us. Retrieved April 13, 2008, from http://www.renlearn.com/aboutus/

Todd, R. J. (1999, March). Transformational leadership and transformation learning: Information literacy and the World Wide Web. *National Association of Secondary Principals Bulletin, 93,* 4–12.

Todd, R. J. (2008). Hearing the voices of those we help: Finding the natural, multidimensional perspectives on the value of school libraries [Electronic Version]. *School Library Media Research* Retrieved April 6, 2008, from http://www.ala.org/ala/aasl/aaslpubsandjournals/slmrb/slmrcontents/volume10/editors_choice.cfm

Todd, R. J., & Heinstrom, J. (2006). Report of phase two of Delaware school library survey: "Student learning through Delaware libraries": Part 2 Summary of findings and recommendations. Center for International Scholarship in School Libraries, Rutgers University. Retrieved July 22, 2010, from http://www2.lib.udel.edu/taskforce/study/phasetwo.pdf

Whelan, D. L. (2006). School libraries benefit from federal grants: Improving literacy through school libraries helps disadvantaged libraries make headway. *School Library Journal, 52,* 16: Retrieved February 14, 2010, from http://www.schoollibraryjournal.com/article/CA6296511.html

Whelan, D. L. (2007, January). Wonder woman: Eliza Dresang, winner of the Scholastic library publishing award [Electronic Version]. *School Library Journal, 53,* 34–37. Retrieved July 22, 2010, from http://www.schoollibraryjournal.com/article/CA6463501.html

Wofford, A. (1940). School library evolution. *Phi Delta Kappan, 22,* 285–188.

10

Public Libraries in the Lives of Young Readers

Past, Present, and Future

Paulette M. Rothbauer

University of Western Ontario

Virginia A. Walter

University of California, Los Angeles

Kathleen Weibel

Chicago Public Library (Retired)

Youth services in public libraries have always been characterized by good intentions and commitment to patrons' personal choice: to select, to question, and to know. The public library has changed and grown since its Progressive Era beginnings, and the leadership for much of this change has come from youth services librarians through their work on behalf of young library users, whether this involves summer programming or digital media development. This chapter's three scholars bring a wealth of public library experience to this endeavor, as they describe the past, present, and future of public library service to young people in the United States and Canada.

For over a century, young people's literature has been a central focus of public library service to youth. In the past, youth services librarians' leadership in supporting and facilitating young people's reading and use of literature has focused on texts in the traditional print-on-paper format. The young people of today and tomorrow will continue to read and connect with texts in traditional formats. However, with the rapid expansion and growth of electronic resources in the virtual online environment, young people are becoming "digital natives" who look to online resources to meet their informational and recreational reading needs. The public library has taken a leadership role in facilitating overall public access to the internet and online resources.

Public library youth services have taken a similar leadership role in enabling young people to connect with literature as it exists in the online environment's virtual world. Although the actual and virtual worlds are increasingly intertwined, Part 1 of this chapter focuses on the history and foundational roles that the public library has played in facilitating young people's connections with literature. Part 2 focuses on the present and future worlds of young people's literacy and literature as resources in the virtual world of information-seeking and social networking, dubbed the "kidlitosphere," are used, created, and directed by youth themselves.

Part I: Public Libraries in the United States

Our discussion of the history and roles of U.S. public libraries begins with the numbers: There are more public libraries in the United States than McDonald's restaurants—16,604 public library buildings (Henderson et al., 2009, p. 4) compared to over 13,000 McDonald's outlets (McDonald's, 2008, p. 34). Managed by 9,214 administrative units, these 16,600 plus public library buildings are scattered across rural, suburban and urban areas in all 50 states and the District of Columbia. Ninety-eight percent of all U.S. counties have at least one public library, and 97% of the American population has access to a public library. These public libraries are supported primarily through locally generated tax funds. The average total per capita (household) operating revenue for all public libraries was $37.66 in FY 2007, the year for which we have the latest data. Of that, the majority, $31.68, was from local sources, $2.52 was from state sources, $0.16 from federal sources, and $3.29 from other sources such as private foundations (Henderson et al., 2009, p. 12).

The governance of each public library "takes place within the interlocking contexts of local, regional, state and national political jurisdictions" (McCook, 2004, p. 107). Eighty-five percent of public libraries are public agencies; the remainder (15%) is operated by nonprofit associations/agencies. The latter are privately controlled but meet the legal definition of a public library in the states in which they are located. Typically, public libraries are governed by elected or appointed citizen boards, commonly known as trustees, but there are also public libraries which are municipal departments or are governed by other elected or appointed boards.

Almost all public libraries offer collections and services for youth, and these services and collections are in continual use. In 2009 the American Library Association (ALA, 2009) reported "children are among the heaviest users of public-library resources" (p. 5). In the same report ALA cited a 2008 Harris Poll that found that 70% of the respondents saw the public library as a family destination. The latest US Institute for Museum and Library Services survey of public libraries reports the circulation of children's materials was 739.7 million nationwide, or 34% of total public library circulation (Henderson et al., 2009). Children's programs account for 69% of all public programming offered by public libraries. Approximately 59 million children attended the over 2 billion children's programs in 2007. In a 2002 National Center for Education Statistics study, 66% of the households surveyed with children under 18, and 69% of households with a high school student, used a public library in the past year (Glander & Dam, 2007). Numbers are telling us that libraries both define their services as and produce the sustainable support for the literacy access, programming, and community engagement that youth seek. How did such an extensive system for literature circulation and literacy development come into existence?

History and Development of Youth Services

Public library service to children began in the United States and in England in the 19th century, when both countries experienced the increased urbanization and industrialization brought by the Industrial Revolution. In addition, the United States experienced a large influx of immigrants whose labor was essential to the growing economy and whose assimilation was viewed as crucial to class harmony and national unity. These shifts led to compulsory public education, enhanced the value of childhood literacy, and led to an increase in books and periodicals designed specifically for young readers (Jenkins, 1994).

Early U.S. public libraries serving children existed in isolated instances in New England during the early 19th century, primarily as the result of gifts from wealthy individuals. For example, the founding of the Bingham Library for Youth in Salisbury, Connecticut, in 1803, was "the first instance in which a municipal governing body contributed active financial assistance to public library service" (Shera, 1949, p. 160). Thus, the first American public library, as the term is currently understood, was a library created specifically for young people. Thirty-one years later in 1834, the Peterborough, New Hampshire, Town Library was founded and became a far more well-known claimant to the "earliest public library" designation. Although the Peterborough library was for residents of all ages, Shera notes that more than half of its inaugural collection—approximately 200 books out of 370—were described as "the Juvenile Library," or books for young readers (pp. 64–65). Thus, from the very early years, children have been a significant constituent group of public library users.

Public library service to children as we know it today emerged during the Progressive Era, a time during which the first generation of professional child welfare advocates began supervising children's physical and moral well-being within institutions like settlement houses, juvenile courts, public playgrounds, public health programs, and public libraries. Advances in higher education for women and waged work for middle-class women led to the development of female-intensive child welfare professions, including children's librarianship. The Anglo-American model of children's public librarianship, as created by the "first generation" of American children's librarians at the turn of the last century, was characterized by several essential elements: specialized collections, separate areas or rooms, specially trained personnel, and services designed to bring children and children's books together, all existing in a network of relationships with other child welfare agencies. This model has proved so durable it became an international standard for library service (Thomas, 1982).

However, despite its centrality within American public librarianship, service to children has been largely ignored in the profession's research agenda. Like many other activities involving children, and carried out primarily by women, library service to young people has been simultaneously revered and ignored (Jenkins, 2000, p. 104). Librarians gather and report quantitative data on youth services (circulation of children's materials, in-library use of children's materials, children's program attendance, etc.), but research utilizing qualitative or mixed methods to investigate research questions is still less common.

What Happens in Public Libraries?

What happens for children and teens in public libraries? Pretty much everything from homework help to story hour to craft programs to video game contests. Authors visit. Musical groups perform. Parents select books, records, and DVDs with their children. Or children and teens come in alone to read magazines, access the Internet, check out materials, ask questions of staff, meet and work with or enjoy their friends. Teens put on programs and serve as Advisory Board members. Librarians and other library staff advise and assist the children and teens. Through their collections and all these activities, collectively called "services," public libraries encourage children and teens to connect with books. Both collections and services are developed in response to one core principle: personal choice.

Walter (2010) identifies six principles and values derived from over 100 years of the practice of public library youth services:

1. Reading good books contributes to a good life.
2. Readers' advisory services, storytelling and booktalks are the key strategies for promoting reading.
3. The individual child is the primary user of children's library service.
4. The library children's room is an integral element in library service to children.

5. Children's librarians are the appropriate specialists who can best deliver library service to children.
6. Children's librarians are advocates for library service to children. (pp. 22–23)

Walter (2010) further identifies two themes that have emerged more recently: (a) Libraries provide children with information as well as pleasure, and (b) Library service to children can be optimized through partnerships and collaborations (p. 23). In the same review, she also identifies two themes that have "waxed and waned" over the years depending on views of the social role of the public library and current conditions: (a) library use is a civic activity, and (b) Americans and American libraries have a responsibility to look beyond their borders and to adopt a global perspective (p. 23). All of these themes to varying degrees are present in the six core public library youth services functions we will discuss for the remainder of this chapter.

An Aside: Public Library and School Library Practices

Before continuing with this section on public libraries, it is important to clarify the distinction between public and school library services and practices. Natalie Reif Ziarnik's (2003) *School & Public Libraries: Developing the Natural Alliance* offers a comparison of the strengths of both facilities. Ziarnik recognizes, for example, the differences in guidance related to youth and adults: School libraries offer frequent librarian-teacher interaction while public libraries offer frequent librarian-parent interaction. The categories of difference most significant for understanding a youth perspective, we believe, have to do with the relationship between learning and community engagement that school and public libraries offer.

School libraries tie literacy skills to daily schoolwork and the library collection and instruction are strongly connected to a school district's specific educational goals. In contrast to, (and increasingly in concert with) school libraries, public libraries encourage self-directed learning and discovery, opportunities to witness modeling of library use by people of all ages, and a library collection and programs that are strongly connected to a local community's needs.

Six Core Functions of Youth Services Librarianship

There are six core functions common to youth services librarianship: collection development, readers' advisory service, reference service, summer reading program, year-round programming, and space. At the basis of everything that youth services librarians do is the evaluation of books and other materials to provide collections chosen to reflect the community and a particular philosophy about children's and teens' reading. This philosophy is typically stated in a collection development policy approved by the library's board of trustees or other governing body. Librarians generally refer to this process as book selection or collection development.

The second core youth services function is called readers' advisory services. Librarians and other staff members advise children and teens, their caregivers and other adults, on books that will meet specific reading needs or on other materials that will be of interest to the individual library user. They may do this through one-on-one encounters, or by producing reading lists and guides, displays, etc., either in the library, on the web, or in some community venue.

Youth services librarians and other staff also answer informational questions, a function termed "reference service." This may be done in the library, over the phone or via the Internet through email or chat. Both advisory and reference questions may be motivated by the child's or teen's personal interests (self-generated) or come from an external agent (imposed queries) such as a teacher (Gross, 2006).

Almost every public library offers a summer reading program, a series of enrichment activities, often with small rewards built in, designed to keep children reading during the summer vacation from school and thereby lower "summer learning loss." In addition to the summer reading program, library staff develop programs throughout the year that respond to the specific needs and interests of the age range they serve. The purpose of these programs, which include storytelling, craft activities, baby lapsit programs, booktalks, etc., is to promote reading and encourage library use. Finally, the spaces set aside in public libraries for children and teens are important community resources for youth in and of themselves.

In addition to these six core functions, many public libraries develop specialized programs such as homework assistance, support for home schooling, and parent or teacher resource centers. More and more public libraries are also engaged in teaching information literacy, computer and library use. As Walter (2010) notes, this instruction may take place informally (in contrast with the formal programs offered by school libraries), but is a conscious concern for public library youth service librarians.

Collection Development

Children's literature scholar Anne Pellowski (1968) notes "the history of U.S. children's libraries cannot be separated from that of children's literature" (p. 391). Collections predate the other elements of youth services librarianship, and the librarians' knowledge of the books and other materials in their collections is the bedrock of expertise upon which the profession rests.

Young people have varying needs based on age, ability, educational needs, and reading interests. Building and maintaining relevant collections to meet the needs of young library users is one of the key missions of the youth services librarian. Librarians receive guidance in their selection decisions from the library's collection development policy which will reflect the mission of the library; outline the types of materials that will be available and general selection criteria; and provide guidance for dealing with challenges to library materials, with materials that are worn or outdated, with materials that come to the library as gifts, and so on (Cerny, Markey, & Williams, 2006).

The librarian makes decisions based on reviews, reader requests, community needs, and other criteria that go into creating a collection that reflects the information and recreational reading needs and interests. Books are evaluated for their individual value, their value in relationship to other materials in the collection, and for their potential for use by library users. The goal is "a balanced collection" that includes a range of subjects and a range of points of view (Walter, 2001, p. 23). As stated in ALA's (1999) treatise, "Libraries: An American Value": "We celebrate and preserve our democratic society by making available the widest possible range of viewpoints, opinions and ideas, so that all individuals have the opportunity to become lifelong learners—informed, literate, educated, and culturally enriched."

Among the many considerations for librarians as they develop their collections is the age-old debate between quality and popularity. On the one hand, there are the high-minded aims of literature for children held by children's librarians of the past, as reflected in Walter de la Mare's oft-quoted "only the rarest kind of best in anything can be good enough for the young" (Silvey, 2004, p. xv). On the other hand, the popularity of mass-market series with many young readers is undeniable. In earlier days, libraries would have refused to purchase *Tom Swift and His Photo Telephone* (Appleton, 1912) or *Nancy's Mysterious Letter* (Keene, 1932). Collection policies have changed since then, however, and children's rooms will have whole shelving units containing full sets of series books arranged in numbered order.

Researchers have been asking specific and general questions about library collections for as long as there have been libraries. Fortunately, from the card catalogs of yesterday to the online catalogs of today, many questions about books and collections may be studied through the readily-available data found in these catalogs.

A Number of Questions

For example, librarians use book reviews to make selection decisions. Indeed, at one time it was common for libraries to require at least two positive book reviews before a book was acquired for the collection. So what impact do reviews have on the collection development process? One factor is number of reviews a book receives. But what if the book receives negative reviews? Are they less likely to be added to library collections? This question was investigated by Judith Serebnick (1981), who found that the more reviews a book received—whether they were positive or negative—the more likely it was to be added to the public library collection.

Readers' Advisory Services

Joyce Saricks' (2005) definition of readers' advisory services was developed through her work with adults but is equally applicable to work with children and teens: "A successful readers' advisory service is one in which knowledgeable, nonjudgmental staff help fiction and nonfiction readers with their leisure-reading needs" (p. 1). According to Walter (2001), "children's librarians have elevated readers' advisory, or reading guidance, almost to an art form," (p. 29) by melding knowledge of children's developmental stages and children's books so that the individual child finds a book perfect for him or her, a book that is engaging and at the right reading level. This may be a book like another in pacing, plot, underlying emotional theme, setting, characterization or style, known as a "read alike." Or it may be a book on a personal passion like dinosaurs or Disney princesses (no other princesses will do) or a "good book," a "thin book," or an "easy book" to meet a school assignment.

Children's librarians practicing the art of readers' advisory make the connections between the book and the child, or the adult acting on behalf of the child. They learn when to push and when to pull back, when to just

> leave a pile of books on the table for a child to examine with no pressure at all, when to reassure a child that it won't hurt their feelings if he or she doesn't take any of the books they recommended. They learn to know the "regulars" who gobble up books like popcorn and which children are still unsure of their reading skills or unconvinced about the pleasures of literature. They learn which parents worry about violence in children's stories and which ones need to be weaned from some limited understanding of the definition of a "classic." They learn which teachers will take a risk on a controversial new title and which ones cannot be budged from a very literal-minded, objective view of the world and the curriculum. They learn, too, if they are very good at this, to listen for the silent, "unasked" questions that children sometimes pose. Children don't formulate questions well, and they usually aren't aware of their own deepest and most important information needs. (Walter, 2001, p. 31)

Heather Booth (2007), author of the first book-length treatment of readers' advisory work for teens, sees that "many of the issues relevant to readers' advisory for children are also applicable to working with teens, such as the need to assess reading level, working with proxies (parents or caregivers), and the distinction between reading for recreation and reading for school" (p. 100). Angelina Benedetti (2001) admonishes that "before a librarian can become a successful reader's advisor for teens, he or she must have some connection to the literature published for young adults, to what teens actually read, and to the library's collection" (p. 239). Benedetti also points out that many U.S. public libraries have no designated Young Adult or Teen Librarian, and if they do, that person or persons are not always available, so readers' advisory work with teens is more likely to be done by a librarian with another age specialty or someone who is a generalist.

Booth (2007) also reminds librarians that:

> readers' advisory for teenagers differs from readers' advisory for adults not just in the selection of materials that we offer but also in the manner in which we conduct ourselves. Whereas an easy rapport may form between two adults discussing a book, we must remain aware that because teens most often encounter adults as teachers, parents, or supervisors, they may be caught off guard or surprised by our usual manner, be it poised professionalism or more laid-back joviality. (p. 28)

In readers' advisory work with both children and young adults, as in reference service, librarians deal with the issues of "imposed queries" and "proxy inquiries." In her review of children and young adult readers' advisory services, Jessica Moyer (2008) notes that librarianship tends to draw on the literature of education for research on reading. Because of the high value placed on personal choice in public librarianship, youth librarians have embraced as their own *The Power of Reading* by Stephen Krashen (2004). With his emphasis on choice and reading for enjoyment, known in educational circles as "Free Voluntary Reading," Krashen justifies and affirms what public librarians have been doing for years and provides a guide to understanding and translating the educational research into public library practice.

Because of the reliance on education research, public youth services have "only a limited amount of research... conducted on how youth services and young adult librarians provide readers' advisory for their patrons" (Moyer, 2008, p. 77). Ross, McKechnie and Rothbauer (2006) reviewed the education research from a library perspective in *Reading Matters*. They point out that "The research...indicates that pleasure and free choice are both key elements in the making of readers....With their large collections of books and magazines and newspapers that are free to all, promoting leisure reading for all ages is a role that public libraries are ideally suited to fill" (p. 7). Despite the paucity of research on youth reader advisory services, youth services librarians have been talking and writing at the practice level about "getting the right book for the right reader at the right time" since the beginning of public libraries and this is a fruitful area for further examination.

Reference Service

The informational needs of youth were not given much attention in public library youth services literature and research until the 1990s despite the fact that youth librarians have been building reference collections and answering informational questions for years. Reichel's (1991) book, *Reference Services for Children and Young Adults*, marks a sharpened focus on meeting the informational needs of children and the articulation of techniques for doing this akin to those developed in the larger literature of reference service to adults. In a later analysis of reference services, Walter (2001) contends that children "ask for more help at the library reference desk than grownups do" (p. 29) and further notes that "the conventional wisdom is that most children making use of public library reference services today are there for homework purposes" (p. 31). In offering practical advice for public library staff not trained to work with children, Steele (2001) posits that the "people skills" and "professional expertise" needed to work with youth and adults are the same. "Good reference service to children differs only slightly in approach and communication" (p. 12). But these services are more complex than Steele suggests.

The nature of children and childhood, teens and adolescence, adds complexity to the already complex communication process known as the "reference interview," the questioning approach librarians use to assist library users in person, over the phone or online, and to meeting the information needs of youth. Working with British youth, Shenton (2007) found five reasons why children and teens failed to find the information they needed: (a) need-source mismatch or inappropriate source, (b) knowledge deficiency or inability to formulate a search based on lack of knowledge, (c) skill shortcomings, (d) psychological barriers such as being overwhelmed, and (e) social unease and inhibition that makes it difficult for the child to approach an adult (pp. 328–342). Shenton particularly emphasizes the psychological dimension in developing strategies for assisting young people to find information.

Jones, Gorman, and Suellentrop (2004) take a similar approach to teens in their practical advice manual: "[D]evelopmental tasks play a huge role. The self-consciousness of YAs (young adults) is a major barrier; after all, a reference question is admission of not knowing a particular element" (p. 78). Focusing on electronic resources, Druin (2005) notes, "Today's digital landscape can also be problematic for young people. Children see the world differently than adults; they have very different needs for technology and are quite diverse in their abilities, even in the age span of a few short years" (p. 173).

Also complicating the youth reference process are what Gross (2006) terms "imposed queries," when a child's information need is generated externally, typically a school assignment, and "double imposed inquiries" when a parent seeks information on behalf of his or her child, again typically for an assignment. Gross distinguishes these queries from "self-generated queries" where a child's or teen's personal interests motivate the question. Shenton (2007) found that for both "older and younger informants when information was being sought on matters of personal interest" (self-generated queries) the results were "markedly more effective" than for the imposed queries (p. 352). In discussing "double imposed inquiries" from a practical perspective, Jones et al. (2004) acknowledge that

> almost universally, the one type of patron loathed by many librarians, is the parent doing research for their child…. Often the parent will come in with the child, but the parent will do all the talking. Focus your eyes on the student and

ask him or her the follow-up questions, because that is who will help you complete the reference transaction. (p. 345)

Youth needs for school related assistance are not new. Mediavilla (2001) notes that as "early as 1898…Linda Anne Eastman admonished that (for public librarians) one of the requisites for working successfully with children was a thorough knowledge of the school's curriculum" (p. vii). Public library youth service literature is full of tips for working with teachers and school librarians to get information about homework assignments. Many public libraries have set up "homework centers," programs "dedicated to meet the curricular needs of students by providing: staff or volunteers who are trained to assist students with their homework, space designated for student use during specific days and times, and a multiformat collection of materials related to the curricular needs of students" (p. x). To this must be added web-based services typically made available to a public library's constituency through a contract with a commercial service such as Tutor.com. (Tutor.com, 2010). However, as Walter and Mediavilla (2005) found, there are significant limitations in these contract services when judged using the standards for effective reference service.

Research in the area of public library youth reference service and youth information needs has been steadily underway since the publication of Reichel's (1991) groundbreaking book on reference service to youth. Chelton and Cool (2004, 2007) have ably charted this growing research agenda in their two editions of *Youth Information-Seeking Behavior.* The 2005 issue of *Library Trends,* edited by Druin, focuses on Children's Access and Use of Digital Resources, an important area of research in youth reference service. This is an area where significant work can be done on the information needs of children and teens at various developmental stages, effective communication strategies for helping children and teens articulate those needs and develop successful search strategies, and appropriate resources and services to meet these needs.

Summer Reading Programs

Summer reading programs have been a core public library function almost since the inception of youth services in the late 19th century. Carolyn Hewins, a pioneer of youth services, for example, began a summer program of book talks at the Hartford Public Library in 1898 (Locke, 1988). A similar program at the Cleveland Public Library included a letter to teachers from the library director, lists of books read during the summer, and bookmarks with suggested titles (Eastman, 1897; The library in vacation days, 1898). The purpose of these early programs was to encourage children to use the library, read during the summer, and develop a lifelong habit of reading. And this purpose has remained remarkably consistent over the past 110 years. However, public librarians now emphasize educational benefits and cite research on summer learning to justify the programs (Wisconsin Department of Public Instruction, n.d.).

Today 95% of all public libraries offer some sort of Summer Reading Program (National Center, 1995). This program is such a hallmark of American public library youth services and requires such a high level of planning and commitment from the youth services staff that we believe it to be a core function separate from the broader year-round programming function in public libraries. In his handbook on public library youth services, Sullivan (2005) characterizes the Summer Reading Program as "the most intensive period of activity for children's services, and for the library as a whole" (p. 166). In many public libraries the Summer Reading Program has spread from children to teens and in some libraries includes adults as an audience.

Walter (2001) identifies three typical elements of the Summer Reading Program: theme, reading incentives, and programming. We believe that partnerships have also become a key element of successful summer reading programs. While many libraries carry out their functions on their own, partnerships and collaboration are increasingly essential to serving children and teens in a community setting. Walter (2010) identifies two reasons that collaboration will continue to be of importance to youth services librarians: (a) the funding climate and (b) the fact that these librarians "are still passionate advocates and missionaries who believe so strongly in the importance of their work that they will usually leap at any opportunity to develop alliances to spread the good word" (p. 47).

The Summer Reading Program theme may be locally generated, developed at the state or consortia level, or purchased from a commercial outlet. The theme may generally promote books and reading such as the 1992 state of Missouri theme "Leap into Books" (Fiore, 1998, p. 150), connected to an event like the Olympics, or appealing to the current interests of children or teens such as the 1996 Florida state theme "Rhythm and Books—Feel the Beat!" (p. 54). A good theme gives a focus to what otherwise might be unconnected activities and also aids in publicity that preferably reflects the life of children who will participate.

The effort it takes to develop and support an annual Summer Reading Program, including designing and producing materials, has led many public libraries to work together. The Collaborative Summer Reading Program, a grassroots consortium of states, contracts with a vendor to produce materials and resources. Their children's theme for 2010, with materials designed to prepare "children for continued success through the development of early language skills" is "Make a Splash—Read!" The teen theme with activities and materials designed to integrate "differentiated literacy activities to motivate young adults to read and discuss books" is "Make Waves at Your Library" (Collaborative summer reading program, n.d.).

Reading incentives or prizes for completing all or part of the Summer Reading Program are "a touchy issue" according to Sullivan (2005, p. 163). Those opposed to prizes generally believe that reading should not be competitive. Some are also opposed to the commercialization of the Summer Reading Program. Sullivan argues that more reluctant readers will be attracted by prizes. Fiore (1998) suggests that "rather than thinking of incentives as prizes, think of them as another means of promoting" (p. 78) the Summer Reading Program. And Walter (2001) notes "most librarians now prefer to avoid the kind of competitive summer reading program that rewards the children who read the most books" (p. 34); thus many programs encourage participants to set their own goals relative to an overall completion goal. In addition, incentives can be tied to a community goal such as the "Read a Ton" program Sullivan (2005) describes, where books read were weighed to contribute to a community goal (p. 164).

Programmed activities during the Summer Reading Program may have several purposes according to Walter (2001): an end in itself, providing educational or cultural enrichment, motivation to read, or a means to generate publicity. Some programs suit all of these purposes. The 2006 Summer Reading Program partnership between the Chicago Public Library and the Field Museum of Natural History, called "Wrapped Up In Reading," celebrated Ancient Egypt, highlighting the life of King Tut, and included a free visit to the Tut exhibition for the families of children who completed the program.

More and more, the successful Summer Reading Program for youth is characterized by community partnerships. Public library staff may visit classrooms or assemblies, materials for teachers and school librarians who will promote the program, work with school librarians and teachers on reading lists, inform principals of children and teens who complete the program, and meet with the local school parent organization (Minkel, 2003). Local business partners provide fiscal support for the program often in the form of incentives or prizes to motivate reading. Partnerships with other community organizations such as parks may take the program outside of the library building. Partnerships with local church and other youth groups provide readymade programs for these organizations.

Successful Summer Reading Programs for teens partner with the teens themselves. Jones et al. (2004) advise that "a summer reading program for YAs should allow participating teens to be directly involved in the creation of the program, providing an opportunity for teens to provide input during the developmental phase as well as during the program itself" (p. 230). They also identified five common characteristics of successful Summer Reading Programs for teens: (a) keep it simple, (b) make it possible for teens to get involved on many levels, (c) allow free choice when it comes to selecting reading materials, (d) incorporate the Internet in some way, and (e) have great prizes that teens would enjoy (p. 230). Fiore (2005) also suggests the incorporation of online participation options in Summer Reading Programs for all ages of youth with online reading logs and reports and online incentives, making it possible to participate in the Summer Reading Program without coming to the physical library.

The key research question for all the Summer Reading Programs is how effective are they? Fiore reviews Summer Reading Program effectiveness research and public policy responses to summer learning issues through 2005; Shin and Krashen (2008) review the research from an education perspective but do acknowledge public libraries in *Summer Reading: Program and Evidence*. All research concludes that summer reading results in better achievement for students but there are significant differences based on how readily available reading material is for children and teens and how much their personal choice enters into reading.

In a frequently cited study of Pennsylvania public libraries, Celano and Neuman (2001) found that children who attend library summer programs spend significant amounts of time with books—a first step toward reading. These programs also encourage parents of these children to play greater roles in their child's literacy development—another factor leading to reading achievement. They conclude that, "children who attend library summer reading programs read significantly better than those children who attend a camp program, suggesting that time spent in the library significantly enhances children's reading achievement when compared to activities more purely recreational in nature" (p. 48).

Dominican University Graduate School of Library and Information Science (Roman, Carran, & Fiore, 2010) recently completed Institute for Library and Museum Services funded research focusing on third and fourth graders addressing the question: "Do public library summer reading programs impact student achievement?" (p. 1). Preliminary findings indicate that Summer Reading Program participants, who are more likely to be girls, are engaged and active readers with books in the home and with parents who are involved in their reading and other literacy activities. Despite research advances there remains a myriad of questions to be addressed about Summer Reading Program impact.

Year-Round Programming

It is safe to say that the majority of the literature of public library youth services librarianship, whether monograph or periodical, consists of practical advice on, tips and guides to, and resources for programming. Unlike services such as reference and readers' advisory, which are available to individuals on demand, programs are typically scheduled events. Jones et al. (2004), in their essential "how-to-do-it" manual for teen service define programming as "a library-sponsored activity that takes place outside the context of reference service (and we would add readers' advisory service) and is designed to inform, entertain, or enrich users, as well as promote the use of the library and its collection. With teen users, put the accent on entertain and add the word 'fun'" (p. 219).

Programming Skills is one of the seven Association for Library Service to Children 1999 Competencies for Librarians Serving Children and Youth. These skills are broken down further to address public library children's services:

1. Designs, promotes, presents, and evaluates a variety of programs for children of all ages, based on their developmental needs and interests and the goals of the library.
2. Identifies and utilizes skilled resource people to present programs and information.
3. Provides library outreach programs, which meet community needs and library goals and objectives.
4. Establishes programs and services for parents, individuals and agencies providing childcare, and other professionals in the community who work with children.
5. Promotes library programs and services to underserved children and families. (Association, 1999)

In *Outstanding Library Service to Children: Putting the Core Competencies to Work,* the chapter on programming skills opens with this prideful statement: "Children's librarians in the public library do more original programming than their colleagues who serve other age groups, and they are well known both within the profession and among the general public for the skill sets behind the programming" (Cerny, Markey, & Williams, 2006, p. 50). In contrast, there is no specific set of programming competencies in the seven recently revised Young Adult Library Services Association (2010) *Competencies for Librarians Serving Youth*. Rather programming, as we have defined it, is integrated into: leadership and professionalism, communication, marketing and outreach, administration, and services. Children's librarians most often plan and deliver book programs on their own without significant input from their clientele, while teen librarians often seek to engage their clientele as programmers or through participation on advisory boards.

The Concept of Youth Development

Year-round programming is designed to enrich and engage children and their parents and caregivers, and teens; to promote reading and library use; to provide free organized activities for individual teens, children and their families; and to market the library. This programming is often tied into cyclical events like holidays and sport seasons; known interests of children and teens like games, popular culture, hobbies, or continual areas of fascination like snakes; but can also be tied to community activities or celebrations, or current events. Sullivan (2005) divides programming into two categories: literature based programs that have reading at the core; (a) story hours, book discussion groups, and booktalking; (b) and non-literature based programs which "deal with ideas and information not directly tied to the printed word" (pp. 120–121) such as a fire truck demonstration or chess games. It should be noted that children's librarians will typically try to tie books to all non-literature based programs through indirect methods like book displays and reading lists. Because of the scope of this volume, we will focus on three types of literature-based programming: storytelling, book discussion programs, and booktalking. While it is possible to offer all these three types of programs to teens, it is more likely that storytelling or story hours are offered for younger children, and booktalking and book discussion to teens and tweens.

Walter (2001) notes that "there is probably less storytelling provided for school-age children than there once was" despite the fact that story times are conducted in 90% of all libraries. "Most of these are probably story hours for children under the age of five" with the focus on emergent literacy and infant brain development leading to an increasing emphasis on programs targeting infants and children under ages three to four, the traditional pre-school story hour audience (pp. 36–37). Infant programs, sometimes known as "baby lapsit programs" include rhymes, songs, and physical activities and are viewed as a way of teaching parents how to interact with their babies as well as stimulating the children. Programs for toddlers and family groups are short and typically include a variety of activities: picture-book reading, flannel board stories, fingerplays, songs, nursery rhymes, and lots of audience participation. All of these programs are usually broadly based on a theme, as much for program promotion as program continuity.

Book discussion groups are common for school-age children and teens. Sullivan (2005) cautions that the "composition of a book discussion group for children is more complicated than for adults" (p. 136). Among factors to consider in forming a group are: age-range, reading-level, gender, and whether adults are welcome or not. Jones et al. (2004) identified two types of book discussion groups for teens: (a) everybody reads the same book or (b) everybody reads what they want and discusses the story or genre their books share.

Sullivan (2005) defines booktalking as standing "before people and telling them why they would want to read a book…. Booktalking is promotion, and especially with children, you must remember that you are not just promoting the book but also promoting reading in general" (p. 141). Writing for young adult librarians, Jones et al. (2004) define a booktalk as "a paperback blurb as performance" and admonish "don't tell, sell" (p. 167). Common types of booktalks according to Sullivan (2005) include: plot summary, character sketch, reading a vignette or dialog, author or media tie-in, or theme based; whereas Jones et al. (2004) suggest booktalks that focus on mood, plot, character and scene.

Walter (2010) notes that booktalks are more typically part of a program for children or teens rather than the whole program. She also notes the significance of book-talking titles while working with individuals in the library, what book sellers call hand selling, a function she sees as integral to readers advisory service.

As with the questions for Summer Reading Programs, all of this effort and engagement begs the question of impact. What works and what does not, according to what criteria?

Space

Sociologist Ray Oldenburg (1999) devotes a chapter of his landmark survey *The Great Good Place* to the problems of a society that segregates youth and does not provide appropriate spaces for them. In most communities, the public library and the parks are the only two public spaces open year round at little or no cost to all ages. People may think of the local mall, a favorite teen hangout place, as public space but it is not—it is privately owned and operated. Those walking the mall hallways do not necessarily have the same rights as those walking a sidewalk or park pathway. As Oldenburg points out, the mall as shared space also implies a culture of consumerism. While there are often fees for park programs, especially summer activities, this is generally not true for use of the public library or most public library programs. The concept of the public library as a public space, "a great good place" is an increasingly important concept even in the virtual age. In the influential analysis *Better Together*, Putnam and Feldstein (2003) characterize public libraries as "third spaces" not work or school, not home, where people can spend time together. This is true for all ages but particularly true for children and teens who do not have the options adults have for other "third spaces."

The Harris Interactive Poll of 8- to 18-year-olds (2007) identified two place/space-related variables which impact public library use: 38% of the respondents said they would use the public library more often if "it was closer to where I live," and, 22% indicated they would use it if "the library had a comfortable, welcoming atmosphere." Four of the nine responses in the same poll to the question "what do you go to the library for?" were related to space use: 34% go to the library to read, 26% to study, 20% go for events, and 18% go to hang out with friends.

Librarians have always attended to space: "From the beginning, the children's room was intended to send a clear message to children: this is your space" (Walter, 2010, p. 32). "The children's corner of the 1890s, specially fitted with low tables and chairs, was replaced in theory and in practice by completely separate reading rooms for children by 1900" (Van Slyck, 1995, p. 176). This clear territorial message is also true of any space set aside for teens after the opening of the first room for young adults at the Cleveland Public Library in 1925. "A teen space sends a message, if done right, that 'this is not your father's library' by blowing away the stereotypes of libraries, and librarians, by presenting a fresh, fun, and flexible environment" (Jones et al., 2004, p. 254).

For early childhood areas, "size, scale, and access dominate the discussion of the physical environment from the perspective of safety and from the way features communicate encouragement and welcome" (Feinberg, Kuchner, & Feldman, 1998, p. 31), but this is also true for all ages. Furniture and shelving appropriate to the age level and a welcoming atmosphere are essential parts of the entire children's room or teen space. Today, this space must accommodate the solitary reader, computer users, group study and assignment needs, children with parents or caregivers or teens with their friends, as well as youth who are at the library because there is no adult at home or they have nowhere else to go.

For children, Walter (2010) identifies three trends that are changing the way we think about library space for children: homework centers, renewed emphasis on early literacy and the library as a destination place like Disneyland. Feinburg et al. (1998) identify the need for active learning in the public library, especially for young children, and encourage the development of family centered and developmentally appropriate spaces where children and their caregivers can learn and interact together. Walter and Meyers (2003) suggest the use of the architect W.G. Clark's views on physical space, cultural space, and spiritual space when thinking about teen places in the public library. Library building design expert Nolan Lushington (2008) reviews trends in youth services spaces for children with some reference to teens and provides an annotated list of readings on the topic in *Libraries Designed for Kids*.

In a White Paper for the American Library Association's Young Adult Library Services Association, Bolan (2008) reports "a transformation in library facility design for teenagers" with renewed emphasis on teen space because of increasing use.

> This reevaluation of priorities is supported by the fact that kids are not only using the library, they are visiting frequently. Seventy-eight percent of children ages 8 to 18 have library cards.... According to the Public Agenda in June 2006, three-quarters of Americans believe it is a high priority for local public libraries to offer a safe place where teenagers can study and congregate. Equally relevant is the Harris poll response to the question, "I would use my local public library more often if...?" Twenty-six percent of the respondents replied, "If there was a space just for teens." (p. 136)

Bolan (2008), like Walter and Meyers (2003), advocates for young adult involvement in all phases of planning and developing teen space. She argues further "the ratio of teen area to the overall library should be equal to the ratio of the teen population of that community to the overall population of that community" (p. 137). This is not the case in most American public libraries.

For many children, teens and their parents, the public library is viewed as a "safe place." Some children and teens are routinely told to go to the library after school or on weekends because there is no adult at home. The needs of these children or teens may become a major issue for library staff, but many libraries have developed programs to meet the needs of these youth and policies to aid staff in working with them. There is also a creative tension between keeping order in space for youth and their free and creative use of this space. Maintaining that balance through space utilization and appropriate staffing is essential to the public library as a "safe space."

Conclusion

In 2001 Virginia A. Walter called for addressing two research needs in public library youth service. "One is the codification of best practices in our field. We need more than anecdotal evidence and common sense to determine what works and what doesn't. The second need is for tangible evidence of the outcome of our work" (p. 120). Although more progress has been made on the codification agenda than on the outcome agenda, both agendas are still relevant today. A later summary of research (Walter, 2003) on public library services for children and teens recognized four "significant and unanswered questions: (a) How have public library services to children and young adults developed over time? (b) How and why do young people use the public library? (c) How can we evaluate the effectiveness of public library service to young people? (d) Why should policy makers fund public library services for children and young adults?" (p. 572). Despite some progress, particularly in the area of historical studies and youth information seeking, these questions remain relevant to the development of a research agenda for public library service to children and young adults. Added to this agenda will be studies on the changing use of online and digital media services, which have altered the access, roles, and guidance youth seek in public libraries.

Part II: Youth, Literature, Public Libraries, and the KidLitosphere

In recent years, some librarians have moved their advocacy for young people's literature and for young readers to a variety of online venues. In a chapter that examines the ways that public libraries and librarians support children and young adults as readers, we would be remiss to neglect the webs of influence and advocacy that comprise the "kidlitosphere" (Bird, 2007) on the World Wide Web. From early awareness of the utility of the multimedia online platforms for promoting children's and young adults' literature to "live" play-by-play online updates of major awards ceremonies, children's and youth services librarians appear to have been early and ongoing adopters of interactive internet tools such blogs, wikis, video-hosting sites, and popular online social networking sites such Friendster, MySpace, Facebook, and Twitter. In articles published in the professional literature, readers were urged to learn more about these new online tools to investigate new opportunities for working with young people and to promote library materials and services.

Given how ubiquitous and pervasive such tools are today Agosto and Abbas (2009) remind us that sites like Friendster, MySpace, and Facebook are quite recent entities, established in 2002, 2003, and 2004, respectively. Youth services librarians were among the first in the library world to herald the value of online journals and blogs. For example, Sara Ryan (2002) wrote a short article in *Voice of Youth Advocates* (VOYA) about the value of new online journal and blog hosting sites, allowing teens to connect with others through public writing. In another article published in 2002, this time in *Teacher-Librarian*, Clyde provided concise definitions and samples of relevant weblogs as she introduced the technology and its possibilities to school librarians. It is worth noting that in 2002, Clyde was unable to identify any school libraries that were using blogging software, however by 2009, Agosto and Abbas were able to report that "there were more than five hundred Facebook search results with 'public library' in the page name" and that a search "using the keywords 'public library' did return 62,000 pages with the phrase included somewhere in the page content" (p. 34). In the span of just a few years, there would seem to be evidence of an impressive attempt to embed libraries into the social networking landscape.

While empirical research on the uptake and effects of the use of such tools in terms of reading promotion is scarce, it is, nevertheless, possible to identify four important trends in the online world of children's and young adult literature and librarianship: an energetic renaissance in reviewing of and writing about children's and young adults' literature spurring online book discussions that cross multiple populations including young people, librarians, authors and illustrators and book industry professionals; digital libraries and the rise of electronic books; interactive sections of more traditional library websites for children and teens including digital booktalks, book trailers, and interactive spaces for youth reviewers and bloggers; and online awards competitions.

Online Reviewing and Reading Promotion. Perhaps the most noticeable aspect of online promotion of children's and young adult literature concerns the rise of review websites and blogs that feature a range of library materials although with a clear emphasis on novels and picture books. There are now a number of bloggers who have made reputations as discerning writers and reviewers and who have a wide and growing readership. Publishers took notice of these renegade, non-affiliated reviewers as concern mounted about the effects that unsolicited, unedited, non-filtered reviews could have in terms of marketing and readership (see Bird, 2009, on challenges and tensions associated with this kind of extra-professional work). Professional divisions such as the Association for Library Services to Children (ALSC) also responded to the

growing online reviewing practices among its members by implementing policies directly related to the online writing practices of its members: for example, by curtailing reviews of award nominees and contenders (Bird, 2007).

For librarians responsible for collecting children's and young adults literature for library collections and for promoting it to library users, there are several other online modes for professional awareness and development aside from blogs. Interactive and collaborative wikis, designed for use with multiple writers and editors are another way that librarians are developing their professional competencies related to children's and young adult's literature. For example, the Child Lit Wiki and Book Recommendation Engine (Berman, 2010) invites any user to write and submit book reviews following posted reviewing guidelines. The Children's Literature Web Guide, a collaborative project of the University of Calgary similarly invites reader-generated additions to a number of categories related to children's literature including awards, other web guides and book lists, illustrator and author resources and more. The Association for Library Services to Children and the Young Adult Library Services Association (YALSA), divisions of the American Library Association, both maintain open wikis for its members and other interested users.

While online fora devoted to children's literature discussion have grown and diversified in recent years to include blogs and wikis, Facebook and MySpace, notable online antecedents are still active. To name just two examples, PUBYAC (Public Libraries Young Adults and Children) and Child_Lit are listservs that were established in 1997 and 1993, respectively, and for over 15 years, both have constituted active, informative, and collegial venues for hundreds of subscribers for discussions about children's literature. However, as blogging advocates will point out (Beaman, 2006), the new online technologies permit a wider readership, reaching people who may not subscribe to more esoteric or professional listservs—children, teens, parents, and those not directly connected to the children's book industry.

Digital Collections and E-Books. The International Children's Digital Library (http://childrenslibrary.org) is one of the most exemplary digital collections of children's materials designed for a wide audience of child readers with ongoing attention to both ease and openness of access (see Collen, 2006, for a review of a recent study using ICDL with children). However, digital and multimedia materials for children and teens are being integrated into the most traditional library collections of printed and bound books. Public libraries offer a spectrum of multimedia stories from telephone-based story times for very young children to streaming story videos. For example, in one of her regular American Libraries columns Jennifer Burek Pierce (2007) features Tumblebooks and Tumblereadables from an electronic children's book service that sells subscriptions to public libraries, but allows library card-free access to young people. Electronic books have been on the children and young adult's literature scene for a number of years but with advances in the design, functioning and portability of digital readers we can expect continued interest in developing e-book access for young people through public library collections.

Interactive Library Websites. As public librarians continue to explore the viability of electronic and digital collections for children and teens, there is evidence that library websites are integrating more and more interactive online content for young people as well. Online homework help centers for young people have been offered by public libraries for several years, sites that guide students to useful library resources and to tutorials on how to use them, along with online reference services. However, newer modes of online engagement with children's and young adult literature are supported on library websites as well. Digital booktalks and booktrailers can support multiple literacy skills and reading enjoyment among young people who produce and view them.

In fact, researchers Gunter and Kenny (2008) have found that the production of video booktalks can play a positive role in changing attitudes towards reading among reluctant youth readers. Several public librarians now work with teen patrons on digital booktalks, posting the products of this kind of programming to video hosting sites like YouTube and Google Video. YALSA hosts its own video channel at bliptv (see http://yalsa.blip.tv) featuring a range of videos including award-winning booktalks of young adult titles. Digital and audio booktalks are just one type of interactive online activity; many public libraries now also dedicate a portion of the their library webpages to creating interactive spaces for youth patrons giving them a forum for reviews, feedback, and commentary on library issues and events of interest to them. These spaces can be links to Facebook and MySpace pages or to blogs that feature teen input. For example, Seattle Public Library maintains a teen-run blog, accessible from their homepage called "Push to Talk," along with online homework help and an online newsletter for teens (Seattle Public Library, 2010). Online book discussion groups for young people are gaining ground as well with invitation for youth participants announced on library website homepages. Paulette Stewart (2009) provides a detailed account of one teacher-librarian's experience of developing a virtual reading group with teenagers, reporting on an increased degree of engagement among participants.

Online Awards. In 2006, the Children's and Young Adult Bloggers' Literary Awards (Cybils) was established; it is a singular new award for children's and young adult materials voted on by children's literature bloggers ("There's a new award" 2008; Cybils). Nominations are taken from anyone who submits titles, and then a second round of judging occurs among assigned bloggers who

evaluate the short list of finalists to arrive at a winner. Although the Cybils is the only award to date that operates entirely online, other awards are capitalizing on the interactive engagement made possible with online tools. For example, the Forest of Reading and Festival of Trees comprise the Ontario Library Association's very popular literacy initiative and readers' choice awards. By visiting the association's website, young readers are able to interact with other readers and with authors as well as read online previews of chapters of nominated titles (Ontario Library Association, 2010).

The establishment of the Newbery Medal signaled the arrival of children's literature as a distinct and identifiable presence within the larger field of literature. It also signaled the arrival of children's librarians as those uniquely qualified to determine the year's "most distinguished contribution to children's literature." Online readers' choice awards, likewise, signal young people as uniquely qualified to judge their own literature. We are currently witnessing a consolidation of established library practices in the online world of children's and young adult's literature, strengthening already existing connections and forging new ones among librarians, authors, illustrators, publishers and young readers and their advocates.

Academic References

Agosto, D. E., & Abbas, J. (2009). Teens and social networking: How public libraries are responding to the latest online trend. *Public Libraries, 48*(3), 32–37.

American Library Association. (1999). Libraries: An American value. Retrieved on June 22, 2010, from http://www.ala.org/ala/aboutala/offices/oif/statementspols/americanvalue/librariesamerican.cfm

American Library Association. (2009). *The State of America's libraries.* Retrieved March 4, 2010, from http://www.ala.org/ala/newspresscenter/mediapresscenter/presskits/2009stateofamericaslibraries/2009statehom

Appleton, V. (1912). *Tom Swift and His Photo Telephone.* New York, NY: Grosset and Dunlap.

Association for Library Service to Children. (1999). *Competencies for librarians serving children in public libraries.* Retrieved March 9, 2010, from http://www.lita.org/ala/mgrps/divs/alsc/edcareeers/alsccorecomps/ALA_print_layout_1_506107_506107.cfm

Beaman, A. (2006). YA Lit 2.0: How technology is enhancing the pleasure reading experience for teens. *Knowledge Quest, 35*(1), 30–33.

Benedetti, A. (2001). *Leading the horse to water: Keeping young people reading in the information age.* In K. Shearer & R. Burgin (Eds.), *The readers' advisor's companion* (pp. 237-248). Englewood, CO: Libraries Unlimited.

Berman, M. (2010). *Child lit wiki and book recommendation engine.* Retrieved March 10, 2010, from http://childlit.info/

Bird, E. (2007). Blogging the kidlitosphere. *The Horn Book Magazine, 83*(3), 305–309.

Bird, E. (2009). This blog's for you. *School Library Journal, 55*(11), 26–29.

Bolan, K. (2008). *The need for teen space in public libraries: YALSA White Paper Number 1.* In A. Alessio (Ed.), *Excellence in library service to young adults.* (5th ed, pp. 136-138). Chicago, IL: American Library Association.

Booth, H. (2007). *Serving teens through readers' advisory.* Chicago, IL: American Library Association.

Celano, D., & Neuman, S. (2001). *The role of public libraries in children's literacy development: An evaluation report.* Harrisburg, PA: Pennsylvania Library Association. Retrieved March 10, 2010, from http://www.ifpl.org/junior/studies/Role%20of%20Libraries.pdf

Cerny, R., Markey, P., & Williams, A. (2006). *Outstanding library service to children.* Chicago, IL: American Library Association.

Chelton, M., & Cool, C. (Eds.). (2004). *Youth information-seeking behavior: Theories, models, and issues.* Lanham, MD: Scarecrow Press.

Chelton, M., & Cool, C. (Eds.). (2007). *Youth information-seeking behavior II: Context, theories, models, & issues.* Lanham, MD: Scarecrow Press.

Child_Lit. (2006). Retrieved March 10, 2010, from http://www.rci.rutgers.edu/~mjoseph/childlit/about.html

Children's and young adult bloggers literary awards (the Cybils). Retrieved March 10, 2010 from http://dadtalk.typepad.com/cybils/

Clyde, L. A. (2002). Shall we blog? *Teacher-Librarian, 30*(2), 7–9.

Collaborative summer reading program. (n.d.). Retrieved on March 4, 2010, from http://www.cslpreads.org/

Collen, L. (2006). The digital and traditional storytimes research project: Using digitized picture books for preschool group storytimes. *Children and Libraries, 4*(3), 8–18.

Druin, A. (2005). Children's access and use of digital resources. *Library Trends, 54*(2), 173–177.

Eastman, L. (1897). Methods of work for children – Cleveland Library League. *Library Journal,* (22), 687–688.

Feinberg, S., Kuchner, J., & Feldman, S. (1998). *Learning environments for young children.* Chicago, IL: American Library Association.

Fiore, C. (1998). *Running summer reading programs.* New York, NY: Neal-Schuman.

Fiore, C. (2005). *Fiore's summer library reading program handbook.* New York, NY: Neal-Schuman.

Glander, M., & Dam, T. (2007). *Households' use of public and other types of libraries: 2002* (NCES 2007-327). Washington, DC: U.S. Department of Education. National Center for Education Statistics. Retrieved March 3, 2010, from http://nces.ed.gov/pubsearch/pubsinfo.asp?pubid=2007327

Gross, M. (2006). *Studying children's questions: Imposed and self-generated information seeking at school.* Lanham, MD: Scarecrow Press.

Gunter, G., & Kenny, R. (2008). Digital booktalk: Digital media for reluctant readers. *Contemporary Issues in Technology and Teacher Education, 8*(1). Retrieved March 10, 2010, from http://www.citejournal.org/vol8/iss1/currentpractice/article1.cfm

Harris Interactive, Inc. (2007). Youth use of public and school libraries. Retrieved March 5, 2010, from http://www.ala.org/ala/mgrps/divs/yalsa/HarrisYouthPoll.pdf

Henderson, E., Miller, K., Craig, T., Dorinski, S., Freeman, M., Isaac, N., Keng, J., McKenzie, L., O'Shea, P., Ramsey, C., Sheckells, C. (2009). *Public Libraries Survey: Fiscal Year 2007* (IMLS-2009–PLS-02). Washington, D.C.: Institute of Museum and Library Services.

International Children's Digital Library. (n.d.). Retrieved March 10, 2010, from http://en.childrenslibrary.org

Jenkins, C. A. (1994). History of public library services to children. In W. Wiegand & D. Davis (Eds.), *Encyclopedia of library history* (pp. 127-131). Hamden, CT: Garland, 1994.

Jenkins, C.A. (2000). The history of youth services librarianship: A review of the research literature. *Libraries & Culture, 35* (1), 103-140.

Jones, P., Gorman, M., & Suellentrop, T. (2004). *Connecting young adults and libraries* (3rd ed.). New York, NY: Neal-Schuman.

Keene, C. (1932). *Nancy's Mysterious Letter.* New York, NY: Grosset and Dunlap.

Krashen, S. (2004). *The power of reading: Insights for research* (2nd ed.). Westport, CT: Libraries Unlimited.

Locke, J. (1988). *The effectiveness of summer reading programs in public libraries in the United States.* Doctoral dissertation. Pittsburgh, PA: University of Pittsburgh.

Lushington, N. (2008). *Libraries designed for kids.* New York, NY: Neal-Schuman.

McCook, K. (2004). *Introduction to public librarianship.* New York, NY: Neal-Schuman.

McDonalds's annual report. (2008). McDonald's Corporation Oakbrook, IL. Retrieved March 4, 2010, from http://www1.mcdonalds.com/annualreport/index.html

Mediavilla, C. (2001). *Creating the full-service homework center in your library.* Chicago, IL: American Library Association.

Minkel, W. (2003). Making a splash with summer reading. *School Library Journal, 49*(1), 54–56.

Moyer, J. (2008). *Research-based readers' advisory.* Chicago, IL: American Library Association.

National Center for Education. (1995). *Services and resources for children and young adults in public libraries.* Washington, DC: US Department of Education, Office of Education Research and Improvement.

Oldenburg, R. (1999). *The great good place.* New York, NY: Marlowe & Company.

Ontario Library Association. (2010). Forest of reading programs. Retrieved on March 10, 2010, from http://www.accessola.com/ola/bins/content_page.asp?cid=92

Pellowski, A. (1968). *The World of Children's Literature.* New York, NY: R. R. Bowker.

Pierce, J. B. (2007). Booting up book lovers. *American Libraries, 38*(10), 61.

Public Libraries Young Adults and Children (PUBYAC). 2010. Center for Children's Books, Graduate School of Library and Information Science, University of Illinois at Urbana-Champaign. Retrieved March 10, 2010, from http://www.pubyac.org/

Putnam, R., & Feldstein, L. (2003). *Better together: Restoring the American community.* New York, NY: Simon and Schuster.

Reichel, R. (1991). *Reference services for children and young adults.* Hamden CT: Library Professional Publications.

Roman, S., Carran, D. T., & Fiore, C. D. (2010). *The Dominican study: Public library summer reading programs close the reading gap.* River Forest, IL: Graduate School of Library & Information Science, Dominican University. Retrieved July 21, 2010, from http://www.dom.edu/academics/gslis/downloads/DOM_IMLS_book_2010_FINAL_web.pdf

Ross, C., McKechnie, L., & Rothbauer, P. (2006). *Reading matters: What the research reveals about reading, libraries, and community.* Westport, CT: Libraries Unlimited.

Ryan, S. (2002). Not under the mattress: Revelations from online journals. *Voice of Youth Advocates, 25*(2), 103.

Saricks, J. (2005). *Readers' advisory service in the public library* (3rd ed.). Chicago, IL: American Library Association.

Seattle Public Library. (2010). *Seattle Public Library: Teens.* Retrieved March 10, 2010 from http://www.spl.org/default.asp?pageID=audience_teens

Serebnick, J. (1981). Book reviews and the selection of potentially controversial books in public libraries. *The Library Quarterly, 51*(4), pp. 390-409.

Shenton, A. (2007). Causes of information-seeking failure: Some insights from an English research project. In M. Chelton, & C. Cool (Eds.), *Youth information-seeking behavior II: Context, theories, models, & issues.* Lanham, MD: Scarecrow Press.

Shera, J. H. (1949). *Foundations of the public library: The origins of the public library movement in New England, 1629–1855.* Chicago, IL: University of Chicago Press.

Shin, F., & Krashen, S. (2008). *Summer reading: Program and evidence.* Boston, MA: Pearson Education.

Silvey, A. (2004). *100 Best Books for Children.* New York, NY: Houghton and Mifflin.

Steele, A. (2001). *Bare bones children's services: Tips for public library generalists.* Chicago, IL: American Library Association

Stewart, P. (2009). Facebook and virtual literature circle partnership in building a community of readers. *Knowledge Quest, 37*(4), 28–32.

Sullivan, M. (2005). *Fundamentals of children's services.* Chicago, IL: American Library Association.

The Library in vacation days. (1898). *Library Journal, 23*, 279.

There's a new award in town. (2008). *School Library Journal, 54*(3), 20.

Thomas, F. (1982). *The genesis of children's library services in the American public library, 1876–1906.* Unpublished doctoral dissertation. Madison, WI: University of Wisconsin-Madison.

Tutor.com (2010). *Learning and career services for your library.* Retrieved on March 8, 2010 from http://www.tutor.com/libraries

University of Calgary. (2010). *Children's literature web guide.* Retrieved March 10, 2010, from http://wiki.ucalgary.ca/page/ChildrensLiteratureWebGuide

Van Slyck, A. (1995). *Free to all: Carnegie libraries & American culture 1890–1920.* Chicago, IL: The University of Chicago Press.

Walter, V. (2001). *Children & libraries: Getting it right.* Chicago, IL: American Library Association.

Walter, V. (2003). Public library service to children and teens: A research agenda. *Library Trends, 51*(4), 571–589.

Walter, V. (2010). *Twenty-first century kids, Twenty-first century librarians.* Chicago, IL: American Library Association.

Walter, V., & Mediavilla, C. (2005). Teens are from Neptune, Librarians are from Pluto: An analysis of online reference transactions. *Library Trends, 54*(2), 209–227.

Walter, V., & Meyers, E. (2003). *Teens & libraries: Getting it right.* Chicago, IL: American Library Association.

Wisconsin Department of Public Instruction. (n.d.). *Research on the importance of summer library programs* Retrieved on March 4, 2010, from http://dpi.wi.gov/pld/slp-research.html

Young Adult Library Services Association. (2010). *YALSA's competencies for librarians serving youth: Young adults deserve the best.* Retrieved March 9, 2010, from http://www.ala.org/ala/mgrps/divs/yalsa/profdev/yadeservethebest_201.pdf

Ziarnik, N. (2003). *School & public libraries: Developing the natural alliance.* Chicago, IL: American Library Association.

11

Becoming Readers of Literature with LGBT Themes

In and Out of Classrooms

Mollie V. Blackburn and Caroline T. Clark

The Ohio State University

Who gets to feel safe as a reader in school? What if the selected reading and literature are actually intended to be for your benefit; and yet you remain invisible, or worse, the subject of disdain? Conversely, what is it like to be in the company of friends and allies who want to know what it's like to be *you*—who seek your insights so they can learn from you, laugh with you, and live with you? In this groundbreaking chapter, Mollie Blackburn and Caroline Clark provide a framework for understanding what gets asked of books, readers, and the places where reading happens—whether the focus of this reading is situated in school or out of school, with LGBTQ youth, teachers, and allies in mind.

In this chapter, we ask where and how young people become readers of literature with lesbian, gay, bisexual, and/or transgender (LGBT) themes in and out of classrooms in contemporary contexts. We begin by discussing the theoretical framework that guides our interpretations of LGBT-themed literature and contexts. Then, we consider *where* youth read by reviewing scholarship on reading LGBT-themed texts situated in elementary through secondary classrooms. However, the primary focus of our chapter will be on adolescent and young adult readers of LGBT-themed literature. We next turn to the scholarship documenting readers of LGBT-themed literature beyond classrooms to review the few studies that focus on the reading of this literature in out-of-school contexts intended to support LGBTQ[1] people. Then, we focus on *how* a particular group of LGBTQ and allied adolescents and adults, including ourselves, are working together to become readers of literature with LGBT themes outside of classrooms.

In asking how readers and texts are defined in each of these contexts, we examine what happens in and out of school spaces that limit or invite students to be particular kinds of readers with particular allowances and expectations for engaging with texts. We then analyze how texts are selected in each context, what readers do with these texts, and what kinds of work readers ask these texts to do. In doing so, we draw on Bishop's (1992) concept of literature serving as windows and mirrors for its readers and Cart and Jenkins's (2006) heuristic for describing changes in depictions of LGBTQ characters in young adult literature: homosexual visibility, gay assimilation, and queer community. We conclude each section with questions about the consequences of becoming a reader across these contexts.

Ultimately, we look across the work being done in and out-of-schools around LGBT topics and themes in order to name key practices that teachers, youth service providers, and librarians can enact and enable in order to help people become readers of literature with LGBT themes and thus work against homophobia in and out of schools.

Interpreting LGBTQ Literature and Contexts

Drawing on Bishop (1992) and Cart and Jenkins (2006) to examine how readers and texts are defined in classrooms, in LGBTQ-friendly out-of-school communities, and in our book discussion group for LGBTQ students and teachers and their allies, is appropriate for several reasons. Like these scholars, we locate our work in the field of multicultural literature for children and young adults. Moreover, Sims (Bishop) laid the foundation for chronological categorizations of characters in such literature, in her germinal book, *Shadow and Substance: Afro-American Experience in Contemporary Children's Fiction* (1982). Cart and Jenkins built on this foundation, and in doing so, focused specifically on LGBT characters, instead of African American characters, and literature for young adults, rather than children. These shifts in foci brought Sims's significant scholarship even closer to our foci in this chapter.

Bishop also provides the metaphor of texts as mirrors and windows as a way of understanding opportunities provided by multicultural children's literature for readers both to see themselves and their own lives reflected in texts as well as to see through windows into other worlds (Smith, 1997). For example, let's say a reader of this chapter identifies as a straight teacher of the English Language Arts who generally considers herself to be LGBTQ-friendly, who interrupts homophobia when she encounters it in her classroom, but who does not use LGBT-inclusive curricular materials in her work. This reader may experience this chapter at times as a mirror in which she sees herself reading texts with students in classrooms and discussing content that is sometimes quite contentious. There are other times, however, when she may experience this chapter as a window into a world where adults read LGBT-themed texts with young people in ways that add depth and significance to anti-homophobia efforts.

Cart and Jenkins's (2006) heuristic contributes to what fictional texts might accomplish in representing the experiences of LGBTQ people. Stories of *homosexual visibility* (HV) typically portray a single character, assumed to be straight, who comes out or is outed as gay or lesbian. The responses, or potential responses, of other characters are the problem that drives the story. For example, in *Keeping You a Secret* (Peters, 2003), Holland, the main character, comes out when she falls in love with an out and proud lesbian named Cece. After coming out, Holland's family and friends ostracize her. As the story unfolds, her familial, social, and even academic life essentially falls apart. As she tries to continue her life as a lesbian she encounters overt homophobia and support through a center for gay youth. Cart and Jenkins categorize the book as HV, because Holland's homosexuality becomes visible in her predominantly homophobic world. *Gay assimilation* (GA) stories, however, present gay/lesbian characters as no different from straight characters, aside from their sexuality. They portray sexual identity as just another characteristic, much like being left handed or having red hair, suggesting that underneath the superficial differences that distinguish all people, gay people are just like straight people.

Such a character is central in *The Perks of Being a Wallflower* (Chbosky, 1999). Written as a series of letters from the main character, Charlie, to someone addressed only as "Friend," this popular young adult novel chronicles Charlie's life in high school, including his friendship with Patrick, who is out and gay, and his sister, Sam, with whom Charlie falls in love. The story is told with stunning attention to the details of high school life and the importance of music, sex, freedom, and friendship in negotiating adolescence. The author's depiction of Patrick as a kind, loving, flawed character, just like Charlie and Sam, seems to us to be the reason that Cart and Jenkins place *Perks of Being a Wallflower* in the GA category. Cart and Jenkins call their final category *queer consciousness/community* (QC), however, their application of this term emphasizes community over consciousness. QC books portray multiple LGBTQ characters within supportive communities and families, including families of their own making. They show the diversity of LGBTQ characters and dispel the myth that being gay means being alone.

This is evident in *Finding H.F.* (Watts, 2001), particularly when the narrator, H.F., and her best friend Bo go on a road trip from their small, rural community in Kentucky to Atlanta, where they encounter diverse communities of LGBTQ people. They meet people in a bookstore and a park; they meet young and old people, Black and White people, and even some religious people who embrace their LGBTQ identities. Thus, they find themselves in a queer community (QC). It should be noted that despite the important distinctions Cart and Jenkins (2006) identify, they do not assume that any one book belongs in only one category; rather, a book can be appropriately placed in one, two, or even all three categories.

Cart and Jenkins's analysis (2006) shows that the majority of LGBT-themed children's and young adult literature falls into the HV category. They also point out that there is some, although significantly less, LGBT-themed children's and young adult literature that falls into the second category, GA. There is, however, a dearth of LGBT-themed children's and young adult literature that shows queer youth in queer communities, categorized as QC. Together, Bishop's metaphor and Cart and Jenkins's heuristic are useful in understanding the work that readers ask texts to do.

Reading LGBT-Themed Literature with Young People in Classrooms

There is a significant body of research documenting the hostilities that LGBTQ and non-gender-conforming youth face in U.S. and international school contexts (see, e.g., Hillier, Turner, & Mitchell, 2005; Kosciw, Diaz, & Greytak, 2008; Ryan & Rivers, 2003; Wyss, 2004). However, scholarship focused on reading and becoming readers of LGBT-themed children's and young adult texts, whether in U.S. or international school-settings, is incredibly sparse. Increasingly, scholars have argued that literature study can be an important place to counter homophobia and heterosexism. They argue for expanding text selections in schools to include LGBT-themed young adult literature and for increasing the visibility of lesbian and gay readings of more traditional literature (Blackburn & Buckley, 2005; Cart & Jenkins, 2006; Gallo, 2004; Reese, 1998).

Scholars have also gone beyond questions of why and whether or not to include such texts to consider questions of *how* these texts might be used in school. They provide strategies for working in primary and secondary classrooms through reading, writing, and classroom talk, and identify curriculum frameworks and detailed multi-week plans for particular texts (Hammett, 1992; Harris, 1990; King & Schneider, 1999). Despite arguments for the inclusion of LGBT-themed literature in schools and efforts to show possibilities for *doing* this work in K–12 classrooms, detailed descriptions of how readers and texts are defined during these engagements are limited.

In this section, we provide a summary of studies that describe readings of LGBT-themed literature in classrooms. We highlight this work to show what is (and is not) happening in classrooms and schools, not to demonize these classrooms or the important, and even ground breaking, work that occurs in them. Rather, we aim to trouble this scholarship, arguing that reading and becoming readers of LGBT-themed literature in classrooms may be limited by the very context of school. The contextual framing we provide for each study, however, is limited, in part due to the brevity of the contexts provided in the original studies themselves, and in part due to our framing of this chapter. Our analytic focus is on classrooms as *one* of the places where young people become readers of LGBT-themed texts.

After summarizing, we treat the studies collectively and focus on (a) how readers and texts are defined, (b) what was done to and with texts by readers, and 3) what texts were asked to do as windows or mirrors and as HV, GA, or QC representations. We conclude by considering the implications of this analysis for young people becoming readers of LGBT-themed literature in classrooms.

The studies we review take place in elementary, middle, and high school settings, although mostly in U.S. high school English classrooms. For example, Carey-Webb (2001) describes the work of Tisha Pankop, an English teacher in an ethnically mixed, inner-city, U.S. high school (students, age 15–18). As part of a short story unit on the theme of "fear," Pankop offered her students blue triangles to wear prior to engaging in a read-aloud of Bruce Coville's "Am I Blue?" the title story in a collection of young-adult, lesbian, and gay-themed stories (Bauer, 1994). As the meaning of "blue" was revealed in the story (indicating how "exclusively queer" a character was) several of Pankop's students ripped off their taped-on triangles and threw them across the room, while some of the female students quietly kept them on, and others proclaimed that they were "tricked" by their teacher. When Pankop probed into students' responses, those who rejected the triangles expressed: "I'm not gay. I don't want anybody to think I am," and "It's okay for girls to be gay, but not guys" (p. 45). In their discussion, students tied their responses back to the topic of the unit—"fear"—and talked about homophobia, as well as the fears that a young person who is gay or lesbian might face. Carey-Webb states that the students came to no final conclusions "except that it was 'sad about the way that the kid in the story was treated'" (p. 45).

Athanases (1996) also describes students reading LGBT-themed texts in a high school English class in the United States (students age 15–18). He focuses on Reiko Liu, a teacher in a multi-ethnic, urban high school in the San Francisco Bay area. As part of Athanases's multi-year study of Liu's use of ethnic literature with her Honors English class, Athanases documented Liu's students' reading of and responses to the essay, "Dear Anita: Late Night Thoughts of an Irish Catholic Homosexual," by Brian McNaught (1988)—a text taken up, in part, because of the Euro-American ethnicity of its writer.

Greenbaum (1994) and Hoffman (1993) describe their own work as high school English teachers engaging students (ages 15–18) in LGBT-themes. Greenbaum sought to challenge the assumed absence and invisibility of lesbian and gay content, students, and experiences in schools. As a closeted teacher, she did so through the examination of gay and lesbian subtexts in canonical works (e.g., *Catcher in the Rye*, *Julius Caesar*, *Cat on a Hot Tin Roof*). In contrast, Hoffman (1993) taught a text in which gay and lesbian themes were prominent. He taught Harvey Fierstein's (1988) play *Torch Song Trilogy* to his high school creative-writing students in Houston, Texas, in response to his work with pre-service teachers who felt that reading gay-themed texts with students in public high schools was unimaginable.

Engaging student readers with LGBT-themed literature, though, is not limited to high school. Hamilton (1998), for example, taught the young adult novel, *Jack* (Homes, 1990), to his New York city middle school students (ages 11–14) in response to an eighth grader's letter to the faculty complaining about the problem of homophobia in the school. Kauffmann, who was a teacher in an elementary, multi-age, structured English immersion classroom in a large Tucson, Arizona, school district, introduced literature with gay and lesbian characters to her students (ages 6–10) in a one-day literature study that was documented by a colleague. Like Hoffman, Schall and Kauffmann (2003) were prompted by their work with pre-service teachers who argued such books were "inappropriate" and that children did not and could not know about or understand issues of homosexuality.

In a more comprehensive study, Epstein (2000) describes the complicated negotiations of gender and sexuality in a Year 5 (ages 9–10) ethnically-mixed classroom in a working-class school located in north London. Working with a popular, out-to-his-colleagues, gay teacher, Mr. Stuart, Epstein examines Stuart's teaching on the topic, "Me, My Family, and My History." Focal texts for the topic included *Asha's Mums* (Elwin, & Paulse, 2000) and the photopack, *What is a Family?* Although selected texts were important to the study, Epstein (2000) documented, both in the classroom and on the playground, the role that other texts played in signifying gender and normalizing heterosexuality, including skipping rhymes and playground games that reinforced strongly dichotomized gender roles and lines. Hence, while Mr. Stuart worked hard to encourage students to see possibilities that were anti-heterosexist and anti-homophobic, the dominant discourses around gender and (hetero)sexuality prevailed.

Looking across these classrooms reveals some subtleties relative to how young people as readers of LGBT-themed texts are positioned in schools. It also helps us see the possibilities and the limitations for young people as readers of LGBT-themed young adult literature in these spaces.

Defining Readers

Within school contexts—whether public or independent, and regardless of geographic location—students are invariably positioned as straight and often homophobic. While many people in schools would acknowledge that students might have a loving relationship with someone who is lesbian or gay—an aunt, uncle, sibling, cousin, or the like—students are addressed by text, teacher, or institution as presumably straight and often aggressively homophobic.

For example, in Athanases's (1996) study, Liu's expressed goals were to teach an attitude of sensitivity toward diversity and help students find common ground across marginalized groups. She wanted "especially some of the more homophobic members of our class to under-stand where this [gay] person is coming from" (p. 232). Despite this goal for homophobic students to understand a gay person's perspective and experience, there was still a tacit suggestion that maintaining a position of homophobia was acceptable in Liu's classroom. In starting the unit, for example, Liu chose a chapter from Martin Luther King Jr.'s (1958/2010) book, *Stride Toward Freedom*, in part because King "brings to life the age-old notions of love as a unifying force, of hating the sin, but not the sinner" (Athanases, 1996, p. 237).

This rationale suggests several problematic positionings of both gay and straight students as readers of LGBT-themed texts in this classroom. One positioning suggests that homosexuality is a "sin" and that gay and lesbian people are sinners; a second positioning suggests that straight students, who are understood to be homophobic students, are free to both view their gay peers as sinners and to "hate" their fundamental sexual orientations and gender identities. This is not to say that all of Liu's students were homophobic or even straight. In fact, one student in the class came out as a lesbian a year and a half after the reading, but all students were positioned as straight, and generally homophobic.

This positioning was not unique to Liu's classroom. Hoffman (1993) even went so far as to say, in describing his students, most of whom were racial minorities identified with intellectual gifts, "it is hard to imagine a more homophobic group" (p. 56).[2] In the classroom Schall and Kauffmann (2003) examined, students were positioned as straight and were allowed the choice of not engaging with the texts at all if they felt uncomfortable—a choice that was made by four of the children in this class of 29. Thus, students were empowered to maintain a homophobic position.

Only Epstein (2000) and Greenbaum (1994) complicate the positioning of students as readers of LGBT-themed literature in schools. For example, Greenbaum's aim was to reach both gay/lesbian and straight-identified students, helping the former hear their voices actively in texts, and helping the latter see the range of "ways to be sexual in the world" (p. 71). Even with these expressed goals, however, Greenbaum's only gay-identified student, who was not out to his peers, felt he could only enter a class discussion and raise issues related to homosexuality in homophobic disguise, asking in a discussion of Conrad's (1910/2007) *The Secret Sharer*, "Is this about faggots?" (p. 72). Similarly, in Epstein's study, Mr. Stuart encouraged students to see possibilities that were anti-heterosexist and anti-homophobic. Even so, as in Greenbaum's school, the dominant discourses around gender and (hetero)sexuality prevailed in positioning the students and urging them to position themselves as straight and/or homophobic.

Across all of these studies, then, students are either positioned, or position themselves, as straight, homophobic, and lacking any real knowledge of lesbian or gay issues.

Defining Texts

The actual use of LGBT-themed young adult and/or children's literature across these studies was complicated and limited as well, as was the assumed work that these texts did in each classroom. How texts were selected and positioned seems clearly related to the positioning of young people as readers.

How Texts were Selected.   In all of these studies, texts were selected by adults—generally by teachers, or by teachers in collaboration with research partners. While several of the selections were children's and young adult literature, many were not. Often a text's form was instrumental to legitimizing its uptake in classrooms. For example, Hoffman's (1993) use of *Torch Song Trilogy*—a play, written for an adult audience—was aimed, in part, at disguising its LGBT themes and focusing, instead, on its form. Because of his plans to introduce playwriting, among other genres, Hoffman felt that *Torch Song Trilogy* (Fierstein, 1988), with its innovative structure, would be an acceptable text in a creative writing class. Similarly, Reiko Liu's (Athanases, 1996) use of the essay "Dear Anita" stemmed in part from its form. McNaught's (1988) persuasive essay, like the form of *Torch Song Trilogy*, provided a model for subsequent student writing and positioned the text as a legitimate choice in the high school English classroom. Finally, Greenbaum's (1994) use of canonical texts to explore gay and lesbian subtexts was legitimized by the form and stature of these texts as "classics" (p. 72).

Selections of LGBT-themed children's and young adult literature included Hamilton's (1998) use of the young adult novel *Jack*, Pankop's (Carey-Webb, 2001) use of the short story, "Am I Blue?," and the children's picture books used by Schall and Kauffmann (2003). Epstein (2000) departed from the usual text mode through her use of the photopack, *What is a Family?*, a collection of photographs of families, including a photo of two women, a baby (and a cat), which the students steadfastly resisted reading as a lesbian couple and their child.

What was Done to, and with Texts.   When readings of LGBT-themed literature happen in schools, they typically occur behind the closed door of a classroom, where teachers work quietly alone against the institutional grain in order to provide students access to texts that they hope will, at best, challenge heterosexism, homophobia, and oppressive gender norms, or at least provide exposure to issues and encourage tolerance among students (Carey-Webb, 2001; Greenbaum, 1994; Hoffman, 1993). In some instances, such work is institutionally embraced and supported by colleagues and/or administrators (Athanases, 1996; Epstein, 2000; Hamilton, 1998; Schall & Kauffmann, 2003). In all of the classrooms studied, reading LGBT-themed texts was a singular event. Typically, such readings occurred only once in the school year, and at times on a single day—as in the case of Schall and Kauffmann (2003) and Pankop (Carey-Webb, 2001). Indeed, many of these studies chronicle the single time that an LGBT-themed text was ever taken up in the course of a student's K–12 schooling. In Greenbaum's (1994) case, LGBT-themed texts were not taken up at all; rather, canonical texts were read to uncover hidden subtexts, including for the first time, possible homoerotic ones.

In many of these classrooms, the curricular focus was often the force that shaped how LGBT-themed young adult and children's literature was used and to whom it was addressed. In Epstein's (2000) study, for example, Mr. Stuart's work with LGBT-themed texts was part of a unit on "Me, My Family, and My History"—a unit specifically intended as an opportunity for children to engage in anti-racist, anti-sexist, and anti-heterosexist work. Pankop's (Carey-Webb, 2001) use of Bruce Coville's "Am I Blue?" occurs in a unit on "Fear," a topic that presumes homophobia in its basest terms ("fear of gay people"), along with the fear-filled lives that gays and lesbians are presumed to face (as experienced by Vincent in the story). Likewise, Schall and Kauffman (2003) embedded their use of children's literature with lesbian and gay characters in a unit on "Survival" with a focus on name-calling on the playground—a real issue in the lives of the children. Students were invited to engage with a wide-range of quality picture books, but the unit framing caused some confusion as the children were expected to recognize that calling someone "gay" was an insult; at the same time the class's discussion focused on positive portrayals of gay people required them to use these terms in positive ways. Positioning the children as straight and possibly homophobic outsiders to this discourse seemed to make it difficult for the children to engage more positively with the selected texts.

In Hoffman's (1993) teaching of *Torch Song Trilogy*, the focus was on creative writing, and Hoffman described the play to his students as a "daring" text that "might shock or upset them" in places, and tried to focus on the structural aspects of the play. Yet, he also felt this text was one that could serve as a useful vehicle to change students' perceptions and attitudes towards gay males and lesbians. This focus on the text as daring, shocking, and upsetting, as well as holding the potential to change students' minds links directly to the positioning of Hoffman's students as overtly and determinedly homophobic.

Reiko Liu's (Athanases, 1996) choice of the essay "Dear Anita" was similarly focused on her sense of her students as homophobic, and the notion that their homophobia was linked, in part, to their religious beliefs. Her choice was aimed explicitly to expose her students to an author, McNaught, who was simultaneously family-oriented and religious, traits he shared with many of her students and also gay—an identity that was apparently at odds with nearly all of her students at the time of the assignment.

In Hamilton's (1998) case, *Jack* was taken up specifically to address a student-identified concern about homophobia in the middle school. Finally, while Greenbaum (1994) used canonical texts to explore gay and lesbian subtexts, she was careful to address "all the subtexts, not just homoerotic ones" (p. 72) so as to protect herself as a closeted lesbian teacher and to engage her students in reading for "racism, sexism, and cultural differences" and to learn to do these kinds of readings on their own. In all cases texts were chosen as a means toward a didactic end of exposing students to issues pertinent to LGBTQ people so as to provoke empathy, understanding, and a sense of commonality across differences. While using texts in such didactic ways in classrooms is neither "bad" nor uncommon, it concerns us that LGBT-themed literature seems to be used in *only* these ways. That these texts might provoke pleasure, humor, or self-recognition in their readers was rarely, if ever, a consideration.

What Texts were Asked to Do. Since all of the students were assumed to be or positioned as straight, texts in these classrooms were typically employed as "windows" (Bishop, 1992; Smith, 1997) through which students might peer into a different world, vicariously experience oppression, and gain empathy for an "other's" experience. Only in the case of Hamilton's (1998) use of *Jack* were students asked to see themselves in the story, and then, only in relation to Jack, the straight adolescent protagonist who learns that his father is gay after his parents' divorce. So, while readings of these texts were sometimes framed as a "mirror" for straight students, students were rarely asked to see reflections of themselves in LGBTQ or homophobic characters (e.g., the bully in "Am I Blue?"). This is particularly troubling since students across all studies were regularly positioned as homophobic. In Liu's (Athanases, 1996) class, students were even allowed to maintain their homophobia while reading "Dear Anita," not actively but silently, by failing to discuss the problems implicit in "hating the sin and not the sinner."

Because students were presumed to be straight and/or homophobic (either by teachers or in Epstein's case, by themselves or their peers), the use of texts as windows or mirrors was particularly problematic for queer or questioning youth because they were effectively erased from visibility in discussions or presumptions about the audience for the books. In their presumed absence, a teacher could not mediate students' gaze through a window at straight characters or into a mirror at LGBTQ characters. Aside from Greenbaum's hope that any lesbian or gay students might hear their voices in the subtexts of canonical literature, students were never invited to see themselves or their possible queer selves in the texts.

Most of the LGBT-themed children's and young adult literature in these classrooms, including *What is a Family?*, would fall into Cart and Jenkins' (2006) category of HV, *homosexual visibility*. In other words, almost all of the texts were asked to make homosexuals visible, but they were not asked to show either that gay and lesbian people are just like straight people or to represent queer communities. The single exception to this is Bauer's "Am I Blue?," which was used in Pankop's urban high school class (Carey-Webb, 2001). This short story, we argue, has a more developed sense of queer consciousness (QC), because several of the stories in this collection show "GLBTQ characters in the context of their communities of GLBTQ people" (Cart & Jenkins, p. xx).

Consequences

School is a significant site where young people become readers, both collectively and individually, and where readers, acts of reading, and texts themselves are defined and redefined. Scholarship on reading LGBT-themed literature in schools, however, is sparse. The studies that do exist suggest that these contexts are severely limited and limiting in terms of the possibilities they allow for readers and texts. The homophobic and heterosexist institution of schooling shapes and limits how readers are defined by others and by themselves. In all of the studies, readers in schools were presumed to be straight and often homophobic. This positioning, combined with the limited ways that texts are read—often in isolation from broader curricula, and typically toward didactic ends—may lead, at best, to sympathetic responses in straight student readers who feel sorry for gay people. However, this response leaves LGBTQ students in the classroom positioned as pitiable. Moreover, by exposing students to LGBT-themed literature in schools without an end goal of actively combating homophobia and heterosexism, teachers fail to hold themselves and their students accountable for the injustices and inequities experienced by LGBT youth. Teachers can say they have done their work by raising issues and making texts available, but that it is not their job to impose their beliefs on homophobic, heterosexist students (see, e.g., Schneider, 2001). In effect, by positioning students as straight and even homophobic and then leaving their beliefs unchallenged, teachers tacitly affirm and even promote heterosexism and homophobia in schools.

The severe limitations that currently surround readers and reading of LGBT-themed texts in classrooms, as documented in recent scholarship, provoke the following questions:

- What would it look like to read LGBTQ-themed literature with LGBTQ people, rather than people presumed to be straight if not homophobic?
- What would it look like to do this reading in contexts that are more queer-friendly than typical school and classroom contexts?

The next section addresses these questions by examining recent scholarship on LGBT-themed reading (and writing) outside of the institution of schooling.

Reading LGBT-Themed Literature in Out-of-School LGBTQ Youth Communities

Contexts in which LGBTQ youth engage with literature reflecting their experiences are distinctive from in-school contexts in both positive and negative ways. Although the opportunity to understand how readers of LGBT-themed literature are mindful of conflicting values among stakeholders, such as administrators, parents and guardians, and other community members is lost, the opportunity to interpret literature while less encumbered by heterosexism and homophobia is gained. We review several projects that focus on LGBT themes using literary and non-literary forms in queer-friendly, out-of-school contexts: Blackburn's (2002/2003, 2003a, 2003b, 2005a, 2005b) work at The Attic (or sometimes named with the pseudonym, The Loft) a youth-run center for LGBTQ youth; Halverson's (2007) work with About Face Youth Theatre (AFYT), a youth theatre program dedicated to working with LGBTQ adolescents; and de Castell and Jenson's (2007) work on the Pridehouse project, which was a study with street-involved LGBTQ youth.

The project at The Attic was a three-year literacy ethnography (Street, 1995) that documented the literacy performances of youth who identified as LGBTQ and ranged in age from 12 to 23 years old. The youth were diverse in terms of race, class, and gender, but the majority were African American males who were poor and working class. The youth were predominantly urban, being born and raised in Philadelphia, Pennsylvania. The project captures literacy performances in a variety of situations associated with The Attic: a literacy group called Story Time (Blackburn, 2002/2003, 2005a), a speakers' bureau (2003b), and working with individuals outside of formal groups (2002/2003, 2003a, 2003b). Although the purposes of the literacy performances varied from situation to situation, Blackburn was particularly interested in documenting reading and writing for social change. Young adult literature was not her focus per se, but this literature was present and sometimes prominent in the work of Story Time.

Halverson (2007) documented AFYT's program in Chicago, Illinois during a full season, starting with the initial storytelling workshops—in which LGBTQ youth talk about the stories of their lives to generate ideas of what might be scripted, rehearsed, and performed—and ending with the final performance. Of the 60 participants, ranging in age from 13 to 19 years old, she focuses on six who were diverse in terms of race and gender, although predominantly White and female. The stories, scripts, and performances in this project provided a means for "exploring, understanding, and trying on identities" (p. 171). As will be discussed later, even though the texts were not young adult literature the stories and performances produced in this project further our understanding of readers of LGBT-themed young adult literature.

The Pridehouse project was a "short-term, ethnographically based, peer-to-peer study to identify the conditions and assess the needs of street-involved 'queer and questioning youth'" (de Castell & Jenson, 2007, p. 131) that took place in Vancouver, British Columbia. The entirely queer team of researchers comprised a balance of university-affiliates and youth who were or had been living on the streets. Over five months, they trained together; developed, distributed, collected, and analyzed surveys; observed and took field notes; conducted and recorded interviews and focus group discussions; and photographed and videotaped "sites of safety and danger" (p. 136) and the people in them. Later, they produced a web page that features a video presenting their data. Like the other projects, de Castell and Jenson's does not include young adult literature, but the authors make a compelling argument for what self-produced multimedia and multimodal texts, rather than more typically schoolish texts, have to teach us in terms of working with "youth for whom formal mainstream schooling had been a hostile and exclusionary environment" (p. 146). In heterosexist and homophobic societies, it is worth looking at the texts youth *produce* outside of school in addition to the texts they *consume*, both in and out of school.

Defining Readers

As described above, all of the youth in these three projects identified, at least at the point of data collection, as not-straight. Some of them identified as lesbian or gay, and others as bisexual. Some of the people who were bisexual were in heterosexual relationships, but unquestionably identified as not-straight. There were youth who had transitioned from one gender to the other, and in doing so went from experiencing same-sex desire to opposite-sex desire, but these young people did not identify as straight. Some identified as queer, an identity that allows for fluidity among various sexual identities, behaviors, and desires; but, again, these youth did not identify as straight.

The researchers in all of these projects acknowledge the impact of the youth's non-straight identities on their social status by including descriptors such as vulnerable (Blackburn, 2005b), neglected, abused, harassed (Blackburn, 2005a), marginalized (Blackburn, 2005a; de Castell & Jenson, 2007), stigmatized, disenfranchised, traumatized (Halverson, 2007), and at-risk (de Castell & Jenson, 2007; Halverson, 2007). The researchers do not, however, let these descriptors stand alone. All three of the projects are based on the understanding that these young people are knowledgeable about themselves, their experiences, and their worlds, and are, therefore, described as powerful, educated, and artistic. Blackburn even recognizes the privileges these young people have and sometime assume by performing straightness and, sadly, homophobia. Moreover, these researchers portray the young people as leaders and valued employees. De Castell and Jenson (2007) even position the youth as co-researchers, and Blackburn (e.g., 2005a) portrays them as agents for change or activists.

Their complicated positionalities had implications for their status as students. Although the youth in Halverson's project were predominantly students, those in both Blackburn and de Castell and Jenson's projects were sometimes students, sometimes not students, but almost always had troubling relationships with schools. Student status is important to consider in thinking about readers of LGBT-themed young adult literature because even though the theme is not sanctioned at school, the genre is recognized and valued. Some teachers may consider young adult literature to be barely-school texts, but the young people in these projects understand young adult literature as decidedly school texts, and, as such, are not drawn to them.

This tension between teachers and students' understandings of young adult literature in classrooms is significant since many teachers use young adult literature primarily to engage students who are less interested in school. Still, De Castell and Jenson (2007) found that "school-based discourses and text-based literacy practices," including but not limited to young adult literature, can "be powerfully disenfranchising for a population already marginalized" (p. 132). They explain that traditional academic literacies "have worked less *for* than *against*" (p. 137) the young people in their project. With this in mind, we shift our focus from defining youth in these projects to defining texts.

Defining Texts

The texts used in the Attic, AFYT, and Pridehouse do not fit neatly within those categories typically understood as children's and young adult literature. These alternative texts are related to the negative school experiences of the young people and the consequences of these experiences on youths' perceptions of schoolish texts. Here, we examine how texts were selected, what was done with them, and what the texts were asked to do across the three contexts. We conclude this section on out-of-school reading, by considering the consequences of these practices for LGBTQ youth and their reading.

How Texts were Selected. In the Story Time project, both the adult facilitator, Blackburn, and the participating youth selected texts to share at Story Time, generally, independently of one another. Blackburn documented their weekly meetings over the course of a year, during which the facilitator shared texts at 82% of the meetings, and youth shared at 47% of the meetings. Of the texts the facilitator shared, 80% were texts that would generally be considered literature. These texts included poems, short stories, picture books, excerpts from novels, and excerpts from graphic novels, among others. Although the intended audience of this literature ranged from children to adolescents to adults, a good portion of it came from the anthology for young adults entitled *Am I Blue? Coming*

out from the Silence (Bauer, 1994). Of the texts the youth shared, 67% were authored by those sharing them. These texts included journal entries, poems, short stories, videos, art, and photographs, among other things. The texts chosen by the youth included a broader range of texts, including journal entries, for example, and other text forms, such as art and photographs.

Texts in the other two projects were even further removed from what is traditionally conceptualized as children's and young adult literature. AFYT worked from stories told by youth, mostly orally, although some were submitted on-line and via email. These stories were then synthesized and organized thematically and preliminary scripts were created and revised. Later, scenes were rehearsed and ultimately performed as the theatrical production *Up Until Now*. The AFYT process was a dramaturgical one. In contrast, the Pridehouse process was an ethnographic one in that youth stories were gathered via surveys, photographs, interviews, and focus groups and then transformed into a video on a webpage representing the lives of these street-involved queer youth.

Across these three projects, texts authored by others were replaced by performative, multimodal, and multimedial ones authored by youth themselves. The transition from written to alternative texts can be understood in the context of youth working to distance themselves from school, an institution they have come to know as hateful. The shift in authorship, in our view, can be understood as a move toward the pleasurable, as we discuss in the next section; as well as a shift toward self-portraiture and queer consciousness and communities (Cart & Jenkins, 2006).

What was Done to and with Texts. Reading LGBT-themed texts in schools was framed as an isolated event, something that happened once during the school year and perhaps only once during the students' K–12 lives. This is quite distinct from the reading of LGBT-themed texts in out-of-schools contexts, where such texts were taken up across the span of the project. LGBT-themed texts were framed, in these contexts, as a part of everyday life.

Moreover, the framing of LGBT-themed texts in out-of-schools projects was built around entertainment and pragmatic political action. This is not to stay that political action was not an implicit goal of the teachers and researchers conducting in-school work. However, the explicit framing in the out-of-school projects stands in stark contrast to the framing of fear, bullying, and survival, which is how LGBT-themed texts have been framed in schools. In Story Time at The Attic, texts were framed as entertainment. They were selected and shared with the pleasure of the participants in mind. Of course, what was pleasurable to some was not pleasurable to others, so not all texts pleased all participants, but the primary criteria for selection was pleasure. The AFYT project also centered around pleasure, but rather than the pleasure of its participants, the participants aimed to create a pleasurable text for the audience members of their play, *Up Until Now*.

The explicit goal of political action is most clearly articulated in the texts produced by The Attic's speakers' bureau and the Pridehouse project. The Attic's speakers' bureau created documents designed to educate youth and youth service providers about the experiences of LGBTQ youth. The Pridehouse documentary was designed "to better inform a community-based housing development organization about the conditions, needs, and expressed desires of the specific population for whom they sought to improve existing housing support" (http://www.sfu.ca/pridehouse/) ,which was street-involved queer and questioning youth. Thus, LGBT-themed texts taken up in these out-of-school projects were framed both in terms of pleasure and political action.

What Texts were Asked to Do.   LGBT-themed literature read and discussed in classrooms seemed mostly to offer a window through which to observe LGBTQ people, since the readers were defined as straight and even homophobic. In these out-of-school settings, though, the readers were defined as LGBTQ, and the literature read tended to serve as a mirror, a way of seeing themselves, as LGBTQ youth, in literature. The majority of the texts, however, were distinctive in that they were produced by those engaging with them. In other words, most of the LGBT-themed texts taken up in out-of-school contexts were neither windows nor mirrors; rather, they were self-portraits. Of course, these self-portraits could serve as mirrors or even windows for participants in the groups, but their primary purpose was more about representing themselves, their experiences, and their worlds.

The transition from texts written *about* queer youth to texts produced *by* and about queer youth, we argue, is related to Cart and Jenkins's (2006) typology of LGBT-themed children's and young adult literature. We argue that the most prominent category of literature, promoting homosexual visibility and gay assimilation, would not have been of particular interest to the LGBTQ youth in the out-of-school projects. Literature that increases homosexual visibility would not engage these young people because they were already visible. They knew LGBTQ people existed, that they were such people, and that there were other people like them. Likewise, the literature that does gay assimilationist work would have been of little use to the young people in these projects, particularly those in Blackburn and de Castell and Jenson's work because they were not, for a variety of reasons, assimilating. The experiences being captured in these texts were neither reflective nor informative of their own.

Although literature categorized as queer consciousness and community would have been quite interesting to LGBTQ youth in these out-of-school projects, Cart and Jenkins point out that not very much children's and young adult literature falls into this category. Therefore, it

seems to us, these LGBTQ youth created their own texts that incorporated queer consciousness and communities because they did not find much young adult literature that provides images of LGBTQ people at least connected with, if not immersed in, communities accepting of them, like The Attic, AFYT, and Pridehouse.

Consequences
A significant impact of the creation of these texts was that it allows the young people in these projects to define texts rather than being defined by them. So, for example, Justine, in Blackburn's (2002/2003) project at The Attic, combined words from a love poem, images from a non-fiction historical text, a photograph of her girlfriend and her, and a bit of prose she wrote herself to produce a video in which she was not positioned in stereotypical ways but in ways that she defined. She was not a vulnerable lonely lesbian but an "empowered dyke" among gay rights activists.

The work that LGBTQ youth have accomplished in out-of-school LGBTQ youth communities, as represented by The Attic, AFYT, and Pridehouse, is significant, but it raises a couple of questions:

- What would it look like to do this work with readers who are both LGBTQ people and their allies?
- Is it possible to do such work in ways that foreground young adult literature as it is typically conceptualized, to frame this literature in terms of pleasure and political action, while being cognizant of how the reading is being accomplished?

These questions and those raised by the classroom-based research will guide the following section.

Reading LGBT-Themed Literature in Queer-Friendly Contexts among LGBTQ People and Their Allies
We turn, now, to a project that we have been working on since the spring of 2006. The project is an offshoot of another in which teachers committed to combating heterosexism and homophobia in classrooms and schools through literature and film have been meeting monthly since the fall of 2004 (Blackburn, Clark, Kenney, & Smith, 2010). We have come to call ourselves the Pink TIGers. In our meetings, we struggle together to figure out whether to use LGBT-themed young adult and children's literature in our classes, and if so, how to do so. As a part of our learning, we decided to bring together students from our various schools to read and discuss LGBT-themed literature. This chapter examines the seven meetings that we participated in during 2006 and 2007.

In part, this project is important to consider because it takes place in a queer-friendly context. Unlike the scholarship located in classrooms and schools but like that located in out-of-school contexts, this book discussion group takes place in a context that at least strives to be queer friendly. Although we considered meeting in the high schools of students and teachers involved and the university with which several of us are affiliated, we opted for the local queer youth center because it provided some privacy from classmates who may not approve of involvement in the group, and it introduced participants to a space specifically designed to meet the needs of queer youth.

Still, even this place was not perfectly queer-friendly. After our first meeting a furious, homophobic, and threatening father came to get his daughter away from the "gay teacher" who gave her a "gay book" and invited her to a "gay establishment." We considered relocating after this meeting, but instead, the center implemented a policy prohibiting the admittance of adults who are not escorted by youth affiliated with the center. This space with this policy provided the group with a queer-friendly context in which to discuss LGBT-themed young adult literature. Beyond context, this project offers important insights on becoming readers of LGBT-themed young adult literature because of the ways that readers and texts are defined. We turn to those in the following portions of this section.

Defining Readers

Across seven meetings, a core group of about ten people attended. The majority of the youth were freshman and sophomores, with the exception of one eighth-grader and one senior, both of whom only attended a single meeting. The adults included three high school English teachers and facilitators of their schools' Gay Straight Alliances, three university faculty members, two doctoral students, and two pre-service teachers. The English teachers and faculty members attended regularly.

The majority of the participants were White. There were two African American youth participants, one of whom is a boy, and the other who is transgender. One girl self-identifies as Mexican American and another as African American and Middle Eastern. One woman identifies as a person of color, specifically African American and German. Of the 21 participants, three boys either stated or suggested they were gay, three women identified as lesbian, and one girl implied she was a lesbian.[3] Another youth sometimes identifies as male and other times as female but seems to be consistently attracted to females. If any of the participants identify as bisexual, they have not articulated this identification in the group. Of the eight people who are lesbian, gay, or transgender, three are people of color; two of whom are youth. These two only attended once during the period being reported here. Of regularly attending participants, there are four White adult allies; four White gay or lesbian people, two of whom are youth; and two youth allies who are people of color.

The readers of LGBT-themed young adult literature in this group are defined neither as entirely straight nor LGBTQ, thus distinguishing this project from those located in schools, which overwhelmingly define readers as straight and sometimes homophobic. The project is also distinguished from those located in out-of-school contexts, which define readers as LGBTQ. Of the ten regular participants in this group, four identify as lesbian or gay and six identify as straight allies for LGBTQ people. None of them identify as homophobic. This holds true across all 21 participants.

Because the group comprises LGBTQ people and their allies but not homophobes, it provides a unique opportunity for LGBTQ people to talk about their lives openly and for allies to gain insights about the ways heterosexism and homophobia impact the population with whom they are in alliance. In addition, members of this group are teachers and students but in a non-school setting. People come together to talk about young adult literature with LGBT-themes because they want to. Our identities as teachers and students cannot be dismissed, though, because the ways we know one another are through our roles as teachers and students. Although these roles provide the foundation for our relationships, the dynamics are different.

Teachers were not responsible for designing and/or implementing particular curricula, syllabi, and lesson plans; and students were not responsible for completing assignments or passing assessments. Neither was there pressure, aside from our own habits, as teachers and students, to direct conversation toward literature conventions, poetic devices, literary themes, and the like. Our discussions typically centered on what we liked and didn't like about a book and how certain stories in the literature reminded us of stories in our lives. As a result, we were all positioned as knowledgeable; that is, knowledgeable enough to work together to present, select, read, and discuss LGBT-themed young adult literature in ways that would allow us to reflect on our lives as LGBTQ people and their allies.

Defining Texts

Most of the texts we selected as a group reflected conventional understandings of young adult literature; however, the actual selections, how we engaged with them, and what we asked texts to do and enable in our group were often unconventional. Here, we will discuss these issues, along with the consequences we see for working with LGBT-themed young adult literature in queer-friendly out-of-school settings.

How Texts were Selected. Across the 2006–2007 meetings, our group read eight books. Youth and adults selected texts together, with adults generally deferring to youth's choices. Starting in the autumn of 2006, we began with David Levithan's (2003) *Boy Meets Boy* in which Paul, a gay high school student, attends a school where the quarterback and the homecoming queen are the same person and the town supports the "Joy Scouts" instead of "Boy Scouts." Through Levithan's fictional world, readers can imagine what it might be like if homophobic values were greatly diminished and how Paul's friendships and romantic relationships unfold in such an imaginary world.

At the end of each meeting, we talked together to determine what we would read for the next meeting. After *Boy Meets Boy*, we read Stephen Chbosky's (1999) *Perks of Being a Wallflower*, Julia Watts's (2001) *Finding H.F.*, and Joe Babcock's (2002) *The Tragedy of Miss Geneva Flowers*. The latter book features Erick, a young, gay male growing up and attending Catholic school in Minneapolis. His search for identity and acceptance from his family leads him into a life-changing friendship with Chloe, a drag queen, and time on the streets where he encounters drugs, alcohol, and their consequences. He also develops his own drag personae, Miss Geneva Flowers, and develops the courage, in the end, to accept himself and demand acceptance from his parents.

The last book selected at the end of the 2006 school year was Kim Wallace's (2004) *Erik & Isabelle: Freshman Year at Foresthill High*. This is the first of a series of four books about two best friends, both of whom are gay. Erik is academic, athletic, and being raised in a homophobic household. Isabelle's family, in contrast, is open and accepting of her lesbian identity. Across the first and second books (Wallace, 2004), Erik and Isabelle support each other as they endure homophobia and fall in and out of love. We read *Erick & Isabelle* over the summer and it was the first book discussed in autumn of 2007, followed by David Sedaris's (1997) *Holidays on Ice*, a collection of short stories related to Christmas. Many of the stories are autobiographical accounts by the out gay author with a presumed adult readership.

The last books selected were Peters's (2003) *Keeping You a Secret* and Bauer's *Am I Blue*. All books were selected collaboratively by youth and adults and on the basis of sincere interest and a desire to share a reading experience with others. Often, books were suggested because someone in the group had already read the book and thought the entire group might enjoy reading it. This was the case for *Boy Meets Boy, The Perks of Being a Wallflower, Finding H.F., Holidays On Ice, Keeping You a Secret,* and *Am I Blue*. Of these, *Holidays on Ice* would not be categorized as a young adult text, or even LGBT-themed per se, but as adult short fiction. Likewise, *The Tragedy of Miss Geneva Flowers* was written for and marketed to an adult audience. In the case of *Holidays on Ice*, many of the adult participants had read or heard this text read and thought the humorous essays would be fun to share as a group, particularly when everyone met in December.

The Tragedy of Miss Geneva Flowers, on the other hand, was youth-selected. After reading Levithan's love story set in a queer-inclusive world, Chbosky's epistolary novel, and Watts's novel based in rural Kentucky, several youth participants suggested we read a realistic LGBT-themed book set in a suburban context more reflective of their own experiences. One of the youth participants did an online library search and found several titles and descriptions that sounded appealing to him. He brought the list to a meeting, read the descriptions to the group,

and together, the group chose *Miss Geneva*. Similarly, Kim Wallace's series was chosen because its title and description sounded like it would reflect the life-situations of many of the group participants who, after reading *Miss Geneva*, wanted to focus on LGBT issues in schools, featuring both male and female characters. This time, an adult participant brought in titles after an online search, and Wallace's *Erik & Isabelle* series was chosen by the group. Interestingly, while *Erik & Isabelle: Freshman Year* was a favorite of many of the youth (and read near the end of their own freshman year), *Erik & Isabelle: Sophomore Year* was received much more critically, and the group, lead by the youth participants, opted not to read any more books in the series.

What was Done to/with Texts.   Reading and discussing LGBT-themed literature was the primary purpose of our group. Unlike classrooms, where reading an LGBT-themed text might happen only once, if ever, our readings occurred over time. And, unlike the out-of-school, queer-centered contexts, where LGBT-themed texts were framed as part of the everyday lives of the participants, reading LGBT-themed-literature was a new, but welcome experience for several of the group participants. David Levithan's *Boy Meets Boy*, for example, was the first piece of LGBT-themed young adult literature read by many youth members of the group, either gay or straight. In addition, our group included queer and straight youth and adult readers, all of whom were actively non-homophobic. As a result, texts were never selected for didactic purposes, as they often are in classrooms. Texts were not actively read for their form (e.g., play or essay) or their place as a "classic" in the literary canon. Instead, as in the out-of-school, queer-centered spaces, LGBT-themed literature was read, primarily, for entertainment. What *entertainment* and *pleasure* came to mean, however, was negotiated through conversation in the group.

No book was automatically embraced simply because it was deemed *good* by either a youth or an adult reader. Instead, participants typically pointed out what they liked in the text, often quoting passages that were marked ahead of time, or reading favorite scenes aloud to others in order to share what was most appealing—or not. One young ally, for example, was often drawn to writing style. She would frequently read particular passages aloud in order to showcase what she admired in an author's word choice, use of imagery, or humor. For example, in the discussion of Julia Watts's *Finding H.F.*, this female, youth ally shared, "There's just so many little funny parts. On page 66, 'One time...' —talking about her grandma—'One time she lost her dentures and we finally found them in the breadbox.' I just did little chuckles out loud," to which a lesbian, adult participant replied, "Yeah, you can picture the author having her own little writer's notebook and being like, 'Oh, I've got to write this one down. This is going to fit in somewhere.'"

At times, passages were selected for sharing by youth or adults because they triggered a memory of a similar situation. In *Perks of Being a Wallflower*, Chbosky's frequent references to song titles elicited discussions of specific songs and musical groups (e.g., Pink Floyd, Fleetwood Mack, the Smiths, Bright Eyes), and events that group members associated with key songs. Similarly, scenes from *Perks*, of characters driving at night and listening to music with the windows down, triggered pleasurable memories across the group. A young ally pointed to one such scene, "The woman driving the car," to which an adult, lesbian participant responded, "Another great scene," followed by a gay youth replying, "I really like that part too. Because it's so real. It's happened before. You just find yourself sitting in the car with your favorite people and this song comes on and suddenly your whole outlook on life just changes."

While texts could trigger feelings of humor and pleasure, what was pleasing could also trigger complex discussions of identity, sexuality, and love. In the discussion of *Finding H.F.*, for example, a gay youth participant shared,

> I really like the part in the movie, too…when they meet Dee and Shantell, and they see those two guys holding hands and walking through. And they find themselves following in shock. And H.F. notices that Bo, once they walk away, is kind of sad. You can imagine that because when you—I know this from experience—but when I first came out and everything and seeing other people together in real life.

A young man who was, at the time, questioning his sexuality, continued, "It made you so sad." The gay youth participant then continued, "Because, you're like, I'm alone, so when am I going to find someone." To which the questioning youth responded, "Yeah." An adult ally added, "Actually, I relate to that too because even when you see straight couples, you're like, ohh," and the gay youth who initiated the discussion stated, "Everyone can [relate to that]."

Texts, then, were discussed, at times, in schoolish ways, with participants pointing to specific page numbers, chapters, or scenes to substantiate a claim (of humor or realism, for example) or to highlight a word choice. Unlike school, however, this kind of talk was not required or directed towards an academic or pedagogical end. Rather, the primary purpose for specifying particular passages and scenes was to revel in the craft of writing and the pleasure that writing brought to the reader, or to share a feeling—of joy, humor, or pathos—with other readers. And, unlike school, both youth and adults took the lead in finding and sharing these passages, and in sharing their emotional responses to these texts. Moreover, these responses were shaped by explicit references to one's own identity and sexuality. Rather than hiding these identities, both youth and adults could draw on these identities in order to make meaning from texts and extend one another's understand-ings of the texts and the negotiations of similar issues and situations in life.

Beyond the purposes of entertainment, then, we would argue that there was a form of political action occurring in this out-of-school reading group. While reading LGBT-themed texts in the out-of-school, queer-centered contexts was clearly oriented towards pragmatic, political action, as characterized earlier, the political action of this group was more subtle, but equally important. First, unlike virtually all classroom-settings, young people and adults in the book discussion group were free to share their sexual identities openly with one another, if they chose. Doing so allowed both youth and adults to share experiences and explore possibilities (both real and imagined) for being in the world. In the case of responding to *Finding H.F.*, for example, two young people, one out and gay, the other questioning his sexuality, could identify with Bo's longing to be in a loving relationship, as could the straight, adult ally who responded to the same scene with a similar kind of longing.

This is not to say that all discussions resulted in reaching across differences. There were certainly many conversations that highlighted distinctions between queer and straight people and a few were even grounded in homophobia. However, in this case, the fact that all three could respond openly from a shared place of longing, created a space for them to see connections across their situations in that moment, and explore potential meanings in the text more deeply. Such possible connections are currently prohibited in classroom situations where heterosexism is the presumed norm, and where naming of one's sexuality outside of compulsory heterosexuality is typically taboo for both students and teachers.

Second, in the current climate of testing and accountability in schooling, opportunities for young people—regardless of sexual and gender identities—to read with adults in ways that promote pleasure and community are rare. Unfortunately, out-of-school literacy opportunities at libraries and elsewhere are, likewise, increasingly justified solely for academic ends. So, in this queer-friendly context where LBGTQ people and their allies came together frequently to read and talk about books, another significant end was to reconnect around reading for pleasure.

What Texts were Asked to Do. In this mixed group of readers, where participants were LGBTQ or straight, and youth or adult, texts were employed in myriad ways. Across readers, texts served at times as mirrors—reflecting queer, possible queer, or ally selves for both young people and adults. At other times the books worked as windows, allowing queer readers and their allies to see through windows into the worlds that are (or could be realized) around them. Aside from *Holidays on Ice*, which does not represent either conventional LGBT-themed or young adult literature, and *Perks of Being a Wallflower*, which Cart and Jenkins (2006) categorize, in part, as HV, all of the texts read in the reading group can be classified as either GA or QC. *Boy Meets Boy, Perks of Being a Wallflower, Keeping you a Secret,* and *Erik and Isabelle: Freshman Year* and *Sophomore Year* all fall into the GA category, showing that gay and lesbian people are just like straight people in most ways. *Boy Meets Boy, Finding H.F., The Tragedy of Miss Geneva Flowers,* and *Erik and Isabelle: Sophomore Year* can all also be categorized as QC because all, to varying degrees, show LGBTQ people finding and participating in larger, extended queer communities.

As windows and mirrors, these books enabled readers in the group to understand similarities across lines of difference relative to age, sexuality, and gender. Through shared responses to texts, or the sharing of memories and experiences that were provoked by the texts, participants were able to see that all of us, LGBTQ or straight-ally, youth or adult, are alike in most ways, reflecting Cart and Jenkins GA category. But, because this was a group of LGBTQ and straight allies, where LGBTQ people could talk openly about their lives and experiences, important differences could also be highlighted, revealing the significant ways that heterosexism and homophobia impacted LGBTQ participants, but not allies.

For example, in a discussion of *Miss Geneva Flowers,* an adult lesbian participant brought up how queer characters in the book discuss their conscious choice to take cabs, which cost more and depleted their already limited incomes, instead of public transportation. She shared, "Yeah, it was interesting to me when they chose to get a cab versus public transportation. How they would talk about was it worth [not] getting their asses kicked." Two adult allies responded, "Definitely" and "Right, for safety," to which a youth ally added, "Better than walking." Here, the adult lesbian participant agreed, but clarified why her point is decidedly about people perceived to be lesbian or gay and gender non-conforming people protecting themselves from homophobia and/or transphobia that could lead to physical abuse. She stated, "But I liked, the thing I appreciated is that it wasn't just about walking or not walking. It was about protection. That kind of thing that I feel like you have to do all the time, deciding when to be how, where. Just like the everydayness of it." Her response helped to show that, what felt common and understood across readers, LGBTQ and straight, was distinctly different to her as a lesbian reader. Her response both validated Babcock's (2002) rendering of the scene and revealed to ally-readers how LGBTQ people have to make many more conscious decisions about how to present themselves publicly, all of the time, in order to protect themselves from possible attacks.

This discussion prompted an adult ally to share a passage from the book, where an older, gay character shares with the main character how he came to embrace his sexual identity. She read,

I remember my childhood, but my memories are tweaked, you know, it's like I remember what I did but forgot who

I was. I'd forgotten what it was like to look at boys before I actually allowed myself to. I forgot what it was like to control my voice from sounding flamboyant. Or to make a conscious effort to sit like a man. I see myself and all my memories the way I see myself now, super gay. (Babcock, 2002, p. 91)

For another adult ally, this passage and the prior discussion of protecting oneself caused her to wonder aloud about what can be hidden or covered: "Seeing the connections. When to cover, when not to cover, and you just said, it's so hard to cover your voice." A male youth participant, who at this point may have been questioning or may have been identifying as gay, responded, in his soft, high-pitched voice, "The way you talk, yeah. The flamboyancy." A youth ally then asked, "Is it like, have you talked like that since you were a kid?" to which he responded, "Yeah." He went on to share how he is sometimes quiet because of his voice, and how he used to feel like he had to change his speech patterns in some situations:

Yeah, sometimes I don't even talk. I just let people say whatever they want. But other than that, I don't feel I have to hide my voice, that much. I really don't. But when I did, it was the hardest thing to do, like it was just, God, totally against what I had to do.

Across these discussions, texts as both mirrors and windows enabled important learning and sharing for LGBTQ and ally participants alike. In her sharing in response to the passage on taking cabs for safety, the adult lesbian participant provided a window to ally participants, helping them understand how seemingly simple decisions have potentially dire consequences for LGBTQ people, and how these have to be considered in nearly every situation.

Through her sharing, ally participants could begin to understand the kinds of complex decisions relative to identity and presentation of self in a homophobic world that LGBTQ people have to carry out all of the time in their daily lives, and consider ways to use this knowledge to be more informed, supportive allies. Her sharing also provided a mirror to LGBTQ people in the group, prompting them to share their own experiences with figuring out how to navigate a complex, often homophobic world. The discussion around her response, for example, led one youth participant to talk about his own experiences of covering his voice and how very, very difficult this was. Again, his sharing provided yet another window through which ally-participants could see and understand the kinds of daily work and decisions that LGBTQ do and face in a homophobic world.

Consequences

Reading LGBT-themed young adult literature with readers who are both LGBTQ people and allies in an expressly queer-friendly context revealed opportunities that are currently missing from both classroom-based settings and exclusively queer-settings outside of schools. Unlike in classroom settings in schools and exclusively queer-settings outside of schools, readers in these discussion groups were defined as both LGBTQ people and straight allies, and no one was positioned as homophobic. Not only were these identity positions explicitly available in this group, they were also openly claimed by group members in ways that were rarely, if ever, allowed in classroom settings—without negative consequences for both young people and adults. Because LGBTQ and straight ally positionings were clearly sanctioned in our group, the possibilities for reading LGBT-themed texts were expanded, including what we asked these texts to do and what readers could do with them.

Our group was a place where readers could engage with LGBT-themed texts in academic ways, but toward pleasurable, political ends, distinguishing this group's aims from those in classroom and exclusively queer settings. For example, academic work around texts was certainly an option in classrooms, and generally the most invited, if not the only, way to engage with texts—LGBT-themed or otherwise. In contrast, in the out-of-school settings at the Attic/Loft, AFYT, and Pridehouse, working with texts for entertainment and political action was always encouraged and often central to the groups' goals. In our group, academic ways of taking up texts (e.g., through attention to language, imagery and writing craft) were common; however, this was never for the purpose of teaching or learning about language, imagery or writing craft. Rather, they were intended to point out lines, passages, or phrases that brought us pleasure, be it through humor, shared sadness, or connected memories.

Most importantly, because this group allowed participants to name explicitly and talk about their sexual identities, texts could serve as both mirrors and windows for LGBTQ and straight ally participants. Viewed as knowledgeable and able to speak about their lives, including their sexuality, all participants, youth and adult alike, could help to mediate textual encounters for other participants and extend them in ways that could reveal the commonalities across experiences while making evident the important ways in which they differed. Unlike in classrooms and exclusively queer out-of-school settings, this group provided a unique opportunity for LGBTQ people to talk about their lives openly and for allies to gain insights about the ways heterosexism and homophobia impact the population with whom they are in alliance.

Conclusion

When we look at the work young readers of LGBT-themed literature accomplish in and out of classrooms, we notice several key practices that teachers, youth service providers and librarians can enact or enable in order to help young people become readers of literature with LGBT themes and thus work against homophobia. One key practice that we notice being enacted is in terms of the range of read-ing positions that are offered to and/or assumed by young readers. In classroom spaces, reading positions are limited and students are uniformly positioned as straight and/or homophobic. In contrast, both the out-of-school LGBTQ-only youth communities and the out-of-school queer-friendly contexts enabled a variety of reading positions. Readers could assume positions of straight, homophobe, queer, victim, agent, ally, and activist, among others.

We are struck by the value of this range of reading positions. Making space for these many reading positions enabled the diversity of readers to enter the discussion and expanded the work that could be done with and through texts. The diversity of readers, whether this diversity is defined by sexuality, gender, race, class, age, ability, and/or religion enhances the experience of the reading and discussion. The fluidity of reader identities promises more opportunity for change as it enables queer readers to talk about both the commonality across reading experiences with readers positioned as allies, as well as the discontinuities in experience. These opportunities enabled the enactment of queer community within a group of readers, as well as allowing ally readers to hear and learn about queer experiences in ways that would inform and enable them to enact ally identities with greater insight in the future.

Other key practices relate to text selection, the amount of time spent with LGBT-themed texts, and the uses of these texts as ways to see into another world and/or reflect on one's own. We have come to appreciate the importance of collaboratively selecting and creating diverse literature, not only to connect with curriculum, but primarily to experience pleasure and ultimately to pursue explicitly named political action. We recognize the importance of engaging in this work across time so that young readers can reflect on, and respond thoughtfully to, what they are encountering. We understand that asking literature to work as both windows and mirrors allows for, but also demands diversity and fluidity in its readers. We can foster engagement with these demands by deliberately selecting literature with an acknowledgement of readers' identities but not such that literature always reveals alternative identities or reflects similar identities; rather, that such literature sometimes does one and/or the other. For example, by sometimes but not always selecting LGBT-themed, or any other identity-themed, literature. Finally, we value literature that contributes to homosexual visibility and gay assimilation but recognize the need for literature that represents queer people in communities.

This review of research and examination of our own work leads us to encourage teachers, librarians, and other adults working in queer-inclusive contexts with young people to be open in allowing a range of fluid reading positions to be taken up around texts. This means that teachers and other adults will need to be clear and assertive in making their workplaces safer for participants to assume a range of reading positions. And, it means that adults doing this work must be critically self-aware and self-reflective about their own attitudes and deeply held assumptions around sexuality and gender identity. Opening up spaces—classrooms, libraries, and queer-inclusive community-based settings—to this range of reading positions, textual forms, and work around texts provides a promising range of possibilities for young people to become readers of LGBT-themed literature and, by extension, to work with adults against homophobia and transphobia.

Notes

1. We use the acronym LGBT to describe themes and LGBTQ to describe people because even when literature includes characters questioning their sexual and/or gender identities, LGBT themes are still present. People, however, who are questioning, are not necessarily more or less likely to identify as LGBT than they are straight. Also, we recognize that the vast majority of the children's and young adult literature represented in this chapter focuses on gay and lesbian identities. We include bisexual and transgender identities because a few of the texts focus on characters who embody these identities. To be clear, we are not assuming that bisexual and transgender identities are the same as, or close enough to, each other or lesbian and gay identities. We recognize the distinctions among these identities and that all four get taken up to varying degrees in the literature discussed in this chapter. Moreover, our exclusion of I, for intersexed, from the acronym represents the absence of such identities in the literature included here.
2. We recognize that our quoting of Hamilton implies a correlation between racial minorities and homophobia. This is not a correlation that we understand to be true.
3. Here we mark people's identities in overly simplistic ways to give readers a sense of the diversity of the group. Some of what gets lost is when participants shifted identities across time. For example, one participant shifts from questioning his sexual identity to identifying as gay. Here, we name him as gay. In our discussion of this participant, later, we sometimes describe him as questioning and other times as gay, depending on how he seemed to identify during the time represented.

Literature References

Babcock, J. (2002). *The tragedy of Miss Geneva Flowers*. New York, NY: Carroll & Graf.

Bauer, M. D. (1994). *Am I blue? Coming out from the silence*. New York, NY: Harper Collins.

Chbosky, S. (1999). *The perks of being a wallflower*. New York, NY: MTV Books/Pocket Books.

Conrad, J. (2007). *The secret sharer*. Las Vegas, NV: FQ Publishing. (Original work published 1910)

Elwin, R., & Paulse, M. (2000). *Asha's mums* (D. Lee, Illus.). London: The Women's Press.

Fierstein, H. (1988). *Torch song trilogy*. New York, NY: Signet.

Homes, A. A. (1990). *Jack*. New York, NY: Vintage.

King, M. L., Jr. (2010). *Stride toward freedom: The Montgomery story*. Boston, MA: Beacon Press. (Original work published 1958)

Levithan, D. (2003). *Boy meets boy*. New York, NY: Alfred A. Knopf.

Peters, J. A. (2003). *Keeping you a secret*. New York, NY: Little, Brown, and Young Readers.

Sedaris, D. (1997). *Holidays on ice*. New York, NY: Little, Brown, and Company.

Wallace, K. (2004). *Erik & Isabelle: Freshman year at Foresthill High*. Sacramento, CA: Foglight Press.

Wallace, K. (2004). *Erik & Isabelle: Sophomore year at Foresthill High*. Sacramento, CA: Foglight Press.

Watts, J. (2001). *Finding H.F.* Los Angeles, CA: Alyson Books.

Academic References

Athanases, S. Z. (1996). A gay-themed lesson in an ethnic literature curriculum: Tenth graders' responses to "Dear Anita." *Harvard Educational Review, 66*(2), 231–256.

Bishop, R. S. (1992). Multicultural literature for children: Making informed choices. In V. Harris (Ed.), *Teaching multicultural literature in grades K-8* (pp. 37–54). Norwood, MA: Christopher-Gordon.

Blackburn, M. V. (2002–2003). Disrupting the (hetero)normative: Exploring literacy performances and identity work with queer youth. *Journal of Adolescent & Adult Literacy, 46*(4), 312–324.

Blackburn, M. V. (2003a). Losing, finding, and making space for activism through literacy performances and identity work. *Penn GSE Perspectives on Urban Education, 2*(1). Retrieved on February 7, 2010 from http://www.urbanedjournal.org/articles/article0008.html

Blackburn, M. V. (2003b). Exploring literacy performances and power dynamics at The Loft: Queer youth reading the world and word. *Research in the Teaching of English, 37*(4) 467–490.

Blackburn, M. V. (2005a). Disrupting dichotomies for social change: A review of, critique of, and complement to current educational literacy scholarship on gender. *Research in the Teaching of English, 39*(4) 398–416.

Blackburn, M. V. (2005b). Co-constructing space for literacy and identity work with LGBTQ youth. *Afterschool Matters, 4*, 17–23.

Blackburn, M. V., & Buckley, J. F. (2005). Teaching queer-inclusive English language arts. *Journal of Adolescent & Adult Literacy, 49*(3), 202–212.

Blackburn, M. V., Clark, C. T., Kenney, L. M., & Smith, J. M. (Eds.), (2010). *Acting out: Combating homophobia through teacher activism*. New York, NY: Teachers College Press.

Cart, M., & Jenkins, C. (2006). *The heart has its reasons: Young adult literature with gay/lesbian/queer content, 1969–2004*. Lanham, MD: Scarecrow Press.

Carey-Webb, A. (2001). *Literature and lives: A response-based, cultural studies approach to teaching English*. Urbana, IL: National Council of Teachers of English.

De Castell, S., & Jenson, J. (2007). No place like home: Sexuality, community, and identity among street-involved queer and questioning youth. In M. V. Blackburn & C. T. Clark (Eds.), *Literacy research for political action and social change* (pp. 131–152). New York, NY: Peter Lang.

Epstein, D. (2000). Reading gender, reading sexualities: Children and the negotiation of meaning in 'alternative' texts. In W. J. Spurlin (Ed.), *Lesbian and gay studies and the teaching of English: Positions, pedagogies, and cultural politics* (pp. 213–233). Urbana, IL: National Council of Teachers of English.

Gallo, D. (2004). The boldest books. *English Journal, 94*(1), 125–130.

Greenbaum, V. (1994). Literature out of the closet: Bringing gay and lesbian texts and subtexts out in high school English. *The English Journal, 83*(5), 71–74.

Halverson, E. R. (2007). Listening to the voices of queer youth: The dramaturgical process as identity exploration. In M. V. Blackburn & C. T. Clark (Eds.), *Literacy research for political action and social change* (pp. 153–175). New York: Peter Lang.

Hamilton, G. (1998). Reading *Jack*. *English Education 30*(1), 24–43.

Hammett, R. F. (1992). A rationale and unit plan for introducing gay and lesbian literature into the grade twelve curriculum. In

P. Shannon (Ed.), *Becoming political: Readings and writings in the politics of literacy education* (pp. 250–262). Portsmouth, NH: Heinemann.

Harris, S. (1990). *Lesbian and gay issues in the English classroom: The importance of being honest.* Philadelphia, PA: Open University Press.

Hillier, L., Turner, A., & Mitchell, A. (2005). *Writing themselves in again: 6 years on. The 2nd national report on the sexuality, health & well-being of same sex attracted young people in Australia* (Monograph series no. 50). Melbourne: Australian Research Center in Sex, Health, & Society.

Hoffman, M. (1993). Teaching "Torch Song": Gay literature in the classroom. *The English Journal, 82*(5), 55–58.

King, J., & Schneider, J. (1999). Locating a place for gay and lesbian themes in elementary reading, writing, and talking. In W. Letts & J. Sears (Eds.), *Queering elementary education* (pp. 61–70). Lanham, MD: Rowman and Littlefield.

Kosciw, J. G., Diaz, E. M., & Greytak, E. A. (2008). *The 2007 National School Climate Survey: The experiences of lesbian, gay, bisexual, and transgender youth in our nation's schools.* New York, NY: Gay, Lesbian, and Straight Education Network.

McNaught, B. (1988). Dear Anita: Late night thoughts of an Irish Catholic homosexual. *On being gay: Thoughts on family, faith and love* (pp. 72–75). New York, NY: St. Martin's Press.

Reese, J. (1998). Teaching tolerance through literature: Dealing with issues of homosexuality in English class. *International Schools Journal, 17*(2), 35–40.

Ryan, C., & Rivers, I. (2003). Lesbian, gay, bisexual and transgender youth: victimization and its correlates in the USA and UK. *Culture, Health & Sexuality, 5*(2), 103–119.

Schall, J., & Kauffmann, G. (2003). Exploring literature with gay and lesbian characters in the elementary school. *Journal of children's literature, 29*(1), 36–45.

Schneider, J. J. (2001). No blood, guns, or gays allowed!: The silencing of the elementary writer. *Language Arts, 78*(5), 415–425.

Sims [Bishop], R. (1982). *Shadow and substance: Afro-American experience in contemporary children's literature.* Urbana, IL: National Council of Teachers of English.

Smith, E. B. (1997). Reflections and visions: An interview with Rudine Sims Bishop. *Journal of Children's Literature, 23*(1), 62–65.

Street, B. V. (1995). *Social literacies: Critical approaches to literacy in development, ethnography and education.* London: Longman.

Wyss, S. E. (2004). 'This was my hell': The violence experienced by gender non-conforming youth in US high schools. *International Journal of Qualitative Studies in Education, 17*(5), 709–730.

12

Immigrant Students as Cosmopolitan Intellectuals

Gerald Campano

University of Pennsylvania

María Paula Ghiso

Teachers College, Columbia University

As they describe young immigrants in U.S. cities and classrooms, Gerald Campano and María Ghiso recognize their students' capacity to savor new words and meanings and their commitment to learn—and record—the stories of sacrifice, dignity, and resilience passed along through families and communities. For Campano and Ghiso, these multilingual, transnational, multivoiced stories form the core of a cosmopolitan approach to teaching reading and literature. Through their analysis of Shaun Tan's *The Arrival* and a child's 20-page narrative of her family's literacies and activism, a new vision of reading unfolds that places young, emerging voices and their literary legacies at the center of educational reform.

Genius has no country. It blossoms everywhere. Genius is like the light, the air. It is the heritage of all.

—José Rizal (1884)

Taking as an inspiration the Filipino writer and activist José Rizal, this chapter argues that we should regard immigrant students—and all students—as cosmopolitan intellectuals. José Rizal's transnational intellectual odyssey inspires how we might think about the role of literature and the literary imagination in diverse 21st century classrooms. In our work with immigrant, migrant, and refugee populations, we have learned that students' literacy practices and knowledge are not merely relevant for their respective communities, but also have value for the world we share. We understand this capacity to make claims of universal significance as part of what it means to be a cosmopolitan intellectual.

In his comparative study on the early stages of globalization, *Under Three Flags: Anarchism and the Anti Colonial Imagination*, Benedict Anderson (2007) charts the range of forces—Avant-Gardism, Marxism, transoceanic migrations, imperial repression, independence movements, etc.—and the "vast rhizomal networks" (p. 4) of people and places that shaped the writings of turn of the century intellectuals such as Rizal. Two aspects of Rizal's life and work have particular salience for helping us better understand students and reconceptualize the literary curriculum. First, Rizal read capaciously and opened himself up to a wide range of experiences. Although he is an icon of Philippine nationhood, his work was fertilized by a range of intellectual influences and social dynamics which traverse national boundaries and reified genres. For example, he incorporated oral traditions from his homeland as well as European literary styles in order to create one of the first great novels of the Eastern hemisphere, the politically catalytic *Noli Me Tangere*. Rizal spent significant portions of his life away from his native land—as a student, tourist, and political exile. His flexible intellect both absorbed and transformed what he experienced in his travels. A polyglot, Rizal wrote in several different languages, including Spanish, Tagalog, Italian, French, and English. He also knew Latin, Greek, and Hebrew. Rizal wrote for multiple audiences through a number of outlets such as novels, essays, and editorials. Similar to intellectuals in other colonized contexts, such as the poet José Martí in Cuba, Rizal was quintessentially a cosmopolitan intellectual. His concerns and commitments had as a focus his native land, but his work had global resonance. The connections he made across contexts only deepened more local understandings. Anderson (2007) discusses how Rizal fictionally transposed political dynamics and aesthetic sensibilities from what was considered the European center to the colonial periphery.

The second related issue, also powerfully rendered by Anderson, has to do with the radically procreative powers of words. Rizal's proleptic second novel, *El Filibusterismo,* went beyond commenting on or reflecting the corruption of the friars and imperial rule; it gestured toward an alternative world without Spanish domination. That is, it helped *imagine into existence* an ideal of Philippine independence, which subsequently ignited the anticolonial aspirations of younger generations of Filipinos. Anderson (2007) writes: "What Rizal had done in *El Filibusterismo* was to imagine the political landscape of this society and the near-elimination of its ruling powers. Perhaps no Filipino had ever dreamed of such a possibility till then, let alone entered the dream into the public domain. It was as if the genius's genie was out of the bottle…" (p.165). Rizal's writings took on a life of their own beyond even their creator's ability to fathom.

The invitation of this chapter is to view immigrant students in the current age of "late globalization" (Anderson, 2007, p. 234) as cosmopolitan intellectuals themselves, geniuses whose literary genies can potentially transfigure our own educational, aesthetic, and political realities. This simple proposition goes against the grain of dominant ways immigrant students are thought of and treated in language arts curricula, which often involves two seemingly contradictory, yet actually complementary impulses: The first involves a pervasive "discourse of deprivation" (Campano, 2007, p. 3), which remediates students and homogenizes their experiences through standardization;

the second approach slots individuals into prefabricated social and ethnic categories that correspond, often in a one-to-one reductive relationship, with culturally appropriate texts and pedagogies. Both constrain the types of literacy experiences students are provided, while denying how their existences and creative forms of literary and cultural production are not easily contained by our classifications.

Many articles on children's literature and immigrant students provide lists of books that address the experiences of Latina/os, Asian Americans, and, more rarely, African or Middle Eastern immigrants, and often grapple with issues such as the complexity of authenticity. Our approach in this chapter is a different one: We place the accent on the creative alchemy of student literary agency, and emphasize the ways in which our youth draw on disparate experiences and texts to imagine worlds and bring these new conceptions into existence. We begin by reviewing how the diverse identities in 21st century classrooms are still invisible to the world of children's literature and educational research, despite strides in multiculturalism and culturally responsive pedagogy. Next, we provide a rationale for our use of the cosmopolitan intellectual as a working ideal for a literary curriculum, following Harste (1992) in defining curriculum as "a metaphor for the lives we want to live and the people we want to be" (p. 3). In the spirit of cosmopolitanism, we suggest that educators should open up, rather than restrict, textual possibilities, so that students can draw on and make connections with books in ways that are not always predictable. We take a close look at how "writerly texts" (Barthes, 1970/1974), such as Shaun Tan's *The Arrival* (2007), foster cosmopolitanism by resisting easy identification and instead providing a platform for children to articulate their own intellectual and physical migrations in order to constantly "arrive" at new understandings of particular histories and overlapping experiences. We then build on the notion that engaging with literature involves not only response, but also authorship and creation, by focusing on the work of a fifth-grade student who used reading and writing to both give shape to and realize a cosmopolitan identity that was largely invisible to the dominant discourse. We conclude by offering recommendations for educators as they strive to co-construct school learning environments that are in synergy with the budding cosmopolitanism of their immigrant student body.

The Context of 21st Century Classrooms

There is a growing consensus about the value of having students read high-quality literature that speaks to their identities (e.g., Beach, Thein, & Parks, 2007; DeNicolo & Fránquiz, 2006; Landt, 2006; Medina, 2006). Multicultural literature is considered a platform for students to expand their knowledge of the world, interrogate their social locations, and challenge discrimination (Cai, 2002). It is important to note, however, that the literature doesn't teach itself, but must be situated within pedagogical contexts. As Enciso (1997) emphasizes, teachers have the ability (and responsibility) to support discussions of equity and critical examinations of multicultural literature, a stance that can interrupt whose knowledge is and is not valued in the classroom. In addition, there have also been significant strides in providing a cultural range of literary representation for children and young adults, though literature by and about people of color continues to account for a small percentage of the number of children's books published yearly (Cooperative Children's Book Center, n.d.) and is less likely to be widely advertised and available (McNair, 2008).

Despite progress in the publishing field, the world of children's literature does not reflect the world of many 21st century schools, which increasingly house students who communicate in numerous languages, claim multiple identities, and often have ties which extend beyond our nation's borders to diaspora communities. How, then, do teachers create culturally responsive literacy pedagogy when there are simply very few books which speak to students who are, for example, of Filipina, Laotian, Bengali, Costa Rican, or Quechua heritage? How do students who claim *mestiza* or mixed identities—such as Mexipino or Korean-Argentinean-American relate to the children's literature canon, multicultural or otherwise? What literary curriculum would address the experiences of, for instance, a student of Chinese ancestry born in the country of Jamaica whose family migrated to Jamaica, Queens in New York City and who now attends public school with children from over 50 different countries speaking over 30 different home languages? This profile is, in fact, a familiar part of life in the borough of Queens, where the 2000 census data indicate that 138 language are spoken, with many more added since then (Office of the State Deputy Comptroller, 2000).

How do researchers understand the lives and learning of students who are illegible to conventional research categories? For example, how do the designations "voluntary" and "involuntary" minorities (Ogbu & Simmons, 1998) explain how a Vietnamese family's ostensibly voluntary migration shades into an effect of colonialism? What does it mean to be at once "invisible" within a curricular context, while at the same time hyper-visible in the current immigration discourse, which linguistically dehumanizes (with ascriptions like "illegal") many who are already dehumanized by the global economic system?

We offer these questions to underscore the complexities of teaching and learning in today's diverse school contexts. One possible avenue for addressing students' identities is the continued commitment to providing texts that echo students' experiences and portray a multiplicity of cultural, linguistic, and migratory representations within any given community. The project of expanding the canon, including what constitutes a literary text, needs to

continue with vigor. At the same time, however, educators can approach the heterogeneity of 21st century classrooms through cultivating a stance of cosmopolitanism. This honors our students as future authors of literature and of the world we share.

Why Cosmopolitanism?

In her examination of patriotism and cosmopolitanism, Martha Nussbaum (1996) argues for a notion of global citizenship rather than for allegiances merely bounded by historically contingent national borders. The foundation for this cosmopolitanism is the moral responsibility to the human community as a whole. Our memberships in a particular group, while important to individual and collective identity, are also accidents of birth that do not mitigate the equality of all people by virtue of their humanity or our sense of justice for others. Cheah (2008) notes:

> Cosmopolitanism is primarily about viewing one-self as part of a world, a circle of belonging that transcends the limited ties of kinship and country to embrace the whole of humanity. However, since one cannot see the universe, the world, or humanity, the cosmopolitan optic is not one of perceptual experience but of the imagination. World literature is an important aspect of cosmopolitanism because it is a type of world-making activity that enables us to imagine a world. (p. 26)

For all students, whether recent immigrants or established in a context for generations, literature can serve as a rich source for cultivating a cosmopolitan stance: Engaging with texts that portray ways of being different than our own local instantiations sensitizes us to global diversity and well-being, defamiliarizes what is taken as "natural" and "commonsense," and assists in the "enact[ment] of the love of humanity" (Nussbaum, 1996, p. 140). For students from immigrant experiences, however, cosmopolitanism is not just an imagined possibility, but often a perceptual and lived reality as well. By virtue of their diverse vantage points and transnational negotiations, they are uniquely positioned to educate their peers and teachers about the world. If, as Nussbaum contends, the role of education is to "cultivate the factual and imaginative prerequisites for recognizing humanity in the stranger and the other" (p. 133), then multilingual and multicultural students can lead the way.

The Vantage Point of Epistemic Privilege

Much like Rizal, whose intellectual and political labor drew from a vast range of transnational influences and experiences, immigrant students are themselves cosmopolitan citizens. Their perspectives, derived from familiarity with multiple and often contrasting settings, offer understandings of the human condition—including the suffering of many worldwide—that may not be readily available to individuals whose frame of reference has never been unsettled. Because of their identities and life experiences, immigrant students have unique vantage points from which to interpret and generate knowledge about the world. This knowledge, what theorists have called "epistemic privilege" (Mohanty, 1997; Moya, 2000), may be embedded in personal and group legacies and struggles for human rights and self-determination. Unfortunately, the current educational climate of standardized curricula and monolingual practices reifies the insularity of national experiences, creating increasingly polarized notions of belonging that work to dichotomize the experiences of students rather than seek opportunities for fostering nuanced mutual understandings and commitment to the human condition.

There are several reasonable reservations with the idea of the cosmopolitan intellectual as a working model and curricular metaphor. One charge might be that a global point of view potentially devalues local knowledge, privileging an overly abstract notion of humanity over the specificities of difference. As we hope our examples illustrate, we believe the literacy curriculum is driven by a dialectic between the particular and general, and that students' subjective experiences may contribute to more comprehensive knowledge about the world we share, which may, in turn, inform local understandings and identities. In addition, if individuals at the turn of the century had access to global phenomena, we can only begin to fathom how technology increases access to world-wide information. Many young people, for example, are involved in activist organizations that employ what scholars have labeled "new literacies" in order to draw connections between social issues and injustices at home and abroad.

Equity and Cosmopolitanism

Attention to cosmopolitanism is in no way meant to transcend the particularities of ethnicity or group experience. Rather, we suggest that the particular and the cosmopolitan exist in a mutually informing relationship. For example, many identity-based movements were also about human rights issues that had more universal resonance (Alcoff, Hames-García, Mohanty, & Moya, 2006). Likewise, a phenomenon such as nationalism was the product of cosmopolitan dynamics. Nussbaum (2008) herself has recently argued for the need to reconcile a progressive, "globally sensitive" patriotism with cosmopolitan human rights commitments, lest we concede patriotism to the forces of nativism and fear. Cosmopolitanism is also not intended to prematurely posit a romanticized ideal of a world where difference has been transcended. On the contrary, examining issues of inequality and conflict is a critical aspect of global justice.

There may also be concern that the ideal of the cosmopolitan intellectual is elitist. We suggest, rather, that it is an antidote to the pervasive ways children from migrant and refugee backgrounds are stigmatized by labels and sorted in schools. Researchers have critiqued how the teaching of culturally and linguistically diverse students is commonly

viewed as a "problem" (Gutiérrez & Orellana, 2006), when instead such diversity necessarily improves conditions for inquiry. The idea that our youth are cosmopolitan intellectuals is a radical break from convention precisely because it asserts the fundamental universal capacities of all students to engage in profound intellectual and creative labor. Our use of cosmopolitanism takes issue with deficit characterizations of immigrant students. This framing is not meant to construct another, albeit different, classroom hierarchy. We believe that cosmopolitanism is a working ideal for *all* students. However, cultivating a cosmopolitan stance in educational contexts can begin from the ground up: by valuing and learning from the radically hybrid experiences of historically disenfranchised and immigrant communities.

Cosmopolitanism in Community

Finally, it might be suggested that a cosmopolitan stance dilutes our obligations to our most immediate communities. The logic implies that we have a natural affinity with those with whom we have most in common. However, it must also be remembered that "commonality" itself is an ideological construct which often entails processes of exclusion and scapegoating, that indeed there is nothing natural about common. One tragic irony with othering categories such as "the foreigner" is that too often they prevent us from socially and intellectually bonding with people with whom we may actually have shared interests and passions. We believe there is the ethical imperative for educators to think about all human beings, and equally respect all students who walk through their classroom doors. Caring and respecting everyone is not just a sentimental matter. It entails being mindful of one's own presuppositions and not putting students' experiences in boxes or designating a particular literature as exhaustively suited for their identities. For example, an urban student might be attracted to Milton's *Paradise Lost* and the quote "The mind is its own place, and in itself, can make heaven of Hell, and a hell of Heaven" as a way of coping with the material realities of street life as well as structural forms of discrimination. This attraction to Milton would not exist in contradiction to the student's love of the poet and hip-hop artist La Bruja. Similarly, an affluent suburban student's interest in reggaeton should not necessarily be read merely as a cynical appropriation of urban culture—although such impulses ought to be subject to ongoing critical self-reflection—but may also serve to mark his own feelings of alienation within a homogenous community and help him to engage in productive forms of dissent. As educators, we need to care about all our students and recognize their profound creative potential to make literature their own as well as their abilities to broaden their own identities and epistemic horizons through transactions with other forms of cultural expression.

There is also a political rationale for a cosmopolitan stance in the curriculum, articulated by Stew, the author and composer of the Tony Award-Winning *Passing Strange*. The musical, written with the assumption that "everyone has a little outsider in them" (Hannaham, 2008, para 5), is a Brecht and Baldwin inspired semiautobiographical *bildungsroman* about a young man from South Central Los Angeles who travels to Europe as part of his aesthetic and political awakening. Stew comments that his play was inspired by an American president who "had never been to Europe until he became president…a guy who actually owns planes who never went outside his own country." He goes on to explain, "that incuriosity informs our politics …I was comparing my curiosity about the world, my hunger to know about the world to him, who had the world at his feet…I wanted to write about curiosity, about travel, about thinking outside your neighborhood, your neighborhood of a country" (Goodman, Lee, & Stew, 2008, para 23). Many schools have in their mission statements the need to prepare students for the challenges and possibilities of globalization. We believe helping to cultivate the curiosity to engage in productive cross-cultural and transnational exchange is necessary for educating future critical democratic citizens of the world.

Cosmopolitanism and Curricular Responsibility

It should not be incumbent on young people to eventually find the intellectual and artistic resources to broaden their horizons on their own. This should be a curricular responsibility that can begin in elementary grades. Fortunately, there has been much important work about pedagogy that encourages the epistemic value of diverse perspectives. While classrooms are contested spaces with competing ideologies and practices, Gutiérrez, Baquedano-López, and Turner (1997) note that "these tensions may be productive—if they become the means through which richer linguistic, sociocultural, and content knowledge is created" (p. 374). Alluding to Bhabha, this postcolonial "third space" (Gutiérrez, Rymes, & Larson, 1995) is a site of negotiation and translation that is fundamentally procreative and cannot merely be reduced to its prior influences. Guerra (2008) places his emphasis on the agents that negotiate these tensions through what he terms "transcultural repositioning": how students from historically marginalized communities are able to "make use of the prior knowledge and experiences they have accumulated and the rhetorical agility they have developed in the course of negotiating their way across the various communities of practice to which they currently belong, have belonged in the past, and will belong in the future" (p. 299). Anne Haas Dyson (1993, 2003) reminds us that students draw from and remix their linguistic, cultural, and intertextual resources, and that school curricula should be "permeable" to these creative social and intellectual projects.

These educational theorists promote an alchemy between the curriculum and a community of learners. In this spirit, while we don't intend to be prescriptive, we would like to highlight several texts that may be well-suited for a hybrid, permeable, and transcultural pedagogical approach. Following our discussion of these literature examples, we focus on one student reader and author who enacts a cosmopolitan ideal.

A Look at *The Arrival* and Other Cosmopolitan Books

Shaun Tan's (2007) *The Arrival* is a powerful example of the potential of literature for children and adolescents to take up the topic of immigration in ways that make visible its varied characteristics without essentializing the experience into a single narrative or resolving its contradictions. Told strictly through a visual medium, and in the absence of a narrating voice that pulls together any intended interpretation, *The Arrival* constitutes an invitation for readers to create meaning through immersion into a world that is both familiar and strange. The detailed series of pictures in the first opening show a father packing his belongings to leave his family for a new land—his house, possessions, and family easily recognizable—but subsequent illustrations portray him entering a futuristic, alien city with features unknown to the reader. In large part, the power of Tan's text lies in this shifting of the reader's position. Through a variety of semiotic resources, *The Arrival* works to deconstruct the legally sanctioned dichotomy between individuals already living in a particular country and newcomers from other nations, critically interrogating notions of belonging. From the beginning of the text, the reader is made to identify with the immigrant protagonist as the character attempts to navigate his new surroundings and procure basic necessities. For instance, in his search for something to eat—with the help of a dictionary entry featuring a loaf of bread—the man only encounters foreign, and seemingly unpalatable, food items, many with a number of protruding tentacles. As readers, we do not clamor for him to assimilate or disdain him for not desiring the food of his new home, but understand his unfamiliarity, hesitation, and yearning for recognizable tastes.

Throughout the images of *The Arrival*, Tan embeds a written language of his own invention, which populates the signs, maps, advertisements, and overall environmental print of the futuristic setting. As a result, this foreign world is literally unintelligible to readers; they, like the protagonist, cannot rely on knowledge of reading and writing to make sense of the surroundings. One poignant scenario entails the main character's search for employment. After being repeatedly turned down for jobs, he is hired to affix posters. The textual images track his careful labor, until his boss's return alerts both the immigrant man and readers themselves that the signs have been posted upside down. In a subsequent job, he cannot decode a "Danger" sign, which results in a close encounter with a monstrous creature. Eventually, the protagonist ends up working in a factory assembly line. Set against prevalent national and international conceptions of immigrants as uneducated, unwilling to learn the language of a new country, and especially suited for sweatshop labor, this characterization instead makes explicit the difficulty of negotiating and acquiring a new language, the limited options available to the majority of immigrants, and the perseverance of many despite adverse—often inhuman—working conditions.

The Arrival provides an opening to explore immigration without circumscribing the experience or suggesting a uniform trajectory, and as such is a departure from much of children's literature on this topic. The images in Tan's texts work by "recognition, not evocation" (Tan, 2001) and thus are permeable to the range of circumstances of transnational migration. When Tan depicts the homeland of the main character as a cluster of buildings overpowered by the giant tails of unseen creatures, the oppressive climate is left intentionally vague, thus allowing for multiple readings of his motivation to emigrate. Having journeyed to a new country, the protagonist encounters other immigrants who relate their own varied experiences in a similar fashion. The multivoiced perspectives provide ample testament to the diversity of immigration as well as identify possible points of connection across particular histories.

The Arrival underscores how living in uncertainty—continually negotiating possible opportunities, enduring hardships, and crossing linguistic, relational, and national borders—is part of the phenomenology of migration. This essence is in itself productive. Students from immigrant, migrant, and refugee backgrounds are cosmopolitan intellectuals well-versed in navigating multiple contexts and with honed global sensibilities. Educators can learn from their students to engage in a degree of uncertainty within the classroom. Fostering school communities based on students' epistemic privilege requires the unsettling of educators' own identities and of the rigid categorizations imposed on immigrant students, challenging notions of English Language Learners as a subgroup in need of "intervention" and of multicultural literature and culturally responsive pedagogies as solely for students of color. This stance necessitates advocating for teaching and learning relationships based on the premise that knowledge does not travel uni-directionally, and that in many cases students, by virtue of their lived experiences, may have more nuanced understandings than educators.

In authoring this cosmopolitan book, Shaun Tan's creative process was informed by a multiplicity of textual and relational resources. Tan (n.d.) notes that *The Arrival*'s genesis dates back to his father's history of immigration and to grappling with his own identity in the homogenous and often discriminatory suburbs of Western Australia. The narratives of immigration his father shared with him resonated with other accounts Tan uncovered while conducting further research on the topic. In the artist's note of *The Arrival*, and on his website (n.d.) Tan describes some of his influences, such as photographs of transatlantic voyages,

inspections at Ellis Island, New York, at the turn of the century, post-war Europe, and of a newsboy announcing the sinking of the *Titanic*; first-hand accounts of immigration in Lowenstein and Loh's *The Immigrants* and Davies and Dal Bosco's *Tales from a Suitcase*; the 1886 painting *Going South*; and the movie *The Bicycle Thief*. Additional influences on *The Arrival* include, but are not limited to: the short story "Won Chu and the Queens Letterbox" by T.A. Hungerford, which connected to Tan's interest in "the somewhat invisible history of the Chinese in Western Australia;" Raymond Brigg's *The Snowman*, which inspired the layout—and in many ways the essence—of the text; references about graphic novels and comics; and Tan's own experiences as a traveler in foreign countries. These various frames of reference oscillate among local understandings such as family narratives and the specificity of the Western Australian context, and collective, transnational experiences of immigration.

Much like the influences on Tan's creative process, the genre and audience of *The Arrival* disrupt clear characterizations. Originally begun as a picturebook, the work took on the shape of a graphic novel. This text is one that can be accessed by individuals across a range of ages, and the nature of readers' interactions is shaped by understandings of immigration and belonging that may result from personal or family histories, insights gained from the school context, or perspectives present in media characterizations. Tan has argued that there is nothing inherent in the picturebook genre that delimits use of such texts to children or merits their classification as strictly children's literature. Rather, he contends that "simplicity certainly does not exclude sophistication or complexity" (2001, p. 2), thus making the genre appropriate for a broad audience. The layered configuration of *The Arrival* recognizes the cosmopolitan resources of students from immigrant backgrounds and provides an invitation for readers with less direct transnational experiences to defamiliarize and interrogate their own understandings.

There are other compelling examples of literature for children and adolescents that showcase the hybridity of immigrant experiences and the phenomenology of migration, providing openings for fostering a cosmopolitan stance. *American Born Chinese* by Gene Yang (2006), another graphic novel, explores issues of transnational identities and discriminatory practices by weaving together three seemingly distinct tales: the Chinese myth of the Monkey King who wishes to be one of the Gods; the experiences of Jin Wang, the only Chinese American student in his school; and the story of Danny, an all-American teen whose perfect life is only marred by the periodic visit of his cousin, Chin-Kee, an embodiment of racist stereotypes. Wildly imaginative, this text interlaces multiple and multifaceted voices of Asian and "native-born" Americans, making visible existing implicit and explicit racism and challenging rigid categories of immigration. Identities that initially appear dichotomized are actually revealed as contradictory and fluid. Jin Wang and Danny, the two human protagonists, might seem to be on opposite sides of the tolerance spectrum: Jin Wang is consistently subject to discrimination because he is Chinese American, while Danny, a White student, is embarrassed and even revolted by his Chinese cousin. As the narratives progress, however, these two characters are shown to be one and the same, and readers witness how Jin Wang's attempts to fit in and reject his Chinese heritage result in his transformation into Danny. The text skillfully captures the time-space compression (Harvey, 1990) that shapes immigrants' consciousness, with ancient myths becoming lived realities affecting possible selves.

The cosmopolitanism of another community, the Hmong, is the focus of three extraordinary texts, the picture books *Dia's Story Cloth: The Hmong People's Journey to Freedom* (Cha, 1996) and *Whispering Cloth: A Refugee's Story* (Shea, 1999) and the young adult novel, *Tangled Threads: A Hmong Girl's Story* (Shea, 2003). These stories convey the subaltern histories of a refugee population and, in making public their epistemic privilege, disrupt deficit characterizations of Hmong students as "at-risk" due to interrupted schooling and "lack" of literacy. Each text highlights the narrative *pa'ndau*, or storycloth, as an intricate literacy practice stitched in Thai refugee camps and used to record a buried history. The *pa'ndau* depict the (forced) geographic movement that has characterized Hmong communities and the resistance embodied in authoring this perspective. *Tangled Threads* follows the character Mai, also the protagonist of *Whispering Cloth*, as she negotiates the realities of the refugee camp and of a new home in Providence, Rhode Island. The juxtaposition of contexts provides a dual lens through which to understand the cosmopolitan identities of immigrants like Mai. One of many poignant vignettes is a scene in newly arrived Mai's middle school cafeteria: Having experienced starvation in Thailand, where food was strictly rationed, Mai is horrified when she witnesses students throwing away uneaten food. As someone discards an apple that is whole save for one bite, Mai grabs it with lightning speed, intending to eat it, and is stopped by a Hmong classmate and mentor who recounts how she was called "pig" and ostracized when she had done something similar. Having followed Mai through her escape from Laos to Thailand and her journey to the United States, readers must necessarily recognize her worldly frame of reference (in contrast to classmates who are unaware of global inequities) and may even reflect on their own possibly sheltered practices. Mai's ability to discern this reckless and pervasive wastefulness is an incisive example of her epistemic privilege.

We have selected a group of texts that complicate and unsettle immigrant experiences, and could add a number of additional examples. Taken together, the books convey movement. The historical accounts of the *pa'ndau*, with figures that cross rivers and geographical borders stitched in multicolored thread, are not anomalous to one group,

but an essential part of the human condition. Immigrant students, far from having deficits, are cosmopolitan intellectuals who continually navigate border spaces as productive tension. They are the new *mestiza* vividly described by Anzaldúa (1987): "she has a plural personality, she operates in pluralistic mode—nothing rejected, nothing abandoned. Not only does she sustain contradictions, she turns the ambivalence into something else" (p. 101). On a more disturbing note, the various texts also speak to the capacity of all people to exclude and stigmatize, even those who have suffered such inequities: Jin Wang turns on his Taiwanese friend, the Hmong have a history of persecution by the Chinese. Scapegoating and discrimination are not portrayed as character flaws of villains, but as a potential in all people, which must be guarded against with vigilance.

A Look at a Cosmopolitan Student: Maria's Writing

In his college and graduate level courses, Gerald often shares two writing samples from his former multilingual and multiethnic fifth-grade class. He asks his adult learners to consider who the students producing the work might be and to imagine the characteristics of a literary curriculum that would speak to their identities.

The first piece is a note given to Gerald that inquires into his well-being and shares updates from the student and her family (see Figure 12.1).

The second selection consists of excerpts from a piece titled, "The War that Gave New Perspectives and Started New Lives (Historical Fiction Inspired by My Grandfather's Stories)." This lengthy work—amassing 20 single spaced typed pages—unpacks one family's immigration to the United States from the Philippines. The first few lines alert the reader that there is much beneath the surface in the act of coming to America:

> In the year 1922, a family immigrated to America. No big deal, right? Wrong! They didn't come here by choice; they came here for their lives. Their lives were at serious risk, because the American Embassy threatened to prosecute them, and their whole community. The community contained nearly 1,800 people. Fortunately, some families fled the land and the country, but some got beaten, were treated like slaves, and were persecuted.

The student goes on to document colonization, including the violent subjugation of the Filipino people, through the experiences of the Gallias family. Written primarily in English, the piece also includes dialogue in Ilocano, ranging from hushed family conversations to the cries of the public during an attack on their community: "Most families yelled, 'Nalpas ti biyag ti itoy Ilocos Norte!' 'All our lives are finished. All the lives of Ilocos Norte!'"

A powerful moment in the narrative occurs when the Gallias, faced with the brutality and persecution of their people at the hands of American military power, make the difficult decision to leave from their homeland. The son, John Ray, who until this point has been described as

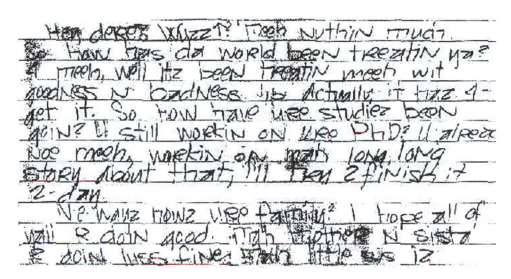

Figure 12.1 Student letter to Gerald

"idle" and "tumultuous," devises a plan for escape. This image of John Ray as a savior to his family, able to think creatively and rationally amid the direst of circumstances, contradicts how he had been construed by the institutional system and even by those closest to him:

> He didn't pay much attention to education. They thought he wouldn't get into college, and they even thought he would drop out of high school. What his friends and family didn't know was that he loved to read and write.
>
> He wouldn't take it serious at school, but he took it serious at home. Reading was one of his virtues, and so was writing. One of his favorite authors was José Rizal. He loved to read his book. That one book changed his perspective on Filipino life. It was about freedom: "Writing comes from the heart and soul, and the soul of your heart should get written on blank pieces of paper," John Ray would say to himself. He was just too timid to tell people of his other side.

When confronted with these two writing samples—the letter and the historical fiction narrative—readers typically respond by creating very different portraits of the students in question. The author of the letter is generally described as more fluent in vernacular forms of literacy but in need of remediation on the conventions of Standard English. The author of the second piece is considered a good student with sophisticated vocabulary and writing style. The two samples are often assumed to represent different worlds, with children who have mutually exclusive literacy practices.

The obvious twist is that these authors are one and the same—a 10-year-old girl named Maria. Her identity and intellectual capabilities (like those of all immigrant students) disrupt possible reductive characterizations. Throughout her writing, Maria challenges monolithic understandings of immigration: She begins by denouncing the reader "wrong" to think it "no big deal" for a family to come to America, and continues to provide nuanced representations of various characters, including John Ray, who was thoughtful and intellectual despite school, and Carl, a member of the American military who questions

the massacre of the Filipinos and secretly begins to work in opposition to his superiors. Her writing samples urge us to reconsider narrow portrayals of the students who populate our classrooms.

What insights can we derive about reading and the literary curriculum from Maria's writings? First, we might build on the commonly held position in literacy research and reader response theories that the social and pedagogical practices surrounding texts matter as much as the texts themselves. These practices, we find it important to add, should foster less-alienating forms of authorship and cultural production than is typically endorsed in schools.

It has become all too apparent how students are reading for purposes other than their own, whether it is to glean a predetermined interpretation, passively consume representations of others (or themselves), perform well on a standardized test, or assume an academic persona similar to that of their teachers. It is commonly argued that these goals are important—especially for supposed "non-traditional" students such as those from immigrant backgrounds—because they provide access to the power codes. One caveat is that educators need to be self-reflective about the ways in which students identify (or do not identify) with particular books or how the subject positions of both the teacher and students invariably color their transactions with literature. From this perspective, one may rush to conclude that Maria's community "self," as expressed in the first writing sample, is at odds with who she is asked to be in school. A critical approach to teaching would at least ensure that she does not labor under a "false-consciousness" about why certain modes of literate expression are privileged over others.

However, as we hope has become clear, Maria's readings and writing were not at odds. They were just different valences of a creative intellect that singularly blends a range of experiences. Students will feel conflict to the degree to which the school imposes too rigid categories onto their experiences and practices. Maria's historical fiction itself constantly subverts expectations. Does the

171

reader think this is a "No big deal" traditional immigrant narrative? "Wrong!" It is a tale that must be understood within the too often elided history of American colonization of the Philippines. Is the main character a sluggard of a student, devoid of intellectual proclivities? On the contrary, outside of school he had "another side" inspired by Rizal that loved to read, write, and contemplate freedom. Is this story written in Standard English? It is also written in Ilocano and youth vernacular.

Maria culled from a range of textual, linguistic, and cultural resources to recover her past in order to arrive at and name her present. Truly demystifying and gaining access to power codes goes beyond exposing and even learning to navigate the assumed or naturalized ideological underpinnings of a text or textual practice; rather, it involves fundamentally transforming relationships students have with texts so that they can make them their own, so that they can *assimilate the books* into their own experiences, identities, writings, and processes of imagining and becoming. True power, Maria teaches us, entails creating one's own power codes. This will look different for every student; it can't happen in a standardized classroom, whether the students are all writing five paragraph essays with objectives on the plays of Shakespeare (the Bard), the poems of Tupac Amaru Shakur (the hip-hop icon), or the sayings of Túpac Amaru II (the indigenous revolutionary leader from the Andes). The learning community of which Maria was a part was immersed in all types of literary traditions: She and her peers read José Rizal, Dr. Martin Luther King Jr., Sandra Cisneros, Carlos Bulosan, Dolores Huerta, June Jordan, Salman Rushdie, Langston Hughes, William Blake, and many others, alongside rich examples of literature for children and adolescents. These texts may all be part of a students' intellectual universe, which, if explored, can help them inscribe their own literary constellations.

Suggestions for Cosmopolitan Teaching

A fundamental dilemma for teachers is how to cultivate literacy curricula that recognize our commonalities without compromising our attention to singular or particular experiences. In this section, we offer recommendations for K–12 educators, teacher educators, librarians, policymakers, and researchers as we collectively work to provide more equitable learning opportunities for immigrant students and tap into the cosmopolitan energy of our diverse school populations.

Be Aware of How Our Identities Blend

The poet Audre Lorde (1984) famously asserted, "I am not one piece of myself. I cannot simply be a Black person, and not be a woman, too, nor can I be a woman without being a lesbian" (p. 262). A cosmopolitan stance entails a queering of identity, an acknowledgment that students should not be reduced to a single aspect of themselves when educa-

tors make curricular decisions. In any particular context some ever-evolving dimensions of a student may be more salient than others, more socially ascribed and visible, or less visible and chosen (such as a self-identified feminist male), but often they blend. This includes pedagogical contexts such as literature discussion groups. It is not always predictable how a student will identify or not identify with any particular text—e.g., one year Gerald's male fifth graders nominated *Heidi* (Spyri, 1880/1998) as their most influential book. Designing a literary curriculum is not a matter of matching certain texts with certain people. It is about employing a plurality of texts to individually and collectively fashion identities and investigate our shared realities.

Just as there may be a plurality of experiences within any particular person, groups do not merely occupy separate, insular spaces. We need to explore with students "the imbrication of our various pasts and presents…how our differences are intertwined and, indeed, hierarchically organized" (Mohanty, 1989, p. 13). Students' literacy practices are often an enactment of a complex history. For example, Maria's work is inflected with a colonial legacy that implicates American imperialism, Spanish rule, and Filipino nationhood; the braided experiences of Filipino and Mexican migrant workers; the polyvocality of the playground; popular culture; and the rich variety of literature she reads. A critical component of cosmopolitanism entails cultivating a meta-awareness of these layers of history and experience.

Embed Texts Within an Inquiry Approach to Teaching and Learning

Cochran-Smith and Lytle (2001) characterize an inquiry stance as a matter of "building, interrogating, elaborating, and critiquing conceptual frameworks that link action and problem-posing to the immediate context as well as to larger social, cultural, and political issues" (pp. 51–52). This suggests that access to texts, and the power codes they embody, is not an end in itself. Texts might also serve as a means for students to investigate issues, cultivate critical perspectives, and engage in processes of (self) authoring and creation. Embedding reading within an inquiry approach does not contradict a close reading of a book—whether in a New Critical or Deconstructive spirit—but, rather, it is complementary. Students gain proficiency in certain academic conventions in order to appropriate, challenge, and even supersede them for their own purposes, ones which ideally rise organically out of particular teaching and learning situations.

For example, one generative activity we have done with *The Arrival* follows Serafini's (2004) suggestion that the pages of a picturebook be spread out on the wall to allow readers a different vantage point from which to inquire into visual aspects of the text. Students and teachers respond by writing and drawing around the pictures, noticing details, making connections, and posing questions, which may be taken up by others in the classroom community. This multimodal and potentially multilingual exploration of the text is open to the diversity of participants' prior experiences and insights, and can serve as a platform for inquiry into the topic of immigration. Participants not only draw on their own histories but also transform their understandings by learning from peers. Just as important as who students *are*—is who they *might become*. Many of us may have had the uncanny experience that we might more fully realize ourselves and our relationships to the world through our transactions with alterity, or that we feel more at home in a space that is distant and foreign. A literary curriculum based on inquiry helps to unleash students' capacities to enter into and imagine new worlds that are more conducive for ethical and intellectual growth.

Read Literature from the Postcolonial South

Part of exposing students to a wide array of texts includes attending to literature and art from formerly colonized regions in Latin America, Asia, and Africa. For example, award winning author Monica Brown has several picturebooks that introduce readers to influential literary figures: *My name is Gabriela: The life of Gabriela Mistral* (2005) and *My name is Gabito: The life of Gabriel García Márquez* (2007). Melodic bilingual prose and evocative illustrations (by John Parra and Raúl Colón) bring to life the personal histories and artistic and intellectual contributions of two Latin American Nobel Prize winners. Brown (2008) emphasizes that these texts showcase the rich cultural and linguistic heritage of Latin America overlooked in more conventional literary historiographies. They can help students think about intellectual traditions that supersede national borders, for example, a "hemispheric" network (Moya & Saldívar, 2003) that may connect Whitman with Neruda.

Advocate for Multilingualism

Like José Rizal and 10-year-old Maria, students from immigrant backgrounds have the ability to navigate multiple languages and language varieties. Too often, schools are inhospitable to these resources, delineating Standard English as the only viable means of communication and in the process compromising native language facilities and hampering English acquisition. As St. Lucian poet and Nobel Prize winner Derek Walcott noted, "The English language is nobody's special property. It is the property of the imagination" (quoted in Hirsch, 1997, p. 73). Language is not for an institution to harness, deliver, and evaluate, or for a privileged group to own and sanctify. Gloria Anzaldúa's (1987) *Borderlands* is such a powerful work in part due to its use of multiple Englishes and Spanishes to articulate an identity that cannot be contained within prescriptive categories. If multilingualism is an essential component of a cosmopolitan ideal, it should not be the case that our immigrant students, who arrive in schools already proficient (and in many cases literate) in a variety of international tongues, leave the educational system further away from this goal. Educators are uniquely positioned to recognize their students' expertise by honoring the value of being multiliterate and providing opportunities for students to engage with and create texts that cross linguistic boundaries. There is an emerging body of children's literature that is written in several languages, explicitly addresses language learning, and illustrates the connection between language and identity (e.g., *La Mariposa* by Francisco Jiménez, 1998, *Dear Juno* by Soyung Pak, 2001, and *America is her name/La llaman America* by Luis Rodriguez, 1998).

One timely example is the recently published *Return to Sender* by Julia Alvarez (2009). This young adult novel tells the story of a family of migrant workers whose composition reflects many of the contradictions of capitalism and nationhood: The family was brought over to work on and save a Vermont farm, and two of the daughters are U.S. citizens while the eldest sibling and parents are undocumented. Alvarez eloquently examines how language can affect and dehumanize communities through labeling (i.e., "illegal"), but also shows the linguistic resourcefulness of individuals who negotiate multiple affiliations, including native English speakers who learn Spanish to connect with the family, the U.S.-born Latino children who gravitate to English over the family language, and the father's efforts to preserve Spanish in the home. Novels such as *Return to Sender* potentially inspire students to embrace more than one language.

Take a Learner's Stance

Schools have much to learn from immigrant students and communities, a process that entails disrupting institutional tendencies to arbiter and deliver information. Educators who encourage immigrant students to generate knowledge from their own locations may encounter situations that are multiply unintelligible to them: in instances where students read texts or discuss content material in their native languages or when they name experiences that are outside educators' lived realities. Apprehension about incorporating material that may be out of the cultural or linguistic range of a teacher's body of knowledge is mitigated when we recognize the students in our classrooms as experts who can teach us—and each other—about individual and collective histories that are invisible to the educational arena, the publishing field, and the national discourse. For example, allowing students to share testimonials, a genre of political witnessing, can provoke others in the classroom community to learn about social issues which may be outside the ambit of their everyday thinking.

Be Wary of Standardization

Though the push to replicate educational experiences across an array of contexts is claimed to provide equal services to all students, standardization in fact promotes hierarchies by setting up rigid notions of an ideal student and ideal academic work. The reality of students' intellectual capacities and school endeavors is much more varied and multifaceted: In Maria's classroom, for instance, many of the children wrote powerful texts, but these pieces were unique and quite different from each other. Embodying a cosmopolitan stance in teaching necessitates that we not entrap students within an arbitrary image of what it means to be an intellectual, and instead nurture the flowering of multiple geniuses. We should aspire to create schools that are, in the words of the Zapatistas, "un mundo donde quepan muchos mundos" (a world that encompasses many worlds).

Conclusion: Queens' Englishes

We began the chapter with the turn of the century cosmopolitan intellectual and political visionary, José Rizal, and we will conclude with a contemporary writer in the current age of "late globalization," the activist and Pulitzer winner Junot Díaz. Díaz, himself multiliterate, born in the Dominican Republic and raised in New Jersey barrios, is acclaimed for literature that transgresses traditional linguistic, national, and cultural boundaries: For example, his depictions of translocal spaces, ear for "street" and "academic" sensibilities, and poignant renderings of the simultaneity of the tragic and comic, all evidence what the literary critic Jahan Ramazani (2001) might call a "Hybrid Muse." But, of course, one has to wonder if there is any other kind of muse, if there ever has been. It is significant that Díaz's work isn't merely executing an abstract idea or artifice onto paper. His words reference a real world, and he writes for a real audience who embody the textured, multifaceted, yet coherent experiences of any community. That is, what may be coded either negatively as "non-standard" or positively as something like "an instance of postmodern mixing" may simply be one of many possible representations of peoples' actual lives. And if our imaginations will invariably lag behind the poets and artists, it has been the argument of this chapter that our imaginations as educators may also fall short of those of our students, whose intellectual interests and forms of expression are often not contained by our narrow pedagogical categories.

At an event at Haverford College, Díaz (2008) discussed the irony of giving a talk at Princeton University as an esteemed Pulitzer winner, in a town where his mother used to clean professors' homes (noting a further irony that many of the "Marxist" professors were stingiest with their tips). Knowing that her son was an avid reader, Díaz's mother would jot down the names of books on the professors' shelves so he might later take them out of the local neighborhood library. Her advocacy stance for her child existed in stark contrast to that of the public school, where Díaz was tracked into special education. One message of this story is that many students gain access to rich literature and literacy curricula in spite of schools.

We offer the following neighborhood portrait of people and places in Queens, New York City—where we both have family roots—to give a sense of the cosmopolitan energy that can potentially inform and transform the reading curriculum, not just for immigrant students, but for all students. Imagine the following youth and the rich legacies and "vast rhizomal networks" they bring to a typical public school classroom representative of Queens demographics: a student raised with Confucian philosophy who knows about labor history because of her parents' participation in the custodial union; a Caribbean student who has watched Shakespeare productions that have been Africanized and won contests reciting Louise Bennett's dramatic monologues in Creole; students whose histories include Balinese puppetry or Brazilian *literatura do cordel* (string literature), literacy practices steeped in political traditions and grass-roots movements; a Colombian American teenager who was born and raised in New York and takes the F train on the weekend to the Nuyorican Poets Café in the Lower East Side to hone her spoken word skills; a newly arrived Hungarian immigrant who is more studied in American literature, history, and government than the vast majority of native-born Americans; a student from Mexico City who loves science fiction and punk music. The list is seemingly inexhaustible.

This is the plenitude of our student populations, which defy strict categorizations, and whose robust intellectual bounty may entice our own capacities to wonder about (and wander in) the literary curriculum. Many of our students experience the world osmotically in their own neighborhoods, a collective genius that, to quote Rizal (1884) from the epigraph of this chapter, "is like the light, the air" and "blossoms everywhere." Unfortunately, the assimilationist impulses of schools often frame such student legacies and potentials from a deficit perspective or in dichotomous reductive terms (such as standard versus non-standard English, school versus home literacy practices, or power codes versus vernacular literacies). Many local institutions, however, have tapped into the vibrancy of these multilingual and multicultural communities. For instance, the Queens' public library system houses print and online texts in international languages, and offers services that include story hours, tai chi, ESL courses, information regarding jobs and heath care, tax assistance, and multilingual workshops addressing labor rights in Spanish, parenting in Chinese, or understanding the school system in Urdu, among other topics (O'Connor, 2008). This dynamic community center, so attuned to the resources of its population, unfortunately faces risks of underfunding as public services are continually undermined in our privatized economy (Dominus, 2008).

The educational system could learn a great deal from the communities in which they are embedded. Schools need to celebrate the opportunity for epistemic growth that the prodigious diversity of our immigrant population affords. One avenue towards this goal is to allow students like Maria to self-fashion their identities through interactions with literature that represent less alienating, more cosmopolitan practices. The writing of José Rizal—essential to generations of readers and part of the literary repertoire of Maria and her peers—imagined possibilities for Filipina/o nationhood and ushered in an anticolonial movement. Our students' literary practices may not (or may) have revolutionary effects of that magnitude. But in schools across the United States, students have the opportunity to foster creative literary work, which may broaden our own provincial understandings of individual and collective identity. Through their transactions with books, students may articulate buried histories, enlarge our aesthetic sensibilities, redraw boundaries, rethink what it means to be American, and cultivate human rights commitments that transcend national borders.

It may be worth mentioning that we wrote this chapter during a political season in the United States. Daily headlines about the fear of "foreign" ideas and names, suspicion of those "who don't think like us," the attempted censorship of books, and anti-immigrant sentiments served as a constant reminder that provincialism and xenophobia are more instruments of power than characteristics of communities. And precisely because they are not essential characteristics, we believe that there is even more of an urgency to nurture, revise, and vigilantly defend the working ideal of cosmopolitanism in the literary and literacy curricula to provide an alternative vision of "the lives we want to live and the people we want to be" (Harste, 1992, p. 3). We also realize that this is a rather unconventional chapter for this volume. It is not a rehearsal of the canon, multicultural or otherwise, and it is not organized around fixed genres or prescriptive categories. Instead, we have tried a more rhizomatic approach ourselves, connecting ostensibly disparate texts and experiences that could potentially inform the intellectual makeup of so many contemporary students who have been displaced by the realities of neoliberalism, war, and natural disaster. At the same time, what we are suggesting is in many ways a traditional and rigorous humanities approach, with the exceptions that humanity encompasses everyone—all humans in the full complexity and imbrication of their experiences—and that tradition is understood as something that students create as well as inherit.

Literature References

Alvarez, J. (2009). *Return to sender.* New York, NY: Knopf.

Brown, M. (2005). *My name is Gabriela: The life of Gabriela Mistral/Me llamo Gabriela: La vida de Gabriela Mistral.* Flagstaff, AZ: Luna Rising.

Brown, M. (2007). *My name is Gabito: The life of Gabriel García Márquez/Me llamo Gabito: La vida de Gabriel García Márquez.* Flagstaff, AZ: Luna Rising.

Cha, D. (1996). *Dia's story cloth: The Hmong people's journey to freedom.* New York, NY: Lee & Low Books.

Jiménez, F. (1998). *La mariposa.* New York, NY: Houghton Mifflin.

Pak, S. (2001). *Dear Juno.* New York, NY: Puffin Books.

Rodríguez, L. (1998). *América is her name/La llaman America.* Willimantic, CT: Curbstone Press.

Shea, P. D. (1999). *Whispering cloth: A refugee's story.* Honesdale, PA: Boyds Mills Press.

Shea, P. D. (2003). *Tangled threads: A Hmong girl's story.* New York, NY: Clarion Books.

Spyri, J. (1880/1998). *Heidi (Children's Classics).* New York, NY: Random House.

Tan, S. (2007). *The Arrival.* New York, NY: Arthur A. Levine Books.

Yang, G. L. (2006). *American born Chinese* (L. Pien, Color). New York, NY: Macmillan.

Academic References

Alcoff, L., Hames-García, M., Mohanty, S., & Moya, P. (Eds.). (2006). *Identity politics reconsidered.* New York, NY: Palgrave Macmillan.

Anderson, B. (2007). *Under three flags: Anarchism and the anticolonial imagination.* New York, NY: Verso.

Anzaldúa, G. (1987). *Borderlands/La frontera: The new mestiza* (2nd ed). San Francisco, CA: Aunt Lute Books.

Barthes, R. (1970/1974). *S/Z: An essay.* New York, NY: Hill & Wang.

Beach, R., Thein, A., & Parks, D. (2007). *High school students' competing social worlds: Negotiating identities and allegiances through responding to multicultural literature.* Mahwah, NJ: Erlbaum.

Brown, M. (2008). From a writer's perspective: Recreating images of community in multicultural children's books. *Language Arts, 85*(4), 316–321.

Cai, M. (2002). *Multicultural literature for children and young adults: Reflections on critical issues.* Westport, CT: Greenwood Press.

Campano, G. (2007). *Immigrant students and literacy: Reading, writing, and remembering.* New York, NY: Teachers College Press.

Cheah, P. (2008). What is a world? On world literature as world-making activity. *Daedalus: Journal of the American Academy of Arts & Sciences, 137*(3), 26–38.

Cochran-Smith, M., & Lytle, S. L. (2001). Beyond certainty: Taking an inquiry stance on practice. In A. Lieberman and L. Miller (Eds.), *Teachers caught in the action* (pp. 46–60). New York, NY: Teachers College Press.

Cooperative Children's Book Center at the University of Wisconsin-Madison. (n.d). *Children's books by and about people of color published in the United States: Statistics gathered by the Cooperative Children's Book center, School of Education, University of Wisconsin-Madison.* Retrieved October 18, 2008, from http://www.education.wisc.edu/ccbc/books/pcstats.htm

DeNicolo, C., & Fránquiz, M. (2006). "Do I have to say it?" Critical encounters with multicultural children's literature. *Language Arts, 84*(2), 157–170.

Díaz, J. (2008, April). Talk presented at Haverford College, Haverford, PA.

Dominus, S. (2008, April 11). A place of neighborhood vitality may be in budget cutter's sights. *New York, NY Times,* pp. B1, B4.

Dyson, A. H. (1993). *Social worlds of children learning to write in an urban primary school.* New York, NY: Teachers College Press.

Dyson, A. H. (2003). *The Brothers and Sisters learn to read and write: Popular literacies in childhood and school cultures.* New York, NY: Teachers College Press.

Enciso, P. E. (1997). Negotiating the meaning of difference: Talking back to multicultural literature. In T. Roger & A. O. Soter (Eds.), *Reading across cultures: Teaching literature in a diverse society* (pp. 13–41). New York, NY: Teachers College Press and Urbana, IL: National Council of Teachers of English.

Goodman, A. (Interviewer), Lee, S. (Interviewee), & Stew (Interviewee). (2008, July 17). *Spike Lee to film Tony-award winning musical 'Passing Strange' as show comes to a close on Broadway* [Interview transcript]. Retrieved October 18, 2008, from http://www.democracynow.org/2008/7/17/spike_lee_to_film_tony_award

Guerra, J. (2008). Cultivating transcultural citizenship: A writing across communities model. *Language Arts, 85*(4), 296–304.

Gutiérrez, K., & Orellana, M. F. (2006). The 'problem' of English Learners: Constructing genres of difference. *Research in the Teaching of English, 40*(4), 502–507.

Gutiérrez, K., Baquedano-López, P., & Turner, M. (1997). Putting language back into language arts: When the radical middle meets the third space. *Language Arts, 74*(5), 368–378.

Gutiérrez, K., Rymes, B., & Larson, J. (1995). Script, counterscript, and underlife in the classroom: James Brown versus Brown v. Board of Education. *Harvard Educational Review, 54*(3), 445–471.

Hannaham, J. (2008, June 11). Strange but true. *Salon*. Retrieved October 18, 2008, from http://www.salon.com/ent/feature/2008/06/11/stew/index.html

Harste, J. (1992). Inquiry-based instruction. *Primary Voices, 1*(1), 3–8.

Harvey, D. (1990). *The condition of postmodernity: An enquiry into the origins of cultural change*. Cambridge, MA: Blackwell.

Hirsch, E. (1997). The art of poetry (1986). In R. Hamner, R. (Ed.), *Critical perspectives on Derek Walcott* (pp. 65–83). Boulder, CO: Lynne Rienner.

Landt, S. (2006). Multicultural literature and young adolescents: A kaleidoscope of opportunity. *Journal of Adolescent Literacy, 49*(8), 690–697.

Lorde, A. (1984). My words will be there. In M. Evans (Ed.), *Black women writers, 1950–1980: A critical evaluation* (pp. xx–xx). New York, NY: Anchor.

McNair, J. C. (2008). The representation of authors and illustrators of color in school-based book clubs. *Language Arts, 85*(3), 193–201.

Medina, C. L. (2006). Identity and imagination of immigrant children: Creating common place locations in literary interpretation. In J. Jasinski-Schneider, T. P. Crumpler, & T. Rogers (Eds.), *Process drama and multiple literacies: Addressing social, cultural and ethical issues* (pp. 53–69). Portsmouth, NH: Heinemann.

Mohanty, S. (1997). *Literary theory and the claims of history: Postmodernism, objectivity, multicultural politics*. Ithaca, NY: Cornell University Press.

Mohanty, S. (1989). Us and them: On the philosophical basis of political criticism. *Yale Journal of Criticism, 2*(2), 1–31.

Moya, P. (2000). Postmodernism, "realism," and the politics of identity. In P. Moya & M. Hames-Garcia (Eds.), *Reclaiming identity: Realist theory and the predicament of postmodernism* (pp. 67–101). Berkeley: University of California Press.

Moya, P., & Saldívar, R. (2003). Fictions of the trans-American imaginary. *Modern Fiction Studies, 49*(1), 1–18.

Nussbaum, M. (1996). *For love of country: Debating the limits of patriotism*. Boston, MA: Beacon Press.

Nussbaum, M. (2008). Toward a globally sensitive patriotism. *Daedalus: Journal of the American Academy of Arts & Sciences, 137*(3), 78–93.

O'Connor, M. (2008, January). *Multicultural populations*. Presentation retrieved on April 25, 2008, from http://jaguar.intrapoint.no/bibliotekforeningen/site/flerspraklig/downloadfile.php?i=1679091c5a880faf6fb5e6087eb1b2dc

Office of the State Deputy Comptroller for the City of New York, NY. (2000). *Queens: An economic review*. (Report 11-2000). Albany, NY.

Ogbu, J., & Simmons, H. D. (1998). Voluntary and involuntary minorities: A cultural-ecological theory of school performance with some implications for education. *Anthropology and Education Quarterly, 29*(2), 155–188.

Ramazani, J. (2001). *Hybrid muse: Postcolonial poetry in English*. Chicago, IL: University of Chicago Press.

Rizal, J. (1884). Brindis speech (E. Medina, Trans.). Retrieved February 14, 2010, from http://www.bukisa.com/articles/33984_the-brindis

Serafini, F. (2004). *Lessons in comprehension: Explicit instruction in the reading workshop*. Portsmouth, NH: Heinemann.

Tan, S. (n.d.). *Picturebooks*. Retrieved April 6, 2008, from http://www.shauntan.net/books.html

Tan, S. (2001, July). *Picturebooks: Who are they for?* Paper presented at the Joint National Conference of the Australian Association for the Teaching of English and the Australian Literary Educator's Association. Hobart, Tasmania, Australia. Retrieved February 15, 2010, from http://www.shauntan.net/images/whypicbooks.pdf

Part 2

THE BOOK

In 1968, John Rowe Townsend (1969) made a now famous distinction between "book people" and "child people" (p. 407) that has haunted the field of children's and young adult literary criticism ever since. "Book people," he argues, are authors, publishers, and critics, while "child people" are teachers and parents, with librarians falling somewhere in between. In this volume, we have consciously attempted to abrogate the distinction; our goal, as we note in the preface, is to encourage crosstalk among people who study children's texts in their various disciplines and from their necessarily focused perspectives—after all, without focus, we have a hard time seeing anything clearly.

However, it is clear that Townsend's binary is still operative in the way we go about our work. This is perhaps most evident in the different kinds of analyses that emerge from Departments of English versus Colleges of Education. Literary scholars tend not to care all that much about issues of engagement, which is the focus of the first section of this *Handbook*, and only in certain ways about access, which is the focus of the third section. Instead, they look at texts, crafting their analyses from a range of theoretical perspectives and "isms" that are sometimes very relevant, even crucial, to the concerns of educators and parents, and sometimes only relevant to other scholars who map literary and cultural trends.

Textual critics tend to have preferred emphases when it comes to working with literature. Some focus on what might broadly be called textuality. These critics look at the way language and images are shaped into story; they map genre qualities and distinctions, and focus on the special features of literary language. Since the 1970s, these critics have paid particular attention to the ways in which language communicates cultural value, and how stories and character types participate in the naturalization of common sense and perpetuate belief systems on conscious and unconscious levels. Often, these critics concern themselves with subtextual elements—story patterns and ideological assumptions that never quite announce themselves, but seep into the reading experience nonetheless.

In this emphasis, critics whose main concern is textuality are closely aligned with those who focus on subjectivity, which is a broad category that includes identity, both of the author and the reader. Traditional single-author studies fall into this category, but so too do ethnicity studies, transactional criticism, and psychoanalytic interpretations that seem to focus on the effects of books on their child readers. But the kind of focus on the reader practiced by literary critics does not entirely bridge the gap between book people and child people. Instead, literary critics who focus on subjectivity are more concerned with representations of certain identity markers such as ethnicity or gender, subject positions offered to the readers by literary mode or point of view, and characteristics of implied readers. Sussing out authorial intention is currently out of favor in English departments, having been replaced with a notion argued by Roland Barthes (1967) among others that a text is incomplete until it is read. But the readers that literary critics care about are those who are imagined or idealized through the text, rather than those who actually pick up the book. Moreover, these readers are cultural amalgams rather than individuals, so that even the dynamism proposed by critics who imagine a child reader in the Barthesian sense of one who completes the reading is not grounded in an ethnographic experience of an actual child interacting with a book.

A third category of critics who focus on the texts

themselves are the literary and cultural historians. Their concern is how a genre or type of literature has developed and changed over time, and what conditions from the culture at large have contributed to those changes. As both a product of culture and a visionary artistic form, literature both reflects the conditions of the time in which it is produced, and also acts as an agent of cultural change and development. General agreement among critics regarding the constructedness of the category of childhood complicates our understanding of children's literature over time because the genre must be defined at the intersection of authorial and publishing intention and actual readership. The work of literary historians is crucial to other kinds of textual critics because it sets their understandings of textuality and subjectivity into more refined contexts.

So, while these book people may have little interaction with either children themselves or their child people counterparts in other disciplines, they still find themselves with plenty to do. Generally speaking, literary critics of children's literature do all of the same kinds of work that literary critics of, say, Victorian literature or British Romanticism do, and they use the same tools with which to do it. This has been a hard-won battle in academic circles. Townsend laments in 1968 that, in Britain at least, "[n]o university English department will look at [children's literature]" (p. 417). But by 1972, the Children's Literature Association had formed in the United States, and now we have robust undergraduate and graduate programs in English departments in many countries, with people coming from all over the world to study in these programs. At Illinois State University alone, for instance, graduate students from Belgium, Cyprus, Indonesia, Japan, Nepal, South Korea, Taiwan, Tanzania, Thailand, Venezuela, and Zimbabwe have taken their degrees and returned to their home countries to expand offerings there. Strong children's literature graduate programs flourish at Eastern Michigan, Hollins University, Kansas State, Roehampton University, San Diego State, Simmons College, University of Cambridge, University of Florida, University of Pittsburgh, and University of Winnipeg. Professional organizations promote ever more sophisticated scholarship, and there are a number of widely respected international journals that will publish it. Textual studies in children's literature is a going concern.

What may be distinctive about textual studies in children's literature, however, is an underlying anxiety not shared by other kinds of literary studies. Perry Nodelman's (2008) *The Hidden Adult* focuses on the chronic anxiety that there is a shadow text present in children's books that seeks to manipulate its vulnerable readers. Indeed, he argues that children's literature ultimately teaches readers to "accept your dependence on wiser and more careful adults and their right to control your environment and manipulate your thinking for your own good" (p. 35). Literary critics ostensibly hate this kind of prescriptive imposition; they analyze, and often evaluate on the basis of that analysis, but they see it as a flaw to argue by assertion or rhetorical manipulation. Ostensibly. Indeed their efforts are to expose this sort of manipulation so that child readers won't be vulnerable to it, but that indicates precisely a deep-seated fear that they will. What is different about children's literature may in fact be the presence of a hidden adult, but we would argue that what is distinctive about children's literature criticism is the presence of a hidden child. Despite its best efforts to escape the reader and focus purely on the literature as literature, there is almost always a touch of moralism or at least worry on behalf of a child latent in the criticism. Various critics might see this child as a Romantic innocent, a subversive sneak, a neutral sort of developmental project, or a noble (or not so noble) wild thing, but there is always a distinct attitude toward children that guides the interpretation of the text.

There are, then, multiple ironies in the critical response to a children's literature that strives "to keep children statically and safely childlike by working to preserve their ignorance of the knowledge the adults possess" (p. 54). The work of textual critics is to expose these kind of ideological blinders, but not only are they not writing their critical work for children, they are also not actively trying to communicate with educators or librarians or parents who might work with children, either. And this is the gap that we would like to see bridged: for book people to acknowledge the unconscious child for whom they write, and for child people to approach what the book people have to say with the view that texts operate on levels that children may not be able to articulate, but that are transforming them all the same.

Academic References

Barthes, R. (1967). The death of the author. *Aspen, 5+6*. Retrieved June 22, 2010, from http://www.ubu.com/aspen/aspen5and6/threeEssays.html#barthes

Nodelman, P. (2008). *The hidden adult*. Baltimore, MD: Johns Hopkins University Press.

Townsend, J. R. (1969). The present state of English children's literature. In S. Egoff, G. T. Stubbs, & L. F. Ashley (Eds.), *Only connect: Readings on children's literature* (pp. 407–418). Toronto, Ontario: Oxford University Press. (Original work published 1968)

13

History of Children's and Young Adult Literature

Deborah Stevenson

University of Illinois, Urbana-Champaign

Literary histories, like literary theories, begin with a particular perspective. Ideological conceptions of what constitutes literature, material conditions, and prior histories are among the forces that shape how one writes the history of a particular genre. Deborah Stevenson walks readers through the considerations necessary for forming and critiquing a history of children's and young adult literature before embarking on her own meta-reflective rendering of how literature for youth evolved from classical times to the advent of modern children's literature. Personal perspective returns as Lois Lowry reminds us that we each have our own history of the literature that drew us in as readers, regardless of what the literary historians say we should have paid attention to.

No genre history is simple and objective. Literary historians always face decisions about what's worth noting and why, and what gets left out and why, and previous histories either mark their paths or provide a view they wish to counter. So it has been with children's literature, a genre blessed—or cursed—with complicated audience issues and a handful of magnetic and influential literary historians. This chapter will therefore first explore the issues that have influenced the literary history/ies of the genre, and then proceed to an historical overview, from classical times through the 19th century and to the dawn of modern children's literature, that acknowledges the forces behind the perceived significance of the titles and authors chronicled. I rely largely upon the histories that have been taught, quoted, argued with, and assigned with the greatest frequency over the years, narrative works that allow authors' opinions and contexts full rein for expression. To these I add material from works that are more specialist, or more recent, but nonetheless possess sufficient significance either in their scholarship or their impact to provide a solid source of illumination. While this exploration touches on various kinds of children's literature, from folktales to poetry to picture books, nonfiction to novels, it's the fictional prose narratives that receive the main focus; they have largely been the popular ambassadors of children's literature and the primary subject of the genre's historians, and as such they provide the most fruitful site for historiography.

Complications in Crafting a Genre History

The Issue of Definition

The genre's primary challenge is categorization. To define children's literature we need, at bare minimum, to define a child and to define literature, and then to define what combination of their meeting counts as the genre.

Defining children isn't always as simple as it would seem. Some materials aimed predominantly at young readers, such as the 18th century's novels, target people we'd now consider fully adult, and the 20th century's creation of the young adult genre expanded the categories of non-adult readers. Ultimately, though, historians of the literature tend to agree fairly amicably on the definition of a child. More significant, however, is the question of which children? Literate children have often been a minority; even among them, many have had neither money with which to buy books, other opportunities to access them, especially in the pre-library days, nor the school or the leisure time in which to read them. The tidbits of incidental information, personal recollection, or historical documents that offer us snapshots of child readership confirm the fact that until quite recently, the "children" in "children's literature" have been a privileged subset of a much larger group. Defining "literature" is even more complicated. Does the term mean only finely written material, or can texts better known for their popularity than their writing quality count as well? Can literature be nonfiction, informational, even institutionally educational, or must it be a pure and pleasurable continuous narrative?

Defining "children's literature" is most complicated of all, and the openings of genre histories invariably contain a definition—combined with a defense of exceptions to the definition. While this chapter will go on to explore those complexities in more depth, let's assume a highly imperfect working definition of *books associated with children and important in their reading history.*

Arguably the most important historian of children's literature, F. J. Harvey Darton (1932/1982), opens his masterwork *Children's Books in England* with this definition of children's books: "printed works produced ostensibly to give children spontaneous pleasure, and not primarily to teach them, nor solely to make them good, nor to keep them *profitably* quiet" (p. 1, italics Darton). One of his successors, Percy Muir (1954), similarly states that his history is "mainly concerned with books produced for children's entertainment" (p. 217), while E. M. Field (1891), who assessed the genre before either of them, discussed the challenge of keeping her work a literary history and not an educational one as well. Darton (1932/1982) in his preface describes children's literature as "the scene of a battle between instruction and amusement, between restraint and freedom, between hesitant morality and spontaneous happiness" (p. vii), and that polarization becomes a largely unchallenged tenet of the literature, providing the spectrum that underpins nearly every genre history prior to the 21st century.

The Issue of Didacticism

The result is that many things children have read don't meet all historians' standards for children's literature. Historic books designed for use in schooling or lessons, to teach children writing or philosophy or comportment, have clear descendents in contemporary textbooks rather than the trade books one finds in bookstores or libraries, and they are thus omitted from histories with enjoyment-based definitions of children's literature. One could argue that that's fair enough—the history of educational literature could well be considered a separate topic, and explorations of contemporary children's literature don't focus on textbooks either. Yet, the division between recreation and education is not always crystal clear, especially when we're looking back at eras when schooling and schoolbooks look very different, and such an omission would suggest that children prior to the 18th century did much less reading than they actually did. As a result, a convention seems to have tacitly arisen: Educational materials merit inclusion in places and times when few other books are published for children, only to lose that consideration after the 18th century when a literature develops that's expressly geared for children's pleasure.

Even when it's not explicitly acknowledged, the convention of including some but not all educational material is at least fairly easily discernible and relatively understandable—it maps reasonably well onto treatment of current children's books (you don't find the textbooks shelved with the Newbery winners), and the educational texts make a pretty massive subject in their own right. The issue becomes much cloudier when we start looking at scholars' treatment of moral didacticism, at children's literature that's written to "make them good" (Darton, 1932/1982, p. 1). The literary historians' stated prioritization of pleasure reading would suggest marginalizing or ignoring such texts, and sometimes they do; historians sometimes dispose of the discussion by discussing the theme generally rather than individual titles specifically, or, as Cornelia Meigs (1953) does with martyr tales, by obviously shuddering and holding their noses as they write, lest readers think their documentation indicated approval.

Ultimately, though, the devaluing of morally aimed children's literature is cheating; it requires a denial not only of children's literature past but children's literature present. Didacticism remains a strong element of contemporary children's books ostensibly designed for pleasure (Dr. Seuss, for instance, is one of the most unflaggingly moralistic authors in children's literature history), and children's literature remains an important instrument of education; even the library science advocacy for reading often boils down to encouraging children to find pleasure in books so that they may progress better in their education. French academician Paul Hazard (1944), author of one of the 20th century's most influential championings of children's literature, spoke passionately about the value of morality: "I like books that contain a profound morality…. I like books that set in action truths worthy of lasting forever, and of inspiring one's whole inner life…. I like books that have the integrity to perpetuate their own faith in truth and justice" (pp. 44–45). Nor is this inclination limited entirely to children's literature: The most admired works for adults remain those that bring readers a greater understanding of ourselves or of the world.

In general use, "didacticism" has become a synonym for overt preachiness of the kind that imbued much of children's literature prior to the 20th century. To some extent the contemporary resistance to the notion of didacticism is a reaction to specific literature, realistic stories by writers such as Maria Edgeworth and lesser imitators that taught children clear, unambiguous lessons in realistic situations (it's worth noting that there's still more sensitivity to preachiness in realistic literature than in fantasy, despite the latter's inclination to be even more overtly moralistic). The real objection, therefore, isn't so much to books that educate as it is to books that educate in an old-fashioned way. In contemporary literature, morality is rather a Goldilocks problem, avoiding too much (and being like literature of the past) and too little (and being too lightweight) to get it *juuust* right. When children's literature scholars and practitioners claim to reject texts that teach, what we actually reject is writing that gets *caught* at teaching. As a result, accounts that devalue the didactic falsify the literature's history and create a myth about the present. We've never been in it just for the fun.

The Issue of Audience

Children have never been as concerned as scholars with definitions, and they've always complicated the categorization of children's literature by happily reading books written for adult audiences. Historians don't generally consider a title to be children's literature merely because a child has read it, but they must decide how to approach "crossover books," those works that begin as titles for adults and then become the reading matter of children. Classics such as Swift's (1726) *Gulliver's Travels* and Defoe's (1719) *Robinson Crusoe* figure prominently in the history of children's reading, but do they count as children's literature if their intended audience wasn't children? Most historians feel obliged to include them: Darton (1932/1982), for example, argues simply that any picture of children's literature would be incomplete if it omitted such works on a technicality; he notes, in case justification is required (which he clearly believes it isn't), that these works spawned editions clearly intended for a child audience soon after they were published, which indicates a publisher awareness of the child audience for the original title. Such a crossover can even happen to an entire kind of narrative, as it has with folklore, once the domain of adults, now more commonly associated with children. These works are not just adult texts that have become popular with children, these are adult books that become so predominantly the reading fodder of children that they are perceived by adults as children's literature.

It's worth noting two significant aspects of such texts'

treatment: Their inclusion is felt to be necessary, and their inclusion is felt to need defending. It's interesting that Darton and his ilk would rather include texts that don't fit their initial definition (books designed for children to read for pleasure) than change their definition—there is something so pervasive about that essential belief of children's literature as designed for children, not adults, and for pleasure, not education, that historians are resistant to finding a definition that encompasses the materials they actually view as important. The result is an implication that the for-children-and-for-pleasure condition is actually the genre's goal and pinnacle of achievement rather than its actual membership requirement, despite initial claims to the contrary.

The Issue of Practicality

It's also fascinating to consider how much simple practical issues, not just literary ones, can affect literary history. It's difficult to determine how many children could read at any given time; overall estimates generally, until recently, focused on adults, and "literacy rate" is often an ill-defined term that can mean as little as the ability to sign one's name. It's therefore impossible to ascertain exactly how many children in a given period would be able to read non-scholarly books even if they had access to them. While oral materials could be transmitted during work activities, pleasure readers need to have the leisure in which to read, not a situation all groups or ages of people could historically count on as we witnessed in Arizpe and Styles's opening *Handbook* chapter on reading in the home. Since such leisure time often occurs after dark, readers need light sources, not always easy to obtain in households with no electricity and little budget for candles. Readers also need access to books, which means having funds to afford them (or family with same), having access to a vendor, or having access to somebody or some institution from which they can borrow materials. Many of us can take these conditions for granted in the contemporary industrialized world, but children's literature began back when such opportunities were luxuries, when books were hand-copied and hand-carried. The development of the printing press, which allowed for mechanical and therefore considerably cheaper reproduction of a work, is therefore an important watershed for children's literature as well as for adult literature, and the printing press's English pioneer, William Caxton, thus earns a place in children's literature history for chroniclers such as Darton (1932/1982), Smith (1937/1980), and Thwaite (1972). National infrastructure affects readership: The building of roads and canals, and, much later, the development of the railroads, eased books' ability to penetrate areas beyond major cities in numbers above those that a roving peddler could carry in his pack. The absence of copyright laws or the ability to successfully apply them can allow for much lucrative imitation: Copyright piracy allowed for the free reprinting of successful British material in the United States, until

20th-century crackdowns on intellectual property cut into the profitability of such unauthorized borrowing.

And scholars can only document reading of which they have record, which is why early books and early references to children's readings, whether they be Roger Ascham's (1570) Tudor warnings against what he considered mischievous literature (thus indicating that there was enough of the stuff to raise his concern) or Richard Steele's (1709) early 18th-century celebration of his god-children's reading tastes, are pure gold to historians. Unfortunately, children's reading hasn't always been considered worthy of discussion by adults, so early mentions are few and far between. Even more frustratingly, scholars are severely limited in their primary material when it comes to early children's reading. Books in general are fragile things, and children's books are notoriously prone to destruction; books regularly get loved to death, or at least loved out of collectability. Ironically, better survival rates may be obtained by books considered "too nice" to be regularly handled by children; early volumes with color illustrations by landmark artists such as Arthur Rackham, Kay Nielsen, and Edmund Dulac, for instance, were too pricey for regular mauling by sticky little hands. Conversely, cheaply produced and more widely disseminated items such as chapbooks fell apart with fewer readings, and the cheapness that brought them within children's independent reach meant greater wear on the individual copies, leaving scholars of later centuries with less material to study. As a result, historians may be missing considerable amounts of literary history; Darton (1932/1982) even posits the existence of nearly a whole genre of early children's books that have since been lost to scholars save in its undetected influence on orally transmitted narrative or on later works.

The Issue of Human Nature

It's also important to remember that literary historians are only human, and they bring their own subjectivity and biases, so that their judgments of historical significance are never objectively factual. Literary history is influenced by historians' views of the current literature and of class, by historians' field of study and home country, and by the needs of those who disseminate that history. Early historians of the literature were mostly male and mostly from the publishing industry, and for many decades publishers, librarians, and educators, each bringing the slant of their own discipline, chronicled the literature. Later in the 20th century academic literature scholars in English departments and elsewhere dove in, bringing their own approach to their explorations. We're even influenced by the simple fact that we study children's literature, since we benefit from its existence and thus from its significance. Views of the literature can be affected by the fortunate existence of unofficial publicists (one of Newbery's first and most admiring biographers, Charles Welsh (1885), was a publisher in a firm that directly descended from Newbery's, so Newbery's increased profile

would redound to Welsh's benefit) or by dominant scholars. Brian Alderson (Darton, 1982) leaves a considerable mark through being the editor of the most available version of Darton's seminal history and in his translation/adaptation of Bettina Hürlimann's (1968) classic German-language account of European children's literature, *Three Centuries of Children's Books in Europe*.

While we can't avoid influence, we can attempt to be aware of our biases. Even this idea, however, is more popular in our time than previously, and some literary historians have clearly been blind to their own inclinations. One of the most difficult biases to overcome is what one might term "presentism," the tendency to view the present day as the norm. Some historians write as if present-day literature weren't simply the genre's current state but the goal the genre had been working towards, and they judge past titles on the basis of their resemblance to current works. Even figures of speech can reveal such tacit assumptions of an underlying purpose and direction, as when Cornelia Meigs (1953) characterizes the literature as a plant that has finally, at the time of her writing, grown into a beautiful tree, or when Paul Hazard (1944) chides the past when its "juvenile literature had gone astray" (p. 34).

Writers with a presentist bias sometimes even suggest that children with no contemporary-style reading had essentially nothing to read at all. Hazard, for instance, draws a dramatic picture of a world where adults "were satisfied to let a few crumbs—books of piety, of manners—fall from the upper tables" and where children had to "beg for tales from their nurses, from the servants, the kitchen folk, the common people" (p. 6), while other historians describe the time before the 18th century as "prehistory." Similarly, present-day writers can find it difficult to accept that children might have found pleasure in what brings them only boredom or revulsion. But refusing to acknowledge the different tastes of historical readers, including children, misleadingly skews the literary history we write. The result are histories that imply that children frustratedly gnawed at hand-me-down adult books and religious texts, sulking at the injustice of living before Captain Underpants and paging through Puritan tales of martyrdom in the disappointed hope that they would be as good as Gossip Girls. Whether we like these children's books or not, many of their young readers clearly did, and they and the literature deserve to have such tastes honestly recorded.

Fortunately, quite a few historians consider historical literature within its time rather than in contrast to their own. These writers range from the 19th-century chronicler Mrs. Field (1891), who thoughtfully notes that "on the whole ... in these days, when books were scarce and costly, a great deal was done for the young and ignorant, all drawbacks considered" (p. 35) to Elva Smith (1980), Percy Muir (1954) to F. J. Harvey Darton (1932/1982), all noting the extensive practice of children's reading well before the mid-18th century. Darton also explicitly argues that children of previous eras quite likely enjoyed many works that contemporary readers wouldn't and contemporary scholars clearly don't. In *Behold the Child: American Children and Their Books, 1621–1922*, Gillian Avery (1995) takes up that notion and explores it with cogent thoroughness on behalf of the much-derided Puritan author James Janeway (1671), whose stories of martyred Christian children horrify several 20th-century literary historians but were immensely popular in his day, and she points out the seductive centrality of the children in these stories and their literary descendents in subsequent literature. Ultimately, the 18th century's importance in the history of children's literature and publishing doesn't mean that previous eras were starving for reading matter.

It's also important to note that different kinds of books can fare differently with historians, as with contemporary children's literature practitioners. On the one hand, nonfiction for children doesn't tend to seize adult imagination in the same way fiction and picture books do, whether we're talking about adults giving awards to contemporary children's books or adults writing about children's books of the past. On the other hand, some reading material is treated as too slight, rather than not slight enough. Even now, we in the book field still argue about the merits of mass market books (usually paperbacks, often series books, as noted in Chapter 14 of this volume), and such titles are silently excluded from much award consideration (Children's Choice awards, which allow young readers to choose their favorites from a group of books pre-selected by adults, are excellent examples of such a deliberate and unacknowledged slant). Our histories of the genre have displayed a similar bias. Some writers aren't prepared to consider popular materials literature at all: Thwaite (1972), for instance, refers to broadsheets, inexpensively printed and widely available, as "trash" (p. 16) and considers publishers of inexpensive marvels and gossip "less reputable" (p. 39). Yet, several authors either overlook their reservations about content or lack such reservations, with Darton (1932/1982) noting that the chapbook "contained all the popular literature of four centuries" (though he, a respectable trade publisher himself, does term the more cheaply produced popular genre "a rude and degenerate form" [p. 81]). Muir (1954) attested to the "abundant evidence of the buying and reading of these cheap little books [chapbooks] by children" (p. 27), and even early historian Field (1891) chronicled the popular as a key part of children's reading in her "Books from the Conquest to Caxton" chapter. As noted earlier, survival of material is important to its later understanding; such inexpensively produced reading as chapbooks and broadsheets fall apart more readily, and their very inexpensiveness can often lead to less careful treatment. Moreover, literary histories tend to focus on identifiable and individual texts, and materials such as chapbooks make their effect en masse, like books of Garfield cartoons (e.g., Davis, 1980) or trivia compilations such as Uncle John's Bathroom Reader (e.g., Bathroom Readers' Institute, 1988).

They may not have been improving works or literature written with great care for style or eloquence—they were made to sell, and sell they did. But young people, like adults, enjoy popular literature and media; such material is often their first or main source of classic narratives, and even when it's not, it can constitute an important and significant portion of their reading. Just as children now (and, it's important to acknowledge, adults as well) read paperbacks and chick lit and magazines and fluff, so too did children of past eras eagerly devour cheaply produced tales of popular heroes such as Robin Hood and Dick Whittington. If we focus only on the officially authored, singly produced titles, we again draw a false picture of the historical reading practices of children.

As if there weren't enough influences shaping what we call "history" already, the very practical needs of the scholarly historians can influence the histories they create. Ultimately, we declare beginnings in literature not because it must have had a specific starting point but because they're convenient, allowing scholars and students to pick people and titles out of a considerable mass of past books. The desire to counterbalance previous material, offer original claims, or even, frankly, to make a flashy argument that will establish an individual's professional standing can lead to overemphasis of less significant material; more notable in literary history, however, is the tendency toward self-replication. Literary historians generally build on extant work, so a single individual's view of importance can affect genre histories for years to come. Every work that singles out John Newbery, the mid-18th-century London publisher often considered the originator of children's literature, ensures the continuation of his status and expands the number of people who will learn his primacy as a fact.

The simpler and more compact the overview, the more likely it is to repeat the high points of the best known histories—potted histories in textbooks for college and graduate students, for instance, still tend to present Newbery as a lonely innovator, despite the fact that more in-depth critical discussion treats him very differently. Such overviews probably reach the largest audiences of any reading about children's literature, and they're likely to be the most conservative of all, often being simply reprinted from edition to edition without reflecting the critical changes to the view of the literature's history taking place outside of their publication.

Classrooms are another fruitful place to find scholarly convenience at work. Faced with the challenge of reducing part or all of a genre into twelve weeks of reading, professors must choose texts so as to cover as much ground as possible. It's therefore an advantage to assign material that can provide connection points to thematic as well as chronological topics, to favor titles that offer easy stepping off points for discussion of publishing, cultural movements, adult literature, or ways to connect to contemporary works. A title's significance in the classroom can therefore be greater than its significance in its own time, especially since students will infer a text's importance from its inclusion in their course. Even simple availability will determine a text's use in a class, since a text in print is going to be taught in more classes than one that isn't—another self-sustaining situation, since in-print works sell, and thus are likelier to stay in print.

It's also worth admitting that taste plays a role here, and that the affections of scholars are as variable as anybody else's; forced to choose between two books that offer similar opportunities of discussion and elaboration, we'll often choose the one we simply prefer, leaving generations of students and their following students believing that our selected book is more significant than the omitted text. Additionally, teaching anthologies, which are hotly contested markers of canonical significance in other genres, have in the last few years become available for children's literature, so the *Norton Anthology of Children's Literature* (Zipes, 2005) may come to affect the picture of children's literature much as other Norton anthologies have done for their genres.

Toward a History, Then

Literature from the Classical Era to Gutenberg

So far, our earliest indications of children's reading date to the classical era, wherein records suggest that young people were largely reading adult texts or adaptations thereof, and this is the era least explored by historians of children's literature. The Roman rhetorician Quintilian, in the 1st century CE, argued for the importance of children's literary education, advocating the reading of Homer, classic drama, and the fables of Aesop in Greek as well as the Latin works of notables such as Virgil and Horace. St. Augustine, musing on his childhood reading in the 4th century, recalls a similar curriculum, not wholly with delight. Historian Seth Lerer (2008) notes a 3rd century CE text, inscribed on a wooden tablet, wherein a teacher has written out a portion of the *Iliad* in very large print for his young students; a fragment of papyrus text for the same era offers an illustrated and simplified account of Hercules's adventures, probably a nice break from denser material.

Schoolbooks, usually in Latin, often remaining the possession of the schoolmaster rather than the child, were still likely the only reading material for European and English children for some centuries. The 4th-century grammarian Donatus became a schoolroom standard, with a brand recognition akin to Roget's thesaurus or Webster's dictionary that lasted well into the next millennium. The monk Aelfric, one of the great teachers of his era, offered at the beginning of the 11th century an educational Latin dialogue (amended to include an Anglo-Saxon translation) between master and pupils, which gives a glimpse into the teacher-student relationship as well as the students' reading matter. (Monastery schools were the predominant institutions of

learning for young boys; nuns also taught, to mixed groups of girls and boys as well as girls on their own.)

A book children were likelier to pick up on their own was the *Gesta Romanorum* (Acts of the Romans), a Latin compilation of tales that probably first appeared around 1300. The title is misleading, since it encompassed material from all over—Greek, European, and Asian legendry in addition to Roman—and its accounts became fodder for writers from Chaucer to Shakespeare. Its contents varied from edition to edition, as transcribers and, later, printers would add or subtract material to suit their needs or tastes. Though it ostensibly had a moral goal, it was the lively stories that kept this compilation in use for centuries and led children to it despite its being officially an adult work. The printing press gave its circulation an additional boost, and the text appeared in German, French, and English in the 15th and 16th centuries, flourishing in multiple editions well into the 18th century.

Otherwise, reading for children was still largely educational in nature, even if their subjects weren't academic. In the 15th century, books of courtesy, guiding young gentlemen in the ways of gentility, became prominent, and texts such as *Stans Puer ad Mensam* (Table Manners for Children), first appearing in English in 1479, and *The Babees' Book* (ca. 1475), gave stern, often rhymed, advice about comportment in the face of one's elders and betters.

Early Print to the Puritans

Literature changed radically in the mid-15th century with the introduction of the mechanical printing press by Johann Gutenberg, a technology brought to England by William Caxton in 1476. The press enabled the mass production and mass ownership of books, and thus the publishing industry itself. Caxton printed what may be the oldest material still available to children today, *Aesop's Fables,* in 1484, translating from a French edition. While the fables were valued for their ability to teach reading, they were clearly entertaining as well as educational, and the endless numbers of subsequent editions testify to their enduring popularity. Though Caxton's edition wasn't explicitly aimed at children, it's clear that Aesop was read by the young as well as the old; inscriptions on extant editions reveal child ownership. The great educator John Locke (1693) recommends Aesop as the pinnacle of useful and entertaining literature, and editions designed for students and other children appear as early as the 17th century.

Fables in general and Aesop in particular contribute one of the elements still beloved in children's literature today: the anthropomorphized animal. Caxton turned to a very different piece of traditional lore in 1485 with his printing of Sir Thomas Malory's *Le Morte d'Arthur,* the only one of his printings that rivals his Aesop for long popularity with youth. This classic romance of stirring chivalric adventures was sufficiently enjoyed by young readers that Roger Ascham (1570), schoolmaster to the Tudors, complained in the 16th century of its bad influence on children.

Aside from fables and romances, children in the 15th and 16th centuries read their reading primers and their horn books (a small sheet, containing the alphabet and a few other details, often religious verses, printed on paper that was affixed to a wooden backing and protectively covered by a flat, clear piece of horn) and alphabets, which were often religious in their inspiration. Inarguably a religious work was John Foxe's (1563) *Actes and Monuments of These Latter Perilous Times Touching Matters of the Church*, known familiarly as Foxe's *Book of Martyrs*. This work was a lengthy collection of stories of Protestant martyrs, filled with vivid dialogue and dramatic, gory executions; save for its considerable length, it probably would translate effectively into a graphic-novel format. As with most books published for adults, it's difficult to ascertain when it gained a young readership as well, but one author was recommending it as ideal youthful reading a century later, and the early 19th century saw an official adaptation for children (at least one lucky student received a copy as a school prize in 1900, so enduring has its reputation been). Outside of the Bible, this was the single most approved text for Anglophone Protestant children until James Janeway (1671) brought martyrdom directly to child readers a century later.

Not all the significant works of the 17th century were religious in nature, however; one of the era's most important contributions was *Orbis Pictus* (Comenius, 1658, first English edition 1659), a wonderfully encyclopedic guide to myriad aspects of the world in Latin and the vernacular, illustrated with helpful woodcut diagrams. Authored by Jan Amos Komensky, usually Latinized to Johannes Amos Comenius, it sold well in European languages and in English, and it remained available and periodically reprinted for two centuries. Bettina Hürlimann (1968) devotes a chapter to Comenius and his legacy, specifically noting the *Orbis Pictus* as a watershed moment, the inception of "children's books as objects of pleasure" (p. 246) While this statement, like all absolutes about children's literature, probably requires some fudging, it seems likely that this was the first popular secular book that pleased young children as the author intended, a fairly momentous development. With its combination of text and pictures to convey information, it's classified both by French critic Isabelle Jan (1974) and American critic Margaret Hodges (see Smith, 1980) as the first picture book for children, and it's also the first big informational book for children. It's thus the forerunner of a large segment of subsequent children's literature.

The case of Comenius is revealing, because the *Orbis Pictus* is a book for which scholars tend to feel real fondness—it still exerts a genuine fascination nearly four centuries later, with its spreads categorizing items with the same matter-of-fact thoroughness as contemporary texts such as the *Facts on File Visual Dictionary* (Corbeil, 1986)—and Comenius himself is an engaging and sympathetic man, receiving in Hürlimann's (1968) book the sort of personal encomium usually reserved for John Newbery, star of many literary histories. The National Council of Teachers of English has an important award named for the Orbis Pictus, a historical honor that usually both indicates and consolidates an honoree's historical position. Why, then, do many literary historians rush past him to reach the 18th century's literary productions?

There are two main reasons. Though continental historians such as Hürlimann note his influence on subsequent generations, writers describing English literary history tend to see him as an uncle rather than a direct ancestor, someone who is remarkable for his uniqueness rather than his influence. You can't trace Comenius's influence on contemporary picture books the way you can trace Newbery's on publishing; he seems to have been the creator of an important book rather than the originator of an important phenomenon. It's also nonfiction, and historians of children's literature—and, often, contemporary practitioners in the field—prefer fictional narrative, books that seize the imagination by telling stories. It is Comenius's ill fortune, in terms of literary history, to be educationally significant.

The late 17th century brought the Puritans to the fore in children's literature. James Janeway's (1671) *A Token for Children* has a full title, *A Token for Children: Being an Exact Account of the Conversion, Holy and Exemplary Lives, and Joyful Deaths of Several Young Children*, which effectively describes the material within: account after account of children finding piety and serving as examples to their elders as well as their peers, usually prior to their dramatic end. As Darton (1932/1982) notes, Janeway, after John Bunyan, "had the widest and longest popularity as the author of works read in English nurseries; read, and, sometimes, as they were meant to be, enjoyed; real children's books of one period in particular, and in the background of others" (p. 52).

Yet the intervening centuries have made the *Token* a rather tough sell to scholars attempting to focus on literature that children read for pleasure. Stories of children weeping in self-recrimination about sinfulness and slowly expiring as they bring godliness to those around them are highly unsavory to the contemporary palate; Janeway's work is a classic example of the kind of historic children's text that later historians can only envision gaining popularity for want of competition. Seventeenth-century philosopher Locke (1693), whose highly influential attitude toward children and their education is considerably more congenial to us, never deigned to recommend the *Token* despite its popularity in his time. Even the Victorians, fond of a histrionic death scene themselves, found Janeway's excess repellent; Mrs. Field in 1895 refers to his work as "strangely unhealthy reading" (p. 189)

Sixty years later, gentle, sunny Cornelia Meigs (1953) echoes the sentiment, referring to the *Token* with revulsion as the "most dreadful example" of "a whole group of terrifyingly unwholesome writings" (p. 124). Yet, as Gillian Avery (1995) shrewdly points out, Janeway's work was a genuinely child-centered landmark: novelistic narratives (however truth-based they may—or may not—have been, they read with a fictional verve) filled with domestic details of childhood and starring children in roles so important that they even overshadow and instruct adults. Darton (1932/1982) points out that the *Token,* unlike virtually any of its predecessors, was designed for children to read at their leisure, and he makes the important observation that the difference between the pleasures it may bring and the childish joys of later eras in no way precludes it from having pleasure as its goal. Its more secular enjoyability even raised a few eyebrows, since, as Mary Jackson (1989) notes, its resemblance to fiction aroused the suspicions of those who considered non-factual narratives to be sinful lies.

Ultimately, the *Token* is probably the greatest shock to the contemporary student of the genre's history, and it is the book most demanding of a move outside of one's contemporary viewpoint. It is useful in understanding two important factors: the considerable differences in taste in different eras, and the similarities that may not be easily apparent. Languishing children who teach lessons are by no means bereft of popularity in the modern era; their secular approach tends to disguise their kinship with the *Token,* but the readers of Lurlene McDaniel's (e.g., 1985) tearjerkers about dying young people find much of the same satisfaction as Janeway's audience.

Another 17th-century Puritan also wrote a book that became a children's literature landmark, but literary historians have treated John Bunyan's (1678) *Pilgrim's Progress* more kindly than Janeway's *Token.* Though Bunyan produced some works explicitly for a child audience, *Pilgrim's Progress* wasn't among them; this allegorical tale of a hero's journey through obstacles and tests in order to reach the Celestial City, exemplifying the struggles of a Christian (the hero's name), initially reached its greatest popularity with adults. However, Bunyan's plainspoken writing, colorful images, and touches of humor made the story broadly accessible not only to reluctant adult readers but also to children, and soon abridged versions were created specifically for young audiences. Though the title long remained a popular adult work, over the next 200 years it became increasingly associated with the child audience; it inspired and influenced many other works for children, most famously Louisa May Alcott's (1868, 1869) *Little Women,* which repeatedly quotes and refers to the work. As the Alcott example would suggest, Bunyan's work was read in both Britain and America, and it was translated into dozens of other languages as well. Even after it stopped being widely read, it remained common cultural currency in incarnations from Sunday school prizes to subjects for films, and new editions still appear (2008 saw an adaptation by Gary Schmidt, with illustrations by esteemed illustrator Barry Moser). For literary historians, *Pilgrim's Progress* is a bit of a relief. It seems to help writers such as Meigs (1953) wash away the taste of the earlier Puritans, and it gives them a chance

to discuss the Puritans without being perplexed at their considerable literary significance.

The Western side of the Atlantic initially imported its books for young people, but soon it began to create its own, and one of the first significant publications was the *New England Primer.* This title first appeared somewhere between 1686 and 1690 in Boston, and it was a compilation; though its contents varied from printer to printer and edition to edition, it generally contained spurs to reading (alphabets, syllabaria) and spurs to Godliness (biblical texts and prayers from the Puritan contributors). The earliest surviving editions date from 30 years after its first publication, it wasn't the work of a single author, and it was more in the nature of an anthology than an original narrative, all characteristics that make it difficult to identify its discrete role to children's literature. It was, however, a literary phenomenon that shaped the youth of New Englanders for over a century, making it the most important early American contribution to children's literature.

Enlightenment-era Works: Folklore, Novels, and Poetry

The late 17th and early 18th centuries saw the inception of one of most enduringly important areas of children's literature, print folklore. Some children's literature specialists go so far as to claim folklore as the literature's source, making the print genre an outgrowth of oral culture, a suggestion made by the title of Roger Sale's (1978) *Fairy Tales and After: From Snow White to E. B. White,* one of the first children's literature histories to come out of an English department rather than library science or education. Certainly both nursery rhymes and folktales have a venerable history with children, and both appear early in the literature's print timeline. Charles Perrault's (1697) *Histoires, ou Conte du Temp Passé, Avec les Moralitéz,* known popularly as *Contes de Ma Mère l'Oye* (Tales of My Mother Goose), contains some of the folktales best known today: In English, they're usually titled "Sleeping Beauty," "Red Riding Hood," "Bluebeard," "Puss in Boots," "Diamonds and Toads," "Cinderella," "Ricky with the Tuft," and "Hop o' My Thumb." This collection arrived on English shores in 1729 in a translation by Robert Samber known as *Histories, or Tales of Past Times, Told by Mother Goose.*

Perrault is actually a somewhat ironic starting place for folklore-favoring historians, because folklore's importance, in this focus, lies in its ostensibly oral, unrefined, told-around-the-fireplace vigor. It's arguable how much folk there is in any of the classic folk collections (the Grimms, collecting in 19th-century Germany, deserve special notice for their perpetuation of the myth of hardy peasant sources while gathering material from the well-educated and middle class), and Perrault's highbrow reputation stood behind his tales from the start, while each story concluded with a motto of considerable courtly flavor. On the other hand, the tales proper were compact and energetic, and the tension between oral folklore traditions and written adaptations exists throughout children's literature, so perhaps it is fitting that this early entry in the history exemplifies the contradictions that exist to this day.

Perrault has other reasons for his popularity with scholars, too. Perrault tales are still widely available in contemporary retellings and provide the engine behind many a Disney cartoon. His work remains enjoyable reading even today; though the language is a little outside of the usual contemporary child's vocabulary, the tales are among the earliest writing for children that will still be read with genuine pleasure by modern readers with non-scholarly motivations. From the standpoint of a curriculum or anthology that seeks to give an overview of the literature, Perrault is also useful as an early marker for print folklore in general, a vitally important aspect of children's literature. Though the *Contes* are by no means the earliest print examples of folklore, they're the first to gain a significant child audience. Perrault therefore operates in the vanguard of folktales for young people, followed in the 19th century by such stalwart collectors as the German Grimms, the Scandinavian Asbjørnsen and Moe, and England's Joseph Jacobs, all of whom put into print tales that still feature regularly in children's literature. And, as Bettina Hürlimann (1968) points out, folklore has "long been the subject of distinguished research" (p. 21), earning the attention of scholars long before the general run of children's literature, making Perrault important in the history of the genre's scholarship as well as in the genre itself. Folklore also gains significance from its close relationship with fantasy, one of the most important genres within children's literature; since more contemporary forms of fantasy narratives appear only in 19th century (save for fabulous talking animals in Aesop and other moral tales), the discussion of folklore allows for the overt exploration of imaginative, rather than reality-based fiction, which holds an important place both in children's literature and in people's perception of it.

In a very different vein is the writing of another significant figure in this key century in the genre's history, the poet Isaac Watts (1715), another in the series of Puritan principals of children's literature, whose best-known work was *Divine Songs Attempted in Easy Language for the Use of Children.* Muir (1954) singles Watts out as the first to write for children in their own idiom, and his verse proved enduring, selling briskly in America as well as in Britain and remaining a viable publisher's title for 200 years. In fact, his poems became such chestnuts of recitation that he began to be more associated with plodding schoolwork than with pleasure reading, an outcome that could not help but color his profile in literary history. As a result, he's probably better known today through Lewis Carroll's (1865) parodies of his poems in *Alice's Adventures in Wonderland* ("How doth the little crocodile" is a parody of Watts' "Against Idleness and Mischief," and "'Tis the voice of the lobster" a take on "The Sluggard") than in his

original verses for children, and even that legacy fades as Alice too slips away from center stage.

Though Watts' own work remained prominent enough for mocking a century and a half later, he didn't immediately spawn successors to carry his legacy with similar popularity. He undoubtedly influenced many writers for young people who grew up reading his works, but his own reputation eclipsed most of theirs, and literary histories generally leap past him nearly 100 years to get to the next prominent writers of verse, sisters Ann and Jane Taylor (author of "Twinkle, Twinkle, Little Star"). Watts therefore requires the literary historian to face the choice: Put him with the 18th-century prosodists, where, due to our intense focus on form and genre, he sticks out awkwardly; or put him in with the poetry, and conflate hugely time-separated eras. It's notable that Watts is one of the few historic authors for young people who has managed to maintain his fairly high profile based entirely on the writing of poetry.

Having an even longer influence than Isaac Watts' poetry are two significant novels of the same era. Both Daniel Defoe's (1719) *Robinson Crusoe*, the story of a shipwrecked sailor who eked out a living on a desert island, and Jonathan Swift's (1726) *Gulliver's Travels*, the account of a ship's doctor who traveled to a series of strange lands, left a legacy that still exists in literary and popular culture (a Crusoe television series was broadcast in the U.S. in 2008, and actor Jack Black has been slated to play Gulliver in a 2010 film retelling of Swift's novel). Though both novels were initially penned for adult readers, their effects on children's literature have been incalculable. *Robinson Crusoe* was a runaway success, prompting translations and adaptations and imitations right from the start, and it has even given its name to the robinsonnade, the classic survival story, a plot successful for centuries in incarnations as varied as Scott O'Dell's (1960) *Island of the Blue Dolphins* and E. L. Konigsburg's (1967) *From the Mixed Up Files of Mrs. Basil E. Frankweiler.*

Gulliver's Travels moved more selectively into the realm of children's reading, with the first voyage, Gulliver's trip to Lilliput, the land of the little people, becoming the most often excerpted or adapted for young readers (Andrew Lang even adapted it for his 1889 folklore collection, *The Blue Fairy Book*). Young readers with little interest in Swift's political satire and burlesquing of contemporary luminaries marveled at the sheer fantasy of his protagonist's journeys. Since children themselves are usually the tiny among the large, they undoubtedly found particular appeal in seeing the world itself miniaturized as they, through Gulliver, strode among it as giants. The term "Lilliputian" itself, however, became, understandably, associated with the small and thus with children, as in the children's periodical *Lilliputian Magazine,* produced by John Newbery in 1751 and 1752.

These two novels, significant in the early history of the novel as well as in children's literature, offer an excellent example of crossover titles, books that started as adult works but have since become considered the property of children. Such crossover titles challenge the chronicler's conventional emphasis on the "written for children" rule, because children's literature history simply can't be told without Defoe and Swift, and these novels have been longer successful with children than adults. The crossover phenomenon also points up an irony in the attempt to limit materials to those intended for children: The adult's intention for a text outweighs the child reader's own vote.

Beginnings of Publishing for Children

Books intended explicitly for children's amusement, though, were starting to appear in the early 18th century. One of the earliest and least celebrated such landmarks is *A Little Book for Little Children,* by "T.W.," published sometime between 1702 and 1712. This title took a sufficiently different tone from previous works as to be notable; though it included a rhyming alphabet, its main goal was clearly pleasure rather than intellectual betterment. It is a hard place to plant a flag for a genre beginning, though. The mystery of the author's identity makes it difficult to place the title societally and culturally, and it's a fairly isolated work. It doesn't play a substantial role in any literary genealogy (none of its verses made much of a later or earlier splash), and its creator seems never to have contributed anything else. It's nonetheless significant that it was published and that it was reasonably successful.

The strongest candidate for a near-miss at being the father of children's literature, who would probably have snagged Newbery's "first" title had there been no Newbery, is Thomas Boreman, who began publishing material for young readers in the 1730s, and who is considered by scholar Mary Jackson (1989) to be a genre founder alongside Newbery and Mary Cooper. Boreman was the publisher and presumed author of 10 or 11 books for young people. Most notable are his "Gigantick Histories" titles, beginning in 1740, which described historic landmarks of London, and which were cheerfully copied by Newbery several years later; he also favored the flowered Dutch binding later associated with Newbery's books. He was sufficiently successful to have a reputation that spread to the American colonies, where he had subscribers to the Gigantick Histories. There's a touch of "what might have been" about Boreman: He lacks Newbery's general publishing prominence and reputation-puffing authors and business descendents; he also simply published considerably less. (Brian Alderson, in his notes for Darton's [1982] *Children's Books in England,* theorizes that Boreman probably died in 1743, which would have restricted him to a drastically short career in which to make a publishing mark [p. 355]). Yet, it still seems a little harsh to imply, as Darton does, that he was not a "genuine 'children's publisher'" (p. 123), and other historians definitely consider him a groundbreaker as such.

Not long after that, in 1744, Mary Cooper published *Tommy Thumb's Pretty Song Book,* the first known collection of English nursery rhymes in print. Advertising dates suggest this title preceded Newbery's *A Little Pretty Pocket-Book* (1744) by several months, thus chronologically pipping Newbery to the post, if indeed the post is to be found in this era at all. Cooper was the widow of Thomas Cooper, publisher, who in 1742 produced a playful reading guide called *The Child's New Play-thing,* which Mary Cooper brought out in another edition after her husband's death. While two child-themed titles may be insufficient to label Mary Cooper a children's publisher to the degree of Newbery, she had clearly confirmed the existence of the market for such works.

Children's literature as we now identify it was becoming an established marketing genre in the mid-18th century; sightings of children's texts appear closer together, the documenting of a local population rather than the celebration of a glimpse of a rara avis. Publishers even find it profitable to flatteringly imitate (or lazily steal from) their competitors, suggesting that the market was large enough to absorb copies and readalikes as well as originals. As Percy Muir (1954) says, "The thing was in the air" (p. 67), and the audience was clearly ready to buy what the publishers could concoct to sell. And John Newbery quickly grasped what that could mean.

John Newbery

Newbery, born in 1713, began his professional life as a printer's assistant and became a partner in the business by marrying his master's widow. An enthusiastic businessman, he actively sought to expand his firm's profile and moved it to London in 1743 or 1744, in 1745 settling it in St. Paul's Churchyard under the soon-to-be-famous sign of the Bible and Sun. It's in 1744 that he produced the book considered by Darton (1932/1982) and many others to be the first children's book from the first real children's publisher: *A Little Pretty Pocket-Book,* which contained sprightly rhymes, the occasional tip of the hat to education and morality, and a guest appearance by the folkloric character Jack the Giant Killer. In a presaging of modern packaging, it was also available, for a slightly higher price, packaged with a toy ("the use of which will infallibly make Tommy a good Boy, and Polly a good Girl" [as cited in Darton, p. 1]). It's an interesting but not startlingly original title, but it reflects the blend of commercial savvy, understanding of parental taste, and provision of genuine entertainment for children that was to mark Newbery's publishing oeuvre.

He published between 20 and 30 non-educational books for children (surviving copies are rare, and advertisements, business records, and other mentions can be inaccurate and inconsistent in their use of titles, so the exact number is difficult to discern) and a further number of more factual nonfiction titles, which are sometimes quite engaging in their own right. As previously noted, he published a periodical, *The Lilliputian Magazine* (1751–52), also available in a compiled volume. His most significant single publication for young people was probably *The History of Little Goody Two Shoes* (1765), the tale of a young farmer's daughter early left orphaned along with her brother, her travails in the face of villainous landowners and privation, and her self-education to the point where she became able to support herself as a teacher.

That's a pared-down summary of a book in which a great deal happens and many digressive points are made, ranging from the plight of the poor in the face of the powerful to the evils of animal abuse. A success right from the start, it was widely read for a good half-century and in print for at least 50 years beyond that, and it got rather a new lease on life in the 19th century as a subject of traditional British pantomime, though the plot, as is usual in that genre, was considerably altered. Newbery paid attention not only to the content of his titles but also to their appearance, employing attractive engravings and flowered Dutch paper covers, creating a distinctive house style that foreshadowed contemporary tendencies for publishers to stamp their own individual design on their books. He sold near, in his fabled bookshop, and far, across the Atlantic Ocean, and he dabbled in marketing strategies such as the book-toy combination and the two-tier pricing system that presaged the paperback/hardback pricing strategies.

It's certainly a considerable contribution to the genre of children's literature. Newbery has received encomiums from the majority of genre historians, including French academics Isabelle Jan (1974) and Paul Hazard (1944), and Gillian Avery (1995) notes his considerable influence on early American literature (he was advertising his children's wares in an American newspaper soon after he began publishing in the genre). It's particularly interesting that this watershed figure isn't really a writer (though he may have penned some of the texts he sold), and his books aren't significant for their individual art or thematic implications. Newbery is important because he establishes the possibility of children's publishing as an industry, and an industry that was so profitable that others wished to engage in it as well.

He's also a figure of importance beyond children's literature: Seemingly known by every Londoner who put pen to paper, he's the recipient of a shout-out in the novel *The Vicar of Wakefield*, written by Oliver Goldsmith (1766), who was the occasional beneficiary of Newbery's financial generosity. And he gets affectionately satirized by literary lion Samuel Johnson (1758) as "Jack Whirler," the man who's always affable and is always on his way to somewhere else. (He even had a family connection to the writerly world, in that his stepson-in-law was the celebrated, if troubled, poet Christopher Smart.) The breadth of his business doings allowed his publishing to have a scope and a success unmatched by his contemporary competitors such as Boreman and Cooper. His name lived

on in the publishing world even after his death in 1767, and in fact more than one branch of his family ended up in publishing, resulting in a familial-professional dynasty that kept his name and achievements—or perhaps more accurately, his legend—alive.

From an academic standpoint, Newbery is a curricular dream: There're masses of material on him in his time, in our time, and in between, and because of his scope and connections he's a terrific vessel for discussion of a variety of relevant literary issues. He's an entrée to discussion of novels, literary criticism, journals, publishing, patronage, and religious divisions (he was a Protestant, his wife Catholic, and his daughters were raised Catholic and sons Protestant). With his commitment to marketing and tendency toward gleefully hyperbolic statements ("See the Original Manuscript in the Vatican at Rome and the Cuts by Michael Angelo," loftily advises the title page of *Goody Two Shoes*) and his use of product placement (his other business concern, a patent medicine, gets in-text approbation in *Goody Two Shoes*), he's an easy figure to link to contemporary publishing practices. He's also a character, an easy man to storytell, with his broad interests and lively approach to business and publicity (his famous motto, "Trade and Plumb Cake for ever. Huzza!" celebrates both business and pleasure). As a religious tolerant in an age where it wasn't the norm and a busy businessman focused on financial growth in an age where that was often considered vulgar and unacceptable, he's particularly appealing to Americans, and it's therefore not surprising that the major American children's literature award bears his name—and, of course, bolsters his reputation further. Even historians distancing themselves from the notion that John Newbery is to children's literature what 1066 is to English history find him an easy figure to discuss.

The Newbery dominance has become such a convention, in fact, that there's a modest backlash—not against his significance per se, but against the perception of his single-handed creation of the genre of children's literature. While most serious historians avoid giving him lone credit, the strong emphasis on Newbery and his tendency to appear as a watershed in timelines and other brief overviews leaves many with the suggestion that Newbery all on his own brought into being what we now know as children's literature. Percy Muir (1954) especially takes aim at this false lionization, trimming Newbery down to actual size by pointing out the narratives he published were fairly lackluster and, more importantly, that many titles that sounded like Newbery works were actually published elsewhere, so his perceived output was larger than his actual, while Mary Jackson (1989) devotes nearly an entire book to the point that he was but one among several. Ironically, though, even these counterarguments end up planting Newbery all the more firmly in his historical place by establishing him as the man to beat—and then never managing to beat him.

After Newbery: 18th-Century Growth

After Newbery, the histories become more finely granulated, the significant events closer together. While recency bias makes this technique inevitable, it's also reasonably valid in children's literature: The discovery and creation of a market and the spread of that discovery beyond Britain did genuinely result in considerably larger numbers of children's books and the growth of what we'd now term the industry, a world wherein people could earn their living as writers, artists, publishers, and critics of children's literature. It therefore becomes useful at times to examine not just individual titles but subgenres and themes as they begin to appear and flourish.

For instance, another landmark of the era was Sarah Fielding's (1749) *The Governess*, which was perhaps the first children's novel; this title is the originator of the still-popular subgenre of the school story. Especially in light of the author's prominent connections (she was the sister of Henry Fielding, author of *Tom Jones* [1749] and one of the pioneers of the genre of the novel) and her other literary achievements, it's a little surprising that her work doesn't receive more attention in histories of children's literature. Mostly she's mentioned en passant, or in comparison to *Goody Two Shoes;* perhaps more significantly, she's mentioned in discussions of 19th-century responses to *The Governess,* whether by the eminent early critic Mrs. Trimmer, who scorned the narrative's included fairy tales, or by the 19th-century writer Mrs. Sherwood, who published a revised version of the novel that removed interludes she felt objectionable and added new emphases.

Despite these developments, didacticism remained a strong force in 18th-century children's literature. What changed were its influences, with godliness no longer the primary message, and its flavor, with the lessons increasingly incorporated into narratives effective for their writerly skill. The influence of the French philosopher Jean-Jacques Rousseau (1712–1778), who in his landmark *Émile* (1762) described the ideal upbringing of a fictional child (an upbringing that included only one book—*Robinson Crusoe*), was felt across the continent and into Britain. Author Thomas Day legendarily attempted to follow Rousseau's teachings in life, making two attempts, both failures, to guide a young preteen girl along Rousseauian lines in order to make her into a suitable wife for him and dying as the result of an attempt to bring Rousseauian principles to an apparently unimpressed young horse. Day's (1783) *Sandford and Merton* is a novel about the development of two young boys, one spoiled by privilege, one naturally virtuous, with their experiences and maturation providing cause for exploration of social and political theory. Dire as that sounds in summary, the book had sufficient color, if not believable character, to involve young readers of its day, and Darton (1932/1982) calls the book "a great work, in its queer little way" (p. 145). It retained sufficient prominence to be worthy of a parody nearly a century later, but it seems to have been particularly damned for its difference from later fashions, being the subject of indignant contempt (Muir [1954], in several pages of excoriation, at one point calls the book "a feast of nausea"[p. 91]) rather than embarrassed affection. More gently treated by later generations is Maria Edgeworth (1796), best known for her short moral tales in *The Parent's Assistant* and elsewhere, who was deeply influenced by her father, a disciple of Rousseau and an educational theorist. Edgeworth's stories were fluid and clean, edged with telling detail, and they evinced some of the absorbing miniature human drama of letters to advice columnists. Darton (1932/1982) writes of her with admiration and gleefully plunges into a heartfelt exploration of her best-known story, "The Purple Jar," that involves his partisan siding against the didactic adults therein.

Edgeworth heralds another important development of the late 18th century: the growing number of women entering the world of children's literature and development. Charles Lamb later famously blasted them as "the cursed Barbauld crew" (as cited in Clarke, 1997, p. 91; Anna Letitia Barbauld being one of the most prominent children's writers of the era), a condemnation that may be children's literature's equivalent to Nathaniel Hawthorne's excoriation of the "damned mob of scribbling women" (as cited in Gilbert & Gubar, 1985, p. 185) in its indication both of the market significance of female authors and the opposition in some quarters to same.

Another influential woman of the time was Mrs. Sarah Trimmer, who became famous in writing about children as well as for them. Not just about children, in fact, but about children's books—Mrs. Trimmer is arguably the first notable practitioner of children's literature reviewing and criticism, offered in her popular periodical *The Guardian of Education* (1802–1806). Yet, she was not, in the Maria Edgeworth sense, a theorist, and her audience for her criticism was largely parents and governesses. In contemporary terms, she was a popular writer rather than a scholarly one, and it's indicative of the growing importance of children's books to the middle class that she was able to influence such a readership on the topic.

19th Century: Folktales, Fantasy, and Fun

While various incarnations of the moral tale continued strong through the 19th century, other strands of children's literature begin to edge it from center stage. Folktales made a strong return with Jakob and Wilhelm Grimm, keen folklorists and nationalists eager to uncover (or, more accurately in light of their misrepresented collecting habits, create) a folk literature. They published their two-volume collection of tales, *Kinder- und Hausmärchen,* in Germany in 1812 and 1815 (English edition 1823 and 1826), and it not only became popular in its own right, it paved the way for much later literature, not just folktale retellings, but the literary fairy tale, exemplified by Hans Christian Andersen's collections and practiced by major writers from Nathaniel Hawthorne to Oscar Wilde. Though adaptations for children would still massage folktales away from the more adult details and toward those that would develop children in accordance with adult wishes, they nonetheless retained their celebration of the strange and magical.

Realism began to change as well, finding an appreciation for playfulness among the morals. Catherine Sinclair's (1839) *Holiday House,* a high-spirited family story, was cited by Edwardian author E. V. Lucas as offering "the first example of modern nursery skepticism" (as cited in Darton, 1932/1982, p. 220); Darton calls it "the first example of real laughter and a free conscience" (p. 220), and Roger Lancelyn Green (1965) considers it the beginning of the "revolt against the old kind of children's books" (p. 21). It might well be the earliest children's novel that could still be enjoyed by contemporary young people for its literary rather than historical merits (the odds of any 21st-century child's pleasurably perusing *Goody Two Shoes* or *The Governess* are slim indeed). It was the earliest book that seems not just to acknowledge contemporary sensibility but to share it and side with it. Yet, for all it's a precursor of humorous family stories such as Hilary McKay's, *Holiday House* didn't immediately elicit imitation—instead, playfulness turned sideways, slipping into the literature through parody, nonsense, and fantasy.

The parody came from Heinrich Hoffmann's (1845, English translation 1848) *Struwwelpeter,* which took cautionary moral tales to a satirical and poetic extreme. The fates of the heedless children, who set themselves ablaze with matches or lose their favorite, much-sucked thumbs to a digit-slicing tailor, are so drastic that they're often found rather horrifying despite the humor, but the German author's rhymes presage the blend of savagery and humor in writers such as Roald Dahl as well as the growing and now firmly established impulse to satirize the didactic. A similar tension between the grotesque and the humorous appeared in Edward Lear's (1846) *A Book of Nonsense,* which gave nonsense its first big break. This compilation of absurd limericks, illustrated with drawings by Lear himself, sold well in several printings and received favorable attention from critics. After a nearly 20-year gap, Lear produced several more collections of nonsense, which included more limericks plus longer nonsensical works in poetry ("The Owl and the Pussycat" probably the most famous) and prose.

The book that many literary historians seem to spend their chronicle waiting for, however, is Lewis Carroll's *Alice's Adventures in Wonderland* (1865). Cheerfully praised by one critic on the grounds that "it has no moral," (as cited in Carpenter, 1984, p. 17), the book, with fanciful yet intensely detailed illustrations by John Tenniel, was an immediate success; it sold quickly in Britain and crossed the Atlantic for an American edition the following year. Carroll's book wasn't the first popular fantasy, but it was the most lasting and influential one; without *Alice,* it's unlikely that the era would receive the admiration critics tend to bestow on it. *Alice* confirmed the completely imaginary with no point but amusement as legitimate fodder for children's literature.

Global Growth

Realism, however, continued to develop as well. Louisa May Alcott's (1868, 1869) *Little Women,* a fictional story drawn largely from Alcott's own New England childhood, was by no means the first example of domestic realism, but it has become the best known; much as *Alice's Adventures in Wonderland* (Carroll, 1865) operates as the first standard-bearer for the fantastical thread in children's literature, *Little Women* represents the domestic thread. And, like *Alice,* it's a book that 20th-century critics may have encountered in their own childhood and thus recalled with affection. Cornelia Meigs (1934), in fact, authored a biography of Alcott for young readers, *Invincible Louisa,* ensuring it a place in critical history even as its contemporary readership diminishes. *Little Women* also became popular not only nationally but internationally, becoming perhaps the first American children's classic and a key representative of American life to readers abroad.

Similarly, other countries and regions began to produce literature that reflected their own cultural sensibility, a direction particularly apparent in the British colonies. Canada's Catherine Parr Traill (1826) wrote about the country before she even moved there, in *The Young Emigrants*, and then published what might be considered the first Canadian children's novel, *Canadian Crusoes: A Tale of the Rice Lake Plains,* in 1859. Interestingly, she had difficulty finding a Canadian publisher for her Canadian works, which were therefore generally published in England. Australia began to develop its own voice in children's literature late in the century in works that reflected not only a distinct identity but a distinct idea of childhood. The most famous example of these is Ethel Turner's (1894) *Seven Little Australians*, which may have been influenced by *Little Women* in its lively depiction of everyday girls' lives and its focus on a female character who chafes at the restrictions of proper womanhood. However, its nature remains essentially Australian. Similarly, Johanna Spyri's (1880, English edition 1884) *Heidi* became the face of Switzerland to readers of children's literature worldwide; Spyri took the traditional Swiss story of village life and individualized it into a compelling story of a young girl's contrasting experiences in town and in country, with the peaceful rural existence celebrated for its beauty.

It was England, however, that propelled the picturebook into new and exciting form in the 19th century. The key creative force behind this development was Edmund Evans, technically a printer, but performing work that today might be associated with art design and publishing. His advances in color printing enabled what were then called "toy books" to be inexpensively yet beautifully produced, and he's associated with three of the great 19th-century picturebook artists, the elegant Walter Crane, the picturesque Kate Greenaway, and the boisterous Randolph

Caldecott, after whom the American Library Association's Caldecott Medal was named.

The American Library Association, founded in 1876, was also the source of children's librarianship, a professional category that is probably the single biggest force behind children's literature as we know it today: It has provided editors when publishing houses decided children's literature was worthy of a separate division, it has provided the critics who reviewed the books, and it has provided the thousands of librarians who bring books together with young readers. Its founding marks the beginning of the modern age of children's literature, with its thousands of books per year, its awards, and its bestseller lists.

Conclusion

It's a strange and complicated journey from Latin readers to new-millennium medal winners, and it's far from complete, since our contemporary version of the genre is just a stop along the way. Ultimately, the literature isn't a single, fixed organism but a large number of texts grouped together under a rubric, and that categorization is always dependent on the eye of the beholder. This overview too is a product of bias, culture, time, and practical exigencies—stuffing the entire history of children's literature into a chapter requires the merciless excision of most of it, after all. Nonetheless, there's still great meaning in the collection of texts and discernible connections between its elements, changeable though their interpretation may be. Examining the past, these nearly two millennia of history, of adult hopes and intentions and children's duties and pleasures, allows us to better understand the texts, conventions, and assumptions in our current world of children's literature, even as it itself becomes history.

Literature References

Alcott, L. M. (1868, 1869). *Little Women.* Boston, MA: Roberts Brothers.

Bathroom Readers' Institute. (1988). *Uncle John's bathroom reader.* New York, NY: St. Martin's Press.

Boreman, T. (1740–1743). Gigantick histories series. London, England: T. Boreman.

Bunyan, J. (2008). *Pilgrim's progress* (Adapted by G. Schmidt). Grand Rapids, MI: Eerdmans Books for Young Readers.

Bunyan, J. (1678). *The pilgrim's progress.* London, England: Nathaniel Ponder.

Carroll, L. (1865). *Alice's adventures in wonderland.* London, England: Macmillan.

The child's new play-thing. (1742). London, England: Cooper.

Comenius, J. A. (1659). *Orbis pictus* (C. Hoole, Trans.). London, England: J. Kirton. (Original work published 1658)

Corbeil, J. C. (1986). *The facts on file visual dictionary.* New York, NY: Facts on File.

Davis, J. (1980). *Garfield at large: His first book.* New York, NY: Ballantine.

Day, T. (1783). *The history of Sandford and Merton.* London, England: Stockdale.

Defoe, D. (1719). *Robinson Crusoe.* London, England: W. Taylor.

Edgeworth, M. (1796). *The parent's assistant.* London, England: J. Johnson.

Fielding, H. (1749). *The history of Tom Jones, a foundling.* London, England: A. Millar.

Fielding, S. (1749). *The governess, or the little female academy.* London, England: A. Millar.

Foxe, J. (1563). *Actes and monuments of these latter perilous times touching matters of the church.* London, England: John Day.

Goldsmith, O. (1766). *The vicar of Wakefield.* London: B. Collins for F. Newbery.

Grimm, J. & W. (1823). *German popular stories translated from the kinder- und hausmärchen.* Vol. I. (E. Taylor, Trans.). London, England: C. Baldwyn. (Original work published 1812)

Grimm, J. & W. (1826). *German popular stories translated from the kinder- und hausmärchen.* Vol. II. (E. Taylor, Trans.). London, England: J. Robins. (Original work published 1815)

The history of Little Goody Two Shoes. (1765). London, England: J. Newbery.

Hoffman, H. (n.d) *Slovenly Peter or cheerful stories and funny pictures for good little folks.* Philadelphia, PA: John C. Winston. (Original work published 1845)

Janeway, J. (1671). *A token for children: Being an exact account of the conversion, holy and exemplary lives, and joyful deaths of several young children.* London, England: D. Newman.

Konigsburg, E. L. (1967). *From the mixed-up files of Mrs. Basil E. Frankweiler.* New York, NY: Atheneum.

Lang, A. (1889). *The blue fairy book.* London, England: Longmans.

Lear, E. (1846). *A book of nonsense.* London, England: Thomas McLean.

Little Pretty Pocket-Book. (1744). London: John Newbery.

Malory, T. (1485). *Le Morte d'Arthur.* Westminster, England: Caxton.

McDaniel, L. (1985). *Six months to live.* Worthington, OH: Willowisp.

Meigs, C. (1934). *Invincible Louisa.* Boston, MA: Little, Brown.

O'Dell, S. (1960). *Island of the blue dolphins.* Boston, MA: Houghton Mifflin.

Perrault, C. (1697). *Histories, ou contes du temps passé, avec les moralitéz.* Paris, France: Barbin.

Rousseau, J-J. (1762). *Emile ou de l'éducation.* Paris, France: Duchesne.

Samber, R. (1729). *Histories, or tales of past times, Told by Mother Goose.* London, England: J. Pote & R. Montagu.

Sinclair, C. (1839). *Holiday house.* London, England: Ward, Lock, & Tylor.

Spyri, J. (1884). *Heidi, her years of wandering and learning* (L. Brooks, Trans.). Boston, MA: De Wolfe, Fiske, & Co.

Swift, J. (1726). *Gulliver's travels.* London, England: Benjamin Motte.

Tommy Thumb's pretty song book. (1744). London, England: Cooper.

Traill, C. P. (1859). *Canadian Crusoes: A tale of the Rice Lake Plains.* London, England: A. Hall, Virtue.

Traill, C. P. (1826). *The young emigrants.* London, England: Harvey & Darton.

Turner, E. (1894). *Seven little Australians.* London, England: Ward, Lock & Bowden.

W., T. (ca. 1702). *A little book for little children.* London, England: publisher unknown.

Watts, I. (1715). *Divine songs attempted in easy language for the use of children.* London, England: M. Lawrence.

Academic References

Ascham, R. (1570). *The scholemaster.* London, England: John Daye

Avery, G. (1995). *Behold the child: American children and their books, 1621-1922.* Baltimore, MD: Johns Hopkins.

Carpenter, H. (1984). Alice's adventures in wonderland. In H. Carpenter & M. Prichard (Eds.), *The Oxford companion to children's literature* (pp. 15–18). Oxford, England: Oxford University Press.

Clarke, N. (1997). The cursed Barbauld crew: Women writers and writing for children in the late eighteenth century. In M. Hilton, M. Styles, & V. Watson (Eds.), *Opening the Nursery Door: Reading, Writing and Childhood 1600-1900* (pp. 91–116). London, England: Routledge.

Darton, F. J. H. (1982). *Children's books in England: Five centuries of social life* (3rd ed.). B. Alderson (Ed. and Rev.). Cambridge, England: Cambridge University Press. (Original work published 1932)

Field, Mrs. E. F. (1891). *The child and his book.* London, England: Wells, Gardner, Darton, & Co.

Gilbert, S. M., & Gubar, S. (1985). *The Norton anthology of literature by women: The tradition in English.* New York, NY: Norton.

Green, R. L. (1965). *Tellers of tales* (Rev. ed.). New York: Franklin Watts. (Original work published in 1946)

Hazard, P. (1944). *Books, children & men* (M. Mitchell, Trans.). Boston, MA: Horn Book.

Hürlimann, B. (1968). *Three centuries of children's books in Europe* (2nd ed.) (B. Alderson, Trans.). Cleveland, OH: World.

Jackson, M. V. (1989). *Engines of instruction, mischief, and magic: Children's literature in England from its beginnings to 1839.* Lincoln, NE: University of Nebraska Press.

Jan, I. (1974). *On children's literature.* New York, NY: Schocken.

Johnson, S. (1758, August 12). Whirler's Character. *The Idler, 19.*

Lerer, S. (2008). *Children's literature: A reader's history, from Aesop to Harry Potter.* Chicago, IL: University of Chicago.

Locke, J. (1693). *Some thoughts concerning education.* London, England: A. & J. Churchill.

Meigs, C. (1953). *A critical history of children's literature.* New York, NY: Macmillan.

Muir, P. (1954). *English children's books: 1600 to 1900.* New York, NY: Frederick A. Praeger.

Sale, R. (1978). *Fairy tales and after: From Snow White to E. B. White.* Cambridge, MA: Harvard University Press.

Smith, E. S. (1980). *The history of children's literature* (Rev. by M. Hodges & S. Steinfirst). Chicago, IL: American Library Association.

Steele, R. (1709, November 15-17). *The Tatler, 95.*

Thwaite, M. F. (1972). *From primer to pleasure in reading* (2nd ed.) London, England: The Library Association. (Original work published 1962)

Welsh, C. (1885). *A bookseller of the last century.* London, England: Griffith, Farran, Okeden, & Welsh.

Zipes, J. (Ed.). (2005). The Norton anthology of children's literature: The traditions in English. New York, NY: W.W. Norton.

Point of Departure

Lois Lowry

I've been asked to comment a bit on the history of children's literature, after reading this very erudite essay. I'm not sure that I can. I'm completely unscholarly myself. I dropped out of graduate school.

But since you asked. Here's the way I see it: a long time back, even before I was a child, children's literature was designed to turn children into better-behaved and more religious adults, sometimes by scaring them and making them cry. For the most part, this was boring and didn't work. But because children, including me, have always liked stories, and didn't have any other options, we read that stuff anyway. Our great aunts gave it to us for Christmas, and we dutifully wrote them thank you notes because our mothers said we couldn't go to the Roy Rogers movie on Saturday afternoon until we did.

Later—much later—we turned into great aunts ourselves, and into grandmothers, and we discovered that for the most part writing thank you notes has gone out of fashion, but books are still around, and we still give them as gifts. But they have changed. There are still talking animals, like the ones in the Aesop fables of our childhood; but they no longer advise us on how to become worthy children. Now they say very funny stuff, often, and they do some pretty sophisticated things.

Foxes, for example. When I was a child, I read about a fox who couldn't reach some grapes that he wanted. So he pretended he didn't want them. There was apparently a lesson there somewhere, but I could never figure out what it was, and it made me irritated at foxes in general.

Years later, I read to my own grandchildren a story in which there was a fox. He had a toothache and went to the dentist, who was named Doctor De Soto. Doctor De Soto happened to be a mouse, and the fox planned to eat him, after his toothache was fixed. But the mouse, who wore a small white dental uniform, perceived this plan and, ah, out-foxed him.

This is a very funny story, and it teaches the reader absolutely nothing.

The Aesop story purportedly has a lesson in it somewhere, and is not funny at all.

In my opinion this is the major breakthrough in the history of children's literature: the awareness that children would rather laugh and be entertained, than to be instructed and improved.

I didn't dislike the preachy books I read as a child, any more than I disliked my knee socks or my corn flakes. They were there, and they were what I had, and I read them, wore them, ate them, without questioning their merits.

As a matter of fact, I did love orphans, for some reason. There were many orphans in my childhood bookcase. (I vowed, when I was eight or nine, never to visit India, since Sara Crewe and Mary Lenox had both lost their mothers there, to cholera.) But to be honest, my interest in them always waned when the no-nonsense housekeepers and the wealthy benefactors appeared, and things began to change. I think I wanted my orphans to remain waiflike and needy. They were always so *boring* after their circumstances improved. And pious! I just checked—and yes, it is true, not a grotesque fabricated memory on my part—in the next-to-last chapter of *The Secret Garden*, the children sing the Doxology ("Praise God from whom"... etc.) while tears roll down the weather-beaten cheeks of Ben Weatherstaff, the gardener.

And so, while reading, when I got to the inevitable *thank-you-lord-for-this-happy-ending* parts, like Chapter XXII in *Heidi* (which is titled, "Something Unexpected Happens," a totally fraudulent title, since everything is so predictable it puts the reader to sleep), which contains the sentence "Both children said their prayers, and each thanked God in her own way for the blessing He had bestowed on Clara, who had for so long lain weak and ill," I would set the book aside, make sure no one was watching, and turn to....

Oh dear. This has been a deeply hidden secret for so many years. It began, I think, when I was eight or nine and lasted until I was eleven, ending then only because we left the United States and I no longer had access to my hidden vice. It was Little Lulu comic books. Officially, on the cover of each issue (for which I paid 10 cents at the drugstore on Main Street) the title was "Marge's Little Lulu." I did not know, or care about, or wonder about, the identity of Marge (research now tells me that a woman named Marjorie Henderson Buell created Lulu in 1935); it was Lulu I loved—with her springy black ringlets, her triangular red dress, and the odd little hat she always wore, which seemed to be shaped like the bell on my fourth-grade teacher's desk—and whom I hid behind the books in my bookcase, sensing somehow that she was not literature, that she was for little kids, that I was lesser for my passion and should keep it under wraps, the way a successful businessman might fall for a sluttish waitress but never introduce her to his family back at the ancestral estate.

And here is why I had a crush on Lulu (and why I wish *The History of Children's Literature* would confer some kind of status on her): She was pragmatic, devious, and capable of outwitting boys. She was a hell of a storyteller; she often used that skill to make her way out of scrapes. She was not pretty, not pious, not good. But she had a great dignity. And she was very, very funny, like Doctor De Soto.

She's part of the past, now, and perhaps a scholar would find her interesting only because she was a graphic novel before anyone dreamed up that name for it. But Little Lulu is showing up again in other guises (didn't I say she was devious?) with new identities, and oh, I am glad to see her counterparts in the books I give to my grandchildren these days!

14

Dime Novels and Series Books

Catherine Sheldrick Ross

University of Western Ontario

Fittingly, Catherine Ross's chapter on the history of dime novels and series books follows Deborah Stevenson's chapter on the history of children's and young adult literature, as the relationship between series books and children's literature is symbiotic. Despite the concerns of educators, librarians, and parents voice over children's active and abiding interest in what adults consider junk food for the mind, series books commonly provide the newly literate with compelling stories and fast-paced reading experience that enable them to become fluent readers. Although often dismissed as the products of "fiction factories," series books are in fact created by writers who fashion stories in the manner of professional journalists. As a young reader, Point of Departure author Candice Ransom was inspired by *Trixie Belden* mysteries to write the adventure stories she loved to read. She is still writing them; her 100+ titles include more than a dozen in the perennially popular *Boxcar Children* series.

Dime novels and series books have, for a century and a half, provided the terrain for a contest over children's reading. Taking the high ground are reading experts—teachers, librarians, and some children's authors—who agree that dime novels and series books should not be counted as "real reading." On the other side are the child readers themselves, who have been enthralled by dime-novel characters such as Deadwood Dick and have avidly read about the exploits of youthful series-book heroes such as Tom Swift and Nancy Drew, Encyclopedia Brown, the Famous Five, the Boxcar Children, the Sweet Valley Twins, the Baby-sitters Club, and the Animorphs.

For generations, children have blithely discounted the advice of teachers and librarians, turning their forbidden reading into a clandestine pleasure. When they couldn't borrow their favorites from the public library, they built their own private collections, which were energetically discussed with friends, traded, saved, and passed on to the next generation. Grown-up readers recall with nostalgic fondness the dime novel and series book reading of their childhoods, and many are now turning to online communities and booksellers to share memories and reacquire long-lost favorites. Successive generations of young readers become fans and avid collectors of the latest series craze. For example, Margaret Mackey (1990) has described the neighborhood ferment as the latest book in the *Baby-sitters Club* series by Ann M. Martin (e.g., 1995) hit the stands.

So uniformly have dime novels and series books been a lightning rod for the social anxieties of the guardians of culture that it is easy to lose sight of what they really are: one of the first forms of popular literature produced on a mass scale, bought by millions of readers, and read repetitively for the pleasure provided. As a widely-shared source of popular stories, stereotypes, and social mythology, dime novels were the 19th century equivalent of television in the second half of the 20th century.

The obvious point about both dime novels and series books is that there were so many of them and they were so cheap. They were a standardized product with high appeal to their readers, whose interest was satisfied by the regular and seemingly inexhaustible supply of new stories. Once readers have experienced the entrancement of Nick Carter or Nancy Drew or Captain Underpants or Junie B. Jones or Lemony Snicket's (e.g., 2000) *Series of Unfortunate Events*, they can repeat the predictable, pleasurable experience as often as they wish. And they do. Teachers and librarians have noted this repetitive reading and found it inexplicable and alarming. The closest they could come to an explanation relied on analogies to states of altered consciousness: being under a sorcerer's spell, being drawn into a dream life, or being addicted to a mind-altering drug. Critical attacks linked reading popular fiction to social disorder and moral breakdown. Dime books were denounced from the pulpit, along with cards, dancing, movies and booze, recalls Leslie McFarlane (1976), the first ghostwriter of the *Hardy Boys* series: "We found it puzzling that the iniquity seemed to be determined by cash outlay" (p. 159).

Any account of dime novels and series books needs to pay attention to these linked themes of cash outlay, adult disapproval, the entrancement of story, and the shared experience of clandestine reading. The first scandal of dime books and series books was their cheapness: children often could bypass the official guardians of taste and acquire the books themselves. Written initially for a working-class adult readership but enjoyed by children, dime novels told stories about the frontier, Indian captivity, pirates on the high seas, detectives in disguise, telephone boys who succeed in business, orphaned sewing girls who find love, millionaires disguised as millhands, and so on. These 10 cent and 5 cent formats were the 19th-century forerunners of the 20th-century series books for children and were produced by the same "fiction factory" methods (Cook, 1912) in which the writer was just one node in an industrial production line that depended upon Fordist principles of quantity, uniformity, and speed.

Hence the second scandal: the affront offered by these works to accepted notions of the autonomous author who is supposed to produce works of creative genius with no thought of cash return. Some commentators make invidious distinctions between "books in a series" such as L.M. Montgomery's (e.g., 1908/2008) *Anne* books, Beverly Cleary's (e.g., 1975) *Ramona* books, J.K. Rowling's (e.g.,

1998) *Harry Potter* books or Stephanie Meyer's (e.g., 2006) *Twilight* books, which at least are all written by the same author, and "series books," such as the Stratemeyer series or Francine Pascal's (e.g., 2008) *Sweet Valley High* and *Sweet Valley Twins* (e.g., 1989) books, which are a franchise written by many hands.

Almost all accounts of dime novels and series books emphasize the theme of speed and acceleration—the speed in the writing, the speed in the reading, and the speed in the unfolding of plot incidents. Writers could write these stories very quickly because in a sense they had already been written. The conventions of popular fiction, popular for over 2,000 years, were ready to hand and available to be used again for an audience of readers new to literacy for whom the motifs of hereditary insanity, identical twins, disguised identity, malevolent guardians, the quest for lost treasure, etc. were unfamiliar. And while the conventions were old, stories were given a modern, up-to-date flavor by incorporating details of city life or of the new technology that was shrinking distances and accelerating travel. Speed was often what stories were about, as characters with names like the Speedwell Boys, the Motor Girls, or Dave Dashaway were propelled through space on galloping horses, trains, ice-boats, cars or, in the case of Tom Swift, futuristic vehicles such as an electric runabout, skyracer, or skytrain.

Popular Fiction and the Expansion of Reading

Whatever else they were, dime books, penny dreadfuls (the British equivalent of the dime book), and series books were compelling stories that keep their readers reading by tricks and formulas developed over centuries by writers of popular stories. The bulk of popular literature—what readers read for their own pleasure—belongs to a genre that Northrup Frye (1976) calls romance. Frye's *The Secular Scripture*, which is about principles of storytelling, provides a comprehensive account of the conventions and formulas of romance. By romance, Frye means stories in which the elements of narrative design clearly stand out, as they do in folktales from which popular romance descended.

The building blocks of popular stories have showed little change over the course of centuries. Frye points out that in the old Greek romances, we find stories "of mysterious birth, oracular prophecies about the future contortions of the plot, foster parents, adventures which involve capture by pirates, narrow escapes from death, recognition of the true identity of the hero and his eventual marriage to the heroine" (p. 4). Fifteen centuries later, concerning Walter Scott's *Guy Mannering*, Frye notes that it turns out also to be a story "of mysterious birth, oracular prophecies, capture by pirates and the like" (p. 4). *Seth Jones*, probably the most popular of all dime novels, is about guess what?—capture by Indians, narrow escapes from death, disguise, the recognition of the true identity of Seth Jones, and the final pairing off of partners. The popular motif of twins, one bad and one good, turns up again with Jessica and Elizabeth Wakefield in Sweet Valley High School in California (Pascal, 2008). "Romance is the structural core of all fiction," Frye (1976) claims (p. 15), and romance motifs are the enduring building blocks of popular stories.

You know that you have wandered into romance territory when the story you are reading includes stereotypical elements. Just to give a few examples: a lost child stolen away at birth but recognized years later by birth tokens; an orphan whose origins are mysterious; identical twins or doubles, one good and one bad; matched opposing heroes or heroines, one dark and one blond; sacrificial heroines who are falsely accused/ beseiged by suitors/ imprisoned by malevolent uncles/ kidnapped by pirates or Indians/ threatened with rape and death; a brotherhood of comrades who go on a perilous journey to undo a wrong/ find a lost kingdom/ discover a secret; and of course escape from the imprisoning lower world, deliverance, recognition of identity, and rewards, including marriage and treasure.

These motifs and plot elements provide a huge pool into which storytellers dip their buckets to draw out the materials for their stories to which they add, in greater or lesser degree, details drawn from everyday life. Dime novels told stories of quests for a lost precious object or a kidnapped heroine, characters in disguise, orphans who discover their identity, and sudden shifts in fortune, where the plot reversal often depends upon coincidence. Some series books, especially tamer books for younger children such as the early Rollo books, the Bobbsey Twins, and school stories such as Junie B. Jones, emphasize everyday experience, sometimes enlivened with a hint of romance in the form of a buried treasure at the seaside or a mysterious stranger.

Others, especially those set in worlds historically or geographically remote from the world of the reader give more play to romance elements, including the heightened contrast of good and evil, the use of disguise and coincidence, strong patterning and design, and the use of non-representational plots and characters that do not pretend to correspond to the way things are in the outer world. The sensational stories that Louisa May Alcott wrote in the 1860s under the pen name A.M. Barnard provide a compendium of romance motifs: inherited insanity, mind control, the foundling, the malevolent guardian, the beleaguered heroine, the pretended wedding, the death-like trance induced by drugs, murder, suicide, disguises, and false names (Stern, 1995; Stern, 1996). In the case of fairy stories and folktales, the plots and motifs are sufficiently conventionalized and formulaic that they have been indexed by folklore specialists such as Stith Thomson (1955-1958).

Northrup Frye (1976) says that the conventionalized structures of folktales are what you get when the imagination is left to itself. When the imagination struggles to take into account the outer world, which is separate from itself, it has to adapt its formulaic units to the demands of external plausibility. "The fundamental technique used," claims Frye, "is what I call displacement, the adjusting of formulaic units to a roughly credible context" (p. 36). The more "realistic" a work seems, the further it has moved in the direction of the displaced and the representational.

The concept of displacement is a useful conceptual tool to help us find appropriate criteria by which to judge a literary work. Much of the criticism of dime novels and series books, as we shall see, involves the application of standards for realism—i.e., plausibility and probability—to stories that are nearer to the pole of romance than to the pole of realism. The closeness of these popular fictions to undisplaced fairy tales accounts is reason for their popularity with children and with beginning readers. On the other hand, the displacement of these fairy tale plots by the use of details drawn from daily newspapers give the stories the appearance of realism and up-to-dateness.

The story of the enormous popularity of dime novels and series books is in many ways an account of the expansion of literacy itself. In 19th-century America and elsewhere, a number of factors came together that transformed the book from a rare cherished object, like the family Bible, to a disposable commodity. The manual press gave way to speeded-up, mechanized printing. New paper-making machinery was developed that produced a continuous web of paper; the rotary press was invented into which the web was fed; the composition of type was speeded up by composing machines. The building of canals and railroads sped up the process of distribution and made it possible for newspapers and books to be printed in New York City and shipped efficiently to dispersed markets.

These developments in the production and distribution of popular fiction brought cheap, recreational reading within the economic reach of young working-class readers. In *Mechanic Accents*, Denning (1987) makes the case that the bulk of the readers of dime novels and story papers were working class—apprentices, sewing girls, craftspersons, factory workers, servants and domestic workers. For these readers, cheap fiction did not so much displace other and more literary reading as inaugurate reading for people whose parents had not been able to read at all. According to Stern (1980), the 19th-century American publishers who "built their houses upon the thesis that the millions had the right to affordable literature" launched a "literary revolution" (p. ix) that transformed reading and made diverse reading materials far more widely available to all classes of readers.

Similarly, series books for children became for many an important part of their apprenticeship in learning to read. From Jacob Abbott's (1835) first *Rollo* to Enid Blyton's (e.g., 1942/2001) *Famous Five*, R.L. Stine's (1989) *Fear Street*, and Francine Pascal's (2008) *Sweet*

Valley High, series books have accounted for a large bulk of the voluntary reading that children choose to do for pleasure. Silk Makowski's (1998) *Serious about Series*, which annotates and evaluates 62 contemporary paperback series for young adult readers, demonstrates the continuing appeal of series books. Along with Catherine Barr's (1999) *Reading in Series: A Selection Guide to Books for Children*, which includes more than 800 series for children in grades K–8, these two bibliographic guides are helpful to teachers and librarians wanting to get a handle on the large and growing output of series books.

What keeps young readers reading is the pleasure of the experience itself, as dime novels and series books introduce their readers to the tried-and-true formulas of popular storytelling. Young readers who read dime books or series books are introduced to the shape of stories as a whole. It is not the individual title that is important but rather what the entire convention is saying and doing through the particular work. From the point of view of literacy, dime novels and series books are important for what they teach the readers about the universe of storytelling and how stories function.

"Books for the Million!"

Because accounts of children's literature are often silent on the subject of dime novels and series books, it can be a surprise to realize the enormous size and scale of the phenomenon. According to Cox (2000), there were several thousand writers in North America who wrote dime novels between 1860 and 1915. Of these, some were amazingly prolific. For example, Gilbert Patten was the professional name of the principal writer of Street & Smith's Frank Merriwell stories. In 17 years, Patten produced 777 stories of 30,000 or so words each under the house name of Burt L. Standish (Cox, 2000). Another Street & Smith author, Frederic Van Rensselaer Dey, was the principle author of the Nick Carter detective series, producing a 25,000-word story a week for 17 years (Cox, 2000; Reynolds, 1955). Laura Jean Libbey published 82 romances for female readers that sold between 10 and 15 million copies in her lifetime (Cox, 2000). Her plots retell the story of an orphaned or abandoned mill girl who, despite being beset by a blocking parent figure or kidnapped by a villain, retains her integrity and wins the love of a man far above her in class and wealth. Horatio Alger, Jr. published some 125 novels for boys about industrious apprentices who succeed by pluck, luck, virtue, and hard work (Bennett, 1980). Alger's titles indicate the typical shape of his plots, which usually involve an upward bounce from a lower world: *Luck and Pluck; or, John Oakley's Inheritance* (1869); *Bound to Rise: or, Harry Walton's motto* (1873); *Risen from the Ranks; or, Harry Walton's Success* (1874); *Struggling Upward; or, Luke Larkin's Luck* (1890). Bishop (1879), a reviewer in *The Atlantic Monthly,* argued that the dime novel and story paper literature are,

an enormous field of mental activity, the greatest literary movement, in bulk, of the age, and worthy of very serious consideration for itself. Disdained as it may be by the highly cultivated for its character, the phenomenon of its existence cannot be overlooked. (p. 383)

Overlooked at the time, dime novels eventually attracted the attention of fans and collectors and scholars. Albert Johannsen (1950) published the first scholarly treatment of dime novels in his three-volume study *The House of Beadle and Adams and its Dime and Nickel Novels*. Johannsen's bibliography provided the listing of the 3,117 dime novels published between 1840 and 1900 that were microfilmed for the University Microfilms International (UMI) collection.

Growing interest in popular culture and leisure studies has given a boost to those who regard dime novels and their publishers, writers, readers, and detractors as a crucial part of the history of 19th-century literacy and taste. The description of the UMI project characterizes dime novels as a valued source for the student of mass media entertainment, revealing "the ideals of the times" and "typically American trends of patriotism, rugged individualism, frontier virtues, and faith in hard work as the road to success." Enstad (1999) in *Ladies of Labor* argues that working-class women found in dime novels a melodramatic defence of women's position as wage earners and that they were able therefore to read themselves into a heroic identity denied by the culture at large. Other valuable work on dime novels has been done by a growing group of scholars, including Edward T. Leblanc (1996), Lydia Cushman Schurman, and Deidre A. Johnson (2002).

Michael Denning (1987) has described the dime novel as one of the three dominant formats for popular fiction in America between the 1840s and 1890s, the others being the story paper and the cheap library. These three formats were interconnected, sharing the same authors and publishers and system of distribution. The term "dime novel" started off as a brand name in *Beadle's Dime Novels* (1860–1874) and became a catch-all name for several, related formats that flourished between 1860 and about 1900. "Dime novel" was used for any sensational story sold serially in cheap pamphlet form, irrespective of actual price—in fact many, especially those directed to children, were sold in nickel libraries for five cents.

Beadle's original dime novels were booklets of some hundred or so pages and 70,000 to 80,000 words, with illustrated, salmon-colored paper covers— not in fact yellow, although dime novels were often pejoratively called "yellow-backs." Beadle's Half-dime Library books were typically 35,000 to 40,000 words. Varying in size, the dime books were about 4.25 inches by 6.5 inches, convenient for carrying in a pocket or reading concealed behind a schoolbook or devotional text. According to J. Randolph Cox (2000), whose invaluable *Dime Novel Companion* contains 1,200 alphabetical entries relating to dime books and their producers, there were eventually five major publishing companies that dominated dime story production as well as many other smaller publishers who tried to cash in on the popular trend. The Big Five were Beadle & Adams, George P. Munro, Norman L. Munro (brothers and rivals from Nova Scotia), Frank Tousey, and Street & Smith.

By the 1860s, dime novels were reaching an audience of unprecedented size, created by the general expansion of literacy and the strong demand for cheap reading by Civil War soldiers. The slogan of dime novel publishers Beadle & Adams was "Books for the Million! A dollar Book for only a Dime!! 128 pages complete, only Ten Cents!!" (Reynolds, 1955, p. 72). It took a few dozen issues of Beadle's Dime Novels before the dime story conventions stabilized. The first 28 were published in salmon wrappers, without the cover illustration that later became such an important element in selling the books. From number 29 onwards, covers featured black woodcut illustrations depicting such dramatic scenes as a heroine in deadly peril, an Indian warrior brandishing an axe or clutched by the throat by the hero, or masked bandits on horseback holding up a train.

By the 1880s, advances in color printing using a combination of red, yellow, and blue, allowed for covers with vividly colored lettering and images. Just as the illustrations became more vivid—detractors called them lurid and garish—the writing became less descriptive and more plot-driven. As Pearson (1929) pointed out, dime-novel writers took some time to hit upon the formula of plunging the main character immediately into exciting action with a prototypical opening such as "Bang! Bang! Bang! Three shots rang out on the midnight air!" (p. 3).

Written initially for a working-class adult readership, dime novels were enjoyed by children and eventually many were written and marketed specifically for a youthful readership. In *Virgin Land*, Smith (1950) noted that with the launching of the Beadle Dime Novels "An audience for fiction was discovered that had not previously been known to exist" (p. 100). In short, dime novels translated the conventions of popular fiction into new world settings making them available to a new audience of children and working-class readers.

An examination of the story types given separate entries in Cox's (2000) *Dime Novel Companion* suggests that frontier and western stories were only one genre among a list that includes: Bandit, Outlaw, and Highwayman Stories; Circus and Carnival Stories; Civil War Stories; Detective and Mystery Stories; Sea Stories; Temperance Stories; and War Stories among others.

Newly literate readers could choose thrilling stories about the frontier, Indian captivity, revenge, western heroes and outlaws such as Kit Carson, Wild Bill, Daniel Boone, and Calamity Jane. But they could also read stories about detectives such as Old Cap Collier, "Old Sleuth," and Nick Carter, road-agents such as Deadwood Dick, or "detective queens" such as Denver Doll who did battle against road agents. Or they could read about industrious apprentices and other "Boys Who Succeed"; stories of aristocratic children stolen away and raised by gypsies; or impoverished girls whose love for a rich young man is thwarted by his aristocratic father. In Charlotte M. Braeme's (1877) *Dora Thorne*, young Ronald protests stoutly when warned by his father that a "simple rustic, the daughter of my lodge keeper" is no fitting wife for "my son, the heir of Earlescourt." And he responds, "What mesalliance can there be, father? I never have believed and never shall believe in the cruel laws of caste. In what is one man better than or superior to another save that he is more intelligent or more virtuous?" (p. 12).

Series Books, Stratemeyer, and the Fifty-center

By the end of the 19th century, when the dime novel was tapering off, a related publishing phenomenon was getting its second wind: series books written and marketed for children and featuring young people as central characters. Johnson (2002) traces the successful formulae for contemporary children's series to early 19th-century origins in the multiple series generated by Jacob Abbott, author of nearly 200 books for young readers including the Rollo, Jonas and Cousin Lucy series books. Starting with *Rollo Learning to Talk* (1835) and *Rollo Learning to Read* (1835), the 14-volume Rollo series follows the everyday life of its hero from about five years old to the end of his education and beyond. In the continuum from everyday realism to the heightened effects and designing power of romance, Abbott stands at the pole of realism. Johnson (2002) points out that Abbott was the first to use marketing strategies that later became standard: the use an established character to kick off a new series; the launching of a parallel girls' series to capitalize on the popularity of an already existing boys' series; the selling of the series by including a list of all previous titles in each new one; and an anticipatory reference to the next book in the series at the end of the current one. The 40 volumes that were published in the Rollo, Jonas and Lucy series sold an estimated 1,250,000 copies in 25 years (Mott, 1947, quoted in Johnson, 2002).

Abbott's success demonstrated that readers are attracted to books with continuing characters. For novice readers, series books provide scaffolding. It is easier to get into a new book if some of the central characters are familiar and if the reader knows in advance the kind of story to expect. On the other hand, too much familiarity and predictability is boring. Producers of series books have struggled with this problem of finding the right balance between familiarity and novelty. Over the years, they have experimented with different structures that link stories together while providing something new in the next book: chronological variety as the central character grows older and progresses through various stages of education and rites of passage into adulthood; geographic variety as the same characters travel to different locations, often on the trail of something secret or stolen; and problem-based variety as the same characters solve a succession of puzzling cases.

Many series are hybrids. Hence we may find the school story combined with mystery or travel elements in the Rover Boys or an education/apprenticeship story combined with mystery in the Cherry Ames series or in Margaret Sutton's Judy Bolton series. Less common is the series with changing characters but a common locale or atmosphere or theme. One such example is R.L. Stine's (e.g., 1989) Fear Street, where the Fear Street atmosphere is carried over from one book to the next while the characters change. As Silk Makowski (1998) remarked in her helpful guide to YA paperback books in series, "any family that moved there might as well kiss their teenagers goodbye! ...something evil inhabits Fear Street" (p. 43).

The detective story proved to be the most resilient and popular formula for juvenile series books because, among other virtues, it solves a key problem of seriality: how to achieve both continuity and variety. This problem presents itself most starkly in school stories and stories of apprenticeship, where plot interest centers on growing up and rites of passage. After Rollo has learned to read, in the next book he needs to be older and achieve a new milestone. Martha Finley's (e.g., 1867) 28-title Elsie Dinsmore series follows Elsie's lachrymose development from a motherless eight-year-old suffering injustice in the schoolroom right through to marriage, motherhood, and grandmotherhood. The danger is that, as the characters age, they outgrow their audience. Once the Rover Boys got to Wall Street, Edward Stratemeyer had to start over with a second generation. The detective story genre avoids the problem of aging characters who outgrow their readership, variety being provided instead by the succession of baffling cases. Enid Blyton's (e.g., 2001) Famous Five solve mysteries and hunt treasure summer after summer but don't grow any older. The Hardy Boys and their friends never graduate; Nancy Drew has remained 16 (and later 18) in each book, living in what her first author Mildred Wirt Benson (1995) called a "time capsule" (p. 65).

Series book momentum was building as the 20th century began, with 160 new series launched between 1900 and 1909 and almost 500 additional series started in the following two decades (Johnson, 2002). What turned the series book phenomenon into "The Series Book Problem" was the stunning popularity of Edward Stratemeyer, which as early as 1901 had prompted a backlash—the Newark Public Library removed Stratemeyer books from its shelves, along with those of Horatio Alger and Oliver Optic (Rehak, 2005). The Stratemeyer books were under suspicion because Stratemeyer's background as a dime novelist highlighted for librarians the connection between series books and the hated dime novel. Dizer (1996) points out that many wrote both dime novels and series books for juvenile readers, the most successful being Edward S.

Ellis, W. Bert Foster, Harriet Irving Hancock, William G. (Gilbert) Patten, and Edward Stratemeyer.

Stratemeyer got his publishing start in the 1890s, writing and editing dime novels for Street & Smith, where he met many of these dime novel greats. According to McFarlane (1976), "He learned from the inside. He rid himself of any fancy notions about literature as an art" (p. 48). He made his biggest impact as a book packager and founder of the Stratemeyer Syndicate. According to Johnson (1993), who has written the definitive book on Stratemeyer and his Syndicate, Stratemeyer series books have sold over 200 million copies. Stratemeyer generated new series for different market segments—boys, girls, young children, adolescents— and in many different genres— the school story, the family story, travel adventure, the sports story, science fiction, the western, the outdoor and campfire story, and the detective story—and waited for the market to decide. How many titles, series, house names, and writers? A staggering number. In an online article, "The Stratemeyer Syndicate Pseudonyms," James D. Keeline (n.d.) reports that he is working on a major project tentatively titled *The Series Book Companion*, in which he hopes to address "the sheer volume of the material."

Billman (1986) notes that what Stratemeyer did in the field of children's publishing was not new—in fact, it was "representative of the workings of the juvenile publishing world after the turn of the century" (p. 4). Stratemeyer stands out because he did what others did, but did it better. He set the pattern for the modern series for boys and girls by adapting and combining elements developed by his predecessors, including Jacob Abbott's marketing strategies and Street & Smith's production and distribution methods, but adding his own special understanding of the kinds of stories that turn young people into repeat readers. Stratemeyer's practice was to devise series concepts, market them to publishers, and recruit ghostwriters to write the books. He was clear about what style he wanted. In a 1904 interview, he declared, "I have no toleration for that which is namby-pamby or wishy-washy in juvenile literature. This is a strenuous age.... [The boys and girls] of today are clever and up-to-date" (Johnson, 1993, p. 5).

Writers who could produce vigorous, "up-to-date" copy were paid from $75 to $150 for a manuscript (Rehak, 2005), or about what a journalist would be paid for two or three weeks of work. Stratemeyer generated a title and brief plot outline, the ghostwriter expanded the outline into a book of some 200 pages, and Stratemeyer edited the manuscript, always having the final say. The book was published under a Syndicate house name such as Arthur M. Winfield (Rover Boys), Laura Lee Hope (Bobbsey Twins), and Carolyn Keene (Nancy Drew). Individual writers could come and go, but the author names beloved by readers stayed with the Syndicate. Information about the ghostwriters has only gradually emerged, as accounts have been published about Howard Garis (1966), who wrote Bobbsey Twins and Tom Swift books; Leslie McFarlane

(1976) who wrote the first Hardy Boys books; and Mildred Wirt Benson (Lapin, 1994; Rehak, 2005) who wrote the first Nancy Drews.

At a time when hardcover fiction for children was selling for $1.00 or $1.25 a book, Stratemeyer invented an economic model for children's publishing that did an end-run around cultural gatekeepers. Soderbergh (1974) reports that Stratemeyer was fond of saying, "Any writer who has the young for an audience can snap his fingers at all the other critics" (p. 866). In 1906, he approached publisher Cupples & Leon with a proposal: a set of breeders for a new series, "The Motor Boys," and a plan for selling cloth-covered, hard-bound books directly to kids by lowering the unit price. The profit margin for an individual book would be low, but publishers would make up for it in volume.

By the 1930s series books were selling for 50 cents and were referred to as Fifty Cent Juveniles or fifty-centers. According to anonymous *Fortune* magazine reviewer identified by Rehak as Ayers Brinser (1934), Grosset & Dunlap was printing 3 million fifty-centers a year and its major competitors Cupples & Leon and A.L. Burt were printing 1 million apiece. Stratemeyer became known as the Henry Ford of children's publishing: he speeded up production by the use of ghost writers; he achieved uniformity by controlling the story outlines and retaining editorial control; and he kept unit costs low through large production runs and economies of scale.

The image of this rising tide of cheap books triggered the usual anxieties associated with mass media: that the counterpart to the assembly-line form of production is a mass audience conceived of as passive dupes, made supine by the meretricious pleasures of mass consumption. The designation "fifty-center," like "dime novel" and "penny dreadful," became a term of opprobrium used by critics who associated cheap purchase price with cheap content. Indignation over the fifty-center was heightened by the respectable, hard-cover binding of the books. Some felt that at least the dime novel was honest: a shoddy product in a shoddy and lurid package. The fifty-center was a wolf in sheep's clothing, an imposter in the fold of children's literature duping unwary children who mistook series books for the genuine article.

Setting aside the child-as-dupe explanation, we could ask what, then, is the appeal of series books to children? The key seems to be that series books find the right balance for their particular audience of familiarity and novelty, safety and danger, comfort and challenge. Boredom, argues Margaret Meek (1991), is frequently the result of a misalignment between the reader and the text: boring texts are usually either too difficult or too easy for the reader. Series books succeed with novice readers by providing a lot of scaffolding that makes reading easy enough to be successful and pleasurable. The predictability of the conventions that bores practiced readers helps novices get into the story. The series in effect provides a contract with readers, guaranteeing the kind of experience they can expect. Repeat readers come to regard the continuing characters as friends. At the end of each book, readers are alerted to the next adventure—hence at the end of *Cherry Ames at Spencer* (Tatham, 1949), we read "Don't miss *Cherry Ames, Night Supervisor*—the exciting story of how Cherry outwits a shrewd criminal and solves the hospital's financial problem" (p. 213).

Readers are taught by the books themselves how to distinguish good guys from bad guys, how to size up the significance of events, and how to know that apparently unrelated plot lines will eventually come together (Ross, 1995). In an excellent discussion of the Baby-sitters Club and its role in supporting literacy, Mackey (1990, p. 484) argues that children make "valuable reading discoveries, almost without noticing"—reading for the story but learning about "the value of practice in prediction, extrapolation, and pattern-making."

The guaranteed happy ending makes it safe to enjoy the vicarious adventure—from the tamer excitements of finding treasure in Bobbsey Twins books to ghosts, skeleton fingers, haunted attics, submarine caves, etc. in Nancy Drew, Judy Bolton, and the Hardy Boys. In a nutshell, the familiarity of the characters, settings, and conventions, together with the happy ending, makes series book reading a safe experience for new readers. The reader comes to know that, however desperate the hero's situation seems at the end of a cliff-hanger chapter, the next chapter will begin with some variant on, "And then, with one bound, he was free!" Novelty is provided by plot elements that invite the reader to turn the page. Formulas such as threats looming out of the fog, rescues "in the nick of time," miraculous escapes from impossible situations, the pursuit of lost, precious objects and the discovery of secrets and hidden identities—these were the devices that cultivated the repeat readers of boys' series books (some of whom were girls).

Girls' series books tended to be tamer affairs. In the late 19th century, series such as Little Prudy, Dotty Dimple, Flaxie Frizzle told stories about the daily adventures of childhood (Johnson, 2002). Clearly, girls responded strongly to the appeal of books that celebrated the comforts of home, domesticity, school, and friendship (Ross 1994). But, as Mason (1975) suggests, after decades of Little Prudy and Elsie Dinsmore, there was an evident need for fiction about girls who "did things" (p. 10).

Initially, they did things in groups. By 1910, go-ahead girls had taken to the open road and skies in various series produced by Stratemeyer and his competitors: The Motor Girls, The Automobile Girls, The Motor Maids, The Flying Girl, and The Girl Aviators (Romalov, 1997). Other up-and-doing girls were learning woodcraft, singing camp songs, building fires, and wearing feathered headdresses in multiple series about Camp Fire Girls, Outdoor Girls and Girl Scouts (Inness, 1997a; Tarbox, 2000). In the girls' series, however, the motor trips and camping excursions are understood as an interlude, a time to acquire and practice skills that will be useful later in the domestic sphere. Knowing camp fire skills such as how never to be without a knife and matches, how to rig up a temporary winter shelter, how to bandage a sprain, etc., turns out to be a good preparation for the serious work of housekeeping.

But the image of the series book heroine was changing. In 1919, Stratemeyer chided Howard Garis for his "tendency to fearful and fainting girls and women. Better cut it—in these days the girls and women have about as much nerve as the boys and men. The timid, weeping girl must be a thing of the past" (Rehak, 2005, pp. 80–81). The real change came with Nancy Drew, full-time sleuth who ventures alone as she searches with her flashlight for clues in an attic, castle tower, hidden staircase, or locked chamber. As one person exclaimed in an online discussion of Nancy Drew, "Oh, my goodness, you've NEVER READ a Hardy Boys book????...They're just as good as Nancy Drew except it takes two boys to do what Nancy could do on her own."

We Owe It All to You, Nancy Drew

In publishing circles, everyone knew that girls' series don't sell as well as boys' series—not until Nancy Drew exploded on the scene and has became a one-of-a-kind phenomenon. Four years after the 1930 debut of the first three Drew books, an article in *Fortune* magazine reported, "Nancy is the greatest phenomenon among all the fifty-centers.... In the six weeks of the last Christmas season Macy's sold 6,000 of the 10 titles of Nancy Drew compared with 3,750 for the runner-up Bomba, which had 15 volumes to choose from" (Brinser, 1934). By the mid-1980s, estimated cumulative sales of the Nancy Drew series were some 80 million books (Billman, 1986), with annual sales of a million a year. In the 2007 movie *Nancy Drew* from Warner Brothers (Beeson & Brennan, 1995), Nancy was still being Nancy more than 75 years after her first appearance in *The Secret of the Old Clock* (Keene, 1930)—perfect at everything she does, stylish, independent, level-headed, gutsy, and able to face down bad guys without turning a hair. One scene in the movie trailer shows Nancy finding a bomb in her car and saying, "Excuse me, I have to defuse this bomb." Over the years, Nancy has been imprisoned in towers, locked in car trunks, shoved into ravines and down elevator shafts, and has frequently found herself going around a mountainous curve with the brakelines on her roadster cut (Plunkett-Powell, 1993). The Nancy Drew series became a pattern book that later series used even when they chose to deviate from the pattern. Girl sleuths sprang up in abundance: Judy Bolton (1932–1967), Dana Girls (1934–1979), and Trixie Belden (1948–86) just to name a few.

Because of her enduring popularity and her pioneering role beating the boy heroes at their own game, Nancy Drew herself has become a cultural icon unmatched by any other series book character. In addition to the original Grosset & Dunlap series and its sequels and spin-offs, there have been multiple films and television shows, Nancy Drew lunch boxes, puzzles, comic books, cookbooks, and recently Nancy Drew websites, online discussion groups, and computer games. Several generations of readers have grown up reading Nancy Drew, with collections of the blue, cloth-covered and later yellow-spined books passed on from mother to daughter to granddaughter and niece. Nancy Drew is widely considered a feminist role model—and for some a lost leader.

The Nancy Drew series has attracted far more than its share of scholarly work. In *The Girl Sleuth: A Feminist Guide*, Mason (1975) was the first to give book-length attention to girls' series books, tracing the genealogy of the girl sleuth and outing Nancy as a preserver of class distinction and old money privilege. Mason asks, "Why is solving mysteries the special domain for girl adventurers in fiction? And have these 'liberated' heroines liberated their readers?" (p. 7). In subsequent articles and books that consider Nancy's effect on readers, the answers given to the liberating-the-reader question are mixed. In *The Secret of the Stratemeyer Syndicate*, Billman (1986) emphasizes the gothic motifs in the Drew books—moldering castles, decaying aristocracy, hidden staircases, and buried secrets. But in the end she suggests that these same romance elements that give the Drew books their readerly appeal also undermine the felt correspondence between Nancy's world and the outer world. Thus Nancy is disqualified for the role of "helpful fictional model of successful womanhood" (p.119).

Literary critic and mystery writer Carolyn Heilbrun (1995), on the other hand, calls Nancy "the model for early second-wave feminists" (p. 17). Heilbrun claims that what the original Nancy Drew books were all about was "the mystery of overcoming gender expectations and *doing* something in the world" (p. 18). A surprisingly large percentage of the critical work on Nancy Drew replay the central questions also asked about dime novels: What kind of human experience is being represented? What impact will reading this fictional representation have upon readers? Won't young readers of Nancy Drew get false views of the ideal life as white, Anglo-Saxon, heterosexual, and privileged?

Among the critiques of Nancy as role model are some from the perspective of those whom the text seems to exclude: people of color and lesbian readers. In "Fictions of Assimilation: Nancy Drew, Cultural Imperialism, and the Filipina/American Experience," Melinda L. de Jesus (1998) reports that growing up in a gritty city of eastern Pennsylvania in the 1970s she and her friends immersed themselves "in the world of Nancy Drew: unflappable, sophisticated Nancy [who] always outsmarted the boys and got things done.... Our love for Nancy bordered on an obsession" (p. 228). By the time she was 16, however, she repudiated the unattainably perfect Nancy in a poem that began: "Fuck off, Nancy Drew" (p. 229). Her article explores the tensions of identification experienced by a young Filipina girl who chose a WASP girl detective as a beloved role model. Reading now as a feminist cultural critic, she views these series books as a site of colonization and hegemonic power, beguiling non-WASP readers with an invitation to identify with whiteness and wealth, against their own race and class interests.

Some critics, on the other hand, have argued that Nancy is an ambiguous figure—both feminine and masculine, a perennial teenager with adult powers—whose very ambiguity requires the reader to fill in the gaps. Inness (1997b) in "Is Nancy Drew Queer?" makes the case that works of popular culture offer the potential for excluded readers to read themselves into the text in ways that can be empowering. Taking the Nancy Drew books as her specific example, she describes how some lesbian readers construct their own meanings from texts targeted to a largely heterosexual readership, "reading against the grain of the implied text" (p. 82) and finding lesbian subtexts. These lesbian subtexts are available to readers of the series, but Mabel Maney (Gardner, 1998) makes them explicit in three parodies featuring Nancy Clue, Cherry Aimless, and the Hardly Boys, all of whom turn out to be gay: *The Case of the Not-So-Nice Nurse* (1993), *The Case of the Good-for-Nothing Girlfriend* (1994), and *The Ghost in the Closet* (1995). This re-writing of texts provides a dramatic example of what readers do all the time as they read themselves into texts and read the texts back into their own lives. Research that focuses on the activity of readers rather than solely on texts indicates that pleasure-readers are poachers: they opportunistically take up whatever speaks to their immediate lives, they forget or simply skip over the parts they don't find meaningful, and they rewrite unsatisfying endings (c.f. the slash fiction that Dutro and McIver discuss in an earlier *Handbook* chapter). This readerly agency makes it difficult to predict on the basis of the text itself what significance a particular reader will take from a text, whether colonizing or liberating.

"The real Nancy Drew mystery," says Nancy Pickard (1995), "may be the Mystery of the Appeal of Nancy Drew herself, and of her phenomenal attraction for successive generations of American girls." Pickard suggests the answer when she calls *The Hidden Staircase* "a rich and nutritious feast of psychological archetypes" which "assumes the quality of fairy tale and myth." In effect, Nancy's descent into the underground looking for her lost father and her "journeying deeper and deeper in a really quite frightening tunnel" is so powerful because it taps into a fundamental story motif: the descent into a subterranean world and the return.

More recently, R.L. Stine (e.g., 1989) tapped this same vein with great success. In Fear Street, the subterranean world visited in the *Hidden Staircase* becomes more menacing and more overtly connected with death as Stine superimposes the underworld of the nightmare on the everyday world of the school story. In an interesting twist, many Fear Street titles suggest a traditional school story—e.g., "The New Girl," "The Prom Queen," "The First Date" but seasoned readers know that, because these stories happen on Fear Street, they will contain as many chills as the more ominously titled stories, such as "Who Killed the Homecoming Queen?" In such stories, the central characters enter a lower world where they experience growing isolation and immobility: they may be trapped in a labyrinth or prison; they may meet human beings who have been turned into sub-human, animal forms; clocks and mirrors become objectifying images of death; the descent to the night world may be accompanied by a loss of identity. Frye (1976) devotes a whole chapter, "Bottomless Dream: Themes of Descent" (p. 97), to the elaboration of this descent theme in two thousand years of popular literature. Beginning readers, however, often have their first encounter with the underground journey when reading about Nancy Drew's exploration of hidden staircases, the Hardy Boys' penetration of deep ocean caves, or the supernatural terrors of Fear Street. As we have seen, series books become the reader's first introduction to powerful literary forms.

Scorned Literature and Pernicious Reading

Tom Sawyer imagined running away to sea and returning triumphant as "Tom Sawyer the Pirate—the Black Avenger of the Spanish Main." "False views of life," sniffed all those cultural authorities who worried about the effects of popular fiction on impressionable minds. The dime book and later the series book became a lightning rod for anxieties about uncultivated readers with low tastes reading too many books, enjoying it too much, and acquiring false views of life. To some extent this uneasiness can be explained as the worry by a cultural elite that things were getting out of hand.

Mightn't a newsboy read a Jesse James dime novel and aspire to becoming an outlaw or at the very least lose respect for figures of authority? Mightn't a sewing girl read Cinderella stories about factory girls marrying the sons of rich mill owners and get ideas above her station? Stories that enact wish-fulfillment dreams are thought to be unruly, subversive, just waiting to cause a bust-out in unregulated ways. The metaphor underpinning many accounts is that popular fiction is a drug: reading dime books or series books is like consuming opium or alcohol (Ross, 1987). Commentators wrote of readers being "intoxicated" with Tom Swift, suffering from an "overstimulated" imagination, being "addicted" to the repetitive pleasures of "the series habit."

Some thought more regulation and control was required. Popular literature is what people read, says Frye (1976), "without guidance from their betters" (p. 23). Popular fiction, including dime books, penny dreadfuls, and series books, provides pure entertainment, is not intended to instruct, and is therefore considered a waste of time. But worse than that, popular fiction is "sensational," deliberately seeking out violent stimulus. Reading (or excessive reading) of popular fiction was variously said to be injurious because, on an increasing scale of harm, it does some or all of the following:

1. Wastes precious time.
2. Provides models of poor writing, faulty grammar, and non-standard spelling (especially in the case of dialect used as a marker for uneducated or foreign characters).
3. Injures the mind, fosters mental laziness, and renders the brain unwilling or unable to read serious fare.
4. Instills false views of life and unfits readers for everyday life (the *Emma Bovary* effect).
5. Over-stimulates the passions and/or the imagination and creates a morbid love of excitement that is addictive, establishing a habit that must be fed by ever-increasing doses of stimulation.
6. Lessens the reader's horror of crime and wickedness by providing glamorous representations of highwaymen, outlaws, and criminal life.

Taking the long view, John Springhall (1998) has provided an analysis of successive waves of "moral panics" that have accompanied each new, commercially-successful form of mass entertainment. Emphasizing the British experience, Springhall looks at responses to mass culture from penny gaff theatres and penny dreadful novels to horror comic books, Gangsta-Rap, and violent videos. A common set of elements appear in each case: a young or proletarian audience; a popular entertainment thought to be sensational, sexy and/or violent; a link made between reading/ watching the entertainment and taking up a life of vice or crime; and an alarmed response from social guardians including a call for censorship.

At the root of the worry is the proletarian and youthful status of the consumers of these forms of entertainment. Springhill (1998) argues that, during these periodic outbreaks of censorship, the mass entertainment was turned into a scapegoat for larger social problems of poverty and an excluded underclass. Springhall quotes police in England in 1859 as saying that regulars at penny gaffs were "young thieves and prostitutes, whose morals are still further vitiated by the scenes nightly enacted at these sinks of infamy and vice" (p. 20). Dime novels, the North American counterpart of penny dreadfuls, were similarly targeted as breeders of crime.

Twentieth-century critical attacks on series books tended to be less panicky. The story of these attacks has been told from different perspectives (e.g., Soderbergh, 1974; Dizer, 1982; Kaye, 1990; Deane, 1991; Bierbaum, 1994; Ross, 1995; Romalov, 1995). Chamberlain (2002) points out that on balance the critique of series book was less shrill than one would guess by "the tone of moral outrage that marks the most-often-quoted scorners of series books" (p. 189). Children's librarians, especially as they struggled in the early years of the 20th century to establish their domain as a genuine area of professional expertise, began to make their case against series books on the basis of the imperative to weed out the "mediocre" and promote "the best." A newly emerging profession of children's librarianship was beginning to define itself by what it was not. It was *not* a friend of series books, trash, or mediocrity (Beckman, 1964; Bowman, 1921; Root, 1929).

As it turns out, the campaign to promote "the best" did not need to attack dime novels and series books. It is not either/or but both/and when it comes to readers reading popular fiction and literary fiction. Adult denigraters have overlooked the experience of the child reader and the role of dime novels and series books in the making of pleasure-readers. Research based on interviews with avid readers suggests that series books play a vital role in literacy just because they are so pleasurable and because they help novice readers build up the bulk of reading experience needed to become a confident reader. Ross (1995) reported that the majority of adults who consider themselves readers said that they devoured series books as young readers. Case studies confirm the role of series books in helping struggling readers: for example, Carol D. Wickstrom, Curtis, and Daniel (2005) describe how Ashley, a special needs child, made her first genuine connection with books through listening to Barbara Park's (1993) *Junie B. Jones and Her Big Fat Mouth* followed by others in the series about the rambunctious kindergartner, memorizing recurrent lines or patterns from the books, connecting with the character of Junie B., and eventually reading by herself the books that had been read to her. Librarians and literacy specialists are now paying more attention to the reader and to the context of reading and are more likely to consider "the best for whom" and "the best for when." Series books have gained acceptance in libraries and in library selection guides (Barr, 1999). But not everywhere. With more than 43 million copies in print (Grossman, 2007), the Junie B. Jones books, for example, still come in for some familiar anti-series criticisms. Junie B. is a poor role model (she is too mouthy, impulsive and rude; she is a troublemaker who is disrespectful of authority and gets away with it). Junie B.'s first person narrative style, which uses constructions such as "funnest," "beautifuller," and "runned," exposes children to faulty grammar and non-standardized spelling. But readers will ultimately have the last word regarding the real value of series books. Consider two comments from Junie B. Jones fans who have posted online reviews on Amazon.com about readers' engagement with the series:

> I was a little worried at first because [my 9 year old daughter] didn't seem interested in reading at all. But now that Junie

B. has entered her life, she reads non-stop. (November 6, 2001)

We read these Junie B. Jones books at my school. I have checked them all out from the library and just keep reading them. Junie is so funny! I just love the way she talks. She makes me laugh and laugh. (By a 7-year-old reader. Nov 12, 2001)

Children love them and often learn to love reading through them, and parents come to appreciate them for turning their children into readers. No matter the critique, both past and present, of cheap construction, worthless literary quality, and pernicious perils in terms of children's development, it appears that series books (and the dime novels that preceded them) are here to stay.

Literature References

Abbott, J. (1835). *Rollo learning to read.* Boston, MA: Thomas H. Webb.

Abbott, J. (1835). *Rollo learning to talk.* Boston, MA: Thomas H. Webb.

Alger, H. (1869) *Luck and pluck; or, John Oakley's inheritance.* Boston, MA: A.K. Loring.

Alger, H. (1873). *Bound to rise: or, Harry Walton's motto.* Boston, MA: A.K. Loring.

Alger, H. (1874). *Risen from the ranks; or, Harry Walton's success.* Boston, MA: A.K. Loring.

Alger, H. (1890). *Struggling upward; or, Luke Larkin's luck.* Philadelphia, PA: Porter & Coates.

Blyton, E. (2001). *Five on a treasure island.* London, UK: Hodder Children's Books. (Original work published 1942)

Braeme, C. (1877). *Dora Thorne.* London, UK: W. Stevens.

Cleary, B. (1975). *Ramona the brave* (A. Tiegreen, Illus.). New York, NY: Avon.

Finley, M. (1867). *Elsie Dinsmore.* New York, NY: Dodd & Mead.

Keene, C. (1930). *The hidden staircase.* New York, NY: Grosset & Dunlap.

Keene, C. (1930). *The secret of the old clock.* New York, NY: Grosset & Dunlap.

Maney, M. (1993). *The case of the not-so-nice nurse.* Berkeley, CA: Cleis Press.

Maney, M. (1994). *The case of the good-for-nothing girlfriend.* Berkeley, CA: Cleis Press.

Maney, M. (1995). *The ghost in the closet.* Berkeley, CA: Cleis Press.

Martin, A. M. (1995). *The baby-sitters club: The truth about Stacey* (R. Telgemeier, Illus.). New York, NY: Graphix: Scholastic.

Montgomery, L. M. (2008). *Anne of Green Gables.* New York, NY: Putnam. (Original work published 1908)

Park, B. (1993). *Julie B. Jones and her big fat mouth.* New York, NY: Random House.

Pascal, F. (1989). *Jessica on stage (Sweet Valley twins).* New York, NY: Sweet Valley.

Pascal, F. (2008). *Sweet Valley High.* New York, NY: Laurel Leaf.

Rowling, J. K. (1998). *Harry Potter and the sorcerer's stone.* New York, NY: Scholastic.

Snicket, L. (2000). *The miserable mill (A series of unfortunate events—Book the fourth)* (B. Helquist, Illus.). New York, NY: HarperCollins.

Stine, R. L. (1989). *The new girl.* New York, NY: Pocket Books.

Tatham, J. C. (1949). *Cherry Ames at Spencer.* New York, NY: Grosset & Dunlap.

Academic References

Barr, C. (Ed.). (1999). *Reading in series: A selection guide to books for children.* New Providence, NJ: R.R. Bowker.

Beckman, M. (1964). Why not the Bobbsey Twins? *Library Journal, 89*(20), 4612–4613, 4627.

Beeson, D., & Brennan, B. (1995). Translating Nancy Drew from print to film. In C. S. Dyer & N. T. Romalov (Eds.), *Rediscovering Nancy Drew* (pp. 193–207). Iowa City, IA: University of Iowa Press.

Bennett, B. (1980). *Horatio Alger, Jr.: A comprehensive bibliography.* Mt. Pleasant, MI: Flying Eagle.

Benson, M. W. (1995). Fulfilling a quest for adventure. In C. S. Dyer & N. T. Romalov (Eds.), *Rediscovering Nancy Drew* (pp. 59–65). Iowa City: University of Iowa Press.

Bierbaum, E. G. (1994). Bad books in series: Nancy Drew in the public library. *The Lion and the Unicorn, 18,* 92–102.

Billman, C. (1986). *The secret of the Stratemeyer syndicate: Nancy Drew, The Hardy Boys, and the million dollar fiction factory.* New York, NY: Ungar.

Bishop, W. H. (1879, September). Story-paper literature. *Atlantic Monthly, 44,* 383–393.

Bowman, I. K. (1921). Why the American Library Association does not endorse serials for boys and girls. *Iowa Library Quarterly,* 212.

Brinser, A. (1934, April). 'For it was indeed he.' *Fortune,* 86-90.

Chamberlain, K. (2002). 'Wise censorship': Cultural authority and the scorning of juvenile series books, 1890–1940. In L. C. Schurman & D. Johnson (Eds.), *Scorned literature: Essays on the history and criticism of popular mass-produced fiction in America* (pp. 187–211). Westport, CT: Greenwood Press.

Children's Literature Research Collections, University of Minnesota Libraries. (1992). *Girls series books: A checklist of titles published 1840–1991.* Retrieved February 23, 2010, from special.lib.umn.edu./clrc/girlsseriesbooks.html

Cook, W. W. [John Milton Edwards, pseud.] (1912). *The fiction factory.* Ridgewood, NY: Editor Company.

Cox, J. R. (2000). *The dime novel companion: A source book.* Westport, CT: Greenwood Press.

de Jesus, M. L. (1998). Fictions of assimilation: Nancy Drew, cultural imperialism, and the Filipina/American experience. In S. A. Inness (Ed.), *Delinquents & debutantes: Twentieth-century American girls' cultures* (pp. 227–246). New York, NY: New York University Press.

Deane, P. (1991). *Mirrors of American culture: Children's fiction series in the twentieth century.* Metuchen, NY: Scarecrow Press.

Denning M. (1987). *Mechanic accents: Dime novels and working-class culture in America.* London, UK: Verso.

Dizer, J. T. Jr. (1982). *Tom Swift® & company: "Boys' books" by Stratemeyer and others.* Jefferson, NC: McFarland.

Dizer, J. T. (1996). Authors who wrote dime novels and series books, 1890–1914. In L. E. Sullivan & L. C. Schurman (Eds.), *Pioneers, passionate ladies, and private eyes: Dime novels, series books, and paperbacks* (pp. 73–85). New York, NY: Haworth Press.

Enstad, N. (1999). *Ladies of labor, girls of adventure: Working women, popular culture, and labor politics at the turn of the twentieth century.* New York, NY: Columbia University Press.

Frye, N. (1976). *The secular scripture: A study of the structure of romance.* Cambridge, MA: Harvard University Press.

Gardner, J. D. (1998). 'No place for a girl dick': Mabel Maney and the queering of girls' detective fiction. In S. A. Inness (Ed.), *Delinquents & debutantes: Twentieth-century American girls' cultures* (pp. 247–265). New York, NY: New York University Press.

Garis, R. (1966). *My uncle was Uncle Wiggily: The story of the remarkable Garis family.* New York, NY: McGraw-Hill.

Grossman, A. J. (2007, July 26). Is Junie B. Jones talking trash? *New York Times.* Retrieved February 23, 2010, from http://www.nytimes.com/2007/07/26/fashion/26junie.html

Heilbrun, C. G. (1995). Nancy Drew: A moment of feminist history. In C. S. Dyer & N. T. Romalov (Eds.), *Rediscovering Nancy Drew* (pp. 11–21). Iowa City: University of Iowa Press.

Inness, S. A. (1997a). Girl scouts, camp fire girls, and woodcraft girls: The ideology of girls' scouting novels, 1910–1935. In S. A. Inness (Ed.), *Nancy Drew® and company: Culture, gender, and girls' series* (pp. 89–100). Bowling Green, OH: Bowling Green State University Press.

Inness, S. A. (1997b). Is Nancy Drew queer? Popular reading strategies for the lesbian reader. In S. A. Inness. *The lesbian menace: Ideology, identity and the representation of lesbian life* (pp. 79–100). Amherst: University of Massachusetts Press.

Johannsen, A. (1950–1962). *The House of Beadle and Adams and its dime and nickel novels: The story of vanished literature* (3 vols.). Norman: University of Oklahoma Press.

Johnson, D. (1993). *Edward Stratemeyer and the Stratemeyer syndicate.* New York, NY: Twayne.

Johnson, D. (2002). From Abbott to Animorphs, from godly books to goosebumps: The nineteenth-century origins of modern stories. In L. C. Schurman & D. Johnson (Eds.), *Scorned literature: Essays on the history and criticism of popular mass-produced fiction in America* (pp. 147–165). Westport, CT: Greenwood Press.

Kaye, M. (1990). The twinkie collection: Books that have no apparent redeeming value but belong in the library anyway. In A. M. Fasick, M. Johnson, & R. Osler (Eds.), *Lands of pleasure: Essays on Lillian H. Smith and the development of children's libraries* (pp. 49–61). Metuchen, NJ: Scarecrow Press.

Keeline, J. D. (n.d.). Stratemeyer syndicate pseudonyms: Bobbsey Twins, Tom Swift, Hardy Boys, Nancy Drew. Retrieved February 23, 2010, from http://www.trussel.com/books/strat.htm

Kinlock, L. M. (1935, January). The menace of the series books. *Elementary English Review, 12,* 9–11.

Lapin, G. S. (1994). The outline of a ghost. *The Lion and the Unicorn, 18*(1), 60–69.

LeBlanc, E. T. (1996). A brief history of dime novels: Formats and contents, 1860–1933. In L. E. Sullivan & L.C. Schurman (Eds.). *Pioneers, passionate ladies, and private eyes: Dime novels, series books, and paperbacks* (pp. 13–21). New York, NY: Haworth Press.

Mackey, M. (1990). Filling the gaps: 'The baby-sitters club,' the series book, and the learning reader. *Language Arts, 67*(5), 484–489.

Mason, B. A. (1975). *The girl sleuth: A feminist guide.* Old Westbury, NY: Feminist Press.

Makowski, S. (1998). *Serious about series: Evaluations & annotations of teen fiction in paperback series.* Lanham, MD: Scarecrow Press.

McFarlane, L. (1976). *Ghost of the Hardy Boys: An autobiography by Leslie McFarlane.* Toronto, ON: Methuen/ Two Continents.

Meek, M. (1991). *On being literate.* London, UK: Bodley Head.

Meyer, S. (2006). *Twilight, Book 1.* New York, NY: Little Brown.

Mott, F. L. (1947). *Golden multitudes: The story of best sellers in the United States.* New York, NY: MacMillan.

Pearson, E. (1929). *Dime novels: Following an old trail in popular literature.* Boston, MA: Little Brown.

Pickard, N. (1995). I owe it all to Nancy Drew. In C. S. Dyer & N. T. Romalov (Eds.), *Rediscovering Nancy Drew* (pp. 208–211). Iowa City: University of Iowa Press. Retrieved February 23, 2010, from http://www.nancypickardmysteries.com/nancydrew.htm

Plunkett-Powell, K. (1993). *The Nancy Drew scrapbook: 60 years of America's favorite teenage sleuth.* New York, NY: St Martin's Press.

Rehak, M. (2005). *Nancy Drew and the women who created her.* New York, NY: Harcourt.

Reynolds, Q. (1955). *The fiction factory; or, from Pulp row to quality street: The story of 100 years of publishing at Street & Smith.* New York: Random House.

Romalov, N. T. (1995). Children's series books and the rhetoric of guidance: A historical overview. In C. S. Dyer & N. T. Romalov (Eds.), *Rediscovering Nancy Drew* (pp. 113–120). Iowa City: University of Iowa Press.

Romalov, N. T. (1997). Mobile and modern heroines: Early twentieth-century girls' automobile series. In S. A. Inness (Ed.), *Nancy Drew® and company: Culture, gender, and girls' series* (pp. 75–88). Bowling Green, OH: Bowling Green State University Press.

Root, M. E. S. (1929). Not to be circulated. *Wilson Bulletin, 3*(17), 446.

Ross, C. S. (1987). Metaphors of reading. *Journal of Library History, Philosophy, and Comparative Librarianship, 22*(2), 147–163.

Ross, C. S. (1994). Readers reading L.M. Montgomery. In M. H. Rubio (Ed.), *Harvesting thistles: The textual garden of L.M. Montgomery* (pp. 23–35). Guelph, ON: Canadian Children's Literature.

Ross, C. S. (1995). If they read Nancy Drew, so what?: Series book readers talk back. *Library and Information Science Research, 17*(3), 201–236.

Schurman, L. C., & Johnson, D. (2002). *Scorned literature: Essays on the history and criticism of popular mass-produced fiction in America.* Westport, CT: Greenwood Press.

Smith, H. N. (1950). *Virgin land: The American west as symbol and myth.* New York, NY: Vintage Books/ Harvard University Press.

Soderbergh, P. A. (1974). The Stratemeyer strain: Educators and the juvenile series book, 1900–1973. *Journal of Popular Culture, 7*(4), 864–872.

Springhall, J. (1998). *Youth, popular culture and moral panics: Penny gaffs to gangsta-rap, 1830–1996.* New York, NY: St Martin's Press.

Stern, M. B. (Ed.). (1980). *Publishers for mass entertainment in nineteenth century America.* Boston, MA: G.K. Hall.

Stern, M. (Ed.). (1995). *Louisa May Alcott unmasked: Collected thrillers.* Boston, MA: Northeastern University Press.

Stern, M. B. (1996). Dime novels by 'The children's friend.' In L. E. Sullivan & L. C. Schurman (Eds.), *Pioneers, passionate ladies, and private eyes: Dime novels, series books, and paperbacks* (pp. 197–213). New York, NY: Haworth.

Tarbox, G. A. (2000). *The clubwomen's daughters: Collectivist impulses in progressive-era girls' fiction.* New York, NY: Garland.

Thomson, S. (1955-58). *Motif index of folk literature: A classification of narrative elements in folktales, ballads, myths, fables, medieval romances, exempla, fabliaux, jest-books, and local legends* (6 vols.). Bloomington, IN: Indiana University Press.

University Microfilms International (UMI) collection of dime novels. (n.d.). Retrieved February 23, 2010, from http://www.proquest.com/en-US/catalogs/collections/detail/Dime-Novels-410.shtml

Wickstrom, C. D., Curtis, J. S., & Daniel, K. (2005). Ashley and Junie B. Jones: A struggling reader makes a connection to literacy. *Language Arts, 83*(1), 16–21.

Point of Departure

Candice Ransom

Enjoying series books has always been considered poor taste, like reading at the table. Witness the criticism leveled at nine-year-old Amy Carter for doing both: reading *Nancy Drew* and *Three Investigators* books at state dinners in the late seventies.

As Catherine Ross noted, series books were often missing from library shelves, certainly when I was growing up. Endorsed by the American Library Association or not, these books somehow managed to fall into the eager hands of readers.

My first encounter with a series book could have been spun from the plot of a Judy Bolton mystery. I was home sick from school that day. Bored, I draped a bedspread over a card table for a hideout. Because I had read the print off my Golden Books, the only books I owned, I browsed my mother's book club selections like the promisingly titled *Panther Moon*. Wedged behind was a book called *Trixie Belden and the Mysterious Visitor*. Whose book was this? The glossy cover showed a girl kneeling before a fireplace, a sinister-looking man leaning over her.

After the first two sentences, I knew I had found my fictional doppelganger— unruly-haired, math-hating, mystery-loving Trixie Belden. Like me, Trixie lived in the country and would rather solve cases than do chores. We might have been separated at birth, except Trixie had rich friends while I had no friends and she unearthed real crimes while I planted clues to fake mysteries so obvious even my cat figured them out.

How I longed to move to Sleepyside in upstate New York, join Bob-Whites of the Glen, and wear a red jacket with B.W.G. cross-stitched on the back! Criminals were thin on the ground in Virginia and our five acres lacked the requisite run-down gatehouse to convert into a club-house.

Kresge's, where cello-bound Trixies could be had for 59 cents and a lot of whining, provided my ticket to a country where Rip Van Winkle, the Mendelian theory of heredity, and Bennington pottery were in juxtaposition with the grittiness of Hawthorne Street and other unsavory places jewel thieves lurked. In my world, Hawthorne Street took the form of Camp 30, a minimum security facility on the other side of our woods. Only a scrim of trees and weeds divided me from the skulking conmen just beyond. Though I was itching to trap a footpad, I weighed sixty-three pounds and had "adenoids." Such heroics, I learned, were best encountered in the safety of books.

In my day, librarians did their part to "promote 'the best'," as Ross noted.

Newbery winners were branded with an "N" on their spines. Associating "N" books with vitamins, I bucked the notion that someone would dictate what was good for me. Trixie Belden filled a need in me that, say, *Wheel on the School* could not.

When her adopted daughter glommed onto a cheap "totally expendable" book, reviewer Elaine Moss was forced to redefine a "good book." In her essay "The Peppermint Lesson," Moss recognizes that any book a child lays personal claim to is "… a matter of identification not just for the duration of the story but at a deep, warm comforting and enduring level."

Trixie kept me company throughout a difficult childhood. I tried to continue the experience of stand-alone books by poring over the illustrations, endpapers, dust jacket, even the Library of Congress cataloging information, but when the book was over, it was over. Whenever I picked up *Trixie Belden and the Secret of the Mansion*, I was immediately welcomed into a community where I could stay for the duration of that book and others in the series.

Like most popular fiction addicts, I ventured into other series territory. A cousin introduced me to a titian-haired shamus. I tore through Nancy Drew books like greased lightning, but felt Nancy was like my older sister—pretty, exotic, and untouchable.

Trixie's tomboy actions validated my preferences for chemistry sets to dolls and bird-watching to jump rope. While I knew a souvenir teacup wasn't a priceless heirloom in danger of being swiped or the builder of our house wasn't a *real* crook as my parents often claimed, the books satisfied my craving for adventures that *could* happen. Bobby Ann Mason relates a similar experience in *The Girl Sleuth*. Comparing Trixie to the glamorous Nancy Drew, she says, "The Trixie stories had a healthy, restraining effect. They … weren't calculated to make an ordinary little girl unhappy." Of all the female gumshoes, Mason adds, "Trixie is one of the most liberating."

The Trixie Belden series was created by Julie Campbell Tatham, a literary agent who answered Western Publishing's call for writers to produce fast-paced, well-written mysteries. She set the series in her beloved Hudson River Valley. Trixie's Crabapple Farm was based on Tatham's own farmhouse, Wolf Hollow. Unlike many stiffly-written series stories, Tatham's books brim with nature details, a celebration of rural living, and realistic characters.

Tatham quit after writing titles one through six. Subsequent Trixies were penned by different authors under a house pseudonym, Kathryn Kenny. The first of the Kenny books, *The Mysterious Code,* inspired me to pass classroom notes using the stick-figure alphabet cipher. The mild romances introduced in later books left me a bit queasy since I planned on staying eleven forever. Then I reasoned if Trixie could nab bad guys wearing a little mascara on her sandy lashes, maybe leaving my childish self behind a bit at a time wouldn't hurt.

Years ago I came across a Trixie Belden *autographed* by Julie Campbell Tatham in a used bookshop. As I lunged for the copy, the owner told me Mrs. Tatham lived in Alexandria. I nearly lost consciousness. The great author lived *less than 20 miles* from me. When I got home, I ripped through the phone directory and lo! there was her listing. I pounced on the receiver, then paused. What would I say? That her books saved my life when I was a kid? Offer to spend the rest of my born days tending her every need? I didn't dial her number.

From time to time I'd remember Trixie's creator lived only a short drive away. Yet I never called. Suppose she told me Trixie was "just a character?" I couldn't ruin the illusion that my truest friend existed only on the printed page. Julie Campbell Tatham died in 1999, never knowing how much her books had meant to me. I'm sure she must have known Trixie Belden helped guide other hoydenish girls over the steep, slippery bridge to teenagehood.

With the veil of "wickedness" stripped from series books, reading specialists recognize series like the Boxcar Children, Magic Tree House, and the Hardy Boys free independent readers from the spadework of new settings, characters, and styles. In *Beyond Leveled Readers*, Karen Szymusiak and Franki Sibberson state, "Allowing children to linger in books they can easily read can provide them with the context and support they need to become more effective readers." Series books can also plant the seeds for future careers. The wobbly mysteries I scribbled in elementary school became sturdier when I modeled them after Trixie Belden. And my future desire shifted from detective to writer.

Mamas (and daddies), don't let your children grow up without sharing Trixie Belden with them. Slip into a card table reading tent filled with pillows and snacks and head for Sleepyside, where there are gardens to weed, codes to crack, and a red B.W.G. jacket just their size, hanging on a nail inside the gatehouse.

15

Folklore in Children's Literature

Contents and Discontents

Betsy Hearne

University of Illinois, Urbana-Champaign

What could Cinderella and Brer Rabbit possibly have in common—a seemingly passive pawn and a sly trickster? As Betsy Hearne, noted library science professor, children's book author, and folklorist explains, both tales emerge from the oral tradition, appear in a variety of guises as they move onto the written page, and comment boldly on the human condition. Whether dressed in rags or sporting rabbit ears, the characters of folklore in books for the young demonstrate the subversive potential in all of us, and the tales themselves survive by adapting to ever-shifting sociopolitical climes. Hearne's perceptive chapter adds depth to the extensive research surrounding folklore by commenting extensively on the personal relationship between researcher and story. And Julius Lester's Point of Departure commentary adds further insight into social history by reminding us that folklore is transformed in the mouth of the teller, for princesses and rabbits were never expected to lie passively on the page, but step out and teach us all a bit more about life.

Those who engage with children's literature professionally or academically often have a secret that started in childhood: story addiction. Grown up, we may disguise our addiction in a variety of institutional codes: postcolonial discourse, ethnography, child development, pedagogy, performance studies, information access, and theoretical frameworks ad infinitum. But underneath it all, we are story listeners, story takers, story givers, storytellers, story stealers, story dealers. Whatever distance stretches between our adult story-work and childhood story-experience, between our objective and subjective understanding, can become a journey of insightful connections. For this reason, I've used both telescopic and microscopic approaches here: to review some landmark work done in the field, to indicate complexities of contemporary children's literature as a print vehicle for folklore, and—incorporating specific examples—to suggest the importance of scholars' social and personal relationships with the folkloric children's literature we study.

How do we explain a story, when the essence of story is mystery? Partly, we circle around it, because a story never has just one side. We follow tracks to see where it came from, where it is now, where it might go, as well as where it has not been, isn't now, and won't go. All the tracks criss-cross, so they're hard to read. Eventually we get inside the story, but all the while, it has been inside us—something that may take a long time to discover.

Research on storytelling, folklore, and fairy tales in children's literature is challenging because the best way to approach stories is one at a time, and each time is different. A textual study could involve detailed word-by-word and image-by-image comparative criticism, as well as contrasts with mass-market books and popular media. A folkloric field study could involve collection, transliteration, narrative history, and interpretation of setting and interaction during a telling. An educational study could involve analysis of children's responses to the stories as read aloud, read alone, or re-told in their own words. Any one of these approaches, or an interdisciplinary combination, could fill a book.

Part I Background: Folklore, Storytelling, and Brave Cinderellas

> Close reading, so called, can become a bad habit, possibly a vice, where simple appreciation is concerned, but never does it start more quarrels than when the folk are involved. (Bontemps, 1958, p. viii)

Folklore is the birthplace of literature. Historically, oral texts preceded written, print, or electronic texts and were rooted in communal memory and performance. Like Caesar's Gaul, folklore is divided into three parts: verbal, as in stories, chants, and songs; customary, as in parades, birth celebrations, and other rituals; and material, as in handmade buildings, tools, and even manufactured goods altered by homemade art. However, unlike Gaul, these three parts are not discrete but intertwined and interactive. For instance, a pre-World-War II East European epic, shown by Albert Lord (1960) to be related formulaically to Homeric epics, would involve all three parts: the singing of the stories (verbal), male rituals of drinking and smoking (customary), and coffee house interiors with traditional instruments and other handmade objects (material). Thus, the folkloric text must be considered in context of audience, event, and setting, and a study of the text would necessarily involve anthropological observation as well as literary knowledge. Although verbal lore dominates the study of folklore in children's literature in the form of folk and fairy tales, customary and material lore lurk behind every text, and it is important to be aware of the broader scope of folkloric study, which analyzes narrative as part of a living tradition grounded in community.

Even today, the oral tradition coexists and interacts with the written, as elements of folklore such as family, work, or playground stories become culturally embedded, contribute to the common lore of a group, and affect individuals. Folktales, whether formally published or informally told, are part of this environmental matrix; they have been a staple of children's literature since its beginning, but because critical studies so often focus intensely on literary

or theoretical aspects of text, socio-cultural details have sometimes been neglected. Yet, these details are significant in examining distinctive oral variants and print versions, interpreting their meanings, and understanding controversial folkloric issues, such as questions of ownership and appropriation of Native American stories by non-Native authors and illustrators unfamiliar with specific tribal lore (Bruchac, 1992; Hearne, 1993b, 1999; Stott, 1992; Toelken, 1996b).

Although the purveyors of English- and European-language children's literature have historically favored folktales from nineteenth-century collections such as those by Jacob and Wilhelm Grimm (German), Peter Asbjørnsen and Jørgen Moe (Norwegian), Aleksander Afanasyev (Russian), and Joseph Jacobs (English), it is imperative to remember that: first, folklore is not frozen in the past but either survives in a changing context or lives not at all; and second, folklore is ubiquitous. Storytelling is a universal activity, in person if not in print. Countries and cultural groups without the resources for a published body of children's books nevertheless have rich traditions of oral literature crucial to their children's development and heritage; and industrial nations, despite their wealth of literature in print, also host folkloric narratives as part of daily life.

We are all folk, and in multicultural societies and global economies, text and context interact in increasingly complex ways as folk groups diversify, communicate online, reflect or shape popular culture, and find expression in children's and young adult literature. Picture books, fiction, and even nonfiction for youth host folkloric content of which critics need to be aware, from the misguided adaptation of major mythologies (Hercules tamed), to the misrepresentation of archetypal tricksters (Coyote defanged), to the perpetuation of nationalistic legends (Lincoln unprejudiced), to the adulation of family history (mail-order brides romanticized).

The very identification of children as a primary audience for folklore creates a challenge for narrative once considered intergenerational or sometimes adult-only. Certainly the use of children's literature as a tool to instill value systems raises questions among those who view folklore as embedding children's books with demonic imagery, fantastical magic, sexism, racism, violence, and a range of other elements variously viewed as dangerous to the moral development of the young. Thus folklore is not only inherent in children's literature but also inherently controversial as a genre that requires interdisciplinary critical scrutiny.

Complicating the fact that folkloric research demands scholarship in both the humanities and the social sciences is the common lack of folkloric training in three of the fields that deal most often with children's and young adult books: education, literature, and librarianship. The difficulty of academic boundary crossing can prevent specialists from getting a fully rounded view of the folkloric issues involved in children's literature. In fact, many folklorists have taken a dim view of children's literature as hosting inauthentic "fakelore"—of failing to distinguish, for instance, between tales from oral and literary sources. However, this becomes a less than clear-cut distinction given the re-writing that many folktales such as those by the Grimms underwent during publication and sequential editions, not to mention the widespread disagreement over defining what folklore is. Despite all these barriers of differing orientation, folklore in children's literature has received a growing amount of attention to match its consistent and insistent presence.

Developmentally, folklore is born with a child. Children begin their pre-literate lives as part of the oral tradition, hearing and remembering rhymes, songs, games, images, and stories, incorporating them into play and daily activities, and retelling or referring to what they've heard told or read aloud with peers as they socialize. We have not only valid anecdotal evidence of this from parents and other experienced caregivers, but also carefully monitored collections and analytical field studies (Butler, 1980; Opie & Opie, 1959; Wolf & Heath, 1992), along with extensive work on narrative practices and the social construction of self (Alexander, Miller, & Hengst, 2001). Few of these studies limit observations to folklore per se but reveal the way children take what they want from narratives—folk, family, and literary—and use it to survive and thrive.

Children reclaim stories from family and cultural traditions—whether delivered in person, print, or electronic media—and make them their own, selecting, adapting, and appropriating various elements as needed in a process that reflects the oral formation of folktales. Jump-rope rhymes and play chants transmute with the substitution of new names or other elements, as do camp songs, popular jingles, and urban legends youngsters tell each other on overnights. Storytelling of all kinds is pervasive in children's lives, and although family lore enters increasingly into the world of picture books (e.g., Hearne, 1997b; Rylant, 1992; Say, 1993; Woodson, 2005), storytelling in libraries, daycare, and schools depends heavily on folktales in print and electronic media, either as sources for oral delivery or for reading aloud. Canadian storyteller Dan Yashinsky (2004) remarks, "For most contemporary storytellers the local library is our elder" (p.122). Various studies have traced the influences on, and of, storytelling in recent history (Birch & Heckler, 1996; MacDonald, 1999; Pellowski, 1991; Sobol, 1999; Stone, 1998). Annual American events like the National Storytelling Festival, organizations like the National Storytelling Association, journals like *Storytelling, Self, and Society*, and publishers like August House have all focused growing attention on storytelling. Guides both classic (Sawyer, 1942/1976) and contemporary (Haven & Ducey, 2007) help students get started, while websites like the National Storytelling Network (www.storynet.org/) provide easy access to information.

Traditional storytelling—as opposed to reading aloud or alone—has unique power derived from the teller's flexible adaptation of a tale to audience response, eye contact without intermediary graphics, and the exchange of creative communal energy between teller and listeners, who participate through actively intense silence as well as verbal and postural expression.[1] The fact that folktales fall into culturally familiar patterns built on common motifs and tale types makes them easy to remember for both teller and listener, from the simplest cumulative stories to fairy tales, legends, myths, and religious parables; even family stories often incorporate folkloric archetypes of hero, trickster, and villain in everyday roles and situations (Stone, 1988).

Structuralists once tracked motifs and tale types in a research paradigm based on narrative elements relatively independent of cultural context (Thompson, 1955–58; Uther, 2004). Indexes for folklore of Europe, North America, China, Africa, and so on, have facilitated access to and comparison among a vast range of stories. For instance, "Cinderella" is classified as ATU 510A, ATU referring to the classification system published by Aarne, Thompson, and Uther. Included in this tale type are "Cendrillon" (French), "Aschenputtel" (German), "Cenerentola" (Italian), and many other tales from different cultural and ethnic groups.

In fact, "Cinderella" is a good example of the enrichment that awaits anyone interested in exploring a canonical fairy tale. I had always thought of it as a relatively boring story until I began researching some of Cinderella's cousins and ancestors at the start of my doctoral work on fairy tales in 1978. Subsequently, one of my students at the University of Chicago, a counselor at Bruno Bettelheim's famously controversial Orthogenic School, did a case study of an autistic girl who obsessively asked to be read three Cinderella books she had brought with her—one by Disney, one by Perrault, and one by the Grimms—depending on what kind of day she had had and whose part she had enacted. From that time onward, I began to realize that Cinderella was not about magic solutions, but about the courage, kindness, and/or tenacity that "earned" magic. In an autobiographical essay, Ann Trousdale (1992) identified truthfulness as the element that originally drew her to the Canadian "Indian Cinderella," a variant that was anthologized in a widely used text by Clarkson and Cross (1980), and in later research she co-authored the enchantingly titled "'Cinderella was a wuss': A young girl's responses to feminist and patriarchal folktales" (Trousdale & McMillan, 2003).

One of the most widely distributed fairy tales in the world (Cox, 1893; Rooth, 1951), Cinderella permeates popular culture in the form of everyday verbal lore from jokes to jump-rope rhymes: "Cinderella dressed in yella went upstairs to kiss her fella." Typing "Cinderella" into the Google search engine produces—as of this writing—37,200,000 references, and more will materialize. Fantasy novels such as the Newbery Honor book *Ella Enchanted* (Levine, 1997) fictionalize it. Popular films like *Pretty Woman* are based on it. Literature as diverse as William Shakespeare's play *King Lear*, Charlotte Brontë's novel *Jane Eyre*, and George Bernard Shaw's play *Pygmalion*, have reflected Cinderella themes. The Broadway musical *My Fair Lady*, based on *Pygmalion*, was a smash hit, and the subsequent film starring Audrey Hepburn and Rex Harrison won Best Picture, Best Actor, and Best Director.

The Cinderella most commonly known to today's children is Perrault's (1697/1961), on which Walt Disney based his film (1950), and it portrays the weakest heroine. But braver Cinderellas are legion and serve as a good example of how different oral variants and literary versions can reveal contrasting value systems. As Michael Levy (2000) points out in "What If Your Fairy Godmother Were an Ox? The Many Cinderellas of Southeast Asia,"

> It's hard to imagine the codependent Cinderella of Perrault, the passive beauty of Walt Disney, or any other western Cinderella (prior, of course, to Drew Barrymore's depiction of Cinderella in *Ever After* [1998]) having the nerve to stand up to her stepsister and stepmother, let alone take up a sharp-edged weapon in her own defense. (p. 185)

Cinderella, known in folkloric parlance as "The Persecuted Heroine," centers a basic story pattern featuring a young orphan (mostly female but sometimes male) whose mother or both parents are dead and who is persecuted by a parent, step-parent, siblings, and/or step-siblings. S/he undergoes tests of endurance, fidelity, courage, and/or wit; receives magic help, usually from the spirit of a dead mother; is identified as the true hero/ine despite disguises of rags, filth, or animal skins; wins a prince/princess; and either lives happily ever after or has to undergo one more trial after marriage. The cruel treatments of Cinderella vary from impossible chores inflicted by a stepmother to threatened incest by a father who cannot find anyone to marry more beautiful than his dead wife—except the daughter who looks just like her. (This tale type, Peau d'Asne or Donkey Skin, is classified as 510B and is portrayed in McKinley's [1993] novel *Deerskin* as rape by her father.)

The slipper motif appeared 2000 years ago with Rhodopis, a Greek slave girl whose golden sandal was seized by an eagle and dropped in the lap of a Pharaoh who finds and marries her. The Chinese orphan Yeh-shien receives, like many other Cinderellas, the support of an animal helper (a fish) who is killed by the jealous stepmother but whose bones provide magical assistance. The German orphan Aschenputtel's dead mother helps her by means of a hazel tree growing over her grave and inhabited by doves that actually warn the prince of the stepsisters' deceit and pluck out their eyes at the end of the tale. The dying mother of the Russian girl Vasilisa gives her a doll which, if Vasilisa shares with it a bit of food and drink, will advise the girl through tests at the hands of the dangerous witch Baba Yaga. The Irish lass Trembling is swallowed by a whale and spat up again, while the Irish lad Billy Beg runs away from his cruel stepmother on the magical bull given him by his real mother. Cap o' Rushes from England is cast out by her father, like Shakespeare's Cordelia, when she tells him how much she loves him—like meat loves salt—in contrast to her sisters' extravagant claims; but Cap o' Rushes wins her way in the world with hard work and assertive cleverness. The Japanese orphan Benizara proves her worth by composing an exquisite poem. The Little Rag Girl from the Republic of Georgia makes herself known by sticking her needle into the king's backside through the basket where her stepmother has hidden her.

Judy Sierra's (1992) valuable compendium of 25 Cinderella tales includes both common and uncommon versions from around the world. What we find in most of these stories is an active heroine who draws strength from a spiritual connection with her mother, even after the death that was common to women in earlier times when childbirth claimed so many of their lives. True power comes from the mother's love and the daughter's strength. Physical beauty is a manifestation of inner goodness, and the prince is icing on the cake.

In contrast to these many brave Cinderellas of folkloric tradition, Disney's ubiquitous film and book spin-offs feature a sentimental pawn, with the heroine less in a state of suffering than in a state of insufferable cheeriness. The first 20 minutes of the 76-minute production are about cute birds and mice. Folkloric "doubling" becomes "folkloric multiplication," which, in our American obsession with excess, tends to bury folktales' powerful simplicity. Gus, Lucifer, Bruno, and company become main characters; the king and minister provide slapstick distraction from conflict. The fairy godmother's power is diminished by her absent-minded, befuddled demeanor. Cinderella does not have to seek her out, stay loyal to her, remain steadfast, or otherwise prove herself. What she has to do is GIVE UP. That's the moment—when she throws herself on the garden bench sobbing that dreams are no use—when the fairy godmother finally shows up and fixes everything, Bippity, Boppity, Boo.

Children's literature offers many alternatives. At a medium-size midwestern library where I spoke about Cinderella in 2008, 83 different versions were available for young readers and listeners to browse, including collections, novels, and pictures books with wide-ranging artistic interpretations of the story retold from different ethnic traditions. Folklorists such as MacDonald and Sturm (2001; MacDonald, 1982,) have identified a huge range of tales that appear in children's books, resuming indexes that were started in 1926 but eventually outdated. Yet, all of these textual connections, valuable as they are, only begin the research story. Equally important to interpreting, re-creating, and evaluating Cinderella variants such as "Ashpet" (Appalachian) or "The Invisible One" (Micmac)—in, say a picture book or illustrated collection—is not only an awareness of its other variants but also a contextual understanding of the culture from which the tale came and the specific circumstances of its collection, including occasion and teller. Such cultural comprehension increased among folklorists from the late 1960s but did not really penetrate folkloric research in children's literature till the 1990s.

Some cultures are strict about defining how a story can be told and who tells it, while others encourage—both aesthetically and financially—artistic freedom for storytellers to take what they want, make something new, and discard the rest. Cultural appropriation can be a problem both in multicultural societies with tension between ethnically and politically divided subgroups, and in more homogeneous societies "invaded" by dominant outside popular culture. While folk cultures have always borrowed from each other to some extent, writers and artists claiming authorship, copyright, and royalties add a different dimension. Books, film, television and video exert corporate power more far-reaching than earlier formats of communication. Current children's literature—especially since the early 1990s—often features parodies that satirize conventional values, as well as fantasy novels that elaborate folk and fairy tales with fictional strategies *persuading* readers to a willing suspension of disbelief, where their folk predecessors *assumed* suspension of disbelief. While we accept the magical events in the folktale "East of the Sun and West of the Moon," for instance, the novel *East* (Pattou, 2003) develops an elaborate history, set of motivations, and rules of internal logic for its fictionalization of the folktale.

As complex as the relationship is between oral and literary forms and their cultural contexts, the analytic interpretations that seek to gain perspective on them reveal even more intricate and often contradictory relationships. Research on folktales in children's literature becomes a tale within a tale, or at its most abstract, a tale without a tale; in extremis, theory can become disconnected from the practice of storytelling and the observation of dynamic child life.

In fact, theory and practice increase each other's value, and synthesizing variant theoretical viewpoints can deepen insight into the complexity of folk and fairy tales in children's literature, culture, and lives. A few touchstone titles serve as examples of critical dialectic and show an encouraging arc in the awareness of such complexity. One of the most famous studies to call attention to "the meaning and importance of fairy tales" in children's lives was Bruno Bettelheim's (1976) *Uses of Enchantment*, a Freudian analysis that stressed the developmental value of parents telling their children "classic" Grimms' tales. Unfortunately Bettelheim universalized his conclusions based on a limited selection of stories, an overgeneralized representation of "the Child," a culture-bound monomyth of psychological interpretation, and ignorance of contemporary children's literature.[2] Directly challenging his ideas, Jack Zipes (1979/2002) criticized Bettelheim's

psychoanalytic distortions and repressive social constructs. Zipes went on in many other books, including anthologized selections with socio-historical commentary, to skewer patriarchal aspects of European folk and fairy tales, offer cultural critiques of their reconstruction in children's literature, and recommend revisionist versions (e.g., Zipes 1983/1993, 1986, 1997, 2002, 2006).

From a different perspective, folklorist Alan Dundes (1982) combined a global knowledge of folk and fairy tales with his own psychoanalytic approach that did not foreclose other theoretical orientations. His *Cinderella: A Folklore Casebook* hosted a renowned international cast of essayists, including Jungian psychologists, anthropologists, educators, and literary critics. As debates waxed warmer, historian Robert Darnton (1984) suggested that the psychological interpretation of fairy tales missed the point that many stories were actually depicting literal situations in children's lives, including exploitation, violent abuse, and abandonment during periods of famine. If the parents starved, the whole family starved; if a child died, there was still the possibility of the parents having more children, who were therefore dispensable. "The human condition has changed so much since then that we can hardly imagine the way it appeared to people whose lives really were nasty, brutish, and short." (p. 29)

Few research publications during this period focused on actual children's book publishing or on interaction with children as related to folklore and storytelling, though Yolen (1981a) discussed, along with her own picture books and fantasy that drew on folklore, a few representative icons such as contrasting versions of "Snow White" by Randall Jarrell and Nancy Burkert (Grimm, 1972), Paul Heins and Trina Schart Hyman (Grimm, 1974), and Walt Disney (1938). Two important international conferences—"Fairy Tales and Society: Illusion, Allusion, and Paradigm" at Princeton University in 1984 and the International Bicentenary Symposium on the Brothers Grimm at the University of Illinois in 1987—produced only one paper (Hearne, 1988) relating to the onslaught of children's book editions of folk and fairy tales being published in the 1980s. There had been and continue to be some publishing histories of European fairy tales, from chapbooks onward (Opie & Opie, 1974; Tatar, 2002) as well as studies of single fairy tales such as "Beauty and the Beast" (Griswold, 2004; Hearne, 1989).

However, noticeably absent from this rich cross-section of folkloric scholarship on European fairy tales in juvenile literature has been assessment of children's book folklore from Latin America, Africa, Asia, and the Pacific Rim. This is due partly to Western ignorance of languages in these areas, partly to uneven book distribution, and partly to the fact that non-canonical—especially non-award-winning—children's books go out of print so quickly that their quality and impact are difficult to assess. All these factors contribute to a lacuna, despite the renaissance in feminist research on European folktales (Stephens & Mc-

Callum, 1998; Stone, 1975; Tatar, 1992; Warner, 1994) and feminist folktale collections by Angela Carter, Virginia Hamilton, Alison Lurie, Rosemary Minard, Ethel Phelps, Kathleen Ragan, James Riordan, and Katrin Tchana. There have been, of course, myriad picture books and collections from all corners of the globe, especially in answer to a demand for multicultural materials; but although the best of these do involve some research on the part of authors and illustrators, it is rarely at the level of academic scholarship. Calls for careful background research on folktales appropriated by children's book authors and illustrators who are unfamiliar with cultures from which they "borrow" have led to relatively little in-depth scholarship about particular indigenous lore in children's literature. To this extent, colonialism—of which, as we shall see, I am an unwitting example—continues to dominate children's book publishing.

The American Folklore Society (AFS) has a Children's Folklore Section that has awarded, since 1992, an Aesop Prize and an honor list called "Accolades," comprising children's books that folklorists consider well adapted and authentically sourced; the featured folklore is international in scope, and a few titles are even bilingual. AFS also sponsored an important early bibliography of folklore for children (Ramsey, 1952), and of course its *Journal of the American Folklore Society* has included many articles on folk and fairy tales, as does the journal *Marvels and Tales*. The International Board on Books for Young People (IBBY) often features authors and illustrators (such as Tololwa Mollel, an Arusha Maasai from Tanzania) who work with their member countries' folktales, and some scholarship on children's book folklore appears in IBBY's publication *Bookbird*. Websites such as Heiner's *SurLaLune* and Ashliman's (N.D.) *Folklinks* focus primarily on European/American folk and fairy tales that commonly appear in children's books, but the Internet offers growing potential for access to and evaluation of such material by scholars in diverse cultures.

Why is any of this important to children and their literature? What do they care when all they really want to know is what happens next, and how it happens? These are valid questions. What attracts most young listeners and readers to folk narrative in children's books is the aesthetic power of its telling: the fast-moving, highly structured elemental plots; clearly delineated archetypal characters; engaging voice; selectively spare detail; rhythmic language patterns; and reassuringly familiar formulae. Entertainment value is fundamental to the success of story, rhyme, or song. The space for imaginative play offered by these sturdy verbal forms is what attracts children, authors, illustrators, and scholars. It is this space that allows each individual to glean different emotional, socio-cultural, intellectual, spiritual, and physical connections with a tale. Reading and listening are not passive activities but active constructions of information and meaning. All of us have selective hearing, and we retain what fits our individual psychic patterns,

which makes it difficult to generalize about the impact of children's book folklore.

Do children's books represent the characters in canonical fairy tales as stereotypical, archetypal, or simply heroic in different ways? Do children take these stories literally, symbolically, or subversively? Although it is undeniable that socio-economic forces, including corporate organizations and educational institutions, wield tremendous power, one popular form of resistance is folk art and narrative, along with their subversive re-creations. No sooner has Sleeping Beauty settled down for a long rest than up pops *Sleeping Ugly* (Yolen, 1981b). Beauty recasts her name and nature in *Beauty* (McKinley, 1978, 1997). Hansel and Gretel's witch gets exonerated in *The Magic Circle* (Napoli, 1993), and Rapunzel's witch gets a complete personality makeover in *Zel* (Napoli, 1996). Rumpelstiltskin accrues six different character readings in *The Rumpelstiltskin Problem* (Vande Velde, 2000). Rampaging porkers burst out of their story for a hypertextual romp by Caldecott Medal winner David Wiesner (2001) in *The Three Pigs* (For an extensive analysis of picture book versions, see Stewig, 1992; Smith, 2006).

These examples in U.S. children's books mirror a multitude of similar revisions in British, German, Italian, and French literature for youth. And this is not only a current phenomenon. Almost as soon as folk and fairy tales began to appear in children's books, they received humorous popular-culture treatment. British educational writer Sarah Trimmer (1741–1810) took folk and fairy tales very seriously indeed because she opposed their fantastical elements and excoriated the potential effects of frivolity on children's development. She would surely have turned over in her grave at the sight of spoofs such as Planché's (1841) *Beauty and the Beast: A Grand, Comic, Romantic, Operatic, Melo-dramatic, Fairy Extravaganza in Two Acts*, which piled levity on top of fantasy. Folk and fairy tales have inspired equal measures of ideological critique and riotous mirth, offending different sensibilities in every age. This cyclical history suggests that a sense of balance and even humor can give crucial perspective on children's exposure to folklore, which often—notwithstanding violent and chauvinistic elements—pokes fun at the status quo and abounds with tricksters, fools, and nonsense. Many folk and fairy tales were originally subversive—the weak defy the powerful to achieve success—and throughout cycles of critical disapproval, they have survived by adaptation.

All folklore, I believe, is about survival in one way or another, and survival *requires* adaptation, keeping what's valuable and changing what's not, balancing the past and present, the old and new. This paradoxical tension between preservation and innovation is what folklorist Barre Toelken (1996a) calls the dynamic of folklore, which plays out in children's books as well as in the oral tradition. To respect the elements of text and context, researchers and re-tellers need both cultural and self-knowledge. That is to say, they need to locate the text in context, and themselves in relation to both text and context, because all stories are personal constructs as well as narrative constructs. Every listening, changed by the listener's new experience, is a story reconstituted. Every retold or re-contextualized story is a re-creation. Researchers are in fact retellers who reconstitute and even re-create stories as they listen ever more deeply to what they study.

Part II Foreground: Text, Context, and Elusive Rabbits

Supporting multiculturalism forces an individual to engage in a great deal of critical self-reflection. (Harris, 2003, p.131)

Let me tell you a story.

It is a particular story because, as Isaac Bashevis Singer (1985) says, the general must begin with the particular. To be more exact:

…there is no literature without roots….In literature, as in life, everything is specific. Every man has his actual and spiritual address….Without folklore and deep roots in a specific soil, literature must decline and wither away. This is true in all literature of all times. Luckily children's literature is even now more rooted in folklore than the literature for adults. And this alone makes children's literature so important in our generation. (pp. 334–335)

This story I'm telling started out with an address in the deep South. I chose it because it reveals many research issues related to folklore in children's literature and childhood, but also because it involves me personally, and a researcher's connections to a story are personal as well as professional. It is important to be aware of what draws you to exploring a story because whatever that is will invariably affect your work on it. Scholars are human and therefore subjective, no matter how broad and deep their knowledge. Sometimes it takes as long to understand your connection with a story as to understand the story itself, since the two searches are intertwined. In a book titled *A Narrative Compass: Stories that Guide Women's Lives* (Hearne & Trites, 2009), I have examined my life-long relationship with "Beauty and the Beast" and its connection to my family lore, arguing that:

Authentic, enduring engagement with a story involves getting inside it and letting it get inside you, internalizing as well as analyzing it. You cannot tell or even know a story from the outside. Jean Cocteau called "Beauty and the Beast" the archaeology of his soul. People are drawn to different stories for idiosyncratic reasons that can enlighten both the stories and their lives. It is a challenge to find, know, and understand your own stories, bearing in mind that a story means different things at different times of life. (pp. 207–208)

For this discussion I have chosen to focus on Brer Rabbit stories because they reflect so controversially the importance of socio-political context in cultural and aesthetic analysis—and because they offer a good example of understanding a personal relationship with story. The Brer Rabbit stories are not only about universal human dynamics of power and subversion but also about specific dynamics of racism, with roots in slavery and the subsequent oppression of segregation. They are also about deep connections to African folklore, as modified by the slaves who brought them to the United States and the Caribbean, adapted them to different life situations, and grafted new stories onto them to increase their relevance and usefulness. They feature a trickster who delivers different messages from those of his Wakaima and Anansi predecessors because of context, and their birth in African American history does not necessarily make them acceptable to African Americans today.

To begin with, many were taken from the oral tradition but published in newspaper columns (later book collections) for the amusement of White readers by a White man, Joel Chandler Harris, who framed them in running commentary by an Uncle Tom-like figure, Uncle Remus, who tells them to White children on a southern plantation. There are other sources for some of these stories, including a few in Zora Neale Hurston's (1935) influential *Mules and Men*, but Harris's collections are the largest and serve as the canonical source for most later adaptations, especially in children's and young adult books.

I first heard these stories in the pine-woods of central Alabama where I grew up during the 1940s, when the respectful word was not Black or African American but Negro or "Colored." You can imagine the disrespectful word used by many Whites in rural Alabama. Illiteracy was pervasive and books were not, though oral lore was plentiful. Material poverty dominated the region, and most residents, Black and White, did not enjoy amenities more common elsewhere—indoor plumbing, electricity, telephones, and automobiles. As the daughter of a doctor who started the only clinic in the region (treating both White and Black patients), I had access to all of these. I did not hear the Brer Rabbit stories from African Americans, who instead told me other stories, mostly calculated to scare the hell out of me—a wildly successful enterprise. No, Brer Rabbit stories entered the household when I was five years old via a 1947 recording based on the controversial Disney (1946) film *Song of the South* and narrated by the first actor ever hired by Walt Disney for a full-length, live-action film, African American James Baskett as Uncle Remus and the voice of Brer Fox. (Being first did not mean that Baskett was able to attend the film's gala premier in Atlanta, where no hotels would accept him.) We had no movie theater, so I did not see the images but played the record on the "Victrola." As in the oral tradition, I absorbed these stories by listening to them over and over again, a good girl allowed to express her bad self through identifying with mischievous tales. The "Brother" and "Sister" animal characters were especially familiar: I shared my room with a possum, a de-scented skunk, and a raccoon that teased them mercilessly; a baby alligator inhabited our bathtub until we moved it to the pond; two owls lived on the porch; a pet snake served as mousetrap; my best friend was a dog; and the farm and woods animals offered a congregation of domestic and wild companions. My sense of animal kinship was powerful and authentic.

With no idea that Disney's recorded tales were not "the real thing" but aware at some level that they offered commentary on the violently racist environment against which my Yankee mother and India-born father railed, I carried them around in my psyche until it came time to let them out to a crowd of children in an Ohio county library where I was presenting a storytelling program seventeen years later. This was my first real job, which I had landed in 1964 by telling the library director that I could tell a story. It was, as Zora Neale Hurston's informants would say with admiration, a "big old lie," "lie" and "story" being honorably synonymous among some of the folk from whom she was collecting. (My missionary grandmother, called *my* stories lies, but not with admiration.) I had no training and no idea how to tell a story, so I told what I remembered and the children, starting with three attendees the first day in September and building to 125 by Halloween, were mesmerized. When I switched my finger like Brer Fox switched his tail, they did too. When I snarled and showed my teeth like Brer Fox, they snarled back. One even threw up on my shoes. Whether this was the result of narrative power or flu, the programs were a hit.

I did have the intellectual decency to bypass Disney and consult Joel Chandler Harris—the 1880–1906 versions, compiled and introduced by folklorist Richard Chase in 1955—but it was not until I began politically radicalized 1960s graduate library school work in folklore and storytelling that I discovered the complex background of these stories, further complicated when I began to review them as children's books in *Booklist* and later in the *Bulletin of the Center for Children's Books*, which made recommendations to librarians, teachers, and parents. Such recommendations often determined whether children's books would be bought for institutional collections and thus determined the survival of the book and, in this case, a newly adapted oeuvre of African American tales in school and library programs. The century-long role of librarians as both storytellers and book evaluators is a subject of research unto itself (Del Negro, 2007; Smith, 1996).

Meanwhile, evaluative questions about Brer Rabbit multiplied in this order: Whose version was the right one? Twentieth-century White children's book writers as dissimilar as Margaret Wise Brown and Enid Blyton, White illustrators as disparate as Beatrix Potter and Edward Gorey, had worked with Brer Rabbit stories. Did non-African Americans have the right to tell these African American stories generated by slaves of a racist system? What does an adapter do with dialect when it has often been associated with stereotypical representations? One African American author, William J. Faulkner, with whom I spoke at a book signing in 1977, was as decisively anti-dialect as he was anti-Uncle Remus. I had just reviewed (and starred) his

book *The Days When the Animals Talked: Black American Folktales and How They Came to Be*, which featured forewords by Spencer Shaw, a distinguished African American library professor and storyteller, and Sterling Stuckey, a noted African American historian. In my conversation with Faulkner, he reiterated the same strong opinions expressed in the introduction to his book:

> In retelling Simon Brown's stories, I have retained some dialectal words, but have largely used standard English. Although I feel that something is lost in the translation [from Gullah dialect], I am opposed to allowing children, black or white, to use dialectal speech in school, and I would not want this book to encourage such language patterns. (1977, p. 7)[3]

Faulkner had no such problem with dialect in books for adults, as recorded in his "Slave's Riddle," included in Langston Hughes and Arna Bontemps's (1958) anthology *Book of Negro Folklore*. Faulkner was a PhD from the Chicago Theological Seminary, a Minister and Dean of Men for 19 years at Fisk University, where Bontemps was a librarian for 22 years. A self-styled folklorist, Faulkner (1977, p. 189) collected "stories the way some people collect stamps," and the stories he retold came from oral tradition:

> Dr. Faulkner's first encounter with black folk literature came in 1900, when he was a boy of ten, and a gifted storyteller named Simon Brown was hired to work on his widowed mother's farm in Society Hill, South Carolina. Simon Brown had been a slave in Virginia, and he enthralled young William with his true tales of slave life and his imaginative tales of talking animals. (p. 189)

Faulkner's language was straightforwardly focused on action, with an occasional light-hearted note: "Throw me in the fire. That's a good way to die. That's the way my grandmother died, and she said it's a quick way to go. You can do anything with me, anything you want, but please, sir, don't throw me in the briar patch" (1977, pp. 126–127). Troy Howell's pen-and-ink drawings offered sly visual asides, as in the cover portraying Brer Rabbit's head in fine lapin detail and work-worn brown hands holding a corncob pipe. (Brer Wolf's hands are conspicuously White!)

Four years after Faulkner's book appeared, White author Priscilla Jaquith (1981) published *Bo Rabbit Smart for True: Folktales from the Gullah*. She noted the exact source for her versions, with comparative references to other variants. Though no field collection of her own was involved, Jaquith's bibliography indicates solid archival research, including work by Adolph Gerber (1893), Elsie Clews Parsons (1923), and Albert H. Stoddard (1949). The text is liberally sprinkled with Gullah dialect, sound effects, and transitional slides between past and present tense: "By and by in the sun-hot, Elephant gets tired. He gives back slack. Whale gives a jerk, KPUT, and pulls till he's back in the deep" (p. 20). The words appear in short sections arranged vertically beside Chinese American illustrator Ed Young's soft black-and-white pencil drawings, which often break out of the slender brown frame and seem to dance with their shadows. This innovative picture book format sets up a dialogue between illustration and text that projects dramatic interaction, with phrasing and pauses suggested by creamy space between words and images. The tone is comically clever with no cruel edges of ridicule or violence. The success of the book in terms of aesthetics, child appeal, and responsibly researched source notes proves that those three elements are not incompatible in children's book folklore.

Four years later (is this folkloric repetition?) African American author Virginia Hamilton (1985) published her award-winning collection *The People Could Fly: American Black Folktales,* including several Brer Rabbit stories, a rich bibliography, and helpful notes, though a lack of specific sources listed for each tale hinders comparative analysis. Hamilton's *People Could Fly* is an adventure in language and art, with folkloric sensitivity to both. Leo and Diane Dillon's highly patterned black-and-white illustrations, one or two per story, use design to create an archetypal dimension, while Hamilton's playful juggling of dialect with her own experimental style results in a musical text: "'Hot lettuce pie! This is where I want to be,' Doc Rabbit hollered for happiness. He was square in the middle of the briar patch. 'Here is where my mama and papa had me born and raised. Safe at last!'" (p. 19).

In 1986, 1987, and 1989 White Mississippi composer and musician Van Dyke Parks published a sequence of books based on his album and theatrical production: *Jump! The Adventures of Brer Rabbit*, all drawn from Joel Chandler Harris and illustrated by Barry Moser. The book jacket claims that Parks "vividly remembers listening to the Brer Rabbit stories when he was a little boy," but there are no notes on who might have told him the stories or indication of background research for the adaptations. Were those who told him the stories so unimportant that he could not remember or find out their names? Parks's texts are very close to Harris's, though grammatically smoothed out, and violence always lurks around the corner of these animal-people's lives. Nor does illustrator Barry Moser's art diminish the constant threat to creature survival. His watercolor portraits and scenes indelibly delineate each tale. The slightly demonic, hyperactive rabbit and sleazy fox, usually with a tooth or two showing, add a depth of interpretation that matches the tales' sharp social commentary and made the second volume a New York Times Best Illustrated Children's Book. Indeed, part of what distinguishes Parks's books is the luxurious packaging, a high-gloss performance more assertive than any of the preceding books and unsurprising given its origins in the entertainment business and Parks's background on stage.

Between 1987 and 1994, African American professor and writer Julius Lester, who had already published *Black Folktales* (1969) and *The Knee-High Man and Other Tales* (1972) and has drawn on folklore in his fiction, published

four volumes (1987b, 1988, 1990, 1994), beginning with *The Tales of Uncle Remus: The Adventures of Brer Rabbit* introduced by trail-blazing African American librarian and storyteller Augusta Baker. These were all illustrated by Jerry Pinkney and collected into one book, *Uncle Remus: The Complete Tales* in 1999, a feat of wit and patience. Obviously children will prefer Lester's more manageable separate volumes, while storytellers consider the collected set a prime resource. His introductions consider the tales' folkloric background and themes, his decisions about language and dialect, the contentious racial issues of voice and ownership in retelling the stories, and the relationship between oral and literary culture: "Don't mistake the tales in this book for the tales themselves. The tales will live only if they flow through your voice" (1987b, p. xxi). In the introduction to his last volume, he reminds us that "As the function of storytelling has been taken over more and more by books, the voice of storytelling has become a disembodied one" (1994, p. x), and he discusses the role of storytelling as part of a living community.

Note the use of "Uncle Remus" in these titles, which amounts to laying down a gauntlet. Lester (1987a) addresses the issue directly in his Foreword to the first volume of the series:

> There are no inaccuracies in Harris's characterization of Uncle Remus. Even the most cursory reading of the slave narratives collected by the federal Writer's Project of the 1930s reveals that there were many slaves who fit the Uncle Remus mold.
>
> Uncle Remus became a stereotype, and therefore negative, not because of inaccuracies in Harris's characterization, but because he was used as a symbol of slavery and a retrospective justification for it. (p. xiv)

A thoughtful essay by Anthony Manna (1992) to some extent agrees with this statement, and the book in which it appears, Schmidt and Hettinga's *Sitting at the Feet of the Past: Retelling the North American Folktale for Children* also features brief comments by Jaquith on the "Folktale Decisions" that she made in retelling Bo Rabbit stories. Indeed, this book was a landmark in acknowledging issues related to Native American, African American, western European, and European American folktales in children's literature from the viewpoint of both writers and critics. Although no folklorists, oddly, were represented as authors in the book, references to folkloristic research did appear in some of the essays, and the appearance of the book itself signaled a broader folkloristic awareness, even an occasional healthy discomfort with the status quo in children's book publishing of folklore.

By the time the book came out in 1992, I had been circling the stories as a professional critic since the 1960s in an effort to understand and articulate the issues they raised socially, aesthetically, and personally. All of the Brer Rabbit books during this period retained core plot structures, but varied in selection, voice, narrative frame, format, cultural authenticity, and source attribution. I had favorably reviewed Faulkner's, Jaquith's, Hamilton's, Parks's, and Lester's books in either *Booklist* or the *Bulletin of the Center for Children's Books* and had used them all with children. However, my primary folkloric research focus at the time was European fairy tales, especially variants of "Beauty and the Beast" (Hearne, 1993a), and I circled Brer Rabbit stories warily despite my past involvement with them. I now understand that they brought up difficult personal conflicts, including the contradiction of loving, as a child, "fake" versions by Disney, whom I have excoriated here and elsewhere (Hearne, 1997a), and more important, the recollections of racism that I witnessed early on. In fact, it was not until I explored my own family lore and its relationship to other folklore that I was able to perceive and overcome this barrier.

Can we ever really understand the Other without first understanding ourselves? Oddly, this may require some distance of time and place. In the case of Brer Rabbit and the racism of its setting, the Uncle Remus stories were at first too close to home for me to engage. Initially, it was not until I studied anti-Semitism at the Hebrew University in Jerusalem that I really began to understand the racism I grew up with in Wilsonville, Alabama. And while I could, through a formal European tale like "Beauty and the Beast," eventually understand my own "brave woman" inheritance and polarized family situation, the Brer Rabbit stories have taken many more years of perspective. I. B. Singer's (1985) comment, slightly altered for gender, again comes to mind: "Every [woman] has [her] actual and spiritual address." Knowing that address can keep us from getting lost when we foray into other worlds, but our travels may also clarify the address. There is, of course, a folktale about this (ATU 1645), featuring dreamers who seek treasure abroad but find it at home.

Yet, such perspective often comes with hindsight, and hindsight is not always a possibility in evaluating new books for new children. The speed with which versions of even canonical tales go out of print is a paradoxical situation for scholars who are interested not only in historical textual criticism but also in the mercurial relationship between current books and current culture. In tracking these books as they appeared, it helped to be familiar with basic folklore references such as Karl Kerényi's (1956) germinal essay on the trickster, and African American folklore collected by Richard Dorson (1967), Roger Abrahams (1985), Zora Neale Hurston (1935), and, of course, Joel Chandler Harris. However, there are hundreds of folkloric traditions dashing in and out of the 5,000-plus children's books published every year, and not even a devoted children's literature specialist with folkloristic background can acquire grounding in each. Children, meanwhile, are waiting to hear the story while adults argue over gatekeeping.

In a letter responding to African American writer June Jordan's (1987) *New York Times Book Review* criticism of his "misbegotten resurrection" of the Brer Rabbit stories, Julius Lester (1987a) says:

[Jordan] describes Brer Rabbit as being lazy and a liar, "a pathological hustler, a truly bad rabbit." She characterizes the tales as being filled with "knavery," "premeditated violence, compulsive cruelty, exploitation of children, and regular opportunism." Well, of course! This is no surprise to anyone familiar with folktales, myths, and children's literature. It is only surprising that Ms. Jordan does not recognize Brer Rabbit as the figure known in practically every culture as the Trickster. (p. 37)

Lester (1988) reinforces his position in the introduction to his second volume: "Whether we are black or white, slave or free, child or adult, Brer Rabbit is us" (p. viii). Lester (1987b) respects Harris's integrity as:

…exemplary and remarkable. All of the tales were collected from blacks. Often Harris collected two or three versions of the same tale, and then chose the best version to publish. If he doubted a story's Afro-American roots, he did not use it…. Possessing a remarkable ear, he recognized that the tales could not be divorced from the language of the people who told them. Thus, he made a conscious and diligent effort to put this language on paper. In the absence of actual recordings, the Uncle Remus tales as put down by Harris are the most conscientious attempt to reproduce how the slaves talked, at least in one area of the South. (pp. xiii–xiv)

Despite this admiration and fidelity to the storylines, Lester (1988) shapes his own language with a carefully articulated currency of idiom, as in this rhythmic passage:

Brer Alligator twitched his tail, stretched, and laughed. "Nothing don't bother me. I catch shrimp. I catch crab. I make my bed when the sun is shining hot. Yes, Brer Rabbit, I enjoy myself! I be proud to see trouble."

"I wouldn't be too sure about that if I was you. Trouble come upon you when you have your eyes shut; he come on you from the side you can't see. He don't come on you in the creek, he come on you in the broom grass."

"If he do, I'll shake his hand and tell him howdy." (pp. 83–84)

Like others before him, Lester (1987b) picks up on Harris's reference to "bobbycue" in "Brer Rabbit and the Tar Baby" when Brer Rabbit says, "Getting barbecued is almost a blessing compared to being thrown in that briar patch on the other side of the road. If you got to go, go in a barbecue sauce. That's what I always say. How much lemon juice and brown sugar you put in yours?" (p. 15).

Brer Rabbit is pushing it here, and so is Lester. He's surrounded. What would Richard Dorson say about folklore and fakelore? What would Alice Walker say about retaining Uncle Remus? We can hypothesize, based on Dorson's (1976) theories and Walker's (1988) criticisms in "The Dummy in the Window: Joel Chandler Harris and the Invention of Uncle Remus." Uncle Remus seemed, after all, the opposite of a trickster. He appeared to accept the outrage of slavery and passed on his priceless traditions to a patronizing White boy. Or was he and did he? These stories are the soul of subversive irreverence, and maybe

Joel Chandler Harris/Uncle Remus had a trick up his sleeve in targeting a gullible White audience that dominated the marketplace and made sure the stories stayed alive—all unawares of being the butt of the joke. Could that still be happening? Who's the tricker, and who's the trickee? Any psychologically attuned folklorist (or folkoristically attuned psychologist) will tell you the same thing Lester (1987a) does in replying to Jordan, "...the trickster is in each of us. He is created in our image. Our task is to receive him and thereby uncover our humanity—if we dare" (p. 37).

Lester (1994) describes his own relationship with the stories, along with background information about them, and then proceeds to retell the tales with the natural narrative flow that characterized their oral predecessors.[4] Indeed, the narrator is one of the most vivid characters as he admonishes, perhaps self-reflexively, "Nothing in this world will get you in trouble quicker than your mouth" (p. 22). A brief passage from "Why the Earth Is Mostly Water" exemplifies the casual style laced with satire:

> I don't have to tell you that when an Elephant steps on you, you have been stepped on. When the Elephant lifted up his foot, there was not even a memory of the Crawfish left. To make matters worse, the Elephant didn't even know he had done it. All the other Crawfish got mad. They had a caucus, which is a little meeting which nobody could come to except crawfish. (p.10)

Will children ever forget that definition, or fail to appreciate its irony as they get older? The humor ranges from sass to slapstick. Everybody gets a fair share of back-handed ridicule, including feminists, chauvinists, ageists, and racists. Sometimes the storyteller confines himself to sideswiping one group: "that's how men can be—adding two and two and coming up with seventy-seven" (Lester, 1994, p. 22). Sometimes he manages to insult two with one blow, as in his under-the-breath indictment of both politicians and voters; "You don't have to be smart to be king or president, (I could name presidents who didn't have *any* brains)" (p. 82). Ultimately, like Brer Rabbit, Lester makes fun of just about anything on two, four, or eight legs.

Jerry Pinkney partners the narrative with realistically detailed watercolors to illustrate the rustic world of talking animals invaded by the occasional stray human. His drafting is as relaxed, smooth, and mellow as a good story gets over time, and he manages to underscore Lester's sly tone by treating the cast of characters with deadpan respect. Respect is a key word here. You can't get any more respectful of a cultural tradition than recharging the elements that helped it survive and that, at the same time, affirm its commonality with other peoples of the world—including storytellers, folklorists, cultural critics, and children's literature specialists. Lester respects history by acknowledging the outsider who collected the stories and is thus part of the story; at the same time he defies history by transforming that outsider's work with his own insider voice. It's quite the trick, involving a balance of creative and critical powers. The children and adults who hear, remember, and retell these stories in new contexts bear witness to Lester's returning folklore to the folk.

So where is Brer Rabbit now? He has been beatified, co-opted, exempted, argufied every which way...and maybe, now, accepted. Hamilton's was, in many ways, a breakthrough book in the sense that her audacious language, folkloric fidelity, and established reputation—coupled with the star-studded Dillons' restrained but haunting images—drew awards that brought the book, and therefore the subject, admiring attention. It was starred right and left in review journals and won a place as an ALA Notable Children's Book as well as numerous other honors, including a Coretta Scott King Award. Faulkner's book went quietly out of print, and Jaquith's was an ALA Notable book for children but still did not fare as brilliantly as the post-Hamilton books by Parks and Lester, which, in addition to being ALA Notable books, attracted other honors and major media attention; Lester's received a Coretta Scott King Honor, among other accolades. Various factors contributed to this arc of success in parading Brer Rabbit before new children, including packaging and illustration, changes in socio-political awareness, the dynamics of award committees, and the momentum of authorial/artistic reputation. There was no question that the Brer Rabbit stories, since the 1940s primarily perpetuated for children in Walt Disney's disputed *Song of the South*, had acquired new stature in children's literature.[5]

Do the print versions in children's literature defuse the bittersweet power of Brer Rabbit, as so many do Coyote's? That depends on interpretation of their respective places in history and culture. Both tricksters reveal a dark force as well as a humorous sense of human absurdity. However, Coyote is bound—literally—by different rules and rituals. Among some tribal heirs of those who originated them, Coyote stories are dangerous if told out of the winter season that limits his destructive action, which words can initiate. Brer Rabbit had no such rules and rituals. His tellers allowed him to do whatever he could do, however and whenever he could do it. To that extent, Brer Rabbit can be scary, and to that extent, Lester is the only one who has dared to retell the entire canon, where Brer Rabbit not only does funny things but also lies, cheats, steals, and manipulates others to death. It was the only way he—and the slaves who told about him—could survive. Whether survival tactics are amoral in such circumstances is a question these stories don't answer. Each of us must do that for ourselves. Sometimes Brer Rabbit is a victim of his own arrogance, as when he beats up the Tar Baby for not saying hello and gets away by the skin of his teeth. Sometimes he victimizes others and exacts cruel revenge on their arrogance, as in the story where he starts a fire around complacent Alligator—turning him from smooth to rough, *White* to *Black*—to show him what Trouble is like.

Does that mean these stories should be confined, as June Jordan (1987) suggested, to the historical era that generated them? Such a confinement would imply that we don't act that way any more, but folktales are true to human nature as well as historical situations. Unlike some children's literature, unlike what most adults try to protect children from, they tell what is, not just what should be. They are often not models of human behavior but reflections of human behavior. Perpetuating them requires narrative perspective, which in turn requires narrative knowledge.

I did grow up in the deep South; I did hear much African American folklore in the oral tradition, though not the Brer Rabbit stories themselves. I have researched enough background on them, both in folkloric and children's literature sources, to feel confident analyzing them and telling a few, though I am not comfortable with the famous "Tar Baby" story because back in 1940s Alabama I heard Black children referred to derogatorily as "tar babies." You don't find out that kind of information in a children's book that features the story. "The Tar Baby" (ATU 175) has a long, culturally rich, and academically researched folk history of variants in Europe and Asia as well as Africa and the American South, but my social and personal context keeps it from fitting into my particular mouth, no matter how naturally I fall into a southern accent. In Faulkner's, Hamilton's, Parks's, and Lester's mouths, the story fits fine (Jaquith doesn't include it). This is a decision about understanding and using text, and I've elaborated on it here to show how many layers of consideration surround books of folklore in children's literature. After all, whatever their research potential, children's books are meant to be used with children.[6]

As a storyteller, I have no problem using other Brer Rabbit stories such as "How the Gator Got Black," which I've often retold to children and even in an autobiographical novel, *Listening for Leroy* (1998), which deals with racism in the pre-Civil Rights South. Another of my favorites is "Sheer Crops" (Hughes & Bontemps, 1958), a Brer Rabbit story that shares elements with "How Bobtail Beat the Devil" (Chase, 1948) from the Appalachian mountains where I lived in the 1950s after moving away from Alabama. But I have a long way to go with Brer Rabbit stories. It took years to puzzle out why I was so consistently attracted to learning and telling trickster tales; it turns out there's an inner price for behaving yourself all the time! Not until I had taught storytelling and folklore to hundreds of students did I clearly see how the stories that claim us tell who we *really* are, inside as well as outside. Understanding stories is a matter of subjective experience as well as objective study, in a mutually enlightening process.

As a critic, I owe it to children and their books to track variants and background controversies when I'm considering a new (or old) edition of Brer Rabbit stories in picture books, collections, or fiction. Though Toni Morrison's (1981) adult novel *Tar Baby* makes a children's novel based

on that story unlikely, some brave soul—even Morrison herself—may write a children's novel based on another Brer Rabbit tale or two; the genre of fairy tale fiction has set a rampant precedent.[7] Whatever the future holds, children's literature hosts a rich brotherhood and sisterhood of rabbits (not to mention other creatures both animal and human) just waiting in the briar patch to fool and inform us folk of all ages and origins, if we dare to investigate.

Notes

1. Brian Sturm (2000) has documented a kind of trance experience among story listeners. Folklorists who have contributed famously to performance studies include Roger Abrahams, Richard Bauman, Dan Ben-Amos, Dell Hymes, and Dennis Tedlock.
2. Bettelheim also plagiarized his material, in some cases word for word, from a book first published in German, Julius Heuscher's (1963) *A Psychiatric Study of Myths and Fairy Tales: Their Origins, Meaning, and Usefulness*, but that is another story.
3. Thirty years later, African American storyteller, poet, and children's book author Janice Harrington expressed the same opinion in a personal conversation (January 13, 2008).
4. For a rich comparison of insights into narrative voice, see Lester's (1989) essay "The Storyteller's Voice: Reflections on the Rewriting of Uncle Remus" and Malcolm Jones's (1989) essay "The Talespinner's Mind."
5. Brer Rabbit's rise in children's literature is clearly reflected in Phyllis E. Church's (1991) summary "Sassy as a Jaybird: Brer Rabbit in Children's Literature."
6. Annie Ruth Leslie (1998) has done research on the specific use of Brer Rabbit tales, as reported in her article "What African American Mothers Perceive They Socialize Their Children To Value When Telling Them Brer Rabbit Stories."
7. Like many other writers for adults during the last decade, Toni Morrison has written several children's books, including *Who's Got Game? Poppy or the Snake?* (2004). Illustrated in comic-book format, the story is related to ATU 155 (Ungrateful Serpent Returned to Captivity), which appears in Jaquith's book as "Rattlesnake's Word" (pp. 43–50) and in Faulkner's as "Brer Possum and Brer Snake" (pp. 99–101).

Literature References

Grimm, J., & Grimm, W. (1972). *Snow White and the seven dwarfs* (R. Jarrell, Trans., N. Burkert, Illus.). New York, NY: Farrar Straus Giroux.

Grimm, J., & Grimm, W. (1974). *Snow White* (P. Heins, Trans., T. S. Hyman, Illus.). New York, NY: Farrrar Straus Giroux.

Hamilton, V. (1985). *The people could fly: American black folktales* (L. & D. Dillon, Illus.). New York, NY: Alfred A. Knopf.

Hearne, B. (1997b). *Seven brave women* (B. Andersen, Illus.). New York, NY: Greenwillow/HarperCollins.

Hearne, B. (1998). *Listening for Leroy*. New York, NY: Margaret K. McElderry/Simon & Schuster.

Lester, J. (1969). *Black folktales* (T. Feelings, Illus.). New York, NY: Grove Press.

Lester, J. (1972). *The knee-high man and other tales* (R. Pinto, Illus.). New York, NY: Dial.

Lester, J. (1987b). *The tales of Uncle Remus: The adventures of Brer Rabbit* (J. Pinkney, Illus.). New York, NY: Dial.

Lester, J. (1988). *The tales of Uncle Remus: The further adventures of Brer Rabbit, his friends, enemies, and others* (J. Pinkney, Illus.). New York, NY: Dial.

Lester, J. (1990). *Further tales of Uncle Remus: The misadventures of Brer Rabbit, Brer Fox, Brer Wolf, the Doodang, and other creatures* (J. Pinkney, Illus.). New York, NY: Dial.

Lester, J. (1994). *The last tales of Uncle Remus* (J. Pinkney, Illus.). New York, NY: Dial.

Lester, J. (1999). *Uncle Remus: The complete tales* (J. Pinkney, Illus.). New York, NY: Penguin Putnam.

Levine, G. (1997). *Ella enchanted*. New York, NY: HarperCollins.

McKinley, R. (1978). *Beauty: A retelling of the story of Beauty and the Beast*. New York, NY: Greenwillow/HarperCollins.

McKinley, R. (1993). *Deerskin*. New York, NY: Ace Books.

McKinley, R. (1997). *Rose daughter*. New York, NY: Greenwillow/HarperCollins.

Morrison, T. (1981). *Tar Baby*. New York, NY: Alfred Knopf.

Morrison, T., & Morrison, S. (2004). *Who's got game? Poppy or the Snake?* (P. Lemaitre, Illus.). New York, NY: Scribner.

Napoli, D. J. (1993). *The magic circle*. New York, NY: Dutton.

Napoli, D. J. (1996). *Zel*. New York, NY: Dutton/Penguin Putnam.

Parks, V. D. (1986). *Jump! The adventures of Brer Rabbit* (B. Moser, Illus.). San Diego, CA: Harcourt Brace Jovanovich.

Parks, V. D. (1987). *Jump again! More adventures of Brer Rabbit* (B. Moser, Illus.). San Diego, CA: Harcourt Brace Jovanovich.

Parks, V. D. (1989). *Jump on over! The adventures of Brer Rabbit and his family* (B. Moser, Illus.). San Diego, CA: Harcourt Brace Jovanovich.

Pattou, E. (2003). *East*. San Diego, CA: Harcourt Books.

Perrault, C. (1961). *Perrault's complete fairy tales* (A. E. Johnson, Trans.). New York, NY: Dodd Mead.

Planché, J. R. (1841). *Beauty and the Beast: A grand, comic, romantic, operatic, melo-dramatic, fairy extravaganza in two acts*. London: G. Berger.

Rylant, C. (1992). *When I was young in the mountains*. New York, NY: Dutton.

Say, A. (1993). *Grandfather's journey*. New York, NY: Houghton Mifflin.

Vande Velde, V. (2000). *The Rumpelstiltskin problem*. Boston, MA: Houghton Mifflin.

Wiesner, D. (2001). *The three pigs*. New York, NY: Clarion.

Woodson, J. (2005). *Show way* (H. Talbot, Illus.). New York, NY: Putnam/Penguin.

Yolen, J. (1981b). *Sleeping Ugly* (D. Stanley, Illus.). New York, NY: Coward, McCann & Geoghegan.

Zipes, J. (2002). *Breaking the magic spell: Radical theories of folk & fairy tales* (Rev. Ed.). Lexington, KY: University of Kentucky Press. (Original work published 1979)

Academic References

Abrahams, R. (Ed.). (1985). *Afro-American folktales: Stories from Black traditions in the New World*. New York, NY: Pantheon.

Alexander, K., Miller, P., & Hengst, L. (2001). Young children's emotional attachments to stories. *Social Development, 10*(3), 374–398.

American Folklore Society. Children's folklore section. Retrieved August 1, 2008, from www.afsnet.org/sections/children/

Ashliman, D .L. (N.D.). *Folklinks: Folk and fairy-tale sites*. Retrieved August 1, 2008 from www.pitt.edu/~dash/folklinks.html

Bettelheim, B. (1976). *The uses of enchantment: The meaning and importance of fairy tales*. New York, NY: Alfred Knopf.

Birch, C., & Heckler, M. (Eds.) (1996). *Who says? Essays on pivotal issues in contemporary storytelling*. Little Rock, AK: August House.

Bontemps, A. (1958). Introduction. In L. Hughes & A. Bontemps (Eds.), *Book of Negro folklore* (pp. vii–xv). New York, NY: Dodd, Mead.

Bruchac, J. (1992). Storytelling and the sacred: On uses of Native American stories. In B. Slapin & D. Seale (Eds.), *Through Indian eyes: The Native experience in books for children* (3rd ed.). Philadelphia, PA: New Society.

Butler, D. (1980). *Cushla and her books*. Boston, MA: Horn Book.

Chase, R. (1948). *Grandfather tales* (A. B. Frost, F. S. Church, J. M. Condé, E. W. Kemble, & W. H. Beard, Illus.). Boston, MA: Houghton Mifflin.

Church, P. E. (1991). Sassy as a jaybird: Brer Rabbit in children's literature. *Journal of Youth Services, 4*(3), 243–248.

Clarkson, A., & Cross, G. B. (1980). *World folktales: A Scribner resource collection*. New York, NY: Charles Scribner's Sons.

Cox, M. R. (1893). *Cinderella: Three hundred and forty five variants of Cinderella, Catskin, and Cap o' Rushes, abstracted and tabulated*. London: David Nutt.

Darnton, R. (1984). *"Peasants tell tales: The meaning of Mother Goose" in The great cat massacre and other episodes in French cultural history*. New York, NY: Basic Books.

Del Negro, J. M. (2007). *A trail of stones and breadcrumbs: Evaluating folktales published for youth in the 20th century, 1905–2000*. Unpublished doctoral dissertation, University of Illinois at Urbana-Champaign.

Disney, W. (Producer), & Geronimi, C. (Director). (1950). *Cinderella*. [Motion picture]. USA: RKO Radio Pictures.

Disney, W. (Producer), & Jackson, W. (Director). (1938). *Snow White*. [Motion picture]. USA: Disney Studio.

Disney, W. (Producer), & Foster, H. (Director). (1946). *Song of the South* [Motion picture]. USA: RKO Radio Pictures.

Disney, W. (1947). *Song of the South*. [Recording]. Hollywood, CA: Capitol Records.

Dorson, R. (Ed.). (1967). *American Negro folktales*. Greenwich, CO: Fawcett.

Dorson, R. (1976). *Folklore and fakelore: Essays toward a discipline of folk studies*. Cambridge, MA: Harvard University Press.

Dundes, A. (Ed.). (1982). *Cinderella: A folklore casebook*. New York, NY: Garland.

Faulkner, W. J. (1977). *The days when the animals talked: Black American folktales and how they came to be* (T. Howell, Illus.). Chicago, IL: Follett.

Gerber, A. (1893). Uncle Remus traced to the old world. *Journal of American Folk-lore, 6*, 245–257.

Griswold, J. (2004). *The meanings of Beauty and the Beast: A handbook*. Toronto, Canada: Broadview.

Harris, J. C. (1955). *The complete tales of Uncle Remus* (R. Chase, Ed.). Boston, MA: Houghton Mifflin.

Harris, V. J. (2003). The complexity of debates about multicultural literature and cultural authenticity. In D. L. Fox & K. G. Short (Eds.), *Stories matter: The complexity of cultural authenticity in children's literature* (pp. 116–134). Urbana, IL: National Council of Teachers of English.

Haven, K., & Ducey, M. (2007). *Crash course in storytelling*. Westport, CT: Libraries Unlimited.

Hearne, B. (1988). Booking the Brothers Grimm: Art, adaptations, and economics. In J. McGlathery (Ed.), *The Brothers Grimm and folktale* (pp. 220–233). Champaign, IL: University of Illinois Press.

Hearne, B. (1989). *Beauty and the Beast: Visions and revisions of an old tale*. Chicago, IL: University of Chicago Press.

Hearne, B. (1993a). *Beauties and Beasts: The Oryx multicultural folktale series*. Phoenix, AZ: Oryx.

Hearne, B. (1993b). "Cite the source: Reducing cultural chaos in picture books, Part I" and "Respect the source: Reducing cultural chaos in picture books, Part II." *School Library Journal, 39*(7&8), 22–27, 33–37.

Hearne, B. (1997a). Disney revisited, or, Jiminy Cricket, it's musty down here! *The Horn Book, 73*(2), 137–146.

Hearne, B. (1999). Swapping tales and stealing stories: The ethics and aesthetics of folklore in children's literature, in "Folkloristic approaches to library and information science." *Library Trends, 47*(3), 509–528.

Hearne, B., & Trites, R. (Eds.). (2009). *A narrative compass: Stories that guide women's lives.* Champaign, IL: University of Illinois Press.

Heiner, H. A. *SurLaLune fairy tales.* Retrieved August 1, 2008, from http://www.surlalunefairytales.com

Heuscher, J. (1963). *A psychiatric study of myths and fairy tales: Their origins, meaning, and usefulness.* Springfield, IL: Charles C. Thomas.

Hughes, L., & Bontemps, A. (Eds.). (1958). *Book of Negro folklore.* New York, NY: Dodd, Mead.

Hurston, Z. N. (1935). *Mules and men.* New York, NY: J.P. Lippincott.

Jaquith, P. (1981). *Bo Rabbit smart for true: Folktales from the Gullah* (E. Young, Illus.). New York, NY: Philomel.

Jones, M. (1989). The talespinner's mind. In C. Otten & G. D. Schmidt (Eds.), *The voice of the narrator in children's literature: Insights from writers and critics* (pp. 74–77). New York, NY: Greenwood.

Jordan, J. (1987, May 17). A truly bad rabbit. *New York Times Book Review,* p. 32.

Kerényi, K. (1956). The trickster in relation to Greek mythology. In R. Radin (Ed.), *The trickster: A study in American Indian mythology* (pp. 173–191). New York, NY: Schocken.

Leslie, A. R. (1998). What African American mothers perceive they socialize their children to value when telling them Brer Rabbit stories. *Journal of Comparative Family Studies, 29*(1), 173–185.

Lester, J. (1987a, June 14). "Letters," *New York Times Book Review,* p. 37.

Lester, J. (1989). The storyteller's voice: Reflections on the rewriting of Uncle Remus. In C. Otten & G.D. Schmidt (Eds.), *The voice of the narrator in children's literature: Insights from writers and critics* (pp. 69–73). New York, NY: Greenwood.

Levy, M. (2000). What if your fairy godmother were an ox? The many Cinderellas of Southeast Asia. In C. W. Sullivan (Ed.), *The Lion and the Unicorn* (Folklore In/And Children's Literature), *24*(2), 173–187.

Lord, A. (1960). *Singer of tales.* Boston, MA: Harvard University Press.

MacDonald, M. R. (1982). *Storyteller's source book: A subject, title, and motif index to folklore collections for children.* Detroit, MI: Neal-Schuman/Gale.

MacDonald, M. R. (Ed.). (1999). *Traditional storytelling today: An international source book.* London: Fitzroy Dearborn.

MacDonald, M. R., & Sturm, B. (2001). *Storyteller's source book: A subject, title, and motif index to folklore collections for children, 1983–1999.* Detroit, MI: Gale Group.

Manna, A. (1992). Br'er Rabbit redux. In G. D. Schmidt & D. R. Hettinga (Eds.), *Sitting at the feet of the past: Retelling the North American folktale for children* (pp. 94–108). Westport, CT: Greenwood Press.

Opie, I., & Opie, P. (1959). *The lore and language of school children.* London: Oxford University Press.

Opie, I., & Opie, P. (Eds.). (1974). *The classic fairy tales.* London: Oxford University Press.

Parsons, E. C. (1923). *Folk-lore of the Sea Islands, South Carolina* (Memoirs of the American Folk-Lore Society, 16). Cambridge, MA: American Folk-Lore Society.

Pellowski, A. (1991). *The world of storytelling: A practical guide to the origins, development, and applications of storytelling* (Rev. ed.). New York, NY: H. W. Wilson.

Ramsey, E. (1952). *Folklore for children and young people: A critical and descriptive bibliography for use in the elementary and intermediate school.* Philadelphia, PA: American Folklore Society.

Rooth, A. B. (1951). *The Cinderella cycle.* Lund, Sweden: Gleerup.

Sawyer, R. (1976). *The way of the storyteller.* New York, NY: Penguin. (Original work published 1942)

Schmidt, G. D., & Hettinga, D. R. (Eds.). (1992). *Sitting at the feet of the past: Retelling the North American folktale for children.* Westport, CT: Greenwood Press.

Sierra, J. (Ed.). (1992). *Cinderella: The Oryx multicultural folktale series.* Phoenix, AZ: Oryx Press.

Singer, I. B. (1985). *Stories for children.* New York, NY: Farrar Straus Giroux.

Smith, D. M. (2006). *What is a wolf? The construction of social, cultural, and scientific knowledge in children's books.* Unpublished doctoral dissertation, University of Illinois, Urbana-Champaign.

Smith, K. P. (Ed.). (1996). Imagination and scholarship: The contributions of women to American youth services and literature [Special issue]. *Library Trends, 44*(4), 679–895.

Sobol, J. (1999). *The storyteller's journey: An American revival.* Urbana: University of Illinois Press.

Stewig, J. W. (1992). The interlinking of text and pictures: A study of "The Three Pigs." In G. D. Schmidt & D. R. Hettinga (Eds.), *Sitting at the feet of the past: Retelling the North American folktale for children* (pp. 155–170). Westport, CT: Greenwood Press.

Stephens, J., & McCallum, R. (1998). Folktale and metanarratives of female agency. In *Retelling stories, framing culture: Traditional story and metanarratives in children's literature* (pp. 201–228). New York, NY: Garland.

Stone, E. (1988). *Black sheep and kissing cousins: How our family stories shape us.* New York, NY: Penguin.

Stone, K. (1975). Things Walt Disney never told us. In C. Farrer (Ed.), *Women and folklore* (pp. 42–50). Austin, TX: University of Texas Press.

Stone, K. (1998). *Burning brightly: New light on old tales told today.* Toronto, Canada: Broadview Press.

Stoddard, A. (1949). *Animal tales told in the Gullah dialect.* Washington, D.C.: Archive of folk song recordings, Library of Congress.

Stott, J. C. (1992). Native tales and traditions in books for children. *American Indian Quarterly, 16,* 373–380.

Sturm, B. (2000). The storylistening trance experience. *Journal of American Folklore, 113,* 287–304.

Tatar, M. (1992). *Off with their heads: Fairy tales and the culture of childhood.* Princeton, NJ: Princeton University Press.

Tatar, M. (Ed.). (2002). *The annotated classic fairy tales.* New York, NY: W.W. Norton.

Thompson, S. (1955–58). *Motif index of folk literature: A classification of narrative elements, exempla, fabliaux, jest-books, and local legends* (Rev. ed., 6 vol.). Bloomington, IN: Indiana University Press.

Toelken, B. (1996a). *The dynamics of folklore.* Logan, UT: Utah State University Press.

Toelken, B. (1996b). The icebergs of folklore: Misconception, misuse, and abuse. In C. Birch & M. Heckler (Eds.), *Who says: Essays on pivotal issues in contemporary storytelling* (pp. 35–63). Little Rock, AK: August House.

Trousdale, A. M. (1992). "My Cinderella: An autobiographical essay." In G. D. Schmidt & D. R. Hettinga (Eds.), *Sitting at the feet of the past: Retelling the North American folktale for children* (pp. 33–38). Westport, CT: Greenwood Press.

Trousdale, A. M., & McMillan, S. (2003). "Cinderella was a wuss": A young girl's responses to feminist and patriarchal folktales. *Children's Literature in Education, 34*(1), 1–28.

Uther, H. (2004). *The types of international folktales: A classification and bibliography based on the system of Antti Aarne and Stith*

Thompson. Vols 1–3. FF Communications No. 284-86, Helsinki: Academia Scientiarum Fennica.

Walker, A. (1988). "The dummy in the window: Joel Chandler Harris and the invention of Uncle Remus." In *Living by the word: Selected writings, 1973–1987* (pp. 25-32). San Diego, CA: Harcourt Brace Jovanovich.

Warner, M. (1994). *From the Beast to the blonde: On fairy tales and their tellers.* New York, NY: Farrar, Straus and Giroux.

Wolf, S. A., & Heath, S. B. (1992). *The braid of literature: Children's worlds of reading.* Cambridge, MA: Harvard University Press.

Yashinsky, D. (2004). *Suddenly they heard footsteps: Storytelling for the twenty-first century.* Jackson: University of Mississippi Press.

Yolen, J. (1981a). *Touch magic: Fantasy, faerie and folklore in the literature of childhood.* New York, NY: Philomel.

Zipes, J. (Ed.). (1986). *Don't bet on the prince: Contemporary feminist fairy tales in North America and England.* New York, NY: Methuen.

Zipes, J. (Ed.). (1993). *Trials and tribulations of Little Red Riding Hood: Versions of the tale in sociocultural context* (Rev. Ed.). New York, NY: Routledge. (Original work published 1983)

Zipes, J. (1997). *Happily ever after: Fairy tales, children, and the culture industry.* New York, NY: Routledge.

Zipes, J. (2006). Why fairy tales stick: The evolution and relevance of a genre. New York, NY: Routledge.

Point of Departure

Julius Lester

In his essay, "To what Extent Does Language Prescribe Thinking?" the German philosopher, Hans-Georg Gadamer writes, "Reading is already translation, and translation is translation for the second time. The process of translation comprises in its essence the whole secret of human understanding of the world and of social communication."

Although Gadamer was writing of translation as being from one language to another, his words are also an accurate description of the process involved in translating folktales from the oral tradition into written form. Any writer who undertakes the retelling of folktales is, first of all, a reader. As reader, what the writer perceives in a given folktale depends on the range and breadth of the knowledge and experience he or she brings to the act of reading.

A folktale is not just any story. As Betsy Hearne observes, "…it is important to be aware of the broader scope of folkloric study, which analyzes narrative as part of a living tradition grounded in community." Perhaps no book illustrates this better than Zora Neale Hurston's *Mules and Men.* Instead of merely presenting the tales she collected in the South, Hurston places them in their social settings—a front porch, outside a dance hall, at a community center. We are given not only the tales, but the social interactions between the storytellers and those listening. We see how one tale provokes someone to remember another tale, and who is storyteller and who are listeners is constantly shifting.

Of particular significance in *Mules and Men* is that the audience is not children. Hearne is correct when she writes, "The very identification of children as a primary audience for folklore creates a challenge for narrative once considered intergenerational or sometimes adult-only." I grew up in Black communities in the Midwest and South at a time before television and movies had become our primary storytellers. My father was a minister, and I learned much about the White world from listening to him and his ministerial colleagues tell stories about John and "ol' Massa'." But they were telling the stories to each other, not me. My presence was accepted only as long as I kept very still and very quiet.

These ministers also told stories about Brer Rabbit and other animals, but I did not hear them as being "about specific dynamics of racism, with roots in slavery and the subsequent oppression of segregation," as Hearne contends. This interpretation sees only the clever creature (slaves) who outwits his adversaries (Whites). The other side of Brer Rabbit is, as Hearne also observes, a creature that "also lies, cheats, steals, and manipulates others to death. It was the only way he—and the slaves who told about him—could survive. Whether survival tactics are amoral in such circumstances is a question these stories don't answer."

But Brer Rabbit is not as much the slave's surrogate as he is the trickster, an archetypal figure. To see Brer Rabbit's amoral cruelty as a reflection of what slaves had to do to survive is to diminish the complexity of the trickster. As I wrote in my introduction to the second volume of my *More Tales of Uncle Remus,* Brer Rabbit permits us to experience behavior that is not socially permitted. When we identify with the trickster's cruelty, we are made whole.

Among the tales I overheard as a child were ones in which the anger was not disguised. My father and those ministers told stories filled with open contempt for White people, stories that bragged about how easily Blacks manipulated Whites into believing what Blacks wanted them to believe. I recall hearing one minister tell how he found himself driving the wrong way on a one-way street. Before he could correct his mistake, he was stopped by the police. The policeman, using the N-word, said, "You goin' the wrong way on a one-way street." "No, suh," the minister protested. "I was only going one-way." The minister kept repeating this until the policeman called him "a dumb n----r" and let him go.

Many of the stories in Hurston's *Mules and Men* and *Black Folktales*, my first book of retellings, are similar in their disdain for Whites. The group of tales about High John the Conqueror were stories Blacks told among themselves while they told stories about Brer Rabbit to Whites. In one such story High John tricks his master into letting himself be drowned because the master thinks he will make a lot of money. In this story the slaves reveal a keen awareness of how rapacious slave owners were.

It is ironic that folktales are now relegated to children's books. Unfortunately, all too many printed tales are presented in disembodied voices, as if these are just stories. They are not. As Hearne states, "…all stories are personal constructs as well as narrative and social constructs."

When I began work on retelling the Uncle Remus stories, the challenge was to find the right voice. Because I had grown up listening to master storytellers, I had in my ear the rhythms, cadences, and music of the voices of my father and the other ministers. Hearne understands that the narrator of my Uncle Remus tales "is one of the most vivid characters…." I wanted the reader to be engaged equally by the story and the storytelling experience. Although folktales today exist primarily on paper, tales only come to life when they flow from the tongues of people who love the tales so much that it brings them joy to share the tales with others.

Reading a tale in a book is a solitary experience.

Reading/telling a tale to another or others establishes a human connection, creates a sense of community. The disembodied voice in which so many published folktales are presented cannot do this. The voice of the storyteller is as important as the story.

Having said this, I need to make clear that I do not believe that only Blacks can tell the Uncle Remus tales. People who've listened to the recordings I made of *The Complete Tales of Uncle Remus* (Recorded Books) invariably say, "I could never tell the stories the way you do." Of course not. Neither could a Black person who grew up in the North and went to prep schools. I grew up in an environment and at a time that doesn't exist anymore. But just because my way of telling the stories has its own authenticity, this doesn't mean that I "own" the tales.

Ownership of folktales has become an important issue in children's literature. However, no one can stop others from doing what they want with traditional stories. The most I can do is what I have done, namely, to present the stories in books and on recordings in a way that reflects the social milieu from which they came.

It is my hope that others, regardless of race or background, who want to tell the stories will fill the stories with their love and passion as I have. In so doing the stories will go from their hearts and souls into the hearts and souls of the audience, be that audience one child at bedtime, or a room full in a class or library.

In folktales lies one element of our core humanity. Those of us involved with tales in any capacity serve as bridges from a scarcely remembered past to the present and into the unknown future. I will not be around in 100 years, but I hope that the tales about High John the Conqueror in *Black Folktales* will be historical relics.

Brer Rabbit, however, well, Brer Rabbit will live forever.

16

African American Children's Literature

Researching Its Development, Exploring Its Voices

Rudine Sims Bishop

The Ohio State University

The artistry and literary legacy created by African American authors, illustrators, and editors is recognized, today, as a treasure for children around the world. Renowned scholar and educator, Rudine Sims Bishop, asks what processes and ideals brought this literature into production. Bishop takes readers inside the creative and scholarly process she followed to trace the lines of convergence among those adults who persisted, across two centuries, in making a literature "in their own words." This history leads to a deeper understanding of Black adults' visions for children's experiences of history, family, community, and justice that extend from pre-Civil War oral stories to present day picturebooks and novels. In her Point of Departure essay, Jacqueline Woodson describes what those books have meant to her as a writer who discovered that her stories could be told, read, and shared, from one generation to the next, as part of the journey that enables so many authors, artists, and readers not only to walk tall—but to fly.

When I wrote those words … I was just reminiscing about the necessity for literature, the necessity for African Americans to make their own art in their own words. (Morrison, 2008, pp. B1, B6)

The Need for African American Children's Literature

The history of American children's literature attests to the legitimacy of Toni Morrison's claim that an African American literature—literary art by African Americans in their own words—is a necessity, no less for children's literature than for literature addressed to an adult readership. Up until the mid-1960s, the world of American children's books could be characterized as largely homogeneous and fundamentally mono-cultural. For much of the 19th and 20th centuries, when people of color did appear in children's books, they were, with a few notable exceptions, most often presented from a cultural perspective that viewed them as inferior in some way—comical, primitive, pitiable, or in need of paternalistic care. So common were these representations early in the 20th century that even kindergarten-age Black children understood that the popular and dominant images of Black children in books had little to do with their own reality. In the early 1930s, teacher/author Eva Knox Evans reported that when she read to her Black kindergarten children the draft of a book she was writing about a young Black girl much like themselves, her pupils did not realize, in the absence of the illustrations, that the main character, Araminta, was "colored" because she did not speak and behave the way "colored" children in books typically did (Evans, 1941).

The first literary studies that confirmed the need for African Americans to make their own literature were conducted by critics such as Sterling Brown (1933) whose notable study examined the ways "Negro" characters were portrayed in White-authored books published between 1832 and the early 1930s. Brown concluded that for those 100 years the literary portrait of Black people in American literature was comprised primarily of seven stereotypes, which in a sense paralleled the history of Black people in America—from slavery (e.g., the contented slave, the wretched freeman) to the Harlem Renaissance (e.g., the exotic primitive). Although the books Brown examined were aimed at adult readers, because the writers of children's books are steeped in the same social and cultural milieu as those who write for adults, the scholarship on African Americans in adult literature was and to a certain extent continues to be relevant to children's books as well. Once scholars turned their attention to children's literature, it became clear that historically American children's books echoed many of the same stereotypical images described in Brown's study. Juvenile versions of at least two of the stereotypes Brown identified—the "comic Negro" and the "local color Negro"—were appearing in popular children's books as late as the 1950s.

Although from early in the 20th century on, there had existed a few books that realistically portrayed Black people as ordinary, recognizable human beings, the quantity of such books was relatively small even as late as the mid-1960s. By the 1930s, scholars, librarians, and writers had begun calling for change. In a 1932 article, Harlem Renaissance poet and author Langston Hughes (1932) expressed his concern: "Faced too often by the segregation and scorn of a surrounding white world, America's Negro children are in pressing need of books that will give them back their own souls" (p.110). By the end of the 1960s, old, blatant stereotypes were fading away and a new era was dawning in the development of African American children's literature. Spurred by several coinciding factors and changes in the social climate, including the Civil Rights Movement, urban unrest, and the timely availability of government funds for library books, the numbers of Black-inclusive children's books began to increase substantially. The door was opened to a new era that would include the kind of literature that Morrison asserted was necessary.

Morrison's observation was that African Americans needed to make "their own art in their own words," but children's books focusing on African American characters,

African American history, or African American cultural themes has never been the exclusive province of African Americans. Rather, the call for such books in American children's literature has been treated as an invitation to any and all interested writers of children's books. Data from the Cooperative Center for Children's Books (2007) at the University of Wisconsin indicate that, even in the 21st century, on average, nearly half of the children's books published each year about African Americans are produced by non-African Americans.

Given that circumstance, and given the sad history, particularly prior to the 1960s, of Black images in children's books, it should not be surprising that disagreements and controversies have arisen around issues such as the effect of an author's cultural background or perspective on the text he or she produces; the extent to which cultural perspectives matter or should matter to the reader, the writer, and the critic; and who has the "right" to tell the stories of a group that has been marginalized by the dominant culture. Numerous articles, critiques, and studies have been devoted to those issues, and it is not my intention to cover that territory here. Rather, working from the assumption that a literature that responds to what Morrison identified as a necessity—African American art "in their own words"—would carry its own distinctiveness, I argue here for expanding critical perspectives on children's literature by taking into account the ways that it is shaped by the cultural context from which it emanates. African American children's literature is the exemplar, but I would contend that the same arguments could be made concerning children's literature from other parallel cultures. The essay begins with a discussion of two significant research studies that critically surveyed the field and reported on representations of African Americans in children's books published from the 19th century to the end of the 1970s. These studies help to confirm the need for African American voices and perspectives in children's books featuring African Americans. A second section describes two studies that examine significant historical and modern works by African Americans in their own voices, confirming the impact of approaching the creation of literature from differing cultural perspectives. The third section focuses on some conclusions and observations derived from my own study of the development of African American children's literature.

Searching for African Americans in American Children's Literature: Surveying the Landscape

Arguably the first important comprehensive critical and analytical study of Black characters in American children's literature didn't come until the early 1970s when librarian and educator Dorothy Broderick, published *Image of the Black in Children's Fiction* (1973). Based on her Ph.D. dissertation, Broderick's "historical, literary, and critical analysis" (p. vii) in a sense paralleled Brown's study, covering children's books published between 1827 and 1967. Not surprisingly, she discovered that the images of Black characters in the early books were very similar to those identified by Brown, although by the end of the period of Broderick's study, portrayals of Black characters were becoming more realistic. Nevertheless, Broderick concluded that the books in her study could have been characterized primarily as one of two types: condescendingly racist books or traditionally liberal, do-gooder books. Writing, she noted, as "a white for other whites" to "provide an analysis that may possibly help us to avoid repeating past mistakes" (p. viii), Broderick argued that the image of Black people in children's fiction, as revealed in her study, "represents what the adult white establishment wished white children to know about Black people" (p. 6). It is telling that, even though her study included a small number of books by a few Black writers such as Arna Bontemps, Broderick implies both a White authorship and a White readership for the books in her study. In her view, neither Black writers nor Black readers were taken into account, as a general rule, by the white establishment. Studies such as Brown's and Broderick's serve to document the historical need for an African American literature that reflects what African Americans would want all children to know about Black people.

Broderick ended her study with books published in 1967, just about the time that the numbers of Black-inclusive books began to increase noticeably. My own research journey began as an attempt to analyze and describe the ways African American experiences were represented in children's literature published in the first decade and a half of the modern (i.e., post-1965) era of Black-centered contemporary children's fiction. *Shadow and Substance: Afro-American Experiences in Contemporary Children's Fiction* (Sims, 1982) was a survey and analysis of 150 Black-inclusive books of contemporary fiction published between 1965 and 1979. Although the sample did not include every such book published in those years, it included the overwhelming majority, and as such yielded a defensible picture of the status of Black literary images in American children's fiction at the end of the 1970s.

My analysis was guided by three main questions: (a) To whom do these books appear to be primarily addressed? That is, do the books address Black children as readers or do they use Black characters to address others? Broderick had asserted that the image of Black people in her sample represented what "the white establishment wanted white children" to know about Black people. My question asked whether that statement was still true. (b) How does the term *Afro American experience* appear to be understood? Do the books appear to treat Black culture as distinctive or do they tend to embrace the idea of a single homogeneous American culture? If treated as distinctive, does the fictional portrayal seem true-to-life? (c) What cultural perspective(s) appear to inform the creation of the fictional worlds and their inhabitants? That is, does the fictional world appear to be viewed through the eyes of someone who is an inhabitant of that world or through the eyes of a visitor or tourist?

Based on those questions, the 150 books fell into three categories, which I labeled (a) *melting pot* books, (b) *social conscience* books, and (c) *culturally conscious* books. Briefly, I concluded that the melting pot books appeared to be intent on a literary assimilation of African Americans into the American middle class, ignoring or dismissing racial and cultural differences. The social conscience books appeared intent on raising social awareness, developing sensitivity, and pricking the consciences of White readers. The culturally conscious books appeared to recognize and to try to reflect, with varying degrees of success, some aspect of distinctively African American ways of living, believing, and surviving. I also identified five Black writers of contemporary fiction who could be considered *image makers*, because as a group they had published the bulk of the culturally conscious books in the study and had drawn on their own cultural sensibilities to re-shape the literary image of Black people in children's books. This group was part of the vanguard of Black writers of modern African American children's literature.

The *Shadow and Substance* analysis indicated that children's fiction centered on African American characters was developing in parallel streams, driven by different aims and informed by different perspectives. It resembled the Broderick study in that it attempted to examine a substantial portion of the extant body of Black-inclusive children's fiction, without regard to the cultural affiliation of its authors. But in addressing the culturally conscious books and identifying the five image makers, it also moved in the direction of examining the kinds and characteristics of texts that were produced when African Americans created for children "their own art in their own words."

"In Their Own Words"

One of the first in-depth research studies to critically examine African American children's literature as an African American creation was Violet Harris's doctoral dissertation, *The Brownies' Book: Challenge to the Selective Tradition in Children's Literature* (1986). Harris analyzed the 24 issues of a children's periodical published by W.E.B. Du Bois and Augustus Dill in 1920–21. Du Bois—a sociologist, author, civic leader, and a founder of the NAACP—declared that the magazine was for all children, but especially for "ours, the children of the sun." Thus, *The Brownies' Book* was the first significant 20th-century literary enterprise produced by African Americans and directed explicitly, though not exclusively, to African American children. Harris viewed the magazine as an effort to establish a new tradition in children's literature as well as a challenge to dominant literary perspectives and beliefs about African Americans.

Harris adopted Raymond Williams's concept of the

selective tradition to label this dominant literary perspective and used it to explicate the cultural and historical factors that motivated the creation of *The Brownies' Book*. These factors are implicit in the seven objectives Du Bois listed for the magazine, which were about instilling race pride, bolstering Black children's positive self image, helping them develop coping strategies; educating them about Black history; and inspiring them to become informed, productive adults. To develop and publish a magazine with such objectives was to indict both the prevailing social environment and the common curricula in public schools engaged in what historian Carter G. Woodson (1933/1968) would later call the "miseducation of the Negro." Harris also demonstrated, through identifying and discussing the eight prominent themes she found in *The Brownies' Book*—race pride, duty and allegiance to the race, Black intelligence, Black beauty, respect for African cultures, political and social activism, moderation, and values such as kindness and truthfulness—that the magazine was indeed an explicit challenge to the accepted literary tradition and to existing Black stereotypes. It was clearly an effort to provide a counter story to the prevailing societal narrative. Harris was not the first to write about *The Brownies' Book* (see Sinnette, 1965), but her in-depth study and her subsequent scholarship based on that study and published in professional journals (e.g., Harris, 1987, 1989) provided an important historical context, a powerful reminder that well before the 1960s African Americans had been attempting, through literature, to address educational, cultural and aesthetic needs of African American children. It also invited inquiries into the relationship between *The Brownies' Book* and subsequent African American children's literature.

In *Telling Tales: The Pedagogy and Promise of African American Literature for Youth*, Dianne Johnson (1990) demonstrated something of the nature of that relationship. She conducted close readings of *The Brownies' Book*, as well as the books for youth written by Harlem Renaissance writers Arna Bontemps and Langston Hughes in the 1930s and 1940s. In addition she analyzed picture books created by contemporary poet Lucille Clifton, beginning in 1970. Citing *The Brownies' Book* as a forebear of contemporary African American children's literature, Johnson demonstrates the ways in which the more contemporary works reflect and build on the forms and themes, as well as the inclination towards pedagogy, that were revealed through her examination of *The Brownies' Book*.

Defining African American children's literature as that created by African Americans and focused on Black experiences, Johnson also argued strongly for treating African American children's literature as worthy of literary study and criticism. In her view, most previous discussions having to do with African Americans and children's literature had not been focusing on African American children's literature as she defines it, but on the negative and misguided portrayals and stereotypes of African Americans

in so-called "mainstream" children's literature. Johnson's goal was to steer critical discussion towards an examination of the ways African Americans portrayed Black lives and experiences—in their own voices and for their own purposes. Her close readings of these representative examples of African American children's literature document the purposeful nature of the literature and the strategies authors use in their attempts to both fulfill their purposes and create literary art.

Keepin' On Keepin' On: The Journey Continues

Building on *Shadow and Substance* and on the work of researchers such as Harris and Johnson, I set about to trace the development of an African American children's literature from its early roots to the end of the 20th century. For purposes of this study, I defined African American children's literature as that created by African Americans, focused on African American characters and experiences. The result of this work is reported in *Free Within Ourselves: The Development of African American children's Literature* (Bishop, 2007). My exploration was guided by the following general questions: How has the collective historical experience of African American within the American socio-cultural context influenced the shape and direction of African American children's literature? What distinguishes African American children's literature from other American children's literature? What elements or features of the literature recur across texts, authors, time, and genres? Who have been the major influential African American writers and artists, and how can their work be characterized? What landmark or milestone works or developments have advanced the African American children's literature canon, and what was their significance? What insights or inferences can be drawn from African American authors' and artists' statements about their work, their sense of its purposes, and the ideological or philosophical perspectives that underlie it? I explored these questions along three main pathways: readings in African American history, particularly as it pertained to literacy and literature; examining or reviewing African American children's books; and studying the published essays and interviews and commentaries of African American writers, artists, and critics. This study was informed not only by the research for *Shadow and Substance*, but beyond that, another quarter century of teaching, learning, and writing about African American and multicultural children's literature. In a sense then, it represents both new research and the culmination of years of following the development of African American children's literature.

The Research Process: Creating a Historical Framework

One purpose of this study was to connect African American children's literature to the historical, literary, political, cultural, and social contexts from which it emanated, and to which it owes its identity as a distinctive component of American children's literature. I began by searching for the foundations of African American children's literature in pre-20th-century African American history. Based on the premise that a prerequisite for the development of an African American children's literature was a population of literate African Americans, I searched classic works of African American history, such as John Hope Franklin's *From Slavery to Freedom* (Franklin & Moss, 1994) and Fishel and Quarles's *The Negro American: A Documentary History* (1967), for information on pre-20th-century education and literacy among African Americans. I also found more detailed information about the lives and literacy experiences of enslaved African Americans in works such as Genovese's *Roll Jordan Roll: The Lives the Slaves Made* (1976), and in various published accounts related by former slaves. In his well-known study *Deep Like the Rivers: Education in the Slave Quarters* (1978), Thomas Webber identified a set of salient attitudes and values, which he called cultural themes, some of which continue to be echoed in African American children's literature. Janet Cornelius' study, *When I Can Read My Title Clear: Literacy, Slavery, and Religion in the Antebellum South* (1991) and Carter G. Woodson's *Education of the Negro Prior to 1861* (1919/1968) were also valuable sources of information about literacy among antebellum Black Americans.

A search for early Black writing addressed to children led to periodical literature and inevitably to the Black church, the first African American publishers. Early issues (1852–1864) of *The Christian Recorder*, the official newspaper of the African Methodist Episcopal Church, stood as the exemplar of church-sponsored publications. From the beginning a portion of the *Recorder's* content, which was not exclusively religious, was regularly addressed to children and families. Another valuable resource, *The Afro-American Press and Its Editors*, by I. Garland Penn (1891/1964) reports on African American newspapers and magazines published from 1827 to 1890, and includes one section devoted to women writers and editors, many of whom wrote magazine articles and other material intended for children.

Synthesizing this historical material on life, literacy, and education among pre-20th-century African Americans led to the conclusion that the roots of African American children's literature indeed lie deep in the soil of African American history. These roots were nourished by such factors as a vital oral tradition, the high value placed on acquiring literacy, and African Americans' early writing addressed to children, especially by women. Further, it also became clear that African American children's literature stems from a tradition in which literacy and literature served a number of functions in addition to "purely literary" ones, including self-affirmation, protest, disseminating information, and racial uplift.

For the first half of the 20th century, one of the main incentives for the creation of an African American children's literature was the perceived need to remake the literary image of African Americans in children's books. Up through the 1950s there existed a body of popular Black-inclusive literature that represented African Americans in negative or distorted ways and stimulated efforts to contradict those representations. To demonstrate how this body of work would have been one incentive for African Americans to create an alternative children's literature with realistic and affirmative representations, I examined several "bad examples," such as books from the *Little Brown Koko* stories (Hunt, 1951) and the *Nicodemus* series (Hogan, 1932, 1941).

I also examined some more positive Black-inclusive children's books by non-African Americans, published in the 1930s to the 1950s, to discern what aspects of the larger social context might have accounted for positive changes and helped to pave the way for acceptance of an African American children's literature created by African Americans. For example, the influence of the Intercultural Education Movement of the 1930s and 40s is evident in books such as Marguerite De Angeli's *Bright April* (1946), which espouses WWII era democratic values in the context of a story of a middle-class Black girl and her encounters with bigotry. I also reviewed other 20th-century social political, economic, educational, and literary movements (e.g., the Harlem Renaissance, the Black Arts Movement, the Civil Rights Movement, multicultural education) that affected the development of an African American children's literature. The influence of such movements was reflected not only in the content and themes of the children's books produced during those times, but explicitly in various journal articles, essays, and other publications produced by writers/critics, librarians, and educators. For example, during the heyday of the Intercultural Education Movement, articles with titles such as "Intercultural Books for Children" (Trager, 1945) and "Mosaic" by Florence Crannell Means (1940) were appearing in the professional literature.

Although African American children's literature differs in important ways from African American literature addressed to an adult audience, both are informed and shaped by the same socio-cultural contexts. It was important, therefore, to view African American children's literature in the context of the larger body of African American literature. I was particularly interested in critics' views on what might constitute a Black cultural aesthetic, and how that might manifest itself in the literature. To that end I perused references such as *The Oxford Companion to African American Literature* and the *Norton Anthology of African American Literature*, as well as the work of particular scholars from different time periods, such as W.E.B. Du Bois, Ralph Ellison, Toni Morrison, and Henry Louis Gates, Jr. These readings offered insight into the ways African American scholars, for the most part, have seen Black literature as an expression of Black culture and as part of a larger Black social and political struggle for liberation and social justice.

The Research Process Continued: African American Children's Literature and Its Creators

The history of 20th-century African American children's literature can be divided into two periods, with the dividing line at 1967, when Virginia Hamilton's first book marked the beginning of a new era. Between 1920 and the 1960s, African American children's literature was either written or published by just a few pioneering individuals, including W.E.B. Du Bois, Langston Hughes, Arna Bontemps, Ellen Tarry, and Carter G. Woodson. Because of their importance as milestones, I devoted considerable attention to Du Bois' magazine, *The Brownies Book,* and to the groundbreaking work of Arna Bontemps, who was the most prolific, most versatile, and critically acclaimed writer of African American children's literature of his day. Because of Bontemps and a few other authors, this was an era of "firsts" for African American children's books—the first modern picture books, the first poetry anthologies or collections, the first novels with racial conflicts as a central theme, the first "urban novel," to name a few. Fortunately, most of these writers also published essays about their work and their perspective on it, which helped to place the literature in its social and political contexts.

Tracing the development of African American children's literature after 1967 was complicated by the greatly increased quantity of books by African American writers and artists. To focus and organize my reading and analysis, I chose to concentrate on poetry, picture books, contemporary fiction, and historical fiction published through the end of the 20th century. I also chose to concentrate on literature directed to elementary and middle school age children, although it was necessary to pay some attention to African American literature for young adults. It was my intention to examine as much of the body of African American children's fiction and poetry as I could find. My aim was to identify the major contributors to African American fiction and poetry for children, to analyze and describe their major contributions, and to identify—within and across authors, across time, and across genres—recurring themes, motifs, stylistic devices and cultural references. The idea was to describe some of the characteristics of African American children's literature that make it distinctive. In the end my reference lists included more than 600 children's and young adult books.

I organized the reading of post-1965 books by genre, and within genres by author or artist and by decade, moving from the late 1960s, through the 70s, 80s, and 90s. I concentrated on writers and artists who had published several children's books and who continued to publish over a period of years. I also included writers or artists who may not have been prolific, but whose works represented a milestone, a trend, or a contribution unique to its time. Within each genre and each decade I read or reviewed the work of those writers, as well as their published statements about their work and, when available, critiques of their work. As I examined the children's books, I took note of literary elements such as plot lines, themes, and settings (geographical, socio-economic, chronological). I also looked for what I will call "cultural markers," such as the use of Black vernacular language or rhetorical styles, and references to values, customs, beliefs, attitudes and manners associated with African American culture. For example, I noted numerous references to Black music, religion or spirituality, Black heroes, Black achievements, Black history, and African heritage.

Sorting out picture books was complicated by the fact that I had defined African American literature as that created by African Americans. But picture books are often created by two different individuals and in the case of picture books featuring African Americans, those two individuals—the writer and the artist—have not always both been African American. Because I was interested in the work of African American writers and artists, my solution was to first examine picture books *written* by African Americans, regardless of who had illustrated them. Second, I examined the work of important African American illustrators, identified both by the quantity of their work and by the recognition they have received from various sources, such as awards and honors (e.g., Coretta Scott King Award, Caldecott Medal). Most, but not all, of their books had also been written by African Americans. I looked for ways to describe their illustrations and for similarities across artists, such as recurring images. As with the authors, I also sought out artists' statements about their work.

Observations and Conclusions

African American children's literature has been a purposeful literature, even as it has aspired to literary artistry. In the late 1960s, African American writers and artists initially set out to fill a void. Beyond simply including Black children in books, however, these creative artists sought to pass on knowledge and transmit values while engaging readers in well written stories that are both specific to Black experiences and recognizable as human experience. Through imaginative writing and illustration, African American writers and artists have sought to bear witness to African Americans' nearly 400 years of struggle and survival. There is, of course, diversity within that experience, and that diversity is reflected in the body of African American children's literature. Nevertheless African Americans as a group have in common a historical experience burdened by the effects of racism, but redeemed by a sense of hope, resulting in what writer Ralph Ellison (1964, p. 131) called a "concord of sensibilities" through which the group has coalesced. Premier African American author Virginia Hamilton (1981) subscribed to a similar idea:

> The life of the people is and always has been different in a significant respect from the life of the majority. It has been made eccentric by slavery, escape, fear of capture, by discrimination, and by constant despair. But it has held tight within it happiness, and subtle humor, a fierce pride in leadership and progress, love of life and family, and a longing for peace and freedom. Nevertheless there is an uneasy, ideological difference with the American majority basic to Black thought. (p. 57)

This concord of sensibilities, this eccentricity of experience, is reflected in the goals stated by many creators of African American children's literature in essays, articles and interviews. One of the premier African American writers, Eloise Greenfield (1975), articulated a set of goals for her writing that echoed W.E.B. Du Bois' objectives for his 1920 magazine and was in turn echoed by numerous writers in the last third of the 20th century. Greenfield wrote of wanting to (a) encourage children to develop positive attitudes towards themselves; (b) help children learn how to overcome negative experiences and seek new ways to solve problems; (c) familiarize children with Black history and achievements, and Black heroes; (d) encourage children to reflect on the strength of Black families and respect the contributions of elders; (e) inspire children to enlist in the struggle for freedom and equality; (f) engender a love for the arts.

The goals articulated by Greenfield and others are reflected in the overarching thematic emphases that have come to characterize much of African American children's literature. Among the most important of those themes are celebrating family relationships, learning to love oneself, and taking pride in Black history and achievements. Woven throughout the literature are references to familiar African American cultural values, attitudes, customs and practices. For example, Black music such as jazz, blues, or gospel music, is often referenced in poems and stories. Some poems and stories in fact, have Black music in one form or another as their central topic or as a structural device. For example, Eloise Greenfield's poetry collection *Nathaniel Talking* (1988) celebrates rap in the opening poem, "Nathaniel's Rap." The collection also includes a blues poem and at the end an explanation of twelve bar blues along with a guide to help interested students create their own blues poem. Walter Dean Myers has written picture books celebrating both blues and jazz music (*Jazz*, 2006; *Blues Journey*, 2003). Some African American literature also reflects African American speech patterns and rhetorical styles and conventions, in the dialog of their characters or in the narration itself or in both.

One of the most important goals outlined by Greenfield relates to portrayals of African American families. She expressed a desire to reflect the strength of Black families and in particular to encourage respect for the contributions of elders. Although picture books focusing on family relationships are hardly exclusive to African American literature, the numbers of such books written by African Americans across three and a half decades and their proportion within the body of the literature, particularly picture books, suggest that the theme carries particular importance among African American writers of children's books. Not surprisingly, a number of these books are about parent-child relationships, as in *Tell Me a Story, Mama* (A. Johnson, 1989), *Saturday at the New You* (Barber, 1994), or *Kevin and His Daddy* (Smalls, 1999). Sometimes the adult is an aunt, as in *Just Us Women* (Caines, 1982), *The Aunt in Our House* (A. Johnson, 1996) or *The Jones Family Express* (Steptoe, 2003). Sometimes the adult is a generation older than the parents, but not a grandparent, as in a great-great aunt—*Aunt Flossie's Hats—and Crab Cakes Later* (Howard, 1991) or great uncle as in *Uncle Jed's Barbershop* (Mitchell, 1993). When the relationship is with a grandparent, it is most often a grandmother, as in *Grandmama's Joy* (Greenfield, 1980), *The Glass Bottle Tree* (Coleman, 1995), *Louise's Gift* (Smalls, 1996), *Just Right Stew* (English, 1998), *We Had a Picnic This Sunday Past* (Woodson, 1997), but grandfathers appear as well, as in *Grandpa's Face* (Greenfield, 1988), *When Jo Louis Won the Title* (Rochelle, 1994), or *When I Am Old With You* (A. Johnson, 1990). What follows is a discussion of three picture books that focus on loving relationships between young children and elders, with a view to pointing out some of the ways that theme plays out in the context of a developing African American children's literature tradition.

Honoring the Elders: Three Picture Books

First published in 1975, Sharon Bell Mathis' *The Hundred Penny Box* was a 1976 Newbery Honor Book. Michael is 9; Aunt Dew is 100. Dewbet Thomas is Michael's great-great aunt. She had raised Michael's father John after his parents drowned accidentally when he was a young child. Now John has brought Aunt Dew from Atlanta to live with his family. Michael and Aunt Dew have developed a special loving relationship. On the other hand, Michael's mother Ruth tries to care for Aunt Dew with patience and kindness, but also feels free to dispose of Aunt Dew's possessions, since Ruth believes that Aunt Dew no longer needs them. Ruth's life has become difficult as Aunt Dew struggles to hold onto her things, her dignity, and what's left of her independence. Her most prized possession is her hundred penny box, a beat up old wooden box that contains a sack of pennies—one for each year of her life. She and Michael have made a game of counting the pennies as Aunt Dew tells stories of the events of a given year—beginning with 1874, the year she was born. When Ruth threatens to burn the hundred penny box, Michael defies his mother and searches for a way to save it. Aunt Dew has said, "When I lose my hundred penny box I lose me" (p. 19). When the book ends, the box is safe for the moment, but all Michael can do is to stay close to Aunt Dew to let her know how much he cares.

The Hundred Penny Box was among the first modern African American children's books to highlight the special relationship between a young child and an elderly relative. The book is uncommon, if not unique, in its treatment of the family dynamics. It is honest about the tension that can result when a family is suddenly faced with having to care for a very old person who may or may not be confused and who resents having to give up her home and her independence. Furthermore, Aunt Dew clearly favors the males in the household, making Ruth feel a bit like an outsider in her own home. The story covers just part of a day, and so in a sense the ending is unresolved, as it must be.

The Hundred Penny Box also shares characteristics with other African American intergenerational books. Often these are stories of extended families in which more than one generation share a household. One of the cultural themes that Thomas Webber (1978) identified in his study of the life of people living in slave quarters was the importance of family. He also identified family as an important instrument or agent for educating the children. In the circumstances in which people in the slave quarters lived, family almost always included people beyond the immediate nuclear family, even people who were not related. Elders were often the caretakers of the children, the source of knowledge of local and past history, the tellers of stories, and the transmitters of wisdom. The desire of African American writers to foster a respect for elders and their contributions, then, may be a long-standing cultural attitude.

Aunt Dew at age 100 sometimes calls Michael by his father's name, and thus appears to be confused about whether Michael is himself or his father John as a child. It may be, however, that she is not so much confused as she is making a statement to the effect that Michael looks so much like his father—"Look like John just spit you out" (p. 21)—that he must be mis-named. She is never confused, however, about the history that she relates as she and Michael count out the pennies. The first penny, representing 1874, elicits commentary about Black men in Congress running things. "They was in charge. It was the Reconstruction" (p. 27). The narrator then states that she talked about Reconstruction through twenty-seven pennies/years. Her journey through history begins with a sense of pride in Black achievements and includes personal and family history in the context of general American history. Thus Aunt Dew fulfills the role of family and cultural historian that is often assigned to elders in these books. And it should be noted that her history is passed on through story.

One of the things closest to Aunt Dew's heart is the gospel hymn "Take My Hand, Precious Lord," a song as familiar to most church-going African Americans as "Amazing Grace" is to much of the American public. (It has been reported that Dr. Martin Luther King's last request, just before he was assassinated, was for saxophonist Ben Branch to play "Precious Lord" at a meeting scheduled for that evening.) It is "her" song; she often sings it, has Michael play a recording of it over and over while she hums along, and sometimes stands up and moves to it. Mathis' inclusion of this song and its meaning to Aunt Dew speaks not only to the music but to the spiritual or religious beliefs embraced by many African American elders.

The Hundred Penny Box is narrated in Standard English, but the speech attributed to various characters reflects informal, vernacular speech patterns associated with Black cultural contexts. For example, Michael's father employs one grammatical strategy common to Black vernacular when he negates every possible element in his sentence: "And when I didn't have nobody…I didn't have nothing" (p. 11). Aunt Dew's language reflects the vernacular speech of some older Southern African Americans. She asks Michael "What your momma name?" (p. 20)— leaving out the verb "to be," and leaving the possessive unmarked, as is characteristic of the syntax of some African American vernacular speech. Other expressions that reflect Black speech or rhetorical styles are sprinkled through the dialogue (e.g., "it didn't make them no never mind…"; they couldn't get the suitcase in the house good before he was climbing and falling out the trees. We almost had to feed him up them trees!" (p. 23). John's attempt to reassure his wife through sweet talk also displays African American rhetorical conventions, "Baby, baby, sweet woman, you doing fine" (p.11). Mathis also uses something of a non-linear structure. As a way of relating one incident between Ruth and Aunt Dew, Michael recalls a conversation between his parents that he had overheard some time before the day of the story. And, of course Aunt Dew's stories have the effect of mixing past and present. In *The Hundred Penny Box*, Mathis presents a complex story of family love, warmed by framed illustrations rendered in brown watercolors by Leo and Diane Dillon.

Valerie Flournoy's *The Patchwork Quilt* appeared in 1985, a decade after *The Hundred Penny Box*. Tanya's grandmother, who lives with Tanya's family, is determined to create a patchwork quilt as her masterpiece. Tanya's mother thinks it is easier to go and buy a quilt, but Grandma prefers the old ways. A quilt, she says, can tell your life story. Tanya, who is very close to Grandma, offers to help, not realizing that it would take a year. Grandma starts work on her masterpiece, cutting patches from items belonging to each family member. When Grandma's progress on the quilt is stopped halfway through by illness, Tanya takes over cutting patches, and sewing them together with her mother's help. Even her brothers help to cut squares, but it is Tanya who does most of the work. When the quilt is finished, she discovers that it has one square on which is embroidered, "To Tanya from Your Mama and Grandma." The tradition of handing down a family quilt from one generation to another continues.

The Patchwork Quilt, like *the Hundred Penny Box,* presents another extended family with a live-in elder who has a special relationship with a young child. Grandma is teacher, and through her quilt, family historian. Since this picture book covers an entire year, there are not many detailed conversations between Tanya and Grandma, but it is clear that they are very close. Grandma, like Aunt Dew, displays some feistiness. When Tanya's mother calls her "Grandma" and tries to get her to move away from a drafty window, she reminds her daughter that she, Grandma, is not her grandmother, but her mother, and asserts her right to sit where she pleases. Grandma stubbornly insists on sitting "in the Lord's light" to do her sewing. Again, there is that reference to religious belief that appears frequently in the characterization of Black elders. Grandma is clearly the matriarch of the family. At Christmas time, "All Grandma's sons and daughters and nieces and nephews came to pay their respects."

Grandma's language, like Aunt Dew's, sometimes reflects informal Black vernacular: "A year ain't that long, honey. Makin' this quilt gonna be a joy." Mostly, however, the narration and the dialogue reflect an informal variety of what is referred to as Standard English. On the other hand, Flournoy's treatment of the quilt evokes an African American cultural context. Although quilts and quilting are not exclusive to African Americans, there is a tradition of African American quilting to which this story alludes. Quilts and quilting appear fairly frequently in African American literature, and the quilt is sometimes a metaphor for the improvisational aspects of Black life and art. It is also notable that Grandma believes that quilts are made to be used. When Tanya describes the quilt on Grandma's bed as "old and dirty," Grandma reminds her, "It ain't dirty, honey. It's worn, the way it's supposed to be." The quilt may be a work of art, but it is not art for art's sake.

Although *The Patchwork Quilt* is cited here as an example of the thematic emphasis on the relationship between an elder and a young child, the award-winning illustrations are noteworthy as well. Pinkney (1999) notes that while he was working on a project just prior to this book, he discovered what became his signature approach to his illustrations. *The Patchwork Quilt* is his first picture storybook to take full advantage of this discovery. His approach involves, among other things, the staging of scenes using models and photography. As a result, his characters always look like ordinary, real people. They are individualized and reflect the natural diversity of appearance among Black people. The history of Black imagery in children's books, and the desire to affirm the beauty and worth of Black people make the portrayal of Black characters in children 's books an important consideration. Pinkney (1999) expressed a desire to portray Black people with dignity.

The illustrations of *The Patchwork Quilt* also include an image that recurs in African American picture books—a grandmother hugging her granddaughter close, the child's head resting on the grandmother's shoulder, her face towards the reader. This image appears in at least six of the picture books that feature intergenerational relationships.

In the context of these stories, such an image may not be surprising, but given the fact that in most cases the embrace is not described in the text, and given the artist's freedom to choose what scenes to depict, it seems significant that six or more different artists would choose to create that particular image of shared love.

Narrated in the voice of an unnamed young girl, Francine Haskins' *Things I Like About Grandma* (1992), as the title implies, details the activities she enjoys participating in with her grandmother. Unlike *The Hundred Penny Box* and *The Patchwork Quilt*, the book focuses only on the two characters and on no other family members. There is no real plot, but a series of descriptions of situations in which the narrator and Grandma interact.

The descriptions and the illustrations offer examples of the ways an African American author or artist can situate a story squarely in a Black cultural context. The first thing the narrator says she likes about Grandma is that Grandma tells stories of the "old days," including stories about Africa and slavery. This reference to African American history and the implicit positive association with Africa is common in the literature. The first illustration in the body of story is the characteristic one of Grandma holding and hugging her granddaughter, echoing *The Patchwork Quilt*. In another echo of *The Patchwork Quilt*, Grandma is also a quilter. She is making one of her "wonderful quilts" that "tell the story of our family." This one, too, is a patchwork quilt, and the narrator helps to choose the patches.

Although the central theme of *Things I Like About Grandma* is the relationship between grandmother and granddaughter, it is also about a sense of community. This Grandma is active, and is out and about. When she does her errands around the neighborhood, "Everybody says 'hello' to Grandma. They think she's special." On Sundays Grandma and granddaughter attend Sunday School and church. The illustration shows Grandma's friends outside the church dressed in their Sunday best, wearing hats that match their outfits, as has been traditional among church-going Black women, and is still customary for many, especially older Black women. Some of Grandma's friends are also wearing gloves, another older tradition. The traditional attitude has been that one dresses in one's best to go to church out of respect for what is considered a holy place.

Grandma takes her granddaughter along when she visits friends in the senior citizens' home to chat, eat snacks, and play cards. The senior citizens' home is named Banneker House, after Benjamin Banneker, the well-known African American mathematician, astronomer, surveyor, and almanac author who is often credited with helping to lay out the city of Washington, D.C. As part of the effort to call attention to African American heroes or achievers, African American writers often take the opportunity to drop names into the text. Grandma also takes her granddaughter along to the beauty shop where she has a blue rinse applied to her hair, which is then pressed and curled.

Pressing and curling refers to using a hot comb and then a hot curling iron to straighten the hair and curl it. This beauty shop is very much an African American cultural setting, where the ladies "laugh and gossip and listen to gospel music."

The lively illustrations, which are colorful and expressionistic, seem childlike, and very appealing. African Americans are shown with attractive faces with broad noses and full lips. The young narrator wears hairstyles typical of young Black girls with thick hair. Each illustration is full of details, often including those that indicate an African American cultural setting. Black dolls appear in many scenes, either on display or being held by the granddaughter. There is a patchwork quilt hanging on a wall in one of Grandma's rooms. Even the coloring book granddaughter takes to the senior citizens' home depicts African Americans. All the passengers pictured on the bus downtown are African American. This is a picture of an African American community as viewed by one for whom the community is "home."

In her author's note, Francine Haskins (1992) sums up what appears to be the main point of these African American picture books focusing on the relationship between a grandparent and a grandchild:

> It's a special relationship. It's teaching, telling, giving, bonding. It's learning family histories and traditions, things that have been passed from generation to generation. It's building the foundation—giving the child a basis to grow on and come back to. It's love shared.

The review of these three picture books provides just a snapshot of some aspects of an African American children's literature tradition, including some of the ways the literature can reflect the cultural context from which it emanates. These particular books are about love in a family; as such they are open to readers across social boundaries, and can possibly be read by critics and reviewers as universal stories, paying little or no attention to the cultural context in which they are situated. These books, however, do emanate from a specific cultural context and a full and fair reading of them demands some understanding of that context and the books' relationships to it. It is the specifics that enrich the story and ultimately allow for both universality and particular cultural substance.

It should be pointed out that, in spite of the existence of a small number of overarching thematic concerns and the recurrent thematic, stylistic and cultural threads woven throughout, the children's and young adult literature that has resulted from African Americans creating "their own art in their own words," is diverse and varied and complex and dynamic. Over time the scope of the literature has expanded to reflect a wide range of African American life. The cadre of African American authors and artists who create for young people has also expanded to include persons with various life experiences, differing views of their roles as African American literary artists, and, of course,

different creative interests and talents. Nevertheless, their stories are informed, and often driven, by the knowledge and understandings that they have acquired from living in a racialized society on the undervalued side of what Du Bois (1903) called the color line. At the heart of the literature remains the perceived need for African American literary artists to bear witness for young people—in their own words—to African Americans' unique journey across the landscape of American history.

And In Conclusion...

Most of my research has been about surveying the landscape of African American children's literature, trying to paint a big picture of the body of work that fits under that umbrella and the history of its development. I hoped that such research would enhance our understandings of the need for literature rooted in and emanating from the unique experiences of Americans of African descent, and also move in the direction of defining the aesthetics of that literature by identifying aspects of its distinctiveness and highlighting its cohesiveness across texts. It is also my hope that this research has helped to clear the way for continued in-depth literary and critical scholarship on African American texts and on the work of particular African American writers and artists who create for children and young adults. To that end, it is encouraging to note the existence of a number of edited volumes such as Karen Patricia Smith's *African American Voices in Young Adult Literature* (1994), the 1998 special issue of *African American Review,* edited by Dianne Johnson, and *Embracing, Evaluating, and Examining African American Children's and Young Adult Literature*, edited by Wanda M. Brooks and Jonda C. McNair (2008). A few book-length studies also have appeared in recent years. Michelle Martin (2004), for example, published *Brown Gold,* a historical and critical analysis of picture books focused on African Americans. In addition, some scholars have undertaken book-length studies of African American authors, including Angela Johnson (Hinton, 2006) and Sharon Draper (Hinton, 2008). There remains much to examine as social and political contexts change and newer writers and artists, with newer vision, enter the field.

Further I hope that my work, along with that of scholars from underrepresented groups, has helped to create a critical context for examining the children's and young adult literatures emanating from diverse groups within our nation. In that regard, it is gratifying to note, for example, that my work for *Shadow and Substance* provided a framework that Michael Cart and Christine Jenkins (2006) adopted for their study *The Heart Has Its Reasons: Young Adult Literature with Gay/Lesbian/Queer Content, 1969–2004.* In the past few decades, in the wake of a focus on multicultural education, a body of scholarship on so-called multicultural literature has emerged. Numerous journal articles, book chapters, critical reviews, and annotated bibliographies (some book-length) have been focused on the literatures of parallel culture groups such as Native Americans, Latinos, and Asian Americans (I am aware that diverse social groups are subsumed under those labels, making the terms oversimplified at best, but for the sake of brevity I ask the reader's indulgence). For example, Darwin Henderson and Jill May (2005) edited a volume that includes chapters devoted to various aspects of literatures from such groups as well as issues relating to images of women and religious minorities. Another example is Paulette Molin's *American Indian Themes in Young Adult Literature* (2005), which provides a critical look at the ways American Indians have been portrayed. The door is open to much more scholarship that would enrich our understandings of the stories that American socio-cultural groups deem important to share with young people through their literature, as well as the distinctive ways they may choose to tell those stories. No doubt scholars and writers from those groups would embrace Toni Morrison's notion that literary art is a necessity and her assertion of the need for a literature created "in their own words." By studying such literature, and situating it in its social and political contexts, scholars can open the way for more attention to diverse literatures in schools, deeper understanding of their richness, and greater awareness of their importance to making whole the body of American literature for children and youth.

Literature References

Barber, B. (1994). *Saturday at the New You* (A. Rich, Illus.). New York, NY: Lee and Low.

Caines, J. (1982). *Just us women* (P. Cummings, Illus.). New York, NY: Harper.

Coleman, E. (1995). *The glass bottle tree* (G.G. Carter, Illus.). New York, NY: Orchard.

De Angeli, M. (1946). *Bright April*. New York, NY: Doubleday.

English, K. (1998). *Just right stew* (A. Rich, Illus.). Honesdale, PA: Boyds Mills.

Flournoy, V. (1985). *The patchwork quilt* (J. Pinkney, Illus.). New York, NY: Dial.

Greenfield, E. (1975). Something to shout about. *The Horn Book Magazine*, *41*, 524–626.

Greenfield, E. (1980). *Grandmama's joy* (C. Byard, Illus.). New York, NY: Philomel.

Greenfield, E. (1988). *Nathaniel talking* (J. S. Gilchrist, Illus.). New York, NY: Black Butterfly.

Greenfield, E. (1988). *Grandpa's face* (F. Cooper, Illus.). New York, NY: Philomel.

Haskins, F. (1992). *Things I like about grandma*. San Francisco, CA: Children's Book Press.

Hogan, I. (1932). *Nicodemus and his little sister*. New York, NY: E. P. Dutton.

Hogan, I. (1941). *Nicodemus laughs*. New York, NY: E.P. Dutton.

Howard, E. F. (1991). *Aunt Flossie's hats (and crab cakes later)* (J. Ransome, Illus.). New York, NY: Clarion.

Hunt, B. F. (1951). *Stories of Little Brown Koko* (D. Wagstaff, Illus.). Chicago, IL: American Colortype Co.

Johnson, A. (1989). *Tell me a story, Mama* (D. Soman, Illus.). New York, NY: Orchard.

Johnson, A. (1990). *When I am old with you* (D. Soman, Illus.) New York, NY: Orchard.

Johnson, A. (1996). *The aunt in our house* (D. Soman, Illus.) New York, NY: Orchard.

Mathis, S. B. (1975). *The hundred penny box* (L. Dillon and D. Dillon, Illus.). New York: Viking.

Mitchell, M. (1993). *Uncle Jed's barbershop* (J. Ransome, Illus.). New York, NY: Simon and Schuster.

Myers, W. D. (2003). *Blues journey* (C. Myers, Illus.). New York, NY: Holiday House.

Myers, W. D. (2006). *Jazz* (C. Myers, Illus.). New York, NY: Holiday House.

Rochelle, B. (1996). *Louise's gift* (C. Bootman, Illus.). New York, NY: Little, Brown.

Smalls, I. (1994). *When Jo Louis won the title* (L. Johnson, Illus.). New York, NY: Houghton Mifflin.

Smalls, I. (1999). *Kevin and his dad* (M. Hays, Illus.). New York, NY: Little, Brown.

Steptoe, J. (2003). *The Jones family express*. New York, NY: Lee and Low.

Woodson, J. (1997). *We had a picnic this Sunday past* (D. Greenseid, Illus.). New York, NY: Hyperion.

Academic References

Bishop, R. S. (2007). *Free within ourselves: The development of African American children's literature*. Portsmouth, NH: Heinemann.

Broderick, D. M. (1973). *Image of the black in children's fiction*. New York, NY: R.R. Bowker.

Brooks, W. M., & McNair, J. C. (Eds.). (2008). *Embracing, evaluating, and examining African American children's and young adult literature*. Lanham, MD. Scarecrow Press.

Brown, S. (1933). Negro characters as seen by white authors. *Journal of Negro Education*, 2(2), 179–203.

Cart, M., & Jenkins, C. (2006). *The heart has its reasons: Young adult literature with gay/lesbian/queer content, 1969–2004*. Lanham, MD: Scarecrow Press.

Cooperative Children's Book Center (2007). *Children's books by and about people of color published in the United States*. Retrieved February 3, 2010, from http://www.education.wisc.edu/ccbc/books/pcstats.htm

Cornelius, J. D. (1991). *When I can read my title clear: Literacy, slavery and religion in the antebellum South*. Columbia: South Carolina University Press.

Du Bois, W.E.B. (1903) *The souls of Black folk*. New York, NY: New American Library.

Ellison, R. (1964). Twentieth-century fiction and the black mask of humanity. In R. Ellison (Ed.). *Shadow and act* (pp. 60–76). New York, NY: Random House.

Evans, E. K. (1941, August 30). The Negro in children's fiction. *Publisher's Weekly*, *140*, 650–653.

Fishel, L. H. Jr., & Quarles, B. (1967). *The Negro American: A documentary history*. New York, NY: William Morrow.

Franklin, J. H., & Moss, A. (1994). *From slavery to freedom: A history of African Americans* (7th ed.) New York, NY: Knopf.

Genovese, E. (1976). *Roll, Jordan, roll: The world the slaves made*. New York, NY: Vintage Books.

Hamilton, V. (1981). Changing woman, working. In B. Hearne & M. Kaye (Eds.), *Celebrating children's books* (pp. 54–61). New York, NY: Lothrop.

Harris, V. J. (1986). *The Brownies' Book: Challenge to the selective tradition in children's literature*. Ph.D. Dissertation. University of Georgia, Athens.

Harris, V. J. (1987). Jessie Fauset's transference of the "new Negro" philosophy to children's literature. *The Langston Hughes Review*, 6(2), 36–43.

Harris, V. J. (1989). Race consciousness, refinement, and radicalism: Socialization in The Brownies' Book. *Children's Literature Quarterly, 14*(4), 192–196.

Henderson, D. L., & May, J. P. (2005). *Exploring culturally diverse literature for children and adolescents: Learning to listen in new ways.* Boston, MA: Pearson.

Hinton, K. M. (2006). *Angela Johnson: Poetic prose.* Lanham, MD: Scarecrow Press.

Hinton, K. M. (2008). *Sharon M. Draper: Embracing literacy.* Lanham, MD. Scarecrow Press.

Hughes, L. (1932). Books and the Negro child. *Children's Library Yearbook, 4,* 108–110.

Johnson, D. (1990). *Telling tales: The Pedagogy and promise of African American literature for youth.* New York, NY: Greenwood Press.

Johnson, D. (Ed.). (1998). A selected bibliography for the study of African American children's literature. *African American Review, 32*(1), 157.

Martin, M. (2004). *Brown gold: Milestones of African American children's picture books, 1845–2002.* New York, NY: Routledge

Means, F. C. (1940). Mosaic. *The Horn Book Magazine, 16,* 35–41.

Molin, P. (2005). *American Indian themes in young adult literature.* Lanham, MD: Scarecrow Press.

Morrison, T. (2008, July 28). Lee, F. R. Bench of memory at slavery's gateway. *New York Times,* B1, B6.

Penn, I. G. (1891/1969). *The Afro-American press and its editors.* New York: Arno Press and the New York Times.

Pinkney, J. B. (1999). Profile: A conversation with Jerry Pinkney. In H. Smith (Ed.), *The Coretta Scott King Awards book, 1970–1999* (pp. 64–66). Chicago, IL: American Library Association.

Sims, R. (1982). *Shadow and substance: Afro-American experience in contemporary children's fiction.* Urbana, IL: National Council of Teachers of English.

Sinnette, E. D. V. (1965). The Brownies' Book: A pioneer publication for children. *Freedomways, 5,* 33–142.

Smith, K. P. (Ed.). (1994). *African American voices in young adult literature.* Lanham, MD: Scarecrow Press

Trager, H. (1945). Intercultural books for children. *Childhood Education 22,* 138–145.

Webber, T. (1978). *Deep like the rivers: Education in the slave quarter community,* 1831–1865. New York, NY: Norton.

Woodson, C. G. (1933/1968). *The miseducation of the Negro.* Washington, D.C.: Associated Publishers.

Woodson, C. G. (1919/1968). *The education of the Negro prior to 1861.* New York: Arno Press and the New York Times.

Point of Departure

Jacqueline Woodson

Reading To My Son On A Winter Morning

In another month, my daughter will turn eight and our baby boy, who lies when people ask and says he's six years old, will turn two. Why are the ages of my children important? Because now, well into my forties, I've begun to look behind—to see where I've come as a reader and a writer and to bear witness to the road my children have walked. It moves quickly, time does—and looking back at my past while at once, looking ahead into my children's and my own future, I am again stunned at how far we've come. And how much further we have to go.

This morning, my son brings Virginia Hamilton's *The People Could Fly* downstairs with him, struggling beneath the weight of the heavy book in his small hands. He gives the command he gives many times in a given day "Mommy! Read it!" Then after a moment, he adds "Please...!" As he's been taught to do. Again and again. My daughter, pauses over her breakfast and says, "You know we used to could fly Jackson. Before me or you or Mommy and Mama were born." The baby stares at the cover for a long time. Then slowly says, "I want flying. "So after Toshi leaves for school and it's just the two of us, we open the pages of Virginia Hamilton's book—and begin to fly.

When I look back—into my world at eight years old, there was no Virginia Hamilton yet (I would discover her book *Zeely* two years later, a battered copy in our meager classroom library. My public school was a poor one without a school library so the books we had access to came from class or the public library around the corner) there was no Mildred Taylor or Nikki Giovanni. What existed in that underserved school (I would many times over the course of my childhood hear it referred to as "ghetto" and would come to despise that word) were the stories of middle-class White families living in worlds I couldn't even imagine, where the biggest struggle was a torn pocket, a missing doll, a friend moving away. And yes, I'd torn pockets in my life and had my grandmother give me a good talking to about clothes not growing on trees. And while I'd never lost an actual doll, I'd been known to misplace a limb, a tiny patent leather doll shoe, or sometimes (but I still blame my brothers for this) whole dolls' heads. But the worlds in those books were solidly White worlds, and the world I lived in was not.

But at eight, I discovered an amazing book that would remain a part of my library from that moment till this day. *Stevie* by John Steptoe was the story of an African American family living in a world that looked very much like my world. And from the book's opening line—"One day my momma told me, 'You know you're gonna have a little friend come stay with you.'" I knew I had just entered a world that would change me forever. Not only did the characters in the book look like the people I loved, the way they spoke reminded me of my own family and the many families living around me.

This is how a door opens—a child picks up a book and finds a part or many parts of their lives on the page. And because of this, the child keeps reading. And keeps reading.

And turning the pages of Stevie lead me to the pages of *She Come Bringing Me that Little Baby Girl* and onward to *Zeely, A Hero Ain't Nothing but a Sandwich, The Me Nobody Knows, Roll of Thunder Hear My Cry*—the list goes on and on...

Leading me to this moment, years later, a writer who has been brought to this place in my life and my career by the Black writers who were not there when I was a child—allowing me to grow up with a hunger I had no name for but wanted to satisfy. And the writers who finally were—who simply by being on the page and out in the world said to me "Tell YOUR story." And I do.

My son stares open mouthed at the page in *The People Could Fly* where Leo and Diane Dillon's illustration de-picts Sarah, a slave woman with a baby on her back as Toby, looks on.

"The baby Mama flying?" he asks, looking up at me as he points to the page. "Mommy! Her flying?!"

I stare at the illustration for a long time. More than 30 years have past since I opened the first book I'd ever read by an African American. The book that would start me on my journey. In my children's library, it is hard not to pull a book off the shelves and see either illustrations or text or both by a person of color. The absence of my childhood is not a part of the world they know. Of course, there is still so much work to do, so many gaps to fill in the road to each of us being able to be fully human in this place called America. But as I pull my son closer to me and look down at Sarah about to lift off, as I think of the books my daughter will open and find herself in again and again, as I think of the children out in the world who won't have to see themselves in the absence of themselves, who won't feel invisible, illegitimate, un-thought of, I can't help but feel a tremendous pride for the body of work my people have put into the world of children's literature. And sitting with my baby boy on this cold winter morning, I smile as the sun suddenly pours in through the kitchen windows.

"Yep, Jackson-Leroi," I say. "The baby's mama is flying."

17

The Art of the Picturebook

Lawrence R. Sipe

Graduate School of Education, University of Pennsylvania

Picturebooks blend words and illustrations. The two dance together, in what Maurice Sendak once famously called the "seamless" style of these two modes of expression. Lawrence Sipe—who specializes in the analysis of this genre—has specifically chosen to highlight the relationship by using picturebook as one word rather than two, for it is the combination of art and language that together create the aesthetic object. Still, he argues that the picturebook is ever transforming, drawing in other visual and written genres from the comic book to the novel. And like all transformations, each decision—from the peritextual features to the drama that occurs at the turn of the page—is freighted with ideological and sociocultural implications. Caldecott award-winning artists, Chris Raschka and David Wiesner, echo Sipe's argument with detailed insights into their own creative processes, including their often surprising results as they work with gutters, end pages, and margins to best tell their stories.

"Sequential art," to use Will Eisner's (1985) term, is nothing new. Think of Hogarth's (1735) popular series of eight prints limning the rise and demise of a headstrong and greedy young man, *A Rake's Progress,* and you will see that the idea of a series of visual images connected together by a narrative thread is not something that originated recently. Indeed, we can trace this idea much further back to ancient Egyptian, Greek, and Roman murals, Chinese and Japanese scroll paintings, and to medieval art such as the Bayeaux tapestries and stained glass windows. Some (Kiefer, 2008) argue that we can go even further back, to prehistoric sequential cave paintings. Often, these earlier pieces of art rely almost exclusively on visual images; Hogarth's series has no words except for the titles of the images.

In picturebooks, however, we *do* have a new literary/visual format—a series of pictures with corresponding words, where the words and pictures, equally important, stand in complex relationships with each other, and where the pictures do not merely "illustrate" what's already said in the verbal text, but add something different and new, so that the synergy (Sipe, 1998) between words and pictures adds up to something greater than the sum of its parts. This intricate dance between words and visual images is, according to many scholars, the unique contribution of children's literature to the whole of literary endeavor, and in modern times begins with the work of Randolph Caldecott (1846–1886).

In a famous example of this synergy, in one of his

"toy books," Caldecott takes the nonsense nursery rhyme "Hey Diddle Diddle" and transforms it. Perhaps the most brilliant passage of this ground-breaking exemplar is the last line of the rhyme: "and the dish ran away with the spoon." In Caldecott's illustrations, the dish, presented as a male suitor, "spoons" on a bench with the object of his affections. Moreover, the next illustration shows the tragic result of the dish's attentions: he lies broken in pieces on the floor, while the indignant knife and fork (the spoon's parents) lead her off, while the dish's crockery groupies raise up an almost audible wail of mourning. Thus, Caldecott's visual images, when combined with the words, produce a charmingly inventive expansion, while the words anchor the illustrations by telling us what we should pay attention to. The words tell us things that the pictures omit, and *vice versa*; in addition, readers/viewers must fill in the gaps that neither the words nor the illustrations contribute. This, in a nutshell, is the art of the picturebook.

I have chosen to begin with this example because it not only defines the nature of the picturebook so well; it also gestures toward many of the points I want to make in the rest of this chapter. Caldecott's art, and its reproduction in his books, demonstrate the great technological advances that have been made in the "means of production" of picturebooks since the late 1800s. Caldecott relied heavily on Edmund Evans and his team of expert engravers to transfer his fluid and supple line drawings to small blocks of boxwood, one of the hardest of woods, and the blocks were then assembled tightly together, inked, and the images printed one by one. This incredibly laborious process of reproducing illustrations and combining them with text has changed dramatically over the last 125 years. My point is that art is always *embodied* in some form, whether as paint on canvas, bronze castings for a statue, or in a well-crafted book. There is a materiality about art that we must take into consideration, and the art of the picturebook is no exception.

As light and amusing as Caldecott's dish-and-spoon illustrations are, they also show that art always has a serious side. As well, there is the subtlest of ideological messages in the failed relationship of the dish and the spoon: *stick to your own kind*. Art invariably reflects the political and sociocultural contexts in which it is made, and Caldecott's toy books, as well as our contemporary picturebooks, always express these contexts, however surreptitiously or unconsciously. In other words, in addition to what we might broadly call considerations of "aesthetics," all art has an ideological, political, and social dimension that I want to address.

Finally, my reference to Caldecott indicates that picturebooks today have one foot in their historical context, with all the conventions and techniques that have evolved over time, but they also stand on the cutting edge of publishing, more than holding their own against exotic technologies such as cyberformats and hypertext. Picturebooks, along with these other invitations to "new literacies" are both

re-inventing themselves and transforming the way we view the processes of reading and seeing, inviting us to think of ourselves—especially our identities as readers/ viewers—in new ways. All art both informs us and has the potential to transform us.

This chapter is divided into four sections. First, I describe the process of making a picturebook and address advances in the technology of reproduction that have allowed an unprecedented blossoming of picturebooks with illustrations in many different media. The second section discusses the qualities and affordances of picturebooks as aesthetic objects. In the third section, I turn to the sociocultural and ideological issues related to contemporary picturebooks. Finally, I explore possible new directions in picturebooks, including the ways in which they will continue to blur into other visual formats.

The Process of Producing a Picturebook and Advances in Technology

Picturebooks, like any other art form, have both conventions and formal qualities that are incarnated in doing and making, which result in a physical, aesthetic object. Unlike the objects (paintings, sculpture, etc.) produced by individual artists, picturebooks are the result of a process involving a number of people: authors, illustrators, editors, designers, and all the technically savvy people who know how to produce excellent reproductions of the original art and bind the resulting pages into a book.

In addition, picturebooks are produced in quantities, unlike a unique painting or piece of sculpture crafted by one artist. In this regard, picturebooks have a greater similarity to the limited edition prints often made by the artist herself or in conjunction with a printer who reproduces the original work. As Marantz (1977) reminds us, the picturebook *itself* is the aesthetic object, not the original set of illustrations for it. In other words, though the original art is desirable and collectible, it is always in the service of making the book we hold in our hands. This gives a new twist to Walter Benjamin's (1936/2000) observations about the means of mass-reproduction that have become commonplace in the last two centuries. Benjamin reflected on the ways in which practically everyone could have a copy or reproduction of the *Mona Lisa*, even though there is only one original, hanging in the Louvre, which obviously has much higher value and social cachet. By contrast, picturebooks are in this sense more important than the set of "original" illustrations. In the case of the *Mona Lisa*, the painting is the original, and the copies/reproductions are spinoffs. With picturebooks, the reverse is the case—the book itself is the "real thing," and the work of the artist (and author, editor, and designer) are subsidiary.

I can do no more than sketch the process of making a picturebook from start to finish; much detailed description exists in the books mentioned at the end of the chapter on the business of children's literature in this handbook, and even in some books meant for children (Aliki, 1988; Stevens, 1995). However, it's necessary to at least limn the outline of the process. Generally, what happens is this: an author composes a text and sends the manuscript to an editor, who reads the manuscript, and suggests changes. When this back-and-forth negotiation is complete, the author and editor divide the text into segments, which will appear on each page. Then the editor usually has the responsibility of assigning the text to an illustrator, who produces illustrations for each page, first creating a "dummy" book—a thumbnail size version with sketches of the illustrations for each page. Curiously, and surprisingly, the author often has no input into the choice of an illustrator, nor do the author and illustrator usually communicate with each other. This lack of communication may result in a less integrated final product; Salisbury (2004) suggests that the best picturebooks may be those where the author and the illustrator are the same person. Salisbury (2008) calls these people "authorstrators," borrowing the coined word of one of his students. On the other hand, some editors defend the practice of assigning an illustrator to a text without any input from the author, asserting that this gives illustrators more freedom of artistic choice.

Meanwhile, the designer often chooses the font used for the words of the story, the placement of the words on the page, the size and shape of the book (portrait or landscape), and determines what the elements that "surround" the story look like—the dust jacket, the cloth or board cover (called the case), the title page, dedication page, etc. Then the book is ready to go into production. This involves reproducing the illustrations by a number of different means, usually photo-offset, which involves photographing the illustration through a successive series of fine screens or filters that separate the illustration into four parts (yellow, cyan [blue], magenta [red], and black), which will then be printed on top of each other so that the finished reproduction will be as close to the original colors as possible. The filters not only separate the colors, but also reduce the illustration to an incredibly large number of tiny dots, which makes the printing possible. The type of magnifying glass called a printer's loupe can be used to see this matrix of dots, and adults as well as children are fascinated by this sight—what appears as solid color is actually a complex array of tiny pinpoints.

This is where the length of the manuscript comes into play. The length is usually limited to the amount of text that can be printed on 32 pages, including a proportionally greater space for the illustrations. Why the magic number 32? Simply because of the means of production: When the final printing is done, the standard procedure is to print eight pages on each side of a very large piece of paper, which is then folded and cut so that there are sixteen pages (counting the front and back) called a signature. Larger presses can handle even larger sheets of paper, so sixteen pages may be printed on each side, and divided into two sixteen-page signatures. Two signatures are most often used in picturebooks—thus 32 pages. Although books can be as few as 24 or as large as 40 or even 48, most picturebooks have a limited number of pages, and that number is always divisible by eight. Pull a picturebook off the library shelf and count the pages to check this for yourself. In an interesting newer development, some picturebooks are printed with only four pages to a side, so as to have more control over the color values. Norman Juster's (2005) and Chris Raschka's Caldecott-winning *The Hello, Goodbye Window* was printed in this way (Raschka, personal communication, 2007). When the signatures are ready, they are either sewn or glued together on the spine of the case cover. The dustjacket is printed and folded around the case, and—voila!—the picturebook is ready to be distributed to bookstores.

Reproduction techniques have improved dramatically, even in the last decade. Well before this, there were paradigm-shifting improvements in the 1960s. Before that time, artists had to do their own color pre-separations; in other words, instead of relying on a machine to separate the colors, artists had to produce a separate image for each color (and black) in each illustration—what an arduous process! This is why, if you look at picturebooks that are more than 40 or 50 years old, you will see a much simpler style and range of color values. The advances in reproduction give artists a virtually unlimited choice of what media and techniques they can now employ to illustrate picturebooks.

Qualities of Picturebooks: The Picturebook as an Aesthetic Object

Color, Line, Shape, and Texture

The illustrations in a picturebook are meant to be seen in sequence; however, we can only look at one *opening* (also called a *double page spread*) at a time, so some mention must be made of the traditional elements of visual design—*color*, *line*, *shape*, and *texture*—common to all visual art rendered in two dimensions. Color has natural associations and cultural associations. Blue is almost universally associated with calm, detachment, serenity or (in its darker moments) melancholy, for example. But the color for grief and mourning in most of western society—black—is replaced in some Asian countries with white. Illustrators' use of these associations will therefore depend on their own cultural backgrounds. Colors have three aspects—hue, tone, and saturation. *Hue* refers to the pure color, unmixed with anything else. Hues may be combined with black, which results in *shades*. Or they may be combined with white (or water, in the case of water-based media), which results in *tints*. *Tone* refers to the amount of darkness or brightness of a hue, and *saturation* is the intensity or purity of a color. For example, highly saturated hues are predominant in Christopher Myers's clever version of the famous nonsense poem *Jabberwocky* (Carroll, 2007); there are very few dilutions of pure color in either the text or the illustrations, in keeping with the energy, tension, and triumph of the story. As reimagined by Myers, the Jabberwock is a huge, threatening basketball player, challenged by the much smaller (but faster) hero, who beats him and takes the basketball (the Jabberwock's "head") home in celebration. Marisa Montes's (2007) *Los Gatos Black on Halloween* contains highly shaded hues and dark tones, with very few saturated colors, appropriate for a story that takes place at night and combines the Mexican Day of the Dead with Halloween.

Line can vary in "weight" from thin and wispy to thick and solid. The fine ink lines in *The Wall* (Sis, 2007) make possible a great deal of detail, even in small illustrations. *Cross-hatching*, where fine lines criss-cross each other, can darken certain areas of an illustration and gives a feeling of energy or tension, palpable in that most classic of all picturebooks, *Where the Wild Things Are* (Sendak, 1963). Shape is discussed very clearly in Molly Bang's (1991) *Picture This*, which explains several general principles of shapes in pictorial art. Horizontal shapes, for example, give us a sense of "stability and calm" (p. 56), while vertical shapes are more exciting and suggest energy. Diagonal shapes are the most energetic and dynamic of all, evoking a sense of motion or drama. Pointed shapes create anxiety and dread, because of their association with objects that may hurt us, whereas rounded shapes act in the opposite way, soothing us with their safety and comfort. The placement of shapes is also important; Moebius (1986) and Bang (1991) suggest that placement on the top half of an illustration gives an impression of lightness, freedom, happiness, or spirituality, whereas placement in the bottom half signifies greater weight or "down-to-earth-ness" and may also mean seriousness or sadness. Kress and Van Leeuven (1996) suggest that shapes on the left (*verso*) side of the double page spread indicate the status quo and stability, whereas those on the right (*recto*) side suggest the possibility of change or motion, since they are near the place where we will turn the page. Shapes near the center get our attention first, and often signal importance or domination (Moebius, 1986).

Texture is difficult to represent on the smooth paper in picturebooks, but the *illusion* of texture—in three dimensions—as rough or smooth, hard or soft, is made possible by the exacting reproduction techniques discussed above. The variety of highly textured hand-made papers of Bulgarian illustrator Sibylla Benatova's backgrounds for the illustrations in *The Magic Raincoat* (David, 2007) contrast nicely with the slick, shiny smooth renditions of a little girl in her raincoat, rendered on mylar. The overlapping surfaces of the various textured papers fool our eyes into perceiving a three-dimensionality on the two-dimensional space of the page.

Style, defined by Nodelman (1988) as "all the aspects of a work of art considered together" (p. 77) results from the combination of color, line, shape, and texture; the artistic medium or media the illustrator uses; and common motifs or themes. Some styles (such as Tomie dePaola's) are so consistent that children can recognize the work from across the room; other artists purposefully vary their styles according to the content/subject matter of the story. Even young children can grasp the concept of style if practitioners begin by contrasting two very different styles, such as the fluid, loose watercolor style of Jerry Pinkney, with its pencil underdrawing, and the outline style of dePaola, with its rounded shapes, minimalist depictions of characters' facial expressions, and extensive use of acrylic or watercolor tints rather than fully saturated colors. After discussing these differences, we can then distinguish more subtle differences in style, and help children to perceive these differences. For example, Pinkney, E. B. Lewis, and Ted Lewin all use watercolor as their primary medium. Pinkney's style is the most loose and flowing; Lewin has a very tightly controlled style; and E. B. Lewis's style falls somewhere in between these extremes.

Taking a Tour of a Picturebook

I want to give a sense of the various parts of picturebooks by giving directions for examining these elements closely. I will be referring to a few examples from Ashley Bryan's (2007) *Let it Shine*, a picturebook version of three popular spirituals: "This Little Light of Mine," "When the Saints Go Marching In," and "He's Got the Whole World in His Hands." I'll also share some insights about the design elements of *Los Gatos Black on Halloween* by Marisa Montes (2007). It would be most useful if you had these books in front of you as you toured the books with me. First, take a look at the front and back dust jacket cover, and ask whether they comprise a single illustration. Or are there different illustrations on the front and the back? What does the dust jacket suggest about the tone, possible characters, or topic of the book?

Next, remove the dust jacket, and look at the front and back board covers in a similar way. Are they the same as the dust jacket (as in *Let It Shine*) or are they different (as in *Los Gatos*)? Why do you suppose the designer made these choices? The circular shapes on the dust jacket of *Los Gatos* are paralleled by the circular shapes of the circular frames for the images on the board cover.

Then open the book, and examine the endpapers. The endpapers of *Let it Shine* are as colorful and exuberant as the front cover, with wavy stripes of various colors, suggesting the lines of a staff of music as well as a horizon line; two large hands; and what appear to be photographs of two pairs of scissors on top of the hands. The hands suggest both the spiritual "He's Got the Whole World in His Hands" and the illustrator's own hands. In contrast, the endpapers of *Los Gatos* are appropriately plain black, for a story that combines the Mexican Day of the Dead and Halloween. Take a look at the front and back endpapers; are they alike or different? In both *Let it Shine* and *Los Gatos*, they are alike, but this is not always the case. See Sipe and McGuire (2006a) for a fuller discussion of endpapers.

Turn the flyleaf of the front endpapers and examine the next page, which may consist of a dedication page and "front matter" (publishing information) or perhaps a frontispiece (an illustration opposite the title page that sets the tone for the book). Is there a half-title page (a page with only the words of the title) followed by a full title page (which gives the title plus the author, publisher, and copyright date), as in *Let it Shine*?

Ask yourself how all these surrounding elements prepare you to read and understand the story that follows (Sipe & McGuire, 2006b). Also ask yourself how all the design elements of the book (the color palette, the major shapes utilized, and the artistic medium or media) are arranged to make the book an artistic whole, rather than a miscellaneous collection of elements. How do the size and shape of the book match the story or the perspectives used in the illustrations? How are the words and pictures arranged? For example, are the words always at the bottom of the page, or are there variations in the ways in which the words and pictures relate to each other physically? In *Los Gatos*, the many curved shapes in the illustrations are echoed by the curved lines of the text, whereas the text of the spirituals in *Let it Shine* are invariably printed in horizontal lines at the bottom of each page, suggesting the way that texts for music are printed below the musical notations. Are all the illustrations double page spreads, with the illustration going across both pages, or are there smaller illustrations, perhaps even a series of smaller illustrations? Do the illustrations "bleed" (extend all the way to the edge of the pages) or is there a border or white space? A border always gives a feeling of distance, whereas illustrations that bleed to the edge of the page give us a sense of involvement and engagement. How is the font chosen for the words appropriate to the tone and setting of the story? In general, how do all these elements work together to produce a satisfying and harmonious aesthetic whole?

The Relationship of Words and Pictures

As I mentioned in the introduction, the intricate dance between text and pictures is the *sine qua non* of the picturebook. There are many ways in which the various relationships between words and pictures have been described. In one category, we have a wide range of *metaphors*. Moebius (1986), for example, speaks of the "plate tectonics" of the word-picture relationship, and Miller (1992), continuing the scientific metaphor, writes of the "interference" patterns between the visual and the verbal, in reference to physics and wave theory, for two waves may combine to form an entirely new pattern. Musical metaphors are also employed; "counterpoint" or a "duet" are used by Pullman (1989) and Cech (1983–84), respectively, and Moss (1990) refers to Janet and Allan Ahlberg's idea of words and pictures as having an antiphonal or fugue effect on each other.

Other writers use more developed *concepts* to describe the relationship. Lewis (1996) writes of the

"polysystemy"—"the piecing together of text out of different kinds of signifying systems" (p. 105). Lewis also uses the term "interanimation," following Margaret Meek's (1992) observation that the words and pictures interanimate each other. My own term is "synergy," referring to the effect that text and pictures produce together that would not be achieved if either were missing. I have also used semiotic theory to describe the ways in which reader/viewers engage in "transmediation" (Suhor, 1984), translating, as it were, one sign system to another and back again—interpreting the words in terms of the pictures and the pictures in terms of the words (Sipe, 1998). Nodelman (1988) suggests that the words "limit" the pictures by telling us what to pay attention to in the visual image, and that the pictures "limit" the words by telling us exactly what visual image to think of when we read a word. For example, if the story is about a princess, the illustration limits that word by showing us exactly what this particular princess looks like. Doonan (1993) argues that there is always some tension: the words always drive us to keep reading to find out what happens, whereas the pictures pull us in the other direction by inviting us to linger and slow down.

Finally, there are numerous *taxonomies* of word-picture relationships; these may be the most useful because they make the point that words and pictures do not have just one type of relationship with each other, but many (Agosto, 1999; Golden, 1990; Lewis, 2001). Nikolajeva and Scott's (2001) typology is perhaps the most complex. They suggest that there are five distinct word-picture relationships: (a) symmetry (there is a virtual equivalence between words and pictures); (b) complementarity (words and pictures form one narrative, but contribute independently); (c) enhancement (the words and pictures extend or expand on each others' meaning); (d) counterpoint (the words and pictures tell different stories, which may have an ironic relationship with each other); and (e) contradiction (words and pictures flatly contradict each other).

All of these typologies make the point that, in the same picturebook, the words and visual images may interact in one way on one opening, and in entirely different ways in other openings. Lewis (2001) thus refers to the "ecology" of the picturebook, since all these relationships are not merely present independently, but are related *to each other* in complex ways, in the same way a biosystem consists of a complicated set of relationships among the various plants, animals, and their environment. The typologies also suggest that if the relationships between words and pictures are so complex, the relationships added by other modalities (movement in pop-up books and sound or light produced by small computer chips inserted in the book) must be even more interconnected and complicated. This is another argument for revisiting, re-reading, and re-viewing picturebooks. In general, word-picture relationships integrate sign systems: Steiner (1982), writing about illustrated books (and, by extension, picturebooks), observes that they are "a gesture toward semiotic repleteness" (p. 144) much in the way that an opera combines music, visual interest, drama, and narrative in a multisensual way.

Other Important Elements of the Picturebook Format

The Page Breaks/Turns. Unlike a novel, in which the words on one page flow seamlessly onto the next, the page breaks (sometimes called page turns) are very carefully considered in picturebooks. Authors, illustrators, and editors pay close attention to the movement from one double page spread to the next. Barbara Bader (1976) suggests that the excitement and the aesthetics of a picturebook depend, in part, on "the drama of the turning of the page" (p. 1). Although authors and illustrators talk about the importance of page breaks in picturebooks, this characteristic is an under-theorized and under-researched part of the elements of picturebook format (Sipe & Brightman, 2009). There is not only a pause as we turn the page; there is likely to be a gap or indeterminacy (Iser, 1978) in the narrative. Consider, for example, the fourth and fifth openings of Asma Mobin-Uddin's (2007) *The Best Eid Ever*, the story of Aneesa, a Pakistani Muslim girl who discovers two refugees in the mosque during the celebration of Eid, the most festive holiday in the Islamic year. On the fourth opening, Aneesa's grandmother gives her a bite of lamb korma in their well-appointed American kitchen. Grandmother says, "I'm glad you like it. Now let's hurry and get ready so we're not late for prayers." When we turn to the fifth opening, the illustration depicts Aneesa sitting in the mosque with her grandmother, trying to pay attention, but thinking about her parents, who have gone to Saudi Arabia for the Hajj pilgrimage. What happens between these two openings? We could speculate about the grandmother and girl putting on their good clothes, riding or walking to the mosque, and having conversation. The setting changes from the kitchen of grandmother's house to the mosque. The mood also changes from one of delight in tasting the delicious lamb korma to the reflective mood in the mosque, where Aneesa misses her parents. Speculating about these things allows reader/viewers to piece together each successive double page spread into a seamless narrative. This is crucial in order to understand the flow of the story. As reader/viewers, we are invited to be co-authors of the narrative, filling in the indeterminacies between the spreads with interpretative inferences. Although all texts have indeterminacies, the page breaks in picturebooks seem an ideal place to speculate, hypothesize, and infer what happens in the liminal space (Turner, 1969) "in between." Simply asking the question (to children or to one's self) about what might have happened from one opening to the next is natural way to encourage active meaning making.

Connections to Other Works of Art—Intertextuality. No art is *sui generis*; it comes from a tradition and either continues that tradition or breaks from it. Some picturebooks, however, make a special point of referring to other famous works of art or the style of particular artists or time periods. Paul Zelinsky's (1997) gorgeous illustrations for *Rapunzel* give a nod to the traditions of Renaissance Italian painting. Author/illustrator Anthony Browne is well known for including imitations and parodies of well-known works of art in his books. For example, in *Willy the Dreamer*, Browne (1997) wittily references the works of many paintings and painters, including Salvador Dali, Winslow Homer, and Henri Rousseau. The entire plot of *Picturescape* (Gutierrez, 2005) takes the protagonist on an intertextual art adventure, as he "enters" one painting after another as he visits a museum. These types of books may be used to teach the history of art (Sipe, 2001). They provide an entrée into the fascinating world of art, and there is a pleasure in recognizing how the illustrator has imitated or parodied a style or a particular work of art in a picturebook.

Borders and Breaking the Frame. One critical aspect of illustrations' appearance on the space of the double page spread is the ways in which designers and illustrators use borders (or the lack of them). As I indicated above, the full bleed of every double page spread of *Let it Shine* (Bryan, 2007) invites our participation. When there is a frame, illustrators may "break" it by extending part of the illustration beyond the outside border of the frame. On the ninth and eleventh openings of *Rainstorm* (Lehman, 2007), for example, there are illustrations with white borders and black line frames that include images of a lighthouse. In both cases, the top of the lighthouse breaks the frame, adding visual interest by interrupting the straight lines of the frame, but also giving us an idea of the great height of the lighthouse. In *How We Are Smart* (Nikola-Lisa, 2006) each double page spread recounts the biography of one of 12 famous people of color who contributed to a variety of fields, from ballerina Maria Tallchief to singer Marian Anderson. In many cases, the straight line of the illustration is broken. For example, the illustration for Marian Anderson includes a depiction of her famous concert on the steps of the Lincoln Memorial in 1939. She is pictured standing in front of the enormous sculpture of Abraham Lincoln, and one of Lincoln's arms and the chair it rests on break the frame, again giving us an indication of the size of the sculpture. In the illustration of Maria Tallchief, a silhouette of a ballerina breaks the frame by extending the ballerina's arm outside the frame, suggesting freedom of movement.

The Problem of the Gutter. One aspect of picturebooks that illustrators and designers must take into account is that if an illustration is to cross the gutter (the place where the pages join and are bound into the spine), there needs to be special care taken so that important parts of the illustration (e.g., a face) do not cross this space, lest some of the illustration be covered in the binding process. This is a problem unique to the picturebook, and requires careful handling, in addition to the usual challenges of balance of shape and areas of color. Text almost never crosses the gutter, because some of it would be obscured. In his Point of Departure essay for this chapter, Chris Raschka recounts an unfortunate experience he had when he neglected to take note of the gutter.

Ideology and Sociocultural Aspects/Contexts of Picturebooks

Language (and indeed any sign system, including systems of visual respresentation) "is endemically and pervasively imbued with ideology" (Stephens, 1992, p. 1). There is no such thing as value-free art, whether it is purely literary art or the combination of visual and verbal art that constitutes the picturebook. One of the aspects of the art of the picturebook that we must address, therefore, is how the modes of representation in picturebooks are necessarily freighted with sociocultural and political significance. Marriott (1998) asserts that this is especially true in texts intended for children. It is therefore important to examine how picturebooks represent all the cognitive/affective tasks of childhood. Kidd (2004) asserts that "the successful picture book speaks its own psychological truth about childhood" (p. 155). To add even more weight to the burden that picturebooks carry, according to many theorists, visual representation always trumps verbal representation (Kress & Van Leeuwen, 1996), making it all the more important to examine the power of visual images in conveying messages to readers/viewers. Thus, the hoary debate about what is proper to read to/with the young (which had its inception with the very beginnings of a special literature for children in the eighteenth century) continues unabated, and picturebooks, with their primary association with young children, receive a great deal of scrutiny and critique. At the same time, we must be cautious: it is simply not possible for one picturebook to convey the riches and nuances of any culture in 32 pages.

We are seeing an increasing diversity and melding of cultures in picturebook illustrators and authors. *Picturescape* by Elisa Gutierrez (2005) narrates the story of a Canadian boy's trip to a Toronto art museum, and his subsequent fantasies of entering a series of paintings and prints by 12 famous Canadian artists. Although she currently lives in Vancouver, Gutierrez "graduated in 1996 from La Salle University in Mexico City with a degree in Graphic Design" (back endflap). This is just one example of many picturebooks that have multiple cultural influences, and are not limited to the somewhat rigid categories we have invented. This increasingly international scene makes judgments about what is or is not representative of a particular culture problematic.

Ever since the publication of Nancy Larrick's (1965) famous essay, "The All-White World of Children's Books,"

the world of children's literature has experienced a significant increase in the number of "multicultural" books, and picturebooks are no exception. Nevertheless, as Rudine Sims Bishop (2007) reminds us, the proportion of books that deal with children of color remains sadly low. Even so, we now have children's publishers (i.e., Lee & Low; Arte Público Press) that specialize in books by/for/about people of color, and the mainline publishers seem to be increasingly amenable to dismantling the White middle-class cultural hegemony that was in place for so many years. However, White privilege still operates in the world of children's picturebooks, as McNair (2008) demonstrates in her analysis of the lamentably low proportion of books for/by/about people of color in Scholastic Book Clubs for young readers.

Two words that most often surface in debates about representation of any group, culture, nationality, or ethnicity, are "authenticity" and "authority": what constitutes an authentic representation of a culture, and who has the authority to do so? We should not assume that any picture "about" Mexican Americans will reflect the values, ideology, and social practices of any particular person who identifies as Mexican American, for example. Therefore, as Smolkin and Suina (1997) show in their analysis of various Southwestern Pueblo Native American critiques of McDermott's (1974) Caldecott Medal-winning *Arrow to the Sun*, who has the right to "speak" for an entire culture or ethnic/racial group is a difficult question: "No culture…is monolithic; therefore, no single member of that culture can be seen as able to issue a final assessment of cultural authenticity of a text" (p. 315). We should also be aware that more and more people are identifying themselves as having several ethnic/racial identities, so that it is no longer viable to think about categories such as Native American, African American, or Asian American as having rigid demarcations. We need to be careful not to reify "Whiteness" any more than we can reify "Blackness"—Caribbean and African are not the same as African American, and African American is not one solid category, either. Nor is Puerto Rican American culture the same as Mexican American culture, though they are often lumped together as "Hispanic." Nor are "Native American" cultures the same—there are vast differences between South Western Native cultures and North West and North East and Southern Native American cultures. We need a new sophistication and awareness about the subtleties of cultural difference, and we must move beyond simple broad labels. Nevertheless, from the vantage point of the United States, contemporary society is still very much constructed around rigid demarcations of racial and ethnic groups, and some picturebooks will continue to reflect this rigidity. If children's literature is to be a transformative force for society, however, publishers should continue to press for the broadest possible range of representations of the increasing diversity of the populations that constitute their audience.

Martin (2004), in her important analysis of African American children's picturebooks, suggests the following questions (applicable to depictions of all cultures, races, and ethnicities) to assist students in interrogating a picturebook's ideology when read in conjunction with similar picturebooks:

- What sorts of ideological messages does this text convey about individual African Americans or African Americans as a people/group?
- In what way do the illustrations in these African-American picture books uphold or attempt to dismantle racial stereotypes?
- What can you surmise about African-American cultural values after reading this book that you might not have concluded before your exposure to it?
- Who do you think is the audience for this text, and why? If you are not the intended audience for this text, how might your response to it differ from the response of its intended readers?
- What difference does the ethnicity of the author and/or illustrator make to your reception of the text?
- And how has one text in this unit "spoken to" other texts in this unit? (p. 194)

The issues surrounding the representation of gender in picturebooks are complex and varied (Lehr, 2001) as well. We know that the socialization of gender occurs very early in children's lives (Davies, 1990), and that picturebooks generally continue this socialization, so that it is clear to even very young children that boys learn how to act (and do not act) in certain ways, and that the same is true for girls. In picturebooks that resist this rigid socialization, there seem to be two approaches, described by Altland (1994). Either the picturebook is a parody, inverting the power relations so that girls have agency and control, or the picturebook presents a world where both genders share power and agency equally; this second option is called "poesis" by Altland, who asserts that parodies such as *The Paperbag Princess* (Munsch, 1999), as much as they give agency to girls, do so at the expense of boys, so that there is still a hierarchy of power relations, but that girls are at the top. Altland argues that this is not the best way to represent true gender equality. Rather, stories that do not give girls power at the expense of boys are needed. Another aspect of gender representation is the research, summarized by Cherland (1992) that girls tend to be attracted to what is termed the "discourse of feeling," with emphasis on character relationships, whereas boys tend to be attracted to the "discourse of action," where the story is plot-driven. Naturally, this is a binary that is better understood as a continuum, and there are books that may embody the discourse of action and the discourse of feeling equally. As well, to employ a common philosophical distinction, the fact that something *is* the case says nothing about what we think *ought* to be the case; so even if it is true that there are gendered differences in response to plot-driven or character-driven picturebooks, we are still left with the question of whether we might want to work to broaden the preferences of both boys and girls.

There is little research about representations of gay/lesbian characters in children's picturebooks, nor are there many examples (Chick, 2008). Schall (2007) identified 64 picturebooks (of varying quality) with gay or lesbian characters; "different" families including same-sex parents; and picturebooks that could be read as gay or straight. *And Tango Makes Three* (Richardson & Parnell, 2005), about two male penguins who build a nest and eventually hatch an egg that has been abandoned, has the distinction of both being an informational book based on actual occurrences in New York's Central Park Zoo *and* being excoriated by homophobic fundamentalists as a veiled valorization of homosexual relationships. Even facts about penguins, it would seem, are not exempt from the fundamentalists' ire. Clearly, however, mainline publishers are skittish about the appropriateness of any representation of same-sex relationships for an audience of young children. A more common and acceptable stance—to present the relationship either obliquely or as doomed—is present in *Caleb's Friend* (Nones, 1993), a picturebook about a friendship (with obvious overtones of love and romance) between a merboy and a human boy named Caleb. Having no common language—a metaphor for the "love that dare not speak its name"—the two can communicate only by gestures. Caleb, for example, gives the merboy a rose, which the merboy then presses to his heart. As Kidd (2004) comments, "The merboy's liminality eroticizes the friendship but also ensures its innocence. Their distance keeps the bond mythical and chaste; the merboy could not survive in Caleb's world, or Caleb in his, suggesting a painful separation of self and other....Certainly the book's management of same-sex love tells us much about the heteronormativity of the picture book genre" (p. 165).

Finally, it is important to consider the sociocultural contexts of the school situations in which picturebooks are often used. In *Art as Experience*, Dewey (1934/1980) lamented the fact that, in modern times, art was divorced from everyday life, pointing out that it was literally and figuratively put on a pedestal in museums and galleries, and that people did not have access to it in the same way that they had in previous ages (in churches and other public buildings, outdoor sculpture, etc.). Picturebooks, available in virtually every primary classroom (and some classrooms in higher grades where teachers value and know the potentials of the picturebook form) bridge this gap that Dewey felt was lacking. It is often the case that children's first experience of truly excellent and high-quality art happens when picturebooks are shared with them. It is this aesthetic experience that is so critically important, now more than ever in the current sterile educational climate of high-stakes testing (No Child Left Untested!) and approaches to schooling that devalue the arts and have very narrow definitions of both literacy and "the basics." It is quite ironic that, in the age that is according increasing importance to visual representation, we have a school system in the United States that places such a low value on visual modalities of teaching and learning, as well as a dismally low view of the arts in general. This is especially distressing for children of color and low SES children, whose schools have cut back significantly on the arts—if indeed they ever stressed them (Gadsden, 2008). I doubt whether this is going to change any time soon; however, the persistence and presence of picturebooks in classrooms allows the possibility for them to be seen and used as aesthetic objects, in addition to the purposes more commonly employed for them in teaching the skills of reading and as models of writing. It is not that these purposes are unimportant, but rather that we should advocate for using picturebooks as more than mere tools for teaching literacy–narrowly conceived in what Elliot Eisner calls "the tightest most constipated terms" (as cited in Considine & Haley, 1999, p. xvii).

Art both reflects current cultures, identities, and ideologies, while at the same time challenging them, pushing their assumptions and proposing a deep "seeing" and intellectual engagement that leads to new ways of conceiving of ourselves and the world. Socio-politically, art always engages us in the tension of how the world is perceived and understood, and therefore how it can be changed. Ideally, art should be a spur to political and social action. Picturebooks and other literature will not automatically accomplish this, but they can provide a catalyst for shifts in our thinking. Art always makes the familiar strange and the strange familiar (Shklovsky, 1925/1966), freeing us from the contingencies of everyday life. But that freedom can also be used to imagine new possibilities for human life, especially in this age of post-structuralism, where we find ourselves fragmented both socioculturally and individually.

New Directions for Picturebooks (and Other Sequential Art)

A Growing Recognition of the Aesthetic Importance of Picturebooks

Salisbury (2007) states that "In recent years the field of children's book illustration has attracted an expanding range of artists, drawn to the area by the potential for authorial creative design and by the elevated status of artists working in picturebooks (it would appear that it's no longer uncool)" (p. 6). "That's not art—it's illustration" is a demeaning critique heard much less these days, partly because of the breaking down of the distinctions between high and popular culture in the postmodern era, but also because of the growing artistic merit of picturebooks themselves. Some (e.g., Salisbury, 2008) have observed that European, Australian, and Asian picturebooks seem to be more on the cutting edge when it comes to the subjects, styles, and sophisticated quality of illustrations than

American picturebooks (though there are of course notable exceptions). This assertion, of course, is not capable of empirical proof, for it depends on aesthetic taste, which can vary widely. However, there may be some reasons why picturebooks that are not published in the United States are considered superior. As Joel Taxel points out in his closely argued chapter in this volume, United States publishers are perhaps more subject to the "bottom line" philosophy of the multinational corporations that have changed the landscape of American children's publishing so drastically over the past two decades. Other countries, for whom children's publishing has assumed greater importance in recent years, may have considerable subsidies provided by governmental arts councils, which could encourage high levels of experimentation and creativity on the part of authors and illustrators. As Salisbury (personal communication, 2007) comments, "The long tradition in children's illustration here can be seen as something of a burden as well as a strength" in the United States and the United Kingdom. In other countries, there may be also less of a developed concept of what is proper fare for young children, and an openness to a broader range of subject matter that would appeal to a wider range of ages. In any case, a trip to one of the yearly international exhibits of children's illustrated books drawn from a worldwide perspective, such as the famous Bologna Book Fair, might allow each scholar of picturebooks to draw her own conclusions about this matter.

This growing interest both reflects and advances the so-called "pictorial turn" (Mitchell, 1994) of the last four or five decades: the ascendancy of television, the Internet, gaming (Mackey, 2007), and the increasing immersion of society in visual images from advertising/marketing have all contributed to a decrease in the "verbocentric" quality of Western society, and picturebooks have been a part of this larger change. One sign of the burgeoning interest in picturebooks is the museums and collections devoted to them, for example the Oshima Museum in Japan; the Eric Carle Museum in Massachusetts; and the Marantz Collection of picturebooks at Kent State University in Ohio, as well as the Seven Stories Collection in the United Kingdom, all of which Elizabeth Hammill well describes in her chapter in this volume.

Another indication of the "pictorial turn" is the increasing sophistication of wordless picturebooks and the prizes that they have been awarded. For example, some of David Wiesner's most successful and captivating picturebooks have been wordless, or nearly so, with words appearing only in the illustrations themselves or with extremely sparse text: *Tuesday* (1991) and *Flotsam* (2006) tell their stories with very little or no resort to words, and both won Caldecott Medals. Barbara Lehman is another master of the wordless picturebook format. She won the Caldecott Honor for *The Red Book* (2004), but that is merely one of her many examples. In most of her books, the visual sequence of illustrations is similar to slow-motion film or a selection of stills from a larger film in which the reader/viewer must fill in the gaps in order to construct a coherent narrative.

Appeal to a Wide Range of Reader/Viewers

It's been a number of years since picturebooks were considered interesting fare only for young children (Benedict & Carlisle, 1992). However, I believe we will continue to see a growing number of picturebooks whose topics, style, and general complexity (in terms of format and narrative) are meant for an ever-broadening audience. The Japanese fascination with manga, for example, points to a potential expanding adult audience for all types of sequential art.

Woolvs in the Sitee (Wild & Spudvilas, 2007), originally published in Australia, is a tour de force of this appeal to older readers. Purposefully ambiguous, it is set in a city where something cataclysmic—a nuclear war? an epidemic? an extreme societal upheaval?—has taken place. Ben, the narrator, appears to be a young teenager. He begins his story ominously: "There are woolvs in the sitee…And soon they will kum…No won is spared." The phonetic spelling used throughout the story adds to the pathos: perhaps Ben has been unable or unwilling to go to school for many years. Ben's only friend is "Missus Radinski," an older woman who lives in the same building as Ben. It's unclear whether she shares his deep fears, though she does come to rescue him when he mistakes a newly painted wall for the blue skies he has not seen in years and spontaneously rushes outside, only to be paralyzed by his fear of the "woolvs." When Missus Radinski disappears, Ben makes a courageous resolve: he will not "scrooch" in his cave-like room any more, but will go to find her. The last illustration of this almost unbearably powerful book depicts Ben, his head turned back, his eyes looking directly at the reader, with an expression of profound longing and invitation: "Joyn me." The illustrations verge on the terrifying, with a dark palette and figures depicted in half-shadow; and the endpapers are jet black, with child-like scribbled drawings of wolves. Is this picturebook a metaphor for violence, poverty, and other intractable social problems, especially in large cities, that drive people to trust no one and to lose any sense of community life? Or is it something even more sinister, a futuristic dystopia that admits of no hope for humankind except the quixotic courage of a few young people? Readers of *Woolvs* must accept these ambiguities.

The content of some contemporary picturebooks certainly addresses serious sociocultural themes and problems. At the same time, we must not underestimate the ability of younger readers to navigate these complexities. It is also important to note that any picturebook—no matter what the subject matter or topic—can be examined and enjoyed as an aesthetic object by older readers. Older readers can evaluate and critique any picturebook's integration of text and pictures and the ways in which all its constituent elements complement and inform each other in order to achieve artistic wholeness.

The Postmodern Picturebook

Metafictive or postmodern picturebooks, though continuing to be a very small fraction of the total number of picturebooks published, have increased in importance as children's literature scholars, practitioners, and librarians have become intrigued with their characteristics (Sipe & Pantaleo, 2008). These types of books, with their subversion of traditional picturebook (and narrative) conventions; their parodic play, their self-referentiality, and their ambiguity and lack of resolution seem to have great potential for increasing children's abilities to interpret both words and pictures (and their complex combinations) in new ways. Although postmodernism is not easily defined, a synthesis based on the work of a number of picturebook theorists suggests that there are five defining characteristics of these exciting new books: (a) playfulness (the text functions as a playground for readers and does not take itself seriously, drawing attention to itself as a work of fiction); (b) multiplicity of meanings (multiple possible pathways for readers' interpretation because of nonlinear plots, a high degree of indeterminacy, ambiguity, and lack of resolution); (c) intertextuality (a pastiche of references to many other visual and verbal texts); (d) subversion (a general tone of sarcasm, parody, or irony); and (e) blurring distinctions between "high" and popular culture, between authors and readers, and demarcations among literary genres (Sipe & McGuire, 2008). According to Lewis (2001), the most characteristic feature of postmodern picturebooks is their metafictive qualities. Unlike traditional stories, which tend to draw the reader into the secondary world (Benton, 1992) of the narrative, metafiction pushes us away, as if to say, "don't forget that what you are reading is an artifice—it's not real" (Waugh, 1984).

Some of the best (and award-winning) exemplars of this type of picturebook are *Black and White* (Macaulay, 1990), which, according to the title page, may be read either as four separate stories or one complex unified tale; *The Stinky Cheese Man and Other Fairly Stupid Tales* (Scieszka & Smith, 1992), which parodies a number of traditional stories as well as playing with the conventions of picturebooks themselves; David Wiesner's (2001) version of *The Three Pigs*, in which the wolf's huffing and puffing blow the pigs out of their own story and into a series of other stories; and *Wolves* (Gravett, 2005), a book-within-a-book that states baldly "It is a work of fiction," and gives an alternative ending for squeamish readers after Rabbit (the main character) is eaten by a wolf.

Postmodern picturebooks afford readers the possibility of being co-authors; they seem to invite an even higher level of intellectual engagement from readers than traditional picturebooks. As well, postmodern picturebooks stimulate children to think about their own cognitive processes as they read; in other words, metafiction may encourage children to be metacognitive about their own reading/interpreting process. Ambiguous, nonlinear narratives drive readers/viewers to new and more intellectually sophisticated levels of interpretation. Parody assumes familiarity with older forms and conventions of style, narrative structure, and the conventions of picturebooks themselves, so that readers/viewers can get the joke.

Finally, postmodern picturebooks question almost all established theories of text-picture relationships and reader response. Glasheen (2007) suggests that a book like *Bad Day at Riverbend* (Van Allsburg, 1995), which turns out to be populated by the characters in a coloring book, and ends with a realistic rendition of a child's hand scribbling on the page, cannot be explained by existent theories of the relationships between words and pictures, because none of these theories contemplate "a picturebook whose text and illustrations are initially intended to confound the reader" (p. 3). *Bad Day* goes far beyond Nodelman's (1988) idea that text and pictures stand in an ironic relationship to each other, and suggests a far more subversive relationship: words and pictures continually destabilize each other. In other postmodern picturebooks, there is no real distinction between words and pictures because the words are so integrated into the illustrations themselves that the distinction blurs and finally fades away. It is perhaps no accident that one of the favorite media of postmodern picturebook illustrators is the collage (often incorporating seemingly random scraps of words), a perfect way to represent our fragmented, non-unified world and us as non-unified subjects.

Informational Picturebooks

There is a growing importance of the picturebook as a format for informational books. Steve Jenkins (Page, 2003) is one of the masters of the information picturebook, with his stunning paper collage illustrations. In her careful research, Christine Pappas (2006) has done the field a great service with her carefully crafted typology of different types of informational books.

Photographs are a natural medium for informational books. One excellent example is *Where in the Wild? Camouflaged Creatures Concealed and Revealed* (Schwartz & Schy, 2007). The message of the book is that if you can't be seen, you might "avoid a prowling predator." Color photographs appear opposite well-written poems that give hints about what's hiding in the picture. In a smaller version of the photograph, readers can find the animal or insect. For example, on one of the photos, a ladybug appears on a flower petal.

For older readers, another important example of the beauty and sophistication of informational picturebooks is Molly Bang's (2000) *Nobody Particular: One Woman's Fight to Save the Bays*. The book concerns Diane Wilson, a woman whose family were (and are) shrimpers. They fish in the bays of the eastern Texas coast. When legal-sized shrimp started to disappear because of the pollution

from six chemical plants in the area, it became critical for something to be done. Although Wilson was not an environmentalist or a politician, she took up the cause to save her community's livelihood. The reader opens the book and immediately the account of this fight to preserve and maintain the fragile environment begins. The bibliographic information faces the title page—the endpapers begin the story. Bang creates a color background image for each double page spread showing the water and the land that is the setting for this account. She overlays each color painting with two black and white images (one on the verso and one for the recto) that resemble cells in a comic book. The images and the text sometimes break the edge of these overlays; this creates a dynamic quality and adds a sense of action. The story is told in the first person voice of Diane Wilson. Borders are created on each double page opening by these black and white overlays on the color paintings. In the color borders, in small white type, there is information about shrimp, what they need to thrive, and what their place is in the ecosystem of the bays. The double spread paintings that constitute the front and back endpapers are virtually identical, except that on the flyleaf of the back endpaper, there is "An Update on the Story;" on the pastedown, there are figures of two people walking toward the right-hand edge of the page. The speech balloons suggest that Diane could be off to fight another environmental issue. In this way, Bang has used all the space available to convey her message.

Incorporation of Multi-Modalities

Picturebooks, even the most traditional, are by nature multi-modal: visual and verbal sign systems constitute two semiotic modes of communicating thought and emotion to reader/viewers. However, it is becoming increasingly common to see the incorporation of light (as in *The Very Lonely Firefly*, 1995) and sound (as in *The Very Clumsy Click Beetle*, 1999), both by Eric Carle. These additional modalities are made possible by the incorporation of small computer chips in the books. Pop-up books (the more formal term is "movable books") add an element of motion and surprise, often on every double page spread, as the illustration becomes three-dimensional. Robert Sabuda and his partner Matthew Reinhart (2008)—truly paper engineers— are indisputably the masters of this form. David Carter (2008) is another up-and-coming movable book artist, whose ouvre often consists of abstract designs in contrast to Sabuda and Reinhart's representations of real scenes and objects.

It is not a recent innovation to include an audio cassette or CD with a picturebook, so that children can listen to the words of the story (sometimes with the inclusion of sound effects) while they follow along by looking at the illustrations and turning the pages. However, this common addition has been given new life in recent years. For example, the story *The People Could Fly* is now published (Hamilton, 2004) as a separate picturebook well after its incorporation into Virginia Hamilton's (1985) collection of African American folktales with the same title. Superbly designed with Leo and Diane Dillon's evocative illustrations, the book is further enriched with a CD of the story narrated by Hamilton and James Earl Jones. Hamilton's voice lives on in this narration (she died in 2002), and the alternation of her lilting, magical tone with Jones' *basso profundo* makes this a duet of sound that is truly remarkable. In *Jazz on a Saturday Night*, also illustrated by the Dillons (2007), there is an interesting variation on the use of an accompanying CD. Rather than simply reading the story, the Dillons take turns in introducing jazz as an American musical style, as well as describing the various instruments (echoed in the endpapers) that are used by the performers. Another example of an innovative use of a CD that accompanies a picturebook is Don Sheen's (2002) *Yellow Umbrella,* a beautiful wordless book in which the CD includes one track with music composed specifically for listening while viewing the picture sequence; another track with an accompanying song with lyrics printed at the end of the book; and a final set of tracks that expand the music for each double page spread, for a slower and more contemplative "reading."

A much more far-reaching use of multi-modalities is present in Elisa Gutierrez's (2005) *Picturescape*, already described as the story of a Canadian boy's experience at an art museum. The title itself can be read as a pun (Hornberger, personal communication, 2006): this book is a "picture-scape" in that it recounts the boy's magically entering a series of landscape paintings and prints, traversing all of Canada, from the Pacific to the Atlantic. The title can also be read as "picture escape," because the boy's world, depicted monochromatically in tones of gray, is greatly expanded by his magical trek from colorful painting to painting: he has escaped the dull world of the quotidian and into the world of art. The intriguing endpapers chronicle this change: the front endpapers are a series of vertical stripes in shades of black and grey, whereas the back endpapers continue the series of stripes, which are rendered in colorful shades and tints of blue, yellow, green, and red. What is even more interesting about this book is that is has its own website (www.picturescape.ca), which has a wonderful array of extensions. Thus, the almost infinite resources of the Internet, with links leading to other links—a limitless hypertextuality—are part and parcel of this inventive and beautifully designed picturebook.

More Restrained and Sophisticated Use of New Media

After the initial (almost giddy) fascination with the powerful means of reproducing color, picturebook illustrators have started to purposely tone down their exuberance and use technological advances in more discretionary ways. The *Olivia* books (e.g., Falconer, 2000), and *The Secret Olivia Told Me* (Joy, 2007) hark back to a retro look of 1950's illustration with their spare use of color. Another example of this restraint is Peter Sis's (2007) *The Wall,* in which bright red, an icon for the repressions of communism, is the only color on most pages. The influence of Western ideas and freedom is always signaled by a wider range of colors. The Prague Spring of 1968, in which there was a tremendous opening to Western musicians and poets and an intense feeling of liberation, is symbolized by the single double page spread that is in full color, imitating the "psychedelic" palette of the late 1960s. This single spread is made all the more powerful by the absence of color (other than the ubiquitous red) in the other illustrations.

Adobe Photoshop's influence, initially greeted with great enthusiasm by illustrators and perhaps overused as a gimmick, has also been used in more sophisticated ways, and in concert with more traditional methods of producing images. As Salisbury (2007) makes clear, "the early days of Photoshop were dominated by the layering aesthetic, as so many designers were infatuated with the new toy. But where the artistic vision drives the work, the tool becomes less and less visible" (p. 7). For example, William Low's illustrations for *The Day the Stones Walked* (Barron, 2007), a story about the last days of the Easter Island civilization, seem to have been produced with a paintbrush and acrylic or oil paints in a quite painterly style. It's surprising to read the publishing information and to discover that the images have been executed solely with Adobe Photoshop.

Blurring of Formats and Hybrid Formats

The distinctions among comics, graphic novels, and picturebooks are blurring. I predict that this trend will continue, until the distinctions become less and less useful, and we begin to think of picturebooks, comics, and graphic novels as forms of "sequential art." We are in need of theories of sequential art that take into consideration the similarities and the differences among comics, graphic novels, picturebooks, and digital media of various types (games, hypertextual visual arrays, etc.). Without these theories, we will be left trying to fit new and ground-breaking works of visual/verbal art into the Procrustean beds of our old definitions of these forms and formats.

It was an intense pleasure for me to be present when the American Library Association announced the 2008 book award winners. One of the great surprises—perhaps *the* surprise—of the awards ceremony was that the Caldecott Medal—given "to the artist of the most distinguished American picture book for children" was won by Brian Selznick (2007) for *The Invention of Hugo Cabret*. I think this will come to be considered a historic moment in the evolution of both the picturebook and the Caldecott Award, because, for the first time, a book looking very unlike the standard picturebook was the judges' choice. Selznick's book is well over 500 pages in length, and consists of passages of text, some almost as long as the standard chapter in a novel, interspersed with black and white drawings whose layout resembles a graphic novel. The illustrations are never accompanied by text on the same page, however. Thus, we can see in the choice of this innovative book a sterling example of the blurring of genres and formats that I have described. Is this book a picturebook? The 2008 Caldecott Committee clearly thought so. Certainly it shares some of the qualities of traditional picturebooks, the most important being the necessity of both words and pictures to tell the story. The verbal text of *Hugo Cabret* would be impossible to understand without the visual text, and the illustrations, by themselves, would make no sense, either. So the *sine qua non* of the picturebook—the synergy and equal weight given to both words and pictures—is clearly present. However, the sheer length of the book—it's about three inches thick—suggests a novel. And the layout of the illustrations resembles the cells in comic books or graphic novels. Our normalized categories are not terribly useful in describing this book: it is a brilliant hybrid of elements from all these genres and formats. Thus, the Caldecott decision represents a watershed in the ways in which we think about the combination of text and pictures, and it promises to spur artists and authors to even more creative departures from the standard format of the picturebook.

Another example of the blurring of formats is the Australian author/illustrator Shaun Tan's (2007) *The Arrival*, a breathtaking tour de force that tells the story of an immigrant to a foreign land, with all the adventure, challenge, despair, and triumph of learning an entirely new culture. See the chapter by Campano and Ghiso, this volume, for further discussion of this remarkable book. Is this book a very long wordless picturebook? A wordless graphic novel? An imitation of a film? A wordless, cell-less comic book? Again, the categories we have constructed do not do justice to this book.

The implications of the new forms of sequential art (including innovative forms of the picturebook) for literacy—what we mean by literacy for children in the twenty-first century as well as how literacy is used—are enormous and far-reaching. More than twenty years ago, Margaret Meek (1988) wrote a small but extremely influential and subtle booklet called "How Texts Teach What Readers Learn." If we take Meek's title seriously, we are driven to the conclusion that, as the types of texts children encounter change and proliferate, so will the lessons they learn from them. The more active engagement of the types of readers/viewers I have been referring to will no doubt rise to ever-higher levels. This, in turn, has profound implications for how literacies (in the plural) are acquired both in and out of school (Anstey & Bull, 2006). The picturebook, as a format, arose as something new with Caldecott, and it will continue to change and merge with other forms and formats as it evolves. Paradoxically, picturebooks stand both in the traditional historical evolution of children's literature, and are poised to be on the cutting edge, promoting all types of new literacies.

Literature References

Aliki. (1988). *How a book is made*. New York, NY: HarperTrophy.
Bang, M. (2000). *Nobody particular: One woman's fight to save the bays*. New York, NY: Henry Holt.
Barron, T. A. (2007). *The day the stones walked* (W. Low, Illus.). New York, NY: Philomel.
Browne, A. (1997). *Willy the dreamer*. Cambridge, MA: Candlewick Press.
Bryan, A. (2007). *Let it shine*. New York, NY: Atheneum.
Carle, E. (1995). *The very lonely firefly*. New York, NY: Philomel.
Carle, E. (1999). *The very clumsy click beetle*. New York, NY: Philomel.
Carroll, L. (2007). *Jabberwocky* (C. Myers, Illus.). New York, NY: Hyperion Jump at the Sun.
Carter, D. (2008). *Yellow square: A pop-up book for children of all ages*. New York, NY: Little Simon.
David, R. (2007). *The magic raincoat* (S. Benatova, Illus.). Asheville, NC: Front Street.
Dillon, L. & D. (2007). *Jazz on a Saturday night*. New York, NY: Blue Sky Press.
Falconer, I. (2000). *Olivia*. New York, NY: Atheneum Books for Young Readers.
Gravett, E. (2005). *Wolves*. New York, NY: Macmillan.
Gutierrez, E. (2005). *Picturescape*. Vancouver: Simply Read Books.
Hamilton, V. (1985). *The people could fly: American black folktales*. New York, NY: Alfred A. Knopf.
Hamilton, V. (2004). *The people could fly* (L. & D. Dillon, Illus.). New York, NY: Alfred A. Knopf.
Joy, N. (2007). *The secret Olivia told me* (N. Devard, Illus.). New York, NY: Just Us Books.
Juster, N. (2005). *The hello, goodbye window* (C. Raschka, Illus.). New York, NY: Hyperion.
Lehman, B. (2007). *Rainstorm*. Boston, MA: Houghton Miflin.
Lehman, B. (2004). *The red book*. Boston, MA: Houghton Mifflin.
Macaulay, D. (1990). *Black and white*. Boston, MA: Houghton Mifflin.
McDermott, G. (1974). *Arrow to the sun*. New York, NY: Viking.
Mobin-Uddin, A. (2007). *The best Eid ever* (L. Jacobsen, Illus.). Honesdale, PA: Boyds Mills Press.
Montes, M. (2007). *Los gatos black on Halloween* (Y. Morales, Illus.). New York, NY: Henry Holt.
Munsch, R. (1999). *The paperbag princess* (M. Martchenko, Illus.). New York, NY: Scholastic.
Nikola-Lisa, W. (2006). *How we are smart* (S. Qualls, Illus.). New York, NY: Lee & Low.
Nones, E. J. (1993). *Caleb's friend*. New York, NY: Farrar, Straus & Giroux.
Page, R. (2003). *What do you do with a tail like this?* (S. Jenkins. Illus.). Boston, MA: Houghton Mifflin.
Richardson, J., & Parnell, P. (2005). *And Tango makes three*. New York, NY: Simon & Schuster.
Sabuda, R., & Reinhart, M. (2008). *Encyclopedia prehistorica: The complete collection*. Cambridge, MA: Candlewick Press.
Schwartz, D. M., & Schy, Y. (2007). *Where in the wild? Camouflaged creatures concealed and revealed*. Berkeley, CA: Tricycle Press.
Scieszka, J., & Smith, L. (1992). *The Stinky Cheese Man and other fairly stupid tales*. New York, NY: Viking.
Selznick, B. (2007). *The invention of Hugo Cabret*. New York, NY: Scholastic.
Sendak, M. (1963). *Where the wild things are*. New York, NY: HarperCollins.
Sheen, D. I. (2002). *Yellow umbrella* (J. S. Lin, Illus.). La Jolla, CA: Kane-Miller.

Sis, P. (2007). *The wall: Growing up behind the iron curtain*. New York, NY: Farrar, Straus and Giroux.

Stevens, J. (1995). *From pictures to words*: A book about making a book. New York, NY: Holiday House.

Tan, S. (2007). *The arrival*. New York, NY: Scholastic.

Van Allsburg, C. (1995). *Bad day at Riverbend*. Boston, MA: Houghton Mifflin.

Wiesner, D. (1991). *Tuesday*. New York, NY: Clarion.

Wiesner, D. (2001). *The three pigs*. New York, NY: Clarion.

Wiesner, D. (2006). *Flotsam*. New York, NY: Clarion.

Wild, M. (2007). *Woolvs in the Sitee* (A. Spudvilas, Illus.). Honesdale, PA: Boyds Mills Press.

Zelinsky, P. (1997). *Rapunzel*. New York, NY: Dutton Children's Books.

Academic References

Agosto, D. E. (1999). One and inseparable: Interdependent storytelling in picture storybooks. *Children's Literature in Education, 30,* 267–280.

Altland, A. E. (1994). Parody and poesis in feminist fairy tales. *Canadian Children's Literature, 73*(20), 22–31.

Anstey, M., & Bull, G. (2006). Teaching and learning multiliteracies: Changing times, changing literacies. Newark, DE: International Reading Association.

Bader, B. (1976). *American picturebooks: From Noah's ark to the beast within*. New York, NY: Macmillan.

Bang, M. (1991). *Picture this: Perception & composition*. Boston, MA: Little, Brown.

Benedict, & Carlisle (Eds.). (1992). *Beyond words: Picture books for older readers and writers*. Portsmouth, NH: Heinemann.

Benjamin, W. (1936/2000). The work of art in the age of mechanical reproduction. In M. G. Durham & D. M Kellner (Eds.), *Media and cultural studies keywords* (pp. 48–70). London: Blackwell.

Benton, M. (1992). *Secondary worlds: Literature teaching and the visual arts*. Buckingham, UK: Open University Press.

Cech, J. (1983–84). Remembering Caldecott: *The Three Jovial Huntsmen* and the art of the picturebook. *The Lion and the Unicorn, 7/8,* 110–119.

Cherland, M. (1992). Gendered readings: Cultural restraints upon response to literature. *The New Advocate, 5,* 187–198.

Chick, K. (2008). Fostering an appreciation for all kinds of families: Picturebooks with gay and lesbian themes. *Bookbird: A Journal of International Children's Literature, 46,* 15–22.

Considine, D. M., & Haley, G. E. (1999). *Visual messages: Integrating imagery into instruction*. Portsmouth, NH: Teacher Ideas Press.

Davies, B. (1990). Lived and imaginary narrative and their place in taking oneself up as a gendered being. *Australian Psychologist, 25,* 318–333.

Dewey, J. (1934/1980). *Art as experience*. New York, NY: Perigee.

Doonan, J. (1993). *Looking at pictures in picturebooks*. Exeter, UK: Thimble Press.

Eisner, W. (1985). *Comics and sequential art*. Tamarac, FL: Poorhouse Press.

Gadsden, V. L. (2008). The arts and education: Knowledge generation, pedagogy, and the discourse of learning. *Review of Research in Education, 32,* 29–61.

Glasheen, G. (2007). Might as well read it backwards: The subverted text-picture relations in *Bad Day at Riverbend*. Unpublished manuscript.

Golden, J. (1990). *The narrative symbol in childhood literature: Explorations of the construction of text*. New York, NY: Mouton de Gruyter.

Iser, W. (1978). *The act of reading: A theory of aesthetic response*. Baltimore, MD: Johns Hopkins University Press.

Kidd, K. B. (2004). *Making American boys: Boyology and the feral tale*. Minneapolis: University of Minnesota Press.

Kiefer, B. (2008). What is a picturebook, anyway? In L. R. Sipe & S. Pantaleo (Eds.), *Postmodern picturebooks: Play, parody, and self-referentiality* (pp. 9–21). New York, NY: Routledge.

Kress, G., & van Leeuwen, T. (1996). *Reading images: The grammar of visual design*. London: Routledge.

Larrick, N. (1965, 11 Sept.). The all-white world of children's books. *Saturday Review, 48,* 63–65.

Lehr, S. (Ed.). (2001). *Brains, beauty, and brawn: The construction of gender in children's literature*. Portsmouth, NH: Heinemann.

Lewis, D. (1996). Going along with Mr. Gumpy: Polysystemy and play in the modern picturebook. *Signal, 80,* 105–119.

Lewis, D. (2001). *Reading contemporary picturebooks: Picturing text*. London: RoutledgeFalmer.

Mackey, M. (2007, December). *Narrative understanding: Book, film, game*. Paper presented at the National Reading Conference, Austin, TX.

Marantz, K. (1977, October). The picturebook as art object: A call for balanced reviewing. *The Wilson Library Bulletin,* 148–151.

Marriott, S. (1998). Picture books and the moral imperative. In J. Evans (Ed.), *What's in the picture? Responding to illustrations in picture books* (pp. 1–24). London: Paul Chapman.

Martin, M. (2004). *Black gold: Milestones of African American children's picture books, 1845–2002*. New York, NY: Routledge.

McNair, J. (2008). The representation of authors and illustrators of color in school-based book clubs. *Language Arts, 85,* 193–201.

Meek, M. (1988). *How texts teach what readers learn*. Stroud, Gloucestershire, UK: Thimble Press.

Meek, M. (1992). Children reading—now. In M. Styles, E. Bearne, & V. Watson (Eds.), *After Alice: Exploring children's literature* (pp. 172–187). London: Cassell.

Miller, J. H. (1992). *Illustration*. Cambridge, MA: Harvard University Press.

Mitchell, W. J. T. (1994). *Picture theory*. Chicago: University of Chicago Press.

Moebius, W. (1986). Introduction to picturebook codes. *Word and Image, 2,* 141–158.

Moss, E. (1990). A certain particularity: An interview with Janet and Allan Ahlberg. *Signal, 61,* 20–26.

Nikolajeva, M., & Scott, C. (2001). *How picturebooks work*. New York, NY: Garland.

Nodelman, P. (1988). *Words about pictures: The narrative art of children's picture books*. Athens: University of Georgia Press.

Pappas, C. (2006). The information book genre: Its role in integrated science literacy research and practice. *Reading Research Quarterly, 41,* 226–250.

Pullman, P. (1989). Invisible pictures. *Signal, 60,* 160–186.

Salisbury, M. (2004). *Illustrating children's books: Creating pictures for publication*. London: Quarto.

Salisbury, M. (2007). *Play pen: New children's book illustration*. London: Lawrence King.

Salisbury, M. (2008). The artist and the postmodern picturebook. In L. Sipe & S. Pantaleo (Eds.), *Postmodern picturebooks: Play, parody, and self-referentiality* (pp. 22–40). New York, NY: Routledge.

Schall, J. (2007, November). *Celebrating or subverting difference: Comparing gay characters with characters that are "different" in children's picture books*. Paper presented at the National Reading Conference, Austin, TX.

Shklovsky, V. (1925/1966). Art as technique. In L. Lemon & M. Reis (Eds.), *Russian formalist criticism: Four essays* (pp. 3–24). Lincoln, NE: University of Nebraska Press.

Sims Bishop, R. (2007). *Free within ourselves: The development of African American children's literature.* Portsmouth, NH: Heinemann.

Sipe, L. R. (1998). How picture books work: A semiotically framed theory of text-picture relationships. *Children's Literature in Education, 29,* 97–108.

Sipe, L. R. (2001). Using picturebooks to teach art history. *Studies in Art Education, 42,* 197–213.

Sipe, L. R., & Brightman, A. E. (2009). Young children's interpretation of page breaks in picture storybooks. *Journal of Literacy Research, 41,* 1–36.

Sipe, L. R., & McGuire, C. E. (2006a). Picturebook endpapers: Resources for literary and aesthetic interpretation. *Children's Literature in Education, 37,* 291–304.

Sipe, L. R., & McGuire, C. E. (2006b). *Young children's meaning making from picturebook peritexts.* Paper presented at the National Reading Conference, Los Angeles, CA.

Sipe, L. R., & McGuire, C.E. (2008). *The Stinky Cheese Man* and other fairly postmodern picturebooks for children. In S.

Lehr (Ed.), *Shattering the looking glass: Challenge, risk, & controversy in children's literature* (pp. 273–288). Norwood, MA: Christopher-Gordon.

Sipe, L. R., & Pantaleo, S. (Eds.). (2008). *Postmodern picturebooks: Play, parody, and self-referentiality.* New York, NY: Routledge.

Smolkin, L. B., & Suina, J. H. (1997). Artistic triumph or multicultural failure? Multiple perspectives on a "multicultural" award-winning book. *The New Advocate, 10,* 307–322.

Steiner, W. (1982). *The colors of rhetoric.* Chicago, IL: The University of Chicago Press.

Stephens, J. (1992). *Language and ideology in children's fiction.* New York, NY: Longman.

Suhor, C. (1984). Towards a semiotics-based curriculum. *Journal of Curriculum Studies, 16,* 247–257.

Turner, V. (1969). *The ritual process: Structure and anti-structure.* Chicago, IL: Aldine.

Waugh, P. (1984). *Metafiction: The theory and practice of self-conscious fiction.* New York, NY: Routledge.

Point of Departure

Chris Raschka

As it turns out, simple picture books are not so simple after all. Even for those of us who spend our days writing them, painting them, editing them, and doing everything else to make them, it is extraordinarily helpful and instructive to read it stated so well and thoroughly by Professor Sipe. While it is true that we sometimes go to seemingly endless pains over the smallest of details of book making, pains we know only too well, we often forget why we do it.

Professor Sipe reminds us why. And he presents forthrightly the idea that I have always held dear, that is, that it is the book itself which is the work of art, not the illustrations, not the text, and not anything else, but the book as an object, in all of its materialness. It is not an ethereal idea but an embodied idea, an object, a sculpture, and for some four-year-olds I know, a bit of performance art as well.

William Wordsworth put this idea this way: "The matter always comes out of the manner." For me, the manner is the picture book, and it is this manner that Professor Sipe has so well detailed.

Let me describe how I have been tripped up over the years by a couple of these details.

The first involves the basic idea of the gutter, that spot in the middle of a two-page spread where the pages come together at the spine. This is perhaps the first thing that is pointed out to any would be illustrator—mind the gutter.

In my sixth picture book, *Mysterious Thelonious,* I had set for myself the task of rendering, at least in part, some aspect of the music of the great jazz composer, Thelonious Monk, in a picture book. The means I struck to achieve this

were to map very exactly the 12 tones of Western classical music (A A♯(B♭) B C C♯ etc.) onto the 12 hues of the chromatic color wheel (red, red-orange, orange, orange-yellow, etc.) and to apply this to a favorite Monk composition, *Mysterioso.* Each double-page spread was to cover a four beat measure of music in a 12 measure phrase.

Consequently, I laid out a grid dividing each spread into eight vertical columns in order to break each beat in half as dictated by the eight notes of the piece, i.e., half a quarter note, there being four quarter notes to a measure in 4/4 time. I then split the columns into squares to mimic the up and downness of pitch, matching each square to its appropriate color, surrounded by the corresponding harmonic color. Then, to complete the book, I created a text, the individual syllables of which appearing over each colored square.

A number of months of dedicated work passed until I had created a perfectly true, by my own paradigm anyway, translation of aural-time symbols (music) into graphic-spatial symbols (art). I was very pleased.

Only one problem: I had forgotten about the gutter. On the afternoon before I was to deliver the completed art to the publisher (Orchard), a worry flickered to life somewhere in the back of the more practical half of my brain: What if the middle text-fragments, positioned as they were, crashed into each other at the gutter? I made a tissue overlay with the text traced onto it and slipped this over another book to check; my worst fears were realized.

To say I was distraught is to say Rumpelstiltskin was a little miffed. I was beside myself.

In the end, after some consultation with a patient production manager, I decided to carefully slice each precious (to me, anyway) painting into two pieces along a zigzag line following the lines of the design, then cut an exactly corresponding piece of paper to add precisely one and five-eighths inches to the spread, which is the amount I calculated I needed, and then match this to the oddly shaped hole I had created, finally adding color to blend with its surroundings and gluing the now three pieces of paper onto a stiffish board. The result in the published book was to create the impression that when laid open, the bend of the paper and the plunging of the gutter produced a visually even beat of the eighth-note color-squares across the one bar, two-page spread (see above).

I sincerely hope that I never have to do that again.

The second instance really came before this, but I mention it last because it has affected each book project since. I was painting the finished art for another picture book about a great jazz musician—*Charlie Parker Played Be Bop.* Again, it was the formulation of the style and manner of art that kept tripping me; I knew that the art had to flow and not be so detailed and interesting that it slowed down the cadence of the text, which in this case was paramount, and yet it couldn't be too abstract because I was presenting a real person, Charlie Parker.

I brooded about this again for many weeks. But I did not stop my ordinary life. For instance, I did the laundry across Broadway Avenue from my apartment. I put in a load to wash. I returned to my studio and drew a picture of a cat in charcoal. I put the load in the dryer. I returned to my studio and looked at the cat. I liked the cat. But then I worried: Was it all right for an illustration, the drawing of it anyway, to take only the time it takes for a rinse cycle?

I decided—Yes.

Thank you, Larry, for your work, which makes my own seem a little less silly.

Point of Departure

David Wiesner

Professor Sipe gives a wonderfully thorough overview of the world of the picturebook. I would like to draw attention to one aspect of the picturebook that is so obvious as to be taken for granted—its length. The brevity of the picturebook lets children easily hold the complete story experience in their minds. The limited length also lets me, as an author and illustrator, have a vision of the book as a whole in *my* mind throughout the creation process.

When I am writing and designing a book, I am simultaneously working on the layout for the entire book and on individual double page spreads. Each spread must convey a specific piece of the story. It must also move readers to the turn of the page and set up their reaction to the next spread. Do I want to build suspense at the page turn? Do I want readers to be surprised when they see what's on the other side? Do I want them to laugh? Because there are so few pages in a picturebook, the act of turning those pages is one of the most important considerations in creating one.

I must have an overarching design for the spreads to work within. I try to come up with a layout that is visually elegant and has a direct relationship to the story. In my book *Sector 7*, the story takes place in two locations—on the ground and high in the sky at the Sector 7 Cloud Dispatch Center (where the clouds get, via blueprints, the assignments for the formations they make each day). The first and final one-third of the book take place on the ground, in the real world. The middle third takes place in the sky, the fantasy world.

I wanted each place to have its own look and feel. In the earthbound sections, the images on each page are contained within a rectangle surrounded by a three-quarter-inch white border. The rectangle can be a single image or divided into smaller panels. When the story moves into the sky, the format changes to full-bleed double page spreads, i.e., the pictures now extend all the way to the edge of the paper. Some of these spreads have an inset rectangle that is a single image or divided into smaller panels.

Framing the images in the earthbound sections with a white border puts the story at a distance. The reader is observing the action from outside. When the story moves into the fantasy world, the frame is removed. As the pictures expand to the edge of the page and beyond, the reader is drawn into that world and made a part of it. It is a simple but effective way to visually separate the two realities of the story. The design of a picturebook can encompass not only the pages where the story takes place, but also the cover, the title page, the endpapers, and even the binding. Apparently these things have a name, the *peritext*. Who knew? They can be used in many ways to help set up the story or add inviting or complementary imagery. I had an idea for the title page of *Sector 7* that I was really excited about. The story is wordless, so the only text that needed to be typeset was the title, my name, the publisher's imprint, and the copyright material. It occurred to me that I could avoid using any type at all by making the information on the title page part of a picture. If I made the title page a close-up view of a blueprint—like the ones the clouds used—I could draw all the text as part of the art: My name would be listed as the architect, the copyright material as building specs, etc.

Sector 7 is 48 pages long and contains a lot of complex imagery. My drawing for the title page was also very complex. There was a lot for the eye to absorb. In fact, there was too much in the context of the rest of the book. The eye needed to land in a simpler, quieter place before entering into the intricacies of the story. So, instead of the blueprint, the title page became a simple neutral-toned background, with the few necessary words typeset in a classic font. I loved the concept of the blueprint, but it didn't serve the visual flow of the book.

Had I chosen to make *Sector 7* longer—a graphic novel, say—I could have used that blueprint title page. I would have had the room to surround it with blank pages to create a cushion for the eye. A longer book allows for the fuller exploration of picture elements and narrative tangents. But in a picturebook the author and artist must pare a story down to its essential elements. It is the concise nature of the storytelling that is unique to picturebooks. One of the hardest parts of creating a picturebook is deciding what to leave out, my blueprint title page being a case in point. I am often heartbroken about omitting great images or sequences that, in the end, were not central to the story or did not move the story forward.

I think of the picturebook as a kind of Chinese tangram puzzle. Like those puzzles, a picturebook has a few basic elements that have to fit together perfectly to reveal their simple, precise shape. When I am working, I strive to reach the point where there is nothing I could take away from the story and there is nothing I need to add.

18

Comics and Graphic Novels

Robin Brenner

Brookline Public Library

As the story of comics has shifted across time, continents, and formats, so too have readers' interests and tastes. Robin Brenner details the history of creating and marketing comic books, in all its forms, from the mid 1800s to the present, while never taking her eye off the readers who, today, keep the books circulating at breakneck pace through libraries, bookstores, and online sources. The rise and popularity of this multi-faceted form—among adults and children, critics and consumers—suggests that its literary and artistic qualities hold endless potential for reshaping what and how we read stories. Following Brenner's descriptive history and analysis, Gareth Hinds' illustrated essay takes readers through the creative process of transforming well-known stories into a visual, graphic novel format. The chapter concludes with a comic essay, "The Beginning," by Raina Telgemeier, that brings into focus a young reader's first, deeply felt, encounter with a book-length comic.

Skeptics voice many concerns over comics and graphic novels, wondering why anyone would read them in the first place, and why they should be considered "real" reading. I have been challenged as to why avid fans of the format should be indulged by library collection policies, giving comics that stamp of approval. Many feel that reading graphic novels and comics will delay readers in seeking out quality literature and lead them away from inspiring or educational tales.

When I was first building a collection of graphic novels for the teen section of a public library, I sought out the opinion of our local graphic novel and comics readers as much as possible. I quickly grew to know the variety of readers we had. I met children poring over *Calvin and Hobbes* (e.g.,Watterson, 2005), teens desperate for the next volume of *Naruto* (Kishimoto, 2003), and adults discovering the format through bestsellers like *Persepolis* (Satrapi, 2003) and *Watchmen* (Moore, 1987). I got to know one teenage girl who in her reading habits fit all the stereotypes that skeptics seemed to fear would lead her astray. She loved Japanese manga (print comics), and amid the hundreds of volumes to choose from, she sought out almost exclusively girls, or shojo, manga. Devouring stories of school romance and epic fantasy, she rarely read outside the sub-category, and although she did also read prose novels, she usually checked out stacks of the latest swoony manga soap.

One day, she surprised me by asking about a comic she'd just finished: *The Golden Vine* by Jai Sen (2003). *The Golden Vine* is an alternate history of Alexander the

Great, veering off from history to speculate on how Alexander might have proceeded if he had not razed the Persian city of Persepolis to the ground but instead integrated the Persian empire into the greater collective he dreamed was possible. The art was created by three Japanese artists, each tackling a different chapter of Alexander's life, and this teen picked up the book entirely because of the Japanese art. The tale of Alexander told in its pages is rich in history, political intrigue, and the challenges of integrating cultures. Those familiar Japanese lines had led her miles away from her customary school romances and melodramas. She quizzed me about Alexander, about what had really happened and what was speculation, and we ended up chatting for over 40 minutes about ancient history and Alexander's influence. By the end of our talk, we had consulted reference books, and I sent her home with a recommended reading list of more novels and nonfiction on Alexander and his time.

Discovering an innovative story or comprehending a confusing topic is a key appeal of the graphic format. We learn very early that reading is defined by parsing letters, understanding words, and relishing a well-turned phrase, but as picture books too often fade into childhood, we forget that images have just as much power, subtlety, and information packed into them as prose. Graphic novels and comics integrate both words and images so completely that the story cannot be told another way. The format itself appeals to the learned joy of reading text and whirls it together with the instinctive, emotional connections images bring a reader. Graphic novels and comics are a different way of both telling and digesting stories, neither better nor worse than prose as a delivery method for stories, and as they challenge how reading is defined, their addition to canon increases the variety and reach of storytelling.

Terminology and Definitions

Vocabulary describing comics, comic books, and graphic novels is still fluctuating, and while a few terms have settled into pop culture awareness, the exact definitions can and do change depending on the perspective of the user. I have heard the format referred to as *comics, comix, graphic novels, graphic fiction, graphica, graphic albums,* and *manga*. Some underground artists in U.S. counterculture prefer comix, the "x" distinguishing their work from mainstream superhero titles, indicating mature content and a willingness to push artistic and social boundaries (Sabin, 1996). Many readers and educators are annoyed by the term "novel" in the identifier graphic novel as it incorrectly implies that all titles are fiction, and therefore adopt other terms such as *graphica* instead. Manga can be used to identify any graphic novel that mimics the style of creators from Japan, although in translation manga is simply the Japanese word for print comics. In the United States, manga means comics originating from Japan, whereas in

Japan manga means everything in the format no matter the country of origin.

In interacting with the general public, as I do every day, the most recognized terms are "comics" and, for bound books, "graphic novels." Despite their flaws as all-encompassing terms and the connotations each bring to the table, these are the names most readers use and will recognize. In the course of this chapter, I use the term "comics" as an umbrella term: the one that contains all other permutations of the format. This term hopefully also acts as a reminder that all comic strips, comic books, and graphic novels are essentially the same format. The shift between these are not differences in storytelling technique but in length, from (approximately) four panels to 30 pages to anywhere from 100 to 1,000 pages. The literacy required for reading these formats grow more complicated as the stories get longer, and require more close reading in between the panels, but the structural elements are the same.

All versions of the format, from comic strips to graphic novels, contain the same trademark parts, usually but not always including images, text, word and thought balloons, sound effects, and panels. In *Understanding Comics,* Scott McCloud (1993) clarified Will Eisner's (1985/2008) term from his landmark work *Comics and Sequential Art,* defining sequential art as "juxtaposed pictorial and other images in deliberate sequence intended to convey information and/or to produce an aesthetic response in the viewer" (McCloud, 1993, p. 9). The most important terms in this definition are juxtaposition, images, and sequence. Variations exist, from wordless tales to prose-heavy tomes, but the essential nature of comics is that they use pictures to convey information and story, and they do so by placing images next to each other in a sequence on a page. Wordless comics, and wordless sequences, show that while the reader may not be processing words in the final product, a writer or artist did construct that visual sequence, using images to "write" a narrative sequence even if no words are ultimately on the page.

A number of titles have appeared in recent years to challenge the accepted definition of graphic novels, from Jeff Kinney's (2007) charming hybrid series starting with *The Diary of a Wimpy Kid* to Brian Selznick's (2007) substantial combination of prose and filmic images, in *The Invention of Hugo Cabret.* What makes these titles graphic novels or not graphic novels? There are arguments to be made from both sides: *The Invention of Hugo Cabret* undoubtedly contains images in sequence (propelled forward by flipping the page, akin to the films it is intended to mimic), but does not include other trademark elements like word balloons, panels, or sound effects. *The Diary of a Wimpy Kid* is a true hybrid in that portions of the story are told as comics and portions are told in prose. Is it simply a question of how much comics content there is? If it is more than 50%, does that make a text a graphic novel? Many of these questions are still being debated, as they should be, and we may never see a resolution that satisfies all interested parties. The one conclusion that seems most important is this: it matters very little to the readers what we call it—if it's a strong story and well told, then they will read it, and readers care less and less about distinctions unless someone asks them to examine the format itself.

Comics Literacy

Graphic novels have elements that are similar to everything from picture books to video games to traditional prose, but they function differently in what they demand from the reader. There is still the idea that comics aren't "real" reading. Our definition of literacy benefits from broadening rather than denying the skill it takes to comprehend a graphic novel. Teenagers can instinctively read graphic novels, even if they've never read one before, much more competently than many adults. Our world is filled with media that breaks apart and integrates text and images in new ways, from television and film to the Internet to video games. Kids and teens learn from an early age to parse combinations of images and text in a variety of ways, and so reading a graphic novel feels new but within their scope of understanding.

Previous generations, particularly those who have much less experience with visual media in general, can be baffled by what they should be doing, feeling there must be a correct way to read a graphic novel that unlocks all of its mysteries (Rudiger, 2006). Reading comics requires self-direction: the reader chooses what to look at first, the images or the text, and chooses how much of the page to concentrate on. Some readers take in the whole page, read the text, and then go back to re-read the text with the context of images. Some read the images first, getting a sense of the sequence, and then add in the dialogue in a second run-through. Some do a lightning quick combination of both techniques. The self-direction required in reading a graphic novel can be intimidating, especially for prose readers used to little variation in how you are supposed to read words: left to right, top to bottom. Artists and writers have different techniques for leading a reader through the page, and the best of them do so with compelling dexterity. Yet, ultimately it is up to the reader to create the story out of its presented parts.

If inexperienced in processing the format, there are a number of adjustments new readers have to make. The main difference in reading is paying attention to the visual portion of the story. Readers more accustomed to prose start by reading only the text, consciously or unconsciously ignoring the visual aspect until they finish the words on the page. Graphic novels are constructed so that the text cannot make sense without the images and vice versa, so it is vital to process the images. In the images are the description, asides, and background information that are found in traditional prose, and skimming over them leaves readers with the impression of a lack of detail, character development, or world-building.

Panel progression can be simple or complicated. It's up to the artist to lead you to the logical next panel, but it's also part of the format's conventions. As Scott McCloud (1993) articulated in *Understanding Comics,* the types of panel transitions are vital to comprehension and the deeper awareness of how comics work. Panel transitions can be divided into six types: moment to moment, action to action, subject to subject, scene to scene, aspect to aspect, and non-sequitur (pp. 72–75). Film uses many of the same edits, and new readers can get a more immediate grasp on reading graphic novels by thinking of them in cinematic terms. Moment to moment is a function of time, showing the shift of a character or scene from one second to the next—a blink or a hand wave.

Action to action is cause and effect, showing a character throwing a punch in one panel to see his opponent fall down in the next. Subject to subject is familiar from movies, where the camera flips back and forth between two speakers, or the view shifts from a man drinking coffee in a diner to a ticking bomb under the table. Scene to scene directs the reader from one place to another, as when you flip to a different set of characters at another location. Aspect to aspect is the hardest to articulate partially because it is not used as prevalently in U.S. comics or cinema (though it is a staple of Japanese manga).

Aspect to aspect uses the view of each panel to highlight a different element of a scene: a character's angry expression, a slammed down coffee cup, a jostled flower in a vase, and retreating feet might all come together to indicate a character's abrupt departure from dinner. This kind of transition requires connections be made by the reader in a more active process than more instinctive transitions, and is partly the reason Japanese manga can seem more incomprehensible to new readers (McCloud, 2006).

Aside from the most noticeable aspects of comics including text, images, and panels, a myriad of smaller elements further distinguish the format and become a code new readers must break to get the most out of their reading. Symbols of all sorts, many culturally defined, have taken on significance of their own in comics. Most readers start off with an awareness of some comics elements. Most know what signifies a speech balloon, a thought balloon, or that somebody yelling is shown by lettering in all caps. Accepted symbols include a lightbulb going on over someone's head, birds circling around after someone's been bonked on the head, or a tiny thundercloud showing anger. Caricature and exaggeration are also familiar parts of graphic narrative, especially in defining character traits. Characters who are evil will look evil, although traditions may also be subverted to confound or surprise the reader. Other visual elements are left up to the reader to interpret including how the words are lettered— for example, in Neil Gaiman's (e.g., 2006) *Sandman*, the lead character of Dream speaks in elegant, looping black speech balloons lettered with white text. Every reader is left to interpret what his voice might sound like from those speech bubbles, but you know immediately he does not sound like everyone else.

Sound effects add a cinematic layer to graphic novels and take on a life of their own, acting as asides and jokes in their own right. Many readers already know the twang of an arrow being released, or the ka-pow of a solid punch, but more subtle sounds include the pounding of rain, the rattle of a teaspoon, and the crinkle of a food wrapper. Sound is integrated to an even greater degree in Japanese manga where thousands more words are used for sound effects that English cannot approximate, including making a dramatic entrance (*za!*), a heartbeat (*doki doki*), and blushing (*po*).

A Brief History of Comics

Cartoons and comics have a long artistic legacy, arguably reaching back to Egyptian heiroglyphs and ancient Greek pottery, but the first landmark cartoons in the modern European tradition appeared in the 1730s with the publication of *A Rake's Progress* by noted satirist, painter and engraver William Hogarth (see also Sipe's commentary in the preceding chapter of this volume). *A Rake's Progress* includes illustrations and captions presented in sequence and is a prime example of the kind of cartooning accepted as satire and criticism in the newspapers and magazines of the day (Sabin, 1996). By the 1840s, a Swiss gentleman named Rodolphe Töpffer produced a number of what he termed picture stories, complete with panels in sequence, dialog, and captions. Akin to *A Rake's Progress*, Töpffer presented a satirical view on his society, and though most were made to entertain his acquaintances, they proved quite popular with the general public (Willems, 2008). In 1841, the British political humor magazine *Punch* launched, and the artistry and variety of cartooning visible in its pages propelled comics forward as a powerful critical medium. In the 1880s and 1890s, a number of comic strips and stories appeared in Europe led by the 1860s German comic strip *Max und Moritz* by Wilhelm Busch. These strips in turn inspired *The Katzenjammer Kids* by Rudolph Dirks in the United States and during the same period the *Ally Sloper* comics magazine series in England (Becker, 1959; Sabin, 1996). R. F. Outcault can claim popularizing the first major comic strip character in the United States with his creation of the Yellow Kid in the strip *Hogan's Alley*, and his work is notable for the first use of color as well as his famous struggle for rights to the character between William Randolph Hearst and Joseph Pulitzer (Silverman, 1994).

From Comic Strips to Comic Books

Out of comic strips were born comic books, and once again Europe lays claim to initial innovations in expanding the form. In the 1920s, the Belgian comic *Tintin* by Hergé (e.g., 1994) was published in a special supplement to the newspaper, *Le Petit Vingtième*, and was soon collected and on sale bound in book form. European comics, particularly francophone comics published mainly in Belgium and France, are to this day most commonly sold as bound volumes rather than anything approximating the more ephemeral comic book. Their immediate shift into bound volumes demonstrates the long-standing respect for the medium that has led France to count comics as fine art rather than low culture (Sabin, 1996).

In the United States, as comic strips and Sunday supplements gained in popularity, including Windsor McKay's *Little Nemo*, George Herriman's *Krazy Kat*, Milton Caniff's *Terry and the Pirates*, and Chester Gould's *Dick Tracy*, the reading audience was primed for longer form comics (Becker, 1959). The first American comic book superhero, *Superman*, created by Jerry Siegel and Joe Shuster, appeared in Action Comics #1 in 1938 by Detective Comics—soon to be known as DC (Weiner, 2003). The appeal of superhuman heroics in the late 1930s, with the world already embroiled in the conflicts that would become World War II, cannot be emphasized enough and undoubtedly drove the immediate success of superhero tales. Masked vigilantes began to crop up from a variety of publishers, including the still dominant DC Comics and Marvel Comics, keen to cash in on the immediate demand for more.

Introducing the Comics Code

Comics flourished in the 1940s, and while superheroes intended for kids and teens initially dominated the market, adult science fiction, fantasy, mystery, and crime comics skyrocketed in popularity once they were introduced. Action-packed, lurid series published by EC Comics including *Weird Science, Crime Does Not Pay*, and *The Vault of Horror* exemplified this trend. This broadening of the market, however, was short-lived. Widespread anti-comics sentiment, best captured by child psychologist Frederick Wertham's (1954) *Seduction of the Innocent*, a well meaning but misguided indictment of comics as a major cause of juvenile delinquency, placed extreme pressure on the United States comics industry (Hadju, 2008). Amid public outcry and Senate hearings on the negative impact of their work, the comics industry created the internal regulations known as the Comics Code Authority. The Comics Code was similar to the Hayes Code in the film industry, intended to ensure appropriate content for young readers. Its creation, paired with comics publishers simultaneous loss of a major distributor, effectively squashed adult-oriented comics. As comics continued into the 1950s, they narrowed their aim exclusively to children and teens. The lingering conviction that these are the only appropriate audiences for comics is still powerful in American culture today (see McGillis, Caswell, Filipi, & Smith, this volume).

Superheroes: Gods and Geeks

The waning popularity of comics in post-War culture in the United States led to a boom in the one genre still considered acceptable: superhero comics. The war-driven need for heroes was replaced by a new range of heroes, with science fiction origins rather than magical destinies, and DC Comics introduced reinvented heroes, including the Flash, Green Lantern, and the entire Justice League of America. Marvel Comics responded by launching in quick succession some of their most popular characters, many created by Stan Lee: The Fantastic Four, Spider-Man, the X-Men, and assembling their own superpowered team in The Avengers, led by a revived Captain America. The defining element of these comics is a shift toward character driven stories and Marvel's decision to make their heroes more human and fallible (Weiner, 2003). Spider-Man was not, like the previous generation's Superman, an invulnerable alien, but instead a geeky teenager from Queens: young, awkward, and not at all sure of himself. Marvel's intent was to explore heroics that came from ordinary men and women, not the unreachable ideal of gods, and Spider-Man remains one of the most iconic superheroes of our time.

Finding Comics: Underground and Direct Markets

Underground comics, also known as comix, arose from a reaction against both mainstream superhero comics and the Comics Code Authority and are represented by the imaginations of R. Crumb, Harvey Kurtzman, Art Spiegelman and as unleashed in the pages of *MAD* magazine, *RAW,* and *Zap Comix*. The "x" added to comic implied both their difference from mainstream comics, including the artistic investigation of the form, a desire to reject the Comics Code, and frequently x-rated content. Comix were a strong part of the 1960s counterculture, including the hippie movement as it grew in San Francisco. Famous for publishing just what the Code opposed, artists and publishers purposefully skirted submitting any content to the Comics Code Authority by distributing comics through non-comics outlets including head shops, i.e., stores selling drug paraphenalia (Sabin, 1996). When the counterculture movement waned at the start of the 1970s, comix lost their sites of distribution, but their legacy lived on in alternative comics, still thriving in opposition to the comic shop mainstream today and represented by such creators as Charles Burns, Chris Ware, Daniel Clowes, Adrian Tomine, and Harvey Pekar.

By the 1970s, the Comics Code had lost much of its grip on the industry; opening the way, by the late 1980s, for the direct market, which became the main distribution point. Comics stores sold both approved and non-approved comics. At this time, comics were marketed mainly to collectors: those avid fans who would buy issues of comics series every Wednesday at their local comics store, read it once if at all, and then carefully store it in a plastic sheath for posterity and potential future profit. While collectors kept the market afloat, aiming only for the collector limited publishers' ability to appeal to new readers.

A few landmark moments jolted publishers out of this trend. Will Eisner, legendary creator of *The Spirit* (see 2005) and one of the first well known graphic novels, *A Contract with God* (1978/2006), was a determined champion of the format as a worthwhile medium for long form stories (Eisner, 2008; Gravett, 2005). Eisner also rejected the idea that comics should be limited to any particular genre, including superheroes; or age range, writing expressly for adults in *A Contract with God.* In 1986, Frank Miller *(The Dark Knight)* and Alan Moore *(Watchmen)* dismantled the expectations of the superhero genre and pushed the format into psychological and literarily complex territory (Wolk, 2007). Art Spiegelman (1986) winning the Pulitzer Prize for his Holocaust memoir *Maus* in 1992 provoked readers to recognize that prejudices against the format were no longer valid (Weiner, 2003). Despite the accolades associated with Speigelman's and others' creative works, it would take more than a decade for comics to gain the widespread acceptance in the literary world that would bring them to be reviewed and acclaimed in literary bastions like *The New Yorker, The New York Times Book Review,* and *Time Magazine.*

The shift toward the bookstore market happened gradually and was less a demand from readers than a result of innovations from publishers and corporate buyers. Borders Group graphic novel buyer Kurt Hassler is credited for leading the charge in 2000 to get graphic novels stocked at bookstores, a move that led to the format's greater visibility and acceptability in the world of bookstores and libraries. Bookstores were dubious about the potential success of a graphic novel section, but as a fan of both graphic novels and manga, Hassler had a strong sense of what the graphic novel audience was looking for, and made smart selections that turned a largely ignored bookstore section into a money-maker (see, for example, Icv2.com [Internal Correspondence version 2]: "ICv2's Top Ten," 2006). At the same time, Japanese manga publishers made two major decisions that led their titles, and businesses, to tremendous success: they decided to publish mainly paperbacks, rather than continuing to attempt enticing traditional comic book readers with comic book versions; and they decided to leave titles "unflipped," in the traditional, right to left Japanese reading order. This allowed Japanese manga publishers to print more titles at a lower cost for both themselves and their readers. At the same time, publishers like Tokyopop decided to publish shojo manga—manga targeting girls and women rather than adult men, drawing in an as-yet untapped market: teenage girls.

A Brief History of Japanese Manga

During the 1950s, comics were taking off in another vital region key to readers today: Japan. When Japan opened its borders to the West in the late 1870s, all types of Western culture and arts quickly flooded the country, embraced by a government determined to become a modern nation as quickly as possible. Amid all of the influences of Western culture, Japanese artists devoured Western comic strips and political cartoons such as those seen in London's *Punch* magazine. An Englishman, Charles Wirgman, started the *Japan Punch* in 1862, and while at first Japanese cartoonists mimicked their English counterparts, creators quickly learned to alter the style of Western comics by introducing Japanese art traditions and symbols. Artists drew from diverse sources including ukiyo-e, the vivid woodblock prints of the 1600s through the 1800s, and the long history of Japanese caricature and sequential storytelling that began in the Choju Giga, a caricature scroll drawn by a Buddhist monk around the 12th century (Schodt, 1983).

Comic Strips to Magazines

The history of comics in Japan follows much the same path as Western comics, starting with political cartoons and cultural critique in the late 1800s, then moving on to comic strips and full page stories in magazines in the 1920s and 30s (Gravett, 2005). Japanese comic strips are created as four-panel sequences, often vertically aligned, and are known as four koma tales. Initially comic strips gained popular attention, including the everyday life of a young housewife in Hasegawa Machiko's (1926) *Sazae-san*. With the rise of ultra-nationalism in the 1930s, comics became a powerful medium for the Japanese public, and the arrival of conflict led to the government giving creators limited choices for continuing their work: create comics as propaganda for the government, give up creating comics, or leave the country to create comics elsewhere (Schodt, 1983). World War II had an indelible effect on the creative output of Japan, not in the least because the atomic bombings of Hiroshima and Nagasaki became a cultural touchstone for the following generations of artists (Drazen, 2003). Post-war culture in Japan was particularly receptive to manga, or print comics: childrens and adults alike thirsted for low-cost, high-value entertainment (Schodt, 1983). Reading manga provided a quiet, absorbing past-time that neither bothered your neighbors nor required a lot of money. The manga supplements in children's magazines proved to be enormously popular in the 1930s, and so when creators decided to begin creating manga post-war, they quickly determined that comics anthology magazines were the most popular and affordable method for distributing comics. Beginning with comics magazines aimed at boys, starting in the late 1940s and expanding into major titles like 1959's *Shonen* magazine (shonen meaning boy), anthologies were and continue to be the main way to publish manga (Gravett, 2005). These anthology magazines range from 100 to close to 1,000 pages, all printed in black and white on cheap newsprint and collecting multiple different series in one phone book sized collection. Magazines come out monthly and weekly, and are marketed by age, gender, and niche audience. Japanese creators, once they realized the strength of the market, also quickly recognized that there were audiences worth pursuing aside from young men. Comics magazines aimed at girls began with the collections *Nakayoshi* (1954) and *Ribon* (1955), and the first comics aimed at adult men arrived with *Young Comic* (1967) as well as more experimental manga published in *Garo* (1964). By the end of the 1960s there were stacks of manga magazines for a broad range of age and inclination.

Redefining Manga's Audiences

Tezuka Osamu is revered as the "God of Manga" in Japan, and his profound influence on manga as a creator is palpable even today. Starting in the late 1940s and early 1950s, Tezuka defined manga's form in a variety of ways, including emblematic character design (drawn from Western cartoon inspirations including Disney and the Fleischer Brothers' Betty Boop), extended pacing and editing techniques drawn from film, and the feeling that a story of any length could and should be told, leading to manga works thousands of pages long. Tezuka's first hit was *Astro Boy* (see Tezuka, 2002–2004), starting serialization in 1951, and from there he created iconic manga series including *Princess Knight* (2003–2008), *Buddha* (2003–2005), and *Phoenix* (2001). Tezuka can also be given credit, much like Will Eisner in the United States, for recognizing early on that manga should not be limited in audience or appeal: He and his mostly male colleagues are responsible for manga quickly growing to include titles for adult men (Gravett, 2005).

On the side of female creators and audiences, a group still largely ignored by mainstream U.S. comics, many of the trademark elements of today's shojo (or girls) manga are inherited from tales like Ikeda Riyoko's (1981) *Rose of Versailles* and the output of the Year 24 Group, a group of young female artists hired in the 1970s to boost interest in shojo manga. Shojo manga was varyingly successful in the 1950s and 1960s, but as most tales were created by male artists they failed to resonate with the young female audience. *Rose of Versailles* burst onto the manga scene, telling the tale of a young woman, raised as a man and now captain of the royal guard, who is caught up in the court politics of Marie Antoinette. Romance, sweeping historical melodrama, and lush art engaged readers' imaginations, especially girls. At the same time, the Year 24 Group (named for the fact that most of the women involved were born in Showa year 24, or 1949) marked the first time women were given relatively free reign to create comics for girls and women. Their intensely emotional, psychologically complex stories set a new standard for girls manga. Their work, ranging from Takemiya Keiko's (2007–2008) science fiction epic *To Terra* to Hagio Moto's (1974) romance between boys, *Heart of Thomas,* pushed boundaries narratively and artistically. The Year 24 Group focused on emotions and character-driven stories, and their page and panel design was at once breathtakingly beautiful and formally nontraditional (Gravett, 2005). This new type of shojo manga was embraced enthusiastically by teenage girls and adult women, and from that time on female creators have dominated the shojo market.

From the 1970s onward, the manga industry has maintained a steady presence in Japanese culture, and while there are periodic public criticisms of risque content, the industry never suffered the backlash U.S. comics experienced in the 1950s. Manga is an accepted part of everyday entertainment in Japan, similar to the ubiquity of television here in the United States, and everyone from businessmen to senior citizens to students indulge in their weekly manga fix. Unlike the U.S. market, Japanese manga were and continue to be written on any topic, from sports comedies to romance to nonfiction guides to the workplace, and no one genre (like superheroes) dominates the market. The general age categories today are shonen manga (boys), shojo manga (girls), seinen manga (adult men), and josei manga (adult women) (Schodt, 1983).

As manga are created via a strong partnership between the editor and the main artist, who in turn is supported by a group of artistic assistants, manga series are notable for being the product of one or two imaginations rather than the committee of creators often required in superhero comics (Kinsella, 2004). Manga publishers produce comics at a much higher rate, with your typical manga artist and cadre of assistants expected to produce anywhere from 50 to 150 pages of comics a week (Brenner, 2007). When a creator is finished with one tale, they can easily decide where to head next: a shojo manga artist may decide to take a turn at seinen audiences, or a writer known for romances may give sports a try. Manga are thus creator-driven, rather than character-driven, and fans follow creators from work to work rather than just seek out the latest X-Men or Batman comic. The structure of the industry allows series to begin and end when the creator feels the story is finished, leading to an expectation for new stories rather than stories about the same character or within the same world.

Reading Comics: Stereotypes and Misconceptions

When readers are initially introduced to comics, from comic strips to graphic novels, most react with cultural preconceptions that skew their impressions. U.S. readers think of comics as being solely humorous, fluffy stories for kids, or else make immediate connections to superhero comics, given their dominance in the U.S. pop culture scene for decades. As a result, stateside readers have little sense of the variety of subject and style currently available. Readers from France consider comics on par with great literature and as one of many fine arts. Readers from Japan dive into comics as a release from the pressures of a busy life focused on work or study; and they read them at all stages of life in the same way many U.S. viewers take a break with TV (Gravett, 2005).

Adults in the United States still consider comics as a juvenile medium, unaware that comics have, for the past 30 years, been primarily aimed at adult readers, not children or teens. On the flip side, adults worry that comics are wildly unsuitable for their children, full of either pornographic sexuality or excessive violence, startled by pages taken out of context from Alan Moore's (1987) *Watchmen* or an adult-oriented Japanese manga volume like Koike Kazuo's (2000–2009) *Lone Wolf and Cub* or Shirow Masamune's (2004) *Ghost in the Shell*. New readers begin reading comics with the idea that all comics are fine for children. However, while one title they pick up will confirm this belief, if they venture further into the format they discover content aimed at mature adults without understanding the creator's intended audience. The creation of the Comics Code Authority in the 1950s and the ensuing inoffensive superhero comics aimed at kids and teens still dominate the Baby Boom generation's sense of what comics should be. While the later generations, especially those who were kids in the 1960s, are more aware of comics' breadth, only the most recent generations of comics readers come to the medium without the "comics are for kids" preconception.

Book Challenges

The continuing strength of these stereotypes can be seen in the well-publicized challenges to graphic novels in library and school collections. In 2006, Alison Bechdel's (2006) *Fun Home* and Craig Thompson's (2003) *Blankets*, both award-winning titles, were requested to be removed from the public library by local patrons in Marshall, Missouri, for being pornographic (Simms, 2006). That particular incidence of challenges was resolved by the library in creating a collection development policy and, after a public meeting allowing townspeople to speak, they decided to keep the titles in the collection in the open stacks (Harper, 2007). That same year, in Victorville, California, a mother of a 16-year-old boy demanded the removal of Paul Gravett's (2004) academic work on the history of Japanese manga, *Manga: 60 Years of Japanese Comics,* and by contacting a local politician she succeeded in getting the title pulled from all of the county's libraries ("Suburban LA County"). In Sioux Falls, South Dakota, in October 2009 the comic anthology *Stuck in the Middle: Seventeen Comics from an Unpleasant Age,* edited by Ariel Schrag (2007) was removed after a challenge from the circulating collection of two middle schools. In a troublesome incident, in Nicholasville Kentucky, two library staff members saw fit to remove *The League of Extraordinary Gentlemen: The Black Dossier* from the collection for over a year and then, when a patron requested the title, to cancel the request so that no patron could see the title they deemed inappropriate (Wilson, 2009). News stories covering a parent's outrage at discovering what they consider inappropriate content in a comic book or graphic novel, as happened in June 2009 in Charlotte, North Carolina, (Ruebens, 2009) are almost always accompanied by admissions that adult readers presumed most comics were fine for their children to read.

Challenges and visual art. Part of the issue that arises with content concerns is the fact that comics are, by their very nature, visual. In a culture where videogames, television, and films are rated for appropriateness, it should come as no surprise that consumers are concerned with the images presented in comics as more problematic than the same events presented in prose. There is no standard ratings system for comics, though individual publishers have created their own systems for indicating content and suggesting intended audiences. Additionally, the sting of the memory of the Comics Code Authority crackdown has made many comics publishers resistant to stricter or overarching attempts to rate their products.

Publishing Comics: Collectors Versus Readers

Libraries have been a part of what is a distinct shift in the recognized market for graphic novels. As more trailblazing graphic novels like Craig Thompson's (2003) *Blankets* and Marjane Satrapi's (2003) *Persepolis* arrived and were discovered by book clubs and adults who had either never read or forgotten why they read comics, readers became a vital audience for graphic novels. Readers in this case, as opposed to collectors, are consumers interested not in the physical object of the book or comic issue but in the content. They are driven to read comics in a package most similar to novels: bound volumes of longer stories that may be serial, yet still contain a significant portion of plot per volume. Comics publishing has been traditionally driven by characters: profits are made from having Spider-Man or Batman continue on indefinitely, and the universe of each character and publisher are frequently rehashed and reinvented to draw in new readers and invigorate creators. Starting in the late 1970s and early 1980s, creators and publishers broke with the traditional model and produced graphic novels with limits, complete in one volume like Will Eisner's (2006) *A Contract with God* or Don McGregor's (1998) *Sabre*, or with at least a definite beginning and end, as with Neil Gaiman's (e.g., 2006) *Sandman* series or Alan Moore's (1989) *V for Vendetta* (Sabin, 1996).

Book publishers, including Random House, entered into the domain of specialty comics publishers, bringing out more stand alone titles that departured from the canon-driven superhero serials that remain the bread and butter of the mainstream comics industry as represented by Marvel and DC Comics. Collectors still account for a large portion of what's known as the direct market sales in speciality comics stores, whereas readers have become at least an equal if not more substantial force for both bricks and mortar and online booksellers. There is still a substantial divide between the direct market and the bookstore market, and the two have yet to win over each other's core audiences. Traditional superhero comics fans are often unaware of the works and creators arriving on the book market, and traditional prose readers can be unaware of the artistic quality or literary work going on within the comics industry and thus disdainful of the idea that comics could ever produce anything as worthy as the latest literary novel.

The comics industry's reliance on direct market sales leads to missed opportunities in gaining new audiences as titles are deemed failures and canceled before they even reach graphic novel readers who browse bookstore and library shelves rather than the comic book racks at their local specialty shop.

The most integrated location to find graphic novels, from mainstream comics to alternative comics to manga, are the bookstores, both bricks and mortar and online. Chain bookstores, most notably Borders and Barnes and Noble, show that highlighting the format and particular works meets a heretofore unrecognized demand, and independent bookstores have also taken up the charge. Libraries, by turn, have become a place where, like the dime store racks and newsstands of the past century, children first encounter comics and develop their interest in pictures into a strong love of story. As more and more libraries stock collections in Children's, Teen, and Adult departments, they meet their patrons' demands and encourage an awareness of the range and depth of what the format offers readers.

A Graphic Novel for Every Reader

In looking at who reads graphic novels today, perhaps the more apt question should be who doesn't read graphic novels? Certain audiences have been recognized as notable consumers of comics and graphic novels: initially, teenage boys and adult men, and more recently teenage girls, as the manga boom dominated the market. Kids up to age 12 have been left out of the major publishers' market equations for decades, and only now are publishers and creators creating and marketing comics expressly for children. The format in itself appeals to a broad range of readers, especially those who are visual learners, and for today's generations raised with the visual diversity of television, film, and the Internet, comics are a natural combination of forms, not a confusing language to be decoded.

Given the history of comics, it's been heartening to witness the boom of publishing diversity in the past 10 years paired with the growing awareness of the validity of the format in popular and literary culture. Libraries and schools have played, and will continue to play, a substantial role in advocating for the format. Most generation Xers and Millennials had no reason to see or read comics, with the exception of the Sunday funnies still prevalent in newspapers. Comic books had disappeared from the corner stores, grocery stores, and magazine racks that once propelled their popularity. Fans were created by word of mouth: if you had a comics fan around you, you would likely at least see a comic book, and potentially join the ranks of fans. If not, there was no easy way to discover the format, and the narrowing of the market appeal to adult men in the 1980s meant there was no obvious way to hook new readers.

Graphic novels have long been included in library and school collections for one reason: they circulate in high numbers (Raiteri, 2003). Some of the volume of circulation can be adjusted by the understanding that graphic novels are faster reads than novels and, akin to DVDs, are checked in and out much faster. If you take into account the internal circulation, or how many times a graphic novel is read in-house, the circulation jumps even higher. Within my own library's teen collection, graphic novels in 2008 made up for 35% of the collection's total circulation, beating out even the DVDs and paperbacks as the most popular format in the collection. In pure circulation counts, 16 of the top 20 circulating titles in the entire collection are graphic novels, 13 of those manga volumes. The most popular titles in each have circulated over 23–28 times, compared to the most popular hardcover fiction, including Stephenie Meyer's *Twilight* volumes, clocking in at 17–25 circulations each. Each graphic novel averages 9 circulations per volume, whereas hardcover fiction averages 3 circulations per volume. Graphic novels and comics are by far the books the library staff must clear up and put away at the end of the day, their only close rival being magazines. In addition, comics anthology magazines, like *Shonen Jump,* and magazines about comics are the magazine titles most read.

Adult graphic novel collections are just starting to be separated out in terms of placement and statistics, but even in our library's smaller collection, circulation has gone up over 50% in the last year. As comics in the library and education world were first collected as a way to appeal to teenagers, particularly teenage boys, for a long time comics and graphic novels have been relegated to teen collections. There has always been an awareness of adults as an audience for graphic novels and comics, but because adults are not as vocal about their fandom as teens, adult graphic novel collections have been slower to establish in libraries and universities. Adult fans have become more and more visible recently, especially when the release of feature films like *Sin City, 300, V for Vendetta,* or *Watchmen* spark adult readers' interest in the source material and inspires them to seek out similar types of comics. As more and more libraries collect specifically for adults, more adult patrons recognize the library collecting a format they desire and take advantage of their own power in requesting more titles be added to the collection.

Similarly, the demand for comics for children keeps rising, and while superhero titles are no longer automatically the go-to titles for children, favorites embraced by adult readers and children, like Jeff Smith's (2005) *Bone,* have paved the way for the success of Jennifer and Matthew Holm's (2005) *Babymouse,* Andy Runton's (2004) *Owly,* and Scott Morse's (2008) *Magic Pickle* series. Many titles for children come from independent creators

and book publishers rather than traditional comics publishers. Independent creators, including Jimmy Gownley (2006), Joshua Elder (2007), Kean Soo (2008), Kazu Kibuishi (2008), and Raina Telgemeier (e.g., Martin, 1995), have all led the charge in creating comics targeted for younger readers. Book publishers getting in on the action have successfully lent more credence to comics for kids, especially as notable titles including Shaun Tan's (2007) *The Arrival* have caught the attention of both the children's literature world and the comics world (Bickers, 2007; Lyga, 2006; see also Campano & Ghiso, and Sipe, this volume). In 2008, legendary wife and husband team Francoise Mouly and Art Speigelman launched TOON books, a publishing venture devoted entirely to titles for the youngest audiences, children ages four and up. Their hard work was rewarded when one of their titles, Eleanor Davis's (2008) *Stinky,* was awarded as an honor book for the Theodor Seuss Geisel Honor Award in 2008 ("'Stinky' Named Geisel 'Honor Book'," 2009), and in 2009 Geoffrey Hayes's *Benny and Penny in the Big No-no* won the award. Currently, demand for kids comics is outpacing production, but publishers and creators are poised to release more quality titles into the market.

Current Trends

Today's comics readers are an eclectic group. Many of the expected divisions remain: superhero fans still seek out their favorite spandex clad crime fighters, and manga devotees leave with stacks of volumes of their favorite series. Independent comics fans still gravitate toward the comics' equivalent of literary fiction, while kids still embrace the humorous action of *Calvin and Hobbes* (Watterson, 2005) alongside Jeff Smith's (2005) *Bone* family. At the same time, browsing collections allows for more crossover, and more and more readers are discovering the format itself through its inclusion in library and school collections, not to mention the local Barnes and Noble.

Superheroes are still a dominant form, though their main audience is arguably the adult fans who follow the universe-driven story lines from Marvel and DC Comics, and while younger readers cheerfully list their favorite superheroes, many know them from films or television rather than the pages of their favorite comic. The visible demand from young audiences, both kids and teens, is for Japanese manga, and the appeal of manga continues to attract and challenge U.S. publishers. Manga's presentation of stories and genres that appeal strongly to female readers has been vital in proving the power of an audience previously ignored by mainstream comics, demonstrating the buying power of teenage girls (Thompson, 2007).

The continuing acceptance of graphic novels into the literary and high culture sphere has helped weaken the impression that reading comics is not "real" reading, and lent the format a respectability it could never previously claim. The lessening of superhero tales' hold on the market has led to a welcome variety of genres and subgenres, especially outside the direct market. Alison Bechdel, an independent creator most known for her long-running comic strip *Dykes to Watch Out For*, gained critical acclaim for her literary memoir (2006) *Fun Home*, named Time Magazine's Book of the Year in 2006. Gene Luen Yang's (2006) *American Born Chinese* was the first graphic novel to win the top literary award for teen literature, the Printz Award, in 2007. In March of 2009, the *New York Times* debuted a new best seller list, this time tracking graphic books sales divided between hardcover, softcover, and Japanese manga (Gustines, 2009). Films based on comics, including such diverse fare as *Ghost World* (Clowes, 1998), *Road to Perdition* (Collins, 2002), *A History of Violence* (Wagner, 2004), *Batman Begins* (Franco & Nolan, 2005), *300* (Miller, 1999), *Sin* City (Miller, 2005), *Speed Racer* (2008) and *Watchmen* are rolled out by Hollywood at an increasing pace, which in turn feeds viewers' desire to uncover the source material.

The participatory and vibrant fan culture of the internet has unleashed a variety of opportunities for comics creators. The internet allows for the creation of everything from Munroe's (2006) stick figure characters in *xkcd* to Kurtz's (1998) full color *PvP* comics; in either short form traditional comic strips or long form comic book or graphic novel length. Starting online also means building an audience without the intermediary of either a publisher or editor—anyone can and does create their own comics. The freer structure of a webpage does not confine creators to a traditional page size or reading order, allowing for increased innovation in how webcomics are both presented and read.

Publishers are also venturing into releasing more and more content online. Initially most publishers concentrated on posting mainly previews and brief excerpts to advertise their print editions, but more and more publishers are testing the waters of releasing substantial material online. In 2007, DC Comics introduced ZudaComics, a site devoted to independent content that depends on site visitor voting and ratings to succeed ("DC Plans," 2007). The same year, Marvel created a subscription service, Marvel Digital Comics Unlimited which allows readers, for either $9.99 a month or $59.98 a year, to read over 2,500 comics, although titles must be at least 6 months old to appear via the service ("Marvel Launches," 2007). In 2007, they also announced they would be publishing content exclusively online ("Marvel Launches Original," 2007). In May 2009, VIZ ventured online with five titles from a monthly magazine from Japan, *IKKI*, as a way to build audiences for their adult-oriented VIZ Signature line and test popularity of titles before they go into print ("VIZ Launches," 2009). VIZ was able to release Rumiko Takahashi's (2009) new manga, *Rin-Ne*, at the same time as the title was published in Japan by releasing the title online at their Shoneny Sunday site, set up on the IKKI model ("New Takahashi," 2009).

One of the major problems facing publishers also arises directly out of participatory online fan culture: the distribution of comics, especially Japanese manga, via various channels on the Internet. Fans, driven by enthusiasm for the format, are easily able to scan and publish favorite comics online for other fans to read. Similar to music file-sharing and the legal wrangling over Napster faced by the music industry, the comics industry has been challenged by fans file-sharing their own favorite comics with no regard for copyright or legal permission. U.S. companies have attempted to deal with scanned titles by sending cease and desist letters to websites hosting scans of copyrighted works, but it seems to be a losing battle given the ease with which new sites pop up ("Marvel and DC Target," 2007).

Japanese manga publishers have faced a much more entrenched fan culture. Works still only available in Japanese, are "scanlated": fans scan in the pages, translate the text, and publish the results online for reading or download. These practices do have a positive side for publishers, raising an awareness of a property before it officially arrives and even allowing manga publishers to gain a strong sense of how popular a series would be were it licensed and published in the United States. Nonetheless, although scanlation has been a part of manga and anime fan culture for years, the ease of digital sharing has made the practice much more threatening to the business of anime distributors and manga publishers.

As publishing online continues to gain ground, the future of comics and graphic novels is likely to spread across platforms including PDAs, cell phones, and digital book readers. Ultimately, the hope is that graphic novels will become as ubiquitous and as accepted as any other format like television, audiobooks, or prose. The format, however, will remain the same, and while the delivery device may shift from paper to screen, there is no sign of readers' fondness for the format slowing down.

Literature References

Bechdel, A. (2006). *Fun home: A family tragicomic*. Boston, MA: Houghton Mifflin.

Clowes, D. (1998). *Ghost world*. Seattle, WA: Fantagraphics.

Collins, M. A. (2002). *Road to perdition*. New York, NY: Pocket Books.

Davis, E. (2008). *Stinky: A toon book*. New York, NY: Little Lit Library.

Eisner, W. (2005). *The best of the spirit*. New York, NY: DC Comics.

Eisner, W. (1978/2006). *A contract with God and other tenement stories*. New York, NY: W. W. Norton.

Elder, J. (2007). *Mail order Ninja* (Vols. 1–2). Los Angeles, CA: Tokyopop.

Gaiman, N. (2006). *The absolute Sandman* (Vol. 1). New York, NY: DC Comics.

Gownley, J. (2006). *Amelia rules! The whole world's crazy*. Harrisburg, PA: Renaissance Press.

Hayes, G. (2009). *Benny and Penny in the big no-no*. New York, NY: Toon Books.

Hergé. (1994). *Adventures of Tintin.* (*Adventures of Tintin Series:*

Three in one #1, Vol. 1). (M. Turner & L. Londdale-Cooper, Trans.). New York, NY: Little Brown & Co.

Holm, J. L. (2005). *Babymouse: Our hero*. New York, NY: Random House.

Ikeda, R. (1981). *The rose of Versailles* (Frederik L. Schodt, Trans.; Vols. 1–2). Tokyo, Japan: Sanyusha.

Kibuishi, K. (2008). *Amulet: The stonekeeper*. New York, NY: Graphix: Scholastic.

Kinney, J. (2007). *Diary of a wimpy kid: Greg Heffley's journal*. New York, NY: Amulet Books.

Kishimoto, M. (2003). *Naruto* (Vols. 1–47). San Francisco, CA: Viz.

Koike, K. (2000-2009). *Lone Wolf and cub* (Dana Lewis, Trans.; Vols. 1-28). Milwaukie, OR: Dark Horse Comics.

Martin, A. M. (1995). *The baby-sitters club: The truth about Stacey* (R. Telgemeier, Illus.). New York, NY: Graphix: Scholastic.

Machiko, H. (1926). *Sazae-san*. *Fukunichi Shimbun*. Tokyo: Kodansha.

McGregor, D. (1998). *Sabre*. Fullerton, CA: Image Comics.

Miller, F. (1999). *300*. Milwaukie, OR: Dark Horse Comics.

Miller, F. (2001). *Batman: The dark knight returns*. New York, NY: DC Comics.

Miller, F. (2005.) *Frank Miller's Sin City: The hard goodbye*. Milwaukie, OR: Dark Horse Comics.

Moore, A. (1987). *Watchmen*. (D. Gibbons, Illus.). New York, NY: DC Comics.

Moore, A. (1989). *V for Vendetta*. New York, NY: DC Comics.

Morse, S. (2008). *Magic pickle*. New York, NY: Graphix: Scholastic.

Moto, H. (1974). *Heart of Thomas*. Weekly Shoujo Comic. No.19-52. Tokyo: Shougakkan.

Runton, A. (2004). *Owly*. Marietta, GA: Top Shelf.

Satrapi, M. (2003). *Persepolis: The story of a childhood*. New York, NY: Pantheon Books.

Schrag, A. (Ed.). (2007). *Stuck in the middle: Seventeen comics from an unpleasant age*. New York, NY: Viking.

Selznick, B. (2007). *The invention of Hugo Cabret: A novel in words and pictures*. New York, NY: Scholastic Press.

Sen, J. (2003). *The golden vine*. Delhi, NY: Shoto Press.

Shirow, M. (2004). *Ghost in the shell* (Frederik L. Schodt, Trans.) Milwaukie, OR: Dark Horse Comics.

Smith, J. (2005). *Bone: Out from Boneville*. New York, NY: Graphix: Scholastic.

Soo, K. (2008). *Jellaby*. New York, NY: Hyperion Books for Children.

Spiegelman, A. (1986). *Maus I: My father bleeds history*. New York, NY: Pantheon.

Takemiya, K. (2007-2008). *To Terra* (Dawn T. Laabs, Trans.; Vols. 1-3). New York, NY: Vertical.

Tan, S. (2007). *The arrival*. New York, NY: Arthur A. Levine Books.

Tezuka, O. (2001). *Phoenix* (Frederik L. Schodt, Trans.; Vols. 1-12). San Francisco, CA: VIZ Media.

Tezuka, O. (2002-2004.) *Astro Boy* (Frederik L. Scodt, Trans.; Vols. 1-23). Milwaukie, OR: Dark Horse Comics.

Tezuka, O. (2003-2005). *Buddha* (Jacques Lalloz, Trans.; Vols. 1-8). New York, NY: Vertical.

Tezuka, O. (2003-2008). *Princess Knight* (Yuriko Tamaki, Trans.; Vols. 1-12). New York, NY: Kodansha International.

Thompson, C. (2003). *Blankets: An illustrated novel*. Marietta, GA: Top Shelf.

Wagner, J. (2004). *A history of violence*. New York, NY: Vertigo: DC Comics.

Watterson, B. (2005). *The complete Calvin and Hobbes*. Kansas City, MO: Andrews McMeel.

Yang, G. L. (2006). *American born Chinese*. New York, NY: First Second.

Academic and Media References

10 Best. (2006, December). *Time.com*. Time, 17 December 2006. Retrieved on February 25, 2010 from http://www.time.com/time/magazine/article/0,9171,1570768,00.html

Becker, S. (1959). *Comic art in America*. New York, NY: Simon and Schuster.

Benny and Penny gets Geisel. (2010, January 25). ICv2.com. Retrieved February 25, 2010, from http://www.icv2.com/articles/news/16688.html

Bickers, J. (2007, February 2). The young and the graphic novel. *Publishers Weekly 254*(8). Retrieved January 29, 2010 from http://www.publishersweekly.com/article/396386-The_Young_and_the_Graphic_Novel.php

Brenner, R. (2007). *Understanding manga and anime*. Westport, CT: Libraries Unlimited.

Cart, M. (2007, March 15). "You go, graphic!" *Booklist*, *43*. Retrieved January 29, 2010 from http://www.booklistonline.com/default.aspx?page=show_product&pid=1909652

DC plans webcomics site. (2007, July 9). ICv2.com. Retrieved January 29, 2010, from http://icv2.com/articles/home/10877.html

Drazen, P. (2003). *Anime explosion: The what? Why? And wow of Japanese animation*. Berkeley, CA: Stone Bridge Press.

Eisner, W. (1985/2008). *Comics & sequential art: Principles and practices from the legendary cartoonist*. New York, NY: W. W. Norton.

Franco, L. (Producer), & Nolan, C. (Director). (2005). *Batman begins* [Motion picture]. United States: Warner Bros. Pictures.

Gravett, P. (2004). *Manga: Sixty years of Japanese comics*. New York, NY: Harper Design International.

Gravett, P. (2005). *Graphic novels: Everything you need to know*. New York, NY: Collins Design.

Gustines, G. G. (2009, March). Introducing *The New York Times* graphic books best seller lists. *New York Times*. Retrieved January 29, 2010, from http://artsbeat.blogs.nytimes.com/2009/03/05/introducing-the-new-york-times-graphic-books-best-seller-lists/

Hadju, D. (2008). *The ten-cent plague: The great comic-book scare and how it changed America*. New York, NY: Farrar, Straus and Giroux.

Harper, R. (2007). Library board approves new policy/Material selection policy created, controversial books returned to shelves. *Marshall Democrat News*. Retrieved January 29, 2010, from http://www.marshallnews.com/story/1193923.html

ICv2's Top Ten Most Powerful People in American Manga Publishing. (2006, October 18). ICv2.com. Retrieved on February 24, 2010, from http://www.icv2.com/articles/news/9478.html

Kinsella, S. (2004). *Adult manga: Culture and power in contemporary Japanese society*. Honolulu: University of Hawai'i Press.

Kurtz, S. R. (1998-) *PvP: Player vs. Player*. Retrieved February 25, 2010, from http://www.pvponline.com

Lyga, A. A.W. (2006). Graphic novels for (really) young readers: Yowly. Buzzboy. Pinky and Stinky. Who are these guys? And why aren't they ever on the shelf? *School Library Journal*, *52*(3), 56-61.

"Marvel and DC target BitTorrent downloads." (2007, November 23). ICv2.com. Retrieved February 24, 2010 from http://www.icv2.com/articles/news/11676.html

Marvel launches original webcomics. (2007, September 17). ICv2.com. Retrieved January 29, 2010, from http://www.icv2.com/articles/news/13313.html

Marvel launches subscription site. (2007, November 13). *ICv2.com*. Retrieved January 29, 2010 from http://www.icv2.com/articles/news/11623.html

McCloud, S. (1993). *Understanding comics: The invisible art*. New York, NY: HarperPerennial.

McCloud, S. (2006). *Making comics: Storytelling secrets of comics, manga, and graphic novels*. New York, NY: Harper.

Munroe, R. (2006). *xkcd*. Retrieved February 24, 2010, from http://www.xkcd.com

New Takahashi manga to debut on web. (2009, April 15). ICv2. com. Retrieved February 24, 2010, from http://www.icv2.com/articles/news/14755.html

Reid, C. (2003, October). Manga is here to stay. *Publisher's Weekly, 20*. Retrieved January 29, 2010, from http://www.publishersweekly.com/article/419550-Manga_Is_Here_to_Stay.php

Raiteri, S. (2003). Graphic novels. *Library Journal, 128*(1), 80.

Rudiger, H. (2006, March/April). Graphic novels 101: Reading lessons. *The Horn Book Magazine*, 126-134.

Ruebens, L. (2009, June 20). Uncaped crusader in comic causes concern—Parents surprised at images they find in Batman comic bought at the local library. *Charlotte Observer*. Retrieved on January 29, 2010, from http://docs.newsbank.com/s/InfoWeb/aggdocs/NewsBank/128F97EF5B497D28/0EB90D8C549AE593?p_multi=CHOB&s_lang=en-US

Sabin, R. (1996). *Comics, comix, & graphic novels*. London: Phaidon.

Schodt, F. (1983). *Manga! Manga! The world of Japanese comics*. Tokyo: Kodansha International.

Silverman, F. (1994). Tracing the history of America's first modern comic character. (the Yellow Kid). *Editor & Publisher 127*(48). Retrieved January 31, 2010, from http://www.virtuemag.org/articles/the-yellow-kid

Simms, Z. (2006, October 6). Library board hears complaints about books/Decision scheduled for Oct. 11 meeting. *Marshall Democrat News*. Retrieved January 29, 2010, from http://www.marshallnews.com/story/1171432.html

"'Stinky' Named Geisel 'Honor Book'." (2009, Janaury 25). *ICv2. com*. Retrieved on January 29, 2010, from http://www.icv2.com/articles/news/14166.html

"Suburban LA County Pulls Manga Text from Libraries." (2006, April 14). ICv2.com. Retrieved February 26, 2010, from http://www.icv2.com/articles/news/8510.html

Thompson, J. (2007, October 23). How manga conquered the U.S., a graphic guide to Japan's coolest export. *Wired*. Retrieved January 29, 2010, from http://www.wired.com/special_multimedia/2007/1511_ff_manga

"VIZ Launches Webcomics Site." (2009, May 21). ICv2.com. Retrieved February 25, 2010, from http://www.icv2.com/articles/news/14998.html

Weiner, S. (2003). Faster than a speeding bullet: The rise of the graphic novel. New York, NY: NBM.

Wertham, F. (1954). *Seduction of the innocent*. New York, NY: Rinehart.

Willems, P. (2008). "This strangest of narrative forms: Rodolphe Töpffer's sequential art." Mosaic, 41(2). Retrieved January 30, 2010, from http://www.accessmylibrary.com/article-1G1-181165017/strangest-narrative-forms-rodolphe.html

Wilson, A. (2009, November 10). "Library employees fired over censorship of graphic novel." Lexington Herald-Leader. Retrieved January 29, 2010, from http://www.mcclatchydc.com/2009/11/10/78655/library-employees-fired-over-censorship.html

Wolk, D. (2007). *Reading comics: How graphic novels work and what they mean*. Cambridge, MA: Da Capo Press.

Point of Departure

Gareth Hinds

Figre 18.1 The one-man film crew

Drawing a graphic novel is kind of like making a whole film by yourself. The artist becomes the writer, director, production and costume designer, art director, location scout, cinematographer, ALL the actors, the special effects team, and the editor!

Unlike in film, however, the images are static. Time, motion, and sound are implied by logical sequences of pictures, or by descriptive text (such as "We waited for hours" or "WHAM!").

The basic idea of telling a story in pictures is really quite natural, and has a long tradition going back to primitive cave paintings—but doing it really well is still pretty tricky. The artist has to decide which information is best conveyed by text, and which by pictures. How much dialogue is enough, or too much? What's the clearest way to show a scene, and what's the most dramatic? How much can the drama be heightened before it becomes melodrama? There are thousands of such decisions that have to be made in the course of drawing a graphic novel. Ultimately, I make most of these decisions in an intuitive manner, but I'll try to explain how I approach them.

Since comics is a storytelling medium, a comic or graphic novel will usually only be as good as the story it tells. When I first set out to create graphic novels I decided that instead of writing original stories myself, I would work with the very best writers in history. Homer. Shakespeare. The anonymous authors of orally transmitted epics like *Beowulf*. This lets me focus my energy on the thing that really fascinates me: how to (re)tell a story in pictures.

The first step for me is to get really comfortable with the work I'm adapting, reading it through several times and taking preliminary notes on the themes and scenes I want to emphasize, while simultaneously starting to visualize how I want the story to look.

Here's part of an outline of *Romeo & Juliet*. The scenes are underlined to show how I'm thinking about their relative importance. As you can see, on the same piece of paper I'm starting to brainstorm visually by making rough sketches. I have to figure out how the book is going to look—the main characters, setting, and also the style of the drawing and coloring. I adapt my artistic style to each

Figure 18.2 Outline and character sketches for *Romeo & Juliet*

book, partly because I enjoy visual experimentation, but mostly because I feel strongly that each story has different visual needs. *The Merchant of Venice* is not the same kind of story as *Beowulf*, or for that matter, *Spider-Man*™ or *Archie*™. Each demands a different level of realism, a different mood, color palette, style of lettering or type, and even different composition and storytelling techniques.

I continue to sketch and do visual research throughout the writing stage, as I move from rough outline to script, trimming out non-essential narration and dialogue, identifying and refining the most important passages, and making sure the result flows well. My compass here is simply my own sense of what makes the original text great. I want to share with the reader everything I love about the original.

Next comes the layout stage, and this is really the heart

269

The Odyssey – Books 3-4

Book 3

<The ship arrives at Pylos. 9 guilds of 450 men are making sacrifice of 9 bulls each.>

Athena/Mentor: Don't be shy; speak plainly to Nestor and he will tell you the truth.

<they are greeted by the Pylians, seated near Nestor, and given food.>

Pisistratus: Strangers, welcome. Join our feast. Make an offering to Lord Poseidon, for this feast is in his honor.

Athena: Lord Poseidon, whose dominion embraces all the earth, hear our prayer: glory to Nestor and all the line of Neleus; good fortune to all the men of Pylos in exchange for their sacrifice; and swift success to Telemachus and myself in our mission.

<eating>

Nestor: Now that we have put aside our hunger, tell me who you are, guests, and from what port you sailed -- are you merchants, perhaps, or men of war?

Telemachus: Nestor, son of Neleus, pride of Achaea, I will answer you. I come from Ithaca, but my business here is personal. I seek news of my great-hearted father, Odysseus who fought with you at Troy.
We have heard the fate of every other Achaean general, returned home or dead and buried before the walls of Troy; but of Odysseus' fate no one seems to know. I have come to beg you: tell me what you know, if you saw him fall in battle or heard of his end from any traveller. I pray, do not soften it out of pity, but tell me everything.

of the comic medium—figuring out which moments to show and how to compose them. Comic artists often use the same terminology as film directors, speaking in terms of close-ups, establishing shots, low and high angles, two-shots, and so on. But we also have to figure out how to place these shots together on a page, leave the right amount of room for text and sound effects, lead the reader through the panels in the right order, and create a sense of things happening quickly or slowly as the scene requires. I created the layouts for *Beowulf* traditionally, but for *The Odyssey* I created them digitally (see detailed videos showing the process of creating *The Odyssey* at gare-thhinds.blip.tv). This made editing and text placement much easier and more precise.

After the rough layouts are edited and

Figure 18.3 (left) *Odyssey* script sample.

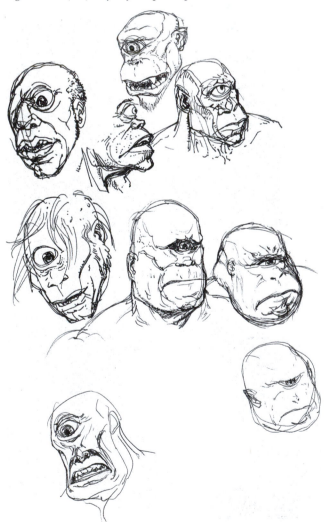

Figure 18.4 (below right) Rough page layouts for *The Odyssey*. Credit (this page): THE ODYSSEY. Copyright © 2009 by Gareth Hinds. Reproduced by permission of the publisher, Candlewick Press, Somerville, MA.

Figure 18.3a (below left) Concept sketches for *The Odyssey*.

Figure 18.5 Inked Beowulf page.
Credit: BEOWULF (Unpaginated) © 1999, 2000, 2007 by Gareth Hinds. Reproduced by permission of the publisher, Candlewick Press, Somerville, MA.

approved, I transfer them to big sheets of heavy paper and start drawing/painting the final illustrations. The challenges at this stage are basically the same as with any other kind of representational art (accurate and expressive drawing, selection of color, capturing light, form, and depth, etc.); but there are a few special issues. First, the prodigious number of drawings involved in a graphic novel means that I have to work fast. Second, I have to maintain continuity: From one panel to the next, each character must look the same, have the same costume and coloring, and have body language and expression that matches the dialogue or action.

I scan the finished art back into the computer. Sometimes I fix mistakes or add color to the art digitally. Then I add the sound effects, speech balloons, and panel borders, also digitally. This keeps them editable, in case there are copyedits or the book later gets translated into another language.

Finally, I deliver it all to my publisher on a DVD (or two, in the case of *The Odyssey*). This begins a 12- to 14-month waiting period, during which time I review copyedits, proofs and cover designs, make big marketing plans… and hopefully complete another book!

Figure 18.6 Finished King Lear panels with balloons and sound effects.
Credit: KING LEAR, p. 67. Copyright ©2007 by Gareth Hinds. Reproduced by permission of the publisher, Candlewick Press, Somerville, MA.

Point of Departure

Raina Telgemeier

The Beginning

When I was nine my dad gave me this comic book, <u>Barefoot Gen</u>, and told me I should read it. He said it was about a kid who lived through the atomic bombing of Japan. I dunno. I guess I thought it was sort of interesting, but nothing special— not better than reading <u>Calvin and Hobbes</u>, anyway. I stuck with it simply because of my dad's encouragement.

In the book, the actual bomb doesn't fall till the last 20 pages or so, and the thing is like 300 pages long. By that point you've begun to like the characters.

I think my family was camping when I finally reached the end of the book.

HEY!!

19

A Burgeoning Field or a Sorry State

U.S. Poetry for Children, 1800–Present

Laura Apol and Janine L. Certo

Michigan State University

Scholarly critical attention to children's poetry waxes and wanes, but the poetry itself continues to flourish and evolve, continually open to innovations in form and the inclusion of new voices. Laura Apol and Janine Certo, both poets themselves as well as teacher educators, begin by working through what distinguishes children's poetry as an art form in children's lives, and then chart the history and critical reception of children's poetry in the United States from 1800 to the present. Janet S. Wong, author of more than 20 books of poetry for children, talks about her poetic process, a process which includes thoughtful revision and careful attention both to personal detail and cultural sensitivity.

Since the days of the *New England Primer* (1687/1777), poetry for American children has occupied an ever-changing place in the world of children's literature: It has been viewed as central to language learning and reading instruction, as a means of political and religious indoctrination, as a tool for Americanization and socialization, as a stepping stone to the "real" world of poetry for adults, and as a source of linguistic pleasure and subversive fun. Over the centuries, the debate over the health and status of poetry for children has swung between claims that it is either a burgeoning field or a sorry state—and sometimes, that it is both at the same time.

Burgeoning or sorry, poetry for children has been, across generations, a sometimes powerful, sometimes invisible force in schools, churches, homes, playgrounds, and community events, and though it is often marginalized in American classrooms and curriculum, both its history and its current state are of interest to those who work with children, literature, and, of course, children's literature.

The topic of poetry for children is much larger than a single chapter can contain. These, then, are the parameters we have necessarily put in place: Ours is a look at U.S. English-language poetry for children as it has evolved over time since the 1800s. Reluctantly, we limit our discussion to the poems most often found in U.S. schools and how they have been used, which keeps us from including other English-language or translated poets or poems, as well as including the kind of cultural or diverse representation that was excluded for centuries from the schoolroom canon. It is only late in the 20th century that children in U.S.

schools began to be given poems by poets who represent racial, ethnic, or religious range or diversity; therefore, in the sections of the chapter devoted to contemporary poets and poems we have tried to include some of this diverse representation.

Poetry for Children: The Definition

One of the most troubling questions for poets and literary scholars alike is that of definition—not only what is poetry for children, but what is poetry itself? Poets have given a range of definitions—from "the best words in the best order" (Coleridge, 1836, p. 45) to "...a short, lyrical response to the world. It is emotion under extreme pressure or recollection in a small space. It is the coal of experience so compressed it becomes a diamond" (Yolen, as cited in Johnson, 2009, p. 241). Children's literature scholars have put forward their own definitions. For example, Charles Elster (2000) relies in part on the purpose of poetry to aid in the definition: "Poetry, perhaps more than any other form of language, has the potential to convey intense and new ways of experiencing the world. In poetry, the formal features of language [i.e., rhythm, rhyme, alliteration, imagery, word play] become a means of drawing the reader into these intense experiences of the world and the pleasures of language itself" (p. 71). In defining poetry, some educators and poets (see, especially, Barr, 2006) find it helpful to distinguish "poetry" from "verse"; according to the authors of one textbook of children's literature, verse is much less emotionally intense than poetry, and while verse is often amusing and light-hearted in content and form, poetry uses poetic techniques to call attention to something in a fresh and compelling manner (Galda, Cullinan, & Sipe, 2009).

Perhaps the most well-known definition of poetry is provided by Emily Dickinson: "...if I feel physically as if the top of my head were taken off, I know that is poetry" (as cited in Bianchi, 1924, p. 276). Yet, if definitions of "poetry" are complicated, equally so are definitions of "child" and the boundaries of childhood, particularly as it changes across history and is located within an ongoing and unresolved debate about childhood as a social construction. As for the parameters of "poetry for children"—such a question can get mired endlessly in questions of intents of authors, ways poets and poems have been co-opted by and for child audiences, motives of publishers and booksellers, and the educative desires of teachers and other adults. In their textbook, *The Pleasures of Children's Literature*, authors Perry Nodelman and Mavis Reimer (2003) write of the difficulty of determining what can be considered "poetry for children" in the following way:

> We suspect that no one would want to assert that all adult poems are equally suitable for children. But that raises an interesting question. Which ones are? The poems specific adults think suitable for child readers reveal much about their attitudes toward children .... These choices also re-

veal something of adult ideas about what poetry is. (pp. 267–268)

Even the idea of "audience" when it comes to poetry for children is vexing, given that poetry published for children is always mediated by adults. As Lissa Paul (2005) asks of poetry for children: "Who is the text for? Adults or children? Who publishes it? Who buys it? Who knows best?" (p. 258).

Given the persistent challenges of defining the boundaries of "children's poetry," for this paper our working definition of poetry for children is determinedly unpoetic and largely utilitarian; it is historically and culturally constructed rather than organically or intuitively derived. Rather than debate the definition of the genre or the audience, we take as poetry for children the definition that Hall (1985) puts into practice in *The Oxford Book of Children's Verse in America*: those pieces that have, over time, been recognized as poetry for children by poets, editors, anthologizers, educators, and—most importantly—by children themselves. As Hall points out, this definition can include traditional material like Mother Goose, as well as "verses clearly intended by their authors for the entertainment and edification of the young. It can also include poems not written for children, which children have enjoyed" (p. xxiv).

Clearly, the notion of poetry for children is complicated and rich; still, we believe our utilitarian definition can function as a workable boundary. That this boundary has shifted across time and generations goes without saying. As a result, part of our purpose in this chapter is to outline, in broad strokes, some of the historical and cultural shifts that surround what has come to be known as "poetry for children."

Poetry in the Lives of Children

Across multiple disciplines and fields of study, theorists and practitioners agree: Humans are born with a predisposition toward the elements of poetry. Eric Havelock (1986) maintains "oral societies have commonly assigned responsibility for preserving speech to a partnership between poetry, music and dance" (p. 72). Poetry became the repository for cultural information and supplied an important structural framework for retrievable knowledge. "It was memorable because it was formulaic, repetitious, and participatory" (Apol-Obbink, 1990, p. 228).

In considering the history of poetic thought, poet Donald Hall (1985) links these cultural aspects of poetry to the developmental aspects. Hall sees poetry emanating from a set of elements that he terms "sensual pleasures" that are "primitive, both personally (back to the crib) and historically (back to the fire in front of the cave)" (p. 149). The three elements Hall identifies function both culturally and individually: the sensual pleasures of form, rhythm and sound. Hall locates these three pleasures in the infant body—Twinbird is our pleasure with form, balance, and opposition in poetry, deriving from the infant's perception of its hands as independent/dependent twin birds that are exactly alike but exactly unalike, mirror images of one another; Goatfoot is the pleasurable thrill of rhythm and motion in poetry that derives from the infant's use of its legs, which contract and expand in a rhythmic beat; and Milktongue is the oral pleasure of the texture of poetic language, derived from infant babbles, from the way the infant's tongue curls around sounds.

Apol-Obbink (1990) connects Hall's sensual pleasures to the earliest forms of oral poetry—forms originally used by preliterate societies to preserve and transfer information (Havelock, 1986; Ong, 1982), but later preserved for children in the form of Mother Goose rhymes. These rhymes began orally as proverbs, weather lore, charms and incantations, pieces of historical ballads, anecdotes about historical personages, popular street songs, and fragments of political and religious diatribes (Baring-Gould & Baring-Gould, 1962). However, they have been preserved *because of* the poetic elements that made them memorable, and therefore valuable, to a preliterate society, and they connect in multiple ways to the expanding world of poetry for children.

This developmental link between Mother Goose and other forms of poetry for children is well documented by scholars of children's literature. As *Children's Literature Association Quarterly* editors Anita Tarr and Richard Flynn (2002) put it, "No one needs a reminder of how prevalent poetry is in children's lives, ranging from nursery rhymes to advertising jingles to song lyrics to poetry in the classroom" (p. 2).

Thus, the origins of poetry for children meet at the intersection of historical and developmental literacy, and continue to exist in homes, classrooms, and playgrounds. However, beyond this understanding of the cultural and developmental history of language play and versification, there is another strong correlation that is made between children and poetry—that is, the romanticized notion that young people "live closer" to the language and perceptions of poems, that by virtue of their youth they are more in touch with the sources of language, that they possess a freshness of vision and expression that is central to the production of poetry.

This is not a new notion. In an 1882 sketch for the highly popular 19th-century periodical for children, *St. Nicholas*, Lucy Larcom wrote,

> …both children and poets see things in the same way,—simply, with open eyes and hearts, seeing Nature as it is, and finding whatever is lovable and pure in the people who surround them…. The little child is born with a poet's heart in him, and the poet has been fitly called "the eternal child." (as cited in Sorby, 2005, p. xxi)

Even in more contemporary times, Leonard Clark (1980), author of many books for children and adults, articulated a similarly romantic view of the connection between children and poetry.

For decades, ongoing debates have occurred between those adults who believe that because children live close to the world of poems, they have an innate appreciation for poetry and an inborn ability to create poetry, and those adults who believe that—at least when it comes to poetry creation—the title of "poet" must be learned and earned. Most notably, these discussions have taken place between two individuals, themselves authors of poetry for children, both of whom have worked with children in the schools: Kenneth Koch and Myra Cohn Livingston. Koch is the author of numerous collections of poetry for adults, as well as collections of poetry by and for children, and books detailing how to get children to write poems. He is convinced of the innate ability young children have to appreciate and produce high-quality poems, based on "their own strong feelings,[…] their spontaneity, their sensitivity, and their carefree inventiveness" (Koch, 1970, p. 25).

Livingston, also a poet and the author of many books of poetry for children along with many books theorizing poetry for children, believes quite the opposite: that the writing of poetry is hard work, requiring training, practice, and experience. The mantle of poet must be learned and earned, rather than granted too easily and too early in life. She writes, "…I have never told children that they are *poets*, for I know only too well the years and work it takes to be considered a poet" (Livingston, 1976, p. 29). Livingston repeatedly demands quality in poetry written for children; she advocates that rather than letting a child believe that poetry is something that naturally emerges from a poet-child self, we should instead "teach [the child] …something of the craft of poetry and its tools by using examples of the finest poetry written, so that, eventually, the child can find a form best suited to his own thought and feelings" (p. 30). This attention to models and craft in working with children and poetry has been elaborated more recently by Certo (2004).

Joseph Thomas, Jr. (2007), in his book-length study of poetry for children, *Poetry's Playground: The Culture of Contemporary American Children's Poetry*, addresses not only the work of poets *for* children, but also the poetry *of* children themselves in the form of the playground poetry (rhymes, jingles, etc.) that children routinely produce in play. Thomas maintains that this should be included as a part of a comprehensive study of American children's poetry as "belonging to a rich poetic tradition" (p. 40). He associates playground poetry with the Bakhtinian notion of carnivalesque—that is, "a playfulness which situates itself in positions of non-conformity" (Stephens, as cited in Thomas, 2007, p. 44), including hierarchical inversion, the rejection of authority and mockery of authority figures, defiance of the constraints and restraints of the social order, and the use of abusive language and insulting words.

Whether children are by nature "nearer" the world of poetry, and whether adult intervention harms or helps the child-as-poet, the fact remains that poetry and childhood are inexorably linked, if not in the production of poetry then certainly in its reception—both outside and within the classroom. We turn, then, to poetry for children—the history, the role in 20th-century American culture and education, contemporary views, and, finally, recent trends.

U.S. Poetry for Children: The History

In recent years, serious scholars of the history of poetry for children have insisted on contextualizing their studies both within the wider world of poetry for adults, with its movements and progressions, as well within the fields of literary criticism, politics, American history and cultural studies (e.g., Flynn, 2000, 2003, 2006; Paul, 2005; Sorby, 2005; Styles, 1998). In the past, such contextualization has rarely been the case; as Thomas (2007) writes, "Many critical treatments of children's poetry, particularly U.S. children's poetry, divorce the object of their study from its larger, poetic [and, we would add, political] context" (p. xiii). Thus, those who take up this challenge have provided thick descriptions of the complex cultural and educative role poetry has played in the lives of generations of children.

18th Century and Early 19th Century: From England to America

In colonial America, most poetry for children would have originated in England—including, often, the couplets included in the *New England Primer* (1687/1777). Frequently, English verse was printed—nearly verbatim—by American sources, with "Boston" substituted for "London" (Hall, 1985, p. xxv). Across the successive printings, the rhymes that made up the primer alphabet "altered according to the politics and religious fervor of the moment" (p. 289).

In the mid- to late 18th century in America, school readers such as McGuffy's, along with Sunday School magazines and children's gift books, became sources for children's poetry, thus creating an identifiable history of American children's poetry—written by American authors for an audience of American children. At school, where memorization and recitations remained the chief pedagogy, rhymes emphasized piety, morals, and early literacy (i.e., the alphabet in didactic couplets). However, school rhymes were not limited to morality and alphabeticism; they were also used to teach other subject areas such as geography and mathematics, as well as patriotism and nationalism. According to Hall (1985), the push for nationalism spurred a distinctly "American" poetry for children, for nationalism provided the desire to promulgate an "American culture" (p. xxxi), bound at first by piety, later by patriotism.

Nineteenth century children's periodicals such as *The Youth's Companion* (1827–1929) and *St. Nicholas* (1876–1941) served as a source for early American poetry for children—much of which was authored by women—and the quantity of early 19th-century verse for children attests to the popularity of this genre of literature for children.

For poets in the 19th century, the link between childhood and poetry was a given: Childhood was romanticized, explored, and celebrated through poems. In writing about the "child-centeredness of American poetry" (p. xviii), Hall (1985) writes that "in the popular culture of the nineteenth century, to be a poet was to be childlike" (p. xxxiv), linking this infantilization of poetry to the feminization of American literary culture. In reviewing the results of a study of New England authors between 1770 and the Civil War, historian Joan Shelley Rubin (2007) concludes that the numbers:

> suggest that women were more likely than men to define themselves "primarily" as writers because they lacked alternative sources of income.... But women also sustained amateurism because prescribed gender roles discouraged their economic independence and because critics disdained the sentimental mode in which most women poets wrote. (p. 30)

Thus, women writers were both more numerous and more "amateur" than male writers—creating a confluence of the feminization and the infantilization of popular American poetry in the early 19th century.

Mid-19th Century to Early 20th Century: Schoolroom Poets

Recent scholarship that examines the post-bellum period of American poetry studies the role of poetry in schools and other institutions responsible for training young people. Poems were an important means of socialization and education, learned not only as a genre of literature, but learned "by heart" to be recited in schools, homes, churches, and at various public events. As Sorby (2005) writes in her study of schoolroom poets: "Once upon a time, within living memory, but just barely, people knew poems, repeated them, and wove them into their daily lives" (p. xi). Nineteenth- and 20th-century popular poetry, then, was truly *popular*.

Clearly, this was a time where poetry for children could be viewed as a burgeoning field (though the poems read and learned by children were not children's exclusive domain), for poetry played a central role in middle class American life. Poems were learned, memorized, and performed on a regular basis. Given this role, popular poetry functioned not only as entertainment and literature, but also, more centrally, as a pedagogical tool used for socialization, education, and indoctrination.

The poets of antebellum United States—particularly Henry Wadsworth Longfellow, John Greenleaf Whittier, James Russell Lowell, and Oliver Wendell Holmes—have come to be known as the New England "schoolroom poets" because of the important role they played in 19th-century classrooms, creating a common canon of literature that was familiar, and that served in community building and acculturation. In the process of memorization, the individual learning the poem could become part of a larger community with shared experience, repertoire, and language.

Rubin (2007) confirms the multiple social roles of poetry in 19th-century America—particularly in the arena of schools and public performances. According to Rubin, poems functioned as vehicles to deliver moral lessons, to promote citizenship, to create a shared sense of community, to develop an American identity, to allow for language acquisition, to supplement religious instruction, to serve as acquired cultural capital, and to increase aesthetic appreciation. Through poetry, communities were united (both locally and across the country) by a shared body of poems—a canon of schoolroom poetry—linking schoolchildren across the nation and across the generations.

In this way, the poetry of the mid- to late 19th century came to define, enliven, but also limit most people's understanding of poetry from their earliest days. Every poem in the schoolroom canon was used extensively as a performance piece, which meant the poem had to be easy to read—that is, easy to read *aloud*. As well, the multiple functions of the schoolroom poem dictated "that it be accessible by, and useful to, ordinary middle-class people; this meant that it should rhyme, that its meter should be regular, and that its language should be easy to understand, to remember, and to repeat" (Sorby, 2005, p. 185). And, due to the genre's functions as "didactic rite," there was an ongoing expectation that "poetic language should be transparent in every instance" (Rubin, 2007, p. 23).

This transparency of form and content was not, however, matched by accuracy of historical record. Because schoolroom poems were intended to turn readers into citizens, the poets themselves believed they had a mandate, and license, to have their poems do democratizing as well as poetic work. Longfellow felt free to fabricate histories in poems that celebrated American values and contained not only memorable narratives, but memorable means of carrying those narratives. Thus a poem like Longfellow's "Hiawatha" became a tale of assimilation and indoctrination, linking the audience members' own childhoods to the childhood of a nation, but relying very little on historical accuracy. The unvarying trochaic tetrameter mimicked the sound of far-off drums and, with the chant-like repetition of lines, lent itself to oral performance. At the same time, the notion of the "noble savage" who at the poem's conclusion endorses the arrival of Christian missionaries reinforced a popular (and sanitized) version of America's past that masqueraded as "history." Likewise, "Paul Revere's Ride," published in 1860 when America was on the brink of the Civil War, created a story of brave citizenship in establishing a unified nation. Carried forward by galloping anapestic lines that create poetic tension while aiding in memorization, the poem co-opts both the listening audience and the speaker into a narrative of patriotism concluding with a rousing call to arms that was intended to be not only historical, but contemporary as well. However,

once again the narrative line contained little documented historical "truth."

The popularity, educational importance, and cultural impact of the New England schoolroom poets was undeniable, and with time they paved the way for the Western schoolroom poets (John Whitcomb Riley and Eugene Field), creating a widespread, although limited, understanding of what poetry was and what it could accomplish. However, by the end of the 19th century, American poetry had reached a "crisis of rhyme and meter, a crisis in popular poetic forms" (Sorby, 2005, p. 96). The schoolroom poets were still respected and imitated, seen as role models for the young and as worthy namesakes for elementary schools, but much of their power had been lost to prose and the rise of the modern novel. And although early in the 20th century people still read the schoolroom poets, and teachers still taught them, no longer was "everybody" exposed to the same few poems. As the 20th century wore on, middle-class people became much less likely to know, and to be able to quote from, a stable archive of popular verses. Indeed, in the later 20th-century, middle-class people (outside a tiny group generated by English departments) barely read poetry at all.

Poetry for Children in 20th-Century American Culture and Education

Even as canonical "schoolroom poetry" declined in power, poetry for children took its own path, as pedagogy and popularity—once synonymous—parted company. In part, this split took place at the hands of the most popular periodical published for children during the late 19th and early 20th centuries: *St. Nicholas,* edited by Mary Mapes Dodge. Dodge was famous for her emphasis on literary offerings for children that allowed for entertainment rather than insisting exclusively on instruction. In the magazine, she established a 3-tier system to differentiate "poems" from "verses" from "jingles," which diminished in importance, value, and virtuous qualities (Sorby, 2005, p. 72). As the magazine became more geared to children, though, the serious poetry of the magazine gave way to "age-appropriate" light verse and nonsense. As a result, the gap between "serious" adult poetry and "light" children's poetry began to be more clearly defined. Increasingly, adult poetry was dominated by the aesthetic of modernism, which banished the conventions of schoolroom performance and repetition in favor of formal experiments and novelty. This does not mean that the galloping meters and overt rhymes of "Paul Revere's Ride" were banished entirely, however. Instead, it meant that they were relegated to the now-compartmentalized realm of children's poetry.

This splitting of a poetic aesthetic that had previously been intergenerational into "adult poetry" and "children's poetry" ushered in a new era of poetry for children, and a new set of names became canonical in that world: Robert Frost, Carl Sandburg, Gwendolyn Brooks, Randall Jarrell, Theodore Roethke, and John Ciardi. Many of these were also considered poets for adults (some were primarily poets for adults), but for the first time, noted adult poets were writing poems specifically with a child audience in mind.

A New Form of "School" Poetry: Frost, Sandburg, and Brooks

In the vacuum left behind as the schoolroom poets lost favor, questions arose about whether the arts in general—and poetry in particular—were going to exist as marginal or central to American public life and education (Rubin, 2007). On such a stage, figures such as Frost, Sandburg, Brooks, Jarrell, Ciardi, and Roethke assured that poetry for children occupied a place of prominence in the American poetry scene of the middle of the century. As these poets grappled, both publicly and privately, with the role of the poet in society (a spokesperson? a figurehead? a political rabble-rouser?), they also produced a body of work that allowed poetry for children to separate from the wider world of poetry writ large.

In *Poetry's Playground*, Thomas (2007) contends that during the mid-20th century, there became two kinds of poetry for children—the officially sanctioned and therefore studied "school poetry" of Frost (conservative, safe, uncontroversial, White, and middle class, as opposed to the more political and edgy poetry of Sandburg and Brooks), and, eventually, a "poetry of the playground" (p. x) that was more experimental, playful, and child-centered in its use of humor, initiated by Ciardi and Roethke and eventually leading to the poetry of Jack Prelutsky and Shel Silverstein.

In laying out the early stages of poetry written expressly for children during this time, Thomas traces the poetic histories of Frost, Sandburg, and Brooks, who rose to prominence during the middle of the century. According to Thomas, American politics and pedagogy privileged Frost at the expense of the others. In the 1930s and 1940s, Sandburg was considered to be "the poet of the future, the poet of America" (Niven, 1991, p. 376), but he eventually was eclipsed by Frost in the 1950s, and in 1961, it was Frost who was invited to present the inaugural poem when Kennedy was sworn in as president of the United States.

Thomas maintains that it was Frost's poetic conservativism and traditionalism that led him to surpass Sandburg in popularity and to become the most influential poet for students in the mid- to late 20th century and beyond. Frost, a New England poet acknowledged as "probably the greatest traditionalist in twentieth-century American poetry" (Gray, 1990, p. 131), produced work that lent itself to interpretive strategies that privileged certain types of poetic complexity and that deemed as "high quality" those poems that were appropriate for explication using New Critical methods, allowing for structured extraction of an ethical principle, equating theme with meaning, and rewarding formal textual features over voice, and universalism over regionalism.

Indeed, one of the reasons Frost's work has found such

a home in primary and secondary education is its teachability. Randall Jarrell (1996) explains, "metre, stanza form, rhyme, alliteration, quantity, and so on" are the least important qualities of poetry—qualities that "criticism has paid…an altogether disproportionate amount of attention [to]—partly, I suppose, because they are things any child can point at, drawn diagrams of, and count" (p. 697). We would add that they are also matters on which teachers can lecture, test and evaluate—much more easily than they can teach and evaluate the political leaning of poets and poems that seek to disrupt the existing social order or introduce "troublesome" topics in the classroom.

In contrast to Frost, whose work was viewed as "universal" in theme and structure, Sandburg and Brooks were viewed as limited by geography and politics. Sandburg was a midwesterner who wrote in free verse, and was—along with being a poet—both an activist and an author for children, while Brooks, an African American poet who looked unflinchingly at the lives of children in the south side of Chicago, was considered a "regional" black poet (when her work was included in anthologies or taught, it was accompanied by reassurances that it would have appeal *in spite of* her race). Because the poetry of Sandburg and Brooks (along with the poetry of Langston Hughes, and later June Jordan and Nikki Giovanni) was highly political in theme and form, it was rarely included in anthologies for children and was seldom taught by teachers in American schools; as poets, they were excluded or marginalized largely because of the overtly political nature and historical situatedness of their work.

Thomas (2007) notes that in classrooms in the middle of the century, "Brooks's poetry was depoliticized, Sandburg's poetry fell from esteem, and Frost's poetry replaced Sandburg's as a necessary part of all American children's poetic diet" (pp. 16–17), mostly because "the United States public…saw Frost primarily as an apolitical poet who spoke timeless truths in clear, finely wrought lines" (p. 9). Thus, the privileging of Frost over Sandburg and Brooks gives an indication of what was considered to be an appropriate "fit" between public poetry and politics, as well as what it meant to be "American."

Domesticated Playground Poetry: From Ciardi and Roethke to Silverstein and Prelutsky

In addition to the "official school poetry" of Frost, the later 20th century saw the ascendancy of a different sort of children's poetry in the U.S., Britain, and Australia. It is poetry produced for children *as children*: adult-produced "playground poetry" (Thomas, 2007). If official school poetry is notable for its apparent teachability and its use of literary devices, then, by contrast, the poetry of the playground defies this sort of canonical categorization. It is the playful, irreverent, sometimes offensive poetry that culminates with the work of contemporary poets Prelutsky and Silverstein, but that marks the transition from canonical poetry to what has been labeled "urchin poetry"—the poetry of the street, the poetry of resistance and subversion that delights the child reader. Thomas (2007) sees this playground poetry as "domesticated" (p. 61) because although it contains elements of child-produced playground poetry (subversion, anarchy, mockery, irony, and edgy play), it is not truly children's *own* poetry—that is, poetry produced by children. Instead, it is created, published, disseminated, and purchased by adults with differing agendas. Still, it is read by children for the sake of pleasure and delight, as well as for resistance to authority and the undermining of adult values, rules, and perspectives—even if this resistance and undermining occurs in a controlled and adult-determined way.

In her history of poetry for children, scholar Morag Styles (1998) traces this urchin poetry back to the work of British poet Michael Rosen in the 1970s; leaving behind the pastoral themes of previous generations of poetry written for or given to children, this poetry depicts the authentic underside of life for young children (particularly urban children) with its complexities, nastiness, and subversive humor. X.J. Kennedy (1994) traces the origins of urchin verse even further back, to the shift from mid-century light verse and nature poetry to the U.S. poet John Ciardi. In *The Reason for the Pelican* (1959), Ciardi—who was a lauded poet in the world of "adult poetry"—positions his work in contrast to the pastoral countrysides of Frost's New England to explore the suburbs with irreverent playfulness. As Thomas (2007) says, "Ciardi's poetry does not yoke the child to nature, nor does it idealize or fetishize the child" (p. 63). Yet, Ciardi did intend for his poetry to educate his young readers; the voice he uses for his poetry for children is different from the voice he uses for adults—his tone is straightforward, with internal and end rhymes and surprising use of enjambment, as if, according to Thomas, he wishes to *teach* his child readers the musical vocabulary of poetic craft.

Ciardi's entrance into the world of poetry for children helped modify how the establishment viewed this poetry, even as his poems offered a prototype for urchin poetry to come. Ciardi was responsible to a large extent for the change in climate that allowed a poet for adults to publish a collection of children's verse without being exiled from the literary world at large. Within two years, another poet highly regarded in the world of poetry for adults published a collection of poetry for children: *I Am! Says the Lamb*, by Theodore Roethke (1961)—a collection in which he borrowed from nursery rhyme symbols and other appeals to the child's unconscious. Roethke's poetry for children does not continue in the vein of urban "urchin" poetry; he writes of the natural world, and even his nonsense verse resists the urban focus of most urchin poetry. Where Ciardi seemed to tease the young reader, Roethke seemed more protective and inclusive of his young audience. According to Thomas (2007), "Ciardi's and Roethke's success, coupled with their interest in the folk tradition, in playground poetry, nursery rhymes, and their insistence on including

violence and unpleasantness, created the environment in which subsequent children's poets could thrive" (p. 77). Such subsequent poets include Silverstein and Prelutsky in the United States, Michael Rosen in Britain, Dennis Lee in Canada, and Steven Herrick in Australia, all of whose works mark early forays into the territory of adult-produced playground poetry.

In moving from Ciardi and Roethke (as well as contemporaries Randall Jarrell and Richard Wilbur) to Silverstein and Prelutsky, it is tempting to adopt an attitude of condescension. With their rhymed undercutting of authority and their celebration of topics that border on off-limits to adults, Silverstein and Prelutsky are exceedingly popular with young readers, but are often disdained by adults. They actually *make money* writing rhyme and meter—something few poets for adults manage. And although Silverstein has done some publishing for adults, the work for which they are most known is aimed at children. They are, first and foremost, poets for children—not simply the most famous authors of *urchin poetry* in the United States; they are also the most famous authors of *children's poetry* in the United States—and, perhaps, in the world. This presents a bit of a problem: Although contemporary poetry for children is much wider than the hyper-popular work of Silverstein and Prelutsky, researchers have found that preservice teachers coming into their poetry course were hard-pressed to name a poet for children beyond these two super-powers (Certo, Apol, Hawkins, & Wibbens, 2009). Moreover, these were almost exclusively the only poetry works these future teachers reported planning to bring into the classroom with their future students.

But while critics may feel justified in dismissing these writers as "merely" popular, Sorby (2005) sees these poets as part of the history of linking children and poetry (that is, verse) that reaches back to the 19th century, maintaining that "These authors echo and extend the innovative, playful uses of rhyme, meter, and illustration introduced by *St. Nicholas*, and their tremendous popularity takes for granted (and perpetuates) a 'natural' connection between children and poetry" (p. 188). She continues, "The infantilization of American poetry began in the nineteenth century, but it did not end there; popular verse forms became—and remain—forms of American childhood" (p. 189). And Thomas (2007) urges a more thoughtful consideration of Silverstein's and Prelutsky's work as examples of a tradition that borrows from, participates in, and in some ways resists the older traditions of poetry used to assimilate, to indoctrinate and to instruct.

Regardless of their liabilities or merits, it is certainly true that these poets have tapped into the most primitive roots of poetry for children—that is, oral performance and the ongoing appeal of Goatfoot, Milktongue and Twinbird. Their rollicking rhythms and rhymes delight children, and their irreverent content promotes the spirit of youthful anarchy (or at least pseudo-anarchy), providing children with an occasion to test the rules and to imagine pushing against them. Nevertheless, both poets are aware of the socializing function of poetry and are not above moralizing. They are always adults, writing for children—"domesticated," in part, because the adult-driven world of poetry for children demands such domestication (Thomas, 2007, p. 81).

Contemporary Poetry for Children

Although Prelutsky and Silverstein dominate on home bookshelves, in bookstores, and in public and school libraries, they are often not the poets included in basal readers, in university textbooks created for pre-service teachers, or in professional journal articles for teachers of the English Language Arts. There are currently many other poets who write for children. Some of these poets produce rhymed verse; some write in forms that resist the heavy rhythm and rhymes for which the adult-sanctioned playground poets are known. As Sloan (2001) has observed, "At the beginning of the twentieth century, the number of poets whose works were intended solely for children was relatively small. At the century's end, however, poetry and verse for children is a burgeoning field, the roster of writers lengthy and growing" (p. 47).

The question, however, is whether all this activity in the past 50 years (and, in particular, in the past 10 years) is positive activity. In the last several decades, almost every article on poetry for children has lamented the sorry state of the field, with ongoing jeremiads filling the pages of publications for teachers, teacher educators, and scholars of children's literature. Before examining the field of contemporary writers and their poetic contributions, we present this ongoing debate about the current state of poetry for children.

Views of Poetry for Children in Contemporary Society

Many of the adults who would bring poetry to children, and many of the children for whom these poems are written and published, have little sense of the range and the scope of the field of contemporary poetry for children. They view "poetry" and "verse" as interchangeable, and there is no question that there is plenty of "verse" that is currently published for children. Certainly Silverstein and Prelutsky fall into this category, but so do dozens of books released each year—with some books of verse being fresher and more clever than others. In 1980, in a special issue of the *Children's Literature Quarterly* devoted to poetry, noted scholar of children's literature Alethea Helbig had the following to say about contemporary versifiers:

> While it is good that nonsense continues to be recognized as a valuable and exciting part of a child's literary diet, enough is enough.... It makes one wonder whether those responsible for putting out [collections of verse for children] have a sense of the difference between good and bad poems, or whether they feel that almost anything is good enough for the young as long as it jingles, is easily assimilated, and, especially, is short and funny. (p. 39)

When Helbig lamented the sorry state of poetry for children in the United States, she was only adding her voice to a chorus that sounds throughout the second half of the 20th century and continues into this century as well. For example, Tarr and Flynn (2002) assert that

> Unquestionably, we live in anti-poetic times. Poetry has become dispensable in an age that values information over art, and consequently fewer and fewer of our teachers seem equipped to teach poetry to our children. We have become shortsighted, paying less and less critical and pedagogical attention to children's poetry. (p. 2)

Such observations are not limited to children's literature scholars writing in professional journals. In 1991, in *The New York Times,* poet and anthologizer Liz Rosenberg writes, "Verse is childlike—but in our childish age, childlike things are despised" (para. 10), the result being that "Children's verse seems, partly by default and partly by definition, to be poetry too silly, trivial, old-fashioned or slack for adult readers" (para. 3).

Two themes seem to echo across the years: the poor content of contemporary poetry for children and the shoddy presentation of contemporary poetry for children. "Poor content" extends both to the choices of topic, as well as to the choice of form for poetry for children. In 1975, poet and critic Myra Cohn Livingston wrote, "Teachers, educators, and commercial publishers catering to schools often foster shabby, poorly rhymed, didactic, and Truth, Beauty, and Wisdom poems" (p. 579). And 16 years later, Rosenberg (1991) wrote, "many children's anthologies restrict themselves to short, lyric poems about the seasons, furry animals and national holidays—as if children never thought about God, love, death or any of the other great themes of poetry" (para. 6). No wonder poetry is viewed as something childlike and childish, as something that is "outgrown" by most adults, left behind in the nursery or the elementary school, and revisited seldom if at all.

In addition to bemoaning the content of poems for children, scholars of children's literature also bemoan the presentation of that poetry for children. Helbig (1980) herself addressed this when she wrote that the trend in over-illustrating children's poetry was "embarrassing because it implies… that poems no matter how good need fetching pictures to bolster them…and… if they're bad, some pretty illustrations will compensate for their poetic inadequacy" (p. 39).

Livingston (1984) lays the blame for the lack of high quality poetry on society at large when she writes, "Poetry dies in the schools too often because in this society it is not respected. It is tacked onto language arts, it is mutilated by gimmickry, it is castigated as a frill. It is thought of as some esoteric region of the mind, as a luxury" (p. 309).

And, of course, there is the base assumption—even on the part of well-meaning teachers, parents and librarians—that uninspired rhyme and narrative free verse are age appropriate for and popular among children. These beliefs on the part of adults about what children will like and understand become self-fulfilling prophecies; after years of encountering poems with thumping rhythms and rhymes, children *do* come to believe poems must adhere to predictable patterns and that they are about nature, funny stories, or love (Apol & Harris, 1999). And once children associate certain characteristics with poetry, they are more likely to resist the introduction of poetry that is more substantive, that has depth and craft, that challenges readers with both its content and its form. Flynn (1993) suggests that although children may initially be drawn to poetry that is simplistic in content and form, "we are doing them a disservice if we encourage them to retain that preference into adulthood" (p. 41).

In fact, for many contemporary scholars of poetry, the line between adult and children's poetry is—and always has been—blurred. Flynn maintains, "The idea that an innocent and separate realm of children's poetry should exist at all is questionable at best, and it has led to a narrower, more circumscribed notion of poetry reflected in contemporary anthologies" (pp. 40–41). At the very least, if children's poetry is going to exist in a category of its own, it should have the potential to remain important to the reader well beyond childhood.

Poems that children can appreciate into adulthood *can* be found, but for most parents and educators, the challenge is separating the wheat from the chaff. Who are the poets whose work grows with readers and allows those young readers to grow? To begin to answer this question, we turn to the world of contemporary poetry for children: the awards provided; the innovations taking place; the inclusion of wider audiences, forms and themes; and the return to oral and aural experiences of poetry.

Awards for Poetry for Children

As poets, scholars, educators, and publishers have begun to recognize the important role poetry can play in the lives of contemporary children, several literacy and literature organizations have created awards to encourage, identify and reward quality and excellence in poetry for children. In this section, we include only awards given exclusively to poets or collections of poems for children, though many works of poetry for young people have won other literary awards, such as the Newbery or Caldecott (which are examined in detail by Junko Yokota in her chapter in this volume).

In 1977, The National Council of Teachers of English established an Award for Excellence in Poetry for Children to honor a living American poet or anthologist for his or her work for children ages 3–13. The award is presented every other year for a poet's aggregate work—its potential for growth and evolution in terms of craft and its overall excellence. Although the appeal to children of a poet's or anthologist's work is an important consideration, the art and craft of the poetry is the primary criterion for evaluation.

The Lee Bennett Hopkins Promising Poet Award is given by the International Reading Association every three years to a promising new poet of poetry for children up to Grade 12. The award is for published works only, and to fit the designation of "new," the poet may have published no more than two books of poetry for children. Poetry in any language is considered, though non-English poetry must be accompanied by an English translation. Many of the early winners of this award have gone on to become highly regarded contributors to the world of poetry for children.

Perhaps the most interesting of the awards given to poetry for children is granted by the scholarly journal of children's literature, *The Lion and the Unicorn*, which initiated a poetry feature modeled on the annual poetry award essays published between 1979 and 2001 in the British children's literature journal, *Signal*. When *Signal* ceased publication in August 2003, *The Lion and the Unicorn* continued the *Signal* tradition of publishing the award along with a discussion about each year's publications of poetry for children—though the focus shifted from poetry collections published in the United Kingdom to those from North America (the Centre of Literacy in Primary Education continues with a British poetry award, but with no accompanying essay). As with the *Signal* essays, the long essays published in *The Lion and the Unicorn* deal with Winners, Honor Books, books of note, and some notably disappointing patterns in the publication of poetry for children. Across the years, the essays have had a profound influence on poets and publishers, as well as on the people charged with choosing and circulating poetry among children, calling attention to new work that might otherwise have been overlooked.

Undoubtedly, the most prestigious award in the world of poetry for children is the honor of being named Children's Poet Laureate by the Poetry Foundation—an award granted to Jack Prelutsky as the first children's poet laureate in 2006, and to Mary Ann Hoberman in 2008. According to the Poetry Foundation press release (2006), the findings from the Poetry Foundation's research study, *Poetry in America*, demonstrate that "a lifelong love for poetry is most likely to result if cultivated early in childhood and reinforced thereafter." Therefore, during laureateship, the Children's Poet Laureate gives two major public readings for children and their families, teachers, and librarians. He or she also serves as an advisor to the Poetry Foundation on children's literature, and may engage in a variety of projects and events "to help instill a love of poetry among the nation's youngest readers." The Poetry Foundation makes the appointment with input from a panel of experts in the field of children's literature.

Recent Trends in Poetry for Children

In recent years, there are many changes that have taken place in the world of poetry for children. In looking at recent trends, we see several themes that run across the last decade of poetry for children: changes of authorship, changes of imagined audience, reconfiguration of poetic forms, inclusion of a range of cultures, and the re-emphasis on poetry performance.

Authorship. The debate that raged between Koch and Livingston about whether or not young writers should or should not be termed "poets," and whether the writings they produced should be considered "poetry," continues. Most teachers of writing and most poets who work with young people in the schools seem to lean in the direction of affirmation of young writers. And in spite of Livingston's passionate disavowal of children's work as "poetry," there are some recent collections of poetry authored by young writers that contain notable poems in the voices of young writers—two, in particular, edited by Betsy Franco: *You Hear Me?: Poems and Writing by Teenage Boys* (2001a) and *Things I Have to Tell You: Poems and Writing by Teenage Girls* (2001b). As well, Bill Aguado and Richard Newirth (2003) have edited a collection called *Paint Me Like I Am: Teen Poems from WritersCorp,* Lee Francis (1999) has collected the voices of Native American youth in *When The Rain Sings: Poems By Young Native Americans*, and Naomi Shihab Nye (2000) has collected responses to her poetry workshops in the schools in *Salting the Ocean: 100 Poems by Young People.* Younger writers are collected in an anthology by Davida Adedjouma, R. Gregory Christie, and Lucille Clifton (1998), entitled *The Palm of my Heart.* In addition to book publications, there are several published periodicals (such as *Cricket, Spider, Stone Soup,* and *New Moon*) that showcase the talents of young writers. Mostly, however, today's young writers are publishing their work online on websites too numerous to list.

Intended Audience. If once the border between poems for adults and poems for children was blurred because adult poems were adopted by (or imposed upon) children in schools, in the last decade, writers of fine poetry for children have earned the attention of the literary world beyond juvenile booklists. One writer in particular, Marilyn Nelson, has done more than any other poet to blur the line between poems published for children (that is, identified as "children's poetry" on publishers' lists, in libraries and in bookstores), and those that are read, studied and awarded by adults.

In all her recent work for children, Nelson (2001, 2004, 2005, 2008) writes within and often manipulates traditional poetic forms and line structures. For example, *A Wreath for Emmett Till* (2005) is a poetic retelling of the story of Emmett Till, the 14-year-old African American boy who was lynched in Mississippi for supposedly whistling at a White woman. Nelson re-creates Till's story in a heroic crown of sonnets—15 poems in the Petrarchan rhyme scheme, with the last line of one poem being the first line of the next, and each of the first lines of the first 14 poems making up the entirety of the 15th poem.

While certainly there are other poets whose work for

children is picked up and appreciated by adults, perhaps none so skillfully blur those boundaries as Nelson, effectively countering any claim that poetry for children is too simple, silly, uninspired, childish, or childlike for adults.

Forms. In addition to the blurring of notions of authorship and audience, publication of poetry for children in recent years has also blurred notions of poetic genre or form. Parodies, concrete poems, poems based on music or art, poems for multiple voices, themed anthologies, linked poems, and novels written in the form of poems are just a few of the ways poetry for children is re-defining its boundaries. Many of the awards for children's literature and children's poetry have gone to these various hybrids (or slippages) of genre: Newbery awards for poems for two voices and verse novels, IRA awards for linked poems, and *The Lion and the Unicorn* awards going to parodies, concrete poems, poems for multiple voices, and verse novels.

When done well (which is often the exception rather than the rule) each of these forms and genres (or cross-genres) offers something of value to the world of poetry for children. Parodies do not simply imitate the structure of the original poem on which they are based; they bring young readers back to those poems to allow children to hear the dialogue (in play or in conflict) between poets and poems; they call attention to the inter- and intra-textual nuances of language; and they expand the expectations children have for experimenting with the language of poems. Concrete poems make visible the form of poems, the interplay of text and space, the ways the meaning of language expands beyond its symbolic boundaries. Poems based on music or art cross artistic media, helping turn art into words that reflect, expand on, and engage with non-verbal media. Poems for multiple voices call attention to the weaving of sound and silence, the aural and oral qualities of Goatfoot, Milktongue and Twinbird being spoken aloud. And themed anthologies put poems in conversation with one another, creating an over-arching sense of connection and (sometimes) progression between and among groups of poems.

Finally, the "verse novel," which is perhaps the most popular (for writers and for readers) of the genre-blurring forms of poetry for children, and the one that has exploded on the poetry scene in the past two decades, makes explicit the narrative qualities of a series of poems. Mike Cadden, in this volume, examines the verse novel as a special category of the novel, but because it also represents such a recent innovation in the world of poetry for children, we will give it some attention here as well.

The verse novel is characterized by a series of short, individual poems linked by topic, character, and plot, though it is the inclusion of *plot* that differentiates this form from a collection of poems on a theme. Most often, the poems are arranged in chronological order, though occasionally the novel may be comprised of "a collage of fragments without a meta-narrative" (Alexander, 2005, p. 272). While it is possible to read each poem individually, the ordering of the poems is important to the developing narrative line; thus the reader of the text is encouraged to proceed in a linear fashion just as the reader of a prose novel is encouraged to read chapter by chapter as the novel unfolds. In this way, novels in verse formalize the way a book of poetry is read. As Flynn, Hager, and Thomas (2005) explain,

> By highlighting the paths that lead from one poem to another, verse-novelists draw attention to the book as a constructed whole, with a pattern and a logic to its design. Similarly, verse-novels guide the reader from one poem to the next, privileging the plot of the collection and celebrating the way in which one poem leads (or doesn't seem to lead) to the next. (p. 429)

While many teachers have turned to verse novels as a straightforward, brief and "non-threatening" way to lure reluctant readers into books (as Cadden notes, Chapter 21, this volume), we would argue that this is a serious misunderstanding of the complexity and power of verse novels. Indeed, even the designation of "verse novel" is a misnomer, since most of these novels exhibit regular speech patterns rather than the rhythm and rhyme implied in the term "verse" (see Apol, 2005). When done well (that is, when comprised of "real" poetry rather than prose that is merely indented and lineated to appear to be a poem), verse novels are generally *more* rather than less difficult to read and comprehend. The multilayered nature of the verse novel encourages readers to explore what is implied rather than what is simply described or stated in any single poem; as a result, there is not only density of meaning within each poem, but also in the juxtaposition of the poems within the novel sequence that allows for meaning to lie between (or across) the poems (Halliday, 2003).

Because these novels are often internal monologues, they can contain "crafted language and memorable story-telling" (Alexander, 2005, p. 281). However, the same elements that give the form its richness of possibility also present the writer with particular challenges:

> The handling of the verse may be sloppy, inadequate, uninteresting, arbitrary. The plot may be ineffectively realised through the medium. The verse-novel foregrounds the fact that the narration is voiced, which can give rise to difficulties…. The form lends itself to the confessional and to the expression of feelings, which raises the spectre of banality or melodrama. (p. 281)

Ultimately, the poetic form may serve as nothing more than a plot delivery device, where the only thing that marks the narrative as "verse" is the length of the lines and the ways ordinary sentences have been chopped into something that *looks* like a poem.

That is not to say that there are not verse novels that demonstrate both engaging story-telling and good poetry. For instance, Virginia Euwer Wolff's (1993) *Make*

Lemonade—a book that is often considered to be the first verse novel—captures the intimacy and immediacy of the narrator's thoughts through poems that attend to the voice, the ear, and the breathing rhythms of the speaker. Karen Hesse (1997) tells the story of the Oklahoma Dust Bowl in *Out of the Dust* in a way that is as spare and emaciated as the bare bones of the poems themselves. And Sharon Creech emphasizes a sort of pedagogy of poetry as her protagonist learns to write his own poetry through the use of models in *Love that Dog* (2001) and *Hate That Cat* (2008).

Culture. If, in the past, poems were written by white men and recited by schoolchildren in an effort to create like-minded citizens and shore up a unified democracy, then in recent years there has been an acknowledgement that the voices of poetry (read and heard) should represent a variety of cultures expressed in poetic form, language, and experience. And if, in the past, the poems focused on the glorification of American history (with silence around issues of the genocide and extermination of Native peoples and African slaves, along with a reluctance to examine the immigrant experience and ongoing discrimination based on gender, race, culture or religion), then it has only been in the late 20th century that children in schools have begun to be given poems by poets who represent racial, ethnic, or religious diversity. James Damico (2005) explains that children now have access to poems that feature political and social themes with a speaker narrating or describing an experience of discrimination. Once considered "troublesome topics" in classrooms, the themes of slavery, violence, racism, and immigration are now part of a wider world of poetry for children through poems by and about people with diverse cultural and linguistic backgrounds, and there is a growing canon of poetry for children on issues of social justice. This represents a major development in the world of poetry for children.

Poets in recent years have introduced English-speaking children to a range of cross-cultural poetic forms. From the haiku of Issa, to Japanese sijo (Park, 2007), to Middle Eastern ghazals (Nye, 2000), poets and anthologists have published collections of poetry from around the world, speaking in the words and conveying the experiences of culturally and ethnically diverse national and international groups.

Presentation. The roots of poetry are in orality, for poems were intended to be chanted or sung. While English-language poetry was moving away (both developmentally and culturally) from its oral roots toward literate and literary abstraction, toward "words-on-the-page," visual play, and what Fahamisha Patricia Brown (1999) calls "psychological self-probing" (p. 63), African American poetry, along with other poetic traditions rooted in oral cultures (e.g., Caribbean poetry), maintained or returned to the larger traditions from which they came. Brown explains "African world cultures value word skills, poetry making, story telling, and the literacy extensions of… public activities; they rely on an audience that is hearing as well as reading" (p. 29).

Rooted in oral cultures from around the world, there is a growing, widespread, renewed interest in spoken poetry, as signaled by the emergence of poetry slams and the re-emergence of the spoken word (Eleveld & Smith, 2004; Glazner, 2000). Much of this oral and aural renewal hearkens back to the Harlem Renaissance in the 1920s when there was a focus on the intimate relationship between the oral and the literate through African American expression in poetry, prose, music, dance and theatre (Fisher, 2003). Publishers are responding by making available hip-hop, rap, and spoken word poetry, with publications often accompanied by a CD.

Conclusion

Poetry for children—feast or famine? A burgeoning field or a sorry state? Across the generations, the ongoing development of poetry *for children*—sometimes distinct from, sometimes synonymous with, always in relationship to the wider world of poetry—has both linked and recognized the already-existing link between children and poems. Sometimes a tool, sometimes a treat, to educate or to delight, a way of instructing, informing, celebrating, and engaging—poetry has offered much to children of the past and continues to offer much to contemporary children as well. The reinvigoration of the field is heartening; the persistent challenge for literary critics, educators, librarians, and poets themselves is to deepen our critical explorations as our understandings of poetry, children, and poetry for children continue to evolve.

Literature References

Adedjouma, D., Christie, R. G., & Clifton, L. (1998). *The palm of my heart*. New York, NY: Lee & Low.

Aguado, B., & Newirth, R. (2003). *Paint me like I am: Teen poems from WritersCorp*. New York, NY: HarperTeen.

Baring-Gould, S., & Baring-Gould, C. (Eds). (1962). *The annotated mother goose*. New York, NY: Bramhall.

Bianchi, M. D. (1924). *The life & letters of Emily Dickinson*. Boston, MA: Houghton Mifflin.

Ciardi, J. (1959). *The reason for the pelican* (M. Gekiere, Illus.). Philadelphia, PA: Lippincott.

Coleridge, S. T. (1836). *Specimens of the table talk of Samuel Taylor Coleridge* (2nd ed.) H. N. Coleridge (Ed.). London, England: John Murray.

Creech, S. (2001). *Love that dog*. New York, NY: HarperCollins.

Creech, S. (2008). *Hate that cat*. New York, NY: HarperCollins.

Francis, L. (1999). *When the rain sings: Poems by young Native Americans*. New York, NY: Simon & Schuster.

Franco, B. (Ed.). (2001a). *You hear me?: Poems and writing by teenage boys*. Cambridge, MA: Candlewick Press.

Franco, B. (Ed.). (2001b). *Things I have to tell you: Poems and writing by teenage girls*. Cambridge, MA: Candlewick Press.

Hall, D. (1985). *The Oxford book of children's verse in America*. New York, NY: Oxford University Press.

Hesse, K. (1997). *Out of the dust*. New York, NY: Scholastic Paperbacks.

Kennedy, X. J. (1994). Afterword. In J. Ciardi. *The reason for the pelican* (pp. 61-64). Honesdale, PA: Boyds Mill.

Nelson, M. (2001). *Carver: A life in poems*. Honesdale, PA: Front Street.

Nelson, M. (2004). *Fortune's bones: The manumission requiem*. Honesdale, PA: Front Street.

Nelson, M. (2005). *A wreath for Emmett Till*. Boston, MA: Houghton Mifflin.

Nelson, M. (2008). *The freedom business: Including a narrative of the life and adventure of Venture, a native of Africa*. Honesdale, PA: Front Street.

New England Primer. (1777). Retrieved on February 12, 2010, from http://www.sacred-texts.com/chr/nep/1777/index.htm (Original work published 1687)

Nye, N. S. (2000) *Salting the ocean: 100 poems by young poets*. New York, NY: Greenwillow.

Park, L. S. (2007). *Tap dancing on the roof: Sijo*. New York, NY: Clarion.

Roethke, T. (1961). *I am! says the lamb*. Garden City, NY: Doubleday.

Wolff, V. E. (1993). *Make lemonade*. New York, NY: Henry Holt.

Academic References

Alexander, J. (2005). The verse-novel: A new genre. *Children's Literature in Education*, 36(3), 269–283.

Apol, L. (2005). The politics of genre: Content and form in the poemic novel. Paper presented in the panel, "Where have all the narratives gone?: Children's novels in the form of poetry, police report, and online entry," (L. Apol, chair). Modern Critical Approaches to Children's Literature Conference, Nashville, TN.

Apol, L., & Harris, J. (1999). Joyful noises: Creating poems for voices and ears. *Language Arts*, 76(4), 314–322.

Apol-Obbink, L. (1990). The primacy of poetry: Oral culture and the young child. *The New Advocate*, 3, 277–234.

Barr, J. (2006, Sept. 18). Is it poetry or is it verse? Retrieved February 20, 2010, from http://www.poetryfoundation.org/journal/article.html?id=178645

Brown, F. P. (1999). *Performing the word: African American poetry as vernacular culture*. Piscataway, NJ: Rutgers University Press.

Certo, J. (2004). Cold plums and the old men in the water: Let children read and write "great" poetry. *The Reading Teacher*, 58, 266–271.

Certo, J. L., Apol, L., Hawkins, L., & Wibbens, E. (2009). The case for poetry in teacher education: Preservice teachers' genre knowledge and development in a university-based course. Proceedings from AERA '09: *The Annual Conference of the American Educational Research Association*. San Diego, CA.

Clark, L. (1980). Poetry unfettered. *Children's Literature Association Quarterly*, 5(2), 10–13.

Damico, J. (2005). Evoking hearts and heads: Exploring issues of social justice through poetry. *Language Arts*, 83(2), 137–146.

Eleveld, M., & Smith, M. (2004). *The spoken word revolution: Slam, hip hop & the poetry of a new generation*. Naperville, IL: Sourcebooks.

Elster, C. A. (2000). Entering and opening the world of a poem. *Language Arts*, 78(1), 71–76.

Fisher, M. (2003). Open mics and open minds: Spoken word poetry in African Diaspora Participatory Literacy Communities. *Harvard Educational Review*, 73(3), 362–389.

Flynn, R. (1993). Can children's poetry matter? *The Lion and the Unicorn*, 17(1), 37–44.

Flynn, R. (2000). "The kindergarten of new consciousness": Gwendolyn Brooks and the social construction of childhood-critical essay. *African American Review, 34*(3), 483–499.

Flynn, R. (2003). Consolation prize. *SIGNAL Approaches to Children's Books, 100*, 66–83.

Flynn, R. (2006). The "infantilization" of American poetry. *Children's Literature, 34*, 222–227.

Flynn, R., Hager, K., & Thomas, J. T. Jr. (2005). It could be verse: The 2005 *Lion and the Unicorn* Award for Excellence in North American Poetry. *The Lion and the Unicorn, 29*(3), 427–441.

Galda, L., Cullinan, B., & Sipe, L. (2009). *Literature & the child.* Belmont, CA: Wadsworth Cengage Learning.

Glazner, G. M. (2000). *Poetry slam: The competitive art of performance poetry.* San Francisco, CA: Manic D Press.

Gray, R. (1990). *American poetry in the twentieth century.* New York, NY: Pearson Longman.

Halliday, A. (2003). Poetry in Australia: A modern dilemma. *The Lion & the Unicorn, 27*(2), 218–234.

Havelock, E. (1986). *The muse learns to write: Reflections on orality and literacy from antiquity to the present.* New Haven, CT: Yale University Press.

Helbig, A. K. (1980). The state of things: A question of substance. *Children's Literature Association Quarterly, 5*(2), 38–45.

Jarrell, R. (1996). Levels and opposites: Structure in poetry. *Georgia Review, 50*(4), 697–713.

Johnson, D. (2009). *The joy of children's literature.* Boston, MA: Houghton Mifflin.

Koch, K. (1970). *Wishes, lies, and dreams: Teaching children to write poetry.* New York, NY: HarperPaperbacks.

Livingston, M. C. (1975). But is it poetry? (Part 1). *The Horn Book Magazine, 51*, 571–580.

Livingston, M. C. (1976). But is it poetry? (Part 2). *The Horn Book Magazine, 52*, 24–31.

Livingston, M. C. (1984). *The child as poet: Myth or reality?* Boston, MA: The Horn Book.

NCTE. (2009). NCTE award for excellence in poetry for children. Retrieved on February 25, 2010, from http://www.ncte.org/awards/poetry

Niven, P. (1991). *Carl Sandburg: A biography.* New York, NY: Charles Scribner's Sons.

Nodelman, P., & Reimer, M. (2003). *The pleasures of children's literature* (3rd ed.). Boston, MA: Allyn & Bacon.

Ong, W. (1982). *Orality and literacy: The technologizing of the word.* New York, NY: Methuen.

Paul, L. (2005). "Writing poetry for children is a curious occupation": Ted Hughes and Sylvia Plath. *The Horn Book Magazine, 81*(3), 257–267.

Poetry Foundation. (2006). Poetry Foundation names Jack Prelutsky first Children's Poet Laureate. Retrieved on February 25, 2010, from http://www.poetryfoundation.org/foundation/release_092706.html

Rosenberg, L. (1991). Has poetry for kids become a child's garden of rubbish? *New York Times Book Review, 55.* Retrieved on February 25, 2010, from http://www.nytimes.com/1991/11/10/books/children-s-books-has-poetry-for-kids-become-a-child-s-garden-of-rubbish.html?pagewanted=1

Rubin, J. S. (2007). *Songs of ourselves: The uses of poetry in America.* Cambridge, MA: The Belknap Press of Harvard University Press.

Sloan, G. (2001). But is it poetry? *Children's Literature in Education. 32*(1), 45–55.

Sorby, A. (2005). *Schoolroom poets: Childhood, performance, and the place of American poetry, 1865–1917.* Durham: University of New Hampshire Press.

Styles, M. (1998). *From the garden to the street: Three hundred years of poetry for children.* Herndon, VA: Cassell.

Tarr A., & Flynn, R. (2002). "The trouble isn't making poems, the trouble's finding somebody that will listen to them": Negotiating a place for poetry in children's literature studies. *Children's Literature Association Quarterly, 27*(1), 2–3.

Thomas, J. T., Jr. (2007). *Poetry's playground: The culture of contemporary American children's poetry.* Detroit, MI: Wayne State University Press.

Point of Departure

Janet S. Wong

In 1992, I signed up for Myra Cohn Livingston's "Beginning Class in Poetry" through UCLA Extension. I had no intention of writing poetry. I wanted simply to learn about rhyme, repetition, and rhythm—a poet's tools—so that I could write the next *Goodnight Moon*. I had heard Myra speak at a one-day seminar and her reading of "There Was a Place" made me blink back tears. It was a sad poem in plain, simple language about the loss of a father. This was not the kind of poem I read as a child. Those poems were full of complicated phrases that made my brain shut down. Poetry was the flowery stuff that flowed out of the mouth of Maurice, the warlock-father of Samantha on *Bewitched*. Any seven-year-old could see he was one weird guy; if Maurice liked poetry, I surely did not.

Myra did not talk much about her poems but simply read or recited them in a regular, non-dramatic voice. This, too, was new to me. I began to suspect what I would know with certainty a year later: When I decided in fourth grade that I hated poetry, I was wrong. What I hated was poetry homework, reciting poems in a "poetic voice," picking poems apart to find the "true meaning." I realized I hadn't known enough poetry to hate it. If someone had introduced me in second grade to Lucille Clifton's *Everett Anderson*, I would not have become a poetry-hater. If only I had known Arnold Adoff or Eve Merriam or Karla Kuskin or Myra Cohn Livingston, or any of the NCTE poets!

The first 50 or so poems that I wrote in Myra's class were silly verses about made-up things. I figured that I

JANET S. WONG

should try to write poems that could sell someday, in a book. What sold? Shel Silverstein and Jack Prelutsky, so I decided to try to write in their style. Myra gave these poems no praise at all; I wondered if she was even reading my work. About 100 poems into the class, I wrote "Waiting at the Railroad Cafe," a serious poem about race discrimination—specifically, an incident in which my father and I were not served in a restaurant. This earned a "v.g." from Myra—"very good"—the ultimate compliment. Instantly I knew what I needed to do: I had to dig for childhood memories.

"Campfire" sprang from a sliver of a memory of my first camping trip. From quick notes, two possible poems emerged: one about my dad, struggling with our tent, and another about my mom who, squatting by our campfire, told me that she grew up in the country, "real country," where she roasted chestnuts and grasshoppers as a child.

Being the child of Asian immigrants and one of a handful of Asians at two of my schools, my parents often reminded me that my whole people (or peoples, as I am both Chinese and Korean) would be judged by what I did. And so, between my handwritten notes and early scribbled drafts and my first typewritten draft, I chose to forget about grasshopper-eating and focus on chestnuts. Besides, Myra was not fond of "disgusting" poems. Here is Computer Draft #1:

Real Country
"This is the real country,"
my mother explains,
picking her teeth
as she squats near
the fire, pants rolled up.
We are roasting chestnuts.
"Here," she says, picking one
up with a thick green leaf.

This is the real country.

I stuck with chestnuts in Drafts #5–10. By Draft #10, I thought that poem was finished. I moved on, writing more poems for *A Suitcase of Seaweed*. Finished as I thought I was, though, the poem itself told me otherwise. Part of the poem-making process is fermentation, and as the poem sat in the computer, it started to stink.

Serious rethinking occurred in Draft #11. "Real country": those are the exact words that my mother uses when she describes her rural Korean village, Kum San, where tigers ate babies in the woods. But "real country" means nothing to most people. Real as opposed to what—"fake country"? How could I "show not tell" the reader about "real country"? Roasting chestnuts is authentic, and my mother has always enjoyed roasting them at holidays. But roasting chestnuts wasn't the interesting thing about her story. Besides, sophisticates from Seoul eat roasted chestnuts. New Yorkers eat chestnuts! But if you grew up in the "real country" of old Korea, you might find yourself eating something a little more unusual. Downright disgust-

ing. Knowing that Myra would approve of my adherence to authenticity, the grasshoppers came back.

Draft #11:

Campfire
Prodding the fire
with a strong thin
branch I found
when wandering
in the forest,
I squat next to Mother,
my pants rolled up
like hers, still wet
from washing dishes
in the river.
When she was my age,
she used to catch
grasshoppers,
build a fire
with the sparks
from rocks
and dry straw,
and eat them,
fresh, char-roasted,
whole, soft, succulent
grasshoppers.

When the fire is
spitting ready,
Mother gives me
the sign to go
get them.

Fresh, char-roasted,
whole, soft, succulent
marshmallows—
my kind of
grasshopper.

I didn't know, when I started writing that draft, that I would end the poem with the marshmallow stanza. I thought of it only when I sent my child-self to retrieve the grasshoppers. How could I—raised in Los Angeles on pizza, burgers, and burritos—possibly stomach grasshoppers? And would my mother, now so American, ever be able to chew a grasshopper again? No matter what they ate once upon a time in the old country, here we eat marshmallows.

Another significant change happened by the final draft, Draft #15: I deleted the squat. Having opened my people(s) up to some ridicule with the grasshoppers, I couldn't also subject them to the embarrassment of the squat. The Squat: This is something that I've seen dozens of Asians do—squat, rather than sit on the ground, where there isn't anywhere else to sit. Squatting is cleaner than sitting on the ground, but it looks so awkward. Maybe some non-Asian people squat this way, too, but I have never seen them. (Baseball catchers do not count.) It was time to dump the squat.

Draft #15 (almost final draft):

Campfire
Just think—
when Mother was my age,
she could build a fire
with sparks from rocks,
catch a bunch of
grasshoppers and
roast them whole
for a summer
night's snack!

"Get me a good stick,"
she says, "thin but strong,"
and I bring her one
from the woods
behind our tent.
On the way back
I see a brown bag
by her feet—
could it be?

When the fire is spitting
ready, she reaches in the bag,
rustling, and hands me
one big, fat, luscious
marshmallow.

The final change was made after my editor Margaret McElderry bought my manuscript. I don't remember if it was she or the copyeditor who made the suggestion, but someone thought that the word "ready," fourth line up from the bottom, should be moved up a line.

It took 10 months to write *A Suitcase of Seaweed*, mainly from 9 p.m. to 2 a.m. Not every poem in that book went through so many drafts, but usually I do write at least 10 drafts of each poem, and sometimes—especially when playing with alignment—up to 50. Even if I love the first draft, I try a second draft. I'm not trying to make it better, but simply to make it different. This was a lesson that Myra burned into us (as do all good teachers of writing): revise, revise, and revise again. One of her favorite exercises required us to change a poem from the narrative voice to the lyrical voice to the dramatic voices of apostrophe, conversation, and the mask. Some people practice writing until they get tired; we practiced getting tired of writing, which made a tenth draft seem quite regular and a fifth draft seem like we were just getting started.

With so few Asian American poets, I worry when I write something like "Campfire." I fear that I am reinforcing stereotypes—in this case, the stereotype that Asians eat strange things. But, (some) Asians (in Asia) do eat strange things. And when my mother was young, during the time of the Japanese occupation of Korea, it would not have been such a strange thing for a spunky farm girl, starving for a snack, to roast a handful of grasshoppers. I rely on my readers to read carefully, all the way to the last word. For this reason I write as plainly and simply as I can, hoping that my readers will see exactly what I mean.

Or, the magic of poetry: Maybe they will see something entirely different, see what they need to see. A middle school student once said, "The fire in 'Campfire' is supposed to represent the warmth of the family, right?" The idea had never occurred to me, but I liked it. I answered, "I guess you could think of it that way—why not?"

20

Nonfiction Literature for Children

Old Assumptions and New Directions

Barbara Kiefer and Melissa I. Wilson

The Ohio State University

In a literary world that foregrounds fiction, writers and illustrators of nonfiction often receive limited criticism—or praise—except from the young and adult readers who avidly pursue these books for topics of interest across the disciplines. Barbara Kiefer and Melissa Wilson ask what qualities distinguish nonfiction as a literary art form; and point out that for child audiences, the genre is often oriented to entertainment—so much so, that the facts may be distorted or mistaken altogether. They conclude their analysis, however, by pointing to promising research and criticism on the distinctive characteristics of nonfiction that authors, illustrators, and readers find notable and malleable for their own artistic—and learning—goals. In her Point of Departure essay, noted author, Penny Colman, approaches the questions raised by Kiefer and Wilson from a writer and educator's perspective on the making of literature—with facts.

The working title for this chapter, "Nonfiction: Going After the Facts," made us uncomfortable from the beginning—uncomfortable with the idea that nonfiction is limited to facts, but equally uncomfortable with writing about nonfiction at all. Over the years our experience and enthusiasm lay with fiction and picturebooks. However, interactions with colleagues over time have increased our appreciation for nonfiction literature for children. In addition, the current emphasis on educational standards for nonfiction in classrooms convinced us that nonfiction *literature* was well worth exploring. We describe here our somewhat circuitous and often contradictory journey into the genre to share the questions that arose and to try to challenge the prevailing paradigms regarding nonfiction.

We found our first forays into the field were like opening a Russian nesting doll; questions gave rise to more questions rather than to any definitive answers. Coming at this topic from our general children's literature scholarship, our first question was "What do we mean by literature and what do we mean by nonfiction?" This question led to others including "What is the history of nonfiction literature for children?"; "How does reporting and writing about adult nonfiction differ from reporting and writing about children's nonfiction literature?"; "What is the state of criticism and scholarship in children's nonfiction?"; "What disciplines are interested in children's nonfiction literature?"; and "What new directions might we propose for the study of nonfiction children's literature?" We found ourselves asking the sorts of questions that graduate students new to the field might pursue as part of a scholarly study; these questions, in turn, guided us on the journey we took for this chapter.

Defining Literature in Nonfiction

The Dictionary of Literary Terms and Literary Theory (Cuddon, 1991) states that "If we describe something as literature as opposed to anything else, the term carries with it qualitative connotations which imply that the work in question has superior qualities: that it is well above the ordinary run of written works" (pp. 505–506). If we agree that literature has superior qualities, then is nonfiction literature? To answer this we turned to our understanding of aesthetic objects—literary, visual, and other forms (Kiefer, 1995) to argue that works of literature, fiction and nonfiction, whether written for adults or for children, stand above the ordinary due to the quality of writing. Good nonfiction, like fiction, is an art form, designed to give pleasure, and enlightenment, to arouse wonder, and to reveal our capacity for self awareness and understanding.

Although many sources agree that nonfiction can be literary, we found it difficult to find a comprehensive or even a clear definition of nonfiction. *The Dictionary of Literary Terms and Literary Theory* (Cuddon, 1991) does not even include an entry for nonfiction. Many resources tend to define nonfiction by what it is *not*. *Webster's New Collegiate Dictionary* (1980), for instance, defines nonfiction as any literature that is not fictional.

Definitions of works of nonfiction for children are not much more enlightening. In a survey of children's literature textbooks Kristo, Colman, and Wilson (2008) quote definitions that include, "a genre created mainly to inform," (Mitchell, 2003, p. 326); "The term nonfiction describes books of information and fact about any topic" (Galda, Cullinan, & Sipe, 2010, p. 304); "Nonfiction-informational texts [are] about the way things are" (Nodelman & Reimer, 2003, p. 128). Moreover, for many years children's trade publishers, unlike adult trade publishers, seem to have accepted the notion that science or history is only palatable to children in the guise of a story. Laurie Mack's (2008) *Animal Families* for example, includes photographs with speech bubbles in which animals talk directly to the child reader. Pam Conrad's (1995) *Call Me Ahnighito* tells of Admiral Peary's discovery of a meteorite and its journey from Greenland to New York City. It is told in the first person by Ahnighito, the meteorite.

Even library classification systems for organizing nonfiction are confusing. The Dewey Decimal system includes many works of fiction under the subcategories of Social Sciences (e.g., folk and fairy tales) or Literature (e.g., poetry). Even more confusing, perhaps, is the Library of Congress system which separates children's books into two main categories, juvenile fiction and juvenile literature. Juvenile literature encompasses those topics that we would generally assume to be informative or factual (hydrology, waterworks) but designates as "juvenile literature" books such as Joanna Cole's (1986) *Magic School Bus at the Waterworks*. However, this book and others in the series present information alongside the pure fantasy, for example, that a school bus can shrink and fly.

The Magic School Bus at the Waterworks, Animal Families, and *Call Me Ahnighito* are representative of what has been termed hybrid structures in nonfiction (Anderson, 1989). In adult nonfiction the term hybrid is synonymous with "creative nonfiction" and "new journalism," where authors incorporate traditional nonfiction forms (essay, explanation/exposition) with fictional elements such as narration, attention to place, setting, theme, and characterization (Druker, n.d.).

However, authors of adult hybrid nonfiction are expected to "rein in our impulse to lie" (Gerrard, 1996, p. 5). In other words, they should not invent or change facts or events (Lounsberry, 1996). Authors of nonfiction for children, however, do not seem to be bound by the same principles. Thus, in nonfiction for children it is acceptable for school buses to fly, animals to speak, and rocks to tell their life stories.

To further compound the difficulty in defining children's nonfiction, such works are often referred to as information or informational books, breaking with traditions in nonfiction for adults. Colman (1999) argues that the widespread use of these terms began in the 1970s with the writings of Zenna Sutherland and Margery Fisher. It is still common to find that textbooks in children's literature relegate discussion of nonfiction to a single chapter titled "Information books." In addition, professional books and articles often use the term (see Kristo et al., 2008).

With all these conflicting labels and definitions, we have tried to find a framework for children's nonfiction literature that fits with our understanding of literature in general. We found Russell Freedman's (1992) explanation a good place to start. He argues, "Certainly the basic purpose of nonfiction is to inform, to instruct, hopefully to enlighten. But that's not enough. An effective nonfiction book must animate its subject, infuse it with life. It must create a vivid and believable world that the reader will enter willingly and leave only with reluctance. A good nonfiction book should be a pleasure to read" (p. 3).

How, then, can we expand and deepen our understanding of the art of nonfiction literature for children? Scholarship from the disciplines of rhetoric and exposition that study nonfiction literature for adults has been most helpful; especially Barbara Lounsberry's description in *The Literature of Reality* (Talese & Lounsberry, 1996). She begins by listing the categories into which nonfiction can be divided:

Lives (diaries, memoirs, autobiographies, biographies)
Events (histories, journalism)
Places (travel writing, nature writing, science writing)
Ideas (essays, including religious and philosophical works)
(p. 29)

She then argues that within each of these categories "nonliterary" and "literary" works can be found; and that the literary nonfiction within each category is "artful," characterized by exhaustive research, style, and the writer's ability to enlarge our understanding of the world.

We believe that Lounsberry's explanation works just as well for studying children's nonfiction as it does for adult nonfiction. However, we would add one more qualification for critiquing nonfiction, and that is the author's intent. As author Penny Colman (2007) states, "Nonfiction is writing about reality (real people, places, events, ideas, feelings, things) in which nothing is made up" (p. 260). While many books for children may blend fantasy and narrative with information and facts, this may be confusing to children who are only just beginning to sort out what is real. This tension in purpose could be a fertile starting point for future criticism and research in children's nonfiction literature.

The History of Children's Nonfiction Literature

Views of what matters in nonfiction for children have changed over the history of this genre. However, determining a clear historical timeline for nonfiction literature is difficult because historical research in children's literature has tended to focus on its fictional forms such as stories. Even so, it is likely that children in classical times and in the Middle Ages read nonfiction as well as fiction (Lerer, 2009). Zipes, Vallone, Hunt, and Avery (2005) classify nonfiction of the medieval period as books of instruction and mention *The Babees Book* (1475) as an early example of one such book intended to teach children how to behave properly using rules of courtesy.

Scholars generally agree that one of the first nonfiction picturebooks written and published for children was the *Orbis Sensualium Pictus* (The Visible World) written by Johannes Amos Comenius and published in 1658 (translated into English in 1659). In the preface, Comenius seems to be in harmony with many of today's writers of nonfiction when he states that

The Pictures are representations to all visible things, of the whole world...and that nothing very necessary or of great concernment is omitted.

The Descriptions are the explications of the parts of the picture... (Comenius, 1658, p. xv)

Indeed, Comenius's "Descriptions" are presented in the expository style or scientific register that we find in many nonfiction books today. Using numbers in the text, he creates explanations for corresponding line drawings of a field of cereal plants:

Title: Corn.
Text: Some Corn grows upon a straw parted by knots as Wheat, 1. Rie, 2. Barley, 3. in which the ear hath awnes (spikes or heads) or else it is without awnes and it nourish the corn in the Husk. Some instead of an ear have a rizom (or plume) containing the corn by bunches as Oats, 4. Millet, 5. Turkey Wheat,... (p. 23)

Comenius's approach to nonfiction proved so popular that for the next century and a half many of the nonfiction books published for children followed the same form; i.e., pictures accompanied by brief descriptions. In fact this 450-year-old text is remarkably similar to many of today's nonfiction books for children. Compare the Orbis Sensualium Pictus text to the words and images found on page 12 in Gail Gibbons' (2008) *Corn* or page 7 in Charles Miccuci (2009) *The Life and Times of Corn*. These author-illustrators show a cross section of the corn plant with labels for the parts of the plant. Smaller illustrations depict the parts of the ear. Such examples serve to emphasize the point that illustrations and visual displays seemed to be essential elements of nonfiction for children from its inception.

According to Zipes, Vallone, Hunt, and Avery (2005), in the 18th century more children were exposed to formal schooling and societies were becoming more democratic, more industrialized, and more scientific. "Books of instruction" were produced to respond to this trend. One example from among John Newbery's many books for children was a ten volume *The Circle of Sciences* (1745–1748).

Then, in the early 19th century, although still focused on presenting facts for children, nonfiction began to be presented in a new format. Whalley and Chester (1988) state, "Rationalism and knowledge were the guiding factors of the new style of children's books. To contain this wealth of information, books had to become bigger and more lavishly illustrated" (p. 37). With titles such as *The Geographical Guide: A Nautical Trip Round The Island of Great Britain with Entertaining And Illustrative Notes In Prose* (Harris, 1805), *Rural Scenes: Or, A Peep into the Country for Good Children* (Taylor, 1806), *Scenes of British Wealth in Produce, Manufactures and Commerce* (Taylor, 1823) "publishers showed that almost every aspect of life and work were considered suitable for portrayal," (Whalley & Chester, 1988, p. 37). Harris's *Geographical Guide* for example is 77 pages long and includes pleasing etchings and descriptions and definitions of places around the coast of the United Kingdom.

Also in the 19th century "life writing" in the form of biography, letters, memoirs, and personal essays became more common. Zipes et al. (2005) note that John M. Darton's (1864) *Famous Girls Who Have Become Illustrious Women: Forming Models for Imitation for the Young Women of England* was one example of a collective biography of the times. As with the earlier "books of instruction," these works were as much about proper social and moral behavior as they were about scientific and biographical facts.

In the 20th century, interests in human development brought the recognition that children were naturally curious and actively sought information. Where previously facts were often hidden in some type of narrative or story format, now publishers began to acknowledge that children enjoyed facts, and that they eagerly accepted information given to them in a straightforward manner. E. Boyd Smith created *Chicken World* (1910), and *The Railroad Book* (1913) both of which included large, colored, double-page illustrations filled with detail. W. Maxwell Reed, a former professor at Harvard, answered his nephew's questions about scientific topics in a series of letters that resulted in *The Earth for Sam* (1932) and *The Stars for Sam* (1931). These books exemplified the beginnings of nonfiction books written by recognized authorities in the field (Kiefer, 2010).

As a result of the preschool movement and its emphasis on the "here and now," very young children became the audience for nonfiction or concept books. Mary Steichen Martin and her father, Edward Steichen, produced *The First Picture Book: Everyday Things for Babies* (1930), with pictures of such common objects as a cup of milk with a slice of bread and butter, a faucet with a bar of soap, a glass holding a toothbrush, and a brush and comb set. No text accompanied these pictures, which were clear enough to provoke recognition and discussion for the child. Their books paved the way for the use of photography in today's nonfiction such as Seymor Simon's (2003) *Spiders* and Nic Bishop's (2009) *Butterflies and Moths*.

Biographies also flourished in the 20th century. Ingri and Edgar Parin d'Aulaire presented idealized images in their large picturebook biographies *George Washington* (1936), and *Abraham Lincoln* (1939), notable for their accessibility for younger children. Biography was one of the first genres to represent people of color to children. The 1940s saw biographies of such international figures as Nehru and Sun Yat Sen. In 1951 Catherine Owen Peare's *Mary McLeod Bethune*, a biography of the noted American civil rights pioneer, was published.

By the 1960s, nonfiction about historical events and biography reflected more current social attitudes. Alex Bealer's *Only the Names Remain: The Cherokees and the Trail of Tears* (1972/1996) was representative of a new emphasis on readable, carefully documented history that attempted to balance recorded history with a different point of view, in this case by presenting a Cherokee perspective.

As we enter the 21st century, children's nonfiction literature seems to be thriving. Although accurate accountings of the number of nonfiction children's titles that are published each year are difficult to find, Hepler (2003) reported that, according to The Library of Congress, by the 1990s, 60% of their juvenile cataloging was nonfiction. If that trend still holds true, then we might assume that of the 17,650 books published for children in 2005 (Bowker, 2007, p. 487), nonfiction titles account for a substantial share of children's publishing. Many of these titles, however, may belong to the somewhat formulaic series marketed to school libraries. Creative Publishing, for instance, offers such series as *Big Outdoors* and *Machines that Build*. Each series consists of at least six titles with page length ranging from 24 to 48 pages.

On the other hand, *Booklist* magazine reports an increase in the number of high-quality nonfiction series since they began their bi-annual "Spotlight on Nonfiction Series" in 2000 (Ott, 2009). These include series such as Houghton Mifflin's "Scientists in the Field" and National Geographic's "Face to Face with Animals" and "How to Get Rich" series. HarperCollins has published titles in the "Let's Read and Find Out" series for over 40 years, and Holiday House continues to publish one or two of Gail Gibbons' titles annually.

Reporting and Writing about Adult Nonfiction and Children's Nonfiction Literature

Awards and Reviews

As we looked at the realm of nonfiction literature, we found very different approaches between the world of adult nonfiction and children's nonfiction in reporting and writing about the genre. For example, major literary prizes such as the National Book Award or The Costa (Whitbread) Award that are given to writers of adult literature have long singled out works of fiction *and* nonfiction. In the children's literature field, however, it wasn't until 1990 that the National Council of Teachers of English established a special award for children's nonfiction, the Orbis Pictus Award. Two awards from the American Library Association followed the creation of the Orbis Pictus Award. In 2001 the Robert F. Sibert *Informational Book Medal* (italics ours) was established and in 2010 the first YALSA (Young Adult Library Services Association) Award for Excellence in Nonfiction for Young Adults was awarded. Prior to the founding of these awards, nonfiction titles showed up only occasionally on Newbery or Caldecott Award lists.

Adult and children's nonfiction trade books are also reviewed very differently. For instance, book review magazines such as the *New York Times Sunday Book Review* or *The New York Review of Books* give comparable coverage to works of fiction *and* nonfiction, and reviews of both run about 800 words (an entire page). In some of the journals that review children's literature, reviews of nonfiction do appear, but generally they are brief—only 200–250 words. Further, publications like *The New York Times* or *Publishers Weekly* post both fiction and nonfiction bestseller lists for adult trade books. *The New York Times*, however, only posts children's bestsellers about once a month and then limits titles to categories such as Picture Books, Chapter Books, and Series Books. *Publisher's Weekly* also divides children's bestsellers into three types,

Picture Book Bestsellers, Children's Series and Tie-Ins, and Children's Fiction Bestsellers.

Scholarship and criticism also differ between adult and children's nonfiction. Adult nonfiction holds a place of prominence alongside fiction in Colleges of English (see Anderson, 1987, 1989). However, children's nonfiction literature is often neglected as a subject of scholarship at all. Indeed, works such as *The Aesthetics of Children's Literature* (Nikolajeva, 2005) and *Criticism, Theory and Children's Literature* (Hunt, 1991) whose titles lead us to hope for in-depth critical analyses of nonfiction, do not cover the genre. In fact, in textbooks on children's literature, nonfiction is usually covered in one chapter, often placed toward the end of the book, almost as an afterthought (Galda et al., 2010; Kiefer, 2010; Lukens, 2007; Norton, 2006). Furthermore, these professional texts and others like them tend to suggest that evaluation of nonfiction should focus on such qualities as accuracy and authenticity, content and perspective, style, organization, and illustrations and format rather than on literary qualities of the books. Readers are asked to determine if the author is sufficiently qualified to write about the topic and whether the book fosters "the spirit of inquiry" (Kiefer, 2010, p. 497) rather than how the book function as literature or aesthetic objects. Although "style" is usually one of the criteria categories, readers are asked fairly superficial questions like, "Is the terminology appropriate?" (Galda et al., 2010, p. 306) or is "information presented clearly and directly?" (Kiefer, 2010, p. 497). In the 12-page section devoted to criteria for evaluating nonfiction, aspects of style are covered in approximately a page and a half.

Scholarship Focused on Children—or Books

Another incongruity exists between the scholarship surrounding nonfiction for adults and nonfiction for children. In two of the three disciplinary fields represented in this handbook, critical or empirical writings are largely focused on the genre of fiction. An informal survey of articles from the 2008 *Children's Literature Quarterly*, the publication of the Children's Literature Association of The Modern Language Association, reveals that almost all relate to fiction. *School Library Media Quarterly* articles are also largely devoted to fiction. Further, *Children's Literature in Education*, whose market is educators and librarians, describes itself as publishing "articles on fiction, poetry, drama and nonfictional material" with a clear emphasis on the analysis of fictional works (Springer, n.d). Even educational journals such as *Language Arts, Research in the Teaching of English,* and *Reading Research Quarterly*, which include reports of empirical research on nonfiction (Donovan, 2001; Pappas, 2006, 2009; Smolkin & Donovan, 2001; Tower, 2002), tend to focus more on children's responses to nonfiction texts than on the texts themselves.

A survey of professional titles that do focus on nonfic-

tion indicates that scholars in the field of education are the ones largely responsible for published articles and books about children's nonfiction literature. The one exception is *Nonfiction for Young Adults: From Delight to Wisdom* (Carter & Abrahamson, 1990), whose authors, notably, hail from the disciplines of Library Service *and* Education. Often articles or books from educational scholars focus on teaching the writing or comprehension of nonfiction structures that will be measured on standardized tests. Other titles by educators do provide useful overviews of the genre and criteria for evaluation but their main focus is still on the presence and use of nonfiction in classrooms rather than on critical analysis (Bamford & Kristo, 2000, 2004; Duke & Bennet-Armisted, 2003; Freeman & Person, 1998; Hoyt, 2002). Two excellent resources on children's nonfiction literature include edited volumes by Freeman and Person's (1992), *Using Nonfiction Trade Books In The Elementary Classroom: From Ants To Zeppelins*, and Bamford and Kristo's (2003) *Making Facts Come Alive: Choosing Quality Nonfiction Literature K-8*; sadly, both are currently out of print.

Across our survey of articles and books on nonfiction for children we found four authors who have expanded our own understanding of the genre and whose work, we believe, suggests promising possibilities for future research in education, English, and Library and Information Studies. These include Pappas (2006) and Pappas, Kiefer, and Levstik's (2006) research on the structure of nonfiction science texts, Kerper's (2003a) "Examining Aspects of Visual Displays," and "Examining Aspects of Design" (2003b), McClure's (2003) "Examining Aspects of Writing Style," and the essays of nonfiction by author Penny Colman (1999, 2007). We will briefly review their ideas in the next section.

New Directions for the Study of Nonfiction Children's Literature

Thinking about Textual Structures

If we are to accept that nonfiction *is* literature, and if we are to better appreciate how the genre works as an aesthetic object, an analysis of different typical structures and types of nonfiction may inform and expand our understanding. Western scholars have long maintained that stories (in the Western tradition) have a fairly straightforward grammar or structure. In a story there is a formal beginning, a problem, action is taken to resolve the problem, the problem is resolved and there is a formal ending (see Mandler & Johnson, 1977; Propp, 1968; Stein & Glenn, 1979). We believe readers intuitively apply story or grammar structures or the author's digression from those structures when they analyze fiction.

Nonfiction, however, is more diverse in story form insofar as it makes use of a variety of patterns including compare and contrast, cause and effect, sequence of events, and description and embedded definitions of concepts.

Furthermore in children's nonfiction literature we may encounter a wide variety of formats including alphabet books, photo-essays, experiment books, survey books, and specialized books (Hepler, 2003) such as Jerry Stanley's (1992) *Children of the Dust Bowl: The True Story of the School at Weedpatch Camp,* as well as the many hybrid formats of which the Magic School Bus Series is just one example.

Pappas (1993, 2006, 2009), who has studied children's retelling and writing of nonfiction, has also done extensive work in analyzing the generic structure of nonfiction science books, as well as the language characteristics of the writing. Pappas has contributed to our understanding of the typical structure of science nonfiction books (which she refers to as information books) for young children, a structure that many would describe as expository writing. Her careful analysis provides a description of the obligatory elements and their organization. In the following chart (Figure 20.1) these are shown with examples from Gail Gibbons's *The Honey Makers* (1999).

Pappas's scheme also includes optional elements authors may use such as comparisons between members of the class or historical events. Further, she has identified linguistic features common to these texts. For instance, in typical science nonfiction the author uses plurals when referring to categories (honeybees, bee keepers) and present tense or timeless verb constructions (are building, ripens). This "scientific register" is in opposition to a single, named main character and the past tense narrative we would find in a typical narrative story (Price, van Kleek, & Huberty, 2009).

Pappas's analysis of typical nonfiction science texts invites future scholars to consider in-depth analysis of other registers and types of nonfiction literature for children. It also raises questions for educators about ways to use nonfiction within classroom reading settings or as mentor texts in children's and adolescents' writing. Her work also indicates the importance of visual elements in nonfiction which we consider next.

Christine Pappas, Generic Structure Potential	Gail Gibbons, The Honey Makers
A topic presentation:	It is Springtime. Two bee keepers have placed a beehive on a hill.
A description of attributes:	Honeybees are social creatures.
A description of characteristics or activities:	Inside the beehive honeybees are building a honeycomb.
A final summary:	Finally the wax-making bees cap, or seal the cell with wax. Slowly the nectar ripens into honey.

Figure 20.1 Pappas's Scientific Register Examples

Thinking about Visual Elements

Until very recently little attention has been given to the visual aspects of today's nonfiction texts even though visuals have been a major aspect of children's nonfiction since its inception. However, by the beginning of the 21st century, the interest in multimodal literacy has led researchers to reconsider the illustrative materials in nonfiction and to develop descriptive structures or grammars of illustration. Kerper (2003a), Moline (1995), Pappas (2006), and Unsworth (2001) all provide analytic schemes for analyzing the potential of the illustrations to convey information. We offer an outline summary, below, of the structures proposed by Pappas et al. (2006), Pappas (2006) and Unsworth (2001).

Meaning-making Through Visual Images: Pappas and Unsworth

Representational and ideational structures. These structures verbally and visually construct the nature of events, the objects and participants involved, and the circumstances in which they occur. They ask the question, *"What is happening?"* and include the following visual elements:

- Images that show events—these include pictures that show participants involved in actions (a frog confronting its prey) or a single participant in action (a picture of a frog jumping)
- Images that classify—tree diagrams, taxonomies, flow charts
- Images that show part whole relationships—diagrams, picture glossaries
- Timelines

Interactive and interpersonal structures. These verbal and visual resources construct the nature of relationships among speakers, listeners, reader, writers, and viewers and what is viewed. They ask the question, *"Who is taking part?"* and include the following elements:

- Visual demands on and offers to readers—such as direction of gaze
- Social distance—close-up, medium, and long shots
- Attitude—involvement, non-involvement with viewer
- Power—point of view (e.g., worm's eye view, bird's eye perspective)
- Realism—color, contextualization of image
- Objective image—cutaways, cross sections

Compositional and textual means. These meanings are concerned with the distribution of the information and the value or relative emphasis among elements of the text or image. They ask the question, *"What role is communication playing?"* and focus on:

- Information value—left or right of page, familiar vs.

new, generalized, abstract vs. familiar, concrete, center, or margin
* Framing—how objects are joined or separate
* Salience—prominence as illustrated by size, placement in foreground

Access Features, Iconography, and Aesthetic Choices: Kerper

Kerper's (2003a) work on access features (indexes, glossaries, bibliographies) and visual displays (photographs, diagrams, maps) in nonfiction has also contributed to our understanding and appreciation for the visual elements in nonfiction and how they contribute to meaning. Kerper calls these features in nonfiction "iconographic materials;" and include photographs, diagrams, flow charts, tables, and maps. He discusses how these displays enhance and explain concepts and processes described by the written text. He shows, for example, how Lynn Curlee's (2001) diagram of the Brooklyn Bridge "shows relationships and complexity more easily than a pure linguistic form could" (2003a, p. 54).

Kerper (2003b) builds further on his previous work with nonfiction iconography in his chapter "Choosing Quality Nonfiction for Children: Aspects of Design." With this work Kerper opens up the potential for an *aesthetic* reading of the art of nonfiction. Kerper discusses such qualities of design as the book's size and shape, its front matter, its page layout, its typography, and its paper and ink; he goes on to show how these factors can enhance our aesthetic pleasure as well as our intellectual understanding in a work of nonfiction. For example, he describes how the shape of a book like Jean Fritz's *Leonardo's Horse* (2001) "echoes the content of the narrative and visually enriches the linguistic and pictorial presentation" (p. 68).

Kerper's work offers an invitation to other scholars to consider nonfiction picturebooks as art objects in the ways that others have attended to picture storybooks (Kiefer, 1995; Nodelman & Reimer, 2003). Following Kerper's lead we might look at Janet Schulman's (2008) *Pale Male: Citizen Hawk of New York City* as much more than a recounting of red-tailed hawks' attempt to nest on an apartment building in Manhattan. While Schulman provides a wealth of interesting information about nesting patterns and behaviors of red-tailed hawks, Meilo So's beautiful watercolor illustrations exemplify the wonder the human watchers must have felt at seeing this species return to New York after an almost 100-year absence. Beginning with a close-up of wings in the endpapers, So's flowing watercolors capture the airy spaces these wondrous birds inhabit. With close-ups and distance shots she creates the rhythm of wing flaps and glides. She varies the color schemes to add dramatic intensity to events. Because of the beauty of the illustrations we can easily accept Janet Schulman's explanation of how a group of citizens took the time and trouble to fight the powers-that-be to allow two birds to remain nesting on the edge of an elegant Fifth Avenue apartment building.

Thinking about Style: McClure

Kerper's work also raises the issue of style in nonfiction. As we have seen, style receives major attention in the scholarship of adult nonfiction. Our own analysis of illustrations in picturebooks (based on the artist's stylistic choices) leads us to conclude that style, or "manner of expressing" (Kiefer, 1995, p.120) is a primary factor in engendering aesthetic response. Yet, as we looked at the scholarly writing about children's nonfiction, we found style was seldom given prominent place in critical discussions. An exception was Amy McClure's (2003) "Choosing Quality Nonfiction Literature: Examining Aspects of Writing Style." In her thorough and thoughtful chapter, McClure discusses such features as clarity and coherence; use of figurative language; emotional involvement/voice; tone; language; and leads and conclusions. McClure helps us appreciate the poetic language in Sayre's (2008) book *Trout are Made of Trees*: "In fall, trees let go of leaves which swirl and twirl and slip into streams" (p. 6); or the humorous tone in Schaefer and Miller's (2008) *Look Behind!:* "Did you know that animal butts are amazing?" (p. 5). Her examples drawn from many works of children's nonfiction illustrate her point that "well-written nonfiction goes beyond facts to present eloquent, informed and well crafted discussion" (p 79).

A Continuum of Form and Style: Colman

By drawing our attention more directly to style in nonfiction writing, McClure (2003) opens up new avenues for the literary criticism of children's nonfiction. Author Penny Colman takes us a step further by proposing a model for analyzing both fiction and nonfiction. Colman writes as both an educator and an author with a lifelong love of nonfiction. She has long argued that nonfiction *is* literature (Colman, 1999); she was the first person to introduce us to the techniques of "creative nonfiction" or "literary nonfiction"—techniques that have dominated scholarship in the adult nonfiction world since the late 1960's (Wolfe, 1970). In creative nonfiction, style is a major concern for the writer. According to Lounsberry (1996), these stylistic elements can include scenic constructions, interior monologues, imagery, allusion, humor, and artfulness in language and form. Although the writing may include these literary features, the admonition remains to "never invent or change fact or events" (p. 30).

Using these ideas, Colman (2007) has created a model that allows us to look at features such as made-up material, organizational structure, textual structure and literary devices across literary types (see Figure 20.2).

Colman's model allows us to acknowledge the role that information may play in engendering our aesthetic response to a novel such as Jean Craighead George's *Julie*

Instructions: Assess the text, e.g., book, poem, essay, article for each element. Starting at the left side, fill in the bar to show the extent to which each element is present in the text. If an element is not present, leave the bar blank.

No made-up material	All Made-up Material

Made-up material is material that is fictionalized or unverifiable.

Minimal Information	Lots of Information

Information includes facts, events, biographical accounts, etc. that are real, actual, and verifiable.

Simple Structure	Complex Structure

Structure is how the material is organized, e.g., chronological, thematic, episodic, etc. Simple structures have one layer of organization. Complex structures have multiple layers.

No Narrative Text	All Narrative Text

Narrative text tells a story.

No Expository Text	All Expository Text

Expository text conveys information or explains something.

No Literary Devices	Many Literary Devices

Literary devices are techniques, such as diction, metaphors, repetition, telling details, etc.

Minimal Author's Voice	Intense Author's Voice

Author's voice is when the reader senses the presence of a distinct author by the style and/or voice in the text.

No Front/Back Matter	Copious Front/Back Matter

Front matter appears before the main text. Back matter appears after it.

No Visual Material	Copious Visual Material

Visual material includes illustrations, maps, graphs, diagrams, etc.

Figure 20.2 A visual model for analyzing fiction and nonfiction texts

of the Wolves (1972) that details the behavior of arctic wolves or Joyce Sidman's (2005) poems in *Song of the Water Boatman* that offer insight into and close observations of insect life. The model also allows us to appreciate Colman's (1997) use of voice and structure in *Corpses, Coffins, and Crypts*; for example, we note her use of the first person as she writes of death: "My great-aunt Frieda Matousek called me with the news her husband, Willi, was 'having another attack'....When I arrived, Frieda met me at the door. 'He's dead,' she said. 'Come and see him'" (p. 15). Likewise, in April Pulley Sayre's (2008) *Trout are Made of Trees* we can appreciate the use of alliteration and onomatopoeia:"Trout join in. Swim and snap! Fins flick. Rush. Zap!" (n.p.).

Conclusion

In the beginning of this chapter, we suggested that a Russian nesting doll might be a good metaphor for our exploration into nonfiction literature for children. But with a nesting doll we come to an end at some point—the last

little doll is eventually revealed. In fact, although some of our initial questions have been answered, during our research we kept finding more and more ideas, and texts and histories to explore. Nonfiction is indeed a fertile field for scholars who wish to study such texts and the classroom contexts for using them.

We couldn't help but think of some possible titles related to style, visual, and multimodal dimensions, that we might find in imaginary scholarly tomes in the future such as, "Voice in the Nonfiction Books of Jim Murphy"; "Tone across Topic: Fiction and Nonfiction about Animal Behaviors"; "The Aesthetics of Nonfiction Picturebooks"; "Visual Modes and Digital Media in Nonfiction"; "A Feminist Lens applied to Women's Biographies by Male Writers"; or "Nonfiction for Children in the 19th Century." Classroom-based researchers might study "Children's Understanding of Information and Concepts in Hybrid Nonfiction," "The Aesthetic Response of Young Readers to Nonfiction," or "Nonfiction Genres and Lessons on Writing." We hope that our curiosity about nonfiction will spread to other scholars in other disciplines. We can indeed go beyond the idea that nonfiction is only "going after the facts."

Literature References

Bealer, A. (1972/1996). *Only the name remains: The Cherokees and the Trail of Tears* (K. Rodanas, Illus.) Boston, MA: Little, Brown Books for Young Readers.

Bishop, N. (2009). *Butterflies and moths*. New York, NY: Scholastic.

Cole, J. (1986). *Magic school bus at the waterworks* (B. Degan, Illus.). New York, NY: Scholastic.

Conrad P. (1995). *Call me Ahnighito*. New York, NY: HarperCollins.

Colman, P. (1997). *Corpses, coffins, and crypts*. New York, NY: Holt.

Curlee, L. (2001). *Brooklyn Bridge*. New York, NY: Simon and Schuster.

D'Aulaire, I., & D'Aulaire, E. P. (1936). *George Washington*. New York, NY: Doubleday.

D'Aulaire, I., & D'Aulaire, E. P. (1939). *Abraham Lincoln*. New York, NY: Doubleday.

Fritz, J. (2001). *Leonardo's horse* (H. Talbot, Illus.). New York, NY: Putnam.

George, J. C. (1972). *Julie of the wolves*. New York, NY: HarperCollins.

Gibbons G. (1999). *The honey makers*. New York, NY: Morrow.

Gibbons G. (2008). *Corn*. New York, NY: Holiday House.

Harris, J. (1805). *The geographical guide: A poetical nautical trip round the island of Great-Britain; with entertaining and illustrative notes, in prose, descriptive of its principal ports, havens, rivers, creeks and inlets; cities towns, forts and mountains, and a particular view of the country as viewed from the sea.* Retrieved February 23, 2010 http://www.archive.org/details/geographicalguid00londiala

Mack, L. (2008). *Animal families*. New York, NY: DK.

Miccuci, C. (2009). *The life and times of corn*. Boston, MA: Houghton Mifflin.

Schulman, J. (2008). *Pale male: Citizen hawk of New York City* (S. Meilo, Illus.). New York, NY: Knopf.

Sayre, A. P. (2008). *Trout are made of trees*. Watertown, MA: Charlesbridge.

Schaefer, L. M., & Miller, H. L. (2008). *Look behind!* (J. Manning, Illus.). New York, NY: Greenwillow.

Sidman, J. (2005). *Song of the water boatman and other pond poems* (B. Prange Illus.) Boston, MA: Houghton Mifflin.

Simon, S. (2003). *Spiders*. New York, NY: HarperCollins.

Stanley, J. (1992) *Children of the Dust Bowl: The true story of the school at Weedpatch Camp.* New York, NY: Crown.

Academic References

Anderson, C. (1987). *Style as argument: Contemporary American nonfiction*. Carbondale: Southern Illinois University Press.

Anderson, C. (Ed.). (1989). *Literary nonfiction: Theory, criticism, pedagogy*. Carbondale: Southern Illinois University Press.

Bamford, R. A., & Kristo, J. V. (2000). *Checking out nonfiction K-8: Good choices for best learning*. Norwood, MA: Christopher Gordon.

Bamford, R. A., & Kristo, J. V. (2004). *Nonfiction in focus. A comprehensive framework for helping students become independent readers and writers of nonfiction, K-6*. New York, NY: Scholastic.

Bamford, R. A., & Kristo, J. V. (Eds.). (2003). *Making facts come alive: Choosing quality nonfiction literature K-8*. Norwood, MA: Christopher Gordon.

Bowker. (2007). *Bowker annual of library and trade book information* (52nd ed.). New York, NY: Bowker.

Carter, B., & Abrahamson, R. F. (1990). *Nonfiction for young adults: From delight to wisdom*. Phoenix, AZ: Oryx Press.

Colman, P. (1999). Nonfiction is literature too. *New Advocate, 12*(3), 215–223.

Colman, P. (2007). A new way to look at literature: A visual model for analyzing fiction and nonfiction texts. *Language Arts, 84*(3), 257–268.

Comenius, J. A. (1658). Translated by C. Hoole. 1887 Edition by C. W. Bardeen Retrieved February 18, 2010, from http://www.gutenberg.org/files/28299/28299-h/28299-h.htm

Cuddon, J. A. (1991). *Dictionary of literary terms and literary theory* (3rd ed.). New York, NY: Penguin.

Donovan, C. A. (2001). Children's development and control of written story and informational genres: Insight from one elementary school. *Research in the Teaching of English. 35*, 394–447.

Druker, P. (n.d.). What is creative non-fiction? Retrieved on February 18, 2010, from http://www.class.uidaho.edu/druker/nonfic.html

Duke, K., & Bennet-Armisted, V. S. (2003). *Reading and writing informational texts in the primary grades: Research based practices*. New York, NY: Scholastic.

Freedman R. (1992). Fact or fiction. In E. B. Freeman & D. G. Person (Eds.), *Using nonfiction trade books in the elementary classroom: From ants to zeppelins* (pp. 2–10) Urbana, IL: National Council of Teachers of English.

Freeman E. B., & Person, D. G. (Eds.), (1998). *Connecting informational children's books with content area learning*. Needham Heights, MA: Allyn and Bacon.

Freeman, E. B., & Person, D. G. (1992). *Using nonfiction trade books in the elementary classroom: From ants to zeppelins*. Urbana, IL: National Council of Teachers of English.

Galda, L., Cullinan, B. E., & Sipe, L. (2010). *Literature and the child* (7th ed.). Belmont, CA: Thomas Wadsworth.

Gerrard, P. (1996). *Creative nonfiction*. Cincinnati, OH: Story Press.

Hepler, S. (2003). Nonfiction books for children: New directions, new challenges. In R. A. Bamford & J. V. Kristo (Eds.), *Making facts come alive: Choosing and using quality nonfiction literature K-8* (pp. 3–20). Norwood, MA: Christopher Gordon.

Hoyt, L. (2002). *Make it real: Strategies for success with informational texts*. York, ME. Stenhouse.

Hunt, P. (1991). *Criticism, theory and children's literature*. Oxford, UK: Basil Blackwell.

Horning, K. T. (1997). *From cover to cover: Evaluating and reviewing children's books*. New York, NY: HarperCollins.

Kerper, R. (2003a). Choosing quality nonfiction for children: Examining access features and visual displays. In R. A. Bamford & J. V. Kristo (Eds.), *Making facts come alive: Choosing and using quality nonfiction literature K-8* (pp. 41–64). Norwood, MA: Christopher Gordon.

Kerper, R. (2003b.) Choosing quality nonfiction for children: Examining aspects of design. In R. A. Bamford & J. V. Kristo (Eds.), *Making facts come alive: Choosing and using quality nonfiction literature K-8* (pp. 65–78). Norwood, MA: Christopher Gordon.

Kiefer, B. Z. (1995). *The potential of picturebooks: From visual literacy to aesthetic understanding*. Columbus, OH: Merrill.

Kiefer, B. Z. (2010). *Charlotte Huck's children's literature*. New York, NY: McGraw-Hill.

Kristo, J. V., Colman, P., & Wilson, S. (2008). Bold new perspectives: Issues in selecting and using nonfiction. In S. S. Lehr (Ed.), *Shattering the looking glass: Challenge, risk and controversy in children's literature* (pp. 339–360). Norwood, MA: Christopher Gordon.

Lerer, S. (2009). *Children's literature: A reader's history from Aesop to Harry Potter*. Chicago, IL: University of Chicago Press.

Lounsberry, B. (1996). Anthology introduction. In G. Talese & B. Lounsberry (Eds.), *The literature of reality* (pp. 29-31). New York, NY: HarperCollins.

Lukens, R. A. (2007). *A critical handbook of children's literature*. New York, NY: Pearson.

Mandler, J. M., & Johnson, N. S. (1977). Remembrance of things parsed: Developmental differences in story structure and recall. *Cognitive Psychology, 9*, 111–151.

McClure, A. A. (2003). Choosing quality nonfiction literature: Examining aspects of writing style. In R. A. Bamford & J. V. Kristo (Eds.), *Making facts come alive: Choosing and using quality nonfiction literature K-8* (pp. 79–96). Norwood, MA: Christopher Gordon.

Mitchell, D. (2003). *Children's literature: An invitation to the world*. Boston, MA: Pearson.

Moline. S. (1995). *I see what you mean: Children at work with visual information*. York, ME: Stenhouse.

Nikolajeva, M. (2005). *Aesthetic approaches to children's literature*. Lanham, MD: Scarecrow Press.

Nodelman P., & Reimer, M. (2003). *The pleasures of children's literature*. Boston, MA: Allyn and Bacon.

Norton, D. (2006). *Through the eyes of a child: An introduction to children's literature*. Boston, MA: Allyn and Bacon.

Ott, B. (2009). Spotlight on nonfiction. *Booklist, 105*(15), 1.

Pappas, C. C. (1993). Is narrative primary? Some insights from kindergartener's pretend reading of stories and information books. *Journal of Reading Behavior, 25*, 97–129.

Pappas, C. C. (2006). The information book genre in science: Its role in integrated science literacy research and practice. *Reading Research Quarterly, 41*(2), 226–250.

Pappas, C. C. (2009). Young children's multimodal books in integrated science literacy units in urban classrooms. *Language Arts, 86*(3), 201-211.

Pappas, C. C., Kiefer, B. Z., & Levstik, L. S. (2006). *An integrated language perspective in the elementary school: Theory into action* (4th ed.). White Plains, NY: Longman.

Price, L. H., van Kleek, A., & Huberty, C. J. (2009). Talk during book sharing between parents and preschool children: A comparison between storybook and expository book conditions. *Reading Research Quarterly, 44*(2), 171–194.

Propp, V. (1968). *Morphology of the folk tale* (2nd ed.). Austin, TX: University of Texas Press.

Smolkin, L. B., & Donovan, C. A. (2001). The contexts of comprehension: The information book read aloud, comprehension acquisition and comprehension instruction in a first grade classroom. *Elementary School Journal, 102*(2), 97–22

Springer.com (n.d.). Children's literature in education. Springer science and business media homepage. Retrieved February 23, 2010, from http://www.springer.com/education/linguistics/languages+%26+literature/journal/10583

Stein, N. L., & Glenn, C. G. (1979). An analysis of story comprehension in elementary school children. In R. Freedle (Ed.), *Multidisciplinary approaches to discourse comprehension* (pp. 53-120). Hillsdale, NJ: Ablex.

Talese, G., & Lounsberry B. (Eds.). (1996). *The literature of reality*. New York, NY: HarperCollins.

Taylor, I. (1823). *Scenes of British wealth in produce, manufactures and commerce*. London: J.Harris.

Taylor, J. (1806). *Rural Scenes: Or, A Peep into the Country for Good Children*. London: Harvey Darton.

Tower, C. (2002). "It's a snake you guys!": The power of text characteristics on children's responses to information books. *Research in the Teaching of English, 37*, 55–88.

Unsworth, L. (2001). *Teaching multiliteracies across the curriculum: Changing contexts of text and image in classroom practice*. Buckingham End, UK: Open University Press.

Webster's New Collegiate Dictionary. (1980). Springfield, MA: G. & C. Meriam Company.

Whalley, J. I., & Chester, T. (1988). *A history of children's book illustration*. London, UK: Victoria and Albert Museum.

Wolfe, T. (1970). *The new journalism*. New York, NY: Harper & Row.

Zipes, J. P., Vallone L., Hunt, P., & Avery G. (Eds.). (2005). *The Norton anthology of children's literature*. New York, NY: W.W. Norton.

Point of Departure

Penny Colman

Full disclosure: I avidly read nonfiction; the current stack of nonfiction books by my reading chair measures seventeen inches and includes the laugh-out-loud *The Curse of the Labrador Duck: My Obsessive Quest to the Edge of Extinction* by Glen Chilton; the dramatic *The World is Blue: How Our Fate and the Ocean's are One* by Sylvia A. Earle; the Pulitzer Prize winning *What Hath God Wrought: The Transformation of America, 1815–1848*; and *The Best American Essays 2009* edited by Mary Oliver.

I prolifically write nonfiction, having published a slew of articles, essays, and books for all ages. I fervently teach a course in nonfiction children's literature to graduate students in education; in fact, my first formal lecture on this topic was in Barbara Kiefer's class at Teachers College, Columbia University in 1997, which resulted in my first scholarly article, "Nonfiction is Literature Too." Given that string of adverbs—avidly, prolifically, fervently—what is my response to "Nonfiction Literature for Children: Old Assumptions and New Directions"?

First, my compliments to Barbara Kiefer and Melissa Wilson for tackling this subject. In particular I greatly appreciate their sections on the history of children's nonfiction literature and their discussion of how reporting, writing, and scholarship in the world of adult nonfiction differs from what happens regarding children's nonfiction literature. As someone who works in the worlds of nonfiction literature for both children and adults, I am constantly astonished by the yawning gap between the two. Considering that nonfiction is the currency of the real world—i.e., most of what students and adults need to comprehend and produce–I am frequently infuriated by the hegemony of fiction reading and writing in most classrooms.

Second, there are some issues in the preceding chapter that raised questions for me.

> The authors appear to assume that story equals fiction, an assumption that excludes nonfiction stories; yet, the first stories we tell are nonfiction— who we are, who our family is.

The bulk of the stories we relate in everyday life are nonfiction—the stories my six-year-old granddaughter relates when I pick her up from school, or those my partner and I share over dinner. Nonfiction is the source, the seedbed, the spark for fiction. We know fiction is fiction by its relationship to nonfiction, i.e., real phenomena—people, clouds, dogs, birthdays, deaths, etc. When I first uncovered the definitional morass that Kiefer describes, I asked myself—having written both fiction and nonfiction—as a writer, what do I do differently?

The answer is that I either do or don't make up material, which is how I formulated my definition of nonfiction: Nonfiction is writing about reality (real people, places, events, ideas, feelings, things) in which nothing is made up. My definition for fiction is writing in which anything can be made up. My third genre category is hybrid, which is comprised of books that are designated "juvenile literature" but contain made-up material, such as *Magic School Bus at the Waterworks*, which has both made up text and illustrations, and *Remember: The Journey to School Integration* in which Toni Morrison made-up captions for iconic photographs.

I also consider illustrated picture books hybrids, even if there is not made-up text, because the art work has been made-up by an illustrator, such as in *Wanda Gag: The Girl Who Lived to Draw*, by Deborah Kogan Ray. I do this because I think it is important for children to learn how to discern what is and is not made-up. In addition, understanding that an illustration is made-up by an artist offers a potential aesthetic experience by giving readers the opportunity to analyze or respond to the artist's interpretation of a particular text.

> Their statement that "in adult nonfiction the term hybrid is synonymous with 'creative nonfiction' and 'new journalism'" does not match my writerly experience.

Many of us who write creative nonfiction and new journalism are squeaky clean about not blurring the boundaries. Yes, we employ literary elements, but we rigorously eschew making up interior monologues, creating dialogue, inventing characters or creating composite characters, altering a chronology, or employing any of the other fictional devices that would put our writing in the hybrid category.

I was interested in Keifer and Wilson's discussion of Barbara Lounsberry's categories: "Lives (diaries, memoirs, autobiographies, biographies); Events (histories, journalism); Places (travel writing, nature writing, science writing); Ideas (essays, including religious and philosophical works)." While I agree that Lounsberry's categories can be useful in examining nonfiction, they do not appear to acknowledge the interconnectedness of categories that is found in many nonfiction texts.

For example, in one my favorite books, *Without Reservations: The Travels of an Independent Woman,* the author, Alice Steinbach, weaves together places and lives. In another terrific book, *The Worst of Hard Times,* Timothy Egan connects events and lives. Lounsberry's categories also problematically conflate topics with formats. For example, diaries and essays are formats while science writing is a topic. For me, the concept of "variety," is more reflective of the nature of nonfiction. For my graduate students, I developed a handout titled "A Variety of Nonfiction Texts" with examples under each of these headings: Motives, Topics, Modes, Structures, Media, Modalities of Delivery, Formats, Visuals, Designs, Professions. Under "A Variety of Motives," for example, I list "Storytelling, advocating, exposing, self-expressing, educating."

> In their discussion of textual structures it appears that story structure belongs to fiction and that text structures, such as compare and contrast, sequence, description or cause and effect, are found in nonfiction; both formulations are only partly accurate.

Narrative nonfiction—think Jim Murphy or Sy Montgomery—is all about the story. My forthcoming book, *Elizabeth Cady Stanton & Susan B. Anthony: A Friendship that Changed History,* is a nonfiction story with a beginning, middle, end, replete with problems, solutions, dialogue (i.e., quotations), setting, place, themes, characters, etc. As for text structures, fiction writers use them too. For example, examine this brief excerpt in Kevin Henkes's fictional story *So Happy!*, illustrated by Anita Lobel:

The seed was thirsty.
The rabbit was lost.
The boy was bored
Then . . . the rain came.
The creek got bigger.

> I also notice an exclusive focus on expository nonfiction.

That, of course, is not surprising since most nonfiction books in classrooms are expository in the form of "All About" and "How-To" books and textbooks. Most literary writing (nonfiction and fiction), however, is comprised of all four traditional modes of writing: narration, exposition, description, and argumentation. In my teaching, I use my book, *Corpses, Coffins, and Crypts: A History of Burial,* to demonstrate these modes. For example, chapter one is a narrative account of my great-uncle's death interspersed with segues into expository material about related topics, such as the task of determining if a person is dead and a discussion about why do people die. There is description, dialogue (i.e., quotes), and argumentation, related to the fact that people deal with death in a variety of ways.

In addition to writing my books, I also do the picture research and take photographs. In that capacity, I have delighted in packing my books with visual material; there are 74 photographs in *Rosie the Riveter: Women Working on the Home Front in World war II*, a map and microphotographs in *Adventurous Women; Eight True Stories About Women Who Made a Difference,* and a chart in *Thanksgiving: The True Story*, to name a few. Recently, however, I have been rethinking the use of visual material in nonfiction because discussions with students have sensitized me to readers' struggles with how to read a book with lots of visual material. Yes, it can aid in understanding, but it can impede the actual reading of the text. If we want students to actually read nonfiction texts and/or use them as model texts for writing nonfiction, it is important to assess whether or not they can find the text under the all too frequent blizzard of boxes slanted every which way, diagrams, charts, fonts of all sizes, and colors galore.

In conclusion, I would add to Kiefer and Wilson's list of "imaginary scholarly tomes in the future" the following titles: "Finding the Facts in Fiction: A Guide to Meticu-lously Researched Information-Rich Fictional Books"; "Down with Dichotomies: A Guide to Discerning Character, Setting, etc., in Nonfiction and Information and Text Structures in Fiction"; and "Powerful Nonfiction: Books, Articles and Essays that Made a Difference." As for their suggestions of areas of study for classroom-based researchers, I would like to see the following: "On Teaching Information—"What it is, Where it's found"; "Who Reads Author's Notes: Why and Why Not"; "The Nonfiction Baskets: What's in it and Why"; "Given Free Rein, Which Books Do Students Choose to Read (assuming there's an ample supply of both fiction and nonfiction)?"; "Graphic Nonfiction: What is It and How to Use It"; "How to Spot Made-Up Material"; "How to Fact-Check What You Read and Write"; "Overcoming Anxiety About Using Nonfiction Trade Books in The Classroom"; "How To Know What I Need To Know To Teach Content With Nonfiction Books"; and "Do Readers Really Need 'a Spoonful of Sugar' to Make Nonfiction 'Go Down'?"

Barbara Kiefer and Melissa Wilson have written an important chapter that clearly puts forth key issues in nonfiction children's literature that demand continued discussion, examination, and advocacy. I look forward to continuing the dialogue.

Colman's Nonfiction References

Chilton, G. (2009). *The curse of the Labrador Duck: My obsessive quest to the edge of extinction.* New York, NY: Simon & Schuster.

Colman, P. (1999). Nonfiction is literature too. *New Advocate, 12*(3), 217.

Earle, S. A. (2009). *The world is blue: How our fate and the ocean's are one.* Washington, D.C.: National Geographic Press.

Egan, T. (2006). *The worst of hard times: The untold story of those who survived the great American Dust Bowl.* New York, NY: Houghton Mifflin.

Howe, D. W. (2007). *What hath God wrought: The transformation of America, 1815-1848.* Washington, D.C.: Oxford University Press.

Oliver, M. (Ed.) (2009). *The best American essays 2009.* New York, NY: Houghton Mifflin Harcourt.

Steinbach, A. (2000/2002) *Without reservations: The travels of an independent woman.* New York, NY: Random House.

Children's Literature

Cole, J. (1986). *Magic school bus at the waterworks.* New York, NY: Scholastic.

Colman, P. (2008). *Thanksgiving: The true story.* New York, NY: Henry Holt.

Colman, P. (2006). *Adventurous women: Eight true stories about women who made a difference.* New York, NY: Henry Holt.

Colman, P. (1997). *Corpses, coffins, and crypts: A history of burial.* New York, NY: Henry Holt.

Colman, P. (1995). *Rosie the riveter: Women working on the home front in World War II.* New York, NY: Crown.

Henkes, K. (2005). *So happy!.* (A. Lobel, Illus.). New York, NY: Greenwillow.

Morrison, T. (2004). *Remember: The journey to school integration.* New York, NY: Houghton Mifflin.

Ray, D. K. (2008). *Wanda Gag: The girl who lived to draw.* New York, NY: Viking.

Figure 20.3

21

Genre as Nexus

The Novel for Children and Young Adults

Mike Cadden

Missouri Western State University

In considering the many factors that go into the definition of the children's novel, literary critic Mike Cadden addresses a range of issues that link his discussion to other chapters in this volume. How, for instance, do children's novels engage their readership in ways that are different from picturebooks? What distinguishes a children's novel from a young adult novel? Why and for whom do these distinctions matter? What remains the same when surface features of children's books change and new forms emerge? His discussion of mode is especially helpful in bringing a conscious and critical awareness to the question of just how we know a children's novel when we see one, even when the children's novels in question are as complex and challenging as Philip Pullman's work. Pullman's Point of Departure, then, picks up the discussion from the point of view of an author whose work has been challenged with the same vexing question: Is this really a children's book?

When literary critics look at children's novels, they often struggle with what defines the genre: What makes a book marketed to children and packaged in a certain format a children's novel, and not something else? What are the characteristics, formal and thematic, that distinguish it from other kinds of writing for children or adults? Are all of the various categories, modes, and forms traditionally and historically identified in the study of "the novel" present and accounted for in books written for children? Whereas librarians, educators, publishers, and children themselves might know a "chapter book" when they see one, and be content to distinguish it from a picturebook or a YA novel, literary critics are keen to parse fine distinc-

tions and come up with definitions and genre categories that place children's books within the larger contexts of literary studies. This kind of work helps them understand their field better, and tracking changes and innovations in literary genres gives scholars insight into shifting cultural and aesthetic values as well.

But genre distinctions are also important to readers. Even if they don't consciously study or articulate the mechanisms of how genres work, readers use their experiences of generic conventions to set expectations for their reading, which is particularly important for people new to tracking longer narratives, a process which may include attending to multiple plot strands, keeping track of lots of characters, and positioning themselves with respect to various types of narrators and points of view. Genre also helps readers find what they like, which is no small consideration if the goal is to encourage lifelong reading for pleasure as well as information.

In this study of children's novels, I begin by offering a succinct look at some of the considerations involved in defining the children's novel as a genre. I then discuss the idea of the chapter book as it relates (or doesn't) to the novel for young readers and address the question of book length as both a literary and literacy value for adults. Following that I will address the rarely discussed question of literary mode as it affects the question of what is possible in novels for the young and then look at some matters of genre, specifically epistolary and verse novels, the role of growth and change in novels for the young, some common and distinguishing features of children's and young adult novels by genre, and lastly the vexing phenomenon of fake or superficial realism in novels for the young reader.

Defining the Children's Novel

As a genre category, the novel for young readers is a nexus—a core of connections and links. It is a nexus of other genres, including not only those more structurally-defined like science fiction or mystery but also the age-based genre categories of children's and young adult literatures. When a hierarchy is made of those categories, it changes what a book can be. If the hierarchy starts with "novel" and is followed by "mystery" and then "children's," the novel of mystery for children exists next to those for adults, and mystery novels next to other genres of novels that, presumably, can be distinguished by the age of the audience. When the hierarchy begins with "children's" and is followed by "novel" and then "mystery," there are created structural and ideological expectations and limitations on what "novel" means, and further "mystery." The secondary and tertiary descriptors bend to the ideological and structural expectations established by the first. There are separate children's sections in bookstores, libraries, and clothing stores—and that means that there will not be children's versions of adult items next to them in the adult section—nor the reverse. The category "children's" set off by itself makes the alternative "adult" invisible—or at least a minor challenge to find up or down some stairs and hallways. One implication for children's literature is that, as Perry Nodelman (2008) argues, "for the child readers for whom it is intended, children's literature cannot be identified or understood as a genre" (p. 131) because they don't see it—or, rather, it's all they see. The term has no "use value" when its opposite isn't provided. When a child writes a poem, she isn't writing a "children's poem." Only adults do that because only adults see the binary.

Despite the fact that the novel has been the favorite literary genre among the reading public for over a century, the genre itself remains notoriously difficult to define, having been born in the nexus of different traditions and circumstances. Since the English novel's development in the 17th century and its rise in the 18th century (and because of arguments all along about its various lines of descent from traditions like English prose fiction, French Heroic Romance, Spanish picaresque, and Epic), critics have tried to define "novel" on the basis of verisimilitude, length, imagination, and even readership, but it remains the elusive form it ever was. The genres of children's and young adult literature are themselves fuzzy sets, culturally and structurally protean like the novel and resistant to a satisfying poetics in spite of the limitations of genre that I discuss above (and despite heroic attempts by critics like Roni Natov [2003], Maria Nikolajeva [2005], and Zohar Shavit [1986] to pin it down through poetics). This resistance is a result of the competing textual, subtextual, and contextual approaches and agendas of critics, parents, librarians, and teachers. And yet, I would argue that this indeterminacy has allowed both the novel and literature for the young to stay relevant and alive in culture; their respective and combined ambiguity keeps it/them from becoming static and ultimately irrelevant, too specific in use or audience, or dated in style and structure. As it is with any species, evolution equips it to survive. A recent adaptation, as noted by Laura Apol and Janine Certo in this volume as an innovation in poetry as much as I see it here as an innovation in the novel form, is the verse novel for young adults, which would seem to bring us back in many ways to one argued origin of the novel species, the epic—but I'll address that later on in the chapter.

The Chapter Book and Length

A curious ambiguity that I note in this discussion of children's books is the use of the term "chapter book." Is there a difference between a chapter book and a novel? *The New York Times* bestsellers categories as seen on the Barnes & Noble website include "children's chapter books," "children's series," "children's picture books," and "children's paper backs"; these are hardly mutually exclusive terms. The chapter book bestseller list includes fiction by Sherman Alexie (2007) and Jeff Kinney (2007) as well as nonfiction for children by conservative pundit Bill O'Reilly (O'Reilly & Flowers, 2007) and former First Daughter Jenna Bush (2007), respectively (Bush's book is categorized "young adult," which seems to be included on the children's list). In contrast, the adult bestseller section does distinguish between fiction and nonfiction, a distinction not made within children's chapter books. I would guess that a bestselling poetry collection would appear under a chapter books category given this organization. It appears that a chapter book is simply anything that is not a picturebook, which suggests that it's really all about the age of the reader, or should I say it's about a presumed reading level, however divined, rather than actual readers.

"You're too *old* to read picturebooks, Stevie—wouldn't you like a nice *chapter book* about spiders?"

This idea that genre is associated first (or perhaps only) to age and reading level is unfortunate for the way it moves readers along a series of genre canal locks. Once readers get to chapter books, they can't go "back." To read a picturebook is to regress. The novel is at the end of the literary canal—the final destination in reader development. The irony here is that never has the picturebook been more inclusive of readers by age due to its own use of irony, allusion, intertextuality, metafiction and other crossover techniques, as explored by Lawrence Sipe in his *Handbook* chapter as well as by Rod McGillis when he addresses *The Invention of Hugo Cabret* (Selznick, 2007) in his chapter. In her discussion of YA literature in this volume, Karen Coats uses the metaphor of the gateway drug to make a parallel point. She decries the tendency of various camps to think of YA as a transitional rather than a destination literature, a place to which one might go intentionally and not as a way to work up to something else. The two metaphors of the canal lock and the gateway drug are useful to contrast: one might still return to the gateway drug as a milder form of pleasure without giving up the "harder stuff"; but once the ship is through the lock, it doesn't back up without a great deal of trouble. The YA novel can be taken as a book for adults, especially in genres like fantasy and science fiction in which there is much less of a distinction made between YA novels and those for adults; teachers and other well-meaning adults are much more likely to ask a child with a picturebook why he or she is reading below level.

Of the novel characteristics noted earlier, the length of a book is for many people a determination of the age reader for which the book is meant (or *best for*, which isn't the same thing at all). As picturebooks are not considered by many adults as advanced as novels, the length of the novel is sometimes erroneously assumed to be a measure of the relative precociousness of the middle elementary reader, and parents take greater pride in the length of the books their children read (and without pictures, of course) than in their literary merit. So, a child is pushed from the picturebook lock to float in the waters of the easy reader; then the lock opens, spilling the reader toward the chapter book of different lengths and reading levels; increased length and lower picture-to-word ratios become the standards for moving a child from one lock to the next. The irony is that picturebooks are often at a higher reading level than easy readers, and short and illustrated folktales may well be more demanding than some episodic, comedic novels for children.

It should come as no surprise, however, that the children's novel shows great variety in length, and it is absolutely true in this particular case that size doesn't matter; the problem, of course, is that many parents think it does. The Newbery-winning *Sarah, Plain and Tall* (MacLachlan, 1985), the story of a motherless 19th-century midwestern farm family and the woman who comes to make her home with them, is a little more than 70 pages, and its beauty is the simplicity of language that happens to result in its brevity; though perhaps its brevity is considered by some to be a sign of its being simplistic instead. Two other well-regarded and very short chapter books for children are all the more truncated in terms of story events because much of the books are given over to multiple narrators that go over largely similar events but from different vantage points. *Seedfolks* by Paul Fleischman (1997), a novel comprised of 13 vignettes about gardening in a single city garden plot, runs about 70 pages. Michael Dorris's (1992) *Morning Girl*, the story of two siblings in the just-barely pre-Colombian Caribbean, is an 80-page novel that alternates between the two siblings' respective narration; the book often describes the same events from both of these two different perspectives.

I'm afraid that the *Harry Potter* (e.g., Rowling, 1997) books have been a double-edged sword for the development of the novel for young readers. That kids can read long books has always been undeniable (one would think that J. K. Rowling had single-handedly invented fantasy, long books, as well as the English boarding school story). The claim that a book is too long and will defeat a modern child's presumed mayfly-like attention span can be countered with the success of the Harry Potter series. Once the child has read the Potter series, will he or she ever again be given a small and beautiful novel, or anything more on the order of an illustrated short story? There are reasons that children's and young adult historical fiction and fantasy have been typically longer than children's novels of realism: there are worlds to build for the reader that can't be assumed. The recent and wonderful Revolution era fictional slave narrative *The Astonishing Life of Octavian Nothing* by M.T. Anderson (2006) closes in on 400 pages and provides a great deal of historical context for the implied reader. But it isn't better or more advanced than Sandra Cisneros's (1991) 110-page collection of lovely vignettes in *The House on Mango Street*. It's a matter of genre, not reading level. Adults who choose their own books make their judgments based on other things (unless they're eager to impress the folks on the subway with the girth of their reading material); whether we're up to a book, we know, goes beyond measures of mass—but do people consider this for their young literary charges in the same way? What is challenging and worthwhile about Philip Pullman's *His Dark Materials* novels (1996–2000) isn't a function of (or at least not simply limited to) the trilogy's 1,000 pages but of the demand it places on the young reader's intellect on each page. In a parallel area, I can remember tackling some of Scott Joplin's ragtime on the piano as a kid. After seeing the mass of notes on the sheet music, my father was proud. For a while after that he was disappointed to see a Billy Joel song on the music stand because it contained more white than black on the sheet music. He feared regression rather than recognizing variety. I think it's true that the quick-glance assessment of a book by size is often the measure of whether junior is progressing. Aesthetic worth is hard to see across the living room and out of the corner of one's eye.

The measures of whether young readers are up to Pullman's trilogy include, for one, their ability to adapt to a challenging style of mixed fantasy that presents to them their world, but that world altered and amid other worlds. This is more challenging than the usual children's "portal" fantasies such as Lewis's Narnia books or the Oz books in which there is a clear here and there. Another challenge to readers of Pullman's trilogy is the way he complicates what seem to be character types within the larger hero story. Lyra's parents, for instance, are dark but less clearly evil than, say, Voldemort (despite Rowling's [2005] attempts to contextualize him in view of his childhood in *Harry Potter and the Half-Blood Prince*). It's difficult to be dismissive of Mrs. Coulter or Lord Asriel as simple bad guys, despite the invitation of the story type to consider them as such—they have complicated motives, which include love and the desire for truth. Young readers of Pullman also need to be up to his demand that they cope with ambiguities regarding key ideas, such as Dust, and accept that there is a certain necessary mystery to this (and our) world, partly due to the limits of Lyra as focalizer in many cases, unlike the Harry Potter series in which all answers are provided. Readers able to cope with the demands Pullman places on them will thus be rewarded with a richer experience.

Another consideration of difficulty as a gauge of a novel's merit is the episodic plot—or what is done with length. The Ramona books by Beverly Cleary (e.g., *Ramona Quimby, Age 8*, 1981) along with *The House on Mango Street* (Cisneros, 1991), *Seedfolks* (Fleischman, 1997), and *Morning Girl* (Dorris, 1992), as different as they are in terms of character development, are novels episodic in their telling. The novel of episodic plot has long been a standard of children's literature. The episodes provide good closure for reading aloud with the early-to-middle elementary school child, and it does demand less on the part of the reader in terms of keeping plot points straight, but it also puts a premium on character—which may be why children's novels and chapter books in general have such a memorable cast of characters. And with the episodic plot, especially in the mode of comedy, comes a satisfying stasis that makes it possible to return to characters over and over in book series, a phenomenon especially prevalent in literature for the young. Ramona, Amelia Bedelia, Junie B. Jones, Pippi Longstocking, and so many others stay reliably the same while they become better and better known, giving the reader a trustworthy focus from episode to episode. This is less seen in literature for adults (if we contrast postmodern fragmentation in plots to the use of clear and complete episodes) and, perhaps, one reason for the comparable paucity of series books for adults, especially in realism. Mystery/detective fiction is

a notable exception here, as is chicklit. Series fiction, as Catherine Ross indicates in this volume, has long been considered a more likely home of the less literary novels, with notable exceptions.

But this is more a matter of mode than it is of merit. While the comedic lends itself to the episodic, the romance or hero novel, such as the Newbery Medal-winning *Holes* (Sachar, 1998) and *The Tale of Despereaux* (DiCamillo, 2003), is much more likely to offer the reader a multistranded narrative, or any sort of rearrangement of narrative time, as a result. In *Holes*, Louis Sachar offers us multistranded narration that isn't clearly linked until later in the book as the increasingly tightening narrative strands of the tales of his grandfather, Kissin' Kate Barlow, and his own life become one tale with a clear chain of chronological events. In DiCamillo's *The Tale of Despereaux*, the narrative relies on understanding the stories of three parallel characters whose stories are told one after another until the second and third narratives' respective intersection with the first is clear.

Absent this sort of narrative complexity, an episodic plot can still create, through the sum of its parts, a sense of progression and even character growth. After a catalog of Caddie Woodlawn's tomboyish escapades in the eponymous novel (Brink, 1935), there is something poignant in the conclusion that Caddie is to leave the foolish things of childhood behind, including acting like a tomboy in their late 19th century Wisconsin town. A more contemporary example is Jack Gantos's Joey Pigza, whose four-book series begins with *Joey Pigza Swallowed the Key* (2000), a novel that reads episodically and which manages to draw on our developing attachment to Joey in order to touch us at the end when he seems to be saved from falling through the cracks of the education system.

Literary Mode and Novel Subgenera

The larger question of mode is pretty interesting as it plays out in novels for children and young adults. Northrop Frye (1957) and his successors have explained the modes of irony, comedy, romance, and tragedy in great detail, so any summation will be necessarily inadequate, but we can consider the differences among this circle of stories (for they are always to be thought of as a compass that shows by degrees how a story shifts toward a different quadrant of the compass). As we move from irony toward comedy, characters move from being ridiculous or even less moral than ourselves to what we might think of as "like us," or empathetic. The move from comedy to romance pushes the main character towards someone typically better than we are in a number of ways (differences in heroism); as we move toward tragedy we add to that superior character the ability and willingness to sacrifice him or herself. As we swing toward irony from there, otherwise admirable characters are laid low by fate and absurd circumstances, introducing less control by the character.

Death in these modes, therefore, takes on different qualities. Beginning in irony, death is absurd and importantly so—it is random and we have no control over it, making it disturbing. The comedic still maintains death's absurdity, but removes its importance and focuses on its ridiculousness (and, very likely, its unreality—characters don't always stay dead). As comedy shifts towards romance, death becomes important, but it is actually triumphant and desired as the "bad guy" is thwarted by the superior character. As the compass moves toward tragedy, the death is a sacrifice of the hero rather than a disposal of a villain and is meant to establish a new order. As we swing back toward irony, the tragedy (in which the death of the hero is decided on by the hero as true sacrifice) moves toward tragic irony (in which the death becomes more fated, absurd, out of control). Comedy and romance are at the heart of a conservative world view of returning to a previous order—things "go back to normal." Part of what makes irony and tragedy more upsetting is that they are modes of change—either random and absurd in the ironic or as the rebirth of a new order as in tragedy.

As I've argued elsewhere (Cadden, 2005), while one *can* find novels of all four modes (comedy, irony, tragedy, and romance) for children, only comedy and romance are consistently published. We can find exceptions that prove the rule, but even when we have the makings of irony (Leslie's story in Katherine Paterson's [1977] *Bridge to Terabithia*) or tragedy (Charlotte's story in E. B. White's [1952] *Charlotte's Web*) the stories are tempered with co-protagonists whose stories outlast and recast the modality of the story by providing the "opposite" mode (Jess's story as romance in *Bridge to Terabithia* and Wilbur's as comedy in *Charlotte's Web*). Comedy and tragedy are opposite directions on the compass, as are romance and irony. Jonathan Stroud's (e.g., 2003) *Bartimaeus* trilogy ends with one of the main characters, Nathaniel, sacrificing himself so that Bartimaeus might live. Nathaniel is a character who grows from selfishness to this final act of selflessness over the course of the trilogy. But, as we'll see with *Harry Potter* below, the trilogy is an ensemble piece featuring a core trio (without as many secondary figures, but with more equality among the primary trio than in the *Harry Potter* series): Bartimaeus, Nathaniel, and Kitty. Bartimaeus and Kitty survive, tempering the loss (indeed, an unexpected loss, as we aren't sure Nathaniel has this in him) and providing that combination of heroic triumph and tragic sacrifice. We aren't asked to absorb the loss of the sole protagonist but are asked to deal with it to a degree, as in *Charlotte's Web*. There may be so many children's chapter books rather than novels of change or development for children specifically because the modalities at authors' disposal (or demanded by publishers)—romance and comedy—don't require (or present much opportunity for) change or growth on the part of either protagonists or readers. Traditional romance may feature unchanging heroes on a series of adventures, and comedy

in turn may feature rather minor misunderstandings that are cleared up and return us to the status quo. In many ways, the two modes of romance and comedy—of the quest and the cleared up misunderstanding—are more different by degree in children's stories than by kind, and their combination often yields quests that seem to result in defeating characters or situations reduced to ridiculousness rather than stories of real physical or, more important, moral heroism. For example, the Newbery Medal-winning *The View From Saturday* (Konigsburg, 1998) is ultimately about a group of four kids, each of whom has an experience or journey in which they come to some understanding (they live in the fictional town of Epiphany, NY) only to use this collective wisdom to win a quiz bowl. This isn't to say that there are no children's romances that require real demands from protagonists— there are a great many (any heroic quest narrative serves as an example here, whether in realism or in fantasy)—but children's fiction always has an available out of keeping the narrative about external and safe adventures. "This will end up alright," we want to be able to reassure our children, or at least low-risk, and romance and comedy always provide this in different degrees. The expected happy ending of a children's tale is a function of providing the romantic and comedic (especially in combination, using the latter to temper the former) more than it is an accurate account of what folktales tend to do. People tend to think of folktales as children's stories with happy endings; what is the case, however, is that we've only given children the ones that have such endings, or changed them to end this way, and we simply don't read folktales as adults, and so don't know about the ironic and tragic folktales. It is no accident, therefore, that Disney prefers its folklore to be of the fairy or Märchen variety as well as its modes either romance or comedy.

Both tragedy and irony, however, are more likely to force revelation and discomfort in the reader, even if the characters in ironic novels fail themselves to grow. The publishing industry tends to play it safe and follows a fairly Romantic view of childhood. Children, the Romantic argument follows, are to be protected from the chaos or nihilism of irony and the sadness of tragedy, however inspiring. Comedy offers a conservative if not completely static world view and the romantic hero quest thrills with adventure in which all will, we know, be well at the end, however dicey things seem to get. I usually put the chapter books we've read in my children's literature course side-by-side and contrast them by genre—alternative world fantasy, historical fiction, contemporary realism, autobiography, whatever it might be—and get students to agree how different they are, how separate they are on the scale of genre, but this is a set-up; we then discuss how irony, tragedy, romance, and comedy work and place the same books side by side: the dramatic differences argued for just minutes before disappear. They are usually bunched together within a few degrees of each other: All are either romance tinged with the comedic or comedy tinged with romance. They all provide different contexts (genre) for similar presentations of the nature of character and the world (mode). So, while the animal fantasy *The Tale of Despereaux* (DiCamillo, 2003) and the nonfiction account of the Iditarod in *Woodsong* (Paulsen, 1990) seem pretty different by genre, they are both romantic hero journeys that convey remarkably similar subtexts about the value of difference, the power of the individual, and the justified faith that any obstacle can be overcome in the service of a worthy goal. Whether of mice or men, the worldview of romance varies little.

Let's dwell on the Harry Potter series (e.g., 1997) on this point for a moment. Harry Potter is the story of the Boy Who Lived, an outcome that has a great deal to do with mode. If we think of the series as one long story, as it is meant to be, we can see how mode is the most important consideration of all—not genre (it is many genres, from portal fantasy to school story to family novel) or children's book, even (it is read by all ages). What all readers of all ages, friends to different genres, ultimately care about is how the thing will end, and in that ending we will have our answer to how we should feel, for Rowling has swerved along all modes over the course of the series, giving us three legitimate possible endings. It is the ending, and perhaps the last book as it sets up that ending, that will tell us what this story has been about, after all—it recasts our relationship to the seven books. And what ultimately happens is what we all wanted to happen, perhaps against misgivings by many readers: we get romance. The Hero ("chosen one," after all) defeats the Evil One. Rowling has prepared us for other possibilities, to her credit. The irony of Harry the Horcrux argues for one direction: Irony demands that, after all this time, he has been fated to be defeated since the day he was given his scar because he has been, all along, a container for part of Voldemort's soul. On the other hand, his final decision to face and likely be killed by Voldemort is the ironic tragedy of Jesus allowing Pilate to do what must be done to fulfill prophecy and make things right. That Harry somehow survives the attack (Dumbledore is seldom wrong, after all), is able to fool all that he is dead, and then is able to strike out against and defeat his much older opponent has the ultimate David and Goliath ending that we have expected, hoped for, and perhaps felt a bit guilty about being so relieved that it ends this way. I think as a children's series, though, tragic death might have been acceptable, especially if Voldemort is taken down with Harry, because the rest of the "family" is safe and the other main characters, Hermione and Ron, are safe and can play Horatio to Harry's Hamlet. Comedy was long out of the question as a choice, as the characters are too much larger than life, though Rowling has played the "he's just a mischievous boy, after all" card enough to make Harry likeable and not insufferably superior to us all, which could have been fatally off-putting. Irony, though deliciously present, is ultimately unthinkable in

the context of a children's book—especially as the end of a long series.

I think it is clear that Rowling has taken the safest, and ultimately the most satisfying route for a children's series, and one that will ensure that it is bought and read for years to come by parents who know things will end well and can reassure their children to that end. Rowling has saved parents the decision of whether or not to share a ripping good story that ends in a way that they know will give their children emotional pain, even if uplifting through sacrifice in tragedy. The epilogue to the series goes even further, almost asking for the comedic ending after all, complete with the double marriage resolution so common in comedies of error. The epilogue reassures us all that the right people marry, reproduce, and provide for their children the names of those who died in the struggle, thereby allowing them to live on. Its presence makes it certain that Rowling is aiming to please at the end of this epic series, not challenge the reader emotionally. For despite ending up as YA novels, the series begins and is considered a children's series, and will almost certainly be marketed in children's sections, next to C.S. Lewis, Ursula K. Le Guin, and Susan Cooper—not Stephanie Meyer.

Young adult novels, in contrast, much more fully represent all modal possibilities; a tragic novel like Lois Lowry's (1993) *The Giver* or a dystopic irony like M.T. Anderson's (2002) *Feed* are good examples of how the YA novel will venture into modes left unexplored in children's literature. This is one important way that young adult novels are closer to novels for adults than they are to novels for children. In fact, it might be fair to say that the YA novel is different than the novel marketed to adults more by degree than kind. Despite having thematic and structural tendencies of its own, the YA novel blends with the novel for adults in its employment of, for example, themes and scenes of sexuality and the presence of science fiction. This isn't to say that sex and spaceships are the simple dividers, but by mode, genre, and theme there is more in common between the YA novel and novel for adults than between the children's and YA novel. There could be a real theoretical argument that the YA novel is a subset of the novel for adults while the novel for children is its own creature.

To extend an implication made above, while fantasy is a major subgenre of the children's novel, there are very many fewer actual science fiction novels for children, and when we can think of examples we usually end up realizing that they are borderline young adult novels that share the middle school reader as the target audience. There are humorous science fiction stories, for instance, by Bruce Coville or Daniel Pinkwater—usually categorized for the middle elementary reader, and these are usually simply devices for comedy rather for pursuing truly speculative fiction. Exceptions are works by Margaret Mahy, Eleanor Cameron, Virginia Hamilton, Diana Wynne-Jones, and Monica Hughes. But little serious speculative science fiction appears before a target audience of sixth-graders. Ironically, however, it is young adult literature that Farah Mendlesohn (2004) believes has principal thematic differences with science fiction, not children's literature. While young adult literature focuses on the evolving adolescent's inner journey in the world, it is the changing larger world that is the primary concern of science fiction. This suggests an antagonistic relationship between what YA and science fiction focus on, respectively, despite the tendency of many to consign science fiction as an entire genre to the category of adolescent literature—damning them both as "popular literature" along with equally-maligned genres of the Western and the Mystery Novel. In any case, ironic or not, science fiction makes itself available as a choice for the young adult reader, who it seems has a choice between reading the inwardly focused young adult or outwardly focused science fiction novel.

As I mention above, the modes of comedy and romance provide the basic story patterns for children's novels. The science fiction that is available for younger readers will thus either follow the comedic pattern of misunderstanding resolved which leads to a return to the status quo at home, or it will feature the romantic narrative of heroic adventure or quest which provides a stable home (a return to one's own or to a "true" home) and a happy ending as well, as we see in the *Mushroom Planet* books of Eleanor Cameron (e.g., 1954), Isaac Asimov's *David Starr: Space Ranger* books (e.g., 1952), or even Madeleine L'Engle's (e.g., 1962) *Wrinkle in Time* books. The story patterns of the children's and young adult novel, respectively, differ based on the prevalence of the circular narrative found in children's novels and the prevailing linear pattern of the young adult novel. Critics such as Jon Stott (1978), Christine Doyle Francis (Stott & Francis, 1993), Virginia L. Wolf (1990), and Chris Clausen (1982) have noted the Odyssean pattern of the children's novel, the reaffirmation of home as the best place to be for the returning hero (of whatever size quest or hero). In contrast, the story of the young adult is often a story of getting away from home. Frank Kermode (1966) calls this linear trajectory, fully realized in the YA novel, an "apocalyptic" plot. While in romance the "events derive their significance from a unitary system" (p. 5), the apocalyptic plot is more time-conscious and crisis-driven. Kermode tells us that "the story that proceeded very simply to its obviously pre-destined end would be nearer myth than novel or drama" (p. 5), and the novel for children is more likely to follow that mythic system than those for the YA novel, which is often a crisis driven narrative covering a clearly defined portion of a school year. In this sense, children's novels have always been closer to folklore (though not *necessarily* fairy tale, as Disney prefers) and YA novels to the novel proper. Chris Clausen (1982) has illustrated the difference by pointing to two of Mark Twain's most famous novels. *The Adventures of Tom Sawyer* (1876) is a children's novel; its sequel, *The Adventures of Huckleberry Finn* (1884), is

not. Tom's adventures, presented by an external narrator, are episodic and comic, ending safely at home, Huck's and Jim's, narrated by the young adult himself, are comic in a picaresque and satiric way, ending with both protagonists charting new directions for themselves and their lives. Tom Sawyer's story idealizes childhood as an idyllic time in an antebellum United States, unconcerned with the divisions to come; while Huck's story is written after the war, it takes as its subject the human bondage that is outlawed as a result of the war and is hardly an idyllic look at anything. In fact, while Hemingway famously claimed that *Huck Finn* is the first great American novel, many point to *Huck Finn* as a precursor, if not initial instance, of the YA novel, and Roberta Seelinger Trites (2007) points to the novel, along with Louisa May Alcott's (1868, 1869) *Little Women* as an early example of the adolescent novel of reform.

The Epistolary and Verse Novels

There are other oppositional categories separating novels for children and those for adolescents. Two important trends in the YA novel are the epistolary and verse novels. The YA epistolary tradition begins, arguably, with Jean Webster's (1912) *Daddy-Long-Legs* and has continued to enjoy a healthy sampling in the market ever since, culminating in the Internet age with the recent text message novels of Linda Myracle (e.g., *ttyl,* 2004). Notable differences between the different media represented in Webster's and Myracle's respective novels include the story time between missives and the length of the letters. The move from actual letters to text messages changes the dynamic of what is possible in terms of the development of thought over time as well as the sense of the exchanges as conversation or dialogue rather than instances of monologue exchanged over greater time. One doesn't send one-sentence letters hoping for a response in the next half hour. The text message epistolaries have more in common with a telephone transcript than with "snail mail." However, the letters sent by Judy to her benefactor in *Daddy-Long-Legs* are no more or less successful in terms of her constructing an identity than what we see created by the text messages of the easily distinguishable three main characters of Myracle's novels.

Emily Wasserman (2003) notes that YA epistolary reflects what the young adult is engaged in as well as providing teenagers with fictional characters with whom they can identify. Unlike the children's novel, which isn't usually about crises of identity apart from identity theft or surprise (being found to be a lost prince or wizard or the only mortal who can help us or a changeling or some other way of making the child artificially important), the YA novel's primary subtext is usually about identity construction. A contemporary cult-classic is the MTV sponsored novel *The Perks of Being a Wallflower* by Stephen Chbosky (1999), in which an abused teen seeks out a stranger to send anonymous letters that serve as a diary or journal in which he can work out his thoughts. The successful series of diaries of Georgia Nicolson by Louise Rennison (e.g., *Angus, Thongs, and Full-Frontal Snogging*, 2000), Sue Townsend's Adrian Mole series (e.g., *The Secret Diary of Adrian Mole, Age 13 ¾*, 1985), and the Newbery Medal-winning diary *Catherine, Called Birdy* by Karen Cushman (1994) are other examples of the YA diary novel.

In fact, the character written text, as opposed to texts spoken to the narratee as in *The Catcher in the Rye* (Salinger, 1951), includes books like Jerome Foxworthy's summer-long journal about the previous year with his pal Bix (Bruce Brooks's [1984] *The Moves Make the Man*), S.E. Hinton's (1967) *The Outsiders* (the longest English paper ever written), the novel-long letter by the protagonist of Sylvia Engdahl's (1970) *Enchantress from the Stars* to her cousin about her interstellar journey, and Aiden Chambers's (1978) *Breaktime* in which the character Ditto records his own life as a story. The propensity for YA novels to be character narrated presents writers with the problem of how to contextualize the telling, and so these examples above point to the some of the ways it is handled, however awkwardly, apart from the epistolary or diary form. Typically, however, the character narration simply takes the form of an oral recount of events that span, usually, the previous school year. Few people seemed concerned with the mystery of the narratee and his or her writing occasion, it seems, so grateful are they for the identifiable voice of a young adult protagonist.

The verse novel for young adults is an even more recent phenomenon, and it has become something of a publishing trend. A quick look at one of the lists of verse novels for young adults on the net reveals that very few verse novels appeared before the late 1990s, making this format the first big development within young adult literature in the 21st century. If one buys that the novel itself is directly descended from epic (about which there is plenty of debate), it should surprise no one that a long narrative for young adults can be told through verse. But most verse novels, the vast majority, do not follow the oral tradition of rhymed verse. The contemporary verse novel is mostly a free-verse exercise, making it more closely akin to the prose novel.

When done well, the verse novel provides readers with brief, lyrical glimpses of character and thought. They are always character-driven as dramatic monologues even when there's a clear plot. Like matter itself, the verse novel is mostly air, and we see that even in the textual nature of the layout. When the form flops, we get a fragmentation whose parts never make a satisfying whole and "poetry" that is reformatted prose—free of poetry rather than free verse. But usually the whole is more than the sum of its dramatic monologues, and readers can begin to get a full sense of the story as either perspectives shift from speaker to speaker or as the single speaker returns again and again, as in diary or journal fiction. The monologue form is rich

with thought and action without going into overmuch exposition; as this makes most character narrated fiction interesting, it also works in the verse novel. It is as if all of that white space left on a page is where much of the exposition might have been, and readers fill it in through association or create it on their own. I think sometimes that the effect of reading a verse novel is not unlike watching a movie in subtitles: As I remember the film long after seeing it, I remember it in English rather than as something I read while a pleasing but inaccessible language is spoken in the background. Finishing a verse novel, I think I remember the exposition, though it was really just implied and I read it in the white spaces. And all of that free space on the page can be heartening to a reader otherwise intimidated by, say, the over 400 pages of Allan Wolf's (2004) wonderful verse rendering of Lewis and Clark's journey, *New Found Land*. Here we have an interesting compromise between the need for increased page counts (as discussed in my questionable canal lock metaphor above) and the desirability for beautiful and simple brevity. The verse novel is a book that reads "faster" than one might expect and might well satisfy adults who place a page count on reading success (see Apol and Certo, this volume, for a conflicting view). While I agree with Karen Coats that YA literature should be its own destination rather than a workout to ready the reader for the real stuff of literature for adults, the YA verse novel is a useful transitional literature for moving to another genre entirely. Success and pleasure at reading a verse novel might lead YA readers to be more accepting of poetry itself, and if we have more best-sellers in the poetry category we may have the YA verse novel to thank. In fact, the YA verse novel may well make young readers more open to language play and the unconventional in general, perhaps allowing them to see lyrical vignette (like Sandra Cisneros's [1991] *The House on Mango Street*) or lyrical surrealism (such as Francesca Lia Block's [1989] *Weetzie Bat*) as a legitimate option to the prosaic realist novel.

Notable practitioners and authors who have written at least two successful novels in verse include Sharon Creech, Helen Frost, Mel Glenn, Nikki Grimes, Sonya Harnett, Steven Herrick, Karen Hesse, Ellen Hopkins, Angela Johnson, Ron Koertge, Margaret Wild, Allan Wolf and Virginia Euwer Wolff, among others. The verse novel comes in different forms, but it has tended to be true to the YA narrative emphasis on character narration. This has meant that the books cross over into the diary genre, as do Karen Hesse's (1997) Newbery Medal-winning *Out of the Dust* and Ron Koertge's (2003) *Shakespeare Bats Cleanup*. The genre includes historical and multicultural fiction, contemporary sports, and even biography (Marilyn Nelson's [2001] *Carver: A Life in Poems*). Voices range from the single to the multiple; Allan Wolf's (2004) *New Found Land* employs thirteen different speakers. Nikki Grimes's (2002) *Bronx Masquerade* mixes prose with poetry (the poetry is read by the characters during class time). These novels range from simple strings of poems by one speaker after another (Patricia McCormick's [2006] *Sold*) to a novel like Mel Glenn's (1997) *Jump Ball: A Basketball Season in Poems*, which is divided in four parts, involves multiple speakers, and provides mixed temporal play through flash forward, or prolepsis.

Novels of Growth and Change

Young adult books are typically not called chapter books when they are discussed as a discrete category apart from children's books (the *New York Times* bestseller list shows they are often lumped together). Their categorization seems to parallel the divisions seen in literature for adults. One reason that the term "chapter book" isn't used in relation to YA literature is because the genre evolved out of the novel tradition of the *Bildungsroman*. While the picturebook dominates the world of children's books, the novel is the major genre of YA literature (a trip to any bookstore will confirm this). While YA books can be both episodic and comedic, it is far more likely that a YA book will be about change and growth, reflecting Romantic, modern, postmodern, and notions of self that can combine all of these movements. The YA novel is often either a full blown novel of growth (*Bildungsroman*) or of character change (*Entwicklungsroman*), as Roberta Seelinger Trites (2000) notes, and continues to be the story of enlightenment through personal struggle and reflection, as we see in novels by such authors as Robin McKinley, Gary Paulsen, and Annette Curtis Klause. The goals of the YA novel can be, alternatively, the triumph of the unified self able to grow, the integration of a self partly determined by society, or the discovery of a self (self-consciousness) that is almost purely socially determined. "Almost" is key, for even when they tend toward dystopia they show the capacity of the character for self-recognition. Trites has pointed out that the YA novel is the postmodern inheritor of a Romantic impulse. There is a tension, even in the most postmodern of YA novels, between the desire to create a romantic figure in search of self and of depicting society as the inscriber of the adolescent self.

Children's novels are still rarely postmodern, which I say as a matter of description rather than as indictment; in fact, it's almost certainly true that many adults appreciate this about children's novels. The children's novel will privilege a protagonist that is a unified self (variously static, changed, or grown by the novel's end) with the goal of being integrated into society—or, more usually and locally, achieving a home. Interestingly, there are some decidedly postmodern picture books in the market because they have a rather conflicted sense of implied audience (are they cool coffee table parodies for adults rather than children's books?), but chapter books and novels for children are rarely postmodern. Children's novels, despite showing children afloat in a world they don't control, don't argue for a deterministic view of society, as would be the

case for a more postmodern sensibility. At least not yet; it's still pretty early in the 21st century, after all.

Common Genres

Young adult novels and children's novels continue to share some elements and tendencies, though perhaps fewer than one might think. The young adult novel, caught in the continuum between childhood and adulthood, is parallel to children's literature mostly as a genre named for an implied audience. There are times when the young adult novel is more closely allied with the novel more generally, as I discuss above, and times when novels for children or young adults are indistinguishable. In what ways do the children's and young adult novels continue to be comparable? Clearly, fake or superficial realism is alive and well in both and fantasy is the great unifier.

The fantasy novel has always been popular for children and young adults. The circular movement of children's novels discussed above, and of children's literature generally, accounts for why we see so much of quest fantasy for children—and even makes possible something as odd (and oddly popular) as *The Brave Little Toaster*, a 1987 animated film that features earnest appliances in search of their master (oh, to have been a fly on the wall of the board meeting in which that idea was pitched). The quest fantasy for young adults, and ultimately for adults, seems to be a simple continuance. Really, it's the case that fantasy readers are famously unconcerned with distinctions between age groups, as opposed to readers of realism, and this is perhaps the greatest connection between children's, young adult, and "grown-up" novels—especially as it relates to what is called alternative world fantasy, or "high" fantasy. Adult readers are happy to pick up Lloyd Alexander's *Prydain Chronicles* (e.g., 1964) just as young readers have always tried to tackle Tolkien. The elements remain the same. High or alternative fantasy is set in an entirely different world from our own—there is no traffic between there and here. Readers of Tolkien, Le Guin, Lloyd Alexander, and Paolini rarely worry about whether they're the right age for the book.

Portal fantasy, however, has always been a staple of the children's novel. By "portal" fantasy I mean any narrative that begins in the world that the child character and child reader mutually identify and share as their real world, even if that world may not be of the same historical time. This starting point leads the characters across a threshold and into a fantastic dimension. This seems to be prevalent for a few reasons, not least of which is that this pattern matches up nicely with the mode of romance, which provides the heroic quest pattern of many children's novels, as well as the way such a pattern implies a safe sealing off of the fantasy world from the real world for the possibly anxious child reader. In any case, the portal fantasy is the stuff of classics, and seems still to be the accepted format for many children's fantasies. Obvious precursors to the contemporary portal fantasy novel for children include *Alice's Adventures in Wonderland* (Carroll, 1865) and *The Wonderful Wizard of Oz* (Baum, 1900). More modern classics include the *Narnia* series (Lewis, e.g., 1950), *The Phantom Tollbooth* (Juster, 1961), and *The Neverending Story* (Ende, 1983). In the portal fantasy, the child is able to shuck off all adult authority in his or her world and be a mover and shaker—often a "chosen one"—and have the sort of adventure that is reserved for adults in our world. The child hero of the portal fantasy always returns home, even if it takes a while; to do otherwise is to die in the world and stay in the dream. Children's fantasy rarely offers this particular kind of escapism, and adults (always the primary audience/purchaser of children's books) would be uncomfortable with the novel ending in the child's preference of the fantasy world over home. Cornelia Funke's recent *Inkheart* series (e.g., 2003) is a clear exception to this trend, whereas the Narnian Chronicles end with the children leaving both the real and the fantasy world for a "heaven" shared by both, so it hardly counts.

"Mixed" fantasy has also been a genre shared between children's and young adult literature, though this mixture of the fantastic and real dimensions can lead us into the subgenera of horror and stories of the supernatural, which aren't as prevalent in children's literature. Mixed fantasy for children tends toward the use of (often random) anthropomorphism rather than true invasion of the world by outsiders. In these novels animals in our world have a human consciousness and speech (at least among themselves, but often with humans as well), such as in *The Wind in the Willows* (Grahame, 1908), *Charlotte's Web* (White, 1952) and *Stuart Little* (White, 1945). The *Harry Potter* novels start off as more of a portal fantasy. There's a clear demarcation between the Muggle world and Hogwarts, and the wizards in power at that particular moment work to keep it that way. As the novels progress and Harry becomes more a young adult, the novels become more mixed—part of the darkness and horror of the later books is due to this mixture of the wizarding world and our Muggle world; not coincidentally, the novels become more YA in theme and scope. But the *Spiderwick* series (e.g., Black & DiTerlizzi, 2003), *Green Knowe* books (e.g., Boston, 1955), *The Indian in the Cupboard* series (e.g., Banks, 1980), *The Dark is Rising* series (e.g., Cooper, 1973), *The Moorchild* (McGraw, 1996), *Winnie-the-Pooh* (Milne, 1926), Dahl's novels, and any number of other examples show that we do share this mixture of the real and fantasy with children with as much regularity, if not the same degree of subtextual darkness, as books like Annette Curtis Klause's *The Silver Kiss* (1990) and *Blood and Chocolate* (1997) offer the adolescent market.

Fake Realism

A form of fantasy that children's literature seems to be more inclined toward doesn't look like fantasy at first blush—it's a sort of false reality, though presented as "realism." Fake realism (Le Guin, 1989) or superficial realism (Lewis, 1966) is ultimately wish-fulfillment fiction. Le Guin points to soap operas and pornography as examples of this sort of thing for adults; children's fake realism is typically set up as novels of development, but they are rather scripted and formulaic transformations. They give the reader what she wants, as romance does, but without earning it through building superior characters, in whatever way, who succeed believably—and this is a requirement of romance whether in fantasy or realism. The children's versions might come in the form of the sports stories in which a home run hit or goal scored is all that it takes to make the protagonist popular (unlike in real romance, we know this gimmick won't stick; the child needs more than a swing of the bat to deserve lasting happiness); it might also come in the form of the bully defeated (or converted) against all odds, requiring just a little pluck on the part of the protagonist ("I like your moxie, kid!"). Sports fake realism is a common form of wish fulfillment for all ages, and the children's/adolescent sports novel, such as those by Matt Christopher, has been offering young readers the thrill of the game-winning (and popularity-securing) basket/hit/touchdown/goal for decades. Young adult fake realism also features versions of the bully story, especially the novel in which "mean girls" are defeated.

For girls, then, our fake realism of today comes largely from Alloy Entertainment. These are the folks who bring the tweeners the wildly popular series about *Gossip Girls*, *The Clique*, *The A-List*, and *It Girls*—and what seems to be the whole YA gossip-oh-my-gawd-he's-so-cute-but-can-you-believe-what-that-bitch-said industry. It's clearly an entertainment company and would be a target for those concerned with representations of adult behavior and what is/should be important to adolescent girls. I guess you could say that they're the guilty beach-reads for adolescents, though we could argue that it's without the guilt. But hey, at least those kids are reading, right? These are novels that, unlike more clearly comic and contemporary realism like *The Princess Diaries*, haven't a tongue within miles of the cheek—at least not one's own.

Fake realism as a form of wish fulfillment would seem to be especially seductive, and well-meaning parents might mistake fantasy as the escapist fiction when in many cases it is fake realism that entices young readers to wallow in unrealistic expectations about their lives as well as others'. As long as novels are divided by genre, readers will tend to point to realism as the more relevant genre, not realizing that the line between realistic fiction and fantasy fiction is less what they mean to draw than the one between fiction and nonfiction—and as if any of it were free of manipulation. As there is at one end of the scale of relevance the generic sword and wizard fantasies there is the wish-fulfillment realistic tale at the other—neither has much to offer the reader in terms of learning about human nature or the human condition. But, unlike poor fantasy novels, bad realism novels can often be accepted as useful because they are set in some semblance of the real world, though they are no more real than the hyberbolic and idealized worlds of soap opera or pornography. So, instead of making the distinction between good books that fall in any of the categories of fiction and nonfiction, parents and children often draw the line of relevance between the true and the untrue regarding setting. This, I think, is no new trend or development as much as the continuation of an old problem.

Novels for children and adults will continue to evolve, much as the concepts of "novel" and the implied readership of young people will. As we now see the development of online novels, cyberfiction, hyperfiction, multimodal texts, and the e-book, new forms of the novel for young readers will continue to emerge, and in all of those new forms, children's novelists will have to decide what sorts of modal (and therefore, emotional) experiences to provide the child. These new forms may seek to innovate on generic conventions, but they will also be limited by what stories we as a culture want to tell our children, and even what we value as an acceptable experience of text—the canal might gain a few more locks as the book itself is supplanted by the screen. But while we might advance in electronic forms, we will likely still be limited to the pleasing and reassuring cycles and stasis of comedy and romance when we consider a novel suitable for children.

Literature References

Alcott, L. M. (1868, 1869). *Little women*. Boston, MA: Roberts Brothers.

Alexander, L. (1964). *The book of three*. New York, NY: Henry Holt.

Alexie, S. (2007). *The absolutely true story of a part-time Indian*. New York, NY: Little, Brown.

Anderson, M. T. (2002). *Feed*. Cambridge, MA: Candlewick Press.

Anderson, M. T. (2006). *The astonishing life of Octavian Nothing, traitor to the nation, Volume 1: The pox party*. Cambridge, MA: Candlewick Press.

Asimov, I. (1952). *David Starr: Space ranger*. Garden City, NY: Doubleday.

Banks, L. R. (1980). *The Indian in the cupboard*. Garden City, NY: Doubleday.

Baum, F. (1900). *The wonderful wizard of Oz*. Chicago, IL: George M. Hill.

Black, H., & DiTerlizzi, T. (2003). *The field guide*. New York, NY: Simon & Schuster.

Block, F. L. (1989). *Weetzie Bat*. New York: HarperCollins.

Boston, L. M. (1955). *The children of Green Knowe*. New York, NY: Harcourt, Brace.

Brink, C. R. (1935). *Caddie Woodlawn*. New York, NY: Simon & Schuster.

Brooks, B. (1984). *The moves make the man*. New York, NY: Harper & Row.

Bush, J. (2007). *Ana's story: A journey of hope*. New York, NY: HarperCollins.

Cameron, E. (1954). *The wonderful flight to the mushroom planet*. New York, NY: Little, Brown.

Carroll, L. (1865). *Alice's adventures in wonderland*. London, England: Macmillan.

Chambers, A. (1978). *Breaktime*. London, England: Bodley Head.

Chbosky, S. (1999). *The perks of being a wallflower*. New York, NY: Pocket Books.

Cisneros, S. (1991). *The house on Mango Street*. New York, NY: Vintage.

Cleary, B. (1981). *Ramona Quimby, Age 8*. New York, NY: Morrow.

Cushman, K. (1994). *Catherine, called Birdy*. New York, NY: Clarion Books.

Cooper, S. (1973). *The dark is rising*. New York, NY: Atheneum.

DiCamillo, K. (2003). *The tale of Despereaux: Being the story of a mouse, a princess, some soup, and a spool of thread*. Cambridge, MA: Candlewick Press.

Dorris, M. (1992). *Morning girl*. New York, NY: Hyperion Books.

Ende, M. (1983). *The neverending story* (R. Manheim, Trans.). Garden City, NY: Doubleday.

Engdahl, S. (1970). *Enchantress from the Stars*. New York, NY: Atheneum.

Fleischman, P. (1997). *Seedfolks*. New York, NY: HarperCollins.

Funke, C. (2003). *Inkheart*. (A. Bell, Trans.). New York, NY: Scholastic.

Gantos, J. (2000). *Joey Pigza swallowed the key*. New York, NY: HarperTrophy.

Glenn, M. (1997). *Jump ball: A basketball season in poems*. New York, NY: Lodestar Books.

Grahame, K. (1908). *The wind in the willows*. London, England: Methuen.

Grimes, N. (2002). *Bronx masquerade*. New York, NY: Dial Books.

Hesse, K. (1997). *Out of the dust*. New York, NY: Scholastic.

Hinton, S. E. (1967). *The outsiders*. New York, NY: Viking.

Juster, N. (1961). *The phantom tollbooth*. New York, NY: Random House.

Kinney, J. (2007). *Diary of a wimpy kid: Greg Heffley's journal*. New York, NY: Amulet Books.

Klause, A. C. (1990). *The silver kiss*. New York, NY: Delacorte Press.

Klause, A. C. (1997). *Blood and chocolate*. New York, NY: Delacorte Press.

Konigsburg, E. L. (1998). *The view from Saturday*. New York, NY: Aladdin.

Koertge, R. (2003). *Shakespeare bats cleanup*. Cambridge, MA: Candlewick Press.

Kushner, D., & Wilhite, T. L. (Producer), & Rees, J. (Director). (1987). *The brave little toaster* [motion picture]. USA: Hyperion.

L'Engle, M. (1962). *A wrinkle in time*. New York, NY: Farrar, Straus, & Giroux.

Lewis, C. S. (1950). *The lion, the witch, & the wardrobe*. London, England: Geoffrey Bles.

Lowry, L. (1993). *The giver*. Boston, MA: Houghton Mifflin.

MacLachlan, P. (1985). *Sarah, plain and tall*. New York, NY: Harper & Row.

McCormick, P. (2006). *Sold*. New York, NY: Hyperion.

McGraw, E. (1996). *The moorchild*. New York, NY: Margaret K. McElderry Books.

Milne, A. A. (1926). *Winnie-the-Pooh*. London, England: Methuen.

Myracle, L. (2004). *ttyl*. New York, NY: Amulet Books.

Nelson, M. (2001). *Carver: A life in poems*. Asheville, NC: Front Street.

O'Reilly, B. & Flowers, C. (2007). *Kids are Americans, too*. New York: William Morrow.

Paulsen, G. (1990). *Woodsong.* New York, NY: Bradbury.

Paterson, K. (1977). *Bridge to Terabithia.* New York, NY: HarperCollins.

Pullman, P. (1996). *The golden compass.* (*His dark materials*, Book 1). New York, NY: Alfred A. Knopf.

Pullman, P. (1997). *The subtle knife.* (*His dark materials*, Book 2). New York, NY: Alfred A. Knopf.

Pullman, P. (2000). *The amber spyglass.* (*His dark materials*, Book 3). New York, NY: Alfred A. Knopf.

Rennison, L. (2000). *Angus, thongs, & full-frontal snogging.* New York, NY: HarperCollins.

Rowling, J. K. (1997). *Harry Potter & the philosopher's stone.* London, England: Bloomsbury.

Rowling, J. K. (2005). *Harry Potter and the half-blood prince.* New York, NY: Arthur A. Levine.

Sachar, L. (1998). *Holes.* New York, NY: Farrar, Straus, & Giroux.

Salinger, J. D. (1951). *The catcher in the rye.* New York, NY: Little, Brown.

Selznick, B. (2007). *The invention of Hugo Cabret.* New York, NY: Scholastic.

Stroud, J. (2003). *The amulet of Samarkand.* (*The Bartimaeus Trilogy*, Vol. 1). New York, NY: Hyperion.

Townsend, S. (1985). *The secret diary of Adrian Mole, Age 13 ¾.* London, England: Methuen.

Twain, M. (1876). *The adventures of Tom Sawyer.* Hartford, CT: American Publishing.

Twain, M. (1884) *Adventures of Huckleberry Finn.* New York, NY: Charles L. Webster.

Webster, J. (1912). *Daddy-long-legs.* New York, NY: Grosset & Dunlap.

White, E. B. (1945). *Stuart little.* New York, NY: HarperTrophy.

White, E. B. (1952). *Charlotte's web.* New York, NY: HarperCollins.

Wolf, A. (2004). *New found land: A novel.* Cambridge, MA: Candlewick Press.

Clausen, C. (1982). Home and away in children's fiction. *Children's Literature 10*, 141–252.

Frye, N. (1957). *Anatomy of criticism.* Princeton, NJ: Princeton University Press.

Kermode, F. (1966). *The sense of an ending: Studies in the theory of fiction.* Oxford, England: Oxford University Press.

Le Guin, U. K. (1989). Why are Americans afraid of dragons? In *The language of the night: Essays on fantasy and science fiction* (pp. 34–40). New York, NY: HarperPerennial.

Lewis, C. S. (1966). On three ways of writing for children. In W. Hooper (Ed.), *Of other worlds: Essays and stories* (pp. 23–27). New York, NY: Harcourt.

Mendlesohn, F. (2004). Is there any such thing as children's science fiction?: A position piece. *The Lion & the Unicorn 28*(2), 284–313.

Natov, R. (2003). *The poetics of childhood.* New York, NY: Routledge.

Nikolajeva, M. (2005). *Aesthetic approaches to children's literature.* Lanham, MD: Scarecrow Press.

Nodelman, P. (2008). *The hidden adult: Defining children's literature.* Baltimore, MD: The Johns Hopkins University Press.

Shavit, Z. (1986). *Poetics of children's literature.* Athens, GA: University of Georgia Press.

Stott, J. C. (1978). Running away to home—a story pattern in children's literature. *Language Arts 55*(4), 473–477.

Stott, J. C., & Francis, C. D. (1993). 'Home' and 'not home' in children's stories: Getting there—and being worth it. *Children's Literature in Education 24*(3), 223–233.

Trites, R. S. (2000). *Disturbing the universe: Power and repression in adolescent literature.* Iowa City: University of Iowa Press.

Trites, R. S. (2007). *Twain, Alcott, and the birth of the adolescent reform novel.* Iowa City: University of Iowa Press.

Wasserman, E. (2003). Epistolary in young adult literature. *ALAN Review 30*(3), 48–51.

Wolf, V. L. (1990). From the myth to the wake of home: Literary homes. *Children's Literature 18*, 53–67.

Academic References

Cadden, M. (2005). Simultaneous emotions: Entwining modes in children's books. *Children's Literature in Education 36*(3), 285–298.

Point of Departure

Philip Pullman

Mike Cadden's essay deals with a number of issues very deftly. The question of what a children's book really is does engage critics, and not only critics: many adults who are probably not literary critics have asked me who the intended audience of *His Dark Materials* is, and what they mean, as I discover when I ask them to elucidate, is "Is this really a children's book?"

What I say in response varies according to the occasion. But if I have time, what I tend to say is that I write for anyone who is kind enough to want to read me, and that I don't want to shut any reader out. That's always been an instinctive reaction on my part, and I didn't have to think through what it meant till 2008, when many UK children's publishers declared that they were going to put an age-guidance figure on all their books. The original impulse for the idea clearly came from supermarkets that wanted to know which shelf to put a book on without having to pay someone to think about it.

Like many other British authors, I was outraged by this unilateral declaration (nobody had asked us what we thought about the matter). Several of us joined together to set up a website in opposition, and we were able to encourage many writers to stand up to their publishers and say "Not on my books, you're not." Many writers told us that their publishers had said, in effect, "It's all right for X and Y to object, because they're best-sellers, but frankly, dear, you're not in that league, and you'd better toe the line."

I mention that affair in this context because I have never known any issue, in my 30 years or more of being published, that raised more passion among my fellow-writers; and because it's evidence that it clearly matters a great deal to many people, and for many reasons, whether such-and-such a book is really a children's book, and if so, for what age it's suitable. As I say, it made me think through my attitude to my own work: did I have an audience in mind? If I did, what sort of audience was it? The conclusion I came to was that I very much wanted an audience, and a big one, please, but that I didn't believe I had the right—and I certainly didn't have the desire—to say what sort of audience it was to be. I didn't want to turn anyone away who wanted to read me.

That meant welcoming everyone, of any age, who was able to make out the words; which in turn meant playing fair with them, and not, for example, making fun of some readers by winking over their heads at others. Mike Cadden refers to some "postmodern picture books" which "have a rather conflicted sense of implied audience (are they cool coffee table parodies for adults rather than children's books?)," which describes exactly the sort of thing I mean. Even in my most "postmodern" story, *Clockwork, or All Wound Up,* I tried to keep every strand of the multiple narratives free of the acid of irony, which has such a delightful tang when you're grown-up, but makes you feel unfairly got-at before you're used to it. There is a little drop of it in the last paragraph but one, though.

I find it interesting that whereas many adults have, as I said, quizzed me about the intended audience for *His Dark Materials,* no children have. Young readers seem to be content to read that book, at least, without wondering whether they're doing so licitly, as it were. I don't know what that says about readership or implied audience or whatever, but if a book doesn't positively say "Keep Out," it seems that children will be prepared to tackle it. And there are several ways to say "Keep Out," including dull cover design, unskillful typesetting, poorly executed illustrations, a rebarbative prose style, and, of course, those age-guidance figures we authors made such a fuss about a couple of years ago. They have all been tried, and they all work.

I'd take slight issue with one aspect of Cadden's essay, and that's the word "genre." I think that's a bit misleading when applied to books that children read. "Fantasy" is a genre, and so is "historical fiction"; but I don't think a genre is best defined in terms of those who are expected to read it—or if it is, there is almost always an element of condescension involved: "chicklit," for example. Every writer of "children's fiction" knows that condescension intimately, from the receiving end. Surely a genre is something else. One of the processes involved in becoming a reader is the discovery of a genre that seems to speak to the very core of your being, and many a young person has become an adult reader by getting drunk on science fiction or ghost stories. That sort of passion isn't likely to be stirred into life by some large bland category called "books for children."

However, Cadden knows this, and he's quite right to stress the "Nexus" part of his title. The shelves we set aside for children are those where connections are made, and we need to protect them and give children plenty of time and plenty of opportunity to make those connections for themselves. But protection doesn't mean exclusion; it seems a shame that so many very good books remain neglected on those shelves, books that would find a keen readership among older readers, if only they were free to roam the library and take up residence in the adult section. But that's my current obsession: everyone should be welcome. "Children's fiction" should shut no one out.

22

Young Adult Literature

Growing Up, In Theory

Karen Coats

Illinois State University

While children's literature often plays a central role in elementary school curriculum, young adult literature journeys toward secondary schools, but rarely arrives. Here Karen Coats, literary critic and Lacanian scholar, argues that like young adults themselves caught in a liminal state, YA literature frequently experiences a failure to launch, not simply in curriculum as Lewis and Dockter argue in their chapter of this volume, but in literary criticism as well. Coats explores the reasons that books for young adults should be a "destination literature," rather than characterized as a short sidetrack before stepping into more sophisticated material designed for adults. She further analyzes the polyphonic, dialogic, culturally conditioned, ever changing, and emotionally laden qualities in current YA literature. In his Point of Departure essay, Markus Zusak, the astonishing author of *The Book Thief,* affirms Coats's arguments in his desire to write "the right book at the right time in that ridiculously raw period of a person's life."

As a sixth grader in a small, rural middle school, I finished my math book in six weeks. Not knowing what to do with me, the powers that be put me to work in the school library. Looking back, I realize that if they would have introduced me to a more advanced math curriculum, my professional life might have turned out very differently. Instead, I found a cache of books on a shelf in the library workroom that very likely set the course of my career. They were young adult books, they were banned, and I read every one of them.

These books full of questionable material about sex, drugs, and antiwar protests taught me what it meant to be an American teenager in the 1970s. From Nat Hentoff (1968), Judy Blume (1975), S. E. Hinton (1967), Robert Cormier (1974), and John Donovan (1969), I learned what was going on in the world outside my sheltered community, and I got some insight into the people who sat across from me at the lunch table. It wasn't until I went back to those books as an adult that I realized how much of my own everyday speech, expressions, thought patterns, and values had been influenced by their words and ideologies. Young adult literature exerts a powerful influence over its readers at a particularly malleable time in their identity formation, and yet we still pay more critical scholarly attention to *Antigone* (Sophocles, c. 442) and *The Great Gatsby* (Fitzgerald, 1925) than we do to the potentially life-changing books our teens read on their own. It seems to me that if we believe that literature has something to say about what it means to be human, and if we further nuance that belief with the idea that national, ethnic, and women's literatures say something about the character and preoccupations of nations and the experience of being of a certain ethnicity or gender, then we ought to approach YA literature with the same careful scrutiny, even if it is written about and to young adults rather than by them.

It may seem, of course, that I am speaking to the choir here; after all, this *Handbook* is evidence that there is a group of people who take YA literature very seriously. However, this volume also contains evidence that there are different kinds of choirs who sing in different keys and with different kinds of harmonies to different audiences. I am currently in the literary theory choir, but I have some experience singing education and library sciences tunes through my history as a secondary teacher and my current work as a reviewer. Hence, what I want to address in this chapter are the various critical debates that emerge from different disciplinary standpoints.

I will begin by briefly exploring the status of YA literature in secondary and postsecondary educational settings, that is, by thinking about the ways YA literature is legitimized as appropriate reading material in high schools and as a fit subject for literary criticism. For the bulk of the chapter, however, I will look at the literature itself from a literary and cultural theory perspective by exploring some of the many tensions that can be found by analyzing the tendencies that these texts share. As a body of literature, YA fiction is organized around the same sorts of tensions that preoccupy the physical bodies and emotional lives of its intended audience: tensions between growth and stasis, between an ideal world we can imagine and the one we really inhabit, between earnestness and irony, between ordinary bodies and monstrous ones, and, perhaps most importantly, between an impulsive individualism and a generative ethics of interconnectedness. To explore these tensions, I will adopt a librarian's approach of including many references to YA books in an attempt to demonstrate the dialogues at work in this body of literature. Unfortunately, space will not allow the extended close readings of the texts that literary critics favor and teachers encourage; instead my aim is to sow the seeds for further thinking about the many thematic dimensions at work in contemporary YA literature and the critical dialogues surrounding it.

YA Literature in Secondary and Post-Secondary Contexts

In her 1996 article, "Young Adult Literature Evades the Theorists," Caroline Hunt threw down a gauntlet of sorts to literary critics engaged in the teaching and study of YA literature. She called on critics to theorize their subject, to bring YA literature into the wider dialogue that had come to characterize the work of English departments, namely, literary and cultural theory. She believed that the main reason YA literature had not been considered theoretically is because courses on YA literature were usually service courses for Education and Library Science majors, and hence focused on topical lists and trends, analysis of literary elements, pedagogical applications, and issues of censorship. Indeed, the definitive textbook in the field, Donelson and Nilsen's (2008) *Literature for Today's Young Adults*, first published in 1980 and now in its eighth edition, provides exactly that material for preservice teachers and librarians. The focus in this text and these courses, as it is for most work done with literature in Education and Library Science, is on the interaction between texts and readers. Thus the academic study of young adult literature in these disciplines is primarily, and quite rightly, concerned with engagement and response.

In English Education, young adult literature is often viewed as a gateway drug used to entice readers to try the harder stuff. There is even a textbook entitled *From Hinton to Hamlet: Building Bridges between Young Adult Literature and the Classics* (Herz & Gallo, 2005) that champions and provides resources for this approach. For teachers as dealers, it's not a bad scam. If I want my students to read and understand what's at stake in *Othello* (1755/1969), I have to work against the foreignness of Shakespearean language, the gaps of history and culture, and the strangeness of distant characters (what the heck is a Moor anyway, or a standard-bearer for that matter?). But if I can introduce them to Tim Blake Nelson's *O* (2001) first, they can immediately see the relevance of the story to their lives and the conflicts they face on a daily basis. Alternately, if I am trying to introduce a new and sometimes alienating critical vocabulary to my students, it makes good pedagogical sense to rub the theory up against literature that they can readily access.

Roberta Seelinger Trites (2000) describes a technique for getting her students to understand the literary concepts of polyphony and dialogism through a role-playing exercise where students answer questions from the perspectives of Tehanu, Tenar, and Ged from Ursula K. LeGuin's (1990) fantasy novel *Tehanu*. According to Bakhtin (1981), who first introduced the concepts of polyphony and dialogism, literature can sometimes be monologic, offering a single, authoritative viewpoint through flat characters who are designed as mere vehicles to express or embody that viewpoint. In children's and YA circles, we would scorn such works as overtly didactic. Meaningful literary texts, like all meaningful cultural interactions, function polyphonically. Such "dialogic" novels create a living dialogue between a variety of voices, styles, and intertextual references and allusions that add to the richness of the reading experience by enabling readers to share in the making of meaning and encouraging them to situate themselves within the themes under consideration.

As Trites's students realize the difficulty of crafting a single answer, even from a single character's perspective, to a moral or ethical question, they begin to understand the multiple voices and contradictions that are involved in the creation of a believable, multi-faceted character. This exercise would work well for any number of complex characters that students can readily empathize with in contemporary realistic novels, such as Steve from Walter Dean Myers' (1999) *Monster* and Keir from Chris Lynch's (2005) *Inexcusable* or Violet from M. T. Anderson's (2002) dystopic science fiction novel *Feed,* and it works considerably better than taking them straight to Bakhtin and Dostoyevsky to learn the same concepts.

The goal in such exercises is that students will then be able to apply the theory they have learned to more sophisticated adult texts. Anna O. Soter (1999) has written a textbook that seeks to help teachers apply various literary theories to young adult texts, and Bushman and Haas (2006) make eloquent and compelling arguments for using young adult literature rather than adult classics in secondary English classrooms in order to engage students in the critical process through literature that they actually enjoy. Countless journal articles have appeared that offer readings of particular texts through various theoretical lenses as well as ways of using YA literature to approach social and cultural problems. Yet, despite this show of support for the value or at least the utility of the literature to teach other things, there remains a sense that YA literature is a house you pass on the way, and not a destination in and of itself.

It may be because YA literature is in fact the literature that I would prefer to read even if I didn't make a living doing so that I would argue strenuously for a shift in this perspective. That is, just as children's literature is viewed as both an entrée into more sophisticated reading for its intended audience and a viable area of academic study in and of itself, so literature aimed at young adults should be afforded the same dual valuation. Like Hunt (1996), I would like to see a more robust critical conversation emerge that treats YA literature as a destination literature, rather than an in-between phenomenon that is useful for pedagogical applications and/or diverting entertainment before readers enter into the more serious work of studying capital L literature. Instead of moving from Hinton to *Hamlet,* I would argue for a productive move from Hinton to, say, Zusak, where readers might consider, among other things, the role of physical violence in the complex rhetoric of loyalty, masculinity, and fraternal love that comprises coming of age for Ponyboy (*The Outsiders,* 1967) and Cameron Wolfe (*Fighting Ruben Wolfe,* 2001 and *Getting the Girl,* 2003). It's certainly not a question of sacrificing richness in character portrayal, beauty of the language, or depth of thematic significance. All of these things can be found in carefully chosen YA literature. The major difference seems to rest in the assignation of cultural value to certain texts and genres and not others,

and the development of a critical literature than keeps texts and ideas circulating in academic contexts. To consider YA literature as a viable destination literature, the terms of traditional theoretical conversations surrounding the study of literature would need to be recast.

YA Literature as a Destination

Certainly, traditional methods of literary study, such as applied theoretical discussions of single texts or sets of texts using the various "isms" that have become standard fare in literary and cultural criticism, are a growing and necessary part of that critical conversation. So are historical studies that map trends in the development of the literature, such as Anne Scott Macleod's (1997) "The Journey Inward: Adolescent Literature in America, 1945–1995" and Roberta Seelinger Trites' (2007) *Twain, Alcott, and the Birth of the Adolescent Reform Novel.* Establishing a history of YA literature and even, dare we say it, a canon of significant texts, and showing those texts' ability to stand up to the rigors of critical scrutiny are all part of the process of legitimizing a marginalized literature in the field of literary studies. What remain rare in the critical discourse are studies that seek to theorize YA fiction as a type of literature that has its own constellation of concerns that mark it as distinctive from literature for either children or adults.

Two such studies do exist, their authors having found controlling themes that act as paradigms for understanding YA literature's distinctiveness. In her definitive work *Disturbing the Universe: Power and Repression in Adolescent Literature,* Roberta Seelinger Trites (2007) argues that while adolescent literature may seem to be about growth, that growth always takes place in the context of power—who has it, who doesn't, and what must be negotiated in order for the adolescent to gain power in his or her culture. By exploring the relationship of the teen protagonist to various institutions of cultural power as well as the biological imperatives of sex and death, Trites views adolescent literature as a staging ground for power struggles whose outcomes determine the ethics and delimit the possibilities for agency of the young adult as an actor in his or her world. Using a primarily Foucauldian paradigm, Trites expands her theoretical field to include insights from poststructural theory generally, and invites teachers of YA literature to do the same in order to empower their students to question the narratives that often, under a slick cover of cool or edgy plotlines and characters, seek to interpellate them into oppressive cultural mandates.

In *Ideologies of Identity in Adolescent Fiction: The Dialogic Construction of Subjectivity,* Robyn McCallum (1999) focuses on the dialogic construction and representation of the adolescent self in literature for young people. She emphasizes how the self is constructed and mediated through interaction with ideology, cultural and social forces, and other selves. Her approach is Bakhtinian, exploring and deconstructing the conceits of a liberal humanist emphasis on individual agency that is so prevalent in young adult fiction. The cheese doesn't stand alone after all, Mr. Cormier; the notion of the individual has been revealed in postmodern discourse and representation as a fiction, to be more precisely understood as what René Girard (1987) has called an interdividual. To counter the liberal humanist ideology of the essentialized self as agent, McCallum (1999) offers a model of reading that seeks to place "implied readers in active subject positions" (p. 259) by emphasizing the analysis of texts that employ mixed genres, multiple narrative strands, and varied modes of discourse through Bakhtinian concepts of heteroglossia, polyphony, and intertextuality.

I often teach Virginia Walter's (1998) *Making Up Megaboy* in precisely those terms. In this mixed-genre, mixed media book, the main character is the decentered subject of postmodern discourse *par excellence*. He never speaks for himself, and those who would speak for him know strikingly little about him. We learn the facts: On his 13th birthday, Robbie Jones takes his father's gun, bikes to a local liquor store, and murders the Korean shopkeeper in cold blood. The rest of the book proceeds in a documentary style, with news and police reports, interviews of friends and family members, photo montages, and finally, a comic drawn by Robbie that seems to have nothing to do with the incident, and provides no insight into who Robbie is, other than the fact that he feels alienated and alone. Readers are often frustrated and deeply disturbed by the gaps in the narrative line of this text—there is no cause and effect, no foreshadowing, no way to profile this kid as a potentially violent shooter. And although this text predates Columbine and other high profile school shootings that followed as well as 9/11, it offers an eerily prescient picture of how a criminal adolescent subject is created for mass consumption through various soundbites, documents, and retrospective profiles.

As readers, we learn about the ways characters, indeed people, are constructed through their actions and the way society views those actions, through the impressions of others which are always more than half embedded in narcissistic self-impressions, and through more nebulous and abstract cultural expectations that help us fill in gaps in our experience with prefabricated subject positions. Unpacking these last is often the most disturbing for readers, as in doing so they unearth unconscious prejudices that filter into our ways of perceiving the world.

Considering these prejudices in secondary and postsecondary classrooms through the "classics" or through works that feature adult protagonists from times past allows for the possibility that students may distance themselves from what they are reading. The experiments with narrative form in classic texts may fail to register with today's students as new or innovative. The contexts are often alien, particularly to marginalized groups, because of the predominance of dead white male perspectives; there is

the sense that that was then, this is now; those characters are the kinds of adults we will never be; it's all different today. Contemporary YA literature, on the other hand, stages an up-to-the-minute confrontation with a mirror they can't look away from, and thus makes moral, social, and cultural problems both accessible and urgent.

What YA Literature Teaches Us about Itself

I find it revealing that both McCallum and Trites look to Bakhtin's theory of dialogism as key to the study and pedagogy of YA literature. That they find this theory so useful suggests to me that there is something about the literature that requires a paradigm of mutual and multilayered imbrication to understand the construction of its subjects. YA texts tend to appear in thematic clusters, revealing an intertextuality that responds to the market, which in turn responds to prevailing cultural and personal fantasies. For instance, YA shelves in the early 21st century are littered with mean girl novels featuring obscenely rich protagonists doing what they can to make life hell for those outside their circles. On the other hand, ensemble friendship novels, such as *The Sisterhood of the Traveling Pants* (Brashares, 2001) and its sequels, feature girlfriends who make each others' lives bearable.

While books about girls have always located their characters in relationship-intensive plotlines, gone are the days where getting the guy ends the story with a happily or a tragically ever after. Girls today are generally encouraged to be more savvy in negotiating objectifying discourses, even standing against mainstream feminism in their quest to chart their own destinies. In Randa Abdel-Fattah's (2007) *Does My Head Look Big in This?,* for instance, Amal, an Australian-born Muslim Palestinian with a passion for pop culture, must thread her way through social, political and spiritual ideals of gender in her decision to wear the hijab in a post 9/11 secular high school context. What is most interesting in her decision is the way the hijab intersects with her desires to be pretty and flirt with cute boys while asserting her commitment to sexual purity. The protagonist from E. Lockhart's (2008) *The Disreputable History of Frankie Landau-Banks,* plays in a similar space of ambiguity, where she wants to be recognized as a sexual being but also as someone more substantial and deserving of recognition for her ingenuity in disrupting the masculine traditions of her school, in particular a secret society that excludes girls from membership.

In books that feature male protagonists, the idea of dialogism has emerged as a self-reflexive theme of identity construction. The 1970s myth of the lone male standing against peer pressure and shaping his own destiny has given way to an exploration and frank acknowledgement that identities are in fact shaped by our participation in groups, rather than our standing apart from them. Markus Zusak's character Cameron Wolfe, for instance, is a working-class boy who is struggling to emerge as himself rather than as an indistinct shadow of his brother in *Fighting Ruben Wolfe* (2001) and *Getting the Girl* (2003). His quest is individual, but it is defined through and through by his being a member of the Wolfe family, his pack. Both he and Ruben are guided by the strong examples of their parents who have implicitly taught them to fight their way through adversity and setbacks, and Cameron knows that the key to his identity is finding meaningful connectedness with the people he loves, rather than standing alone against them. Arnold Spirit, in Sherman Alexie's (2007) *The Absolutely True Diary of an Part-Time Indian,* is self-consciously caught in the space between life on the rez, where he is brutally bullied and his future prospects are dim, and life among White people, which his best friend Rowdy reads as the ultimate betrayal of his heritage. He works out his identity by laying claim to a number of tribes to which he belongs:

> I realized that, sure, I was a Spokane Indian. I belonged to that tribe. But I also belonged to the tribe of American immigrants. And to the tribe of basketball players. And to the tribe of bookworms.
> And the tribe of cartoonists.
> And the tribe of chronic masturbators.
> And the tribe of teenage boys.
> And the tribe of small-town kids.
> And the tribe of Pacific Northwesterners.
> And the tribe of tortilla chips-and-salsa lovers.
> And the tribe of poverty.
> And the tribe of funeral-goers.
> And the tribe of beloved sons.
> And the tribe of boys who really miss their best friends.
> (p. 217)

Even though he is making a boldly individual choice by leaving the reservation to pursue his future, he still recognizes and needs the sense of connection to others to help him understand who he is.

Helen Frost (2003) uses poetic form to highlight this sense of connection as an ideological shift between generations. In *Keesha's House*, a novel in verse, the teenagers, each with his or her own clichéd problem, speak in sestinas, while the adults use sonnets. The sestina is a fluid form that emphasizes connectedness among its six-line verses through the repetition of the last words of each line, and their reappearance in a final, three-line stanza. Frost furthers the theme of connectedness and fluidity by repeating the number six in the number of kids that end up mutually imbricated in each other's lives, and by varying the number of syllables in the lines of her sestinas, making it a less rigid form.

The sonnets of the adults, on the other hand, are formally composed, following the rules of iambic pentameter and the rhyme schemes of either English or hybrid sonnets. These poems, like the adults who voice them, are isolated; thematically and structurally, they stand alone. The maturity that the teens gain through their experiences is signaled by a shift to the sonnet form for the final section of the book, but unlike their adult counterparts, who have problems that they feel they must face alone, the teens have formed a community of support for one another. Thus they stay connected through a crown of sonnets, acknowledging that their strength in the face of overwhelming obstacles comes from their mutual interdependence.

In David Levithan's (2003) *Boy Meets Boy* the character of Infinite Darlene, who is both homecoming queen and star quarterback, stands out as exemplary of this new paradigm of the self in community:

> She seems very full of herself. Which she *is*. It's only after you get to know her better that you realize that somehow she's managed to encompass all her friends within her own self-image, so that when she's acting full of herself, she's actually full of her close friends, too. (p. 41)

If the hallmark of the teen character has traditionally been Holden Caulfield's narcissistic self-involvement, then Infinite Darlene represents a kind of expansive narcissism that admits of embeddedness in community as integral to the self.

Examples of the need for interconnection, multiple perspectives, and mutuality abound. Through form, content, and intertextuality, the myth of the atomistic, liberal humanist self is being satisfactorily debunked in YA literature. But the key player is still, more often than not, a figure who positions him or herself as cultural outsider. In my own work (Coats, 2004), I have used a Lacanian paradigm to identify contemporary adolescent literature as a site of working through the physical, psychic, and social abjection of the teenage body seeking meaning and value in a culture that places that body in a liminal space between childhood protection and adult responsibility. Characters who operate on the social rim situate themselves as observers not fully integrated into the culture they tend to view with equal parts longing and disdain. I have further identified a common character type in adolescent literature, the abject hero, who forces the reader to confront his or her own complicity in the creation and maintenance of those oppressive cultural and psychic systems, not as victim, critic, or mere spectator, but as someone who stands by and lets victimization occur at best, a victimizer herself at worst.

The complex relationships between characters like Jerry Renault and Archie Costello in Robert Cormier's (1974) *The Chocolate War* and Tulip and Natalie in Anne Fine's (1997) *The Tulip Touch* expose the coextensive, almost erotic relationship between the victim and the victimizer, and the way these perverse relationships prop up the cultural system as a whole. Archie comments that his activities with the Vigils, which amount to cruel manipulations of the teachers and the students, keep the school from being torn apart by outside forces. The tension that he holds to a slow simmer through his pranks keeps the students focused on the inner world of their school, rather than on any larger forces that may be at work in their world. The book explicitly highlights the way Archie uses his power to manipulate and abuse Jerry, but what goes unsaid is the way Jerry needs Archie to abuse him. Jerry's guilt over his inability to grieve his mother needs to be assuaged. He longs to be punished for his indifference to her death in order to be able to feel it properly, so he seeks physical pain to break through the emotional ice block. The pain of football doesn't serve, because it is random and part of the game, but Archie's campaign of oppression, in both its unfairness and Jerry's ability to place himself in positions where it will intensify, is just what Jerry needs to work through his own issues.

Natalie, on the other hand, uses Tulip's shocking cruelty as a way to distinguish herself as a good person; she builds her sense of self by abjecting that part of her that identifies with and is fascinated by Tulip. And yet she continues to need Tulip in her life to remind her where the lines are. These stories show a darker side to dialogism—it's kind of a warm fuzzy to think that our subjectivities are interconnected with the others in our lives, that we are not existentially singular as liberal humanist ideology would have it, and that we are embedded in communities. But the presence of an abject hero reminds us that part of that self-construction in community depends on abjecting others that we or our communities revile while continuing to use them for our own purposes.

Each of these literary critical studies dedicated to YA literature—Trites's, McCallum's, and Coats's—identify and offer descriptions of the key players in the game. They include the young adult, social others, culture and its institutions, ideology, language, narrative conventions, the body, and they insist on the importance of their dynamic interaction in the creation and study of YA literature. However, their substantive conclusions are necessarily contingent, because the nature of their subject is always changing, or more precisely, the nature of their subject *is change*, both personal and cultural.

For instance, if the holy trinity of the teenage years, at least since Elvis and the Beatles, has been sex, drugs, and rock 'n' roll, then postmodern surveillance and Internet culture has added fame to the mix. In 1989, Peter Dickinson wrote *Eva*, a novel where a young girl's brain is transplanted into the body of a chimp, resulting in her development of an increased social conscience and concern for the environmental devastation caused by overpopulation. In 2008, Meg Cabot traversed similar ground in *Airhead*, but her protagonist's brain is transplanted into the brain of a supermodel, whose major concerns then become how to balance multiple love interests, pick the right color lip gloss, and deal with paparazzi. Robin Benway's (2008) *Audrey, Wait* details the viral and invasive nature of sudden fame in a way that both interrogates and affirms the desire to be a household name. The strange illusion of intimacy afforded by "reality" TV programs and the overexposure of celebrities has added a new space of yearning for teens, and YA publishers have exploited that space by providing an alarming number of glitzy, wish-fulfilling titles such as *The Clique* (Harrison, 2004) and *Gossip Girls* (Von Ziegesar, 2002) series that feature wildly rich and remarkably unsupervised teens behaving badly.

Young adult literature thus responds to and helps contextualize cultural trends for its readers. In this way, it is itself dialogic—that is, it participates in the vibrant and constantly shifting cultural dialogue regarding what we value and how our lives might be lived both responsibly and responsively in the face of increasing globalization, perspective-altering technologies, and ideological challenge and change.

To Grow or Not to Grow

It is this quality of constantly changing cultural conditions and definitions, I suspect, more than the pedagogical sites of its dissemination, that makes YA literature tricky to theorize. Julia Kristeva (1990) makes the argument that the novel form itself, as least the classical liberal humanist novel, is by definition adolescent insofar as it is always concerned with chronicling the growth—moral, cognitive, emotional—of a character. But this definition is limited in its application. Existential and postmodern novels for adults often no longer fit this definition, as there we find stories of characters who stay the same, or even devolve or regress in their developmental path from beginning of the book to the end. YA novels, for the most part, still operate under the imperative of growth, but more and more we are seeing books, like the series book cited above, that simply tell stories.

To take an example from an emergent and as yet understudied national YA literature, critics of the recent explosion of Chinese books for young adults by young adults decry these books as unworthy of the tradition of Chinese literature because they are simply entertaining stories. Wildly popular, these books, by a group of writers dubbed the "post-80s writers" because of when they were born, show no commitment to social issues or improving moral philosophy, nor are they very original. Instead, they tend to feature kids with diagnoses such as bulimia and depression who are just struggling to get out of their teenage years alive.

The writers themselves don't care what the critics say, however, nor do their readers. Most, however, do object to the convenient appellation of "post-80s writer," considering it demeaning, but it is culturally significant because it means that they were all born after China implemented its one-child policy in 1979. Teddy Carey (cited in Rui & Dalby, 2007) dismisses the older critics, claiming a different purpose for his writing than literary glory: "I don't care about things like these official writers' congresses or associations; I don't care if these old men accept me. Their formalism doesn't concern me. I just use my words to record my life, and find those who understand me." That sort of reaching out for understanding is crucial for the one-child generation, many of whom, as these writers attest, grew up feeling lonely and isolated. It's especially telling that the most successful writer in China today is Guo Jingming, whose editor decided to publish Guo's first book, *City of Fantasy*, "because it would appeal to the lonely children of China's one-child generation" (King, 2008, p. X). Guo and other post-80s writers, such as Han Han, Zhang Yueran, Sharon, Ming Xiaoxi, and GirlneYa (Gou Ni) are writing for a new Chinese youth culture (that looks remarkably like British, American, Canadian, Japanese, Australian, and European youth culture)—fashion and celebrity conscious, rebellious, tech savvy, and iconoclastic. They are as much pop icons as they are writers, which is another reason why the writing establishment hates them and the teens love them. They are trendy and hip, and Guo and Han are particularly yummy eye candy, a feature they self-consciously play up to attract young fans to their work.

Although the majority of novels by the post-80s writers engage adolescent problems such as eating disorders, abuse, depression, drug use, other forms of Chinese YA lit take a decidedly lighter view of contemporary culture (Martinsen, 2006). Shen Hanying, the managing editor of a new Chinese form for young adults, the "'mook'"or magazine-book, explains:

> I want to give a dream world to girls who like to dream: a rose colored fable, a glittering crystal conservatory, an extravagantly lovely pumpkin carriage, miraculous rose magic books, candy houses overflowing with fragrance and love, a place where you can drink your afternoon tea in the sunlight while reading lucid, transparent, romantic fairy tales. (Cited in Martinsen, 2007)

Many of the post-80s writers have created or invested in mooks, which have a tremendous audience even though (or perhaps because) they are decidedly frothy. Their light-hearted approach to teen life and culture is a large and important part of their appeal, as well as the appeal of much commercially successful young adult literature.

Teenagers think differently than either child readers or adult readers. That is, it is demonstrable that they think with a different part of their brains. Recent research into brain activity during adolescence shows that, in addition to radical hormonal fluctuation, teenagers are subject to significant brain development and growth (Spinks, 2002). Their physical and mental coordination is undermined by an underdeveloped but rapidly growing cerebellum, rendering them physically clumsy and making it difficult to stabilize their emotions through cognitive processes, and their first responder to stimuli tends to be their amygdala, the emotional or gut reaction center of the brain, rather than their frontal cortex, which is responsible for calculating risk, moral considerations, and consequences. Thus, a large part of the success of these Chinese works of adolescent literature is due to the fact that they engage readers on an emotional level.

This may be particularly important for kids who have grown up without siblings to mirror and amplify, and thus validate, their emotional responses to the world, but it is a crucial factor for all teens as they develop the affective and imagistic aspects of their identity. Unfortunately, these vital components of identity are often dismissed as unimportant or even silly and distracting in institutional settings such as formal schooling, where concern for linguistic, intellectual, and cognitive growth outweighs attention to other aspects of development. Young adult fiction that considers extremes of emotion and focuses on impression management rather than challenging moral or social problems may not seem "serious" or overly invested in the project of growth toward maturity, but if viewed in light of a more complex formulation of identity, one that takes into account emotions and image perception as well as ethical and intellectual development, it clearly deserves theoretical attention, if not traditional critical acclaim.

Claiming the Popular

Chinese young adult literature, like much pop cultural production, is unapologetically not engaging deep philosophical or moral truths, but rather working at the level of identification, emotional mirroring, and fantasy, all of which we hope teens will grow out of, or at least come to view with some sort of mature perspective. A similar claim could be made for most popular YA lit produced in the United States, Britain, and Australia as well, which brings us to yet another problem in the theorization of YA literature: How does one think seriously about texts that are apt to have a short shelf life because their success depends on their responsiveness to a readership who are, by definition, in a state of flux? Should we only study those texts like Cormier's (1974) *The Chocolate War,* Walter Dean Myers's (1988) *Fallen Angels,* or Markus Zusak's (2006) *The Book Thief,* which engage in weighty philosophical and ethical questions? Or should we find ways to think about the more ephemeral books, the ones that are widely read, but probably won't outlast their generation? While books like Per Nilsson's (2005) *You & You & You* scream symbolism! allegory! deep meaning!, others like Jennifer Lynn Barnes' (2008) *The Squad* series about cheerleaders who are also highly trained government operatives are just good fun.

To be successful in a critical enterprise that makes room for both the serious literature and the merely popular means taking into account the peculiar response needs of the audience. Ethics and ideology are largely matters of emotion and image with teens, and yet as adult critics we tend to treat emotionalism, sentiment, and melodrama with disdain. Successful adult authors of YA texts, however, have no such prejudices; instead, they honor the energy of the emotions of the period through both representation and intervention, and critics may be wise to follow their lead. Indeed, developing critical frameworks that are adequate to the range of the contemporary textual field of YA will often set YA literature critics, as feminist critics before them, against the grain of established protocols, as it will likely entail taking on some of the characteristics of adolescence itself. That is, critics, like teens, will need to rebel against established theoretical orthodoxies and adult-inflected expressions of value, to be constantly attentive to innovation, to follow cool, to take risks, to be unapologetically presentist, to reach strong but always provisional conclusions, to adapt our critical identities to the objects we study, to be fickle in our pleasures.

That said, we will need to resist other qualities of adolescence, namely, the hyper-narcissism of judging others by our own experiences, and an unreflective immersion in and advocacy for those things that please us in the moment. If these sorts of methodological commitments sound a lot like the Cultural Studies advocated by Grossberg (2006) and cited by McGillis in this volume, then I would say, yeah, it's a Zeitgeist thing—as culture becomes more youth-oriented in its emphases, values, and entertainments, the lability that characterizes youth has become part of the way we study culture and the literature a culture produces. Such a model of critical inquiry requires a context of continual refreshment; studies like Trites's and McCallum's provide us with the terms we need to consider and reconsider as we build our "political histor[ies] of the present" (Grossberg, 2006, p. 2).

The Problem of Definition

Still, a persistent obstacle to the serious study of YA literature that might be worth considering is the lack of a clear demarcation of the field. Where does children's literature end and adolescent literature begin? Is a text like *Tehanu* (LeGuin, 1990) even considered by most critics to be YA, and if so, what makes the crucial distinction? Does authorial intention matter? Robert Cormier's (1974) *The Chocolate War,* for example, was never intended for a young adult audience, but was rejected as an adult novel and has since become one of the most acclaimed YA books of all time. If not author intention, then what about reception? Books such as *The Lovely Bones* (Sebold, 2002) and *The Secret Life of Bees* (Kidd, 2002) were written for adults but have become staple fare for teen readers. And of course, crossover happens in the other direction as well, as with Pullman's (1996) *Dark Materials* trilogy and J. K Rowling's (1997) books about a young wizard. Many scholars simply defer the question to the marketers, but savvy marketers have tapped into the crossover phenomenon by creating alternate covers and trim sizes that correspond to consumer expectations to house the same texts, so is form what really matters? Reviewers take the marketing into consideration, but at the *Bulletin for the Center for Children's Books,* for instance, publisher-indicated age ranges are sometimes modified as the team of reviewers, which includes working librarians as well

as academics in the fields of English and Library Science, consider format, likely appeal, length, vocabulary, and sophistication of the subject matter as factors in deciding a recommended age range.

Pragmatic considerations also enter into the mix in academic study. For instance, at my university, we have separate courses for preadolescent and young adult literature. Hence, my colleagues and I can argue about the fine (or less fine, depending on perspective) distinctions between those two categories. While we agree that the age of the protagonist is important to making the distinction, my colleagues Anita Tarr and Roberta Trites both cite sex as a key determining factor between YA literature and preadolescent texts—if a book has sex in it, it's YA; if it doesn't, it's preadolescent. My own distinctions tend to be more ideological in nature— I argue that a book that has what I call a closed moral universe, that is, a plot line that features punishment for the wicked and reward for the good, is more likely to be preadolescent, whereas a book that calls that moral universe into question, such as *The Chocolate War, I am the Cheese,* oh, anything by Cormier really, or *Monster* by Walter Dean Myers, is clearly YA. Thus, sex or no sex, I tend to follow Trites' (2000) argument in *Disturbing the Universe* where she argues that YA novels tend to be more interrogative of social constructions, as well as critical of the notion of a responsive universe beyond what might be readily identified as social institutions.

My criterion rests on my belief that most contemporary literature for young people operates on the overly-simplified modernist assumption that children develop their moral judgment through a series of stages that roughly correspond to age categories, and that ambiguity in the moral fabric of represented worlds is detrimental to that development in its earlier stages but quite necessary in developing an ethical framework and a sense of moral agency in the teenage years. Most universities don't have the opportunity to separate preadolescent and YA literature, and hence include the middle grade novel in their YA courses; McCallum (1999) also includes what I would consider middle grade fiction in her discussion of adolescent literature, so it may be that fine distinctions are more fiddly and pedantic than necessary for developing the critical conversation regarding YA literature, but it seems to me that the concerns of a sixth grader (bored library aides aside) are quite different from the concerns of a 16-year-old, and so their literature would differ in significant ways. It also seems that defining the field by its concerns is helpful in establishing the boundaries of one's critical arguments.

Constructing Contemporary Adolescence

It is important, for instance, to think about how adolescence is constructed in YA literature, including its distinctiveness from childhood and preadolescence. This is a strong focus in Trites's work, but since its primary characteristic is that it is a state of change, it is a component that needs to be continually re-examined. Even 10 short years after the appearance of Trites's and McCallum's studies, our cultural narratives about adolescence have changed. Significantly, even though their books appeared after the Columbine shooting, because of publication cycles, the bulk of their writing and the books they include in their studies predate that watershed event, at least in an American context. More globally, the events of 9/11, a generalized fear of contagion that began with the AIDS epidemic in the 80s and continued through SARS and vague threats of chemical warfare, have left behind a legacy of fear that has seeped into YA literature in veiled ways as an increase in the exploration of the monstrous and the panopticon of surveillance culture. Additionally, personal technologies have changed the way adolescents interact and interface with their world. New rhetorics have developed around instant messaging and texting, and if we take poststructural claims about the significance of language in the creation of identity seriously, then changes in the way we use language and the way it uses us will alter who we imagine ourselves to be. If we expand the definition of language to include multiple semiotic systems, then we could say that today's youth generate their identities and subjectivities through an increasingly visual, iconic, and virtual web of images that has largely been stripped of traditional modes of authority, including the authority of an Oedipal family structure and its contingent conflicts.

Like children's literature, YA literature is traditionally defined by its audience, not its writers. Hence, adult writers use a combination of memory, observation, and belief to convey their sense of the world as it appears to an adolescent consciousness, as well as to craft characters who are believably adolescent in their approach to that world. Writers who are insensitive to language and semiotic system shift rarely create believable teen characters, not simply because their fictional worlds lack verisimilitude if they don't include cell phones, brand names, and computers in their contemporary YA novels, but because teens who have instant access to images, information, and communication think differently than teens did 10 years ago. Even dystopian YA fantasies must respond to the kinds of thinking made possible by current developments, such as the extreme technologies of beauty that are the focus of Scott Westerfeld's (2005b) *Uglies* series and Melvin Burgess's (2007) *Sara's Face* and changes in the human/machine interface detailed in *Feed* (Anderson, 2002), a text I will take up in more detail later.

While these futuristic novels often act as satire, warning, and critique, contemporary realist novels tend to engage new technologies without accompanying social commentary. For instance, in her very successful novels *ttyl* (2004), *ttfn* (2006), and *l8r g8r* (2007), Lauren Myracle tells her story entirely through text messages. She effects character development in these books not so much through first-person introspection or third person description as through the use of online personality quizzes, font styles, and predictable responses to common scenarios. That adolescents feel an attachment to these characters suggests something about the changing nature of relationships. Communication between friends is constant but largely without substance, and it is mediated by technologies that subordinate individuality and thought to the straitened rhetoric of profiles and icons. This, like the notion of abjection, can be tied to the concept of dialogism in negative ways. The voices of others, as well as the big Other of mainstream culture, that become part of the conversation through which we construct our selves have lost the qualities of truly meaningful dialogue and interaction. Instead, they have been largely replaced by a homogenized, hive-based, aesthetically and semantically bankrupt shorthand that offers little scope for meaningful innovation or self-exploration. OMG!):

Repeat Offenders

Likewise, the images teens access through their technologies are ubiquitous in their repetition—the same shots of Britney Spears, for instance, appearing on every channel and magazine cover and website over and over again, the obsessive coverage of celebrities, the white noise of commercials repeated so often that their slogans and jingles become part of our everyday lexicon. According to Freud, repetition of a trauma is part of the process of working-through the trauma's aftereffects; the intense popularity of Lurlene McDaniel's oeuvre with many teen readers demonstrates this nicely. As Trites (2000) points out, "… in adolescent literature, death is often depicted in terms of maturation when the protagonist accepts the permanence of mortality, when s/he accepts herself as Being-towards-death" (p. 119). The trauma of facing your own mortality requires some working through, and many teens do this work by seeking out books where the characters face the death of a loved one or a sibling. By repeatedly facing this trauma in fiction, they fortify their mental defenses against its occurrence in real life. McDaniel's texts, which include such titles as *Six Months to Live* (1985), *Too Young to Die* (1989), *Sixteen and Dying* (1992), and dozens more like these, also play out a more subtle drama of traumatic acceptance as well. In book after book, the character faces the terminal illness or unexpected death of his or her teen lover. Hence, she thematizes the impossibility of a perfect romance; you can only have a perfect love if one or the other party dies before everyday problems or annoying little tics can infect the romance. Not only does she repeat the trauma of death for her readers, but she repeats, on an unconscious level, the trauma of lost idealism in the realm of love.

While the kind of repetition that teens access through media may facilitate the working through of some personal and cultural traumas, it also seems to create a perceived need for more repetition—the comforting buzz of the same. Hence, teens in the 1960s and 70s were actively looking for the new and shocking, and today's adult librarians and reviewers come to disdain the repetition of the same themes, character types, and conflicts, looking instead for something fresh. Yet, contemporary teen readers are increasingly more likely to seek out sequels, series, parodies, and books with familiar plot lines to meet their media-saturated libidinal needs. If you liked *Twilight* (Meyer, 2005), here are five books just like it, and they are overtly marketed that way. In sum, because contemporary teens' sense of identity, relationships, and libidinal needs are in many ways quite different than they were 10 or 20 years ago, writers and critics who depend on their own memories of their teenage years are unlikely to capture the concerns of their contemporary audiences.

Innovators, On the Other Hand

Those who are successful, on the other hand, tap into rich veins of ideological concerns. For instance, M. T. Anderson's (2002) *Feed* is a complexly imagined vision of a time in the future when humans are wet-wired to the internet through microchips implanted in the base of the skull. Without the use of any external devices, they can "chat" with each other, shop, access information, watch TV and movies, and get high. When Titus wants a pair of pants, for instance, he simply thinks his desire, and advertising banners scroll through his head, announcing sales, product availability, and new products, all tailored to Titus's unique sales profile, which knows his size and what he might be interested in based on what he has purchased in the past. When he has made his selection, money from his bank account is instantly transferred to the store's account, and the pants are shipped.

This level of shared information points to a theme that is developing in response to increased technology and new forms of communication. Whereas in the 1960s, 70s, and 80s, privacy was a key value in the development of the liberal humanist version of an independent, autonomous self, today's teens have a different attitude toward the private self. While many people still experience consumer profiling as a creepy invasion of privacy, Violet and Titus experience it as a form of care. Someone is actually paying attention to what they like, and they want them to have more things they will enjoy. When Violet learns that no corporation will pony up for the cost of her health care because her consumer profile is too random (she has, in fact, sabotaged it deliberately, without anticipating this consequence), the reader is forced to consider his or her own attitude toward consumer profiling in light of Anderson's strong rejection of it. Less subtle is Nancy Werlin's (1998) vision of a community that regularly exchanges shopping cards so that stores can't get a lock on consumer spending patterns in *The Killer's Cousin*. It's a small plot detail, but these two examples show that adult writers

are less ambivalent about profiling than their adolescent readers may be, and seek to get their readers thinking about the practice.

Anderson does remarkable things with language in his book, inventing new slang, for instance, and depicting the degradation of precision in technical communication among the doctors: "[The doctor] said, 'Okay. Could we like get a thingie, a reading on his limbic activity?'" (p. 57). In a world where information is available at the speed of thought without the intervention of a device, people no longer need to accumulate stores of traditional knowledge; they can simply pose a question and the answer appears in their head. This doesn't make them smarter, however, and Anderson is careful to have his main character, Titus, be the only character besides Violet to think and talk in metaphors, rather than instructional or functional language. When Titus frets about this ability as a problem, his parents assure him that he is not stupid, merely a nontraditional learner, the new "tradition" being the unimaginative consumption of immediately pragmatic knowledge, rather than the ability to innovate, synthesize, or produce new knowledge. Furthering his not-so-parodic parody, Anderson has Titus's parents comfort him by assuring him that he is beautiful, and by buying him a car, the ads for which they send directly into his head, taking retail therapy to a new, but very familiar, level.

Anderson also pays attention to other semiotic signs as markers of identity. The girls, for instance, follow trends slavishly, going into the bathroom to change their hairstyles the minute a new look comes across their feed. Most disturbing, though, are the presence of skin lesions, which become aestheticized body markings when they start showing up on pop stars. The lesions are vaguely linked to some sort of environmental contamination, possibly caused by the feed, but are clearly a metaphor for the trendiness (and ultimately ugliness) of body marking and piercing in contemporary culture, as well as a nod to the viral nature of trends. When I teach *Feed* to my students, they find themselves deeply disturbed by the analogues to their own culture that Anderson chooses to augment in his vision of the future, mostly because they know that this is how cool works: a trend or fashion is innovated, taken up by early adopters, blown out by media representation and repetition, and then more quietly adopted by all but the laggards in a progression that seems formidably inevitable—adapt or die. What disturbs them most is their desire to have the things that will ultimately lead to their destruction.

The Worst of Times

YA literature thus constructs as well as reflects an idea of adolescence, just as children's literature does for childhood. Unlike childhood, however, adolescence is not usually remembered with fond nostalgia, nor is it imbued with mythic status as a place of idyllic stasis. Rather, adolescence is a threshold condition, a liminal state that is fraught with angst, drama, and change anxiety. The burden of adolescent literature has always been to achieve synchronicity with the concerns of an audience that is defined by its state of flux and impermanence. Adolescence is a phase someone one goes through. It's a problem if you get stuck there, or at least, it used to be. And this is an added dimension of adolescence's provisionality—its status in culture undergoes change as well. Consider Swedish author Per Nilsson's (2007) *Seventeen*, which features a father talking to his unconscious son, Jonatan, in an emergency room, detailing a life that is in many ways the requiem for an age of rebellion. He tells the story of being a hippie in Sweden, of meeting a rebellious girl at a demonstration, and how the two of them attempted to live out the communal ideal of the countercultural movement. Jonatan's mom, however, has managed to grow up, channeling her idealism into a career in law where she works for social justice, while his father became a jealous drunk, and eventually went home to live with his parents. Clearly, the inability to accept adult responsibility and negotiate a way to keep one's social commitments after the heyday of protest marches, free love, and drug experimentation ended is presented as a dead end.

Nilsson's book is a first-person memoir, an adult recounting what life was like for him as a teen; it also offers a counter-perspective as Jonatan's mother gives her impressions of her ex-husband and their life together in decidedly less romanticized terms. This makes for a strongly authentic narrative, as the voices of the characters correspond with the age, insight, and hindsight of the writer. Most narrators in YA literature, however, do not take this backward looking perspective. Mike Cadden (2000) encourages us to be suspicious of such constructions, especially when they appear in the guise of first person narration, which makes its own claims for authenticity through the pretense of immediacy. Adult writers are projecting a consciousness that has at least the wisdom of having been there done that, so any guise of naivety, of being in the moment and not knowing if and how things are going to work out, is a fiction. This can be read as a bad faith manipulation, or it can be read as a comforting reassurance that however bad the situation, it is ultimately surmountable.

For instance, rarely do teens have the perspective of Dipsy in Gordon Korman's (2003) *Jake, Reinvented,* who self-consciously fashions himself as a remora in a world of high school sharks. The remora, according to Dipsy, attaches itself to the underbelly of the shark and feeds off of his leftovers. Dipsy uses the metaphor to justify the way he is bullied by the football players at F. Scott Fitzgerald High School. He is the butt of all their jokes, but in return, he gets invited to all of the good parties, has a wide circle of friends, and enjoys quite a bit of high school fame. Because the shark never eats his remora, Dipsy feels protected in his role, rather than abused, and he has accepted it because it is a way of getting through the shark-infested waters of high school to something better. Adult writers know that most of the awfulness of high school is temporary, and they can offer perspectives that help readers find their own metaphors for getting through.

Another voice of the bullied comes from Tom Henderson, the protagonist of Frank Portman's (2006) *King Dork.* Adopting a post-Columbine ironic stance to his plight of being continually harassed by the cool people at his school, he takes to wearing military garb and publicly reading weapons magazines in order to make his enemies wary that he might go off on them at any time. Oddly, his strategy works, and he is generally left alone to complain, Holden Caulfield style, about the phoniness of the people and institutions that surround him, especially those who valorize Holden Caulfield as the spokesperson of an age. Although his self-absorbed navel-gazing is very similar to that of Holden's, Tom has a diametrically opposed view of childhood and adolescence as a protected space that he is loath to leave. In considering Holden's desire to protect kids from plummeting out of the childhood fields of rye over the cliff into adulthood, Tom recalls the many incidents of bullying that his youth and social position have made him powerless to fight and concludes:

> I'm sorry, but I'm rooting for the kids and hoping they get out while they can. And as for you, Holden, old son: if you happen to meet my body coming through the rye, I'd really appreciate it if you'd just stand aside and get out of my fucking way. (p. 246)

Tom's perspective on childhood and adolescence is one of the most prevalent ones in contemporary YA literature; when authors go about constructing adolescence, it seems that most of them construct it as angsty and awful. Perhaps, however, it is more accurate to say that books that construct adolescence as angsty and awful are the ones that get taken most seriously by critics and educators.

In the past two decades, however, and particularly since the turn of the 21st century, YA literature has found the fun in being young, beautiful, and relatively carefree. Adult chick and Chica Lit, with their comic takes on body image, ethnicity, relationships, and shopping, have trickled into YA lit in the works of Sue Limb (2004), Louise Rennison (2000), Sherri Winston (2008), Alisa Valdes-Rodriguez (2008), and Michele Serros (2006), among others. Adolescent male humor rocks from the pages of Christopher Paul Curtis's (2004) *Bucking the Sarge,* Derrick Barnes's (2006) *The Making of Dr. Truelove,* and Sherman Alexie's (2007) *The Absolutely True Diary of a Part-Time Indian*, where the humor augments the poignancy. David Levithan (2008) and Walter Dean Myers (2007) have found both the sweet and the funny in all kinds of romantic relationships in novels and short story collections. Even books like Laurie Halse Anderson's (1999) *Speak*, which deals with the aftermath of the rape of an eighth grade girl, treat their subject with a good deal of dark humor. In YA literature, it would seem that the importance of being earnest in the 1970s and 80s has taken a decided turn to the importance of being ironic.

There are, of course, multiple ways to account for this shift from earnestness to irony. One would be that the issues involved require significant emotional investment: the sprouting of adolescent body parts, the management of identity in the seething cauldron of high school, the negotiation of moral agency in a complex and often hostile and unfair environment. Certainly, the emotions we invest in these things can be serious, intense, and unpleasant. Indeed, for several decades, the emotions that predominated in YA literature were quite devastating, as authors worked through problems of body image, eating disorders, failed romance, sexual and physical abuse, parental death, racial oppression. The problem is that unpleasant emotions are, well, unpleasant. For the most part, healthy people seek pleasure in their emotional states, so humor is a way to maintain an emotional investment in a difficult situation, but to keep that investment pleasant rather than unpleasant.

Another more complex way of thinking about this shift is to tie it to ideological change. It is generally accepted that we live in what is called a postmodern era, even if no one can quite agree on what that means. In literary and cultural studies, we follow the work of Jean Francois Lyotard (1984) in linking the idea of postmodernism with the demise of a belief in grand narratives; that is, the notions of transcendent, universal ideals of Truth, Beauty, Family, God, etc., that characterized modernist thinking have been supplanted by the understanding that these things are culturally determined and local in their application. What isn't widely recognized is that vestiges of these grand narratives persist in our belief systems, and that no matter how much we raise our consciousnesses about certain things, archaic impressions from the unconscious push back against cognitive, rational determinations. As a result, dissonance, which is mostly but not quite completely cognitive, results between the fractured worlds we inhabit and the whole, ideal worlds we imagine and wish for. Humor is one way of negotiating that dissonance; making fun of our ideals and our attempts at heroism softens our disappointment at their failure.

Another way that we cope with this sort of dissonance is by engaging in the kind of fantasies that stage conflict and violence in an exaggerated way. When earnest effort fails to bring us to the place in the world we wish for, we manage our anger by imagining aggressive scenarios that lead to the vicarious release of real tension. Again, this operates at both a personal and a cultural level. In the heyday of the European Enlightenment, there was much optimism about the continued development of human society if we could simply find the right formula for social relations; advances in medicine, technology, and cultural exploration were enough to convince us of our evolution and ultimate perfectability as a species.

Didn't happen. Instead, technology devolved into more efficient means for destroying larger numbers of people, and human society fell apart on a grand scale not once, not even twice, but continually throughout the 20th and into the 21st century.

Teenagers in postmodern culture thus find themselves in a paradox of potentiality. Children's and most young adult literature closes with a message of possibility and resilience, and this narrative is shored up by politicians who talk incessantly about hope, peace, and change while simultaneously loading the next generation down with financial, environmental, and emotional debt and continuing to engage in both violent conflict and meaningless political squabbling and gamesmanship. More unsettling, however, is the brand of violence rightly called terrorism, because it operates outside of a system of bloodless political disagreement and staged warfare. Combat troops know, to some degree, what they've signed on for; people killed in subway trains or in their workplaces or schools cause us to remember that there are real monsters among us. More disturbingly, these acts tend to bring to the surface our own murderous impulses, as we are more likely to contemplate revenge than compassion, understanding, or even justice for the attackers. There are monsters among us, and there are monsters within.

The late 1990s and early 21st century saw an explosion of vampire and other monster texts for young adult audiences, largely, I would argue, in response to the increasing sense that we live in a dangerous world where evil is lurking in the shadows, and where we sometimes have to become monsters ourselves in order to protect what we care about. The grand narratives of patriotism and clear poles of good and evil that dominated the public discourse of the World Wars largely dissolved in the protests of the 1960s and 70s, leaving behind a legacy of self-doubt and ambiguity regarding who is the aggressor and who is the victim. Representations of monsters in literature operate in part to stage these ambiguous positions and explore the possibilities of continued violence versus understanding and redemption.

At the level of embodiment, the figure of the monster makes for a remarkably apt image of the changing adolescent body; growth spurts, lurching clumsiness, and new oozings and protruding body parts are all things we associate with both monsters and puberty. The changes are scary, and I (Jackson, Coats, & McGillis, 2007) have argued elsewhere that girls in particular experience a Gothic moment at menarche, where the comforting narratives of becoming a woman or a medicalized understanding of what puberty means pale before the archaic fear of the issue of blood from one's own body. Elsewhere, the figure of the vampire, with its sadistic, overwhelming need to penetrate and feed off the flesh of another, provides a powerful analogue for the adolescent body just awakening to its not-yet-under-control sexual appetites and desires, as well as many of the attendant problems of coming of age.

For instance, the traditional reading of a vampire as someone who has lost its reflection has particular resonance for the teen, for whom appearance is everything in a lookist culture. The idea of not having a reflection resonates with the loss or mutation of identity, of not seeing oneself as others do. Chris, in M. T. Anderson's (1997) *Thirsty,* is devastated by the idea that he is turning into a vampire; he is the Holden Caulfield of vampire world, reluctant to take up adult responsibilities especially when they require sexual activity, which he cannot separate from his predatory feelings. He much prefers his metrosexual fantasy, like Holden's, of a sophisticated celibacy, a meeting of minds, hearts, and passions but where no actual fluids need be exchanged. Anderson goes out of his way to link Chris's change to a recognition that he is gay: "You gonna come out of the coffin?" (p. 202) a girl vampire taunts, and Chris worries that his mother will not be able to accept his vampire identity. But his obsession with Rebecca multiplies interpretive possibilities, and the peculiar poignancy in Chris's predicament becomes how to remain human in the grand battle between good and evil, even when every instinct you have screams for you to give in to your predatory desires.

Teens are often scripted in contemporary culture as fearsome creatures, especially when they roam in packs, like the Five in Annette Curtis Klause's (1997) *Blood and Chocolate.* But much contemporary YA literature, in keeping with the trend toward dialogism and community discussed above, sets out to redeem that image. The Scoobies in *Buffy the Vampire Slayer* (1997–2003) are in fact a formidable pack, but they use their powers for good. Likewise the vampires in Scott Westerfeld's (2005a) *Peeps.* Peeps are people who are parasite-positive; that is, they have a parasite that, when ingested, presents with the symptoms of vampirism, including a revulsion for mirrors, an enhanced sexual appetite, superhuman strength, a hatred of light, and cannibalism. If a victim is merely a carrier, or if a victim can be given a course of medication to control the more virulent and socially unacceptable symptoms, then he or she can join in the war against a horrible, ancient evil that exists underground; indeed that is why the parasites exist, to keep the creature in check so that humanity can flourish.

Melissa de la Cruz (2006) places her vampires as the first families of New York City, the Blue Bloods who shaped and still sustain the economy of a nation. They came to this country to escape persecution, but were followed by an even older order of vampires, who destroyed one of the settlements and left only a word—Croatan—as a warning. Both de la Cruz and Westerfeld offer shades of humor in their "now you know the rest of the story" explanations for the origins of vampirism, which answers to a contemporary appetite for debunking myth and legend in favor of pseudo-scientific explanations, but they also present their vampires as attractive, special, and able to save the world, which is a very affirming and redemptive

message indeed for teens who feel a kinship with the monstrous.

Many contemporary vampire and monster novels, then, are deeply concerned with the ethical development of young adults. Their teen characters are cast as both the plague and its cure; their bodies are powerfully and potentially monstrous, but they have the ability and the responsibility to hold their power in check, and use it for good. They are at a threshold of possibility, and the fate of the world rests on their ability to respond ethically and with restraint in the face of profound obstacles, including their own inner demons.

The Best of Times

This kind of ethical engagement is not limited, of course, to fantasy novels. Since human society continues to persist despite its crisis of faith in itself, it has had to develop new narratives, and these narratives bear within them the history of their construction; that is, they face the lack of perfection not as an incomplete state of development, but as an impossible dream, and thus adopt an ironic or wondering stance toward it. Nevertheless, these narratives, particularly ones intended for YA audiences, tend to express the belief that progress is possible if in fact we can cultivate what Erik Erikson (1964) called the impulse of "generativity." Erikson believed that "the fulfillment of…identity" (p. 131) manifests itself in the desire to reach out to others, to engage in the kind of selfless caring for others that we ourselves received in infancy. So central is this impulse to human identity that he asserts that "we are the teaching species" (p. 130). Don Browning (1973) elaborates further that "it is the great task of generative [people] to develop the 'ethical potential of our older youth'—those who are so close to their own childhood, so close to full adulthood, and so intensively sensitive to the ethical and generational needs of both" (p. 207).

In other words, we might say that adolescents are at a threshold of emotionally engaged understanding that makes them particularly susceptible to the development of a generative identity, especially if that kind of identity support is found in their cultural and artistic artifacts. Markus Zusak (2005) takes this kind of generative engagement as his explicit subject in *I am the Messenger* by staging its lack as protagonist Ed's central problem. In his late adolescence, Ed suffers from a failure to launch, spending his days working as a cab driver and playing cards with his equally stalled friends. It isn't until Ed begins to take responsibility for the welfare of others, acting on mysterious messages that direct him to people who need something only he can give, that he begins to find value and direction in his life. His identity development thus depends on his enacting generativity.

Zusak's (2006) amazing historical novel, *The Book Thief,* offers another such narrative that shows the intergenerational progression of generativity. The main character, Liesel, experiences generosity and love from her adoptive parents as they enact their desire to teach her to read and encourage her to tell her story. Their love comes in various guises, and hers reaches out in equally various ways to others in her community. Her generative response comes when the family shelters Max Vandenburg, a Jew, in the basement of their home. She reads with him, writes with him, prays for him, and ultimately, loves him in a way that is clearly the fulfillment of her identity as one who had been well-loved.

The Book Thief also exemplifies a sustained version of the stance of wonder in the face of human wreckage. The narrator, Death, takes more than a passing interest in the fate of Liesel, whom he first encountered when he took her brother from her in childhood. Death has a perspective on humanity that allows him to see it at its most noble and most ignoble, and he marvels at the human capacity to sustain love in the face of crushing grief, and the power of words to hold the world's beating heart against the relentless drive of forces that would stop it. Death's grim humor reflects his idealist stance with regard to people; he expects them to be more or less than they are, and they continually surprise him, prompting a humorous response to the incongruity of what he sees. In his words, "I wanted to explain that I am constantly overestimating and underestimating the human race—that rarely do I ever simply *estimate* it. I wanted to ask [Liesel] how the same thing could be so ugly and so glorious, and its words and stories so damning and brilliant" (p. 550).

Like Death, young adults are faced with idealist expectations sold to them in the narratives of childhood, but must also face the incommensurability of the lives and bodies they inhabit with the representations they imagine as ideal. But Zusak's Death provides literary critics with much to consider as well. As readers, educators, and critics, we must take care that we do not over or underestimate our teens, but rather estimate them, and work to understand the ways in which the literature they encounter provides identity support at multiple levels so that we may contextualize more fully the ugly, the glorious, the damning, and the brilliant.

Obviously, there is much more happening in the world of YA literature than can be covered in a single chapter. What I have attempted to do here is to point not only to structural necessities for the critical study of YA literature, which include attention to the distinctive emotional life and embodiment of teens, the historical, social, and cultural environments in which they live, and the prevailing metaphors for the construction of adolescence, but also to fill in some of those structures with content from contemporary YA literature. The very nature of the genre and its readership prevents the saying of any critical last word, and yet while the first critical words have been well-spoken, much remains to be articulated in this vibrant conversation.

Literature References

Abdel-Fattah, R. (2007). *Does my head look big in this?* New York, NY: Orchard.

Alexie, S. (2007). *The absolutely true diary of a part-time Indian.* New York, NY: Little, Brown.

Anderson, L. H. (1999). *Speak.* New York, NY: Farrar, Straus, and Giroux.

Anderson, M. T. (1997). *Thirsty.* Cambridge, MA: Candlewick.

Anderson, M. T. (2002). *Feed.* Cambridge, MA: Candlewick.

Barnes, D. D. (2006). *The making of Dr. Truelove.* New York, NY: Simon Pulse.

Barnes, J. L. (2008). *The squad: Killer spirit.* New York, NY: Laurel Leaf.

Benway, R. (2008). *Audrey, wait.* New York, NY: Razorbill.

Blume, J. (1975). *Forever.* Scarsdale, NY: Bradbury.

Brashares, A. (2001). *The sisterhood of the traveling pants.* New York, NY: Delacorte.

Burgess, M. (2007). *Sara's face.* New York, NY: Simon & Schuster Books for Young Readers.

Cabot, M. (2008). *Airhead.* New York, NY: Point.

Cormier, R. (1974). *The chocolate war.* New York, NY: Knopf Books for Young Readers.

Cormier, R. (1977). *I am the cheese.* New York, NY: Dell.

Curtis, C. P. (2004). *Bucking the Sarge.* New York, NY: Wendy Lamb Books.

De la Cruz, M. (2006). *Blue bloods.* New York, NY: Hyperion.

Dickinson, P. (1989). *Eva.* New York, NY: Delacorte.

Donovan, J. (1969). *I'll get there, it better be worth the trip.* New York, NY: Harper & Row.

Fine, A. (1997). *The Tulip touch.* Boston, MA: Little, Brown.

Fitzgerald, F. S. (1925). *The great Gatsby.* New York, NY: C. Scribner's Sons.

Frost, H. (2003). *Keesha's house.* New York, NY: Farrar, Straus, and Giroux.

Harrison, L. (2004). *The clique.* New York, NY: Little, Brown.

Hentoff, N. (1968). *I'm really dragged but nothing gets me down.* New York, NY: Dell.

Hinton, S. E. (1967). *The outsiders.* New York, NY: Dell.

Hinton, S. E. (1971). *That was then, this is now.* New York, NY: Viking.

Kidd, S. M. (2002). *The secret life of bees.* New York, NY: Viking Adult.

Klause, A. C. (1997). *Blood and chocolate.* New York, NY: Delacorte.

Korman, G. (2003). *Jake, reinvented.* New York, NY: Hyperion.

LeGuin, U. K. (1990). *Tehanu: The last book of Earthsea.* New York, NY: Atheneum.

Levithan, D. (2003). *Boy meets boy.* New York, NY: Knopf Books for Young Readers.

Levithan, D. (2008). *How they met, and other stories.* New York, NY: Alfred A. Knopf.

Limb, S. (2004). *Girl, 15, charming but insane.* New York, NY: Delacorte.

Lockhart, E. (2008). *The disreputable history of Frankie Landau-Banks.* New York, NY: Hyperion.

Lynch, C. (2005). *Inexcusable.* New York, NY: Atheneum.

McDaniel, L. (1985). *Six months to live.* Worthington, OH: Willowisp.

McDaniel, L. (1989). *Too young to die.* New York, NY: Bantam.

McDaniel, L. (1992). *Sixteen and dying.* New York, NY: Bantam.

Meyer, S. (2005). *Twilight.* New York, NY: Little, Brown, & Co.

Myers, W. D. (1988). *Fallen angels.* New York, NY: Scholastic.

Myers, W. D. (1999). *Monster.* New York, NY: HarperCollins.

Myers, W. D. (2007). *What they found: Love on 145th street.* New York, NY: Wendy Lamb Books.

Myracle, L. (2004). *ttyl.* New York, NY: Amulet.

Myracle, L. (2006). *ttfn*. New York, NY: Amulet.

Myracle, L. (2007). *l8r g8r*. New York, NY: Amulet.

Nelson, T. B. (Director). (2001). *O* [Motion picture]. United States: Lions Gate Entertainment.

Nilsson, P. (2005). *You & you & you* (T. Chace, Trans.). Asheville, NC: Front Street.

Nilsson, P. (2007). *Seventeen* (T. Chace, Trans.). Asheville, NC: Front Street.

Portman, F. (2006). *King dork*. New York, NY: Delacorte.

Pullman, P. (1996). *The golden compass*. New York, NY: Alfred A. Knopf.

Rennison, L. (2000). *Angus, thongs, and full frontal snogging*. New York, NY: HarperCollins.

Rowling, J. K. (1997). *Harry Potter and the sorcerer's stone*. New York, NY: Scholastic.

Sebold, A. (2002). *The lovely bones*. New York, NY: Little, Brown.

Serros, M. (2006). *Honey blonde chica*. New York, NY: Simon Pulse.

Shakespeare, W. (1969). *Othello*. London: Cornmarket Press. (Original work published 1755)

Sophocles. (2000). *Antigone*. Translated and with Introduction by Marianne McDonald. (2000). London: Nick Hern Books. (Original work published c. 442)

Valdes-Rodriguez, A. (2008). *Haters*. New York, NY: Little Brown Young Readers.

Von Ziegesar, C. (2002). *Gossip girl #1: A Novel*. New York, NY: Poppy.

Walter, V. (1998). *Making up Megaboy* (K. Roeckelein, Graphics). New York, NY: DK Ink.

Werlin, N. (1998). *The killer's cousin*. New York, NY: Delacorte.

Westerfeld, S. (2005a). *Peeps: A novel*. New York, NY: Razorbill.

Westerfeld, S. (2005b). *Uglies*. New York, NY: Simon Pulse.

Whedon, J. (Executive Producer). (1997–2003). *Buffy the vampire slayer*. [Television series]. United States: The WB (1997–2001), UPN (2001–2003).

Winston, S. (2008). *The Kayla chronicles*. New York, NY: Little, Brown.

Zusak, M. (2001). *Fighting Ruben Wolfe*. New York, NY: Arthur A. Levine.

Zusak, M. (2003) *Getting the girl*. New York, NY: Arthur A. Levine

Zusak, M. (2005). *I am the messenger*. New York, NY: Alfred A. Knopf.

Zusak, M. (2006). *The book thief*. New York, NY: Alfred A. Knopf.

Academic References

Bakhtin, M. M. (1981). *The dialogic imagination: Four essays* (Michael Holquist, Ed.; Caryl Emerson, Trans.). Austin: University of Texas Press.

Browning, D. (1973). *Generative man*. Philadelphia, PA: Westminster Press.

Bushman, J. H., & Haas, K. P. (2006). *Using young adult literature in the English classroom*. New York, NY: Allyn & Bacon.

Cadden, M. (2000). The irony of narration in the young adult novel. *Children's Literature Association Quarterly, 25*(3), 146–154.

Coats, K. (2004). *Looking glasses and Neverlands: Lacan, desire, and subjectivity in children's literature*. Iowa City: University of Iowa Press.

Donelson, K. L., & Nilsen, A. P. (2008). *Literature for today's young adults* (8th ed.). Boston, MA: Pearson Education.

Erikson, E. (1964). *Insight and responsibility*. New York, NY: Norton.

Girard, R. (1987). *Things hidden since the foundation of the world* (Stephen Bann & Michael Metteer, Trans.). Stanford, CA: Stanford University Press.

Grossberg, L. (2006). Does cultural studies have futures? Should it? (Or what's the matter with New York?). *Cultural Studies, 20*(1), 1–32.

Herz, S. K., & Gallo, D. R. (2005). *From Hinton to Hamlet: Building bridges between young adult literature and the classics* (2nd ed.). Westport, CT: Greenwood.

Hunt, C. (1996). Young adult literature evades the theorists. *Children's Literature Association Quarterly, 21*(1), 4–11.

Jackson, A., Coats, K., & McGillis, R. (2007). *The gothic in children's literature: Haunting the borders*. New York, NY: Routledge.

King, A. (2008) "China's Pop Fiction." *The New York Times Sunday Book Review*. Retrieved May 25, 2009, from http://www.nytimes.com/2008/05/04/books/review/King-t.html?ref=review

Kristeva, J. (1990). The adolescent novel. In J. Fletcher & A. Benjamin (Eds.), *Abjection, melancholia, and love* (pp. 8–23). New York, NY: Routledge.

Lyotard, J. F. (1984). *The postmodern condition: A report on knowledge*. (G. Bennington & B. Massumi, Trans.). Minneapolis, MN: University of Minnesota Press.

MacLeod, A. S. (1997). The journey inward: Adolescent literature in America 1945–1995. In S. L. Beckett (Ed.), *Reflections of change: Children's literature since 1945* (pp. 125–130). Westport, CT: Greenwood Press.

Martinsen, J. (2006). Writing and packaging young adult fiction for teenage girls. *Danwei: Chinese Media, Advertising, and Urban Life*. Retrieved May 25, 2009, from http://www.danwei.org/books/writing_and_packaging_young_ad.php

Martinsen, J. (2007). Colorful mooks for Chinese teens. *Danwei: Chinese Media, Advertising, and Urban Life*. Retrieved May 25, 2009, from http://www.danwei.org/magazines/teen_magazines.php

McCallum, R. (1999). *Ideologies of identity in adolescent fiction: The dialogic construction of subjectivity*. New York, NY: Garland.

Rui, J., & Dalby, C. (2007). Writers from the 1980s: A golden generation tarnished. China.org.cn. Retrieved May 25, 2009, from http://www.china.org.cn/english/photo/196127.htm

Soter, A. O. (1999). *Young adult literature and the new literary theories: Developing critical readers in middle school*. New York, NY: Teachers College Press.

Spinks, S. (Director, Producer, & Writer). (2002). Inside the teenage brain. In D. Fanning (Executive Producer), *Frontline*. Boston, MA: WGBH.

Trites, R. S. (2000). *Disturbing the universe: Power and repression in adolescent literature*. Iowa City, IA: University of Iowa Press.

Trites, R. S. (2007). *Twain, Alcott, and the birth of the adolescent reform novel*. Iowa City, IA: University of Iowa Press.

Point of Departure

Markus Zusak

There's nothing academic in the words, the thought, or the heartfelt statement when I say: "I wanted to be Ponyboy."

Even here, in a city as far away from Tulsa as Sydney is (there's south and then there's *really* south), I think I could make that statement to 100 people my own age and at least half of them would reply with something like, "*The Outsiders*, right?" or "You wouldn't rather be Dally?" or "Filthy greaser, get the hell away from me"...

The point is not so much that even in the 1980s we still grew up on a book that was written in the 60s, but that teenagers in Australia were reading books written *for* and *about* teenagers. For a lot of us, it was the first time we had that magical experience of *being there*, inside a book, and all of us were turning pages without knowing it. The mechanics of it were left way behind, in that cinema mentioned on page one of S. E. Hinton's book, or with "Paul Newman and a ride home." It was one of the first times I didn't want to turn off the light when I went to bed. I was a reader, and I didn't want it to stop.

I think I can safely say that without Young Adult literature, I wouldn't be a writer; I certainly wouldn't have written the books that I have—because as a teenager I was fairly typical in that I kept a lot of what I felt and thought completely to myself. I didn't talk to people about what I truly wanted or believed, or how I wanted things to be. In the end, I had those conversations with books. And they were Young Adult books.

For this reason, I think the role of Young Adult literature is often undermined in one crucial way from *within*. Yes, I often find that we're most guilty of it ourselves—in our own sense of inferiority to what is often perceived as the main event of *Adult Fiction*. It's incredible the amount of times I've heard two writers chatting at a festival and have it start out with something like this:

"So, what do you write?"

"Oh...just Young Adult."

I've caught myself doing it, too, as well as countless friends and sparring partners, many of whom I *know* have written many a teenager's favorite book. Of course, it's the word *just* that I object to. If someone was to tell me that S. E. Hinton was just a Young Adult writer, I'd probably do everything I could to keep from screaming, "You're talking about the woman I love!" None of her work is *just* a book. Nor is a Robert Cormier book, or a John Marsden book, or a David Almond or Melina Marchetta, or Chris Crutcher. These are writers of the highest order, who could all stand toe to toe with anyone on the planet when it comes down to the ethic of a bloody good story, bloody well told. These are writers to look up to, and to emulate.

One of the most commonly asked questions I receive about my book, *The Book Thief*, is whether it's a novel for adults or for young adults. At times there's also a more interesting moment when someone intimates that the book is done a disservice by being classified as a YA novel. "It won't get enough attention," they say, with the view that being a Young Adult writer is some sort of ticket to the underclass. My own view has always been the opposite. Do we really loathe and disrespect teenagers to such a degree that we'd herd together all the pretty hopeless writers and say, "Right, you bunch of uncoordinated losers can write for the teens. They're pretty stupid, after all, and they won't really know the difference." Imagine suggesting that to Sonya Hartnett or S. E. Hinton. Or, if we really want to stir the pot, who would be game enough to say it to Harper Lee or J. D. Salinger? You wouldn't dream of it.

Sometimes, after complaining about how difficult it is to have the self-belief required for the job, I remind myself that it's a privilege to be a writer. But it's an even greater privilege to be a *Young Adult* writer. When I think of how I was at that age, I think of myself at my most vulnerable, my most heartfelt, and probably my most *everything*. What an honor to write for that audience. To be a part of a person's life with a story at that time is surely something special. In my identity as a reader, I know it's something I cherish as one of the highlights of my life.

As a writer, however, I rarely need reminding that it's also an incredible challenge to write for a Young Adult audience. As a writer for that age group, there's surely a desire to create a book that lights a fire—the right book at the right time in that ridiculously raw period of a person's life. Achieving that is no easy task. A Young Adult writer who thinks it's easy deserves to call him or herself *just* a Young Adult writer. A superb Young Adult novel sits comfortably next to all great works of fiction, surely.

Ultimately, it truly *is* an honor and a privilege to be a Young Adult writer, and not only for the depth of emotion within the hidden thoughts of our audience, but in the quality of authors who have come before us—who have raised the bar to such a distinguished level. We owe it to them, as much as to ourselves, to always make our goal simple and single-minded—to write someone's *favorite* book. If that is the goal, to fall short is no disgrace.... But to succeed, well, can you imagine? You get to be S. E. Hinton, if only for a moment, and it doesn't get much better than that.

23

Reading Indigeneity

The Ethics of Interpretation and Representation

Clare Bradford

Deakin University

The transmission of indigenous stories is a fraught enterprise. In contrast to Western practices of the free circulation of ideas, many indigenous cultures view their stories as sacred, and have strict rules about who may tell certain tales, and in what settings and with whom they may be shared. Indigenous storytellers and novelists who want to tell contemporary stories also face the minefields of a history of (mis)representations of their cultures' values and practices. Australian literary scholar Clare Bradford picks her way carefully through this minefield, identifying its perils and proposing a self-reflexive practice that enables scholars to approach these works with sensitivity; Abenaki children's author Joseph Bruchac adds his own impressions and frustrations as an author to Clare's frank assessment of the possibilities of criticism, cross-talk, and mutual understanding in the field.

I begin this discussion with a disclaimer: I am not a member of an Indigenous minority. I am a white scholar who has lived and worked in two countries (New Zealand and Australia) where Indigenous populations were dispossessed and subjugated by colonial rule during the heyday of British imperialism. As a non-Indigenous scholar I am an outsider to Indigenous textuality, so that when I read texts located in Indigenous cultures I am positioned differently from audiences whose ancestry and experience align them with the world views and values of such texts.[1]

My experience of living in postcolonial societies has given me a keen interest in relationships between Indigenous and non-Indigenous peoples and cultures, and the histories of these relationships. Growing up as a white, middle-class child living in a region of New Zealand populated by many Maori, I was conscious of the differences between the lived experience of my family and that of many of the Maori children with whom I went to school. Whereas I was always warmly dressed during cold winters, many Maori students came to school shoeless and without jackets; while most of the adults in my family were farmers or teachers, the parents of my Maori school friends typically worked in low-paid menial occupations. I sensed, too, that the differences between Pakeha (white) and Maori culture went far deeper than economic and class distinctions, and extended to values and world views. At school I performed Maori songs and dances along with my classmates, and I learned about the armed conflict between Maori and British settlers which occurred during the 19th century in my district, leaving behind local stories and the artefacts my brother loved to collect, such as bullet shells and stone axes.[2] My perspective of Maori history and culture was, then, always mediated by my whiteness and by my sense of the distance between Maori and Pakeha.

My university studies in history enhanced my understanding of the historical and contemporary influences that have contributed to the continuing disadvantage of Maori and other Indigenous populations. When I moved to Australia in the 1970s, I encountered what is now regarded as the renaissance of Aboriginal writing during that decade, when Aboriginal novelists, poets, and playwrights wrote out of their experience, introducing members of the majority white culture to Indigenous histories, knowledge, and world views. The political struggle for recognition and land rights which had been conducted by Aboriginal people for decades informed and was informed by the poetry, fiction, and drama of the 1970s, raising the consciousness of many non-Indigenous Australians.

By experiencing the differences between two postcolonial societies, I learned that colonial histories and contemporary race relations are situated and specific. For instance, in New Zealand it would be almost impossible for a Pakeha (white) citizen not to engage with Maori first-hand, since Maori constitute 14.6% of the population, or 1 person in 7. In contrast, people of Native American and Alaska Native descent comprise only 1% of the population of the United States, and in Australia the Indigenous population (comprising Aboriginal and Torres Strait Islander peoples) constitutes just 2.5% of the total population. In New Zealand, then, Pakeha children typically learn about Maori people and cultures through interaction with Maori. In the United States and Australia, most non-Indigenous children encounter Indigenous cultures through representations in fiction, film, and television; and most such representations are produced by non-Indigenous people.

It is not a part of my argument that non-Indigenous authors should not write about Indigenous themes and characters; however, my reading across Australian, New Zealand, Canadian, and American texts for children has convinced me that many non-Indigenous authors and illustrators draw upon assumptions and stereotypes which are invisible to them because they are cultural givens. For instance, it is common for Indigenous characters in children's books to conform to a limited number of types, including the old sage, the young activist, the disturbed teenager (often prone to substance abuse), and (in historical fiction) the noble savage, whereas non-Indigenous characters are accorded far more diversity and complexity. Moreover, most accounts of Indigenous cultures by non-Indigenous producers are filtered through the perspectives of white culture, so that Indigenous characters are generally the objects of discourse and not subjects. For this reason Indigenous children rarely encounter texts produced within their own cultures. There are notable examples of non-Indigenous texts whose representations of Indigenous cultures are complex and nuanced, and these tend to be produced by people with close and longstanding connections to Indigenous people.

Since the 1970s, Indigenous authors and artists have increasingly produced children's texts, often through Indigenous publishing companies, although (given the small proportion of Indigenous to non-Indigenous writers and artists) these texts still comprise a minority of works for children. Because Indigenous producers write out of their experience and cultural knowledge, they offer Indigenous children experiences of narrative subjectivity by accepting as normal the values of minority cultures. Non-Indigenous children who engage with such narratives may develop an appreciation of cultural difference and a realization that many ideologies that they thought to be natural and universal are culturally constructed. It is often the case that Indigenous texts present challenges to readers unfamiliar with the cultures in which they are located. As I have read Indigenous texts, I have frequently experienced moments of perplexity or uncertainty when I have struggled to understand language, character motivation, or cultural contexts. Such moments are powerful reminders that I am an outsider to these texts, and that while I can develop an enhanced understanding through research into the cultures and histories that have shaped them, a full understanding of their cultural meanings will always elude me.

I return now to the topic with which I began this discussion, how I locate myself as a scholar and writer. I have always been sharply conscious of this question and have frequently struggled to negotiate the difficult terrain of race relations across different national settings. A key component in discussions of representation is that of positioning—that is, where and how scholars position themselves in relation to Indigenous texts. As I have explained, I am an outsider to Indigenous textuality by virtue of my ancestry and cultural background. This does not mean that I am prohibited from writing about Indigenous texts or about representations of Indigenous people and cultures; it does mean, however, that my scholarly work in this area requires different theoretical and interpretive frames. Above all, working in this field requires a reflexivity which I will attempt to model as I discuss Indigenous and non-Indigenous textuality. That is, I will endeavour to be specific about the reading strategies I adopt and the limitations of my understanding.

"Traditional" Texts and the Ethics of Retelling

There exist important distinctions between "traditional" Indigenous narratives—that is, those which have been transmitted over thousands of years within particular communities and clans, and contemporary fiction by Indigenous authors. The first category comprises stories which articulate the fundamental beliefs and values of Indigenous clans and communities and are directed toward Indigenous audiences. In contrast, contemporary fiction by Indigenous authors usually seeks a general audience and deploys genre types and narrative strategies drawn from Western traditions. Such fiction, produced from within Indigenous cultures, is likely to advocate Indigenous values and perspectives even as it exploits some of the possibilities of Western forms such as the novel and the picture book.

From colonial times, Indigenous stories have been retold by non-Indigenous authors and storytellers, many of whom having "[made] free with the cultural resources of native peoples in order to achieve European self-definition" (Boehmer, 1995, p. 218). I take a hard-line position on such retellings, explaining as follows in *Unsettling Narratives:*

> I believe that traditional narratives are best retold by those to whom they belong, whether directed at Indigenous or non-Indigenous audiences, and that the processes of retelling should accord with practices of authorization and custodianship of stories as they are observed in…diverse Indigenous cultures…. My reasons for this position are, first, that traditional narratives are woven into cultural values and beliefs and are apt to be reduced or distorted when they are treated in isolation from Indigenous traditions; secondly, that the history of colonization is littered with instances of appropriation of stories and the time for such practices is now over; and thirdly, that Indigenous people are best equipped to determine which of their stories should be retold and by whom, and which versions are authorized by individuals and communities. (Bradford, 2007, p. 51)

Western readers, socialized to accede to the view that stories, like other products, circulate freely within an open marketplace, frequently struggle with the idea that some societies observe strict rules about who can tell and hear stories. In many Indigenous societies, narratives are not merely vehicles for instruction or modes of entertainment, but form an integral part of a culture's systems of belief. Certain secret and sacred stories may be attributed with transformative and regenerative effects, such as connecting contemporary people with spirit beings, or maintaining traditions of initiation. These stories are very often restricted to particular kinship groups, or to those who have been initiated, to men or to women (Bradford, 2001, 2003). Through the appropriation and retelling of Indigenous stories, sacred stories are reduced and debased. Moreover, many Indigenous peoples believe that the loss of stories, or their inappropriate use, result in negative consequences for individuals and groups.

It should not be imagined that all Indigenous narratives are off-limits to non-Indigenous people, since very many narratives do not fall into the categories of restricted and sacred material, but are available to children and adults,

Indigenous and non-Indigenous. Even so, Indigenous communities often observe practices of custodianship whereby stories are located within particular clans or communities, so that certain people have the right to tell them or to pass them on to other storytellers according to ancient protocols.

The field of children's literature includes many retellings, by non-Indigenous authors, of traditional stories. Such retellings are often highly contentious, including Paul Goble's body of work. While Goble claims that a close relationship with the Lakota elder Chief Edgar Red Cloud has provided him with the authority to undertake retellings of Lakota and other Plains narratives, Native American scholars have made strong and compelling criticisms of his approach (see Reese, 2009).

Regimes of power and knowledge are central to publishing processes. In general the weight of power is with established non-Indigenous authors, valued by publishers for their capacity to produce books that sell to large markets. In this context, Goble's invocations of his friendship with Chief Edgar Red Cloud cover over the fact that as a privileged and successful white author he is in a powerful position as one who claims to speak for Native Americans (see Bradford, 2007). In the author's note in *Brave Eagle's Account of the Fetterman Fight,* Goble (1972) states that he publishes his retellings primarily in order to make traditional stories available to Native American children. Doris Seale's (2001) response is: "Along with many anthropologists, [Goble] assumes, apparently, that we have so lost our traditions, cultures, and histories that we must be taught them by a white person" (p. 119).

Another form of appropriation occurs when non-Indigenous authors make use of mythic figures and story elements. The Australian novelist Patricia Wrightson takes this direction in her highly regarded novels (Bradford, 2001; Bradford, 2007), which incorporate Aboriginal spirit figures in their narratives. Like Goble, Wrightson relied on the authority of an Aboriginal elder for "permission" to draw upon Indigenous traditions; namely, the instance, in 1978, when the poet and playwright Jack Davis publicly supported her approach. Other Indigenous scholars, however, have taken issue with Wrightson's deployment of Aboriginal spirit figures (see, for instance, Collins-Gearing, 2002).

Such differences of opinion within Indigenous communities can be confusing to non-Indigenous people. Colonial discourses characteristically homogenized Indigenous peoples, treating them as other to Europeans and enforcing the binary distinctions on which colonial discourses were based, such as those between civilized and savage; active and passive; modern and ancient; religious and pagan. This tendency to homogenize is common in political and media discourses which foreground differences of opinion and values within Indigenous communities, as though such differences invalidate what all Indigenous people say. Perhaps this insistence on Indigenous uniformity derives from white anxieties about what can be regarded as "true" or "authentic": if some Australian Aboriginal people endorse Wrightson's work and others do not, what are non-Aboriginal people to think? This dilemma is most evident in relation to canonized and highly regarded works which have been extensively used in schools and libraries and whose authors have received significant prizes and awards. Wrightson's novels are in this category, although most of her books are no longer in print and are little read by contemporary Australian children.

Reading Indigenous Texts

In this section I consider how non-Indigenous readers might approach Indigenous texts, and explore some of the ethical and interpretive issues that arise. I am most familiar with Australian Indigenous texts and cultures, and I do not imply that all Indigenous peoples everywhere have the same practices and beliefs, even if there exist striking similarities across diverse Indigenous peoples.

As a white scholar trained in the methodologies and theories of Western scholarship in literary and cultural studies, I necessarily bring these epistemological and interpretive practices to bear upon Indigenous texts. However, there are serious dangers in applying Western theoretical paradigms to non-Western texts. Within children's literature research the two most prominent paradigms deployed in discussions of traditional narratives are humanist and Jungian frameworks, both of which emphasize the common features of tropes and story schemata from different places and cultures. Joseph Campbell's (1949/2008) formulation of the hero's progress through the stages of separation, initiation, and return has been particularly influential. Since the 1960s the fields of literature, history, ethnography, and anthropology have taken up many of the tenets of postcolonial theory, which focuses on local and particular forms of textuality, situating narratives in relation to places and cultures and resisting the universalizing effects of humanist and Jungian approaches.

Poststructuralism, too, has shaped the directions of literary studies over the last few decades, emphasizing the multiplicity of meanings that surround any texts, and foregrounding the role of readers in constructing texts. Indigenous texts resist both humanist/Jungian and poststructuralist readings, since they are located in specific places and derive their significances through their connections with particular groups of people. Moreover, they are not open to interpretation in the way that Western texts are, but are often subject to strict rules concerning the accuracy and exactness of retellings. While poststructuralist theories reject the concept of an authoritative cultural tradition that validates stories and storytellers, Indigenous cultures often insist on just such a tradition and its associated protocols.

How, then, might Western readers approach Indigenous texts and avoid incorporating them into Jungian and humanist generalizations? A key strategy is to observe a self-reflexive style of reading, in which non-Indigenous readers are alert to the signs of difference in these texts, and to the ways in which their own habits and assumptions are challenged. The most powerful way to understand Indigenous beliefs and values is to consult Indigenous people, either first-hand through professional and friendship associations, or by consulting websites developed and maintained by individuals, clans, nations or tribes, or by seeking out the work of Indigenous scholars working in anthropology, education, history, literature, and Indigenous studies. Such scholars provide valuable information about Indigenous epistemologies and textual traditions and include Jace Weaver (Cherokee), Craig S. Womack (Creek/Cherokee), Thomas King (Cherokee, Canada), Linda Tuhiwai Smith (Maori), Martin Nakata (Torres Strait Islands), and Marcia Langton (Yiman and Bidjara Nations, Australia). Many non-Indigenous postcolonial theorists and critics have produced important work on Indigenous textuality, although here it is important to be judicious, selecting authors who do not assume the mantle of experts on Indigenous peoples or speak on their behalf.

In her essay "Ethical Reading and Resistant Texts," Patricia Linton (1999) discusses the experience of "cultural outsiders" (p. 42), those who read the work of minority authors while not belonging to the cultures of such authors. Linton observes that merely because "an ethnic or postcolonial writer hopes to be read by a broad or varied audience does not mean that he or she invites all readers to share the same degree of intimacy" (p. 32). It is common, she says, for cultural outsiders to experience a sense that minority texts incorporate silences and omissions on certain topics and details, so constructing boundaries that alert cultural outsiders to their outsider position. In this way cultural outsiders are reminded that they are not entitled to understand all that there is to know of the worlds of these texts. In Linton's words, these texts "require a readerly tact that recognizes boundaries and respects them" (p. 43).

Dust Echoes: A Case Study

As a case study of how Indigenous narratives work, I now turn to a series of animated films based on stories from Wugularr (Beswick), a remote Aboriginal community in the Northern Territory of Australia. Early in 2005 I worked on a project that involved collaboration between the Wugularr community, my university (Deakin, in Melbourne, Australia), and the Australian Broadcasting Corporation (ABC), Australia's national public broadcaster. The *Dust Echoes* project was initiated by a Deakin University staff member, Adrienne Campbell, who worked in the Northern Territory during 2004, establishing websites in remote Aboriginal communities, and by Tom E. Lewis, an actor, singer, and artist who lives at Wugularr and who acted as our translator and liaison. The aims of the project were: to develop an archive of stories by Wugularr elders; to showcase the narrative and cultural practices of the Wu-gularr community; to make Wugularr stories available to Indigenous and non-Indigenous children across Australia, with an emphasis on stories previously not circulated beyond the Wugularr community; to investigate how new technologies can assist in making ancient stories available to contemporary audiences; and to develop a prototype for the dissemination of other Indigenous stories. With a filmmaker and sound technician, we collected video and audio footage of four Wugularr stories: *The Morning Star, Namorrodor, The Be,* and *The Wagalak Sisters.* The ABC employed animation companies to produce short films, using voiceovers by Tom E. Lewis and other Indigenous actors, and music developed for the project. My role was to collect information about the stories, their country, and their custodians for the *Dust Echoes* website (http://www.abc.net.au/dustechoes/). In the following year the ABC together with Tom E. Lewis produced eight further stories to arrive at a collection of twelve animations, which have been screened on ABC Television and at film and animation festivals in addition to their availability through the ABC website.

Although I had read all that I could find about Northern Territory history and about the many clans of this region, it was when I heard and saw the Wugularr elders telling their stories in their ancestral languages that I gained a deeper understanding of the complex cultural meanings of these narratives, and of their embeddedness in country.[2] As I walked with a Wugularr elder, Jimmy Wesan, through the river country to a location where he was to tell one of the stories, I noticed that Jimmy sang quietly and clapped his hands at intervals. When I asked him why he did so, he explained that although he had lived in the Wugularr community for many years, this was not strictly speaking his homeland, which is Dalabon country, around 200 kilometres north of Wugularr. It was therefore his duty to alert the spirits of the place that he was walking through their country and that he intended to do no harm to it. The presence of spirits in country is entirely unremarkable and natural to Jimmy and his people, and relations between humans and spirits are foundational to many stories.

Again, I was familiar with the practices and protocols whereby Aboriginal people distinguish sacred stories from those available to wider audiences long before my involvement in the *Dust Echoes* project. But I learned about the material effects of these practices when Victor Hood, another Wugularr elder, expressed his deep anxiety about his telling of the story *The Morning Star,* which describes the first death among humans. Victor's unease stemmed from the fact that although he was the correct custodian of this story, and although the version he was to tell took a form that made it suitable for all to hear, it is similar in some ways to other secret and sacred stories which deal with the same events. He worried that if he inadvertently used words or phrases that belonged to these sacred stories, he might be guilty of passing on

knowledge to the wrong audiences, something which would have negative consequences for him and his community. The series title *Dust Echoes* derives from Victor's explanation of his story, that it came "from the dust" (V. Hood, personal communication, January 16, 2005); that is, that it is an ancient and important story originating in the Dreaming, a time-space when the Ancestors, the spirits who created the land, moved around country establishing relations between humans and the natural world and between different groups of humans.

Aboriginal stories do not exist as discrete cultural items, but within a chain of related stories, some of which may be sacred and others available to diverse audiences. The story *Namorrodor* exemplifies some of the complexities of Aboriginal narrative practices. This story, told by the Wugularr elder Pamela Weston, concerns a creature, Namorrodor, who lives in a cave and preys on babies and old people. Taking the form of a flying serpent, Namorrodor sniffs out meat cooked at night and snatches babies, ripping out their hearts. A shooting star in the night sky tells that Namorrodor is roaming about.

Like many Aboriginal narratives, *Namorrodor* is concerned not with individuals but with representative human and spirit figures. Thus, no named mother or baby features in the story, and in the animated version the mother and her child stand for all such community members. Individuality is thus subsumed into communal values and concerns. I first understood *Namorrodor* as a cautionary tale warning of the dangers of cooking meat at night when animals and other creatures might be attracted to a camp, and of the perils to children who left camps at night. That is, I instinctively located the story within a Western schema, drawing upon traditions with which I am familiar from my childhood. The inadequacy of this conceptual framework was made clear to me when Pamela Weston created two paintings of Namorrodor figures, one of whom was visibly female. Pamela explained to me that there existed many stories about the female Namorrodor, who was benign and never harmed humans. My surprise at this revelation is indicative of my lack of understanding of the complexity of Aboriginal traditions, where multiple stories exist about the same spirit figure, with each story occupying a distinct place in a web of narratives, told by a particular custodian and available to prescribed audiences.

A further complexity became apparent to me when Glen Wesan, another Wugularr elder, told me about stories which describe how Namorrodor can be killed: that only a cleverman (one endowed with secret knowledge and powers) could kill him, only at a certain time of the night, and only with a spear made over a fire and "sung" with magic words. Although Glen could tell me *about* the existence of these stories, she could not narrate them because she was not their custodian. The words used in the singing of the spear would be available only to a senior person with specialized knowledge and powers. My access to the Namorrodor story and the narratives and traditions associated with it is, then, limited to what I am entitled to know according to the protocols which apply within the Wugularr community.

I have described the *Namorrodor* story in some detail because it exemplifies some of the most crucial distinctions between Western and Indigenous stories. Whereas Western folktales are located in settings understood as universal (castles, forests, villages) and can be narrated by anyone, the Wugularr stories belong to particular tracts of country and can be told only by those identified as their custodians. Western stories are available to all audiences; the Wugularr stories belong to a complex system of narratives with differential availability to audiences. While the Wugularr stories are part of a chain of narratives, Western folktales can stand alone as self-sufficient story events. Most significantly, the Wugularr stories, like the ceremonies, rituals and artworks with which they are linked, connect members of the community to their kin, their country, and to cultural traditions based on the Dreaming.

My experience of the Wugularr stories provided me with enhanced insights into the cultures that inform them. These stories also taught me about my own expectations and assumptions as a reader, and the limitations of my knowledge. Like other Indigenous stories, the Wugularr narratives are of enormous significance to their community since they embody values, articulate worldviews, and locate contemporary people within their cultures. These stories assert the continuity of Wugularr culture despite the despoliation wrought by colonization, and they exemplify the readiness of the Wugularr elders to share their stories with a global audience. When stories are retold by non-Indigenous authors, on the other hand, they are wrenched away from the contexts which give them meaning and are swept into a domain of undifferentiated stories.

Reading Contemporary Indigenous Fiction

My discussion so far has centered on questions of reader positioning and appropriation in relation to traditional narratives. I now focus on a growth area in Indigenous writing for children over the last two decades: fiction dealing with contemporary Indigenous protagonists. Fictions by Indigenous writers necessarily deploy many of the narrative strategies of mainstream fiction; but this does not mean that they are mainstream texts. In her essay "A Different Drum: Native American Writing," Cynthia Leitich Smith (2002) describes an episode in which a white author took her to task because Smith's picture book *Jingle Dancer* (2000) is built on a sequence where Jenna, the protagonist, visits four women in turn to ask them for help with the preparation of a dress sewn with jingles (conical metal shapes sewn onto dresses worn by girls and women performing jingle dances at powwows). Smith (2002) explains that she built the narrative of *Jingle Dancer* around the number four because this number is central to Native American traditions: "that oh-so-indig-

enous number (four winds, four stages of life, four colors of man, four seasons)" (p. 409).

The "living legend" told Smith: "It's three. Three because that's the tradition. Three pigs, three wishes, three goats. The Father, Son, and the Holy Ghost. It's three, always three, because that's what feels right" (2002, p. 410). This is, of course, a deeply Eurocentric view of what is normal, built on Western folktale schemata and Christian beliefs. A narrative built on four rather than three was experienced as "wrong" not because it is wrong but because it does not accord with the experience and socialization of the "living legend."

As Smith (2002) also points out in her essay, Indigenous authors face dilemmas in writing for non-Indigenous audiences. Mainstream publishers seeking the widest possible markets for texts by Indigenous authors may exert pressure through the processes of selection, translation, editing, and marketing, effectively shaping Indigenous texts into mainstream products. Nor is it always feasible for Indigenous authors to publish with Indigenous publishing companies, which are generally small-scale operations producing limited numbers of children's books. Indigenous fiction always implies two audiences: Indigenous children, for whom the world of the text may offer a sense of narrative subjectivity; and non-Indigenous children who are, in Linton's (1999) terms, "cultural outsiders" (p. 42). Strategies such as the use of Indigenous language, the provision of glossaries, and the use of parenthetical explanations of words or expressions serve to foreground linguistic and cultural differences, reminding non-Indigenous readers that they do not have the kind of direct and unproblematic access to textual meanings that they experience when reading literature founded in their own culture (Ashcroft, 2001; Ashcroft, Griffiths & Tiffin, 1989).

Rather than merely inserting the significances and thematics of Indigenous cultures into Western forms and genres, Indigenous authors claim narrative authority by "reinventing the enemy's language," a term used by Joy Harjo and Gloria Bird in their book title (1997). Harjo and Bird note that "the language of the colonizers was forced on us.... It was when we began to create with this new language that we named it ours, made it usefully tough and beautiful" (p. 23). I now turn to three Indigenous novels in order to discuss some of the strategies through which they engage in this process of reinvention.

Sherman Alexie's (2007) *The Absolutely True Diary of a Part-time Indian*, Lee Maracle's (2002) *Will's Garden*, and Meme McDonald and Boori Monty Pryor's (2002) *Njunjul the Sun* (respectively, American, Canadian, and Australian) are structured by a focus on the identity-formation of Indigenous male protagonists. All incorporate first-person narration and all involve sequences in which Indigenous protagonists move between settings where Indigenous cultures are normative, and mainstream locations such as schools and neighborhoods. The movement of characters back and forth between these settings allows for comparisons between cultures and examinations of the negotiations involved in cross-cultural friendships. In *The Absolutely True Diary* (Alexie, 2007), the protagonist moves between a reservation ("the rez") where he is known as "Junior," and a mainstream school in the town of Reardon where he is known by his full name, Arnold Spirit Junior. In *Will's Garden* (Maracle, 2002), Will attends a high school in the town near his home in the Sto:loh reserve; and in *Njunjul the Sun* (McDonald & Pryor, 2002), Njunjul shifts from the ironically named Happy Valley, an Aboriginal community on the outskirts of a country town, to Sydney where he lives with his uncle Garth and Emma, Garth's non-Aboriginal partner.

The physical journeys of these protagonists symbolize the distances between cultures, positioning non-Indigenous readers as outsiders to Indigenous perspectives of both cultures. Language is at the core of cultural difference; it is also the means of negotiation between cultures and individuals. In *The Absolutely True Diary* (Alexie, 2007), Arnold/Junior provides explicit and entertaining explanations of aspects of Indian culture, including language, humor, and cultural practices. Before his first fight at his new school, Arnold outlines a list of "THE UNOFFICIAL AND UNWRITTEN (but you better follow them or you're going to get beaten twice as hard) SPOKANE INDIAN RULES OF FISTICUFFS" (pp. 61–62). When Roger, one of the school jocks, makes a racist joke at Arnold's expense, Arnold follows the rez rules by punching Roger in the face, adhering to the rule "IF YOU GET IN A FIGHT WITH SOMEBODY WHO IS SURE TO BEAT YOU UP, THEN YOU MUST THROW THE FIRST PUNCH, BECAUSE IT'S THE ONLY PUNCH YOU'LL EVER GET TO THROW" (p. 82). However, Roger does not retaliate, and Arnold realizes that there exists at the school another set of rules that he does not comprehend. Indeed, when Arnold asks Roger, "What are the rules?" Roger responds, "What rules?" (p. 66). This comical mismatch of assumptions points to how concepts of appropriate behavior are naturalized through processes of socialization. It also produces a comparison between the rez culture, where options are few and violence normalized, and the culture of the school, where many more choices (including non-violence) are available to Roger.

Both *The Absolutely True Diary* and *Will's Garden* (Maracle, 2002) address the complexities of cross-cultural negotiations by tracing the progress of friendships between protagonists and non-Indian classmates. At school Arnold and Will align themselves with figures marginal to the dominant student groups, reasoning that they will have common interests with other outsiders. Arnold engages with the class nerd Gordy, who teaches him how to study efficiently. Through the figure of Gordy the novel undercuts Arnold's tendency to succumb to discourses of hopelessness and victimhood. When Arnold tells Gordy that he is regarded by his best friend Rowdy as a traitor because he has left the rez to attend school, and that "Some

Indians think you *become* white if you try to make your life better," Gordy responds, "If that were true, then wouldn't all white people be successful?" (Alexie, 2007, p. 131). Gordy's remorseless logic points to the deficiencies of a conceptual system that assumes that all white people are successful and all Indians unsuccessful.

The dark and deadpan humor of *The Absolutely True Diary* is liable to confront cultural outsiders reading this book. For instance, after Arnold has been accepted into the Reardon basketball team he plays in a game against his former team on the reserve, the Willpinit Redskins. Before the game he reflects, "Jeez, I felt like one of those Indian scouts who led the U.S. Cavalry against other Indians" (p. 183). When the Reardon team wins the game, Arnold is overcome with a sense of shame because of the pivotal role he has played in Willpinit's loss, and emails Rowdy to commiserate:

> "We'll kick your asses next year," Rowdy wrote back. "And you'll cry like the little faggot you are."
> "I might be a faggot," I wrote back, "but I'm the faggot who beat you." (p. 197)

As Arnold notes, "that might just sound like a series of homophobic insults" (p. 198), but within the discursive framework of rez language as it is represented in the narrative, the boys' use of the term "faggot" bridges the estrangement between them. The chapter ends with the self-reflexive irony that characterizes the humor of the book: "I was a happy faggot!" (p. 198).

The eponymous protagonist of *Will's Garden* (Maracle, 2002) similarly moves between the reserve and the mainstream school, aligning himself with the nerds because, as Will's cousin Sarah comments, the nerds are "usually the thoughtful ones" (p. 39) who are open to cultural difference. Like *The Absolutely True Diary* (Alexie, 2007), *Will's Garden* both deploys and reflects on the particular brand of humor common on the reserve. Will develops a friendship with Joseph, one of the nerd group, who joins Will and other community members as they build a community center on the Sto:loh reserve. The moment when Joseph makes a Sto:loh-style joke is also the moment when the two boys recognize both their difference and their capacity to reach across that difference:

> "How are you getting home, Joseph?" Thomas [asked]....
> Don't worry. My dad is still here."
> "We might as well hang out 'til you leave. If I know my pop, we will be the last to go."
> "You want to work 'til then?" Joseph asks.
> "Are you kidding?" I reply with a little too much intensity.
> Joseph laughs. He caught us. It was his first crack at an Indian joke. He nailed us. (Maracle, 2002, p. 149)

In this exchange is encapsulated a complex range of meanings and references. By observing and participating in Sto:loh sociality Joseph has come to understand the influence of elders in the community, the mixture of resentment and loyalty demonstrated by the Sto:loh young men, the high priority attached to communal effort, and the oblique, self-mocking humor of the reserve. That Joseph can make even an elementary "Indian joke" is emblematic of his openness to other ways of seeing the world.

Language operates in these novels, too, as a signifier of loss and confusion. When Njunjul attends a city school for the first time in *Njunjul the Sun* (McDonald & Pryor, 2002), he notices a sign that says "Welcome" in the many languages of this multilingual setting:

> I can read "Welcome," that's it, but. I'm trying to get my head around all these other languages written up there. What is this place? The United Nations?… Now I'm wishing I had my language. Mine got taken away, but. (pp. 62–63)

The school setting, with its signifiers of multiculturalism, functions in the narrative as a homologue of the nation, suggesting that national celebrations of cultural diversity conceal Australia's colonial and assimilationist past, when Aboriginal people were prohibited from speaking their languages.

The novels I have discussed are, like many mainstream novels, built on coming-of-age narratives and rely on strategies such as focalization, dialogue, and the ordering of events, which are common to mainstream fiction. Arnold, Will, and Njunjul are located in settings where they must forge Indigenous identities while engaging with mainstream culture. For all this, they are not constructed as hybrid subjects or unhappy figures torn between cultures. When Arnold struggles to come to terms with a series of tragic deaths in his family, he consults dictionaries for the meaning of the word "grief" but no definition fits the extremity of his feeling until Gordy shows him Euripides' *Medea*. As soon as he reads Medea's words, "What greater grief than the loss of one's native land?" (Alexie, 2007, p. 173), he realizes that the losses he has experienced commenced with the colonial loss of land and spiraled into loss of languages, customs, and relationships. Medea's despair affords an analogy for his own depression: "And, after Eugene's funeral, I agreed with [Medea]. I could have easily killed myself, killed my mother and father, killed the birds, killed the trees, and killed the oxygen in the air" (p. 173). Euripides, a "way-old dude" (p. 172), provides Arnold with a way of thinking about his experience and that of his family and community. Just as Indigenous subjectivities are not a combination of Western and Indigenous elements, so Indigenous texts are not a combination of tropes and discourses but "reinvent the enemy's language" (Harjo & Bird, 1997) to engage in processes of self-representation.

Representing Indigeneity from the Outside

So far I have focused on aspects of Indigenous textuality. As I have already noted, however, most representations of Indigeneity in children's literature are produced by non-Indigenous writers and illustrators. In her essay "The Problem of Speaking for Others," Linda Alcoff (1991) notes that it is difficult to "distinguish speaking about from speaking for in all cases" (p. 9) because representation does not unproblematically produce the truth about a culture or individual, but is shot through with interpretations and judgments. Alcoff advocates that those speaking for others should be conscious of the power relations involved in acts of textual production, that they should take responsibility for what they say, and that they should "analyze the probable or actual effects of the words on the discursive and material context" (p. 26).

In writing about Indigenous cultures, many children's writers manifestly do not take the measures suggested by Alcoff, as is evident from the stereotypical and limited representations that abound across national literatures. Yet, making judgments about books is not simply a matter of lining up "good" against "bad" representations, or of distinguishing positive from negative depictions. Criticism of texts incorporating representations of Indigenous peoples and cultures has the potential to identify the cultural work carried out by these texts, how they position child readers, and what they have to tell us about relations between Indigenous and non-Indigenous people and concepts of national identity. As Brooke Collins-Gearing (2002) notes in her discussion of Australian 19th-century texts, it is not sufficient to label colonial texts as racist, since such generalizations "overlook the complexity of nineteenth-century representations which were not uniformly misinformed" (pp. 16–17; see also Bradford, 2001). Marcia Langton (1993) points out that merely to reverse colonial binaries by "using a positive/negative cultural formula (e.g. blacks are superior or more compassionate) does not challenge racism. It may, in fact, corroborate racism" (p. 41).

If categorizing books as good or bad does not provide a solid foundation for critique, nor does the much-debated concept of authenticity (Bradford, 2007). The principal problem with this term as it is used in discussions of race is that it almost always invokes a state of Indigenous purity that is accepted as genuine by non-Indigenous cultures. The racist practices whereby colonized people were categorized as "half-caste," "full-bloods," "mulattos," or "half-breeds" continue to haunt contemporary postcolonial societies in representations that identify Indigenous cultures with an idealized, romanticized past prior to colonization. In such formulations, Indigeneity is treated as fixed and static, and Indigenous people and practices associated with modernity are regarded as inauthentic. A further problem with notions of authenticity is that they never address the question "Who determines what is authentic?" but rely on representations which circulate within white culture.

To move beyond categorizations of good/bad books, or invocations of "authentic" modes of Indigeneity, I have found it useful to combine cultural theories (particularly postcolonial literary theories) with close attention to the linguistic and narrative features of texts. The narrative strategies of point of view and focalization are crucial to how readers are positioned by texts, since in John Stephens' (1992) words, "point of view is the aspect of narration in which implicit authorial control of audience reading strategies is probably most powerful" (pp. 26–27). In order to construct Indigenous focalizing characters, non-Indigenous authors must imagine how such characters think, value, and feel, a highly demanding exercise. It is not surprising, then, that most texts by non-Indigenous authors represent Indigenous cultures through the focalizing perspective of non-Indigenous protagonists.

A particularly common narrative pattern is that in which non-Indigenous protagonists derive psychological or spiritual benefits from engagement with Indigenous cultures. Ben Mikaelsen's (2001) *Touching Spirit Bear* is a symptomatic text, in which the protagonist, Cole Matthews, agrees to spend a year alone on an island in Southeast Alaska as part of the Circle Justice process whereby offenders are given alternatives to custodial sentences. Cole has been regularly beaten by his alcoholic and violent father, and has seriously assaulted Peter, a younger boy. Two Tlingit men, the parole officer Garvey and Edwin, an elder who has volunteered to assist in the Circle Justice process, are charged with guiding Cole through his period of banishment.

The novel's point of view shifts between an external third-person narrator and focalization through Cole's perspective, so that Garvey and Edwin are depicted from outside, accorded no subjectivity. Indeed, they are indistinguishable from each other except in regard to their age and physical build. They are given to gnomic utterances coded as Native: "The sky, this stick, hot dogs, life, it's all the same. It's what you make of it. What you focus on becomes reality. Everybody carries anger inside. But also happiness" (p. 145). That is, Garvey and Edwin are treated as stock Indian figures following the long tradition of such representations from colonial times. They function as spiritual guides without reference to a system of Tlingit beliefs except within the banal, New Age terms of the novel. Cole is unproblematically inducted into rituals of dance, physical tests, and carving, and is ultimately healed of his anger. It is as though the two Tlingit men, like the Spirit Bear who mysteriously appears to Cole, exist purely for Cole's benefit. They have no social or cultural contexts, no history apart from sketchy accounts of past emotional and psychological problems, no identities apart from responding to Cole's need for healing.

In *Touching Spirit Bear*, Tlingit culture is treated as a commodity, a substitute for religious and spiritual traditions missing from Cole's life and that of his family. In this way the novel, like many texts, responds to contemporary anxieties over the rootlessness of modern Western culture and its thoughtless exploitation of the natural world. The figures of Edwin and Garvey are clearly intended to valorize Tlingit culture; however, what may seem like a benign representation is, finally, a stereotype. As Homi Bhabha (1994) observes, "Stereotyping is not the setting up of a false image which becomes the scapegoat of discriminatory practices. It is a much more ambivalent text of projection and introjection, metaphoric and metonymic strategies, displacement, over-determination, guilt, aggressivity" (p. 81). Spiritual guides like Edwin and Garvey are ambivalent figures because they encapsulate vestiges of colonial guilt as well as contemporary desires for a purer and less materialistic life.

A very different approach to Indigenous spirituality is apparent in an Australian text, Leonie Norrington's (2004) *The Last Muster*, written by a white author who spent her childhood living in Aboriginal communities. The action of the novel centers on the discovery of a cache of old bullet heads by Shane, the son of the manager of a cattle station in the remote Kimberley region of Western Australia. The Aboriginal protagonist, Red, is the grand-daughter of Lofty, the head stockman on the cattle station. Like Edwin in *Touching Spirit Bear* (Mikaelson, 2001), Lofty is an elder of his clan; unlike Edwin, he is not merely a stock sage figure but plays out a political role in the highly charged context of land rights negotiations at a time when large landholdings are being purchased by corporations. To Lofty, no matter who "owns" the land, he and his Bunuba people are its custodians, and the bullets discovered by Shane turn out to have been directly implicated in an episode of colonial violence when Jandamarra, a warrior and leader of the Bunuba, was trapped and shot.

In *The Last Muster* (Norrington, 2004), focalization shifts among several characters: Red, Shane, Lofty, and Shane's father. The narrative is predominantly in the present tense, which has the effect of bringing together past and present, recalling colonial events in a way that emphasizes their real and immediate consequences for the contemporary protagonists. Added to this, the novel deploys a variety of dialects and languages in conversational exchanges, thus achieving a dialogical effect whereby cultural differences and memories play off against one another. An example of some of these techniques occurs in an episode when Shane and Red, pursuing a wild stallion in the mountainous area where Shane discovered the bullet heads, find themselves suddenly hemmed in by great towers of rock:

Don't panic. Panic's what gets people killed. Shane hears his father's voice. If you're in a car, stay with it. Someone will find you. If you have to move, think clearly before you do and stay on the track. His body's suddenly weak, heavy, pressing him down, his legs jittering so much he has to crouch down and gammon check the ground for footprints before he falls.

Red leans her leg against Shane's arm. She pulls herself up tall and, looking out at the country, says softly in language, "I'm Redeleenia. Granddaughter for that old man Lofty, working station long time. Head stockman. Law man. Countryman. I come here by mistake. I mean no offence." (pp. 26–27)

Shane's thoughts at the beginning of this excerpt recall his father's voice, authoritatively advising Shane as to what to do if he is lost in the vast spaces of the Kimberley region. With "His body's suddenly weak," the narrative modulates into a description of Shane's panic and awe, suggesting his idiolect in "he has to crouch down and gammon check the ground." The term "gammon" is an Aboriginal English word which means "pretend," and its use by Shane (or, more accurately, in a narrator-focalized account of his language) constructs him as familiar, and indeed intimate, with Aboriginal culture. Whereas Shane relies on his father's pragmatic approach to the strangeness of his surroundings, Red's response is to address the land and its spirits directly, introducing herself in relation to her kinship with Lofty, whom she describes in relation to his status in white and Aboriginal worlds: in the world of the cattle station as one who has been "working station long time" and is "head stockman"; but, more significantly, as "law man" and "countryman." In describing Lofty in this way she claims kinship with one who is an elder, a fully-initiated man with access to sacred and secret knowledge of the laws established by the ancestors of the Dreaming; and a traditional owner of Bunuba country, hence "countryman." Red's behavior here is that of a person who (whether for reasons of gender, lack of standing as an initiated member of the clan, or because of the sacredness of the place) does not have the right to enter this region of her country. Her apologetic "I come here by mistake. I mean no offence," together with her declaration of kinship with Lofty, seeks to placate the spirits and seek safe passage. Discursive features characteristic of Aboriginal English, such as the use of the preposition "for" rather than "of" in "granddaughter for," and Red's use of the demonstrative pronoun "that" in "that old man Lofty," distinguishes her language from Shane's, so foregrounding difference even as the episode constructs the two as close and empathetic friends.

In *The Last Muster* (Norrington, 2004), Lofty's knowledge of country and colonial history is the key to a process of remembering that brings together black and white inhabitants of the cattle station. This knowledge is grounded and historicized, unlike the New Age imaginings of *Touching Spirit Bear* (Mikaelson, 2001). The novel's interplay of languages and worldviews acknowledges the complex and symbiotic relationships of the colonial past and the contemporary setting, advocating an enhanced understanding of how the past shapes the present. Importantly, the novel treats Aboriginal traditions with respect and not as a resource to be plundered, while clearly differentiating characters' access to sacred and secret traditions. Norrington's (2004) deft treatment of Shane's and Red's responses to an inexplicable event pulls back from interpretation or explanation, but foregrounds the boundaries between cultures and systems of knowledge.

The Problem with History

To read a large number of settler society historical novels located in the colonial period is a peculiarly depressing experience. Many of these novels are informed by the conviction that the displacement and destruction of Indigenous societies was a necessary, inevitable consequence of colonization. They often represent Indigenous peoples as victim populations whose pathetic resistance to imperialism gives way to resignation, and who fade into obscurity at the end of the narrative, while white protagonists advance to prosperous futures. Many novels feature a pair of characters, one white and the other Indigenous, who become friends; however, the weight of these narratives generally falls on the identity-formation of the white character, who typically gains skills, insight, or tolerance from an encounter with Indigeneity.

Elizabeth George Speare's (1983) *The Sign of the Beaver* is a paradigmatic example of this style of representation. Like most novels of the colonial period, places and events are filtered through the perspective of a white protagonist whose encounters with Indigenous people are treated as symptomatic of white ascendancy. Matt Hallowell's first encounter with the Indian boy Attean and his grandfather occurs when they rescue him from swarming bees. As this incident suggests, the Indians have access to knowledge and skills that are of benefit to Matt, and the narrative follows a trajectory during which Matt becomes expert at many of these skills. On the other hand, Attean shows no interest in learning to read, although his grandfather wishes him to do so in order that he can understand the language of treaties. One implication is that whereas Matt is adept at learning the skills required to live off the land, Attean clings to the old ways and can see no advantage in accessing literacy. This distinction between the two boys points to a larger disparity between European and Indian cultures: that Europeans are capable of higher-order intellectual pursuits, but Indians are not. By the end of the novel Matt is, in his mother's words, "so brown I'd have taken you for an Indian" (p. 134). He is, in effect, indigenized, being completely at home in the new world, and having taken on the "Indian" practices he has been taught. Attean and his tribe, on the other hand, have abandoned their traditional lands and moved away to find new hunting grounds.

The narrative pattern that informs *The Sign of the Beaver* is common across historical novels by non-Indigenous authors, constructing Indigenous cultures as less advanced than colonizing cultures and incapable of withstanding the relentless force of imperialism. Another implication is that Indigenous cultures faded into the shadows, clinging to their old ways and resisting change and "progress." This treatment of Indigeneity easily buys into notions of authenticity that allow little room for invention, cultural change, or dialogue between cultures. Discussing the difficulties, for Indigenous authors, of writing historical fiction, Thomas King (2003) remarks that the North American past constructed in fiction, film and television and taught in schools "was unusable, for it had not only trapped Native people in a time warp, it also insisted that our past was all we had" (p. 106).

Although realist historical fiction is produced, in the main, by non-Indigenous authors, texts by Indigenous writers have begun to emerge, especially in the United States, since the late 1990s. Such works include Louise Erdrich's (1999) *The Birchbark House* and its sequels *The Game of Silence* (2005) and *The Porcupine Year* (2008), Michael Dorris's (1992) *Morning Girl*, and Joseph Bruchac's novels, *The Arrow over the Door* (1998), *Children of the Longhouse* (1996), and *March Toward the Thunder* (2008). In Australia, Anita Heiss's (2001) *Who Am I? The Diary of Mary Talence*, set in the 1930s, locates the novel's protagonist in a white family where she is placed after being removed from her family; and Richard J. Frankland's (2007) *Digger J. Jones* is framed as a diary by 11-year-old Digger, tracing his involvement in the campaign leading up to the 1967 referendum which determined that Aboriginal people should be counted as part of the Australian population in the census. These novels offer an important corrective to mainstream accounts of history by drawing upon Indigenous memories, stories, and perspectives of the past. Another approach to the recovery and re-imagining of Indigenous histories is exemplified in picture books such as Thomas King and William Kent Monkman's (1992) *A Coyote Columbus Story* and Gavin Bishop's (1999) *The House That Jack Built*, which exploit the interplay of visual and verbal texts to produce subversive and ironic treatments both of the past, and of received versions of history.

Conclusion

Texts are produced as much by cultural discourses as by individual writers, and often evade the intentions of their producers, recycling assumptions and beliefs that are deeply embedded in national consciousness. Although progress toward more progressive forms of representation of Indigenous peoples has been slow and uneven across settler societies, it is nevertheless true to say that over the last two decades an appreciable difference is discernible. Increased numbers of publications by Indigenous authors and illustrators now circulate; and there has been a gradual expansion of critical works dealing with how Indigenous peoples and cultures are represented in children's books.

Toward the end of Speare's (1983) *The Sign of the Beaver*, Matt and Attean exchange views about the ownership of land. Attean maintains that it is impossible for humans to own land, which is "same as air" (p. 117). Faced with Attean's conviction, Matt experiences a sense of uncertainty: "Somewhere in the back of his mind there was a sudden suspicion that Attean was making sense and he was not. It was better not to talk about it" (p. 117). This moment of textual fissure, which so departs from the confidence with which the narrative has proposed doctrines of Indigenous inferiority to this point, signals the unease that haunts societies founded upon the invasion and destruction of Indigenous peoples. Rather than Matt's remedy, "not to talk about it," the field of children's literature has much to gain from informed critical readings of texts that represent Indigenous cultures.

Notes

1. I use the term "Indigenous" (in upper case) to refer generally to the autochthonous peoples of Australia, Canada, the United States, and New Zealand. In discussions of national literatures, I use the terms that appear in census figures and the constitutions of individual nations. In relation to specific texts, I use the terms they deploy. I use the terms "non-Indigenous" and "white" to refer to people other than Indigenous.
2. When I was a child these conflicts were called "the Maori Wars," as though they were instigated solely by Maori. They are now generally (and more accurately) referred to as "the Land Wars" or "the New Zealand Wars."
3. The word "country" in Aboriginal English refers to particular tracts of land to which Aboriginal people belong through kinship relations and cultural practices.

Literature References

Alexie, S. (2007). *The absolutely true diary of a part-time Indian.* Londo, England: Andersen Press.

Bishop, G. (1999). *The house that Jack built.* Auckland, NZ: Scholastic.

Bruchac, J. (1996). *Children of the longhouse.* New York, NY: Dial.

Bruchac, J. (1998). *The arrow over the door.* New York, NY: Dial.

Bruchac, J. (2008). *March toward thunder.* New York, NY: Dial.

Dorris, M. (1992). *Morning girl.* New York, NY: Hyperion.

Erdrich, L. (1999). *The birchbark house.* New York, NY: Hyperion.

Erdrich, L. (2005). *The game of silence.* New York, NY: HarperCollins.

Erdrich, L. (2008). *The porcupine year.* New York, NY: HarperCollins.

Frankland, R. J. (2007). *Digger J. Jones.* Gosford, New South Wales: Scholastic Australia.

Goble, P., & Goble, D. (1972). *Brave Eagle's account of the Fetterman fight, 21 December 1866* (P. Goble, Illus.). New York, NY: Pantheon.

Heiss, A. (2001). *Who am I?: The diary of Mary Talence.* Sydney, New South Wales: Scholastic Australia.

King, T. (1992). *A Coyote Columbus story* (W.K. Monkman, Illus.). Toronto, Ontario: Douglas & McIntyre.

Maracle, L. (2002). *Will's garden.* Penticton, British Columbia: Theytus Books.

McDonald, M., & Pryor, B. M. (2002). *Njunjul the sun.* Crows Nest, New South Wales: Allen & Unwin.

Mikaelsen, B. (2001). *Touching Spirit Bear.* New York, NY: HarperCollins.

Norrington, L. (2004). *The last muster.* Norwood, SA: Omnibus Books.

Smith, C. L. (2000). *Jingle dancer* (C. Van Wright & Y. Hu, Illus.). New York, NY: Morrow Junior Books.

Speare, E. G. (1983). *The sign of the beaver.* New York, NY: Dell.

Academic References

Alcoff, L. (1991–1992, Winter). The problems of speaking for others. *Cultural Critique*, 5–32.

Ashcroft, B. (2001). *Post-colonial transformation*. London, England: Routledge.

Ashcroft, B., Griffiths, G., & Tiffin, H. (1989). *The empire writes back: Theory and practice in post-colonial literatures*. London, England: Routledge.

Bhabha, H. (1994). *The location of culture*. London: Routledge.

Boehmer, E. (1995) *Colonial and postcolonial literature: Migrant metaphors*. Oxford, UK: Oxford University Press.

Bradford, C. (2001). *Reading race: Aboriginality in Australian children's literature*. Carlton South, Victoria: Melbourne University Press.

Bradford, C. (2003). Oh, how different: Authorship, ownership and authority in Aboriginal textuality for children. *The Lion and the Unicorn, 27*(2), 199–217.

Bradford, C. (2007). *Unsettling narratives: Postcolonial readings of children's literature*. Waterloo, Ontario: Wilfrid Laurier University Press.

Campbell, J. (2008). *The hero with a thousand faces* (3rd ed.). Novato, CA: New World Library. (Original work published 1949)

Collins-Gearing, B. (2002). *When the Hairy Man meets Blinky Bill: The representation of Indigenality in Australian children's literature*. Unpublished Doctoral Thesis, University of Newcastle, Australia.

Harjo, J., & Bird, G. (1997). (Eds.). *Reinventing the enemy's language: Contemporary Native women writers of North America*. New York, NY: Norton.

King, T. (2003). *The truth about stories: A Native narrative*. Toronto, Ontario: House of Anansi Press.

Langton, M. (1993). *Well, I heard it on the radio and I saw it on the television: An essay for the Australian Film Commission on the politics and aesthetics of filmmaking by and about Aboriginal people and things*. Woolloomooloo, New South Wales: Australian Film Commission.

Linton, P. (1999). Ethical reading and resistant texts. In D. L Madsen (Ed.), *Post-colonial literatures: Expanding the canon* (pp. 29–44). London, England: Pluto Press.

Reese, D. (2009). *American Indians in children's literature: Critical perspectives of Indigenous peoples in children's books, the school curriculum, popular culture, and society-at-large*. Retrieved January 30, 2010, from http://americanindiansinchildrensliterature.blogspot.com/

Seale, D. (2001, March). Parting words: The works of Paul Goble. *Multicultural Review*, 119–120.

Smith, C. L. (2002). A different drum: Native American writing. *The Horn Book Magazine, 78*, 409–412.

Stephens, J. (1992). *Language and ideology in children's fiction*. New York, NY: Longman.

Point of Departure

Joseph Bruchac

In many ways, reading Clare Bradford's essay is a breath of fresh air. It's good to discover a scholar who has a sense of the breadth and complexity of indigenous realities. Bradford clearly recognizes how often books by non-Native writers that purport to present Native lives are deeply flawed by either the assumption of the cultural superiority of western culture or a cloying romanticism as the stereotypical images of the noble savage and the vanishing Indian (or whoever) are trotted out and paraded past us yet again... in chains.

She also gets at something that has been bugging me for a while. To express it as my Abenaki grandfather did: "You ought to know what you're talking about before you open your mouth."

Knowledge is not a function of bloodline. Culture is something we learn, not something we're born with. That is why, as Bradford rightly says, you do not necessarily have to be, for example, a Lakota to write well about the Lakota experience for children. But you do need to know a lot! (Quite frankly, every Lakota does not know everything about being an Indian, or even being a Lakota Indian. That's especially so if you're a Lakota who was denied the opportunity to learn your own language by a government boarding school.) Some of us are true elders, honored by our people. Some of us know our languages and our traditions and devote our lives to passing them on. Some of us are gifted storytellers. But none of us are like spiders with the genetically imbued ability to spin a cultural web.

It takes a long time to learn a culture. We are talking years and years of immersion, not just observation. Even expert ethnologists have often failed to really grasp the reality of the people they're studied—and written books about. Margaret Mead never caught on that her informants, who spun tall tales about sexual freedom in Samoa—a Polynesian culture that actually views premarital sex as taboo—were doing what American Indians have done for years—"putting on the anthro." Just making up stories in response to their annoying and impolite questions.

Culture, like language, is very specific. If you do not learn it well, then you end up speaking pidgin at best and either nonsense or insult at worst. That is why, to put it plainly, the vast majority of books for kids "about" so-called indigenous cultures that have been written by white people are stupid or insensitive. Those authors might mean well, but like the inexperienced driver who just accidentally hit you with his car, good intentions don't make up for being run over.

Here's another thing. There's no such thing as indigenous cultures. Just as there's no such thing as an American Indian. Catch phrases like "American Indian" or "Native American" or "Aboriginal People" or "First Nations" (Canada's culturally correct favorite phrase, as they legislate their Native nations out of existence by defining them according to blood quantum and saying your kids are no longer true indigenes once you reach Status 3) are convenient lies. There are, instead, a vast number of culturally and linguistically distinct original nations or communities of people who are different from the majority immigrant cultures in whatever country they exist. And we all have our own names for ourselves. Alnobak, Anishinabe, Aniyunwiya, Dine, Haudenosaunee, Inupiat…

Actually (Do I contradict myself? Why not?), the word "Indian" works pretty well for me if I have to generalize. Hey, most indigenous people in the United States refer to themselves as Indian. Sure, it was an error of labeling by a lousy Italian navigator. But it's been in wide use for centuries and it's not an ethnic insult like Redskins. (Go Skins! Go Wops?) That's why the consensus tribal choice for the new museum on the Mall in Washington, DC was The National Museum of the American Indian.

Lumping us all together may be convenient, but it is not accurate. Being Maori is as different in many ways from being Abenaki as it is from being Polish. (Oh, and by the way, the Poles were also colonized, had their children taken from them, were regarded as inferior to western Europeans, and have had a long struggle to regain their cultural and political identities. So, too, the Irish.)

So rather than talking about being an indigenous writer, let me get more specific to speak about being a writer of Abenaki Indian descent who has often focused on the stories and histories of a number of native nations, in addition to my own. I've shared stories and histories that I have learned not just from books but from years of experience and interaction with living tribal elders and historians, people who've read what I've written and approved of its publication before I've put it into print.

I was not raised on a reservation. I grew up in rural New York at a time when being Indian was not a desirable thing. Indian blood was often hidden to protect your family. My grandfather Jesse Bowman left school in fourth grade—leaped out the window and went to work in the woods because they kept calling him a dirty Indian. In nearby Vermont in the 1930s, Indians and others of "inferior genetic stock" were being sterilized as part of the state's Eugenics Project to breed better Vermonters. New England Indians learned how to hide in plain sight. That's the subject of a novel of mine called *Hidden Roots*.

I've spent much of my adult life learning things about my Abenaki heritage that I was not given as a child. I've occasionally been criticized because of my openness about that long learning process and the fact that I was not raised in a "typical" Indian way. Tough.

I'm also of mixed blood. But don't get me started on that. If the only "real" members of any ethnicity are those who are of "pure blood," then virtually every ethnicity in the modern world will cease to be or be reduced to a handful. But we are always being asked how much Indian blood we have. I've been known to carry a dipstick tucked into my belt. When I get asked that I pull it out and say, "Looks like I'm down a pint."

Is there any other group in this country that is expected to show their papers to prove they are who they say they are? Poodles? It goes along with "looking Indian," especially if when you go to a school as a visiting author you arrive in your everyday attire rather than regalia.

"Mr. Bruchac, you don't look Indian like Chief Red Woodpecker who visited our school last week did. He had on his feathers."

Ah, yes, Chief Red Woodpecker, who is an Italian American hobbyist who sells tipis and wears western Indian regalia on his school visits.

It's amazing to me how, although there is now more sensitivity in the United States about respecting African American culture (and it's about time!) the same stereotypes, insults, and assumptions keep turning up again and again about Indians. That is especially true in children's literature. I've contributed to two of the best books that deal with this, *Through Indian Eyes* and *A Broken Flute*, both edited by Doris Seale and Beverly Slapin. I wish those books were in every school.

Whoa! This is supposed to be a brief response rather than a doctoral thesis. I've already written one of those in my life, so I'll confine myself to a few more stories and end up there.

The first is about a phone call I received from a non-Abenaki, non-Indian who had rewritten as a rhymed poem one of the traditional Abenaki stories I often tell (and had already published).

"I want to publish this as a children's book," the other writer said.

"Don't," I said. I hoped that would be enough, but it wasn't.

"Why not?" Shocked tone.

I sighed inwardly, but then spent the next half hour patiently—but firmly—explaining that I had told that story in the way elders had told me it should be shared. It was a traditional story that should not be rewritten or retold as a clever little rhyming poem. To me it was not just a story, but a living thing that had to be treated with respect. I knew it not only in English, but also in the Abenaki language, and my telling had been done in a way meant to honor that original tongue. It didn't need to be written again by someone outside the culture.

Eventually, I got my point across and—to the other writer's credit—that rewrite of the story was never published.

Not every story is meant to be told by everyone. There are stories that I've been entrusted with that are only to be spoken on certain occasions. And there are stories that

I keep only in my mind and never tell. The possibility of being published is seductive, but it's more important to be honest. That is why, at the end of 2009, I turned down the opportunity offered me to write a book for young people about the history and culture of the Hopis.

"You need a qualified Hopi writer to do that," I replied and made some suggestions, though I'm not sure the publisher intended to take them.

That leads to my last story—which is about publishing and publishers. It's actually more than one story. I've reached the point in my career where it's relatively easy to find a publisher. (Not always, though. I've had a dozen different book ideas rejected by my publishers over the past decade—including a sequel to my novel *Pocahontas*, which was meant to be only the first volume in a trilogy.) However, there are not enough books by Indian writers for kids being published. And it is not because there's a lack of talented Indian authors.

It's hard for any writer to get a first book published, but it is doubly difficult for Indians who have to fight all of those hurdles of stereotypical expectations and cultural obtuseness that Bradford rightly cites, including being asked to rewrite traditional tales or stories that are culturally accurate in ways that might make them more acceptable to a non-Indian editor but render them no longer authentic.

It's pretty well known that I appreciate writing by other people and that I'm willing to help where I can. As a result, every now and then I find myself sent a manuscript by a new Indian writer. I read it and think it would make a great book for kids. I recommend it to some editors and publishers, including some of my own. But none of them accept it. It doesn't fit the mold—which has usually been shaped by a non-Indian writer's vision. It's not cute. It's not commercial. Isn't it enough that we have Alexie and Erdrich and Bruchac? Who needs more Indian writers? Arrghhh.

Sometimes, after years of trying, the book ends up being self-published, accompanied by an intro I've written.

But that's not a losing story. Because the technology has advanced so much so recently and the costs of publishing have gone down, there's more opportunity now for smaller publishers and self-publishing to fill the gap.

And that—if the big publishers can't or won't do the right thing—is what I hope will happen more often.

Bradford ends her essay with the point, a very good one, that we need "to talk about it," no matter how difficult that conversation may be, no matter how uncomfortable it may make some people feel. My final point is that we need to enlighten and educate not just the critics and the reading public, but also editors and presses to the point where more publication of good books by a wide variety of writers accurately representing their own cultures, becomes not a dream, but a reality.

24

Literary Studies, Cultural Studies, Children's Literature, and the Case of Jeff Smith

Roderick McGillis

University of Calgary

It has been nearly 40 years since children's literature courses began appearing as regular offerings in English departments, but their status there is not unchallenged. Noted Canadian literary scholar Roderick McGillis situates the development of children's literature studies within the changing landscape of cultural studies that has redefined the missions of many English departments. He argues that children's literature's challenge to the academic orthodoxy of what constitutes literary art participates in the reinvigoration of the discipline through expanding notions of textuality. In particular, he focuses on Brian Selznick's *The Invention of Hugo Cabret* and Jeff Smith's *Bone*, both groundbreaking graphic novels, as exemplars of "cultural studies at work." This discussion is aptly followed with commentary by Smith himself and his curators, David Filipi and Lucy Shelton Caswell, who demonstrate some of the innovative ways this cultural work becomes available for study.

a vague and baggy monster, Cultural Studies…

(Williams, 1989, p. 158)

I have thought for a long time now that English departments were about to go the way of departments of Classics; they will not disappear, but they will shrink and move to the periphery of important scholarly activity (Deresiewicz, 2008). I see the beginnings in my own university where retention rates for first year students are worst in the Faculty of Humanities, while another faculty, Communication and Culture, grows yearly. Traditional literary studies began to look quaint and rarified at least 20 years ago, although the signs of its fading prestige were apparent in the 1960s. One

obvious indication of things to come was Leslie Fielder's *Playboy* article in December 1969, "Crossing the Border, Closing the Gap," and the creation of the Popular Culture Association in the 1970s. By the time the 1980s rolled in, we were on the verge of the so-called "canon wars," and English departments felt compelled to offer courses in a variety of non-canonical subjects such as fantasy and science fiction, detective fiction, and children's literature.

Children's literature had been around for some years, usually as a course either in colleges of Education or offered as a service to Education programs by English departments. As things have developed, courses in children's literature now appear on course listings in English departments, Faculties of Education, Schools of Library and Information Science, and in foreign language departments. As for English departments, we have evidence that in some universities these departments are changing to accommodate film studies and/or cultural studies. The opening of English departments to new forms of textuality is a survival tactic. Whether it will work remains to be seen. What is clear is the necessity for change; change is a prerequisite for survival.

Once children's literature found a place among course offerings in university calendars, it did not take long for conferences and associations to take notice and establish an academic presence. In 1972, the Children's Literature Association formed, and not long after, the annual MLA conference began offering regular sessions on children's literature. By the 1980s, children's literature was a presence, perhaps not a large presence, but a presence nonetheless in universities throughout North America. The acceptance of children's literature into the academy took somewhat longer in the UK, but we now see that it shares space with other areas of cultural studies, including gender studies and communication studies. Perhaps it was inevitable that a process of forming a children's literature canon should take place, and this is precisely what happened in the 1980s when the Children's Literature Association began to formulate a list of essential children's books. The Association's efforts culminated in the three-volume *Touchstones* series, edited by Perry Nodelman (1985–1987).

Looking back on the *Touchstones* volumes illustrates how far we have come in the past 25 years. In his "Introduction" to the first volume, Nodelman (1985) noted that the books listed and studied in this and the other volumes "almost exclusively represent the European traditions of most well-off North Americans" (p. 10). He went on to say that the titles discussed in *Touchstones* "are the literary equipment of well-educated people, people destined for economic and social success—and so are the values they express. Taken as a whole, in fact, these books are rather singlemindedly concerned with the joys of acceptance of one's lot—with coming to an accommodation with what already is" (p. 10). We have come a long way since Nodelman wrote these words, and a cultural studies approach to children's literature does not pretend to inform people what is necessary to their cultural education. In fact, such an approach is quite willing to take culture in all its unwieldy bagginess. We now discuss canonical works such as *Charlotte's Web* (White, 1952) or *Tom's Midnight Garden* (Pearce, 1958) alongside contemporary slash fanfiction and comic books, as is evident in this *Handbook*, particularly in the chapters by Dutro and McIver as well as Brenner.

Something of an irony exists in the Association's effort to construct a canon of children's books. First, children's literature had been part of an expanding canon from the beginning. For departments of English to offer courses on children's literature was a challenge, either implicitly or explicitly, to traditional course offerings. And yet, here was an association bent on establishing the legitimacy of the study of children's books within literature departments by creating a list of great children's books to rest beside the great tradition in mainstream books. Second, the Association set out to construct a canon of children's books just when the academy in general was engaged in a testy debate over the literary canon, and the advocates of breaking the canon were winning (on the canon, see McGillis, 2003). A third factor complicates my narrative. The canon wars were part of a larger culture war in which the privileged place of the book in both education and the larger cultural context was finding itself challenged. Once the traditional literary canon no longer seemed adequate in the face of insistent resistance from readers and academics who not only read beyond the canon, but who also sometimes argued for the importance of other forms of "reading"—the reading of film or of painting or of other graphic arts (e.g., the comic book)—reading itself came under scrutiny. Why do we think that reading Jane Austen or James Joyce is important and intellectually stimulating whereas reading work by the likes of Stan Lee and Jack Kirby is a waste of time, and perhaps even detrimental in some way? Why is it preferable to read a novel by William Faulkner than to watch a film by John Ford, or—heaven forbid—Roger Corman or Sam Raimi?

Cultural Studies and Changing Curricula

However we might respond to such questions, the canon wars resulted in a breakdown of traditional ways of organizing college curricula in the Humanities. Indeed, even the notion of "Humanities" came under question since it implied a certain ideological way of seeing the world, a way most often encapsulated in the term "liberal humanism." Many of us had been trained to think of the Humanities as the area of knowledge that most effectively prepared students to think critically and hence to take their place as informed and independent citizens. And at the center of the Humanities was the study of English, or perhaps more accurately, Anglo-American literature. In the 1980s, however, the challengers to the literary canon and to the privileged place of the book in liberal studies pointed out that the teaching of literature fit neatly into what we assumed children's literature had been doing for more than two centuries, that is, socializing the reader. The canon worked to capture or interpellate readers, to draw them into a comfortable coterie that would offer little resistance to the reigning ideology. In short, the canon was a conservative force, a means of managing public fantasies. We might use a variety of terms to describe literary study—a state apparatus, a colonial exercise, a symbolic system, or a form of repressive satisfaction—but we are hard-pressed to deny that the study of literature could be (and as often as not was) elitist. Some accept this word—elitist—as the description of a necessary and positive ideal in a civilized society, while others use the word to reflect snobbery and divisiveness.

Cultural studies, as several writers note (e.g., Grossberg, 1992; Xie & Wang, 2002), have somewhat different origins in Britain and the United States, but in both countries the impetus for such studies came from the political left. Both the British and American versions of cultural studies owe a debt to the Frankfurt Institute for Social Research that opened in 1924. The Institute's work focused on a combination of Freudian and Marxist approaches to culture, and gave the study of culture its early leftist leaning. As early as 1964 at the University of Birmingham in the UK, the Centre for Contemporary Cultural Studies was founded (the Centre closed in 2002), and under the direction of Richard Hoggart and Stuart Hall a focus on matters such as youth subcultures, race, gender, and class indicates the Centre's political agenda. In the United States, Ray Browne and Russell Nye organized the fledgling Popular Culture Association in 1971, just about the same time as the Children's Literature Association was forming. The Popular Culture Association took an interest in all aspects of cultural production from formula fiction to film and television to bubblegum wrappers. As things developed, the political interests of the Frankfurt and British versions of cultural studies manifest in the work of American writers such as Frederic Jameson (1981) and (importantly for children's literature) Henry Giroux (1981).

In treating both high and low art with high seriousness, cultural studies, in effect, challenged class systems. At the outset of its acceptance in the academy, cultural studies changed the debate over the negative or positive signification of elitism by doing away with the division between high and low in art. Some, Leslie Fiedler (1969) for example, lauded this breakdown of high and low, whereas others such as Theodor Adorno (1991) saw the merging of high and low as a facet of market economics and a weakening of social critique. In any case, cultural studies argued that everything a culture produced was not only important for us to study, but was also worthy of our study. Books are part of the market economy, and as such are just as important for us to understand in all their aims and targeted audiences as any other product of labor exchange. Children's books, even books for very young children, signify in complex ways, and we learn things about books, children, adults, economics, politics—in short, culture in a broad sense—when we study these books. The picture books of Peter Sis, *Madlenka* (2000), *Madlenka's Dog* (2002), or *The Wall* (2007), for example, combine an interest in history and politics with an interest in growing up and inter-generational relationships. For adolescents, a book such as Markus Zusak's (2006) *The Book Thief* delivers an intense narrative that deals with history, death, and the function of literature in human survival.

Helping in the openness of cultural studies was the turn from a specifically literary theory to a broader notion of "theory." The advent of "high theory" occurred in the late 1960s, just when the study of popular culture (and children's literature) began to nudge its way into the universities, probably as a late result of post-war expansion in university enrollments. Literary theory, as it had existed since at least the mid-19th century, not only privileged the book, but it also assumed that the study of literature could be self-contained, hermetically sealed from the sciences of humanity, always understanding, of course, the moral importance of the book. Theory was not only prepared to turn its attention to anything, but it also insisted that the book was just one object of many produced by a modern culture. Context was now as important as the book itself as content.

Context means placing the book in its historical and social setting, and considering who makes it, who publishes it, and who reads it. Theory nicely brought the within and the without together. We now understand reading as an activity related to both the individual and the community, and we also understand that reading is not an activity isolated to the book. We read our environment, and our environment reads us. Questions of value are less important than questions of manipulation and coercion and complicity. David Rudd (2006) identifies "pre-text" (p. 31), "con-text" (p. 35), and "post-text" (p. 41) in his survey of cultural studies. He thoroughly outlines the theoretical bases of each of these, touching on the whole range of concerns from the new historicism to Foucauldian genealogy to race, class, and national identity. Rudd mentions other areas such as the interest in environment (ecocriticism) and disability studies. His essay closes with a look "beyond the book" (p. 44).

In this brief but expansive essay, Rudd is careful to connect ideology (and its manipulative agenda) and children's literature. Sensitivity to ideology necessitates that we pay attention to subtext and intertext. This means that when we read a book such as Jon Scieszka's and Lane Smith's (1992) *The Stinky Cheese Man and Other Fairly Stupid Tales*, we pay attention to the manner in which the book parodies earlier stories and also to how it markets itself. Marketing is no longer outside the book, as the Captain Underpants series (e.g., Pilkey, 1997) indicates. Books carry a variety of cultural signifiers on their paratextual matter: medals that indicate awards, clips from positive reviews, large-lettered tag lines, allusions to other forms of textuality such as films (cover photos, for example), comic books, and tabloids. Rudd (2006) asserts that an "awareness of ideology is frequently missing in studies of children's literature" (p. 43), but a cultural studies approach will more often than not look for ways in which cultural products set out to hail or manipulate youngsters or to identify subversive and progressive messages.

Cultural Studies and the Unconscious

Mention of manipulation reminds us that one influential direction in theory deserves special mention:

psychoanalysis. Back in the 1950s, perhaps spearheaded by a popular works such as Fredric Wertham's (1954) *Seduction of the Innocent* and Vance Packard's (1957) *The Hidden Persuaders*, people got worked up over the question of the unconscious and how forces in our culture work on this buried part of the human psyche. In the study of literature, this interest in the unconscious turned attention to the ways works of literature might either speak to and hence influence (interpellate) the reader's unconscious or reflect the reader's unconscious. The connection with children's literature and culture is clear: how do books reflect the desires and anxieties of children? More importantly, how do the books to which we expose our children influence the way they think and act as individuals and members of a social group? Simply put: how do books and other cultural products manage our fantasies and our children's fantasies?

Marsha Kinder's (1991) *Playing With Power In Movies, Television, and Video Games* manifests this interest in culture and the controlling of fantasies. Kinder draws on Freud, especially the famous "fort/da" game (see pp. 20–22), and on psychoanalytic theorists such as Jacques Lacan and Julia Kristeva, as well as literary critics and theorists such as Peter Brooks and Umberto Eco. The importance of psychoanalytic work in understanding the significance of textuality in the lives of the young lies in its move beyond the formal properties of text and what we used to think of loosely as the thematic properties of text. To see text as fundamentally a reflection of mind is to follow Freud (1908/1985) in his essay, "Creative Writers and Day-Dreaming," and to understand the complexities of desire. A study of children's literature that pursues the Freudian perspective through its Lacanian pathways is Karen Coats's (2004) *Looking Glasses and Neverlands: Lacan, Desire, and Subjectivity in Children's Literature.* Cultural studies is nothing if not attuned to questions of desire.

Indeed, desire is all. Psychoanalytic theory has, for obvious reasons, taken an interest in children and their emotional and intellectual development. Whatever psychoanalytic perspective we select, desire proves formative. Human beings are creatures of desire, and most narratives relate the onset of desire with the early relationship between mother and child and the inevitable complications to this relationship generated by the father. Desire announces the arrival of consciousness. In terms of children's literature, psychoanalytic theory can help us understand the management of desire that literature sets out to accomplish. To put this succinctly, I quote Slavoj Žižek (1997): "a fantasy constitutes our desire, provides its co-ordinates; that is, it literally 'teaches us how to desire'" (p. 7).

Coats (2004) sets out to explain Lacanian psychoanalysis as it pertains to literary and social (cultural) interpretation. She argues that a Lacanian reading of literature for children and adolescents goes a long way in explaining how young people become subjects, in the full sense of the word. How does the literature they read hail them, bring them into existence as members of their social milieu? I say, "goes a long way," because Coats also argues for a distinction between modernism and postmodernism that necessitates her leaving her argument fluid, unfinished, open-ended. This is nice, in the precise sense of this word. Whereas modernism sees a split subject trying to repair or at least cover over this split, postmodernism accepts fragmentation, lack, multiplicity, *différance*, and so on. She concludes with the possibility for hope emerging from the relative and fluid confusion that appears to be postmodernism's legacy. She not only clarifies difficult concepts, but she also places her psychoanalytic readings in cultural, historical, and contemporary contexts. Her insights connect books for the young with our contemporary struggles with abjection. Current concerns with violence among the young and a disconnection between young people and political urgencies are not answered in Coats's study, but they are contemplated, considered, and cunningly worked. Taking her cue, perhaps, from Freud, she considers books from the canon such as *Through the Looking Glass, and What Alice Found There* (Carroll, 1871) and *Peter Pan* (Barrie, 1911) as well as contemporary texts such as the Weetzie Bat books (e.g., Block, 1989) and the Goosebumps series (e.g., Stine, 1992) (the latter is an example of what Freud (1908/1985) means when he says, "not the writers most highly esteemed by the critics" (p. 137). Coats's (2004) work intersects with such contemporary theoretical approaches as postcolonialism, critical race theory, queer theory, and disability studies.

What interests me is the similarity of much of what Coats has to say with the Romantic insistence on paradox, the paradox of incomplete completeness, of desire as ongoing even in fulfillment. The mind is always in danger of overbalancing into neurosis, perversion, or psychosis. And stories, Coats urges, are "as old as bread," and they are "as indispensable to our survival as food" (p. 1). That she chooses the word "stories" rather than "literature" cues us to the cross-media manifestations of narrative. Romantic writers used different language, but they struggled with the same desire for security in an insecure world—both mental and material – and they equally argued for the centrality of story in human development. Coats's concern is genuinely humane; she sees literature as a force in the acculturation of young people. We do have other books that provide a psychoanalytic or psychological approach to literature for the young—I think of books by the likes of the Rustins (1987) or Holbrook (1991)—but nothing like Coats's study. Nodelman and Reimer (2003), in *The Pleasures of Children's Literature,* do provide some commentary on Lacanian psychoanalysis, and we have also had a few articles on such material, such as "The Loving Father in Disney's *Pinocchio*: A Critique of Jack Zipes" by Paul Nonnekes (2000), or Hamida Bosmajian's (1999) "Reading the Unconscious," but these essays are not as thorough or as useful as *Looking Glasses and Neverlands.*

Literary Studies Beyond the Book

We can see the influence of cultural studies even in the traditional areas of literary studies. Studies in the various periods (Medieval, Renaissance, Augustan, Victorian, and so on) now regularly contain material beyond the strictly literary—for example, the study of the "Pamphlet Wars" of the early 17th century or the study of 17th-century medical practices or the study of 18th- and 19th-century slave narratives and captivity narratives. As the last two examples might indicate, we also have a widening of the canon for literary study, especially in the study of literature that lies outside the Anglo American context and literatures inside that context that mark an emerging of previously silenced voices (African American writing, Native American writing, and so on). Study of authors who are neither American nor British born is now a regular feature of literary study.

Children's literature too has broadened its scope, and we no longer focus on a few canonical works from Britain and the United States along with a select number of translations from various European countries. Not only do we study a greater range of what I'll refer to as genres, but we also study literature along with the other arts. Children's literature has an especially intricate relationship with forms of textuality that go beyond the book. From at least the 18th century, the children's book has taken its place alongside related market products, most obviously toys, but also clothing, games, hygiene products, and more recently videos and food products, as examined by Margaret Mackey in this volume. Obvious and crude examples are the Cheerios board books published by Little Simon. More familiar are the various spin-off products from such series as the Harry Potter books (e.g., Rowling, 1997) or the Spiderwick Chronicles (e.g., Black & DiTerlizzi, 2003). Games, films, action figures, clothing, and other products travel the marketplace in the wake of these books.

Literature and the others arts now consist of "texts." We used to refer to texts as "works" of art or of literature or sculpture, the word "work" suggesting a finely crafted object polished and finished and complete: in a word, unified. The work of art was unified and therefore we could examine its unity and admire the manner in which the artist achieved this unity. We could, in other words, attend to the formal features of the work and admire its "aura" of greatness. "Text," however, suggests something woven, textured, connected to strands that may lead beyond the single text to contexts, intertexts, and subtexts. Cultural studies encourages us to read a book such as *Winnie-the-Pooh* (Milne, 1926) not only as an example of cozy Edwardian children's literature, but also as just one facet of a whole texture (or web) of cultural production that takes us into literary history, into developing media (film and television, and now the Internet), into the areas of market research and advertising, and the shift of an authored book into spin-offs that derive not from the original creator but from nameless corporate agents. What may have begun as an expression of and appeal to middle-class British parents and their children, has now become a marketing industry aimed at cross-cultural and cross-class consumers. The original book now has a great range of consumer products marked with its copyrighted characters. We have, of course, many examples of this from Beatrix Potter's books to J. K. Rowling's.

The Invention of Hugo Cabret and the Literary/Cultural Polysystem

We have an excellent example of just how the "enculturation" of what Zohar Shavit (1986) termed the "literary polysystem" (p. 112) has begun to transform the book itself. I am thinking of Brian Selznick's (2007) *The Invention of Hugo Cabret*. This book is partly a conventional narrative recounting the adventures of an orphan who lives in early 1930s Paris, and partly a history of cinema in that it involves a young protagonist who discovers the wizard of early cinema, Georges Méliès, and learns about his films and other films of the silent period. It combines the written word, pencil drawings by Selznick, sketches and drawings by George Méliès, and film stills. The narrative proceeds verbally and visually. Unlike the comic book or graphic novel and unlike the conventional children's picture book, *Hugo Cabret* separates its verbal telling from its visual telling. We have several pages of prose followed by several pages of drawings. At times the drawings mimic the cutting from one frame to another in film, and they use the close-up, long shot, and reaction shot format that we know from film. A reader of this book, like the reader of a children's picture book or the reader of a comic book, reads on at least two levels—the verbal and the visual. Complicating these two levels is the direct call to filmic experience, as the book asks the reader to recall the experience of watching a film. The text here weaves together multiple forms of textuality. In addition, the book's content combines high and low culture—the high narrative of classic realist fiction by Dickens or highbrow cinema by Rene Clair and Francois Truffaut, and the popular fiction of adventure or popular cinema of Charlie Chaplin, Harold Lloyd, and, of course, Méliès himself. The acknowledgements and credits at the end testify to the scholarship that has assisted in the making of this book. Finally, the plot situates the book in Paris at a certain time, and yet it is the product of an American author/illustrator. Thus this book offers a cross-cultural as well as a cross-media experience.

The Invention of Hugo Cabret is about magic. The preposition "of" in the title cues us to the possibility that this book not only invents Hugo Cabret, but that it is also about Hugo Cabret's invention—the thing he makes. The story recounts the making of clocks and relates such making to the crafting of automata, mechanical bodies that perform amazing feats. The automata are reminders of the past, as well as harbingers of the future. They represent the mechanics of time and space, and they point forward to the animating of bodies and things on film. In short, the "invention" of Hugo Cabret is a new form of magic: automaton, film, clockwork objects, and a book that contains the story of its own invention. Hugo grows up to be the magician, Professor Alcofrisbas, a character who appears in many of Georges Méliès's films. Hugo/Professor Alcofrisbas builds a new automaton that "can produce one-hundred and fifty-eight different pictures, and it can write, letter by letter, an entire book, twenty-six thousand one hundred and fifty-nine words. These words" (p. 511). In other words, the automaton that Hugo devises writes the book that we are reading. Mechanism, magic, writing, science, and art are interconnected in *The Invention of Hugo Cabret*. The invention of the title is—tada!—the book itself.

The reader of this book benefits from exposure to a range of cultural production from 19th-century fiction to early cinema. He or she will also benefit from a sense of history, the history of science and of magic. Although the reader will benefit from such foreknowledge, she or he may enjoy Hugo's adventures without such knowledge. This book, like just about all books, leaves room for the reader to grow. The reader of this book has an opportunity to learn things she or he may not have known. The obvious allusions to historical personages and other works of art, such as *The Trip to the Moon* (Méliès, 1902) and Hal Roach's (1923) *Safety Last!* just might pique a reader's interest to seek out these films and view them. *The Invention of Hugo Cabret* is about Hugo's intellectual adventures, as much as it is about his physical adventures, and the reader too may share the intellectual adventures, the search for the art of the past.

The magic this book delivers just might deflect our attention from another of the book's concerns: thievery and survival on the streets. One of the several magic tricks in the world of this book is the overcoming of poverty, both the poverty of the street child and the poverty of an old man whose fame has fled along with his wealth. The story incorporates the myth of Prometheus to explain and rationalize Hugo's thefts, and also to explain the importance of both Hugo's activities and those of his exemplar, Méliès. Prometheus suffered endlessly for stealing fire from the gods to warm mankind, initiating science and civilization. Fire was a kind of magic, as was the science it inaugurated. Science, magic, and art are all brought together in the myth of Prometheus/Georges Méliès/Hugo Cabret. The magician/artist/writer/filmmaker keeps civilization energized. This is a book about art and its importance to survival. This book delivers a cultured world, and it seeks to cultivate its reader. It reminds us that in order to create, to enjoy the pleasures of magic and invention, suffering, and constant resistance are necessary.

The name, Alcofrisbas, gives us another clue. Alcofrisbas is an anagram of the French writer, François Rabelais;

Alcofrisbas Nasier is the pseudonymous name of the writer of *The Life of Gargantua and Pantagruel* (Rabelais, 1928/1532–1564). Invoking Rabelais in *The Invention of Hugo Cabret* inevitably suggests the magic associated with carnival. Hugo, like the book in which he appears, lives on the edge, within the walls, outside the law, and to live outside the law he must be honest. His last name, Cabret, suggests "cabaret," the site of a mixture of performances. In other words, this book performs a cultural studies dance. What Cultural Studies examines, this book performs. In a full sense, *The Invention of Hugo Cabret* traces the transformation of cultural studies from its initial "stealing" of academic space, its sympathy with the disenfranchised, its subversive intentions, and its Marxist leanings to its more recent toothless focus on form. Selznick's achievement is to foreground form, but also to manipulate form in the service of carnival.

Hugo/Professor Alcofrisbas continues his life of theft, the theft of the mundane. The sleight of hand of the magician, the special effects of the movies, the mechanical wonders of the automaton, and the strange evolution of the book steal our sense of the possible and keep us alive to change. The book closes with the diminishing of light, moonlight, until we have black pages. But these pages are not completely black. The final pages of the diegesis are black with large white letters spelling the words "THE END." The next pages give us the Acknowledgements and Credits. The book mimics film, and we know that, as in any film (just as in any narrative), the "end" is never an end. The end is always just the beginning of another exploration, another trip to the pole or to the moon or to the cinema itself. The end credits signal this because they point to other texts and other forms of textuality, other forms of invention. The "invention" of Hugo Cabret is both the discovery and fashioning of the character and the character's discovery and invention. Invention reminds us just how deeply rhetoric is woven into culture.

Cultural Studies at Work with Jeff Smith

How to find ways of saying and of persuading, how to invent, are the features of cultural studies today. And we have a good example of cultural studies at work in Jeff Smith's (2004) epic graphic novel, *Bone*. By "cultural studies at work," I mean that the story of Smith's graphic novel parallels the development of cultural studies as it moves from the periphery of academic syllabi to the center, and as it moves, it gathers momentum and shifts from a position of challenge to a reassuring component of institutionalized literature. The institutionalization of what we have come to call "graphic novels" may reflect the assimilation of potentially subversive material into the mainstream or it may indicate an expanding of possibility and the healthy challenge to the very institution that embraces these works.

The in-text citation after the book's title a few lines above indicates a publication date of 2004, but this hardly begins to tell the story of the creation of *Bone*. I will keep the story brief here because it is available on the Bone website (Smith, n.d). Suffice to say that Smith began creating his black and white comic and publishing it himself in 1991. In fact, he had been drawing the Bone characters since he was "about ten years old" (Smith, 2007, p. 19). In 1982, he entered Ohio State University and began drawing the comic strip "Thorn" for the university newspaper. Then in 1991, he created the publishing house, Cartoon Books, and began producing *Bone*. His willingness to bypass the usual publishing practices suggests an independent spirit, one happy to subvert the way things are normally done. Word of mouth kept demand for the comic strong, and soon the first six issues came out in trade paperback, titled *Out From Boneville* (1995).

By 2005, Scholastic had brought out this volume and several more in both hardback and paperback color versions. The huge single volume black-and-white version of 2004 contains the complete epic story of the three Bone cousins' quest to find their way back to Boneville. And so *Bone* began modestly as an independently produced black-and-white comic, and later became a market product of lavish success. Scholastic's interest in the comic, its willingness to produce colored versions and to market these aggressively, ensured *Bone* a place not only in the commercial market, but also in the educational market. From here, *Bone* has become a franchise with extended products such as action figures (these appeared as early as 1996), lunch boxes, t-shirts, a computer game, and soon (so they say) a film.

When asked how his publishing deal with Scholastic came about, Smith (Allen, 2006) had this to say:

It all started with the librarians. In 2001, after years of trying to get our books into bookstore distribution systems, like Ingram, and having the door slammed in our faces (because Bone was a self-published comic book), one day, Ingram called us. They wanted to start carrying the Bone books. When we asked why, they said their librarians were insisting on it. Apparently, Bone was one of the most requested graphic novels in libraries across the country. By kids! Now, if you've followed my career in comics, you know I've fought against Bone being labeled a children's book. Mostly for marketing reasons (today's comic book readers are mostly adults, and a kid's comic wouldn't survive long), but also because I wasn't writing for kids. I was writing for the same audience I perceived those old Disney animated films were aimed at: the movie going public.

Anyway, the kids found Bone and claimed it. They got enough librarians looking for it, that Ingram called us. And when trade magazines like Library Journal and Publisher's Weekly began reporting on the high circulations of Graphic Novels and teachers' discovery that kids actually were reading them, big publishers like Scholastic took notice. Since most of the articles either featured Bone or at least mentioned it, the people at Scholastic gave us a call and in short order convinced us they understood what Bone was and that they could run with it. Now, a year and five hundred thousand books sold later, I think they were right!

We can see that the spirit of independence and subversion need not be without a desire to succeed in the market place. *Bone* moved from the obscurity of a self-published work to acceptance into both the publishing and educational institutions; it moved from the margins to the mainstream. The move to the mainstream is interesting because the potentially subversive message of both the form and content of *Bone* combines with its literacy work. *Bone* encourages reading and I daresay finds enthusiastic readers who might otherwise be reluctant readers.

Both the diegetic aspect of *Bone* and the history of *Bone* are of interest in any consideration of children's literature and cultural studies. First we have a history of a text that begins both as popular art meant for an audience of adults and young adults. By the time *Bone* first appeared in 1991, comics were no longer simply cheap reading material for children and young teenagers. In the 1980s, the comic industry had changed radically and the comic market targeted readers older than the ones it once targeted, perhaps many of these older readers who had grown up reading Marvel and DC comics in the 1950s and 1960s. *Bone* clearly showed the influence of Carl Barks, best known for his drawing of Donald Duck, and Walt Kelly, creator of Pogo. For inspiration, Smith draws on two comic artists, one who created for a youth market and the other who created for an older reader. In terms of story, the most obvious source is Tolkien's (1954–1955) *Lord of the Rings* trilogy. Like Tolkien (who began his chronicling of Middle Earth with a children's story), Smith looks for a knowing and hence older readership. But, as Scholastic recognized, both the style of Smith's artwork and the humor of his characters lend themselves easily to a youth market. We have, in *Bone*, a work of cross-art, one that appeals to both a child and an adult audience. And we have a work that straddles the popular and the elitist ends of the artistic spectrum. *Bone* reminds me of the work of Tex Avery, and we can see Avery's influence in Phoney Bone's jaw drop in *The Great Cow Race* (2004, p. 219). As a narrative, *Bone* is complex, allusive, and sophisticated; it is also parodic and comic. *Bone* pulls together a variety of strands, both visual and narrative, in a postmodern performance of dazzling originality. It combines epic narrative with comic book art in a story that plays with fantasy—both the fantasies of the characters and the character of fantasy.

The plot concerns three cousins from Boneville, Fone Bone, Phoney Bone, and Smiley Bone, who find themselves lost in a mysterious and dangerous valley that contains forests, fields, a village, and the farm of Gran'ma Ben. Mysterious mountains surround the valley. The Bones have one desire in common: to return to Boneville. They also have desires of their own. Fone Bone has a crush on Thorn, granddaughter of Gran'ma Ben and heir to the throne of Atheia; Phoney Bone, "a selfish little greedbag"

(Smith, 1995, p. 19) according to Smiley, desires money and power; and Smiley desires only companionship and a good cigar. They represent love, lust (for wealth), and loyalty respectively. They form a threesome familiar in American popular culture, reminding us of Dorothy's three companions in *The Wizard of Oz* (Baum, 1900), or the three friends on the Starship Enterprise, or the various threesomes in western films of the 1930s and 40s (e.g., the *Three Mesquiteers*, the *Rough Riders*, and the *Range Busters*). Smith lists his own threesomes in an interview on the Scholastic web site: "there's something about having three—like the three Marx Brothers, the Three Stooges, the three Seinfeld guys (Jerry, George and Kramer!), and of course, Mickey, Donald, and Goofy. There's something about the same three similar characters over and over again. So I kind of went with that" (Scholastic, 2006). As always, the trio represents a composite character.

Again reminding us of American cultural figures, Fone, Phoney, and Smiley are outsiders. Not only are they strangers in a strange land, lost and alone and threatened by vicious rat creatures, a large mountain lion, and the Lord of the Locusts, but they also look different from other sentient beings, the humans such as Thorn, Gran'ma Ben, Lucius, and the others. The Bones come from a place called Boneville, a place probably reminiscent of Duckburg where Donald and his relatives live. Smith's drawing of the Bones and of the other characters who populate his world allude to the comic book, comic strips, and animated cartoons. The Bones remind us of Carl Barks's characters crossed with those of Walt Kelly, the possums and Roderick the Racoon remind us of Disney animals, Gran'ma Ben looks like Popeye, the Veni Yan look as if they walked off a George Lucas film set. At times, the mise en scene looks as if it aspired to the condition of George Herriman, and the Red Dragon and the rat creatures will look familiar to followers of Disney. I think the dragons generally owe something to the visual style of Dr. Seuss. The mixture of places, creatures, cartoon figures, and humans suggests the blend of both forms and ideas that Smith sets out to create. *Bone* is something of a postmodern pastiche.

The plot of *Bone* follows the misadventures of the three Bone cousins as they both try to get back home and assist Thorn and Gran'ma Ben in their battle with the evil Lord of the Locust and the Hooded One. The one strand, the attempt by the Bones to find home, is typical of what I might call "domestic fantasy"; the other strand, the battle between the forces of good and those of evil, is typical of high fantasy. Added to this is the romance between Fone Bone and Thorn. Fone reminds me of a young Bilbo Baggins in love. None of the Bones is particularly heroic, and yet they participate in a heroic battle between forces of good and evil. This is the kind of story that lends itself to cross-fertilization; that is, it crosses cultural boundaries, closes the gap between high and low, between various media, and between generations. It is a cultural product par excellence.

As I implied earlier, the story of *Bone* is, to some degree, the story of cultural studies. Just as cultural studies began as a challenge to both the canonical structure of literary study in the humanities, and then evolved into a safely contained discipline within academic institutions, so too does *Bone* begin as a challenge to traditional fantasy. The three Bone cousins begin their quest to find home in a strangely "othered" world. They are aliens in the valley, "other" by virtue of how they look and what they know or don't know. They bring with them questions of otherness, and the relationship between Thorn and Fone Bone must raise the question of miscegenation. This is heady stuff, and it gets headier when we see the mélange of characters who inhabit and get along in the valley—characters from the bug Ted to the possum family and the gang that hangs out in the Barrel-Haven tavern. We have here a strange multiculturalism, but one that does not develop through the narrative. *Bone* ends safely with everyone in his or her appointed place.

But within the narrative we have cross-cultural intertextuality that keeps the concerns of cultural studies before us. The most obvious of the cultural references is to that most famously unread of American literary classics, Herman Melville's (1851) *Moby Dick*. *Moby Dick* is Fone Bone's favorite novel, and he carries it with him everywhere. He also takes any opportunity to read it or to paraphrase passages from it to anyone who will listen or anyone who will even appear to listen. At one point he tells the story of the novel to Gran'ma Ben as the small group travel to Barrel-Haven. He recounts the first meeting of Ishmael and Queequeg, and he relishes saying that Queequeg is "CARRYIN' SHRUNKEN HEADS!!" Fone assumes that Gran'ma Ben "APPRECIATES FINE LITERATURE" (p. 143). Gran'ma Ben, however, has been asleep all through Fone's narration. Throughout *Bone*, *Moby Dick* has a similarly soporific effect on everyone but Fone. The joke turns on the perceived tediousness of Melville's book, but it also serves to remind us of a couple of significant aspects of *Bone* itself. Like *Moby Dick*, *Bone* presents a story of an epic quest; at one point in the saga, Fone has a dream in which he is Ishmael, Phoney is Captain Ahab, and Smiley is the white whale. Much later, Gran'ma Ben's twisted sister, Briar, activates and controls the dreaming of our heroes and Phoney and Fone become Ahab and Ishmael again. This time, however, Smiley remains his inimitable self, and he explains to the others that what is happening is the result of "the power of the dreaming" (p. 865).

Of interest here is the folding of a cultural experience—the Dreaming or Dreamtime that may derive from Aboriginal culture in Australia—into this fantasy of containment. Perhaps "folding" is less to the point than "appropriation." Just as Fone's dream features Smiley as the whale and absents Queequeg, this later evocation of the Dreaming has Smiley explain the phenomenon as something "caused by the mystical powers of the earth itself" (2004, p. 865). Smith's concept of "dreaming" explains the valley and its mystical connecting of past and present. In a way, "dreaming" in *Bone* demonstrates the gathering in of disparate (and "other") cultural elements to the universal notion of story as quest motif. The hero with a thousand faces is also the chronotope with a thousand manifestations. Otherness in *Bone* is homogenized. What is contained in *Bone* is difference. What is positive in this blending of cultures is the book's championing of modesty, of characters such as Wendell, Euclid, and Lucius, the salt of the earth, the common person. The general tenor of the book celebrates tolerance and mutual understanding.

Another example of the blending of cultures might make the point bluntly. Early in the adventures, Fone Bone and Thorn go to the fairgrounds prior to the running of the Annual Cow Race. Here Thorn meets the honey-seller, Tom, and falls under his spell. Tom dismisses Fone as a "Cupie-doll," a nice reference that places *Bone* and the *Bone* characters in early American cartoon tradition dating back to the Kewpie doll invented by Rose Cecil O'Neill at the turn of the 20th century. Tom resembles Aladdin from the 1992 Disney animated film, but with his floppy hat he also reminds us of Tom Sawyer, yet another powerful connection to the American literary tradition. His flirtatious behavior with Thorn might remind us of Tom and Becky, and his salesmanship might remind us of American entrepreneurship. Thorn is smitten.

On a later visit to the fair, however, Thorn meets Tom with another girl. This girl is distinctly exotic, and Tom introduces her as Jasmine. The intertextual reference is to Disney's (1992) *Aladdin* in which the Princess Jasmine meets the street thief Aladdin in the marketplace. Smith brings together a range of cultural references from canonical literature to popular film. In addition, these references have an orientalist cast—Eastern culture brought into Western culture. Yet, another instance of blending appears clearly in the colored version of this part of *Bone*. Thorn, dressed pertly in green and with distinctive slippers, evokes Peter Pan. Not only does the reference to Peter Pan carry with it the blending of canonical and popular art, and literary and dramatic art, but it also reminds us of gender blending because Peter Pan, more often than not, has been played by a female in the many stage productions of the story.

The point is, then, that *Bone* demonstrates both the strengths and weaknesses of cultural studies. The weakness is as much historical as anything else. As *Bone* develops its postmodern pastiche, bringing together any number of pop culture references and canonical references, it perhaps lessens the force of any critique it might offer of contemporary culture. *Bone* is safe and this is likely why Scholastic found it attractive. *Bone* offers something new and even challenging, but it also offers the familiarity of a safe, closed, and economically sound community based on the rightness of market practices. Cultural studies began 30 years ago or so with a "concern to understand the dynamics of social and cultural inequality and the ways in which these are lived in and through a variety of social categories and ideological identifications" (McRobbie, 1994, p. 39).

In another shifty move, perhaps *Bone* continues to investigate these dynamics. Two of the characters, Gran'ma Ben and her sister, are named Rose and Briar; together they conjure a familiar figure in both folklore and children's literature, Briar Rose or Sleeping Beauty. In other words, Gran'ma Ben and her sister form a composite character, two sides of one person. They engage in a struggle for control; they seek power. The dreaming allows Smith to formulate a Foucauldian vision of power as something that pervades everything and just waits for the motivated person to activate it. The two sisters give us two connections to power, the one a solipsistic relation that wants power for the sake of power, and the other a communal sense of power as that which can develop unity and equality. The vision of equality includes not only the various creatures and the people who inhabit the valley, but also the various intertextual references to a range of cultural products. *Bone* presents a vision of a unified, rather than a uniform, culture.

Finally, we might turn to the pedagogic implications of *Bone* and Cultural Studies. As Henry Giroux (1996) has argued, taking seriously the cultural production that children find interesting serves to engage them in useful thinking. It also shows respect for children. That *Bone* has entered the world of Scholastic does not mean simply that the comic book has been co-opted by an ideological state apparatus; it also means that our classrooms and school libraries are inviting full participation; they are making room for the kinds of texts young students themselves find attractive. Giroux notes that "For many youths, the experience of schooling becomes synonymous with the disciplining of the body and the policing of knowledge" (p. 14). Cultural studies, however, has tended to share the sources of knowledge. It has, according to Giroux, "contributed to the theoretical possibilities for understanding education as a political, pedagogical practice that unfolds in a wide range of shifting and overlapping sites of learning" (p. 15). Children's literature, perhaps more than literature for adults (if such a distinction is fully possible), is both in itself, and in its cultural positioning as one among a series of related products, centrally related to cultural studies. From the beginning, children's literature has, by its very existence, challenged academic authority, challenged assumed notions of what constitutes literature and ideas, and challenged sources of knowledge in pedagogic situations. David Rudd (2006) has identified a number of areas that come under the cultural studies rubric: disability, ecocriticism, race and ethnicity, class, nationalism, and ideology. We can, of course, relate all of these to children's literature.

Recently Lawrence Grossberg (2006) has asserted that cultural studies sets out "to construct a political history of the present" (p. 2). He also asserts that it "has to avoid allowing either theory or politics [to] substitute for analysis" (p. 6). And so "political history" does not mean easy political proselytizing. The political implications of cultural studies have to do with the "vague and baggy monster" I began with in my epigraph from Raymond Williams. Cultural studies is something of a teratology. Freaks loom large in the world of cultural studies, freaks of the kind we meet in Fone Bone or Georges Méliès, creative characters whose day-dreams manage for us both individual and collective dreaming. These characters cross borders and close gaps. They connect various forms of textuality, and they connect children's literature with various forms of textuality. They also connect audiences. Cultural studies and children's literature remind us that our world is no dream, but that it may and perhaps should become one.

Literature References

Barrie, J. M. (1911). *Peter Pan.* New York, NY: Scribner's.

Baum, F. (1900). *The wonderful wizard of Oz.* Chicago, IL: George M. Hill.

Black, H., & DiTerlizzi, T. (2003). *The field guide.* New York, NY: Simon & Schuster.

Block, F. L. (1989). *Weetzie Bat.* New York, NY: Harper Collins.

Carroll, L. (1871). *Through the looking glass.* London, England: Macmillan.

Clements, R., & Musker, J. (Producers and Directors). (1992). *Aladdin* [Motion picture]. USA: Walt Disney Feature Animation.

Méliès, G. (Director). (1902). *A trip to the moon* [Motion picture]. France: Méliès.

Melville, H. (1851). *Moby Dick.* New York, NY: Harper.

Milne, A. A. (1926). *Winnie the Pooh.* London: Methuen.

Pearce, P. (1958). *Tom's midnight garden.* Philadelphia, PA: J. B. Lippincott.

Pilkey, D. (1997). *The adventures of Captain Underpants.* New York, NY: Blue Sky Press.

Rabelais, F. (1928). *The life of Gargantua & Pantagruel.* D. Douglas (Ed.). New York: Modern Library. (Original work published 1532-1564)

Roach, H. (Producer), & Newmeyer, F. C., & Taylor, S. (Director). (1923). *Safety last!* [Motion picture]. USA: Hal Roach Studios.

Rowling, J. K. (1997). *Harry Potter & the philosopher's stone.* London, England: Bloomsbury.

Scieszka, J., & Smith, L. (1992). *The stinky cheese man and other fairly stupid tales.* New York, NY: Viking.

Selznick, B. (2007). *The invention of Hugo Cabret.* New York, NY: Scholastic.

Sis, P. (2000). *Madlenka.* New York, NY: Frances Foster Books.

Sis, P. (2002). *Madlenka's dog.* New York, NY: Farrar, Straus & Giroux.

Sis, P. (2007). *The wall.* New York, NY: Farrar, Straus & Giroux.

Smith, J. (1995). *Out from Boneville.* Columbus, OH: Cartoon Books.

Smith, J. (2004). *Bone.* Columbus, OH: Cartoon Books.

Smith, J. (2007). *The art of Bone.* Milwaukie, OR: Dark Horse Books.

Stine, R. L. (1992). *Welcome to dead house.* New York, NY: Scholastic.

Tolkien, J. R. R. (1954-1955). *Lord of the rings.* London, England: Allen & Unwin.

White, E. B. (1952). *Charlotte's web.* New York, NY: Harper & Row.

Zusak, M. (2006). *The book thief.* New York, NY: Alfred A. Knopf.

Academic References

Adorno, T. (1991). *The culture industry.* J. M. Bernstein (Ed.). London, England: Routledge.

Allen, M. (2006). Jeff Smith interview. *Suspended animation.* Retrieved February 17, 2010, from http://www.starland.com/sus/2006/sus060224.htm

Bosmajian, H. (1999). Reading the unconscious: Psychoanalytical criticism. In P. Hunt (Ed.), *Understanding children's literature* (pp. 100–111). London, England: Routledge.

Coats, K. (2004). *Looking glasses and neverlands: Lacan, desire, and subjectivity in children's literature.* Iowa City: University of Iowa Press.

Deresiewicz, W. (2008, March 11). Professing literature in 2008. *The Nation.* Retrieved February 17, 2010, from http://www.thenation.com/doc/20080324/deresiewicz

Fiedler, L. (1969, December) Cross the border, close the gap. *Playboy,* pp. 151, 230, 252–254, 256–258.

Freud, S. (1985). Creative writers and day-dreaming. In A. Dickson (Ed.), *Art and literature* (Vol. 14, The pelican Freud, pp. 129–141). Harmondsworth, UK: Penguin. (Original work published 1908)

Giroux, H. (1981). *Ideology, culture, and the process of schooling.* Philadelphia, PA; Temple University Press.

Giroux, H. (1996). *Fugitive cultures: Race, violence & youth.* New York, NY: Routledge.

Grossberg, L. (1992). *We gotta get out of this place: Popular conservatism and postmodern culture.* New York, NY: Routledge.

Grossberg, L. (2006). Does cultural studies have futures? Should it? (Or what's the matter with New York?). *Cultural Studies* 20(1), 1–32.

Holbrook, D. (1991). *The skeleton in the wardrobe: C. S. Lewis's fantasies: A phenomenological study.* Lewisburg, PA: Bucknell University Press.

Jameson, F. (1981). *The political unconscious: Narrative as a socially symbolic act.* Ithaca, NY: Cornell University Press.

Kinder, M. (1991). *Playing with power on movies, television, and video games: From Muppet Babies to Teenage Mutant Ninja Turtles.* Berkeley: University of California Press.

McGillis, R. (2003). What literature was: The canon becomes ploughshare. In A. G. Cano Vela & C. P. Valverde (Eds.), *Canon, literatura y juvenil y otras literaturas* (pp. 31–42). Cuenca, Spain: Ediciones de la Universidad de Castilla-La Mancha.

McRobbie, A. (1994). *Postmodernism and popular culture.* London: Routledge.

Nodelman, P. (Ed.). (1985). *Touchstones: Reflections on the best in children's literature* (Vol. 1). West Lafayette, IN: ChLA Publications.

Nodelman, P., & Reimer, M. (2003) *The pleasures of children's literature* (3rd ed.). Boston, MA: Allyn & Bacon.

Nonnekes, P. (2000). The loving father in Disney's *Pinocchio*: A critique of Jack Zipes. *Children's Literature Association Quarterly* 25(2), 107–115.

Packard, V. (1957). *The hidden persuaders.* New York, NY: McKay.

Rudd, D. (2006). Cultural studies. In C. Butler (Ed.), *Teaching children's fiction* (pp. 29–59). London, England: Palgrave.

Rustin, M., & Rustin, M. (1987). *Narrative of love & loss: Studies in modern children's fiction.* London, England: Verso.

Scholastic Web Site. (2006, November 14). Jeff Smith's interview transcript. Retrieved February 17, 2010, from http://content.scholastic.com/browse/article.jsp?id=8068

Shavit, Z. (1986). *The poetics of children's literature*. Athens: The University of Georgia Press.

Smith, J. (n.d.). The history of *Bone* and Jeff Smith. Retrieved February 17, 2010, from http://www.boneville.com/bone/

Wertham, F. (1954). *Seduction of the innocent*. New York, NY: Reinhart.

Williams, R. (1989). The future of cultural studies. In T. Pinkney (Ed.), *The politics of modernism: Against the new conformists* (pp. 151–162). New York, NY: Verso.

Xie, S., & Wang, F. (2002). *Dialogues on cultural studies: Interviews with contemporary critics*. Calgary, Alberta: University of Calgary Press.

Žižek, S. (1997). *A plague of fantasies*. New York, NY: Verso.

Point of Departure

David Filipi

When children's book publisher Scholastic Books released its first color volume of Jeff Smith's *Bone* in 2005, the book was already immensely popular among comic book fans and a phenomenon in the self-publishing movement. The comic, originally in black-and-white, was published from 1991–2004 in 55 individual issues, a run that was punctuated with a 1,300 page "One Volume" edition (also in black-and-white).

On his website, Smith says that *Bone* was one of the most requested graphic novels in libraries across the country. This drew the attention of library distributors, publishing journalists, and, ultimately Scholastic Books. Scholastic partnered with Smith's company Cartoon Books to reprint the entire run of *Bone*, this time in nine full-color volumes. While the Cartoon Books editions have sold more than 1 million copies and the "One Volume" edition has sold more than 150,000 copies, the Scholastic editions have proven even more popular, selling more than 4.6 million copies as of early 2010. The increased popularity can be attributed to Scholastic's marketing and distribution reach, not to mention its reputation as a leading publisher of reading material for children. It's more difficult to quantify the increased appeal due to the addition of color but it must make the book more accessible to a generation accustomed to color everything. (It should be noted that color work on the Scholastic editions has been done by Steve Hamaker, an acclaimed comic artist in his own right). *Bone* is inarguably more popular in the Scholastic editions and, given the timeless nature of the *Bone* story and the ever-replenishing waves of young readers, should only continue to build upon this success.

If the Scholastic editions introduced *Bone* to a much larger, and younger, audience, Jeff Smith's first solo gallery exhibition in 2008 brought him exposure on a completely different stage. The exhibition at the Wexner Center for the Arts, at The Ohio State University in Columbus, Ohio, titled *Jeff Smith: Bone and Beyond*, was the center's first devoted to a cartoon artist. Lucy Shelton Caswell, curator of The Billy Ireland Cartoon Library & Museum at The Ohio State University, and I co-curated the exhibition.

Bone and Beyond was presented in the wake of such major exhibitions of cartoon art as Chris Ware's 2006 solo exhibition at the Museum of Contemporary Art in Chicago and *Masters of American Comics,* which was co-organized by the Museum of Contemporary Art and Hammer Museum in Los Angeles and which toured nationally. These exhibitions, and others like them, are part of a growing trend of museums presenting original cartoon art in their respective galleries.

The rise in cartoon exhibitions can partly be attributed to an ongoing attempt by cultural institutions to appeal to a broader audience. It can also be attributed to a generation of curators and critics who grew up in an era filled with great examples of cartoon art and who see no qualitative difference between it and other mediums just as earlier generations eventually recognized artistry in popular music and films.

This growing practice, while introducing these artists to the "art world," does beg the question: Does a single page, removed from its intended context, adequately convey the work of an artist who creates comic *books*?

Though he was approaching the concern from a different angle, Jeff asked the same question. He constantly reminded us that *this* (pointing to an original page) isn't his work, *this* is (holding a floppy single issue in his hand). But he also understood that we didn't have an exhibition without original art and, philosophical concerns aside, we proceeded to select the best examples from *Bone*'s 1,300 pages.

Lucy and I realized that we needed to address the narrative aspects of cartoon art in general and, more specifically, Jeff's talent as a writer. Therefore, we included every page from the highly regarded *Bone* #16, hung in order along one gallery wall. In it, Grandma Ben, Thorn, and Fone Bone spend the entire issue passing through a rocky patch of forest, trying to elude the ever-menacing rat creatures. Issue #16 is unique in comics in that the action is essentially depicted in real-time and contains many passages with little or no dialogue.

I imagine that every cartoonist would agree with Jeff—

Credit: Jeff Smith Deposit Collection, the Ohio State University. Billy Ireland Cartoon Library & Museum.

that his or her work is the final, mass-produced book and not one of the original pages. But it is also hard to imagine a cartoonist turning down the opportunity to present original work in a gallery.

While the artists one might feature in a gallery likely don't need any additional validation, there is no arguing that an exhibition does introduce an entirely different audience to the work. At the time we did Bone and Beyond, one could probably count the number of contemporary cartoonists that had been given serious, sustained attention by the formal art press on ten fingers or less. An exhibition at a venue like the Wexner Center changes that, for better or worse.

More importantly, a cartoon page on a gallery wall commands a different level of attention. A viewer is compelled to study the illustration and interplay between panels in a manner much more focused than someone reading the book and caught up in the story. Jeff is an unusually gifted visual artist. His ability to suggest movement, emotion, and form hints at the years he spent as an animator, a fact that might go unnoticed by an untrained eye if not for the more sustained appraisal common in an art gallery.

Also, the original pages often give the viewer more access to the artist's craft and creative process than do the final printed pages. Jeff's Bone pages were filled with original blue pencil sketches, white-outs, and strips of paper covering mistakes or indicating changes to dialogue balloons. As Maus creator Art Spiegelman says, "Oddly, the messier the original, the better it tends to look on a wall" (personal communication, July 2, 2009).

Indeed. In May 2009, I saw the scaled down version of Krazy!, an exhibition at the Japan Society in New York. When originally presented at the Vancouver Art Gallery, the show included a wide array of work from comics, video games, and other pop culture inspired art but the Japan Society's version only included examples of Japanese manga and anime. The content of the exhibition was interesting enough but what was missing was that electricity, that "aura" of the original that one gets knowing that Charles Schulz or Will Eisner or Jeff Smith once put pen to this piece of paper. The manga "originals" in the show were digital printouts, reproducible by anyone with access to the original file. I tried to give each page my full attention but quickly found myself skimming. And there was no reason to look for the hand of the artist on these pages because there wasn't one.

The experience was disappointing and unsatisfying to say the least, but it did convince me of the value of presenting *original* cartoon art on a gallery wall.

Note: A variation of this essay appeared in the exhibition catalog *This is a Comic Book* (2009), published by the Mahan Gallery in Columbus, OH.

Point of Departure

Lucy Shelton Caswell, David Filipi, and Jeff Smith

Editor's note: What follows is an excerpt from an interview Lucy Shelton Caswell and David Filipi conducted with *Bone* creator, Jeff Smith. The interview took place on March 14, 2008, as part of the *Jeff Smith: Bone and Beyond* exhibit at the Wexner Center for the Arts at The Ohio State University in Columbus, Ohio. This interview was originally published in the exhibition catalogue *Bone and Beyond* (Columbus, OH: Wexner Center for the Arts, The Ohio State University, 2008).

DF: When you're creating something that you know several different age groups are going to be reading, what things do you have to take into account? What considerations do you have to make? Or do you not even think about it?

JS: I definitely don't categorize what's appropriate for one level and what's appropriate for another level. I just was always turned on by the kinds of stories that worked that way. Bugs Bunny cartoons—or even Disney feature films—work on both levels. One of the reasons parents can take their children to them is because the parents kind of like them, too. I mentioned *Huckleberry Finn* before and *Star Wars*—both of those are stories that are really pretty much for 10-year-old boys, right? They start off with Huck or Luke Skywalker, and they're swashbuckling, but as Huck goes on or as the *Star Wars* movies progressed, they became more sophisticated—became more complex. And the stories had themes that were darker or about dealing with your father, in both *Huckleberry Finn* and *Star Wars*. So it is those kinds of stories that get me excited, and that I want to try to do. I actually might have to wrestle with this a little bit more in *Rasl* than I did in *Bone* because *Rasl* does involve some more failings-of-the-flesh type of subject matter. At this point I haven't actually started writing it yet, so I'm not sure where it's going to go. But my natural inclination as a writer is to tell adventure stories that operate for general audiences. We'll have to see. If Rasl smokes and drinks too much, it may end up being a more adult work. But I don't know that yet. We'll have to see.

DF: In reading about you and other cartoonists, I'm always struck by how so many, almost without exception, seem to have a really strong sense of the people that came before them. In your work you really get a sense of the people that you're influenced by, where I'm not sure you get the same sense of that when you're reading somebody's more autobiographical story, for instance. I'm wondering if you have a sense that, in a way, we're talking about two different traditions. There is more of a cartoonist tradition, where people are a little bit more acutely aware of artists like Winsor McCay, George Herriman, Will Eisner, Jack Kirby, up until the present day, versus people that maybe aren't as interested in that trajectory, and that sequential art just happens to be the art that they're good at—as opposed to painting or…

JS: No. I think that Harvey Pekar, Robert Crumb, Art Spiegelman, and all those guys are unbelievably aware, and I would say even obsessed, with the tradition of cartooning that came before them. And Chester Brown. All those guys do absolutely feel like they can trace their roots through comics history, through Crumb, through Harvey Kurtzman, through George Herriman—very much the same way I would.

But I don't feel any need to conform to any rules of comics, as far as the industry or format is concerned. I broke many rules repeatedly and was told all along that everything I was doing was undermining everything that is good for comics, like collecting my books into graphic novels and putting them out while my number one was worth $300. People said, "If you do that, then you're going to make the number one comic worthless because you just made it available in a cheap format forever, and if you do that then the retailers are going to hate you because that's where they make their real money, in the back issues." So I was told you can't do graphic novels, you can't do collections, and I just didn't care about any of that stuff. So when it comes to the artwork, I am deeply indebted and in awe of everybody who came before me. But in terms of traditions and industry, I haven't the slightest interest at all in that.

DF: Imagine a teenage girl or boy who might be completely unaware of the history and tradition of comic books. Yet, instead of writing in a journal they create a graphic record of what they're going through, completely outside of the trajectory we've been discussing.

JS: There may be a generation right now…we call it the indie comics…where people are getting into it who may not have grown up reading certain people—or even knowing who they are. But these artists see the medium in a new way, which is very exciting to me, because even just 10 years ago it seemed impossible that the medium could be so well known that people would flock to it and think that it is a place that they could do their art. But that could be happening now. And if it is, I would be excited.

LSC: What do you think about the whole conundrum—how do you learn your craft and your art if you don't have a way to judge what is good and not good and the traditions on which the genre is based?

JS: I actually think that's why most cartoonists who have come from comic books know the traditions. I mean, the ones that don't know them really study them, and those who aren't dedicated to that level are going to drop off. You know that's going to happen. But the guys that make it, like Craig Thompson, they know what they're drawing. They've been reading comics, and they're picking the stuff that's good, and they're usually extremely knowledgeable about world comics—not just the stuff you can buy at the grocery store. They have to be, because you can't go to school to become a comic book artist. Well, I guess you can now. But it's rare. It is still up to the cartoonists to learn it themselves by finding the examples that turn them on. And, boy, they have them now. There's every kind of comic. There are autobiographical comics, comics about world geopolitics…

We're at a time in comics that is completely unlike any that has gone before, where we have a radical shift that involves many elements. There's the graphic novel, which started about 20 years ago with *Maus* and *The Dark Knight Returns* and has really come into flower recently with the wholesale acceptance of graphic novels by large chain bookstores like Barnes & Noble, Borders, and Amazon.com. There's also the element of the Internet, which takes the idea of underground comics and indie comics, which I just mentioned, to a whole new level. You don't even have to figure out how to get your comic books distributed or printed. All you have to do is understand your tools and your technology, and you can upload. There is a large and very healthy community that communicates with each other on the Internet. And the Internet is developing its own sets of symbols and languages that incorporate all that went before it.

The teenager you mentioned a minute ago, creating her graphic diary in her room, is exposed to all these things. The introduction of this new technology so deeply into our lives is making that change. I meet people all the time who are on the fan sites. Another element that's changing comics as we speak is manga, which has more in common with traditional American comics like superheroes, in my opinion, because of the factory nature of the production. Manga are commercial products, designed to sell numbers. For the most part, there is an artist and a writer assigned to create a product, although there are auteurs who transcend that. But the numbers are unprecedented. Manga are now at least 50% of all comics published in the U.S.—if not 60, and the numbers are just growing. Manga are turning comics into a mass medium on the level of bestsellers, paperbacks, TV, movies. So we're at a really interesting time. And I'll add one more element that is happening right now, and that's the acceptance by teachers, librarians, and the art world of this as an art form.

25

Ideology and Children's Books

Robyn McCallum and John Stephens

Macquarie University

No matter how simplistic it may appear, no book is innocent of ideological implications. Whether a text seeks to naturalize the belief systems of a culture or challenge them, it always places an ideological imposition on its readers, since ideology inheres in the very language and images from which it is made. Seeking to expose the implicit and explicit ideologies communicated through children's texts has become the primary work of many of us who work with the genre, and we are indebted to the pioneering work of John Stephens and Robyn McCallum for helping us frame those investigations. Here John and Robyn look at current frameworks for exploring questions of ideology. Their arguments are reinforced by M. T. Anderson's brilliant rendering of the questions faced by authors as they write in, around, through, in spite of, and sometimes in defense of their own conscious and unconscious ideological positions.

Ideology emerged as a concern of children's literature criticism during the late 1970s, as discourses interrogating social assumptions about gender, race, and class began to impact upon the production and reception of children's literature. The first major study was Bob Dixon's (1977) *Catching Them Young*, which set out to examine "the ideas, attitudes and opinions which authors convey to children through novels and stories" and "the ways in which this is done" (Vol. I., p. xiii). A decade later, Peter Hollindale (1988) argued that analysis needed to move beyond a focus on explicit negative content to analyze the unaddressed assumptions of texts and the propensity for ideology to inhere in language itself. Underpinning these approaches themselves was a Marxian assumption (largely mediated through the works of Louis Althusser [1971])

that ideology was invariably negative in impact. That this is a limited perspective in relation to children's literature was argued from a critical discourse studies approach by John Stephens (1992), who pointed out that there cannot be a narrative without an ideology: "Ideology is formulated in and by language, meanings within language are socially determined, and narratives are constructed out of language" (p. 8). Whether textual ideology is negative, positive, or more or less neutral will thus be determined by the ideological positioning of a text within culture. Our purpose in this chapter is to explore such positionings from the perspective of the critical discourse studies which have developed over the past two decades, as seen, for example, in Teun Van Dijk's (2001) evolving project on discourse and ideology.

Our grounding assumption, then, is that all aspects of textual discourse, from story outcomes to the expressive forms of language, are informed and shaped by ideology, understanding ideology in its neutral meaning of a system of beliefs which a society shares and uses to make sense of the world and which are therefore immanent in the texts produced by that society. Ideologies may be more or less visible in texts produced for children, which seldom reproduce overt ideology as a thematized component of text, but which will reflect two functions of ideology. The first of these is the social function of defining and sustaining group values (perceptible textually in an assumption that writer and implied reader share a common understanding of value), and the second is the cognitive function of supplying a meaningful organization of the social attitudes and relationships which constitute narrative plots. As Van Dijk (2001) argues, ideologies can be adjudged desirable or undesirable depending on the consequences of the social practices based on them. Thus both racism and antiracism are ideologies. Ideologies may thus serve to establish or maintain social dominance, as well as to organize dissidence and opposition.

While *ideology* may carry negative connotations, especially when applied to the social practices of an "other" society, the sense in which we use it here encompasses the social and cognitive functions that make social life possible. Thus for a child to participate in society and achieve some measure of personal agency within its forms or structures, he or she must learn to understand and negotiate the various signifying codes used by society to order itself. The principal code is language, since language is the most common form of social communication, and the particular application of language that concerns us here is the imagining and recording of stories.

The creation and telling of stories—what we will refer to as *narrative discourse*—is a particular use of language through which a society expresses and imparts its current values and attitudes, and this happens regardless of authorial intention. A narrative may deal with specific social problems as aspects of story or theme and express a more or less overt attitude towards the implications of those problems, or, if it does not have any obvious exemplary intent, it will express an implicit ideology, usually in the form of assumed social structures and habits of thought. Ideologies can thus function most powerfully in books which reproduce beliefs and assumptions of which authors and readers are largely unaware. Such texts render ideology invisible and hence invest implicit ideological positions with legitimacy by naturalizing them. In other words, a book which seems to a reader to be apparently ideology-free will be a book closely aligned to that reader's own unconscious assumptions, and the identification of such ideologies will often require sophisticated reading of the text's language and narrative discourse. Many books are ideological in both senses referred to here, since a conscious attempt to bring about change in attitude will be grounded in any number of contingent presuppositions about the nature of the self, of society, and of ways of being and knowing.

Picture books, for example, often engage in overt attitude formation through their presuppositions, and this may be quite evident in information books for young readers, which are characteristically underpinned by positive ideologies. Janet Halfmann's (2006) *Alligator at Saw Grass Road* and Isabella Hatkoff, Craig Hatkoff, and Paula Kahumbu's (2006) *Owen and Mzee* illustrate something of the range of possibilities. In each, paratextual material supplies additional facts and figures, so readers are effectively assured that information given is authoritative. Published in an environmental series about overlaps in human and animal habitations, *Alligator at Saw Grass Road* delivers a factual account of how an alligator lays her eggs and cares for her young. The focus on mothering implicitly dismantles the common human assumption that alligators are monstrous—the most pejorative remark offered is that "Alligator is a sneaky hunter" (n.p.), where *sneaky* does little to evoke associations of violence or menace. An interesting sub-story relating how a red-bellied turtle surreptitiously deposits her own eggs in the alligator's nest functions as a metonym for the text's assumption that the alligator interacts symbiotically with the environment (see Figure 25.1). Ideologically, then, the discourse avoids the anthropocentrism that pervades most environmental books for children (see Bradford, Mallan, Stephens, & McCallum, 2008), and depicts, without human value judgments, a part of the natural world fulfilling its own cycles.

A more overtly ideological narrative is the retelling of the true story, in *Owen and Mzee* (Hatkoff et al., 2006), of the unlikely affection between an ancient giant Aldabra tortoise and an orphaned baby hippopotamus. Written in the colloquial register of a factual account, the discourse is grounded in a form of analogical modelling whereby represented action is brought into conformity with an anthropocentric norm. Thus the Scholastic Study Guide for the book, *Cultivating Resiliency* (Mandel, Mullett, Brown, & Cloitre, 2006), explicitly articulates an ideology which, we suggest, replicates the social assumptions which self-consciously informed the writing of the book. These assumptions become quite visible as the book comes to a close:

> Owen [the hippopotamus] suffered a great loss. But with the help of many caring people, and through his own extraordinary resilience, Owen has begun a new, happy life. Most remarkable is the role that Mzee has played. We'll never know for sure whether Owen sees Mzee as a mother, a father, or a very good friend. But it really doesn't matter. What matters is that Owen isn't alone—and neither is Mzee. (Hatkoff et al., 2006, n.p.)

This schema for a happy existence is, needless to say, entirely unexceptionable, and that in turn will erase the fact that it is profoundly ideological. The best society embraces altruism and supports those in need, and this action exists as a structure deeper than its everyday mani-

Credit: Excerpt from Janet Halfmann and Lori Anzalone, "Alligator at Sawgrass Road," page 21. Copyright © 2006 Trudy Corporation and the Smithsonian Institution, Washington, DC 20560. Reproduced with permission of Trudy Corporation, Norwalk, Connecticut.

festations (mother, father, friend). Community existence is preferable to solitary existence. Mandel et al. (2006) assume that the function of a book such as *Owen and Mzee* is to offer children a model of values and behaviors which will contribute to the development of individual identity. Hence they value resilience and link it to such qualities as intelligence, competence, independence, self-control, and a high level of self-esteem. The friendship between tortoise and hippo is said to exemplify "the importance of caring for others who may not be similar to ourselves" (p. 3) and the importance of accepting "the natural diversity of our world" (p. 5). In interpreting the book in this way, Mandel et al. reproduce a basic function of children's literature—to socialize its audience by presenting desirable models of human personality, human behavior, interpersonal relationships, social organization, and ways of being in the world. As *Owen and Mzee* and its interpretation indicate, such desirable models are always produced by the ideologies that inform cultural practice.

Ideology can also become overt in an information book if it seems to be advocating a practice which is not generally assumed to be a social norm. Thus *And Tango Makes Three* (Richardson & Parnell, 2005), based on an actual event, attracted controversy because it depicts gay adoption in a positive way. Set in New York's Central Park Zoo, the book recounts the story of two male penguins, Roy and Silo, who bond as a couple, build a nest, and are given an egg to hatch. They do this successfully, and raise the chick, subsequently named Tango. The narrative strategy of *And Tango Makes Three* is to evoke the assumptions that families are a natural occurrence and that there are "families of all kinds" (n.p.). The desire evinced by Roy and Silo to be parents (they share an attempt to hatch a stone) and the existence of "an egg that needed to be cared for" (n.p.) come together when the egg is placed in Roy and Silo's nest. Their parenting of Tango follows the schema for usual penguin parenting practices, and when all three snuggle together in the nest at night they are embraced by a regular family schema: they are "like all the other penguins in the penguin house, and all the other animals in the zoo, and all the families in the big city around them" (n.p.). The logic of the story—that a gay couple parent in the same way as a heterosexual couple—is thus grounded on an everyday ideological premise about parents in ideal families. To make its argument for gay parenting, the text evokes the nuclear family as core social ideology and uses it to frame the account of this particular family. In doing this, it extends the nuclear family schema to include the possibility of "two daddies" (n.p.), and hence argues for a transformed ideology.

The Textual Presences of Ideology

While ideologies are textually pervasive, they are present in different ways. As evidenced by *Owen and Mzee* (Hatkoff et al., 2006), an ideological position may be topicalized: that is, it may appear as an overt or explicit element in the text, expressing the writer's social, political, or moral beliefs. Because children's literature is persistently concerned with social issues and values, books may openly advocate attitudes or positions as desirable for readers to espouse. This possibility is perhaps most evident in books which deal thematically with gender or race. Such advocacy is more likely to be covert, however, in the sense that it is embedded in a narrative which has a primary focus on events and characters. But since fictive actions are broadly isomorphic with actions in the actual world of readers, and the majority of narratives are built upon the principle that the main character(s) will develop by learning something about the world and the place of the self in it, ideologies are never very far away. As the representation of ideologies becomes less apparent, the more desirable it becomes for readers to understand the textual processes that embed ideology within fiction, if reading is to be a critical process. The implicit presence of a writer's assumptions in a text arguably has a more powerful impact in so far as such assumptions may consist of values taken for granted in the society that produces and consumes the text, including children. The assumption in *Owen and Mzee* that no creature should be alone is an example of such a value.

On a wide scale, meaning is influenced by the larger contexts of text and culture within which particular utterances acquire meaning. Ultimately, however, ideology is inherent within linguistic and visual semiotic systems (sentence syntax, lexical selection, topicalization or implicitness, conversational dynamics, and so on; physical appearance, dress codes, placement within scene and in relation to other figures, and so on). Particular utterances are thus affected by the elements which join them together into larger structures. These coherencies are of interest at two levels: first, at the level of more specifically linguistic features, such as the grammatical and other ties which combine sentences together into larger units; and second, at the level of elements often considered to be the domain of a more "literary" purpose—type of narrator, the implied reader who is constructed by the text, point of view, allusion and theme, for example—but which are inextricably bound up with discourse in some more precisely linguistic application. This second element is probably more readily identified by readers.

Ideology operates within all three components of a narrative: the *discourse* (the linguistic and narrative structures); the *story* (characters and the actions they perform), which is ascertained by an act of primary reading, or reading for "the sense"; and the *significance* (organization of social attitudes and values), which is derived by secondary reading from the first two. While readers may attribute quite different significances to a text according to their already held social attitudes and values—and for scholars this will be influenced by the kind of literary criticism they practice—such significance, unless entirely procrustean, emerges as a dialogue between the already-held subject position of a reader and the subject position(s) offered by the text.

Ideology and Subject Position

The concept of subject positions implied within texts is of crucial importance for reading and especially for examining a text's possible ideological impact, because what such positions inevitably seek is reader alignment with or against the social attitudes and relationships that constitute the narrative. Andrea Schwenke Wyile's (1999, 2003) accounts of three types of narration in children's literature chart a very useful way into a central aspect of subject position, especially when it is combined with specific elements of discourse. The crux is always how a narrator's telling of a story is related to a character's perceptions as well as a reader's understanding. Wyile argues that in *immediate-engaging first-person narration*, in which the time of narration is close to or coincident with events narrated, and in which the narrator is also the focalizer, readers align closely with the subjective experience of narrator-protagonists. It follows, then, that readers will be apt to align with the subject position, and hence social attitudes, occupied by such a protagonist. An immediate-engaging third-person narration which is heavily character-focalized produces much the same effect. In Wyile's second type, *distant-engaging narration*, in which the time of narration is considerably later than the time of the events, the narrating self can judge the narrated self from the perspective of experience. The subject position proffered is thus principally aligned with the narrating character, although character focalization will produce alignment with the narrated character. This more dialogic structure builds a position apt to offer a more retrospective reflection on social attitudes.

Wyile defined her types principally in relation to first-person narration, and so did little with her third category, *distancing narration*, which she concluded was "not prevalent in children's literature" and "more suited to adult narratives, particularly stories about childhood that incorporate the adult narrator's reflections" (p. 190). Third-person narration in children's fiction has also been distant-engaging since heavy character-focalization emerged as the predominant practice during the 1960s, but distancing narration is still common: It is a narrative with a non-identified narrator, a predominance of narrator focalization over character focalization, a tendency to represent conversation as tagged direct speech rather than in free or indirect forms, and, recently, inclusion of metafictive elements. Major authors who use the form extensively are Diana Wynne Jones, Terry Pratchett, Philip Reeve, Neil Gaiman, and Gregory Maguire, for example.

The three types of narration are not exclusive, however, and a novel may employ more than one. David Almond's (2008) *The Savage* uses all three. Reader alignment with characters in distancing narration is strong but intermittent, so the subject positions available to readers entail a greater awareness of how stories are imagined and narrated in relation to society's values and attitudes. In this way, certain objectives and outcomes of the story are assumed to be commonsensically natural and desirable—for example, it is only to be expected that the main character of Gaiman's (2008) *The Graveyard Book*, a child raised from infancy by ghosts in a graveyard, will grow up and find his place in the world of the living. His life-course is a fantastic version of a normal social expectation and, as a culturally desirable outcome, it is not recognized as an element of social ideology but is rather presupposed and not textually asserted.

Ideology and Imagination

The ideology implicit in quite simple texts, usually in the form of assumed social structures and habits of thought, can be a powerful vehicle for affirming that "this is the way things are." How a text begins is apt to involve an ideological orientation within the expected narrative orientation, as the following picture book beginning demonstrates:

> You think it's *easy* being the tooth fairy? Well, it's not. It takes skill! It takes daring! Thank goodness I am here to do the job.
>
> Let's get one thing straight, OK?
>
> I *never* wear pink flouncing skirts or twinkling glass slippers! That's Cinderella. She does a lot of sitting around the castle looking pretty.
>
> *Boring!*
>
> Me, I'm an action kind of gal.
>
> I live for danger!
>
> For suspense! (Bell-Rehwoldt, 2007, n. p.)

There are numerous picture books about the Tooth Fairy in the English-speaking world, each book striving for a new angle, which it defines by its linguistic structure, its intertextual relations, and a counterpointing of inclusionary and exclusionary ideologies. This book is immediately grounded in a contrast of types of femininity (the "action kind of gal" opposed to the passive femininity of "pink flouncing skirts"), which are brought into combination with an assumption that work must be valued.

It is common for small children in the English-speaking world to believe that their first teeth, as they fall out, can be left at night (usually under a corner of the child's pillow, or in a glass of water) for the Tooth Fairy to collect. The Tooth Fairy is an anthropomorphic personification of indeterminate form, so her appearance in picture books is commonly drawn from conventional, often kitsch, fairy images or traditional representations of angels. In contrast to such images, Bell-Rehwoldt and illustrator Slonim (2007) have produced a feisty modern girl who is a version of a mountain climber, an inventive, active girl devoid of mystery. Illustrations of tooth fairies don't strive to enhance a numinous imaginative engagement with a childhood imaginary being, but function rather to make the tooth fairy a familiar and benign figure, not someone small children would feel worried about if she crept into their bedrooms while they were sleeping. Through such illustrations, the fantastic is incorporated into the everyday world, and any propensity for the tooth fairy to be a supernatural or numinous being from the realm of mythopoeic thought is erased. Instead, a more mundane, practical message in

these books is that you should clean your teeth carefully, and those perfect teeth will be displayed triumphantly in the Tooth Fairy's palace.

A book such as *You Think It's Easy Being the Tooth Fairy?* is playful and imaginative, but confines the fantastic imaginary to versions of the everyday. The Tooth Fairy determines how to reach the relevant bedroom by using "my Spy-o-Binoculars (patent pending) to scope out your house" (n.p.). A mystery is thereby reduced to a legalism "(patent pending)" and a piece of contemporary slang ("scope out"), with the consequence that early childhood speculation and imagination is contained by means of a strong ideological assumption about what childhood should be.

In her anthropological study of the Tooth Fairy, Santa Claus, and the Easter Bunny within social practice in America, Cindy Dell Clark (1995) argues that belief in these immaterial beings has two important functions. First, it enables children to participate actively in culture, shaping cultural practices rather than being simply acculturated by them. Clark's second point is that mythopoeic thinking and experience are made possible when disbelief is cognitively suspended while trust and creative involvement are engaged. It is then possible for a child to go on, when literal belief has passed, to grasp the distinction between concrete symbols and the referential, transcendent meaning beyond those symbols. Clark's argument finds support in ideas about the imagination proposed by Susanne Langer (1956) and explored in fictive form by Gregory Maguire (2007) in *What-the-Dickens. The Story of a Rogue Tooth Fairy*. Langer (1956) argues that imagination enables a symbolic or conceptual rendering of experience that finds expression in the formation and elaboration of images, grounds language, and furnishes the material for dreaming, myth, ritual, narrative, and the arts.

A rejection of mythopoeic thinking by some characters in *What-the-Dickens* Maguire (2007) comes specifically from religious fundamentalism, which is made an issue early in the frame narrative. During an extreme weather event, which the discoursal mode suggests is part of an end-of-the-world scenario, three children are left in the care of Gage, a 21-year-old distant relative, while their parents go in search of medication for the mother's diabetes. To help survive a dark and stormy night, Gage tells the story of What-the-Dickens, a Tooth Fairy (here a *skibberee*; plural, skibbereen). Zeke, the eldest child, has internalized hostility to any narrative that is other than factual or Biblical, so one strand in the frame story is his development of an interest in mythopoeia. His sister, Dinah, is an imaginative child, however.

> "No, Santa Claus has no website staffed by underground Nordic trolls. No, there is no flight school for the training of apprentice reindeer. No to Santa Claus, period," her mother always said. "Dinah, honey, don't let your imagination run away with you." Exasperatedly: "*Govern* yourself!" (pp. 5–6)

The story Gage tells about the orphan tooth fairy What-the-Dickens functions in a thematic dialogue with the frame story (it is in part about resilience and survival), and this frame and embedded story structure demands imaginative engagement. The embedded story is a *Bildungsroman* in which What-the-Dickens develops quickly from an incompetent cinder lad to a strong, inventive, independent subjectivity. Through this development the narrative traces the evolution from concrete symbols to the referential, transcendent meaning beyond those symbols, as What-the-Dickens's struggle with the meaning of existence and the nature of cathexis leads him to the most valued quality in children's literature: altruism. At the same time, the novel's abundant and extremely playful intertextuality (which Maguire draws attention to in a list of acknowledgements) involves readers in a process of constant recognition and discovery, and invites an active play of imagination. *What-the-Dickens* actively engages in arguments about cultural ideology that have gone on for several decades, and affirms that a function of literature is to express the imaginative processes that govern how lived experience is remembered and retold in language and narrative, and thence shapes our understanding of human actions and their significances.

Intersubjective Relationships, Gender, and Agency

A strong ideological effect can be derived from an interplay between creative imagination and the stereotypic discourses of everyday life, as is signalled by the opening page of David Almond's (2008) *The Savage*, narrated by a young boy, Blue Baker:

> You won't believe this but it's true. I wrote a story called "The Savage" about a savage kid that lived under the ruined chapel in Burgess Woods, and the kid came to life in the real world.
>
> I wrote it soon after my dad died. There was a counsellor at school called Mrs Molloy, that kept taking me out of lessons and telling me to write my thoughts and feelings down. She said she wanted me to explore my grief, and "start to move forward." I did try for a while, but it just seemed stupid, and it even made me feel worse, so one day I ripped up all that stuff about myself, got an old notebook and started scribbling "The Savage." Here's the first bit of it, and I know the spelling isn't brilliant, but I was younger then.
>
> There was a wild kid living in Burgess Woods, I wrote. (p. 7)

The ideology of the text inheres in framing situation, represented patterns of behaviour, interactions between characters, linguistic discourses, and the interpersonal relationship with implied readers. This beginning flags several themes—coping with loss and grief, growing up and developmental narratives, dealing with school authorities, creativity, the power of story—and frames these through the counterpointing of the narrator's own life situation and a feral child narrative. Almond's *Savage* (2008) conforms closely to what Kenneth Kidd (2004) has identified as a symbolic discourse about human and cultural development and the path to manhood, which, in mapping a process of socialization onto a mode of being that is marginal, alien, or subversive to the adult social order, has mostly been complicit with a variety of social institutions in producing the middle-class, White masculine subject. Blue—fatherless, grieving, bullied at school, struggling to express himself—creates a feral child as an alter ego. When his story of the Savage continues, "He had no famly and he had no pals and he didn't know where he come from and he culdn't talk…," (p. 8) Blue is delineating a pattern of behavior which also corresponds to his own self-image. The social ideology against which this pattern emerges is the assumption that whatever lacks agency cannot be desired; thus Blue's attainment of a positively gendered subjectivity will depend on the possibility of attributing agency to that subjectivity.

The failed interaction with Mrs. Molloy will later contrast with the intersubjective relationships with his mother and sister which promote subjective growth, and with his final, deeply moving and emotionally healing encounter with the Savage of his imagination ("we … stared into each other's eyes like we were staring into some great mystery" [p. 74]). The kind of masculine subject Blue develops into is overtly ideological, topicalized by means of his place in a triangular configuration with the Savage and Hopper, the hard, macho bully who has made Blue's life miserable. Blue's developing self-awareness has led him to discover how discourse shapes the world and hence to a realization that creativity is a form of agency. Hence, his attempt to write a scene in which the Savage enters Hopper's bedroom at night and kills him with an axe unravels as he realizes that he cannot write the incident: "I'm not a hard lad and now I knew that the savage wasn't either" (p. 56). So instead, Hopper is beaten and terrorized. After the Savage leaves Hopper's house, he performs two significant actions. First, in the street "he danced like Jess had done in the woods that day and he waved his ax round his head in triumf" (p. 60). Then he enters Blue's house, goes to Jess's bedroom, places his hand on her sleeping brow, weeps, and "tried to say poems" (p. 63). The sequence marks the Savage's final entry into human intersubjectivity, but of particular interest is the text-illustration interaction (see Figure 25.2). Brandishing his hand-ax, the figure evokes the image schema of the dangerous primitive of fiction and film, but the fluidity of his bodily gesture, the delicacy of face and hands, especially the ethereal linking of fingers and ax, and the textual connection with Jess's feminine dancing evoke strong audience empathy. It is not a "triumf" of savagery, but of humanity, and functions as a strong reinforcement of the text's humanist ideology.

There is satisfaction for Blue (and readers) in witnessing Hopper's subdued and abjected state on the subsequent

And the savage growled and snarled and bared his teeth and spat rite in Hopper's face and he waved his fist like a last warnin, then he went back owt into the nite, and he stood out there in the street in the littel town and he danced like Jess had done in the woods that day and he waved his ax round his hed in triumf.

Credit: Excerpt from "The Savage" by David Almond and illustrated by Dave McKean, pages, 60–61. Illustration copyright © 2008 David McKean. Reproduced by permission of Walker Books Ltd., London SE11 5HJ.

day. While, ideally, reducing a bully to inarticulate abjection is not the best outcome, it is endorsed by the popular imagination, and by the inadequacy of the support offered Blue (for example, Mrs. Molloy's advice to "try to ignore it, try to understand that it shows how inadequate Hopper is" [p. 18]). Blue's action in taking responsibility for his own life leads to a form of masculinity widely approved in modern society: It is grounded in a resistance to social constructionism, in moral integrity and a capacity for other-regardingness, and in self-awareness which enables deep interpersonal relations grounded in mutual equality (Stephens, 2002).

The ideological structure of masculinity in *The Savage* (Almond, 2008) emerges from a textual negotiation amongst the various tenets available within the social group depicted in the novel. While the group is uniform in ethnicity and origin, it is not entirely homogenous in attitudes, assumptions, motivations and behaviors. Blue's (masculine) subjectivity thus develops out of a process of self-fashioning through imaginative composition, i.e., his writing is metonymic of self-constitution and subjective agency. As the Savage learns about language, what it feels like to be human, and about "good and bad in people" (p. 51), Blue shapes his own subjectivity by assessing norms and values, evaluating his social position

and relationships, and drawing upon the resources of his family and creativity. His creativity thus articulates subjective agency as a force for expressing emotions and making responsible judgments based on consideration and concern for others.

The triangular configuration of Blue, Savage, and Hopper exemplifies how many contemporary novels which seek to intervene in normative gender constructions interrogate the performance of gendered practices by what Romören and Stephens (2002) refer to as "metonymic configuration" (p. 220). Patterns of gendered behaviors are built up through the simple fictive practice of developing conflict and/or thematic implication through interactions amongst diverse and contrasting characters (often character stereotypes). Such characters function as metonyms because they embody easily recognized, more general patterns of behavior and being.

As Almond's (2008) novel evidences, an author writes in the context of a number of constructions of and attitudes towards gender; he or she may conceptualize a particular social construction of gender as the dominant, filtering this through his or her own attitudes in order to reproduce it or attempt to modify it. An author also chooses a genre to work within, and this will tend implicitly to be always already a gendered genre. This is most obvious with fairy tale, and the modern history of retellings that seek to undo the gendered narratives of fairy tale.

Diana Wynne Jones's (1986/2000) *Howl's Moving Castle* is a good example of how patriarchal ideologies associated with traditional fairy tale and high fantasy may be challenged. The story is narrated from the viewpoint of Sophie, who embodies a form of "subjected" or repressed femininity. Through its allusion to the quest narrative, generally a specifically "masculine" fairy tale paradigm, the opening of the novel attributes Sophie's subjection to the patriarchal discourse, which traditionally informs fairy tales and circumscribes the lives of fairy tale heroines. Sophie herself knows the constraints on her subjectivity from her reading, which is in turn symptomatic of the range of discourses which construct female subjectivities.

To inhabit a gendered body in a gendered space can mean that an individual is constructed, lacking the freedom to be self-fashioning. Writers who consciously resist such positioning of an individual seek to depict characters whose subjectivity will evolve so that by the time closure is reached, subjectivity will be grounded in particular attributes: a resistance to social construction such that allows self-constitution; moral and political integrity; and self-awareness which enables deep interpersonal relations grounded in mutual equality. In other words, gender will be framed within subjective agency.

In fictive representation, two of the key aspects in the constitution of (inter)subjective agency are point of view and intentionality, as narratives model subject positions by depicting characters in relationship with other characters within social structures, and imply particular positions for readers to take up in relation to what is depicted. Jones thematizes the function of subject position by the curse placed upon Sophie at the beginning of the novel, whereby she becomes a teenage girl inside the body of an elderly crone. The resulting bifurcation emphasizes that subjectivity is embodied as well as socially shaped and foregrounds the focalizing perspective that perceives objects or situations. By disclosing that the perception of a given entity may change while what is perceived remains the same, the text presents the possibility of a subjectivity able to rework and reshape norms and givens. Second, the overt adoption of another subject position makes obvious the function of intentionality in subjective agency. Altieri (1994) suggests, "intentionality consists in the ways that agents shape routes within the world and thus provide the bases for defining convictions, expressing priorities, and ultimately accepting responsibility for the routes chosen" (p. 96). When a fictive character is depicted as playing a role, as when Sophie embraces the license permitted to the old and eccentric, what tends to be placed before readers is a knowing and self-aware actor, capable of using discourse with intention in spite of an inability to control the effects of language use. The role-play gives the actor ostensible power over public discourse, which is then manipulated in the service of personal expression. Sophie is a witch and

has a linguistic gift to bestow objects with intentionality, although it takes her the whole novel to discover this. The resultant dialogic relation between public discourse and personal expression is thereby instrumental in gaining assent from the implied community of address to "new" forms of subjective agency.

Such dialogic strategies also make possible interrogative relationships with the texts and genres of the past (what might be loosely called the tradition of children's literature) whereby the discourses of femininity informing fairy story, fantasy, and romance, for example, are made visible as socially constructed and ideologically shaped discourses. Further, in depicting characters whose expectations and behaviors have been shaped by the femininities represented in fairy tales, romance fiction, "high" fantasy, and other cultural discourses, writers can use the constructedness of texts to draw attention to the constructedness of those femininities, and to a great extent the constructedness of masculinities as well.

Howl's Moving Castle (Jones, 1986/2000) is again a useful example because it self-consciously and interrogatively explores how a discourse of femininity is organized in relation to culturally privileged texts, and through its narrative processes and outcomes constructs an implied reader position which in some sense can be called feminist—in this case, the novel constructs a reader position which can be broadly described as a pragmatic liberal-humanist and typically liberal feminist. The concept of "femininity as discourse" was explored by Dorothy E. Smith (1988, p. 37), though in applying it to fictional representations we have to narrow its reference. Smith viewed *femininity* as "a social organization of relations among women and between women and men which is mediated by texts, that is, by the materially fixed forms of printed writing and images" (p. 39). Its discourse has no particular local source and is not embodied or produced by individuals, but individuals "orient themselves to the order of the discourse in talk, writing, creating images (whether in texts or on their bodies), produced and determined by the ongoing order" (p. 40). By performing the discourse, an individual performs gender. Femininity is thus not simply an effect of patriarchal ideology, though in *Howl's Moving Castle* patriarchal practices and assumptions are depicted as playing major roles in orienting the subjectivity of represented female characters towards a "feminine" discourse centered on submission to authority, appearance and behavior codes, guided ambition, and subordination of the self in relationships, including romantic love where this is applicable.

In Smith's (1988) framing of it, the discourse of femininity is always already intertextual because it is a complex of textual relations among magazines, television, advertisements, shop and fashion displays, and (to a lesser extent) books. Within novels this intertextual effect is produced by the relations among (fictive) individual experiences, some of the culturally diverse texts cited by

Smith, and more or less specific literary pre-texts. Hence, the novels explore how forms of gendered behavior are inscribed, and can be resisted, during the transition from child to adult female subjectivity, and thus lay bare the ways in which conservative gendered discourses are inscribed within social and narrative discourses. Resistance becomes possible when oppositional reading positions are constructed as a negotiation of intertextual space, wherein it becomes possible to question and challenge the patriarchal discourses which position female characters within feminine discourse. Such texts construct a narrative in which the focalizing female characters come to recognize this positioning process and the nature of its oppressiveness, and seek alternative and more personally empowered subject positions for themselves. Along the way they will experience misperceptions and misdirections, but the texts' dialogic strategies enable readers to evaluate these. In combination, reader alignment with the point of view of focalizing characters and evaluation of that point of view construct a reading position from which the narrative outcomes are affirmed as narratively coherent and socially satisfactory. Insofar as the outcomes conform to a feminist agenda—for example, "to understand the social and psychic mechanisms that construct and perpetuate gender inequality and then to change them" (Morris, 1993, p. 1)—the implied reading position constitutes a feminist reading position. Whenever feminist texts have emerged in children's literature, it has been as a challenge to, indeed a transgression against, masculinist ideology.

More recent feminisms, however, have challenged presuppositions about how gender is constructed and naturalized, and have moved away from ideologies attributed to second wave (liberal) feminism (Harnois, 2008). Various "third-wave" feminisms now foreground personal narratives that are multiperspectival and intersectional, intersectionality being defined as "the relationships among multiple dimensions and modalities of social relations and subject formations" (McCall, 2005, p. 1771). They draw upon postmodernism to embrace pluralist conceptions of subjectivity, emphasizing "the 'messiness' of their own lives in terms of identities, beliefs, and actions" (Harnois, 2008, p. 133). And they seek to be inclusive and non-judgmental about women's life choices (Hubler, 2000; Marshall, 2004; Snyder, 2008). Such perspectives are gradually emerging in children's fiction (and discussions of it), and thus impacting upon the ideology of texts.

Messiness thus characterizes the life of Sophie O'Farrell, protagonist, narrator and putative author of a distinctively third-wave YA novel, Joanne Horniman's (2008) *My Candlelight Novel*. While the novel is about "birth and death and love and sex" (p. 4), there is little action or conflict. Rather, it is a topography of self and place. On her daily walks, pushing her baby's stroller, the narrator crosses and re-crosses a river in a movement metonymic of the boundary crossings of time and sexuality that make up her life and the novel she is writing. Both self and text are in "a process of becoming" (p. 15), "the body is a leaky thing" (p. 168), sexual desire is polymorphous, and phrases and characters (Becky Sharp, Maggie Tulliver) seep into the text from other literary works. Finally, the novel ends with a bundle of fragments and memories which evoke beginnings and endings in a way that refuses closure. *My Candlelight Novel* demonstrates the ideological importance for children's fiction of third-wave feminist ideas about subjectivity. Subjective agency develops a different nuance when contextualized within notions of ambiguity, multiplicity, contradiction, and even transgression, where the becoming self will not be unified and its gender and sexual identity will remain fluid.

Ideology and Transgression

Representations of *transgression* more generally are an important way children's literature makes ideologies apparent and seeks to redefine or even overthrow them. It does this especially by depicting complex processes whereby characters define the otherness of the world by separating themselves from it through roles or actions involving subversion, deviance, or revolt. Carnivalesque transgression, often flaunting taboo motifs, may go no further than mocking the ways things are, but because transgression is inevitably against some socio-cultural formation, it is inextricably tied up with the ideology of the text, whether overt or implicit. It thus tends to define what ideologies are being depicted as the contemporary status quo, and what are imagined as possible social or individual transformations of behavior in opposition to those ideologies. Transgressive action must evoke the culturally dominant, or it would not be identifiable as transgression, but in doing so its function may be to reinscribe the dominant: In other words, transgression often implies, or even depends on, the strategies that contain it. More often again, transgression defines a conflict between co-existing formations or ideologies, and privileges one over the other. Almost invariably, the privileged ideology is marked as more humane, more socially responsible, more intersubjective, offering a perspective which not only embraces difference but enfolds it within a larger, more comprehensive sphere.

The possibility of transgression is premised on the existence of social, ideological, legal, or cultural codes and conventions, which constitute boundaries or constraints upon a person's actions, speech, thoughts, or sense of identity. These boundaries imply the construction of subjectivity as subjection to a particular set of constraints. The action of either countering or violating them would thus enable the construction of a sense of identity as agent, and as capable of conscious or directed meaning or action which thereby situates a person outside of or in conflict with existing ideology. However, the act of transgressing does not simply constitute agency. Such actions also function to position and construct a person, albeit in a conflictual relation to the received codes or conventions of a society. In other words they also imply the status of that person as a subject. The possibility of transgression thus presumes the co-existence of two aspects of individual subjectivity: a sense of a personal identity as subject—and hence positioned in a relation, of compliance or of conflict, to specific social and discursive practices; and a sense of identity as an agent—and hence as occupying a place or position from which resistance to or transgression of the social boundaries which constrain the subject can be produced (McCallum, 1999).

Because ideologies evolve over time, there are ongoing developments in what children's fiction represents as desirable models of human personality, human behavior, interpersonal relationships, social organization, and ways of being in the world. To examine how transgression opposes ideology, we will compare two very different novels, David Almond's (1999) magical realist *Kit's Wilderness* and An Na's (2001) realist migration narrative *A Step from Heaven*. *Kit's Wilderness* focuses on a specific and local setting to recuperate a dystopian past, while *A Step from Heaven* explores how the main character forges subjective agency out of displacement and subsequent resistance to hegemonic structures.

Both novels envisage a world better than the everyday world the characters inhabit, and as such belong to a large body of children's fiction from the early 1990s to the present in which utopian tropes are evident either within constructions of fantastic or realistic worlds (both utopias and anti-utopias), or implied through their opposites in dystopian narratives. These two novels are stories about kinds of exile or displacement: *A Step from Heaven* (Na, 2001) tells the story of Young Ju, its principal character, from the age of four until the end of her teenage years; *Kit's Wilderness* (Almond, 1999) tells of events that the narrator was centrally involved in over a period of half a year while he was thirteen. The two thus offer contrasting perspectives on the experience of displacement. *Kit's Wilderness* pivots on an internal re-migration, whereby Kit has returned with his parents to Stonygate, the town of their birth, so that Kit is displaced into a quest to comprehend place and origin. *A Step from Heaven* is a story of permanent emigration from Korea to America, narrated by the protagonist, Young Ju, recounting the experiences of an immigrant family, and exploring what it means to be an immigrant.

A common form of transgression in children's literature is transgression against norms of behavior determined by the adult world. Adults in *Kit's Wilderness* (Almond, 1999) are quick to condemn the children's behavior when a teacher discovers the children playing "the game called Death" (p. 6), a game invented by John Askew, a marginalized child from a dysfunctional family. The game involves a form of shamanism, as a child, chosen at random, enters a hypnotic trance which mimics death. For Askew, it is a way to identify which of the children are like him, and

have the capacity to see the spirits of young boys who died in a mine collapse in 1821. He perceives an affinity with Kit, as their grandfathers worked the mines together, and both boys shared their names with "great great great great uncles" (p. 21) who had died in the disaster. As Kit becomes more engaged with Stoneygate, the spirits of these long-dead children begin to appear on the edges of his vision, presences from the past, a metonym of the deep bond of past and present. For school authorities, however, the game signifies "leanings to darkness" (p. 75) and indicates a need to exercise more control over the children: "'You're just children,' [the Principal] said. 'Innocents. It is our duty to protect you'" (p. 76). The children are quickly polarized into those who excuse themselves by claiming Askew was evil and had threatened them, and those, consisting of Kit and his friend Allie, who assert that the game was meaningless. Power prevails, however and Askew is expelled from school and rendered even more marginal. Kit himself is given a gentle warning to curb his powerful imagination and channel it into writing.

Since the valorizing of imagination in the Romantic era, there has been a persistent controversy over the imagination: education systems in English-speaking countries, for example, have privileged imagination over mundane learning, but have also sustained a suspicion of imaginations that are overactive, overheated, and unhealthy. As John Sallis (2000) encapsulates it,

> …imagination has a double effect, a double directionality, bringing about illumination and elevation, on the one hand, and deception and corruption, on the other, bringing them about perhaps even in such utter proximity that neither can, with complete assurance, be decisively separated from the other. (p. 46)

In suppressing the game of death and unregulated imagination (and these suppressions are depicted physically as a bulldozer is brought in to destroy the underground den where the game was played), the school authorities play out a process whereby discourse operates and maintains its authorized meanings and ideology exerts control over all visions and judgments. The appropriated duty to protect the innocent proves to be repressive in what it will permit and deny. However, the suppression of this first transgression and the concomitant repression of agency is short-lived, and through its second act of transgression *Kit's Wilderness* affirms the power of artistic expression—visual art (Askew), writing (Kit) and performance (Allie)—to resist the tenets of ideology and become a means to see in new ways. In short, Almond's novel affirms that it is a part of the aesthetic function of literature to encompass the pleasures of creativity, imagination, and a knowledge about self and the world, and thereby provide a critique of ideology.

The second transgressive act occurs towards the end of the novel when Kit makes a night journey to enter a mine-shaft in search of Askew, who has been missing since his expulsion. The action is a much deeper version of the game of death, and a culmination of the magical realist, shamanistic element in Almond's narrative, and hence of the power of imagination to render the world meaningful. In this journey, Kit crosses a border that takes him beyond his sense of being displaced in this setting to becoming deeply embedded in it. More generally, the concept of borders signifies in a variety of ways: It can describe a personality disorder ("borderline"), the effects of experiencing multiple subjectivities, or a liminal space between meanings. Borders are thus also a marker of hybrid or liminal subjectivities, such as those that would be experienced by persons who negotiate among multiple cultural, linguistic, or racial systems throughout their lives. Borders also make space and time ambiguous, as meaning slips metonymically between the literal and the figurative. There is a predominant theme of healing in *Kit's Wilderness*, which is identifiable as a recurrent motif in Almond's novels, and here focused through the unlikely alliance between sensitive Kit and Askew, who is harsh and confused. Askew is drawn by his negative construction of the past into an emotional darkness—expressed metonymically by the way he is drawn to physically dark places such as the mine shaft. The power of Kit's creative imagination enables him to negotiate the border of space and time, to learn there is both light and dark in the world, and to guide Askew back to a new beginning. In this way, the novel affirms the value of an unfettered imagination as superior to a channeled imagination inside a docile body.

A different perspective on ideology and transgression emerges from an examination of fictive characters who are intercultural subjects. Ideologies of multiculturalism have been a vexed issue in any country that has embraced them, and stories narrated from the perspective of a character depicted as experiencing ethnic otherness have a propensity to turn into problem novels. Nevertheless, as Peter Morgan (1998) observed, because Asian American YA novels deal with the question of fitting into the "identity-conscious world of teen society" (p. 18), it becomes easy for readers to subsume them into narratives of maturation and thence into some overarching ideology of childhood and development.

Young Ju, the principal character of *A Step from Heaven* (Na, 2001), feels compelled to transgress against her culture of origin in order to negotiate the border between being American, the culture she primarily knows beyond the domestic sphere of her family, and being Korean, the linguistic and cultural domain of the family. An Na has used the representation of Young Ju's quest for personal and national identity to explore the complexities and contradictions of growing up in a community where independent female relationships are opposed by oppressive patriarchal assumptions. Thus, she has adapted the conventions of the novel of development to a novel about migration, to offer her own narrative about progressive development and coherent identity.

Young Ju feels compelled to lie to her parents about her friendships, which they oppose, and despises herself for concealing her impoverished family circumstances from her friends. Strategically, however, the novel affirms her transgressions by contrasting them with the greater and destructive transgressions of her violent and drunken father. For example, a scene in which the father ("Apa") has beaten her and knocked her to the floor for continuing to see an American friend closes with this injunction: "Do not get up, Apa says, standing over me. Do not get up until you know how to be a Korean girl again" (Na, 2001, p. 112). The scene sharply focuses the underlying clash of ideologies between an open and closed society, and the violent repression confirms the rightness of Young Ju's transgression in quest of the more open society.

Similarly, her mother judges that Young Ju has behaved transgressively in phoning the police during one of her father's drunken rages—it is her husband's prerogative to beat her as violently as he pleases. Readers will not see Young Ju's attempt to save her mother as transgression, and eventually her mother shifts her own view. Thus when her husband, unable to find a way to exist within American society, returns to Korea, she opts to stay in America with her children. After this decision the novel moves toward closure by leaping some years to the great day when the mother and the two children move into their own home on the eve of Young Ju going away to college. By the close of the novel Young Ju has fully achieved an accommodation to the existing society, demonstrating that she has become capable of self-positioning and assessment of both herself and her place in society:

> Uhmma said her hands were her life. But for us, she only wished to see our hands holding books. You must use this she said, and pointed to her mind. Uhmma's hands worked hard to make sure our hands would not resemble hers.
>
> It takes only a glance at our nails, our knuckles, our palms to know Uhmma succeeded. Joon and I both possess Uhmma's lean fingers, but without the hard, yellowed calluses formed by years of abuse from physical labour. Our hands turn pages of books, press fingertips to keyboard buttons, hold pencils and pens. They are lithe and tender. The hands of dreams come true. (Na, 2001, p. 154)

Young Ju's displacement is part of the modern Korean diaspora, as Koreans spread out around the world in search of another kind of life. Her mother, driven by a mixture of ambition and desperation, undergoes great hardship to achieve her dream for her family, working multiple jobs to support them and to ensure they are educated. This almost stereotypical immigrant's dream encapsulates the complex of ideological and socioeconomic structures that produce the protagonist's evolving relationships with society and family. This final state of emplacement is balanced against a photograph Uhmma gives to Young Ju to take with her to college. It is a photograph taken on the day on which the novel opens, when four-year-old Young Ju learned to be brave in the waves of the sea. Her mother offers her the photograph to remind her to be brave, but also to remind her of her heritage. The photograph enacts a nostalgic relationship with, and affirmation of, Young Ju's lost origins. While Young Ju does not feel a desire for Korea as home, the photograph sums up the novel's continuous process of gesturing towards the "source" of identity, towards the grounds of cultural origins, towards conflicting notions and images of what constitutes home.

The literature of multiculturalism and now post-multiculturalism can be read as an ongoing exchange among ideologies or discourses. One effect of this is that the very notion multiculturalism has been produced within this process of exchange and has therefore constantly been a process of becoming. The process becomes very evident when texts incorporate overt advocacy, or, like *A Step from Heaven*, are structured as a progression from lack to well-being; such processes constitute a dialogic relationship between, on the one hand, what the writer conceives of as a current and dominant situation or attitude and, on the other hand, a desirable direction of change for society.

Closure thus has crucial ideological impact. How a narrative resolves the complications of story is of special interest with children's fiction. Here, the desire for *closure*, both in the specific sense of an achieved satisfying ending and in the more general sense of a final order and coherent significance, is characteristically an affirmation of the social function of ideology to sustain or redefine group values. Orientation of the self towards these values controls both actions and interpretations, and in many ways defines how fictive subjects represent themselves, other participants, interpersonal relations, everyday social actions, and the significances of time and place—in other words, the ideological complex that organizes social attitudes and relationships. Narrative fictions then function as models of everyday life experience in the lived world.

Conclusion

Ideologies are the systems of belief which are shared and used by a society to make sense of the world and which pervade the talk and behaviors of a community, and form the basis of the social representations and practices of group members. Literary discourse, on the other hand, serves to produce, reproduce and challenge ideologies more self-consciously; thus, all aspects of textual discourse are informed and shaped by ideology. Texts produced for children seldom thematize ideology, but either implicitly reflect its social function of defining group values or seek to challenge received ideologies and substitute new formations. No narrative is without an ideology, and since narratives for young readers maintain a primary focus on events and characters which are isomorphic with actions in the world inhabited by readers, they are always imbricated with ideological positions.

We have argued here that several concepts are germane to understanding the ideology of text. First, the concept of subject positions implied within texts is of crucial importance for reading and especially for examining a text's possible ideological impact, because what such positions inevitably seek is reader alignment with or against the social attitudes and relationships that constitute the narrative. Reader alignment with unexamined positions can be a powerful vehicle for naturalizing ideologies.

Second, we have drawn attention to the widespread thematizing of imagination as a way of affirming and advocating social metanarratives promoting humane behaviors. A key expression of imagination is in the creativity of represented characters, especially its capacity to articulate the connection of creativity with agency as a force for expressing emotions and making responsible judgments based on intersubjective relations. Underpinning such representations is the social assumption that life without agency is tantamount to abjection.

Third, we have pointed to the intersections of genre and gender, whereby the ideology of a text inheres in framing situation, represented patterns of behavior, interactions between characters, linguistic discourses, and the interpersonal relationship with implied readers. Because particular genres instantiate reading strategies more or less implicitly bound up with that genre, ideological implications are apt to remain implicit or invisible. The interplay of overt and invisible ideologies is most evident in realist texts which thematize social issues, especially representations of bodies and behaviors marked by gender or race/ethnicity.

Fourth, we have stressed that representations of transgression are an important way children's literature makes ideologies apparent and seeks to redefine or even overthrow them. Because transgression is inevitably against some socio-cultural formation, it is inextricably tied up with the ideology of the text, whether overt or implicit, and so tends to define what ideologies are being depicted as the contemporary status quo, what are the problems with or limitations of those ideologies, and what are imagined as possible social or individual transformations of behavior in opposition to them.

Finally, we would reaffirm that ideology inhabits text in the most basic ways, in language structures and narrative forms. Because ideology is formulated in and by language, meanings within language are socially determined, and narratives are constructed out of language, an effective understanding of textual significance must begin here.

Literature References

Almond, D. (1999). *Kit's wilderness*. London, England: Hodder Children's Books.

Almond, D. (2008). *The savage* (D. McKean, Illus.). London, England: Walker Books.

Bell-Rehwoldt, S. (2007). *You think it's **easy** being the tooth fairy?* (D. Slonim, Illus.). San Francisco, CA: Chronicle Books.

Gaiman, N. (2008). *The graveyard book*. London, England: Bloomsbury.

Halfmann, J. (2006). *Alligator at Saw Grass Road* (L. Anzalone, Illus.). Norwalk, CT: Soundprints.

Hatkoff, I., Hatkoff, C., & Kahumbu, P. (2006). *Owen & Mzee: The true story of a remarkable friendship* (P. Greste, Photographer). New York, NY: Scholastic.

Horniman, J. (2008). *My candlelight novel*. Crows Nest, New South Wales: Allen & Unwin.

Jones, D. W. (2000). *Howl's moving castle*. New York, NY: HarperCollins. (Original work published 1986)

Maguire, G. (2007). *What-the-Dickens: The story of a rogue tooth fairy*. Cambridge, MA: Candlewick Press.

Na, A. (2001). *A step from heaven*. Asheville, NC: Front Street.

Richardson, J., & Parnell, P. (2005). *And Tango makes three* (H. Cole, Illus.). New York, NY: Simon & Schuster.

Academic References

Althusser, L. (1971). *Lenin and philosophy, & other essays*. London, England: New Left Books.

Altieri, C. (1994). Intentionality without interiority: Wittgenstein and the dynamics of subjective agency. In C. McDonald, & G. Wihl (Eds.), *Transformations in personhood and culture after theory* (pp. 85–116). University Park: The Pennsylvania State University Press.

Bradford, C., Mallan, K., Stephens, J., & McCallum, R. (2008). *New world orders in contemporary children's literature: Utopian transformations*. New York, NY: Palgrave Macmillan.

Clark, C. D. (1995). *Flights of fancy, leaps of faith: Children's myths in contemporary America*. Chicago, IL: University of Chicago Press.

Dixon, B. (1977). *Catching Them Young;* Vol 1: *Sex, Race and Class in Children's Fiction*; Vol 2: *Political Ideas in Children's Fiction*. London, England: Pluto Press.

Harnois, C. (2008). Re-presenting feminisms: Past, present, and future. *NWSA Journal, 20*(1), 120–145.

Hollindale, P. (1988). Ideology and the children's book. *Signal 55*, 3–22.

Hubler, A. E. (2000). Beyond the image: Adolescent girls, reading and social reality. *NWSA Journal, 12*(1), 84–99.

Kidd, K. (2004). *Making American boys: Boyology and the feral tale*. Minneapolis: University of Minnesota Press.

Langer, S. (1956). *Philosophy in a new key: A study in the symbolism of reason, rite, and art* (3rd ed.). Cambridge, MA: Harvard University Press.

Marshall, E. (2004). Stripping for the wolf: Rethinking representations of gender in children's literature. *Reading Research Quarterly, 39*(3), 256–270.

McCall, L. (2005). The complexity of intersectionality. *Signs: Journal of Women in Culture and Society, 30*, 1771–1800

McCallum, R. (1999). *Ideologies of identity in adolescent fiction*. New York, NY: Garland.

Mandel, J., Mullett, E., Brown, J., & Cloitre, M. (2006). *Cultivating resiliency: A guide for parents and school personnel*. Retrieved on February 14, 2010, from http://teacher.scholastic.com/products/tradebooks/discguide/owen_mzee_dg.pdf

Morgan, P. E. (1998). A bridge to whose future? Young adult literature and the Asian American teenager. *ALAN Review 25*(3), 18–20. Retrieved on February 14, 2010, from http://scholar.lib.vt.edu/ejournals/ALAN/spring98/morgan.html

Morris, P. (1993). *Literature and feminism*. Oxford, England: Blackwell.

Romören, R., & Stephens, J. (2002). Representing masculinities in Norwegian and Australian young adult fiction: A comparative study. In J. Stephens (Ed.), *Ways of being male: Representing masculinities in children's literature and film* (pp. 216–233). New York, NY: Routledge.

Sallis, J. (2000). *Force of imagination: The sense of the elemental*. Bloomington: Indiana University Press.

Smith, D. E. (1988). Femininity as discourse. In L. G. Roman, L. K. Christian-Smith, & E. Ellsworth (Eds.), *Becoming feminine: The politics of popular culture* (pp. 37–59). London, England: Falmer Press.

Snyder, R. C. (2008). What is third-wave feminism? A new directions essay. *Signs: Journal of Women in Culture and Society, 34*(1), 175–196.

Stephens, J. (1992). *Language and ideology in children's fiction*. London, England: Longman.

Stephens, J. (2002). 'A page just waiting to be written on': Masculinity schemata and the dynamics of subjective agency in junior fiction. In J. Stephens (Ed.), *Ways of being male: Representing masculinities in children's literature and film* (pp. 38–54). New York, NY: Routledge.

Van Dijk, T. (2001). Discourse, ideology and context. *Folia Linguistica, 35*(1/2), 11–40.

Wyile, A. S. (1999). Expanding the view of first-person narration. *Children's Literature in Education, 30*(3), 185–202.

Wyile, A. S. (2003). The value of singularity in first- and restricted third-person engaging narration. *Children's Literature, 31*, 116–141.

Point of Departure

M. T. Anderson

Recently I was on a panel with several other children's book writers, and we were asked what lesson we hoped to pass on to children. Almost universally, the answer was that we're not trying to pass on any lesson at all, just trying to tell a good story.

If there is any accusation we fear as writers for children, it is that our books have been somehow instructive, that they have had a *message*. Our own heritage of primers and abecedaria embarrasses us. We all fear Dick and Jane. We cringe at their knee-socks and the plasticine sheen of their cheeks. Confronted with their image, we want to disavow the vacuous sweetness of their moral world. Given the marginalization of children's books that Markus Zusak discusses in his Point of Departure essay, we're eager to prove that we don't play by schoolyard rules. After all, in literary discussions, the charge of didacticism is often precisely what contributes to our marginalization—the dismissive assumption that books for kids are too safe in their scope and limited in their vision.

So writers for children are more troubled by imputations of an ideological dimension to their work than writers for adults are. Most of us were brought up in a literary and critical tradition which suggested that literature is defined by ambiguity—the precise opposite (it would seem) of ideological clarity. Trained in high school and college English Lit classrooms that assumed critical approaches vacillating between the modernist and the postmodern, we are eager to celebrate the sublimity of the artfully unclear and the polyvalent. So one of the reasons I love *Romeo and Juliet*, for example, is that I can never decide whether it's a grand, sweeping love story about a noble passion that shall never fade—or the story of two self-absorbed pubescents who die unnecessary and irritating deaths, meeting their stupid, sticky ends in pools of blood and puppy love. Is Mercutio right about the idiocy of love, or is he just a buzz-kill sidekick? For me, the delight in the play is the instability of these questions.

As the writer sits down at his or her desk, thinking out the next chapter that needs to appear on the blank screen, there is constantly a question of how far ambiguity should reach in a narrative. How far should we try to determine the reader's reactions? How far should we nail down characters' motivations? And to what extent should we be overt about stating our opinions? These questions become more vexed because of embarrassment at the accusations that we, as writers for children, are hacks who just say what we mean, shout out our spiel, and then drag children by their gangly arms into whatever political and ethical side-show we want to ballyhoo.

These craftsman's concerns for the calibration of ambiguity—when we agonize over the clarity of character motivation or the extent to which an abstract narrator should endorse or condemn a character's actions—these concerns should not blind us to the fact that (as the preceding article suggests) ideology is always present, vibrating in the text, whether it's there consciously or unconsciously. We can't escape it. It structures our stories. It informs our cast of characters. It imparts a feeling of rightness or wrongness to our plot resolutions.

Picture a scene from some generic YA novel—the prom, say, and a hunk of cake thrown on someone's lapel, and the outsider boy blushes, and the mean blond girls laugh. When we tell this story, it's embedded in a narrative tradition which we implicitly comment on, and the action is undergirded by a series of tropes and *topoi* on which we subtly take positions: sweet good boy vs. thrilling bad boy, for example, or jock vs. intellectual, or mean stud vs. shrinking sophisticate, or cruel sophisticate vs. gentle rube—and behind those constructions lie other, more deeply buried structures related to whatever ethical and economic and cultural markers we wish to endorse.

And why should that embarrass us? It is those buried debates and struggles that give these narratives their energy. It is our willful desire to prove one thing true or prove another thing false or declare our love for something else that makes our prose dynamic. We are, consciously or unconsciously, always reworking our own histories, our own tensions, our own anxieties, so of course those *topoi* and tropes are propelled by our own tangled subjectivity, our own situation in intersecting ideologies and in stories that came before us and meet within us.

This is true even in the simplest texts. Take a hypothetical board book, say. The whole text is something like, "Up. Down. Farm. Town. Black. White. Day. Night." Already, however, in just these simple phrases, the writer reveals a commitment to a certain kind of educational and developmental methodology—one based on the use of binary oppositions to establish definition, for example. And even just the fact that the author has written a board book is significant: The board book as cultural artifact suggests a certain approach to childhood literacy and development that many of us take for granted in our culture, but which isn't universal. And then we might look at the illustrations in the board book—grinning cows, chickens settling down under blankets—and note that the book partakes of a long association between young children and the American pastoral. While overtly teaching young children word sets, therefore, the book is also introducing them to an oft mythologized and de-historicized image of agricultural production—one which I, for example, as a guilt-ridden but enthusiastic meat-eater, would infinitely prefer to real and historicized images of life on the modern industrial farm. So one could ask, what's at stake in the reproduction of these images? What is being revealed and what is being concealed? This board book couldn't be simpler or more spare, in some ways, and yet it is involved in transmitting all kinds of values to its readers.

So—given that our writing exists in a context of competing ideologies anyway, and reflects those contexts and the struggles between them—why balk at wading into the fray openly? Why not admit that we're girded with a battle-ax to grind? They say to write about your passion—and I'm passionate about questions of ethics, questions of the human capacity for love and for destruction and for genius and for idiocy. Why shouldn't I just plonk down my answers? Why shouldn't I just write non-fiction, in fact—argumentative non-fiction?

And a lot of the answer is that I don't always know the answers before I begin writing. And a lot of the answer is that answers aren't clear. And part of it is that I'm fasci-nated by those moments of disruption when I *don't* know. (Though commitment to pluralistic ambiguity is itself ideological.) And so I'm stranded between knowing and not knowing, uncertain, often, whether to make statements or ask questions.

And in the midst of this, I wonder: *Why, anyway, the commitment to literary ambiguity when writing for a young audience that is still using narrative to construct their world? Don't we want to participate in that construction?* And even: *What's wrong, in some cases, with a little propaganda? What's wrong with telling the lies that might come true if they're believed?* These are difficult times, and worse times may come, and do we really want to abjure our power to argue fervently for what we believe in the forum of the young?

And yet simply to say that causes me shame. How brittle and trivial "lessons" seem.

Oh, who knows? This all hurts my head. And maybe, in the end, that's important. Maybe the books that endure are those that engage us most powerfully in the anxiety of doubt and polemic—narratives that hurt the heads of successive generations, each generation reformulating the story and the issues—so that the author's ideological certainty and ideological doubt both continue to inspire debate within readers, and delight, and despair, and adoration, and awe.

26

The Author's Perspective

Claudia Mills

University of Colorado at Boulder

We suspect that many academics who study and teach children's literature also harbor a secret desire to write children's books themselves. For those that do, Claudia Mills, philosophy professor and prolific children's author, is living the dream. Here she shares an insider's view of the many facets of her "eccentric hobby" from process to publication, full of the wit and charm that characterizes her work for children. She places strong emphasis on working within a community of writers who respect and sharpen each other's work. Although her story may seem somewhat idiosyncratic, Phyllis Reynolds Naylor finds much in common with Claudia's processes, her need for strong connections with characters and situations, and her sense of why a story matters.

When I was a little girl growing up in New Jersey, the first book that I ever bought with my own money was *Someday You'll Write* (1962), by Newbery-medalist Elizabeth Yates. I had checked it out of the North Plainfield public library countless times, but I wanted to have my personal copy to cherish forever. I loved how Yates had written the book to *me*, written it in the second person, starting with the opening line: "You say that you want to be a writer someday, that you dream of being one; but you know, as well I as do, that we cannot dream ourselves into being anything. We can, though, through work and acceptance of the discipline, shape ourselves into being what we want to be" (p. 11). Yes!

I knew I wanted to write children's books, because I loved reading them so much. Even when I became a grownup, I always preferred reading children's books over anything else, especially rereading my beloved childhood favorites over and over again: *A Little Princess* (Burnett, 1905/1963), *Anne of Green Gables* (Montgomery, 1908), *Skating Shoes* (Streatfeild, 1951), *The Middle Moffat* (Estes, 1942), and the Betsy-Tacy books by Maud Hart Lovelace, based on the author's own childhood growing up in Minnesota in the early 1900s. I consider *Betsy and Tacy Go Downtown* (1943) to be the finest novel in the English language! Like me, Betsy wanted to be a writer, scribbling away in her maple tree nook at novels with titles like *The Repentance of Lady Clinton*. On my desk now, as I write this, sits a cross section from that very maple tree, which I purchased from the Betsy-Tacy Society after the aged tree had to be cut down.

In this chapter I want to share a frankly personal account of how one writer became a published children's author and how I go about the wonderful, terrifying, exhilarating task of writing for children. I will also draw on how

374

other writers have written about their creative process in Newbery acceptance speeches over the past 15 years. My account will be representative in many ways, idiosyncratic in others. In the first section, I will tell how I sold my first book (my best story!), and offer some advice for emerging children's book writers on how to get published. In the second section, I will examine my own writing process, from initial idea through final revisions, citing the Newbery speeches to have a reference point for how the truly great writers of my profession have proceeded. In the third section, I will explore how my various worlds—as children's book author, children's literature scholar, philosophy professor, and parent—intersect to form one coherent life. My closing section will take me full circle back to Betsy writing in her maple tree.

Getting Published

While publication is the final stage in the process—after all, a book cannot be published until it has first been written—I want to talk about it first, because if I had never been fortunate enough to become a published children's author, I would not be writing this essay for this volume. I have never heard of anyone else who first became published in the way that I did, but my story nonetheless has some instructive lessons to offer.

Knowing that I wanted to be a writer of children's books, I left my Ph.D. program in philosophy at Princeton in 1979 and accepted my first full-time, grownup job working at Four Winds Press, which was at that time the hardcover trade-book division of Scholastic (I subsequently finished the degree, but not until a full 12 years later, in 1991). I was a secretary to three editors there: Barbara Lalicki, Beverly Reingold, and Susan Albury. Immediately I became inescapably aware of the lowliness of my position. While I had envisioned being taken out to lunch on my first day by the company's vice president, who would chat with me about my trajectory to greatness, instead I was introduced to the other secretaries as "the girl who took Tina's extension." My identity had become a phone extension, and the tasks of my position involved struggling to type letters on an IBM Selectric typewriter so that the carbon copy would appear on the second sheet of paper inserted into the roller, rather than (as happened all too often) on the back of the first. Every day on my long commute from Princeton to Manhattan and back again, I sat on the bus and wrote my own books, chiefly picture books, as at that time I harbored the false belief that picture books were easier to write than novels. I kept collecting form letter rejections from all the major New York publishers.

Desperate for some more helpful feedback on my work, yearning to be a fly on the wall in a publishing house so I could view the actual response to my manuscripts with my own eyes, I suddenly had the brilliant idea of submitting one of my picture book masterpieces to Four Winds under a pseudonym. My manuscript duly arrived in the mail, and Barbara whisked it off into her office with the other submissions of the morning. I toiled away at my desk, heart pounding, sure that any moment now Barbara would burst out of her office with the cry, "I have finally found the manuscript I have been waiting for, for 20 years! I will be known forever as the editor who discovered *Campbell the Tomato*!" Instead, *Campbell the Tomato* was rejected—and I was the one who had to type my own rejection letter. Undeterred, I sent Barbara a second manuscript, which suffered the same fate: I typed rejection letter number two.

But when I sent in a third manuscript, this time Barbara came out of her office, handed me my own little story, and said to me, "Read this. I'd like to know what you think." What did I think? I thought it was a work of matchless genius, destined to be an enduring classic of children's literature. I rolled a piece of paper into my typewriter, ready to write a glowing editorial report. But then I read my story over again, read it as if a stranger had written it, and for the first time I could see flaws in my work I had never seen before. Far from being a shoo-in for the Newbery, the work, alas, wasn't even publishable as written. But it did have promise. I ended up writing Barbara a balanced and thoughtful report, pointing out both the features of the story that worked for me (its vivid characters, its haunting, evocative mood) and those that didn't (it should never have been written as a picture book; it cried out to be developed into a full-length novel). Well, Barbara wrote a letter to the author (me), which her secretary (me) typed (to myself), saying, "I am sending you a copy of my reader's report on your book" (the report I had written about myself). Barbara went on to say, "If you would be willing to revise the book according to these suggestions, I would like to see it again and consider it for publication." Indeed, I was willing to revise it, following all the advice I had the good sense to give myself. The book was published under the title *At the Back of the Woods* (1982).

I had to confess, of course, a confession made easier by the fact that I had also summoned my nerve to show the manuscript of a young adult novel I had completed to another of my three editor-bosses, Beverly Reingold. A couple of weeks later, Beverly stopped by my desk and asked me what I was doing for lunch that day. "Because," Beverly said, "I would like to have lunch and talk about publishing your first book." I told Beverly about my duplicity with my pseudonymous manuscripts, Beverly told Barbara, Four Winds published both books (though rejected my next four full-length novels), and Beverly and I went on to publish close to 40 books together.

Most people are not going to become published in this way. Author friends of mine who have "broken in" to publication in recent years have done so through meeting editors and agents at regional or national conferences such as those put on by SCBWI, the Society of Children's Book Writers and Illustrators. At these conferences, attendees generally have the opportunity to receive a critique of a single page of their work by an editor or agent, who may then express interest in seeing the full manuscript. This opens the crucial door. Contacts never hurt: Cynthia Kadohata's editor was her roommate in graduate school. Other authors have been published after being discovered through writing awards for new talent sponsored by leading publishers: For example, Christopher Paul Curtis's (1995) *The Watsons Go to Birmingham—1963* won the Delacorte Press Prize for a First Young Adult Novel. Some writers still become published by sending in their work "over the transom," either to an editor directly (although fewer and fewer houses now accept unsolicited work) or to an agent, who will then represent their work to houses otherwise closed to an unpublished author. In her Newbery speech, Cynthia Rylant (1993) reports having launched her career by buying "a copy of a book which listed publishers' addresses" (p. 418) and then mailing her stories to them. Linda Sue Park in her 2002 speech thanks her editor for pulling her first book from "the slush pile" (p. 378).

The lesson I can generalize from my own admittedly unusual break-in experience is that my lowly job gave me the opportunity to engage in an extensive, year-long study of what was being currently published by a leading New York publisher, and why it was being published. Every day I read manuscripts and critiqued them; I typed editorial correspondence; I read reviews of the books we published. A reasonable substitute for this would be to spend all the time one can reading *The Horn Book Magazine*, talking to the local children's librarian, searching bookstore shelves, and reading huge stacks of books every week dragged home from the public library—reading as a writer, to analyze what works in each book, what doesn't, and why. Relatively few children's book authors have earned academic degrees in creative writing, although programs are now emerging like the MFA programs in children's book writing at Hollins University and Vermont College. In my view, students at these programs are doing exceptionally well at learning their craft and producing publishable, and even award-winning work. (I spent two weeks during the summer of 2005 as a writer-in-residence at Hollins, and two good friends have completed the program at Vermont College.) Still, many, if not most, children's book authors have no formal, credentialed training in writing. We have learned our craft simply by reading and writing, and by sharing our work with our peers for critique. The best way, and in the end the only way, to publish a children's book is to write a publishable book.

The Writing Process

Getting an Idea

A book begins with an idea. Almost all authors will say that the question they are asked most frequently is "Where do you get your ideas?" (Actually, when I do school programs, the question I am asked most frequently is "How many books have you written?" But still.)

As is the case with many children's authors, most of my ideas in the early years of my career sprang from my extremely vivid memories of my own childhood. I have a sister just twelve months younger, and my scrupulously fair mother treated us as if were identical twins, dressing us alike until we were in junior high school. In *The One and Only Cynthia Jane Thornton* (1986), Cynthia has a sister, Lucy, just one year younger, and the girls are dressed alike by their scrupulously fair mother; the book is about Cynthia's struggle to find her own distinctive identity. (My sister, Cheryl, claims that she wants to write her own book called *Cynthia and Lucy: The Real Story—At Last It Can Be Told*, in which Lucy's side of the story will get a hearing.) An extroverted, even narcissistic child, I was the star of every class play, with the exception of one traumatic kindergarten experience in which I didn't get a part because the teacher thought it was someone else's turn to be the star. I saved that hideous moment and it became the seed for *Dynamite Dinah* (1990), where Dinah does not get to play Becky Thatcher or Aunt Polly in the classroom play of *The Adventures of Tom Sawyer*, but is instead cast only as Village Girl Number Two. The boy Dinah both loves and hates in *Dinah in Love* (1993), Nick Tribble, bears more than a passing resemblance to the boy with whom I fell in love on October 17, 1967, one Dick Thistle. Lizzie Archer in *Lizzie at Last* (2000) is so much like my romantic, poetic, unpopular seventh-grade self that I even dedicated the book "For the girl I used to be." My first 15 books are all about girls: brainy, book-loving girls who get straight A's on their report cards, even though they have a harder time winning social acceptance.

Then I became the mother of two boys. My older son has several diagnosed learning disabilities and struggled in school (well, I'm not sure that he struggled, but I, as his mother, certainly did). My younger son is a strong student but focuses his energies elsewhere, on music and video games rather than on reading and impressing his teachers. I began writing about boys: boys who are average in school (*Losers, Inc.*, 1997), boys whose mothers are disappointed in their academic performance (*You're a Brave Man, Julius Zimmerman*, 1999), boys who have trouble mastering the times tables (*7 x 9 = Trouble!*, 2002) or completing a school biography unit (*Being Teddy Roosevelt*, 2007). My Gus and Grandpa books are based on the relationship my boys have had with their only surviving grandfather, my father-in-law who is now 98, but each book also features some challenge Gus is trying to overcome. Gus can't think of anything good to bring for show-and-tell, he is the last kid in the neighborhood to give up training wheels on his bike, he loses his focus during basketball games, he forgets his memorized piece during his piano recital. These are all experiences of my boys that I now share with my readers.

I do not take these experiences whole, however, and simply write them down. I write fiction, not nonfiction with events slightly altered and the names slightly changed (though the substitution of Nick Tribble for Dick Thistle suggests otherwise!). The vast majority of events in my books never happened in real life. Although my boys were late to give up training wheels, they didn't get help in this department from their grandfather, and he never came to show-and-tell or attended a basketball game or piano recital. Dinah, so much like me in her narcissism, has a baby brother; I had a one-year-younger sister. There may not be a single actual incident in any of my 40-plus books that is taken directly from real life. What real life provides is the seed from which the book then grows in its own organic, self-impelled way.

Many of the Newbery speeches give examples of these seeds, little bits and pieces of the author's life that consciously or unconsciously played a role in the genesis of their award-winning book. Reflecting on the origins of *The Giver* (1993), Lois Lowry (1994) remembers bike rides she took at age 11, from her "comfortable, familiar, safe American community" (p. 415) in Tokyo beyond its boundaries to the "Elsewhere" of the genuinely Japanese city; she remembers being part of a college clique thoughtlessly excluding a girl who was different; she remembers her own instinctive reaction to a reported shooting, as she blurted out, "It's all right. It was in Oklahoma" (p. 418). While reluctant to over-analyze the mysteries of the creative process, Sharon Creech (1995) writes that her family provided inspiration for many of the characters in *Walk Two Moons* (1994). She recalls a family road trip she took from Ohio to Idaho when she was 11; on her birthday during that trip, July 29, 1957, she bought a pair of leather Indian moccasins ("Don't judge a man until you've walked two moons in his moccasins" [Creech, 1995, p. 422]). Part of the inspiration for *Bud, Not Buddy* (1999) was stories told at a family reunion about Curtis's grandfather's Depression-era Big Band. In writing her Newbery acceptance speech, Kate DiCamillo (2004) was struck for the first time by uncanny similarities between some of the events in *The Tale of Despereaux* (2003) and a disturbing childhood memory of a traumatic trick she and her father played on her timid brother on a darkened staircase. Cynthia Kadohata (2005) observes, "Out of our homes…grow our stories" (p. 412), sharing how her family, like the family in *Kira-Kira* (2004), moved to the South, where her father worked as a chicken sexer in a poultry plant. Perhaps the most common inspiration for the Newbery books, judging from the acceptance speeches, is a sense of place: the West Virginia mountains for Cynthia Rylant, a love affair with the Kansas plains for Karen Hesse, the heat of a Texas summer for Louis Sachar, the small midwestern town where his real-life grandmother lived for Richard Peck, the deep South for Cynthia Kadahota, and a "hardscrabble town in the high desert of the Eastern Sierras" for Susan Patron (2007, p. 330). (Note to self: if I want to win the Newbery, I need to focus more on place!)

All published children's book writers I have ever known are united in their view about where ideas for books should *not* come from: the desire to teach a lesson or preach a moral. Didacticism is perhaps the leading danger of writing for children: Too many beginning writers come up with, not an idea for a book, but a lesson they want to teach, a moral they want to preach. It has taken literally centuries for children's book writers to overcome our roots in instructive, moralizing Sunday School tracts. That said, perhaps because I am a philosophy professor as well as a children's book author, I have always harbored the seemingly heretical view that message is important, that a book does need to say something. As a reader, I read for the epiphany moment where the character finally *gets* it, finally garners some hard-earned nugget of wisdom that tells her something about how the world works and allows her to take the next step forward toward maturity. I don't read as much to find out what is going to happen, as to find out what it all means: What is the point? Why has this stretch of a character's experience been singled out to enclose within the covers of a book? The epiphany moment is the moment at which I, as a reader, get tears in my eyes, the "Aha!" moment that sends me forward different from the person I was when I began reading the book. So as an author I do think a lot about the theme of my books. But I know that there is a danger here. I hope my messages are complex and interesting, rather than banal platitudes; I hope they unfold in an independently interesting way. But unlike many authors, I do care passionately and unabashedly about the point of my books.

In beginning to write *Losers, Inc.* (1997), I knew that the central issue of the book would be competition. Ethan Winfield lives in the shadow of his extremely successful older brother, Peter, a star both academically and athletically. Ethan decides that if he can't be a winner like Peter, he'll be a loser, and proud of it! So he and his best friend, Julius Zimmerman, form a losers club, Losers, Incorporated, vowing to have the worst science fair experiment, the dumbest book reports, and so on. Obviously, the resolution of the book had to turn on how Ethan would develop a new self-understanding and a new view of his relationship with his brother. When I go to schools, kids often tell me that they wanted the book to end with Ethan discovering the thing that *he* was best at, the area where *he* would excel; he would find something that he was better at than Peter. The message of the book then would have been: Everybody is best at something. This is a cheering and heartening message. The only problem is that it is false. In fact, the opposite is much closer to being true: For whatever you are good at, there is almost certainly somebody else in the world who is better. So as I wrote the book I groped toward a different underlying message: Maybe who we are isn't best grasped comparatively; maybe the game of "Who is best?" is one that we would be better giving up altogether. I still get tears in my own eyes when I reread the scene in which Ethan's student teacher, departing after her time at West Creek Middle School, says goodbye to

Ethan and tells him what a "remarkable young man" he is. "But I'm *not*," he blurts out. "My brother's the one who's remarkable, not me." And the teacher tells him, "I don't know your brother. I only know you" (pp. 147–148).

For most of my books, at least my books for middle-grade readers, message in some way is key. Dinah is wrestling with the question of how much space one person is allowed to take up in the world; in *Dinah Forever* (1995), she ponders the question of whether life has any meaning if the sun is going to burn out in a mere five billion years. *Standing Up to Mr. O.* (1998) deals with Maggie's disillusionment in her idolized teacher after she refuses to do dissections in his biology class. *Trading Places* (2006) builds toward the seemingly simple, but (in my biased view) powerful, conclusion: "People are complicated." In the book I'm working on now, *One Square Inch* (2010), Cooper learns that the only way he can cope with his mother's mental illness is to keep some small place of strength and safety within himself.

As I reread all of the recent Newbery speeches to write this essay, I saw the authors falling on a spectrum in terms of their concern with the message or theme of their book. Louis Sachar (1998) is withering about the conscious insertion of any message into a story:

> It's hard to imagine anyone asking an author of an adult novel what morals or lessons he or she was trying to teach the reader. But there is a perception that if you write for young people, then the book should be a lesson of some sort, a learning experience, a step toward something else. (pp. 416–117)

He cites a recent letter from a kid who had obviously been told to write a letter to an author saying what lessons he had learned from a book: "Your book taught me that the acts of your great-great-grandfather can affect your life." Sachar comments, "Well, I didn't write the book for the purpose of teaching kids that something their great-great-grandparents did long ago might have cursed them and their descendants for all eternity" (p. 417). Instead, *Holes* "was written for the sake of the book, and nothing beyond that. If there's any lesson at all, it is that reading is fun" (p. 417).

But Lois Lowry (1994) seems clearly to have constructed *The Giver* (1993) to communicate a heart-felt message about resisting conformity and embracing complexity:

> If I've learned anything through that river of memories, it is that we can't live in a walled world, in an 'only us, only now' world, where we are all the same and feel safe. We would have to sacrifice too much. The richness of color would disappear. Feelings for other humans would no longer be necessary. Choice would be obsolete. (p. 420)

While she deliberately provided an ambiguous closing scene that would allow young readers to provide their own ending to Jonas's story, Lowry's own creative process makes clear that her purpose in writing *The Giver* (1993) was to explore both the seductive appeal and the ultimate horror of a world in which difference is eradicated.

Other Newbery writers fall in between on the theme/message spectrum. The fact that Sharon Creech (1995) began with the fortune cookie message "Don't judge a man until you've walked two moons in his moccasins" (p. 421) shows that she did not judge message to be irrelevant. Karen Cushman (1996), noting that children "are what they read," says that this is why she writes what she does: "about tolerance, thoughtfulness and caring; about choosing what is life-affirming and generous; about the ways that people are the same and the ways they are different and how rich that makes us all" (p. 418). Karen Hesse (1998) was prompted by her editor to answer the question, as she was revising *Out of the Dust*, "What is it about, really?" And Hesse came up with the answer: "And I knew. It was about forgiveness. The whole book. Every relationship. Not only the relationships between people, but the relationship between the people and the land itself. It was all about forgiveness" (p. 426). It is interesting here that Hesse apparently didn't set out to write a book about forgiveness—indeed, she says that her first seed for the book was research into "agricultural practices on the Great Plains" (p. 423). But she needed to understand her theme before she could bring the book to completion. Richard Peck (2001) said that all fiction has the same underlying message: "In the long run you will be held responsible for the consequences of your actions" (p. 400). (Hmmm—maybe even your great-great-grandchildren will be held responsible?)

My critique group goes away for a retreat every summer, up to Lake Dillon in the Colorado Rockies, and we always spend our first night together discussing that year's Newbery winner. Since our purpose is to work together to develop our craft, we think it's worthwhile to give a close examination to what has been recognized by the library community as the most distinguished children's book of the year. Interested in process, we also share the winner's Newbery Medal acceptance speech, in a beloved ritual where we read the speech aloud page by page, passing my copy of *Horn Book* around in a circle, each taking a turn at reading. Then we vote to rank all the Newberys since we started reading them together, back in 1994. The two that consistently emerge at the top of the lists every single year are still *The Giver* (1993) and *Holes* (1998)—the most theme-driven book of the bunch and least theme-driven (at least according to its author). Go figure.

Writing the Book

There is no one correct way to write a book. At writing conferences, I have heard talks by successful authors who insist on the value of outlining and by equally successful authors who say that if they had a detailed outline of what was going to happen next, they wouldn't bother to write the book at all. Some writers take years to write what seem like deceptively simple stories; others are amazingly prolific, pouring out an enormous volume of everything from picture books to complex historical novels.

Here is how I write.

For one thing, I write by hand. I have written all my books by hand, always using the same battered clipboard (now missing its clip) that I have had since college, always writing on pads of white, narrow-ruled paper with no margins, always using the same kind of pen, a Pilot Razor Point fine-tipped black marker pen. And I always drink Swiss Miss hot chocolate while I write as well, the beverage that seems to awaken my muse and alert her to the fact that it is time to create. I am writing this essay directly onto my computer, as I write all my academic papers whether in the field of philosophy or of children's literature criticism, but I write my children's books by hand. I don't know that I have a reason why I do this. Partly it is because of the importance of creative ritual (as dancer and choreographer Twyla Tharpe [2003] wonderfully explains in her book *The Creative Habit*). This is how I've always done it. This is how I always plan to do it. This is simply how I write a children's book.

Not only do I write my books by hand, I think of my ideas by hand, as well. Sometimes I view myself as having no actual inner life at all; it seems that there is nothing going on inside my head, nothing that happens internally until I actually pick up the pen. I will lie on my couch with my clipboard, pad of paper, and pen, and write at the top of my blank page: IDEAS FOR A BOOK. For years, worried that I was writing only about girls, I would write at the top of my blank page: IDEAS FOR A BOOK ABOUT A BOY. Then I would begin brainstorming on the page. When I wrote *7 x 9 = Trouble!* (2002), I knew I wanted to write a third-grade chapter book, because I wanted to have books for kids in between the reading level of my easy reader Gus and Grandpa books and my middle-grade novels. So on my blank page I wrote down everything I could remember about my own third-grade year, and the third-grade experiences of my boys. Both my boys had to memorize all 12 times tables by a certain date in order to receive the reward of an ice cream cone: one was the last in the class to get his ice cream cone, and one was the first. Ooh! I might have the material for a book here!

As the idea begins to emerge, I brainstorm things that can happen in the story. My early books were heavy on introspection, short on action. Now I am keenly aware that in a book, something has to *happen*. The main character has to *do* things. So I start thinking of things that he or she can do, things that can be developed into *scenes*.

For my book, *How Oliver Olson Changed the World* (2009), I began with a cluster of ideas. Wandering the hallways in a school I had recently visited, I saw a display of student essays on "How I Would Change the World." My favorite idea of the ones posted (which made its way verbatim into the book) was: "I would give food to poor people so they wouldn't die, and if they died, I would go their funerals." That was seed number one. I always keep

in the forefront of my consciousness an awareness of how the story has to be structured: If I'm going to write about a kid with an idea about how to change the world, the kid has to be initially unlikely to change the world. Okay, I would write about a boy with "helicopter parents," hovering over him, supervising all his schoolwork, unable to let him have any independence or freedom. I had ample material from the family of one of my younger son's friends. Indeed, his mother (my own dear friend) ruefully told me, "If you need any more material on over-protective parents, just come over to our house." So far, so good, but this is not yet a book. I decided to incorporate our elementary school's third grade unit of study of the solar system, culminating in the third-grade space sleepover, to structure the story. I have found that it is hard to come up with anything more lively and original than the curriculum created by good and committed teachers. I knew Oliver would have the assignment to make a diorama of the solar system; I knew his parents would be making it for him; and I knew that something would have to change for him through the course of the book: He would have to make his own diorama! And I also knew that Oliver would have another school assignment to come up with a world-changing idea, and his idea would somehow get recognized publicly in a way that would contribute to his struggle for independence.

I love to work with the formal element of structure. When I wrote poetry back in junior high and high school, I wrote sonnets, glorying in the liberating constraint of these fourteen lines in iambic pentameter. So when I write a book I start by thinking of what kind of physical form the book will have. The manuscript of a chapter book will have ten chapters of five pages each. (This is a rule I have invented for myself: Somebody else's chapter book might have eight chapters of six pages each. But not mine.) I'm looking now at my first notes for Oliver Olson. For Chapter 1 I have written "introduce Oliver—space study—big idea." For Chapter 2 I have written "Oliver at home—starting diorama?—parental supervision." For Chapter 3, "mention big idea campaign—sleepover—or mention sleepover in chapter 1?—yes!" I have nothing yet for Chapters 4 through 8, except "make diorama. Go to Crystal's house." (I knew Oliver would need help in securing independence from his parents, so he would end up working on his diorama not alone, but with a lively and bossy girl at school, Crystal.) For Chapter 9, "assembly with speaker—BIG SURPRISE when O's suggestion [for changing the world] is revealed." Chapter 10: "sleepover—can't change *the* world, but can change *your* world." At this point I don't yet know what Oliver's big world-changing idea is going to be. I don't know anything about what the diorama is going to look like. But, more like Lois Lowry than like Louis Sachar, I do know my theme. Other notes on the page (I said earlier that I don't have any thoughts that aren't written down) say: "is this too depressing? I need some funny energy! I need another plot element? SCENES!"

At this point, I stop outlining and begin writing, confident that the rest will emerge as I put pen to paper. And it does. A classroom discussion about the demotion of Pluto as a planet leads Crystal and Oliver to plan a protest diorama on behalf of Pluto, with Pluto positioned outside their diorama holding a little sign pleading, "Let me in!" The scenes I was hoping for become scenes of working on the diorama first at Crystal's house (where her dog makes off with Pluto) and then at Oliver's house (where his hovering mother inadvertently throws Pluto away). Observations about Pluto provide much of the humor of Oliver's thoughts: "Pluto would be the only planet not inside the space diorama. Oliver would be the only kid not going to the space sleepover. He would never have guessed that he and Pluto had so much in common."

Generally, I begin to write the actual book when I have perhaps five or six closely written pages of notes. It is important at this point for me to start writing the book itself, to see the character come alive on the page and begin to shape his or her own story. I spend a lot of time trying to get the first chapter right, with the help of my critique group (more on which, below). Until I have a solid foundation in my first chapter, I don't really know if I have a book at all. I have given up on ideas because I couldn't get the first chapter right. But I have never given up on an idea once that first chapter was in place.

Most authors, perhaps all authors, experience the surprises that come to us as we write, things that our characters do or say that lead the story into a completely unexpected direction. My most striking example from my own work is *Dinah in Love* (1993), the third book in my Dinah series. As I planned out the book, I knew I wanted to write a book about unrequited sixth-grade love. My own love for the aforementioned Dick Thistle was certainly unrequited. I called Dick Thistle "Apollo," wrote him sonnets from Clytie (the girl in Greek mythology who turns into a sunflower from pining for the sun god), and generally made his life miserable by my unstinting devotion throughout the years we were together in high school. I had long wanted to write about unrequited love, and I had the basic idea of what the message of the book would be, some variant on the classic idea that it is better to have loved and lost than never to have loved at all. But every time I began thinking of a book about unrequited love, I was struck by how unappealing and pathetic the "loveress" would be: this poor, drippy girl! Dinah, however, had already been established in the first two books of the series as a force to be reckoned with. And Dinah's narcissism would provide a fresh and interesting angle on unrequited love: Dinah wouldn't be in love with Nick Tribble as much as in love with the idea of being in love, in love with her own self as a lover. It seemed perfect! Yet, when I began to write the first chapter, in which Dinah was supposed to fall in love with Nick, something unexpected happened: Dinah met Nick, yes, but she didn't fall in love. Instead, she fell in hate! Far from pining for Nick, she hated the very marrow

of his moldy bones! I tried writing chapter two, hoping that she'd feel some tingle of affection for Nick at that point, but her hatred of him only intensified. So I realized that I didn't have a novel of unrequited love after all. Instead, I had a traditional romantic comedy, where the two characters hate—or at least think they hate—each other until the moment when they realize that they love each other instead. The book earned me my favorite review of my career, from Deborah Stevenson (1993) at the *Bulletin of the Center for Children's Books*: "It's predictable, sure, but so were Tracy and Hepburn" (p. 217).

Sometimes I'll begin writing only with a strong sense of the structure of the book. I know the kind of thing that has to happen, but not the specific instance of that thing. In *You're a Brave Man, Julius Zimmerman* (1999), I began writing the book knowing that I had two parallel story lines: Julius takes a summer French class, and he has a summer babysitting job, both activities the result of his mother's efforts to "improve" Julius over the summer following sixth grade. I knew that the two story lines would have to intersect both in terms of plot and theme: Something would have to happen in the babysitting job, which would interfere in some way with what was happening in the French class, which would only intensify Julius's mother's disappointment in her son, but which would also lead to a deeper understanding between the two of them. But what would it be? I didn't find out until Julius arrived at the first day of his babysitting job and was horrified to discover that Edison was not yet potty-trained. Pleased to have this possibility for kid-pleasing humor in the story, I kept on writing, and was tickled myself when Julius has to leave the French class play of Cinderella to help Edison make his first tinkle in the potty. Thank you, universe! Finally, as I noted above, I began to write *How Oliver Olson Changed the World* (2009), knowing that Oliver would have a school assignment to come up with a world-changing idea, and that his world-changing idea would get special recognition from the state senator who comes to speak at a school assembly, but I had no idea what this great idea was going to be. I knew, however, that if I kept writing, I would find out. Or rather, if I kept writing, Oliver would find out, and I could write it down.

And so I keep on writing. My goal for myself is a page a day, written in an hour a day. This is all that I am able to do, given the demands of my full-time job as a professor at the University of Colorado and of my family. But when I had the opportunity to spend two magical weeks as writer-in-residence at Hollins University's graduate program in children's literature, I discovered that even when I had all day to write, one hour of writing was enough. I need to let what I have written settle; I need to give my subconscious time to work as well. I love the rhythm of writing an hour a day so much that I even have a beautiful cherry-wood hourglass that I use to mark my hour, to define the boundaries of my time to create.

Revision/Critique

All authors, except the most unlucky ones, have somebody with whom they can share their work before sending it off to an editor. I have never shared my work with my family—I want love and support from my family, not criticism—but many children's authors say that their family, especially their children, are their first and best critics. In the Newbery speeches, Curtis (2000) and Park (2002) both write that they first share their work with their own children. Although support and criticism from writing groups are not mentioned specifically in this batch of Newbery speeches, I know that Newbery medalist Phyllis Reynolds Naylor relies heavily on her long-standing critique group. And I know that I couldn't write without mine.

I have been in two critique groups. The first was in Maryland, drawn from members of the marvelous Children's Book Guild of Washington, D.C. My writing group there was called the Soup Group: we met every other Tuesday for lunch, and we ate, yes, soup. One of our members didn't like to drive on the Beltway, and in exchange for our coming to her house for our meetings, she served us home-made soup and home-made bread. The best of the soups, as I remember, was her cream of cashew. When I moved from Maryland to Colorado in 1992, I approached someone I had met through the Society of Children's Book Writers and Illustrators, and she invited me to join her critique group, then in the process of formation. I have been a member of that group ever since. We meet every other Monday evening from 7 to 10, rotating houses, and have no distinctive profile of refreshments. We had eight members at first; now we have five, but the other three still join us for our annual Christmas dinner.

Different critique groups operate with different mechanisms. This is how we do it. Anyone who has something to share brings it to the meeting, with copies printed out for us to read there. Even though it might save time at the meeting to have read the submitted manuscripts in advance, it would smack of homework, and we don't like homework. It is also especially gratifying to hear fellow members of the group laughing aloud at funny bits—and especially revealing when they don't. We read silently, unless the manuscript is a picture book manuscript, or poetry, when it is so important to hear the work read aloud (by someone other than its author). The exception to this practice of reading only at the meetings is that sometimes we will read the full, completed manuscript of a novel when it is all done, because we need to be able to see the story in its entirety rather than critiquing it piecemeal, chapter by chapter.

Our group has rules that are fairly ironclad regarding the order in which we read the manuscripts and how we critique them. To correct a tendency which we once had to straggle in to the meeting late, we now read manuscripts in the order in which people have arrived; latecomers will get their manuscripts critiqued last, when the rest of us are becoming either tired or silly. Now we all come ridiculously early, jostling each other to be first through the door. After the manuscript has been read, we begin the critiques proceeding in order clockwise around our circle, beginning with the person next to the manuscript's author. No one speaks twice until each person has spoken once. This rule is an excellent one for preventing any member of the group from coming to dominate; it both evokes and enforces our equality and respect for one another. It is important, as we go around the circle, that each member repeat or at least endorse previous criticisms with which she agrees. Although it can be painful for the author to have to hear the same criticism several times (in our early years, SEVEN times), if criticisms are not repeated, the author can leave the meeting thinking, "Well, this one part bothered Ann, but it didn't seem to bother anyone else, so I'm not going to change it."

Some critique groups have the rule that all critiquers should begin with something positive. We don't have that as a formal rule, but it is our informal practice. Seasoned professionals that we all are, with well over 130 books published among the remaining five of us, we still feel vulnerable and exposed as we share our work; we still have sensitive feelings that are easily hurt. So we try to begin with some appreciative remark about the work. Some groups also have the rule that the author of a piece isn't allowed to defend herself against criticism of it; he or she is only supposed to listen, say "Thank you," and then let the next person speak. We don't have that rule. It can be helpful for the rest of us to hear what the author was trying to do, why she made the artistic choice we think is problematic. Still, it is a terrible act of ingratitude when an author tries to refute a piece of critique. Critique is a gift and must be received as such. On the rare occasions when my fellow critique group members have openly rebuffed some critical comment of mine, I want to say, "Fine! Don't change this! Write a bad book! And then see who publishes it!" But I don't say this. Ultimately, each of us knows that there is no refuting a reader. If the reader doesn't laugh, there is a limit to how much the author can insist that the piece really, truly is funny. And if the reader doesn't believe in the reality of the story, it is beside the point for the author to insist that in real life this really, truly happened. The story has to be funny, and touching, and believable in itself, regardless of the author's claims on its behalf.

I was at a writing conference recently where an adult-book author (we call them "adult books," but we don't mean X-rated, just books for grown ups) was speaking; he boasted that he had revised one crucial scene for his recent novel 88 times. The audience gasped admiringly. But I wasn't admiring. "You don't have a critique group, do you?" I asked. Of course, he said no. "Well," I told him, "a critique group would have saved you 80 of those drafts."

Given the care with which my critique group has reviewed each of my books, when I send one of them off to my editor, Beverly Reingold, at Farrar, Straus & Giroux, I am always confident that *this* time, there will be nothing left for her to criticize, nothing at all. After publishing over 40 books, I still think this, every single time. And yet, every single time, without fail, she writes me an editorial letter—a long editorial letter—filled with comments and suggestions that hadn't occurred to me, or to any of us. Perhaps this is because she is coming to the manuscript completely fresh, whereas my critique group has been living inside the world of the book with me for so many months, keenly aware of how much better the book is now than it used to be, and blinded to how much better it could be still. I'd like to be able to say that as soon as I get Beverly's comments, the scales fall from my eyes, but instead I get Beverly's comments and begin several months of sullen sulking. I speculate about how much easier my life would be if I had a less nitpicky editor—or if I gave up writing and publishing children's books altogether. Sometimes I doubt Beverly's comments so much that I ask (in a nice way, of course) for a second opinion from her editorial assistant—who invariably confirms all of Beverly's criticisms of the manuscript and adds half a dozen huge ones of her own.

In my book *Trading Places* (2006), for example, I was given these comments to address: (a) why does crybaby Violet cry so much? (b) the whole story seems to lead up to a big fight that never happens; (c) the scene where Julia and Kelsey come to Amy's house and are made uncomfortable by the sight of her father unshaven and in his pajamas needs to be shown, not mentioned as happening offstage; (d) the pacing regarding Wiggy the dog's illness is unsatisfying—the whole episode happens too quickly; (e) the message of the book as presented isn't right—the idea shouldn't be that Todd and Amy change in character (becoming this, NOT that), but grow in potential (becoming this AND that). Yikes! But at some point I do sit down to revise, tackling the small, easy problems first, and then gradually closing in on the bigger ones. I have learned that sometimes my resistance to revision comes because I feel uncomfortable with Beverly's specific suggestion about how to deal with a certain problem in the story. I have learned that she is sometimes wrong about how to fix a problem, but she is never wrong that there is a problem that needs to be fixed. My revisions invariably end up being far easier than I had dreaded, and actually, once I have made up my mind to face them, tons of fun. When I finally send the manuscript back to Beverly, it is always with overwhelming gratitude for how much better she has helped me to make it.

Intersecting Worlds

I am a children's book author, a children's literature scholar, a professor of philosophy, and the mother of two teenaged boys. I have been asked how all these different worlds and lives fit together—or collide.

One way that all my other worlds and lives impinge on my world and life as a writer is that I have less time to write than my writer friends who aren't parents or who don't have other full-time jobs. Perhaps, though, not that much less: most writers who don't work full-time at another profession spend their "extra" time not writing, but engaging in other writing-related, income-generating activities, such as speaking or book promotion. Nonetheless, it is because of the other demands on my time that I have become an hour-a-day writer, faithful to my hourglass. Having less time to write has made me more efficient as a writer, in ways that are both good (I don't have a lot of time to sit around wallowing in self-doubt) and bad (I also don't have a lot of time for what Brenda Ueland (1938/1987), in her marvelous book *If You Want to Write,* has called "moodling—long, inefficient, happy idling, dawdling and puttering," (p. 32). Ueland says that people who are "always briskly doing something and as busy as waltzing mice…have no slow, big…noble, shining, free, jovial, and magnanimous ideas" (p. 32). I don't have time to write 100 pages of a novel and then throw it away because I'm not satisfied with the direction the book is going. I get an idea, get a contract, write my book, have my writing group critique it, have my editor critique it, revise it, and publish it. My process is more linear than that of the Newbery winners. But I have to say that I don't think my books would be significantly better if I spent significantly more time on them. Anthony Trollope (1883/1947), my writing idol, wrote his novels while working full-time for the British post office. In his splendid autobiography he writes, "My novels, whether good or bad, have been as good as I could make them. Had I taken three months of idleness between each they would have been no better" (p. 104).

My philosophy career and my children's book career have reinforced and enriched each other in many ways. My background as a philosophy professor has made me especially sensitive to the importance of theme and message in my books, as I discussed above. Two of my middle-grade novels are overtly philosophical. In *Dinah Forever* (1995), Dinah has an existential crisis about the meaning of life when she realizes that the sun is going to burn out in a mere five billion years. In *Standing Up to Mr. O* (1998), Maggie refuses to dissect animals in her biology class; the novel presents both sides of the question about the morality of this practice, with heated debate between Maggie and her pro-dissection lab partner, Matt.

My children's book career has also influenced my teaching and scholarship as a philosophy professor, specializing in ethics and political philosophy. When I teach my favorite freshman course, Introduction to Ethics, I begin on the first day by reading aloud to the students from *Stuart Little* (White, 1945), the chapter where Stuart is a substitute teacher leading his students in a discussion of what is important in life; this is a springboard to our own classroom discussion about what is important. When we get to our two weeks on Nietzsche, I read the students Marcus Pfister's (1992) picture book *The Rainbow Fish*, and we talk together about how much Nietzsche would have hated that book. Far from viewing it as a sweet little story about the virtue of sharing, he would have seen it as a tale about how the rainbow fish is pressured by "the herd" to give up everything that makes him special and distinctive, so that he ends up being just like everyone else. For the final exam, I have the students read Phyllis Reynolds Naylor's (1991) Newbery-winning novel *Shiloh* and write an essay examining Marty's moral dilemma from the perspective of the philosophers we have read together in the course. At the university, I sometimes do independent studies with students in creative writing or education who are interested in children's literature; once I even did an independent study with a computer engineering major who was working on the narrative for the video game she was designing. I have heard stories about professors who were also writers of genre fiction who had to publish under a pseudonym because otherwise they wouldn't be taken seriously at tenure time by their colleagues. But my colleagues have always viewed my children's book writing with interest and affection. Philosophers are supposed to have an eccentric hobby. This is mine.

One important subfield within ethics is professional ethics, and I have published two philosophical articles on the overlooked topic of the professional ethics of authors. In both articles, I examine the particular question of what obligations authors have to individuals who are used as material for their stories. I argue for the importance of the sharing of stories and conclude that the writing of fiction would be impossible without the author's license to borrow from real life, including the real life stories of those she knows and loves, of those she knows and hates. But the more the author's treatment of her "material" is in tension with ordinary moral requirements, the harder it is to justify it. Authors have no special license to harm others, either by damaging their reputation or by causing them pain; authors have no special license to invade others' privacy or violate their confidentiality; authors, who are after all first and foremost human beings, need to respect their relationships with those whom they write about. Although it might seem that the greatness of a work of literature could justify considerable harm caused in its production, in actuality, harmful portraits—in virtue of the very features that make them harmful—fall short of the kind of greatness needed to justify such harm. So the formula for justifying harm by greatness turns in upon itself: The greater the work, the more harm it justifies; but the more harm it needs to justify, the less its claim to greatness. The harm, then, remains unjustified.

This leads me to the question of how my family reacts to my need to use our lives together as material for my books. As I noted above, I change so much when I write that I really draw from my family only inspiration and ideas; I don't write about my boys as characters in my stories,

or take actual events from their lives without significant alteration. Perhaps luckily for me, my boys don't read my books! (Although my younger son's best friend is my biggest fan.) Maybe they would rather just not know.

Back in Betsy's Maple Tree

I want to close with one last anecdote. Several summers ago, my older son had just gotten his driver's license and wanted to take a family road trip. I said, fine, so long as I get to pick where we go. I picked a circuit from Boulder, Colorado, where we live, to De Smet, South Dakota (Laura Ingalls Wilder's Little Town on the Prairie), and then on to Mankato, Minnesota, the Deep Valley of the Betsy-Tacy books. There, I had the climax of my career as a children's book author, and of my entire life, when I did a book signing at Tacy's House, maintained as a small museum by the Betsy-Tacy Society. Earlier in my career, I had the opportunity to pay homage to Elizabeth Yates's (1962) *Someday You'll Write* by having my character Cynthia read it in *The One and Only Cynthia Jane Thornton* (1986). It was a thrill for me to contact Elizabeth Yates to ask permission to quote from her book in mine. The little girl who had read Yates's book and grown up to be a writer was now writing a book about another little girl reading Yates's book as part of her own journey to be a writer. And the little girl who had read *Betsy and Tacy Go Downtown* (1943) and identified with Betsy's yearnings to write was now a writer sitting at her own book signing across the street from Betsy's house.

Literature References

Burnett, F. H. (1963). *A little princess*. New York, NY: J. B. Lippincott. (Original work published 1905)

Creech, S. (1995). *Walk two moons*. New York, NY: HarperCollins.

Curtis, C. P. (1995). *The Watsons go to Birmingham—1963*. New York, NY: Delacorte.

Curtis, C. P. (1999). *Bud, not Buddy*. New York, NY: Delacorte.

DiCamillo, K. (2003). *The tale of Despereaux*. New York, NY: Candlewick.

Estes, E. (1942). *The middle Moffat*. New York, NY: Harcourt, Brace.

Hesse, K. (1997). *Out of the dust*. New York, NY: Scholastic.

Kadohata, C. (2004). *Kira-Kira*. New York, NY: Atheneum.

Lovelace, M. H. (1943). *Betsy and Tacy go downtown*. New York, NY: Thomas Y. Crowell.

Lowry, L. (1993). *The giver*. Boston, MA: Houghton Mifflin.

Mills, C. (1982). *At the back of the woods*. New York, NY: Four Winds Press.

Mills, C. (1986). *The one and only Cynthia Jane Thornton*. New York, NY: Macmillan.

Mills, C. (1990). *Dynamite Dinah*. New York, NY: Macmillan.

Mills, C. (1993). *Dinah in love*. New York, NY: Macmillan.

Mills, C. (1995). *Dinah forever*. New York, NY: Farrar, Straus & Giroux.

Mills, C. (1997). *Gus and Grandpa*. New York, NY: Farrar, Straus & Giroux.

Mills, C. (1997). *Losers, Inc*. New York, NY: Farrar, Straus & Giroux.

Mills, C. (1998). *Standing up to Mr. O.* New York, NY: Farrar, Straus & Giroux.

Mills, C. (1999). *You're a brave man, Julius Zimmerman.* New York, NY: Farrar, Straus & Giroux.

Mills, C. (2000). *Lizzie at last.* New York, NY: Farrar, Straus & Giroux.

Mills, C. (2002). *7 x 9 = trouble!* New York, NY: Farrar, Straus & Giroux.

Mills, C. (2006). *Trading places.* New York, NY: Farrar, Straus & Giroux.

Mills, C. (2007). *Being Teddy Roosevelt.* New York, NY: Farrar, Straus & Giroux.

Mills, C. (2009). *How Oliver Olson changed the world.* New York, NY: Farrar, Straus & Giroux.

Mills, C. (2010). *One square inch.* New York, NY: Farrar, Straus & Giroux.

Montgomery, L. M. (1908). *Anne of Green Gables.* Boston, MA: L. C. Page.

Naylor, P. R. (1991). *Shiloh.* New York, NY: Atheneum.

Pfister, M. (1992). *The rainbow fish.* New York, NY: North-South Books.

Sachar, L. (1998). *Holes.* New York, NY: Farrar, Straus & Giroux/ Frances Foster.

Streatfeild, N. (1951). *Skating shoes.* New York, NY: Dell.

Trollope, A. (1947). *An autobiography.* Berkeley: University of California Press. (Original work published 1883)

White, E. B. (1945). *Stuart Little.* New York, NY: HarperTrophy

Wilder, L. I. (1953). *Little town on the prairie.* New York, NY: HarperCollins.

Academic References

Creech, S. (1995, July/August). Newbery Medal acceptance. *The Horn Book Magazine,* 418–425.

Curtis, C. P. (2000, July/August). Newbery Medal acceptance. *The Horn Book Magazine,* 386–396.

Cushman, K. (1996, July/August). Newbery Medal acceptance. *The Horn Book Magazine,* 413–419.

DiCamillo, K. (2004, July/August). Newbery Medal acceptance. *The Horn Book Magazine,* 395–99.

Hesse, K. (1998, July/August). Newbery Medal acceptance. *The Horn Book Magazine,* 422–427.

Kadohata, C. (2005, July/August). Newbery Medal acceptance. *The Horn Book Magazine,* 409–417.

Lowry, L. (1994, July/August). Newbery Medal acceptance. *The Horn Book Magazine,* 414–22.

Mills, C. (2000). Appropriating others' stories: Some questions about the ethics of writing fiction. *Journal of Social Philosophy, 21*(2), 195–206.

Mills, C. (2004). Friendship, fiction, and memoir. In P. J. Eakin (Ed.), *The ethics of life writing* (pp 101–120). Ithaca, NY: Cornell University Press.

Rylant, C. (1993, July/August). Newbery Medal acceptance. *The Horn Book Magazine,* 416–419.

Park, L. S. (2002, July/August). Newbery Medal acceptance. *The Horn Book Magazine,* 377–384.

Patron, S. (2007, July/August). Newbery Medal acceptance. *The Horn Book Magazine,* 327–335.

Peck, R. (2001, July/August). Newbery Medal acceptance. *The Horn Book Magazine,* 397–401.

Sachar, L. (1999, July/August). Newbery Medal acceptance. *The Horn Book Magazine,* 410–417.

Stevenson, D. (1993, December). Review of Dinah in love. *Bulletin of the Center for Children's Books.* Urbana-Champaign, IL: Center for Children's Books.

Tharpe, T. (with M. Reiter). (2003). *The creative habit.* New York, NY: Simon & Schuster.

Ueland, B. (1987). *If you want to write.* Saint Paul, MN: Graywolf Press. (Original work published 1938)

Yates, E. (1962). *Someday you'll write.* New York, NY: E. P. Dutton.

Point of Departure

Phyllis Reynolds Naylor

As I began reading Claudia Mills's perspective on writing children's books, I thought, "How can I add anything to this? She's writing about *me!*" *I'm* the mother of two boys; *I* write novels by hand using the same battered clipboard on which I began my writing career; *I* write my nonfiction stuff on the computer, and I'll bet that my *Danny the Drainpipe* was every bit as good as her *Campbell the Tomato,* though she had the better title.

Unlike Claudia, however, I never dreamed, when I was young, about becoming a writer because I didn't know you could make a profession of it. My love of stories began with my parents, who read aloud to us for an hour or so every night until long after we had learned to read ourselves. Mother read the Bible Story book several times over, *Alice in Wonderland, The Wind in the Willows, Mother West Wind's Children,* but the real treat was listening to my father read books by Mark Twain. Both parents read with great drama, and when I was invited to sleepovers, I longed for story hour—feeding time for the imagination.

I wrote my own little books on the backs of scratch paper, stapled them together, put a pocket and index card in each one, and signed them out to neighbor children. I wrote about everything that entered my world at that time, and when Mother explained the facts of life to me, I even wrote a book titled *Manual for Pregnant Women,* with illustrations by the author.

When I was 16, a former Sunday School teacher wrote to me, saying that she was now editor of a Sunday school paper for children. She remembered how much I loved stories in her class, and wondered if I would write one for her paper. Thrilled, I wrote a baseball story called

"Mike's Hero," and received a check for $4.67. For 15 years I wrote short stories for a variety of publications before I considered writing a book. And then, afraid to risk it, I simply collected nine of my short stories—each taking place in a different country—and sent the manuscript off to Abingdon Press, figuring that if Methodists sent missionaries to foreign countries, they might be interested in publishing it, though most of my stories were "character-building," rather than religious. The book was accepted, and I was ecstatic. *The Galloping Goat and Other Stories* was published in 1965.

Claudia's story of how she was first published is so much more interesting than mine, but both of us learned our craft primarily by "doing"—over and over again—getting the feel for conflict in plot, timing in humor, for suspense, motivation, mood, dialogue, character and all the other things you think about when writing a novel.

Unlike Claudia, things are going on inside my head all the time. Waking or sleeping. The only way I know I've been asleep is whether or not I dream. There seems to be a troop of noisy chattering characters who travel around with me, each loudly demanding a place in a book. I do not think a lot about the element of structure, and I do not glory in the liberating constraint of iambic pentameter. But I do feel, as Claudia does, that in some way the main character should change, or why write about him at all?

Most of my books start with a situation. When I came across the thin, cowering dog which was the inspiration for my *Shiloh* trilogy, I asked myself, "What if I knew who the abusive owner was, and the dog kept running away, coming to me? What would I do?" Then I think about the types of characters who would most likely be found in this situation, and with that comes a decision as to voice. Since writing is my sole occupation, I have the luxury of writing for as long as I like, and I usually keep going until I feel the story becoming dry on the page. The moment that happens, I stop.

Like most authors, I find that friends and even strangers want to offer me ideas. For an idea to be something I can use, however, there has to be a connection with me; I must be able to add something of myself in order for an idea to take root. Sometimes the original idea may be only a small part of the story, but it's like kindling; it's the thing that gets the fire, the excitement, going.

Meryl Streep once said that she knows a script is right for her when she feels a "ping of commonality." I've always been struck by the similarities between writing and acting. A first draft, to me, is like a director assembling his characters onstage. Each is merely reading his lines, though with as much feeling as he can manage, and the director is figuring out who goes where and what the stage setting will be. In the second rehearsal, more is demanded of the characters. The props may be changed. The scenery may be all wrong, and perhaps an argument between two boys will be less heated, more a glimpse of things to come.

Most of my books go through six or seven drafts—*Ice* was revised 18 times. And with each new draft (two or three on my clipboard, before it is typed up on the computer), the dialogue is distilled a bit further, the setting made more distinct, the characters more vivid. A next draft may heighten the conflict or make it more subtle. The writing may be more elegant or the dialogue more folksy. With each print-out I'm struggling for unity, for clarity, for making each part a necessary component of the whole.

I find outlines too restrictive, but I do write a summary of each book and this is my map through the story. There is no list a writer follows (suspense, check; motivation, check)—it's inside a writer's head. That's why we read it again and again as we go along—sometimes silently, sometimes aloud. If it's supposed to be sad but brings no tears to my eyes—if it's supposed to be funny and I don't even smile—how can I expect it of a reader?

For me, the best part about writing occurs when a character comes alive on the page and I know I've got him; when a place that existed only in my head becomes real. There are no trumpets playing at this moment, no audience applauding—a very solitary time, actually—but it's what I like most.

27

Archives and Special Collections Devoted to Children's and Young Adult Literature

Karen Nelson Hoyle

Children's Literature Research Collections (including Kerlan), the University of Minnesota

Archives and special collections provide a physical history of the field of children's and young adult literature. As curator of the Children's Literature Research Collections for over 40 years, Karen Nelson Hoyle is well prepared to explain how such collections enable researchers to seek—and hopefully to find—a "story behind the story" that may be revealed through an examination of the materials held in such collections. These materials may include draft and final manuscripts and artwork; correspondence; first and variant editions of published books; and other materials relevant to the creation and publication of texts for young readers. As a historian of children's literature, Leonard Marcus takes his Point of Departure opportunity to describe some of the resources he has found and assistance he has received at the Kerlan as well as other special collections.

The focus of this chapter is on archives and special collections devoted to children's and/or young adult literature. They go by various institutional names—Archive, Center, Institute, Library, Society or Special Collection—but each is devoted to the subject of children's and young adult literature. "Archives" hold manuscripts and personal papers apropos to the writing, illustrating, editing, and producing of books. The American Library Association (ALA) defines a special collection as "a collection of library materials separated from the general collection because they are of a certain form, on a certain subject, of a certain period or geographical area, rare, fragile, or valuable" (Young, 1983, p. 211). "Special Collections" contain the books themselves, frequently signed by the author and

acquired in variant editions, along with related artifacts. Historically, these institutional and material entities have fuzzy parameters and often gravitate across categories. And finally, although the books and other materials were intended for children and/or young adults, youth archives and special collections exist for adult researchers of varying degrees of research experience.

Locating Archives and Special Collections

The Association of Library Service to Children (ALSC), a division of the American Library Association, has a long-standing committee, the National Planning of Special Collections Committee (established in 1965), devoted to gathering and disseminating information about these resources. This committee has been responsible for the three most comprehensive directories of special collections in children's and young adult literature. The two earlier editions were edited by Carolyn Field (1969, 1982), and the most recent by Delores Blythe Jones (1995). The number of collections that were included in each edition grew from 133 in 1962, to 267 in 1982, to 300 in 1995. Some of this growth is due to the fact that more collections were reporting their holdings. However, it is clear that the increase in numbers is also due to an actual increase in numbers of archives and special collections devoted to children's and young adult literature.

The arrangement of the directories reflects the access points most commonly used by researchers whose work is conducted in archives and special collections, that is, the subject (author, illustrator, editor, publisher, etc.) and the geographic region. A researcher who is writing a biography of a children's author or illustrator may visit an archive to which their subject donated some or all of their papers: rough drafts, manuscripts, editorial correspondence, royalty statements, and so on. Or the researcher may visit a special collection that includes original editions, subsequent editions, translated editions, etc. However, a researcher's visit to an archive may also be a sort of "fishing expedition" for information that *might* be located in the collection.

Leonard Marcus's Point of Departure essay provides several examples of this type of fishing, which may take into account the subject's family, the various places the subject lived, the organizations they may have belonged to, their colleagues and collaborators, friends and loved ones, editors and publishers they worked with, and other special insights. For example, Marcus (1999) used the Kerlan Collection to enhance *Margaret Wise Brown: Awakened by the Moon*. He found that the original story and drawings by Clement Hurd for *Goodnight Moon* (Brown, 1947) depicted a boy, not a rabbit. Marcus (2007) also traced the apocryphal story that editor Ursula Nordstrom demanded that artist Hurd remove the udders on the cow jumping over the moon. In preparing *Golden Legacy*, Marcus (2007) did research at the Bank Street School of Education, the Brooklyn Museum, the Charles M. Schultz Museum and Research Center, HarperCollins, and the universities of Connecticut, Illinois, Minnesota, Oregon, and Texas Wellesley College among others. As Marcus will demonstrate, a thorough—or perhaps simply serendipitous—search may reveal unexpected resources that shed new light on hitherto unanswered questions.

Archives and Special Collections—United States

As noted above, there are over 300 archives and special collections devoted to children's and young adult litera-

ture. The collections featured below are located in the United States, but such collections exist throughout the world. The largest and most well-known U.S. collections include the following.

Arne Nixon Center for the Study of Children's Literature

The Center was founded in 1995 by Arne John Nixon (1927–1997), a member of the faculty of California State University, Fresno, where he taught children's literature and storytelling. Nixon donated the initial collection of 22,000 books and left a bequest that supports the Center's activities. The Center's collection focuses on American and British books published from 1865 to the present. Strengths of the collection include fiction for young adults, Nordic and Finnish language books, *St. Nicholas Magazine*, as well as books about California and the West. The Center is part of the Henry Madden Library at California State University, Fresno.

The Baldwin Library of Historical Children's Literature

The Baldwin Library was founded in 1977 and began as the private collection of Ruth Baldwin (1917–1990), a member of the faculty of Louisiana State University in Baton Rouge from 1956 to 1977. The collection contains over 100,000 books published in Great Britain and the United States from the mid-1600s to the present. Strengths of the collection include English and American editions of the same title, 200 editions of *Robinson Crusoe,* 100 editions of *The Pilgrim's Progress,* Little Golden Books, and the publications of the American Sunday School Union. The Baldwin Library is in the Department of Special Collections of the George A. Smathers Libraries at the University of Florida in Gainesville.

Cotsen Children's Library

The Cotsen Library is based on a donation of children's books by Lloyd E. Cotsen, former CEO of Neutrogena Corporation. The over 100,000 items in the Cotsen Library include rare illustrated children's books, manuscripts, and artwork from the 15th century to the present in over 30 languages. Strengths include medieval manuscripts, an extensive collection of books published by John Newbery, dime novels, and Soviet picture books. The Cotsen Children's Library is a unit within the Department of Rare Books and Special Collections at the Princeton University Library in Princeton, New Jersey.

De Grummond Children's Literature Collection

Founded in 1966 by Dr. Lena Y. de Grummond, the Collection holds the original manuscripts and illustrations of more than 1200 authors and illustrators, as well as 100,000+ published books dating from 1530 to the present. The de Grummond Collection is a special collection of the McCain Library and Archives on the campus of The University of Southern Mississippi in Hattiesburg.

Children's Literature Center at the Library of Congress

Founded in 1963, the Children's Literature Center at the Library of Congress is ensconced in the Rare Books and Special Collections. The Children's Literature Center assists users in gaining access to all children's materials dispersed throughout the Library. The Library of Congress holds approximately 200,000 children's books and related items, such as boxed and board games, sound recordings, maps, and illustrations. Children's fiction, poetry, and folklore are classified and grouped together. However, nonfiction children's books are shelved in their respective subject areas. In short, children's materials are scattered throughout the Library's complex collections of more than 130 million items. The Center is located in the Thomas Jefferson Building of the Library of Congress in Washington, D.C.

Children's Literature Research Collection

The CLRC is an internationally recognized resource in the field of children's literature, and it contains six core collections (including Kerlan and Hess) and several smaller collections. They include collections of comic books, dime novels, story papers, series books, Paul Bunyan books, Oziana, and editions of *Treasure Island*. The CLRC is housed in the Elmer L. Andersen Library, located on the campus of the University of Minnesota in Minneapolis.

The Kerlan Collection of Children's Literature

The Kerlan Collection is the oldest and most well-known of the collections within the CLRC. It contains more than 100,000 children's books as well as original manuscripts, artwork, galleys, and color proofs for more than 13,000 children's books. One-eighth of the books are inscribed by the author or illustrator. The Collection includes books that are significant in the history of children's literature, as well as over 300 periodical titles, 1,200 reference titles, and other items (posters, toys, photographs, figurines) related to children's literature.

The May Massee Collection

In addition to the larger and more comprehensive archives and special collections, there are also many other special collections that contain very specific materials. One of the most interesting of these in terms of scope and depth is the May Massee Collection at Emporia State in Kansas, named for a prominent children's book editor. The collection holds the 930 books she oversaw over a 40-year period. Even her New York City office was reconstituted. Moreover, the collection contains extensive correspondence and manuscripts by authors such as Rumer Godden, art by illustrators such as Kate Seredy, and both art and manuscripts by Robert McCloskey.

Archives and Special Collections— International

Archives or special collections exist in many corners of the world. Public holdings abound in Western nations, residing primarily in national libraries, institutions of higher education, and large public libraries. Private collections are scattered internationally, yet lack of language expertise and communication curtails gathering names and descriptions of such entities.

Collection sites permeate all corners of the globe. Jella Lepman founded the largest—the International Youth Library (IYL)—in Munich, Germany, in 1949, inspiring a similar library in Osaka, Japan. Each seeks books from the entire world; subject specialists work with each geographic or language section. The IYL is the largest library for international children's and youth literature in the world. Its collection is more than a half million volumes in 130 languages, including reference books. Its program includes their coined phrase "reading museums," exhibitions, children's lending library, adult training courses and seminars, publications, study library, and scholarships. The International Institute for Children's Literature, Osaka, formally opened in 1984. Incorporating Professor Shin Torigoe's 19th-century books and periodicals, it expanded to approximately 260,000 volumes and 190,000 issues of 4,700 of periodical titles.

Lepman also encouraged the collecting of books by national sections as part of her vision for the International Board of Books for Young People (IBBY). Its IBBY chapter headquarters in Mexico and Nigeria possess substantial numbers of indigenous books.

As a requirement of the law, publishers in most countries send new titles to their national deposit libraries. In a few of them—such as Sweden, Singapore, and Japan—the law directs children's books as published to a designated alternate library. In Sweden, the children's books transfer to the Swedish Children's Book Institute, located next to a university library. An electronic catalog offers immediate access to the world. Singapore also collects the publisher's books in the four national languages—Chinese, English, Malay, and Tamil. Some are exclusive regarding language.

The National Diet Library in Tokyo incorporated children's books from the Imperial Library. The children's section ultimately separated from the national library and moved to a building located in Ueno Park, Tokyo in 2000. For this section there are two reading rooms—one for Japanese children's books and one for those of other languages. Rules require registration and reader cards. An exhibit gallery on an upper floor showcases historic and contemporary books on subjects such as Canadian Picture

Books and the sun, moon, and space. A slightly different approach occurs in France. For each copy of a children's book deposited at the Bibliotheque Nationale, another also is placed at the Centre National de la Littérature Pour la Jeunesse—La Joie Par les Livres in Paris.

Books may focus on language and even further on time period of publication. The D. J. Williams Collection at the National Library of Wales in Aberystwyth holds 500 volumes in Welsh from 1800 to 1949. Centro Internacional del Libro Infantil y Juvenil in Salamanca collects editions in all languages spoken in Spain, along with books published in Latin America. Estonian and Lithuanian collections limit themselves to those Baltic languages. The National Library of New Zealand in Wellington owns Maori and Pacific Island language editions.

The National Library of Ireland in Dublin collects Irish authors' books and Irish-themed books, if published abroad. Displays during the IRSCL conference in 2006 featured 19th-century chapbooks and contemporary manuscripts and illustrations. Discussion about an archive and book collection at a conference in 1995 was the impetus for the University of South Africa's "Children's Literature Research Unit." It collects books in all South African languages and recently sent loans of books for exhibition to Prague, Mumbai, Jerusalem, Sao Paulo, Lisbon, Hanoi, and Tunis.

Canadian author Lucy Montgomery's manuscripts, journals, scrapbooks, personal papers, and artifacts are not, as one would expect, on Prince Edward Island, the setting for her *Anne of Green Gables* (e.g., Montgomery, 1908) books. Instead, they reside in Ontario at the University of Guelph. That university also holds the largest collection of Scottish books, including children's writers, outside of Scotland.

Tales of Acquisition

Along with collectors, curators shape acquisitions by reaching out to particular potential donors. Curators hear the horror stories of work lost in fire and flood or discarded after the death of a creator. Passionate about the field, staff members go to great lengths to acquire materials. Each collection contains not only the stories within children's and young adult books, but also the stories behind those stories—the stories of the journey that the materials took on their way to the special collection. One such stroy of my own follows.

In 1970, I visited the recently widowed Mallie Tenggren and asked if she would be willing to donate the art of Gustaf Tenggren's more than 50 children's books to the Kerlan Collection. Among them were Little Golden Books including *The Poky Little Puppy* (Lowrey, 1942) and the larger format of *The Night Before Christmas* (Moore, 1955). Mrs. Tenggren shared information about her offer to the University of Maine that the estate, located on Dog's Head Bay in Maine, become a Tenggren museum and student summer art center. In the course of this discussion, I gave an account of the many Swedish Americans who had been and continued to be prominent in Minnesota's immigrant and political history and the fact that the University of Minnesota's Scandinavian Department kept language and literature on the forefront.

A decade passed and the East coast university took no interest in Mrs. Tenggren's museum-center proposal. As a result, Mrs. Tenggren requested that the University of Minnesota curator serve as the executor of all her husband's art, and she bequeathed the children's book art and paintings to the University of Minnesota. In the mid-1980s, the executor for the entire estate telephoned to tell me that the house in Maine needed to be vacated immediately for impending repairs and eventual sale.

In response, I flew with my husband to Boston, rented a car, and headed to the Boothbay Harbor area. Art was scattered throughout the huge house and attached studio, some formally framed and hung on walls, but others stashed in the attic, under the beds, and in closets. Meanwhile, a curator from Sweden wandered about the rooms looking for the folk art pieces that would be shipped in containers to a museum in Dalarna to which they had been promised. A representative of Maine's university picked up paintings and prints by Mexican artists such as Rivera. Unaware of what had transpired years before, he commented that the property and buildings would make an ideal summer program setting.

Typical of a short time frame to swing into action, I retrieved, sorted, and organized the art by title and listed the images for each book. Thirty-two-paged books with unique covers predominated. Some fragile illustrations required hand carrying on the airplane. Others were packed in 54 boxes by my husband, who drove with them to the small local post office where he lifted each one on the scale for the postmistress. He built crates for the larger paintings and transported them to the nearby town's transport company. The last crates were shipped from the Boston airport. On arrival in Minneapolis, the paintings transferred to the University of Minnesota's art museum and the children's book art to the University's library. And here the story ends, happily ever after. The Tenggren art is now available at the Kerlan Collection for study, reprints, and exhibits, and royalty checks from Tenggren's books and reprints fund the collection's preservation and promotion.

Tales of Discovery

A wide array of individuals from various fields and backgrounds come to archival collections with a myriad of questions, seeking access to materials that may satisfy their queries. Those who examine and study the collections include faculty, students, independent scholars, authors, artists, gallery exhibitors, and many other members of the general public. Their interest in particular texts, or the work of specific authors and illustrators, often lead them to surprising and intriguing discoveries, as well as completed theses, dissertations, and published books.

For example, Frances Trice examines children's literature from a design process point of view. Informed by perspectives from the field of Human Ecology, her dissertation "Drawing and the Design Process: An Examination of Design Methods Used by Award-Winning Illustrators of Children's Books" (2004) examined the design processes of Nancy Carlson and Chris Van Allsburg. Data about their design processes were gathered from interviews, articles from scholarly and popular magazines, and web sites. In addition, the illustrators' original working drawings, which are housed in the Children's Literature Research Collection (CLRC) at the University of Minnesota, were included in the study.

As the curator of that collection, I had visited author/illustrator Chris Van Allsburg. During my visit, he told me I could have the items that he'd created and tossed on the floor. I gathered up the wadded tracing papers, ironed them flat at home, and slipsheeted them with acid free paper. In time, it became clear that I had preserved the preliminary drawings for the 1982 Caldecott Medal winner *Jumanji* (Van Allsburg, 1981). They are now protected with mat board for travel on loan. These drawings, among other documents, were thus available to Frances Trice as she completed her work.

Sharon McQueen is a cultural historian of youth literature. Her award-winning dissertation work, *The Story of "The Story of Ferdinand": The Creation of a Cultural Icon* (2010), is multidisciplinary. The goal of McQueen's study is increased insight into the creation and reception of the picture book, *The Story of Ferdinand* (Leaf, 1936). To answer these questions, Sharon McQueen traveled to well over a dozen research sites in six states and Canada. Libraries, archives, special collections, rare book departments, and a publishing house provided a wealth of empirical sources. Over 10,000 documents were digitally recorded and examined. Archival documents included versions of *The Story of Ferdinand* (primarily translations), manuscripts, visual art works, contracts, correspondence (letters, notes, greeting cards, and telegrams) photographs, sound recordings, newspaper and magazine clippings, Disney animated movie cells, store displays, and realia (jewelry, fabrics, toys, etc.).

The Kerlan Collection of the CLRC contained a number of first editions of Munro Leaf and Robert Lawson books, signed to Dr. Irvin Kerlan. These inscriptions revealed that Kerlan was well-regarded by both men. But McQueen was most interested in documents that substantiated her findings that Munro Leaf and Robert Lawson's books had been used by Franklin Publications, a Cold War organization financially aided by the U.S. government, as well as various foundations, to assist in the translation and publication of U.S. books abroad.

The Free Library of Philadelphia holds both the Munro Leaf and the Robert Lawson collections, the former the author and the latter the artist of the picture book. McQueen spent several weeks with these collections, exploring such items as the original manuscript and the dummy. She traveled to New York to visit the Morgan Library and Museum, which contained the original art of the book, and to explore the archives of Viking Children's Books. McQueen spent a week at the May Massee Collection at Emporia State University. May Massee was the book's editor at Viking. As a result of this research, McQueen decided that the creation of *The Story of Ferdinand* could best be told through biographies of those most involved in its creation: Munro Leaf, Robert Lawson, and May Massee. Each comprise a chapter in McQueen's dissertation, and each will eventually be expanded to book-length works.

Sharon McQueen's research has shed light on myths surrounding the book's creation and reception. For example, scholars of children's literature have long believed that *The Story of Ferdinand* was written to convey a political message. McQueen has provided evidence to refute this through the presentation of papers at several conferences of the Children's Literature Association. When Sharon McQueen was awarded the American Library Association's Jesse H. Shera Award for the Support of Dissertation Research, an award intended to provide recognition for dissertation research employing exemplary research design and methods, she was interviewed in an article for *School Library Journal*. She said:

> I think the notion that the book was written as some sort of reaction to the Spanish Civil War was an assumption that was so oft repeated as to now be considered fact... I have yet to find any evidence that supports the notion. Yet, children's literature scholars have often referred to Ferdinand as a "political text." The 2005 first edition of The Norton Anthology of Children's Literature states that Ferdinand is "possibly the most famous example of the picture book as political text" and goes on to state that "Ferdinand was written during the Spanish Civil War." In the journal, *Children & Libraries*, a professor of English states, "Leaf's book about the bull who refused to fight was prompted by the outbreak of the Spanish Civil War."
>
> In fact, Munro Leaf wrote the story in October of 1935. The Spanish Civil War broke roughly nine months later, in July of 1936, and *The Story of Ferdinand* was published in September of 1936. It was clearly not written during the Spanish Civil War, and it was not prompted by its outbreak. The author and illustrator—as well as their wives and children—have always denied that the book had any political origins or intentions. (Whelan, 2008, para 3,4)

Despite the controversy, McQueen's scholarship demonstrates that what many take as "givens" can be unmasked through careful scholarship. Yet, the book's intended audience, *children*, who are often blissfully unaware of adults' academic arguments, continues to clamor for the book. Asked whether the book would maintain its classic status, McQueen responded, "…Ferdinand is most definitely alive and well. As Munro Leaf used to say, 'A little bit of bull goes a long way!'" (para 8).

As a final example, Professor Peter Neumeyer from the University of California Los Angeles (UCLA) perused the manuscript drafts and notes of E. B. White for his book about Charlotte, the spider who was a true friend and a good writer, and Wilbur, the runt pig. *Charlotte's Web* (White, 1952) won a 1953 Newbery honor and became a classic of children's literature. In *The Annotated Charlotte's Web,* Neumeyer (1994) wrote:

> …there is information from White's eight manuscript drafts for *Charlotte's Web* that are deposited at the Cornell University Library, Division of Rare & Manuscript Collections. From these, we may obtain insights into the craftsmanship of a highly conscious and self-aware artist, and gain an appreciation for the difficulties of writing beautiful prose fiction. (p. xvii)

In terms of annotated texts, Neumeyer's text has now become a classic in its own right, a model for scholars intrigued with the possibilities of tracing an author's steps through the process of creating a masterpiece.

Preliminary and On-Site Procedures

The more procedures the researcher understands in advance about research in archives and special collections, the more efficient the experience will be. Prior to a visit, the researcher completes a literature search and identifies the appropriate collection to use. While university and public libraries in the United States tend to be open to the public, private libraries tend to be more restrictive. Land grant universities in the Midwest by law serve the public. The Huntington in Pasadena, California, and the Pierpont Morgan in New York City are private libraries that serve senior scholars. As a result, neophytes in the study of children's books gravitate toward land grant universities. Then the researcher follows the procedures for that particular institution.

In the exploratory stage, the researcher conducts a literature search to ascertain what other research has been published on their topic. Few ongoing projects are confidential, so the curator might share this proprietary information.

To find the appropriate site, the searcher might consult the paper or electronic copy of *Special Collections in Children's Literature: An International Directory* (Jones, 1995). Occasionally a donor restricts access for a designated number of years or until his or her death. Researchers can explore possible fellowships at the institution or other sources for research support and request a lodging list.

On site procedures to use archives and special collections vary and may seem counter intuitive for regular library users. A delicate balance exists between openness and protection, so usually there is no access to shelves, no individual browsing, no checking out books and materials, and no self-service photocopying. Some special collection web sites list holdings, procedures for researchers, and staff information. A few require a letter of introduction on letterhead, an appointment, and a fee. Finally, many request that a copy of an article or book resulting from research in the collection be donated when published.

Some predictable steps follow selection of a site. There are a myriad of forms to complete, from registering to signing a statement regarding the understanding of copyright law to photocopy or digital camera use. Retrieval may take additional time, so patience on the part of the researcher is necessary. Most collections require registration on site, usually supported by a government issued official photo identification and a stated purpose for research. For distant users, electronic registration and requests for reproduction may be possible.

Second, after registering, the user requests materials. The researcher may request an appointment with a staff member who may assist with descriptive wording or holdings. Archives, associated with organization or personal papers, use terminology such as "finding aids" and "processing" to define the description of holdings and procedure for organizing. Special Collections prefer the words "catalogs" and "cataloging."

Staff members may know of materials not yet processed, which may lead to other collections with similar subject matter or other researchers with similar research interests. Unique materials demand original descriptions for their features such as the notes and correspondence for Francesca Lia Block's books. Special collections and archives handle materials differently; the former may provide a "catalog record" for books by Karen Cushman or Lois Lowry and then a "finding aid" for the manuscript drafts.

Third, security measures may require placing one's personal belongings in a locker and bringing only a pencil or a laptop computer into the reading room. Only after hand washing may one proceed to the reading room. Once there, the researcher works in only one box at a time and removes one folder from the box at a time, retaining the order. No food and beverages, cell phones, or conversations are allowed. Using some materials may necessitate gloves or special equipment, such as a book cradle or microfilm reader.

Fourth, each archive has regulations regarding hand held scanners, digital camera use, and photocopy machines. Staff may photocopy or digitize for a fee for a researcher's personal use, but written permission must be granted for further rights, such as using a publication beyond "fair use." Materials published since a particular date may be protected by copyright regulations. The researcher may need to show evidence of permission in writing from an author or publishing company department of rights and permissions before acquiring a reproduction or taking a digital no-flash photograph. Scholarly publishers may insist that the author provide evidence of permission and even pay for the rights to reprint a picture. Heirs who hold literary or artistic rights may insist on substantial payment.

Conclusion

Researchers in archives and special collections include academics, graduate students, undergraduate students, independent scholars, curators of museums and exhibits, and the general public. Scholars, practitioners, and students committed to a career involving children's books can help by visiting an archive or special collection devoted to children's and young adult literature. The options are simultaneously historical and contemporary, broad and narrow, cursory and deep. I would urge scholars of children's and young adult literature in all disciplines to seek out such opportunities and then share what they learn with students and the public on all levels. Such communication should lead to better understanding of the background, depth and uniqueness of book history, and behind the scenes in children's book formulation. In this way, scholars will ensure that archives and special collections will retain their relevancy and thrive in the 21st century.

Literature References

Brown, M. W. (1947). *Goodnight moon* (C. Hurd, Illus.). New York, NY: Harper & Brothers.

Leaf, M. (1936). *The story of Ferdinand* (R. Lawson, Illus.). New York, NY: Viking Penguin.

Lowrey, J. S. (1942). *The poky little puppy* (G. Tenggren, Illus.). New York, NY: Simon & Shuster.

Montgomery, L. M. (1908). *Anne of Green Gables*. Boston, MA: L.C. Page.

Moore, C. C. (1955). *The night before Christmas* (G. Tenggren, Illus.). New York, NY: Simon & Schuster.

Van Allsburg, C. (1981). *Jumanji*. Boston: Houghton Mifflin.

White, E. B. (1952). *Charlotte's web* (G. Williams, Illus.). New York, NY: Harper & Row.

Academic References

Field, C. W. (Ed.). (1969). *Subject collections in children's literature* (1st ed.). National Planning Committee for Special Collections. Children's Services Division. American Library Association. New York, NY: R.R. Bowker.

Field, C. W. (Ed.). (1982). *Special collections in children's literature* (Rev. ed.). National Planning for Special Collections Committee, Association for Library Service to Children, American Library Association. Chicago, IL: American Library Association.

Jones, D. B. (Ed.). (1995). *Special collections in children's literature: An international directory*. National Planning for Special Collections Committee, Association for Library Service to Children, American Library Association. Chicago, IL: American Library Association.

Marcus, L. S. (1999). *Margaret Wise Brown: Awakened by the moon*. New York, NY: W. Morrow.

Marcus, L. S. (2007). *Golden legacy: How Golden Books won children's hearts, changed publishing forever, and became an American icon along the way*. New York, NY: Golden Books/Random House.

McQueen, S. (2010). *The story of "The story of Ferdinand": The creation of a cultural icon*. Unpublished doctoral dissertation, University of Wisconsin-Madison.

Neumeyer, P. F. (1994). *The annotated Charlotte's web*. New York, NY: HarperCollins.

Trice, F. (2004). *Drawing and the design process: An examination of design methods used by award-winning illustrators of children's books*. Unpublished doctoral dissertation, University of Minnesota.

Whelan, D. L. (2008, June 11). Sharon McQueen talks about her fascination with *The story of Ferdinand. School Library Journal*. Retrieved March 10, 2010, from http://www.schoollibraryjournal.com/article/CA6569531.html?nid=2413&rid=88962601

Young, H. (1983). *The ALA glossary of library and information science*. Chicago, IL: American Library Association.

Point of Departure

Leonard S. Marcus

My work over the last 25 years has taken me to most of the major American research collections in children's literature as well as to many other, less frequented repositories, both public and private, with holdings of original source materials of interest to me. I have arrived at some archives knowing precisely what I wanted to see, but more often the experience has been more in the nature of a fishing excursion: a patient trolling through a body of manuscripts or photographs or letters in hopes either of simply immersing myself more deeply in my subject of the moment or of coming away with a sack load of keepers—elusive answers perhaps to a list of long puzzling questions; or fresh insights gleaned from a study of images or documents that somehow bring my project a step closer to completion. While writing *Golden Legacy*, my history of Golden Books, for example, my editor and I visited the Kerlan Collection where we pored over the contents of more than 100 boxes of illustrator Gustav Tenggren's artwork. We knew Tenggren's finished art well but were thrilled to discover a series of preliminary studies for *Shy Little Kitten* that vividly confirmed the knowledge of animal anatomy that underpinned even the more "adorable " side of Tenggren's varied and prodigious output.

Louise Seaman Bechtel, the founding director of Macmillan's Department of Books for Boys and Girls nearly a century ago, bequeathed a stash of her correspondence to her alma mater, Vassar College. A number of years ago, as I read through the thick sheaf of letters written to her by her friend and author Elizabeth Coatsworth, I became keen to find the other half of the correspondence. The pre-Internet search tools then available to me all came up dry. But knowing that Coatsworth had lived in Maine, I telephoned a few likely Maine repositories and on my third try—a call to the Maine Women Writers' Archive at the University of New England, Portland—I hit pay dirt. Until then, neither archive knew the whereabouts of the other half of a substantial 50-year-long exchange of letters whose ownership they shared. More and more such links between collections are sure to emerge; let's hope that information about them will be freely shared.

I have had my share of fruitless searches. Seemingly useless material, however, can sometimes prove to be of unexpected value. While researching my biography of Margaret Wise Brown I visited the Archives of American Art, in Washington, D.C., to scan the diaries of illustrator Charles G. Shaw for references to his friendship with Brown. I knew from the printed finding aid that Shaw's diaries ran to dozens of volumes—a promising sign, I thought. It soon became apparent to me, however, that the author of *It Looked Like Spilt Milk* was a wholly pedestrian diarist. Typical entries gave the times of day he rose and went to bed, a weather report, the number of hours spent painting, the names of lunch and dinner companions, but with almost no descriptive detail or reflective commentary. Shaw was no Anaïs Nin!

My first reaction was one of extreme disappointment. Then I realized that Shaw's diaries might in fact help solve a vexing problem I had. A friend of Brown's had recently sent me a boxful of her letters. Exasperatingly (for me), Brown had not dated most of them, and I needed to know when the letters had been written in order to know where to place them in her life story. Gradually, by cross-referencing the letters with Shaw's matter-of-fact mentions of Brown's "new apartment," impending trips to Maine, etc., I succeeded in dating much of that treasure trove of correspondence. I have always been grateful that Shaw's "boring" diaries were preserved, and I think my experience makes the case for saving more rather than less whenever possible, and for not presuming that the importance of a document can be judged once and for all.

The first years of my career predated the Internet. In 1980, I began my quest for information about Margaret Wise Brown by publishing an old-fashioned author's query in the *New York Times Book Review*. Nine letters came back in response: eight from *Times* readers who loved *Goodnight Moon* and wanted to tell somebody; the ninth, typed on heavy, engraved stationery, was from a man who introduced himself as a college friend of Clement Hurd. That last letter, it turned out, was all I needed to start me on my way, as its author helped arrange a meeting with Hurd and his wife, who introduced me to *their* old friend Leonard Weisgard, who introduced me to his friend Alvin Tresselt, and on and on, with each of these friends and colleagues of Brown having much to tell me that illuminated the Brown materials to be found at the Kerlan Collection and more than a dozen other libraries.

Now that special collections have web sites on which are sometimes posted detailed finding aids and even virtual exhibitions, it has become easier to scope out the archival portion of the research landscape and to decide in advance whether a trip to a far-flung collection is likely to be worth the time and expense. The more such information becomes available online, the better it will be for all concerned.

While archives will inevitably compete with each other from time to time for the stewardship of this or that mother lode of material, ultimately all stand to gain the most from cooperation and a commitment to open access that allows scholars to do the hard but rewarding work of putting the pieces together.

Part 3

THE WORLD AROUND

Children's and young adult literature is not simply a vehicle for helping young people acquire conventional and cultural literacies, nor is it merely a site for scholarly cogitation. It is also a major player in popular culture and a prospering economic concern. In recent years, for instance, books like the *Harry Potter* and the *Twilight* series have become global points of reference with millions of readers worldwide, but other books in the past, such as *Anne of Green Gables* and *Pippi Longstocking*, have also found international audiences and spawned their own industries of tourism, merchandise, and adaptations. Comprehensive research into children's and young adult literature, then, must examine the contexts in which these books exist and travel through the larger world.

At the heart of this research are questions surrounding publishing, marketing, and distribution practices. As with most products, the end user doesn't get to decide what gets produced to meet needs and satisfy desires, but through clever marketing and manipulation, we are taught to desire what manufacturers and marketers make available to us. A feedback loop develops, where what sells gets replicated, products are refined or innovated according to market research, and a balance between the new and the familiar is maintained. A lot of children's and young adult literature is like that—variations on familiar plot lines and character types, often aligned in trends that flare, burn brightly, and then fade, all packaged to sell.

Children's and young adult literature, then, is undeniably a commodity. This consequence of robust consumerism both increases its value in certain contexts and limits its accessibility in others. Actual books in the hands of children have come to be understood as a fairly undeniable good, but academics are more mixed in our responses to the kinds of consumerism that surround the production of books. What happens when the books become ads for expensive dolls, plush toys, play sets, movies, UGG boots, costumes, games, decorating themes, etc.? Doesn't the book itself get lost, its value as literature cheapened and reduced to a brand through flashy merchandising? Or, on the other hand, does this resituate the book —meaning its story, its characters, its setting—at the center of a community of individuals who enter its world and live in and through it in creative ways? Whether one considers it a boon or bane, aggressive cross-marketing of children's books and related products is a booming business that begs for thoughtful research and analysis.

But of course, literature is so much more than a product; it is an art form as well. Authors and illustrators have something important and fresh to say to their audiences, many work continually to expand the boundaries of their art form, and editors and publishers are seeking luminous works to bring to their intended audience. This desire to produce quality literary art is heightened by the knowledge that these works are specifically aimed at young people. Always, always, there is the sense of that end user, that child or teen who will find in the book some nugget that will open her eyes to the world as possibility and wonder.

Because this sense of a child audience and our obligations to it varies across time and culture, levels of access to children's and young adult literature vary as well. Advocates of children's and young adult literature chafe against barriers of economic necessities and/or inequities that prevent widespread publishing of translated books as well as getting books into the hands of children at all. Countries without a robust publishing industry for adult books are even less likely to spend their scant resources on publishing children's books, while the difficulty of finding skilled, committed translators combines with a concern for publishers' bottom lines to mitigate against the availability of either indigenously produced books or quality translations for children in many places in the world.

Grassroots efforts, NGOs, and other non-profit organizations work tirelessly to improve access to books and create reading cultures in their countries. The Astrid Lindgren Memorial Award has supported the efforts of two such organizations—Banco del Libro in Venezuela and Tamer Institute for Community Education in Palestine—while others, such as Ethiopia Reads, the Little Hands Trust, and Stories Across Africa to name but a few, have sought through local and online networking to generate donations and increase awareness and involvement. Clearly, more work needs to be done to improve access to books everywhere in the world, and this work is being undertaken by academics in the field who adopt activist roles to complement their scholarly ones.

In developed countries, questions are more likely to arise about limiting access to books in the form of censorship, and exploring the effects and politics of awards and reviewing on what counts as literature that adults feel ought to be read by today's youth. The motivations for these discussions stem from similar roots—a concern for children's vulnerability on the one hand, and for the kinds of values and taste that we wish to cultivate in our children on the other. In the midst of this complex swirl of voices that protest, critique, and/or celebrate books, a single note emerges: We believe in the power of children's and young adult literature to transform lives, for better or worse, and hence our responses to the literature always proceed from moral and ideological dimensions as well as aesthetic ones.

Yet, for many of us, the aesthetic dimension is the most powerful. We come to the study of children's and young adult literature for many reasons and from many backgrounds, but mostly, we come out of love. Perhaps because these books contain the stories that have shaped our imaginary geographies, we want to visit them again and again, and in various ways. Who among us doesn't have an object of some kind—be it a doll, a mug, some stationary, a puppet, or a plush toy —on our office bookshelves that reminds us of a favorite character? And who among us, given the chance, wouldn't go to the spaces that have been lovingly set aside to honor the authors whose voices echo in our own voices, whose landscapes feature prominently in our own inner views? Museums, author's homes, and even theme parks can offer us one more layer of experience, often overlooked, in our scholarly journeys.

Children's and young adult literature thrives in a variety of contexts, making interdisciplinary research a rich venue for study. Tracing a text through its incarnations, translations, adaptations, and contextualizations can afford not only fruitful possibilities for publication, but also for pleasure. And understanding the difficulties that many have regarding simple access to those sorts of pleasures can spur us to activism as well.

28

Where Worlds Meet

Ana Maria Machado

In this chapter, two recipients of the Hans Christian Andersen Award share their views on reaching across worlds with stories that contribute to our shared humanity.

Ana Maria Machado and Katherine Paterson first presented their essays at the 8th IBBY Regional Conference (2009). Through her understanding of translating literature and having her own writing translated, Machado traces the meeting of ideas and imaginations across the expanse of national borders, the shrinking time and space of digital worlds, and the artistry of stories. In turn, Paterson expresses the difficulty—and the ultimate value—of reaching across worlds, and into her own emotional memory, to discover the words and images that will bring a Kosava refugee family's experience to life. Both authors asks us to make our passion for international literature "contagious."

Where worlds really meet, it makes no difference if someone is different. Because in such meetings, differences are part of the fun. They make it possible for one to complete the other, by mutual supply of what is missed on each side. They make it possible for one to attract the other and so, to fall in love. They arouse curiosity and so they make learning easier and they build understanding. They show the immense variety of humankind and so they challenge an inward journey, in search of common features.

Ideally, every human being, from an early age, should have the opportunities of crossing frontiers, meeting neighbors, going abroad, getting to know different people and landscapes, listening to other languages, eating different food, being in touch with the beautiful diversity of cultures. But this is not so fully possible, for the whole process is not as easy as it appears when saying it. So, this need

must be met by other means. That's where imagination and symbolic language begin their work.

Throughout history, people have gathered around those who travelled and, upon their return, told what they had seen on their journeys, brought souvenirs, showed images of every kind and shared with them the meetings they had with others. And even more, travelers began writing about what they had seen, or painting landscapes that had impressed them, or singing songs or playing music they had heard. Later on, with technological developments, movement and stories between worlds continued, with the help of photography, slides, prints, films, radio, telephone, television, videos, and audio recordings. Now, in our day, with the web and the possibility of instant accessing any point on the planet, with camera and sound, even with the help of small devices that fit in one's hands, worlds can meet more easily than ever. Information now can be shared so completely and so quickly through digital means that the situation would be perfect for worlds meeting—if information were enough.

But something else is required in order to get at true meetings: something that goes beyond hard facts, concrete data and rational features; something that touches emotions, feelings, personal identification, longing for closeness, mutual sympathy or compassion. That's where personal expression comes in. Objective data are not enough. Subjective touches are needed. That's where a good story, well told, can bring characters alive, in situations that make it possible for different worlds to meet. That's where literature is needed—the art of words, able to express ambivalences and alternative experiences, able to move, to touch one's heart, or to give pangs and thrills, by the mere use of language—an everyday resource—in surprising ways, through an aesthetic approach to words and clauses.

This is possible because art goes beyond everyday life. In art, other worlds meet—beginning with inner and outer worlds. When an author, a painter, a musician, or any artist creates his or her work, it is always as an inner response to an outer provocation, directed to an outer expression. Second, in building this inner response, the artist mixes different worlds, working at different levels. In creating, the artist delves into feelings, reasonings, previous knowledge, new research discoveries, dialogues with lifelong readings, memories, dreams, fears, intuitions, intentions, emotions, unconscious factors, conscious writing devices and so on. This dynamic interplay gives the work its strength, by means of a series of psychological mechanisms that involve projection and identification and make it possible for a reader to recognize that work of art as being also, at least partially, his or her own expression of inner worlds.

This is also called the appropriation of a work of art by its reader, spectator, or consumer—who incorporates the artist's work as his or her own property, as part of oneself. When a reader goes through this process and appropriates a text, for instance, the feeling is that it speaks through the reader's voice and, in doing so, it gives shape and sense to some deep, blurred and unexpressed perceptions that begged to come to the surface. Some analysts, such as Roger Chartier (1996), for instance, tend to associate this quality with the definition of literature itself, described as a written piece that deals with language in such a way that it allows multiple re-appropriations at different readings. In other words, in the literary process, different worlds also meet—the writer's worlds and the multiple readers' worlds—or different worlds inhabited by the same reader in different moments of his or her life. It is all part of the process and mystery of literature.

Another mystery in this writing and reading process involves an author being able to imagine a different self. Sometimes this is done with such talent that the story convinces the reader of being the other. In doing so, someone who has never killed anyone—like Dostoyevsky or Albert Camus and all of us, the readers of their novels—are able to have an insight into a murderer's mind. Or someone who has never turned into an insect—such as Kafka—can write a book like *The Metamorphosis*. Factual realism is not a prerequisite for literature. But to achieve that excellence of imagination, art and talent are required. Good intentions are not enough. And trying to be literal is almost always a wasted effort.

When we were small children and listened to a story like *Hansel and Gretel*, for instance, we could imagine what it means to face starvation or to be abandoned in the dark among beasts and all the night dangers, by those on whom we counted and who should care for us. For a child living in the streets of an African or Latin American city, this feeling is fully understood, even though the story was written in Germany centuries ago. Worlds meet in a story like *Hansel and Gretel*. Like its characters, this story journeys deep into fear, despair and the faint hope of being able to overcome all that awful and harsh reality in spite of the adults—be they parents, stepparents, absent parents, bosses, or rulers … or the witch.

"Meeting the Other" in Art

Lately, in the context of postcolonial studies, it has become almost an obsession to approach literature with eyes trying to discover messages, subjects, intentions, and packaged formula, while only limited concern is given to literary qualities. Such an attitude may have been very useful in the deconstruction of a colonial canon imposed on others. But it is not enough. Maybe today it runs the risk of becoming a new kind of enforced imposition, an artificial pressure that demands the occurrence of certain cultural features. It may be time to come to a more balanced view, that is not concerned only with stressing individual cultural differences, but may allow our common humanity to blossom and to flow more freely. In doing so, we may even discover the existence of certain rather naïve assumptions about what we had been doing, in depicting those cases where worlds were *supposed* to meet. Some years ago, Edward Said (1979) called our attention to the fact that *orientalism* managed to build a certain false idea of the East, through writings by non-Easterners, who tried to picture the other's culture and finally led to views that were charged with exoticism, Eurocentrism, and patronizing attitudes. They might even have been well-intentioned, but the result did not help worlds to really meet and appreciate or understand each other.

If our aim is to shift the representation of the other, it seems to me that the best way to do so would be to listen to what the other really has to say: Hear, see, feel the other's voice in the other's words. Instead of trying to write or use different media to create an *interpretation* of otherness, why not meet otherness through what otherness creates? Of course, if one meets different worlds, gets near them and mixes with others in everyday life, one's creation will naturally reflect those meetings; it cannot be avoided. It is highly desirable and should be promoted—in life. Any artist who lives under those conditions will probably bring its reflections to his or her work. But if it is not the case, the best would be to translate and read what others are already writing and creating, instead of trying to speak for them. To be in touch with the other's productions can be a richer experience than insisting on presenting ourselves disguised as the other and projecting our voices on the other.

An Author's Worlds

Working from my own experiences as an author, I want to show how this process of being in the relation with otherness may make its appearance in a story, even when we are not thinking about it—just by reflecting the background of meetings, readings, and feelings from my life in Brazil, being a Brazilian. Let me introduce my books translated into English.

Like *Nina Bonita* (2001), for instance. As described in the publisher's catalogue, "enchanted by Nina Bonita's black skin, a white rabbit determines to find a way to have children as beautiful and black as she is." With hints at the worlds of ancestors and descendants, of black people and white people, the story also deals with different ideas of beauty in different worlds, with the meeting of different continents, and of children's and adults' points of view.

Me in the Middle (2003) deals with shifts in time and makes three different centuries meet, each one with its own world. But it also weaves a story in which girls' worlds and boys' worlds must meet as they grow up, in times when gender roles are changing. A certain kind of time shifting is also present in *From Another World* (2006), a kind of ghost story. Contemporary children spend some time in a country guesthouse, in a former plantation. And they meet the ghost of a slave girl who lived and died there. This is not only a meeting between past and present worlds, but also between our world and another one, a world that considered it normal to rely on slavery and to treat people as merchandise. It is also a meeting that shows that, contrary to what most would like to believe, those two worlds are not so far apart, even today.

But I would like to take a closer look at another book, still not available in English. It is a book of mine called *Mas Que Festa!/What a Party!* (1999). When I started the book, I meant to develop a kind of philosophic reasoning, along the lines of a linguistic challenge, under the cover of a language play, exploring the richness of if-clauses, subjunctive clauses, possibilities, risks, and consequences, etc. In the process of writing, it followed its own path and became a playful book about worlds meeting. A rough translation from Portuguese to English would be:

WHAT A PARTY!
Be careful!
If your birthday is near and your mother says:

—I guess I'll bake a cake. Why don't you invite some friends to come and play with you?
You may remember that Bob has a nice brother. Then, you may ask:
—May my friends bring someone?
If your mother is absent-minded, she may just say:
—Of course! Whatever you want...

And so, if you are not careful, you may write an invitation just like mine:
Come to my birthday party. On Saturday.
Bring whoever you want. And whatever you want.

If Bob brings his brother Simon, they may want to bring a football. And their mother may send some coconut candies, to share at the party.

If Moacir comes with Maíra (who may bring her parakeet), of course Dona Iracema will take the chance and send a boxful of cashew cupcakes...

If Miguel brings his sister Fatima, they may bring their dog. And their mother Munira will certainly send some homus and kekab for everyone...

If Giovani brings his cousin, maybe they leave the cat at home, but I am sure Dona Gina will bake at least six big pizzas for them to bring. And send some ice cream for dessert...

If Elisa and Frederico come, maybe Frau Hilda doesn't like their idea of bringing the canary. So, she may bake a pie and some biscuits, to apologize...

If Dona Maria knows about it, the least Manuel and his parrot are bringing is a bowl of egg sweets and a lot of small codfish cakes...

And Mrs. Yoko will insist on preparing some sushis for Toshiro to bring, even if his turtle doesn't come along also...

And if Doña Carmen has no time to prepare a paella, at least she will send different kinds of olives, because she thinks that Pedro and Rosa always miss some olives in the pastry and spring rolls that Chang's mother generally cooks...

It may be very difficult to find some place on the table with all that, with Dona Nieta's cheese bread, Dona Vicentina's beans, Dona Esther's *couscous*, Dona Flor's *vatapa,* Dona Iara's *açai,* Dona Rita's fish stew, Dona Sonia's *strogonoff...*

Rodrigo may arrive too early, in order to prepare the barbecue...

But Zabele may arrive too late, and bring along a whole afro-band...

By then, Severino's friends may already have been dancing *forró* for hours...

And Edmond's gang may be in other room, dancing funk...

If you are not careful, you will have to provide some room for two soccer teams to play. And there will still be lots of people everywhere, laughing and speaking at the same time. A lot of noise, a lot of eating, a lot of dancing.

It may well happen that the night comes and goes, and a new day begins, and the party still goes on—if the parents keep on chatting and having just one more beer before taking the children home.

So, be careful! Very careful!

Or your birthday party may be the craziest and funniest party in the world.

A real Brazilian party.

But it is also interesting to see the Spanish and French translations, adapted to different societies, with different illustrations and references to different immigrant groups in each context. I think that, better than anything else I could say, those different versions *show* what I mean by cultural meetings, intercultural approaches, policentric multiculturalism, the richness of points of view from different cultures. They stress how much, in children's books, there are meetings between the author's and the illustrator's views, or the role an editor may play in those meetings. For instance, in the Spanish edition, it was set in a series. So, the book size was reduced to less than half the size of the French one—the elements in the illustrations (and the meeting of worlds) had to be squeezed to fit and look almost crammed sometimes, but it works beautifully.

On the other hand, the French publisher decided that it should be a big book—to have room for all the worlds to meet. And when the illustrator brought her first works, each one in a page, beautifully framed, side by side with the text, I liked them very much. But the editor rejected them on the grounds that the whole story was about overflowing and exaggeration, frontier-crossing, and culture-mixing. So, we should have text and images together, with no boundaries, no frames at all. He insisted on not having a purely French Cartesian viewpoint, with everything in its right place, but a festive celebration. We can never thank him enough for that decision: the result seems perfect to me, and the illustrator was so happy to take up that challenge. The illustrations are of worlds meeting, in a place far from Brazil, but very much a party for people who enjoy one another's presence.

Point of Departure

Katherine Paterson

There was an article in the *New York Times Magazine* on September 10, 2009 (Thompson, 2009), that talked about social contagion. It seems two researchers are seeking to prove that not only are colds and flu catching, but so are things like obesity and smoking and depression. The good news about social contagion is that thinness and non-smoking and happiness are also catching. Based on evidence gathered from participants in the more than 50-year-old Framingham Heart Study, the participants, it appeared, "influenced one another's health just by socializing." The people you hang around with have, in other words, a lot to do with how you feel and behave. I haven't caught thinness yet from my skinny acquaintances, but the article gave me an additional reason to look forward to this conference. I figure that this weekend (during the 2009 Regional International Board on Books for Young People Conference), I'm catching all kinds of good things from friends near and far, and when we go home tomorrow we'll all be spreading this contagion of enthusiasm for bringing books to children all over the globe.

None of us would be here today if it were not for children's books. More personally, I would never have had the opportunity to meet my friends, Carmen Diana Dearden and Ana Maria Machado if it were not for children's books. Carmen Diana and I met in New Delhi where she, as president of IBBY, handed me the 1998 Hans Christian Andersen medal. I did not know then that that was to mark the beginning of a wonderful friendship now more than 10 years old. Ana Maria's and my connection goes back even further when she chose to translate my book *The Master Puppeteer* (1976) into Portuguese. Can you imagine the thrill of that? Having one of Brazil's leading writers choose to translate your book so that children in her own country could read it? And that was only the first of my books that she went on to translate. I was there in Cartagena, Colombia, when she received her own long overdue Andersen medal, and it is a joy and honor to be sharing the stage with her this afternoon.

I think of Carmen Diana and Ana Maria and I look out at this audience and see more people I have come to know and love through the world of children's books, and marvel today as I often do how one person could be so fortunate. Writing books for American children gave me an introduction to what was then called, "Friends of IBBY," and USBBY, as we are now known, gave me an introduction to IBBY, and then IBBY awarded me the Andersen Medal, which, in turn, gave me an entry to the wide and diverse world of persons united in their desire to give to children everywhere the gifts of knowledge and understanding that literature offers. I am forever grateful.

Not long ago my English editor of many years asked me if I had ever dreamed my life as a writer would turn out as it has. "I never dreamed that I would ever get published," I answered. I have many friends who are very fine writers, and it seems to me that all of them knew by the time they were 10 years old that they had been born to be writers. When I was 10 years old, I wasn't sure whether I wanted to be a movie star or a missionary.

It would be nice to be able to look back and see signs of early promise. Alas, you would search in vain. When I won my first literary prize at the age of 44, a friend, who had also lived in China and attended Shanghai American School during the time I was there, decided to look into her collection of school newspapers and see if I had written anything for the *Shanghai American*. This is what she found and gleefully quoted to anyone she heard congratulate me for winning the National Book Award:

Pat, pat, pat.
There is the rat.
Where is the cat?
Pat, pat, pat.

Right beside this, my first published work, was a letter from the teacher that read: "The second graders' work is not up to our usual standards this week...." So, my first published work was published alongside my first critical review.

I once read a speech by a fine writer who said that the thing that qualified her to be a writer for children was her photographic memory of childhood. I can hardly remember what I had for lunch yesterday, much less my entire childhood, with any kind of precision. But I do have, I think, a good emotional memory. I remember not so much the details of the events themselves, but how they felt to me.

There is one story from my childhood that I both remember and was told, so that I probably cannot disentangle the two. It was January of 1938. The war between China and Japan had begun in earnest the previous summer. We had been caught in the mountains on vacation, and with battles raging, only my father was allowed to go home. After five frightening months of air raids, news of battles and atrocities, not knowing what was happening to our beloved father, he finally returned. Soon afterwards, we went down the mountain and, along with many other foreign families, took a river steamer to Hangzhou where we boarded a specially designated train covered with large Red Crosses.

We traveled from Central China all the way south to British ruled Hong Kong. The seven of us had spent days on the journey. On the train we were crowded into a single sleeping compartment where we both ate and slept. My sister Helen was not quite two and baby Anne was less than five months old. The British authorities had no idea what to do with this trainload of foreign refugees, so while the fathers were out scouring the crowded city for reasonably priced shelter, the mothers and children just sat on their luggage in the vast lobby of the Peninsula Hotel which was then and may still be the grandest of all Hong Kong's grand hotels.

Naturally, the elegant British, European, and American tourists who had paid hundreds of pounds for the privilege of staying in the Peninsula were appalled and offended by this filthy lot of women and children who were cluttering up *their* lobby.

My mother, who was not a bitter woman, could not recall that long day without bitterness. "I watched them as they passed by with sneers on their faces and I wanted to cry out to them: 'Do you think I like being here? Do you think I want my children to be dirty?'" She would shake her head. "They couldn't even smile at the baby," she said. "What kind of person can't even smile at a baby?" And she would always end this story by saying, "I can never see a picture of refugees in the paper without remembering how it feels."

I was only five, but the years since have not cured me of the memory of how it feels. I hope they never do. If you need an explanation of why I write the kind of books that I do, perhaps it is found, at least in part, in the lobby of the Peninsula Hotel. I never want to forget that child. I want to keep her a part of all I write and do.

We had to leave China once more at the end of 1940 and come once again to the country my parents called home. I was frightened by the war, and I wanted America to be my home, too. But America was not my home. I seemed quite as alien to my classmates as they did to me. They made fun of my clothes, my accent, and the country I loved best. I realize that the seeds of some of my best writing go back to miserable days in the fourth grade at Calvin H. Wiley Elementary School, but I can't recall once saying to my forlorn little nine-year-old self, "Buck up, Old Girl, someday you're going to make a mint out of all this misery."

While the playgrounds and classrooms were largely places of terror and anxiety for me, the library was a sanctuary. It was there that the wonderful school librarian introduced me to dozens of friends who never made fun of me, never bullied me. The friends I found in books not only helped me to understand myself better, they made it possible for me to come to understand and reach out to others. I remember how comforted I was, reading *The Secret Garden* (Burnett, 2003). Here was another child in exile from the land in which she had been born. Mary Lennox was so like me. She was terribly lonely and had a fearful temper, but imperfect and unlovable as she was, she was given the key to a secret garden. When I am asked what my goal as a writer might be, my answer is this: I want to write a book that will do for a child what *The Secret Garden* did for me nearly 70 years ago.

But back to the lobby of the Peninsula Hotel. I think it may be responsible for my newest book. Over the years countless people have come up to me and told me they have the perfect idea for me. To which I say: "That's your idea. You write it."

This new book is the single exception. We were taking off our choir robes after church one Sunday when Steve Dale said to me: "I think you should write a book about the Haxhuis."

The Haxhui family were Albanian refugees whom our church had sponsored in 1999 after the horrors of 1998–99 in their native Kosovo. I had been out of town on vacation when they arrived and, since they were nominally Muslim, they hadn't been to church, so I had never met them. Steve and his wife Wendy took me to the apartment the church had rented for them, and I had a delightful afternoon. They served tea and showed me pictures of their old home, but there was not much conversation as their English was poor and my Albanian non-existent. I knew a little of their story from Steve—how a Serbian friend that Mr. Haxhui had served with in the Yugoslav Army with had called him just before the worst of the troubles began and warned him to take his family and get out of Kosovo immediately, that terrible things were about to happen to Albanians. So, the Haxhuis left their relatives and the furniture store that they lived above and fled to Macedonia where they lived in a refugee camp until coming to Vermont.

Some years ago, Avi came up with the idea that, in the tradition of Charles Dickens, we writers for children should begin doing newspaper serial stories. These stories, known as Breakfast Serials, are now carried in papers across the United States. I wrote one of the early stories, and Avi had been asking me to write a new one. So, after months of intensive research, I was able to write a newspaper serial not really about the Haxhuis, but about a fictitious refugee family from Kosovo. There were 15 chapters. Each chapter was three double-spaced pages long, the third page ending in a cliff-hanger to make sure readers would buy the newspaper the following week to find out what had happened. The serial, entitled, "Long Road Home" (2004), was well received and ran in almost 100 newspapers around the country. It would have ended there, but my editor of over 30 years, Virginia Buckley, saw it and wanted me to rewrite the story as a novel.

I didn't think it was possible. I did not speak Albanian, I had never been to either Kosovo or Macedonia. The Haxhui family had moved to Michigan, and I was totally frustrated in my efforts to meet any other Kosovar refugees.

I was on the verge of throwing up my hands in defeat, when one day, desperately surfing the Internet, I came across nearly 200 gorgeous photographs of Kosovo, taken by someone calling himself, Kosova Cajun. I emailed the photographer and told him my problem. I needed someone who really knew Kosovo to answer my questions, read my drafts, and help me understand the people, their culture, and the crisis they'd endured.

Mark Orfila did far more than that. He and his family had lived in Kosovo for seven years and, during the worst of the war, had worked in a Macedonian refugee camp. He read every draft and every re-write of every draft, going through them paragraph by paragraph. If he didn't know the answer to a question, he asked an Albanian friend. I could not have done the book without him.

A bookseller friend asked me if I was as hard on my characters in *The Day of the Pelican* (2009) as I usually am. Well, yes, I am. Blame the Peninsula Hotel if you like for that. But it isn't just a tragic tale; it is a tale of new immigrants finding their place among us, which I believe, is a story for our time and our place.

My first three novels were set in Japan. I lived there for four years and I wanted to share my love of Japan with American children. Ten years after my first novel set in Japan was published, I finally was able to tell a story set in China, my literal native land. I'm very happy to say that this book, *Rebels of the Heavenly Kingdom* (1983), has recently been re-issued by Groundwood Books. Now I'm well aware that I am not Japanese or Chinese much less Albanian Kosovar. There are those who feel that I have no right to tell these stories. But neither am I the foundling son of a slave in 19th-century Vermont or the daughter of a prison inmate or a child of a striker calling for bread and roses in 1912. I'm not even a boy of a poor white family in rural Virginia. I have met and become all these people through the world of my imagination. Of course, there is always the danger that I will get it wrong, but believe me, when I do, there is never any shortage of folks out there to set me straight.

If 40 years ago I didn't believe I would ever be published, I certainly didn't dare dream that children across the world would be reading my stories, but because other countries believe in translation, and gifted writers like Ana Maria are willing and able to take on this task, this miracle has happened. The lament that we in the U.S. seldom translate and publish stories from other countries is a constant refrain in IBBY and USBBY gatherings. To be sure there are a few daring North American publishers, our own Patsy Aldana at Groundwood Books in Canada foremost among them, that will take the risk to do this. But we all know how infrequently this happens. I think we have to find more creative ways to persuade publishers to publish translated books and teachers and librarians to buy them when they are published. Those of you who know of books from other cultures that American children would enjoy as well as profit from, please bring them to the attention of sympathetic editors. And those of you who buy books for libraries and school systems, please ask the publishers for such books and then buy them and introduce them to young readers.

When Jimmy Carter was asked the most life changing experience of his presidency, he said it was his friendship with Anwar Sadat. He, a devout Southern Baptist, and Sadat, a devout Muslim, spent time at Camp David talking about faith—not trying to convert each other, but seeking to know and better understand the mind and heart of the other.

Not many of our children would have the opportunity that our former president had, but one way they can have friends in other countries is by giving them books that bring children of other lands and cultures alive. Jella Lepman, founder of IBBY, dreamed that through books the children of the world might be able to make peace. It's not a pipe dream. Because how could you bear the thought of bombing the home of a friend?

If you're not sure where to start finding these important books, please consult the USBBY website and sample something not on your usual read aloud list or list of books you suggest for children to read (www.USBBY.org). The USBBY list is important for breaking out of the usual list of books (good as they are) that U.S. students read year after year.

The USBBY website also links to an annual listing of outstanding international books translated and available in the United States. That's a good starting point. If those books sell well, publishers will be encouraged to publish more translations. Enthusiasm for books from other cultures is surely as contagious as thinness. We already have, through USBBY and IBBY a community of support and caring. All we need to do, friends, is spread the contagion.

Literature References

Burnett, F. H. (2003). *The secret garden.* New York, NY: Signet. (Originally published in 1911)

Machado, A.M. (1999). *Mas que festa!/What a party!* (G. Lima, Illus.) Rio de Janeiro, Brazil: Editora Nova Fronteira.

Machado, A. M. (2001). *Nina Bonita* (R. Faria, Illus.). San Diego, CA: Kane/Miller.

Machado, A.M. (2003). *Me in the middle* (C. Merola, Illus.). Toronto, Canada: Groundwood Books.

Machado, A.M. (2003). *From another world* (L. Brandâo, Illus.). Toronto, Canada: Groundwood Books.

Paterson, K. (1976). *The master puppeteer* (H. Wells, Illus.). New York, NY: HarperTrophey.

Paterson, K. (2004). *The long road home* (E. A. McCulley, Illus.). Denver, CO: Breakfast Serials.

Paterson, K. (2008). *Rebels of the heavenly kingdom.* Toronto, Canada: Groundwood Books (Originally published in 1983)

Paterson, K. (2009). *The day of the pelican.* Boston, MA: Clarion.

Academic References

Chartier, R. (1996). *On the edge of the cliff: History, language, and practices.* Baltimore, MD: The Johns Hopkins University Press.

Said, E. (1979). *Orientalism.* New York, NY: Vintage.

Thompson, C. (2009, September 10). Are your friends making you fat? *The New York Times Magazine.* Retrieved on March 8, 2010, from http://www.nytimes.com/2009/09/13/magazine/13contagion-t.html

29

Translation and Crosscultural Reception

Maria Nikolajeva

University of Cambridge

The translation of children's literature is a specific art form beset with a number of material and ideological challenges. Prolific literary scholar Maria Nikolajeva sets forth two opposing theories of translation studies to contextualize some of the particular problems of translating for children. She also defends her own preferences with regard to the issues of foreignization and domestication of texts. Her extensive bibliography provides an invaluable resource for scholars in the field, canvassing nearly all of available literature on children's translation studies. Her essay is followed not only by translator Tara Chace's Point of Departure, which focuses on the business aspects of translating for children, but also by Petros Panaou's and Tasoula Tsilimeni's essay on translation and the implied reader, which provides an opposing view of the domestication/foreignization debate.

Children's literature is an international phenomenon. Not only are there books devoted to children in developed countries all over the world, but also, the most outstanding and successful children's books usually get translated into other languages. The *Harry Potter* books are a recent and convincing example. Such major children's classics as *Alice in Wonderland, Winnie-the-Pooh, The Little Prince,* and *Pippi Longstocking* have been translated into dozens upon dozens of languages including Latin, Esperanto, Frisian, Catalonian, Kymrian, and Zulu. *Alice in Wonderland* exists in innumerous translations and adaptations in French, German, or Russian.

There is, however, no universal agreement among scholars of children's literature, or even more specifically, among scholars of translations of children's literature, concerning what a translation is, what a "good" translation is, whether there is any radical difference in translating books for children and for adults (O'Connell, 1999/2006; Rieken-Gerwing, 1995; Rutschmann & von Stockar, 1996), and not least, whether and why translated children's literature is a valuable part of any child's reading. Concerning the last issue, much effort has been recently taken in the English-speaking world to introduce international children's classics and modern works, and these endeavors stress the importance of making, for instance, North American children aware of the existence of other countries and cultures (see Beckett & Nikolajeva, 2006; Stan, 2002; Tomlinson, 1998).

Although the process of transposing a literary text from culture to culture may seem independent of the audience, the difference between translating for children and for adult readers is strongly governed by the adults' idea of the implied reader, which in its turn follows from the views on the essence and function of children's literature at any given time in any given culture, as Petros Panaou and Tasoula Tsilimeni demonstrate in the chapter following this one. If the premise is that literature must be adapted to the young audience in terms of its linguistic competence, life experience, practical and encyclopedic knowledge, cognitive capacity and psychological maturity, translation policies will also take these aspects into consideration. Translated texts are also likely to be adjusted to cultural conditions depending on the concept of the child and childhood. What is acceptable in one culture may be offensive in another; what is considered sufficient literary competence in one culture may be perceived as far too advanced in another. As a result, some children's books can be rejected altogether within another culture, while others may be subjected to substantial alterations in the process of translation and publishing. Polysystem theory (Even-Zohar, 1990) can be used to explain how participating in different cultural and social systems affects the value and significance of a literary text.

The word "translation" is in children's literature research (and often otherwise) used to describe two widely different phenomena. The field of analytical, or literary-oriented, translation studies focuses on the process and results of transposing a text originally written in one language, called the source language, into another, called the target language. These studies, that might be considered a branch of comparative literature (O'Sullivan, 2005a), investigate various translation strategies through close reading of texts, and, especially in the case of children's literature, offer evaluative and normative issues connected with pedagogical views.

Another area also often referred to as "translation" involves examination of more general aspects, such as publishing policies, choice of international books for translation, and quantitative studies. This area is actually where studies of translated children's literature started. One of the first volumes devoted to the subject, *Children's Books in Translation. The Situation and the Problems* (Klingberg, 1978), emerged from the proceedings of an international symposium. A more advanced approach is a semiotically framed study of integration of translated books into the target culture (Shavit, 1986/2006). I propose to label this area crosscultural reception, to distinguish it from translation in the former sense. It can also be considered as socially oriented translation studies. It is, however, quite frequent that the two aspects are treated within the same study.

For obvious reasons, translation and crosscultural reception are mainly studied within smaller cultures, such as Holland, Sweden, and Finland, but also Germany is among the leading European countries in the field. Several investigations have been conducted in the English-speaking world. The present chapter offers an overview of this scholarship and highlights its most central issues. For a similar earlier outline, see Reinbert Tabbert's essay (2002/2006). There is also a vast number of unpublished BA, MA, and PhD theses on the various aspects of translations, far too many to include here.

Children's Literature across Borders

The area of crosscultural reception, or sociological translation studies, is relatively new within children's literature criticism, even though the subject appears recurrently during debates at professional conventions and children's literature festivals. The existing empirical studies focus on the reception of foreign books in a specific country, for instance, Australia (Nieuwenhuizen, 1998), Argentina (Alvstad, 2003), the Arab countries (Mdallel, 2003), former East Germany (Thompson-Wohlgemuth, 2003), Taiwan (Desmet, 2005), or Poland (Borodo, 2006). They may also deal with children's books from a certain country in another country: English-language (Fernández López, 1996) or Canadian literature in Spain (Pascua, 2003), Australian (Frank, 2005) or Swedish (Lindgren, Andersson, & Renauld, 2007) in France, American in Japan (Kobayashi, 2005), Canadian in Germany (Seifert, 2005). From these examples it becomes obvious that no comprehensive studies have been made so far; the examinations are mostly of a limited scope that nevertheless add substantially to our knowledge and understanding of the problems.

Moreover, there are studies of the reception of a particular author, for instance, Astrid Lindgren in Spanish (Valado, 2002) or Hans Christian Andersen in English (Hjørnager Pedersen, 2004). Still narrower investigations may concentrate on one single book, such as Heinrich Hoffmann's *Slovenly Peter*, translated into English by Mark Twain (Stahl, 1996/2006), *Alice in Wonderland* (Weaver, 1964) or Roberto Innocenti's controversial *Rose Blanche* (Stan, 2004; O'Sullivan, 2005b). It may also be a matter of reception of a certain type of translated literature, such as crossover books (Cascallana, 2004). It may further be a question of national identity as expressed in a certain book and thus its cultural translatability, in this case *Pinocchio* (O'Sullivan, 1992/2006a). There are quite a few studies showing how national children's literature in its historical development has been influenced by other cultures (e.g., Kuivasmäki, 1995; Li, 2006) or how two cultures have cross-fertilized each other through translation (Colin, 1995; Teodorowicz-Hellman, 2004).

Crosscultural reception studies frequently state the fact that in the English-speaking world less than 1% of all published children's books are translations, while in many European countries, such as Sweden, Denmark, or the Netherlands, roughly half of children's books are translated, mostly from English. In fact, until the 20th century, the overwhelming majority of children's books published in most European countries as well as in North America were translations, often translations of classics such as Aesop's fables, *Tales of the Arabian Nights, Mother Goose,* or Grimms' fairy tales. Translation and reception of these works are therefore quite a dominant subject for scholarship (Blamires, 1989/2006; Dollerup, 2003; Grotzfeld, 2004; Inggs, 2004; Kyritsi, 2006; Malarte-Feldman, 1999; Seago, 1995/2006; Zipes, 2006). Yet still today, many countries that are just starting to develop their national children's literature are filling gaps with translations.

The studies also notice the random nature of books chosen for translation and the dominance of mass-market literature. A closer look at publishing statistics from various reading-promotion organizations and reference libraries is revealing (see, for example, the Swedish Children's Books Institute homepage). About half of the translated books are reprints, among which we find classics, such as *Robinson Crusoe* and *Captain Grant's Children,* as well as series, such as the *Famous Five* and *Nancy Drew* and the newcomers: *Sweet Valley* books, *Sabrina the Teenage Witch, Animorphs,* and Lemony Snicket. Books that are in their country of origin appraised as innovative and challenging, both in their subject matter and in artistic form, have huge problems in establishing themselves on the international market. Some countries have higher esteem; for instance, Swedish children's novels are appreciated in Germany and Japan.

Considering translated books by category, picturebooks are by far the most translated type of children's book. This may be due to the fact that images are believed to be easily transposed from culture to culture. Co-publishing is also frequently practiced. However, the facts behind the statistics are not that satisfactory. The overwhelming majority of translated picturebooks are internationally adapted Disney spin-offs and other mass-market books, where the author of the text is perhaps never mentioned, much less the translator. Such books are often flat and mediocre, portraying sweet anthropomorphic animals engaged in everyday activities, books that do not stimulate children's imagination and still less appeal to adult co-readers. For publishing houses, however, they are safe investments, since such books are significantly cheaper in production, distributed through book clubs, sold in supermarkets and at gas stations, and ensure profits. Works of high individuality, that perhaps do not fit into the national market, are seldom selected for translation and publication. Recently, a whole new category of products have appeared, hybrids of books and toys, such as Pooh birthday books and Peter Rabbit counting books, Babar painting books, and Little Mermaid board books. Negligibly few of these in any given country are likely to be reviewed, noticed, adopted by teachers and librarians, or receive awards. This said, it must be admitted that publishers also bring out foreign books of the highest quality, with the incentive of filling gaps in their own culture, attempting to introduce other cultures, and provide readers with the best of international literature.

While in many countries the bulk of translations are from English, often up to 80–90%, this does not mean that books from Canada, Australia, New Zealand, or South Africa appear frequently among these; the overwhelming majority of translations from English have the United States as the country of origin. During the last few years, Japanese has climbed high in all statistics of source languages, but the secret is the flood of manga. Likewise, the steady high figures for translations from French are explained by comics such as *Tin-Tin* and *Asterix* (with Belgium as the country of origin). French reprints are most likely of the *Babar* franchise.

The proportion of books translated between major European languages is uneven: Considerably more books are translated from Swedish into Finnish or Danish than the other way round. Many Dutch books are translated into German, but not into French. Books from Iceland, Greece, Lithuania, Slovenia, and even Spain are almost as rare in any other European country as they are in the English world.

Yet another remarkable fact is that, even though a book may be translated, it often remains unknown in the target culture. Translated books seldom become part of the canon in the English-speaking world. On the other hand, a book or author may become more famous and appreciated in the target country than in the country of origin, such as Aidan Chambers in Dutch. Further, as the Astrid Lindgren Centennial Conference in Stockholm in May 2007 showed, children's literature characters often become known and popular in other countries through film and television rather than through translated books. What books are translated and achieve international success is often a matter of serendipity, but factors such as major awards and world-wide marketing are frequently decisive.

Something rarely pointed out, and where there is no systematic research at all, is the fact that far from all translations of children's books are done from the original language. A common practice in China from the 1950s through the 1990s was translating via Russian. Partly this guaranteed approval by the Communist regime in the Soviet Union, but most often merely depended on the absence of qualified translators from Western languages, while Russian was mandatory in all secondary schools in China. The same happened in the Soviet republics and partly in the Eastern European satellites, where Western children's books were translated from Russian, which governed the selection and created a somewhat distorted canon. Still today, countries such as Estonia, Lithuania, Poland, Slovenia, or Croatia are filling the gaps concerning major children's literature classics that have not been translated before because they were not available in Russian.

Translated books can be difficult, not to say impossible, to obtain outside the country of publication. Only the International Youth Library in Munich collects children's books translated, for instance, from Dutch into French or from Swedish into Italian; the collection is far from complete and quite random. Books in translation published in the U.K. or even Canada are not always easily available in the United States. Books translated into Spanish or Portuguese in Europe do not necessarily reach Latin America and the other way round. There is no coordinated distribution of translated books in the Arab world. As a result, there is no reliable information about books translated from and to different languages. The Library of Congress, the British Library, and national databases are good places to start. Various reference volumes are invaluable (Stan, 2002; Tomlinson, 1998), yet they frequently only contain a selection and become outdated quickly. Amazon.com and other Internet bookstores are of great help if you know what you are looking for, such as the author's name, but can be inconvenient for browsing.

Literary Translation Studies

The art of translation is perhaps as old as literature itself, and the most important translations in the Western world have been the translations of the Bible. Because the Bible was supposed to be the true words of God, great importance has always been attributed to the "correct" translation, and the debates of what exactly is the most correct translation have occupied learned men throughout the centuries. Some of the recent translations of the Bible in a number of languages reveal significant differences from the older versions not only concerning modernization of language, but also the interpretation of decisive passages.

As noted above, the central terms used in translation studies are source language (the language from which the translation is made) versus target language (the language into which the text is translated), as well as source reader/audience/culture and target reader/audience/culture. These concepts are indispensable in any discussion of translation. Since words in any language are polysemantic (have several different meanings or shades of meaning), the process of translation does not simply imply substitution of one word for another. A translator is faced with the necessity of choosing between several meanings of a word in the source language and finding the adequate word in the target language. Further, translation implies not only conveying denotation (the literal, dictionary meaning of words), but also connotation, that is, contextual meaning that may change from text to text (see e.g., Baker, 1992; Bassnet, 1980; Eco, 2001; Toury, 1995). It is often in this contextual area that translation for children becomes different from translation for adults. Adult readers can be assumed to be familiar with the phenomena of foreign cultures or at least accept that names, places, ways, and habits described in a book they read come from another country. Young readers are supposed to lack both the knowledge and the tolerance for unfamiliar elements in their reading, but this is far from proved; reader-oriented research is needed to show the degree to which children can accommodate cultural differences in their reading.

Some of the most basic problems of translation, for adults and children, arise from the difference in the structure of languages (Baker, 1998), which implies that few words and expressions in the source language have direct correspondence in the target language. Subsequently, word-for-word translation is in many cases impossible (therefore any attempts to apply computerized translation to fiction are doomed to fail). However, one of the two radically different approaches to translation propagates equivalence, that is, a maximal approximation of the target text to the source text. A translation, in this view, should be "faithful" to the original, and no liberties are to be taken. The opposite view suggests that the translator should take into consideration the target audience, whereupon changes may not only be legitimate, but imperative, if the translated text in its specific context is to function somewhat similarly to the way in which the original functions in its initial situation. This view can be called dialogical, since it presupposes an active dialogue, or interaction, between the target text and its readers. The key question in dialogical translation is "For whom?" as opposed to the question "What?" in the equivalence theory. Normally, the attitude of any particular scholar will lie somewhere within the spectrum of the two polarities; just as the strategies of a practitioner are likely to combine the two approaches. Neither are the two theories mutually exclusive. I will, however, for the sake of clarity, in the following resort to these two theories to illustrate the extremities of approaches.

The two views, also elaborated in general translation theory, acquire special significance in connection with children's fiction, once again due to the issues of implied audience. Translation studies within children's literature scholarship have grown from two schools, although few of the recent researchers have strictly adhered to any of them. Swedish scholar Göte Klingberg (1986) in *Children's Literature in the Hands of the Translator* condemns all deviations from source text, including adaptation and abridgement, purification, and similar intrusions. These corruptions are, according to Klingberg, based on the idea that young readers lack the ability to understand phenomena from foreign cultures, such as food, currency, habits, child/parent relationships, and so on. Omissions in translated texts are also the result of ideological values and views on child education, when, for instance, inappropriate behavior is altered or deleted. Klingberg and his followers emphasize instead the use of translations to support young readers' understanding of and tolerance for foreign cultures; that is, they advocate translation as a pedagogical vehicle.

The opposite view, best represented in the Finnish Riitta Oittinen's (1993) *I Am Me – I Am Other: On the Dialogics of Translating for Children* and *Translating for Children* (2000), has been named dialogical, since it is based on a creative dialogue between the source and target cultures. The main goal in dialogical translation is to offer the target-culture readers a similar experience to that which the source-culture readers meet in texts. This strategy not only allows but encourages liberties in translation of children's books in particular, adapting source-culture phenomena that may alienate the reader to more familiar target-culture references. For instance, a certain food or game might be very prevalent in the source culture, but completely unheard of in the target culture. If the translator sticks with the original reference, the target-culture reader will experience the reference as exotic or foreign, thus having a completely different experience than the source-culture reader. Rather than adhering firmly to the source text, then, dialogical translations pay attention to the reference frames of the target-culture readers.

These opposite views can be summarized as the former being true to the text, and the latter being true to the reader. It is not coincidental that Klingberg is a pedagogue while Oittinen is a literary critic and a practicing translator. The views of the "Klingberg school" (equivalence school) are normative and prescriptive. Oittinen's theory is based on the dynamic relationship between the text, the translator, the implied audience and the context. In general translation studies, the dialogic view comes from modern linguistics, semiotics, literary pragmatics, and communication theory. Yet, in the children's literature context, this approach also becomes rather regulative.

Studies from both directions are often devoted to classics where many translations exist, often within the same target culture, such as *Alice in Wonderland* in German (Friese, 1995; O'Sullivan, 1998a, 2001), *Little Women* in French (Le Brun, 2003), or *The Wizard of Oz* in Finnish (Puurtinen, 1994/2006). Many of these studies come with conclusions about a particular translation being a "success" or a "failure." The evaluation is highly dependent on the researcher's adherence to the Klingberg or the Oittinen school, even when these concrete names are not mentioned (see Nikolajeva, 2006). At the same time, as already mentioned, most contemporary scholars go beyond the polarities and are descriptive rather than prescriptive and evaluative.

Translation and Adaptation

Many issues raised by the equivalence school result from the fact that children's books have to a considerably higher extent been subjected to adaptation rather than translation. Adaptation means that a text is adjusted to what the translator believes to be the needs of the target audience, and it can include deletions, additions, explanations, purification, simplification, modernization, and a number of other interventions. It is also common to translate a versified text into prose.

Robinson Crusoe, the text perhaps most often subjected to adaptation, is about 500 pages in the original. It has in some children's editions been cut down to 24 pages. The incentive has naturally been to make the book more acces-

sible to young readers. The nature of the cuts has varied; most frequently, the self-reflexive and religious passages have been removed from this particular book. In the shortest versions, only the very gist of the storyline remains. Quite a few classics, including *Alice in Wonderland*, have been subjected to similar surgery. A frequent form of interference involves periphrasis (retelling), abridgment, text compressions, concisions, and digests. Rather than merely cutting out pieces of text, the translator retells the story, often turning direct speech into summaries, focusing on the central episodes, omitting characterization, and other more complex dimensions of the original. These adaptations often yield interesting insights into the dominant views on childhood and children's literature, as is the case with the analysis of *The Last of the Mohicans* in French (Gouanvic, 2003).

The practice of additions would seem to contradict the drive to make the story shorter and thus more suitable for children, but in some cases, translators have added passages explaining the characters' actions and other aspects of the source text. In one of the most famous adaptations of *Robinson Crusoe*, made by the German pedagogue Joachim Heinrich Campe, a frame story is added, in which a father is telling Robinson's story to his children. This enables the narrator to explain, comment and pass judgment, in accordance with the didactic purpose of the adaptation.

Alterations can include such instances as changing the ending to suit the target audience. The ending of Andersen's "The Little Match Girl" has been in many translations changed from the character's death to her finding a good and loving family (Hjørnager Pedersen, 2004). Omissions and alterations for political, cultural, or religious reasons are called purification: the text is purified from passages that are perceived as offensive (another term is "bowdlerization," after the 19th-century British clergyman Thomas Bowdler, who produced *The Family Shakespeare,* fit to be read in the presence of families). It may be a matter of abusive language, the mention of bodily functions viewed as inappropriate in a children's book, or an expression of ideology unacceptable by the target culture. Studies of translations in, for instance, totalitarian states or countries with strong fundamentalist tendencies illustrate purification, which often borders on censorship. While in the original of the Swedish children's classic *The Wonderful Adventures of Nils*, the protagonist's parents go to a church, in the Russian translation they go to a market. Churches and religion were not supposed to appear in children's books published in the Soviet Union. Most translations (as well as English-language abridgements) of *Gulliver's Travels* omit the episode in which Gulliver extinguishes the fire in the royal palace of Lilliput by passing water.

Simplification implies that a foreign notion is supplanted by something less specific, for instance when a particular dish is simply translated as "food" or the title of a newspaper is changed into the general "newspaper." In *Pippi Longstocking*, her little animal companion is a guenon, a specific monkey species, while in English it is referred to simply as monkey. Rewording means that a metaphor or some other figure of speech, non-existent in the target language, is rendered by a circumscription. Both practices are widely used in children's literature translation and are often ascribed to pedagogical reasons (Stolze, 2003).

Modernization means bringing everyday details, objects, and concepts up to date in translation, including changing or deleting what may be perceived as offensive, such as racism and sexism. Also, purely linguistic modernization is frequent, when, for instance, 19th-century fiction is translated into a more modern idiom. For instance, a comparison between older and contemporary translations from Swedish into English and Finnish demonstrates quite a number of modifications (Rossi, 2003).

Harmonization includes changes in children's behavior, if considered improper in the target culture, or changes in adults' attitudes. For instance, in many cultures adults in children's fiction are supposed to be impeccable, thus any mention of drunkards and the like are eliminated. An infamous example is the first French translation of *Pippi Longstocking* where the three most "offensive" chapters have been deleted, chapters in which Pippi most clearly shows her superiority over the adults.

Embellishment means any form of beautification, from using more high-flown language than the original to adding longish descriptions. In the French *Pippi* translation, additions appear frequently in which Pippi regrets her bad behavior and apologizes. The result is that this French Pippi is much more tame and compliant than the original. Occasionally, the reverse occurs, that is, a possibly offensive element is emphasized in translation, primarily for marketing purposes.

In many theoretical discussions of children's literature, all these practices are unconditionally condemned, since they are perceived as censorship. While we may indeed interrogate the intentions, the practice itself is merely an extreme form of the dialogical approach to translation mentioned above, the one that takes into consideration the target audience. In fact, the use of foul language can be less offensive in some cultures than in others, and the attitude toward nakedness varies substantially between countries and epochs. The practice of adaptation of target texts is then in no way radically different from adapting originals to what authors (or publishers) believe to be the needs and interests of the young audience, which in its turn depends on the views on childhood and education.

Pippi Longstocking provides an excellent example of the various manipulations in translation into different languages (see Blume, 2001; Heldner, 1992; Nikolajeva 2006; Surmatz, 2005). It is a challenging children's book that interrogates the adults' authority and shows a liberated, competent child that may feel alien and threatening

in other cultures. The studies of *Pippi* translations into English, German, and French reveal all kinds of intervention, often connected with supposedly offensive behavior, including not only Pippi's disrespect toward adults, but even more innocent things like drinking coffee. Also the character herself, the strongest girl in the world, appealing to a child's imagination, has been toned down in many translations. Most of the underlying political and ideological issues in the *Pippi* books have been lost in translation into several languages (Surmatz, 2004), either since they were considered insignificant or simply because the translators did not recognize them.

Many examinations of translated children's books point out actual mistakes and faults, which apparently are based on translators' poor knowledge of the source language and/ or source culture. For instance, in the Russian translation of Astrid Lindgren's *Karlsson-on-the-Roof*, the father's Sunday beer has turned into a Sunday tie; the endearment "my little chap" has become "my little goat"; a lady who lives in No. 92 is transformed into a lady who is 92 years old, and so on (Skott, 1977). In many countries such as the Soviet Union with its East European satellites, or China, translators had few possibilities to visit the countries from which the books came to get acquainted with everyday details. In a Russian translation from English, for instance, the translator did not know what bubble-gum was and therefore translated it as a liquid to blow soap-bubbles with. Such mistakes become less frequent as translators today travel more freely and as information becomes accessible on the web.

Translation Strategies: Domestication and Foreignization

In most empirical translation studies, the scholars focus on various alterations made in translations and argue whether the changes are reasonable and justified. Two possible ways of dealing with the elements of source texts that may hamper the target audience's understanding are domestication and foreignization, which reflect the dialogical versus equivalence approaches. In domesticating a translated text, the translator substitutes familiar phenomena and concepts for what may be perceived as strange and hard to understand. It is not uncommon in translations of children's books to change foreign food, clothing, weights and measures, currency, flora and fauna, feasts, customs and traditions, to something that the target readers will more easily understand. In the American translation of *Pippi Longstocking*, for instance, dollars, quarters, and cents are mentioned. In fact, most American translations of children's books have a strong tendency toward domestication. It can be somewhat less significant, but still amazing, when in Sven Nordqvist's *Pancake Pie*, "The Star-Spangled Banner" is played instead of the original Viennese waltzes. Some more sophisticated elements that lie on the border between domestication and pure censorship involve the relationship between children and adults, not least between teachers and students, bodily functions, sexuality and procreation (Nikolajeva, 1996).

Localization implies a form of domestication through changing the setting of a book to a more familiar one. For instance, the German translations of Enid Blyton's adventure novels are set in Germany, as is the Swedish classic *The Wonderful Adventures of Nils* (Desmidt, 2003). The Danish translation of Astrid Lindgren's *Mio My Son* has moved the setting from Stockholm to Copenhagen (Øster, 2003), while the Finnish translation takes place in Helsinki.

In assessing domestication and localization (universally condemned by the adherents of the equivalence theory), we should ask ourselves what the translator's motivation might have been. When a novel for adults is translated, the target audience may be expected to understand that certain objects and concepts are different in a foreign culture. Young readers have less knowledge of foreign countries and cultures. Children are seldom aware that the book they are reading is a translation. While transposing the setting of a British novel to Germany may be an unnecessary interference, some other changes can be fully justified, to make the text more accessible to the target audience.

If a translated text is foreignized, the translator may decide to keep some words untranslated to preserve the foreign flavor. The proponents of this approach maintain that it is essential that young readers become aware of cultural differences as they read translated books. Admirable as it is, the approach may sometimes be stretched too far. In the English translation of *Pippi Longstocking*, Pippi is shown "busy making *pepparkakor*—a kind of Swedish cookie." The motivation behind this translation is apparently to show the American readers that Sweden is a different country with different sorts of cookies. The cookies are, however, nothing more exotic than the universally known gingerbread. By using a foreign word in the English text, the translator focuses the readers' attention on the cookies, thus creating a different effect than is the case with source-text readers. Further, the phrase "a kind of Swedish cookie" is an addition, the translator's explanation of the foreign word, which is unnecessary in the source text, and which would have been superfluous if the word had been translated as "gingerbread." On the other hand, if Pippi were indeed making a cookie that completely lacked a correspondence in the target language (which is more likely with a translation into Chinese or Swahili), would it be motivated to supplant the exotic *pepparkakor* with something more familiar? After all, Swedish readers do not experience a sense of foreignness and exoticism while meeting this word in a text. Some translators of *Pippi* and other Swedish children's books have been confronted with the difficulty of translating the common practice of children drinking coffee, which is acceptable in Sweden, but less so in other cultures. Retaining coffee makes the situation more deviant and attracts the target-text readers'

attention to details, which the source-text reader will not even notice. Many translators have substituted tea or some other drink for coffee, without in any way distorting the meaning of the text. The question in each individual case is whether the cultural detail is indeed significant.

In a dialogic translation, the goal is to approximate the response of the source-text readers, and substituting a familiar notion for a foreign one would be considered more adequate. A famous example can be gathered in the Bible translations: in translating the phrase "God's lamb" into Inuit, the translator changed it into "God's seal cub," since a lamb is an animal unknown to the Inuit. In fact, in a Swahili translation of Astrid Lindgren's *Noisy Village*, spring was changed into the rain season, because spring is an unknown concept for the target audience, and the Noisy Village children's joyful anticipation of spring had to be translated into a similar experience (Nikolajeva, 2006).

Even when a concept in itself is not perceived as foreign, too specific a word in the target text can create a foreignization effect. In a recent English translation of *Pinocchio*, the Blue-Haired Fairy has been changed into Indigo-Haired Fairy, with the motivation that the correct translation for the Italian word used in the original is "indigo" rather than "blue." This may sound reasonable, yet there are some possible counter-arguments. Indigo feels more exotic in English than the neutral blue, and it is unlikely that the author's intention was to be exotic. Further, the character is already known in English as the Blue-Haired Fairy, and whatever the reason might have been for a new translation, it is not desirable to change an established character name, even if the new translation shows greater fidelity to the original. In a recent translation, the name of Hans Christian Andersen's tiny heroine was changed from Thumbelina to Inchelina, which may be a better solution, but is confusing to a reader already familiar with the character.

Translating Cultural Context

Translation does not only imply that a book appears in a new language, but also that it starts functioning within a new culture (see e.g., Fernández López, 1996). Quite a few studies show how texts from particular cultures are adapted to the norms of the target culture. It may be Roald Dahl in Japanese (Netley, 1992), *The Wind in the Willows* in Finland (Hagfors, 2003), *Emil and the Detectives* in English (Lathey, 2006b), Astrid Lindgren's novels in Polish (Liseling-Nilsson, 2006), or *Uncle Tom's Cabin* in Slovenian (Mazi-Leskovar, 2003). Once again, the most common changes include everyday details that have specific connotations in the source culture, but are different or absent in the target culture. They can also convey ideology that is for some reason unacceptable in the target culture and thus has to be adjusted. Even such a simple detail as direct address can turn out to be an insurmountable problem, if the source and the target language have a completely different continuum of polite and informal address (Hirano, 1999/2006). Further, some languages lack diminutives or have different values of diminutives than the source language; for instance, Russian, German, or Dutch have diminutive suffixes, while in English, adjectives such as little, small, and tiny may convey either an endearing or a derogative attitude. Since diminutives are frequently used in children's literature, the issue is highly pertinent.

Some examples of the foreignization of culturally dependent phenomena are also connected to the practice of explanatory additions, strongly questioned by the equivalence theory. For instance, for a Swedish reader, the connotation of "the blue and yellow flag" is as clear as "stars and stripes" for an American reader. In two existing Russian translations of *The Wonderful Adventures of Nils*, two strategies have been employed. The equivalence translator has chosen to write "the blue and yellow flag," providing a footnote with the explanation that the colors of the Swedish flag are blue and yellow. While the solution may seem fortunate, using footnotes in fiction, especially children's fiction, is definitely undesirable. Another translator has circumvented the problem by adding one single word: "the blue and yellow Swedish flag."

Many children's novels contain allusions and other literary and extra-literary references. In translation, it is often pointless to retain the allusion to a text that is completely unknown to the target readers. Dialogic translators may choose to delete the reference or, if it works, to provide another reference that will create a similar effect. Several translations of *Alice in Wonderland* or *Winnie-the-Pooh* have followed either of the two strategies. Naturally, if the text alludes to another text widely known in the target language, this available translation should preferably be used, even if the translator judges it to be poor. For instance, the title of Philip Pullman's trilogy *His Dark Materials* is translated literally into Swedish, ignoring the fact that the Milton quotation to which the title alludes is in Swedish rendered as "the dark element." The readers of the target text have no chance to make the connection between the title and the poem it alludes to. The same goes if a book is explicitly mentioned in the source text, but the title is different from what it is known by in the target text. Especially if the intertext is significant for the understanding of the text itself, the failure to recognize and find the existing title would deny target readers a valuable interpreting strategy. The international bestseller *Sophie's World* by the Norwegian Jostein Gaarder abounds in references to Norwegian literature and culture, which in the English translation have all been changed into more universally known English names, titles, and quotations.

Quite an unusual cultural difficulty arises when a novel taking place in a foreign country is translated into the language of this country, as Vanessa Joosen (2003) notes in the case with the Dutch translation of Aidan Chambers's *Postcards from No Man's Land*. The foreign and "exotic"

elements in the original were no longer that in translation, which naturally affects the way they are perceived by the reader. Other interesting issues are translations within a bilingual country, such as Canada (Le Brun, 2005) or text manipulations within the same language in different countries, significantly East and West Germany (Thompson-Wohlgemuth, 2004). Similar transformations of British books in the United States have not been studied academically (perhaps because the matter is too delicate), but the differences between the British and American editions of the *Harry Potter* books are notorious in their prompt domestication.

Translation of Proper Names

Yvonne Bertills's (2003) book, *Beyond Identification: Proper Names in Children's Literature*, is wholly focused on the translation of names in children's literature and based on modern onomastics, a part of linguistics dealing with proper names. Bertills has examined how names in *Winnie-the-Pooh* have been translated into Swedish and Finnish, Tove Jansson's *Moomin* books into English and Finnish, and a Finnish children's novel into Swedish and English. The results do not only illustrate the different strategies, but also demonstrate a specific aspect of domestication. Similar investigations have been performed with other children's books (Yamazaki, 2002). The numerous French translations of *Alice in Wonderland* pursue different goals in either retaining or changing personal names (Kibbee, 2003), and translators into different languages choose a variety of solutions (Nord, 2003). Incidentally, in the Russian translation of *Alice* by Vladimir Nabokov the heroine's name is russified into Anya.

Personal and geographic names in translation indeed present a special dilemma. The equivalence theory prescribes that names should always be retained as they are in the original. There may, however, be several reasons why names are changed. First, the sound of the name may give undesirable associations in the target language. The name Pippi, for instance, in a number of languages suggests urinating (in Swedish, the connotation is "crazy"). The character is therefore renamed Fifi in French, Pippa in Spanish, and Peppi in Russian. Another reason may be that the name in the target language is already firmly connected with a famous literary character. The hero of Astrid Lindgren's *Emil's Pranks* has been renamed Michel in the German translation, since the name Emil is associated with the protagonist of the German classic *Emil and the Detectives* (Stolt, 1978/2006). A popular Swedish picturebook character Max is renamed Sam in the American translation, obviously to distance him from Maurice Sendak's Max. By contrast, when the name of the title character in Lindgren's *Ronia, the Robber's Daughter* is changed to Kersti, the only motivation seems to be foreignization, since Ronia is just as much a non-existing name in Swedish as in English, or was, before the novel was written. Yet another problem may arise if a name has a specific sound in the source language that gives some associations for the source-text readers. The name Eeyore is an example of onomatopoeia referring to a donkey's neigh. In most translations, it has been changed to match the corresponding sound in the target language.

Many names in the *Harry Potter* books carry associations that critics have tried to interpret: Dumbledore, Malfoy, Lupin, and especially Voldemort. The translators around the world have either retained the names, thus losing the association (equivalence solution), or invented new names with similar associations in the target language (dialogic solution). A controversy between the Swedish and the Norwegian translators is illuminating (Høverstad, 2002). The Swedish translator has invented new words for the Quidditch equipment, but not for the game itself or any other "telling" names. The Norwegian translator has chosen to translate all proper and geographical names, including Dumbledore, Malfoy, Lupin, Sirius Black, the name of the wizard school, Hogwarts, and its houses. Wyler (2003) considers similar strategies in her translation of *Harry Potter* into Portuguese, where she has chosen to change the names in order to give target readers adequate associations. In fact, *Harry Potter* translations have almost grown into a separate branch of children literature translation studies (Fries-Gedin, 2002; Inggs, 2003; Jentsch, 2002/2006; Lathey, 2005).

Finally, names may refer to a phenomenon in the source language known by a different name in the target language. The name of Andersen's figure Ole Lukøje, which means literally "Ole-close-your-eyes" (Ole is a personal name), has in some translations been changed into Willie Winkie. It seems a very sensible solution, since it connects the name with an English folklore character similar to that in the Danish tradition to which Andersen refers. The name of the character in *The Lion, the Witch and the Wardrobe*, Father Christmas, has in the Swedish translation been changed into "jultomten," literally "the Christmas gnome," who performs the function of Father Christmas in Scandinavia. The target readers are thus offered the same association as the source readers. Applying the equivalence theory consistently, all such changes are unacceptable; however, scholars as well as practitioners are quite permissive.

Narrative and Translation

Some more fundamental changes, motivated as well as unmotivated, concern the specific narrative elements of the source text. Just as implied authors of the source text, the translators add their voices to the narrative structure of the target text (O'Sullivan, 2003/2006b). Some significant narrative changes in translation that radically affect readers' perception are the transposition from personal to impersonal narration (such as the many abridged versions of *Robinson Crusoe* retold in the third person, which os-

tensibly makes the text more child-friendly). The change of second-person narration in the first chapter of *Winnie-the-Pooh* into third-person, performed, for instance, in Swedish and Russian translations, destroys the whole narrative frame of the book. The change of gender can be inevitable when the systems of grammatical gender in the source and target language are different, but this can also have catastrophic results if the gender of the characters is significant for the understanding of their relationship. For instance, the neutral ("it") instead of feminine ("she") gender of the tree in the Swedish translation of Shel Silverstein's *The Giving Tree* affects the interpretation of the relationship between the characters: in the original, the tree is clearly a self-sacrificial mother. The change of tense brings the interaction between the narrator and the narratee out of balance (Lathey, 2003/2006a) and occasionally deprives the readers of guidelines when complex temporal switches are involved.

Translating the Untranslatable

There are other difficulties that translators may meet. One is how to deal with humor, nonsense, puns, and other linguistic games often found in children's books (Grassegger, 1985; O'Sullivan, 1998b, 1999). Some critics claim that certain texts are "untranslatable." It is indeed a challenge to translate a title such as *War and Peas* into any language in which the pun will not be possible. Yet, a skillful translator can resort to something called compensatory translation, which implies adding a different pun or word play to compensate for the lost one (O'Sullivan, 1998b). The American translator of *Pippi Longstocking* has basically lost all puns and Pippi's witty comments, either because of incompetence or because dialogical translation, including compensatory, were believed to be disadvantageous.

In many cases, the difference between approaches becomes clearly manifest. In *Alice in Wonderland*, the Duchess says to Alice, among the many platitudes: "Take care of the sense, and the sounds will take care of themselves." For a source reader, the statement alludes to the existing English proverb: "Take care of the pence, and the pounds will take care of themselves." If translated literally, as has been done in many languages, the allusion and thus the humor is lost. All the nonsensical verses in *Alice in Wonderland* are parodies on children's anthology pieces from Carroll's time. The translators of *Alice* into different languages have chosen two opposite strategies. Some have translated the verses literally, which certainly has kept their nonsensical character, but lost the allusion to existing verses. The translations are thus superficially "faithful," yet they are devoid of a deeper equivalence based on the allusion. The adherents of the dialogical theory have chosen to write their own parodies of verses from their own culture. These verses have nothing to do with the source text, yet they evoke the same response in the target-text readers as the original verses evoke in the source-text readers. Such translation strategies may be less faithful to the source text, but instead more loyal toward the target audience. What is a "good" translation is thus a matter closely connected with the general views on what is "good" children's literature.

Specifics of Picturebook Translation

The area where general translation studies are of little use is the translation of picturebooks. With the rapidly expanding field of picturebook theory, constantly growing attention is nowadays paid to the specific significance of the dialogical approach to translation of picturebooks (see Panaou & Tsilimeni, this volume). The characteristic feature of picturebooks as a medium is the interaction of word and image, which creates an inseparable whole where the meaning of the text/image unity, frequently called iconotext or imagetext, is only revealed through the synergy of the two levels (see Sipe, this volume). In countries without a tradition of picturebooks in this sense (even though the art of children's books illustration may be highly sophisticated), a foreign picturebook is often translated and then illustrated by a different artist. The picturebook as an entity is thus ruined, or changed so significantly as to be a completely new text. Alternately, just one or two original images from a picturebook may accompany the target text, as is done in a Russian translation of *Where the Wild Things Are*.

However, even when the target book retains both the verbal and the visual aspects of the source, the specific multimedial nature of the picturebook implies that in translation, the target text should ideally retain the source text's relationship to the illustration (see Nières-Chevrel, 2003; Oittinen, 1995/2006, 2000, 2003, 2004; O'Sullivan, 1999). Unfortunately, presumably because picturebooks are often regarded as simple, but also because the publishers are not aware of the text/image significance, the translation violently interferes with the entity. An analysis of a number of translations of the Swedish Anna-Clara Tidholm's picturebook *Knacka på* ("Knock-knock") into different languages demonstrates horrendous liberties that the Danish, German, French, and some other translators have allowed themselves; liberties that completely destroy the poetic language of the text itself: The incomplete sentences such as "Knock-knock" or "Come in" are translated into conventional "Let us knock on the door" and "Now let us come in" (Rhedin, 2001). In the first place, however, the balance between the words and images, the iconotext, has disappeared.

The different approaches to picturebook translation become especially tangible when comparing two translations (often a British and an American one) of the same book, such as *The Wild Baby*, where, among many other transformations, additional text explains the actions clearly understood from the images (Nikolajeva & Scott, 2001). While in translating verbal texts, intertextual links of the

source text can be difficult to preserve, the problem becomes all the more grave with a picturebook that contains intervisual connections, as Mieke Desmet (2001/2006) observes in her analysis of *The Jolly Postman*. When the source text is not initially illustrated, the various translated and illustrated versions can also be revealing, for instance Spanish illustrations to Hans Christian Andersen's "The Emperor's New Clothes" in connection with nudity (Carvalho & de Azevedo, 2005). Occasionally, the images rather than the words are subjected to purification when they do not fit into the target culture. In the American translation of the nonsense story by the Swedish poet Lennart Hellsing, *The Pirate Book*, a striptease dancer has been changed into a "smashing lady" in the text, and in the picture she has been given a proper black dress (in the original she is nude). In another Swedish picturebook, *Else-Marie and Her Seven Daddies*, by Pija Lindenbaum, the American publisher opposed the illustration in which the protagonist was depicted in a bathtub together with her mother and her imaginary daddies. By agreement with the author/illustrator, a different picture was provided, with the family reading in an armchair.

Other genres and kinds of children's literature have received very little scholarly attention. Poetry for children is highly neglected (some rare exceptions are Bell [1998] and Kümmerling-Meibauer [2003], who explicitly calls poetry translation a stepchild), presumably due to the fact that few works of poetry for children get translated at all. The reason is most probably the specific problems of poetry translation: Poetry should preferably be translated by poets, yet because translating children's literature has such low status this seldom happens. Further, there are few if any analytical tools for studying translated poetry, since the conventional notions of faithfulness to the original are hardly applicable. Yet such attempts have been made, for instance with A. A. Milne's poetry in German (Kreller, 2006).

Translation of drama for children has not been studied, likewise nonfiction, even though the latter comprises a significant part of publishing.

Translators' Voices

One of the many paradoxical phenomena in translation is that theory and praxis seldom go hand in hand. Translation theorists are not necessarily translators themselves, while translators are hardly interested in theory and pay no attention to theoretical debates or even empirical investigations. Practical translation is often a matter of individual choices where decisions are made irrespective of general principles. It is therefore invaluable to partake of what translators themselves say about their work. The renowned British translator Anthea Bell (1979, 1987/2006, 1998, 2001) has repeatedly shared her experience in translating for children, which is revealing considered parallel with studies of "faithful" and "unfaithful" translations. A

Slovenian translator from English also provides valuable insights (Kenda, 2006). The numerous confessions of international translators of the *Harry Potter* books, mentioned above, are equally illuminating.

Conclusion

In conclusion, there are many areas and directions open for future translation studies, in which scholars can both apply research results from general translation theory and from children's literature-specific theory, the latter often based on the concept of the implied reader. The problems delineated above notwithstanding, the art of translating for children develops and improves, and in many cases gains status. Similarly, publishers in many countries become aware of the necessity of translated literature in the age of globalization. As studies of translated children's literature become less evaluative and more analytical, they can in their turn inform children's literature scholarship at large, since translations are frequently more explicit in their didactic and artistic purposes than original texts. Further, translation studies contribute significantly to the area of comparative literature, opening new perspectives for the mutual knowledge of scholars from different cultures.

Literature References

Editor's Note: Because of the many translated texts referred to in this essay, references to primary works and translations are not included. Readers interested in particular translations are referred to the academic sources cited in the text.

Academic References

Alvstad, C. (2003). Publishing strategies of translated children's literature in Argentina: A combined approach. *Meta, 48*(1–2), 266–275.

Baker, M. (1992). *In other words: A coursebook on translation.* London, England: Routledge.

Baker, M. (Ed.). (1998). *Routledge encyclopedia of translation studies.* London, England: Routledge.

Bassnet, S. (1980). *Translation studies.* London, England: Methuen.

Beckett, S., & Nikolajeva, M. (Eds.). (2006). *Beyond Babar: The European tradition in children's literature.* Lanham, MD: Scarecrow.

Bell, A. (1979). Children's books in translation. *Signal, 28,* 47–53.

Bell, A. (1998). Translating verse for children. *Signal, 85,* 3–14.

Bell, A. (2001). Children's literature and international identity? A translator's viewpoint. In M. Meek (Ed.), *Children's literature and national identity* (pp. 232–240). Stoke-on-Trent, England: Trentham Books.

Bell, A. (2006). Translator's notebook: Delicate matters. In G. Lathey, (Ed.) *The translation of children's literature: A reader* (pp. 190–208). Clevedon, England: Multicultural Matters. (Original work published 1987)

Bertills, Y. (2003). *Beyond identification: Proper names in children's literature.* Åbo, Finland: Åbo Akademi Press.

Blamires, D. (2006). The early reception of the Grimms' *Kinder- und Hausmärchen* in England. In G. Lathey (Ed.), *The translation of children's literature: A reader* (pp. 163–174). Clevedon, England: Multicultural Matters. (Original work published 1989)

Blume, S. (2001). *Pippi Långstrumps Verwandlung zur "dame-bien-élevée"- die anpassung eines kinderbuches an ein fremdes kulturelles system: eine Analyse der französischen Übersetzung von Astrid Lindgren's Pippi Långstrump.* Hamburg, Germany: Kovac, 2001.

Borodo, M. (2006). Children's literature translations in Poland during the 1950s and the 1990s. In V. Joosen, & K. Vloeberghs (Eds.), *Changing concepts of childhood and children's literature* (pp. 169–182). Newcastle, England: Cambridge Scholar Press.

Carvalho, J., & de Azevedo, F. F. (2005). El traje nuevo del rey: Semiotic interaction between the iconic and the verbal. *Bookbird, 43*(4), 5–13.

Cascallana, B. G. (2004). Crossing over: The reception of "kidult" fiction in Spain. In P. Pinsent (Ed.), *Books and boundaries: Writers and their audience* (pp. 165–177). Lichfield, England: Pied Piper.

Colin, M. (1995). Children's literature in France and Italy in the nineteenth century: Influences and exchanges. In M. Nikolajeva (Ed.), *Aspects and issues in the history of children's literature* (pp. 77–88). Westport, CT: Greenwood.

Desmet, M. K. T. (2005). Connecting local and global literatures or driving on a one-way street? The case of the Taiwanese Grimm press. In E. O'Sullivan, K. Reynolds, & R. Romøren (Eds.), *Children's literature global and local: Social and aesthetic perspective* (pp. 218–226). Oslo, Norway: Novus.

Desmet, M. K. T. (2006). Intertextuality/intervisuality in translation: *The Jolly Postman*'s intercultural journey from Britain to the Netherlands. In G. Lathey (Ed.), *The translation of children's literature: A reader* (pp. 122–133). Clevedon, England: Multicultural Matters. (Original work published 2001)

Desmidt, I. (2003). 'Jetzt bist du in Deutschland, Däumling': Nils Holgersson on foreign soil—Subject to new norms. *Meta, 48*(1–2), 165–181.

Dollerup, C. (2003). Translation for reading aloud. *Meta, 48*(1-2), 81–103.

Eco, U. (2001). *Experiences in translation.* Toronto, Canada: University of Toronto Press.

Even-Zohar, I. (1990). *Polysystem studies.* Durham, NC: Duke University Press. Alternativt namn: Zohar, Itamar Even-Alternativt namn: Ben Zohar, Itamar

Fernández López, M. (1996). *Traducción y literatura juvenil: Narrativa anglosajona contemporánea en España.* León, Spain: Universidad de León.

Fernández López, M. (2006). Translation studies in contemporary children's literature: A comparison of intercultural ideological factors. In G. Lathey (Ed.), *The translation of children's literature: A reader* (pp. 41–53). Clevedon, England: Multicultural Matters. (Original work published in 2000)

Frank, H. T. (2005). Translating the animal kingdom: Australian titles in French. *Bookbird, 43*(3), 25–34.

Fries-Gedin, L. (2002). Dunkare, Klonken och den gyllene Kvicken: Translating the *Harry Potter* phenomenon into Swedish. *Swedish Book Review Supplement,* 8–14.

Friese, I. (1995). Lewis Carroll's Alice im Wunderland und die probleme mit der Übersetzung. In B. Hürlimann (Ed.), *Klassiker der Kinder- und Jugendliteratur* (pp. 107–130). Frankfurt am Main, Germany: Fischer.

Gouanvic, J. M. (2003). De la traduction à l'adaptation pour les jeunes: Socioanalyse du Dernier des Mohicans de James Fenimore Cooper en français. *Meta, 48*(1-2), 31–46.

Grassegger, H. (1985). *Sprachspiel und Übersetzung: Eine studie anhand der comic-serie Asterix.* Tübingen, Germany: Stauffenburg.

Grotzfeld, H. (2004). Creativity, random selection, and 'pia fraus':

Observations on compilation and transmission of the *Arabian Nights*. *Marvels & Tales, 18*(2), 218–228.

Hagfors, I. (2003). The translation of culture-bound elements into Finnish in the post-war period. *Meta, 48*(1-2), 115–127.

Heldner, C. (1992). Une anarchiste de camisol de force : Fifi Brindacier ou la métamorphose français de *Pippi Långstrump*. *Le Revue Des Livres Pour Enfants, 145*, 65–71.

Hirano, C. (2006). Eight ways to say you: The challenges of translation. In G. Lathey (Ed.), *The translation of children's literature: A reader* (pp. 225–331). Clevedon, England: Multicultural Matters. (Original work published 1999)

Hjørnager Pedersen, V. (2004). *Ugly ducklings? Studies in the English translations of Hans Christian Andersen's tales and stories*. Odense: University Press of Southern Denmark.

Høverstad, T. B. (2002). Å oversette et fenomen: *Harry Potter.*" *Årboka: Litteratur for Barn Og Unge*, 59–69.

Inggs, J. (2003). From Harry to Garri: Strategies for the transfer of culture and ideology in Russian translations of two English fantasy stories. *Meta, 48*(1-2), 285–297.

Inggs, J. (2004). What is a South African folktale? Reshaping traditional tales through translation and adaptation. *Papers, 14*(1), 15–23.

Jentsch, N. K. (2006). Harry Potter and the tower of Babel: Translating the magic. In G. Lathey (Ed.), *The translation of children's literature: A reader* (pp. 190–208). Clevedon, England: Multicultural Matters. (Original work published 2002)

Joosen, V. (2003).Translating Dutch into... Dutch. *Signal, 100*, 106–126.

Kenda, J. J. (2006). Rewriting children's literature. In S. Bassnet (Ed.), *The translator as writer* (pp. 160–170). London, England: Continuum.

Kibbee, D. A. (2003). When children's literature transcends its genre: Translating *Alice in Wonderland*. *Meta, 48*(1-2), 307–321.

Klingberg, G. (Ed.). (1978). *Children's books in translation. The situation and the problems*. Stockholm, Sweden: Almqvist & Wiksell International.

Klingberg, G. (1986). *Children's fiction in the hands of the translators*. Lund, Sweden: Gleerup.

Kobayashi, M. (2005). Which US picturebooks get translated into Japanese? Criteria for choice. *Bookbird, 43*(2), 5–12.

Kreller, S. (2006). Taking a turn for the verse: English-language children's poetry in German translation. In V. Joosen, & K. Vloeberghs (Eds.), *Changing concepts of childhood and children's literature* (pp. 183–194). Newcastle, England: Cambridge Scholar Press.

Kuivasmäki, R. (1995). International influence on the nineteenth century Finnish children's literature. In M. Nikolajeva (Ed.), *Aspects and issues in the history of children's literature* (pp. 97–102). Westport, CT: Greenwood.

Kümmerling-Meibauer, B. (2003). Stiefkind Kinderlyrik: Über dichtende Übersetzer, übersetzende Dichter und warum es Kinderlyrik international so schwer hat. *JuLit, 29*(1), 3–11.

Kyritsi, M.-V. (2006). Taboo or not to be? Edgar Taylor and the first translations of the Grimms' *Kinder- und Hausmärchen*. In V. Joosen, & and K. Vloeberghs (Eds.), *Changing concepts of childhood and children's literature* (pp. 195–208). Newcastle, England: Cambridge Scholar Press.

Lathey, G. (2005). The travels of Harry: International marketing and the translation of J. K. Rowling's *Harry Potter. The Lion & the Unicorn, 29*(2), 141–151.

Lathey, G. (2006a). Time, narrative intimacy and the child: Implications of tense switching in the translation of picture books into English. In G. Lathey (Ed.), *The translation of children's literature: A reader* (pp. 134–142). Clevedon, England: Multicultural Matters. (Original work published 2003)

Lathey, G. (2006b). 'What a funny name!' Cultural transition in

versions of Erich Kästner's *Emil and the Detectives*. In F. M. Collins & J. Ridgman (Eds.), *Turning the page: Children's literature in performance and the media* (pp. 115–132). Oxford, England: Peter Lang.

Le Brun, C. (2003). De *Little Women* de Louisa May Alcott aux *Quatre filles du docteur March*: Les traductions françaises d'un roman de formation au féminin. *Meta, 48*(1–2), 47–67.

Le Brun, C. (2005). Roman pour la jeunesse et sociolectes: Les traductions québécoises de Kevin Major. *Canadian Children's Literature, 31*(2), 60–82.

Li, L. (2006). Influences of translated children's texts upon Chinese children's literature. *Papers, 16*(2), 101–106.

Lindgren, C., Andersson, C., & Renauld, C. (2007). La traduction des livres pour enfants suédois en Français: Lère partie: Choix et transformations. *La Revue Des Livres Pour Enfants, 234*, 87–93.

Liseling-Nilsson, S. (2006). Translating "the already seen" as a Polish guide to Swedish culture: A reflection on intertextuality, play, games and diminutives. In V. Joosen & K. Vloeberghs (Eds.). *Changing concepts of childhood and children's literature* (pp. 209–219). Newcastle, England: Cambridge Scholar Press.

Malarte-Feldman, C. L. (1999). The challenges of translating Perrault's *Contes* into English. *Marvels & Tales, 13*(2), 184–197.

Mazi-Leskovar, D. (2003). Domestication and foreignization in translating American prose for Slovenian children. *Meta, 48*(1-2), 250–265.

Mdallel, S. (2003). Translating children's literature in the Arab world: The state of the art. *Meta, 48*(1–2), 298–306.

Netley, N. S. (1992). The difficulty of translation: Decoding cultural signs in other languages. *Children's Literature in Education, 23*(4), 195–202.

Nières-Chevrel, I. (2003). Traduire *In the Night Kitchen*, ou de la difficile lecture d'un album. *Meta, 48*(1-2), 154–163.

Nieuwenhuizen, A. (1998). Two-way traffic: Translating and publishing children's and young adult books from other countries. *Magpies, 13*(4), 4–8.

Nikolajeva, M. (1996). *Children's literature comes of age: Towards a new aesthetic*. New York, NY: Garland.

Nikolajeva M., & Scott. C. (2001). *How picturebooks work*. New York, NY: Garland.

Nikolajeva, M. (2006). What do we translate when we translate children's literature. In S. Beckett, & M. Nikolajeva (Eds.). *Beyond Babar: The European Tradition in Children's Literature* (pp. 277–298). Lanham, MD: Scarecrow.

Nord, C. (2003). Proper names in translations for children: *Alice in Wonderland* as a case in point. *Meta, 48*(1-2), 182–196.

Oittinen, R. (1993). *I am me—I am other: On the dialogics of translating for children*. Tampere, Finland: University of Tampere.

Oittinen, R. (2000). *Translating for children*. New York: Garland.

Oittinen, R. (2003). *Where the wild things are*: Translating picture books. *Meta, 48*(1-2), 128–141.

Oittinen, R. (2004). Change and renewal: Translating the visual in picture books. In T. van der Walt (Ed.), *Change and renewal in children's literature* (pp. 171–181). Westport, CT: Praeger.

Oittinen, R. (2006). The verbal and the visual: On the carnivalism and dialogics of translating for children. In G. Lathey (Ed.), *The translation of children's literature: A reader* (pp. 84–97). Clevedon, England: Multicultural Matters. (Original work published 1995)

O'Connell, E. (2006). Translating for children. In G. Lathey (Ed.), *The translation of children's literature: A reader* (pp. 15–24). Clevedon, England: Multicultural Matters. (Original work published 1999)

Øster Steffensen, A. (2003). Two versions of the same narrative –

Astrid Lindgren's *Mio, min Mio* in Swedish and Danish. *Meta, 48*(1–2), 104–114.

O'Sullivan, E. (1998a). Alice über Grenzen: Vermittlung und Rezeption von Klassikern der Kinderliteratur. In B. Hürlimann, & K. Richter (Eds.), *Das Fremde in der Kinder- und Jugendliteratur* (pp. 45–57). Weinheim, Germany: Juventa.

O'Sullivan, E. (1998b). Losses and gains in translation: Some remarks on the translation of humor in the books of Aidan Chambers. *Children's Literature, 26*, 185–204.

O'Sullivan, E. (1999). Von Dahl's Chickens zu Himmels Grausen: zum Übersetzen intertextueller Komik in der Kinderliteratur." *1000 und 1 Buch, 4*, 12–19.

O'Sullivan, E. (2001). Alice in different wonderlands: Varying approaches in the German translations of an English children's classic. In M. Meek (Ed.), *Children's literature and national identity* (pp. 11–21). Stoke-on-Trent, England: Trentham.

O'Sullivan, E. (2005a). *Comparative Children's Literature*. New York, NY: Routledge.

O'Sullivan, E. (2005b). Rose Blanche, Rosa Weiss, Rosa Blanca: A comparative view of a controversial picture book. *The Lion & the Unicorn, 29*(2), 152–170.

O'Sullivan, E. (2006a). Does Pinocchio have an Italian passport? What is specifically national and what is international about classics of children's literature. In G. Lathey (Ed.), *The translation of children's literature: A Reader* (pp. 146–162). Clevedon, England: Multicultural Matters. (Original work published 1992)

O'Sullivan, E. (2006b). Narratology meets translation studies, or, the voice of the translation in children's literature. In G. Lathey, (Ed.), *The Translation of children's literature: A reader* (pp. 98–110). Clevedon, England: Multicultural Matters. (Original work published 2003)

Pascua, I. (2003). Translation and intercultural education. *Meta, 48*(1-2), 276–284.

Puurtinen, T. (2006). Translating children's literature: Theoretical approaches and empirical studies. In G. Lathey (Ed.), *The translation of children's literature: A reader* (pp. 54–64). Clevedon, England: Multicultural Matters. (Original work published 1994)

Rhedin, U. (2001). Småbarnsbilderboken och det lilla barnet. In N. Goga, & I. Mjør (Eds.), *Møte Mellom Ord Og Bilde* (pp. 26–49). Oslo, Norway: LNU.

Rieken-Gerwing, I. (1995). *Gibt es eine Spezifik kinderliterarischen Übersetzens? Untersuchungen zu Anspruch und Realität bei der literarischen Übersetzung von Kinder- und Jugendbüchern.* Frankfurt am Main, Germany: Lang.

Rossi, P. (2003). Translated and adapted – The influence of time on Translation. *Meta, 48*(1-2), 142–153.

Rutschmann, V., & Von Stockar, D. (1996). *Zum Übersetzen von Kinder- und Jugendliteratur.* Lausanne, Switzerland: Centre de Traduction Littéraire.

Seago, K. (2006). Nursery politics: Sleeping Beauty or the acculturation of a tale. In G. Lathey (Ed.), *The Translation of Children's Literature: A Reader* (pp. 175–189). Clevedon, England: Multicultural Matters. (Original work published 1995)

Seifert, M. (2005). The image trap: The translation of English-Canadian children's literature into German. In E. O'Sullivan, K. Reynolds, & R. Romøren (Eds.), *Children's literature global*

and local: Social and aesthetic perspective (pp. 227–239). Oslo, Norway: Novus.

Shavit, Z. (2006). Translation of children's literature. In G. Lathey (Ed.), *The translation of children's literature: A reader* (pp. 25–40). Clevedon, England: Multicultural Matters. (Original work published 1986)

Skott, S. (1977). Karlsson på taket i rysk översättning. In M. Ørvig, M. Eriksson, & B. Sjoquist. *En Bok om Astrid Lindgren* (pp. 84–132). Stockholm, Sweden: Rabén & Sjögren.

Stahl, J. D. (2006). Mark Twain's "Slovenly Peter" in the context of Twain and German culture. In G. Lathey (Ed.), *The translation of children's literature: A reader* (pp. 211–244). Clevedon, England: Multicultural Matters. (Original work published in 1996)

Stan, S. (Ed.) (2002). *The world through children's books*. Lanham, MD: Scarecrow.

Stan, S. (2004). *Rose Blanche* in translation. *Children's Literature in Education, 35*(1), 21–33.

Stolt, B. (2006). How Emil becomes Michel: On the translation of children's books. In G. Lathey (Ed.), *The translation of children's literature: A reader* (pp. 67–83). Clevedon, England: Multicultural Matters. (Original work published in 1978)

Stolze, R. (2003). Translating for children—World view or pedagogics? *Meta, 48*(1-2), 208–221.

Surmatz, A. (2004). The topic of cannibalism: Its intertextual, international and interartial reception in children's literature of the 20th century. *Barnboken, 27*(2), 14–31.

Surmatz, A. (2005). *Pippi Långstrump als Paradigma: Die deutsche Rezeption Astrid Lindgrens und ihr internationaler Kontext.* Tübingen, Germany: Francke.

Tabbert, R. (2006). Approaches to the translation of children's literature: a review of critical studies since 1960. In P. Hunt (Ed.), *Children's literature: Critical concepts in literary and cultural studies* (Vol. 4, pp. 100–144). London, England: Routledge. (Original work published 2002)

Teodorowicz-Hellman, E. (2004). *Polsko-szwedzkie kontakty literackie: Studia o literaturze dla dzieci i mlodziezy.* Warszawa, Poland: IBL.

Toury, G. (1995). *Descriptive translation studies and beyond.* Amsterdam, The Netherlands: John Benjamin.

Thomson-Wohlgemuth, G. (2003). Children's literature and translation under the East German regime. *Meta, 48*(1–2), 241–249.

Thomson-Wohlgemuth, G. (2004). Children's literature in translation from east to west. In S. Chapleau (Ed.) *New voices in children's literature criticism* (pp. 119–128). Lichfield, England: Pied Piper.

Tomlinson, C. M. (1998). *Children's books from other countries.* Lanham, MD: Scarecrow Press.

Valado, L. (2002). Astrid Lindgren traducida: Galicia apuesta por 'Os irmáns Corazón de León'. *Cuadernos de Literatura Infantil y Juvenil, 15*, 25–32.

Weaver, W. (1964). *Alice in many tongues: The translations of* Alice in Wonderland. Madison: University of Wisconsin Press.

Wyler, L. (2003). *Harry Potter* for children, teenagers and adults. *Meta, 48*(1–2), 5–14.

Yamazaki, A. (2002). Why change names? On the translations of children's books. *Children's Literature in Education, 33*(1), 53–62.

Zipes, J. (2006). *Why fairy tales stick: The evolution and relevance of a genre.* New York, NY: Routledge.

Point of Departure

Tara F. Chace

Academic studies often completely overlook the business side of the book industry, as Maria Nikolajeva does in her otherwise excellent survey of the schools of thought in translation theory. For example, absurd decisions such as Nikolajeva cites for adapting *Robinson Crusoe* from 500 to 24 pages are made by publishers and editors, never translators.

In fact, translators generally don't choose the books they translate and are often subject to editorial whimsy. At any serious gathering of literary translators, horror stories abound of ignorant, misguided, and injudicious editing—I personally know two established translators who have felt compelled to use pseudonyms on published translations because of egregious editorial changes made without their consent.

Translators who translate into English also face the problem that so many people around the world speak some English: It happens all too frequently that a publisher or author, who is not a native speaker of English, will introduce stylistic problems or outright errors into an English translation. This can lead to agonizing battles and seriously harm the quality of the translation.

Luckily, I have avoided such pitfalls so far. What I do suffer from, like most translators, is lack of time. I have a 400-page novel due back to the publisher in just two months—but let me set that aside for a moment and provide a practicing literary translator's perspective on why more books aren't translated into English, followed by a discussion of why excellent translators don't do more literary translations.

The English-language book market dwarfes the markets for other languages. In 2008, the United States published approximately 500,000 new book titles and editions, the United Kingdom published over 120,000, and Sweden published 4,365. Looking specifically at children's and young-adult books, in 2008 the United States published 29,438 new titles, and Sweden 828. Of those 828, 455 were translations from another language; thus, the pool of Swedish juvenile titles an English-language publisher might even consider translating is miniscule: 373. And of that miniscule pool, the number of titles that are as good as, or better than, what is already available in English is smaller yet.

Publishers also usually incur extra costs for translation when they publish foreign-language titles, so such titles must offer commercial benefit or literary quality beyond what is already available in English to compensate for the extra costs of translation.

The English-language book market is also highly professionalized; I know of many European authors and not a few publishers who think they can get their books published in the United States without an agent, not understanding that most U.S. publishers won't consider blind submissions because of the volume they receive already. The literary landscapes in some countries, e.g., the Nordic countries, are also heavily supported by government arts funding. Competing in the more cutthroat U.S. market often comes as a shock.

Ultimately, one of the most significant reasons more books are not translated into English is that English-language publishers simply don't have people on staff who can read manuscripts in various languages. What publisher wants to purchase rights to a book she can't read and then spend money on translating it only to discover it wasn't as good as the foreign publisher originally claimed? If more publishers could read languages other than English, more foreign books would likely be published in English translation.

Yet, publishers are remiss if they don't explore foreign publishers' tables at book fairs and develop networks of trusted sources to tip them off to good candidates. For very promising books, publishers should commission reader reports and sample translations—and they should be aware of the options available to cover the translation costs. Obviously picking a bestseller is most lucrative, but many U.S. and U.K. publishers are unaware of subsidies and grants (e.g., from the governments of the Nordic countries) that cover most of the translation costs after publication.

Then there is the challenge of finding a good translator. A representative of a large German publishing house I recently spoke with said 30% of the translations she commissioned were unusable, largely because the translation was too close to the source and thus too clunky to read, even unintelligible in spots. She said her second biggest problem with translations was that a surprising number of them are turned in late, sometimes *months* late, throwing off the publisher's lineup. Full-time, experienced translators average about 2,000 words a day. A book can easily run 100,000 words, so if you hire a translator who isn't working on the project full time, or if the translation is more difficult than anticipated, or if the translator can't start early enough, it's not hard to see how publishers' deadlines (and bottom lines) can suffer.

Why, then, don't more excellent translators translate more literature? According to the American Translators Association, the average full-time, professional translator earns between $0.11 and $0.18 per word (depending on language combination) and has an average income of $60,423. However, these successful translators tend to be very busy running their own freelance translation businesses. They also tend not to do too many literary translations, in part because they have trouble finding publishers who want books translated but also because translating literature doesn't pay as well as translating other kinds of material and is very time consuming. Many translators who do translate literature actually earn the majority of their income from another source, e.g., an academic position, retirement pension, or from a spouse's income. In my case, about 30% of my translation work is literary, and the rest is medical/pharmaceutical—I couldn't afford to live on what I make as a literary translator alone.

So, does anyone make a living translating literature? In a few countries, yes. However, it is very rare in the U.S. or U.K. and numerous other countries to find anyone, even the most esteemed translators, who support themselves entirely by translating literature. The European Council of Literary Translators Associations published an international survey in 2008 that spells this out most clearly: "Literary translators earn much less than workers in the manufacturing and service sector" (http://www.ceatl.eu/docs/surveyuk.pdf, p. 69)

Even when a publishing house wants to hire a literary translator, however, they often don't know where to find one. They would never solicit 10 sample translations and choose the best translator to do the job; they almost always rely on word of mouth, networking, or even bilingual people in house to do the job.

In view of these factors, I disagree with Nikolajeva's assertion that "[p]ractical translation is often a matter of individual choices where decisions are made irrespective of general principles." To the contrary, a good translator will have a rationale for just about every translation choice that he or she makes. However, publishers do not always choose good translators and even the best translators are affected by *economic* factors, e.g., tight deadlines or low pay, forcing them to rush through the translation or, perhaps even more disastrously, the proofreading. Add to that editorial considerations entirely outside the translator's control and you will find many substandard translations on bookshelves.

The translator is just one cog in the complex machinery required to bring a book from the author to the reader. As the translator, I have a great deal in common with the author: I hold the copyright, I receive an advance, I earn royalties and subsidiary rights, and I write the book. Well, sort of. I also have a lot in common with the publisher: I'm a serious professional in the business of books, I deal with deadlines, contracts, sales numbers, publicity, and networking. I also have a lot in common with the reader: I love books, I love words, I love great works of literature and some not so great ones, too. You'd be hard pressed to find someone who has read a book as carefully as its translator.

30

The Implied Reader of the Translation

Petros Panaou

University of Nicosia, Cyprus

Tasoula Tsilimeni

University of Thessaly

In this chapter, literary scholars Petros Panaou and Tasoula Tsilimeni approach the translation of children's literature from a different perspective than that of the more academic arguments critiqued by Maria Nikolajeva in the previous chapter. By combining insights from narratology with translation theory and practice, they discuss how translators, when they move from source texts to target texts, translate cultural expectations and ideologies regarding childhood along with the actual words, sometimes distorting the originals and seeking to remove the "foreign" elements that make translated literature so valuable for children in their quest to understand cultural difference. Kostia Kontoleon, in her Point of Departure essay, focuses more on her commitment to preserve the aesthetic qualities of a text, but she too recognizes the importance of translation as an intermediary between diverse cultures.

Considering the Implied Reader

Let us consider this: An author is writing a story from a boy's perspective about the death of his favorite pet. At a crucial point of the story, the boy's father attempts to explain "death" to him. The author ponders two versions of this scene:

(1) "Dead," said Daddy, "is very different from sleeping. Dead is —"

"— NOT alive!" I shouted.

or

(2)"When somebody dies," said Daddy, "it doesn't mean that he is asleep.

It means that…"

"…he is not alive?" I asked.

Which version of the scene will she decide to include in the final draft? What effect will this choice have on her story? A boy protagonist who shouts "NOT alive!" is significantly different from a protagonist who reservedly asks "…he is not alive?" The first expresses anger, an emotion that is part of a series of emotions associated with mourning. The latter avoids expressing intense feelings. How will the author decide? If she thinks that the child reader is capable of processing the intense emotions that accompany loss, then she will probably choose the first. If she believes that children are too innocent and hyper-sensitive to be asked to empathize with such powerful feelings, she will choose the latter.

Now let us consider this: Both choices have been incorporated in published picture books, the first one in the English version of *Goodbye Mousie* (Harris, 2001), and the second one in its Greek translation (translated by Dimitra, 2003, n.p.). Aren't we justified to infer that both a different protagonist and a different reader are implied by each text?

In her comparative analysis of translated versions of Roberto Innocenti's and Christophe Gallaz's (1985) *Rose Blanche*, a picture book portrayal of a young girl who discovers a Nazi concentration camp on the outskirts of her German city, Susan Stan (2004) concludes that

> [...] cultural, aesthetic, national, ideological, pedagogical, and economic issues are all at work in shaping these translations. The Italian saying *traduttóre, traditóre* — "to translate is to betray"— underscores the impossibility of capturing the whole of the original in a translation, but perhaps more to the point in a work for children, where fidelity is not always the main concern, is the Latin motto of the marketplace, *caveat emptor*—"let the buyer beware." (p. 31)

Emer O'Sullivan (2005) asserts that "The implied reader of the translation will always be a different entity from the implied reader of the source text" (p. 105). Perry Nodelman and Mavis Reimer (2003) observe that "All texts have an implied reader. That is, they suggest in their subject and their style the characteristics of the reader best equipped to understand and respond to them" (p. 16). Since the translation of a text, pragmatically, can never preserve the exact same subject and style—let alone that these are often intentionally altered in the case of children's literature translation—the reader best equipped to understand and respond to the new text may be a different reader than that implied by the original.

Building on Whalen-Levitt's (1983) ideas, Nodelman and Reimer describe the implied reader in terms of what the text asks its reader to know and to do while reading it. A text, Nodelman and Reimer tell us, implies a reader with specific tastes and interests, a reader who possesses particular knowledge about literature and life, and a reader who can implement specific reading strategies in order to decode the text at hand (p. 17). A translated children's text, perhaps because of children's assumed inexperience of literature and the world, always assumes that its child-reader in the target culture will not share the same knowledges and strategies with the implied child-reader of the source text. In its anticipation of a reader who knows and acts differently from the reader

of the source text, the translation constructs a different implied reader.

Giuliana Schiavi (1996) was perhaps the first to focus on the difference between the implied reader of the source text and the implied reader of its translation. The process she describes is quite simple: The implied reader of the source text is generated by the implied author; likewise, the implied reader of the translation is generated by the *implied translator*. The translator, according to Schiavi, interprets the original text, follows certain norms, and adopts specific strategies and methods, creating in this manner a new relationship between the translated text and the reader. By doing this, s/he creates a different implied reader from the one in the source text.

Communicating across Cultures

In *Comparative Children's Literature*, Emer O'Sullivan (2005) takes this theoretical framework one step further, presenting a valuable analytical tool, a communicative model of translation which links the theoretical fields of narratology and translation studies. O'Sullivan explains that the communication between the *real author of the source text* and the *real reader of the translation* is mediated by the *real translator*. The *real translator* functions at first as "a receptive agent" (p. 107), an interpreting reader of the source text. S/he then "transmits the source text via the intratextual agency of the *implied translator*" (p. 107). The implied translator, to one degree or another, generates a different *narrator*, *narratee*, and *implied reader* within the target text. O'Sullivan asserts that we should take more notice of the "second voice" in any translated text, "the voice of the translator" (pp. 107–108). Thus, we should persistently ask such questions about translated children's books such as "What kind of translator can be perceived in the text? Where can the translator be located in the act of communication which is the narrative text? How does the implied reader of the target text differ from that of the source text?" (p. 104).

And, of course, the next question is: How have the different cultural contexts influenced these changes? Literary critics have long acknowledged the importance of the cultures and ideologies within which literature is created. Historical and geographical factors often determine both the content and the perspective of a story. Peter Hollindale (1988) claims that a big part of any book is authored, not by its author, but by the world its author inhabits (p. 15). What happens, then, when this book is translated into another world? Shouldn't we also presume that a big part of any translated book is translated, not by its translator, but by the world its translator inhabits?

Critical analysis of translated texts becomes much more meaningful once we begin asking questions like the ones listed above. This is evident, for instance, in Viggo Hjørnager Pedersen's (2008) analysis of Victorian translations of Andersen's fairytales. Professor at Copenhagen University and a literary translator himself, Hjørnager Pedersen begins the introduction of his analysis as follows:

> Unlike plays, books were not censored in Victorian England, censorship having been abolished in 1695. But that does not mean that there were not fairly strict rules governing what might and might not be published, especially for children. As Hans Christian Andersen was generally perceived as a children's writer pure and simple rather than as a writer for both adults and children, such rules were also applied to translations of his stories. (p. 308)

While the source texts produced in Denmark were intended for a dual audience, the target texts in Victorian England were intended for children only. By identifying this pivotal difference regarding the intended audience of each text, Hjørnager Pedersen has paved the way for a productive and well-structured analysis of the translations. The application of Victorian children's literature norms to Hans Christian Andersen's stories inscribed a different implied reader in the target texts.

After a brief discussion of Andersen's own ideas about censorship and the literary climate in early 19th-century Britain, Hjørnager Pedersen moves on to "examples from Andersen's tales in Victorian translation where there is clear evidence of departures from the text that must be due to the publisher's and/or the translator's ideas about decorum where children were concerned" (p. 309). Through these examples, he demonstrates how sexual references, as well as references to violence, death, and religious taboos were toned down by Victorian translators. One such example is found in Caroline Peachey's translation of "The Top and the Ball." A female ball, who had previously rejected a male top, meets him again in a garbage can several years later and tells her story about never getting married and falling into the roof "gutter":

Hjørnager Pedersen's translation of the Danish text:	Peachey's translation:
[...] there I have lain five years, soaking! That is a long time, believe me, for a maid!	I fell into the gutter, and there I have lain five years, and am now wet through. Only think, what a wearisome time for a young lady to be in such a situation!

(pp. 312–313)

Peachey tones down, of course, the sexual connotations, connotations that become even more explicit when Hjørnager Pedersen explains that in Danish the word "Jomfru," which he translates as "maid" and Peachey as "young lady," means both "young woman" *and* "virgin."

Some Revelatory Differences in English-to-Greek Picture Book Translations

But let us test O'Sullivan's (2005) analytical tool in practice, asking the questions suggested by her model in relation to picture books translated from English into Greek, and identifying possible shifts in the constructs of the implied reader. We have intentionally chosen to comment on translated books that deal with "sensitive" issues (i.e., "death" and "difference") in the hope that these translations will be more revealing. While we do not claim that analyzing a few translations will result in broad and irrefutable conclusions, we do agree with Márta Minier (2006), when she writes that

> A translation as a metatext will speak about how an individual culture (and translator) perceives and constructs within its own boundaries the foreignness of another culture; hence, it is determined to reveal a great deal about contemporaneous discourses in a receiving community. (p. 120)

Translations of *children's* books, in particular, are bound to reveal contemporaneous discourses in the receiving community regarding "childhood" and "children's literature." O'Sullivan (2005) suggests that "shifts in the narrative style of the translation provide evidence of the preferences of translators and their assumptions about their readers, and also of the norms and conventions dominating the translation of children's literature" (p. 118). According to Michal Borodo (2006), because of their connection to the child as a specific type of addressee, norms in child-oriented translation and translation studies have proceeded along different lines from mainstream translation.

O' Sullivan (2005) observes that, in translated texts, culture-specific notions of childhood play at least some part in determining the construction of the implied reader. She argues that the implied reader in a translated text can differ substantially from the implied reader in the original, depending on the manner in which a translator in a given time and culture will answer such questions such as: "What do 'children' want to read? What are their cognitive and linguistic capabilities? How far can/should they be stretched? What is suitable for them? What do they enjoy?" (p. 110).

Answers to such questions are often culture-specific. In the Greek translation of Daniela Bunge's (2006) *The Scarves*—translated by Dimitra Simou (2006) from English even though it was originally written in German—different culture-specific answers about the needs of children lead to a major change regarding the main characters and their closeness to the child-reader. Since divorce is still, at least to some extent, a taboo subject in the Greek speaking world, the implied translator makes the separation of the child protagonists' *grand*parents less traumatic by turning them into *god*parents instead. The implied child-reader is one who might be shocked or damaged by representations of disruptions to relations within her/his immediate family. Grandparents are certainly immediate family for Greek children; indeed in some cases they are closer to children than their own parents are. Thus, the implied translator feels that the distance between implied reader and protagonists needs to be increased.

Translation Norms in Reductive and Amplifying Narration

Birgit Stolt (2006) identifies educational intentions in child-oriented translation, which often result in censoring and didacticism, a tendency to adjust the text according to the assumptions about children's needs and capacity, and a "tendency to sentimentalize and prettify" (p. 77). Isabelle Desmidt (2003) proposes a typology of translation norms, distinguishing between:

- **preliminary norms** (in relation to the selection of texts to be translated, etc.);
- **literary and educational norms** (whether 'literary entertainment' or 'the educational aspect' is prioritized);
- **pedagogical norms** (the tendency to simplify the story and to modify elements which are not congruent with the prevalent pedagogical values in the receiving culture);
- **business norms** (the role of the publisher and the market in general). (pp. 168–172)

In *Goodbye Mousie* (Harris, 2003), the example mentioned at the beginning of the chapter, Stolt's (1978) "educational intentions" or Desmidt's (2003) "educational norms" are prevalent. The priority of this translation is not so much to entertain and to preserve the literary quality of the original, but rather to teach the child-reader about death in a subtle and sensitive manner. A tendency to adjust the text according to children's assumed needs and capacity is also apparent. The implied translator constructs a different implied reader by smoothing down the edges, as it were. A more sensitive and gullible child-reader is implied. Besides substituting the boy's shouting with mere questioning, the implied translator also substitutes the taboo word, "dead" (πεθαμένος), wherever she finds it, with a different, smoother word or phrase. Here is an example:

Source text:	Target text translated back into English:
Mousie did NOT die!	Mousie did NOT die!
Mousie is NOT dead!	Mousie **is alive**!

The implied translator also views a shoebox as an inappropriate coffin for Mousie, so she changes it into "a nice carton box" (Harris, 2003, n.p.). And since she finds the use of past tense in the phrase "You were a good mouse" (Harris, 2001, n.p.) too disturbing, she chooses to omit the sentence altogether, minimizing in this manner the boy's realization and acceptance of Mousie's death. Finally, since the implied reader is considered uncritical and easily confused, some potentially confusing phrases are also omitted. Before burying Mousie, the boy places food and toys in the shoebox-coffin, so that Mousie won't be hungry or bored. The translation does not include the phrase "'Now Mousie won't be hungry!' I said" (Harris, 2001, n.p.), keeping only the phrase "'Now Mousie won't be

bored!' I said" (Harris, 2003, n.p.). This is probably due to the translator's eagerness to protect the child-reader from possibly misguiding notions (i.e., that the dead are able to eat). The Greek translation is characterized, for the most part, by substitution and omission, the latter pointing to some extent towards a *reductive narration*:

> …changes in the constitution of the implied reader of the translation made by the implied translator omitting features, cutting sections of text, or reducing several readers' roles inscribed in the source text to only a few in the target text. (O'Sullivan, 2005, p. 115)

Substitution and omission also characterize the translation of Ann De Bode's (1997) *Grandad I'll Always Remember You*, translated from English into Greek by Fotini Peramatzeli (2000), even though the original is in Flemish. This is another text that deals with death. In the scene where Grandma is describing how Grandad died, the phrase "You're an angel, Grandad **said**" (De Bode, 1997, p. 8) is substituted with the phrase "You're an angel, Grandad **smiled**" (De Bode, 2000, p. 8) even though there is not a hint of a smile on Grandad's face in the picture. The implied translator strives to foreground Grandad's tranquility during the last hours of his life. Moreover, the translation omits some phrases that are emotionally charged; one such phrase is: "They [the relatives] are staring into space, and sighing" (De Bode, 1997, p. 5). Educational intentions, which aim to introduce the subject of death and loss as gently as possible to children, are once more prioritized.

The translated picture books analyzed below operate in a completely different manner, but under the auspices of similar norms and assumptions about children. What we have in these target texts is *amplifying narration*:

> Extensive additions to the text, however, can amplify it to the extent that the explanatory voice of the translator as narrator of the translation is so different in nature from that of the narrator of the source text that it drowns out the original narrative voice. We then have a new constitution of the implied reader. (O'Sullivan, 2005, p. 114)

Rather than substituting, simplifying, and omitting, the implied translators of these picture books add, expand, and explain.

In the translation of David McKee's (1989) *Elmer* by Athina Andritsopoulou (1996), perhaps the most important difference between source and target text is found in the title. The English title is a single word, the protagonist's name: "Elmer." The Greek title, on the other hand, consists of the protagonist's name "Elmer" followed by the explanatory phrase "the dappled elephant." This is a twofold change. To begin with, the addition of explanatory text after the elephant's name solidifies his identity, his central characteristic, his essence: *This* is Elmer, the *dappled* elephant. Thus, the Greek picture book "essentializes" Elmer even before the story begins. The English version avoids this "essentializing" notion, using a similar phrase only in Elmer's thoughts: "'Whoever heard of a patchwork elephant?' he thought" (McKee, 1989, n.p.).

One suspects the workings of Desmidt's (2003) "business norms" here. Of course, we can only speculate about the reasons behind this addition. One possible explanation, however, is marketing-related; one could suggest that the change in the title announces a spectacle in the form of an advertisement. From this point of view, the cover calls for attention by inviting prospective readers/consumers to read/buy this intriguing picture book about a strange, *dappled* elephant. The cover invites readers in; just like in the old days a circus director would invite customers into the tent to have a look at a "freak of nature."

As O'Sullivan (2005) explains, many real people usually contribute to the agency of *the implied translator*. The "'translator's consciousness' is not necessarily or exclusively that of the real translator" (p. 107). Joel Taxel (2002) writes that "[w]hile obvious to those *within* the industry, the impact of the business side of children's literature has not been given the sustained and systematic scrutiny it deserves by children's literature scholars and the educational community in general" (p. 146), which he will further explore in his own chapter in this volume. The business impact is observable even in the case of English source texts that get exported from one English-speaking country to another. Perhaps it is even more observable in this case, since the text gets altered in spite of the fact that there is no significant need for linguistic translation. Laura Atkins (2004), reflecting about her work as an assistant editor at Orchard Books in New York, describes a process of "Americanising" British books for children, through which elements such as unfamiliar spellings, words, and locations are edited. These changes are based on the assumption that "the North-American child reader is by and large reluctant, and only wants to read about familiar experiences in recognisable language" (p. 49). We may conclude that, even though these texts are not translated from one language into another, the cultural translation that takes place does result in a different target text with a different implied reader. What is even more important is that Atkins points to market forces that guide the construct of a different implied child-reader. Children's books are usually bought by adults (parents, teachers, and librarians): "The child's needs here are constructed according to the perception of what the majority of teachers and librarians will accept, as perceived by the publisher whose concern is selling to that market" (p. 52).

In relation to the Greek translation of *Elmer* (McKee, 1996), a second market-related issue arises regarding the extension of the title. The translator avoids a word-to-word translation of "patchwork" and chooses instead the Greek word παρδαλός, an adjective that, for lack of a better word, we have translated back into English as "dappled." Παρδαλός usually means both dappled and multicolored, but is also charged with negative or sarcastic connotations: Someone who is παρδαλός is often viewed as too flashy and pretentious. One could claim that this choice of words was probably made by a publisher, an editor, and/or a marketer who intentionally marketed the picture book as "funny" by making fun of Elmer. The new implied reader is expected to read the picture book as a funny book and thus view Elmer from an ironic distance rather than empathize with him.

Yet another noticeable alteration is the employment of *amplifying narration* to foreground Elmer's friendship with the rest of the elephants. In the same manner that negative emotions are toned down in the translations of *Goodbye Mousie* (Harris, 2003) and *Grandad I'll Always Remember You* (De Bode, 2000), in the translation of *Elmer* (McKee, 1996) any unpleasant connotations that might stem from Elmer being different are also toned down. The implied translator achieves this effect by emphasizing the fact that Elmer may be different from the other elephants but he is their friend. Several phrases that point to Elmer's strong friendship with the rest of the elephants are added to the translated text:

Source text:	Target text translated back into English:
[...] and lastly same old elephants.	...the elephants were also the same, **his old friends**.
All elephants must decorate themselves and Elmer will decorate himself elephant colour.	All of us will paint ourselves like him, dappled and **our Elmer** will paint himself in plain elephant color.

(McKee, 1989, 1996, n.p.)

Amplifying narration is found in the translation of *Susan Laughs* (Willis, 1999, translated by Filipos Mandilaras, 2001) as well. Both the Greek and the English text are poems, but the manner in which the Greek poem relates to the images in the picture book, in terms of space and meaning, differs significantly from the relationship between the English poem and the pictures. In terms of space, the English poem is spread out in such a way that each verse is divided in half and each half is linked to a separate picture. In this manner, the number of words that correspond to each picture is kept to a minimum. Also, since 8 out of the 18 verses take up the entire lower part of the open book, the reader is often urged to move on to the next double-spread in order to complete the rhyme; this achieves a fast and animated rhythm. This feature is lost in the Greek translation, where a complete verse is found under each picture and the rhyming verse can be read on the adjacent page.

In terms of meaning, the text-image relation is altered by the implied translator's tendency to allocate more content and power to the text. Things left unspoken by the author are spelled out by the translator, altering the entire viewing and reading process. Regarding the translation of the specific genre of picture books, O'Sullivan (2005) writes:

In this genre combining words and pictures, an ideal translation reflects an awareness not only of the significance of the original text but also of the interaction between the visual and the verbal, what the pictures do in relation to the words; it does not verbalize the interaction but leaves gaps that make the interplay possible and exciting. (p. 122)

This translated picture book does the exact opposite. "Susan waves, Susan grins" (Willis, 1999, n.p.), for example, is translated as "Argiro waves from the car. Argiro goes to the museum for a walk" (Willis, 2001, n.p.), describing the exact actions depicted in the illustrations. We will comment on the name change later, but what is most unfortunate here is the loss of the "training" performed by the source text. The source text seems to be continually preparing the reader for the work s/he will need to do in the end to decode the final page. By leaving things unsaid, it forces the reader to switch to a certain mode of reading, where one has to look for additional meaning in the picture. This is exactly what one needs to do to understand the ending of the book, where the reader has to combine the visual and textual signs on the last page and on all of the preceding pages, in order to realize that Susan can do all these things even though she is in a wheelchair. But the implied translator translates both text and pictures, spelling out almost everything. The markedly different implied reader of this text would find it hard to decode the last page of the book. The implied reader of the translation is perceived as either lazy or incompetent, someone that doesn't seek out additional meaning in the images.

Differences in Narrative Style and Voice

O'Sullivan (2005) asserts that shifts in the narrative style of the translation may be guided by "narrative methods of children's literature more familiar to the target culture" (p. 118). This might be the case here, since the minimal text in the English version of *Susan Laughs* (Willis, 1999) is highly uncommon in children's literature originally written in Greek. Zohar Shavit (2006) explains that in the translation of children's literature, "If the model of the original text does not exist in the target system, the text is changed by deleting or by adding such elements as will adjust it to the integrating model of the target system" (p. 28). The picture book, as a distinctively different genre from the illustrated book, is very new in the system of Greek children's literature. This may be one of the reasons behind the addition of text and the resistance to allocate narrative value and power to the image, observed in the Greek translation of *Susan Laughs* (Willis, 2001). Culture-specific conventions, such as the narrative style of stories addressed to very young children, may have influenced the last translation we will be discussing as well.

In the translation of *Something Else* (Cave, 1995, translated by Tourkolia-Kidoneos, 1997), the implied translator introduces a certain shift in *the voice of the narrator*. In this picture book, the shift in the narrative style is even more evident than in the examples of amplifying and reductive narration discussed so far. Here, on several occasions, the translator modifies words to become what she conceives as more "child-friendly." What we comment on in relation to this translation may seem insignificant, but, as acclaimed translator Anthea Bell (2006) stresses in "Translator's Notebook: Delicate Matters," small changes can often be quite important:

By 'delicate matters', in the context of translation, I mean they are fiddly and may look very minor: choice of tense, use of pronouns, those matters of everyday occurrence in translation work which you would think couldn't possibly make much difference to actual meaning. And yes, translators do take them in their stride every day. Only sometimes one has to stride back again for a second look, and it turns out that quite tiny things can affect meaning a good deal after all. (p. 232)

The use of diminutives, a common practice in Greek stories for very young children, is an illustrative example. The implied translator of *Something Else* (Cave, 1997) applies this convention, inserting diminutives in several parts of the target text. On the first page alone, three diminutives are added. The Greek diminutives "σπιτάκι" (little house), "μοναχούλι" (little and alone), and "φιλαράκι" (little friend) are used:

Source text:	Target text translated back into English:
On a windy hill alone with nothing to be friends with lived Something Else.	Up on a windblown hill, in a **little house**, lived **little and alone** Something Else without a single not even a single **little friend**.

(Cave, 1995, 1997, n.p.)

Ten more diminutives are found in the rest of the translation, bringing into effect a certain narrative shift. The narration is explicitly addressed to very young children and a sweet, sentimentalizing tone is adopted. Stolt's (2006) identification of a tendency to "sentimentalize and prettify" (p. 77) comes to mind. In the above example, the English text is kept simple, straight-forward and minimal (only 13 words), matching the bare hill and the emptiness/loneliness that surrounds it. The Greek text subverts this atmosphere, by introducing diminutives and by using more words than necessary.

A few pages later, *the voice of the translator* is heard once again. When a second "strange creature" (Cave, 1995, n.p.) visits the protagonist's home, the English text strives to communicate a feeling of alienation, by referring to the visitor as "the creature." The translation, on the other hand, refers to him as "το πλασματάκι" (the little creature) (Cave, 1997, n.p.):

Source text:	Target text translated back into English:
"You're welcome," said **the creature**.	"You're welcome," said **the little creature**.
The creature shook its head.	**The little creature** shook its head.
	(n.p.)

When plain and simple "creature" becomes "little creature," it inevitably looks less strange and alien. Another change that tones down the alienation is that the translation allocates the name "Something" to the creature much earlier than in the source text, where the creature is given a name only after it becomes Something Else's friend: "From then on, Something Else had Something to be friends with." (Cave, 1995, n.p.) Also, with the exception of the word "ανεμοδαρμένο" (windblown) on the first page, the implied translator introduces a more oral-oriented language compared to the source text. For example, "You don't belong here" (Cave, 1995, n.p.) is translated into "Your place is not here" (Cave, 1997, n.p.). In this manner, a new implied reader is constructed, one who uses and understands a limited number of words and is closer to the oral than to the written word.

The Translation of Culture-specific Items

The last issue we would like to discuss is the treatment of culture-specific items. These are items that, according to Göte Klingberg (1986), belong in certain categories:

- literary references
- foreign languages in the source text
- references to mythology and popular belief
- historical, religious and political background
- building and home furnishing, food
- customs, play and games
- flora and fauna
- personal names, titles, names of domestic animals, names of objects
- geographical names
- weights and measures (pp. 17–18)

Even though interesting conclusions can be drawn from studies that pay special attention to the treatment of these items in the translation, for the purposes of this short discussion, we refer only to personal names. In two of the picture books we have analyzed, there is "domestication" (Venuti, 2000, p. 16) of the characters' names; they are substituted with Greek names. In the translation of *Susan Laughs* (Willis, 2001), Susan is turned into "Αργυρώ," while in the translation of *Grandad I'll Always Remember You* (De Bode, 2000), Tom becomes "Νικόλας," Martin becomes "Παύλος," and Kate becomes "Έλλη." As Gillian Lathey (2006) observes, this kind of adaptation "rests on

assumptions that young readers will find it difficult to assimilate foreign names, coinage, foodstuffs or locations, and that they may reject a text reflecting a culture that is unfamiliar" (p. 7). However, Lathey then proceeds to argue that

> Once a narrative engages their interest, young readers will persevere with names and localities that are well beyond their ken in myths, legends and fantasy fiction written in their native languages, let alone in translations, and they will certainly never be intrigued and attracted by difference if it is kept from them. (pp. 7–8)

Stolt (2006) agrees with this opinion and supports it, citing both her personal experience and examples like Johanna Spyri's Heidi (1880/1899), a character who managed to became internationally renowned even though—and perhaps *because*—her name was not domesticated.

Child-oriented translation studies have dealt exhaustively with issues that pertain to culture-specific elements and the dilemma of "domestication" or "foreignization":

> Translators may assume two different positions and on this basis they will employ a specific translation strategy. On the one hand they may think that reading a book rich in culture-specific elements enables children to learn and enlarge their knowledge of the world, or on the other they may believe that children cannot deal with a foreign culture because they do not yet possess adequate interpretative and cognitive capacities. (Ippolito, 2006, p. 108)

Göte Klingberg (1986), Márta Minier (2006), Riitta Oittinen (2000), Lawrence Venuti (2000), and many others have participated in heated discussions of this complicated issue. It would certainly take much more than a short chapter to analyze this dilemma in depth. Some scholars even claim that there is no dilemma, since translation inevitably domesticates, at least to some degree, the source text: "Perhaps we should only speak of different levels and dimensions of domestication" (Paloposki & Oittinen, 2000, p. 386).

For the purposes of the present discussion, we agree with scholars like Venuti (2000) and Klingberg (1986), and Ippolito (2006) that "a translation should preserve the cultural values expressed by the original text, because these will promote mutual respect, friendship and dialogue, widen their knowledge of the world and open their minds to new and original ideas" (Ippolito, p. 109). When the culturally different is allowed to remain in the translated text, Helen W. Painter (1968) argues, it can be of charm, interest, and educational value to the child-reader.

Becoming the Implied Reader of a Translation

This brings us back to the *implied reader of the translation*. It should be stressed that the implied reader has a performative effect. Nodelman and Reimer (2003) emphasize that the implied reader, rather than being just a quality of the text, "is a role a text implies *and* invites a reader to take on" (p. 17). Wolfgang Iser (1974), who originally coined the term of the implied reader, explains that the term "incorporates both the prestructuring of the potential meaning by the text, and the reader's actualization of this potential through the reading process" (p. xiii). While reading the text, the real reader is asked to *become*, at least to some extent, the implied reader (Nodelman & Reimer, 2003, p. 17). In the same manner, the *implied reader of the translation* "pulls" the real reader of the translation towards a certain direction. We have already explained, at the beginning of our discussion, that the implied reader is inscribed in the text's expectations about what its reader will know and do. The repeated construction of a particular implied reader of the translation who does not have the knowledge or the ability to decode "foreign" (or "foreignized") texts, may become a self-fulfilling prophecy; it may very well *create* real child-readers who do not have the knowledge, the ability, or even the *willingness* to decode unfamiliar stories.

Our entire discussion so far supports Márta Minier's (2006) claim that, "[r]egarding the manner of the translation, the conflict seems to be between making the outcome of the translation process a visibly borrowed text, or rather a familiar sounding one which could have been originally conceived in the receiving language" (p. 102). We argue in favor of "visibly borrowed texts," not so much because of reverence for the "original," but because young readers should be allowed to experience other cultures than their own, through the reading of translated literature. We acknowledge the fact that a translation's implied reader can never—and perhaps *should* never—be identical to the implied reader of the source text; but we argue for *a foreignizing construct of the implied reader of the translation*. We argue in favor of implied readers that will have the opposite performative effect than the one described in the previous paragraph.

Are we privileging educational norms by taking seriously into account this performative effect? Perhaps, but at the same time we are also emphasizing the aesthetic value of a foreignizing translation, and the pleasure it can bring to a reader in the target culture. We favor translated texts whose implied readers have the knowledge, the ability, and the willingness to read and *enjoy* foreignized texts. In saying this, we emphasize a third aspect of the implied reader: An implied reader is not only what the text asks its reader to know or do, but also, and perhaps most importantly, what it asks the reader to *feel* and *enjoy*. In *Translating for Children*, Oittinen (2000) suggests that a translation should domesticate foreign elements, in order to stimulate within the target text reader the same feelings and impressions that are felt by the source text reader; we are arguing that the target text reader should be allowed to experience *different* emotions, emotions which stem from the very *difference* of a foreign text.

Our use of O'Sullivan's communicative model has indicated that, in the Greek translations we have read, there seems to be an intense effort to bring the text closer to a child-reader who lives in Greece, belongs to a different culture than the one in the source text, and—to use Atkins' (2004) words in a different context—is "by and large reluctant, and only wants to read about familiar experiences in recognisable language" (p. 49). This is why the ideologies, narrative style, and literary conventions of these translated picture books mimic those of children's books originally written in Greek. We suggest that the implied reader of a picture book's translation from English into Greek should indeed be a child who lives in Greece and belongs to a different culture than the one in the source text, but should also be a child who finds joy in reading books that seem "off-key" when compared to other books in her/his mother tongue, and pursues the pleasure of reading stories that were produced within and for "other" cultures.

This means, of course, that the implied reader of the translation will have to work hard to decode the "foreignized" text. O'Sullivan (2005) writes about translated picture books: "The implied reader of the translation should have to do the same work as the implied reader of the original to resolve the complex connections between text and pictures" (p. 122). Perhaps the implied reader of the translation should have to do *more* work than the reader of the original, both in resolving the connections between *foreignized* text and image and in resolving the *dis*connections between what s/he already knows and routinely does and what this book is asking her/him to learn or attempt to do. After all, as described earlier, only then will s/he experience the special kind of pleasure that differs from the one experienced by the reader of the original.

A fusion of narratology and translation studies—translation theories about culture-specific elements combined with what narratology says about the construct of the implied reader—has led to the formation of our argument for *a foreignizing construct of the implied reader of the translation*. Our ideal implied reader would have the following response to a foreignizing translation:

> This text was not written for me. It is a translation. It reflects another culture and the manner in which children and the world they live in are viewed in that culture. It is different and refreshing; this is why I enjoy it. I will pretend to be part of this culture for a while, just to get a glimpse of how it would feel to be a child in that culture.

Literature References

Bunge, D. (2006). *The Scarves*. (K. Bishop, Trans.) New York, NY: Minedition.

Bunge, D. (2006). *Κόκκινο και μπλε μαζί*. (Δ. Σίμου Μετ.). Αθήνα: Καλειδοσκόπιο.

Cave, K. (1995). *Something else*. (C. Riddell, Illus.). New York, NY: Viking.

Cave, K. (1997). *Το Κάτι Άλλο*. (Ρ. Τουρκολιά-Κυδωνιέως, Μετ.; C. Riddell, Εικον.). Αθήνα: Πατάκη.

De Bode, A. (1997). *Grandad I'll Always Remember You*. London, England: Evans Brothers.

De Bode, A. (2000). Παππού θα σε θυμάμαι για πάντα. (Φ. Περαματζέλη Μετ.). Χανιά: Γλαύκη.

Gallaz, C. (1985). *Rose Blanche*. (M. Coventry & R. Garglia, Trans.; R. Innocenti, Illus.). Mankato, MN: Creative Education.

Harris, R. H. (2001). *Goodbye Mousie*. (J. Omerod, Illus.). New York, NY: Simon & Schuster.

Harris, R. H. (2003). Αντίο Ποντικούλη. (Α. Δημητρά, Μετ.; J. Ormerod, Εικον.). Αθήνα: Ελληνική Παιδεία.

McKee, D. (1989). *Elmer*. London, England: Andersen Press.

McKee. (1996). Έλμερ ο Παρδαλός Ελέφαντας. (Α. Α. Ανδρουτσοπούλου Μετ.). Αθήνα: Πατάκη.

Spyri, J. (1899). *Heidi: A story for children and those that love children*. (H. B. Dole, Trans.). Boston, MA: Ginn & Company. (Original work published 1880)

Willis, J. (1999). *Susan laughs*. (T. Ross, Illus.). London, England: Andersen Press.

Willis, J. (2001). Η Αργυρώ Γελάει. (Φ. Μανδηλαράς, Απόδ.; T. Ross, Εικον.). Αθήνα: Πατάκη.

Academic References

Atkins, L. (2004). A publisher's dilemma: The place of the child in the publication of children's books. In S. Chapleau (Ed.), *New voices in children's literature criticism* (pp. 47–54). Lichfield, England: Pied Piper.

Bell, A. (2006). Translator's notebook: Delicate matters. In G. Lathey (Ed.), *The translation of children's literature: A reader* (pp. 232–240). Clevedon, England: Multilingual Matters.

Borodo, M. (2006). Between the global and the local: Child oriented translation today. In P. Pinsent (Ed.), *No child is an island: The case of children's literature in translation* (pp. 138–154). Lichfield, England: Pied Piper.

Desmidt, I. (2003, May). 'Jetzt bist du in Deutschland, Däumling.' *Nils Holgersson* on foreign soil – subject to new norms. *Meta: Translators' Journal, 48*, 165–181.

Hjørnager Pedersen, V. (2008). Self-censorship in Victorian translations of Hans Christian Andersen. In T. Seruya & M. L. Moniz (Eds.), *Translation and censorship in different times and landscapes* (pp. 308–318). Newcastle, England: Cambridge Scholars Publishing.

Hollindale, P. (1988). *Ideology and the children's book*. Woodchester, England: Thimble Press.

Ippolito, M. (2006). Translation of culture-specific items in children's literature: The case of Beatrix Potter. In P. Pinsent (Ed.), *No child is an island: The case of children's literature in translation* (pp. 107–118). Lichfield, England: Pied Piper.

Iser, W. (1974). *The implied reader: Patterns of communication in prose fiction from Bunyan to Beckett*. Baltimore, MD: Johns Hopkins University Press.

Klingberg, G. (1986). *Children's fiction in the hands of the translators*. Lund, Sweden: CWK Gleerup.

Lathey, G. (Ed.). (2006). *The translation of children's literature: A reader*. Clevedon, England: Multilingual Matters.

Minier, M. (2006). Linguistic inventions, culture-specific terms and intertexts in the Hungarian translations of *Harry Potter*. In P. Pinsent (Ed.), *No child is an island: The case of children's literature in translation* (pp. 119–137). Lichfield, England: Pied Piper.

Nodelman, P., & Reimer, M. (2003). *The pleasures of children's literature* (3rd ed.) Boston, MA: Allyn & Bacon.

Oittinen, R. (2000). *Translating for children*. London, England: Garland.

O'Sullivan, E. (2005). *Comparative children's literature*. New York, NY: Routledge.

Painter, H. W. (1968). Translations of traditional and modern material. In H. Huus (Ed.), *Evaluating books for children and young people* (pp. 36–56). Newark, DE: International Reading Association.

Paloposki, O., & Oittinen, R. (2000). The domesticated foreign. In A. Chesterman, N. G. San Salvador, & Y. Gambier (Eds.), *Translation in context* (pp. 373–390). Amsterdam, The Netherlands: John Benjamins.

Schiavi, G. (1996). There is always a teller in a tale. *Target, 8*(1), 1–21.

Shavit, Z. (2006). Translation of children's literature. In G. Lathey (Ed.), *The translation of children's literature: A reader* (pp. 25–40). Clevedon, England: Multilingual Matters.

Stan, S. (2004). *Rose Blanche* in translation. *Children's Literature in Education, 35*(1), 21–33.

Stolt, B. (2006). How Emil becomes Michel - on the translation of children's books. In G. Lathey (Ed.), *The translation of children's literature: A reader* (pp. 67–83). Clevedon, England: Multilingual Matters.

Taxel, J. (2002). Children's literature at the turn of the century: Toward a political economy of the publishing industry. *Research in the Teaching of English, 37*(2), 145–197.

Venuti, L. (Ed.). (2000). *The translation studies reader*. London, England: Routledge.

Whalen-Levitt, P. (1983). Pursuing the reader in the book. In J. P. May (Ed.), *Children and their literature: A readings book* (pp. 154–159). West Lafayette, IN: ChLA.

Point of Departure

Kostia Kontoleon

Competent translators face many difficulties while translating a literary text. I write from the standpoint of an experienced translator, and also from the standpoint of an author, since I believe that creative writing and translation can coexist, without the one working against the other. On the contrary, I would say that they complete each other. I am a "literary translator" and what drives me to engage in this line of work is my love for "beautiful texts."

I have translated more than 80 books and, in a "masochistic" manner, I often set goals that challenge my limits. Philip Pullman's *His Dark Materials* is perhaps the most important and challenging text I have translated to date. Pullman's ambitious work has been something like a school for me, a demanding school, filled with traps and narrow trails that were difficult to follow; I believe, however, that I graduated with distinction. In spite of the difficulties I faced during its translation, I went so deep into Pullman's world that I could not resist the urge to become part of it, to identify fully with the characters in it. I believe that the chance to work with such a text is the dream of every translator. I had to enlist the entirety of my skills in the art of translation—because translation *is* art—while also bringing in all of my imagination reservoirs to match Pullman's imagination. It would not be an exaggeration to say that after completing the translation of his trilogy, I came out of the process feeling wiser and having a better sense of the true meaning of life; feeling overcharged with intense emotions evoked by a journey into unknown worlds filled with mystery, adventure, myth, and fantasy. I consider myself incredibly fortunate to have been given the chance to work with such a text, the translation of which also brought me a translation award.

A lot has changed during the past few years in the field of translation. From a subsidiary enterprise with no particular status, today it seems to be gaining a bigger and more important place in the intellectual milieu of a country. My long relationship with the translation of literature—for adults, as well as for children and young people—combined with my own work as an author, has led me to the conclusion that translation is a multifaceted field; one with sides that are not easily seen by outsiders.

The translation of a text, especially of a literary text, is a peculiar case of "linguistic converging"; it is a channel of information exchange between peoples who speak different languages. The term "translation" includes both the translating process and its result, which is the target text. This result is, of course, valuable and extremely important, since it functions as the intermediary between linguistically diverse peoples or ethnic groups.

The final goal of a translation is to relieve its readers from the harder and more difficult task of reading the original text. In theory, translation replaces the source text with the "same" text in the target language. Transferring a text from one language into another is catalytic for both. The language of the translation reveals the hidden dynamic inscribed in the source text, but it also brings in its own dynamic. The target text cannot be the same as the original, but it cannot be something completely different either. There is a widely known discussion around "unfaithful beauties"—translations which are not particularly "faithful" but are "beautiful" precisely because of their "unfaithfulness." In practice, however, a translation will always be considered incomplete, since it is characterized by a certain loss of information. Thus, the translator is called upon to distinguish between the essential and the trivial and to remain focused on the final recipient, that is, the reading public.

Understanding the age group of a text's readers is also important, but not easy to do. Let's take the addresses of Pullman's work for an example. Because the protagonists are children, people tend to consider it children's literature; however, its symbolic and scientific richness raises particularly bold ethical and philosophical questions, requiring open and unrestrained readings. Thus, one has to wonder if this text is particularly addressed to children and young adults, the very question that vexes Pullman, as he notes in his Point of Departure essay in the this volume. The question should probably focus elsewhere: We should ask ourselves whether true literature can come to terms with an imposed limitation regarding the age of its reader. My answer is no; when a reader meets a text, the relationship or conflict to be developed between them should be based on the reader's choice. At the same instance, I recognize the fact that the reader's will is influenced both by biological age and mental maturity.

As well as sufficient knowledge of the ages the text is targeted to, successful translating also requires an excellent knowledge of both the languages *from* which, and *into* which, s/he is translating. This includes a sufficient grasp of vocabulary, syntax, style, and of idiomatic forms—too often the latter are mistranslated because of ignorance. A competent translator is able to achieve the same level of linguistic competence in the source language as in her/his mother tongue. S/he views literature through a mirror that magnifies details. However, an overly detailed, word-to-word translation is a naïve practice which reveals a translator's ineptitude. It is only natural that a translator may view the original text as "holy scripture," but this entails the great risk of falling into the trap of word-to-word translation.

There are two groups of translators. In the first group belong those who attach themselves to the source text and to the signifiers of its language, focusing their efforts on preserving within their translation as many elements as possible from the source language. The second group includes those who do not pay as much attention to the signifier as to the meaning and the "aroma" of the text they are translating, enlisting every available means of expression from the target language to achieve this. I belong to this second group of translators; I worship the text's "purpose" and not its "source." The translator is a mediator; a mediator who specializes in the field and the authors s/he is working with. S/he also needs to have extensive general knowledge and education and to continuously upgrade her/his expertise in the field of translation.

Publishers often complain about the poor quality of translations and the low competence of translators; however, they seldom consider the fact that the vast majority of translators are very poorly-paid by their publishers. Nor do they take into account the nerve-racking deadlines translators are subjected to by binding contracts, which often force them to neglect the quality of their work in order to become more productive. Moreover, the translator's profession as such does not bring any particular social recognition to those who practice it. Nevertheless, a translator should be personally invested in her/his work.

From the very first book I translated, I felt a powerful attraction to translation; I felt it circulating in my veins, demanding my complete devotion. It was not long before I became addicted to translation. It is an excruciating addiction; one that, even after the completion of an exhausting translation and many sleepless nights, and even after promises to myself that I would stay away from my computer for a long time after that, would push me to throw myself into new translating adventures right away. In these adventures, time and place acquire different dimensions; nothing can come in between me and the text under translation because, without even realizing it, I quickly spin an isolating cocoon around me.

I have my own translating style; being an author as well as a translator makes it inevitable for me to bring in "literariness" in every text I translate. I do not know if translation theorists would agree with such practice, but for me it is enough that readers agree with them. From my perspective, if the final recipient, that is the reader, enjoys what s/he reads, then the purpose of the translation is achieved. Finally, since a big part of my work is translating children's and young adult literature, I always make sure that it is comprehensible—both linguistically and stylistically—by these sensitive age groups.

31

International Communities Building Places for Youth Reading

Michael Daniel Ambatchew

Ethiopian Educational Consultant

Countries in the developing world face tremendous obstacles when it comes to getting books into the hands of children. Ethiopian Educational Consultant and children's author Michael Daniel Ambatchew provides a comprehensive overview of the complex array of challenges that have so far prevented the development of literacy-rich environments in developing nations. Although his primary focus is Ethiopia, the problems he surfaces are all too common in many parts of the world. Fortunately, there are visionary people, such as Yohannes Gebregeorgis and Jane Kurtz, who are making a difference despite the obstacles. Their stories are provided here to show how authors, librarians, and educationists are coming together to open the world to children through books.

Introduction

The choice between a storybook and a basket of bread is one no child should have to make. Yet with four million British children living in poverty, such choices are too near to home anywhere in the world for complacency (Williams, 2004). One in five of the world's people live on less than a dollar a day, making the cheapest storybook an unimaginable luxury to many all over the globe. Yet, purchasing capacity is not the only constraint; issues such as awareness, access, and motivation add to the complexities of the challenge of ensuring that children can and do become readers. A child orphaned by HIV/AIDS and responsible for raising her siblings cannot understand that

learning to read today is a surer way of putting bread into her brothers' and sisters' mouths than performing more immediately remunerative acts.

The question of which language/s should be used for teaching and learning also remains a highly emotive and political issue, with theory and practice at times in direct contradiction with each other. Usually children in developed countries are in a relatively better position than those in developing countries, with better access to a variety of quality reading materials in familiar settings and languages. Public libraries with trained librarians and plenty of adult role models, who have the habit of reading, provide an acquisitionally rich environment for them to learn to read.

However, in the developing countries of Africa, Asia, and Latin America, weak publishing sectors, inadequate distribution mechanisms, and poor purchasing power all contribute to a severe shortage of quality indigenous reading materials, making the acquisition of reading and sustaining of reading nigh impossible for all but the elite. To make matters worse, the lucrative textbook market is often monopolized by state and government-owned enterprises, further discouraging private publishers from producing culturally appropriate materials in local languages at affordable prices.

This chapter focuses on the position of the young reader in Africa, with main reference to one of the poorest countries on the continent—Ethiopia. The first section describes the state of African children with reference to their literacy, educational, and socio-economic status. It raises provocative questions as to whether Africa can solve its educational problems in isolation from its socio-economic and political issues. It questions whether world superpowers really want to see an independent Africa and why developed countries are not meeting their commitments to the Millennium Development Goals adopted by UN member states in 2001.

The second section portrays national language policies regarding the media of education, and the state of children's literature, discussing access, affordability and appropriateness. It queries whether international publishers are more devoted to their profits and thus view Africa as a small export market, rather than as a partner in the publishing arena whom they should support and mentor, and with whom they can collaborate.

The last section scrutinizes the effectiveness of extensive reading projects as well as describing innovative projects aimed at developing children's literature and readers. It discusses how educators, donors, and practitioners have come up with innovative ideas for integrating stories into textbooks, printing stories in newsprint, creating mobile donkey-drawn libraries and setting up pan-African projects that can share stories and illustrations amongst African publishers.

It concludes that in spite of their shortcomings such projects are building up a critical mass that will eventually burst the restraining dam walls of obstacles and flood the near barren plains of the book-drought stricken continent.

In their Point of Departure essays, author Jane Kurtz and librarian Yohannes Gebregeorgis describe their involvement with the grass-roots program Ethiopia Reads, an intervention that emerged out of their personal experience as readers, and in Jane's case as a writer, as well as a commitment to their childhood home. Their stories not only offer hope but also a practical blueprint for similar initiatives that might be undertaken by academics, writers, researchers, librarians, and donors working together to provide access to books for young people in developing nations.

Overview: Who Dare Defy Goliath?

The conclusions and recommendations of research and literature on reading done in developing countries are fairly predictable: Better trained teachers and librarians, affordable, accessible and appropriate reading materials, and enthusiastic and motivated students with effective learning strategies are the main ingredients lacking in most places.

However, such recommendations and conclusions have been on the table for many decades now, yet change is painfully slow. Azubuike (2007) concludes, "the quality of library service available to the average African is grossly inadequate into woefully deficient" (p. 10). He states that the Structural Adjustment Programmes implemented by the World Bank and the International Monetary Fund and forced down Africa's gullet were one of the primary factors for governments having to cut back on their budgets, which in turn has led to poor literacy levels. However, others say that "In African countries the availability of textbooks and other learning materials deteriorated during the 1980's, mainly as a result of economic stagnation, political unrest and competing priorities for social funding" (UNESCO, 2007). Nevertheless, after the Education for All conference held in Thailand in 1990, there was a renewed interest in books and readers.

Greaney (1996) advises, "Persistent, focussed, informed programs; courageous leadership; good management of limited resources; and informed enthusiastic teaching are required if we are to achieve the long-term goal of helping children in developing countries to read" (p. 34).

Yet the scenario remains the same, demanding us to rethink our obvious solutions. Therefore, Larson (2001) calls for a larger vision, citing Wole Soyinka's call for Africa's debt to be abolished as a case in point, and states that a lack of resolution to free Africa of her historical problems is the basis of the crises. Indeed this lack of resolution on behalf of national governments and global superpowers is a highly significant, if not the most significant, obstacle to improving literacy worldwide. Williams (2004) points out that although rich countries agreed to give 0.7% of their national income to assist poor countries, most have not honored their pledges. This is so not because they fear literacy per se, but rather creating acquisitionally rich reading environments requires changes in the power, prestige, and position of the status quo, and such countries are not so eager to relinquish their stronghold and power-grips so readily. Indeed, it is a question of priorities for them; the United States alone has been able to raise over 200 billion U.S. dollars to fight the war on terror (Williams, 2004), yet a fraction of that sum could roll back the frontiers of illiteracy and poverty in developing nations.

The socioeconomic and political reality in most African countries does not foster a conducive environment for all children to have adequate access to nutrition, health services and education. Needless to say, "Literacy does not develop in a vacuum. Reading is taught and learnt within a social context" (Pretorius & Machet, 2004, p. 45). Yet, not enough is being done to improve the existing context.

In Ethiopia, for instance, government figures boast a gross enrollment ratio of 79.8% in primary school (MOFED, 2006), but research into reading skills shows that hardly 2% of Grade 8 students have adequate reading skills to cope with that level of education (Ambatchew, 2003). National literacy figures stood at 38% in 2004 with that of females lagging at 27% for the same period (MOFED, 2006).

Although one may assume more encouraging figures in the developed countries of Africa, one tends to find similar pictures across the continent. In South Africa, for example, apart from the privileged few, the broad majority are still in a highly disadvantaged position; a UN study rated South African fourth-grade students as some of the worst in numeracy, literacy, and life skills even when compared to other African countries (Mtshweni, 2003). The basic difference from the apartheid period being that the privileged few from the middle and upper classes are no longer distinguishable by the tint of their skin. Pretorius and Machet (2004) lament:

> Despite a decade of democratic rule and widespread attempts to level the educational playing fields, gross inequalities still exist within the school system in terms of physical resources, underqualified teachers, poor school management and poor delivery of learning materials to schools. (p. 48)

These educational shortcomings are not isolated, but rather reflect the state of affairs nationally and globally. Many African students may be physically present in a school but are not healthy enough to actually learn enthusiastically and effectively. Williams (2004) points out that although the world produces enough food to feed every one of its citizens, poor distribution of wealth leads to eight hundred million people going hungry every day and two billion people suffering from chronic malnutrition. Such statistics have direct and real effects on the teaching-learning process. Williams (2007) notes that "of Malawi's 1980 university graduates, 25% were dead by 2003" (p. 60).

Other researchers have come across less evident signs of poverty such as a teacher sleeping on the classroom floor at 9 o'clock in the morning (Pretorius & Machet, 2004) and parents tearing out paper from their children's textbooks to roll tobacco (Ambatchew, 1999). Even in developed countries, like South Africa, the poor distribution of wealth leads to many schools lacking the artefacts of school literacy such as textbooks, posters, exercise books, and reading books (Pretorius & Machet, 2004). It is estimated that less than 20% of South African schools have functional libraries (Hart, 2006).

Yet how to go about bringing a drastic change to this dismal picture is open to debate. A shift from individualistic, profit-motivated paradigms to new ones of collective responsibility emerging from high levels of global consciousness and morality is not going to come about in the near or foreseeable future. Noam Chomsky (2003) notes that a dislike for democracy is the traditional stance of all who have a share in power and privilege, so even in the United States there is a severe democratic deficit, whereby major businesses and powers resort to the economic strangulation of competitors.

Such disjunctive relations between Africa and other parts of the world make innovative solutions hard to come by. For instance, while there are 300,000 highly qualified Africans in the diaspora, of whom 10% have doctorates, Africa spends four billion U.S. dollars per year to employ around 100,000 Western experts. Obviously, African governments are also to blame for some of the push factors such as discrimination in appointments and promotions, social unrest and political conflicts, and under-utilization of qualified personnel. Nevertheless, when 50% of Ethiopians who go abroad for training do not return, and there are more Ethiopian-trained doctors in Chicago alone than the whole of Ethiopia, easy solutions such as more training are going to be far from adequate. The South African Network of Skills Abroad, a group formed to link highly skilled South Africans living abroad with local experts and projects in an effort to contribute to South Africa's economic and social development, is just one little step in the search for innovative remedies to the ills of Africa in general and those of the African educational arena in particular.

Whether continental initiatives like New Partnership for Africa's Development (NEPAD) can reverse the global situation in which Japanese cows and European cows are each subsidised by 7.50 US dollars and 2.50 US dollars per day respectively, while 75% of Africans live on less than this amount per day (Williams, 2004), is a question that only time can answer. The question, "Dare the schools build a new social order?" is still pertinent today.

A key factor in Africa's development is thought to be education and in what language it is delivered. At the end of evaluating a Malawian project, Williams (2007) recommends,

> For Africans in general, and Malawians in particular an appropriate point of departure in the debate on education and development may well be to revisit their language education policy, and to consider its implications for the reading behaviours (and for the languages) which they wish to foster in their primary school. (p. 17)

Language Policies and Media of Instruction

The decades following colonial rule in Africa have brought serious challenges to governments and their various partners attempting to instill and sustain widespread reading and writing habits among diverse, largely oral communities living under harsh political and social conditions (Triebel, 2001).

Bloch (2007) points out that language policies forcing the use of ex-colonial languages during and since colonialism have led to a serious neglect and underdevelopment of African languages for high status purposes, particularly as languages for reading. The oral tradition, with its great potential to impart knowledge and to function as a bridge to literacy has been sorely neglected in primary education systems, presumably to a significant extent as a consequence of the low status of African languages and the corresponding loss in perceived value to traditional social and cultural practices that were communicated through these languages. Debates are taking place about issues such as the importance of young children learning in their mother tongue or a familiar language, the benefits of reading for enjoyment, and the need for appropriate storybooks in relevant languages.

Neville Alexander (1996) comments upon the fact that language policies in Africa tend to come up with systematically depressing or disastrous results. This probably emanates from the practice of governments being too willing to absorb and apply "obvious" theories and the inability of the intellectuals to adapt such theories to the practical realities of a certain country and to the felt needs of the people in that region. African countries have varying language policies advocating for monolingual and multilingual media of instruction. Some want a monolingual medium of instruction, most often in an ex-colonial language or, at times, in a national language. Others prefer multilingual media of instruction allowing subtractive or additive bilingualism, where one language gradually takes over from another as medium of instruction or both run together side by side.

However, regarding practice on the ground, the elite often send their children to private schools, where the medium of instruction is an ex-colonial language, and the general public send their children to government schools, where they perceive their children to be getting an inferior education in a local language. Unfortunately, their children often are indeed getting an inferior education, but this is not due to the medium of instruction but rather due to other factors such as disenchanted, poorly trained, and under-paid teachers, inadequate textbooks of limited supply and of dubious quality, and the lack of acquisitionally rich environments at home.

A closer look at the language policies of Ethiopia and South Africa may shed some light on the issue. The Transitional Government of Ethiopia (MOE, 1994) states:

> Cognisant of the pedagogical advantage of the child in learning in mother tongue and the rights of nationalities to promote the use of their languages, primary education will be given in nationality languages.... The language of teacher training for kindergarten and primary education will be the nationality language used in the area.... Students can chose and learn at least one nationality language and one foreign language for cultural and international relations. (pp. 10–11)

A territorial principle was adopted, probably based on the assumption that only such a principle could ensure the survival of minority languages. Hence, children of all ethnic groups would have to learn in the language of the territory in which they dwelled. Although there is mention of "one foreign language" (MOE, 1994, p. 11), only English is taught in the primary schools at present.

After several years the initial exuberant response is fading, as has been observed in other countries (Agnihotri, 1994), and local governments are taking a second realistic look at things. In the capital, almost all families of means are sending their children to English medium schools, which exist despite policies forbidding them and the fact that many of the teachers have inadequate mastery of English to teach effectively in it. Government schools teach in Amharic and there is a relatively good supply of textbooks and supplementary reading materials in Amharic. Outside the capital, though, there are only very few textbooks in local languages and hardly any supplementary teaching materials and storybooks. Therefore, the Afar region and some ethnic groups in the Southern Nation and Nationalities People's Region are retaining Amharic as the medium of primary education and only introducing their local languages as school subjects.

In South Africa, after the end of apartheid, all 11 South African languages were legally given equal status and children's right to be educated in their mother tongues was acknowledged. However, this not only reminded the populace of the former Bantu policies, but was also hampered by the lack of adequately trained teachers and prepared materials in the languages.

The State of Africa's Children's Reading Literature

An abundance of children's reading material presupposes the existence of a thriving publishing sector, children who can and want to read, and parents with adequate purchasing power to buy books. As discussed at the beginning of this chapter, this is a far-fetched supposition as the reality on the ground is rather harsh.

The production of books in African languages has several challenges. It is estimated that Africa imported 769 million US dollars worth of books from the European Union alone between 1988 to 1991 (Walter, 1996), apart from the millions of books donated by organizations like Book Aid International, International Book Bank, and Sabre Foundation. Obviously, Africa provides a small but significant market as well as a dumping ground for international publishers. To make matters worse, Walter (1996) states that the lucrative textbook markets are often monopolized by government owned or affiliated publishers, further dimming the chances of African publishers to become economically viable and to produce a sustained supply of suitable storybooks for developing a lifetime habit of reading. To add insult to injury, several reading projects provide book boxes of imported books in ex-colonial languages.

In the case of Ethiopia, the vast majority of locally produced storybooks are in the national language Amharic. Although this language has a long and illustrious history, the number of titles of children's storybooks is barely 300. A quick visit to any bookstore in the capital and major towns shows that hardly two dozen storybooks are in print at any given time. Although most of the books are fairly priced and cost $1.50 at the most, they still remain well out of the reach of the average Ethiopian. To make matters worse, the number of bookstores outside the cities dwindles to almost nil.

This lack of books obviously places major constraints on any attempts at allowing children to wallow in books. The results of extensive reading projects will be examined hereafter.

Extensive Reading Programmes and Their Effectiveness

With specific references to illiteracy and aliteracy, extensive reading programmes are often touted as a panacea for all the reading ills in Africa. Yet how effective such programmes have really proven to be is open to debate.

One of the solutions vaunted by many experts to encourage the development of reading skills in Africa and other developing regions is the introduction of extensive reading projects. Ambatchew (2003) cites several experts, including Davies (1995), Elley (2000), Krashen (1993), Lituanas, Jacobs and Renandya (2001), and Nation (1997), who have proved that the provision of supplementary readers directly and positively impacts students' reading skills in high profile schemes with catchy names like Book Flood, Uninterrupted Sustained Silent Reading (USSR), Drop Everything and Read (DEAR), Silent Reading for Fun (SURF) and others.

On the other hand, when other researchers evaluated such projects in Africa, they discover a darker picture. Bloch (2007) comments, "One of the great tragedies that is reported repeatedly about reading materials (donations or otherwise) is that even when books have been distributed, they often gather dust in school principals' cupboards or on classroom shelves" (p. 5).

In Ethiopia a very popular project called the Primary Reader Scheme donated 124 readers in book boxes initially to five schools in urban and rural areas in its pilot phase. After positive feedback with requests for more copies of fewer titles, it donated hundreds of book boxes to schools all over the country. However, after a few years when the students' reading skills were compared with those of students in schools which did not receive books, there was no significant difference in their reading abilities (Ambatchew, 2003).

In Guinea, an interesting evaluation project set out to measure the reading skills of Grade 2 and Grade 4 students,

after the government had implemented several interventions in an attempt to make the "Education for All" slogan come true. Using 15 Guinean educators and an expatriate reading recovery expert, they discovered to their dismay that only 10% of the Grade 2 students were able to identify more than 50 letters of the alphabet, while most could only identify 29. Moreover, most students could only recognize 4 of the words that they had already learned in class and write 4 out of 14 correctly. Sadly, 9 out of 10 Grade 2 students were unable to read a 'level 0' text that had explicit illustrations and 16 or fewer frequently used words in it (Diallo & Diallo, 2007).

Similarly, in Malawi, 16,570 book boxes containing 50 books, guidance notes, a record chart, and two dictionaries were provided to 3,440 Malawian government primary schools, after a seemingly successful pilot project. Again when Williams (2007) scrutinized this project with a time-lapse design he concluded, "… the extensive reading initiative had not been successful in boosting reading attainment scores." (p. 14).

So why these disparate results, which show extensive reading programmes as vastly successful or as miserable failures?

Possible Reasons for Results

The first point to consider is the researchers themselves and their degree of objectivity and bias in carrying out the research. Although cynical, many researchers have vested interest in positive results. Most are expatriates performing "parachute consultancy" or living in an African country for a short span of one to three years. Therefore, they transplant foreign practices that might appear to take in the short term, but quickly lead to anti-body rejection. This "taking" is further enhanced by the fact that the project is performed in a highly controlled environment which is not found in the real world. The extensive reading schemes could produce impressive results in experimental situations as they provide abundant facilities and high motivation, but be insignificant when reproduced in the normal schools under everyday situations (Ambatchew, 2003). Williams (2007) also quotes a Commission for Africa report: "… the agency of Africans is key, and that the application of Western-inspired remedies is not guaranteed to succeed" (p. 17).

However, African government employed researchers have integrity and subjectivity issues too. In fact, the study in Guinea (Diallo & Diallo, 2007) openly acknowledges that the researchers felt pressured to present a positive image of the elementary school system and had to be coaxed into presenting the true picture by an expatriate researcher who felt that the purpose of the study was diagnostic and things had to be presented as they were. Interestingly, when they finally presented their study, which gave a negative image of the situation on the ground, the Guinean government forced them to redo the whole evaluation again the next year, only to find the same results. Which country is willing to hire a foreign expert whose previous intervention has not been successful? Which government seeking election votes and popularity is going to admit that the millions spent on a project have not produced the desired results? Which donor is willing to give funds to partners who did not succeed in their previous project? Has the World Bank admitted yet that the Structural Adjustment Programs in Africa were failures? This is why Martin, Oksanen, and Takala (2000) point out that there is a need for independent people outside the whole preparation of projects to carry out more objective evaluations and ensure projects are indeed meeting their set objectives.

A second point is the lack of rigorous research methodology in many of the positive image studies. Rosenberg (2003) notes that "rigorous monitoring and evaluation of reader development activity in Africa is generally lacking" (p. iv). One finds that projects were positively evaluated by the people who implemented the projects themselves, and are thus too close for comfort regarding objectivity. Moreover, several have used subjective qualitative instruments without much concern for the triangulation of their results. A case in point is an evaluation of a reading habit and interest development project in Nigeria, where parents were given questionnaires to fill out after their children had participated in a four-week program to develop their reading skills and attitudes. The researcher discusses "revealing" results:

> All the parents (100%) responded "Yes" to the item, 'Would you want your child to participate next time?' On the item, 'Has the programme enabled your child to read more books than before?' 102 parents (91%) responded "Yes" ... (Udosen, 2007, p. 6)

An even feebler evaluative statement was about a five-day reading clinic for 200 students who could barely read two letters words in Ghana. One of its aims was to "equip the children with skills to enable them to read books meaningfully" (Apenten, 2003, p. 45). It concluded by saying, "By the end of the clinic, it was thought that there had been some improvement." (p. 49).

One finds that research which did not come up with such rosy results often employed highly scientific and objective methodology. For instance, in the Guinean study, separate professional and technical teams were used for instrument design and data collection, data entry, and data analysis. Similarly, in Ethiopia a standardized international reading test was first trialled in the context, and then used (Ambatchew, 2003).

Unfortunately, it is only through carrying out post-mortems on unsuccessful projects that lessons could be gleaned for future successes. The concept of "Successful Failures" will have to get recognition and acceptance by all involved. It is in light of this that Durand and Deehy (1996) state:

> Conducted properly, evaluations provide valuable feedback to all involved in the book donation process, from the do-

nating publishers to the donor agencies and the recipients. The evaluation results, both positive and negative, can be used to improve the overall process of the book donation and to meet the specific—and changing—needs in each country. (p. 163)

Finally, the concept of sustainability, replicability, and continuity must be taken into account by all actors. Introducing beautifully illustrated, expensive books may produce improvements in the short-term, but librarians and teachers simply lock them up as they are deemed priceless and irreplaceable. Williams (2007) pointed to teacher morale and piloting and training deficiencies as factors responsible for the project failures in Malawi, while teacher empowerment, lack of meritology, overcrowding, and resistance to change were factors raised in the Ethiopian case.

Innovative Reading Promotion Projects Across the Continent

Since the 1990 Jomtien Conference, which approved the UN "Education for All" vision, there has been a renewed push to roll back the frontiers of illiteracy in Africa. Numerous projects and programs exist all over the continent, and the following is but a birds-eye view of what is happening.

Take Books to Children

One of the biggest reasons given for poor reading skills of African children is the lack of access to good reading books. Consequently, several projects involve taking books out into inaccessible areas or poorly served rural areas, where the majority of African children are.

In Kenya, for instance, the Kenyan National Library Service raises a financial contribution from a local community, then takes books into these communities using handcarts, public transport, bicycles and motorcycles (Ngumo, 2003).

Similar projects have been run in Zimbabwe and Ethiopia even using donkeys to pull these "mobile libraries," as Yohannes Gebregeorgis describes in his Point of Departure following this essay.

Bring Children to Books

The opposite approach to taking books to children is bringing children to the books. When there are libraries and books that are being under-utilized, this has proved a common approach to attract the children into using the libraries.

An interesting example of such a project is the activities of the Oyo State Library Board in Nigeria, which conducts film shows and even screens football matches, like the African Cup of Nations, to attract readers into the library. Then the librarians try to raise interest in books, at times even re-packaging information to meet their clients' needs. They also sensitize the public through book fairs and handbills (Oyegade, 2003, pp. 62–63).

In Ethiopia, several schools have "library clubs" where members try to get other students to use the library as more than a quiet place to do their homework. As a "reward" the library club members are given borrowing privileges.

Catch Them Early

Another approach, which is just beginning to get acceptance and implementation across the continent, is to target pre-school children with the aim of giving them emergent literacy skills and inculcating a love for reading before they even begin formal education. This is in sharp contrast to the colonial days, when schools would not accept children under the age of seven into school and used to ask the children to touch their left ear by rolling their right arm over their heads as a rough measure of their age. Reaching down to pre-primary level and opening kindergarten and day-care centers has frightening financial implications for many African countries, so it is not surprising to see South Africa as a leader with this approach.

A noteworthy project of this type in South Africa is one called "Born to Read." It is aimed at newborn babies, toddlers and pre-schoolers (2–6). It trains parents and their children on how to develop emergent literacy skills and the newborn and his mother are both rewarded with a book in a local language at the happy event of birth. This project boasts several success stories (Mtshweni, 2003).

Catch the Old Ones Too

An opposite yet complementary approach to training pre-schoolers is to encourage adults, especially parents, no matter what their age, to start reading. Even if they are well past their optimum reading age, they can still be encouraged to read, thereby helping themselves and providing role models for children.

Again in South Africa, an intervention called "Project Literacy" set out to help adults become literate and assist their children in acquiring the reading habit. They used an interactive, group-oriented methodology to keep the adults interested in learning to read. But more innovatively, they used techniques like teaching illiterate parents to "read illustrations" and so enable them to enjoy books with their children (Chetty, 2003).

In Tanzania, the mass literacy program is considered to be one of the most extensively studied ones in the developing world, (Knuth, Perry, & Duces, 1996). Several organizations such as the Tanzanian Library Services, The Children's Book Project, the Book Development Council, and the Tanzanian Library Association are working towards catching both children and adults from falling into and staying in the pit of illiteracy. Recently, a reading tent was set up in the Bagamayo community and participants up to the age of 95 came to participate in a bookfest. Reading competitions and other activities like playing the board game "bao" were used to stir interest in the event. Books were available in Kiswahili and attracted the adults' attention.

Give Them African Books

Chetty (2003) complains about the South African situation saying, "Government policy … has had no impact on the creation or production of books in mother-tongue languages" (p. 19). However, this problem is felt keenly all over the continent and in developing countries all over the globe. Libraries simply do not have culturally and linguistically appropriate materials in either quantity or quality, with a very few exceptions. Knuth, Perry, and Duces (1996) note, "… scarcity of resources has resulted in outdated, haphazard collections, often supplemented by donations and discards of dubious value" (p. 175).

The existence of pertinent storybooks in the mother-tongue of children is not only useful for parents and teachers, but can be effective tools to induce children to learn to read on their own.

> If the child is given rich, diverse and robust texts, the child according to them [transaction model proponents] has the innate capacity to develop finite strategies with which to begin to read without the help or assistance of a teacher. (Onukaogu, 2003, p. 5)

Consequently, it is not surprising to see numerous projects and programs sprouting across Africa aimed at producing interesting books in local languages.

In South Africa, the "Culture of Reading" program of the Project for the Study of Alternative Education in South Africa (PRAESA) produced a range of reading materials for children from early childhood to teens in isiXhosa, English, and Afrikaans, including 16 little books for young children, called Little Hands. As of May 2010, The Little Hands books are now potentially available in Arabic, Amharic, Kiswahili, English, French, Portuguese, Twi , Ciyao, Cinyanja, Emakhuw, Makonde, Kimwane, Kinyarwanda, Mandingue, Xhosa, Zulu, Setswana, Xitsonga, Tshivenda, Sesotho, Isindebele, Siswati, and Afrikaans, with 14,953 little boxes with 239,248 books in them distributed over Africa.In Ethiopia, several NGOs and donors have become involved in the difficult task of producing storybooks in local languages. To begin with, CODE-Ethiopia publishes storybooks and also purchases locally published reading materials for distribution in its community libraries. Next, Irish Aid-Ethiopia has been involved in the production of a local primary reader and the purchase and distribution of locally published readers to underprivileged schools. Similarly, the Swedish International Development Agency was the major supplier of free paper to the government-owned Educational Materials Production and Distribution Agency in the past and is now supporting it to become a commercially viable publishing house through technical assistance.

Conclusion

Looking at the discrete unit of literacy in Africa would be misleading. Within the general framework of Africa's socio-economic context and her position in the new world order of the global village, several inter-related factors, such as national language policies regarding the media of education, the state of children's reading literature, the effectiveness of extensive reading projects and reading promotion initiatives, must all be viewed to give a holistic picture of the reality on the ground.

In this chapter, I have argued that Africa's traditionally marginalized and disadvantaged position on the world scene due to colonialism and other historical events continue to interfere with her current development. Moreover, developed countries still lack a global village mentality and continue to see the improvement of people in the developing world as a secondary priority to their own material interests.

First and foremost, to improve education in Africa, national language policies along with their implementation, acceptance by the public and creation of awareness about them, need to be scrutinized at the national and continental levels.

Next, the provision of diverse and rich texts in several languages with culturally appropriate content must be provided to suit Africa's multilingual and unique context. In relation to this, a vibrant indigenous book market needs to be nurtured with adequate publishing, marketing, and distribution networks.

Finally, a battery of reading development and promotion initiatives must be put in place to create a critical mass to jump-start and sustain the continental reading machinery. Consequently, the view of extensive reading programs as a panacea to Africa's literacy problems needs to be re-examined, especially as most of them are falsely being given positive images.

Despite the shortcomings of the projects and programs described in this chapter, they must be nurtured and strengthened so that they can create the momentum to break through the prison walls of illiteracy. If they don't however, the repercussions, like those of 9/11, will be felt across the globe. Therefore, it is both the duty and the responsibility of all inhabitants of the global village to ensure our youth can and do read and do their best to make the world a better place to read.

Academic References

Agnihotri, R. K. (1994). Campaign-based literacy programmes: The case of the Ambedkar Naga experiment in Delhi. *Language and Education, 8*(1–2), 47–56.

Alexander, N. (1996). Motivation: A circular for a seminar on language in education in Africa. Unpublished manuscript.

Ambatchew, M. D. (1999). Ethiopia: Prospects and possibilities. Unpublished manuscript.

Ambatchew, M. D. (2003). The effect of primary readers on reading skills in Ethiopia. Unpublished doctoral dissertation. University of Pretoria, South Africa.

Apenten, A. (2003). School reading clinics: A programme organized in Accra. In D. Rosenberg (Ed.), *Reader development and reading promotion: Recent experiences from seven countries in Africa* (pp. 47–49). Oxford, England: INASP.

Azubuike, A. (2007). The role of development information in African economies: Issues and policy dimensions related to knowledge, libraries and information services. A paper presented to the Ad-hoc Expert Group Meeting on Development Information in the Economy. Lusaka.

Bloch, C. (2007). Putting little books into little hands in the Year of African Languages: A Stories Across Africa Project initiative. Unpublished manuscript.

Chetty, V. (2003) Post-adult literacy needs and the development of adult literacy. In D. Rosenberg (Ed.), *Reader development and reading promotion: Recent experiences from seven countries in Africa* (pp. 13–27). Oxford, England: INASP.

Chomsky, N. (2003) *Hegemony of survival: America's quest for global dominance.* Crows Nest, New South Wales, Australia: Allen and Unwin.

Diallo, B., & Diallo, M. (2007). Reading competencies of Grade 2 and 4 students in Guinea. A presentation at the 5th Pan-African Conference. Accra, Ghana..

Durand, R., & Deehy, S. M. (1996). Donated book programs: An interim measure. In V. Greaney (Ed.), *Promoting Reading in Developing Countries* (pp. 163–173). Newark, DE: International Reading Association.

Davies, F. (1995). *Introducing Reading.* Harmondsworth, England: Penguin Books, Ltd.

Elley, W. B. (2000). The potential of book floods for raising literacy levels. *International Review of Education, 46*(3/4), 233–255.

Greaney, V. (1996). *Promoting reading in developing countries.* Newark, DE: International Reading Association.

Hart, G. (2006) Educators and public librarians: Unwitting partners in the information literacy education of South African youth? *Innovation, 32,* 74–94.

Knuth, R., Perry, B., & Duces, B. (1996). Libraries, literacy, and developing countries. In V. Greaney (Ed.), *Promoting reading in developing countries* (pp. 174–192). Newark, DE: International Reading Association.

Krashen, S. (1993). *The power of reading.* Englewood, CO: Libraries Unlimited.

Larson, C. R. (2001). *The ordeal of the African writer.* New York, NY: ZED Books Ltd.

Lituanas, P. M., Jacobs, G. M., & Renandya, W. (2001). A study of extensive reading with remedial reading students. In Y. M. Cheah & S. M. Ng (Eds.), *Language instructional issues in Asian classrooms* (pp. 89–104). Newark, DE: International Development in Asia Committee, International Reading Association.

Martin, J., Oksanen, R., & Takala, T. (2000). *Preparation of the sector development program in Ethiopia.* Paris, France: ADEA.

Ministry of Education (MOE). (1994). *Transitional Government of Ethiopia education and training policy.* Addis Ababa, Ethiopia.

Ministry of Finance and Economic Development of Ethiopia (MOFED). (2006). Sustainable development and poverty reduction. Unpublished manuscript.

Mtshweni, D. (2003). Born to read: A programme of the Gauteng Department of Sport, Recreation, Arts, Culture, Library and Information Services. In D. Rosenberg (Ed.), *Reader development and reading promotion: Recent experiences from seven countries in Africa* (pp. 1–12). Oxford, England: INASP.

Nation, P. (1997). The language learning benefits of extensive reading. *The language teacher, 21*(5). Retrieved February 8, 2010, from http://www.jalt-publications.org/tlt/files/97/may/benefits.html

Ngumo, R. W. (2003). The Book-box programme of Karatina Community Library, Kenya National Library Service. In D. Rosenberg (Ed.), *Reader development and reading promotion: Recent experiences from seven countries in Africa* (pp. 50–58). Oxford, England: INASP.

Onukaogu, C. E. (2003). Towards the understanding of reading. In C. E. Onukaogu & O. B. Jegede. (Eds.), *Teaching reading in Nigeria* (pp. 1–35). Newark, DE: International Reading Association.

Oyegade, E. A. (2003) Readership promotion campaign activities of the Oyo State Library Board. In D. Rosenberg (Ed.), *Reader development and reading promotion: Recent experiences from seven countries in Africa* (pp. 59–65). Oxford, England: INASP.

Pretorius, E., & Machet, M. (2004). The socio-educational context of literacy accomplishment in disadvantaged schools: Lessons for reading in the early primary school years. *Journal of Language Teaching, 33*, 45–60.

Rosenberg, D. (2003). *Reader development and reading promotion: Recent experiences from seven countries in Africa.* Oxford, England: INASP.

Triebel, A. (2001). The roles of literacy practices in the activities and institutions of developing and developed countries. In D. R. Olsen, & N. Torrance (Eds.), *The making of literate societies* (pp. 19–53). Malden, MA: Blackwell.

Udosen, A. E. (2007). *VRP: Reading Interest and Habit Development Project for UBE pupils in Akwa Ibom State of Nigeria.* A paper presented at the 5th Pan-African Conference. Accra, Ghana.

UNESCO. (2007). Basic Learning Materials Initiative. Retrieved February 9, 2010. from http://www.unesco.org/education/blm/blmactivities_en.php

Walter, S. (1996) Promoting children's book publishing in Anglophone Africa. In V. Greaney (Ed.), *Promoting reading in developing countries* (pp. 130–147). Newark, DE: International Reading Association.

Williams, J. (2004). *50 facts that should change the world.* London, England: Icon Books.

Williams, E. (2007). Extensive reading in Malawi: Inadequate implementation or inappropriate innovation? *Journal of Research in Reading, 30*(1), 59–79.

Point of Departure

Jane Kurtz

An Icelandic proverb says, "Keen is the eye of the visitor." As a fiction writer, I've found that to be true. But sharp eyesight doesn't mean that a person can put a check mark in the easy-breezy life path column. Usually, quite the opposite.

My parents moved to Ethiopia when I was two years old. I accepted without surprise donkeys on streets, chickens in houses, weird hyena cries slicing up the night air. My parents got busy labeling. Food like an explosion of meat and spices in the mouth: good. Bugs dropping into our beds from the grass roof: bad. I labeled everything—as toddlers do: *home*.

Five years later, I was a shy second grader walking off a ship and onto a New York City dock, peering out windows in the back of the station wagon as our family motored across the United States, living for one year in borrowed and impermanent Idaho spaces. Snow. Grandparents. Brown cows (the slurpy kind). A classroom where I told my fellow second graders that I had a pet crow, which I most certainly did not (although I did have a pet monkey). Everything seemed strange and slightly unreal.

Back in Maji, every day included conversations in at least three different languages, so I was surrounded by swirls of words I mostly didn't understand. Ethiopian girls came to make mud *wat* and *injera* with my sisters and me; in those days, I picked up lots of words in Amharic and a few in Deze. Then girls stopped coming. Boys—and even young men—were seizing the first opportunity they'd ever had to go to school. They arrived every day, sitting on mud benches to learn the Amharic alphabet, wringing the necks of my mother's chickens, and helping my father raise artichokes and plums to make money necessarily for pencils and notebooks. But girls were needed at home as carriers of wood and water, wives in training.

I, although I didn't know it, was a writer in training. For most of my childhood, I hung back, dancing uncomfortably on various sharp edges no matter where I was. My emotions were tangled: Wonder. Yearning. Fear. Observation was survival. If I could interpret body language and expressions and situations accurately, I could sometimes save myself a bit of embarrassment. But I was also learning to gather vivid details, which are, as John Gardner says, the life blood of fiction.

When my own children were young, I haunted the Carnegie Library in my small Colorado town, read out loud every day, and fell in love with children's books. I set goals, dreamed dreams, and spent years figuring out how to write picture books and novels for young readers while ignoring my own childhood. "Write what you know," everyone said. But I was still trying to learn how to be American. I already had one children's book published before I reached back to find the fog and shivery hyena cries that I needed to create the setting of *Fire on the Mountain*, the smell of the emperor's lions I needed for tension in *Pulling the Lion's Tail*, the cloud of pink flamingos I needed to show Desta's change of heart in *Faraway Home*.

I had found my voice. My books gave me a way to talk to those who read to be transported to another time or place. I was touched to see how many people will look open-eyed at a world that is full of astonishing beauty and pummeling pain. A boy who read *The Storyteller's Beads* in a New York City fourth-grade classroom wrote, "Thank you for your book that helped me understand the

438

suffering in the world. You have the coolest vocabulary ever." A Portland sixth grader wrote, "Your book opened the doors and let a hundred worlds in."

Gradually, I was drawn back overseas. In 1997, I did an author presentation in three international schools in Ethiopia. A few years later, in a similar visit to Nigeria, parents and teachers asked me, "How can Nigeria grow a reading culture?" A radio announcer in Uganda, asked me—as a visiting children's book author—along with a Ugandan book publisher and a West African professor the same question. I began to think about how, exactly, it was that a country like the United States where, 100 years ago few households held much printed matter (perhaps a newspaper, a Bible, or Webster's speller), grew a lively reading culture.

If any country in Africa should have a shot at a reading culture, it would be Ethiopia, the only African country that developed alphabets still in use today, a country that has long valued both written and oral texts. But in the period since the time when my parents spent 22 years working on educational and health issues in Ethiopia, life had gone grim for many Ethiopians, their country now statistically lagging behind even other sub-Saharan African countries on many measures.

In 1990, Ethiopia, along with 154 other countries of the world, committed itself to providing universal access to primary education. The problem has been meager financial resources in the face of many needs, and even though immense progress has been made in creating more schools, thousands of children today are learning to read, only to be faced with the problem of no books *to* read. With most of the world's huge NGOs at work in Ethiopia for some time, making a fairly small dent, I didn't think I'd ever have the chance to see girls like the ones I grew up around reading books.

That was before I met Yohannes Gebregeorgis, a man who'd never held a book, outside of school, until he was 19 years old. As he later told me, reading changed his life forever. He had grown up in the southern Ethiopian town of Negelle Borena and first encountered literature, shared by U.S. Peace Corps volunteers, in high school. Then someone handed him the first book he read for pure pleasure—a story that he tells in his own words in the point of departure essay following this one.

As a young man, Yohannes was marked for arrest by the Derg, the military committee then in charge of Ethiopian government. He fled to Sudan, spent eight months at a refugee camp, and was granted political asylum by the United States. While working full time, he earned a B.A. in English Literature and Journalism in 1989 from the University of Buffalo and a Masters degree in Library Science in 1991 from the University of Texas. He was offered a job as a children's book librarian at the San Francisco Public Library.

In that library, he saw books reflecting cultures and languages all around the world—but none in any Ethio-pian language. After a library project introduced him to one of my published re-told Ethiopian folktales, he wrote me an email to say how sad he felt when he visited Addis Ababa and saw children playing in the streets with balls made from discarded plastic bags. Children with no books. Children in Ethiopia, he said, need access to libraries, too.

I thought back to those magical days when I had learned to read, bent over my first Dick and Jane books, in a remote rural area of southwest Ethiopia. The ability to read and write has been shown to lead to greater productivity, better health, longer life, decreased death rates for mothers and children. But could a freelance children's book author and a children's librarian have any kind of impact in one of the earth's poorest countries?

Ethiopia often looks grim even compared to the rest of sub-Saharan Africa. Half of children under five suffer from effects of malnutrition; 78% of citizens lack access to clean water; 87% lack access to decent sanitation; and, between the years 2000 and 2005, 69% of elementary school age children did not go to school. School fees, uniform fees, and book fees still are in place in Ethiopia; school systems either continue to charge tuition for public school, or are so completely overwhelmed by enrollment that children find themselves in classrooms where the student/teacher ratio is 100 to one or worse. Often there are no bathrooms, no running water. (As has been reported in the *New York Times*, the absence of sanitation facilities disproportionately excludes girls from attending school.) Most schools in the country do not own a single book.

Yohannes and I began our efforts with a picture book. Yohannes wrote his own version of a favorite Ethiopian folktale—in English and Amharic—and recruited an Ethiopian illustrator. Some friends (avid readers all) from First Presbyterian Church in Grand Forks, North Dakota, and I raised money for printing and then began distributing and selling what became the first color picture book for Ethiopian children. The San Francisco Public Library and various volunteers helped Yohannes gather 15,000 children's books. We raised another $10,000 to ship them.

In 2003, when I cut the ribbon of the first free library for children in Addis Ababa, I asked Yohannes, "What if we did all this work and nobody comes?" In the first year, the Ethiopian staff recorded 40,000 visits. In 2009, a group of Canadian observers wrote, "We were impressed with the Shola Children's Library as a vibrant central children's library (which runs Saturday morning story times and also has a sanitation center for children to bathe and have their clothes washed). The collection was more balanced between text and trade books and it 'felt' like a children's library we might see in North America."

Yohannes's efforts had proved how welcome books and reading spaces would be. Gradually, as we were ready to think about issues of sustainability and duplication, I realized the answer to that question from Nigerian and Ugandan educators about planting a reading culture probably boils down to three things: books, places to read books, and people.

Books

With funding from two Bay Area projects—Room to Read and Christensen Foundation—Yohannes has published six bilingual children's books and created two bilingual anthologies using traditional Ethiopian tales. Grants from the U.S. Embassy in Ethiopia and the Canadian Book Council have allowed translations into three additional local languages. With English as the language of instruction and textbooks in secondary schools, however, we also focus efforts on providing English-language books to the 20–30 school libraries we've planted.

Places

Ethiopia Reads still sustains Shola Children's Library and another community children's library in the regional capital of Awassa, but our primary focus has shifted to planting school libraries, something Yohannes and his staff are doing at the rate of almost one a month in now three geographic regions. Under the signed agreements, schools provide a clean, well-lighted room; Ethiopia Reads provides furniture, books, and basic training in how to organize those books; the schools appoint a person to be library manager. The only library buildings Ethiopia Reads owns are carts that are pulled by donkeys to several schools and neighborhoods in the Southern Nations, Nationalities, and People's Region. We currently have three donkey mobile libraries with more on the way.

People

As many another NGO has discovered, daunting as it is to deal with the concrete aspects of library planting—building furniture, publishing and gathering and shipping books, recruiting schools, building donkey carts, housing and feeding donkeys—an organization can proudly write check, check, check in those columns and still not have accomplished lasting change. Local leaders and communities must embrace, understand, and become competent with the system demands of innovation. Ethiopia Reads is now trying to think hard and well (and work with such partners as the International Reading Association) about professional development that will share the best literacy practices of educators around the world and help turn the fledgling libraries into true literacy centers and models for other organizations.

In 2008, a panel that included Jane Goodall, Deepak Chopra, and Desmond Tutu named Yohannes one of the top ten CNN Heroes. Yohannes is the first to say that this project has showed him how many other readers are willing to be heroic. Teachers, librarians, school children, adoptive families, and other volunteers have done book drives, stored books, and raised money to ship additional children's books, 20,000 pounds at a time, to build furniture, to employ 27 staff members in Ethiopia, and to continue to financially support Yohannes's explorations. The leadership team in the United States also now includes three Ethiopian Americans; support has steadily built within various Ethiopian American communities.

Today, Ethiopia Reads (www.ethiopiareads.org) reaches at least 100,000 children a year who've never before had access to books. Our literacy efforts are still experimental—and it remains to be seen whether we can be an agent for change in the whole country—but we are sustained by knowing we are changing the world for individual children who, as the author of *Three Cups of Tea* says, want fiercely to learn even though everything has always been mightily stacked against them. The project has inexorably changed my world, too. In the past six years, I've spoken all over the United States and in various other countries about Ethiopia Reads, raised money, recruited volunteers, taken educators to Ethiopia. To my delight, two of my children were among those drawn to volunteer at Shola Children's Library in Addis Ababa. That's how I ended up with two Ethiopian American grandchildren. Whether I'm reading to Ellemae Enku and Noh Iyasu or watching Ethiopian children read books for the first time, I see, over and over, how hungry children are for ideas, for stories, for opening the doors to let a hundred worlds in.

Point of Departure

Yohannes Gebregeorgis

Where do I start? I cannot tell you what I do now without telling you some part of my life as a child. I was born in a small rural village in southern Ethiopia. I grew up with cows and sheep and goats and camels. When I was growing up, there was plenty in Ethiopia; we didn't really have any hunger or any shortage of milk or meat. I had the best childhood. We even had an elementary school in my town, which happened to be a prison house built by Italians when they invaded Ethiopia in 1935.

But there was something missing at that time, and that was books and a library. We didn't even know what a library was, but, of course, we had textbooks that we had to learn from. I remember several textbooks that really impacted me as a young boy. One of these was a British textbook called *The March of Times*. In this book there was one story that has vividly stayed in my mind called "Guy Fawkes and the Gunpowder Plot." Can you imagine what that story has done to me? It has made me a rebel later in my life. You never know when ideas are planted in your mind: That is the power of books and stories.

In my town, there was no high school. The nearest high school was 575 kilometers away, so, in order to go there, a group of kids from the same town would rent a place to live together. And there, in my high school, I had a wonderful encounter with a young American Peace Corps teacher named Douglas. The Peace Corps workers also had to rent a place to live, so we happened to be neighbors. As neighbors, Douglas and other Peace Corps teachers taught us how to play hula hoop and other American games. In my English classroom, Douglas taught us American literature, and I still lovingly remember "Rip Van Winkle" and "The Legend of Sleepy Hollow" and the Headless Horseman. Can you imagine what these stories would do to a young mind? They totally opened up a whole new world of literature.

My encounter with books and stories did not end there, but there weren't many books in my life or in the lives of many young Ethiopian kids at the time. I was 19 years old when I found the book that really transformed my life. I was 19, I was in love—you know if you're 19 and not in love that's not a good sign—and this book called *Love Kitten*, an American romance book, did wonders for me because now I had to look for other romance books to read. I did succeed in finding some, and that led me to reading other books also, other novels, fiction books, crime books from Agatha Christie, and a variety of American authors. At that time, luckily, we had what we called the American Library, the USIS (United States Information Services)

library, right in the middle of Addis Ababa. I was one of the biggest customers of that library. Wherever there were books, I would go at that young age.

But, also, there was revolution in my country. I was involved in that revolution. We had an emperor in Ethiopia, and we wanted to overthrow this emperor because we thought he was a tyrant and had to be replaced by a government of the people, by the people, for the people. But we did not stop there. I think most young people at that time became Communists. As young idealists who wanted change, we wanted to do the best for our countries, so we found this ideology that was made somewhere else, but we embraced it. We read the literature and we ardently fought to dismantle the imperial power of his majesty Emperor Haile Selassie the First. That ended, and we had a military dictatorship in Ethiopia, and then we had to fight it, because we didn't think that it was fair to have a military dictatorship on top of the grave of a monarch. But the military dictatorship was harsh: Most of our compatriots were killed or tortured and, eventually, I had to flee the country.

I went to the Sudan, and from the Sudan, I went to Houston, Texas, in the United States. In Ethiopia I had studied to be a pharmacist, so I was able to get a job in a hospital in Houston. I also went to school at the University of Houston. I got my first degree in English Literature and then I went to the University of Texas and did my Master's in Library and Information Sciences, because I had already decided that what I wanted to do *had* to do with books. I wanted to be a college librarian, but unfortunately, I could not find a job in a college, so I ended up in the San Francisco Public Library, and that was when I started thinking about the children of Ethiopia.

I visited Ethiopia in 1991, but it was devastated. The military was overthrown, but there were no libraries and no books for children. There were no playgrounds; there was nothing at all for children. I said, "I have to do something." But what can a librarian do? Except collect books and send books over and try to establish some place for kids to read. In 1998, I formed this organization called Ethiopian Books for Children, an international foundation which we now call Ethiopia Reads. I left my job, and went back to Ethiopia in 2001 and established the first children's library there in 2003.

How did we do it? We formed an organization with board members, and I found an American lady, Jane Kurtz, who happened to grow up in Ethiopia, and was an author of children's books. I thought, I have to ask this

441

lady to help, so I authored an email, and Jane said, yes, I will help. Ever since, she has been the backbone of this organization as both fundraiser and spokesperson. With her support, I was able to establish our first library, and then after that, we also established other libraries in other parts of the country.

We also established Donkey Mobile Libraries. Ethiopia has more donkeys than any other country in the world except for China. Donkeys are everywhere, all over the countryside, even in cities, in towns, hauling all kinds of things—wood, stone, food, even people in carts or on top of donkeys. They are the most hard-working, humble animals; they will not even kick you when you hurt them. So we started using donkeys to deliver books for children, but we wanted to be fair to these donkeys also, so we said to the kids, these animals are working so hard that they deserve to be treated with respect and dignity. We created a queen of donkeys, called her Queen Helena—Helena means conscience, and she became the conscience of donkeys, the spokesqueen, of all donkeys in Ethiopia. Since there are no other queens of donkeys in the world, I think by extension, she became the queen of all donkeys in the world, including the Chinese donkeys. We created some fun and some excitement when we inaugurated the first Donkey Mobile Library. Thousands of kids followed the procession, including the queen, who was leading the procession with her crown and with her royal robe. The kids were chanting, "Queen Helena, give us books! Queen Helena, give us books!"

Most of these kids had never held a book in their hands. When we started the Donkey Mobile Library and the first library in Addis Ababa, the capital city, they were holding books upside down, even though they were going to school. Some were second graders, third graders, fourth graders, but they had never touched a book because there were no books in their schools. We did a survey in Addis Ababa, and we found that 99% of the schools have absolutely no libraries. None at all, and this was in the capital city. What do you think it is like in the rural areas? One hundred percent or maybe a little less. How can kids be educated without books?

Without ever reading a book? Without ever touching a book? What kind of education would that be? I think it is like eating bland food, food that doesn't have spice, that doesn't have peppers or anything palatable. The spice in education in Ethiopia is missing. The spice of education is books, books that kids read outside of school, or in their classrooms, or in libraries.

So, our organization also started establishing school libraries. As we speak, we have established 35 school libraries. It's not much, but we have functional modern libraries, with shelves and chairs and tables and books. Working with sponsors and donations, we have also published 11 books for children, illustrated picturebooks and anthologies of folktales. I have tried to do as much with all the experience that I've gathered as a librarian in this country and going to different countries to book fairs and conferences. We have established an annual Ethiopian Children's Book Week that is very successful in promoting reading in Ethiopia, and things are changing. Kids are reading books, and I can see that it's absolutely inevitable that kids have books in their schools, in their communities, and if possible, in their homes. During our Book Week, we give most of the books that we publish free to children. We give out thousands of books for children. And this past April when we celebrated our sixth annual Children's Book Week, we were astonished by a presentation from a nine-year-old girl. She came up to the podium and started reading, but didn't see the book—it was an invisible book that she was reading. How could someone read an invisible book? But this nine-year-old girl was reading word by word, word by word. It was one of the books that we had given these kids during our last Book Week, and she had read it so many times, over and over again, that now she could read it without looking at it, word by word without any page in front of her. That's really the power of having books for our children. It transforms their imagination, the way they look at the world, the way they look at themselves. We have a group of brave young kids who have come to our libraries every single day since we opened our doors. And where are these kids going to go to? They are going to reach the stars.

32

Censorship

Book Challenges, Challenging Books, and Young Readers

Christine A. Jenkins

University of Illinois at Urbana-Champaign

Educators and librarians have a long history of energetic work on behalf of young people and their reading. Other people are equally passionate about what children read and what meanings they make but their efforts may be aimed at limiting access to books. Christine Jenkins explores what we do and do not know about the beliefs, goals, and strategies of individuals and groups who would censor books for young readers. Her analysis is central to any discussion of the life of a book as it moves from purchase, to review, to public debate, to bookshelf, and ultimately to young readers; who will, in the end, find their own meanings in the literature they read. Jenkins' overview of censorship is followed by Cart's and Yokota's chapters on book reviews and book awards, all of which extend our understanding of the relationships between society, books, and reading.

Censorship is the removal, suppression, or restricted circulation of literary, artistic, or educational materials—of images, ideas and information—on the grounds that these are morally or otherwise objectionable in light of standards applied by the censor. Frequently, the single occurrence of an offending word will arouse protest. In other cases, objection will be made to the underlying values and basic message conveyed—or said to be conveyed—by a given work…. Americans find censorship odious. Few in our society advocate the banning of all but a tiny handful of materials from sale, circulation, or display to adults. The commitment to free expression is not so clear, however, where minors are concerned.

(Reichman, *Censorship and Selection,* 2001, pp. 2–4)

The principles of intellectual freedom—the idea that a democracy is dependent upon free and open access to ideas—are hallmarks of the library and education professions. But librarians and teachers sometimes face strong opinions regarding what material people think is appropriate for children and teenagers to have access to in a school library, public library, or classroom.

(Cooperative Children's Book Center, n.d.)

In this chapter, I examine the censorship of young people's literature and the published research about it. Many people are not aware of the prevalence of challenges to the right to read in contemporary America. Censorship is associated in the minds of many with dramatic scenes of book burning in other countries or in the past. Further, when people do think of censorship today, they may think first of controversies over rap music lyrics, potty-mouthed radio talk show hosts, or X-rated films. Rarely are cases of attempted book censorship covered as major news stories. The vignettes offered below indicate, however, that challenges to young people's reading options are anything but rare.

Vignettes of Censorship

In 1945, *Ilenka*, a picture book by Lee Kingman, was published to some acclaim. The story about a Russian girl was slight, but the decorative illustrations resembled Matisse's work. *The Horn Book* praised *Ilenka* as an example of a children's book that bridged the gap between book illustration and fine art. The story aroused no suspicions because, in 1945, the USSR was one of the Allied Forces, a valuable partner in World War II. In 1948, however, the Cold War was underway. The members of a veterans' group approached the head librarian of the Philadelphia Free Library to remove *Ilenka* from the children's collection. They objected to its portrayal of a Russian child who "had everything she needed to make her happy" and who was struggling to decide, among many options, what she wants to be when she grows up. The group claimed that the book was factually inaccurate—a little girl could never be happy in Russia (C. Field, personal communication, April 2, 1992).

In 1977, the Illinois Police Association urged librarians to remove William Steig's *Sylvester and the Magic Pebble*, winner of the 1970 Caldecott Medal, from their shelves. Sylvester is a donkey and all the other characters are animals. The policemen are portrayed as pigs. The American Library Association (ALA) reported similar complaints in 11 other states (Haight & Grannis, 1978, p. 87).

In 1980, a school administrator attended a district meeting held in an elementary school library and came across a new book on display, *Body Words: A Dictionary of the Human Body, How it Works, and Some of the Things that Affect It*, by Kathleen N. Daly (1980). The book was illustrated with line drawings of children's bodies and their various systems and organs. She was alarmed by drawings illustrating "erection" and "vulva" and deemed the book more appropriate for a secondary school. However, the book was obviously written for elementary school-aged readers, and the drawings depicting young children would limit its appeal to older students (E. Faye, personal communication, November 18, 1980).

In 1990, a first-grade boy brought home a picture book from his elementary school library. The book, *A Woggle of Witches* (1971), tells a slight story about small witches who fly through the air, sleep in hammocks hung high in oak trees, and are frightened by children in Halloween costumes. The boy's mother testified to the school board:

> I think it is a threat....The presence of the book in school libraries may be interpreted by some children as the school sanctioning the practice of witchcraft. I'm concerned for my family, but my concern goes for those other children who are unprotected because their parents are non-functional, and thus vulnerable to such books' underlying occult and satanic messages. (Brown,1990, 1A)

In 1993, a public librarian recommended *Are You There, God? It's Me, Margaret*, by Judy Blume (1970) to a seven-year old Jewish girl who she thought would be engaged by Margaret's struggle to understand her Jewish heritage. Instead, the girl—who had no previous knowledge of menstruation—was disturbed by Margaret's anticipation of her first menstrual period and asked her parents to explain. They responded by taking the book out of her hands and reassuring her that she needn't worry about this until she was older. Her father, conservative media critic Michael Medved, related this experience to emphasize how vigilant parents must be to preserve their children's innocence. The girl and her parents devised a strategy to help her avoid disturbing books: she would read only books written before 1960. Medved recommended this strategy to other concerned parents (Medved, 1998, pp. 12–13).

In 2006, Cuban exiles living in Miami complained that a bilingual picture book, *Vamos a Cuba/A Visit to Cuba*, by Alta Schreier (2001), one of a series of 24 children's books about life in other countries, was riddled with "inaccuracies" for its positive portrayal of life in Cuba. After a lengthy and politically charged struggle, the school district ordered the books' removal, a move that countered recommendations from the school board attorney, two school review committees (in 7–1 and 15–1 votes) and the district's Superintendent. In November 2009 the U.S. Supreme Court refused to hear *American Civil Liberties Union of Florida, Inc., Greater Miami Chapter, et. al. v. Miami-Dade County School Board*, a lawsuit first filed in June 2006, and the board's decision was sustained. *Vamos a Cuba* was the only book in the series that received a complaint, but all 24 books were removed from school libraries (FLA, 2009).

In 2009, three books with gay/lesbian content in the West Bend, Wisconsin, public library's young adult collection—two fiction and one nonfiction—were challenged by a couple who feared that younger children would read the books. In the ensuing weeks, four school board members lost their seats, the list of challenged books grew longer, the couple and their supporters demanded that the library acquire books that depict homosexuality as a "curable" condition, and the story was picked up by national and international wire services. In the end, the books stayed on the shelf (Hanna, 2009).

Why Are Books Censored?

Book censorship is an act that involves complaints about specific texts. That is, the act of censoring or removing or restricting particular books implies that there are other books that are *not* censored; or that a book that is under attack could be rehabilitated by having the offending portions excised. But the act of censorship implies that there is some sorting procedure in effect. Human history includes many such moments, when powerful people decided that texts written in German (as during WWI in the U.S.), texts written by Jews and Communists (as in Nazi Germany), and all books published before 1949 (the War against the "Four Olds" during the Chinese Cultural Revolution) should not exist. In 1562 in Mexico, Spanish friars burned all Mayan texts to "cleanse" the natives of "devilish" thoughts (and presumably replace them with Christian books written in Spanish). Censorship can also be an extension of "ethnic cleansing," as in 1992, when the Serbs set fire to the National and University Library of Bosnia and Herzegovina in Sarajevo, and destroyed 1.5 million books and manuscripts in a single night (Silvester, 2009).

Indeed, the classic censorship document, the Roman Catholic *Index Librorum Prohibitorum,* is simply a (very long) list of the specific texts denounced by the Church since the 1500s. Contemporary lists, such as the annual *Banned Books Resource Guide* (Doyle, 2007), although compiled for a very different purpose, likewise identify specific titles and the specific reason(s) given for challenging their presence in school and public libraries.

Early censorship attempts, unlike those in more recent times, were rarely based on protecting children. Throughout history, however, the red flags for censors have remained roughly the same: religion, politics, and sexual content. Typically, controversial texts are those that in some way disturb (or are perceived as disturbing) the religious, political, or sexual status quo—from William Tyndale's English translation of the New Testament (1526) to Thomas Paine's *Common Sense* (1776) to Marie Stopes' *Married Love* (1918). Other texts have been challenged not for what they said so much as how they said it. In these cases, the "objectionable language" might be labeled "blasphemous" (religiously objectionable), "treasonous" (politically objectionable), or "lewd" (sexually objectionable), or simply lacking the expected respect or reverence usually accorded these subjects.

Book as Role Model

Books containing words or slurs that demean people on the basis of race, gender, class, sexual orientation, religion, or other characteristics are likewise subject to challenges. Some see the *presence* of such language in books aimed at young readers as indicating tacit approval for the *use* of such language by those readers. If a community's laws or a school's code of conduct prohibits particular actions and behaviors on the part of young people, so the reasoning goes, those actions or behaviors should not appear in the books of that community's public or school libraries. By the same "book as role model" reasoning, books should

not contain profanities that children are punished for uttering, nor depict a young person's disrespect for authority, unless such behavior is shown to have clear and negative consequences. Thus, the argument goes that poor role models have no place in the institutions devoted to the education of young people.

Over the last century, most book challenges have included the complaint that the materials are—or might be—perceived as "harmful to minors." Although high-profile landmark legal cases have involved books for adult readers, such as *Ulysses*, *Lady Chatterley's Lover*, and *The Tropic of Cancer,* the great majority of objections are made for reasons of the perceived vulnerability of the young reader to a text's controversial content and the potential for harm, whether it is depictions of adults having sex, rabid dogs terrorizing humans, teens using recreational drugs, or children playing with matches. Judging from the most recent *Banned Books Resource Guide*, it appears that some version of "harmful to children" is included in the language of nearly every challenge, regardless of the possibility that minors might realistically have access to the book in question. Even when *Of Mice and Men*, *The Grapes of Wrath*, or other books written for adults are challenged, the original audience is not a concern, but rather the reading of minors.

Although restricting access to a book through a challenge or "banning" is an obvious form of censorship, transforming the original text has also been a prevalent practice. Throughout the 20th century, high school students (including this author) have been assigned bowdlerized editions of Shakespeare's plays. Thomas Bowdler wrote versions of Shakespeare's texts entitled *The Family Shakespeare, in Ten Volumes; In Which Nothing is Added to the Original Text; But Those Words and Expressions Are Omitted Which Cannot With Propriety Be Read Aloud in a Family,* which include 24 of Shakespeare's plays, each preceded by an introduction noting the changes to the original text. In Hamlet, the death of Ophelia was pictured as an accidental drowning rather than a suicide. Lady MacBeth's cry of "Out, damned spot!" was changed to "Out, crimson spot!" And so on.

Sexual and Obscene Content: Definitions and Arguments

Although the first U.S. censorship prosecutions on the basis of *sexual* content did not occur until the early 1800s, such prosecutions soon became widespread. Anthony Comstock, the well-known anti-obscenity crusader, spearheaded the YMCA-sponsored Committee for the Suppression of Vice, which later became the New York Society for the Suppression of Vice. From 1872 to 1913, Comstock and his organization were instrumental in over 3,600 arrests for distributing obscene materials, including books, magazines, pictures, and contraceptive devices. Although the Society's concern was not limited to youth and the material it attacked was marketed to adults, "vulnerable minds" were very much at the center of their rhetoric. Comstock's (1883) book, *Traps for the Young*, documented and attacked the "evil reading" available to the young in the form of dime novels, story papers, weekly newspapers, and other obscene materials. As Comstock put it, "Who would go to the state prison, the gambling saloon, or the brothel to find a suitable companion for the child? Yet a more insidious foe is selected when these stories are allowed to become associates for the child's mind and to shape and direct his thoughts" (p. 21).

Former Justice Potter Stewart of the Supreme Court of the United States, in attempting to classify what material constituted exactly "what is obscene," famously wrote, "I shall not today attempt further to define the kinds of material I understand to be embraced….[b]ut I know it when I see it…" (Supreme Court, 1964). However, the 1973 ruling of the Supreme Court of the United States in Miller v. California established a three-tiered test to determine what was obscene—and thus not protected– versus what was merely erotic and thus protected by the First Amendment. Delivering the opinion of the court, Chief Justice Warren Burger wrote,

> The basic guidelines for the trier of fact must be: (a) whether 'the average person, applying contemporary community standards would find that the work, taken as a whole, appeals to the prurient interest, (b) whether the work depicts or describes, in a patently offensive way, sexual conduct specifically defined by the applicable state law; and (c) whether the work, taken as a whole, lacks serious literary, artistic, political, or scientific value. (Supreme Court, 1973)

In fact, "obscenity" in U.S. courts is speech that is by definition unprotected by the First Amendment. Thus, the label of "obscenity" may be applied to texts that contain no depiction of sexual activity, but, for example, include an expletive as an expression of anger, surprise, or disgust. Or Holden Caulfield trying to erase the words "fuck you" from a wall where children might see it (Salinger, 1951, p. 201).

By the turn of the 20th century, the charge of obscenity—that is, objections based on sexual content—had become more common in censorship cases. Among the factors at work in this trend were an increased public discourse about sex (ironically fueled in part by Comstock's campaign), the appearance of more novels of social realism—that described, in addition to other realities, prostitution and out-of-wedlock childbirth—and an increased public awareness of the significant role of sex and sexuality from the dissemination of Freud's theories and the establishment of psychology as a field of study.

Here it must be added that there were also parents, educators, and other adults who saw a need for sex education books written specifically *for children* to support social hygiene and prevent the spread of venereal disease. Finally, technological advances in the paper-making, printing, and publishing industries meant that more books and other printed matter of all types were being produced. All of these factors contributed to an increase in the amount of sexual reading material available to complain about. And for those who would complain, many did.

Public Response to Censorship

To raise public awareness of all of the possible changes in and challenges to literature, Banned Book Week was established with the express aim of affirming the importance of the freedom to read (Doyle, 2007, p. 6). This annual event is now sponsored by a coalition of book industry and professional groups, including the American Booksellers Association and the Association of American Publishers. Many U.S. bookstores, libraries, and schools celebrate Banned Books Week every September by spotlighting books that have been challenged at some point(s) in their histories, from J.D. Salinger's (1951) *The Catcher in the Rye* to Dr. Seuss' (1971) *The Lorax* to J.K. Rowling's (1997–2007) Harry Potter series.

Such awareness of and activism on behalf of readers matters to the public, as in the case of Scholastic Publishing, the leading vendor of packaged school-based book fairs in the United States, that decided against including one of their recent titles in its book fair offerings. The book was Lauren Myracle's (2009) *Luv Ya Bunches*, the first book in a series that chronicles the unlikely friendship between four elementary age girls, one of whom lives with her mother and her mother's female partner. The text had contained some objectionable language (including "crap," "sucks," and "Oh my God"), which the author was willing to remove. However, Scholastic also demanded that all references to that girl's family be omitted so as to avoid complaints from parents. Myracle rejected this demand ("A child having same-sex parents is not offensive, in my mind, and shouldn't be 'cleaned up.'… What, exactly, are children being protected against here?") and Scholastic removed *Luv Ya Bunches* from their book fair distribution list. . After receiving over 4000 emails from people objecting to Scholastic's demand that Myracle turn two moms into a mom and a dad, the publisher relented (SCBWI, 2010).

Selection vs. Censorship: Considering Penguins

Censorship proper is the formal limitation of access to the text, a decision usually made by a school board or a public library's board of trustees. A board or committee charged with making a determination might decide to retain the book in the collection but restrict access to it in some way, or remove the book entirely from the library or classroom. However, the line between censorship and what is described in classic works in library science as selection, are not entirely clear (Asheim, 1953).

Librarianship and Selection

Librarians still agonize over the difference between selection and censorship. Library budgets are rarely sufficient, so the youth librarian makes hard choices with every book order. If, for example, the Jaycees sponsor a free showing of *March of the Penguins* at a local movie house, the librarian can anticipate a run on penguin books. The librarian will begin by noting what books on penguins are already in the collection (several titles, but not sufficient to meet the anticipated demand) and be glad to see that the movie's popularity has inspired publishers to issue several attractive and well-reviewed titles on penguins. So, let's say that there are five titles that would be excellent additions to the collection. One of the five is Parnell and Richardson's *And Tango Makes Three* (2005), a picture book that tells the true story of Roy and Silo, two male chinstrap penguins in New York City's Central Park Zoo who become mates, build a nest together, and find and sit on an egg-shaped stone. When the zookeeper acquires an orphaned penguin egg, he replaces Roy and Silo's stone "egg" with the real one. The two birds successfully hatch and raise a baby penguin that the zookeeper names Tango.

And Tango Makes Three is an engagingly written and attractively illustrated picture book that tells a simple and true story. Originally published by Simon & Schuster in 2005, the book received favorable reviews. Yet from 2006 to 2008 the book topped the American Library Association's list of the year's most challenged books. To no one's surprise, objections focus on the book's depiction of a same-sex pair of penguins raising a baby. Complainants denounced the book as anti-ethnic, anti-family, "not developmentally appropriate," and as "propaganda for gay marriage and the right of same-sex couples to adopt and raise children" (Doyle, 2007, p. 136).

If a librarian or teacher is looking for an attractive, well-written, and well-reviewed picture book about penguins, *And Tango Makes Three* meets all criteria, and many libraries have acquired it. Librarians who do not acquire it are not censors per se, but when a librarian finds positive reviews, notes the positive qualities of the book—and has a ready audience of young penguin fans—but finally decides against its purchase solely because "someone" might object to its presence in the library, then the librarian is not selecting, but rather censoring.

The Public Complainant and Censorship

If it is the public, however, who submit a complaint about a book, another set of definitions—and related responses from librarians and school boards—come into play. Because a book challenge can vary in both intention and intensity, the American Library Association's Intellectual Freedom Committee (n.d.) has developed some standard definitions. At the least stressful level, a book may be the subject of an "expression of concern" by someone who questions the book's presence in the library or classroom. Expressions of concern may have judgmental overtones, but they can also indicate a simple desire to discuss the book in question. The second level is an "oral complaint" regarding the material's presence in the library. At the third level, the library or school receives a "written complaint" that formally challenges the presence and/or appropriateness of the material. Infrequently, there may also be a "public attack," that is, a statement disseminated to the media or others to gain support for the complaint. Since the complainants lack the authority to actually remove or restrict access to the book, all of their actions are technically "challenges" rather than "censorship."

The Challenged Book: What Happens Next

The challenge process, from initial complaint to final outcome, is generally spelled out in a library's selection policy. It can play out like a criminal court case, with the book as the defendant, accused of endangering a minor by threatening to harm or assault them, and/or "rob them of their innocence." The disposition of the challenge with regard to the book is likewise similar to the treatment of a defendant before and after the court's verdict. Those accused of crimes are passed through the legal system, with a hearing, testimony, a trial, verdict, and sentence. Challenged books go through the library's reconsideration process that includes hearings, character witnesses, a prosecutor and defender, and ultimately a verdict and a sentence. A "not guilty" verdict means that the defendant will be released and may return to his or her former life. The book that is retained in the collection is likewise free to resume its former position on the library shelves and thence into the hands of readers.

As noted above, restrictions (or "remedies") proposed by the would-be censor can take several forms, just as a range of sentences, from probation to death, may be handed down to a guilty criminal. Often challengers argue for a solution that seems, on the surface, to be a reasonable compromise. A book could be placed in closed shelving (in these cases a signed note from a parent or teacher would be required for a student to gain access to the materials). It could be moved to the reference collection, where the book can be examined in-house but not checked out, or into a "parenting" collection and circulated to adults only. The book could also be relocated within the library's public collection. This often means that the book is "kicked upstairs" to a section for more mature readers. In school libraries this could mean moving a book from an elementary to a middle school, or from a middle to a high school. In public libraries, juvenile nonfiction or fiction can be reclassified as adult nonfiction or fiction. The good news is that the book remains in the library's collection. The bad news is that the book is no longer located where its potential readers will find it.

Such reclassification practices and intentions can be

viewed through the prism of Dr. Seuss's (1954) *Horton Hears a Who*. Horton the elephant's keen ears enable him to hear calls for help from the Whos–small beings living on a dust speck—so he carefully places the dust speck into the shelter of a clover blossom. The clover is maliciously snatched from him by a family of monkeys and handed off to a black-bottomed eagle, who flies off with it and drops it into an enormous clover field. "'Find that!' sneered the bird, 'but I think you will fail!'/ and he left with a flip of his black-bottomed tail." In a similar manner, teens browsing the young adult fiction shelves might come across a controversial book like Judy Blume's (1975) *Forever,* but when the book is placed in adult fiction (which has happened), only the intrepid teens who go looking for that specific book will ever find it in the midst of thousands of adult fiction titles.

Of course, the most extreme outcome of a challenge is removing the book completely. Whether it is burned, sold, or tossed in the trash, the book is gone. To the censor, the perceived vector of infection has been banished and the community returns to its unsullied state. To the anti-censor, a dissenting voice has been silenced. The book has been tried, found guilty, and executed. In the past, some criminals were sentenced to death by fire. Books too have been burned. It is interesting to note, however, that in the popular imagination, those sentenced to burn were likely to be witches. So, finally the book becomes a witch, with access to supernatural power to do evil. Such is the perceived potential for harm in the pages of a book deemed "forbidden."

Advocacy Groups and Censorship

Those who track book challenges have found that the majority of the books with documented challenges are challenged only once (G.M. Kruse, personal communication, January 17, 1990). However, a handful of books have received numerous challenges. Multiple challenges are generally the result of an organized campaign by an advocacy group seeking to wield its muscle in a public venue.

Many intellectual freedom activists within ALA have stated that all censorship is political. In this context, "political" is defined as social relationships involving authority or power.

According to those who study the history of censorship, there have been various "fashions" in censorship that reflect changing political conditions. Thus, during the 1950s, challenges to Garth William's (1958) *The Rabbit's Wedding*, about the marriage of a black rabbit and a white rabbit, were one small piece of a larger campaign to maintain racial segregation as the Jim Crow laws were being struck down in the American South. In the late 1960s, *Sylvester and the Magic Pebble* (Steig, 1969), a story populated with talking farm animals, provoked challengers who were disturbed that the police in the story

are portrayed as pigs. Later on, when religious concerns about witchcraft and the occult were on the rise, *Sylvester* was against objected to on account of the magic wishing pebble that turns Sylvester from a donkey to a rock (and later turns the rock back into a donkey). As a fear of the occult grew—particularly, but not exclusively, among conservative evangelical Christians—books such as Johanna Michaelsen's (1989) *Like Lambs to the Slaughter: Your Child and the Occult* warned against pop culture products aimed at children (My Little Pony, Smurfs, Care Bears), the possession of which could be the first step down the slippery slope to full-fledged satanic involvement. Each of those toys had books as marketing spin-offs, which were equally suspect. Another popular focus for book challengers is LGBTQ (lesbian/gay/bisexual/transgendered/queer or questioning) content. Thus, challenges to Nancy Garden's (1982) *Annie On My Mind*, Leslea Newman's (1989) *Heather Has Two Mommies*, and Michael Willhoite's (1990) *Daddy's Roommate* demonstrate the initiators' opposition to same-sex marriage, gays in the military, and the perceived "homosexual agenda."

The various challenges to J.K. Rowling's (e.g., 1997) popular Harry Potter books provide an intriguing illustration of current-day efforts to restrict young people's access to books. Those who challenge the presence of Harry Potter in public and school library collections weigh in on both sides of the ongoing "fairy tale wars," a decadeslong debate among librarians and educators as to whether a child's development is best supported by reading fantasy or realistic fiction. Rowling's books have been attacked on several fronts. Some argue that depictions of Harry and company learning spells in order to thwart and conquer evil tempt children with the dangerous pleasures of the occult. Others believe that depictions of Harry and his friends defying authority and disobeying parents and teachers model misbehavior and disrespect toward adults, further undermining the traditional roles of the nuclear family and the authority of those entrusted with the care of children. Furthermore, argue still others, Harry and his allies engage in the timeless struggle between good and evil, battling Lord Voldemort and the death-eaters for control of the world–all without benefit of any organized religion.

Challengers to Harry Potter have described their efforts as a "battle for the hearts and minds" of children. Although the anti-Potter furor has died down since its heyday in the late 1990s, Focus on the Family, Concerned Women for America, the American Family Association, and other Christian Right political groups have made Harry Potter the focus of their considerable energy as they organize on behalf of conservative religious and political "family values." In a 2005 case in the Cedarville, Arkansas, School District, a school board placed Harry Potter books in a restricted area and required students to have written parental permission to check the books out. The school board's restrictions were challenged in federal court, and the court found that the school board had removed the books from its library shelves "for reasons not authorized by the Constitution" (DeMitchell & Carney, 2005, p. 164).

Research on Book Challenges and Censorship

Chronicling and documenting book challenges is the most basic type of research on censorship and has many practical applications. For example, annotated lists of challenged books are consulted to create displays and other publicity during Banned Books Week. As noted above, the foundation for much research on book challenges is the documentation generated by the organizers of Banned Books Week. The most recent compilation of the annual lists describes challenges to over 1,500 titles, gleaned from news sources and incident reports sent to agencies like the ALA's Office for Intellectual Freedom and the National Council of Teachers of English's Anti-Censorship Center (Doyle, 2007). The incident reports are gathered via surveys, report forms, or brief structured interviews and emphasize factual details: What book(s) or materials were challenged? What was the specific complaint? Who made the complaint to whom? When and where did this occur? What happened after the complaint was made?

Each challenge has its own dynamics and trajectory specific to the book, the complainant, the institution, the community, the time and place, and the sociopolitical milieu. But it must be remembered that although the data gathered from self-reports can be rich indeed, unreported book challenges—and there are many—are not included. Still, these incomplete data provide at least a partial picture of the who, what, where, when, why, and how"of book challenges and form the basis for more nuanced and contextualized narratives. An incident report may also describe the type of remedy sought by complainants, and it will most likely report the final resolution of the challenge–whether the book was retained, relocated, restricted, or removed. Rich data of this type were used by Dianne McAfee Hopkins (1991) in her study of significant variables in book challenge outcomes.

In-depth Censorship Studies

In addition to the broad but succinct evidence presented in the Banned Books Week guides, there are also a handful of works that provide more in-depth surveys of banned books. These texts focus primarily on books that have been challenged repeatedly and provide a detailed account of each book's censorship history. Two of the earliest, Lee Burress's (1989) *Battle of the Books: Literary Censorship in the Public Schools, 1950–1985* and Herbert Foerstel's (2002) *Banned in the U.S.A: A Reference Guide to Book Censorship in School and Public Libraries* cover children's and young adult books, while Karolides, Bald & Sova's (2005) *120 Banned Books: Censorship Histories of World Literature* focuses exclusively on books for adult readers. Four volumes in a set published by Facts on File,

taken together, cover approximately 450 titles of both children's and adult literature that have been suppressed on religious, political, sexual, and social grounds (Bald 2006; Karolides 2006; Sova 2006a, 2006b). Two works are notably international in scope: Karolides (2006) focuses entirely on books originating in countries outside the United States, and the revised edition of *The Encyclopedia of Censorship,* includes over 1,000 entries that describe censorship issues throughout the world (Green & Karolides 2005).

Much of the nuts-and-bolts practice-oriented literature pertaining to censorship of children's and young adult literature is written by and published for school and public youth services librarians. Books specific to school libraries and library media specialists include those by Scales (2009), Adams (2008), Kravitz (2002), and Simmons and Dresang (2001).

Dianne McAfee Hopkins's (1998) "Toward a Conceptual Path of Support for School Library Media Specialists" provides a thorough literature review of research on book challenges. This review is a useful starting point for scholars interested in a multidisciplinary approach drawn from research in sociology, psychology, communications, and library and information science. Hopkins's initial questions are practitioner-oriented: "Why do many library media specialists choose to deal with a challenge to school library materials without professional support? What contributions can support make to the library media specialist during the challenge process? What support systems are likely to be most beneficial to the school library media specialist during the challenge? Why? What is known in support research, generally, that can assist in understanding the varying responses of the school library media specialist to a material challenge?"

There are a handful of studies using data gathered from in-depth interviews, including Marjorie Fiske's (1959) classic *Book Selection and Censorship: A Study of School and Public Libraries in California.* Fiske selected 26 communities representing the range of populations, ethnic compositions, locations, rates of growth, and types of library service found in California. She interviewed each community's public library administrator and librarians, the head of the county library system, the superintendent of schools, high school principals, and school librarians, for a total of 204 interviews. She focused on the factors her subjects considered most important in choosing books to add to their libraries; her findings reveal the fear of authority and lack of power felt by many school and public librarians in Cold War era America.

In addition to the literature review described above, Hopkins (1991) also conducted one of the best-known and most influential censorship research studies, by synthesizing findings from quantitative and qualitative data. Hopkins' data sources included surveys, interviews, and "critical incident" reporting to examine censorship and the book challenge process in school libraries. Her research trajectory on censorship and intellectual freedom began with an investigation (via mail surveys to school librarians in three midwestern states) that successfully teased out and examined the factors involved in a book challenge. These factors include: (a) complaint background—the challenged text and the context of the complaint; (b) the initiator of the challenge (parents, other library or school employees, governing board members, or people outside of school/community environment); (c) the characteristics of the librarian (education, years of professional experience, age, amount of pressure felt, perception of support/isolation, and self-esteem); (d) the library's selection policy and degree of compliance with that policy; (e) the institutional environment (support of administrators, co-workers, overall internal support, size of institution); and (f) the community environment (overall external support received during the challenge).

Hopkins' investigations (1991), which culminated in a federally funded national survey, identified the specific factors within those six areas that were significantly correlated to the positive outcome of a book being retained in the collection. Among the significant positive factors Hopkins found were: the librarian's perception of support from colleagues and principal; having a board-approved selection policy in place; and having a complaint instigator from outside the school system. Hopkins also found that a challenge generated by a written complaint was more likely to have a positive outcome than one generated by an oral complaint. Hence her advice to librarians facing book challenges to "get it in writing!" (Hopkins, 1993) .

Research drawn from or aimed toward an LIS audience will necessarily focus on the librarian's role in the book challenge process. Scholars of education, journalism, or communications history examine other aspects of censorship, such as particular types of complaints or particular settings. For example, in *What Johnny Shouldn't Read: Textbook Censorship in America* researcher Joan Delfattore (1992) focuses on the pro-censorship activists, such as Mel and Norma Gabler, who played instrumental roles in the statewide textbook adoption struggles in Texas and California during the 1980s. Other scholars examine censorship by focusing on specific data sources. For example, in *Alien Ink: The FBI's War on Freedom of Expression* journalist Natalie Robins (1992) used Freedom of Information Act requests to examine F.B.I. files on over one hundred U.S. authors and artists who were under F.B.I. surveillance during the 1950s to determine, among other things, what aspect(s) of their lives and works brought them to the attention of the F.B.I.

The most detailed accounts of book censorship are book-length case studies by sociologists, educators, or historians. Among the most well-known of these is James Moffett's (1988) *Storm in the Mountains: A Case Study of Censorship, Conflict, and Consciousness*, an ethnographic study of the 1974 struggle in Kanawha County, West Virginia, over innovative/subversive language arts textbooks.

The controversy involved six months of picket lines and school bus vandalism and ended with the textbooks being withdrawn. Moffett's interviews with key players, which he conducted in 1982, led him to the unsurprising conclusion that the textbooks provided an arena in which rural working-class community insiders and educated middle-class outsiders contended for control of the schools.

At the Schoolhouse Gate: Lessons in Intellectual Freedom takes a more journalistic approach as two high school teachers, Gloria Pipkin and ReLeah Cossett Lent (2002), provide a day by day report of the events, conversations, and legal actions they experienced in defending novels and a school newspaper from administrative censorship. Historian Paul Boyer's (2002) *Purity in Print: Book Censorship in America from the Gilded Age to the Computer Age* takes a different approach by focusing on the activities and campaigns of "vice societies" (an odd name for societies that clearly positioned themselves as "anti-vice") and other pro-censorship movements to trace "the shifting rhythms of censorship" in American legal and cultural history.

Jenkins (2001) used historical methods to look at the years of World War II and the early Cold War to document the impact of McCarthyism on school and public library collections—specifically, the response of youth services librarians to challenges to their collections. In the process of addressing book challenges, these leaders instituted professional practices, such as written book selection policies, and documents, such as the School Library Bill of Rights, that would enable librarians to resist book challenges more effectively.

Youth services library leaders used their status as white middle class professional women to resist censorship successfully through "assertive gentility." Their effective strategies included "quiet resistance" (deliberately ignoring and refusing to publicly acknowledge that an attack has been made); "positive resistance" (countering an attack by including the challenged book in reading lists of recommended books); and "active resistance" (using the attacker's rhetoric to parry the attack–for example, countering an accusation of a book's "treasonous" message by suggesting that seeing treason where none exists is in itself treasonous). As yet, however, there are very few historical studies that combine censorship, intellectual freedom, and youth .

Future research in censorship practices could be informed by the area of media effects; in particular the work of media scholars who have identified a phenomenon, dubbed the "third person effect." In surveys of people on the perceived effect of controversial issues, respondents commonly state that they are not personally disturbed by a particular movie or television program, but they believe it is likely to disturb others (Davison, 1983; Paul, Salwen, & Dupagne, 2000). This way of thinking also seems to be prevalent in cases where books are challenged and could be useful in linking the research methods of ethnography, media studies, and social psychology in studies of perceived threat and social change.

Reading-Effects Research

Librarians and teachers generally take the positive effects of reading as a given. Their task, in the words of the iconic pioneer of youth services librarianship, Anne Carroll Moore, is "to place into the hands of the right child, the right book at the right time"(Jenkins, 1996, p. 815). Other people are equally certain that the effect of reading may be negative and that the wrong book can harm its readers. These opposing viewpoints share a common assumption that reading books or other print materials can indeed change the reader's attitudes, feelings, beliefs, or self-concept. Works such as *Books that Changed Our Minds,* edited by Malcolm Cowley and Bernard Smith (1939); *Caught in the Act: The Decisive Reading of Some Notable Men and Women and its Influence on their Actions and Attitudes,* by Edwin Castagna (1982); and *Voices of readers: How we come to love books* (1988), by G. Robert Carlsen and Anne Sherrill attest to the commonly held belief in the power of reading. What, then, are the facts? Does reading affect people? If so, how? What answers can researchers provide?

Early quasi-experimental studies of the effects of reading sought to determine how particular attitudes or behavior were affected by reading. A typical study included a pretest of subjects—often children—about their attitudes (toward older adults, toward medical settings, etc.). The subjects would then be exposed to a number of stories or books that spoke to these attitudes, including a protagonist's successful negotiation of an uncomfortable setting. This was followed by a post-test. Given what we know now about the individualistic nature of reading response, the flaws in this methodology seem glaring. However, it yielded some interesting results.

A study conducted in 1965 of fifth-graders (ages 10–11 years) in suburban Boston by Joyce Lancaster (1971) is illustrative of this limited approach to research. Boston schools were racially segregated by neighborhood. Lancaster aimed to discover what effect voluntary reading of books with neutral or positive portrayals of African Americans might have on White children's racial attitudes. In this study the pretest/posttest utilized photographic slides of fifth-grade children engaged in various activities (playing football, sewing, reading, etc). There were several photos of each activity, one depicting an all-Black group, one an all-White group, and one a racially integrated group. The slides were shown to the children in pairs, and students were simply asked which of the two groups they would prefer to join. Some students chose on the basis of activity, so that, for example, football would get their vote regardless of the racial composition of the group. Other students chose on the basis of race, choosing the group with the most White children, regardless of

activity. Students who chose by activity were considered "low prejudice" and students who chose by race were considered "high prejudice."

All of the students had multiple opportunities over the next six weeks to select and read children's novels or biographies that included positive or neutral portrayals of African Americans. Significantly, but not accounted for at the time of the study, the books were not discussed among students or by the teacher. Students were simply asked to fill out a form for each book read with their name, the name of the book, and whether they would recommend it to a friend. At the end of the six weeks the post-test was administered.

When the data were compiled, Lancaster (1971) found that for the students with "low prejudice" pretests, the more books they read, the lower in prejudice their post-test scores. For the students with "high prejudice" pretests, the more books they read, the higher in prejudice their post-test scores. Lancaster concluded that reading "operates as a booster to one's attitude rather than as a change agent" (p. 97). The results of Lancaster's study would disappoint those who wish for stories or books guaranteed to make a positive difference in readers' attitudes and beliefs.

Lancaster's (1971) study, while limited, also exposes assumptions about what it means for a young person to read a book. In many ways the methods and questions guiding this study are grounded in the views of would-be censors and their understanding of print media's effects on human behavior. These assumptions include:

1. Reading changes people.
2. Particular content predicts a particular response, and thus a particular effect.
3. One reader's response predicts another reader's response.
4. Forbidding reading materials will diminish reader interest in and desire for the material.

Recent research finds no support for these beliefs; in fact, the opposite is true:

Reading by itself changes people very little, if at all. It may effect small, short-term changes in people's behaviors or attitudes, but people are far more influenced by family, peers, home, school, and socialization than they are by books (Jenkins, 2002).

Textual content does not predict reader response or reading effect. Readers respond to and are affected by texts in ways specific to each individual in the context of a particular time and place. Different people react to the same book differently. Furthermore, the same book may have different effects on the same reader at different times and under different circumstances. As noted above, for example, Steig's (1969) *Sylvester and the Magic Pebble* was read as anti-police propaganda in the 1970s (Haight & Grannis, 1978, p. 87), but read as endorsing a belief in magic in the 1990s (McDaniel, Dec. 1991/ Jan. 1992).

One reader's response does not predict another reader's response. Instead, each reader brings her or his own unique perspective to the reading that is informed, but not dictated, by the reader's personality, gender, education, age, reading ability, and other characteristics (Lancaster, 1971). However, even a relationship between variables does not necessarily indicate cause and effect.

Forbidding reading materials will not diminish reader interest in or desire for the material. Barriers to access are likely to heighten a young person's interest in such a text. The "lure" of the forbidden" has been repeatedly demonstrated by media researchers observing children's responses to "PG-13" and "R" MPAA ratings, who found that perceived age restrictions consistently made children more interested in viewing a program with such a rating (Cantor, Harrison & Nathanson, 1997).

An End to Censorship—or Reading?

A casual perusal of the 2007 *Banned Books Resource Guide* list of 1,724 different books makes it clear that it is not possible to divine which text might upset or offend an individual reader. Even much-loved classics like Wilder's (1932) *Little House in the Big Woods* ("promotes racial epithets") and Kipling's (1902/1942) *The Elephant's Child* ("99% violent")—not to mention newer classics like Lewis's (1950) *The Lion, the Witch, and the Wardrobe* ("depicts graphic violence, mysticism, and gore"), Dr. Seuss' (1971) *The Lorax* ("criminalizes the foresting industry"), and Roald Dahl's (1964) *Charlie and the Chocolate Factory* ("espouses a poor philosophy of life")—have been the objects of challenges. Clearly, adult readers who are invested in finding a problem will work tirelessly to claim evidence for their complaints.

Organizations such as PABBIS (Parents Against Bad Books in Schools) construct websites devoted to highlighting out-of-context quotes and textual nuance that could drum up supporters who are concerned about these "bad books." The Facts on Fiction website, devoted to finding what they perceive to be antisocial or hurtful behavior depicted in children's books, includes charts with detailed reports on several hundred texts, ranging from Cleary's (1955) *Beezus and Ramona* to Huxley's (1932) *Brave New World*. Each book is analyzed in minute detail: "How prevalent are expressions of bad attitudes, anger, and/or moodiness, arguing and/or disrespect without consequences? (Not at all? Brief incident? Multiple brief incidents? Extended incident? Multiple extended incidents? Theme of entire book?)" (Facts on Fiction, 2010).

Is it possible to "censor-proof" a library or school? Librarians or teachers might be tempted to hypervigilance in this regard, making certain that the books available to young readers will not upset any parent or other adult who would act as censor "on behalf of" children. However, as previously noted, the majority of challenges are made by a single individual who is disturbed or offended by a book: Only a book-less library or classroom can be truly censor-proof (Schrader, 1996)

We cannot reliably predict how someone—even ourselves—will respond to a book, as there are multiple factors involved in determining a person's comfort level at a particular time and place. It is not the book that is an active agent, but the reader. The goal of children's librarianship has been stated thus for over a century: "to put the right book into the hands of the right child at the right time." And it is ultimately the child—the reader—who determines what that right book might be.

Conclusion

Censorship is about preventing access. The multifaceted nature of this subject has meant that censorship research can be found in a number of fields of study, including communications and media studies, psychology, history, political science, education, literature, and library and information science. It has often been noted that history is written by the winners. In the case of the censorship of texts, this is doubly true, since the winners—who control the official record—can have the power not only to suppress books, but also to suppress accounts of that suppression. This reality is most evident in non-democratic or totalitarian societies and is a staple of dystopian fiction, such as Orwell's (1949) *1984* and Bradbury's (1953) *Fahrenheit 451*. But as the lengthy annual lists of challenged books prove, the censorious impulse lives in free and open societies as well—even in the United States, where the Constitution's First Amendment protects the freedom to read.

While much of the literature about censorship centers on the fates of individual books, censorship involves causes, beliefs, and goals that are far larger than any particular text. Instances of book censorship represent the tensions of society writ small, a struggle for political, social, and/or cultural power waged in the limited arena of the pages of a book. Books have been restricted, censored, and even destroyed for as long as books and the written record have existed.

In reflecting upon the circuitous and varied paths taken by those who would censor literature for young readers, the significance of the social and historical contexts in which these struggles are played out is striking. The model that is foundational to this volume demonstrates the connection between reader and text surrounded, first, by the specific context of the reading, which is in turn surrounded by the larger world in which that reader, text, and context are located. In addition, because the reader is growing and changing, the specific context in which reader-text interactions occur is ever-changing, as is the nature of the larger world. The social, cultural, and economic factors that affect readers are in constant flux.

When one steps away and considers the dynamic entity that combines reader, text, context, and larger world, there is one element that is actually fairly static and unchanging, and that is the book. The book remains the same and appears motionless within all this activity, like a leaf floating—or sinking—in the moving water of a stream or river. That book, that one static entity, is a mirror. It reflects the worries, the fears, the anger, and the concerns, of each individual who looks into it. We look at a book, but what we see is ourselves.

Author's Note

This chapter is an expanded version of an article that first appeared in the January 2008 issue of *Language Arts* as "Book challenges, challenging books, and young readers: The research picture" (vol. 85, #3, pp. 228–236). Copyright 2008 by the National Council of Teachers of English.

Literature References

Adams, A. (1971). *A woggle of witches.* New York, NY: Scribners.

Blume, J. (1970). *Are you there, God? It's me, Margaret.* Englewood Cliffs, NJ: Bradbury Press.

Blume, J. (1975). *Forever.* Englewood Cliffs, NJ: Bradbury Press.

Bradbury, R. (1953). *Fahrenheit 451.* New York, NY: Ballantine Books.

Cleary, B. (1955). *Beezus and Ramona.* New York, NY: Morrow.

Dahl, R. (1964). *Charlie and the chocolate factory.* New York, NY: Knopf.

Daly, K. N. (1980). *Body words: A dictionary of the human body, how it works, and some of the things that affect it.* Garden City, NY: Doubleday.

Garden, N. (1982). *Annie on my mind.* New York, NY: Farrar, Straus, Giroux.

Huxley, A. (1932). *Brave new world.* Garden City, NY: Doubleday, Doran.

Kingman, L. (1945). *Ilenka.* Boston, MA: Houghton Mifflin.

Kipling, R. (1942/1902). *The elephant's child.* Garden City, NY: Garden City Publishing.

Lewis, C. S. (1950). *The lion, the witch, and the wardrobe.* New York, NY: Macmillan.

Myracle, L. (2009). *Luv ya bunches.* New York, NY: Amulet Books.

Newman, L.(1989). *Heather has two mommies.* Boston, MA: Alyson.

Orwell, G. (1949). *1984.* New York, NY: Harcourt, Brace.

Parnell, P., & Richardson, J. (2005). *And Tango makes three.* New York, NY: Simon & Schuster.

Rowling, J. K. (1997-2007). *Harry Potter* series (7 titles total). New York, NY: Scholastic.

Salinger, J. D. (1951). *The catcher in the rye.* Boston, MA: Little, Brown.

Schreier, A. (2001). *Vamos a Cuba / A visit to Cuba.* Chicago, IL: Heinemann.

Seuss, Dr. (1954). *Horton hears a who.* New York, NY: Random House.

Seuss, Dr. (1971). *The lorax.* New York, NY: Random House.

Stieg, W. (1969). *Sylvester and the magic pebble.* New York, NY: Windmill Books.

Wilder, L. I. (1932). *Little house in the big woods.* New York, NY: Harper & Row.

Willhoite, M. (1990). *Daddy's roommate.* Boston, MA: Alyson.

Williams, G. (1958). *The rabbit's wedding.* New York, NY: Harper & Row.

Academic References

Adams, H. (2008). *Ensuring intellectual freedom and access to information in the school library media program.* Westport, CT: Libraries Unlimited.

American Library Association. (n.d.). *Book challenge definitions.* Retrieved September 7, 2010, from http://www.ala.org/ala/issuesadvocacy/banned/challengeslibrarymaterials/index.cfm

American Library Association. (n.d.). *Intellectual Freedom Q & A.* Retrieved February 28, 2010, from http://staging.ala.org/ala/aboutala/offices/oif/basics/intellectual.cfm

Asheim, L. (1953). Not censorship but selection. *Wilson Library Bulletin, 28*(1), 63–67.

Bald, M. (2006). *Literature suppressed on religious grounds.* New York, NY: Facts on File.

Boyd, F., Boyd, B., & Bailey, N. M. (2009). Censorship in three metaphors. *Journal of Adolescent and Adult Literacy, 52*(8), 653–661.

Boyer, P. (2002). *Purity in print: Book censorship in America from the gilded age to the computer age* (2nd ed.). Madison: University of Wisconsin Press.

Brown, B. (1990). Concern for children led to book-ban request. *Eau Claire [WI] Leader-Telegram.* Nov. 16.

Burress, L. (1989). *Battle of the books: Literary censorship in the public schools, 1950-1985.* Metuchen, NJ: Scarecrow Press.

Cantor, J., Harrison, K., & Nathanson, A. (1997). Ratings and advisories for television programming. In Center for Communication and Social Policy (Ed.), *National Television Violence Study* (Vol. 2, pp. 267–322). Thousand Oaks, CA: Sage.

Carlsen, G. R., & Sherrill, A. (1988). *Voices of readers: How we come to love books.* Urbana, IL: NCTE.

Castagna, E. (1982). *Caught in the act: The decisive reading of some notable men and women and its influence on their actions and attitudes.* Metuchen, NJ: Scarecrow Press.

Children's Cooperative Book Center (CCBC). (n.d.). *Intellectual freedom.* Retrieved February 28, 2010, from http://www.education.wisc.edu/ccbc/freedom/default.asp

Comstock, A. (1883). *Traps for the young.* New York, NY: Funk & Wagnalls.

Cowley, M., & Smith, B. (1939). *Books that changed our minds.* New York, NY: Harbor Press.

Davison, W. P. (1983). The third-person effect in communication. *Public Opinion Quarterly, 47*(1), 1–15.

Delfattore, J. (1992). *What Johnny shouldn't read: Textbook censorship in America.* New Haven, CT: Yale University Press.

DeMitchell, T. A., & Carney, J. J. (2005). Harry Potter and the public school library. *Phi Delta Kappan, 87*(2), 159–165.

Doyle, R. P. (2007). *Banned books resource guide.* Chicago, IL: ALA.

Facts on fiction. (2010). Retrieved February 26, 2010, from http://www.factsonfiction.org

Falk, J. (2001). Censoring school literature in the cyber age. *Reading Today, 18*(4), 22-23.

Fiske, M. (1959). *Book selection and censorship: A study of school and public libraries in California.* Berkeley, CA: University of California Press.

FLA and *Vamos a Cuba* Book Challenge. (2009). In Florida Library Assocation.org. Retrieved July 28, 2010, from http://flalib.org/advocacy_documents/Forehand%20 essays%20for%web.pdf

Foerstel, H. N. (2002). *Banned in the U.S.A.: A reference guide to book censorship in schools and public libraries* (Rev. ed.). Westport, CT: Greenwood Press.

Geller, E. (1984). *Forbidden books in American public libraries, 1876–1939: A study in cultural change*. Westport, CT: Greenwood Press.

Green, J., & Karolides, N. J. (2005). *The encyclopedia of censorship*. Rev. ed. New York, NY: Facts On File.

Haight, A. L., & Grannis, C. B. (1978). Banned books, 387 B.C. to 1978 A.D., 4th ed. New York, NY: Bowker.

Hanna, J. (July 22, 2009). Library fight riles up city, leads to book-burning demand. In CNN.com. Retrieved July 28, 2010, from http://www.cnn.com/2009/us/07/22/wisconsin.book.row/index.html

Heins, M. (2001). *Not in front of the children: "Indecency," censorship and the innocence of youth*. New York, NY: Hill & Wang.

Hopkins, D. M. (1991). *Factors influencing the outcome of challenges to materials in secondary school libraries: Report of a national study*. Madison, WI: School of Library and Information Studies, University of Wisconsin-Madison.

Hopkins, D. M. (1993). Put it in writing. *School Library Journal 39*(1), 26–30.

Hopkins, D. M. (1998). Toward a conceptual path of support for school library media specialists with material challenges. *School Library Media Quarterly Online*, 1-23. Retrieved February 28, 2010, from http://www.ala.org/ala/aasl/aaslpubsandjournals/slmrb/slmrcontents/volume11998slmqo/mcafee.htm

Jenkins, C. A. (1996). Women of ALA youth services and professional jurisdiction: Of nightingales, Newberies, realism, and the right books, 1937-1945. *Library Trends, 44* (4), 813–829,

Jenkins, C. A. (2001). International harmony: Threat or menace? U.S. youth services librarians and cold war censorship, 1946-1955. *Libraries & Culture, 36*(1), 116–130.

Jenkins, C. A. (2002). The effects of reading: A synthesis of research. unpublished paper. Retrieved February 28, 2010 from http://people.lis.illinois.edu/~cajenkin/papers.html

Karolides, N. J., Bald, M., & Sova, D. B. (2005). *120 banned books: Censorship histories of world literature*. New York, NY: Checkmark Books/Facts on File.

Karolides, N. J. (2006). *Literature suppressed on political grounds*. New York, NY: Facts on File.

Kravitz, N. (2002). *Censorship and the school library media center.* Greenwood Village, CO: Libraries Unlimted.

Lancaster, J. W. (1971). *An investigation of the effect of books with Black characters on the racial preferences of White children.* (Doctoral dissertation), Boston University, Boston, MA.

LaRue, J. (2007). *The new inquisition: Understanding and managing intellectual freedom challenges*. Westport, CT: Libraries Unlimited.

McDaniel, T. R. (Dec. 1991/Jan. 1992). On trial: The right to think. *Educational Leadership, 49*(4), 85.

Medved, M., & Medved, D. (1998). *Saving childhood: Protecting our children from the national assault on innocence*. New York, NY: HarperCollins.

Michaelsen, J. (1989). *Like lambs to the slaughter: Your child and the occult*. Eugene, OR: Harvest House.

Moffett, J. (1988). *Storm in the mountains: A case study of censorship, conflict, and consciousness*. Carbondale: Southern Illinois University Press.

Paul, B., Salwen, M. B., & Dupagne, M. (2000). The third-person effect: A meta-analysis of the perceptual hypothesis. *Mass Communication & Society, 3*(1), 57–85.

Pipkin, G., & Lent, R. C. (2002). *At the schoolhouse gate: Lessons in intellectual freedom*. Portsmouth, NH: Heinemann.

Reichman, H. (2001). *Selection and censorship: Issues and answers for schools* (3rd ed.). Chicago, IL: ALA.

Robins, N. (1992). *Alien ink: The FBI's war on freedom of expression*. New Brunswick, NJ: Rutgers University Press.

SCBWI. (2010). Chinook Update: The *Luv-Ya-Bunches* controversy. Retrieved February 28, 2010, from http://chinookupdate.blogspot.com/2009/11/luv-ya-bunches-controversy.html also: http://lauren-myracle.livejournal.com/37145.html

Scales, P. (2009). *Protecting intellectual freedom in your school library: Scenarios from the front lines*. Chicago, IL: ALA.

Schrader, A. M. (1996). Censorproofing school library collections: The fallacy and futility. *School Libraries Worldwide, 2*(1), 71–94.

Shannon, P. (2009). We can work it out: Challenge, debate and acceptance. *Bookbird, 47*(3), 1–8.

Silvester, N. (July 14, 2009). The destruction of libraries in Sarajevo: Book burnings as "culturecide" in the Bosnian War. In Suite101.com. Retrieved July 28, 2010, from http://Serbia-Montenegro.suite101.com/article.cfm/the_destruction_of_libraries_in_sarajevo

Simmons, J. S., & Dresang, E. T. (2001). *School censorship in the 21st century: A guide for teachers and school library media specialists*. Newark, DE: International Reading Association.

Sova, D. B. (2006a). *Literature suppressed on sexual grounds*. New York, NY: Facts on File.

Sova, D. B. (2006b). *Literature suppressed on social grounds*. New York, NY: Facts on File.

Supreme Court of the United States. Jacobellis v. Ohio. 378 U.S. 184 (1964). Retrieved July 28, 2010, from http://laws.findlaw.com/us/378/184.html

Supreme Court of the United States. Miller v. California. 413 U.S. 15 (1973). Retrieved June 21, 2010 from http://www.law.umkc.edu/faculty/projects/ftrials/conlaw/miller.html

Symons, A., & Harmon, C. (1995). *Protecting the right to read: A how-to-do-it manual for school and public librarians*. New York, NY: Neal-Schumann.

Waples, D., Berelson, B., & Bradshaw, F. R. (1940). *What reading does to people: A summary of evidence on the social effects of reading and a statement of problems for research*. Chicago, IL: University of Chicago Press.

Weart, W. W. G. (1949). 9 novels cleared, held not obscene. *New York Times,* March 19, p. 13.

33

Reviewing Children's and Young Adult Literature

Michael Cart

Author and Reviewer, *Booklist*

From Mrs. Trimmer's 19-century *Guardian of Education* to the brave new online world of blogs and social networking sites, Michael Cart charts the history and evolution of reviewing books for young readers. Himself a veteran of 40 years of reviewing, Cart focuses on such considerations as the journalistic and cultural contexts of reviewing, the differences between reviews and literary criticism, the various audiences for reviews and how these affect their tone and content, and longstanding criticisms of reviews themselves from both authors and professional librarians. As befits this consummate educator, Cart concludes with practical advice—and sample reviews—for would-be reviewers of books for young readers.

Though reviews of children's and young adult books typically contain some elements of critical evaluation, they are nevertheless essentially works of journalism, timely reports of the publication of new books. In announcing such publishing events, their function—as Virginia Woolf (1939) famously observed—is "partly to sort current literature; partly to advertise the author; partly to inform the public" (p. 10). And—it must be added—their purpose is to inform that same "public" of the quality of the book, thereby assisting its members in deciding whether or not to purchase or read it. Indeed, this remains the fundamental purpose of contemporary book reviews, whether they are targeted at collection-developing librarians or at parents in search of gifts for children (who are probably hoping for a video game, instead).

At the time of their beginnings in early 19th century England, however, the reviews' "public" was limited almost entirely to parents, governesses, and others charged with the care of children. As a result, reviews appeared primarily in deadline-driven, general circulation magazines and newspapers. With the rise of children's library service at the end of the 19th century, professional review journals also began to appear. Though their target audience was librarians and—to a lesser degree—teachers (instead of parents), the reviews' timeliness remained of paramount importance, since they, too, were designed as guides to purchase. This aspect of timeliness and its relationship to potential purchase are two elements that further distinguish reviews from literary criticism, which tends to be less utilitarian, is more discursive, may appear months or even years after the publication of the book that is its subject, and deals more extensively with analysis and interpretation.

And one final point: whether reviews or criticism and whether published in newspapers, general interest magazines, professional or literary journals, all such writing about books for young readers has been—and remains—targeted at adults, not at the young readers themselves.

In the Beginning, There Was Mrs. Trimmer

The British children's author Mrs. (Sarah) Trimmer (Miyake, 2006) is generally credited with having written the first children's book reviews in her short-lived but influential magazine *The Guardian of Education* (1802–1806). Her review pages—titled "Examination of Books for Children" or "Examination of Books for Young Persons" (Miyake, 2006)—were targeted at parents and governesses and reflected the reviewer's own strong interest in both education and religion. This was further evidenced during the 1780s by her active and influential involvement in the fledgling Sunday School movement, which provided literacy and religious education to working class children. Indeed, no less a personage than Queen Victoria would later invite her to set up a Sunday School at Windsor (Carpenter & Prichard, 1984).

Given Mrs. Trimmer's (1803/1973) brisk concern for morality and books' ability to mold young minds "susceptible of every impression," the reviewer cautioned parents—regarding the then burgeoning number of children's books—that "much mischief lies hid in many of them" (p. 4). And accordingly, "The utmost circumspection is therefore requisite in making a proper selection; and children should not be permitted to make their own choice…but should be taught to consider it as a *duty,* to consult their parents in this momentous concern" (p. 4).

As her reviews reflect, Mrs. Trimmer was concerned not only that books offer moral instruction but also, in an ideological turn, maintain the prevailing social order; thus, she criticizes Newbery's (1766) *History of Little Goody Two Shoes* for its inclusion of "oppressive squires and hard-hearted overseers…in these times when such pains are taken to prejudice the poor against the higher orders" (Trimmer, 1802/1973, p. 6). Similarly, in her review of another Newbery publication, *Renowned History of Primrose Pretty Face,* a tale in which a girl of humble origins grows up to become lady of the manor, she notes it "certainly is very wrong…to put into the heads of young gentlemen, at an early age, an idea that when they grow up, they may, without impropriety, marry servant-maids" (Trimmer, 1803/1983, p. 72). In these moral and societal aspects of her reviews, she approaches a facet of literary criticism that, since the days of Plato, had assumed "that art, as a significant formative agent in man's moral and spiritual development, should be didactic" and that "the relationship between art and society is organic and indivisible" (Beckson & Ganz, 1989, pp. 51–52).

Happily, Mrs. Trimmer was not universally condemnatory in her reviews. She did, for example, laud *Little Goody Two Shoes'* "simplicity of style." "We wish to see this Book continue in circulation," she bountifully concluded but couldn't resist adding, ominously, "as some of these faults *a pair of scissors* can rectify" (!) (Trimmer, 1802/1973, p. 6).

No scissors could rectify her aversion to fairy tales and fantasy, however, and it is for this that Trimmer is best remembered. "We cannot approve," she magisterially wrote in her review of *Mother Bunch's Fairy Tales* (Newbery, 1773), "of those which are only fit to fill the heads of children with confused notions of wonderful and supernatural events brought about by the agency of imaginary beings" (Trimmer, 1805/1983, p. 73). Similarly, she condemned *Little Goody Two Shoes* for its inclusion of a ghost story and an element of witchcraft.

Interestingly enough, however, the most popular of her own stories, *The History of the Robins* (1818) actually featured talking birds, which were further anthropomorphized by being named, respectively, Robin, Jr., Dicksy, Pecksy, and Flapsy. (As Haviland [1973] notes, though, "in her introduction she took pains to explain that the conversations were not real" [p. 4].)

Mrs. Trimmer was not the only 19th-century author-publisher whose magazine featured book reviews. Another was Mrs. (Margaret) Gatty, whose *Aunt Judy's Magazine* was founded in 1866, principally to publish the work of her more famous daughter Juliana Horatia Gatty, better known as Mrs. Ewing ("Aunt Judy" was the daughter's family nickname). Far more receptive to fantasy than Mrs. Trimmer, Gatty published, in her magazine, the work of such well-known fabulists as Lewis Carroll and Hans Christian Andersen, while praising, in her reviews for adults, their respective books *Alice's Adventures in Wonderland* (1865) and *What the Moon Saw* (1866), calling the former "the exquisitely wild, fantastic, impossible, yet most natural history of 'Alice in Wonderland'" (Gatty, 1866/1973, p. 20).

Throughout the 19th century in England occasional reviews of children's books also appeared in adult magazines like *The Quarterly Review, The British Quarterly Review, Macmillan's Magazine,* and more. Many of these were essay or omnibus reviews that gave attention to a number of titles in the context of the author's summary judgment of the prevailing state of children's books. Thus, the author Elizabeth Rigby (1844, cited in Haviland, 1973), also known as Lady Eastlake, castigated, in *The British Quarterly,* "the excessive ardor for *teaching* which prevails throughout" and decried "the interdict laid on the imagination in this mania for explanation" (p. 9). Instead, she called for giving children greater liberty in "promiscuous reading" and "the power of ranging free over field and pasture," eschewing "all the little racks of ready-cut hay that have been so officiously supplied them" (p. 10).

A similar review, entitled "Juvenile Books of the Past" and published anonymously in *The British Quarterly Review* in 1868, condemned the "didactic and dogmatical fashion" in which too many children's books had been written, causing them to be "prosy, tedious, and distasteful" (Rigby, 1868, cited in Bator, 1983, p. 77).

"Turn where you would," the author continued, "it was always the same dreary, monotonous, never-ending dirge—'Naughty, naughty children, you are all utterly lost and wicked'" (pp. 75–76). As a curative, the author recommended—almost categorically—fairy tales, which "afford an endless fund of healthy and hearty amusement" (p. 82) as well as more contemporary work by Mrs. Gatty, R. M. Ballantyne, William Kingston, Phillip Freeman, Edwin Hodder, and others.

Interestingly, this review is also among the first to support the reviewer's flat declarations with specific comments about language and tone (praise for their "exceeding beauty" "yet simplicity"), plot (kudos for "careful composition"), imagination, the qualifications of the author (with the "sound discretion and well-regulated condition of [his] mind"), and potential popularity with young readers ("any boy may read it with gratification and profit to himself" [p. 77])—all considerations that would become staple elements of 20th century reviews.

The Rise of Reviewing in America

Though children's book reviewing may have started in England, it reached new heights in the post-Civil War United States, as Richard L. Darling (1968) has demonstrated in his invaluable book *The Rise of Children's Book Reviewing in America*. Major magazines of politics and culture as *Scribner's Monthly, The Nation, The Dial, The Atlantic Monthly*, and *Harper's Monthly*—along with the now largely forgotten *Literary World*—all regularly published reviews of children's books. They flourished in the second half of the 19th century, though these reviews were all targeted at adults. Among the most influential of these periodicals was *The Riverside Magazine for Young People*, edited by Horace E. Scudder (1837–1902) who was, himself, a children's book author (*Seven Little People and Their Friends*, [1862]). Called by Alice M. Jordan (1948) "one of the two most discriminating editors a children's magazine has ever had" (p. 40), Scudder was passionately devoted to excellence in writing for children as he demonstrated in "Books for Young People," the monthly editorial letter—targeted at adults—that prefaced each issue of *The Riverside Magazine*.

In the inaugural number for January 1867 he wrote, presciently, "A literature is forming which is destined to act powerfully upon general letters; hitherto, it has been little disturbed by critics, but the time must soon come, if it has not already come, when students of literature must consider the character and tendency of *Children's Letters*" (Scudder, 1867/1973, pp. 21–22). "What shall we give our children to read? is the constant cry of anxious parents," he continued. And, in answer concluded, "We may as well discard at once all such unnecessary considerations as when a book was published, or where it was published, and come right at the gist of the matter, and ask if it is *good*, good in itself and adapted to the reader for whom we are buying it" (p. 23).

A decade after Scudder had hailed the formation of a new literature for children, "the first separate children's area in a public library" was created, "a corner with tables designated for children and open shelving, created by Minerva Sanders in the Pawtucket (RI) Public Library" (Jenkins, 1999, p. 547). In her article "Precepts and Practices," Christine Jenkins charts the subsequent development of public library service to children. It is sufficient here to note that 1890 saw the opening of the first separate children's reading area (in the Brookline [MA] Public Library), that 1896 marked the opening of the first architect-designed children's room (at the Pratt Institute in Brooklyn), and that "by the end of the century, library service to children was considered an integral part of public library service" (p. 547).

Such new youth-serving specialists required guidance in selecting books for their patrons and more seasoned professionals, acting individually and in concert, were quick to respond. Thus, in 1882 Caroline M. Hewins, administrator of the Hartford (CT) Public Library, compiled her first booklist "Books for the Young: A Guide for Parents and Children," which was printed in the magazine *Publishers Weekly*, read then—as it is today—by both librarians and booksellers (Melcher, 1963). In 1905 the American Library Association founded its now venerable *Booklist* magazine, which—from the first—contained reviews of children's books recommended for purchase. Indeed, one of its early editors was May Massee, who went on to found the first children's departments at both Doubleday and The Viking Press.

Anne Carroll Moore

It was from this nascent community of children's librarians that the woman who quickly became the most influential voice in American children's books emerged: Anne Carroll Moore, whose career had begun at the Pratt Institute in 1896. In 1901 she became the first chair of ALA's newly formed Children's Library Section and five years later was named the New York Public Library's first Superintendent of Work with Children, a position she held until her retirement in 1941. Meanwhile, her prominence extended from the professional community to the general public when she was asked to launch a children's review page for *The Bookman Magazine* in 1918, the same year that Children's Book Week was founded and the publisher Macmillan launched the first separate children's book department. The *Bookman* pieces appeared approximately every three months. According to Moore's biographer Frances Clarke Sayers (1972), "The years of ACM's contribution to *The Bookman* are generally designated as the era that inaugurated in America the reviewing of books for children on a sustained and continuous basis" (p. 211). Moore (1926) agreed with this assessment.

Moore's association with *The Bookman* continued until 1924 when she was asked to start a children's book review page for *Books,* the newly launched weekly supplement to *The New York Herald Tribune.* This was, coincidentally, the same year that Bertha Mahoney Miller and Elinor Whitney, founders of Boston's Bookshop for Boys and Girls in 1916, launched *The Horn Book Magazine,* which became the first American magazine completely devoted to articles about and reviews of books for young readers. And it was to *The Horn Book* that Moore herself came in 1936 with her column "The Three Owls Notebook" (the *Herald Tribune* page, which lasted until 1930, had been called, simply, "The Three Owls"). In 1932 *The Herald Tribune* resumed its coverage of children's books under the editorship of the estimable May Lamberton Becker (1936), whose book *First Adventures in Reading: Introducing Children to Books* sprang from her *Tribune* reviews. The "Notebook" continued until 1960, the year before Moore's death.

In writing of these early years, Jenkins (1999) has said, "In many ways literary standards have changed very little from that day to this" (p. 549). In the case of Moore it is easy enough to validate this assessment, since her work for that period was not ephemeral but was collected in a series of volumes (*Roads To Childhood* [1920], *New Roads To Childhood* [1923], *Cross-Roads To Childhood* [1926], *The Three Owls* [1925], *The Three Owls. Second Book* [1928], and *The Three Owls. Third Book* [1931]), while Sayers (1972), in her biography, also quotes her subject extensively, in one important instance as follows:

> The instant recognition and detachment of a piece of original work from a mass of ready-made writing and the presenta-tion of one's findings and conviction constitute the reviewer's main chance. His function is to declare the book's quality and give it a place in association with other books. To the degree that the review stimulates the desire of the reader to read the book to confirm or to differ with the critic will it be contributory to thought, discussion, criticism, fresh creative work. And this, as I see it, is the true objective for the reviewer of children's books no less than for the reviewer in the general field. (p. 214)

The need for the reviewer to stimulate the reader—who, remember, has always been an adult—is echoed in the Foreword to *New Roads to Childhood,* where Moore (1923) avers,

> In writing of children's books no less than in personal in-troduction of them to readers, I feel it more important to rouse the spirit of curiosity, to send the reader on a voyage of exploration and discovery—to make books come alive—than it is to outline the subject or present the static grouping by age and grade which leads, in my opinion, straight to the separation of children's books from life as well as from literature. (p. ix)

As for that consideration of "grouping," Moore (1926) resolutely aimed to focus on readers as individuals; hence, in her essay "Entering the Teens," she writes, "There can be no such generalized term as adolescence *without closing a door upon the individual*" (p. 209, emphasis added).

And as for "literature," Moore regarded children's books as being not only a viable part of world literature but also a continuum of its own with which the reviewer must be familiar. As she put it, "I believe it was much reading of the old children's books in contrast to the new that developed and strengthened my powers of appraisal" (p. 45).

The New York Times Book Review began publishing a fortnightly children's book review page of its own in 1930 under the co-editorship of Anne Thaxter Eaton, librarian of the Lincoln School, Teacher's College, and Ellen Lewis Buell of the *Times'* own staff. A number of other major metropolitan newspapers including *The New York Post* and *The Chicago Tribune* soon followed suit, as did such popular, general interest magazines as *The New Yorker* and *The Saturday Review.*

There would be many others over the years, most of them containing reviews of varying quality, since they were often written by working journalists or free lance writers who may, themselves, have had little experience of children's literature. As Selma G. Lanes (1971) has noted, "Even the perceptive critic for the newspapers is unlikely to make a long-time career of reviewing children's books; it is usually an occasional pastime" (p. 150). Lanes was herself such an occasional reviewer for *The New York Times, The New York Herald Tribune,* and *The Washington Post.* Though not a librarian (neither was May Lamberton Becker, for that matter), she was quick to acknowledge, "The librarian's unquestionable value as a judge is that he or she can honestly claim to know the tastes of a wide variety of children on a thoroughly workaday and practical level over a continuous and extended period of time" (p. 150).

Professional Journals

Both Moore and Eaton were slightly anomalous figures: trained librarians who, nevertheless, wrote for a gen-eral audience. Indeed, Eaton's two books—*Reading with Children* (1940) and *Treasure for the Taking* (1946)—are targeted at parents. A third germinal librarian/reviewer, Zena Sutherland, also bridged the gap between the world of general and professional readers but in a slightly dif-ferent way. Although she was, for example, Children's Book Editor of the *Chicago Tribune* from 1972 to 1984 and, from 1966 to 1972, had written the monthly "Books for Young People" column for the *Saturday Review,* she was also, from 1958 until 1985, editor of and sole reviewer for the University of Chicago's *Bulletin of the Center for Children's Books* (BCCB), a professional journal de-voted exclusively to reviews of books for young readers. Prodigiously productive, she is said to have reviewed more than 30,000 children's books during the course of her long career, while also serving as a member of the faculty of the University of Chicago's Graduate Library School from 1972 to 1986 (Harms, 2002).

As one of the most important figures in 20-century children's literature, Sutherland's (1986) thoughts on what "the elements of good children's books are" remain fundamental to an understanding of the form, content, and function of successful book reviews. In that context she wrote, in part,

> In many ways the literary criteria that apply to adult books and children's books are the same. The best books have that most elusive component, a distinctive literary style. A well-constructed plot; sound characterization with no stereotypes; dialogue that flows naturally and is appropriate to the speaker's age, education, and milieu; and a pervasive theme are equally important in children's and adult fiction.... Each book must be judged on its own merits, and each book should be chosen—whether for an individual child, a library or a classroom collection—with consideration for its strength even though it may have some weaknesses. (p. viii)

She was not reluctant to note such weaknesses when they were evident; thus, while praising Virginia Fox (1984) for the "brisk and informative style" she employed in her book *Women Astronauts*, Sutherland (1986) also allowed "its tone (was) marred somewhat by a frequent tone of adulation" (p. 136). Similarly, in her starred review of Paula Fox's (1984) *One-Eyed Cat*, Sutherland (1986) wrote, "Few contemporary writers create their characters with the depth, nuance, and compassion that Paula Fox does." That said, she continued, "and if her story unfolds slowly, it is worth the patience and concentration it takes to follow the many-layered development of the characters" (p. 136).

Beginning reviewers can still learn a great deal of what they need to know about writing exemplary reviews (and analyzing children's and young adult literature) simply by reading Sutherland's reviews, which are collected in the three volumes *The Best in Children's Books, 1966–1972, 1973–1978,* and *1979–1984* (all published by the University of Chicago Press in 1973, 1980, and 1986).

Back to Britain

At about the same time Sutherland became associated with the *Bulletin*, children's book publishing underwent a revival in England, as did children's book reviewing. Before the Second World War, review attention was largely confined to two professional journals, *The Junior Bookshelf* (begun in 1936) and *The School Librarian* (1937). This began changing in the 1960s when "the reviewing of children's books in newspapers and magazines mushroomed" (Watson, 2001, p. 605) and such great names began entering the reviewing arena as Margery Fisher (at *The Sunday Times*), Naomi Lewis (at *The Observer*), John Rowe Townsend (at *The Guardian*), David Holloway (at *The Daily Telegraph*), and Brian Alderson (at *The Times*). In addition, Fisher started her own magazine, *Growing Point*, in 1962. It was then, too, that Aidan and Nancy Chambers (1970) founded their influential magazine *Signal, Approaches to Children's Books.*

While all of these writers became well known and highly regarded in the United States, it is probably John Rowe Townsend who has had the greatest influence here as a reviewer and historian of literature for young readers. His history of children's literature *Written for Children* has gone through at least four editions since its first U.S. publication in 1967 and his two collections of essays, *A Sense of Story* (1971) and *A Sounding of Storytellers* (1979), have found a similarly wide readership among adults. Another measure of the American regard for Townsend is his having been selected as the second Arbuthnot Lecturer in 1971 (the first lecture in ALA's prestigious lecture series was another British writer, Margery Fisher). Of greater relevance to us here, however, is his 1981 essay, "The Reviewing of Children's Books." In it he defines reviewing "as critical or appreciative contemporaneous writing about new books in periodical publications," stressing the word "contemporaneous." "If it isn't contemporaneous, if it isn't about new books, then whatever it may be, it's not reviewing" (p. 177).

His fourfold notion of the *function* of reviewing, which evokes the spirit of Virginia Woolf, is also instructive. It is, first, he argues, "to recognize new work of merit." Second, "it is part of the process by which books are published and distributed." By this, he means there is a kind of quid pro quo relationship between publishers and reviewers, since "publishers support book pages with their advertising, and send copies of books for review, because they hope for publicity, for recommendation, for quotations they can use in their blurbs and advertisements and promotion" (p. 178). Third, reviewing "provides a consumer guide for potential buyers of books" and fourth ("and never to be forgotten"), reviewing is "a branch of journalism" (p. 179). He echoes Moore when he then adds, "The reviewer has a function as a contributor of readable material, as a stimulator of thought…" (p. 179). And Moore's spirit is also alive in his further observation that "Children are individuals, not types or specimens of an age group. I would prefer a reviewer to address herself sensitively to the book there in front of her, rather than crudely to the assessment of its suitability to some broad notional category of child" (p. 186).

And speaking, again, of the reviewer, here is one final unimpeachable thought from Townsend: "One point on which I am not in any doubt is that a reviewer, whether a professional author or not, *must be able to write*" (p. 184, emphasis added).

Meanwhile, Back in America

Fortunately, Zena Sutherland *could* write and under her stylish and vigorous editorship, the *Bulletin* became one of the five major professional sources of book reviews consulted by American librarians; the other four were (and still are): *Booklist* and The *Horn Book Magazine* (founded as we have seen in 1905 and 1924, respectively); *Kirkus Reviews,* founded in 1932 by editor and writer Virginia Kirkus; and *School Library Journal* (1955) (spun off from the venerable *Library Journal*, which had been founded by no less than Melville Dewey in 1876).

A sixth widely used—but more specialized—magazine, *Voice of Youth Advocates (VOYA)*, was started in 1978 by co-founders Dorothy Broderick and Mary K. Chelton to provide a forum for reviews of young adult literature, which had begun appearing with the publication of S. E. Hinton's (1967) *The Outsiders* and Robert Lipsyte's (1967) *The Contender*. Two other sources of young adult book reviews are *The ALAN Review*—published three times per year for members of the Assembly on Literature for Adolescents of the National Council of Teachers of English—and NCTE's own *English Journal*, which is aimed at English teachers (principally at the secondary level).

Lastly, an eighth, *Publishers Weekly*, founded in 1872, is principally targeted at booksellers but, nevertheless, remains widely read by librarians, since its reviews of children's and young adult books generally appear several months in advance of the publication dates of the books under consideration. Such prepublication notice is invaluable to librarians whose purchasing and cataloging procedures are often glacially slow. For this reason a second early noticer of impending publications—*Kirkus Reviews*—was widely read by librarians and booksellers until its apparent demise at the end of 2009 (about which, more later).

Some Summary Profiles

Of all these professional magazines only *The Horn Book Magazine* has been available to a general readership on newsstands. Published six times per year, its eclectic mix of reviews and articles about books for young readers offers intrinsic appeal for anyone interested in literature. Its reviews of children's and young adult books are written by a combination of full-time editorial staff and a small cadre of reviewers from the field. Each of its issues also features a small number of guest reviewers. Though the magazine follows a positive review only policy and is, thus, highly selective in the books it chooses to review, its sister publication, *The Horn Book Guide*, is much more inclusive, claiming to review— either positively or negatively— some 2,000 books in each of its two semi-annual issues, the lion's share of these reviews being written by a group of 60 to 70 field reviewers.

School Library Journal, published monthly, is even more ambitious, aiming to review every book (well, *nearly* every new book) published for young readers each year. Its many reviewers (upwards of 350 at any given time) are all volunteers and almost all are working public and school librarians. *SLJ* also includes numerous articles and columns about library practice.

Also including editorial material about best practice and also using volunteer reviewers is *VOYA*, which is published bi-monthly. Evidencing the magazine's commitment to involving youth in developing the library service targeted at them, *VOYA* is the only one of the journals to feature occasional reviews by teenagers themselves. However, the

number of *VOYA's* reviews is smaller than *SLJ's*, since— as already noted—the magazine's coverage is limited to young adult books (though some adult titles deemed of interest to YA readers may be included, particularly in the area of genre fiction, which has traditionally enjoyed a wide crossover readership). *VOYA* is further distinguished by its use of an elaborate book review code that ranks books on a scale of 1–5 for both quality and popularity and a letter code indicating grade level interest (M for middle school, J for junior high school, S for senior high, and A/YA for adult-marketed books recommended for YAs).

Like *Horn Book*—but unlike *SLJ* and *VOYA*—ALA's *Booklist* is devoted exclusively to book-related content, principally reviews, though the magazine also includes such book-related features as author interviews, thematic bibliographies, and columns. It is one of only two of the magazines (*BCCB* being the other) whose reviews are, in large part, written by full-time editorial staff. However, like *Horn Book*, *Booklist* also utilizes a group of paid field reviewers. Despite its similarities, *Booklist* differs from the other magazines in several ways: in addition to its Books for Youth section it also includes an Adult Books section and each adult review there is tagged if it is deemed of interest to YA readers (the tags are somewhat reminiscent of *VOYA's* codes; e.g., "YA" indicates general YA interest; "YA/C" denotes books with curricular value; "YA/S" is reserved for titles of special subject interest; and "YA/M" for titles with appeal to mature teenagers). The magazine—like *Horn Book*—follows a 'positive review only' policy; i.e., each book submitted for consideration is examined either by a staff member or a field reviewer and if—in their judgment—the book cannot be given a positive review, it is not included. As a result, the number of titles *Booklist* covers is smaller than that of *SLJ* and *The Horn Book Guide*. It is published twice monthly September through June and monthly in July and August.

The Bulletin of the Center for Children's Books (BCCB), which had its start at the University of Chicago, is housed at the Graduate School of Library and Information Science at the University of Illinois, Urbana-Champaign and is published monthly except August by the Johns Hopkins University Press. Most of its reviews are written by editorial staff and recent graduates or current employees of the LIS School. Like *Booklist* and *VOYA*, *BCCB* also employs a coding system for its reviews: "R" is for recommended, "Ad" for additional books of acceptable quality; "M" for marginal titles; "NR" is not recommended; "SpC" denotes books best used in specialized collections; and "SpR" for books having appeal only for "the unusual reader" (*Booklist* boxes its reviews of such titles).

If they use no other symbol, all of the review journals do at least identify works of unusual merit, usually with a star, though *BCCB* uses an asterisk and *Kirkus* (see below) used a pointer.

Until it ceased publication in December 2009, *Kirkus* reviewed approximately 3,000 books for young readers per year (and like *Booklist* it, too, published an adult books section). Though regarded by some as being a trade journal like *PW*, since it was widely read by booksellers and book jobbers, *Kirkus* also counted many librarians among its readers. Occasionally controversial, the magazine was regarded with equal measures of respect and dread, since it was arguably the only one of the major journals to feature notably negative reviews, sometimes, it seemed, gratuitously so (the *Los Angeles Times*, in reporting its passing, called it "a captious beast" [Daum, 2009]). Of course, its reviewers—many of them freelancers—may have felt they had carte blanche to take off the gloves, since *Kirkus* published only unsigned reviews, an inherently controversial practice, though *Publishers Weekly* reviews are also unsigned.

Criticisms and Caveats

Editors and Authors.   The issue of negative reviews has long been a contentious one. Speaking on a panel of reviewers at the 1992 Allerton Park Institute, Betsy Hearne, who was then Editor of *BCCB*, noted,

> What I'd like to speak to is the lack of negative reviewing in this field. Publishers are shocked when they read negative reviews of children's books, partly because they're not used to it. I know that the publishers in the audience will probably disagree with that, but compared to adult books, which get slammed up, down, and sideways by somebody from way out in left field who has no expertise in the subject whatsoever, we are dealing very carefully and idealistically with these books, giving them a lot of time and a lot of space. (Sutton, 1993, p. 14)

As it happened, another speaker at the Institute was Dorothy Briley (1992), then Editor in Chief of Clarion Books, who expressed particular concern about what she called the "unfair negative review," by which, she explained, she meant "one with an agenda other than assessing a book on its merits as literature" (p. 111). As an example, she offered Paula Fox's (1986) novel *The Moonlight Man*, which features a girl whose father is an alcoholic and which one reviewer criticized because "this book does not give acceptable guidance to work on that problem" (Briley, 1992, p. 111). Such social criticism is not uncommon in professional reviews that focus on the utility of a book, especially if it is one of social realism. However, to people who believe the focus should be on the literary aspects, such reviews may recall the proscriptive attitude of Mrs. Trimmer vis-à-vis *Little Goody Two Shoes*. Such attitudes are more pronounced—and controversial—when they arise from a reviewer's concern with political correctness as was the case with a second book Briley cited: Russell Freedman's (1992) *An Indian Winter*, a nonfiction book about the 19th-century Swiss artist Karl Bodmer's watercolor pictures of Native Americans, painted during his 1833–34 expedition to America with German Prince Maximilian. This led the author of an otherwise favorable review to conclude with the words, "though some may question the reliability of two European dilettantes concerning a culture they visited only briefly" (Briley, 1992, pp. 111–112).

It is not only editors and publishers who have been critical of professional reviews, however; authors have also long had reservations. Writing in 1932, Howard Pease (1946), the popular author of boys' adventure books, expressed his own reservations about agendas in reviewing:

> Moreover in criticizing a book, we find it difficult not to reveal our prejudices as well as our enthusiasms, and people who know us well may rightly be skeptical of us on both of these counts. Not many of us are **as** commendably candid as the librarian who faced her colleagues to review a new book. "I didn't like this story at all," she announced, "But then it's all about horses, and I never did like horses." (pp. 96–97)

Instead of prejudice and/or enthusiasm, Pease called for more criticism in reviews of children's books. "We must learn to examine the text itself," he wrote, sounding a bit like one of the New Critics, "and we must do so with less timidity and more discernment" (p. 97).

To that end he advised reviewers to focus on seven elements: (a) Fictional forms (b) Story (c) Characterization (d) Content, i.e., theme (e) Craftsmanship (f) Prose, i.e., style and (g) Response. Writing 25 years later, another writer and—this time—occasional reviewer Selma G. Lanes (1971) observed more succinctly, "That the librarians' journals provide unsatisfactory and inadequate *literary* judgments of children's books cannot be argued" (p. 152).

Fifteen years after that, still another author, Avi (1986), addressed the same perceived inadequacies, noting—in the case of the review media—"standards for criticism are at best vague" (p. 114). His particular censure, however, was reserved for what he termed "the vastly disproportionate percentage of space… given over to textual [i.e., plot] summary. Too often the actual critique is squeezed into one or two sentences" (p. 115). For Avi this practice was rendered even more egregious by the very "brevity of our reviews" (p. 115).

These remarks invited response and they got a practical one from Roger Sutton (1986), who was then working as a branch librarian for the Chicago Public Library. In his article "Reviewing Avi," Sutton suggested the aggrieved author was conflating reviewing with literary criticism. "The first is not entirely the second, which is what I think you are really asking for." Sutton further noted,

> Review reading is utilitarian, part of the process of collection development. In addition to description and evaluation there are other things I like to find in a review: price, bibliographic data, suggested reading level.… While these are extra-literary considerations, they further the goal of the review, to tell librarians about the book. (p. 50)

Sutton would go on a decade later to become Editor of the *Horn Book*, about which Lanes (1971) had earlier—and rather grudgingly—allowed, "The more literary and perceptively written reviews are to be found, on occasion, in

Horn Book, the single independent journal totally devoted to children's books and their authors" (p. 153).

Perhaps an earlier editor of the *Horn Book*, Paul Heins (1970), should, thus, be allowed the last word here. He argued,

> Reviewers do not sift for eternity; they are kept busy selecting the best or the most significant of the books available during a given period of time.... A reviewer does not have to be a prophet, but merely a sensitive reader who is able to perceive the quality of a new book. If the reviewer is in tune with literature, he may often make an uncanny judgment that will be justified by time. (p. 87)

And Librarians. Speaking at the same Allerton Park Institute as Hearne and Briley, Janice N. Harrington (1993), then Head of Youth Services for the Champaign (IL) Public Library, offered a working professional's appraisal of reviews. Starting with the assertion, "Librarians want reviews to appear promptly, to be brief and to select materials assertively," she went on to explain, "They need brevity, because professional librarians place value on their time" (p. 31).

What else do librarians require from reviews? A number of things, it would seem; among them Harrington listed: bibliographical information, authority of the author and publisher, audience, placing the book in context, illustrations, and physical format. In amplifying this, she made the clearest distinction thus far between the needs and expectations of authors/editors on the one hand and librarians on the other:

> For contemporary librarians literary quality is not the sole determinant of purchasing decisions, and often it is not even the major determinant. Perhaps the most valuable part of the review is the information that places the book in context.... Librarians are not just buying books; they are buying books to serve readers. They need specific information about how the book might be used by readers and how it can be used in their own work with children. (p. 31)

What criticisms of reviews do librarians have? Following a survey of the literature and her own interviews with children's librarians from a variety of different libraries, Harrington listed the following:

- inadequate reviewing of foreign language books
- not enough reviews of new books about minority groups
- scanty reviewing of books from new or alternative presses
- too few reviews of books considered for their potential use by the visually handicapped
- not enough identification of high-interest, low-reading level books
- too few suggestions for and too little comment on use of books in the home
- the time lag between the publication of books and the appearance of reviews

- non-fiction does not get reviewed as much as fiction.

Several other less frequent criticisms might also be mentioned:

- reviewers seem out of touch with actual librarians and their needs
- reviewers need to focus more on how the materials can be used (p. 33)

The Present and the (Arguable) Future

Though some of the above observations and criticisms were made nearly 80 years ago, they are still being discussed and hotly debated today. What *has* changed, however, is the venue in which the dialectic is taking place; for over the course of the last decade or so it has moved from the library, classroom, and lecture hall to the Internet, where it continues, now, on countless electronic discussion lists. For example: a recent, fortnight-long (November 1–15, 2009) exchange among the usual suspects (librarians, editors, publishers, and authors) took place at ccbc-net (the listserv of the Cooperative Children's Book Center at the University of Wisconsin, Madison). And many of the issues discussed and debated did, indeed, have a familiar ring: negative vs. positive reviews, the audience for reviews, the (necessary?) brevity of professional reviews; their lack of context; the elements of a good review, etc.

The two matters that excited the most spirited and detailed discussion, however, were (a) the treatment of historically marginalized peoples (especially Native Americans) in books along with the related questions of who is qualified to write the books about Native peoples and—more pertinent to this discussion – who is qualified to review those books? (b) The second—and somewhat overlapping issue—regarded nonfiction or informational books. Discussed here was the lack of review attention given to such books (at a time when the form is newly flourishing), the qualifications of those who review them, the failure to discuss the aesthetic merits of the form, and the necessary haste with which deadline-driven reviews must be written (Carter, 1992).

Surprisingly, another new electronic phenomenon that is changing the world of book reviews—blogs (a contraction of the term "web log")—was little discussed. Though as recently as five years ago, blogs about children's and young adult books were a rarity, the field has since exploded, as a February 2010 search of the website "Kidlitosphere Central" reveals a strapping total of well over 300 active blogs on children's and young adult literature. While many blogs don't feature traditional book reviews, the highly personal, (mostly) unedited, idiosyncratic, sometimes controversial, sometimes ill-informed commentary they do include is already changing the way many people would define reviews (and reviewers).

This is, however, only one change the ascendant digital culture is visiting on America's book reviews. As print has increasingly migrated from paper to digital form, many long-established newspapers have folded while the survivors have dramatically curtailed staff and content to cut production costs or created (as yet) unprofitable versions of the newspaper online. As a result, only one weekly book review section survives in America, that of *The New York Times;* all of the others have been discontinued, though in some cases truncated versions survive online (see *The Los Angeles Times* and *The Washington Post*, for example). A new feature of all of the online newspaper book coverage is at least one blog, none of which features reviews but, instead, a potpourri of book chat, announcements, and literary gossip.

Next to go under will surely be the various book review magazines. Perhaps anticipating that, *Booklist, School Library Journal, Publishers Weekly, The Horn Book Magazine,* and *BCCB* have created online incarnations of themselves and have struggled to create online-only content, much of which is presented in the form of—yes—blogs. To be fair, more—if not all—of these blogs are written by knowledgeable professionals. To cite only one example, author/editor Marc Aronson contributes "Nonfiction Matters" to *School Library Journal*'s website. Whether or not any of these magazines will survive in their traditional paper format is anybody's guess but to consider their prospects is to be irresistibly reminded of the old Agatha Christie (1939) mystery novel *And Then There Were None.*

In the meantime the major review sources have all licensed their reviews to the two major online bookstores, amazon.com and bn.com (i.e., Barnes and Noble) for reprint at their sites. This means that reviews originally written for professional readers are now being read by the general public, many of whom are visiting these commercial websites in search of books to purchase. Since it is the positive review that sparks sales, there is some concern that these two behemoth sites may ultimately influence the nature and content of reviews.

Certainly, they have already introduced another phenomenon to the world of book reviewing: the self-posted reader review. Just as anyone with a computer can start a blog, so can anyone visit amazon.com or bn.com and post a review of any book. It almost goes without saying that the quality and reliability of these reviews varies wildly (since, like blogs, they are largely unedited) and that many of them are written by people who either haven't read the book or are friends of the author or, indeed, are the authors themselves, posting pseudonymously. Meanwhile sites like Teenreads. com and Kidsreads.com—both services of the Book Report Network—offer more reliable online reviews of new and forthcoming books for young readers (many of their reviews being targeted at the young people themselves).

That said, the next major home for book "reviews" is now predicted to be the various social networking sites—both generic ones like Facebook and MySpace and also more subject-specific ones like goodreads.com and librarything.com. But here, too, the problem remains one of reliability. Consider that if you do a Google search for the phrase "children's and young adult book reviews," you will be overwhelmed with 22,100,000 hits. Learning how to select from among this surfeit of…*stuff* and to evaluate one's findings is, clearly, becoming a fundamental part of every nascent librarian's education.

Writing the Book Review and Other Concluding Remarks

And speaking of fundamentals: the avalanche of book reviews and other book-related information on the Internet suggests that the single most important aspect of the book review today has to do with the credentials of the reviewers themselves. And it's important to note that aspiring reviewers, instead of rushing to start a blog or begin posting unedited reviews at unedited websites, would be well-advised to practice the craft first while also establishing credentials. The simplest way to do this remains becoming a volunteer reviewer for a magazine like *School Library Journal* or *VOYA*.

Meanwhile the longstanding and often-criticized problem with reviews—their brevity—may someday be resolved by the burgeoning presence of blogs, which *do* allow for more discursive discussion of individual books. When these blogs are features of established, creditable websites like booklistonline.com or publishersweekly. com, this could represent a positive change. For the moment, however, most traditional professional reviews remain brief (seldom longer than 200 words, if that) and may be getting briefer as production costs continue to escalate as the number of books being published also soars. For the reviewer, this means an endless exercise in economy and self-discipline. In the world of traditional book reviewing, less really is more—particularly now when so many books are being published. Indeed, according to R. R. Bowker (2009), the number of new juvenile (i.e., children's and YA) book titles and editions published in 2008 was nearly 30,000! For older librarians who remember when this total was closer to 2,500, such a statistic is startling and begs careful analysis. Nevertheless, there is no question that the last five years have seen more books for young readers published than ever before in U.S. history, and the growth rate has been particularly steep in the young adult area.

Since this has come at a time when the resources of traditional review journals have become increasingly straitened, the process of selecting which books to review has become ever more important and is, itself, a de facto review. Once that first decision has been made, another decision awaits: deciding which of the many categories the book in hand will fall into. In her indispensable *From Cover to Cover: Evaluating and Reviewing Children's Books*, K. T. Horning (1997) lists the following categories: books of information; traditional literature (e.g., fables, folk tales, myths, etc.); poetry, verse, rhymes and songs; picture books; easy readers and transitional books, and fiction. To this list we must now add comics and graphic novels, one of the most expansive areas of contemporary publishing and one that demands special knowledge and skills on the part of the reviewer (see Brenner, this volume).

Each book category requires a variety of different evaluative skills and, happily, Horning's book is an authoritative source for beginners who need to develop these skills. The differing skills required of their writers aside, it is widely agreed that professional reviews do have some things in common. One is the inclusion of essential bibliographic information, since reviews remain, fundamentally, a guide to selection and purchase. Included in the bibliographic information will be the names of the author, the editor (if an anthology or collection), the illustrator (if any), the publisher, the place of publication (sometimes), the year of publication, the number of pages, the price, and the ISBN (International Standard Book Number). Also to be included is the age range for which the book is deemed suitable. This may be expressed in either age or grade range (and at this point every observer of the field issues a caveat: don't rely on the range the publisher identifies on the jacket flap or in the book itself, simply because the publisher—anxious to sell as many copies of the book as possible—will sometimes unrealistically expand the "suitable" age range). This is where the experience and expertise of the reviewer will be called into play, though recommended age ranges for the same book will still vary to a surprising degree.

As has been indicated, the review that follows the bibliographic information will be a combination of plot summary (with which the review typically begins), critical analysis, and, in some cases, suggestions regarding the uses of the title. All of the individual journals have their own selection policies and style sheets that address these issues, so there is no need to belabor them here.

One thing must be stressed, however: reviews should always focus on the book in hand and not on the cleverness of the reviewer, especially if that is demonstrated at the expense of the author. This is not to say that reviews must be universally sober; many books—especially those with humor—invite a lighthearted touch and many reviews can benefit from an infusion of the style, tone, and spirit of the book being reviewed. Sometimes this can be easily accomplished by quoting a signature line or passage from the book. Sometimes it is a bit more complicated. Here are several reviews I've written for *Booklist* that demonstrate some of these—and other—points we have been discussing.

Let's start with a book for middle-age readers about a British dog named Jack, who tells readers his story in his own idiosyncratic voice, which I echo in my review.

I, Jack.

Finney, Patricia (author), Illustrated by Peter Bailey.

Feb. 2004. 192 p. HarperCollins, hardcover, $15.99 (0-06-052207-0); library edition, $16.89 (0-06-052208-9). Grades 3–6.

First published December 15, 2003 (*Booklist*).

Meet Jack. Hi, hi. Pant, pant. Wag, wag. May I smell…. Oh, sorry. Jack is a yellow Labrador retriever. He tells us 'apedogs' (excuse me, but that's what he calls humans) his story in his own words. Well, the three cats sharing his den (house) help by adding acid commentary in footnotes. A good thing, too, since Jack is very thick and sometimes gets things wrong. But he is sweet. Very, very sweet. He loves Petra, the girl dog next door. They have puppies, and things get complicated. Jack and Petra run away. Jack's pack leader (owner) tries to find them. He has an accident, and Jack gets to be a hero. Oh, wow. Happy dog. Happy readers. Good, funny book. Show British author Finney much respect. Tummy rubs all around.

Next is a review of a picture book that echoes the author/illustrator's visual voice.

Roller Coaster.

Frazee, Marla (author).

May 2003. 32p. Harcourt, hardcover, $16 (0-15-204554-6). PreS–Grade 2.

First published June 1, 2003 (*Booklist*).

A sinuous line of people stretches across two double-page spreads. Everyone, child and adult alike, is waiting to ride the roller coaster. Finally it's time to get into the cars; 12 lucky folks take their seats (a few people have already fallen out of line). Then, seatbelts fastened, off they go, with the picture-book audience brought up close to enjoy the ride. Around and around and up and down, the cars zip and fly across a series of double-page spreads. Frazee does an extraordinary job of conveying motion by the placement of her images, her use of white space, bright colors, and swooshing speed lines. The color of the type changes to red when the ride begins, returning to black when it ends, and the graphite and watercolor art is so dynamic that it practically turns the pages by itself. What will keep children coming back for extra looks, however, is Franzee's clever, dramatic depiction of the 12 riders and their wildly and amusingly different reactions to the stomach-churning experience—before, during, and after. No words are necessary to convey that part of the story; body language says it all. A rambunctious tour de force from an abundantly gifted author-artist.

Reviews are serious business but there's no reason they shouldn't be entertaining, as well as informative, though this obviously requires considerable skill on the part of the reviewer. And, just as obviously, serious books require serious reviews, such as this novel featuring a transgender protagonist.

Parrotfish.

Wittlinger, Ellen (author).

July 2007. 304p. Simon & Schuster, hardcover, $16.99 (1-4169-1622-9). Grades 9–12.

First published April 15, 2007 (*Booklist*).

Angela McNair is a boy! Oh, to the rest of the world she's obviously a girl. But the transgendered high-school junior *knows* that she's a boy. And so, bravely, Angela cuts her hair short, buys boys' clothing, and announces that his name is now Grady and that he is beginning his true new life as a boy. Of course, it's not as simple as that; Grady encounters an array of reactions ranging from outright hostility to loving support. To her credit, Wittlinger has managed to avoid the operatic (no blood is shed, no lives are threatened) but some readers may wonder if—in so doing—she has made things a bit too easy for Grady. His initially bewildered family rallies around him; he finds a champion in a female gym teacher; he loses but then regains a best friend while falling in love with a beautiful, mixed-race girl. Wittlinger, who is exploring new, potentially off-putting ground here (only Julie Anne Peters' *Luna*, 2004, has dealt with this subject before in such detail), manages to create a story sufficiently nonthreatening to appeal to—and enlighten—a broad range of readers, including those at the lower end of the YA spectrum. She has also done a superb job of untangling the complexities of gender identity and showing the person behind labels like "gender dysphoria." Grady turns out to be a very normal boy who, like every teen, must deal with vexing issues of self-identity. To his credit, he does this with courage and grace, managing to discover not only the "him" in self but, also, the "my."

The experienced reviewer will know when to employ humor and when to hold it in reserve. And experience will also prove that writing a review is an art, just as writing a book is. Developing artful review writing skills requires a combination of writing experience and wide reading (and re-reading)—not only of books but also of book reviews. And like all writing that of reviews inevitably requires rewriting and revising, sometimes of the intensive sort. This is never truer than when one is dealing with a potentially controversial book, as demonstrated by this review of a non-fiction title for high school age readers.

Does Illegal Immigration Harm Society?

Barbour, Scott (author).
Oct. 2009. 104p. illus. ReferencePoint, library edition, $25.95 (9781601520852). Grades 8–12. 364.1.
First published October 1, 2009 (*Booklist*).

This title in the *In Controversy* series examines the vexing issue of illegal immigration. Barbour starts with context—an overview of nineteenth and early 20th-century legislative attempts at regulating immigration—and then examines a clutch of contentious issues surrounding the current impact of illegal immigration upon America's economy, culture, crime, and national security. His strategy is to offer the sometimes inflated, sometimes reasonable views of advocates from both sides of the issue(s). The result is generally balanced, though his coverage of crime and terrorism does seem skewed in the conservative direction (could it be the quote Barbour includes from the magazine *New American* without informing readers it's published by The John Birch Society?). One also wonders why, of the five Web sites listed in the appended "For Further Research" section, three are conservative and two libertarian. To be fair, the unbiased Pew Hispanic Center is often cited and readers are also referred to such immigration-friendly sources as La Raza and the Mexican American Legal Defense and Educational Fund. Yes, a controversial issue—and perhaps a controversial book.

No matter how much the field of children's and young adult books changes, one thing will surely remain con-stant: the essential importance of reviews—essential not only to insure that good books never go overlooked but, in a larger sense, also to insure that by identifying and analyzing excellence in books for young readers, reviews and reviewers will stimulate young people to read better books and publishers to issue more works of enduring quality.

In his essay "The Reviewing of Children's Books" the British reviewer and critic John Rowe Townsend (1981) observes, "There is not a great deal of informed comment on the reviewing of children's books; we could do with more" (p. 186). To which anyone embarked upon research into this art (or is it a craft?) can only say, "Hear, hear!" There is, as students will quickly learn, a great deal of critical work extant about children's literature and, finally, an emerging body of critical work about young adult literature, too. But, these nearly 30 years after Townsend wrote his essay, his observation about reviewing remains largely unchanged, even though, as I have tried to evidence in the chapter above, the field itself has been visited by well-nigh seismic changes. One hopes the challenge of these changes might stimulate a larger body of "informed comment" about this essential subject, for it remains sorely wanting.

Literature References

Andersen, H. C. (1866/1840). *What the moon saw, and other tales* (H. W. Dulcken, Trans.). London, UK: George Routledge and Sons.

Barbour, S. (2009). *Does illegal immigration harm society?* San Diego, CA: Reference Point.

Carroll, L. (1865). *Alice's adventures in wonderland*. London, UK: Macmillan.

Christie, A. (1939). *And then there were none*. New York, NY: Pocket Books.

Finney, P. (2003). *I, Jack*. New York, NY: HarperCollins.

Fox, P. (1984). *One-eyed cat*. New York, NY: Bradbury.

Fox, P. (1986). *The moonlight man*. New York, NY: Bradbury.

Fox, V. (1984). *Women astronauts*. New York, NY: Messner.

Frazee, M. (2003). *Roller coaster*. San Diego, CA: Harcourt.

Hinton, S. E. (1967). *The outsiders*. New York, NY: Viking.

History of Little Goody Two Shoes. (1766). London, UK: John Newbery.

Lipsyte, R. (1967). *The contender*. New York, NY: Harper & Row.

Mother Bunch's fairy tales. (1773). London, UK: Francis Newbery.

Trimmer, S. (1818). *History of the robins*. London, UK: N. Hailes, Juvenile Library.

Wittlinger, E. (2007). *Parrotfish*. New York, NY: Simon & Schuster.

Academic References

Avi. (1986). Review the reviewers? *School Library Journal, 32*(3), 114–115.

Bator, R. (1983). *Signposts to criticism of children's literature*. Chicago, IL: American Library Association.

Becker, M. L. (1936). *First adventures in reading. Introducing children to books*. New York, NY: Frederick A. Stokes Co.

Beckson, K., & Ganz, A. (1989). *Literary terms: A dictionary* (3rd ed.). New York, NY: The Noonday Press.

Bowker, R. R. (2009). New book titles and editions, 2002–2008.

Retrieved February 18, 2010, from http://www.bowker.com/bookwire/IndustryStats2009.pdf

Carpenter, H., & Prichard, M. (1984). *The Oxford companion to children's literature*. New York, NY: Oxford University Press.

Cart, M. (2003). Review of the book *Roller coaster*, by M. Frazee. *Booklist, 99*(19), 1768.

Cart, M. (2003). Review of the book *I, Jack*, by P. Finney. *Booklist, 100*(8), 750.

Cart, M. (2007). Review of the book *Parrotfish*, by E. Wittlinger. *Booklist, 103*(16), 40.

Cart, M. (2009). Review of the book *Does illegal immigration harm society?* by S. Barbour. *Booklist, 106*(3), 58.

Carter, B. (1992). Reviewing nonfiction books for children and young adults: Stance, scholarship, and structure. In B. Hearne & R. Sutton (Eds.), *Evaluating children's books: A critical look* (pp. 59–71). Urbana-Champaign: University of Illinois.

Children's books. (1844). *The Quarterly Review, 74* (June-October), 1–3, 16–26. In V. Haviland (Ed.). (1973). *Children and literature: Views and reviews* (pp. 8–18). New York, NY: Lothrop, Lee & Shepard.

Darling, R. L. (1968). *The rise of children's book reviewing in America*. New York, NY: R. R. Bowker.

Daum, M. (2009). *Kirkus Reviews* may have been annoying, but its successors are inane. Retrieved February 18, 2010, from http://www.latimes.com/news/opinion/commentary/la-oe-daum17-2009dec17,0,2074255.column

Eaton, A. T. (1940). *Reading with children*. New York, NY: The Viking Press.

Eaton, A. T. (1946). *Treasure for the taking. A book list for boys and girls*. New York, NY: The Viking Press.

Gatty, M. (1866). Review of the book *Alice's adventures in wonderland* by Lewis Carroll. *Aunt Judy's magazine for young people, 1*, 123. In V. Haviland (Ed.), . *Children and literature: Views and reviews* (1973, pp. 19–20). New York, NY: Lothrop, Lee & Shepard.

Harms, W. (2002). Zena Sutherland, children's literature pioneer, 1915–2002. Retrieved February 18, 2010, from http://www-news.uchicago.edu/releases/02/020614.sutherland.shtml

Harrington, J. N. (1993). Children's librarians, reviews, and collection development. In B. Hearne & R. Sutton (Eds.), *Evaluating children's books: A critical look* (pp. 27–36). Urbana-Champaign: University of Illinois.

Haviland, V. (1973). *Children and literature: Views and reviews*. New York, NY: Lothrop, Lee & Shepard.

Heins, P. (1970/1977). Out on a limb with the critics. In P. Heins (Ed.), *Crosscurrents of criticism. Horn Book essays, 1968–1977* (pp. 72–81). Boston, MA: The Horn Book.

Heins, P. (Ed.). (1977). *Crosscurrents of criticism. Horn Book essays 1968–1977*. Boston, MA: The Horn Book.

Horning, K. T. (1997). *From cover to cover: Evaluating and reviewing children's books*. New York, NY: HarperCollins.

Jenkins, C. A. (1999). Practices and precepts. *The Horn Book Magazine, 75*(5), 547–558.

Jordan, A. M. (1948). *From Rollo to Tom Sawyer and other papers*. Boston, MA: The Horn Book.

Juvenile books of the past (1868, January). *British Quarterly Review, 47*, 128–149. In R. Bator (Ed.), *Signposts to criticism of children's literature* (pp. 74–84). Chicago, IL: American Library Association.

Kidlitosphere Central. (2009–10). Bloggers in children's and young adult literature. Retrieved on February 18, 2010, from http://www.kidlitosphere.org/bloggers/

Lanes, S. G. (1971). *Down the rabbit hole*. New York, NY: Atheneum.

Marcus, L. S. (2008). *Minders of make-believe*. Boston, MA: Houghton Mifflin.

Melcher, F. G. (1963). Introduction to Caroline M. Hewins and

Books for children. In S. Andrews (Ed.), *The Hewins lectures 1947–1962* (pp. 65–66). Boston, MA: The Horn Book.

Miyake, O. (2006). Sarah Trimmer. In J. Zipes (Ed.) *The Oxford encyclopedia of children's literature, Vol. 4* (p. 114). Oxford, UK: Oxford University Press.

Moore, A. C. (1920). *Roads to childhood*. New York: NY: George H. Doran.

Moore, A. C. (1923). *New roads to childhood*. New York, NY: George H. Doran.

Moore, A.C. (1925). *The three owls*. New York: NY: George H. Doran.

Moore, A. C. (1926). *Cross-roads to childhood*. New York, NY: George H. Doran.

Moore, A. C. (1928). *The three owls: Second book*. New York: NY: George H. Doran.

Moore, A. C. (1931). *The three owls: Third book*. New York: NY: George H. Doran.

Pease, H. (1946). An author's view of criticism. In N.R. Fryatt (Ed.) *A Horn Book Sampler* (pp. 96–103). Boston, MA: The Horn Book.

Sayers, F. C. (1972). *Anne Carroll Moore: A biography*. New York, NY: Atheneum.

Scudder, H. E. (1867/1973). Books for young people. *Riverside magazine for young people, 1*(January), 43–45. In V. Haviland (Ed.). *Children and literature: Views and reviews* (pp. 21–24). New York, NY: Lothrop, Lee & Shepard.

Sutherland, Z. (1986). *The best in children's books*. Chicago, IL: University of Chicago Press.

Sutton, R. (1986). Reviewing Avi. *School Library Journal, 32*(5), 50–51.

Sutton, R. (1993). Censorship, negative criticism, glitzy trends, growing publisher output, and other shadows on the landscape of children's book reviewing: A panel discussion. In B. Hearne & R. Sutton (Eds.), *Evaluating children's books: A critical look* (pp. 5–25). Urbana-Champaign: University of Illinois.

Townsend, J. R. (1971). *A sense of story*. New York, NY: J. B. Lippincott.

Townsend, J. R. (1979). *A sounding of storytellers*. New York, NY: J. B. Lippincott.

Townsend, J. R. (1981). The reviewing of children's books. In B. Hearne & M. Kaye (Eds.), *Celebrating children's books* (pp. 177–187). New York, NY: Lothrop, Lee & Shepard.

Trimmer, S. (1802/1973). Art. XVI. The history of Little Goody Two Shoes, with her means of acquiring learning, wisdom and riches. *Guardian of Education, 1,* 430–431. In V. Haviland (Ed.), *Children and literature: Views and reviews* (p. 6). New York, NY: Lothrop, Lee & Shepard.

Trimmer, S. (1803/1973). On the care which is requisite in the choice of books for children. *Guardian of Education, 2,* 407–410. In V. Haviland (Ed.), *Children and literature: Views and reviews* (pp. 4–6). New York, NY: Lothrop, Lee & Shepard.

Trimmer, S. (1803/1983). Art. XXIX. The eenowned history of Primrose Pretty Face. *Guardian of Education, 2,* 184–185. In R. Bator (Ed.), *Signposts to criticism of children's literature* (p. 72). Chicago, IL: American Library Association.

Trimmer, S. (1805/1983). Art. VII. Mother Bunch's Fairy Tales. *Guardian of education, 4,* 412–414. In R. Bator (Ed.), *Signposts of criticism of children's literature* (p. 73). Chicago, IL: America Library Association.

Trimmer, S. (1805/1973). Art. VIII. "Nursery Tales." *Guardian of Education, 4,* 74–75. In V. Haviland (Ed.) *Children and literature: Views and reviews* (p. 7). New York, NY: Lothrop, Lee & Shepard.

Viguers, R. H. (1964). *Margin for surprise*. Boston, MA: Little, Brown.

Watson, V. (2001). *The Cambridge guide to children's books in English*. Cambridge, UK: Cambridge University Press.

Woolf, V. (1939). *Reviewing*. London, UK: Hogarth Press.

34

Awards in Literature for Children and Adolescents

Junko Yokota

National Louis University

A book passes through many hands along its journey to young readers, traveling from author and/or illustrator to editor and from there to designer, publisher, distributor, and booksellers. As described by Michael Cart, the completed book then goes through further evaluation by reviewers, which occurs in the months immediately before and after a book's publication date. Following publication, the book may again be evaluated as it is considered for book awards. Such awards reflect both the excellence of particular titles and the maturity and success of the larger field of children's and young adult literature. In this chapter, book award committee veteran Junko Yokota examines the research related to book awards for what it tells about award processes, what the research may or may not reveal, and raises issues related to awards that remain to be examined.

Awards...the word alone conjures images of banners waving, and celebrations that results in medals, gold stars, and shiny seals on covers of books, announcing their importance to the world.

In recent years, book awards have proliferated, and every year increasing numbers of gold and silver seals are in evidence on the covers of children's and young adult books. Certainly book awards are a meaningful tribute to excellence in writing and illustration, but what precisely *do* they mean? Children are often required to read award-winning literature in school, adults often view award winners as credentials determining worth, publishers see them as moneymakers, and authors and illustrators bask in the recognition.

Awards engender considerable discussion, debate, and written text, both before and after winners are declared,

especially in this age of blogging and listservs. Yet with all that has been talked about and written about, what constitutes research in the area of awards in literature for children and adolescents? In this chapter, I review the research and the issues surrounding awards, and draw considerably on my own experiences of the past 15 years, having served on award committees of 12 different types, some more than once. Through those experiences, I learned many things about how books are considered, debated, and finally selected as award winners, and about the implications of such decisions.

My participation stemmed from volunteering for some committees to being appointed by the organization's president for others, to being nominated and elected by the organization as a whole. The purposes, the processes, the books, the outcomes of these committees were so varied that the experiences are comparable only in the sense that their end result was an award of some type. In particular, the fact is that the award committees I served on span a range of organizations, each representing a different segment of the three fields focused on in this handbook in which literature for children and young adults serves related but varied purposes. Each field sees literature through a different lens, and throughout this chapter I consider those lenses in examining and analyzing the various experiences in order to make recommendations for needed research. Within the section on perspectives on research related to award-winning literature, I delve more deeply into my own experiences and consider their implications for future research.

There are a number of aspects related to awards in literature for children and adolescents that scholars have examined to date, and others that are worthy of study. This chapter examines three: (a) a brief history, description, and process of awarding literature; (b) perspectives on research related to award-winning literature; and (c) researchable issues that may offer considerably more insight into the significance of awards in children's literature.

Part 1: A Brief History and Description of Selected Major Awards

History

The oldest award in literature for children in the English-language world is the John Newbery Medal, established in 1921 at a conference of the American Library Association (ALA) at which publisher Frederick Melcher gave a talk to a group of children's librarians and, in analyzing the response he received, realized that these 300 to 400 people had enormous ability to impact children through their encouragement of the joy of reading. But beyond that, he wanted to go further and elicit librarian interest in the entire process by which books are created for children—how they are produced and brought to children. Although this period in the early 20th century was at a time in the United States when librarians as a group were small in numbers, it was clear to Melcher why he wanted them to be the ones to select the award winners: they worked across many age levels of children (Barker, 1996). The British Library Association established the Carnegie Medal in 1937. Like the Newbery, it sought to improve the literary standards of books for children. And like those in the United States, British librarians were also rare and not considered to be at the forefront of literary innovation. Unlike the Newbery, the Carnegie explicitly states a book's universal appeal as a criterion for the award.

In 1938, the American Library Association established an award for illustration as the Randolph Caldecott Award; in 1955 the British Library Association established the Kate Greenaway Medal for illustration. Both are named in honor of famous Victorian artists. Interestingly, Barker (1996) concluded that the awards for illustration are less

controversial than the debates over the winners and honor books of the awards for writing. He describes this as curious, as if artistic achievement required less intellectual acumen than imaginary writing. He speculates that perhaps it is due to the lack of confidence in artistic evaluation that librarians feel they possess as compared to their confidence in literary judgment, and that much is based on personal reaction to the artistic style of the illustrator.

Considered the most prestigious international award for children's literature, the Hans Christian Andersen Award was established by the International Board on Books for Young People (IBBY) in 1956 for writing, and in 1966 for illustration. It is given on a biannual basis to an author and an illustrator, not for a particular book but for the accumulated body of work created by that person that contributes to children's literature.

Donovan (1986) described how the 1960s was a time of growth in public library services to children and young adults, as well as a time of tremendous expansion of school libraries. He credited part of this growth to the U.S. federal government funding and commitment to materials for children. The desire for librarians to have shopping lists of award winning books perhaps was influential in the development of the series, Awards & Prizes, published biennially from 1969 to 1981, and subsequently every five years in 1986, 1992, 1996. Since then, with the exception of one print version in 2005, it has become an online subscription, listing 322 awards, referencing 8128 books, and 6489 authors and illustrators on the Children's Book Council's web site.

Since the 1960s, a notable trend in awards for children's and young adult literature in the United States has been the establishment of awards that specifically feature particular ethnic groups. The oldest of these, the Coretta Scott King Award, was begun in 1970 and is presented annually to an African American author and an African American illustrator (since 1979) for an "outstandingly inspirational and educational" book. More recently, awards have been added to honor the "Latino/Latina writer and illustrator whose work best portrays, affirms, and celebrates the Latino cultural experience in an outstanding work of literature" (the Pura Belpré Medal, 1996), "to promote Asian/Pacific American culture and heritage, based on literary and artistic merit" (Asian/Pacific American Awards for Literature, 2001), and "to identify and honor the best writing and illustration by and about American Indians" (American Indian Youth Literature Award, 2006).

Another recent notable trend has been the sheer proliferation of awards. In addition to the previously described ethnicity-based awards, over the past two decades at the national level in the United States, book awards have been initiated for specific genres. For example, the American Library Association has initiated awards such as the Theodore Seuss Geisel Award (for the author of the most distinguished American book for beginning readers) and the Robert F. Sibert Informational Book Medal (for the author and illustrator of the most distinguished informational book). The National Council of Teachers of English established the Orbis Pictus Award for Outstanding Nonfiction for Children.

Types of Awards

As can be discerned from this discussion, awards that exist related to children's and young adult books cover a great range of territory. The following outline is provided to give a more complete sense of the different features that characterize the current landscape of children's and young adult book awards:

I. Purpose:
1. Awards bestowed based on popularity
   a. State Book Awards
   b. Children's Choices lists by organizations
2. Awards bestowed on the basis of quality
   a. Text
   b. Illustration
   c. Translation
   d. Author or illustrator's lifetime body of work
3. Awards bestowed on the basis of specific content goals
   a. School subject area: Science, Social Studies, Math, Language Arts, etc.
   b. Peace and social justice
   c. Contests—with the award winner getting published
II. Range of impact:
1. Local awards
2. State awards
3. National awards
4. International awards
5. Special Interest / Needs Population
III. Outcome of award selection process:
1. A collection or list of books
2. A single book (may or may not include runner-up "honor books")

Award Process

The other dimension of importance in this discussion of the nature of book awards is the process by which award winners are arrived at. There is a range of ways that different awards consider, nominate, short-list, and eliminate books. In some cases, all books in a particular time period can be considered by the committee, and committee members are responsible for seeking and selecting eligible books. Other committees only consider books that have first been nominated, vetted, and accepted by a steering committee. In still other cases, the books eligible for consideration by the award committee is a limited short-list that is publicly announced prior to the final discussion.

One path toward an award is that used by the ALA for the Newbery and Caldecott winners: a particular group of people (for these awards, 15 people) choose a particular

book at that particular time. This means that a different group of equally qualified people may have made a different decision. After all, award decisions are made by a group-consensus process and human factors and relations enter into such situations. This is an important point to keep in mind when considering the decision as one that is relative to the circumstances, process, and participants and cannot be considered a definitive and absolute measure of quality.

Although this chapter is on *research* in awards in literature for children and adolescents, what people often want to know is, "What is it *like* to serve on these award committees?" The answer to this question actually does help to frame the consideration of research by examining what people do in the process of making decisions about book awards. I begin with a personal perspective based on my experiences on the various award committees on which I have served. The limitation of this self-reflection for analyzing award processes is that in some cases many years have passed since my actual service on the committee and in other cases the processes have changed somewhat, largely due to developments in digital forms of communication and the resulting possibilities for committee members' virtual engagement. What I describe is based on the experiences of the times on which I served on the various committees.

The International Reading Association's Children's Literature Special Interest Group annually names a set of books to the Notable Books for a Global Society. The National Council of Teachers of English annually names books to the list of Notable Books for Language Arts. The United States Board on Books for Young People annually names a list of Outstanding International Books for Children. All three are selected through a somewhat similar process of having publishers send eligible books to committee members who have been appointed by the sponsoring organization's leadership. In a sense, the publishers are "nominating" books for the list. Each committee member reads, studies, and considers the books that have been sent, and rates them according to the criteria. Then, committee members nominate titles for the final discussion list of the highest-rated books. Committee members meet at length to discuss, debate, and determine the final slate of winning books. Some committees meet face-to-face over an entire day (or two), while others meet in a multi-hour teleconference. After the discussion, each member votes on the specific books that make up the final list of 25 to 35 titles. Because the end product is a group of books rather than a single title, there is less of a sense of high-stakes singular decision for these awards. Rather, one considers the goals of the award (which often reflect the purpose of the organization sponsoring the award), as well as how the set of winning books would look as a balanced whole.

The ALA Association of Library Service to Children's committees such as the Newbery or Caldecott have an elaborate and secretive consensus-building process. Much like other committees, members read throughout a year, and nominate books for final discussion; but the face-to-face meetings are over a period of several days, and the balloting process is a complex formula that reflects the goal of consensus building (a procedural handbook is available online from the Association of Library Service to Children on ALA's website). The intensity of discussion among people who have all read the same set of books makes for lively debate. However, all details regarding the discussions are kept confidential forever. Although only one book is named the winner, honor books can also be named. That group of books (winner and honor books) is considered the winning set for that year's award.

Serving on the Hans Christian Andersen Award Jury was a very different experience for many reasons. First, it is a lifetime achievement award for the body of work created by an illustrator or an author, and each member nation of the International Board on Books for Young People may nominate candidates. Second, because it is an international process as well as an international recognition, jury members are from countries all around the world. Although the language of official communication is English, jury materials and books are submitted in many different languages.

What participation on all award committees have in common is that the initial reading is a fairly solitary act, and note-taking methods and the assessment process is somewhat individualized, although examples and recommendations are often shared by previous committee members. Some committee members prefer to take lengthy, narrative notes that capture nuances of response in journal format, some take very specific and analytical notes directly in books or use post-its to mark passages they are reading, some create forms outlining the criteria with space for remarks, and some create databases with coded notations. I put my data in digitized format because, for me, having searchable files that can be sorted instantly is an important part of how I locate, access, and retrieve information on books that I read. I often assign numerical values and develop coding systems according to the criteria for the award. My notes are brief, but have key words and thoughts that help me remember important points. Others argue that cryptic coding doesn't capture the richness of deep response that should be recalled during discussions. I also need to physically see and move the books around, designating spaces to place the categorized and sorted books by my on-going analysis.

Over the past three years, a significant portion of my award committee work (Hans Christian Andersen, Jane Addams Book Awards) has taken place in online communities. Whereas in earlier years, the transition to the digital communication age entailed moving from sending nominations by postal service to using email, this more recent step has made enormous movement in creating a pathway to instant and constant communication. There are blogs created for the committee that are password protected, and with comments posted by committee members and organized by nominees (whether they are people for

lifetime awards or individual books). This online sharing of information and responses has radically changed the efficiency of award committee work. And certainly, it has changed how conversations about nominees take place. What has yet to be researched is in what ways electronic communication has had (or not had) impact on the outcome of the award winners.

Although some believe that it is the final *product* of books as award winners that is critically important as a means of identifying what gets selected by librarians and teachers to be purchased and read, others believe that it is the *process* of selecting books for awards that is an important lesson by which those on a committee learn more about *how* to critique when evaluating books. Establishing opportunities to practice applying criteria even by those not on the committee is considered a statement of belief about quality for that given award. Participating in various Mock Newbery and Mock Caldecott meetings is an important way to learn *about* the process. How are the various criteria met, and with what enthusiasm? How are "fatal flaws" discovered, discussed, and given credence? How do some books rise to the level of being named as an award winner?

Part 2: Perspectives on Research on Awards in Literature

This volume was developed on the premise that there exist three primary perspectives on research in children's and young adult literature (literary, library and information sciences, and educational) and that these perspectives provide different insights that can profitably complement each other (Coats, K., Enciso, P., Jenkins, C. A., Trites, R. S., & Wolf, S., 2008). So it is also with the topic of research on awards. Scholars from Literature, Education, and Library and Information Sciences have all studied award winning books and, to some degree, the awards/award processes themselves. To an extent, the topics researched vary across perspectives, but in other cases they overlap.

Interestingly, when considering the research on award-winning books, the criteria by which awards are studied often involves factors outside the range of the award's stated purpose. Therefore, these studies are really not research *about* awards, but rather, research on topics such as representation or portrayals of gender, ethnicity, families, etc. in ways that only use the award-winning book as the set of books studied, rather than the reason for the study. This can be a beneficial way to winnow down the enormous number of possible books to study and select a defined set of books that are recognized for their excellence. The high profile of award-winning books also increases the likelihood of recognition, thereby possibly deepening the understanding of the analysis by consumers of the research.

Examination of dissertations studies in the last couple of decades in *Dissertation Abstracts International* reveals that award-winning books were analyzed for their portrayal of gender, character traits depicted, race relations, themes, social class depiction, gender equity, gender representation, portrayal of ethnicity, age, etc. Some study such features as genres that are most popular for certain awards, or settings most predominant in award-winning literature. For example, Parravano (1999) wrote that Newbery winning books tended to portray white, male boys overcoming obstacles. She also found that historical fiction is highly favored. Both findings are intriguing as analysis of award-winning books, but they do not represent research on the award-giving itself. What these kinds of studies have in common is that they all base their study of award-winners ex post facto, or after the fact of the winning books being named.

When researchers decide on the question they ask about award-winning books, do they first consider the criteria by which books were selected for the award? Although it seems a logical step, seldom is there any evidence of analysis in terms of assessing whether books fit/didn't fit the criteria as well as other books. Instead, when researchers consider the sociological impact or the emotional impact of award-winning books, what they study is a completely different reason for selecting the set of books than the angle by which they were selected for the award.

Across all of the disciplinary perspectives that conduct research, studies on awards in literature for children and adolescents have largely focused on content analyses of award winners rather than on the awards themselves (e.g., the processes involved in the awards or the social, readership, or publishing impact of the award).

Perhaps one of the most comprehensive published studies examining a body of award-winning books is Lyn Ellen Lacy's (1986) *Art and Design in Children's Picture Books*, in which she analyzed Caldecott Award winning books from 1938 to 1986, considering the artistic and design elements of line, color, light/dark, shape, and space and how they added up together for the overall visual literacy. After developing an analytical framework, she tested it out with children to make sure that they, too, could grasp those concepts in order to further their understanding.

Preference studies also dominate this field. For example, Flowers (1978) study, "Pupil Preference for Art Media Used in Illustrations of Caldecott Winning Books," showed that first and second graders had a positive and predominant interest in woodcut illustrations. But what becomes of such studies? Do illustrators then go about creating more woodcut illustrations? Do art directors solicit illustrators who are adept at woodcut technique? This is another example of research with award-winning books as the set of books studied, but for which the research study itself was not focused on award-winning at all.

Other types of studies in the field of Library and Information Sciences often focus on the statistical analysis of award winners, e.g., impact of award winners on circulation, relation of award winners to popularity, what types of

books are winning awards, etc. For many years, The Cooperative Children's Book Center (CCBC) at the University of Wisconsin has maintained statistics on approximately how many books for children and teens are published each year in the U.S., and how many of those books are by and/or about people of color. These figures, plus comments on the publishing trends they might represent, are included in the CCBC's annual publication, *CCBC Choices*. Because the librarian field is responsible for the oldest and most highly regarded awards and because the membership is involved in the awarding processes, there is a sense of "ownership" of the awards, and many write reflectively about their own experiences in the process. Some write anecdotal journal-like entries that capture the experience of having been involved in the process (Fiore, 1995; McNeil, 2005). Others write essays that provide information, instruction, and criticism regarding the criteria and selection process for book award committees (Banta, 2004; Erbach, 2008). Although these pieces inform readers about the book award process, they are considered "essays" or "critiques" rather than research.

The work on content analyses of award winners emanating from Literature Departments tends to be analysis of the classic canon of children's literature, and award winning seems to figure as an identifier of a book rather than as the purpose of the research. The literary analyses applied to these older books may not take into consideration the societal and political changes between the time in which the award was given and the time of the analysis. Studies in this area tend to be in such areas as literary elements as developed in award-winning books or comparisons of portrayals in award-winning books across the years.

In the field of Education, the research focuses in large part on the readers themselves, utilizing aspects of reader response to study the ways in which an award-winning book may (or may not) elicit different types of responses from child or teen readers. The award-winning status of books is more a descriptor than a selection factor for research in this area. For example, in Enciso's (1994) research on Spinelli's (1990) *Maniac Magee*, the book seems to have been chosen for specific criteria as a pedagogical tool. The book's Newbery status is significant to this research because of the widespread use of Newbery winners in classrooms, but its Newbery status per se is not the reason or the focus of the research.

Likewise, Ladson-Billings' (2003) research used the same book to examine teacher talk and questioning strategies. The fact that their research focused on children reading a Newbery-Award winning book was not a significant factor to their research or their findings. Sipe's (2008) study of response to literature often features award-winning books as core material that children read and to which they respond. For example, Sipe's research on postmodern picture books features David Wiesner's (2001) Caldecott winner, *The Three Pigs*. Again, the reason for the selection is not the award-winning aspect but rather, the ways in which this book fills the criteria for a central aspect of research on the "postmodern picture book." It is interesting to note that the fact that many of the books featured in studies of reader response are award-winners is rarely mentioned in these studies.

Another type of research in the field of Education focuses on features that are considered important to the teaching of reading. Chamberlain and Leal (1999) examined the readability level of Caldecott winning books because of their belief that while teachers sought beautifully illustrated books, they also needed those books that allowed students "comfortable readability levels." Clearly, their study was pedagogically driven, but "readability" is not included in the determining the Caldecott Award winner as "the most distinguished American picture book for children." Also, as with all readability formulas, the use of the Fry (1977) readability formula is limited to uniformly and objectively measurable features such as sentence length and number of syllables within a passage. On the one hand, the mechanics of such measures are not particularly relevant to determining an award to the illustrator of the year's most distinguished picture book. On the other hand, one can understand this reasoning from a pedagogical point of view to the researchers and teachers who seek such information.

Chamberlain and Leal's (1999) study also evaluated the Caldecott books for cultural focus in order to meet the needs of diversity in education; again, this is of no consideration when awarding a Caldecott Medal. This type of research can be valuable for a number of pedagogical reasons, but they rely on a surface level of content analysis and do not provide much insight for the study of award-winning children's literature.

In the field of educational publishing, considerable attention is given to books that are award-winners, perhaps to give credibility to the pedagogical product created with award-winning books as the basis. Publishers rely heavily on award-winners when selecting the material to be included in reading series and for curriculum support, appreciate the scrutiny given to books that win awards, and value the attention that awards give to books. There is much in-house research done by publishing companies on what awards have been won by the literature they select for reading texts, but because such research is conducted specifically for development and marketing of a single publisher's materials, the results are not found outside the publishing company's internal or marketing papers. Some of this information may be gleaned through an examination of the teacher's guides to reading curriculum materials used in schools.

Finally, there is also a body of research conducted from an historical perspective on award winners. Leonard Marcus's (1998, 2008) work is a prime example. He has studied various aspects of the history of children's literature, and discusses the impact of awards on books, trends, themes, etc. but within the context of the larger picture of the history of children's literature, including the people who played prominent roles within the development of children's literature, and the various sociopolitical and cultural factors that were significant to the development of children's publishing. Kidd (2007) also provides a historical overview of "prizing" in children's literature, the changes over time, and contexts in which prize-giving has evolved. Other studies of a narrower span of years also offer a historical perspective on book awards. For example, Jenkins' (1996) study examined the conflict between librarians and educators regarding children's reading as they played out in an ongoing debate over Newbery Award criteria in the years immediately before and during World War II. Do such historical studies of children's book awards have an impact on the field today? Have such studies influenced award process changes over time?

Part 3: Researchable Issues Related to Children's Literature Awards

One conclusion from this review of the research literature is how little actual research has been published related to the winning of awards in the fields of children's and young adult literature. There have been various analyses of award-winning literature but little attention given to the awards themselves. In this section I highlight and address a number of key issues and questions that could profitably be examined in future research on awards in literature for young readers. I have organized this discussion around what I see as the key issues and research questions that could add a great deal of valuable data and insights to our understanding of awards and children's literature.

Issue: What does it mean to have won an award? What is the impact of awards on what is getting published, noticed, sold, and read?

K. T. Horning (1997) notes the practical significance of awards when she says, "Awards always make a huge difference because they bring people's attention to particular books, no matter what the award is for" (p. x). What does this mean to the children who read the books? The librarians who select them and make them available? The teachers who choose to teach through those books, therefore making them what all students are required to read? The parents who buy them as gifts? The impact of award winning is surely different for creators than it is for consumers.

What impact do awards have on authors, illustrators, and the publishers who create the books? Through conversations and in their talks, authors and illustrators often say that winning an award means their next book is more likely to be seriously considered for publication. Others indicate that winning a major award frees them to try something new— to reconsider their work. The increased name recognition and the assured income from the award winning book sales gives them financial support as well as publisher support in taking some risk to try something different. Winning an award means having a book that may be more likely to stay in print longer. As Donovan (1991) noted, a book that wins a Caldecott Medal can experience a substantial increase in sales and thus remain in print for a very long time. A Caldecott Award can boost book sales by as many as 60,000 additional copies. Other authors and publishers might also look to award-winning books as guides for their future works (Weitzman, 1972). Of course, the level of prestige of the award determines its impact. Publishers consider ALA's awards to be the most important in terms of impacting sales. The news media do as well, demonstrated in the yearly appearance of winners of the Newbery, Caldecott and the Coretta Scott King Awards on *The Today Show* the morning after the awards are announced.

However, Bill Morris, long-time children's book marketing director for HarperCollins publishing company, was known to have said that it was better for a Harper book to be named to the Texas Bluebonnet children's choice list than to win a Newbery or Caldecott. For publishers, winning a Newbery or Caldecott award means hosting dinners, sending author and illustrators on book tours and speaking appearances, and other events at publisher expense. For state awards like the Bluebonnet, children choose the winner from a predetermined list of titles, and librarians purchase multiple copies of each title for children to read and vote on. Sales of the winning title might or might not increase significantly, but all books on the list were already winners from the publisher's perspective in terms of sales.

What does winning an award mean on a global level? How do books get attention for international publication and translation? At the annual Bologna Children's Book Fair, the largest of its kind in the world, or at the Frankfurt Book Fair, or other places where international rights are bought and sold, books that have won awards in their home countries do get attention (although the enormous impact of mass media popularity cannot be overlooked). An award gives the book a distinguished pedigree. Passing the test of this scrutiny means that the book is worthy of international publication possibilities.

Issue: What impact do awards for excellence and ethnicity have on children's book selection?

Horning (1997) noted the value of multicultural awards in helping scholars and teachers get perspectives from cultural insiders as to what constitutes quality and is culturally authentic in multicultural literature. Some, like editor and author Marc Aronson (2001) argue that we should change the ethnic heritage criteria of ethnic-focused awards (i.e., Coretta Scott King, Pura Belpré) because we have come to an era in which the winners of major awards (i.e., Newbery, Caldecott, Printz) have included people of historically underrepresented groups. But Andrea Davis Pinkney (2001) and others continue to see the need, contending that such awards are meant to inspire and lift up the hopes of the

children who need to see "one of their own" as winners; that it is more than the recognition of a book for its merit as a creation alone, but a need to recognize the ethnicity of the creator. One consideration of their debate is to assess whether the purpose of such awards is to honor the book, the person who created the book, or to point to a culturally-vetted list of books that are of high quality from a cultural insider perspective. The Newbery and Caldecott Award winners have long been criticized—and continue to be criticized—for lack of diversity in award winning books. All of the ethnic-based awards have among their goals the advancement of quality in the literature reflecting the lives of the people and increasing the visibility of this literature in children's publishing overall. Will there be a future time when the Coretta Scott King Awards are, like Negro League baseball, a phenomenon of the past?

Contests have been critically important in the development of multicultural literature. Such contests are created to support the publication in focused areas of need and to discover new authors and illustrators. In perhaps the most well-known affirmation of the importance of writing contests, the Council on Interracial Books for Children (CIBC), was founded in 1965 to facilitate and promote high-quality multicultural literature for children. The organization published a journal (the *CIBC Bulletin*) and in 1969 it established an annual writing contest open to "previously unpublished writers in African American, Asian American, and Native American communities." Twenty-one winning manuscripts from the contest's first five years were published by mainstream children's publishers. Several winners (e.g., Virginia Driving Hawk Sneve, Mildred D. Taylor, Sharon Bell Matthis) went on to distinguished careers as children's authors. Winner of the 1974 contest, Taylor's manuscript was published as *Song of the Trees* in 1975, and she went on to win the 1976 Newbery Medal for *Roll of Thunder, Hear My Cry* (Banfield, 1998).

Despite the example of Taylor's remarkable career, it appears that there has been no systematic research on the impact of prizes and contests on the development of careers in children's publishing. How have the winners of the Coretta Scott King Award fared in their subsequent careers as authors or illustrators since the award was established in 1969? What is the career impact of winning the Coretta Scott King Committee's John Steptoe New Talent Award, an award given to authors and illustrators who have previously published three or fewer works (EMIERT, n.d.).

Issue: What is the historical impact of trends in the field on awards and vice versa?

Kidd's (2007) research on the Newbery Medal-winning books notes trends in how the books parallel or reflect the historical and political times during which they are awarded. Such research takes a deep look at a phenomenon, making connections and drawing conclusions based on content analysis. Another example of this kind of work is Leonard Marcus's (1992) biography of Margaret Wise

Brown, in which he notes the ways in which the development of her work was influenced by the educational politics of the time. His recent book, *Minders of Make Believe: Idealists, Entrepreneurs, and the Shaping of American Children's Literature* (2008), is not specially about book awards, but the information he includes about award-winning in relation to publishing industry history makes it clear that awards did play a role in this history of children's literature in the United States. In *Dear Genius: The Letters of Ursula Nordstrom, Marcus* (1998) explores the correspondence between the famous children's book editor Nordstrom and the authors and illustrators with whom she worked, many of whom won book awards.

Issue: What is the effect of gender in the history of awards in literature?

Jenkins (1996) traces the roots of the gender-based debate on the proprietary rights of who administers the major awards in children's literature. She examines the early history of children's librarianship as a field deemed particularly suited to women, whose activities included creating lists of recommended books for children's library collections. By the early 20th century, these recommendations became the basis for critical standards of excellence in children's literature, which eventually led to the establishment of the Newbery and Caldecott Awards. The fact that the field consisted primarily of women who had trained and worked together to establish the key role of children's librarians as arbiters of literary merit did not go unnoticed.

By the late 1930s, the role of children's librarians in determining book awards was being challenged by those who expressed doubt that these female librarians were capable of selecting Newbery and Caldecott winners that would appeal to "the average tousle-headed American boy" (Certain, 1939, p. 828). These challenges to the authority of women to bestow these prestigious book awards were a reflection of a larger effort to defend and maintain the overall male-dominated status quo of the publishing industry. In fact, children's librarianship is still a female-intensive field and the Association of Library Service to Children (ALSC) is still in charge of the Newbery and Caldecott Medals. What role might gender play in future concerns about these and other ALSC-selected book awards?

Issue: What research can be conducted on the awarding process?

Although the basic steps of award processes are clearly articulated at a procedural level, the specific details are strictly confidential. Because the process is not transparent, except procedurally, the part of the process that could be most interesting eludes research potential. However, there are aspects of the award process that are researchable and have the potential to inform various constituents in interesting and worthwhile ways. Research on the process and its dissemination might—or might not—lead to calls for

changes in the award process, criteria, or composition of award committees, depending on what is learned. One potentially interesting area regarding process could be to analyze the people behind the awards. What is the background of committee members? What are their reading preferences? What are their biases? Does the "regional balance" matter in committee appointments as much as individual preferences and biases? Committee members could participate in self-reported studies on their perceptions of the process. Research could be done on and/or by the very people who are the decision makers. At present, researchers can only examine the artifacts and outcomes of book awards.

What about the influence of the opinions of others? Committee members have access to published reviews by professional or volunteer reviewers. They may also read listserv discussions and blogs, participate in book discussions, or solicit children's responses to books under consideration for awards. To what degree do individual committee members bring pre-formulated opinions and responses to award discussions and to what degree do they remain open to others' perspectives within award committee discussions? Are committee members participating on award committees as individuals or as representatives of a wider community?

Issue: Why is there a lack of correlation between awards selected by adults and by children?

Adults select books that they believe children should read. Awards selected by children are usually selected from a master reading list that adults create. But determining popularity with children is as varied a process as with adults. State awards are typically children's choice awards. Depending on the state, children must read 3–5 books from a list of 10–20 titles in order to vote on the winners. Thus the proportion of titles read from the full list varies by state. In Arizona, for example, children must read or have read to them, at least 5 out of the 10 books (50%) to vote for the Grand Canyon Reader Award. In Florida, children must read at least 3 out of 15 books (20%) to vote for the Sunshine State Young Reader's Award. In Illinois, children must read at least 3 out of 20 (15%) to vote for the Rebecca Caudill Award. What is the process by which librarians and teachers decide upon the list of books eligible for each year's children's choice award? What, if any, impact does the variable proportion of titles read have on voting patterns from state to state?

Issue: What is the relationship between award-winning books and popular reading material?

Research on the popularity of award-winning books examines such factors as library circulation and book sales to determine the popularity of books that win awards or receive highly favorable reviews in professional journals. Lamme's (1976) study found that middle school students seldom chose to read award winners or even books that were on lists of high quality literature, but those students who did read from such lists were no better readers than those who read books that were not highly recommended by award committees or adult reviewers. Likewise, when Nilsen, Peterson, and Searfoss (1980) compiled a list of books deemed by critics to be of high quality, the books were usually at the bottom of lists librarians deemed to be popular with children. This is in line with Ujiie and Krashen's (2002) study in which the "home run books" that stimulated children to want to read more were seldom the same as those that had been prize-winners. Their analysis of public library acquisition and circulation led them to conclude that prize winning does not overshadow popularity in librarian purchases, nor does it impact circulation over popular books, such as series books. In a later study, Ujiie and Krashen (2006) found that overall, prize-winning books were not often found on bestseller lists. Interestingly, they also found that bestsellers were no easier than prize-winning books when it came to readability, and in fact, were slightly higher. Librarians in their study reported fewer prizewinners in their collection than popular bestsellers, an indication that perhaps they valued the likelihood of circulation over high critical acclaim. Ujiie and Krashen raised the question whether children simply don't recognize high literary quality or whether judges of Newbery and Caldecott medals have different standards for their selection than do children.

Issue: How fully do award-winning books match the criteria for the award(s)?

Researchers could analyze award winners based on the criteria creating rubrics for which criterion is most prominently represented in the awarding process. When books win multiple awards, which criteria cross over those awards?

Issue: Who defines excellence in children's literature and in what ways? How does a committee define an elusive criterion such as "most distinguished contribution"?

Netell (1990) describes the defensive defiance of award selectors who feel insecure in their own critical abilities and the need to defend their choices as well as the inevitable idiosyncrasy of committee members in selecting the best book. We make different choices, even when criteria are spelled out. Mock Newbery/Caldecotts are examples of such. Therefore, Netell, editor of book reviews for The Guardian and the chair of the Guardian Children's Fiction Award, argues that rather than selecting one best book that he believes is a subjective process, we should be recognizing quality works and authors more broadly. To that end, previous winners are disqualified. Selected books must be ones that are special: they should push the frontiers of children's literature by expanding young imaginations, widening their world, allowing them to explore new ideas, emotions, language, and experiences, and perhaps in doing so demanding something from its readers in return. The

award keeps child readers as the primary audience, but recognizes that by definition of special books they will likely appeal to the more experienced readers.

Miller (1998) raised the issue that authors of Newbery winners and their books' protagonists have been the same race for 21 years. She builds her case on the earlier statement by Parravano and Adams (1996) on 10 years of Newbery winners and authors as not showing diversity (which is not a criteria for the Newbery). But in the context of this discussion, what is interesting to consider is her point as to whether the cause can be attributed to the "interpretive nature of deciding what is 'distinguished'." Therein lies the key question: who decides and how is it decided, and why is it that none of that discussion can be made public, not for the specifics of the secret discussions, but more generally about how "distinction" is noted. Miller's background in having a master's degree in rhetoric is interesting in how she analyzes the wording of the Newbery Award's definition of "distinguished." As individuals who compose a committee, each person brings his or her biases, agendas, and evaluative lenses. Miller cites Scales (1996), Atkinson (1996), and Sutherland (1986), all acknowledging the subjective nature of defining "distinguished." Atkinson (1996) describes committee members as individuals whose backgrounds influence values and priorities and are imperfect people who collectively make a group decision at a particular time and place. If this were to be researched, it could result in recommendations for committee membership.

Arthur Applebee (1993) conducted a study of secondary students and how they responded on questions about literature they had read. Interestingly, African Americans scored well on questions about African American literature, and this was especially notable when you consider that they had done worse on other questions where their ethnic background did not match the literature. What might research reveal on how the background of committee members influenced the ways in which they discussed books and expressed examples about what was "distinguished"? Although there is attempt to balance committees for representation, the gender imbalance is particularly noteworthy. Rarely do the award committees in children's literature have more than one or two men on committees of 10 to 15. In what ways are we considering gender biases in decisions that are made? Speculation exists and is published on these issues; however, research has not been published widely.

Part 4: Conclusion

What do we know about award-winning literature for children and adolescents and what remains to know that is worth finding out? What kinds of research can advance our understanding of awards? Are there cross-disciplinary ways to cooperate on joint research that extends understanding of awards in literature for children and adolescents?

There is a great deal written *about* awards in children's literature, the vast majority of which is perhaps characterized as "informed perspective." These include self-reflections and opinion pieces, and they frequently offer interesting ideas for consideration and insightful perspectives, especially about what it means to be on award committees. Many even suggest promising research questions to be analyzed or even sources of data. But such pieces are not actual research because the data they report on have not been gathered or analyzed following systematic research methodologies.

Part of the reason that the current literature on awards is largely informed opinion is that the authors of such pieces do not write with research methodology as their framework for thinking about analyzing awards. But perhaps more importantly, their careers and their reason for writing are not focused on conducting or publishing research. Rather, they write to participate as professionals, reflect on their roles, and share what they have learned as part of the children's/YA literature community.

It is possible that what has been written as informed perspectives may be useful as data for conducting secondary analysis. One could analyze what various authors have to say in order to identify interesting future research studies and/or ways of collecting new data. Some possibilities include systematically gathering informed perspectives on the processes of committee members. Another possibility is to tap into the rich field of award acceptance speeches. They are frequently recorded, published, and made accessible. They could be used as data sources to research the impact of award winning on the actual creators of the literature. One caveat as to their usefulness is, as Thompson (1988) notes, that out of the context of their celebratory moment of delivery, these speeches alternate between "charming and gossipy" and "critically insightful."

Another way to go about conducting research in areas with topics known to be provocative is to consider what informed opinions have been stated, but not backed up with research. For example, Anita Silvey (1986) wrote an editorial in *The Horn Book* in which she poses the question, "Could Randolph Caldecott win the Caldecott Medal?" She explains that for the first 50 years of the medal, the books awarded honored what he stood for.

But in years immediately preceding her editorial, Silvey notes that "High art, high gloss, decoration, emotionless embellishment seem to be the most recent standards for what we are calling distinguished" (Silvey, 1986; online page), thereby endorsing Bader's (1986) assessment that the definition for what is classified as distinguished has changed.

This is an editorial, and Bader's statement is an essay within for the Newbery/Caldecott volume published periodically by *The Horn Book*. A systematic analysis of the books over the years Silvey referred to would serve to endorse or refute Silvey's and Bader's claims, and that would be interesting research.

In terms of methodologies, studies might document the award-giving processes but with the requirements of reporting data in ways that adhere to triangulation and the writing of "thick description." Interviews and case studies with reflexive analysis are among the qualitative methodologies that may be appropriate for some studies related to the impact of awards in children's literature. Bradford (2009) describes her work in critical analysis of literature as both an examination of linguistic and narrative features but also situated in historical context and cultural forces. This type of research brings together the analytical lenses of cross-disciplinary analysis, and could richly contribute to the study of books that have won awards in children's literature.

Is award-winning still relevant today? With the proliferation in recent years, does the field really need as many as there are? Many people have an opinion in this debate. There is considerable speculation and off-the-cuff theorizing but the thoughts, though adamantly expressed, are not grounded in research. At present, there are many published articles on a myriad of topics related to award-winning, and many are provocatively presented arguments, inviting response and discussion in ways that engage readers to think and take a stance, but seldom yield data that can be considered research (e.g., Aronson, 2001; Grimes, 2009; Pinkney, 2001; Silvey, 2008). In Lillian Gerhardt's 1999 Arbuthnot Honor Lecture (interestingly, an award in and of itself), proposed a study that she described as "needed... wanted...useful[:] a cross-cultural study of the working relationships of all who are involved with children and their books" (p. 22). She called for a level of documentation that ALA has never had for its youth services divisions. She describes the impact of ALA awards in influencing sales. Gerhardt envisions "a cross-disciplinary team of historians, sociologists, anthropologists, statisticians and scholars of children's literature to analyze and evaluate all the forces—social, economic, political, cultural—that affect the selection of books for library collections" (p. 23).

Specifically, there is a need for research that will make a difference in the future of children's literature. Hand in hand with the need for more research is the need for more readers and digesters and learners from that research. In other words, what will make the research worthwhile? I posed this question to editor/author/scholar Marc Aronson (personal communication, January 25, 2010), who speculated that publishers would be interested in research on book awards if it: (a) appeared in accessible and nonacademic journals; (b) was published in a format that would enable the reader to quickly identify and read essential research findings; (c) had significant implications for the work of editors and marketing people, particularly in terms of saving money.

Earlier research on children's book awards was basically market research, but Aronson (2010) believes that we are now in an era of assessment and accountability that requires more relevant research questions and more nuanced data analysis. Speaking as an author of highly regarded nonfiction, Aronson places a high value on rigorous research. Speaking as an editor of books for children and teens, Aronson believes that increasing the quality and rigor of research on book awards could provide better and more useful information that can help publishers develop books for future generations of young readers.

One way to consider this is to do research that builds on earlier studies. In other words, if someone has done a thorough analysis of the portrayal of schools in award-winning literature, the next layer might be to do reader-response research on the impact of such portrayals on readers' perceptions of school, based on what they read. Could such findings be of interest to editors and writers as they consider their work in creating future potential award-winning literature? Could such findings be of interest to teacher educators as they learn how to scaffold student discussion and student learning through their questioning strategies?

There is much potential for conducting research focused on awards in literature for children and adolescents. In addition to the possibilities discussed earlier in the chapter the following have especially interesting potential:

- Relationship between what reading curriculum recommends and criteria for awards;
- Relationship between what children choose and what adults choose;
- Response from children after reading what adults have chosen and what other children have chosen;
- Relationship between awards for traditional books and the future of awards for newer formats of digitized media.

How do awards and lists impact teacher choice for read aloud, classroom libraries and curriculum study support?

Clearly, there is need for more research on the awards in literature for children and adolescents. Perhaps what should be considered first is who the audience is for such research, and what will matter most for that audience. What implications will they have once the research is completed? Will the results of such research impact future authors and illustrators as they create books? Will it guide the editor or art director who "shapes" the direction of a book's development? Will it inform those who are making decisions about the awards themselves? Will studying the process of how award winners are selected demystify the process? How might a more transparent process help us as we recommend award winners to readers? Whatever the answers to these questions, award-winning literature will continue to be introduced to children and young adults. And some of those young people will continue to find in those award winners the books that they will read, reread, and treasure.

Literature References

Spinelli, J. (1990). *Maniac Magee*. New York, NY: Little, Brown.
Taylor, M.D. (1975). *Song of the trees*. New York, NY: Dial Press
Taylor, M.D. (1976). *Roll of thunder, hear my cry*. New York, NY: Dial Press.
Wiesner, D. (2001). *The Three pigs*. New York, NY: Clarion.

Academic References

American Indian Library Association. American Indian youth literature award. (n.d.). Retrieved March 4, 2010, from http://www.ailanet.org/activities/AIYLA_Criteria_5_09.pdf
Applebee, A. N. (1993). *Literature in the secondary school: Studies of curriculum and instruction in the United States*. Urbana, IL: National Council of Teachers of English.
Aronson, M. (2001). Slippery slopes and proliferating prizes. *The Horn Book Magazine, 77*, 271–78.
Atkinson, J. L. (1996). Oh, the places you'll go! (and won't) with Newberys. *Journal of Youth Services in Libraries, 10*(Fall), 46–57.
Bader, B. (1986). The Caldecott spectrum. In L. Kingman (Ed.), *Newbery and Caldecott Medal Books: 1976–1985* (pp. 279–312). Boston, MA: Horn Book.
Banta, G. J. (2004). Reading pictures: Searching for excellence in picture books. In *Association for Library Service to Children The Newbery and Caldecott Awards: A Guide to the Medal and Honor Books* (pp. 9–18). Chicago, IL: American Library Association.
Barker, K. (1996). Prizes and prizewinners. In P. Hunt (Ed.), *International companion encyclopedia of children's literature* (pp. 508–18). London, UK: Routledge.
Bradford, C. (2009, December). *Critical content analysis of children's texts: Theories, methodologies and critique*. Presentation at the 59th National Reading Conference, Albuquerque, NM.
Certain, C. C. (1939). Editorial: Open forum on the Newbery Award. *Elementary English Review, 16*(7), 283. Cited in Jenkins, C. A. (1996). Women of ALA youth services and professional jurisdiction: of nightingales, newberies, realism, and the right books, 1937–1945. (Imagination and Scholarship: The Contributions of Women to American Youth Services and Literature). *Library Trends, 44*(4), 813–827.
Chamberlain, J., & Leal, D. (1999). Caldecott medal books and readability levels: Not just "picture" books. *Reading Teacher, 52*(8), 898–902.
Coats, K., Enciso, P., Jenkins, C. A., Trites, R. S., & Wolf, S. (2008). Schools of thought. *The Horn Book Magazine, 84*(5), 523–536.
Coretta Scott King Award. (n.d). Available at http://www.ala.org/ala/mgrps/rts/emiert/cskbookawards/about.cfm
Donovan, J. (1986). Introduction. *Children's books: Awards & prizes*. New York, NY: The Children's Book Council.
Donovan, J. (1991). Children's publishing on the ascent. *Publishing Research Quarterly, 7*(3), 7–14.
Enciso, P. E. (1994). Cultural identity and response to literature: Running lessons from *Maniac Magee*. *Language Arts, 71*, 524–533.
Erbach, M. M. (2008). The art of the picture book. In Association for Library Service to Children. *The Newbery and Caldecott awards: A guide to the medal and honor books* (pp. 9–17). Chicago, IL: American Library Association.
Ethnic & Multicultural Information Exchange Round Table (EMIERT). (n.d.). American Library Association. John Steptoe New Talent Award. Retrieved February 22, 2010, from http://www.ala.org/ala/mgrps/rts/emiert/cskbookawards/johnsteptoe.cfm
Fiore, C. (1995). Life on the Caldecott committee. In Association

for Library Service to Children. *The Newbery and Caldecott awards: A guide to the medal and honor books* (pp. 10–16). Chicago, IL: American Library Association.

Flowers, W. J. D. (1978). P*upil preference for art media used in illustrations of Caldecott award winning books.* Unpublished doctoral dissertation, University of Oklahoma, Oklahoma City, OK.

Fry, E. (1977). Fry's readability graph: Clarifications, validity, and extension to level 17. *Journal of Reading, 21*(3), 242–252.

Gerhardt, L. N. (1999). The 1999 May Hill Arbuthnot honor lecture: Editorial license. *Journal of Youth Services in Libraries, 12*(4), 22–24.

Grimes, N. (2009). Speaking out. *The Horn Book Magazine, 85*(4), 391–393.

Horning, K. T. (1997). *From cover to cover: Evaluating and reviewing children's books.* New York, NY: HarperCollins.

Jenkins, C. A. (1996). Women of ALA youth services and professional jurisdiction: Of nightingales, Newberies, realism, and the right books, 1937–45. *Library Trends, 44*(4), 813–839.

Kidd, K. (2007). Prizing children's literature: The case of Newbery gold. *Children's Literature, 35,* 166–190.

Lacy, L. E. (1986). *Art and design in children's picture books: An analysis of Caldecott award-winning illustrations.* Chicago, IL: American Library Association.

Ladson-Billings, G. (2003, November). *Still playing in the dark: Whiteness in the literary imagination of children's and young adult literature.* Paper presented at the 93rd Annual Convention of the National Conference of Teachers of English, Detroit, MI.

Lamme, L. (1976). Are reading habits and abilities related? *Reading Teacher, 30*(1), 21–27.

Leal, D. J., & Chaberlain-Solecki, J. (1998). A Newbery medal-winning combination: High student interest plus appropriate readability levels. *The Reading Teacher, 51,* 712–714.

Marcus, L. S. (1992). Margaret Wise Brown: Awakened by the moon. Boston, MA: Beacon Press.

Marcus, L. S. (1998). *Dear genius: The letters of Ursula Nordstrom.* New York, NY: HarperCollins.

Marcus, L. S. (2008). *Minders of make believe: Idealists, entrepreneurs, and the shaping of American children's literature.* Boston, MA: Houghton Mifflin.

McNeil, H. (2005). "Forty hundred books": A single mother's year with the Newbery. *Children and Libraries, 3*(2), 29–35.

Miller, B. J. F. (1998). What color is gold? Twenty-one years of same-race authors and protagonists in the Newbery medal. *Journal of Youth Services in Libraries, 12*(1), 34–39.

Netell, S. (1990). Children's books: Always back of the queue? In M. Hayhoe & S. Parker (Eds.), *Reading and response* (pp. 107–114). Buckingham, UK: Open University Press.

Nilsen, A. P., Peterson, R., & Searfoss. L. W. (1980). The adult as critic vs. the child as reader. *Language Arts 57*(5), 530–539.

Parravano, M. V. (1999). Alive and vigorous: Questioning the Newbery, *The Horn Book Magazine, 75,* 434–444.

Parravano, M. V., & Adams, L. (1996). A wider vision for the Newbery. *The Horn Book Magazine, 72*(1), 4–5.

Pinkney, A. D. (2001). Awards that stand on solid ground. *The Horn Book Magazine, 77*(5), 535–539.

Pura Belpré Medal. (n.d.). Available at http://www.ala.org/ala/mgrps/divs/alsc/awardsgrants/bookmedia/belpremedal/index.cfm

Scales, P. (1996). What the Newbery means to me. *Journal of Youth Services in Libraries, 10*(Fall), 77–78.

Silvey, A. (1986). Editorial: Could Randolph Caldecott win the Caldecott Medal? *The Horn Book Magazine,* Retrieved March 2, 2010, from http://www.hbook.com/magazine/editorials/jul86.asp

Silvey, A. (2008, October). Has the Newbery lost its way? *School Library Journal.* Retrieved March 2, 2010, from: http://www.schoollibraryjournal.com/article/CA6600688.html

Sipe, L. (2008). First graders interpret David Wiesner's *The Three Pigs:* A case study. In L. R. Sipe & S. J. Pantaleo (Eds.) *Postmodern picturebooks: Play, parody and self-referentiality* (pp. 223–237). London, UK: Routledge.

Sutherland, Z. (1986). Newbery Medal Books, 1976–1985. In L. Kingman (Ed.). *Newbery and Caldecott medal books 1976–1985* (pp. 153–164). Boston, MA: The Horn Book.

Thompson, R. A. (1988). Children's books: Awards and medals. *Children's Literature Association Quarterly, 13*(2), 96.

Ujiie, J., & Krashen. S. (2002). Are prize-winning books popular among children? An analysis of public library circulation. *Knowledge Quest, 31*(1) 36–37.

Ujiie, J., & Krashen. S. (2006). Home run books and reading enjoyment. *Knowledge Quest, 34*(3), 33–35.

Weitzman, L. J. (1972). Sex role socialization in picture books for preschool children. *American Journal of Sociology, 77*(6), 1125–1150.

35

The Economics of Children's Book Publishing in the 21st Century

Joel Taxel

The University of Georgia

Joel Taxel has long been for looking at children's literature with a critical eye—an eye keen to discern the subtle and not-so-subtle issues surrounding multiculturalism in children's literature. More recently, he has turned his gaze to the globalization of children's literature, questioning the combination of conglomerates and commercialization in literature for the young. From Harry Potter promoting Coca-Cola to Madonna's foray into the children's book world, Taxel reveals the merchandizing emphasis on controlling consumption from birth to the beyond, with less focus on the aesthetic quality of texts than on the bottom line. Still, Taxel argues that it would be "an error to examine cultural phenomena without reference to human agency." A number of editors and publishers are devoted to producing books of "breathtaking quality" with new and challenging visions for children, and children, who can be quite discerning themselves, are eager to take them up.

Setting the Stage

The past several decades have witnessed momentous changes in the global children's book business. Characterized as "an explosion of almost Cambrian proportions," these changes are a product of "shifts in the economic landscape" that have resulted in a fundamental alteration in publishing practices, including the attraction of "new and diverse entrants to the sector" (Crandall, 2006a, p. 1). In *Children's Book Publishing in Britain since 1945*, Reynolds and Tucker (1998) observed that "there is nothing natural about the children's book scene today," and they noted that children's books are "a product of historical circumstance, ideology, and market forces" (p. xi). Since these factors, forces, and circumstances differ from country to country, the children's book scene varies in each locale, although the publishing industry is connected and interconnected in ways that would have been inconceivable even 50 years ago.

This chapter focuses on how profound changes in market or economic forces have transformed not only the book publishing business, but the larger "culture industry" in which it is embedded. Despite this emphasis, it is necessary to at least point to historical, ideological, and political forces since they often connect directly to the economic realm. In the United States, for example, passage of the National Defense Education Act, a response to the Soviet Union's launching of the *Sputnik* satellite in 1957, provided federal funds for library books and resulted in a dramatic surge in the school market that brought it to the forefront of children's book publication (Epstein, 1996). The shifting political and ideological landscape that led to the U.S. Supreme Court's 1954 decision outlawing segregation in schools gave impetus to the nascent civil rights movement, helped focus attention on what Larrick (1972) famously termed the "all-white world of children's books," and provided the impetus for passage of the 1965 Elementary and Secondary Education Act which infused money to American school and public libraries. This landmark legislation created, for the first time, a viable market for books about Black children (Marcus, 1997).

By 1964, the Labour Government in Britain had increased school and public library funding by 30% (Tucker, 1998), and, while business considerations alone justified this financial support, children's needs clearly were central considerations in fostering the development of children's collections and child-friendly library environments (Reynolds, 1998). The effect of this enhanced support in both countries helped make librarians a dominant influence on the editorial programs at major trade houses (Epstein, 1996), the "arbiters of what children should read" (Eccleshare, 1991, p. 20), a relationship that began to change in the late 1960s and 1970s as government money for libraries was radically reduced. It is important to note that in the United States this was due primarily to the economic downturn during the Vietnam War (Giblin, 1986).

Similar developments in the political and ideological sphere were at work in Canada. Prior to the mid-20th century, Canadian national identity was an amalgam of French, British, and American values and cultures, and tensions between them had existed since the 18th century. In the aftermath of the eclipse of British imperial power following World War II, a strong national identity began to develop, although Canada's continued links to the U.S. economy led to a "double colonial burden-dependence on Britain and on the U.S." (Bainbridge & Wolodko, 2002, p. 21). Seeking to transcend this history and develop a distinctive national identity, Canadians in the latter part of the 20th century created a national canon, a development fostered by subsidies from the Canadian federal government (Bainbridge & Wolodko, 2002; Stan, 1999).

There also are instances around the globe where historical events rapidly and dramatically altered the political and economic landscapes of nations and, as a result, the way children's literature is conceived, written, and published. This occurred most notably in countries where the communist system disintegrated, or was significantly altered. The fall of communism in the former Soviet Union and Eastern Europe, for example, ushered in a political revolution and the beginnings of market-based economies and accordingly paved the way for radically different approaches to children's book publishing in Russia (Frenkel, 1994; Kudriavtseva, 1994), Germany (Stottele, 1994), and Hungary (Lechner, 1994). Likewise, China's tumultuous history has had a discernable impact on its children's literature industry. From the "Fourth of May" cultural movement early in the 20th century when China began to produce a native children's literature (Allsobrook, 2006; Chen, 2006), to the turbulent period of the Great Cultural Revolution (1966–76) when children's literature stagnated and little was produced (Chen, 2006; Rui, 2006), to the current moment when "class struggle" has been supplanted by the "four modernisations" and "ideological purity has given way to pragmatism" (Lijun, 2003, p. 71), the impact of developments in the political sphere has been clear and demonstrable.

My point is that changes in a nation's sociocultural and political arrangements and institutions have a significant impact on cultural institutions, including the manner in which books for young people are written and published. Since these matters often are specific to each country, or group of countries, there is little doubt that discussions of this sort could be the subject of a separate chapter. The focus here instead is on the seismic, world-wide shifts in the economic realm whereby the book publishing industry, as well as newspapers, magazines, television and radio stations, film and record companies, etc., have been absorbed and integrated into giant multinational media corporations whose business practices are transforming the production and consumption of children's literature and popular culture around the world.

While I seek to provide a global perspective on these developments, admittedly much of the discussion does have a distinctly American and British slant. This emphasis is due both to my own limitations and to the enormity of the enterprise of providing even a cursory view of children's book publication around the world. It also speaks to the reality that, for better or worse, the United States and the English language are now dominant cultural forces around the globe. Contemporary media and cultural industries are characterized by accelerating competitiveness, a concentration of ownership, technological convergence, and globalization. As a result, publishing and other media industries increasingly are dominated by a handful of large, multinational companies (Buckingham & Scanlon, 2005) who are able to "synergistically" link their various holdings across national borders and reach countless millions of readers and viewers.

Because many, if not all, of the dominant media corporations have primarily Anglo-American ownership (e.g., the News Corporation, the Walt Disney Company, Viacom) or enormous presences in the English speaking world (e.g., Bertelsmann), many charge that Anglo-American culture is intruding on the cultures of the world, often threatening their existence, and that the United Sates especially is guilty of what is termed cultural imperialism. "Superman, Spider-man, and Batman replace local heroes; Pepsi and Coke replace local fruit drinks; and 'trick or treat' begin[s] to replace Dia de los Muertos" (Sévenier, 2004, n.p.). Even more menacing to some is that in attempting to compete with American cultural imports, local products and varieties seek to mimic American commodities with the result that "the exportation of goods and information from the United States to the entire planet contributes to the exportation of the American culture" (Sévenier, 2004, n.p.). This situation is exacerbated by the rise of English as the primary international language of politics and trade, thus further intensifying the transmission of American culture.

Charges of cultural imperialism are not new and the term currently is contested, even discredited, in some quarters. Historically, U.S. culture has been affected by a variety of social, linguistic, and national influences, and given the U.S. demographic makeup, it is hardly surprising that the country has been very receptive to external cultural influences that in turn have been incorporated into the fabric of U.S. culture. Because of the innumerable foreign influences on U.S. culture, certain "universalistic" elements have crystallized within it that resonate among people all over the world. "Though U.S. popular culture is not alone in this regard, U.S. culture industries have been at the cutting edge of the development of a shared language of popular culture that can, in principle, be communicated without words, in part because of technological innovations" (van Elteren, 2003, p. 174). These factors are intensified by the U.S. government's active support in promoting cultural exports, both "as a source of export income but also as a means of exporting beliefs, values, and practices that favor U.S.-based corporate capitalism" (p. 174). While certainly this is an oversimplification of an exceedingly complex set of issues, even a cursory glance at cultural forces around the world point to the dominating influence of Anglo-American cultural products and forms. The example to follow is a telling illustration of this point.

Children's Literature World Wide: Harry Potter and the Perfect Storm

It is difficult to imagine a more ideal convergence of the forces, a perfect storm, at play in today's global children's culture industry than the remarkable media frenzy that surrounded the worldwide release of *Harry Potter and the Deathly Hallows* (2007), the final book in J.K. Rowlings's phenomenally popular series. The book's release was preceded by the worldwide debut of the fifth film in the series—*Harry Potter and the Order of the Phoenix*. These carefully choreographed events comprised one of the most significant phenomena in popular culture of this, or any, era. Harry Potter is both a marketing and a literary phenomenon that illuminates the ways that literature for the young is being commodified and transformed by conglomerates controlling the mass media (Mackey, 2001; Nel, 2005). According to Zipes (2001),

Phenomena such as the Harry Potter books are driven by commodity consumption that at the same time sets the parameters of reading and aesthetic taste. Today the experience of reading for the young is mediated through the mass media and marketing so that the pleasure and meaning of a book will often be prescripted or dictated by convention. (p. 172)

New Zealand's Margaret Mahy (2001) concurs, noting, "It has become a sort of social necessity to have read them, just as it might become a social necessity to wear certain brand names or to listen to certain music" (p. 17). Harry Potter's status as an international superstar is evidenced by the more than 374 million copies of the seven books that have been sold in at least 64 languages (Glovin, 2008). In China, the success of Harry Potter not only is credited with the surge in the sale of children's books during the early 21st century, it also has inspired Chinese authors and publishers to begin thinking about to how to stimulate sales for domestically produced books. There is little doubt that Chinese publishing has been profoundly influenced by the marketing pattern of the Potter books, resulting in far more commercial books being published than previously was the case (Rui, 2006).

The Harry Potter phenomenon is not limited to the sale of the books or tickets in movie theaters. Nel (2005) describes the impossibility of discussing Harry Potter without considering the marketing that feeds off the immense appeal of the Potter brand:

You can see the movies, you can buy the movies, you can buy Legos, action figures, stickers, notebooks, a card game, a board game, puzzles, address books, calendars, Band Aids®, toothbrushes, toothpaste, t-shirts, sweatshirts, mugs, trading cards, greeting cards, Bertie Bott's Every Flavour Beans, a Nimbus 2000 broomstick, a Harry Potter wallet, wizarding-world money, and even piña colada–flavored "Dementor's Kisses." (p. 237)

Prior to the release of *Harry Potter and the Sorcerer's Stone*, the first film in the series, experts predicted that the scale of the marketing of the brand would dwarf anything seen previously (Bruce, 2001). One of the most remarkable of these agreements was between the Potter brand and Coca-Cola, itself one of the world's most recognizable brands. The partnership called for Coca-Cola to pay for everything from a literacy campaign to a hefty share of the media blitz that preceded the film's opening. Coca-Cola's February 2001 press release illustrates the way that brand identification seeks to convince consumers to select from among the market's myriad choices, inspire trust, and contribute to the construction of consumer identity (Smith, 2007).

Through this relationship, The Coca-Cola Company will combine its worldwide resources and geographic reach to bring the specialness of Harry Potter and Coca-Cola to people and communities around the world. These efforts… will center on helping people discover the magical world of their imaginations through reading while reinforcing the

481

core values and attributes shared by Harry Potter and Coca-Cola. (quoted by Mackey, 2001, p. 184)

Distressed by this assertion of "shared core values and attributes" between a soft drink and Rowlings's boy wizard, Mackey wonders "if Harry Potter is converted into a salesman for soft drink, what is gained—and by whom?" (p. 184).

The Potter books, films, and merchandize stand as a paradigmatic, perhaps impossible to duplicate, example of a children's book becoming the subject of the kind of media orgy previously associated with Disney and *Star Wars* films and, in 2008, the release of the fourth *Indiana Jones* movie. Despite the success of Harry Potter, there are perhaps only a handful of analogues in children's book publishing in which a popular book turned into a blockbuster film (e.g., William Steig's [1990] *Shrek*) that characterize the world of adult publishing. Nevertheless, by the mid-1990s, the once separate worlds of adult and children's book publishing looked increasingly alike as both were dominated by the quest for blockbuster titles, large advances, superstar authors, and media tie-ins (Crandall, 2006a).

Contemporary children's book publishing under the control of multinational corporations has settled into the pattern found throughout our popular culture. A popular book invariably is followed by a sequel, or a series, which often leads to a film or a television program, that leads to a seemingly endless constellation of commodities, or "merch," that advertise the books, that promote the film, that promote the merch in an endlessly repeating cycle. The ultimate objective is to "brand" the books and their characters so that children will return to them to again and again. Hade (2001) captures the essence of this dynamic:

> Today's book publishers look much more like the Walt Disney Corporation than they look like the publishing houses that existed in the '50s and '60s. These publishers understand that they are not in the book business; rather they sell ideas they call "brands," and they market their brands through "synergized" goods designed to infiltrate as many aspects of a child's life as possible. (p. 159)

The Potter phenomenon illustrates the essential elements of the transformation that gained momentum in the last half of the 20th century when a thoroughgoing change in the structure and ownership of the industry, one that parallels developments in the wider economy, began in earnest. These changes radically altered the assumptions and operating procedures that govern the way publishers do business, and even the way many writers write. Although obvious to those *within* the industry, the impact of this business side of children's literature publication has only recently been given the sustained and systematic scrutiny it deserves (e.g., Reynolds & Tucker, 1998).

To be sure, the publishing industry always has been a business designed to make a profit, a point made by editor Richard Jackson in his response to the assertion that "publishers only exist to make money." Jackson's deft reply was, "No, publishers make money to exist" (quoted by Kayden, 1993, p. 265). Although publishing always has been a business, as most of the historically independent publishing companies have been absorbed by giant multinational corporations and become part of the global economy, there has been a dramatic shift in the way books are conceived, commissioned, produced, and sold. While it is essential to recognize that there continue to be many wonderful, extraordinary books published each year, and a growing number of smaller, niche publishers, I am hardly alone in being less than sanguine about the long-term future of the industry. It is to developments in the "political economy of publishing" (Taxel, 2002) that this chapter is devoted.

Global Capitalism in the 21st Century

The new and distinctive form of capitalism spreading across the globe is based on growing concentrations of wealth and power in giant, transnational corporations, and on the ever increasing production of new commodities for consumption (Agger, 1989; Paterson, 2006). This consumer-based form of capitalism, referred to as "Post-Fordism" or as "fast capitalism," involves new business and management theories that "stress competition and markets centered on change, flexibility, quality, and distinctive niches, not the mass products of the 'old' capitalism" (Cope & Kalantzis, 2000, p. 10).

Australian magnate Rupert Murdoch's News Corporation provides a paradigmatic example of the way that diverse segments of an area of the economy are integrated into a single entity. Among the News Corporation's international holdings in what is variously called "culture industry" (Zipes, 1997) or the National Entertainment State (Miller, 2002) are more than 175 newspapers, including the *Wall Street Journal*. The News Corporation also owns magazines (e.g., *The Weekly Standard*), Twentieth Century Fox Films, radio and television networks (e. g., Fox News and Fox TV), the MySpace web site, and HarperCollins Publishers (in the U.S.) and HarperCollins Limited (in the U.K.), which rank among of the world's leading publishers of children's books. Ownership of these diverse media holdings permits the News Corporation and similar conglomerates to synergistically link them in order to enhance and extend the earning power of each element.

This last point relates to "commodification," the proliferation of products or commodities that are "created, perfected, and changed at ever faster rates," another defining characteristic of the "new high-tech-driven capitalism" (Gee, 2000, p. 40). Today's Post-Fordism still is concerned with production, the emphasis of industrial capitalism's Fordist order, but the focus now is more reflexive and able to accommodate variations in the production process. The move away from industrialized capitalism's focus on manufactured products is toward a knowledge-based economy used to sell goods and ideas. This emphasis is visible in the marketing of products tailored to consumers' preferences that reflect the reality that today's capitalism is defined not by a producer mentality but by a consumer ethos (Paterson, 2006). Ideas and goods that are symbolized and personalized as "brands" epitomize this transition. Whether considering such global brands as Oprah Winfrey, Michael Jordon, Coca-Cola, David Beckham, Nike, or Harry Potter, brand identification is designed to help consumers "limit seemingly endless choices provided by the market" and "inspire trust while contributing to the construction of their identities" (Smith, 2007, p. 158). It surely is one of the more remarkable characteristics of our age that citizenship in the 21st century is "increasingly performed through consumption and that people find that identity constructed through consumption is more empowering than through traditional means" (Paterson, 2006, p. 28).

The importance of the identification of young people as a major market has worked in conjunction with marketing and branding "less on the basis of occupation or fixed social status than on self ascribed notions of identity within social groups" (p. 31). Langer (2004) further notes:

> The intimate entangling of brand and identity is nowhere more evident than in the experience of childhood in the last two decades of the 20th century. The colonization of children's 1ives by the entertainment product cycle has woven Disney, Hasbro, Mattel, and McDonald's into the fabric of everyday life for urban children across the globe. (p. 263)

Control of publishing by multinational corporations has led to the proliferation of branded characters and the ubiquitous production of merchandize that capitalizes on children's fascination with well-known book characters such as Curious George (who is enormously popular in Japan), Arthur the Aardvark, or Harry Potter. The well-established pattern is for these commodified characters to become the subject of television programs or films that not only enhance book sales but help to sell the vast array of "spin-off" products including toys, clothing, and bed sheets, etc. These practices speak to the reality of today's environment where "media drives media, and if you have valuable property in one area, like books, you can extend your brand name into others" (Hade, 2001, p. 48). Children's books have become "idea factories" for filmmakers and merchandisers and cross-media synergies often result in books no longer being valued for themselves, but seen instead as "an essential link in a media food chain" (Crandall, 2006a, p. 3).

The Global Children's Culture Industry

The culture industry includes a variety of mass media, including children's literature, that produce and distribute commodities (Pecora, 1998). New markets for these commodities constantly are being sought, and childhood has become a key moment in the formation of consumers as children have become a primary target market for global capital. Not only have corporations "infiltrated the core activities and institutions of childhood," they have encountered little resistance from parents or government (Schor, 2004, p. 11). Efforts to sell to the young begin in infancy as the culture industry "sets the terms of socialization and education in the western world" (Zipes, 1997, pp. 7–8). During the final quarter of the 20th century when children were proving to be "a particularly profitable 'frontier' for global capital," their incorporation into the market demonstrated the broader social logic through which "capitalism reconstitutes life stages as cradle to grave markets" (Langer, 2004, p. 254). This last point was illustrated by the Disney Company's January 2006 introduction of a broadband channel for preschoolers titled "Playhouse Disney Preschool Time Online." Focusing on pre-kindergarten skills, this Internet subscription service was described as part of Disney's "age-banded strategy where we are looking to follow the consumer through all their age levels and have something for them at every age" (Harris, 2006, n.p.). Twenty-first century children are "becoming well-trained consumers able to associate Ronald McDonald with good things before they have learned language" (Pecora, 1998, p. 20).

As the mergers brought previously independent publishers under the umbrella of such giants as the News Corporation, Disney, Viacom, and Bertelsmann, the "articulation of entertainment and product spin-offs," a process that began in the late 1970s, moved into a "new phase of accelerated hyperconsumption" (Langer, 2004, p. 254). Over the past 20 years, the global children's culture industry has sought to balance the "ambivalent fusion of exploitation and enchantment." These efforts led to television/film/merchandise strategies whose goal is to construct children as a "lucrative global market embedded in a culture that holds it to be a universal truth that each child has the right to the pursuit of fun, excitement, and consumer durables" (p. 256). Zipes (2001) provides a less than sanguine appraisal of this state of affairs: "Everything we do to, with, and for our children is influenced by capitalist market conditions and the hegemonic interests of corporate elites. In simple terms, we calculate what is best for our children by regarding them as investments and turning them into commodities" (p. ix).

Economic Power and Individual Agency

The pursuit of a political economy of children's literature runs the risk of falling into the trap of economic determinism that often is endemic in analyses seeking to determine the impact of impersonal macroeconomic forces on cultural institutions, be they schools or publishing companies (e.g., Apple, 1982; Williams, 1977). Among the most persistent and vexing of these problems is to lose sight of the agency of the social actors involved. It is easy, for example, to reduce the women and men working in publishing to helpless pawns in the face of changes wrought when transnational conglomerates assume control of the companies in which they work. This view is both simplistic and a disservice to those who labor to produce the very best books for children. In a similar vein, while it is essential that we be concerned about children being pulled into the marketplace by age 5 or sooner and shaped by the media to be consumers before they've had a chance become citizens (Denby, 1996), children are not passive, helpless recipients of the diverse media messages that pervade their world. Hagood (2001) spoke of the widely held belief that "the culture industry socializes people in common ways by exposing them to mindless drivel" (p. 254). This belief fosters the notion that "people (and especially children) lack the ability to interpret for themselves the messages that mass media produce" and that these messages are "duping them" and doing "little to improve their minds or status in society" (Alvermann, 2006, p. 243). Despite these concerns, we must remember that children actively construct meaning and do not robotically internalize whatever messages are placed in front of them, or that writers and editors are hapless victims in the face of monolithic economic forces.

How Did It Come To This?

The story of how an industry historically owned and operated by individuals dedicated to publishing the "best" books for children while earning enough money to stay in business was transformed into a big business expected to contribute significantly to the bottom line of media conglomerates (Chaikin, 1982) has parallels in industries around the world. Prior to the mergers, publishers sought to balance the cultural and commercial dimensions of their enterprise. In this simplified formulation, culture and commerce were viewed as opposing poles around which the industry was organized. On the one hand were those who eschewed profit because of their earnest commitment to provide "serious" reading and advance culture. On the other were those who focused exclusively on financial concerns and ignored their cultural responsibility (Haugland, 1994). After decades in publishing, Schiffrin (2000) provided a sobering assessment of the shifting culture-commerce fulcrum within the industry:

> In Europe and in America, publishing has a long history as an intellectually and politically engaged profession. Publishers have always prided themselves on their ability to balance the imperative of making money with that of issuing worthwhile books. In recent years, as ownership of publishing has changed, the equation has been altered. It is increasingly the case that the owner's only interest is in making money and as much of it as possible. (p. 5)

The sale of trade books has been viewed as "the most publicly visible of the industry" that brings into sharp focus "the tensions inherent in publishing's status as part of both economic base and cultural production" (Moran,

1997, p. 441). Seeking a balance between these conflicting imperatives is especially difficult in the children's book business since it is "far more complex than the adult book business and has a profile out of all proportion to its market value" (Crandall, 2006a, p. 2). This tension follows from the belief that children's books, despite their commercial dimensions, embody fundamental expressions of society and play a role in shaping young children's values and perceptions. Nevertheless, industry insiders lament the assault on children's book publishing as "corporate acquisitiveness further batters what was once a nice, staid little business" (Roxburgh, 2000, p. 653), while others consider it naïve to "to think that publishing can stand outside or above the market system that produces other commodities" (Stossel, 2001, p. 43).

The inexorable process of integration, consolidation, and downsizing in the industry has led to the integration of individual publishing houses into ever-larger corporate organizations such as The News Corporation. In the 1980s and 1990s, mergers brought the major book publishers into the hands of communication conglomerates with holdings and interests in other highly profitable areas of mass media (Moran, 1997). Schiffrin (2000) contended that a small handful of major conglomerates control 80% of American book sales while their holdings in other sectors of the information and entertainment industries give them their enormous, additional power.

The Key Players

It is critical to note that the dominant media corporations, and their holdings, change with startling rapidity. I have little doubt that the landscape will be altered by the time this book is printed. Nevertheless, at this moment (early 2009), in addition to the previously discussed News Corporation, other key players in the National Entertainment State (Miller, 2002) include the Walt Disney Company, the Pearson Group, Viacom, and Scholastic (an anomaly among the publishing giants as it remains family-owned). Publishing's biggest merger occurred in March 1998 when German-owned Bertelsmann purchased Random House, the largest U.S. trade book publisher. The newly combined company, which retains the name Random House, now is the dominant U.S. publisher, as well as one of Great Britain's (Crandall, 2006b). Speaking of this merger, Alterman (1998) highlights the danger posed by merger mania.

> This big book merger did not tell us anything we didn't already know, except that everything is worse than we thought. The commercial foundations of American culture and its marketplace of ideas are crumbling to dust. The multinational conglomerates that hold its purse strings care for little but the bottom line. The "public trust" aspect of publishing that was once assumed has disappeared. (pp. 5–6)

The search for new and expanded markets is a central business strategy of the media conglomerates. In recent years as China has embraced elements of the market economy, its children's literature industry has begun to merge into the mainstream of international publishing. In addition to unprecedented development, the industry enjoys the support of government policies that encourage development even while it faces the challenges concomitant to the world market of globalized competition. Perhaps the most significant indicator of these developments after decades of government protection is that the Chinese market now is open to foreign capital. Among the major players in this potentially enormous market are the Walt Disney Company, Bertelsmann, and the Pearson Group (Hai Fei, 2006).

Although consolidation is the major development in the evolution of the industry, there are countervailing, contradictory tendencies that require notice. Writing about publishing in the U.K., Crandall (2006b) challenges the conventional wisdom about the state of the independent publishers, pointing out that they actually have increased in number (e.g., Barrington Stoke, Chicken House) over the past decade. She also contends that, "contrary to general opinion, neither conglomerate nor independent publishers has the clear upper hand in terms of the quality of their output, as measured by the success of their authors in winning literary prizes" (p. 215). Reynolds (1998) concurs, pointing out that since 1995 the number of independent publishers of children's fiction has doubled. Candlewick, Holiday House, and Boyd's Mill in the United States and Canada's Groundwood also are able to compete with the corporate giants. Founded in 1991, Candlewick is especially worthy of note. It has won major awards in both the U.S. and U.K. and was described by Patricia Lee Gauch (2008, personal correspondence), former editor-in chief of Philomel Books, as a publisher that creates "aesthetically beautiful books" that dare to "use deckled edges, fine paper, [and] careful printing." She notes as well that this success has "the giants looking at Candlewick, scratching their corporate heads, and wondering exactly how they are accomplishing what they are accomplishing." I personally consider Anderson's (2006) *The Astonishing Life of Octavian Nothing, Traitor to the Nation,* published by Candlewick, to be among the most remarkable, groundbreaking books I ever have read.

As was noted earlier, a defining characteristic of today's Post-Fordist, fast capitalist system is the focus on the production of new commodities tailored to the consumer's preferences or niches (Paterson, 2006). Some believe that global entertainment conglomerates have made book publishing a niche industry, and that children's book publishing occupies a "small nook of that niche" (Roxburgh, 2000, p. 653). This perspective is in keeping with the notion that some of the structures of multi-national conglomerates that swallowed up imprints in the 1980s and 1990s are becoming anachronistic for the 21st century (Reynolds & Tucker, 1998). Multicultural literature exemplifies the phenomenon of niche publishing that is having an increasing impact in the United States and elsewhere. In addition to the multicultural books made available by major publishers

(e.g., Hyperion's Jump at the Sun Books, HarperCollins's Amistad Books), small niche presses devoted exclusively to multicultural literature have proliferated since the late 1980s. These publishers were made possible, perhaps necessary, when the conservatism of 1980s led to a slowdown in the publication of authors and illustrators from parallel cultures. In contrast to the global approach of transnational corporations, these smaller localized enterprises often are owned and run by idealistic individuals acting on a commitment to, for example, bilingual (e.g., Children's Book Press), multicultural (e.g., Lee and Low, Just US Books), or Christian themed books (e.g., Zondervan Publishing House). These companies generally pay authors and illustrators less than major houses and can't compete with them in terms of distribution and publicity, which can result in difficulties for buyers and reviewers obtaining books or even knowing about them. Whether these smaller companies can compete in the U.S. and elsewhere over the long haul, as they seem able to do in the U.K., is a question critical to the future of children's literature.

The Impact of Consolidation

While, again, publishing always has been a business designed to make a profit, it's easy to romanticize the past, to lament the passing of the time when the industry was in the hands of independent, often family-owned companies, and to decry its current domination by impersonal multinational corporations. American children's literature's crassly commercial, courser side included the dime novels of the 19th century and to the mass market empire built by Edward Stratameyer whose series included the Rover Boys, Tom Swift, the Hardy Boys, and Nancy Drew (Keeline, 1995). While women have long played a role in children's book publishing, people of color, until very recently, have been excluded from positions of power and responsibility, especially from editorial positions (Reynolds, 1998), and remain seriously underrepresented. In addition, the canon of children's literature, until recent times, has been governed by a selective tradition that was racist and sexist by commission and omission (Levine, 1997; Taxel, 1981). Substantive change in these practices required the protest and activism of the 1960s and 1970s. Despite some positive changes, publishing has evolved in ways that are of concern to those who long for the days when publishing was an enterprise where, as novelist E. L. Doctorow put it, individuals could "make money and be proud of their contributions to literature and ideas at the same time" (quoted by Coser, Kadushin, & Powell, 1982, p. 14).

Prior to the 1980s when the pace of the mergers accelerated, publishing was a stable and disciplined enterprise. Echoing the culture vs. commerce theme, Crandall (2006a) suggested that making a profit was almost secondary to the stated intention of producing books of the highest quality. Few today would deny that the new corporate publishers are primarily concerned with their profit margins and that previously there was a far healthier balance between the desire to contribute to the culture and the imperative to generate revenue. Revenue generation also is behind the giant publishers' emphasis on the downsizing of existing backlists as publishers began to "asset strip" these lists in search of characters who could be merchandised (Reynolds & Tucker, 1998, p. xii). At the same time, declining sales to the under-funded library systems, whose budgets have been further stretched by the need to purchase computer hardware and software, led to an intensified focus on more commercial, fast-selling books and the cultivation of new sales outlets such as chain bookstores, drug and toy stores, and other retail outlets (Crandall, 2006a; Epstein, 1996; Reynolds, 1998).

The 1980s was the era when the boundary between traditional editorial decision-making and business and marketing began to blur. Business managers increasingly assumed the leadership of publishing houses, and decisions about the design of particular books and whether to publish them no longer were the exclusive province of editors but increasingly that of marketing people. At the same time, editors were expected to adhere to corporate guidelines in the acquisition and shaping of products (Zipes, 2001). Marketing acquired "a new, quasi-scientific—and quasi-mystical—cachet," and "what does marketing say?" became the publishers' mantra as those within the industry sought to satisfy the wishes of the new corporate bosses (Marcus, 2001, n.p.). Many in the business already believe that marketing now influences publishing decisions in ways that would have been inconceivable in the past (Auletta, 1997). Every book, notes British editor Philippa Dickinson, "has to justify its existence in purely financial terms." Like many, she mourns the passing of the days when "I would just have published it because I loved it" where as "now I have to put my personal selection in terms of money" (quoted by Reynolds, 1998, p. 34). Crandall (2006a) makes a similar point when noting, "where editors previously published a book because they loved it, they must now defend their choice to an acquisition committee of accountants and salespeople" (p. 10). Marni Hodgkin, another editor from Great Britain, bemoaned "the move to make the marketing tail wag the publishing dog."

> In times past, the selling titles helped to support those that didn't: the experimental books or those with minority appeal, or by unknown authors. But when books are marketed like soap, each one, we are told, must stand on its own feet. The result is that a title without mass appeal may easily go out of print within the year of its publication, before the hard-pressed librarians have had a chance to assess it or the children are able to have a go. Publishers are less ready to take risks, and new writers and innovative writing go to the wall. (quoted by Reynolds, 1998, p. 34)

One critical institutional change was the 1983 creation at Random House of a first-of-its-kind "Merch Group," a freestanding unit with its own sales force as well as editorial and marketing staff. The Merch Group's exclusive concern was with how the company's books could serve as the basis of licensed merchandize and related spin-offs.

Responding to the decline in government support for libraries in Great Britain and the United States, publishers reassessed the previous balance between the trade and institutional sides of the market. Marketing's ascendant importance also was reflected in the launch by *Publishers Weekly* of a "Marketing Front" column to track these trends (Marcus, 2001). The fact that today's books now are important source material for films and television, which in turn feeds the entertainment licensing market, leads thousands of industry marketers to attend the annual Licensing International Trade Show held in New York (Raugust, 2007). These affairs now are essential to the business of today's children's book industry.

Another manifestation of publishing under multinational control has been the shift from editorial, with complementary salescentered philosophies, to financial-growth and marketing-centered ones, "a pure business model that has never been shown to apply to books" (Simon, 2000, pp. 25–26). This change is demonstrated by the upward shift in expectations of the profits to be garnered from the sale of books. Historically, books were expected to return about 4% after taxes. Such a modest level of return was an indication that money itself was not the sole reason why people entered the industry. This is not to say that publishers were not wealthy. However, the emphasis was more on the steady growth of the firm than on profit itself.

As conglomerates took over publishing, they insisted that each holding generate the same basic rates of profit. In February 1996, Bertelsmann made 15% the target for return on assets for all its new businesses. This figure would apply to Random House, as well as Bertelsmann's holdings in music, television, or computer software (Crandall 2006b). While perhaps not an unreasonable expectation for these other businesses, 15% is an excessive expectation for books. A related step was to "rationalize profits on a title-by-title-basis." In contrast to the long-time practice whereby best sellers subsidized other books, the new world of publishing required that each book "pay its own way" (Schiffrin, 1999, p. 116).

Pantheon's historically profitable children's line, for example, for many years had subsidized its less immediately profitable adult books. However, once the children's department had separate accounting, the practice no longer was possible. The result was that works such as first books or those that were considered "serious" and required time to catch on and find an audience became increasingly difficult to publish. This "logical system" gradually was imposed and accepted throughout the industry where it "became a kind of iron mask" (Schiffrin, 1999, p. 117) that allowed for little variation. "The time when the realm of ideas that historically were exempted from the usual expectations of profit" had passed (p. 103).

What's Good about the Mergers?

Media mergers, of course, have their defenders. Greco, Rodriguez, and Wharton's (2007) analysis of the culture and commerce of publishing in the 21st century provides extensive discussion of the economic benefits of the mergers. They point out that a basic fiduciary responsibility of managers in capitalist enterprises is to maximize revenues for stockholders. Further, the capital accumulation and the ability to grow the company made possible by mergers are central to this effort. Greco et al.'s data suggest that acquisitions were a requirement, indeed an obligation, to support growth and technological advancements and provide the capital needed to improve book publishing efficiency. Mergers also provide publishers with scarce resources that allow them:

1. to find and develop authors and editors;
2. to expand title output and channels of distribution;
3. to bring to the market intriguing and conflicting ideas and opinions;
4. to ensure that the critically important marketplace of ideas remains a vital component of this nation;
5. to publish genres formerly excluded during the golden age of publishing (books on feminism or African American, Hispanic American, and Asian American themes and issues); and
6. to pay dividends to stockholders, wages to hundreds of thousands of employees, and taxes to myriad governmental agencies. (pp. 31–32)

These achievements seem laudable for an enterprise seeking to balance the industry's historic cultural and commercial orientations. However, a number of these assertions, especially those that relate to ensuring that the marketplace of ideas contains conflicting ideas and opinions, are dubious. Some believe that rather than fostering a marketplace for conflicting ideas and opinions, the concentration of power and control of publishing has led to a decline in the diversity of published material given that the same books appear in virtually all stores. A related misgiving is that economic concentration results in only books of national mainstream interest being available. The narrowing of distribution lines is bad for consumers and, when books are concerned, a threat to democracy (Bing, 1999). Finally, when "ideas themselves have become commodities whose value can be measured by the number of potential customers," a form of market censorship ensues whereby "dissenting and counter cyclical ideas" are far less likely to find a publisher (Schiffrin, 1999, p. 120).

Marketing and Merchandising

The concept of the child as a consumer emerged in 18th-century England and was central to the consumer revolution that affected all aspects of English life. It was at this time that John Newbery, widely regarded as one of the founders of modern children's literature, initiated practices to enhance the sale of his books that are the forebears of those that pervade today's global children's culture industry. While not the first to specialize in children's books, Newbery is the first British publisher to see the potential for a profitable and permanent market (Dawson, 1998). Newbery used a variety of "gimmicks" to build and extend his market and his reputation for advertising acumen became almost as great as the fame of his little books (p. 177). How ironic it is that the man whose name graces one of the most prestigious literary awards in American children's literature also pioneered techniques that dominate today's industry and, to many, threaten to undermine its integrity

Marketing and merchandising that exploits the auras (Zipes, 1997) surrounding fantasy characters is a central component of the commodification process and marketing to children. In the late 19th century, Palmer Cox (2008), known as the "Walt Disney of the Victorian age" created immensely popular books about elf-like Brownies (Estes, 1985) and an array of commodities that capitalized on their popularity. A neglected aspect of the legacy of Beatrix Potter (2008) was her interest in merchandising. She patented a Peter Rabbit doll and game and designed a jigsaw puzzle. Potter referred to these items as "merchandising 'side-shows'" and their success continues to this day. As the children's book market expanded at the close of the 19th century, publishers shrewdly began designing book illustrations and covers in an attempt to attract child and adult consumers to the book as an enchanted item (Zipes, 2001).

By the mid-20th century, Walt Disney's prescient understanding of the potential of children as a market for merchandising allowed him to tap into and exploit that market to unprecedented levels. Disney had an uncanny genius for profiting from fantasy and enchantment, and he refined and extended the marketing of the myriad toys derived from his animated features. This commodification led to the licensing of Mickey Mouse, Snow White, and "every other character turned out by the Disney imagineers to every conceivable advertising outlet" (Giroux, 1999, p. 32).

In 1942, Western Publishing licensed the Little Golden Book imprint to Simon & Schuster and became the first major publisher to enter into the lucrative licensing and merchandising market. In another critical development, a major new channel for the sale of Golden Books was opened when Simon & Schuster introduced the 25-cent books to supermarkets. By 1949, the "Golden juggernaut" expanded still further as Simon & Schuster licensed the Little Golden name to manufacturers producing a wide variety children's merchandise. The year 1949 also marked the launch of Les Petits Livres d'Or, French-language editions of Little Golden Books, and the final plans for foreign editions in Spain, Italy, and Germany (Marcus, 2007).

These forebears of today's ubiquitous efforts to capitalize on and promote the popularity of characters from popular books make it clear that today's marketers have several centuries of precedent and experience to build on. Their efforts today are doubtless enhanced by the "hyperconsumption" (Langer, 2004) characteristic of our age.

Children's Books as Idea Factories

The pervasive view of children's books as idea factories that can foster cross-media synergies is visible in the dozens of books that have been optioned to film companies. Transforming a book into a film invariably has a dramatic impact on book sales. The big screen version of *Tuck Everlasting*, while not a blockbuster, provided a substantial bump to the sales of Natalie Babbitt's (1975) classic novel. According to the book's publisher, the novel typically sold 10,000 copies for the month of October; after the release of the film, October 2002 sales were 66,000 copies (Maughan, 2002b). Similarly, despite receiving negative reviews, the filmed version of *The Cat in the Hat* propelled Dr. Seuss's (1957) ever-popular title to the top of bestseller lists (Marcus, 2001). Recent book-based films include: *Because of Winn Dixie; Curious George* (which also has a television program on PBS); *Ella Enchanted; Charlotte's Web* (the second version)*; Stuart Little* (with two sequels); *Holes; The Lion, the Witch and the Wardrobe*; *The Polar Express; Jumanji; Nancy Drew; A Wrinkle in Time; Bridge to Terabithia*; *Horton Hears a Who;* and *The Tale of Despereaux* (Maughan, 2002a).

Other books scheduled for this treatment were on display at the 2007 Licensing Show. The Sony Pictures' booth, for example, was draped in spaghetti in honor of the studio's 2009 release of *Cloudy with a Chance of Meatballs*. Also available for license was Maurice Sendak's (1964) classic *Where the Wild Things Are* (Raugust, 2007).

Authors as Brands

The practice of establishing books and their characters as brands that will attract readers, viewers, and consumers of ancillary products extends to authors. Zipes (2001) contends that authors and illustrators themselves have become commodities as publishers strive to gain for them the name recognition and celebrity that lead to the automatic review of their books, wide publicity, and ready availability in bookstores and other sales outlets. Recent years have brought this sort of fame and brand-name status to children's authors such as Marc Brown, Jan Brett, Tomie de Paola, and, of course, J. K. Rowlings (Marcus, 2001).

William Steig's (1990) *Shrek* is among the handful of children's books that attained the box office success so avidly sought by publishers. After the first film earned three-quarters of a billion dollars, Scholastic didn't need a crystal ball to predict that *Shrek 2* would be one of the biggest movies of 2004 and would spur the sale of books and merchandize. The three Shrek films have grossed over $2 billion and two others are planned. Having secured the rights to publish *Shrek 2* books in multiple formats, Scholastic sought mass-market retailers to capitalize on their license.

Publishers have learned that licensed books, films, and their ancillary products do best in mass-market stores such as K-Mart, Wall-Mart, Costco, etc. As a result, these outlets are increasing space devoted to children's titles, improving their in-store displays, and expanding their selection beyond what were once very narrow parameters (Holt, 2004). Not surprisingly, sales in these stores often depend on impulse buying by consumers who recognize the names of branded authors or films.

The importance of cultivating authors as brands is nowhere more apparent than in the ever-growing trend toward celebrity authors. While not a new phenomenon, within the last decade celebrities have sought to capitalize on their popularity by writing books for children. The reverse also is the case as publishers seek to turn media stars into authors in order to exploit their name recognition. The list of actors and entertainers who have written picture books includes Julie Andrews, Bill Cosby, Jamie Lee Curtis, Whoopi Goldberg, Billy Crystal, Will Smith, Shaquille O'Neal, Jimmy Carter, Paul McCartney, and Duchess of York Sarah Ferguson. Since the appeal of celebrity authors derives from their ability to garner coveted television airtime, finding a publisher usually is rather simple (Marcus, 2001). Unlike the vast majority of authors, celebrities are not dependent on starred reviews to command publicity for their books, and even negative reviews may not affect sales (Austin, 2003).

The September 2003 release of Madonna's (2003) first book, *The English Roses,* was among the more remarkable literary debuts in recent memory. More than 1,000,000 copies in 30 languages were shipped to 50,000 bookstores in 100 countries and backed by a marketing blitz that took the author from London to Paris and to the Oprah Winfrey show. The effect of all of this hype was quickly apparent as *The English Roses* became the fastest-selling children's picture book of all time. In an article for the *Pittsburgh Post-Gazette,* MacPherson (2004, n.p.) explained that Madonna created controversy when she asserted that her decision to become an author began when she started reading to her son and "couldn't believe how vapid and vacant and empty all the stories were. There's, like, no lessons…. There's, like, no books about anything." MacPherson continued with several responses by notable authors and critics. Newbery Medalist Linda Sue Park believes Madonna's comments expose her "shameful ignorance of the world of children's books" and are an "insult not only those of us who dedicate our lives to writing for young people, but also those young readers who have discovered good books and funny books that they love."

Park is not alone in her disdain for celebrity books that, with few exceptions are disparaged by critics who decry their poor writing and frequent didacticism. Book review editor Trev Jones agrees that "most of these books are pretty bad, although it's hard to pan them all" While noting that some celebrity authors can write, many can't "and there is seemingly no connection between whether they can write and whether they will get published." Critic Anita Silvey believes that "celebrity-written children's books are the worst kind of disconnect between a parent—who is attached to a book written by a celebrity they like—and a child, for whom that celebrity is totally meaningless." Jane Yolen points out that despite her many awards and honorary doctorates, she has never been asked to appear on Oprah or spoken to Katie Couric (MacPherson, 2004, n.p.). Other critics fear that if a book sells simply because its author is a celebrity, the distinction between quality and popularity is blurred. Such books also perpetuate the misconception that anyone can write a children's book.

Regardless of what authors and critics say, it is clear that publishers' enthusiasm for celebrity authors only will grow more ardent. While critics complain about "catalogues that read like an issue of *People* magazine," publishers are "too busy counting their money to listen" (Holt, 2004, n.p.). Perhaps the most serious issue raised by the love affair with celebrity authors is that they ultimately limit the opportunities for other, often fledgling, writers to get published. The related problem is that celebrity authors command an inordinate amount of publishers' advertising budgets thus denying needed promotional dollars to less well-known authors. Jane Yolen believes that "celebrity children's books eat up all the available oxygen" (MacPherson, 2004, n.p.).

Series and Sequels

I have discussed some of the ways that publishers seek to brand their authors in order to exploit their name recognition and attract steady and repetitive sales. A ubiquitous strategy toward this end is the publication of sequels to popular books and their development into series. This pattern is evident in films where the success of an initial offering makes a sequel a virtual certainty.

As Catherine Sheldrick Ross points out in her chapter in this volume, children's book publishing has a long and quite lucrative mass-market side that includes the dime novels of the 19th century and later series such as the Rover Boys, the Hardy Boys, the Bobbsey Twins, and Nancy Drew, which have been updated for contemporary audiences (Marcus, 1997). In their heyday, children's librarians banished many of these series, as well as the Little Golden Books, from numerous collections. The prejudice against series was so intense that Wilder's *Little House* books were repeatedly shut out of librarian-administered award competitions such as the Newbery Medal (Miller, 2008). Nevertheless, these series continue to sell and their ranks were swelled in the 1970s by teen romance series such as *Sweet Dreams*, *Sweet Valley High*, and the *Baby Sitters Club* books for preteens. Popular current series include those about Junie B. Jones and the Magic School Bus. Discussing the recent release of the filmed version

of *Kit Kittredge*, one of the titles in the *American Girls* series, Baker (2008) notes that the series had sold 117 million books in 23 years and succeeded in establishing an "emotional connection with this brand" (n.p.).

The difference between books that spawn sequels and those that evolve into series is not easy to discern. While there long have been series of literary distinction and popularity, they are qualitatively different from mass-market romances or popular horror series (e.g., those of R. L Stine). Examples include Lewis's *Chronicles of Narnia* series (e.g., 1994), Alexander's *Prydain* series (e.g., 1999), and Mildred Taylor's books about the Logan family (e.g., 1976). Making distinctions between the "quality" of certain books compared to others, something I have done throughout this chapter, long has been the province of literary scholars and critics. Such distinctions are made explicit by awards such as the Newbery, Caldecott, and Kate Greenway Medals, the Canadian Library Association Book of the Year for Children, and the Australian Children's Book Council Awards.

Judgments about quality also are a defining feature of most children's literature textbooks. Jacobs and Tunnell (2008), for example, state "a good book is one created by a knowledgeable and skilled author in which the elements of literature measure up under critical analysis. Quality is recognized by evaluating different elements of the book including style and language, character, plot, pacing," etc. (p. 11). Referring to the "magnificent texts" discussed throughout *Interpreting Literature with Children*, Wolf (2004) notes that these works have "well drawn characters, absorbing plots, deeply rendered themes, and jewel-like craft in terms of language" (p. 37). Nodelman and Reimer (2003) take a different approach and seek to problematize "old certainties" by asking "new questions" about the difference between "good literary texts and bad ones." For example, they ask, "if good texts are so different from bad ones, why do many people, including literary experts, disagree about these matters" (p. 1). They also wonder, "who decides what is wise and what is beautiful and why should their judgment be trusted" (p. 3)? Despite the provocative importance of these questions, Nodelman and Reimer's volume is full of discussions of specific books that are presented to illustrate literary themes or theoretical issues. The fact that many if not all of these books are, at least in this reader's judgment, "books of quality" points to the fact that while making literary judgments is unavoidably subjective, qualitative distinctions among books can and invariably will be made.

In today's publishing environment, it is the lack of a sequel to a popular book that is likely to elicit surprise, and today's sequels and series usually become enmeshed in the synergistic relations between literature and other media. Sequels to successful high-end trade picture books now are commonplace. For example, the highly successful Caldecott Honor Books *No David* (Shannon, 1998), *Click, Clack, Moo: Cows That Type* (Cronin, 2000), and *Olivia*

(Falconer, 2000) all spawned sequels that are similar in style, content, and format to the predecessor. While these books are not without their charms, they reflect clearly the bottom line imperative and the influence of marketing discussed earlier. Not surprisingly, Falconer, like other successful authors, has utilized the popularity of his literary creation to create a merchandizing bonanza that includes board books, shirts, dolls, umbrellas, paint sets, theatres, tea sets, etc.

The "relentless drive" toward series books and sequels intended to "guarantee larger and more predictable sales" (Crandall, 2006b, p.217) may have a deleterious impact on the creative processes of writers and illustrators. Speaking of films, Ritzer (2000) wonders if the large audiences attracted by predictable film products are offset by the expense of movies based on new characters, ideas, and concepts. Engelhardt (1991) argues:

> The descent of adult methods into children's publishing has also meant the descent of junior versions of distinctly adult genres—the TV soap opera, the woman's romance, and the thriller—deeper and deeper into the world of childhood; and with them, a certain generic sameness has blanketed bestsellerdom. (p. 60)

The veracity of this claim is seen in the announcement that Harlequin, known for its adult romances, has entered the YA market with a new trade paperback imprint aimed at African American teenage girls, a group of readers the publisher says is underserved by commercial fiction.

Looking Ahead

Happily, consideration of the socioeconomic issues related to children's literature and culture no longer is a novelty. These discussions provide us with greater awareness and understanding of the relation between economic forces and the books available to our children. This chapter draws further attention to the escalating pressure that publishers, editors, and authors feel to produce certain moneymakers. This tendency is evident in a variety of factors that comprise the process of commodification: the proliferation of books based on branded characters, the publication of books written by celebrity authors, the generation of series, television programs and movie tie-ins, and the activities of "merch" divisions seeking to parlay a company's books into licensed merchandize and related spin-offs. We can expect more of the same in the future simply because of the enormous amounts of money to be made. Twenty years ago, Shepard (1988) commented on these trends that only have increased with the passage of time: "When big money moves in, creativity, originality, and freedom move out. The reason is risk. When a lot of money is at stake, the investors insist on a safe product. And they get what they want. Formulas reign. Products are geared to the mass market meaning, the lowest common denominator" (n.p.).

It is easy to despair that the market driven impera-

tives discussed in this chapter threaten the existence of the kinds of literature that parents, educators, and other book-lovers have come to take for granted. Clearly, the impact of seemingly impersonal macroeconomic forces on the full range of cultural institutions must never be underestimated. However, as was noted earlier, it is an error to examine cultural phenomena without reference to human agency. It is essential that we always keep in mind that while "people operate within the limits of a variety of constraints, the market being a major example of such constraints, there remains a domain of choices that involves the possibility of "doing otherwise" (Coser, 1984, p. 11). Writing almost 30 years ago, Whiteside (1980) alluded to this point when paying tribute to the handful of editors and publishers "who have shown themselves determined to maintain their standards of excellence and their encouragement of new writing talent." He retained the belief that "even within the most seemingly monolithic companies there are individual editors whose professional skill and energy and devotion to literature are such that they have been able to establish, in effect, their own imprints within these companies" (pp. 121–122).

These editors and writers, along with the publishers of the smaller niche presses, cling tenaciously to the freedom and latitude to make publishing decisions and produce that segment of the many thousands of books published each year, many of breathtaking quality, that are of wonderfully varying styles, genres, and formats. A significant number of these books address complex and controversial issues and themes with an honesty and forthrightness that would not have been possible 20 or 30 years ago. Editor Patricia Gauch (2008, personal communication) insists that the industry still is populated by people who retain the conviction that the industry can, recalling Doctorow, "make money and be proud of their contributions to literature and ideas at the same time" (quoted by Coser, Kadushin, & Powell, 1982, p. 14). Gauch maintains that there are editors, both veteran and novice, who nurture the hope that the industry *can* do both. However, she worries as well that "young administrators tend to be the ones big business has hunted down and [they] put the sword of the bottom-line in their hands."

The primacy of the bottom-line doubtless will continue to challenge all of those who work in, and care about, the industry. One source for optimism is offered by the intriguing notion of the "long tail" promulgated by Anderson (2004) who points to the beneficial impact of on-line vendors. Amazon, for example, unlike chain bookstores and mass-market outlets, is not restricted by the "tyranny of space," the limited amount of shelf space available even in the largest stores. Anderson claims that on the average Barnes & Noble carries 130,000 titles. In contrast, more than half of Amazon's book sales come from *outside* its top 130,000 titles. The implication is that the market for books that are not even sold in the average bookstore (which typically do not stock books published by the smaller niche publishers) is larger than the market for those that are. As a consequence, online distribution and unlimited shelf space is leading to a dramatic shift in the book and entertainment businesses from hit-driven economics to one dominated by niche-driven economics. This broadening of the market has occurred largely because content once considered on the fringe now is finding a market through on-line distribution. Whether books from the new niche publishers get the attention of readers who then go to on-line vendors, or those bookstores that do stock them, remains to be seen.

The ability of authors, editors, and publishers to resist escalating pressures to commodify children's literature further and to maintain their independence in the face of bottom-line imperatives will go a long way in determining the future of children's literature and have a momentous impact on the social, cultural, and political life of our increasingly interconnected world. Books like *The Astonishing Life of Octavian Nothing, Traitor to the Nation* (Anderson, 2006), Alexis's (2007) provocative *The Absolutely True Story of a Part-Time Indian,* and Selznick's (2007) Caldecott Award winning graphic novel *The Invention of Hugo Cabret* are but a few examples from among myriad others illustrating that there is much to celebrate in children's book publishing today. While the continued flowering of wonderfully innovative books in countries around the globe is a cause for optimism, the catalogues of many of the very houses that produce them increasingly are dominated by the kinds of commodified books discussed in this chapter. Over a decade ago, Jane Yolen (1997) confessed to being "appalled" by the "proliferation of pop-up/scratch-and sniff/doll and puppet/paper engineered products" that gradually are "pushing out literature" in the catalogues of major publishers (p. 287). My own cursory inspection of current catalogues suggests that, if anything, the situation has gotten worse, reinforcing the fear that books of quality will be relegated to a smaller niche within the children's literature market. Yolen's apprehension that "if bad books continue to outsell good books, if litter outsells literature, publishers will eventually stop publishing the good" (p. 287) is one that we would do well to take seriously. Zipes (2001) provides a perceptive summary of these conflicting tendencies.

> Children's literature is seeing a flowering of innovative books and illustrations for readers from two to sixteen that are not simply economic ventures. Children's literature needs and thrives on the work of fine writers and artists and fosters experimentation and challenges to the market. Unfortunately, the corporate structure will appropriate the new and sometimes highly unique children's books to quantify and rationalize these works according to market needs and calculations. (p. 48)

Despite the daunting challenges posed by these developments, we are not without power to influence them. Consumers, such as library and school communities, do have power through the sales they generate to influence what gets published. These communities can use their purchasing power to demand that the balance between books of quality and the spin-offs, gimmick, and other mass-market books be redressed. Schools that sponsor book fairs, most now run by Scholastic, can insist that the steady encroachment of mass market books on the lists of books offered for sale be reversed. A critical role also is played by committees who select the Newbery, Caldecott, the Kate Greenway Medal, and other awards. In the U.S., committees that nominate books for statewide awards such as the Georgia Book Award and the Texas Bluebonnet Award share this responsibility. These awards generate a significant boost to sales of books that win or are nominated. We must be aggressive in promoting the kinds of books that receive these awards and appear on these lists.

Central to the dilemma posed by rampant commercialism is whether children will be able to distinguish between books that win prestigious literary awards and the spin-offs and other mass market books I have been criticizing. Like many, I believe that these books are of marginal quality and content. In addition, these books are produced primarily for profit with little regard for literature itself, and the act of reading them is more an act of consumerism than engagement with a literary text (Friese, 2008; Hade & Edmonson, 2003). Similarly, one wonders whether children will be able to differentiate between, for example, Harry Potter as a brand and Harry Potter as a compelling character worth reading about. It is easy, as Mackey (2001) points out, to be so "overwhelmed by the hype and hyperbole" surrounding the release of the Potter and similar books to fear that the books themselves "will disappear into the maw of contemporary publicity and advertising and spin-offs" (p. 185). We must nurture the "global voices" flowing out of books that provide "the power to furnish [children's] heads with individual images that will connect them both to the world in general and their own country in particular" (Mahy, 2001, pp. 18–19).

These voices are an essential counterweight to branded, commodified voices of, to use Mahy's examples, *Pokémon* and the *Simpsons.* Again, educators, parents, and other caregivers must do more than simply lament and rail against the encroachment of products of our commodified culture into all aspects of children's lives. Fortunately, there is a growing body of scholarship offering promising suggestions for the development of a pedagogy that builds on the understanding that young people "are not passive dupes in this process; they have considerable agency in the consumption of these products" (Marsh, quoted by Friese, 2008, p. 78). Alvermann and Xu (2003) and Dyson (1997) point to ways to capitalize on children's fascination with superheroes by using texts found in our popular culture to foster the development of critical literacy skills. Friese (2008) points to work that illustrates that the structure and content of Pokémon texts and cards correspond to many important curricular goals and provide rich opportunities for engagement in mathematics, science, social studies, as well as reading and writing. Children can be taught to analyze critically the wide range of books and films that dominate popular culture (Apol, 1998; Giroux & Shannon, 1997), encouraged to read multiculturally (Hade, 1997; Möller, 2002), and to question the construction of gender in romance novels (Christian-Smith, 1991). Finally, we need to be more aggressive in promoting books that offer genuine aesthetic experiences and provide young people with insight and understanding into the growing diversity and complexity of our society. Careful examination of the wide range of books and films that dominate our popular culture and can attune children to the global voices Margaret Mahy spoke of.

Another issue raised by the commodification of literature and all aspects of our culture is the increasing economic exploitation of children. Roxburgh (2000) fears that they are being exploited today as consumers and wonders if pervasive commercialism is altering our perception of childhood, and even robbing our young of their childhoods. It is difficult not to be terrified that "we have become a nation which places a lower priority on teaching its children how to thrive socially, intellectually, even spiritually, than it does on training them to consume" (Schor, 2004, p. 11), or fear that media shapes children as consumers before they've developed their souls (Denby, 1996). We must work to ensure that developments in critical literacy can address and arrest these alarming developments.

These momentous trends, along with the decline in reading in many countries (Crandall, 2006a; National Endowment of the Arts, 2007) due at least in part to the proliferation of entertainment choices, makes it clear that there are no easy, facile answers to the issues raised in this chapter. To think that there are is naïve, perhaps dangerous. Nevertheless, we are not powerless and can and must foster the development of critical literacies and be unyielding in our commitment to promoting the kinds of books and reading experiences that led us here in the first place.

Literature References

Alexander, L. (1999). *The book of three.* New York, NY: Yearling Books.

Alexis, S. (2007). *The absolutely true story of a part-time Indian.* New York, NY: Little Brown.

Anderson, M. T. (2006) *The astonishing life of Octavian Nothing, traitor to the nation, Volume I: The pox party.* Cambridge, MA: Candlewick Press.

Babbitt, N. (1975). *Tuck everlasting.* New York, NY: Farrar, Straus and Giroux.

Cronin, D. (2000). *Click, clack, moo: Cows that type.* New York, NY: Simon & Schuster.

Falconer, I. (2000). *Olivia.* New York, NY: Atheneum.

Lewis, E. B. (1994). *The lion, the witch, and the wardrobe.* New York, NY: HarperCollins.

Madonna. (2003). *The English roses.* New York, NY: Calloway.

Rowlings, J. K. (2007). *Harry Potter and the Deathly Hallows.* New York, NY: Arthur A. Levine Books.

Selznick, B. (2007). *The invention of Hugo Cabret.* New York, NY: Scholastic.

Sendak, M. (1964). *Where the wild things are.* New York, NY: HarperCollins.

Shannon, D. (1998). *No David!* New York, NY: Blue Sky Press.

Steig, W. (1990). *Shrek.* New York, NY: Farrar, Straus and Giroux.

Suess, Dr. (1957). *The cat in the hat.* New York, NY: Random House.

Taylor, M. (1976). *Roll of thunder, hear my cry.* New York, NY: Dial.

Academic References

Agger, B. (1989). *Fast capitalism: A critical theory of significance.* Chicago, IL: University of Illinois Press.

Allsobrook, M. (2006). Early-20th-century Chinese children's literature: Self, state and story. *Bookbird, 44*(3), 5–12.

Alvermann, D. E. (2006). Afterword: Popular literacies in an era of "scientific" reading instruction: Challenges and opportunities. In J. Marsh & E. Millard (Eds.), *Popular literacies, childhood and schooling* (pp. 241–248). London: Routledge/Falmer.

Alvermann, D. E., & Xu, S. H. (2003). Children's everyday literacies: Intersections of popular culture and language arts instruction. *Language Arts, 81*, 145–154.

Alterman, E. (1998). Random violence. *The Nation, 266*(13), 5–6.

Anderson, C. (2004). The long tail. Retrieved August 15, 2007, from http://www.wired.com/wired/archive/12.10/tail_pr.html

Apol, L. (1998). "But what does that have to do with kids?": Literary theory and children's literature in the teacher education classroom. *Journal of Children's Literature, 22*(2), 32–46.

Apple, M. W. (1982). *Education and power.* New York, NY: Routledge

Auletta, K. (1997). The publishing world: The impossible business. *The New Yorker, 73*(30), 50–63.

Austin, P. (2003). A best-selling picture book by a brand new author: A consideration of the celebrity factor. *Booklist, 41*(2), 6–14.

Bainbridge, J., & Wolodko, B. (2002). Canadian picture books: Shaping and reflecting national identity. *Bookbird, 40*(2), 21–27.

Baker, J. (2008). American Girl heads to the big screen. Retrieved June 19, 2008, from http://www.npr.org/templates/story/story.php?storyId=91680901

Bing, J. (1999). You've got mail. *The Nation, 268*(3), 10.

Bruce, L. S. (2001). Meet Harry Potter … the boy with the $2bn face. Retrieved January 29, 2008, from http://findarticles.com/p/articles/mi_qn4156/is_/ai_n13960892

Buckingham, D., & Scanlon, M. (2005). Selling learning: Towards a political economy of edutainment media. *Media, Culture & Society, 27*(1), 41–58.

Chaikin, M. (1982). What's going on in publishing. *The Advocate, 1*, 144–148.

Chen, D. (2006). Trends in Chinese youth culture and literature. *Bookbird, 44*(3), 13–20.

Christian-Smith, L. (1991). *Becoming a woman through romance.* New York, NY: Routledge.

Cope, B., & Kalantzis, M. (Eds.). (2000). *Multiliteracies: Literacy learning and the design of social futures.* New York, NY: Routledge.

Coser, L. (1984). The publishing industry as a hybrid. *Library Quarterly, 54*(1), 5–12.

Coser, L., Kadushin, C., & Powell, W. (1982). *The culture and commerce of publishing.* New York, NY: Basic Books.

Crandall, N. (2006a). The U.K. children's book business: 1995–2004: A strategic analysis. *New Review of Children's Literature and Librarianship, 12*(1), 1–18.

Crandall, N. (2006b). Children's book publishers in the United Kingdom: New models for a new market place. *New Review of Children's Literature and Librarianship, 12*(2), 215–229.

Dawson, J. (1998). Trade and plumb-cake in Lilliput: The origins of juvenile consumerism and early English children's periodicals. *Children's Literature in Education, 29*(4), 175–198.

Denby, D. (1996). Buried alive: Our children and the avalanche of crud. *The New Yorker, 72*(19), 48–58.

Dyson, A. H. (1997). *Writing superheroes: Contemporary childhood, popular culture and classroom literacy.* New York, NY: Teachers College Press

Eccleshare, J. (1991). Trends in children's fiction in the United Kingdom during the 1980s. *Children's Literature in Education, 22*(1), 19–24.

Engelhardt, T. (1991). Reading may be harmful to your kids: In the Nadirland of children's books. *Harpers Magazine, 282*(1693), 55–62.

Epstein, C. (1996). Children's book publishing in the USA. In P. Hunt (Ed.), *International companion encyclopedia of children's literature* (pp. 478–497). New York, NY: Routledge.

Estes, G. (Ed.). (1985). *American writers for children before 1900.* Detroit, MI: Gale Research Publishing.

Frenkel, P. (1994). Russia: An equation with many, many unknowns. *Bookbird, 32*(1), 11–15.

Friese, E. (2008). Popular culture in the school library: Enhancing literacies through traditional and new. *School Libraries Worldwide, 14*(2), 68–82.

Gee, J. P. (2000). New people in new worlds: Networks, the new capitalism and schools. In B. Cope & M. Kalantzis (Eds.), *Multiliteracies: Literacy learning and the design of social futures* (pp. 43–68). New York, NY: Routledge.

Giblin, J. C. (1986). Children's book publishing in America: 1919 to now. *Children's Literature in Education, 17*(3), 150–158.

Giroux, H. A. (1999). *The mouse that roared: Disney and the end of innocence.* New York, NY: Rowman & Littlefield.

Giroux, H. A., & Shannon, P. (Eds.). (1997). *Education and cultural studies: Toward a performative practice.* New York, NY: Routledge.

Glovin, D. (2008). *Rowling warns of Potter plagiarism in trial testimony (Update4).* Retrieved May 3, 2008, from Bloomberg. com http://www.bloomberg.com/apps/news?pid=20601102&sid=aR2uXKyRcj4

Greco, A. N., Rodriguez, C. E., & Wharton, R. M. (2007). *The culture and commerce of publishing in the 21st century.* Stanford, CA: Stanford Business Books.

Hade, D. (1997). Reading multiculturally. In V. J. Harris (Ed.), *Using multiethnic literature in the K-8 classroom* (pp. 233–256). Norwood, MA: Christopher-Gordon.

Hade, D. (2001). Curious George gets branded: Reading as consuming. *Theory into Practice. 40*(3), 158–165.

Hade, D., & Edmonson, J. (2003). Children's book publishing in neoliberal times. *Language Arts, 81*, 135–183.

Hagood, M. C. (2001). Media literacies: Varied but distinguishable. In J. V. Hoffman, D. L. Schallert, C. M. Fairbanks, J. Worthy, & B. Maloch (Eds.), *Fiftieth yearbook of the National Reading Conference* (pp. 248–261). Chicago, IL: National Reading Conference.

Hai Fei. (2006). Paving a road to the azure sky: The present and future of Chinese children's publishing. *Bookbird, 44*(3), 79–85.

Harris, J. (2006) Disney launches broadband channel for preschoolers. Retrieved August 8, 2007, from http://www.imediaconnection.com/news/7883.asp

Haugland, A. (1994). The crack in the old canon: Culture and commerce in children's books. *The Lion and The Unicorn, 18,* 48–59.

Holt, K. (2004). Mass appeal: The children's book category gets a closer look from mass merchants. Retrieved January 27, 2007, from www.publishersweekly.com/article/CA372595. html?industryid=47139

Jacobs, J. S., & Tunnell, M. (2008). *Children's literature briefly, 4th edition.* Upper Saddle River, NJ: Pearson.

Kayden, M. (1993). Out of print and back in print: A commentary from the publisher's perspective. *Journal of Youth Services in Libraries, 6*, 265–269.

Keeline, J. (1995). The *Stratemeyer syndicate.* Retrieved October 30, 2008, from http://www.keeline.com/StratemeyerSyndicate. html

Kudriavtseva, L. (1994). Other voices: Coping with the caprices of a market economy. *Bookbird, 32*(4), 37–38.

Langer, B. (2004). The business of branded enchantment: Ambivalence and disjuncture in the global children's culture industry. *Journal of Consumer Culture, 4*(2), 251–277.

Larrick, N. (1972). The all-white world of children's books. In D. MacCann & G. Woodard (Eds.), *The Black American in books for children: Readings in racism* (pp. 156–168). Metuchen, NJ: Scarecrow Press.

Lechner, J. V. (1994). The new players in Hungarian children's publishing. *Bookbird, 32*(1), 19–23.

Levine, L. (1997). *The opening of the American mind: Canons, culture, and history.* Boston, MA: Beacon Press.

Lijun B. (2003). Capitalist bears and socialist modernisation: Chinese children's literature in the Post-Mao period. *Children's Literature in Education, 34*(1), 57–73.

Mackey, M. (2001). The survival of engaged reading in the internet age: New media, old media, and the book. *Children's Literature in Education, 32*(3), 167–189.

Mahy, M. (2001). A summery Saturday morning. *Bookbird, 39*(3), 16–19.

MacPherson, K. (2004). Critics, authors chafe as more celebrities join ranks of children's authors. Retrieved February 14, 2008, http://www.post-gazette.com/pg/04308/405539.stm

Marcus, L. S. (1997). Mother Goose to multiculturalism. *Publishers Weekly, 244*(31), 62–70.

Marcus, L. S. (2001). Make way for marketing: From high-minded to hype, the marketing of children. Retrieved on August 17, 2007 from http://www.publishersweekly.com/article/CA159619. html?industryid=47139

Marcus, L. S. (2007). In Golden Times: The story of the beloved Golden Books franchise is one of mid-century verve and innovation that remains relevant today. Retrieved September 28, 2007 fromhttp://www.publishersweekly.com/index.asp?layout=articlePrint&articleID=CA6460295

Maughan, S. (2002a). Hollywood happenings: How some children's books are making it big in show biz. Retrieved January 24, 2007, from http://www.publishersweekly.com/index.asp?layout=article&articleid=CA234550

Maughan, S. (2002b). Moving on up: Fantasy, film tie-ins and farts sell big to kids. Retrieved July 17, 2007, from http://www.publishersweekly.com/article/CA259517. html?industryid=47139

Miller, L. (2008). Review of *Minders of make-believe: Idealists, entrepreneurs, and the shaping of American children's literature* by Leonard S. Marcus. Retrieved June 16, 2008, from http://www.iht.com/bin/printfriendly.php?id=13693048

Miller, M. C. (2002). What's wrong with this picture? Retrieved November 11, 2007, from http://www.thenation.com/doc/20020107/miller.

Möller, K. (2002). Providing support for dialogue in literature discussions about social justice. *Language Arts, 75*, 467–477.

Moran, J. (1997).The role of multimedia conglomerates in American trade book publishing. *Media, Culture and Society, 19,* 441–455.

National Endowment for the Arts. (2007). National Endowment for the Arts announces new reading study. Retrieved December 13, 2008, from http://www.nea.gov/news/news07/TRNR.html

Nel, P. (2005). Is there a text in this advertising campaign?: Literature, marketing, and Harry Potter. *The Lion and the Unicorn, 29*(2), 236–267.

Nodelman, P., & Reimer, M. (2003). *The pleasures of children's literature* (3rd ed.). Boston, MA: Allyn and Bacon.

Palmer Cox: The Walt Disney of the Victorian Age. Retrieved on November 13, 2008, from http://www.gnomesandfairies.com/palmercox.html

Paterson, M. (2006). *Consumption and everyday life.* New York, NY: Routledge

Pecora, N. O. (1998). *The business of children's entertainment.* NY: Guilford Press.

Potter, B. (2008). Retrieved November 10, 2008, from http://us.penguingroup.com/nf/Author/AuthorPage/0,,0_1000025758,00.html?sym=BIO

Raugust, K. (2007). Children's bookshelf: Book-based properties on the rise at this year's licensing show. Retrieved November 2, 2007, from http://www.publishersweekly.com/article/CA6456224.hml?industryid=47139

Reynolds, K. (1998). Publishing practices and the practicalities of publishing. In K. Reynolds & N. Tucker (Eds.), *Children's book publishing in Britain since 1945* (pp. 2–20). Aldershot, England: Scolar Press.

Reynolds, K., & Tucker, N. (1998). *Children's book publishing in Britain since 1945.* Aldershot, England: Scolar Press.

Ritzer, G. (2000). *The McDonaldization of society.* Boston, MA: Pine Forge Press.

Roxburgh, S. (2000). Trilobites, palm pilots, and vampires: Publishing children's books in the twenty-first century. *Horn Book Magazine, 76*(6), 653–660.

Rui, T. (2006). Chinese children's literature in the 21st century. *Bookbird, 44*(3), 21–28.

Schiffrin, A. (1999). When we devoured books. In R. Rosenblatt (Ed.), *Consuming desires: Consumption, culture and the pursuit of happiness* (pp. 111–121). Washington, DC: Island Press/Shearwater Books.

Schiffrin, A. (2000). *The business of books: How international conglomerates took over publishing and changed the way we read.* New York, NY: Verso.

Schor, J. B. (2004). *Born to buy.* New York, NY: Scribner.

Sévenier, G. (2004). American cultural imperialism: Gift or threat?: Retrieved September 25, 2008, from http://gsevenier.free.fr/culturalImperialism.html

Shepard, A. (1988). What's good for the children's book business. Retrieved July 21, 2007, from http://scbwi.org/pubs/scbwi_pubs/shepherd/whats_good.htm

Simon, D. (2000). Keepers of the word. A review of *The business of books* by Andre Schiffrin. *The Nation, 271*(21), 25–32.

Smith, B. K. (2007). Branded literacy: The entrepreneurship of Oprah's book club. In B. Danielle and P. Mortensen (Eds.), *Women and literacy: Local and global inquiries for a new century* (pp. 157–170). New York, NY: Erlbaum.

Stan, S. (1999). Going global: World literature for American children. *Theory Into Practice, 38*(3), 168–177.

Stossel, S. (2001). Bibliosophy. *American Prospect, 12*(2), 40–43.

Stottele, G. (1994). To the point/An imperfect union. *Bookbird, 32*(4), 28–29.

Taxel, J. (1981). The outsiders of the American revolution: The selective tradition in children's fiction. *Interchange, 12*(2–3), 206–228.

Taxel, J. (2002). Children's literature at the turn of the century: Toward a political economy of the publishing industry. *Research in the Teaching of English, 37*(2), 146–198.

Tucker, N. (1998). Setting the scene. In K. Reynolds & N. Tucker (Eds.), *Children's book publishing in Britain since 1945* (pp. 1–20). Aldershot, England: Scolar Press.

van Elteren, M. (2003). U.S. cultural imperialism today: Only a chimera? *SAIS Review, 23*(2), 169–188.

Whiteside, T. (1980, October 6). Onward and upward with the arts: The blockbuster complex-II. *The New Yorker, 56*, 63–146.

Williams, R. (1977). *Marxism and literature.* New York, NY: Oxford University Press.

Wolf, S. A. (2004). *Interpreting literature with children.* Mahwah, NJ: Erlbaum.

Yolen, J. (1997). Taking time: Or how things have changed in the last thirty-five years of children's publishing. *The New Advocate, 10*, 285–291.

Zipes, J. (1997). *Happily ever after: Fairy tales, children and the culture industry.* New York, NY: Routledge.

Zipes, J. (2001). *Sticks and stories: The troublesome success of children's literature from Slovenly Peter to Harry Potter.* New York, NY: Routledge.

36

Spinning Off

Toys, Television, Tie-Ins, and Technology

Margaret Mackey

University of Alberta

When literature becomes marketable both for its stories and its adaptability across mediums and media, one outcome is certainly increased profits and motivation to secure readers' interests and loyalty, as Joel Taxel describes in the preceding chapter. Another outcome, as Margaret Mackey argues, is expanded opportunities for retelling, reshaping, and revaluing a story's original form, content, and audience. In a reach across disciplines, Mackey outlines the questions raised by the "slipperiness" of stories for authors, publishers, educators, and researchers, who all want to know how readers—especially the generation of children who know books as commodities—understand and engage with multiple story forms. While multinational and multimedia enterprises seek ever-narrower storylines for a predetermined market, readers, artists, and entrepreneurs are very busy making up their own spin-offs.

In the world of children's literature, *Harry Potter* stands alone as a singular and astonishing exception to many generalizations. So, perhaps it is reading too much into a one-off phenomenon to be taken aback by a "Special Collector's Issue" of the American publication, *Entertainment Weekly*, a magazine normally focused on Hollywood press releases and gossip. "Goodbye, Harry," reads the headline of the issue of August 3, 2007, and a flash promises readers "36 pages of Pottermania!" The image shows a child with glasses and a scar, immersed in the pages of *Harry Potter and the Deathly Hallows* (Rowling, 2007).

The extraordinary saga of how the *Harry Potter* series developed from ordinary children's books into the kind of pop culture phenomenon that could dominate a whole issue of *Entertainment Weekly* is unique. But Harry is not alone in moving easily between books, movies, Internet sites, magazines, toys, games, Happy Meals, and fan fiction, although not many heroes of print fiction will successfully emulate his total and astonishing fluidity. It is actually Harry's readers who join him in inhabiting a multimedia world, where multiple versions, incarnations, adaptations and spin-offs are completely taken for granted.

The scale of spin has escalated over the past two generations of children. But children's literature and toys have always been partnered; pioneer children's publisher John Newbery (1744) sold balls and pincushions with his

A Pretty Little Pocket Book in the 18th century. Popular authors have often explored the "franchise" possibilities of their successful works; Lewis Carroll approved a Wonderland Postage-Stamp Case (Watson, 2001), and, in the early 1900s, Beatrix Potter was an indefatigable marketer of spin-off commodities (Mackey, 1998). Simultaneously, L. Frank Baum (1900), in the United States, exploited adaptations in both old and very new media (a stage musical, toys and games, even hand-colored film, a breakthrough in 1908) to advertise and re-tell *The Wonderful Wizard of Oz* and its successors (Hearn, 2000/1973).

So adaptations, tie-ins and commodities are not new to the world of children's and young adult literature. Nevertheless, the past few decades, especially in the West, have seen an exponential increase in the re-spinning of stories for young people into a variety of versions, back-stories, and associated objects. The assumption that a story will exist in a variety of shapes and formats is now commonplace, and Fleckenstein (2003) provides a useful phrase for describing this phenomenon. She refers to "slippery texts" (p. 105), a phrase that will serve both as a descriptor and as a heuristic for investigating the mutating shape of contemporary materials.

Slippery texts proliferate on all sides. Correspondingly and appropriately slippery research into this phenomenon is harder to pin down. Different research traditions—literary criticism, education, library science, cultural studies, economics, cognitive narratology—all explore the territory of textual metamorphosis, each using different conceptual lenses and different methodologies. Any overview of this complex challenge is certain to be partial. Nevertheless, in this chapter, in pursuit of this challenge, I will address issues of "slipperiness," focusing on a number of topics:

- Adaptations of children's literature
- Spin-off toys and commodities and services
- The impact on reading of associated forms of consumption
- Consumer-produced adaptations and spin-offs

Slipperiness makes for a varied and fascinating cultural landscape but it creates barriers to the development of manageable yet rigorous methodologies for exploring the contemporary scene of young people's literature, broadly defined. The ever-ramifying extension of spin-off materials makes it difficult to assemble any kind of definitive text-set for content analysis. The exponential rate of diversification in the formats and interactive potential of texts that appeal to young people means that reception studies are often outdated before they can be published. And as cultural, political, and economic structures struggle to keep up with the cultural implications of technological change, the institutional frameworks that support literary experience are also in flux.

To a certain extent, slippery research *tools* are part of the solution. Digitally updated information, particularly about popular culture, is accessible through a variety of websites, listservs, news feeds, blogs, and so forth. Digital forms of analysis and distribution speed the research process—but events invariably move even faster.

With a topic as complex as the spiraling proliferation of adaptations and spin-offs, the research challenges are formidable. There is a need for analytical tools for the principled comparison of adapted versions that take into account both the technical requirements of different media and also the varying ways in which metaphors, themes, subtexts, and ideologies may be translated into new forms (a translation that often must also take account of new times, when one text is antecedent to its adaptations). Textual analysis alone, however, runs the danger of leading to monolithic conclusions unless augmented and contested by reception studies that provide a channel through which to hear the identities and voices of young readers, viewers, players, and collectors; and refined by attention to the commercial imperatives that very often shape and direct artistic choices. Furthermore, the whole intellectual enterprise runs the risk of operating permanently in catch-up mode, as young people adopt new media possibilities at an accelerating rate. Livingstone (1998) encapsulates some of the problem as follows:

> The creation of meaning through the interaction of texts and readers is a struggle, a site of negotiation between two semi-powerful sources. Each side has different powerful strategies, each has different points of weakness and each has different interests. It is this process of negotiation which is central. And through analysis of this process, traditional conceptions of both texts and readers may require rethinking, for each has long been theorized in ignorance of the other. (p. 26)

Livingstone's warning is true enough even in the relatively circumscribed world of print reading, where it is relatively unusual for researchers to combine particular, detailed, and critical textual analysis with thick, rich description of readers' responses to a specified individual text. Add the complications of expanding media versions and the need to capture the behavior of readers as they move between one version and another of a particular story, and the challenge becomes simply gigantic.

Adaptations of Children's Literature

Literary adaptations come in many guises, sometimes but not always involving a change of medium. Print adaptations include stories being abridged, converted into simple English for second language readers or readers younger than the original market, or published in different formats (a picture book story republished as a short story, for example, or vice versa). A shift of medium may involve an audio recording of a reading or a dramatization; or it may entail a transformation into film; less commonly, a children's book may serve as the basis of a digital game. For a short period at the end of the last century, picture books were converted into CD-ROMs, but that technology has now faded. Websites related to selected book titles, however, continue to flourish. A relatively new development involves "transmedia" stories, where the narrative is distributed across a variety of platforms (film, book, TV series, website, for example) and an interpreter needs to follow suit to gain access to the complete story (Jenkins, 2008/2006).

Much of the theoretical literature about adaptation involves the transmutation of a novel into a film, a television series or a stage play (e.g., Cardwell, 2002; Cartmell & Whelehan, 1999; Chatman, 1978; Giddings, Selby, & Wensley, 1990; McFarlane, 1996; Reynolds, 1993). These studies investigate what components of a story are directly transferable between media and what must be re-expressed to suit a new medium. A small number of scholars (e.g., Morris, 2000; Wojcik-Andrews, 2000) and publications (e.g., a special issue of *The Lion and the Unicorn* in June 1996; an edited book of essays [Street, 1983]) look specifically at children's film adaptations.

Pluralities and Pleasures

But today's young people move between many different media versions of their favorite literature, not just back and forth between the print page and the moving image. Not only may they experience and re-experience the same story in many different incarnations, they also live in a world where the trailer, the spoiler, and the YouTube highlight develop an important impact on the concept of the aesthetic whole as a unit of experience in which fragments of a story repeat ever more endlessly.

Lunenfeld (2000) tackles the never-ending plurality of the most popular stories directly, talking about an "aesthetic of unfinish" (p. 7) that arises partly out of the commercial impulse to create successful brands of fiction and partly out of the plethora of media opportunities to tell and re-tell. Hutcheon (2006) also explores this impulse to experience the same fiction over and over again in different instantiations across a wide range of media. "[T]here must," she argues, "be something particularly appealing about adaptations *as adaptations*" (p. 4). She suggests part of the pleasure,

> …comes simply from repetition with variation, from the comfort of ritual combined with the piquancy of surprise. Recognition and remembrance are part of the pleasure (and risk) of experiencing an adaptation; so too is change. Thematic and narrative persistence combines with material variation. (p. 4)

Fidelity and Form: Narrative and Enunciation

The question of fidelity is important to discussions of adaptation, and was often foregrounded, for example, in responses to the first three *Harry Potter* movies. The first two stories were filmed very faithfully by Chris Columbus, but the third, directed by Alfonso Cuarón, branched out into new interpretive territory. A sample critique, drawn at random from an Internet search for the terms "Harry Potter faithful" reads as follows:

Columbus' entries were filmed books, whereas Cuarón creates a film based on a book. That may sound like arguing semantics, but between the two ideas is a huge artistic difference. Cuarón's film is not a reflection but its own image.

In fact, "Prisoner of Azkaban" would be a better film if Cuarón and the writer were freed from the book entirely. The only unsatisfactory portions are the opening and closing 20 minutes, which frantically attempt to keep pace with the novel's dense plot. (Westhoff, 2004, n.p.)

Some core components of a story can and should be transferred between media in order for the story to be recognizable. Some elements of the story are integrally related to how it is told and these elements must necessarily transform when the form of telling changes. McFarlane (1996) provides one set of working vocabulary for discussing these fundamentals when he defines and labels the distinction between:

> (i) those elements of the original novel which are transferable because not tied to one or other semiotic system—that is, essentially, *narrative*, and
> (ii) those which involve intricate processes of adaptation because their effects are closely tied to the semiotic system in which they are manifested – that is, *enunciation*. (p. 20)

McFarlane is discussing the movement of a novel into a film but contemporary stories migrate among a much larger range of media, as Hutcheon (2006) points out:

> If you think adaptation can be understood by using novels and films alone, you're wrong. The Victorians had a habit of adapting just about everything—and in just about every possible direction; the stories of poems, novels, plays, operas, paintings, songs, dances, and *tableaux vivants* were constantly being adapted from one medium to another and then back again. We postmoderns have clearly inherited this same habit, but we have even more new materials at our disposal – not only film, television, radio, and the various electronic media, of course, but also theme parks, historical enactments, and virtual reality experiments. The result? Adaption has run amok. That's why we can't understand its appeal and even its nature if we only consider novels and films. (p. xi)

Nevertheless, though Hutcheon is clearly correct in considering a much broader range of adaptation, the concepts of narrative and enunciation, derived from the print-film nexus, have some general utility in considering the processes involved. Adaptation has indeed run amok, and as a result even very young children have at least a tacit understanding that books can do some things well and some things less well; that movies can take certain components out of books to be re-expressed but that other elements are less readily transferred; that the affordances of an interactive text work differently from the possibilities inherent in a fixed text and so forth. Even very young interpreters of text are at least tacitly sophisticated when it comes to issues of interpreting adaptations. And many understand that a singular fixation on fidelity can unduly restrict a new telling.

Interpreting Adaptations

Research into young people's adaptations explores a number of issues, including the following:

- analysis of specific examples of adapted and adaptable materials for children,
- studies of young people and their understanding of adaptation processes,
- institutional studies of the politics and economics of varied forms of adaptation.

Much of the research into adapted materials focuses on double or multiple instantiations of singular stories. Studies of young people's overt and tacit understanding of adaptation encompass an eclectic disciplinary range and tackle the development of narrative understanding, including the relatively new field of cognitive narratology that explores the "mental tools, processes and activities that make possible our ability to construct and understand narrative" (Scholes, Phelan, & Kellogg, 2006/1966, p. 290). Explorations of the politics and economics of children's adaptations concentrate on the potential and the constraints involved in particular media (film, television, digital games, etc.), the battles over intellectual freedom and copyright, and the impact of commercial frameworks. There is, of course, much overlap among these categories.

Textual Analysis of Adaptations: Bridging the Known and the New

Adaptation is always a form of interpretation and recontextualization. The question of what can be expressed in which medium raises important issues. To take one specific but striking example, a book does not incorporate a soundtrack, but many other formats use music as part of the presentation. David Paterson (1998), discussing his adaptation of Katherine Paterson's (1978) *The Great Gilly Hopkins* for the stage, says, "A song allows for a whole range of emotions that an audience would probably not accept if directed toward them as a speech. Music also allowed us to cover an exposure of time or location during the play" (p. 33). George Bodmar (1992) quotes Maurice Sendak on a 1975 television production of Sendak's (1962) *Nutshell Library* and (1960) *The Sign on Rosie's Door*: "He said of Carole King's music, 'She added her own emotional quality and gave my words a reverberation that they didn't originally have. They've taken on a new edge and weight'" (p. 168). But in opera at least, music creates its own demands; as Bodmer (1992) observes of the opera version of Sendak's (1963) *Where the Wild Things Are*,

> The music is stridently modern, and ends with an ascending phrase, which robs Max's discovery that his supper is still hot of any final resolution or triumph. While Sendak made the decision in the book to present the climax of his story facing a blank page rather than a picture, in opera no such option is open; everything must be sung and shown. (p. 172)

Spike Jonze's 2009 film version of Where the Wild Things Are catered for the possibilities and necessities of a full-length feature film, expanding the story radically with a frame narrative, and exploiting the full potential of computer graphics. In the lead-up to the film's release, it was interesting to see the creative marketing use of a variety of online trailers (themselves an appealing new text form) to whet appetites and prepare devotees for a somewhat different telling.

Adaptation often involves ideological changes as well. Stephens and McCallum (1996), discussing live-action and animated versions of Frances Hodgson Burnett's (1911) *The Secret Garden*, express it as follows:

> The story becomes a site on which the values and assumptions central to one particular cultural formation may be interrogated through the values and assumptions of another cultural formation, so that both self-reflectively and implicitly a new telling reproduces the existential concerns of the pre-text(s) even while it contests and transforms their significance. To put it another way, any particular retelling becomes, at least potentially, a new negotiation between what is textually and culturally already given, and what is new. (p. 357)

The relationship between already given and new may involve changing political perspectives. The attitudes of earlier generations towards racial and/or gender differences are often silently amended in new adaptations, though complete erasure of the original biases is not always straightforward. Diane Carver Sekeres (2005) presents some of the problems in a fascinating study of how the 19th-century popular girls' series Finley's (1867) *Elsie Dinsmore*, set in the slave-owning South, was revised to meet demand in the contemporary Christian market for inspirational fiction:

> The editors eliminated the slave dialect and also softened the interactions between master and slave, but the rewritten edition does nothing to address the racism typical of literature of the time that assumed slaves were content with their lot in life. The new edition's changes only disguised the deeper structures that created the context for the obvious degrading language and mannerisms of African American characters.... While the modern portrayal of the servants may seem more respectful of the African American characters on the surface, it may also reinforce the impression that their servitude was willing and inconsequential. (pp. 15-16, 28-29)

Adaptations may carry with them the assumptions and stereotypes of an earlier text, but the fact that this story is transferred into a "new bottle" may cause young readers to regard the new incarnation as contemporary, even radical. The contemporary nature of the enunciation may camouflage old-fashioned elements in the narrative. Matt Jackson (1997), exploring Marc Brown's (1986) *Arthur's Teacher Trouble* both as paper book and as CD-ROM "interactive book" draws attention to the potential for conflicting messages. He points out that as a mass-market text *Arthur* is heavily dependent on stereotypes, which in the case of this particular story lead to the inclusion of three lessons that might well alarm parents: society draws gender boundaries that are not to be crossed; school is no fun; and we are what we consume. (p. 33)

The designers, says Jackson, took a story that was based on stereotypes and "then added elements that reinforce the patriarchal worldview inherent in the original story" (p. 35). The animations that leap to life under the moving cursor add a veneer of sophisticated playfulness to the story, but Jackson (1997) is not impressed.

Rather than encouraging meaningful interaction with the narrative and the computer, these CD-ROMs merely combine the linear format of a book with the attention-getting sound effects and pratfalls of a television cartoon. No attempt is made to use this technology to foster creative thinking or to explore new methods of constructing a story (p. 35). Yet, the format of the CD-ROM suggests that the story represents a contemporary and exciting new take on the world, a clash that is only partially disguised by the humor in the interactive version of the story.

Martin and Taylor (2006) suggest that some limitations of originating stories may actually foster reincarnation in particular kinds of new media. Looking at digital game versions of J.M. Barrie's (1904) *Peter Pan*, they point out,

> *Peter Pan* clearly fits the basic structure required for adventure and heroism…. Further, *Peter* Pan provides structural and character archetypes that are often used in video games, as well as in oral narratives…. However, *Peter Pan* also parallels video game sensibilities in that both video games and the *Peter Pan* play and novel versions fail to adequately address female characters even when the female characters are pivotal or when they offer new possibilities. This is especially true for video game versions of *Peter Pan* because many of the games rely heavily on video game schemas, which often use only one main male character. (pp. 174–175)

Digital works, suggest Martin and Taylor (2006), "offer a literate return to oral narratives in their modular format, nonlinear structures, participatory requirements, and lack of one definitive version" (p. 180). The complex case of *Peter Pan*, which has always lacked one single definitive version (Rose, 1984), serves as a reminder that some children's texts are shapeshifters from their inception, and that exposing them to what Peter Lunenfeld (2000/1999) calls "the universal solvent of the digital" (p. 14) simply highlights a protean nature that is built into the narrative's specific history.

Adaptions and New Audiences

Altering the medium makes certain changes possible; adaptations may also alter the audience, with different consequences. Davies (2001), exploring movie versions of *The Secret Garden*, observes that Burnett's 1911 book "treats the topic of sexuality, the great, fascinating taboo of early childhood, in a way that is 'safe,' through a series of

narrative events" (p. 51). The 1993 film version "discards this oblique approach and makes the sexual elements more explicit to the extent of changing many of the author's characterizations, narrative events, and descriptions and adding others" (p. 51).

The stage musical version of *The Secret Garden* has similarly been charged with addressing adults more than children, but Phyllis Bixler (1994), discussing this variant rendition, suggests that all adaptations must necessarily "misread" the original text, and that "narratives contain many secrets for a reader to discover—or buried seeds of many other stories, which a reader's imagination can coax into bloom" (p.114).

Clearly, a child audience does not "own" even its most beloved classics, a topic worthy of further exploration. Those who love a book best are often the leeriest of a new version, and we know too little about what may seduce them to take the psychological risks of exploring a different incarnation of that beloved story.

Research into Young People's Comprehension of Adapted Narratives

Studies of how children develop understanding of the conventions of different media need to keep current with evolving technologies, a complication underlined by a poignant comment from Tim Morris (2000) about his own annual childhood viewing of *Peter Pan* on his black-and-white television:

> Watching the same show come round year after year in the cycle of seasons, I did not understand then—as children do today, with VCRs that show them perfect iterations of dramas on command—that the story of *Peter Pan* never changed. So my memories of watching the show are memories of anxiety: Would the children be able to fly? What would Captain Hook do to Wendy when he kidnapped her? And most distressing, would Tinker Bell be saved from death this time? Did America still believe in fairies? I can still feel myself squirming in my pajamas at the suspense of it all. (p. 108)

The shift caused by the first video recordings, which converted the professionally produced moving image into something to hold in your hand and control in your own home, was cultural, economic, and also cognitive. This change was enormous. Children famously learn how to run the video cassette recorder and the DVD player at a very early age (my own children gave me a birthday card which featured a baby showing its mother how to use the remote control), and the impact on their understanding of media affordances is substantial. DVDs with their added extras contribute to the media literacy of very young viewers as they explore the constructed nature of video fictions. Such instruction is not entirely new; *The Wonderful World of Disney* pioneered behind-the-scenes insights into animation, for example, in the early days of television. But the ubiquity and repeatability of the DVD extra makes it much more broadly available.

Studies of children's cognitive development as they master how to interpret both old and new media are not always based on examples from the best of children's literature, nor do they always draw on complex critical analysis of the given texts as part of developing an understanding of the issues. Hodge and Tripp's (1986) excellent work on how children develop an understanding of the modality (degree of fictionality) of television is based on texts such as *Fangface* and *Yogi Bear* rather than literary examples. Their findings about children's growing awareness of how fiction works and how fictionality is marked in televisual terms, are nevertheless broadly and usefully applicable to more literary works as well. Robinson's (1997) study of children's growing understanding of print and television also draws on many popular television texts, not all of them created explicitly for children. It too provides very informative examples of children articulating their developing awareness of such elements as genre constraints and possibilities that could inform their interpretation of both media. Similarly, the work of Anne Haas Dyson (1997, 2003) offers a lens on very young children as they draw on a huge range of textual experiences to develop a broad sense of their own capabilities as textual agents. Lawrence Sipe (2000) explores responses of very young children to picture books. In a 2000 study, he explores the range of intertextual connections from a variety of media upon which these children draw for their interpretation of a particular story. We need more of such detailed work to enrich our understanding of how our capacity to interpret stories in many media develops through childhood and adolescence.

Much current research into young people's multiple responses to variant versions of texts comes from the fields of popular culture and/or education and addresses questions that may be labeled as concerning *literacy* rather than *literary* experiences (e.g., Alvermann, 2002; Buckingham, 1993, 1996, 1998; Davis & Dickinson, 2004; Hilton, 1996; Kinder, 1991, 1999; Marsh & Millard, 2000; McDonnell, 2001). For example, Karen Wohlwend (2009) provides detailed insight into little girls negotiating how to combine the dainty limits of the *Disney Princess* world with the cognitive demands and gender politics of the kindergarten classroom, using skill with adaptable texts as a major tool for asserting an identity.

The degree of overlap between these works and the field of literary studies is far from clearly delineated, and there is much work to be done to draw the strands together. Too often in purely literary studies the idea of the reader is an abstraction (Littau, 2006); too often in literacy work the significance of how the text is composed is overlooked or taken for granted. But we will understand the fluidity of contemporary textual mutations in more sophisticated ways if we make room for research that combines an aesthetic analysis of the text with the individual responses of particular interpreters.

The importance of researching reception as well as production is underlined by a study of eighth graders responding to Anne Frank's (1952) *The Diary of a Young Girl*. Spector and Jones (2007) argue that the stage adaptation of this book and the subsequent movie have created a version of Anne Frank that focuses unduly on her optimistic and unquenchable spirit: "the enshrinement of Anne in American consciousness causes some students to repel thoughts that may shatter the culturally acquired uplifting version they have of Anne Frank" (p. 37). They offer quotes that show readers in action—readers who may be described as every bit as slippery as any text mentioned in this chapter.

Even when students were explicitly told of her cruel death, they still tended to imagine her in hopeful ways. When students answered a question in their textbook… that asked how Anne could have been happy in a concentration camp, Charlotte answered, "Knowing Anne, she was happy in the concentration camps. She didn't have to be quiet anymore; she could frolic outside. She could be in nature. She loved nature. I think this was a welcome relief for her." The basis for Charlotte's version was simply, "Knowing Anne…." (p. 40). Charlotte's classmates unanimously agreed with her prediction, even though they were studying the Holocaust and presumably had some schema of concentration camps.

Readers have always been good at seeing what they want to see in a story, and being able to move between versions of that story may increase this propensity. Spector and Jones (2007) provide an illuminating example of a reader actively imposing meaning on a section of text. Working in a small group, Brooke and a few classmates are asked to describe Anne's most noticeable characteristics. They decide that she is an optimist who loves talking and Brooke turns to the book for support:

> Brooke: Here it is! [She reads] "It's utterly impossible for me to build my life on a foundation of chaos…" Blah, blah, blah. No, here it is, "… ideals, dreams and cherished hopes rise within us, only to be crushed." Blah, blah, blah, "…I still believe, in spite of everything, that people are truly good at heart"….That's it! That's the one. Someone else write that down.
>
> While trying to find the one line that supersedes all other statements Anne Frank made in the Diary, Brooke literally drowned out with "blah, blah, blah" the contradictory material. (p. 43)

The line about people being good at heart, as Brooke's ruminations demonstrate, is just one perspective among many contradictions in Anne's own diary. However, this line provides the inspirational voice-over that concludes the stage show and the movie, shifting the moral compass of the story away from the cruel senselessness of Anne's actual end. Brooke's determination to over-ride those components of the written text that challenge the simplistic "misreading" offered by the dramatized version is startling in its ruthless determination to impose optimism. We need more reception studies that explore the possibility that multiple versions of a demanding story may enable a kind of "mix 'n' match" interpretation in which readers draw the most pleasing components from different incarnations of a story. What is the impact of such potential slipperiness on the growth of literary understanding? Do multiple incarnations of a story add or reduce potential for depth of understanding?

Political and Economic Study of Media Affordances and Limits

Media operate within social and institutional frameworks. The example of television is instructive because different countries make specific national arrangements for the funding of programming, and the range of institutional structures highlights the fact that television's possibilities and constraints are as much socially constructed as inherent in the medium itself. Like most other media, television itself is also in flux, with the onset of cable, satellite, and digital distribution causing substantial change, and such developments apply differential pressure to particular national institutions.

An American example offers a window onto the constraints of the commercial framework. Willis, adaptor of Jill Murphy's (1974) *The Worst Witch* for HBO, lists an assortment of considerations that arise directly from television's perceived mandate:

> What usually makes the adaptation of material for television difficult is not the difference in audience but the constraints that network television puts on the material…. No matter what the audience or material, there are going to be *x* number of commercial breaks, which is one reason why most movies produced for network television are less effective dramatically than they might be. They are written to bring the audience back after each commercial break. (quoted in Freyer, 1987, p. 81)

Willis is speaking prior to the fragmentation of television monoliths and before satellite and cable, personal video recorders, and computer downloads undermined the Big Three American networks. But the constraints of the commercial break are still dominant in American television, even today.

More recently, Davies (2005) discussed the organization of children's television in Britain in terms of "the politics of children's screen provision," listing such institutional conditions as "the legal mandating of the British, terrestrial commercial channel, ITV, to provide children's programming, or the BBFC's (British Board of Film Classification) age-classification of films" (p. 389). British TV institutions for decades supported one significant form of literary adaptation: the classic children's serial. But in 2007, the United Kingdom media regulator, Ofcom, warned that the current systems were failing children, and pointed out that home-grown television accounted for just 17% of children's programming in the UK. In 2006, investment in new children's programs fell from $254 million to $218 million. Jocelyn Hay, chair of a viewers' group, lamented that the corporations supplying entertainment for children were relying on American content, "much of it soaps or animation. Unless swift action is taken to retrieve the situation, future generations will grow up with a Disneyfied view not only of the world, but of their own language and culture" (Clarke, 2007b).

National identity and cultural priority are complex categories. The Canadian government has opposed the illegal importation of ethnic TV programming via satellite, although "Disneyfied" American imports are common in Canada. Beaty and Sullivan (2007) challenge this position as protectionist:

> [T]he Canadian government has positioned its audience as passive consumers marshalled in the service of a massive economic infrastructure…. Under the cloak of cultural sovereignty, Canada continues to promote protectionist measures for the broadcasting industry that undermine diversity and multiculturalism. It also steadfastly refuses to acknowledge that the cultural and technological landscape has changed dramatically since the earlier and still dominant model of media scarcity and border patrol. (p. 66)

Even as the technologies of television diversify, a European study of video platforms, conducted in 2007 by Bain & Co. for Liberty Global, concluded that the popularity of television is likely to be sustained even in the face of new technological options. They predict that even by 2012 "only a fifth of viewing will be on-demand despite the onset of downloaded content via computers and mobile devices" (Clarke, 2007a).

Venues for children's programming that were once stable are manifestly in turmoil, and nobody is entirely clear how it will all work out in the end. As a result, current research into television adaptations is even more likely to be dated by the time it can be published than it has been in the past. Television offers a single, if particularly convoluted and uniquely visible example of a problem that pervades this whole territory of reworking. The institutions that govern production, distribution, and assessment (often in the form of ratings that establish fitness for children) are all in flux.

Not only television but also movies and even books are being recast in the light of commercial pressures. Jennifer Geer (2007) describes the business models that govern movie releases, and suggests that scholars, "would do well…to resist the interpretive paradigms these corporations offer, including the ways in which they encourage audiences to equate their marketing with their films" (p. 194).

Likewise, Philip Nel (2005), discussing the *Harry Potter* marketing phenomenon, warns that when "…the novels and the hype become intertwined, …analyses [may] fail to take into account the full complexity of either…. First of all, conflating the books with the marketing fails to produce a sufficiently sophisticated analysis of the latter. Second, such critical conflation leads some critics to overlook the novels' considerable literary achievements." (pp. 236–237)

Scholars need to explore ways of disentangling the marketing apparatus from the text being sold, in whatever medium (bearing in mind that books are presented, hyped, evaluated, and sold within a framework every bit as commercial as that which sponsors mass market products; they do not exist in some pure high-cultural vacuum). At the same time, reception studies may help to remind us that many children consume the entire package, readily using marketing cues to frame their experience of and response to the aesthetic text.

Spin-off Toys, Commodities, and Services

Saturation marketing of text-related toys and things is a familiar phenomenon to Western children. Whereas their literature strikes adults as an important and benevolent part of children's lives, and their films (at least the good ones) provide insights into the world or, at a minimum, some hours of harmless amusement, the world of toys and commodities is not as culturally sanctified. "Stuff," even literary-related "stuff," makes many adults uneasy. The fact that children in developing countries may actually produce the playthings their Western counterparts carelessly consume and discard does not contribute to an attractive picture. The disposable nature of many commodities (as opposed to the presumed lasting values of literature) also provokes unease.

The layering involved in text-based commodities may be very complex, particularly with those toys that arise from contemporary adaptations of texts created in earlier times under earlier value systems. Sekeres (2004) provides a vivid example of value distortion in her description of an *Elsie Dinsmore* doll. Based on the 19th-century novels discussed above, this slave-owning character (renowned for her pious and feminine passivity) is advertised to a largely Christian market as "not just dolls—'THEY ARE ROLE MODELS!'" (p. 27). Just as the CD-ROM may provide a contemporary veneer to the patriarchal values of *Arthur's Teacher Trouble*, so this present-day incarnation of an old story embodies an outdated and unattractive ideology in ways that are presumably invisible to many purchasers.

Our current era certainly provides an almost infinite supply of spin-offs and commodities, many of them as reductive as the Elsie Dinsmore doll, though in different ways. But commodification of literature is not new. The history of *The Wizard of Oz* supplies an extensive list of merchandise from its earliest days. Richard Flynn (1996), in fact, suggests that commodification began with publication of the original book, and draws our attention to the idea of the book itself as commodity: "Always the consummate salesman, actor, and window-dresser, Baum (1900) must have recognized that his and William Wallace Denslow's investment in the elaborate color plates and textual illustrations (in effect, a form of packaging) would pay off handsomely" (p. 122). "The extensive colorwork in *The Wonderful Wizard of Oz* revolutionized the design of American children's books," says Michael Patrick Hearn (2000). "They would never be so wan and boring again" (p. xlvii).

For nearly 40 years, the print version of *The Wizard of Oz* and its many sequels provided the impetus for a universe of spin-off texts and associated stuff. John Fricke (1999) has assembled a stunning set of images from Willard Carroll's collection of *Oz* memorabilia; items such as an engraved collapsible metal cup in a souvenir box (presented to audience members of the 200th New York performance of the stage musical in 1903), wallpaper panels by Baum's illustrator Denslow, based on the same musical, the *Oz* board game of 1921, and so forth.

Certain texts (many of them aimed at children) have spawned such a spin-off industry of toys and commodities that they have given rise to books devoted to displaying and/or analyzing the range of materials available. Such compilations sometimes veer towards being coffee-table books (e.g., Fricke, 1999, on *The Wizard of Oz*); on other occasions, they serve as vehicles for nostalgia (e.g., Liljeblad, 1996, on TV toys and shows); sometimes they involve a historical overview (e.g., Thwaite, 1992, on *Winnie the Pooh*) or an analysis of the implications for young readers (e.g., Mackey, 1998, on *The Tale of Peter Rabbit*). All such publications share at least a moderate resemblance to a catalogue or bibliography, a distinctive form of research endeavor even when the level of analysis is low; but some of these titles are undeniably oriented to a popular rather than a scholarly audience, and the visual display of "stuff" is often the chief appeal. Nevertheless, they provide a vivid reminder that fiction-related commodities are not a new phenomenon.

In addition to compendiums of materials related to specific texts, more general work addresses some of the issues of commodification in broader terms (see also a related chapter on commodification of children's literature by Joel Taxel in this volume). As in so many arenas, *Harry Potter* often leads the way, numerically, in terms of scope of coverage and occasionally in ingenuity. The numbers themselves are staggering:

AOL Time Warner raked in $1.8 billion in global ticket sales from the first two movies. Coca-Cola paid US$150 million for its food license, Lego $100 million for the construction license. Mattel became the "worldwide master toy licensee for the literary characters"; games, puzzles, trading cards and action figures abound. There is the Harry Potter Robe with built-in fiber optic lights, the Ice Pumpkin Slushie Maker, Late Night Ride Towel, branded school gear, castles, sorting hats, and fake forehead scars. Bertie Botts Jelly Beans are popular with flavors of ear wax, boogers, grass and vomit … Hornby, an almost forgotten maker of model trains, proudly produced a replica Hogwarts Express. Profits soared by forty-five per cent. (Galligan, 2004, p. 37)

It is a commonplace of text-based commodification that authors themselves sometimes become part of the marketing blitz (e.g., Beatrix Potter and the Lake District are promoted as a package deal, as are L.M. Montgomery and Prince Edward Island, and Louise May Alcott and Concord, Massachusetts). The British publisher of *Harry Potter*, Bloomsbury, has gone one step further.

> In a populist gesture, Bloomsbury is splitting seventeen million company shares into four, making them more accessible to parents. At $3.80 each, a few shares might be the next best-ever birthday present for the kids. The synergies created by the Potter brand name are working dynamically to create that extra edge in the marketplace. The consumer can now read the books, watch the movies and videos, play with the toys, master the computer games, and then perhaps, buy into the company. (Galligan, 2004, p. 37)

Waetjen and Gibson (2007) suggest that a disciplinary pincer movement is necessary to understand the implications of a phenomenon as large and complicated as the *Harry Potter* empire. They ask,

> …if popular media texts like the Harry Potter novels are indeed shot through with ideological fissures out of which a wide variety of social meanings can be "activated," then what happens when the *reader* decoding the text is not an individual audience member but rather a multinational media conglomerate? (p. 5)

Pursuing this very interesting line of thought, Waetjen and Gibson (2007) suggest that "…far from simply 'commercializing' Rowling's texts, AOL Time Warner in fact *activated* a reading of the Harry Potter universe that was already present in the texts themselves, particularly within Rowling's complex and often contradictory discussions of class and material life." (p. 7)

Furthermore, Waetjen and Gibson (2007) highlight a contradiction in Rowling's account of commodities and consumption. On the one hand, advertisers rise and fall on their ability to sell the myth that "commodities can change your life, win you friends, and achieve your dreams"; but in Rowling's narrative, commodities have a binary trajectory. "…Dudley's muggle commodities bring him nothing but disappointment…[while] Harry's magical possessions fulfill their promises exactly as advertised" (p. 14). Without a Quidditch broom, for example, Harry would not be able to defeat the aristocratic Malfoys. Although Rowling objects to inequality in general terms, she also (and in contradiction) offers "a more celebratory discourse on the pleasures and power of commodity consumption…. [T]his is a discourse on class and consumption that even AOL Time Warner can get behind" (p. 16). And, of course, AOL Time Warner's interpretation becomes one powerful reading of the story, distributed widely, buttressed with commodities, and taken as a source-text for fan materials.

Sometimes the commodity comes first and the literary materials follow. The *American Girl* empire run by Pleasant Company (acquired by Mattel in 1998), which sells linked dolls and historical novels, claims that the educational power of historical fiction fuels its vast range of dolls and accessories, but it is clear that the force of commodity consumption provides the true dynamic of the project. The impact on the stories is interesting.

Books written about girls who are represented from the very beginning as dolls have their own constraints. For example the plain-faced but fascinating heroine is not the central premise, because as dolls—not just characters—they must be pretty. Talbot (2005) argues that "Some of the most memorable children's book heroines are not pretty—though it is understood that they may grow up to be handsome or striking or even, to the discerning eye, beautiful—which is one reason so many generations of awkward, intellectual girls have loved them…. In a free-standing book, a homely or an unkempt heroine is fine. In a book that supplies back story for a doll, it won't do" (n.p.).

Similarly, American Girl history is focused through a prism of things to buy, and the poor girls in the series own as many items (though they may be humbler) as the richest. Lauren Winner (1998) suggests that this prism also reflects a certain ideology of girlhood as well:

> Pleasant Company relies upon an association of women with consumption that dates at least back to Felicity's time [Felicity is the Colonial character/doll]. That Pleasant Company seeks to undo so many other stereotypes about girls while relying on this very basic construction of girls and women as consumers is, to say the least, troubling. (n.p.)

But Austin Booth (2002) suggests that the multiracial variety of the historical American Girl stories does offer something positive: "Taken as a whole, the series says that what it means to be an American girl is significantly different than the white upper-middle class Victorian girls we are all familiar with from children's literature" (n.p.).

Whatever the impact of the content and the ideologies represented in this phenomenon, there is no question that the historical American Girls stories do offer a complex signifying system, providing book heroines, dolls matched to those heroines, miniature dolls and matching miniature story books (to be "owned" by other dolls), a set of historically accurate accessories for each doll, fictional films featuring some of the main personalities, the obligatory book of "how we made this movie," and books of historical background for each character. The stories themselves may be limited and closed, but the overall system offers rather more potential for cognitive challenge.

The Impact on Reading of Associated Forms of Consumption

In a culture rife with spin-offs, the term connotes the inferior, the second-rate, the commercially meretricious. Even (or perhaps especially) when high literature is involved, noses tend to curl. In an essay by Sutherland (2007) in *The*

503

Times Literary Supplement some of this disdain, mixed with perplexity, is expressed in a discussion of the "extraordinary array of loosely attached commodities" based on Jane Austen's novels. These games, books, kits, toiletries, and movies, "circulate in [Austen's] orbit; and their impact on readers' expectations of the novels themselves can neither be precisely gauged nor denied." (p. 20).

The impact of commodities and adaptations on "readers' expectations of the novels themselves" is a subject of some critical debate. In 1991, Tom Engelhardt wrote a contentious article for *Harper's Magazine*, in which he asserted that "Reading may be harmful to your kids" (p. 55). Engelhardt made a strong case against books as one more commodity. Lamenting the loss of children's librarians and the growth of big-box bookshops where publishers market directly to children and parents, he posited a boom in a different kind of children's literature: "the book designed for the consumer child" (p. 57). From an inspection of children's bestseller lists of 1990, he observed, "a significant number of the picture books and the books for young readers were either Product themselves or enmeshed in a world of Product" (p. 57), concluding pessimistically that "In this newer world of commercial planning for children…early brand loyalty means a lifetime adventure in dependence. This…is what the "habit" of reading is coming to mean in children's books—and the only exit increasingly being offered from such a world is into infantilized best-selling genres for adults" (p. 62). It is not difficult to assume that Engelhardt would regard the commodification of Jane Austen as evidence of continuing infantilization and dependence.

Ten years later, Daniel Hade (2001) took up Engelhardt's gauntlet and explored the impact of the market on children's reading. In an article about "reading as consuming" (p. 158), he discussed the risk that "a book becomes one more kind of product that carries the brand's meanings" (p. 162), and raised a series of questions, particularly about the link between commercialization and education:

> Could it be that what seems to be the reading of literature is really just one of many cross-promotions? The lines between advertising and entertainment, and advertising and education are very blurry lines. It seems we are at a point where we have advertising that thinks it is entertainment or education, and entertainment and education that are really advertising in disguise. (p. 163)

A year later, Hade (2002) returned to the same theme and explored some of the connections between big publishing corporations, licensed spin-offs, and the major reviewing journals, describing a narrowing of the channels that lead to being published and being successfully sold. Again he raised questions about the impact on reading, concluding that " the book and each spin-off piece of merchandise and each retelling across another medium becomes a promotion for every other product based upon that story…. The corporate owners of children's book publishing have successfully turned recreational reading

into a commodity" (pp. 514–515). Jack Zipes (2001) offers a similar conclusion that for young people, reading is mediated through the mass media and marketing "so that the pleasure and meaning of a book will often by prescripted or dictated by convention" (p. 172).

This chorus is singing in unison. But Engelhardt (1991), Hade (2001, 2002), and Zipes (2001) have all based their claims on textual research, analyzing the bestseller lists and the lists of products associated with particular titles. While they make a case that is undoubtedly troubling, they also reveal a gap in our knowledge that badly needs to be filled with serious ethnographic research. What do young readers make of this clutter of commodities? How do they perceive themselves as agents of their own reading in the context of a world of synergy and licensing? Is it possible that as well as (or even instead of) perceiving themselves as the passive victims of marketing overkill, they are actually developing sophisticated and contemporary skills in the new territory of transmedia interpretations and commercial intertexts? We must find productive ways of exploring these questions.

Consumer-Produced Adaptations and Spin-offs

Young people who grow up in a world of adaptation, spin, and digital affordances may naturally turn to the affordances of the computer to help produce their own kinds of adaptation and spin. In exploring research into fan productions, we may well gain oblique answers to some the questions posed at the end of the last section.

It is not long since fan productions were perceived as belonging to the furthest reaches of cultdom, as the products of obsessive Trekkies or Tolkienites, recasting *Star Trek* and Middle-Earth into ever more lurid forms. But the situation is much more complex than this stereotype would suggest (see Dutro & McIver and Lewis & Dockter in this volume for a discussion of literacies and fan fiction). I cast about for a random example of an orthodox work of children's literature that had recently been turned into a movie and came up with Katherine Paterson's (1977) *Bridge to Terabithia*. Google turned up 105,000 fan fiction sites. It would be an interesting project to establish whether the intermediary step of adaptation is essential to the development of a thriving fan base. I suspect the answer to that question would be affirmative (although maybe the prospect of a movie is enough; some weeks before the film premiered, Google found 475,000 hits for *The Golden Compass* fan fiction). Certainly, when I conducted searches for fan fiction of well-known young adult fiction that has *not* been adapted into film, I found little material available. I would certainly not call my exercise a definitive study, but it does raise a question with interesting research potential.

More disappointingly, in pursuing one children's literature reference, what I found was a book title used as an imprimatur of sanitization. *Anne's Diary*, which takes its label from *Anne of Green Gables*, calls itself "the first biometrically-secured social networking site for children in the world. It offers girls in grades 1 to 8 (ages 6 to 14) a secure environment in which to keep a private diary and communicate with their peers around the world. Members can also enter contests, play games, participate in book clubs and receive homework help" (*Anne's diary*, n.d.). A fingerprint reader locks down access to the non-registered, and a perky, winsome and saccharine "Anne" cartoon figure welcomes members. The site encourages a highly policed and strongly framed forum for productive work while implicitly creating a highly reductive, reified, and consumption-oriented reading of the character of Anne.

Nevertheless, in those cases where fan responses to children's texts are available (and here we return full circle to *Harry Potter*, who has spawned an abundance of fan response), we may have a route into the minds of contemporary readers that repays considerable attention. How conventional are fan reactions to the books and movies themselves? More productively, perhaps, how conventional are the parodies and satires? Does a YouTube production like the "Potter Puppet Pals in *The Mysterious Ticking Noise*" (n.d.) tell us anything useful about reader response to the books or the films? This foolish two-minute parody utilizes the musical form of the ostinato (repetition of brief themes) to create a surprisingly catchy song, performed by finger puppets using the names of Hogwarts characters as musical motifs and involving a brief plot in which a pipe bomb destroys everyone but Voldemort. The original video was released in 2007 and has been one of the most popular videos on YouTube. There are now hundreds of parodies of the parody on YouTube, using images ranging from live action Harry Potter movie clips to Legos.

What do these short videos tell us about conditions of reception? That playfulness is a legitimate response to a story, that humor does not have to be critical to be biting, that commercializing a literary commodity is not the only way to spread its influence further. That one proper noun can yoke a variety of images of a character under a single name. That sophisticated play with literature can be shared for pleasure. That the world of adaptation and commodities is itself open to parody—what could be cheaper and more accessible than a set of finger-puppets?

Conclusions

The simplest and most important conclusion from this collection of research is that we have an enormous amount yet to learn. Today's children are at home in a vast world of mutating and slippery literature. Their skills, tacit and explicit, are honed on multiple versions of a fiction. Their understanding encompasses criteria for what makes a good or an inferior adaptation, internal assessments of the play value of assorted toys and spin-offs, essential qualifica-

tions for what must survive as a character changes format, and many other schemata for dealing with variation. Adults have much to learn from these children about embracing mutability.

At the same time, there is considerable scope for children to develop more critical perspectives on what makes their media worlds tick. Their implicit understandings may need external scaffolding in order to blossom into articulated awareness of questions of importance and value. Children also have much to learn.

We need more research that explores the tri-fold nature of literary materials, interpretive responses and institutional enablements and constraints, preferably as they all relate to each other. A complex media world needs complex research approaches; slippery materials sometimes need to be pinned down and sometimes need to be respected in their slipperiness. Much remains to be done.

Literature References

Baum. L. F. (1900). *The wonderful wizard of Oz*. Chicago, IL: G.M. Hill.

Barrie, J. M. (1904/1967). *Peter Pan; or, The boy who wouldn't grow up*. New York, NY: Puffin.

Brown, M. T. (1986). *Arthur's teacher trouble*. Boston, MA: Atlantic Monthly Press.

Burnett, F. H. (1911). *The secret garden*. New York, NY: Frederick A. Stokes.

Finley, M. (1867). *Elsie Dinsmore*. New York, NY: Dodd & Mead.

Frank, A. (1952). *Diary of a young girl*. Garden City, NY: Doubleday.

Murphy, J. (1974). *The worst witch*. New York: NY: Schocken Books.

Newbery, J. (1744). *A little pretty pocket-book*. London, UK: J. Newbery.

Paterson, K. (1977). *Bridge to Terabithia*. New York, NY: HarperCollins.

Paterson, K. (1978). *The great Gilly Hopkins*. New York, NY: Crowell.

Rowling, J. K. (2007). *Harry Potter and the Deathly Hallows*. New York, NY: Scholastic.

Sendak, M. (1960). *The sign on Rosie's door*. New York, NY: Harper & Row.

Sendak, M. (1962). *Nutshell library*. New York, NY: Harper & Row.

Sendak, M. (1963). *Where the wild things are*. New York, NY: Harper & Row.

Academic References

Alvermann, D. E. (Ed.). (2002). *Adolescents and literacies in a digital world*. New York, NY: Peter Lang.

Anne's diary – Setting new standards in online safety. (n.d.). Retrieved February 24, 2010 from http://annesdiary.com/

Beaty, B., & Sullivan, R. (2007). Canadian television and the limits of cultural citizenship. In D. Taras, M. Bakardjieva, & F. Pannekoek (Eds.), *How Canadians communicate II: Media, globalization and identity* (pp. 65–82). Calgary, Alberta: University of Calgary Press.

Bixler, P. (1994). *The Secret Garden* "misread": The Broadway musical as creative interpretation. *Children's Literature, 22,* 101–123.

Bodmer, G. R. (1992). Sendak into opera: *Wild Things* and *Higglety Pigglety Pop! The Lion and the Unicorn, 16*, 176–175.

Booth, A. (2002). *St. James encyclopedia of popular culture*. Gale Group. Retrieved May 25, 2003, from http://www.findarticles.com/cf_0/glepc/tov/2419100033/print.jhtml

Buckingham, D. (1996). *Moving images: Understanding children's emotional response to television*. Manchester, UK: Manchester University Press.

Buckingham, D. (Ed.). (1993). *Reading audiences: Young people and the media*. Manchester, UK: Manchester University Press.

Buckingham, D. (Ed.). (1998). *Teaching popular culture: Beyond radical pedagogy*. London, UK: University of Central London Press.

Cardwell, S. (2002). *Adaptation revisited: Television and the classic novel*. Manchester, UK: Manchester University Press.

Cartmell, D., & Whelehan, I. (Eds.). (1999). *Adaptations: From text to screen, screen to text*. London, UK: Routledge.

Chatman, S. (1978). *Story and discourse: Narrative structure in fiction and film*. Ithaca, NY: Cornell University Press.

Clarke, S. (2007a, September 11). TV is alive and kicking in Europe. *Variety*. Retrieved February 24, 2010, from http://www.variety.com/index.asp?layout=print_story&articleid=VR1117971768&categoryid=19

Clarke, S. (2007b, October 3). British kids' programs disappear: Ofcom warns of crisis. *Variety*. Retrieved February 24, 2010, from http://www.variety.com/article/VR1117973245.html?categoryId=19&cs=1

Davies, M. M. (2001, Fall). "A bit of earth": Sexuality and the representation of childhood in text and screen version of *The Secret Garden. The Velvet Light Trap, 48*, 48–58.

Davies, M. M. (2005, Autumn). "Crazyspace": The politics of children's screen drama. *Screen, 46*(3), 389–399.

Davis, G., & Dickinson, K. (Eds.). (2004). *Teen TV: Genre, consumption and identity*. London, UK: British Film Institute.

Dyson, A. H. (1997). *Writing superheroes: Contemporary childhood, popular culture, and classroom literacy*. New York, NY: Teachers College Press.

Dyson, A. H. (2003). *The brothers and sisters learn to write: Popular literacies in childhood and school cultures*. New York, NY: Teachers College Press.

Engelhardt, T. (1991). Reading may be harmful to your kids: In the Nadirland of today's children's books. *Harper's, 282*, 55–62.

Entertainment Weekly. (2007, August 3). Issue 946. New York, NY: Time.

Fleckenstein, K. S. (2003). *Embodied literacies: Imageword and a poetics of teaching*. Carbondale: Southern Illinois University Press.

Flynn, R. (1996). Imitation Oz: The sequel as commodity. *The Lion and the Unicorn, 20*(1), 121–131.

Freyer, E. (1987. Adapting children's books for television: Interviews with Mary Pleshette Willis and Malcolm Marmorstein. *The Lion and the Unicorn, 11*(2), 73–86.

Fricke, J. (1999). 100 years of Oz: A century of classic images from *The Wizard of Oz* collection of Willard Carroll. (Photography R. Glenn & M. Hill; Design T. Shaner.) New York: Stewart, Tabori & Chang.

Galligan, A. (2004, Winter). Truth is stranger than magic: The marketing of Harry Potter. *Australian Screen Education, 35*, 3–41.

Geer, J. (2007). J.M. Barrie gets the Miramax treatment: Finding (and marketing) *Neverland. Children's Literature Association Quarterly, 32*(3), 193–212.

Giddings, R., Selby, K., & Wensley, C. (1990). *Screening the novel: The theory and practice of literary dramatization*. Basingstoke, UK: Macmillan.

Hade, D. (2001). Curious George gets branded: Reading as consuming. *Theory into Practic,e 40*(3), 158–165.

Hade, D. (2002). Storyselling: Are publishers changing the way children read? *Horn Book Magazine, 78*(5), 509–517.

Hearn, M. P. (2000/1973). Introduction. In L. F. Baum, *The annotated Wizard of Oz*. Centennial ed. New York, NY: W.W. Norton.

Hilton, M. (Ed.). (1996). *Potent fictions: Children's literacy and the challenge of popular culture*. London, UK: Routledge.

Hodge, B., & Tripp, D. (1986). *Children and television: A semiotic approach*. Cambridge, UK: Polity Press.

Hutcheon, L. (2006). *A theory of adaptation*. New York, NY: Routledge.

Jackson, M. (1997). The troubling lessons of *Arthur's Teacher Trouble*: Old stereotypes in a new commodity. *Children's Literature Association Quarterly, 22*(1), 30–36.

Jenkins, H. (2008/2006) Convergence culture: Where old and new media collide. Updated ed. New York: New York University Press.

Kinder, M. (1991). *Playing with power in movies, television, and video games: From Muppet Babies to Teenage Mutant Ninja Turtles*. Berkeley: University of California Press.

Kinder, M. (Ed.). (1999). *Kids' media culture*. Durham, NC: Duke University Press.

Liljeblad, C. B. (1996). *TV toys and the shows that inspired them*. Iola, WI: Krause Publications.

Littau, K. (2006). *Theories of reading: Books, bodies and bibliomania*. Cambridge, UK: Polity.

Livingstone, S. (1998/1990). *Making sense of television: The psychology of audience interpretation* (2nd ed.). London, UK: Routledge.

Lunenfeld, P. (2000/1999). Unfinished business. In Peter Lunenfeld (Ed.), *The digital dialectic: New essays on new media* (pp. 6–22). Cambridge, MA: MIT Press.

Mackey, M. (1998). *The case of Peter Rabbit: Contemporary conditions of literature for children*. New York, NY: Garland.

Marsh, J., & Millard, E. (2000). *Literacy and popular culture: Using children's culture in the classroom*. London, UK: Paul Chapman.

Martin, C., & Taylor, L. (2006). Playing in Neverland: *Peter Pan* video game revisions. In D. R. White & C. A. Tarr (Eds.), *J.M. Barrie's* Peter Pan *in and out of time* (pp. 173–193). Children's Literature Association Centennial Studies Series No. 4. Lanham, MD: Scarecrow Press.

McDonnell, K. (2001). *Honey, we lost the kids: Re-thinking childhood in the multimedia age*. Toronto, Ontario: Second Story Press.

McFarlane, B. (1996). *Novel to film: An introduction to the theory of adaptation*. Oxford, UK: Clarendon Press.

Morris, T. (2000). *You're only young twice: Children's literature and film*. Urbana: University of Illinois Press.

Nel, P. (2005). Is there a text in this advertising campaign?: Literature, marketing, and Harry Potter. *The Lion and the Unicorn, 29*(2), 236–267.

Paterson, D. (1998). Gilly Hopkins: From the page to the stage. *School Library Journal, 44*(7), 32–33.

Potter puppet pals. (n.d.). *The mysterious ticking noise*. Retrieved February 24, 2010, from http://www.youtube.com/watch?v=Tx1XIm6q4r4

Potter puppet pals. (n.d.). *The mysterious ticking noise Lego remake*. Retrieved February 24, 2010, http://www.youtube.com/watch?v=JR2Xbxem5DU

Potter puppet pals. (n.d.). *Mysterious ticking noise presentation!* Retrieved February 24, 2010, from http://www.youtube.com/watch?v=08y-ASp_I2s

Reynolds, P. (Ed.). (1993). *Novel images: Literature in performance*. London, UK: Routledge.

Robinson, M. (1997). *Children reading print and television*. London: Falmer Press.

Rose, J. (1984) *The case of Peter Pan or The impossibility of children's fiction*. London, UK: Macmillan.

Scholes, R., Phelan, J., & Kellogg, R. (2006/1966). *The nature of narrative* (40th anniv. ed.). Oxford, UK: Oxford University Press.

Sekeres, D. C. (2005). Renewed but not redeemed: Revising *Elsie Dinsmore*. *Children's Literature in Education, 36*(1), 15–39.

Sipe, L. R. (2000). "Those two gingerbread boys could be brothers": How children use intertextual connections during storybook readalouds. *Children's Literature in Education, 31*(2), 73–90.

Spector, K., & Jones, S. (2007). Constructing Anne Frank: Critical literacy and the Holocaust in eighth-grade English. *Journal of Adolescent & Adult Literacy, 51*(1), 36–48.

Stephens, J., & McCallum, R. (1996). Ideological re-shapings: Pruning *The Secret Garden* in 1990s film. *Paradoxa, 2*(3-4), 3357–3368.

Street, D. (Ed.). (1983). *Children's novels and the movies*. New York, NY: Frederick Ungar.

Sutherland, K. (2007, April 13). Muddying the hem. *Times Literary Supplement*, 20–21.

Talbot, M. (2005, May 10). American Girl crazy. *Salon*. Retrieved February 2010 from http://dir.salon.com/story/mwt/feature/2005/05/10/talbot/index.html

Thwaite, A. (1992). *The brilliant career of Winnie-the-Pooh: The story of A.A. Milne and his writing for children*. London, UK: Methuen.

Waetjen, J., & Gibson, T. A. (2007). Harry Potter and the commodity fetish; Activating corporate readings in the journey from text to commercial intertext. *Communication and Critical/Cultural Studies, 4*(1), 3–26.

Watson, V. (2001). *The Cambridge guide to children's books in English*. Cambridge, UK: Cambridge University Press.

Westhoff, J. (2004, June 8). *Harry Potter and the Prisoner of Azkaban* Movie Review. Retrieved February 24, 2010, from http://www.rottentomatoes.com/click/movie-1132921/reviews.php?critic=columns&sortby=default&page=1&rid=1287501

Wohlwend, K. E. (2009) Damsels in discourse: Girls consuming and producing identity texts through Disney Princess play. *Reading Research Quarterly 44*(1), 57-83.

Winner, L. F. (1998, September/October). American Girls as we want them to be. *ChristianityToday.com*. Retrieved February 24, 2010, from http://www.christianitytoday.com/bc/8b5/8b5010.html

Wojcik-Andrews, I. (2000). *Children's films: History, ideology, pedagogy, theory*. New York, NY: Garland.

Zipes, J. (2001). *Sticks and stones: The troublesome success of children's literature from Slovenly Peter to Harry Potter*. New York, NY: Routledge.

37

Listening for the Scratch of a Pen

Museums Devoted to Children's and Young Adult Literature

Elizabeth Hammill

Seven Stories: The Centre for Children's Books

Elizabeth Hammill has long been devoted to children and their literature. As bookseller, literary critic, and advocate for the preservation and presentation of the artistic making of texts, she takes us on a round-the-globe visit to the world's greatest children's literature museums. She begins with the house museums of Louisa May Alcott, Lucy Maud Montgomery, and Beatrix Potter, moves to the pioneering work of Dromkeen in Australia and the Chihiro Art Museum in Japan, and then arrives at the more recent creations of the Eric Carle Museum of Picture Book Art in America and Seven Stories, which Hammill co-founded in England. Whether inviting us to contemplate the magic and meaning of a beloved author's home, or the experience of entering the invented worlds of Tove Jansson's Moomins, Colin McNaughton's Preston Pig, or Robert Westall's Machine Gunners, Hammill eloquently puts on display the philosophical, political, and playful spaces devoted to children's literature.

Words and pictures on the printed page look fixed, perfect, immutable—waiting to take our imaginations out into the world. How did they get there? Where did they come from? Searching for their origins, we find fascinating, hidden stories coming into view as we uncover the creative processes that lie behind a book's making to reveal how writers write and artists illustrate. Until recently, such creation stories could only be found, if at all, by researchers in national archives or university and public library special collections. Here, on the whole, they have remained invisible to the world at large as Karen Nelson Hoyle with Leonard Marcus's chapter recounts, unless dedicated exhibition spaces exist where collection treasures can be placed in the public eye. Today, however, in a small but growing number of museums worldwide, the words and images of picture books, stories, and poems for children from first preparatory notes and sketches to finished text and artwork now find themselves not only being collected, but occupying center stage in purpose-built galleries, mounted, framed, and presented to us as independent and meaningful art.

The public role of these new museums in cultivating an appreciation of children's books and their artistic making, and in encouraging reading and scholarship is still in its infancy. Indeed, this chapter is less about *research* on such museums (of which there is little) and more about their appearance on the world stage and the potential for research within. If Dromkeen (1974) in Australia and the Chihiro Art Museum (1978) in Japan were early and inspirational pioneers—particularly in nurturing picture book cultures in their countries, the past decade has seen the emergence of museums like The Eric Carle Museum of Picture Book Art (2002) in the United States and Seven Stories, the Centre for Children's Books (2005) in England, whose very existence signals changing national perceptions about the artistic and cultural importance of children's books. Already, the growing collections of each and the highly individual, often experimental, approaches to using the original materials in them (or on loan) to engross and inspire new audiences, offer rich, yet to be explored research possibilities. This chapter sets the scene.

The homes of writers and artists—the Louisa May Alcott Orchard House or Beatrix Potter's Hill Top Farm, for instance—were the forerunners of today's museums. Here we are invited to step into the preserved domestic worlds of the creators of beloved classics. Such homes have long been sites of pilgrimage, offering us intimate glimpses of literary lives and engaging our curiosity, imagination, and emotions by introducing us to private spaces where reality and imagination once intersected, pen was first put to paper, and iconic works were created.

If we visit house museums to experience a writer's workaday life and to listen, amid threadbare carpets and homespun heirlooms, for the scratch of a pen, we visit the new museums to see the artwork, manuscripts, and work in progress created by the pen. "Nothing," Philip Pullman (2002) declares, "gives us such a powerful sense, both of personal connection and of sheer awe...as seeing the actual paper on which an author or an illustrator we love has made the first marks, the first tentative reaching-out towards what will later become known all over the world." If a writer's or artist's home provides us with a domestic context for those marks, a museum and its collections can open up this story by finding insightful new ways of engaging us with how those words and images came into being, with the creative process itself, with the art and artistry of story making, and with our own creativity. Like a book, a museum offers us a portal into the imagination.

Let's explore—touching briefly on the development of three world famous house museums in the United States, Canada and England. Then, as we trace the unfolding stories of four pioneering museums in Australia, Japan, America, and England, with a fleeting stop in Europe, let us consider how the times and each museum's founding philosophy have shaped how they present themselves as learning environments. From "hallowed home" to "literary playground," as museums choose how to tell their stories, their choices inform—even transform—our conversations about children's literature and its making.

Beginnings: The Writer's Home as Museum

Literary house museums offer us the promise of tangible personal contact with a beloved author or illustrator as we visit the domestic spaces that witnessed their private life and colored their voice, imagination, and art. If a home was also the setting where now classic tales were played out, we find ourselves in a real place, but one that, as readers, we may already have inhabited in our imaginations, imbuing it with emotional associations and meanings.

Within such historic homes, museum staff act as guardians, collectors, and curators but also as storytellers, interpreters, and performers of times and lives long gone—providing us with narratives that are not always fixed. The home as museum becomes the backdrop and point of departure for interpretations that transform these once private spheres into public spaces. As visitors, we anticipate reading a house as a multi-layered story that will illuminate the domestic, cultural, and literary life and legacy of its former inhabitants, both real and fictional. Looking briefly at the evolution of three such museums, however, we discover interpretations initially constructed by their founders to achieve ends that were not purely literary but were steeped in the cultural and political issues of their times, while the re-constructed stories they tell today reflect changes in motivation and critical consensus in tune with our times.

The Louisa May Alcott Orchard House: From an "Agency for Domestic Change" to Living History

The founding of Orchard House in Concord, Massachusetts, in the early 1900s demonstrates just how culturally and ideologically charged creating a house museum can be. As the century turned, Concord, a community deeply identified with its colonial past, faced profound social change. Industrial growth, a huge influx of immigrants, and its incorporation into Boston's streetcar suburbs presented a threat to its traditional way of life. For members of the exclusive Concord Women's Club (CWC), established in 1895 for study and cultural enlightenment, these changes, allied to the divisive issues of women's suffrage and women's domestic role in the era of the New Woman, presented them with "pressing social problems" (West, 1999, p. 56).

Orchard House, the home of Louisa May Alcott and her family from 1858 to 1877, was to provide a potent, ideologically driven, means of response. Offered to the club by Harriet Lothrop, better known as Margaret Sidney, the successful author of the *Five Little Peppers* series, the house and the "little women" who had "lived" there could be seen as "emblems" of a "virtuous and ostentatiously traditional American domesticity that could establish a reassuring stability" at the start of a new uncertain century (West, 1999, p. 65). If Orchard House became a museum presenting Alcott's (2004) life as the story of *Little Women*, much could be achieved. The novel, whose appeal to Lothrop and the CWC lay in its celebration of colonial Anglo-American domestic values and home as "the fountainhead of women's public moral influence," not only provided the literary foundation upon which a "new public meaning for the once-private dwelling could be constructed." It also offered "a model that could provide the basis for social reform" (pp. 65–67)—one that could mold young immigrants into young Americans and define the role of a "proper" (p. 54) home life in achieving this. This was a legacy for an Orchard House museum to build on. In 1911, Lothrop and the CWC formed the Louisa May Alcott Memorial Association (LMAMA) to fundraise, buy, and repair the decaying property.

The re-invention of Orchard House began in LMAMA's emotive fundraising literature. Listen. "The most beloved house in America (is) falling to ruin…. Long…the retreat for the imaginations of countless girls and boys…, its associations are little less than sacred to them…. [It is] an appropriate act of American girlhood and boyhood to preserve this house" (pp. 67–68). This image—one memorializing a nostalgic vision of the traditional American home and the "Alcotts-cum-Marches…[as] the ideal Anglo-American nuclear family" (p. 85) and lynchpin of social stability—was well established when the museum opened in May 1912. Orchard House, re-invented, answered the CWC's need for an "agency of domestic reform" to engage positively with the Anglo-American crisis confronting Concord (p. 78). As a symbol and "reference work for anyone wishing to legitimize their domestic standards" (p. 85), this image would be perpetuated into the late 20th century (West, 1999).

From the beginning, the presentation of Orchard House mixed fact and fiction. LMAMA, in its promotion of a unifying, socializing ideology of American domesticity, significantly ignored parts of the Alcott family history, much as Alcott herself had done in creating *Little Women.* Missing from the interpretative tours carried out by association volunteers in period dress were, for instance, the impoverished childhood of the Alcott girls elsewhere, and the fact that their father Bronson Alcott, a "wild old transcendentalist" (West, 1999, p. 91), had once attacked the ideal single family home now enshrined in Orchard House. The new mythologizing narrative, echoing Alcott's descriptions of family life and home in *Little Women,* was so telling that the *Christian Science Monitor* (August 2, 1913) reported: "Never did a frame surround a picture with more fitness than does Orchard House surround *Little Women*…. It seems like the predestined stage for the March family to occupy" (quoted in Alberghene & Clark, 1999, p. 120).

When Orchard House opened, *Little Women*, published 44 years earlier, was already a best seller. Readers from Jane Addams to Simone de Beauvoir found personal meaning in a novel that supported their ambitions of independence and achievement. By contrast, many immigrants "devoured the book to learn how to become Americans…

(and) part of the American family" (Alberghene & Clark, 1999, p. xix). *Little Women* may have seized the popular imagination, but it was dismissed by the literary establishment as sentimental. Alcott received little serious academic attention until the 1970s when her sensational gothic potboilers, recovered by her biographer Madeleine Stern and Lena Rosenberg in 1943, began to be anthologized by Stern and republished, revealing Alcott's (1975 on) double literary life and provoking a reassessment of the author who now became the subject of feminist, historicist, and children's literature studies.

Significantly, it was in 1975, that LMAMA appointed the museum's first professional staff, and the interpretation of the house began to be revised. Ongoing restoration and preservation programs, initiated in 1979, to save a home built for domestic use (not tourism) from falling down, drew increasingly on a growing body of Alcott scholarship, images in the LMAMA archives, journals in the Alcott Family Archives at Harvard's Houghton Library, and the late Stern herself to present a less conservative, more historically accurate picture of the house, its past, and the personalities of its actual occupants.

Today, the 315-year-old brown clapboard house, a shrine for Alcott lovers the world over, is a designated "National Treasure." Immaculately preserved and enriched, for instance, by the restoration of the pen and ink angels drawn by May Alcott on her bedroom walls and the forthcoming recreation of its landscape, based on plans and observations in Bronson Alcott's journals, the Alcott home—perhaps because some 75% of its furnishings *were* the family's—nonetheless feels unchanged. It is in the ways that the award-winning museum now "brings to life" the Alcott family legacy in literature, art, education, philosophy, and social justice through guided tours by authentically costumed "Alcotts," living history events, a range of educational programs, and an imaginative use of original family furnishings and objects that a new museum agenda appears. The once domesticated and fictionalized interpretation of Alcott's history has been replaced by narratives that situate the story of her creativity and literary contributions within the context of home *and* of her own and her family's wider political, social, and cultural achievements: the focus now firmly on personalities and what *actually* happened. From participating in period activities—amateur theatricals, writing, or keeping a daily journal—enjoyed by the family to learning about their contributions to various 19th-century reform movements, to joining in the annual Summer Conversational Series that echo the lively debates once held in Bronson Alcott's School of Philosophy, we are drawn meaningfully into the house and its inhabitants' past in ways that link that past and the Alcott's legacy to us today.

And yet, as the museum website notes, "a visit to Orchard House is like walking through the book" perhaps with Jo March as our "imaginary and potentially subversive tour guide" (West, 1999, p. 91). It is a strangely intimate experience in spaces that feel familiar but surprise us too as they reveal the literary potential of domestic life—how stories and novels can grow "out of baked bread, mended stockings, and polished silver" (Berne, 1992, p.14).

Green Gables: Tourism and the Creation of a Home as Fiction

Farther north on Canada's Prince Edward Island, two farmhouses, like Orchard House, were to become girls' book literary shrines, but ones with very different histories: the family farmhouse immortalized as Green Gables by Lucy Maud Montgomery (2008) in her first novel *Anne of Green Gables* and the Cavendish homestead nearby where Montgomery was raised by her maternal grandparents and wrote her early work. Within a year of *Anne's* publication in 1908, both homes emerged as sites of pilgrimage—so thoroughly had the passionate, loquacious, red haired orphan Anne Shirley and the rural landscape of Cavendish, depicted as Avonlea, captured readers' imaginations.

Designated a Canadian classic by 1924 with over 50 million sales worldwide today, the novel's appeal, from the beginning, was linked to national identity. Anne, a "born Canadian," but an outsider to Avonlea, successfully settles in a "new cultural space" (Devereux, 2001, p. 12). She makes it hers by renaming it and "capturing its beauty in language," thus creating a "myth of belonging" that has resonated with Anglo-Canadians ever since (Fiamengo, 2002, pp. 232–233). Anne and Avonlea were to become emblems of a "shared Canadianness," icons of a rural, pre-industrial way of life and a "valuable national cultural commodity" (Devereux, 2001, p. 2)—one that Montgomery proved adept at promoting.

From publication on, Montgomery carefully nurtured her public persona as Anne's alter ego and her identification with Cavendish/Avonlea—a pastoral locale that, as book reviewers and interviewers repeatedly noted, "she makes us fall in love with" (Pike, 2002, p. 239). Her journals record the growing tourist appeal of Green Gables and the Cavendish farmhouse, noting, for instance, local dismay when her uncle demolished the dilapidated homestead— "the only 'literary shrine' the Province possessed"—to curb the intrusion of tourists on his property in 1920 and protesting in 1929, at the introduction of road signs for "'Green Gables'…a purely imaginary place" (De Jonge, 2002, p. 256).

By 1936, the popularity of Green Gables and scenic Avonlea sites like "Lover's Lane" was such that the Canadian National Park Service bought the property and the surrounding farm and woodlands to establish Prince Edward Island National Park as a seaside and recreational resort. Tourism, not conservation, was the Park Services' remit. Initially, the outbuildings and agricultural landscape were demolished to create a golf course, but it was Green Gables that drew visitors.

Montgomery's years of marketing herself, her books, and the connection between Cavendish and Avonlea had "created the conditions that [were to give] her fictional world, an independent, commercial existence" (Pike, 2002, p. 250). The Park Services, responding to consumer demand and the public's desire to experience Anne's world, transformed the farmhouse into the imagined home of the feisty orphan (De Jonge, 2002) When it opened as a museum in 1950, the gables had been painted green and green shutters added. The interior, carefully decorated and furnished to represent the 1890's period, was not an exact reproduction of the fictional home. But the bedrooms, once Montgomery's cousins, were now Anne's and Marilla's, with a room for Matthew by the kitchen. The real historical life of the farm had been supplanted by the fictional one. The museum preserved the story.

This interpretative approach continued into the 1980s when the acquisition of Montgomery's diaries and scrapbooks by the University of Guelph in 1981 and the subsequent publication of the first of five edited journals (1985–2004) initiated a critical and academic reappraisal of an author whose work, like Alcott's, was popular but marginalized. Moves to have her novels included in Canada's literary canon were furthered by the establishment of the Lucy Maud Montgomery Institute at the University of Prince Edward Island in 1993.

The Institute plays a dual role as a centre for Montgomery studies and academic scholarship and for the broader promotion of the author. A "cultural gatekeeper," it "carefully balances" Montgomery's promotion as a "valuable and distinctly Canadian author" with a more populist one. Rooting Montgomery and its celebration of her work in *her* celebration of Prince Edward Island as Avonlea, the Institute's activities suggest that "Montgomery's literary value is tied to her tourist value" (Cormack & Fawcett, 2002, p. 188).

The two are certainly linked. These developments, together with the nationwide screening and subsequent export of the first of four televised *Anne* series in 1985, significantly influenced the island's burgeoning Montgomery/Anne tourist industry, fuelling a growing market for Montgomery and Green Gables merchandise and the creation of new tourist sites.

Montgomery's Macneil descendants, for instance, now realized the importance of the Cavendish homestead. It was here, during a difficult and isolated childhood and youth, that Montgomery "took refuge [in] a world of fancy and imagination", in books, writing, and the natural world, much as her Anne would do (De Jonge, 2002, p. 259). The ruined site, sympathetically cleared and excavated, the oldest trees and remnants of the orchard preserved, and interpreted walking paths laid out along routes Montgomery once traversed, now sheds moving light on her life and work. A Canadian National Historical Site, it tells a powerful story about the effects of time (and tourism) on her formative home. The relationship of the ruins and the surrounding setting with its mature trees and view of the fields that Montgomery saw daily from her bedroom window tells another about the natural world that she, like Anne, came to possess, and its power to delight and sustain. Intimately associated with Montgomery's real world, the homestead—or rather its absence—is a grounded counter to Green Gables, inviting us to picture it for ourselves.

Today, the farmhouse is one of Canada's best-known literary landmarks. Redeveloped by Parks Canada in the 1990s, the property and its interpretation now draw on Montgomery's journals and the site's own history, presenting farm life as the author (and Anne) might have experienced it. New out buildings, and reclaimed land recreate some of the farm's former agricultural character. Exhibits and audio-visual presentations in the barn and a new visitor centre focus on Montgomery's life and career and the history of Green Gables, Cavendish, and island farming. But fact and fiction continue to co-exist—particularly at the farmhouse. While the period furnishings reflect the historic farm, details, drawn from the novel, suggest that Anne or Marilla may appear momentarily. Here an apple scented geranium sits on the kitchen windowsill. There an amethyst brooch is pinned to Marilla's pincushion and the slate that Anne broke over Gilbert's head lies on the floor. Crossing the portal, we may wonder who actually lived here, but, lost in the moment, we respond to the place that we have long inhabited in our imaginations.

This Anne experience is not museum bound, but extends to "Avonlea" and "Anne Land" beyond. Whether we "live the life of the story" at Avonlea Theme Park, visit Anne's Lake of Shining Waters or other such sites, we are invited to experience a commodified version of Montgomery's imagination, imposed on the community and landscape that she once knew. Today Anne, Green Gables, and Avonlea are no longer solely emblems of a "shared Canadianness," but instead, of a carefully constructed, almost mythological, shared "nationalism that moves across cultural borders"—even into the global network of cyberspace—to "figure in other nation's iconographies" (Devereux, 2001, p. 12). Shaped by a complex tourist industry managed by tourist authorities, Montgomery's descendants and copyright heirs, and the Institute—each with differing, sometimes conflicting needs—the presentation of Montgomery and her literary landscape is continually evolving to meet local, national, and global ends in which Anne symbolizes nation and Avonlea is an imagined country transportable anywhere. We may not hear the scratch of Montgomery's pen here but, particularly at Green Gables and the homestead, we sense the life and landscape that inspired it.

Hill Top Farm: Beatrix Potter's Self-created Museum or the Writer as Curator

Hill Top Farm, set in the hills of Near Sawrey in England's Lake District, was purchased by Beatrix Potter in 1905 with earnings generated by the phenomenal success of *The Tale of Peter Rabbit,* published three years earlier. A

17th-century farm cottage, it was to be her Lakeland home until she married William Heelis, her local solicitor, in 1913—a home that she retained, nurtured, and developed for the rest of her life as a place to work and entertain the increasing number of literary admirers who sought her out, and, ultimately, as a museum of her life and work in the countryside (Denyer, 2000).

In 1905, Potter, at 39, was living with her parents in London. Her engagement to her editor Norman Warne had just ended most cruelly when he died of leukemia within months of proposing. Potter's childhood and adolescence, while comfortable, had been, like Montgomery's, cold, repressed, and lonely. She found companionship with a wide variety of pets including rabbits, a frog, lizards, guinea pigs, and hedgehogs whose lives she recorded scientifically in her sketchbooks and journals and came to understand completely. She too took solace in nature and the countryside, in stories, in her imagination, and in her art. "I do not remember a time," she wrote, "when I did not try to invent pictures and make for myself a fairyland amongst the wild flowers, the animals, fungi, mosses, woods and streams…in the countryside; that pleasantly unchanging world of realism and romance" (Morse, 1982. p. 147).

This feeling for the natural world laid the foundations not only for Potter's children's books, but also for her choice of Hill Top Farm as a home, and later, for the land management skills and environmental awareness that increasingly shaped her Lakeland life as the farmer Mrs. Heelis. An early supporter of England's National Trust, Potter used the wealth, independence, and freedom that her books secured for her to preserve the landscapes of the Lake District that enriched her life and informed her art. Over the next 38 years, she acquired vulnerable farmland and forest to save it from plunder by wealthy developers, and to perpetuate the traditional agrarian way of life that had shaped it. Her imaginative work, still grounded in her love of nature, shifted away from her books toward the land.

The purchase of Hill Top Farm was an early expression of Potter's "passion for place" (Lear, 2007, p. 7). Here her love of country oak and mahogany furniture and her appreciation of decorative arts and crafts flourished as she created her own independent home. She took inspiration from her memories and sketches of houses that she had loved as a child, eventually incorporating her "sense of comfort and of art and craft into the interiors of her little books." In many senses, she "furnished Hill Top as a set on which she played out her imaginative stories" (p. 374). Nine of her books including *The Tale of Jemima Puddle Duck* (1908a) and *The Tale of Samuel Whiskers* (1908b) were woven around the farmhouse and the surrounding Lakeland landscape.

Over the years, Hill Top became "a work in its own right: a drawing made manifest and part of the way Beatrix wished to project herself" (Lear, 2007, p. 36).

Potter, unlike Montgomery, avoided any personal publicity or public acclaim, yet from early on, enthusiastic admirers—particularly Americans—sought her out. A young Bostonian, aged 13, visiting her with his mother in 1929, recalled that she "opened the door of the farmhouse with 'an enormous key' and let them into the museum that was '*Tom Kitten's* home'" (p. 342). So it was with other visitors.

Despite this growing attention, Potter remained mystified by Peter Rabbit's success at home and abroad, and by her own literary status, turning down a request by Margaret Lane for permission to write a biography in 1941. Her continued mindfulness of Hill Top, however, suggests that she was concerned about how she would be remembered.

Prior to a life threatening operation in 1939, she made her will, adding a list stipulating that "certain favorite pieces of furniture…be kept at Hill Top (in the event of it seeming likely that my rooms there are to be preserved)" (Taylor, 2002, p. 191). Up until her death in 1943, she arranged and rearranged her china, porcelain, artwork, and antique furniture as she wanted them viewed, perhaps imagining sharp-eyed visitors recognizing the hall and its furnishings immortalized in *The Tale of Samuel Whiskers* (Potter, 1908b) and, amongst her treasures in the parlor, the Edward VII coronation teapot that appears in *The Pie and the Patty Pan* (Potter, 1905).

She bequeathed Hill Top Farm and 4,000 acres of land with its farms and cottages to the National Trust, hoping that her "final work" Hill Top would be opened to the public exactly as she had left it (Denyer, 2000, p. 46). When William died in 1945, his will instructed that the house and its contents, "as arranged by his wife or at her direction should if possible remain…and be displayed for all at this permanent memorial" (Lear, 2007, p. 443). Hill Top was opened to the public in 1946. It remains virtually unchanged today, although in 1985, Potter's artwork was removed for conservation. In 1988, Heelis's law office in nearby Hawkshead, became the Beatrix Potter Gallery. Here over 500 of her drawings are displayed on a rotating basis.

The farmhouse—the "shrine that (Potter) set up for herself" (Denyer, 2000, p. 46)—draws us in for it feels familiar. Here, for instance, are the flowered washbasin and caned chair where Tabitha Twitchett washes her kittens. There is Tom Thumb and Hunca Munca's dollhouse. Outside is the fern covered wall where Tom Kitten, Moppet, and Mittens shed their clothes—all recognizable because Potter rendered them so exactly in pen and wash in her "little" books. It is a house and garden to play "I Spy" in—a house with a life both real and imagined.

It is a house that, seen in the light of the stories, displays the intriguing double vision that makes Potter such an original as an author and artist. She could introduce Hill Top to a child as "Tom Kitten's home" and bequeath it to the National Trust as *her* home. Created with the eyes of owner and literary visitor, it became both a private home and public museum, the place of comfort that Potter had long sought but one that she inhabited with a memorable cast of fictionalized animals whose apparent human gloss in the setting of its interiors and gardens invariably slips off when nature and natural events take over. Here we enter a carefully constructed domestic world that was Potter's dream space—an ideal home and landscape that today have come to be synonymous with a particular kind of Britishness.

******

A writer's home, as we see, can be viewed as a blank sheet on which its founders and their successors, or indeed an author herself, can project whatever image or content meets their personal or public needs. It is a space that spans time: we are visiting "now" but experiencing a preserved "then." We may be surrounded and grounded by authentic personal objects and furnishings, but we are also entering the dreaming space of a writer or artist. The house museum is an intriguingly complex, revelatory, and moving place—one that takes hold of our imaginations and often, its country's historical imagination as a shared emblem of home, national character, or nationality. Did publicity-shy Potter imagine, for a minute, that by leaving Hill Top to the National Trust, she was ensuring a worldwide posterity grounded not only in her tales, but also, by remaining visible in the farmhouse, in her association with the Lakeland landscape that she had nurtured and preserved—now known as "Beatrix Potter country"? In the literary house museum, creator, created, and visitor/reader are brought together in once private spaces that witnessed the scratch of a pen—prompting new imaginings, understandings, and an appreciation of how a writer's world shapes the creation of imagined worlds.

The New Literary Museums

Now let's explore the possibilities and potential of children's literary museums. Collectors, interpreters, educators, collaborators, and advocates, they are also catalysts for literary growth, change, and creativity. Their beginnings reveal a response by founders to the status of children's literature in a particular country at a particular time and its relationship to emerging cultural or national identities, and to the subsequent valuing, collecting, and displaying of original material—making them shapers of culture and of visual and verbal literacy.

Dromkeen: A Pioneering "Home" for Australian Children's Literature

Let's begin with some Australian publishing history to set the scene. The first Australian book for children, Charlotte Barton's (1841) *A Mother's Offering to Her Children*, a primer of Australia's flora, fauna, and indigenous people, owed much to Victorian didactic works. This is not surprising, as well into the 20th century most reading matter was imported from England and reflected English tastes and interests. Nonetheless, from the 1890s on, work exhibiting a distinctive Australian character and imagination emerged—blossoming after World War II as the special hold of the new continent's extreme landscapes on writers' imaginations found expression, and Australian publishing houses created children's departments to develop home-grown fiction and picture book lists that were indigenous in every sense. The founding of a Children's Book Council in 1945 and Children's Book of the Year awards in 1946 and the development of school and public libraries and academic studies saw a growing professional and public awareness of the crucial role that literacy and literature play in a child's education for life.

In this newly energized Australian book environment, Joyce and Court Oldmeadow, two enterprising and farsighted educational booksellers, busily expanding a bookselling venture housed in their garage into a nationally respected business, began to dream. They imagined first, exhibiting preliminary and finished artwork in their bookshop to answer the questions that children invariably asked about how books came into being, and then, creating a small permanent collection of such materials. On a book buying trip overseas in 1971, they visited the Osborne Collection at Boys and Girl's House in Toronto, Selma Lagerlof's collection at her home in Sweden, and Hill Top Farm. The farmhouse "enchanted" them and took their vision a step further. A home, not a bookshop, should be the setting for permanent displays of artwork for children's books. It would, however, have to be "just the right kind of home, a place with an aura of history about it" (Prentice & Bird, 1988, p. 16).

Two years later, during a visit to a publishing house in Sydney, the Oldmeadows, viewing original artwork for a contemporary Australian picture book, were struck by a vividness, spark, and immediacy that seemed absent in the printed book, an immediacy that children would respond to. Both were now convinced that the proposed collection should be a "living" one in the sense that work in it would not be shut away from public view as in most collections and archives and only shown on request. Instead, and this was a radical idea at the time, it would be displayed to be enjoyed, examined, and discussed. Most important, it would bring children and books together "'in a more intimate way'" by taking them inside the "hidden," often unrecognized and unappreciated, side of the creative literary process, and making "'their own kind of books'" far more "meaningful and real" to them (Prentice & Bird, 1988, pp. 10–12).

Through their book trade connections, the Oldmeadows had also become aware of the fate of much original material after publication. Manuscripts, sketches, diagrams, and dummies of books, initially filed in publishers' offices and then in warehouses and rarely available for public display, were often lost or destroyed. Artwork for some early classics was in foreign collections. Irreplaceable materials, the "result of so much creativity and expertise," and, as "vital a part of (Australia's) cultural heritage as the published book," were being lost (Prentice & Bird, 1988, p. 11).

It was with these passionate beliefs in mind, as well as business needs for a bulk storehouse, that the Oldmeadows purchased Dromkeen, northwest of Melbourne in rural Riddell's Creek in 1973. A handsome late 19th-century weatherboard homestead, situated on the brow of a hill, with views of the countryside below, extensive gardens and grounds, and a wing added by the previous owner to display his collection of Australian impressionist paintings, Dromkeen was the "right kind of home, a place with an aura of history about it" that the Oldmeadows had dreamed of. Within months, they purchased artwork by Judy Cowell, Peg Maltby, and Ida Rentoul Outhwaite that would form the nucleus of their collection, exhibited it in their dining room, adjacent to a new bookshop, and officially opened The Dromkeen Collection of Australian Children's Literature in October, 1974 to widespread interest and acclaim.

More original art and visitors arrived simultaneously, and the Oldmeadows opened their home to both. The dining room walls were soon covered with works hung three deep, and the collection began to spread into adjoining rooms. Interest in the collection and curiosity about the Oldmeadow's philosophy concerning its uses prompted groups of children and adults, as well as Australian and foreign authors and illustrators, to visit the homestead. A public program of book launches, storytelling sessions, puppet shows, workshops with authors and illustrators, and activities in which children investigated the various stages in the production of a book, using edited manuscripts, galley proofs, and other pre-publication materials in the collection followed.

At Dromkeen, the Oldmeadows had initiated a personally funded and innovative project—one whose national and international importance to children's literature was acknowledged within two years when they were awarded the British Eleanor Farjeon Award. If the couple, at this early juncture, were inspired amateurs in their approach to display and interpretation, to demonstrating the value of original material, to museum making, they were pragmatic in formalizing their creation and recognizing the need for sponsorship. In 1975 they established the Dromkeen Trust to ensure the administration, development, and preservation in readily accessible form of the collection at Dromkeen. After Court's death in 1977, the Trust became the Courtney Oldmeadow Children's Literature Foundation in 1981, and the maintenance and furtherance of the Dromkeen Collection and associated activities were passed to the publisher Ashton Scholastic which purchased Dromkeen in 1985 and, as Scholastic Australia, has imaginatively funded it since.

The Oldmeadow's choice of the Dromkeen setting for

their enterprise was tied to their approach to children and a view of home as a natural intimate space in which to bring children, Australian books, and bookmaking together. An historic homestead, it was also the Oldmeadow's spacious home. Artwork, rare books, an antique printing press and printer's blocks, and other material in the growing collection were all displayed informally in rooms furnished with family antiques. Dromkeen's grounds, in the coming years, were enriched by specially commissioned bronze sculptures of characters from Australian children's literature and a Heritage Trail that ties together different strands of Australian history on fourteen picture boards, each featuring an Australian picture book illustrator and their work.

By early 1976, an education program, linked to the school curriculum and designed to suit different age groups, was in place. The aim, then as now, is to introduce students to the range and complexity of work entailed in the making of a book, the people involved, and the manner in which they work together. The focus is often on the picture book, seen as "an avenue for learning about creativity, art and literature…[that] offers philosophical and theoretical understandings in a very practical and personal way" (Keck, 2008, personal correspondence). Included in all exhibitions and accompanying programs are aspects of the role of author, illustrator, editor, designer, publisher, and printer in making a book. Typically, students role-play these various jobs throughout a visit, sometimes creating illustrations for a set text or a text to support an illustration. Inspiration and approaches emerge after students explore exhibitions designed to develop critical and visual literacy skills by highlighting, for instance, how illustrators view their creative stages and processes, or by introducing them to the changing face and perspectives of Australian picture books *and* to changing techniques and mediums. Workshops with artists and authors further illuminate the creative process. Teacher's notes and resource papers accompany each exhibition.

Early on Joyce, building on previous bookshop work around picture book selection, developed courses for tertiary students and the professional development of teachers and librarians. Her daughter Kaye Keck, Director since 1989, has further positioned Dromkeen as an important educational resource, holding conferences and seminars in a newly built conference facility. Ever responsive to the needs of the Australian book community, Dromkeen is "continually being shaped and developed by those who are linked to it"—offering courses to schools via SOFNET live satellite and creating DVDs such as *Illustrators at Work* to bring the collection and work of artists to a wider audience.

Dromkeen continues to offer public programs from monthly "Meet the Artist" sessions to Dromkeen Dragons for 7 to 12 year olds during the school holidays. The Foundation has inaugurated two prestigious national medals to recognize achievement in Australian children's literature—the Dromkeen Medal in 1982 in memory of Courtney Oldmeadow and the Dromkeen Librarian's Award in 1994

Dromkeen's collection of original art and of Australian children's and reference books continues to grow, via the fundraising activities of the The Dromkeen Society and donations by artists. Now known as the Dromkeen National Centre for Picture Book Art, it currently comprises some 7,000 pieces of pre-publication material with a focus on acquiring work in progress for contemporary picture books—in particular, works showing development and change in a particular illustrator's approach, works demonstrating various artistic styles and media, and works representing the historic development of Australian illustration for children. The collection, open to researchers, is accredited and catalogued. Small exhibitions, shown initially at Dromkeen, have traveled to regional galleries since 1989, making the collection accessible to a wide national audience, while collaborations abroad have brought work to a new international audience. An experimental online exhibition *Picture Book Families* expanded the audience further.

Dromkeen's influence, from a small operational base of some five staff plus volunteers, has been extraordinary. It remains a unique repository for a collection known worldwide and has continually and inventively explored the possibilities of using original artwork and manuscripts to bridge the gap between children and books and engage children with literature through understanding how it came to be made. Its success has inspired the foundation of other Australian galleries with interpretative programs such as The Fremantle Children's Literature Centre in Western Australia and the development of Seven Stories in England. Its collection is of increasing value to researchers exploring the evolution of a national literature. The Oldmeadow's vision of a "living" collection and its realization provided an early model of how a museum celebrating children's literature and picture books in particular might work.

The Chihiro Art Museum: Creating a "Picture Book Culture"

In Japan in the 1970s, Takeshi Matsumoto, the eldest son of the internationally renowned picture book illustrator Chihiro Iwasaki, began to develop a different model. The post-war Japanese publishing industry, like that in Australia, was thriving. Talented artists like Mitsumasa Anno, Shinta Cho, and the sculptor Susumu Shingo were emerging as illustrators. Few, however, recognized the true value of picture book originals. Artists, including Chihiro, formed a union to fight successfully for copyright protection and the return of their originals from publishers—work that was not yet viewed as art and which no museum would exhibit. After Chihiro's death in 1974, Matsumoto (2000), just completing a Fine Arts Degree, determined to create a museum to commemorate his mother's life and work *and,* by demonstrating the value of preserving and displaying original artwork, be instrumental in developing a critically appreciative picture book culture in Japan—a culture that accepted the picture book as "a valid form of artistic expression" (p. 129) and recognized it "as art in its own right" (p. 151).

The Chihiro Iwasaki Art Museum for Picture Books opened in 1977, funded by Chihiro's royalties. Known for her delicate, watery, near abstract style, Chihiro married techniques from Western watercolor painting with those from Japanese and Chinese traditional India ink painting, often creating dramatic and emotive effects by blurring colors. She is best known in the West for her series about Momoko and her re-visioning of Andersen (1991a, 1991b) fairytales such as *The Red Shoes* and *The Little Mermaid.*

The museum stands on the site where Chihiro lived and worked in Tokyo. Designed as an art museum, not a house museum, it included her reconstructed atelier. Initially, changing exhibitions drawn from the Chihiro Iwasaki Collection of approximately 9,300 pieces of artwork focused on her life and work, but soon began to be supplemented with exhibitions of work from overseas artists. Matsumoto, on visits to the Biennial of Illustrations Bratislava and the Bologna Children's Book Fair, realized that picture book originals worldwide were often undervalued and un-conserved. "No matter how historically substantial the works were, they were [in]…danger of being scattered away" and lost (Matsumoto, 2000, p. 2). The museum broadened its collection policy, acquiring work by artists who had influenced Chihiro and by modern Japanese and overseas illustrators. Picture book art crossed borders and offered a universal shared visual language waiting to be explored in one place. The museum also began to collect representative books from various times and places, which could be exhibited as an introduction to the world of picture books. Reflecting the museum's core philosophy and collection aims, it was renamed the Chihiro Art Museum, and became, as Matsumoto intended, a beacon for artists and picture book art as art. It also stimulated the development of other picture book museums in Japan.

As the collection grew and with it the need for increased exhibition space and highly specialized storage facilities to preserve artwork in a humid climate, Matsumoto and The Chihiro Iwasaki Memorial Foundation that managed the Tokyo museum developed plans for a second museum to be located in Chihiro's "spiritual hometown" of Azumino, Nagano Prefecture in the foothills of the Japanese "Alps." In this setting of great beauty where, in 1966, Chihiro had built a cottage and studio, The Chihiro Art Museum Azumino opened in 1997 on the 20th anniversary of the founding of the Tokyo museum. The building and its larch roof subdivided into saddle roofs mirror the surrounding mountains.

Just as Chihiro sought repose and peace here, so the architecture and design of the Azumino museum offer us a relaxed environment in which to explore Chihiro's work within the broader context of the history and development of Japanese and international picture book cultures. Two galleries invite us to "get acquainted" with Chihiro, the person, through her belongings, favorite things, sketches, and works by artists who influenced her, and Chihiro, the artist, through changing displays of her sketches, oil paintings, and picture book originals. Two galleries, drawing on the International Collection of about 12,000 works created by 168 artists from 28 countries, provide an introduction to picture book art, while changing exhibits focus on particular artists and themes. Another offers a history of the evolution of the picture book as an art form from the Egyptian *Book of the Dead* to medieval manuscripts, to Japanese Edo picture scrolls, to rare picture books from the 19th and early 20th centuries. A library containing copies of books by artists represented in the collections allows for extended browsing and exploration and a chance to compare the art on show with the printed book. The collection itself is available for supervised research. There is also a program of guided talks, lectures, films, workshops, and a Storyclub for young children.

Recognizing that picture book artists often create pieces in other mediums, the museum also collects three-dimensional works, displaying these "here and there" at Azumino. Hanging from the roof beams, for instance, as if swimming in an aquarium, are shoals of strange fish made of painted tin plate by the Polish artist Josef Wilkon. Outside in the surrounding Azumino Chihiro Park is a dramatic and intriguing garden, designed by Czech artist Kveta Pacovská from two ponds, six halved stones, paintings and mirrors to marry art, nature, and viewers in an amusing and inventive installation. Nearby is a recreation of Chihiro's cottage and atelier.

Back in Tokyo, the Chihiro Art Museum underwent a complete renovation, reopening in 2002, on its 25th anniversary, having doubled its public space. It now reflects the time that Chihiro actually lived there as well as the history of the former museum. It, like Azumino, invites us to listen for the scratch of Chihiro's pen in her atelier and in the Chihiro Gallery where changing displays reveal her artistic concerns, philosophy, development, and idiosyncratic style. But both museums do more. Here, for the first time, we can contemplate work by the *world's* picture book artists brought together and begin to appreciate and understand the defining individual characteristics of each *and* of their national cultures, to delight in their similarities and differences, and to enjoy their visual dialogue in these most democratic of museums. Matsumoto's vision and its international scope have brought recognition of the artistic and historic value of original picture book art and its place in Japanese and world culture, and of the need to preserve these cultural treasures for future generations. They have inspired the opening of more than 30 picture book museums in Japan. Has their influence been felt elsewhere?

The Eric Carle Museum of Picture Book Art: A First Fine Art Museum

Across an ocean and a continent in Amherst, Massachusetts, the Chihiro Art Museums became models and Matsumoto a mentor for The Eric Carle Museum of Picture Book Art. In the early 1980s, Carle (1969), creator of *The Very Hungry Caterpillar* and other classics, and his wife had been astonished to discover museums in Japan honoring the picture book—an art form largely unrecognized in America. A seed was planted. A decade later, they visited the Chihiro Art Museum Tokyo. The seed began to grow from a small gallery beneath Carle's studio to a purpose-built museum celebrating the art of the picture book and fostering creativity and the confidence to appreciate and enjoy art of every kind in visitors of all ages by exploring the familiar and beloved art of our childhoods. Carle's work would sit at its heart. To realize their vision, they established and endowed The Eric and Barbara Carle Foundation.

Carle's work had always been informed by strong memories of a displaced childhood. Uprooted at six from his American home and a "sun-filled" introduction to school, he was traumatized by the harsh approach at his new school in his parent's native Germany. He dreamt often of building a bridge across the ocean to his old home. Carle's later life-affirming artistic response to this dark, early experience and the liberating notion of himself as a bridge builder were to determine the tenor of his work as a picture book maker. "I am fascinated," he wrote, "by the period in a child's life when he or she…leaves home and goes to school. What a gulf a child must cross then: from home and security, a world of play and the senses, to a world of reason and abstraction, order and discipline. I should like my books to bridge that great divide" (Carle, 1996, p. 38). If his books were bridges between home and school and the new world of literacy, could a picture book museum, he wondered, bridge the worlds of visual and verbal literacy and of picture book illustration and fine art?

In art historian H. Nichols B. Clark, Carle found a director who shared his beliefs. Clark had co-curated *Myth, Magic, and Mystery: One Hundred Years of American Children's Book Illustration* (1996–97), the first major exhibition to survey the history of illustration for children in America. In this pioneering, perception-changing show, artwork was removed from its accustomed context as part of a book and presented on its own with text conspicuously absent. This fine art approach was to underpin exhibition and program design at the planned museum which, as a bridge builder, was to be a "first" art museum for visitors of all ages—an early "step in a journey of museum experiences" (Heller, 2006).

In the museum's architects, Carle found an imaginative firm which drew on the design language of his books for that of the museum, and, as at the Chihiro Azumino, on the "vaulting forms" of the surrounding Holyoke hills.

Set, most appropriately, in an old apple orchard in the cultural quarter of Hampshire College, the museum's white exterior and interior walls echo the white backgrounds in Carle's work where they set the stage for his explosive colored tissue collages of the natural world. Here, they exist like a "welcoming palette awaiting the artist's brush," providing a stage in the central atrium for four large abstract murals in red, blue, green and yellow by Carle—a clear statement of the museum's artistic intent, and in the three galleries, for rotating exhibitions of Carle's work, drawn from the 2,000 pieces in the museum's collection and that of guest artists. Externally, as the orchard blossoms white in spring, the white museum has a dialogue with nature similar to Carle's use of nature in his books, while the atrium windows invite viewers inside and out to contemplate art and nature at once. In a museum about learning to look and looking to learn, this experience begins with the building itself and its relation to the natural world around it

Inside, Carle's vision comes to life through a range of programs built around "hands-on [art studio], eyes-on [galleries], and ears-on [reading library] approaches" (Agoglia, 2008, personal correspondence). The framing focus here is on picture book art, removed from the defining context of a book, as a first experience of fine art—one that is enhanced by offering us a portable toolkit of questions that open up ways of thinking and talking about what we see and can be taken away with us to heighten our enjoyment of art elsewhere.

The separation of image and text in any exhibition gives rise to a curatorial and aesthetic dilemma. The picture book is a collaborative narrative art form, its impact arising from the interactive play of words and pictures. The finished book is the work of art, as Lawrence Sipe affirms in his chapter in this volume. If we remove an image from this frame, what we see on the gallery wall is a still—a frozen moment—out of its own story and placed in a new larger canvas. How are we asked to respond to it? As literature? As fine art? As part of a new artistic or thematic narrative about the nature of picture book making?

At the Carle, literally de-constructing a picture book and re-framing components of it on the gallery walls is seen as a way of demonstrating that the art on show, like all fine art, can invite an aesthetic response on its own. Text and context have no place here, although the relevant picture books are available for reference. The invitation, like that in Carle's *Brown Bear, Brown Bear, What Do You See?* (Martin, Jr., 1996) is to look, look again, and respond creatively to what we see. Our engagement is with the art on show. There are no inter-actives, but videos are occasionally used to illuminate an artist's creative process. Discussion is encouraged, particularly with guided school groups, as we are asked to consider: "What is going on in this picture? What do you see that makes you say that? What more do you see?" There are no labels telling us

ELIZABETH HAMMILL

how to look or what to think, but, for self-guided visitors, there are more specific questions to ponder: "Think about the variety of textures in Carle's work and how they might have been created." or, in a Margot and Kaethe Zemach retrospective: "There are two versions of *The Fisherman and His Wife*. Look at the changes in Zemach's use of line, color and space, and speculate on why they were made…." Personal statements by artists give clues to their approach to their art and the art on show: "The pictures here are finished works and points of departure" (Carle, 2004). "Line is a language—something descriptive as well as functional. You don't just make marks without a reason" (Zemach, 2004).

Here, again, the visual world is being opened up for us, but with a particular slant. What the Carle, as the first full scale museum in America dedicated to the art of the picture book, recognizes and acts on is an understanding, as Clark puts it, that for many people "appreciating art is a very esoteric science…one that makes them nervous…. We provide them with a reassuring entry point…and strategic, bridging tools" (Heller, 2006). Drawing on work in the field of aesthetic and cognitive development by Rudolf Arnheim, Jerome Bruner, and Lev Vygotsky and on the Visual Thinking Strategies (VTS) of museum educator Philip Yenawine and cognitive psychologist Abigail Housen, the Carle provides us with a "toolbox of questions," designed to help us attend to the art on show and find meaning in it. We are encouraged to observe, speculate, make inferences, find evidence for our ideas, and construct interpretations together—just what we do when we think and talk about our reading. There are no right or wrong answers, just different perspectives, different possibilities. We find ourselves reflecting too on an artist's use of color, composition, line, texture, and technique. We are invited to become detectives and compare the art on the wall with the art in the published book—triggering discussions about artistic methods and how books are made as well as introducing us to language to articulate what we see. With work by Carle and at least two other artists on show at any given time, we are also invited to compare very different artistic and national sensibilities, visions, and methods at work.

In the Art Studio, changing, exhibit-related, hands on activities encourage us to take our gallery discoveries about art further by exploring the creative process. In drop-in sessions and workshops, we are introduced to media and artistic techniques and disciplines on view in the galleries and invited to experiment with them ourselves. Drawing on the child-centered Italian Reggio Emilia approach, the emphasis here is on learning to "think" with our hands, eyes, and sensibilities as well as our brain and on problem solving and reflection. As we make our own "works of art", our understanding of how to look at art grows (Agoglia, 2008, personal correspondence).

In the Reading Library housing some 3,000 picture books, our "eyes-on" and "hands-on" experiences join with an "ears on" experience in Carle Storytimes. Shaped by an evolving Whole Book Approach (WBA) that provides a critical framework and pedagogy for the museum's work and draws on whole language instruction, VTS, and the Reggio Emilia discovery model, Storytimes are animated conversation times. Here reader and children share picture book adventures *and* together uncover how the ingredients of a picture book—text, pictures, pacing, design, layout, typeface, and production—interact and play off each other to create an artistic whole.

The Carle, like Dromkeen, offers on-site, outreach, and professional development courses. Staff take art studio workshops and Storytime sessions into regional schools and undertake extended school residencies. They provide teachers, librarians, and others keen to build picture books and visual literacy into their classroom, library, or community work, with a range of book programs that draw on the VTS and WBA methodologies and explore the rich teaching potential of the picture book and its role in developing visual literacy. In a new collaboration with The Center for the Study of Children's Literature at Simmons College in Boston, the museum offers a Master in Fine Arts in Writing for Children. Overseas, the Carle is mentoring staff at the Chihiro Art Museums as they develop education programs, novel in Japan, using VTS and WBA as foundations.

Like Dromkeen, the Carle tours exhibitions nationally—some developed in museum collaborations—to widen the audience for picture book art. It too has inaugurated a set of national awards (2006), The Carle Honors, which celebrate the vital contribution of artists, mentors or champions, financial supporters of its work, and individuals or organizations whose imagination, vision, and dedication to the art of the picture book have furthered art appreciation, early literacy, and critical thinking.

For researchers, the Carle's small but growing collection now contains not only Carle's archive but work by artists including Barry Moser, Gennady Spirin, Steven Kellogg, Robert Ingpen, and Petra Mathers and is available by appointment. So too is the extensive research library of Barbara Elleman, gifted by the critic and former editor of *Booklist* and *Book Links*.

Still in its early years, the Carle's reach and influence is ever-widening as it becomes the bridge that its founder imagined. The museum's ethos, like Carle's caterpillar, is creeping into the American consciousness. Picture book art, once dismissed as a genre, is now the subject of revisionist critical thinking that is breaking down the old walls between art and illustration. "Picture This: Children's Book Art Gains Mainstream Acclaim" announced a *Boston Globe* headline (Reitz) in February 2008. Already then, the Carle is providing us with an important forum for critical debate, one that is changing and developing our aesthetic appreciation both of picture book art and of the picture book as an art form.

Developments in Europe

Meanwhile in Europe, various models for children's literature museums were emerging and injecting a new playful sensibility into the experiences on offer. In Germany, for instance, Europe's first (and only) picture book museum opened at Burg Wissem in Troisdorf in 1982 in an imaginatively converted castle with specially commissioned statues of fairytale characters in its courtyard and fairytale motifs on its staircase walls. The museum houses, exhibits, and tours work from its Alsleben and Bruggermann collections of historical books and its growing collection of modern German picture book art by illustrators including Josef Wilkon, Helme Heine, Jutta Bauer, and Janosch.

Further north, in Finland, in 1987, a museum dedicated to the art of Tove Jansson, creator of the endearingly wayward, iconic Moomins, was created in Tampere's elegant new copper clad library, following her donation of over 2,000 pieces of artwork and an entrancing Moomin House, crafted with artists Tuulikki Pietila and Pentti Eistola to the Tampere Art Museum. The Moominvalley Museum, with its curving galleries hung with a changing selection of Jansson's illustrations for her 13 Moomin books, its enchanting recreation of the floating theatre from *The Exploits of Moominpappa* (Jansson, 1969) where children can dress up and perform to an audience seated in small rowing boats on the "water," and 40 more Moomin tableaux, invites us to experience the artistic shaping of a fictional world which we can imaginatively step inside.

An entry into imagined worlds and play lie at the heart of Junibacken, a theatrical "culture house" for children "full of stories, laughter and mischief" which opened in Stockholm in 1996. Conceived by the actor, director, and producer Staffan Götestam whose career has been built around his interpretations of Astrid Lindgren's work, Junibacken celebrates Lindgren and her fictional worlds but also, at her request, many contemporary Swedish illustrators and their creations.

For Lindgren, play, imagination, and reading were inextricably entwined. "Only children perform miracles when they read," she wrote. Only they, like her young heroes, can "exceed the boundaries of reality" and "unimpededly... move between magic and porridge, between total terror and explosive joy" (Edstrm, 2000, p. 26).

At Junibacken, we are invited to do just that as we embark on a journey of discovery and adventure through a series of 3-dimensional fictional worlds. From Storybook Square to Pippi Longstocking's Villa Villekula, we visit the painstakingly recreated, child-scaled homes of some of Sweden's favorite fictional characters—from urban pre-schooler Alfie Atkins to Old Man Pettson and his cat Findus—and try on and play out their lives and stories for a time.

Arriving at Vimmerby Station and an exhibition about Lindgren's life, the art of her three best known illustrators, and the Astrid Lindgren Memorial Award, we board a small wooden carriage and embark on a breathtakingly inventive, minutely detailed, dramatic, and moving journey through landscapes and scenes from six of Lindgren's books, traveling from Mardie and Emil's sunlit Junibacken to the darker lights of the Brothers Lionhart's Nangilima. The journey lingers in the mind long afterwards.

Junibacken offers us a new kind of literary museum experience. A children's museum, but not a theme park, its inspiration comes from Lindgren's and Götestam's own belief in the power of story, drama, and imaginative play to shape young minds and offer creative entries into other worlds and the world about them. Junibacken enfolds us like a book and like a book, can be re-played again and again.

Seven Stories: The Centre for Children's Books—The Museum as Literary Playground

In the northeast of England, yet another model for a museum of children's literature was emerging in Newcastle upon Tyne. Its roots lay again in a perceived need to establish a new institution—in this case, one with national aspirations—that would collect, preserve, and exhibit a growing collection of the working papers of Britain's modern writers and illustrators for children, and celebrate both the artistry of British children's books and the journeys into the imagination that exploring these original materials and reading itself offer. It was to be developed locally against the backdrop of the culturally fuelled regeneration of the once proud Victorian industrial waterfront of the River Tyne and nationally, against the politics of a shifting arts and education landscape. While its genesis, once more, sprang from personal belief and vision, its realization took place in a political and public arena in which the British Parliament's establishment of a National Lottery (1993) made possible public funding for new cultural ventures that might otherwise have remained dreams. Seven Stories, known initially as The Centre for the Children's Book (CCB), is one such project.

It is here that my part in these stories begins. As an American making my career in Britain from the late 1970s on in the education and book worlds as a children's bookseller, lecturer, and critic, I was increasingly surprised at British reluctance to celebrate their achievements in the field of children's literature. Arriving in Newcastle from New York in 1971, I discovered a rich literary landscape, with children's fiction flourishing in a second "Golden Age" and the modern picture book as an art form coming into its own. Two influential journals—*Growing Point* and *Signal Approaches to Children's Books*—and Aidan Chambers's (1983) *Introducing Books to Children* became my guides, each significantly informing my critical thinking about children's books and about engaging children with books and their making. So too did the philosophy and work of Kaye Webb, editor of Puffin Books, and founder of the Puffin Club. A literary Pied Piper, Webb aimed to turn children into readers by making their relationship with books a "living" one, creating a community of interest, and opening imaginative highways into reading through the Club's iconic magazine *Puffin Post* and activities such as the annual Puffin Exhibition in London, where our family first experienced the heady excitement of meeting authors, stepping into storybook worlds, and seeing original artwork on show.

I became aware, early on, of the ways in which meeting an author can bridge the gap between children and books, and transform their response to reading. Like the Oldmeadows, I was conscious of children's curiosity about how books are made and their fascination with the creative process as they watched an illustrator conjure up imaginary creatures on paper or a writer share notebooks and drafts that were sometimes as untidy as their own. Increasingly over my 16 years as a bookseller, I developed school and public programs in which children and young people could further their development as critically appreciative readers and as apprentice writers learning their craft by meeting and sharing ideas and work with authors and illustrators in mutually rewarding sessions. Work in progress, artists' and children's, always sat at the heart of these programs.

The impetus to develop new approaches and initiatives was furthered throughout the 1980s and 90s by radical changes in the culture and economics of publishing, now multi-national, corporate, commercialized, and prone to overproduction as Joel Taxel's chapter in this volume spells out. The erosion of public and school library services and of school book budgets combined with the introduction of a National Curriculum in 1988 with set English Heritage books prompted controversy. "This government," averred poet Michael Rosen (1993), "in spite of all the rhetoric concerning literacy levels, has declared war on the reading of books" (p. 108). Two years later, Rosen (1995) asked: "How can we intervene to keep what we do more thoughtful, more fun, more useful, more exciting, more dissenting and nonconformist…an alive, hopeful...questioning place to be?" (p. 44). That was a key question confronting the children's book world as the century turned.

One possible answer was already evolving in Newcastle. Prompted by the near loss of the world famous Opie Collection to America in 1988 coupled with the realization that important but neglected parts of our children's literary heritage were disappearing into collections abroad in the absence of any dedicated collection here, and conversations with writers and illustrators lamenting the lack of a British home like Dromkeen for their work, I wondered how this startling gap in Britain's literary provision could be filled. What if a home for a growing collection of books and the original papers out of which they emerged was created, a home that was not only a new national and international resource but also one that could become a kind of National Gallery of Children's Literature?

It was a big, intriguing idea—one that I began to share and develop with the children's book world and local young people. Possible aims, size, scope, activities, and audiences were debated, as was location. Newcastle, on the brink of a cultural renaissance, was already recognized nationally as a champion of children's books through pioneering initiatives like the Northern Children's Book Festival (from 1984 on). High unemployment and low literacy levels made it a place where books and literacy were valued as keys to social, cultural, and economic change, and public investment in a national center could make a difference.

By early 1994, I had written a working proposal for a center whose core vision is realized in Seven Stories today. It echoed Dromkeen in its emphasis on the creation of a home for a living collection to be used in exhibitions and associated school, public, and outreach programs to engage children with literature through understanding how it came to be made. Its broad aims of changing public perception about the value and place of children's books in British culture, cultivating an appreciation of the art, craft, and pleasures of book and story making, and stimulating artistic innovation and creativity within its audiences were akin to those of its developing museum counterparts elsewhere. It differed crucially, however, in its aim to create a national (with a capital N) center to preserve Britain's vital literary heritage of childhood and to transmit it and the reading culture to children. From the beginning, story, story making, and making readers were also at CCB's heart.

The proposal was welcomed by the book world, the English Arts Council (ACE) and Newcastle City Council (NCC). Early support came a year before CCB officially came into existence as an educational charity, when it was offered the literary estate of Robert Westall (2001)—locally born author of *The Machine Gunners* and other prize winning books set in the Northeast—plus £100,000 towards a building. I began to form a steering committee, looked at possible sites, and, by chance, found a local partner for this enterprise—someone who understood politics, public funding, and strategic and business management. Mary Briggs, a co-founder, like me, of the Northern Children's Book Festival, whose career spanned libraries, arts and most recently education, shared my belief in the possibilities of the book as a tool for growth, and recognized the potential of the proposed center to act as a catalyst for change and creativity. If the new Arts Lottery could be a source of capital funding, anything seemed possible. And it was.

But Seven Stories didn't happen overnight. Ten years passed from the day when we each put £10 into a CCB bank account to the day in August 2005 when we opened the £6.5 million center to the public. The decade long journey took us on a roller coaster ride in the politics, economics, and challenges of initiating a new cultural enterprise, but also obliged us to pilot our vision to demonstrate to public funders what a center might be and do.

In 1998 in the first of seven pre-opening exhibitions, our experimental, boundary-breaking approach to exhibition design and interpretation and associated programming emerged. Responding to heated debate around a new National Literacy Strategy that put tests, targets, and national school league tables before reading for pleasure, and to a new Access and Arts for Everyone cultural agenda, we pondered how to display artwork and manuscripts out of their picture book context and place them in a meaningful new gallery frame.

Could a gallery, we wondered, in the spirit of the Puffin Exhibitions of Kaye Webb whose personal archive we had acquired in 1997, be transformed into a setting for an exhibition of original words and pictures that might play to an audience's sense of wonder and fun and fire new readers? Could an exhibition take audiences inside an author or artist's creative world? Could it recreate that immersion in a virtual world that occurs when we say we are "lost in a book"? Could it, in line with funding from the Arts Lottery's "New Audiences" initiative, be framed in such a way that it became a "reassuring entry point" to a key target audience—families unfamiliar with either art galleries or literary events?

An exhibition could and did. Taking our cue from illustrator Colin McNaughton's belief that creating a picture book is like creating a piece of theatre, we designed our first show *Daft as a Bucket: Inside the World of Colin McNaughton* as a giant 3-D picture book—one that invited audiences to step into the artist's pictures. From a Giant's Library, a pirate ship in harbor, Outer Space, to Preston Pig's classroom, theatrical sets provided a dramatic narrative solution to the question of how to display original pictures and words out of their picture book frame—one heightened by an accompanying McNaughton production by a local theatre company. We discovered drama, now a key element of our education, outreach and public programming, as a powerful pathway into story and story making, and found our own curatorial voice. Our experiment in exhibition design and interpretation had generated a literary and artistic experience that was, at once, infectious, playful, fun, eye opening and thought provoking. It, like the best books, was transformational.

Our ensuing pre-opening shows played with design, form, and interpretation in similar ways—always attending to what the work to be displayed suggested, to the story to be told, and to the gallery experience to be offered. We carefully built on our first partnerships—our collaborations ranging from those with local museums, theatre companies, and university graphic arts/design courses to ones with publishers, Tate Gallery's National Programs, Baika Women's College in Osaka, Japan, and Dick Bruna's Dutch publisher Mercis. We began to tour exhibitions and developed outreach programs, working to bring books alive for a variety of new and harder-to-reach audiences and laying the foundations for future projects that, in the spirit of Rosen's query, would be thoughtful, fun, useful, exciting, dissenting, and nonconformist. The newness and

possibilities of what we were doing energized us and took us down many revelatory paths.

In 2002, we initiated a community writing project—*Penning People and Place*—built around two parallel residencies in two sharply contrasting communities linked by walls: Berwick upon Tweed, a walled historic Northumbrian outpost on the North Sea, and Byker in East Newcastle, a declining urban community, centered about a public housing estate known as the Byker Wall. The year-long project introduced CCB to Byker and its people. Here, in the Ouseburn Valley within sight of the Byker Wall, Kate Edwards, now our Chief Executive, had found a home for our project after our hopes of a new £10 million "book palace" were dashed when the Arts Lottery changed its capital funding plans (1999). Leetham's Mill, a listed, semi-derelict seven story Victorian granary backing onto the Ouseburn, a tributary of the nearby Tyne, felt right. The valley, shaped by 19th-century manufacturing and industry, was developing a new life as one of Tyneside's most creative places. Empty warehouses were being converted into artists' studios, and a city farm, riding stables, and regeneration trust had been established. Stepping onto Lime Street with its aging buildings, pigeon crees, and old boats moored on the burn, felt like stepping into another world. We bought the mill and the crisp warehouse next door (2001). Three years and £6.5 million later, conversion of the granary into a modern, family-friendly museum, gallery, performance and workshop space with a literary focus began.

Today, visitors are greeted by a prize-winning building that dramatically marries weathered brick with new polished concrete and glass outside, but retains the integrity and original cast iron structure, timber joists, and beams of the old mill inside. Artwork by eight award-winning illustrators is etched onto the new entrance, shaped like an open book, and an accompanying text of familiar phrases: "Once upon a time…into the deep dark woods." It and the spiraling stair tower invite visitors to embark on a journey into the world of books and their makers. On the river side of the building, a small enchanting boat—*Sea Song Sang*—is moored, another invitation to voyage, created by a community artist whose sculpture grew out of a regional schools' project exploring tales of the sea and children's ideas for a magical Seven Stories story boat.

Inside, the nature of the journey is revealed: "Some people say there are only seven stories in the world but a thousand different ways of telling them. Seven Stories is about the thousand ways." And so it is. From the beamed Artist's Attic on its seventh floor with its winged story chair and children's theatre to the riverside Creation Station, Seven Stories is a kind of captivating literary playground where exhibitions, school programs, drop-in activities, workshops, dressing up, drama, special events with storytellers, performers, authors and illustrators, and a café and bookshop offer visitors of all ages an ever changing landscape for the imagination—one that awakens them to the endless creative possibilities of playing with words and pictures and the ingredients of stories. Like Browser, the Seven Stories' cat, created by illustrator Satoshi Kitamura as a pictorial guide to the building, visitors can become writers, artists, explorers, designers, storytellers, readers, and collectors here as they travel by book.

In the Robert Westall and Sebastian Walker Galleries—the first exhibition spaces in Britain dedicated to children's books, we have played with the graphic framing of shows in different ways to different ends. While words and pictures figure in all our exhibitions, two shows about two North Eastern writers—David Almond and Robert Westall—challenged us to find ways of exploring text-based worlds. For *Westall's Kingdom* (2006), the feel, atmosphere, and dark undercurrents of wartime Tyneside and the bleak beauty of the Northumbrian coast—the landscape of Westall's youth and his favored setting—were evoked, using photographic back drops, period artifacts, and sight, light, and sound effects. At the gallery's center stood the "Fortress," the secret den of the young gang in *The Machine Gunners*, where today's children could imagine and play out, Junibacken-like, Westall's story. Emotive material—photographs, recordings, Westall's typewriter—a novelty today, and a motorcycle, like that in *Devil on the Road* (1996), written after Westall's teenage son died in a biking accident, provided a sometimes gritty realism that brought the writer's notes, manuscripts, and edited typescripts to life.

Winged Tales of the North (2008), a modular touring exhibition, plays inventively with the size and shape of graphic reproductions of original material and an over-arching text by Almond himself as it answers Almond's opening questions: "Where does a story come from? ...Where does it all start?" Traveling via "the universe, the galaxy" to "our house, the kitchen, me…" in his childhood home in Felling-on-Tyne, Almond reveals how stories grow from a known landscape, and how real places, real people, merge with imagined ones to become "living things." The trajectory of *Skellig* from Almond's (2009) childhood belief that shoulder blades are "where your wings were" to a novel, play, film, and opera shows how a story takes flight. Elsewhere, at a desk with Almond's bookshelves reproduced above it, ideas about the writer as reader, literary influences, and authorial voice are introduced and visitors can contribute to a never-ending story. Thus, how this writer writes is meaningfully but magically conveyed.

Other exhibition journeys can be taken at Seven Stories outside the galleries, shows that reflect our commitment to nurturing new talent—work in progress, for instance, by members of the Seven Stories Writer's and Artist's Group, a circle of North Eastern writers and illustrators for children who meet regularly at the center to share work and practice. Or one can view winning entries by graphic arts students for an annual illustration competition, created in partnership with Sunderland University's Graphic Arts Department and poet Gillian Allnutt, which is often the first public showcase for these young artists.

In the Storylab gallery, visitors learn about our collection, currently housed in specialist facilities south of the Tyne, which now contains some 22,000 books and papers for over 70 authors and illustrators. Here, guided by Browser, visitors investigate a Heath Robinsonesque Collection Machine to discover why and what we collect and what happens to work when it enters our collection. Doors open to reveal archive gems—a Philip Pullman manuscript perhaps or a Jan Ormerod rough—and facsimiles of work damaged by bugs, water, and light, in need of conservation. Interactive games illuminate the collecting process further and suggest the kinds of information to be gleaned from a literary collection. The Collection catalogue and 1,000 digitized images of material in it can be accessed here online.

Since its inception, Seven Stories has played an important role in furthering the wider arts, heritage, and education agendas of local and national government bodies. Storylab was created as part of *Storylines*, a pioneering project designed to unlock the potential of our children's literary archive as a new, unexplored, learning resource and to widen access to it and an understanding of its cultural and historical importance School groups, in this and subsequent projects, uniquely work alongside our collection and education teams and our writer in residence. They search works in our collection to discover, for instance, the creative processes of different authors and artists, drawing creative inspiration from their findings, and developing their own responses—through film, drama, or perhaps stories with accompanying personal archives of notes, rough plans, and drafts to document their own creative processes. The resulting works are displayed in Storylab and show us children not just looking over the shoulder of a writer or illustrator but inspired to step into their shoes. For them, magic and meaning come not only from their discovery of the knowledge and information that the collection holds, but also from the self-discovery that their creative responses to it reveal.

We are currently involved in a government initiative that is piloting a new partnership model among schools, libraries, and arts and heritage organizations to create sustained culturally inspiring activities planned with and for young people. Working with teachers, librarians, schoolchildren, artists, storytellers, writers, and actors, we are playing with the possibilities of where different adventures with words and images might take all of us. Projects have included an in-depth-over-time exploration of Michael Rosen's (1993) *We're Going on a Bear Hunt*—its language, sounds, settings, both real and imagined—as an inspiration for new work and new understandings. Another project, *Wonderwords*, has evolved into a traveling poetry writing workshop, that marries performance, travel, contemporary poetry, and writing in ways that are changing children's perception of poetry and of themselves as poets. Out of this has come *Pathways into Poetry*, one of our first professional development courses for teachers, a resource pack and an anthology of participants' poetry.

Building on our belief that sharing books lies at the heart of learning to read and reading to learn, we offer community and public programs designed to engage families with books and reading together and with Seven Stories as a place which can further a love of literature. From school or library based projects to pioneering work with teenage mothers to weekly in-house early years sessions of *Bookworm Babies, Story Party*, and *Yoga Babies*, we are working to foster family relationships with books and the next generation of readers.

Researchers are finding that the papers and books in our collection offer new pathways and insights into the making of modern British children's literature from the 1930s on when our collecting period begins. Our holdings, built from scratch, vary in size from single pieces of artwork to material relating to one or more representative books of an author or illustrator, to the comprehensive archives, including reference and book collections, of writers like Geoffrey Trease, Peter Dickinson, Eva Ibbotson, and Ursula Moray Williams, playwright David Wood, and illustrators Faith Jaques and Judith Kerr.

The academic exploration of this material is an exciting long-term challenge, one being furthered by our partnership with the Children's Literature Unit at Newcastle University, founded in 2004 in response to our creation of a new resource and research facility. Key to this partnership has been an Arts and Humanities Research Council funded project, which has seen three doctoral students basing their research on our Robert Westall and Kaye Webb archives, and working with our collection team to develop our research infrastructure and policy. Seven Stories became an accredited museum in 2008 and aims for our Collection to be of sufficient depth, breadth, and significance to be eligible for formal Designation as a National Collection within five years.

Since the first ideas for a National Gallery of Children's Literature were developed 20 years ago, the public profile of children's literature has changed. We have been part of a movement that has seen children's books make headline news with the works of J. K. Rowling, Philip Pullman, and Jacqueline Wilson. The creation in 1999 of the post of Children's Laureate, awarded bi-annually to an eminent author or illustrator to celebrate outstanding achievement, has given children's literature six influential champions and Seven Stories key advocates and partners. In Bookstart (1992), Britain now has the world's first publicly funded national books-for-babies program. Taken together, these are beginnings that are lodging children's literature in Britain's consciousness as a vital, no longer overlooked, aspect of our national heritage and everyday culture.

Seven Stories, starting from a non-traditional base, is becoming the hub of a new and exciting axis for children's literature nationally. Our evolving approach marries critical reflection with pleasure, new knowledge with questioning, interpretation with changing perceptions, and reading and creativity with adventure, discovery, and growth. We are still so new that the possibilities of being a museum, of collecting, of engaging new audiences with story making, of making books matter, and of being a catalyst of delight, creativity, and change seem infinite.

"Only Connect"

This has been a story about pioneers and new museums working with the same basic materials—manuscripts, artwork, books, and story—but in very distinct ways to place children's literature at the heart of their national literary and artistic cultures. Each has been created in response to the status of children's literature in their countries at a particular moment in time. Each, in its own way, has been and is an agent of cultural politics and cultural change. None has been a neutral space.

Defined in spirit by their framing architecture, be it a home, a traditional art gallery, or a warehouse regenerated as a literary playground, each museum has used its knowledge and the power of the artistic imagination to create what can be transformative spaces and experiences. E. M. Forster's (2002) dictum—"Only connect"—has taken many shapes and sparked many conversations as children's literature comes of age in new museums around the world—museums now reaching across oceans to share their experiences and approaches with each other. Here the politics of art, reading, and pleasure meet and open wide the world of children's literature to all of us. For researchers, they offer an Aladdin's Cave of original materials and original approaches to making those materials matter beyond academia to explore. And to think that it all began with someone listening for the scratch of a pen.

Literature References

Alcott, L. M. (1975). *Behind a mask: The unknown thrillers of Louisa May Alcott* (M. Stern, Ed.). New York, NY: William Morrow.

Alcott, L. M. (2004) *Little women*. New York, NY: Signet Classics.

Almond, D. (2009). *Skellig*. New York, NY: Delacorte.

Andersen, H. C. (1991a). *The red shoes* (A. Bell, Trans., C. Iwasaki. Illus.). Natick, MA: Picture Book Studio.

Andersen, H. C. (1991b). *The little mermaid* (A. Bell, Trans., C. Iwasaki. Illus.) New York, NY: Scholastic.

Barton, C. (1841). A mother's offering to her children: By a lady, long resident in New South Wales. Sydney, Australia: Gazette Office.

Carle, E. (1969). The very hungry caterpillar. New York, NY: Philomel Books.

Forster, E. M. (2002). *Howard's End*. Mineola, NY: Dover.

Jansson, T. (1969) *The exploits of Moominpappa*. London: Puffin Books.

Martin, Jr., B. (1996). *Brown bear, brown bear, what do you see?* (E. Carle, Illus.). New York, NY: Henry Holt.

Montgomery, L. M. (2008). *Anne of Green Gables*. New York, NY: Putnam.

Potter, B. (1902). *The tale of Peter Rabbit.* London: Frederick Warne.

Potter, B. (1905). *The pie and the patty pan.* London: Frederick Warne.

Potter, B. (1908a). *The tale of Jemima Puddle Duck.* London: Frederick Warne.

Potter, B. (1908b) *The tale of Samuel Whiskers.* London: Frederick Warne.

Rosen, M. (1993). *We're going on a bear hunt* (H. Oxenbury, Illus.). London: Walker Books.

Westall, R. (1996). *Devil on the road.* New York, NY: Macmillan.

Westall, R. (2001). *The machine gunners.* New York, NY: Macmillan.

Academic References

Alberghene, J. M., & Clark, B. L. (Eds.). (1999). *"Little Women" and the feminist imagination: Criticism, controversy, personal essays.* New York, NY: Garland.

Berne, S. (1992, August 30). Listening for the scratch of a pen. The New York Times, p. 14. Retrieved March 12, 2007, from www.nytimes.com/1992/08/30/travel/listening-for-the-scratch-of-a-pen.html

Carle, E. (1996). The art of Eric Carle. New York, NY: Philomel Books.

Carle Exhibition. (2004). *The art of Eric Carle.* Amherst, MA: The Eric Clarke Museum of Picture Book Art.

Chambers, A. (1983). *Introducing books to children.* Boston, MA: Horn Book.

Cormack, P., & Fawcett, C. (2002). Cultural gatekeepers in the L. M. Montgomery tourist industry. In M. Robinson & H. C. Andersen (Eds.), *Literature and tourism* (pp. 171–190). London: Thomson.

De Jonge, J. (2002). Through the eyes of memory. In I. Gammell (Ed.), *Making Avonlea: L. M. Montgomery and popular culture* (pp. 252–267). Toronto: University of Toronto Press.

Denyer, S. (2000). *Beatrix Potter at home in the Lake District.* London: Frances Lincoln.

Devereux, C. (2001). "Canadian classic" and "commodity export": The nationalism of "our" Anne of Green Gables. *Journal of Canadian Studies.* Retrieved March 12, 2007, from findarticles. com/p/articles/mi_qa3683/is_200104/ai_n8938663/pg_16/

Edstrm, V. (2000). *Astrid Lindgren: A critical study* (E. Cormack, Trans.). Stockholm: R & S Books.

Fiamengo, J. (2002). Towards a theory of the popular landscape in *Anne of Green Gables.* In I. Gammell (Ed.), *Making Avonlea: L. M. Montgomery and popular culture* (pp. 225–237). Toronto: University of Toronto Press.

Heller, S. (2006). Since when did children's books have a museum? Interview with H. Nichols B. Clark. *Voice.* Retrieved March 15, 2007, from http://journal.aiga.org.content.cfm/

Lear, L. (2007). *Beatrix Potter: A life in nature.* New York, NY: St. Martin's Press.

Matsumoto, T. (2000). *Chihiro Art Museum Collection.* Tokyo: Kodansha.

Morse, J. C. (Ed.). (1982). *Beatrix Potter's Americans: Selected letters.* Boston, MA: The Horn Book.

Pike, E. H. (2002). Mass marketing, popular culture, and the Canadian celebrity author. In I. Gammell (Ed.), *Making Avonlea: L. M. Montgomery and popular culture* (pp. 238–251). Toronto: University of Toronto Press

Prentice, J., & Bird, B. (1988). *Dromkeen: A journey into children's literature.* London: The Bodley Head.

Pullman, P. (2002, May 29). Bank of England speech. Unpublished manuscript.

Reitz, S. (2008, February 243). Picture this: Children's book art gains mainstream acclaim. *The Boston Globe.* Retrieved June 12, 2009, from http://www.boston.com/news/local/connecticut/articles/2008/02/23/picture_this_childrens_book_art_gains_mainstream_acclaim/

Rosen, M. (1993). Books and schools: Books in schools. *Signal, 74,* 103–114.

Rosen, M. (1995.) Raising the issues: On politics and children's literature. *Signal, 76,* 26–44.

Taylor, J. (2002). *Beatrix Potter: Artist, storyteller and countrywoman.* London: Frederick Warne.

West, P. (1999). *Domesticating history: The political origins of America's house museums.* Washington, DC: Smithsonian Institution Press.

Zemach Exhibition. (2004). *Dancing line and merry color: The worlds of Margot and Kaethe Zemach* (Poster). Amherst, MA: The Eric Carle Museum of Picture Book Art.

Coda

Compiling this volume has taken more than three years and the efforts of nearly 130 academics, authors, and illustrators. And still there are gaps: Whole sections of the globe are missing or under-represented, and some of the voices that we had so wished to include were unable to contribute for various reasons. But the histories and present accounts of writing, publishing, marketing, translating, sharing, teaching, and interpreting literature with children that are included here bear the echo of hundreds of other voices who have shaped the research on children's and young adult literature. These pioneering voices have worked against formidable odds to build a scholarly foundation on which our research depends even as it grows in both divergent and overlapping directions.

Why has the scholarly work undertaken on behalf of children's and young adult literature been such a professional struggle? In each discipline where it is studied, many of our colleagues still consider research into books for young people to be a marginal enterprise. The literature itself is often viewed as a subsidiary of popular culture not to be taken all that seriously in terms of theory and criticism, especially not when we might be studying more important things like literacy, or information technology, or literature for adults. Obviously, we believe this attitude to be naïve, or at least dangerously short-sighted. All of the literacy, engagement, and access research in the world means little if young people don't have something worth reading, accessing, and engaging with.

Enjoyment and understanding of literature for adults doesn't happen as a natural outcome of puberty, either. We aren't born with the competencies to sift through the subtle nuances of metaphor, the manipulation of emotion through rhetorical finesse, the complex interplay of the visual and the verbal, the challenge of dramatic irony. Nor do we learn these things the first time we encounter adult literary works. Our encounters with the great works of our literary heritage may be profoundly life-changing events, but our encounters with children's books, even the ones our moms bought us in the grocery store to distract us and pre-empt tantrums, are foundational and formative. We learn the pleasures that can inhere in language through oral stories; we find first delight in language's multivalence and rhetorical force through children's poetry; we map the intersection of the verbal and the visual through picturebooks and comics; we trace complex and sometimes unconscious emotions through novels that introduce us to characters that are both like and unlike us; and all along the way, we are learning what it means to be human in a complex, dynamic world. Examining how texts teach children how to read them, and then how to read beyond them, is a key part of the work we do.

But scholarly research into children's and young adult literature is also crucial to understanding our current cultural values and our social and ideological futures. Along with teaching us the literary competencies necessary to function in our intensely textual world, children's and young adult books contain within them ideological codes that teach children and young adults what matters in a society, and how they "should" feel about things. Texts educate on an emotional level, a phenomenon that is often overlooked in favor of cognitive mastery. Scholars of children's and young adult literature, particularly those who work with children, must attend to the variety of ways that ideologies are communicated through the literature in order to understand their power, and also to intervene by equipping children with the critical thinking skills they need to understand what a text may be asking them to believe about the world they live in.

Given the importance of children's and young adult literature in providing these kinds of formative experiences in accessing multiple literacies and ascertaining cultural value systems, those of us who have and will dedicate our lives to its study will never be convinced of its marginality. But it may mean that we need to look outside of our "figured worlds" to find true kindred spirits. Reading outside of one's own discipline isn't easy. The register of the prose is sometimes different enough to be jarring, but there are other protocols to consider as well. What counts as valid evidence, for instance, as well as the prevalence and use of storytelling, the invocation of particular critics and methodologies, and the focus on texts have all developed differently along disciplinary lines. Whereas an article by an LIS scholar might cite hundreds of titles on a particular issue, a literary scholar could quite happily perform an intensely close reading of just one or two, while an educator might talk about reading experiences in terms of children with little attention to specific book titles. Each of these approaches is going to frustrate somebody. But each offers a crucial piece in a comprehensive understanding of the research possibilities that we can pursue in order to understand children's and young adult literature in an expansive way.

Our early conversations about what to include in the volume and how it should be organized revealed to us the distances between our figured worlds. We found that we valued different things, and we valued the same things differently. The table of contents became a map of our various territories, with each of us feeling more at home in some chapters than in others. We deliberately chose scholars from our own disciplines whom we knew could write for interdisciplinary audiences, and yet, as we discussed first drafts, we were still surprised by the degree to which we all depend on the conceptual shorthand of our respective disciplines. So, we asked authors to illustrate their ideas and define their terms. We don't all agree with the premises, conclusions, and emphases of each chapter, and we found that often those disagreements are as much a result of our disciplinary commonplaces as they are of our personal commitments or aesthetic preferences.

Our work as editors thus sharpened our sensitivity to the way we think and write about literature, and exposed what we take for granted in our own disciplinary conversations. As the project developed and we learned where our interests overlapped and where they remained resolutely separate, we wondered what we might learn from actual travel between our worlds. One key reason why children's and young adult literature scholars don't communicate across disciplines is because we rarely attend the same professional/scholarly conferences. As every academic knows, a lot of scholarly ideas are hatched and professional connections made in restaurants and bars far from home. So, over the space of two years we presented our collaborative work at the annual conferences of the Children's Literature Association, the National Reading Conference, the National Council of Teachers of English (NCTE), the American Educational Research Association (AERA), and the biennial meeting of the U.S National Section of the International Board on Books for Young People (USBBY). Presenting our ideas aloud at these conferences forced us to find the common ground in our research. And where we found it, to no one's surprise really, was in the books themselves.

No matter how large the distances are between our figured worlds, the book becomes a place where we can inhabit a shared world. And this is why we felt it so crucial to include the voices and talents of authors and illustrators in this volume. These creators of the literature we study step in and out of all of our worlds—they go to academic conferences, libraries, bookstores, and schools to share their work; they are intensely aware of the publishing, marketing, reviewing and awards processes; their books fill library shelves and become the subject of the literary analyses around which many of our curriculum vitae are built; their work changes young people's lives. That so many of them were willing to step cheerfully into our world—the world of unpaid academic publishing—attests to the generosity of spirit that undergirds their commitment to share their words and worlds with children. But most importantly, the books these authors and illustrators create form the spaces where people, regardless of academic discipline, theoretical persuasion, or age, can all find true common ground.

List of Contributors

Editors

Shelby A. Wolf is Professor of education and an award-winning teacher and educational scholar at the University of Colorado at Boulder. Her research interests center on children's engagement in literature, particularly through alternative modes of expression. In addition to many research articles, chapters, and monographs, she wrote *The Braid of Literature: Children's Worlds of Reading* with Shirley Brice Heath, and more recently *Interpreting Literature with Children*. Her current work follows young children's engagement in the visual arts with artists from the Tate Modern Museum in London.

Karen Coats is Professor of English and Director of English Education at Illinois State University. She is author of *Looking Glasses and Neverlands: Lacan, Desire, and Subjectivity in Children's Literature* and co-editor, with Roderick McGillis and Anna Jackson, of *The Gothic in Children's Literature: Haunting the Borders*. She publishes widely on the intersections between literary and cultural theory and children's and young adult literature. She is also a reviewer for *The Bulletin of the Center for Children's Books*.

Patricia Enciso is Associate Professor of Literature, Literacy, and Equity Studies in the School of Teaching and Learning at The Ohio State University, where she teaches courses in multicultural literature, sociocultural theory, and literary understanding. She studies the ways youth and teachers mediate diverse cultural knowledge and resources, especially stories, in classrooms and informal settings. In 2007, *Reframing Sociocultural Research on Literacy: Identity, Agency, and Power* (co-edited with Lewis & Moje)

was awarded the National Reading Conference Edward Fry Book Award. As co-editor of *Language Arts* and former Chair of the NCTE Research Foundation, she has promoted deeper understanding of diversity and equity in language arts education across the United States.

Christine A. Jenkins is Associate Professor at the Graduate School of Library and Information Science (GSLIS), University of Illinois at Urbana-Champaign, where she teaches courses in youth services librarianship, young adult literature, and literacy. Her research explores historical and contemporary connections between readers and texts, with a focus on 20th-century youth literature; library history as women's history; and intellectual freedom for young readers. Her work has appeared in numerous venues, and she co-authored *The Heart Has Its Reasons: Young Adult Literature with Gay/Lesbian/Queer Content, 1969–2004*. She is former director of The Center for Children's Books at GSLIS.

Chapter Authors

Michael Daniel Ambatchew is an Ethiopian Educational Consultant who has been working in education in Ethiopia for the last two decades. In addition to doing several pieces of research on reading in Ethiopia, he is one of the leading children's writers in the country. Moreover, he is the advisor to the Stories Across Africa project in South Africa that is in the process of compiling pan-African children anthologies for the various age groups.

M. T. Anderson has written picture books, middle-grade novels, books for teens, and stories for adults. His dystopian satire *Feed* was a Finalist for the National

Book Award and was the Winner of the L.A. Times Book Award. The first volume of his Gothic historical epic, *Octavian Nothing, Traitor to the Nation* won the National Book Award and the Boston Globe/Horn Book Award. The second volume was a Printz Honor Book. He lives outside of Boston.

Laura Apol is an Associate Professor at Michigan State University, where her scholarship and teaching focus on children's literature, issues of diversity in literature, and creative writing. She is the area editor for Literature, Text Analysis and Response for the *Journal of Literacy Research*, and her own poetry has been published in two full-length collections, *Falling Into Grace* and *Crossing the Ladder of Sun* (winner of the Oklahoma Book Award).

Evelyn Arizpe is a Lecturer at the Faculty of Education, University of Glasgow. She has published widely in the areas of literacies, reader response to picturebooks and children's literature. She is co-author, with Morag Styles, of *Children Reading Pictures: Interpreting Visual Texts* and *Reading Lessons from the Eighteenth Century: Mothers, Children and Texts*. She is co-editor of *Acts of Reading: Teachers, Texts and Childhood*.

Rudine Sims Bishop is Professor Emerita at The Ohio State University. She is the author of *Free Within Ourselves: The Development of African American Children's Literature* and numerous other works related to children's literature and cultural diversity. Long active in the National Council of Teachers of English, she was named NCTE's 2007 Outstanding Elementary Language Arts Educator. Also an active member of the American Library Association, she has served on both Newbery and Caldecott Award committees.

Mollie V. Blackburn is an Associate Professor in the School of Teaching and Learning at The Ohio State University. Her research focuses on literacy, language, and social change, with an emphasis on LGBTQ populations. Her scholarship received the Ralph C. Preston and Alan C. Purves Awards and has been published in *Teachers College Record* and *Research in the Teaching of English,* among others. She co-edited *Literacy Research for Political Action* and *Acting Out! Combating Homophobia Through Teacher Activism.*

Clare Bradford is Professor of Literary Studies at Deakin University in Melbourne, Australia. She has published widely on children's literature, with an emphasis on postcolonial literary theory and its implications for reading colonial and postcolonial texts. Her book, *Reading Race: Aboriginality in Australian Children's Literature*, won both the Children's Literature Association Book Award and the International Research Society for Children's Literature Award. Her most recent books are *Unsettling*

Narratives: Postcolonial Readings of Children's Literature and *New World Orders: Utopianism and Contemporary Children's Texts* (with Mallan, Stephens, & McCallum). She is the editor of the Australian refereed journal *Papers: Explorations into Children's Literature*, and she is currently President of the International Research Society for Children's Literature (IRSCL).

Robin Brenner is the Reference and Teen Librarian at the Brookline Public Library in Massachusetts. She was a judge for the 2007 Will Eisner Awards, was a three-year member of the ALA/YALSA Great Graphic Novels for Teens Selection List Committee, serving as Chair in 2008, and has covered graphic novels, manga, and anime for *Library Journal, School Library Journal, Voice of Youth Advocates*, and GraphicNovelReporter.com. Her guide *Understanding Manga and Anime* was nominated for a 2008 Eisner Award. She gives lectures and workshops on graphic novels, manga, and anime across the country. She is a contributor to the group blog Good Comics for Kids hosted at *School Library Journal*. She is the editor-in-chief of No Flying No Tights, a graphic novel review site, www.noflyingnotights.com.

Joseph Bruchac's writing often draws on his American Indian ancestry and New York's Adirondack region where he was raised and still lives with his wife of 46 years, Carol. His poems, articles and stories have appeared in many publications, from *American Poetry Review* to *National Geographic*. Author of over 120 books for adults and children, his honors include an NEA Poetry Fellowship and the Lifetime Achievement Award from the Native Writers Circle of the Americas.

Mike Cadden is Professor of English, Director of Childhood Studies, and Chair of the Department of English, Foreign Languages, and Journalism at Missouri Western State University where he teaches children's and young adult literature. He is the author of *Ursula K. Le Guin Beyond Genre: Fiction for Children and Adults* and editor of *Telling Children's Stories: Narrative Theory and Children's Literature.*

Gerald Campano has taught first, fifth, seventh, eighth, ninth, and 12th grades and adult ESL. He is an Associate Professor in the Reading/Writing/Literacy Program at the Univerisity of Pennsylvania's Graduate School of Education. His scholarly interests include urban education, practitioner research, and immigrant identities in the contexts of schooling. Gerald is a Carnegie Scholar and 2009 recipient of the *David H. Russell Award for Distinguished Research* from the National Council of the Teachers of English.

Michael Cart, a reviewer of children's and young adult books for 40 years, is also the author or editor of 20 books and is currently a columnist and reviewer for *Booklist* magazine. A revised and expanded edition of his critical history of young adult literature, *From Romance to Realism,* will be published in fall 2010. He is the recipient of the 2000 Grolier Award for service to children and literature.

Lucy Shelton Caswell is the founding curator of The Ohio State University's Billy Ireland Cartoon Library & Museum, the largest and most comprehensive academic research facility documenting printed cartoon art in the United States. Professor Caswell's scholarly work focuses on the history of newspaper comic strips and the history of American editorial cartoons. She has curated more than sixty cartoon exhibits and is the author of several articles and books, the most recent being the revised edition of *Billy Ireland*.

Janine L. Certo is an Assistant Professor of Language and Literacy in the Department of Teacher Education at Michigan State University's College of Education. Her research interests include writing instruction, particularly creative writing, with a focus on both teacher and student learning. She is interested in teachers' and students' poetic genre knowledge; teachers' dispositions toward reading, writing and teaching poetry; and analyses of children's poetic texts. A National Writing Project teacher consultant, she is also interested, more broadly, in genre instruction at the elementary level and teachers as writers.

Tara F. Chace translates books from Norwegian, Swedish and Danish. Her translations include both young adult novels—Jo Nesbø's *Dr. Proctor's Fart Powder*, Klaus Hagerup's *Markus* series, Per Nilsson's *You & You & You,* Sara Kadefors's *Are U 4 Real?*, and Gunnar Ardelius's *I Need You More than I Love You and I Love You to Bits*—and books for grownups—Karen Fastrup's *Beloved of My 27 Senses* and Tom Egeland's *Relic: The Quest for the Golden Shrine*. She has a Ph.D. in Scandinavian Literature and has been a full-time translator for 10 years.

Caroline T. Clark is an Associate Professor in the Adolescent, Post-Secondary, and Community Literacies Area of Study in the School of Teaching and Learning at The Ohio State University. Her scholarship focuses on literacy practices across formal/school and informal settings and teaching against heterosexism and homophobia through teacher education and collaborative teacher inquiry. Most recently she has worked with Mollie Blackburn to facilitate and document the work of a book discussion group with high school students who meet to discuss LGBT-themed literature.

Penny Colman is the author of books, essays, and articles, including *Rosie the Riveter: Women Working on the Home Front in World War II*, an Orbis Pictus Honor Book, and *Corpses, Coffins, and Crypts: A History of Burial,* one of the American Library Association's Top Ten Best Books for Young Adults. She also does the picture research for her books, several of which include her photographs. Colman is a Distinguished Lecturer at Queens College, the City University of New York.

Thomas P. Crumpler is a Professor of Reading and Literacy in the Department of Curriculum & Instruction at Illinois State University. His research interests include the changing practices of literacy and literature instruction and assessment in the context of new media. He is a co-author with Rob Tierney of *Interactive Assessment: Teachers, Students, Parents as Partners* and a co-editor with Jennifer Jasinski Schneider and Theresa Rogers of *Process Drama and Multiple Literacies: Addressing Social, Cultural, and Ethical Issues*. He is currently Director of the Mary and Jean Borg Center for Reading and Literacy at Illinois State University.

Jessica Dockter is a Ph.D. candidate in Literacy Education in the Department of Curriculum and Instruction at the University of Minnesota. Her research focuses on how literacy practices shape White racial identities with an interest in helping White students imagine themselves as allies in anti-racist and social justice work.

Eliza T. Dresang holds the endowed Beverly Cleary Professorship for Children and Youth Services at the University of Washington Information School. Formerly she was Co-Director/Founder, Florida State University, of Project LEAD, a federally funded leadership program for school librarians, and Director, School Libraries and Technology, Madison, Wisconsin. She is a widely recognized authority on digital age youth's resources and information behavior, including reading. Among numerous scholarly publications is her award-winning *Radical Change: Books for Youth in a Digital Age*.

Elizabeth Dutro is an Associate Professor of literacy studies in the School of Education at the University of Colorado at Boulder. Her research interests include the emotional dimensions of schooling, the intersections of students' identities and literacy practices, and how issues of race, class and gender affect the school experiences and educational opportunities of children and youth in K–12 classrooms.

David Filipi is the Curator of Film/Video at the Wexner Center for the Arts. He is on The Ohio State University Cartoon Library and Museum Advisory Board and co-curated *Jeff Smith: Bone and Beyond* in 2008.

María E. Fránquiz is an Associate Professor at the University of Texas–Austin where she enjoys teaching courses such as Latin@ Children's Literature for the Bilingual Learner. Her scholarship focuses on the relationship between linguistic and cultural experiences and teacher and student identities. Her co-edited book, *Inside the Latin@ Experience* showcases the work of Latin@ scholars both senior and early career. Another co-edited book, *Scholars in the Field: The Challenges of Migrant Education* is comprehensive in its coverage of this underserved group.

Yohannes Gebregeorgis, born in a small cattle town in Southern Ethiopia, is Founder and Executive Director of Ethiopia Reads. He came to the United States in 1981 after he fled his native Ethiopia from a brutal military dictatorship. While in the United States, Gebregeorgis studied English literature and Library and Information Science and became a children's librarian at the San Francisco Public Library. He has established over 30 school libraries, several Donkey Mobile Libraries, and has published 12 children's books. In 2008, Gebregeorgis was nominated as a CNN Hero and has received several awards for his work in Ethiopia.

María Paula Ghiso is an Assistant Professor at Teachers College, Columbia University. She is a recent graduate from the Reading/Writing/Literacy Program at the University of Pennsylvania and the 2009 recipient of the Morton Botel Award for Outstanding Scholarship and Practice in the Literacy Education of Young Children. Formerly a dual-language kindergarten teacher in New York City, she now supports educators and school districts in their work with linguistically diverse students.

Elizabeth Hammill is the initiator and co-founder of Seven Stories, the Centre for Children's Books. As Artistic and Collection Director, she laid the foundations for the Centre's novel approach to exhibition design and interpretation and its growing, nationally important, collection of original papers and artwork by modern British writers and illustrators for children, drawing on her earlier experiences as a primary teacher, children's bookseller, editor, critic, and university lecturer. She has written distinguished articles for *Signal* and other publications, and she was awarded an OBE in 2007 for services to literature.

Betsy Hearne is former Director of The Center for Children's Books and a Professor Emerita in the Graduate School of Library and Information Science at the University of Illinois, Urbana-Champaign. She has taught children's literature and storytelling for many years; researched and written extensively on folklore, fairy tales, and traditions of children's literature; and authored picture books and fiction for young people. In 2009 she co-edited, with Roberta Seelinger Trites, *A Narrative Compass: Stories That Guide Women's Lives,* an anthology of essays by scholars who discuss how stories—including folktales, fairy tales, children's classics, and family narratives—have shaped their life's work.

Shirley Brice Heath is the Margery Bailey Professor of English and Dramatic Literature and Professor of Linguistics, Emerita, at Stanford University and Professor at Large at Brown University. She has won many awards for her studies of language socialization across cultures as well as her innovative studies of voluntary expertise development among older learners. She is author of the classic *Ways with Words: Language, Life and Work in Communities and Classrooms,* and with Shelby A. Wolf, co-author of *The Braid of Literature: Children's Worlds of Reading.*

Gareth Hinds is the creator of several critically acclaimed graphic novels based on literary classics, including *Beowulf* (which *Publisher's Weekly* called a "mixed-media gem"), *King Lear* (which *Booklist* named one of the top 10 graphic novels for teens), and *The Merchant of Venice* (which *Kirkus* called "the standard that all others will strive to meet" for Shakespeare adaptation). He lives in Massachusetts.

Karen Nelson Hoyle is Professor and curator of the University of Minnesota's Children's Literature Research Collections (including the Kerlan Collection), which holds manuscripts and illustrations for 13,000 children's and YA titles. She is the 2003 recipient of the Minnesota Humanities Commission's Kay Sexton award for "outstanding contributions to Minnesota's book community." Past President of ChLA, she has served on ALA's Batchelder, Caldecott, Newbery, and Wilder Award committees. Her publications include a biography of Wanda Gàg and journal articles in *Bookbird, Children & Literature, Journal of Children's Literature,* and *The Lion & the Unicorn.*

Barbara Kiefer is the Charlotte S. Huck Professor of Children's Literature at The Ohio State University. She has served as member (1988) and elected chair (2000) of the Caldecott Award Committee and has published numerous articles and chapters about reading and children's literature. She is the author of *The Potential of Picturebooks: From Visual Literacy to Aesthetic Understanding,* the sixth through tenth editions of *Charlotte Huck's Children's Literature,* and co-author (with Pappas & Levstik) of *An Integrated Language Perspective in the Elementary School: Theory Into Action.*

Kostia Kontoleon was born in Athens, Greece. Her life is full of literature. She is the author of three novels and a collection of short stories. She has translated over 80 books of literature, for children, young adults, and adults. In 1991, she was honored with the highest national award for her translation of Roald Dahl's *Matilda*. In 2002, she was honored with the award of the best translation of the year for R.K. Narayan's *The English Teacher*. Her translations of Robert Cormier's *I am the Cheese* and Philip Pullman's *The Amber Spyglass* have been written in IBBY's honor list, in 1996 and in 2003 respectively.

M. Bowie Kotrla is an Associate Professor in the School of Library & Information Studies at Florida State University. She has a Ph.D. in Biology and an M.L.I.S. with a youth services concentration. Her areas of research and teaching include school librarianship, children's literature, statistics, and research methodology. She serves on the Intellectual Freedom Committee of the American Library Association and has served on the Research & Development and Intellectual Freedom committees of the Association for Library Service to Children.

Jane Kurtz is an award-winning children's book author, a faculty member of the Vermont MFA in children's and YA literature, and president of the board of directors of Ethiopia Reads, a nonprofit publishing some of the first children's books and planting the first children's libraries in Ethiopia, where she spent most of her childhood.

Julius Lester is the author of more than forty books for children and adults. These books have garnered many awards including a Newbery Honor Book, a Boston Globe Horn Book Award, and the Coretta Scott King Award. He is professor emeritus in the Judaic and Near Eastern Studies Department at the University of Massachusetts at Amherst.

Cynthia Lewis is Professor of Critical Literacy and English Education at the University of Minnesota. Her recent research focuses on the relationship between social identities and learning in English classrooms in urban schools. Cynthia's books include *Literary Practices as Social Acts: Power, Status, and Cultural Norms in the Classroom* and *Reframing Sociocultural Research: Identity, Agency, and Power* (with Patricia Enciso & Elizabeth Moje). Both books were awarded the Edward B. Fry Book Award from the National Reading Conference.

Lois Lowry, author of more than 35 books for young people, two of them Newbery Medal winners, is a mother and grandmother who has worked as a photojournalist as well as a writer of fiction. She divides her time between her residence in Cambridge, Massachusetts and an 18th-century farmhouse in rural Maine.

Ana Maria Machado, novelist, essayist, and children's author, is a member of the Brazilian Academy of Letters and is considered to be one of the most complete and versatile Brazilian contemporary writers. She has won over 40 awards, including the Hans Christian Andersen Medal (2000) and the Machado de Assis prize (2001)— Brazil's most prestigious National Award in Literature, given every year for the whole body of work. Her books are published in 20 countries and have sold more than 18.5 million copies.

Margaret Mackey is a Professor of Library and Information Studies at the University of Alberta. She teaches courses on young adult literature, theories and practices of reading, and multimedia literacies. Her most recent books are *Mapping Recreational Literacies: Contemporary Adults at Play* and a revised edition of *Literacies Across Media: Playing the Text.* She has also published many articles on the changing face of young people's literacies and literatures.

Leonard S. Marcus is a children's literature historian and critic. His books include *Margaret Wise Brown: Awakened by the Moon; Dear Genius; Golden Legacy;* and *Minders of Make-Believe.* He is a frequent contributor to the *New York Times Book Review* and writes a regular column for *The Horn Book Magazine.* Marcus is a founding trustee of the Eric Carle Museum of Picture Book Art and has curated numerous exhibitions of illustration art. He teaches children's books and child development at New York University and lectures widely throughout the United States and abroad.

Carmen Martínez-Roldán is an Associate Professor in the Bilingual Bicultural Education Program at The University of Texas–Austin. Her research addresses bilingual students' literacy development in two languages (Spanish/English) and the use of children's literature to support students' learning. Her work documenting children's responses to literature has been published in national and international journals. Upcoming publications address her more recent work on immigrant children's responses to wordless picture books and teachers' responses to Latina/o literature.

Robyn McCallum is a Lecturer in English at Macquarie University, where she works in children's literature, with a particular focus on adolescent fiction and visual media. Her book *Ideologies of Identity in Adolescent Fiction* received the IRSCL Honour Book Award in 2001. She is co-author of *Retelling Stories, Framing Culture* and *New World Orders in Contemporary Children's Literature.*

Roderick McGillis is in the English Department at the University of Calgary. Recent publications include *He Was Some Kind of a Man: Masculinities in the B Western, George MacDonald: Literary Heritage and Heirs,* and the novel *Les Pieds Devant.* Most importantly, he edited with Karen Coats and Anna Jackson the volume of essays, *The Gothic in Children's Literature.* In spring of 2010, he is guest editing the new journal, *The Journal of Postcolonial Cultures and Societies.*

Monette C. McIver is Assistant Professor in the School of Education at the University of Colorado at Boulder, specializing in literacy. Her research explores the development of classroom teachers' writing identities and the impact these identities have on instruction and student achievement. In addition, Dr. McIver is interested in teacher leadership and how teachers influence policy decisions at local and national levels.

Carmen I. Mercado is Professor of language, literacy, and children's literature at City University of New York – Hunter College. She is also affiliated faculty to the Urban Education doctoral program at the Graduate Center. Her cross-disciplinary collaborations with Latino social scientists from the Center for Puerto Rican studies (CENTRO) has led to working with a vast archival collection that houses the literary contributions of U.S. Latino communities.

Claudia Mills is the author of over 40 books for young readers, including picture books (*Ziggy's Blue Ribbon Day*), easy readers (the *Gus and Grandpa* series), chapter books (*7 x 9 = Trouble!* and *How Oliver Olson Changed the World*) and middle-grade novels (*The Totally Made-Up Civil War Diary of Amanda MacLeish* and *One Square Inch*). She is also an Associate Professor of philosophy at the University of Colorado at Boulder, teaching and writing in the area of ethics and children's literature.

Phyllis Reynolds Naylor's 136 books include novels for middle grades, teens, and adults, as well as picture books, chapter books, and nonfiction. *Shiloh*, the first book of a trilogy, was awarded the Newbery Medal in 1992. A number of her novels have been made into feature-length movies and films for television, and a grant from the National Endowment for the Arts enabled her to do research and to travel throughout West Virginia and Kentucky, producing many of her works. She and her husband, Rex, live in the Washington, D.C. area, the setting for her long-running *Alice* series.

Maria Nikolajeva is a Professor of Education at the University of Cambridge, UK, previously a Professor of comparative literature at Stockholm University, Sweden, where she taught children's literature and critical theory for 25 years. She is the author and editor of many books, the most recent *Power, Voice and Subjectivity in Literature for Young Readers*. From 1993–97 she was the President of the International Research Society for Children's Literature. She was also one of the senior editors for *The Oxford Encyclopedia of Children's Literature* and received the International Grimm Award in 2005.

Petros Panaou is a Lecturer at the University of Nicosia, Cyprus, where he teaches Children's Literature and Language Arts. His work often focuses on picture book analysis and comparative children's literature, while his research is most often interdisciplinary in nature. He has published

several articles and frequently presents at international conferences. He is particularly interested in the intersections between discourses of nation and childhood.

Katherine Paterson is the author of 16 novels, a number of picture books, retellings, and I-Can-Read books. She has twice won the Newbery Medal for *Bridge to Terabithia* and *Jacob Have I Loved*. *The Master Puppeteer* won the National Book Award and *The Great Gilly Hopkins* won the Newbery Honor and National Book Award. For the body of her work she received the Hans Christian Andersen Award, the Astrid Lindgren Memorial Award, and in 2000 was named a Living Legend by the Library of Congress. Most recently, she was named the National Ambassador for Young People's Literature 2010–2011.

Philip Pullman was born in 1946. He graduated from Oxford University in 1968 and became a middle school teacher, finally leaving the classroom at the age of 39 to enter the lecture room. He taught aspiring teachers for 10 years or so, and then left in order to spend all his time writing. His books include *Clockwork, The Scarecrow and His Servant,* and the trilogy *His Dark Materials*. He is interested in every aspect of narrative, and is preparing a book on the subject, which he hopes will illustrate his ideas about how stories work.

Candice Ransom is the author of more than 100 books for children, including her series *Time Spies*. She has published picture books to young adult, board books to biography, historical fiction to nonfiction. Award-winning titles include *The Big Green Pocketbook, Finding Day's Bottom, Seeing Sky-Blue Pink, When the Whippoorwill Calls,* and *The Promise Quilt*. She holds an MFA in writing from Vermont College and an MA in children's literature from Hollins University and is an Assistant Professor in Hollins University's MA/MFA children's literature program.

Chris Raschka is an illustrator and writer of picture books which concern friendship, jazz, life and death and, most recently, a little black crow.

Catherine Sheldrick Ross is Professor in the Faculty of Information and Media Studies at The University of Western Ontario where she teaches in the Library and Information Science and the Media Studies programs. Her research interests include leisure-reading, the reference transaction, readers' advisory, and children's literature. She is currently working on an on-going ethnographic study of avid readers, based on qualitative interviews. Recent books include *Conducting the Reference Interview* and *Reading Matters*.

Paulette M. Rothbauer is Assistant Professor in the Faculty of Information & Media Studies at the University of

LIST OF CONTRIBUTORS

Western Ontario where she teaches courses on young adult literature, media, and library services. Her recent research has focused on the reading practices of young women who claim alternative sexual identities and of rural youth. Currently, she is studying the emergence of the modern Canadian young adult novel and the rise of the discursive construction of the teenage reader in Canada.

Kathy G. Short is a Professor at the University of Arizona in Language, Reading and Culture. Her classroom-based research focuses on reader response, curriculum as inquiry, and international children's literature. Her books include *Creating Classrooms for Authors and Inquirers, Literature as a Way of Knowing, Talking about Books,* and *Stories Matter: The Complexity of Cultural Authenticity in Children's Literature.* She is the director of Worlds of Words (www.wowlit.org), an initiative to encourage dialogue around children's literature to build bridges across global cultures. She is currently President of USBBY, the U.S. national section of the International Board of Books for Young People.

Eva-Maria Simms is Associate Professor and director of graduate studies in the psychology department at Duquesne University in Pittsburgh. As a phenomenologist she studies the psychology of the child in its historical and existential dimensions, and investigates such philosophical themes as embodiment, co-existentiality, spatiality, temporality, and language in light of their appearance in early childhood. She is the author of the book *The Child in the World: Embodiment, Time, and Language in Early Childhood,* and of numerous articles on Merleau-Ponty, childhood, Goethean nature phenomenology, Rilke's existentialism, and the psychology of place.

Lawrence R. Sipe is a Professor at the University of Pennsylvania's Graduate School of Education. His research concerns young children's literary understanding as well the formal qualities of picturebooks. Sipe has won numerous awards from the International Reading Association, the National Council of Teachers of English, and the National Reading Conference. He is the author of *Storytime: Young Children's Literary Understanding in the Classroom* and has co-edited *Postmodern Picturebooks: Play, Parody, and Self-Referentiality.* He is the North American editor of the journal *Children's Literature in Education.*

Jeff Smith, multiple Eisner and Harvey Award winner, broke out on the comics scene in 1991 with the celebrated and well-loved fantasy, *BONE.* U.S. publisher Scholastic brought this indie comic to a whole new audience with a full-color version in 2005, now with over 5 million color graphic novels sold. In 2008, Cartoon Books debuted Jeff's newest adventure series, *RASL,* a sci-fi, noir thriller to critical acclaim.

John Stephens is Emeritus Professor in English at Macquarie University. He is author of *Language and Ideology in Children's Fiction; Retelling Stories, Framing Culture* (with Robyn McCallum); *New World Orders in Contemporary Children's Literature* (with Clare Bradford, Kerry Mallan, & Robyn McCallum); editor of *Ways of Being Male;* and author of about a hundred articles and two other books. He is a former IRSCL President, and currently Editor of *International Research in Children's Literature.* In 2007, he received the 11th International Brothers Grimm Award.

Deborah Stevenson is the editor of *The Bulletin of the Center for Children's Books* and an Assistant Professor at the Graduate School of Library and Information Science at the University of Illinois, Urbana Champaign. A contributor to the *Cambridge Companion to Children's Literature,* a senior editor of the *Oxford Encyclopedia of Children's Literature,* and a co-author, with Betsy Hearne, of *Choosing Books for Children: A Commonsense Guide,* she has published reviews and articles in *Children's Literature, The Children's Literature Association Quarterly,* and *The Lion and the Unicorn,* and she has taught in both English departments and library schools.

Morag Styles is a Reader in Children's Literature at Cambridge University and a Fellow of Homerton College. She lectures internationally on children's literature, poetry, the history of reading and visual literacy. She is the author of numerous books and articles including *From the Garden to the Street: 300 Years of Poetry for Children*; Advisory Editor of *The Cambridge Guide to Children's Books in English*; co-author (with Evelyn Arizpe) of *Children Reading Pictures: Interpreting Visual Texts* and *Reading Lessons from the Eighteenth Century: Mothers, Children & Texts*; as well as co-editor of *Acts of Reading: Teachers, Texts and Childhood.*

Joel Taxel is a Professor in the Department of Language and Literacy Education at the University of Georgia. He has written extensively about the sociocultural, political, and economic issues surrounding children's literature. The founding editor of *The New Advocate,* Joel's articles have appeared in *Curriculum Inquiry, Research in the Teaching of English,* and *Teacher's College Record.* He is co-author, with Peter Smagorinsky, of *Culture Wars in the Classroom: The Discourse of Character Education.*

Raina Telgemeier, graduate of Manhattan's School of Visual Arts, is the author of the graphic memoir, *SMILE* and adaptor and illustrator of the *Baby-sitters Club* graphic novel series, selected by YALSA for their Great Graphic Novels for Teens list in 2007 as well as ALA's Top 10 Graphic Novels for Youth list. Her comics have been nominated for the Ignatz, Cybil, and Eisner Awards, and have appeared in publications by Random House, DC Comics, and *Nickelodeon Magazine*.

Tasoula Tsilimeni is Assistant Professor at the University of Thessaly, where she teaches subjects on children's literature (narration and fiction). Her interests focus on the theory and teaching methodology of children's literature, with an emphasis on Preschool Education. Her work has been presented at various conferences and published in journals, anthologies, but also in books she has authored. She writes books of children's literature, and she is the director of the children's magazine *Delphini*, which is published by the Logos and Culture Workshop of the University of Thessaly. She is also the director of the electronic journal *KEIMENA*.

Virginia A. Walter is Emerita Professor in UCLA's Graduate School of Education and Information Studies (GSEIS). She came to the GSEIS faculty with 20 years of experience as a public library youth services librarian, including Children's Services Coordinator for the Los Angeles Public Library system. She is the author of *Children & Libraries: Getting It Right, Teens & Libraries: Getting It Right*, and *Twenty-first Century Kids, Twenty-first Century Libraries*. She also writes fiction for children and teens.

Linda Wedwick is an Assistant Professor and Coordinator of the Reading Masters program at Illinois State University and former middle school teacher and reading specialist. She is a co-author, with Jessica Ann Wutz, of *BOOKMATCH: How to Scaffold Student Book Selection for Independent Reading*.

Kathleen Weibel began her career in librarianship in young adult services at the New York Public Library in the 1970s. She retired in 2004 from the Chicago Public Library where she served as Director of Staff Development. Throughout her professional career, she has been involved in public library education and advocacy, both nationally and internationally. She is currently involved in a project developing continuing education opportunities for school and public librarians in the Mekong River delta region of Vietnam.

David Wiesner is an author and illustrator of picture books, three of which have been awarded the Caldecott Medal—*Tuesday* in 1992, *The Three Pigs* in 2002, and *Flotsam* in 2006. Two other books of his, *Sector 7* and *Free Fall*, were named Caldecott Honor Books. In 2008, David was the United States nominee, and a finalist, for the Hans Christian Andersen Award.

Melissa I. Wilson is a doctoral student at The Ohio State University having spent 30 years teaching elementary school in Columbus Public Schools, Ohio. She is also a co-director of the Columbus Area Writing Project, an affiliate of the National Writing Project.

Janet S. Wong is the author of 20 books for children and young adults, mainly picture books and poetry collections. In her "Meet the Author" autobiography *Before It Wriggles Away*, Wong discusses her career switch from lawyer to children's author—as well as her accidental passion for poetry.

Jacqueline Woodson is the author of more than two dozen books for children and young adults. She has received many awards including three Newbery Honors, a Coretta Scott King Award and three Coretta Scott King Honors, two lifetime achievement awards, a Caldecott and two National Book Awards. Her titles include *Locomotion, Show Way, The Other Side, After Tupac and D Foster, Feathers, Visiting Day, Peace, Locomotion, If You Come Softly*, and *Miracle's Boys* which was made into a film directed by Spike Lee. Jacqueline lives with her family in Brooklyn, NY. Her website is jacquelinewoodson.com.

Junko Yokota is Professor at National-Louis University in Chicago and directs the Center for Teaching through Children's Books with Gail Bush. Her publications include articles, review columns, editor of *Kaleidoscope: A Multicultural Booklist for Grades K-8* and coauthored textbook, *Children's Books in Children's Hands*. She has served on the Caldecott, Newbery, and Batchelder Award Committees as well as the IBBY Hans Christian Andersen Award Jury. She was president of USBBY and recipient of the Virginia Hamilton Award for Contribution to Multicultural Literature.

Markus Zusak is the author of five novels, including *Fighting Ruben Wolfe, I Am The Messenger*, and the international bestseller, *The Book Thief*. First published in 2005, *The Book Thief* has been translated into over 30 languages, and has been on the New York Times bestseller list for more than three years. He lives in Sydney with his wife and daughter.

Author Index

Subject Index